STO

S0-BWX-558

Advantage: Hoover's Online

With Hoover's Online you get the same high-quality information you've come to expect from Hoover's — updated daily by our industry experts. Plus, even more information from leading sources and timesaving tools that help you manage this wealth of data.

SUBSCRIBE TODAY!
Hoover's Subscription Options:

HOOVER'S LITE
Access to Hoover's proprietary database of in-depth information and basic tools:

▶ 21,000 companies

▶ 180,000+ key people

▶ 600 industries

▶ Eight easy-to-use simple search tools

HOOVER'S PRO
Access to all Hoover's Lite features, plus the following information and advanced tools:

▶ 12 million+ companies

▶ 13 million key people

▶ Company and executive list building tools

HOOVER'S PRO PLUS
Access to all Hoover's Lite and Pro features, plus the following enterprise-class features:

▶ Small business and international list-building tools

▶ Custom report building tools

▶ Data download tools

The information we get from Hoover's ... has been an invaluable resource for us. What a great service!

– Eric Halvorson
Manager, Information Center
Account Planning, Ogilvy & Mather

CALL OR VISIT
1-866-635-9715
www.hoovers.com

About Hoover's

Hoover's, Inc., was founded in 1990 as The Reference Press. The company was renamed Hoover's, Inc., in 1996, and operates Hoover's Online. Today, Hoover's, Inc., is a subsidiary of D&B (NYSE: DNB) and provides comprehensive, up-to-date business information for sales, marketing, business development, and other professionals who need intelligence about U.S. and global companies, industries, and the people who shape them.

Hoover's Handbook of

World
Business

2004

HOOVER'S
BUSINESS PRESS

Austin, Texas

Hoover's Handbook of World Business 2004 is intended to provide readers with accurate and authoritative information about the enterprises covered in it. Hoover's asked all companies and organizations profiled to provide information. Many did so; a number did not. The information contained herein is as accurate as we could reasonably make it. In many cases we have relied on third-party material that we believe to be trustworthy, but were unable to independently verify. We do not warrant that the book is absolutely accurate or without error. Readers should not rely on any information contained herein in instances where such reliance might cause loss or damage. The publisher, the editors, and their data suppliers specifically disclaim all warranties, including the implied warranties of merchantability and fitness for a specific purpose. This book is sold with the understanding that neither the publisher, the editors, nor any content contributors are engaged in providing investment, financial, accounting, legal, or other professional advice.

The financial data (Historical Financials sections) in this book are from a variety of sources. Media General Financial Services, Inc., provided selected data for the Historical Financials sections of publicly traded companies. For private companies and for historical information on public companies prior to their becoming public, we obtained information directly from the companies or from trade sources deemed to be reliable. Hoover's, Inc., is solely responsible for the presentation of all data.

Many of the names of products and services mentioned in this book are the trademarks or service marks of the companies manufacturing or selling them and are subject to protection under US law. Space has not permitted us to indicate which names are subject to such protection, and readers are advised to consult with the owners of such marks regarding their use. Hoover's is a trademark of Hoover's, Inc.

BUSINESS PRESS

Copyright © 2004 by Hoover's, Inc. All rights reserved. No part of this book may be reproduced or transmitted in any form or by any means, electronic or mechanical, including by photocopying, facsimile transmission, recording, rekeying, or using any information storage and retrieval system, without permission in writing from Hoover's, except that brief passages may be quoted by a reviewer in a magazine, in a newspaper, online, or in a broadcast review.

10 9 8 7 6 5 4 3 2 1

Publishers Cataloging-in-Publication Data

Hoover's Handbook of World Business 2004

    Includes indexes.

    ISBN 1-57311-089-2

    ISSN 1055-7199

    1. Business enterprises — Directories. 2. Corporations — Directories.

HF3010 338.7

Hoover's Company Information is also available on the Internet at Hoover's Online (www.hoovers.com). A catalog of Hoover's products is available on the Internet at www.hooversbooks.com.

The Hoover's Handbook series is edited by George Sutton and is produced for Hoover's Business Press by:

Sycamore Productions, Inc.
5808 Balcones Drive, Suite 205
Austin, Texas 78731
info@sycamoreproductions.com

Cover design is by John Baker. Electronic prepress and printing are by Sheridan Books, Inc., Ann Arbor, Michigan.

U.S. AND WORLD BOOK SALES

Hoover's, Inc.
5800 Airport Blvd.
Austin, TX 78752
Phone: 512-374-4500
Fax: 512-374-4538
e-mail: orders@hoovers.com
Web: www.hooversbooks.com

EUROPEAN BOOK SALES

William Snyder Publishing Associates
5 Five Mile Drive
Oxford OX2 8HT
England
Phone & fax: +44-186-551-3186
e-mail: snyderpub@aol.com

Hoover's, Inc.

Founder: Gary Hoover
President: Jeffrey R. Tarr
EVP Operations and Product Management: Russell Secker
VP Advertising and E-Commerce Sales: Joseph B. McWilliams Jr.
VP Enterprise Subscription Sales: John Lysinger
VP Finance and Administration: Jeffrey A. Cross
VP Human Resources: Mike Smith
VP Large Account Product Management: Jonathan Cherins
VP Product Management: Michael Reiff
VP Technology and CTO: Thomas M. (Tom) Ballard

EDITORIAL

VP and Managing Editor: Nancy Regent
Assistant Managing Editor: Valerie Pearcy
Editorial Operations Manager: Rachel Brush
Senior Editors: Margaret Claughton, Paul Geary, Joe Grey, Kathleen Kelly
Senior Editor, Financial Information: Dennis Sutton
Research Manager: Amy Degner
Editors: Sally Alt, Linnea Anderson, Alex Biesada, Larry Bills, Angela Boeckman, Joe Bramhall, James Bryant, Troy Bryant, Ryan Caione, Jason Cella, Jannell Chester, Catherine Colbert, Elizabeth Cornell, Danny Cummings, Lesley Dings, Jeff Dorsch, Michaela Drapes, Bobby Duncan, John Flynn, Adriane Foster, David Hamerly, Stuart Hampton, Jeanette Herman, Guy Holland, Andreas Knutsen, Jay Koenig, Nathan Kokemor, Julie Krippel, Anne Law, Josh Lower, John MacAyeal, Michael McLellan, Rachel Meyer, Barbara Murray, Laurie Najjar, Nell Newton, Peter Partheymuller, Greg Perliski, Anna Porlas, Jennifer Powers, David Ramirez, Kcevin Rob, Melanie Robertson, Matt Saucedo, Amy Schein, Seth Shafer, Joe Simonetta, Daysha Taylor, Vanita Trippe, Tim Walker, Josh Wardrip, Kathi Whitley, Randy Williams, David Woodruff
QA Editors: Jason Cother, Emily Domaschk, Carrie Geis, Allan Gill, Diane Lee, John Willis
Financial Editors: Adi Anand, Chris Huston, Anthony Staats, Matthew Taylor
Editorial Projects Analyst: Audra Martin
Editorial Customer Advocate: Alison Stoeltje
Documents Coordinator: Jim Harris
Library Coordinator: Kris Stephenson
Library Assistant: Makiko Schwartz

HOOVER'S BUSINESS PRESS

Director, Hoover's Business Press: Dana Smith
Distribution Manager: Rhonda Mitchell
Fulfillment and Shipping Manager: Michael Febonio
Shipping Clerk: Paul Olvera

ABOUT HOOVER'S, INC. — THE BUSINESS INFORMATION AUTHORITY™

Hoover's, Inc., a subsidiary of D&B (NYSE: DNB), is a leading provider of business information. Hoover's provides authoritative, updated information for sales, marketing, business development, and other professionals who need intelligence on U.S. and global companies, industries, and the people who shape them. This information, along with powerful tools to search, sort, download, and integrate the content, is available through Hoover's Online (www.hoovers.com), the company's premier online service. Hoover's business information is also available through corporate intranets and distribution agreements with licensees, as well as via print from Hoover's Business Press. Hoover's is headquartered in Austin, Texas.

Abbreviations

AB – Aktiebolag (Swedish)*
ADR – American Depositary Receipts
AG – Aktiengesellschaft (German)*
AFL-CIO – American Federation of Labor and Congress of Industrial Organizations
AMEX – American Stock Exchange
A/S – Aktieselskab (Danish)*
ASA – Allmenne Aksje Selskaper (Norwegian)*
ATM – asynchronous transfer mode; automated teller machine
CAD/CAM – computer-aided design/computer-aided manufacturing
CASE – computer-aided software engineering
CD-ROM – compact disc – read-only memory
CEO – chief executive officer
CFO – chief financial officer
CMOS – complementary metal-oxide semiconductor
COMECON – Council for Mutual Economic Assistance
COO – chief operating officer
DAT – digital audio tape
DOD – Department of Defense
DOE – Department of Energy
DOT – Department of Transportation
DRAM – dynamic random-access memory
DVD – digital versatile disc/digital video disc
EC – European Community
EPA – Environmental Protection Agency
EPS – earnings per share
EU – European Union
EVP – executive vice president
FCC – Federal Communications Commission
FDA – Food and Drug Administration

FDIC – Federal Deposit Insurance Corporation
FTC – Federal Trade Commission
GATT – General Agreement on Tariffs and Trade
GmbH – Gesellschaft mit beschränkter Haftung (German)*
GNP – gross national product
HDTV – high-definition television
HMO – health maintenance organization
HR – human resources
HTML – hypertext markup language
ICC – Interstate Commerce Commission
IMF – International Monetary Fund
IPO – initial public offering
IRS – Internal Revenue Service
KGaA – Kommanditgesellschaft auf Aktien (German)*
LAN – local-area network
LBO – leveraged buyout
LNG – liquefied natural gas
LP – limited partnership
Ltd. – Limited
MFN – Most Favored Nation
MITI – Ministry of International Trade and Industry (Japan)
NAFTA – North American Free Trade Agreement
Nasdaq – National Association of Securities Dealers Automated Quotations
NATO – North Atlantic Treaty Organization
NV – Naamlose Vennootschap (Dutch)*
NYSE – New York Stock Exchange
OAO – open joint stock company (Russian)
OAS – Organization of American States

OECD – Organization for Economic Cooperation and Development
OEM – original equipment manufacturer
OOO – limited liability company (Russian)
OPEC – Organization of Petroleum Exporting Countries
OS – operating system
OTC – over-the-counter
P/E – price-to-earnings ratio
PLC – public limited company (UK)*
RAM – random-access memory
R&D – research and development
RISC – reduced instruction set computer
ROA – return on assets
ROI – return on investment
SA – Société Anonyme (French)*; Sociedad(e) Anónima (Spanish and Portuguese)*
SA de CV – Sociedad Anónima de Capital Variable (Spanish)*
SEC – Securities and Exchange Commission
SEVP – senior executive vice president
SIC – Standard Industrial Classification
SpA – Società per Azioni (Italian)*
SPARC – scalable processor architecture
SVP – senior vice president
VAR – value-added reseller
VAT – value-added tax
VC – venture capitalist
VP – vice president
WAN – wide-area network
WWW – World Wide Web
ZAO – closed joint stock company (Russian)
z o.o. – z ograniczona odpowiedzialnoscia (Polish)*

* These abbreviations are used in companies' names to convey that the companies are limited liability enterprises; the meanings are usually the equivalent of *corporation* or *incorporated*.

Contents

List of Lists

Companies Profiled

Companies Profiled (continued)

About Hoover's Handbook of World Business 2004

It may have a new look, but *Hoover's Handbook of World Business* is as focused on its mission of providing you with premier coverage of the global business scene as it was 11 years ago, when the first edition was published. We have redesigned the cover and the inside pages and moved to a larger format so that we can pack even more information into the pages of the Hoover's Handbooks series. By doing so, we achieved our goal of adding even more value to this already valuable resource.

This book, which features 300 of the world's most influential companies based outside of the United States, is one of the most complete sources of in-depth information on large, non-US-based business enterprises available anywhere.

In addition to this volume, we make available through our catalog many of the best business reference works from other countries around the world. To see our complete selection, call us at 1-800-486-8666 and request a catalog of our products, or see our catalog online at www.hooversbooks.com.

Hoover's Handbook of World Business is one of our four-title series of handbooks that covers, literally, the world of business. The series is available as an indexed set, and also includes *Hoover's Handbook of American Business* (in two volumes), *Hoover's Handbook of Private Companies*, and *Hoover's Handbook of Emerging Companies*. This series brings you information on the biggest, fastest-growing, and most influential enterprises in the world.

HOOVER'S ONLINE FOR BUSINESS NEEDS

In addition to the 2,550 companies featured in our handbooks, coverage of some 40,000 business enterprises is available in electronic format on our Web site, Hoover's Online. Our goal is to provide one site that offers authoritative, updated intelligence on US and global companies, industries, and the people who shape them. Hoover's has partnered with other prestigious business information and service providers to bring you all the right business information, services, and links in one place. Additionally, Hoover's Company Information is available on the Internet at Hoover's Online (www.hoovers.com).

We welcome the recognition we have received as the premier provider of high-quality company information — online, electronically, and in print — and continue to look for ways to make our products more available and more useful to you.

We believe that anyone who buys from, sells to, invests in, lends to, competes with, interviews with, or works for a company should know all there is to know about that enterprise. Taken together, this book and the other Hoover's products and resources represent the most complete source of basic corporate information readily available to the general public.

HOW TO USE THIS BOOK

This book has four sections:

1. "Using Hoover's Handbooks" describes the contents of our profiles and explains the ways in which we gather and compile our data.

2. "A List-Lover's Compendium" contains lists of the largest, fastest-growing, and most valuable companies of global importance.

3. The company profiles section makes up the largest and most important part of the book — 300 profiles of major business enterprises, arranged alphabetically.

4. Three indexes complete the book. The first sorts companies by industry groups, the second by headquarters location. The third index is a list of all the executives found in the Executives section of each company profile.

As always, we hope you find our books useful. We invite your comments via phone (512-374-4500), fax (512-374-4538), mail (5800 Airport Boulevard, Austin, Texas 78752), or e-mail (custsupport@hoovers.com).

The Editors,
Austin, Texas,
January 2004

Using Hoover's Handbooks

SELECTION OF THE COMPANIES PROFILED

The 300 profiles in this book include a variety of international enterprises, ranging from some of the largest publicly traded companies in the world — DaimlerChrysler AG, for example — to Malaysia's largest and oldest conglomerate, Sime Darby Berhad. It also includes many private businesses, such as Bertelsmann AG and LEGO, as well as a selection of government-owned entities, including the British Broadcasting Corporation and Mexico's Petróleos Mexicanos. The companies selected represent a cross-section of the largest, most influential, and most interesting companies based outside the United States.

In selecting these companies, we followed several basic criteria. We started with the global giants, including Toyota and Royal Dutch/Shell Group, and then looked at companies with substantial activity in the US, such as Vivendi Universal and Diageo (33% stake in General Mills). We also included companies that dominate their industries (e.g., Electrolux, the world's #1 producer of household appliances), as well as representative companies from around the world (one Indian conglomerate, Tata; one firm from Finland, Nokia; and two companies from Russia, OAO Gazprom and OAO LUKOIL). Companies that weren't necessarily global powerhouses but had a high profile with consumers (e.g., IKEA) or had interesting stories (Virgin Group) were included. Finally, because of their truly global reach, we added the Big Four accounting firms (even though they are headquartered or co-headquartered in the US).

ORGANIZATION

The profiles are presented in alphabetical order. We have shown the full name of the enterprise at the top of the profile, unless it was too long, in which case you will find it above the address in the Locations section of the profile. Also, full names are provided in the Locations section for some companies, primarily Japanese, that are profiled under their better-known English translations. (The legal name of Nippon Steel Corporation is Shin Nippon Seitetsu Kabushiki Kaisha.) If a company name starts with a person's first name (e.g., George Weston Limited), it is alphabetized under the first name. We've also tried to alphabetize companies where you would expect to find them — for example, Deutsche Lufthansa is in the L's and Grupo Televisa can be found under T.

The annual financial information contained in the profiles is current through fiscal year-ends occurring as late as June 2003. We have included certain nonfinancial developments, such as officer changes, through November 2003.

OVERVIEW

In the first section of the profile, we have tried to give a thumbnail description of the company and what it does. The description will usually include information on the company's strategy, reputation, and ownership. We recommend that you read this section first.

HISTORY

This extended section reflects our belief that every enterprise is the sum of its history and that you have to know where you came from in order to know where you are going. While some companies have limited historical awareness and were unable to help us much and other companies are just plain boring, we think the vast majority of the enterprises in this book have colorful backgrounds. We have tried to focus on the people who made the enterprises what they are today. We have found these histories to be full of twists and ironies; they make fascinating reading.

EXECUTIVES

Here we list the names of the people who run the company, insofar as space allows. We have shown age and pay information where available, although most non-US companies are not required to report the level of detail revealed in the US.

Although companies are free to structure their management titles any way they please, most modern corporations follow standard practices. The ultimate power in any corporation lies with the shareholders, who elect a board of directors, usually including officers or "insiders" as well as individuals from outside the company. The chief officer, the person on whose desk the buck stops, is usually called the chief executive officer (CEO) in the US. In other countries, practices vary widely. In the UK, traditionally, the Managing Director performs the functions of the CEO without the title, although the use of the term CEO is on the rise there. In Germany it is customary to have two boards of directors: a managing board populated by the top executives of the company and a higher-level supervisory board consisting of outsiders.

As corporate management has become more complex, it is common for the CEO to have a "right-hand person" who oversees the day-to-day operations of the company, allowing the CEO plenty of time to focus on strategy and long-term issues. This right-hand person is usually designated the chief operating officer (COO) and is often the president of the company. In other cases one person is both chairman and president.

We have tried to list each company's most important officers, including the chief financial officer (CFO), the chief legal officer, and the chief human resources or personnel officer. For companies with US operations, we have included the names of the US CEO, CFO, and top human resources executive, where available.

The people named in the Executives section are indexed at the back of the book.

The Executives section also includes the name of the company's auditing (accounting) firm, where available.

LOCATIONS

Here we include the company's headquarters, street address, telephone and fax numbers, and Web site, as available. We also list the same information for the US office for each company, if one exists. Telephone numbers of foreign offices are shown using the standardized conventions of international dialing. The back of the book includes an index of companies by headquarters location.

In some cases we have also included information on the geographic distribution of the company's business, including sales and profit data. Note that these profit numbers, like those in the Products/Operations section below, are usually operating or pretax profits rather than net profits. Operating profits are generally those before financing costs (interest income and payments) and before taxes, which are considered costs attributable to the whole company rather than to one division or part of the world. For this reason the net income figures (in the Historical Financials section) are usually much lower, since they are after interest and taxes. Pretax profits are after interest but before taxes.

PRODUCTS/OPERATIONS

This section lists as many of the company's products, services, brand names, divisions, subsidiaries, and joint ventures as we could fit. We have tried to include all its major lines and all familiar brand names. The nature of this section varies by company and the amount of information available. If the company publishes sales and profit information by type of business, we have included it (in US dollars).

COMPETITORS

In this section we have listed enterprises that compete with the profiled company. This feature is included as a quick way to locate similar companies and compare them. Because of the difficulty in identifying companies that only compete in foreign markets, the list of competitors is still weighted to large international companies with a strong US presence.

HISTORICAL FINANCIALS

Here we have tried to present as much data about each enterprise's financial performance as we could compile in the allocated space. Financial data for all companies is presented in US dollars, using the appropriate exchange rate at fiscal year-end.

While the information presented varies somewhat from industry to industry, it is less complete in the case of private companies that do not release data (although we have always tried to provide annual sales and employment). The following information is generally present.

A 10-year table, with relevant annualized compound growth rates, covers:
- Sales — fiscal year sales (year-end assets for most financial companies)
- Net income — fiscal year net income (before accounting changes)
- Income as a percent of sales — fiscal year net income as a percent of sales (as a percent of assets for most financial firms)
- Earnings per share — fiscal year earnings per share (EPS)
- Stock price — the fiscal year high, low, and close
- P/E — high and low price/earnings ratio
- Dividends per share — fiscal year dividends per share
- Book value per share — fiscal year-end book value (common shareholders' equity per share)
- Employees — fiscal year-end or average number of employees

The information on the number of employees is intended to aid the reader interested in knowing whether a company has a long-term trend of increasing or decreasing employment. As far as we know, we are the only company that publishes this information in print format.

The numbers on the left in each row of the Historical Financials section give the month and the year in which the company's fiscal year actually ends. Thus, a company with a September 30, 2003, year-end is shown as 9/03.

In addition, we have provided in graph form a stock price history for companies that trade on the major US exchanges. The graphs, covering up to 10 years, show the range of trading between the high and the low price as well as the closing price for each fiscal year. For public companies that trade on the OTC or Pink Sheets or that do not trade on US exchanges, we graph net income. Generally, for private companies, we have graphed net income, or, if that is unavailable, sales.

Key year-end statistics in this section generally show the financial strength of the enterprise, including:
- Debt ratio (long-term debt as a percent of shareholders' equity)
- Return on equity (net income divided by the average of beginning and ending common shareholders' equity)
- Cash and cash equivalents
- Current ratio (ratio of current assets to current liabilities)
- Total long-term debt (including capital lease obligations)
- Number of shares of common stock outstanding
- Dividend yield (fiscal year dividends per share divided by the fiscal year-end closing stock price)

- Dividend payout (fiscal year dividends divided by fiscal year EPS)
- Market value at fiscal year-end (fiscal year-end closing stock price multiplied by fiscal year-end number of shares outstanding)
- Fiscal year sales for financial institutions.

Per share data has been adjusted for stock splits. The data for public companies with sponsored American Depositary Receipts has been provided to us by Media General Financial Services, Inc. Other public company information was compiled by Hoover's, which takes full responsibility for the content of this section.

In the case of private companies that do not publicly disclose financial information, we usually did not have access to such standardized data. We have gathered estimates of sales and other statistics from numerous sources.

Hoover's Handbook of

World Business

A List-Lover's Compendium

The 100 Largest Companies by Sales in
Hoover's Handbook of World Business 2004

Rank	Company	Sales ($ mil.)	Rank	Company	Sales ($ mil.)	Rank	Company	Sales ($ mil.)
1	Royal Dutch/Shell Group	179,431	36	France Telecom SA	48,892	71	Koninklijke Philips Electronics	33,421
2	BP p.l.c.	178,721	37	Suez	48,408	72	AEGON N.V.	32,764
3	DaimlerChrysler AG	157,107	38	Fortis	48,332	73	Santander Central Hispano S.A.	32,524
4	Toyota Motor Corporation	128,965	39	BNP Paribas	48,116	74	Telecom Italia S.p.A.	31,929
5	Samsung Group	116,800	40	Vodafone Group PLC	48,005	75	Compagnie de Saint-Gobain	31,730
6	Allianz AG	113,236	41	Toshiba Corporation	47,192	76	Veolia Environnement	31,592
7	TOTAL S.A.	107,698	42	Petróleos de Venezuela S.A.	46,250	77	Nokia Corporation	31,526
8	ING Groep N.V.	97,874	43	UBS AG	46,157	78	Enel S.p.A.	31,431
9	Volkswagen AG	91,130	44	Petróleos Mexicanos	45,944	79	EADS N.V.	31,339
10	NTT	91,026	45	RWE AG	45,579	80	Telefónica, S.A.	30,656
11	Siemens AG	82,865	46	Munich Re	45,335	81	Bayer AG	30,415
12	Carrefour SA	72,035	47	Bayerische Motoren Werke	44,316	82	BT Group plc	29,596
13	Hitachi, Ltd.	69,343	48	Deutsche Post AG	44,295	83	Tengelmann	29,511
14	AXA	68,957	49	Tesco PLC	41,615	84	Mizuho Financial Group, Inc.	28,719
15	Honda Motor Co., Ltd.	67,479	50	Tokyo Electric Power Company	41,045	85	Pinault-Printemps-Redoute	28,692
16	Ifi Istituto Finanziario Industriale	66,558	51	NTT DoCoMo, Inc.	40,731	86	Ito-Yokado Co., Ltd.	28,436
17	Royal Ahold N.V.	65,836	52	Zurich Financial Services	40,448	87	Barclays PLC	27,663
18	Credit Suisse Group	65,804	53	HSBC Holdings plc	40,373	88	J Sainsbury plc	27,433
19	Nestlé S.A.	64,258	54	Hyundai Motor Company	40,111	89	IntesaBci S.p.A.	26,159
20	Sony Corporation	63,264	55	HVB Group	39,793	90	Canon Inc.	24,501
21	Nippon Life Insurance	62,197	56	NEC Corporation	39,788	91	Casino Guichard-Perrachon	23,957
22	Assicurazioni Generali S.p.A.	62,102	57	Prudential plc	39,630	92	Norsk Hydro ASA	23,463
23	Matsushita Electric Industria	61,681	58	E.ON AG	38,856	93	Bouygues SA	23,317
24	Vivendi Universal S.A.	61,075	59	Fujitsu Limited	38,529	94	SNCF	23,243
25	Fiat S.p.A.	61,014	60	ABN AMRO Holding N.V.	38,428	95	Novartis AG	23,151
26	Deutsche Bank AG	57,794	61	Repsol YPF, S.A.	38,325	96	Centrica plc	22,960
27	PSA Peugeot Citroën S.A.	57,054	62	Renault S.A.	38,084	97	Nippon Steel Corporation	22,940
28	Nissan Motor Co., Ltd.	56,905	63	British American Tobacco	37,596	98	TUI AG	22,710
29	Deutsche Telekom AG	56,390	64	Japan Tobacco Inc.	37,483	99	PETROBRAS	22,612
30	Nissho Iwai-Nichimen	54,296	65	Robert Bosch GmbH	36,659	100	Deutsche Bahn AG	21,905
31	METRO AG	54,004	66	ThyssenKrupp AG	36,001			
32	Aviva plc	51,128	67	Statoil ASA	34,874			
33	Unilever	50,698	68	GlaxoSmithKline plc	34,183			
34	Electricité de France	50,685	69	BASF Aktiengesellschaft	34,155			
35	Eni S.p.A.	50,332	70	Olivetti S.p.A.	33,447			

SOURCE: HOOVER'S, INC., DATABASE, DECEMBER 2003

The 100 Most Profitable Companies in
Hoover's Handbook of World Business 2004

Rank	Company	Net Income ($ mil.)
1	Royal Dutch/Shell Group	9,419
2	Samsung Group	8,900
3	BP p.l.c.	6,845
4	GlaxoSmithKline plc	6,341
5	Toyota Motor Corporation	6,247
6	TOTAL S.A.	6,240
7	HSBC Holdings plc	6,239
8	Nestlé S.A.	5,451
9	Novartis AG	5,224
10	DaimlerChrysler AG	4,955
11	Eni S.p.A.	4,824
12	ING Groep N.V.	4,726
13	BT Group plc	4,245
14	Nissan Motor Co., Ltd.	4,126
15	Petróleos de Venezuela S.A.	3,993
16	Honda Motor Co., Ltd.	3,612
17	Barclays PLC	3,594
18	Nokia Corporation	3,551
19	BNP Paribas	3,454
20	OAO Gazprom	3,290
21	Millea Holdings, Inc.	3,200
22	E.ON AG	2,912
23	AstraZeneca PLC	2,836
24	Volkswagen AG	2,708
25	Siemens AG	2,561
26	UBS AG	2,560
27	Diageo plc	2,476
28	Statoil ASA	2,426
29	Santander Central Hispano	2,360
30	ABN AMRO Holding N.V.	2,318
31	PETROBRAS	2,311
32	Telstra Corporation Limited	2,287
33	Aventis	2,285
34	Unilever	2,236
35	Bayerische Motoren Werke	2,117

Rank	Company	Net Income ($ mil.)
36	Enel S.p.A.	2,105
37	Renault S.A.	2,050
38	Repsol YPF, S.A.	2,050
39	NTT	1,945
40	BHP Billiton Limited	1,900
41	Teléfonos de México	1,897
42	British American Tobacco p.l.c.	1,856
43	OAO LUKOIL	1,843
44	National Australia Bank Limited	1,832
45	Hutchison Whampoa Limited	1,832
46	NTT DoCoMo, Inc.	1,800
47	Royal Bank of Canada	1,773
48	PSA Peugeot Citroën S.A.	1,771
49	A.P. Møller - Maersk A/S	1,701
50	Pinault-Printemps-Redoute	1,666
51	AEGON N.V.	1,625
52	Canon Inc.	1,590
53	BASF Aktiengesellschaft	1,580
54	BCE Inc.	1,573
55	Anglo American plc	1,563
56	L'Oréal SA	1,526
57	Tesco PLC	1,495
58	Carrefour SA	1,440
59	Tokyo Electric Power Company	1,379
60	Groupe Danone	1,348
61	Norsk Hydro ASA	1,262
62	The News Corporation Limited	1,215
63	Hyundai Motor Company	1,196
64	The Daiei, Inc.	1,152
65	Munich Re	1,133
66	Crédit Agricole S.A.	1,115
67	Bayer AG	1,113
68	RWE AG	1,101
69	Compagnie de Saint-Gobain	1,090
70	Allied Irish Banks, p.l.c.	1,079

Rank	Company	Net Income ($ mil.)
71	Nomura Holdings, Inc.	1,016
72	AXA	997
73	YPF, S.A.	995
74	Sony Corporation	978
75	Bertelsmann AG	973
76	Nippon Life Insurance Company	943
77	POSCO	918
78	Bank of Montreal	910
79	Cadbury Schweppes plc	883
80	Akzo Nobel N.V.	859
81	Heineken N.V.	833
82	The Toronto-Dominion Bank	816
83	Imperial Oil Limited	769
84	Centrica plc	767
85	Scottish Power plc	763
86	Marks and Spencer Group	756
87	Deutsche Lufthansa AG	751
88	Prudential plc	724
89	J Sainsbury plc	715
90	Bouygues SA	698
91	Swire Pacific Limited	693
92	Deutsche Post AG	691
93	Robert Bosch GmbH	681
94	Reckitt Benckiser plc	654
95	Japan Tobacco Inc.	628
96	The Thomson Corporation	615
97	Michelin	609
98	Ricoh Company, Ltd.	605
99	Singapore Airlines Limited	601
100	AB Electrolux	587

SOURCE: HOOVER'S, INC., DATABASE, DECEMBER 2003

The 100 Most Valuable Public Companies in
Hoover's Handbook of World Business 2004

Rank	Company	Market Value* ($ mil.)	Rank	Company	Market Value ($ mil.)	Rank	Company	Market Value ($ mil.)
1	BP p.l.c.	151,615	36	AXA	23,702	71	Norsk Hydro ASA	11,456
2	Vodafone Group PLC	124,197	37	Royal Bank of Canada	23,464	72	Millea Holdings, Inc.	11,421
3	GlaxoSmithKline plc	112,834	38	Allianz AG	23,093	73	Scottish Power plc	11,131
4	HSBC Holdings plc	104,251	39	Philips Electronics	22,559	74	Imperial Oil Limited	10,873
5	TOTAL S.A.	98,268	40	BT Group plc	22,059	75	Ericsson	10,663
6	NTT DoCoMo, Inc.	94,621	41	The Toronto-Dominion Bank	21,847	76	Novo Nordisk A/S	10,251
7	Novartis AG	90,906	42	BASF Aktiengesellschaft	21,797	77	Alcan Inc.	9,490
8	Toyota Motor Corporation	81,135	43	British American Tobacco	21,489	78	Veolia Environnement	9,442
9	Nokia Corporation	74,213	44	Anglo American plc	21,450	79	Gucci Group N.V.	9,418
10	Eni S.p.A.	62,820	45	France Telecom SA	21,149	80	Stora Enso Oyj	9,412
11	AstraZeneca PLC	60,320	46	Teléfonos de México	20,430	81	Akzo Nobel N.V.	9,125
12	Telecom Italia S.p.A.	56,446	47	Nomura Holdings, Inc.	20,308	82	Kyocera Corporation	9,117
13	UBS AG	55,777	48	Matsushita Electric Industrial	20,125	83	Canadian Imperial Bank	9,109
14	NTT	54,105	49	AEGON N.V.	18,534	84	WPP Group plc	8,768
15	Deutsche Telekom AG	53,278	50	Statoil ASA	17,914	85	POSCO	8,086
16	Aventis	43,323	51	Suez	17,801	86	Pearson plc	7,496
17	Telefónica, S.A.	43,049	52	The Thomson Corporation	17,405	87	AB Volvo	6,942
18	Diageo plc	41,514	53	STMicroelectronics N.V.	17,316	88	Allied Domecq PLC	6,780
19	Barclays PLC	40,607	54	Groupe Danone	17,260	89	Gallaher Group Plc	6,386
20	The News Corporation Limited	40,316	55	Vivendi Universal S.A.	17,172	90	Nortel Networks Corporation	6,199
21	BHP Billiton Limited	35,987	56	TeliaSonera AB	16,831	91	Kirin Brewery Company	5,917
22	Santander Central Hispano S.A.	33,617	57	BCE Inc.	16,495	92	Coles Myer Ltd.	5,751
23	ING Groep N.V.	33,557	58	PETROBRAS	16,226	93	Alcatel	5,615
24	Sony Corporation	32,511	59	Royal KPN N.V.	15,992	94	NEC Corporation	5,482
25	Canon Inc.	32,346	60	Repsol YPF, S.A.	15,969	95	AB Electrolux	5,362
26	Honda Motor Co., Ltd.	31,926	61	Bayer AG	15,812	96	TDK Corporation	5,082
27	Enel S.p.A.	31,104	62	Fuji Photo Film Co., Ltd.	15,563	97	SANYO Electric Co., Ltd.	5,080
28	DaimlerChrysler AG	31,042	63	Prudential plc	13,882	98	YPF, S.A.	4,787
29	Siemens AG	29,924	64	Cadbury Schweppes plc	13,170	99	Placer Dome Inc.	4,701
30	Nissan Motor Co., Ltd.	29,723	65	Grupo Televisa, S.A.	12,357	100	Sodexho Alliance, SA	4,691
31	National Australia Bank	27,836	66	Bank of Montreal	12,111			
32	E.ON AG	26,687	67	Allied Irish Banks, p.l.c.	12,061			
33	ABN AMRO Holding N.V.	25,747	68	Royal Ahold N.V.	11,853			
34	SAP Aktiengesellschaft	24,293	69	Hitachi, Ltd.	11,839			
35	Credit Suisse Group	23,750	70	Imperial Tobacco Group PLC	11,576			

*Market value at the latest available fiscal year-end

SOURCE: HOOVER'S, INC., DATABASE, DECEMBER 2003

The 100 Largest Employers in
Hoover's Handbook of World Business 2004

Rank	Company	Employees	Rank	Company	Employees	Rank	Company	Employees
1	Siemens AG	426,000	36	Koninklijke Philips Electronics	170,087	71	Karstadt Quelle AG	104,536
2	Carrefour SA	396,662	37	Toshiba Corporation	165,776	72	Olivetti S.p.A.	104,370
3	Compass Group PLC	392,352	38	Coles Myer Ltd.	165,000	73	EADS N.V.	103,967
4	Deutsche Post AG	371,912	39	Sony Corporation	161,100	74	Ernst & Young International	103,000
5	DaimlerChrysler AG	365,571	40	Accor	157,412	75	Telecom Italia S.p.A.	101,713
6	Royal Ahold N.V.	341,909	41	Fujitsu Limited	157,044	76	BMW	101,395
7	Volkswagen AG	324,892	42	Telefónica, S.A.	152,845	77	Kingfisher plc	99,879
8	Hitachi, Ltd.	320,528	43	NEC Corporation	145,807	78	KPMG International	98,000
9	Sodexho Alliance, SA	315,141	44	Woolworths Limited	145,000	79	Canon Inc.	97,802
10	OAO Gazprom	310,700	45	George Weston Limited	142,850	80	Crédit Agricole S.A.	96,500
11	Veolia Environnement	302,283	46	LG Group	140,000	81	Deutsche Lufthansa AG	94,135
12	Matsushita Electric Industrial	288,324	47	ABB Ltd.	139,051	82	Wal-Mart de México	92,708
13	Tesco PLC	270,800	48	Petróleos Mexicanos	137,134	83	Groupe Danone	92,209
14	Toyota Motor Corporation	264,096	49	Renault S.A.	132,351	84	BASF Aktiengesellschaft	89,398
15	Deutsche Telekom AG	256,000	50	RWE AG	131,765	85	BNP Paribas	87,700
16	Nestlé S.A.	254,199	51	OAO LUKOIL	130,000	86	British American Tobacco p.l.c.	85,819
17	Deutsche Bahn AG	250,690	52	Nissan Motor Co., Ltd.	127,625	87	AB Electrolux	83,347
18	Unilever	247,000	53	Honda Motor Co., Ltd.	126,900	88	Eni S.p.A.	80,655
19	France Telecom SA	243,573	54	Michelin	126,285	89	Bertelsmann AG	80,632
20	METRO AG	235,283	55	Ito-Yokado Co., Ltd.	125,400	90	SANYO Electric Co., Ltd.	79,025
21	Robert Bosch GmbH	224,341	56	PricewaterhouseCoopers	122,820	91	Deutsche Bank AG	77,442
22	Tata Group	210,443	57	Bayer AG	122,600	92	Alcatel	75,940
23	Ifi Istituto Finanziario Industriale	209,141	58	Bouygues SA	121,604	93	IKEA International A/S	75,500
24	NTT	207,363	59	TOTAL S.A.	121,469	94	MAN Aktiengesellschaft	75,054
25	Securitas AB	203,070	60	Deloitte Touche Tohmatsu	119,237	95	Schneider Electric SA	74,814
26	PSA Peugeot Citroën S.A.	198,600	61	Hutchison Whampoa Limited	117,843	96	Ricoh Company, Ltd.	74,600
27	ThyssenKrupp AG	191,254	62	Casino Guichard-Perrachon	115,757	97	Seiko Epson Corporation	73,797
28	Fiat S.p.A.	186,492	63	BP p.l.c.	115,250	98	Nippon Life Insurance	72,784
29	Tengelmann	183,638	64	Pinault-Printemps-Redoute	113,453	99	IntesaBci S.p.A.	72,683
30	SNCF	182,815	65	ING Groep N.V.	113,060	100	Fuji Photo Film Co., Ltd.	72,633
31	Anglo American plc	177,000	66	Royal Dutch/Shell Group	111,000			
32	Samsung Group	175,000	67	Jardine Matheson Holdings	110,000			
33	J Sainsbury plc	174,500	68	E.ON AG	107,856			
34	Compagnie de Saint-Gobain	172,357	69	Bridgestone Corporation	106,846			
35	Electricité de France	171,995	70	BT Group plc	104,700			

SOURCE: HOOVER'S, INC., DATABASE, DECEMBER 2003

The 100 Fastest-Growing Companies in Five-Year Sales Growth in
Hoover's Handbook of World Business 2004

Rank	Company	Annual % Change*	Rank	Company	Annual % Change	Rank	Company	Annual % Change
1	Vodafone Group PLC	72.6	36	LG Group	17.4	71	British American Tobacco p.l.c.	11.6
2	Olivetti S.p.A.	66.6	37	Centrica plc	16.6	72	Munich Re	11.4
3	Lagardère SCA	64.7	38	Imperial Oil Limited	16.6	73	SAP Aktiengesellschaft	11.3
4	Securitas AB	45.1	39	Fortis	16.5	74	Airbus S.A.S.	11.2
5	OAO LUKOIL	40.5	40	Norsk Hydro ASA	16.3	75	Foster's Group Limited	11.2
6	TOTAL S.A.	39.4	41	George Weston Limited	16.1	76	Compagnie de Saint-Gobain	11.1
7	A.P. Møller - Maersk A/S	33.5	42	Sodexho Alliance, SA	15.6	77	Nikon Corporation	11.1
8	Publicis Groupe S.A.	32.6	43	SABMiller plc	15.4	78	Karstadt Quelle AG	11.1
9	Atos Origin S.A.	29.9	44	Repsol YPF, S.A.	15.2	79	Reed Elsevier Group plc	11.1
10	Aviva plc	29.4	45	BNP Paribas	15.2	80	Eni S.p.A.	11.0
11	Gucci Group N.V.	27.3	46	Fuji Photo Film Co., Ltd.	15.1	81	PETROBRAS	11.0
12	BP p.l.c.	27.2	47	Pearson plc	15.1	82	Tesco PLC	11.0
13	GlaxoSmithKline plc	26.7	48	Virgin Group Ltd.	15.0	83	Bertelsmann AG	10.9
14	Statoil ASA	25.3	49	Interbrew S.A.	14.9	84	Kyocera Corporation	10.8
15	Logitech International S.A.	25.2	50	Porsche AG	14.6	85	Rogers Communications Inc.	10.6
16	Deutsche Post AG	24.7	51	AEGON N.V.	14.5	86	Telefónica, S.A.	10.6
17	Japan Tobacco Inc.	23.5	52	Gallaher Group Plc	14.2	87	Pinault-Printemps-Redoute	10.5
18	Compass Group PLC	23.4	53	The Asahi Shimbun Company	14.1	88	STMicroelectronics N.V.	10.4
19	Hyundai Motor Company	23.3	54	Santander Central Hispano S.A.	14.0	89	Tatung Co.	10.3
20	Carlsberg A/S	23.2	55	France Telecom SA	14.0	90	Tokyo Electron Limited	10.2
21	Carrefour SA	22.5	56	Wal-Mart de México	13.9	91	Electricité de France	10.2
22	Petróleos Mexicanos	21.8	57	IKEA International A/S	13.8	92	SAS AB	10.1
23	Anglo American plc	21.7	58	Allianz AG	13.6	93	Heineken N.V.	10.0
24	Imperial Tobacco Group PLC	21.2	59	Vivendi Universal S.A.	13.3	94	Hutchison Whampoa Limited	9.8
25	British Sky Broadcasting Group	21.1	60	Assicurazioni Generali S.p.A.	13.2	95	Tata Group	9.8
26	Royal Ahold N.V.	20.8	61	LVMH	13.1	96	Casino Guichard-Perrachon S.A.	9.7
27	Bombardier Inc.	19.4	62	ING Groep N.V.	13.0	97	PSA Peugeot Citroën S.A.	9.7
28	Sinopec	19.3	63	Samsung Group	12.9	98	Kingfisher plc	9.6
29	Nokia Corporation	19.3	64	UBS AG	12.7	99	Royal KPN N.V.	9.4
30	The Future Network plc	18.8	65	Alcan Inc.	12.6	100	Deloitte Touche Tohmatsu	9.2
31	WPP Group plc	18.6	66	Cap Gemini Ernst & Young	12.5			
32	AstraZeneca PLC	18.2	67	Scottish Power plc	12.2			
33	Hanson PLC	18.0	68	Millea Holdings, Inc.	12.0			
34	Royal Dutch/Shell Group	17.6	69	VNU N.V.	12.0			
35	IntesaBci S.p.A.	17.5	70	NTT DoCoMo, Inc.	11.7			

*These rates are compounded annualized increases, and may have resulted from acquisitions or one time gains. If less than 5 years of data are available, growth is for the years available.

SOURCE: HOOVER'S, INC., DATABASE, DECEMBER 2003

The 100 Fastest-Growing Companies in Five-Year Employment Growth in
Hoover's Handbook of World Business 2004

Rank	Company	Annual % Change*	Rank	Company	Annual % Change	Rank	Company	Annual % Change
1	Airbus S.A.S.	103.2	36	Munich Re	14.7	71	The Asahi Shimbun Company	9.1
2	Espírito Santo Financial Group	75.2	37	Virgin Group Ltd.	14.5	72	Nippon Steel Corporation	9.0
3	Olivetti S.p.A.	57.4	38	Deutsche Lufthansa AG	14.4	73	Reed Elsevier Group plc	9.0
4	Vodafone Group PLC	51.5	39	San Miguel Corporation	14.4	74	Pinault-Printemps-Redoute	8.8
5	Gallaher Group Plc	46.3	40	LVMH	14.4	75	Bertelsmann AG	8.7
6	Gucci Group N.V.	39.7	41	Repsol YPF, S.A.	14.3	76	Credit Suisse Group	8.6
7	Japan Airlines System	35.4	42	SAP Aktiengesellschaft	14.1	77	Deutsche Telekom AG	8.3
8	Imperial Tobacco Group PLC	33.2	43	UBS AG	13.4	78	ING Groep N.V.	8.1
9	Publicis Groupe S.A.	33.2	44	Pearson plc	13.3	79	Tesco PLC	8.1
10	VNU N.V.	32.9	45	ThyssenKrupp AG	13.3	80	Polski Koncern Naftowy ORLEN	7.9
11	Securitas AB	32.2	46	Casino Guichard-Perrachon S.A.	13.2	81	Dentsu Inc.	7.9
12	Atos Origin S.A.	32.1	47	Placer Dome Inc.	13.1	82	Alcan Inc.	7.5
13	Carrefour SA	31.4	48	Hanson PLC	12.5	83	AEGON N.V.	7.4
14	Dai Nippon Printing Co., Ltd.	31.3	49	Isuzu Motors Limited	12.2	84	Bombardier Inc.	7.4
15	Hutchison Whampoa Limited	31.1	50	Aventis	12.1	85	Deloitte Touche Tohmatsu	7.3
16	Yamaha Corporation	27.0	51	BNP Paribas	11.7	86	Molson Inc.	7.1
17	Compass Group PLC	26.2	52	Cap Gemini Ernst & Young	11.1	87	Otto Versand Gmbh & Co.	7.1
18	NTT DoCoMo, Inc.	25.7	53	Computacenter plc	11.0	88	SAS AB	7.0
19	Centrica plc	23.4	54	Wal-Mart de México	11.0	89	HSBC Holdings plc	6.9
20	GlaxoSmithKline plc	22.5	55	Allied Irish Banks, p.l.c.	10.9	90	METRO AG	6.7
21	TOTAL S.A.	20.7	56	Electricité de France	10.7	91	Air France	6.7
22	Interbrew S.A.	20.3	57	Mazda Motor Corporation	10.7	92	Nippon Life Insurance Company	6.7
23	IKEA International A/S	20.0	58	Telefónica, S.A.	10.7	93	Veolia Environnement	6.4
24	IntesaBci S.p.A.	19.5	59	Qantas Airways Limited	10.5	94	Quebecor Inc.	6.4
25	Allianz AG	19.2	60	Rogers Communications Inc.	10.5	95	Kingfisher plc	6.3
26	The Toronto-Dominion Bank	18.5	61	STMicroelectronics N.V.	10.3	96	PSA Peugeot Citroën S.A.	6.1
27	WPP Group plc	18.5	62	France Telecom SA	10.2	97	Sodexho Alliance, SA	6.0
28	Fuji Photo Film Co., Ltd.	17.9	63	Compagnie de Saint-Gobain	10.1	98	Kao Corporation	5.6
29	All Nippon Airways Co., Ltd.	17.4	64	Pioneer Corporation	10.0	99	Dr. Ing. h.c. F. Porsche AG	5.6
30	AstraZeneca PLC	17.1	65	Royal Ahold N.V.	9.8	100	Accor	5.5
31	Anglo American plc	16.1	66	OAO LUKOIL	9.6			
32	Tommy Hilfiger Corporation	15.8	67	Heineken N.V.	9.5			
33	Santander Central Hispano S.A.	15.8	68	Deutsche Post AG	9.5			
34	HVB Group	15.6	69	Toyota Motor Corporation	9.5			
35	Seiko Epson Corporation	15.5	70	BAE SYSTEMS	9.2			

*These rates are compounded annualized increases, and may have resulted from
acquisitions or one time gains. If less than 5 years of data are available, growth
is for the years available.

SOURCE: HOOVER'S, INC., DATABASE, DECEMBER 2003

The World's 100 Largest Public Companies by Market Value

Rank	Company	Country	Market Value* ($ mil.)
1	General Electric	US	294,206
2	Microsoft	US	283,576
3	Wal-Mart Stores	US	259,501
4	Exxon Mobil	US	251,813
5	Pfizer	US	236,203
6	Citigroup	US	222,849
7	Intel	US	187,003
8	American International Group	US	155,382
9	Royal Dutch/Shell	Netherlands/UK	154,194
10	BP	UK	151,431
11	Johnson & Johnson	US	147,194
12	International Business Machines	US	141,713
13	HSBC Holdings	UK	137,526
14	Cisco Systems	US	134,409
15	NTT DoCoMo	Japan	128,766
16	Vodafone Group	UK	124,425
17	Bank of America	US	118,613
18	GlaxoSmithKline	UK	114,811
19	Procter & Gamble	US	112,858
20	Merck	US	112,834
21	Coca-Cola	US	107,201
22	Total	France	105,437
23	Novartis	Switzerland	99,873
24	Toyota Motor	Japan	99,429
25	Berkshire Hathaway	US	98,255
26	Verizon Communications	US	96,368
27	Nestlé	Switzerland	87,872
28	Amgen	US	84,232
29	Wells Fargo	US	83,990
30	Dell Computer	US	83,803
31	Altria Group	US	83,464
32	Nokia	Finland	78,458
33	ChevronTexaco	US	77,831
34	PepsiCo	US	76,525
35	Eli Lilly	US	74,738
36	SBC Communications	US	74,671
37	Home Depot	US	73,891
38	Viacom	US	72,953
39	Roche Holding	Switzerland	72,562
40	Royal Bank of Scotland	UK	71,808
41	United Parcel Service	US	70,628
42	AOL Time Warner	US	70,219
43	Nippon Telegraph & Telephone	Japan	70,048
44	J.P. Morgan Chase	US	69,461
45	UBS	Switzerland	67,766
46	Oracle	US	67,005
47	AstraZeneca	UK	65,896
48	Comcast	US	65,380
49	Fannie Mae	US	63,483
50	Abbott Laboratories	US	62,907
51	Hewlett-Packard	US	60,785
52	ENI	Italy	60,478
53	Medtronic	US	60,234
54	Deutsche Telekom	Germany	59,935
55	Telefónica	Spain	59,540
56	American Express	US	58,790
57	Wyeth	US	56,782
58	Wachovia	US	56,699
59	Samsung Electronics	South Korea	55,843
60	3M	US	55,565
61	Unilever	Netherlands/UK	55,458
62	France Telecom	France	55,357
63	Siemens	Germany	55,153
64	Morgan Stanley	US	52,967
65	Kraft Foods	US	51,450
66	China Mobile	Hong Kong	50,571
67	Merrill Lynch	US	49,851
68	Bristol-Myers Squibb	US	49,143
69	Nissan Motor	Japan	48,412
70	Barclays	UK	47,677
71	L'Oréal	France	47,001
72	BellSouth	US	46,540
73	Bank One	US	45,791
74	US Bancorp	US	45,755
75	Orange	France	44,682
76	BNP Paribas	France	44,651
77	DuPont	US	44,440
78	Anheuser-Busch	US	43,002
79	Lowe's	US	42,695
80	BHP Billiton	Australia/UK	42,465
81	HBOS	UK	41,937
82	Canon	Japan	41,841
83	Walt Disney	US	41,839
84	Telstra	Australia	41,825
85	Goldman Sachs	US	41,554
86	Texas Instruments	US	41,243
87	Sanofi-Synthélabo	France	41,183
88	Tyco International	Bermuda	41,061
89	News Corporation	Australia	40,865
90	Grupo Santander Central Hispano	Spain	40,693
91	Genentech	US	40,506
92	Honda Motor	Japan	39,590
93	Taiwan Semiconductor	Taiwan	39,552
94	ING Group	Netherlands	38,997
95	Aventis	France	38,845
96	DaimlerChrysler	Germany	38,588
97	SAP	Germany	37,812
98	Telecom Italia Mobile	Italy	37,790
99	ConocoPhillips	US	37,743
100	United Technologies	US	37,548

*As of August 29, 2003.

SOURCE: *WALL STREET JOURNAL*, SEPTEMBER 22, 2003

The *FORTUNE* Global 500

Rank	Company	Country	2002 Sales ($ mil.)
1	Wal-Mart Stores	US	246,525.0
2	General Motors	US	186,763.0
3	Exxon Mobil	US	182,466.0
4	Royal Dutch/Shell Group	Britain/Netherlands	179,431.0
5	BP	UK	178,721.0
6	Ford Motor	US	163,871.0
7	DaimlerChrysler	Germany	141,421.1
8	Toyota Motor	Japan	131,754.2
9	General Electric	US	131,698.0
10	Mitsubishi	Japan	109,386.1
11	Mitsui	Japan	108,630.7
12	Allianz	Germany	101,930.2
13	Citigroup	US	100,789.0
14	Total	France	96,944.9
15	ChevronTexaco	US	92,043.0
16	Nippon Telegraph & Telephone	Japan	89,644.0
17	ING Group	Netherlands	88,102.3
18	Itochu	Japan	85,856.4
19	IBM	US	83,132.0
20	Volkswagen	Germany	82,203.7
21	Siemens	Germany	77,205.2
22	Sumitomo	Japan	75,745.2
23	Marubeni	Japan	72,164.8
24	Verizon Communications	US	67,625.0
25	American Intl. Group	US	67,482.0
26	Hitachi	Japan	67,228.0
27	U.S. Postal Service	US	66,463.0
28	Honda Motor	Japan	65,420.4
29	Carrefour	France	64,978.6
30	Altria Group	US	62,182.0
31	AXA	France	62,050.8
32	Sony	Japan	61,334.6
33	Nippon Life Insurance	Japan	61,174.5
34	Matsushita Electric Industrial	Japan	60,744.3
35	Royal Ahold	Netherlands	59,454.6
36	ConocoPhillips	US	58,384.0
37	Home Depot	US	58,247.0
38	Nestlé	Switzerland	57,279.1
39	McKesson	US	57,129.2
40	Hewlett-Packard	US	56,588.0
41	Nissan Motor	Japan	56,040.8
42	Vivendi Universal	France	54,977.1
43	Boeing	US	54,069.0
44	Assicurazioni Generali	Italy	53,598.9
45	Fannie Mae	US	52,901.1
46	Fiat	Italy	52,612.5
47	Deutsche Bank	Germany	52,133.2
48	Credit Suisse	Switzerland	52,121.7
49	Munich Re Group	Germany	51,980.0
50	Merck	US	51,790.3
51	Kroger	US	51,759.5
52	Peugeot	France	51,465.7
53	Cardinal Health	US	51,135.7
54	BNP Paribas	France	51,127.3
55	Deutsche Telekom	Germany	50,759.5
56	State Farm Insurance	US	49,653.7
57	Aviva	US	49,533.3
58	Metro	Germany	48,714.5
59	Samsung Electronics	South Korea	47,605.6
60	Vodafone	UK	46,987.0
61	AT&T	US	46,727.0
62	Toshiba	Japan	46,415.8
63	ENI	Italy	46,328.2
64	Bank of America Corp.	US	45,732.0
65	Électricité De France	France	45,720.3
66	Unilever	UK/Netherlands	45,636.2
67	AmerisourceBergen	US	45,234.8
68	E.ON	Germany	44,941.3
69	China National Petroleum	China	44,864.4
70	Sinopec	China	44,503.2
71	France Télécom	France	44,085.7
72	Target	US	43,917.0
73	Fortis	Belgium/Netherlands	43,597.5
74	Suez	France	43,574.9
75	J.P. Morgan Chase & Co.	US	43,372.0
76	SBC Communications	US	43,138.0
77	Dai-ichi Mutual Life Insurance	Japan	43,134.2
78	Berkshire Hathaway	US	42,353.0
79	UBS	Switzerland	42,329.7
80	AOL Time Warner	US	41,676.0
81	Sears Roebuck	US	41,366.0
82	RWE	Germany	41,114.1
83	Zurich Financial Services	Switzerland	40,638.0
84	Tesco	UK	40,387.2
85	Tokyo Electric Power	Japan	40,370.1
86	Procter & Gamble	US	40,238.0
87	BMW	Germany	39,974.9
88	Deutsche Post	Germany	39,956.0
89	HSBC Holdings	UK	39,730.0
90	Freddie Mac	US	39,663.0
91	Tyco International	US	38,971.3
92	Costco Wholesale	US	38,762.5
93	NEC	Japan	38,531.2
94	Hyundai Motor	South Korea	38,458.5
95	Pemex	Mexico	37,973.9
96	Nissho Iwai	Japan	37,907.8
97	Fujitsu	Japan	37,895.5
98	Crédit Agricole	France	36,745.3
99	HypoVereinsbank	Germany	36,355.8
100	Sumitomo Life Insurance	Japan	36,304.5

SOURCE: *FORTUNE*, JULY 21, 2003

The *FORTUNE* Global 500 (continued)

Rank	Company	Country	2002 Sales ($ mil.)	Rank	Company	Country	2002 Sales ($ mil.)
101	Johnson & Johnson	US	36,298.0	151	J. Sainsbury	UK	26,962.4
102	Royal Bank of Scotland	UK	36,035.0	152	Telefónica	Spain	26,861.0
103	Albertson's	US	35,916.0	153	Lockheed Martin	US	26,806.0
104	Prudential	Britain	35,818.6	154	Prudential Financial	US	26,797.0
105	Dell Computer	US	35,404.0	155	Intel	US	26,764.0
106	Pfizer	US	35,281.0	156	Motorola	US	26,679.0
107	Safeway	UK	34,799.2	157	Barclays	UK	26,589.4
108	SK	US	34,683.3	158	Nippon Oil	Japan	26,492.3
109	ABN AMRO Holding	Netherlands	34,590.6	159	Lowe's	US	26,490.9
110	Repsol YPF	Spain	34,498.9	160	Santander Central Hispano	Spain	26,311.6
111	Renault	France	34,353.3	161	Meiji Life Insurance	Japan	26,228.2
112	MetLife	US	34,104.0	162	Groupe Auchan	France	26,058.1
113	ThyssenKrupp	Germany	33,723.0	163	Groupe Pinault-Printemps	France	25,881.7
114	Robert Bosch	Germany	33,068.5	164	DZ Bank	Germany	25,559.8
115	Samsung	South Korea	32,960.0	165	Walt Disney	US	25,329.0
116	Morgan Stanley	US	32,415.0	166	PepsiCo	US	25,112.0
117	J.C. Penney	US	32,347.0	167	UnitedHealth Group	US	25,020.0
118	Mitsubishi Motors	Japan	31,882.4	168	International Paper	US	24,976.0
119	GlaxoSmithKline	UK	31,874.2	169	AEON	Japan	24,744.8
120	United Parcel Service	US	31,272.0	170	New York Life Insurance	US	24,720.7
121	Kmart Holding	US	30,762.0	171	Viacom	US	24,605.7
122	Statoil	Norway	30,545.4	172	DuPont	US	24,522.0
123	BASF	Germany	30,457.7	173	Société Générale	France	24,205.0
124	Royal Philips Electronics	Netherlands	30,083.8	174	CVS	US	24,181.5
125	HBOS	UK	29,911.7	175	Millea Holdings	Japan	24,037.8
126	Mitsubishi Electric	Japan	29,865.1	176	American Express	US	23,807.0
127	Olivetti	Italy	29,694.2	177	Wachovia Corp.	US	23,591.0
128	Allstate	US	29,579.0	178	Canon	Japan	23,481.3
129	Aegon	Netherlands	29,444.6	179	Archer Daniels Midland	US	23,453.6
130	BT	UK	29,301.4	180	Tyson Foods	US	23,367.0
131	Sumitomo Mitsui Financial	Japan	28,776.2	181	Sysco	US	23,350.5
132	Walgreen	US	28,681.1	182	Georgia-Pacific	US	23,271.0
133	Saint-Gobain	France	28,622.1	183	Arcelor	Luxembourg	23,194.4
134	Wells Fargo	US	28,473.0	184	KDDI	Japan	22,858.7
135	Veolia Environnement	France	28,437.5	185	ABB	Switzerland	22,855.0
136	Nokia	Japan	28,378.2	186	Goldman Sachs Group	US	22,854.0
137	Microsoft	US	28,365.0	187	Mitsubishi Tokyo Financial	Japan	22,753.6
138	Enel	Italy	28,341.3	188	Best Buy	US	22,673.0
139	EADS	France	28,269.5	189	Petrobrás	Brazil	22,612.0
140	Merrill Lynch	US	28,253.0	190	Nippon Steel	Japan	22,563.0
141	United Technologies	US	28,212.0	191	Indian Oil	India	22,506.2
142	Mizuho Financial Group	Japan	28,198.5	192	Ingram Micro	US	22,459.3
143	Bayer	Germany	28,007.6	193	BellSouth	US	22,440.0
144	ConAgra Foods	US	27,629.6	194	Foncière Euris	France	22,424.8
145	Dow Chemical	US	27,609.0	195	Lloyds TSB Group	UK	22,391.0
146	Marathon Oil	US	27,470.0	196	Standard Life Assurance	UK	22,375.6
147	Delphi	US	27,427.0	197	Honeywell Intl.	US	22,274.0
148	Ito-Yokado	Japan	27,206.6	198	Bank One Corp.	US	22,171.0
149	Sprint	US	27,180.0	199	Swiss Reinsurance	Switzerland	22,109.2
150	Valero Energy	US	26,976.3	200	Electronic Data Systems	US	21,782.0

3 1833 04610 6164

The *FORTUNE* Global 500 (continued)

Rank	Company	Country	2002 Sales ($ mil.)	Rank	Company	Country	2002 Sales ($ mil.)
201	Centrica	Japan	21,510.4	251	Crédit Lyonnais	France	18,176.9
202	Kansai Electric Power	Japan	21,462.0	252	Bristol-Myers Squibb	US	18,119.0
203	CNP Assurances	France	21,450.9	253	AstraZeneca	UK	18,032.0
204	Petronas	Malaysia	21,430.1	254	China Telecommunications	China	18,012.6
205	LG International	South Korea	21,394.2	255	British American Tobacco	UK	17,959.7
206	Mitsubishi Heavy Industries	Japan	21,287.6	256	Bridgestone	Japan	17,951.8
207	Alstom	France	21,237.1	257	Sanyo Electric	Japan	17,911.8
208	Franz Haniel	Germany	21,236.2	258	Daiei	Japan	17,884.4
209	Toyota Tsusho	Japan	21,144.4	259	Chubu Electric Power	Japan	17,858.6
210	East Japan Railway	Japan	21,055.9	260	Northrop Grumman	US	17,837.0
211	Bouygues	France	21,033.1	261	LG Electronics	South Korea	17,836.0
212	SNCF	France	20,966.0	262	Nippon Mining Holdings	Japan	17,752.0
213	BBVA	Spain	20,823.2	263	Abbott Laboratories	US	17,684.7
214	Novartis	Switzerland	20,822.5	264	Deutsche Bahn	Germany	17,665.5
215	UFJ Holdings	Japan	20,686.5	265	Dexia Group	Belgium	17,655.1
216	Alcoa	US	20,618.0	266	Sara Lee	US	17,628.0
217	FedEx	US	20,607.0	267	Fleming	US	17,561.5
218	Fuji Photo Film	Japan	20,563.8	268	Banca Intesa	Italy	17,555.8
219	Rabobank	Netherlands	20,508.4	269	George Weston	Canada	17,476.0
220	TUI	Germany	20,431.0	270	Vinci	France	17,437.5
221	Norsk Hydro	Norway	20,412.9	271	Almanij	Belgium	17,410.3
222	Mass. Mutual Life Ins.	US	20,247.1	272	WellPoint Health Networks	US	17,338.5
223	Caterpillar	US	20,152.0	273	Bertelsmann	Germany	17,312.8
224	Johnson Controls	US	20,103.4	274	AMR	US	17,299.0
225	Delhaize Group	Belgium	19,932.2	275	SK Global	South Korea	17,152.0
226	JFE Holdings	Japan	19,917.0	276	LBBW	Germany	17,138.9
227	Cigna	US	19,915.0	277	Japan Airlines System	Japan	17,098.7
228	Aetna	US	19,878.7	278	Tomen	Japan	17,093.9
229	TIAA-CREF	US	19,791.0	279	Korea Electric Power	South Korea	17,074.9
230	China Mobile Communications	Hong Kong	19,783.3	280	Raytheon	US	16,962.0
231	Commerzbank	Germany	19,763.4	281	Pharmacia	US	16,929.0
232	HCA	US	19,729.0	282	Coca-Cola Enterprises	US	16,889.0
233	Royal & Sun Alliance	UK	19,699.7	283	Loews	US	16,827.8
234	Coca-Cola	US	19,564.0	284	Lehman Brothers Hldgs.	US	16,781.0
235	Gazprom	Russia	19,551.5	285	Idemitsu Kosan	Japan	16,587.9
236	Samsung Life Insurance	South Korea	19,536.1	286	Suzuki Motor	Japan	16,539.2
237	Industrial & Commercial Bank	China	19,528.5	287	Japan Tobacco	Japan	16,475.4
238	Aventis	France	19,496.8	288	Sharp	Japan	16,439.9
239	AutoNation	US	19,478.5	289	La Poste	France	16,386.3
240	Mazda Motor	Japan	19,405.1	290	China Life Insurance	China	16,379.3
241	Groupe Caisse d'Épargne	France	19,350.2	291	3M	US	16,332.0
242	Supervalu	US	19,160.4	292	Kingfisher	UK	16,282.1
243	Volvo	Sweden	19,158.8	293	Banco Bradesco	Brazil	16,125.2
244	Denso	Japan	19,144.5	294	Adecco	Switzerland	16,116.0
245	Roche Group	Switzerland	19,096.2	295	Yasuda Mutual Life Insurance	Japan	16,105.4
246	Washington Mutual	US	19,037.0	296	Lufthansa Group	Germany	16,045.4
247	Cisco Systems	US	18,915.0	297	Nationwide	US	15,949.3
248	Sinochem	China	18,763.0	298	Asahi Mutual Life Insurance	Japan	15,933.4
249	Weyerhaeuser	US	18,521.0	299	Publix	US	15,930.6
250	Visteon	US	18,395.0	300	Northwestern Mutual	US	15,916.4

The *FORTUNE* Global 500 (continued)

Rank	Company	Country	2002 Sales ($ mil.)
301	Hartford Fin. Services	US	15,907.0
302	BHP Billiton	Australia	15,906.0
303	FleetBoston Financial	US	15,868.0
304	Xerox	US	15,849.0
305	Endesa	Spain	15,825.6
306	Rite Aid	US	15,800.9
307	Mitsui Sumitomo Insurance	Japan	15,760.2
308	Abbey National	UK	15,744.8
309	Tech Data	US	15,738.9
310	Duke Energy	US	15,663.0
311	Alcatel	France	15,644.1
312	AT&T Wireless Services	US	15,632.0
313	Compass Group	UK	15,609.6
314	American Electric Power	US	15,583.0
315	AdvancePCS	US	15,540.5
316	Nichimen	Japan	15,495.5
317	Mitsubishi Chemical	Japan	15,490.3
318	Qwest Communications	US	15,487.0
319	Federated Dept. Stores	US	15,435.0
320	U.S. Bancorp	US	15,422.3
321	McDonald's	US	15,405.7
322	Kajima	Japan	15,386.1
323	Sun Life Financial Services	Canada	15,311.1
324	Bayerische Landesbank	Germany	15,307.9
325	Michelin	France	15,221.7
326	News Corp.	Australia	15,183.5
327	Man Group	Germany	15,164.8
328	Anglo American	UK	15,145.0
329	Bombardier	Canada	15,115.9
330	Kookmin Bank	South Korea	15,075.3
331	UniCredito Italiano	Italy	15,033.5
332	Bank Of China	China	15,030.9
333	L.M. Ericsson	Sweden	14,999.3
334	Skanska	Sweden	14,979.0
335	Exelon	US	14,955.0
336	KarstadtQuelle	Germany	14,951.7
337	Royal Bank of Canada	Canada	14,771.7
338	Banco Do Brasil	Brazil	14,679.2
339	Household International	US	14,671.6
340	Wyeth	US	14,584.0
341	Liberty Mutual Insurance	US	14,544.0
342	Gap	US	14,454.7
343	Lear	US	14,424.6
344	Onex	Canada	14,424.1
345	Hyundai	South Korea	14,323.7
346	UAL	US	14,286.0
347	Ricoh	Japan	14,266.3
348	Sompo Japan Insurance	Japan	14,261.7
349	Cendant	US	14,243.0
350	Swiss Life Ins. & Pension	Switzerland	14,124.5
351	National Australia Bank	Australia	14,109.6
352	TXU	US	14,086.0
353	Bunge	US	14,074.0
354	Deere	US	13,947.0
355	Tenet Healthcare	US	13,913.0
356	Dentsu	Japan	13,893.7
357	General Dynamics	US	13,863.0
358	Goodyear Tire & Rubber	US	13,850.0
359	Schlumberger	US	13,824.7
360	Emerson Electric	US	13,824.0
361	Lafarge	France	13,812.8
362	PG&E Corp.	US	13,784.0
363	Nippon Express	Japan	13,762.1
364	Gaz de France	France	13,752.3
365	Electrolux	Sweden	13,700.4
366	Old Mutual	South Africa	13,650.1
367	Groupama	France	13,648.3
368	Lucent Technologies	US	13,568.0
369	Anheuser-Busch	US	13,566.4
370	Kimberly-Clark	US	13,566.3
371	China Construction Bank	China	13,539.4
372	Coles Myer	Australia	13,537.7
373	L'Oréal	France	13,508.4
374	Mitsui Mutual Life Insurance	Japan	13,508.1
375	Taisei	Japan	13,497.2
376	May Dept. Stores	US	13,491.0
377	Lukoil	Russia	13,453.0
378	Flextronics International	Singapore	13,378.7
379	Safeway	UK	13,363.2
380	Delta Air Lines	US	13,305.0
381	Anthem	US	13,282.3
382	Legal & General Group	UK	13,239.8
383	Akzo Nobel	Netherlands	13,238.0
384	COFCO	China	13,218.1
385	Diageo	UK	13,215.9
386	KT	South Korea	13,101.5
387	Tohoku Electric Power	Japan	13,080.3
388	Woolworths	Australia	13,075.0
389	Cathay Life	Taiwan	13,071.5
390	BCE	Canada	13,020.7
391	Magna International	Canada	12,971.0
392	Migros	Switzerland	12,968.7
393	Winn-Dixie Stores	US	12,942.9
394	Eastman Kodak	US	12,841.0
395	Royal Mail Group	UK	12,837.7
396	Groupe Danone	France	12,815.4
397	Otto Versand	Germany	12,771.4
398	Shimizu	Japan	12,717.5
399	Air France Group	France	12,619.3
400	Halliburton	US	12,572.0

The *FORTUNE* Global 500 (continued)

Rank	Company	Country	2002 Sales ($ mil.)	Rank	Company	Country	2002 Sales ($ mil.)
401	Sunoco	US	12,550.0	451	Humana	US	11,261.2
402	Alcan	US	12,540.0	452	Central Japan Railway	Taiwan	11,186.1
403	El Paso	US	12,503.0	453	PacifiCare Health Sys.	US	11,156.5
404	Sun Microsystems	US	12,496.0	454	Waste Management	US	11,142.0
405	Lagardère Groupe	France	12,495.3	455	TPG	Netherlands	11,139.1
406	Marks & Spencer	UK	12,494.6	456	Eli Lilly	US	11,077.5
407	Union Pacific	US	12,491.0	457	Isuzu Motors	Japan	11,074.6
408	Comcast	US	12,460.0	458	GUS	UK	11,054.1
409	Dior (Christian)	France	12,449.5	459	Whirlpool	US	11,016.0
410	San Paolo IMI	Italy	12,337.0	460	Obayashi	Japan	11,005.3
411	RAG	Germany	12,314.7	461	Yukos	Russia	10,914.0
412	Solectron	US	12,276.2	462	Telstra	Australia	10,886.0
413	Itaúsa-Investimentos Itaú	Brazil	12,273.7	463	Seiko Epson	Japan	10,853.1
414	Express Scripts	US	12,260.6	464	Canadian Imperial Bank	Canada	10,835.8
415	FirstEnergy	US	12,247.4	465	Edeka Zentrale	Germany	10,818.2
416	Sumitomo Electric Industries	Japan	12,219.2	466	Corus Group	UK	10,801.0
417	BAE Systems	UK	12,135.4	467	Great Atl. & Pacific Tea	US	10,794.4
418	Power Corp. of Canada	Canada	12,108.9	468	Continental AG	Germany	10,785.8
419	Stora Enso	Finland	12,085.1	469	Dai Nippon Printing	Japan	10,742.7
420	Nordea	Sweden	12,068.5	470	Nortel Networks	Canada	10,701.0
421	Alliance Unichem	UK	12,056.5	471	Kinki Nippon Railway	Japan	10,698.2
422	LVMH	France	12,000.4	472	Textron	US	10,658.0
423	Norinchukin Bank	Japan	11,992.4	473	Asahi Glass	Japan	10,627.9
424	Cinergy	US	11,990.1	474	Marriott International	US	10,619.0
425	TJX	US	11,981.2	475	Manpower	US	10,610.9
426	Edison		11,950.3	476	Toronto-Dominion Bank	Canada	10,597.5
427	Amerada Hess	US	11,932.0	477	Southern	US	10,549.0
428	Royal KPN	Netherlands	11,929.5	478	Fortum	Finland	10,539.7
429	British Airways	UK	11,892.6	479	Manulife Financial	Canada	10,526.6
430	Carso Global Telecom	Mexico	11,681.9	480	Thales Group	France	10,499.1
431	Kyushu Electric Power	Japan	11,664.4	481	Kreditanstalt für Wiederaufbau	Germany	10,492.8
432	Bank of Nova Scotia	Canada	11,633.1	482	Sekisui House	Japan	10,481.1
433	Cosmo Oil	Japan	11,609.6	483	Kuraya Sanseido	Japan	10,459.6
434	Staples	US	11,596.1	484	Marsh & McLennan	US	10,440.0
435	Wolseley	UK	11,586.2	485	MBNA	US	10,430.9
436	Accenture	US	11,574.3	486	Vattenfall	Sweden	10,394.9
437	WestLB	Germany	11,573.5	487	AES	US	10,346.0
438	Edison International	US	11,562.0	488	Agricultural Bank of China	China	10,335.3
439	Reliant Resources	US	11,558.0	489	Resona Holdings	Japan	10,334.5
440	Aisin Seiki	Japan	11,555.3	490	Dana	US	10,283.0
441	Sodexho Alliance	France	11,517.3	491	Gasunie	Netherlands	10,282.2
442	Taiyo Mutual Life Insurance	Japan	11,504.6	492	Toppan Printing	Japan	10,271.7
443	POSCO	South Korea	11,472.1	493	AFLAC	US	10,257.0
444	Office Depot	US	11,437.5	494	Xcel Energy	US	10,253.8
445	Pechiney	France	11,395.3	495	Nippon Yusen	Japan	10,252.3
446	Eurohypo	Germany	11,389.1	496	Dominion Resources	US	10,218.0
447	Tokyu	Japan	11,370.0	497	Health Net	US	10,201.5
448	Computer Sciences	US	11,346.5	498	Fluor	US	10,190.4
449	Toys "R" Us	US	11,305.0	499	Schering-Plough	US	10,180.0
450	Fuji Heavy Industries	Japan	11,262.5	500	Kawasaki Heavy Industries	Japan	10,173.1

Business Week's Information Technology 100

Rank	Company	Revenue ($ mil.)	Rank	Company	Revenue ($ mil.)
1	Nextel Communications	9,135.0	51	QUALCOMM	3,785.0
2	Dell Computer	36,870.0	52	Telecom Italia	32,983.4
3	Samsung Electronics	50,216.4	53	Unisys	5,643.8
4	PT Telekomunikasi Indonesia	2,605.0	54	Automatic Data Processing	10,347.5
5	Nokia	32,454.8	55	Symantec	1,406.9
6	Western Digital	2,578.9	56	Synnex Technology International	2,422.1
7	IBM	83,221.0	57	Wanadoo	2,175.1
8	Hon Hai Precision Ind.	7,428.4	58	L-3 Communications Holdings	4,403.4
9	Vodafone Group	47,962.1	59	TeliaSonera	6,823.9
10	Hewlett-Packard	70,444.0	60	Yahoo!	1,043.4
11	Yahoo! Japan	500.5	61	Lite-On Technology	3,850.1
12	Oracle	9,417.0	62	Benq	3,179.0
13	First Data	7,904.9	63	NTT DoCoMo	40,730.8
14	Seagate Technology	6,406.0	64	KDDI	23,590.6
15	Mobile TeleSystems	1,361.8	65	AT&T Wireless Services	15,968.0
16	Compal Electronics	3,377.7	66	Telstra	14,416.0
17	University of Phoenix Online	418.2	67	LG Electronics	18,079.7
18	Microsoft	31,375.0	68	Overture Services	749.6
19	Orange	18,954.0	69	Sharp	16,966.3
20	Rogers Communications	3,036.1	70	BellSouth	22,429.0
21	STET Hellas Telecommunications	794.8	71	KT Freetel	4,512.6
22	Canon	25,436.6	72	Affiliated Computer Services	3,689.5
23	BCE (Bell Canada Enterprises)	13,479.4	73	Pioneer	6,032.6
24	Lexmark International	4,414.2	74	Infosys Technologies	753.8
25	Expedia	673.4	75	Telenor	6,856.1
26	France Telecom	51,668.2	76	Anteon International	861.8
27	China Mobile (Hong Kong)	15,526.7	77	Asustek Computer	3,305.5
28	VimpelCom	768.5	78	Neopost	822.6
29	Level 3 Communications	4,012.0	79	Ricoh	14,723.1
30	TDC	7,766.3	80	Hutchinson Technology	464.3
31	Verizon Communications	67,529.0	81	TELUS	4,797.3
32	Hotels.com	1,057.1	82	Intel	26,734.0
33	USA Interactive	5,041.3	83	Amphenol	1,083.8
34	Quanta Computer	4,465.4	84	Acer	3,093.7
35	América Móvil	5,786.3	85	MSI	1,628.4
36	Accenture	11,428.5	86	China Unicom	4,908.2
37	UTStarcom	1,128.6	87	Benchmark Electronics	1,749.3
38	eBay	1,445.5	88	CDW Computer Centers	4,279.4
39	Electronic Arts	2,482.2	89	Logitech International	1,100.3
40	SAP	7,929.8	90	CASIO COMPUTER	3,731.4
41	SBC Communications	42,949.0	91	CenturyTel	2,129.6
42	Teléfonos de México	10,456.8	92	STMicroelectronics	6,580.0
43	SanDisk	623.1	93	SunGard Data Systems	2,659.6
44	SK Telecom	7,860.1	94	Taiwan Semiconductor	4,766.0
45	Cisco Systems	19,005.0	95	TPV Technology	1,506.2
46	Amazon.com	4,169.1	96	CGI Group	1,667.4
47	ALLTEL	8,056.3	97	Turkcell Iletisim Hizmetleri	2,027.8
48	Tele2	3,844.6	98	Storage Technology	2,063.7
49	Japan Telecom	15,219.1	99	Intuit	1,602.8
50	Elitegroup Computer Systems	1,951.3	100	Fiserv	2,643.5

Note: Rank based on shareholder return, return on equity, revenue growth, and total revenue (revenue for the most recent four quarters available; most recent FY for those companies that do not report quarterly results).

SOURCE: *BUSINESSWEEK*, JUNE 23, 2003

The World's 50 Largest Public Financial Companies

Rank	Company	Country	Assets* ($ mil.)
1	Mizuho Financial Group	Japan	1,128,174
2	Citigroup	US	1,097,190
3	Allianz	Germany	893,722
4	Fannie Mae	US	887,515
5	Sumitomo Mitsui Financial	Japan	880,497
6	UBS	Switzerland	852,618
7	Mitsubishi Tokyo Financial	Japan	834,774
8	Deutsche Bank	Germany	791,348
9	HSBC Holdings	UK	759,246
10	J.P. Morgan Chase	US	758,800
11	ING Group	Netherlands	751,400
12	BNP Paribas	France	744,016
13	Bayerische Hypo Bank	Germany	724,955
14	Freddie Mac	US	721,739
15	Credit Suisse	Switzerland	682,945
16	UFJ Holdings	Japan	675,118
17	Royal Bank of Scotland	UK	663,927
18	Bank of America	US	660,458
19	Barclays	UK	649,442
20	ABN Amro	Netherlands	581,610
21	HBOS	UK	572,175
22	American International Group	US	561,229
23	Credit Agricole	France	530,235
24	Morgan Stanley	US	529,499
25	Societe Generale de France	France	525,777
26	Fortis Group	Belgium/Netherlands	509,519
27	AXA	France	466,401
28	Merrill Lynch	US	447,928
29	Commerzbank	Germany	442,776
30	Lloyds TSB Group	UK	407,284
31	Dexia	Belgium	368,084
32	Resona Holdings	Japan	361,028
33	Goldman Sachs	US	354,774
34	Wells Fargo	US	349,259
35	Wachovia	US	341,839
36	Santander Central Hispano	Spain	340,062
37	Abbey National	UK	331,514
38	Aviva	UK	297,999
39	Banca Intesa	Italy	294,461
40	BBVA	Spain	293,212
41	Prudential Financial	US	292,746
42	Zurich Financial Services	Switzerland	285,856
43	MetLife	US	277,385
44	Bank One	US	277,383
45	Washington Mutual	US	268,298
46	Almanij	Belgium	265,141
47	Nordea	Sweden	261,825
48	Lehman Brothers	US	260,336
49	Aegon	Netherlands	249,854
50	Danske Bank	Denmark	247,671

*Fiscal year 2002 (fiscal year 2003 for Japanese companies).

SOURCE: *WALL STREET JOURNAL*, SEPTEMBER 22, 2003

The World's Top 50 Emerging-Market Companies

Rank	Company	Country	Market Value ($ mil.)
1	China Mobile (Hong Kong)	China	44,899
2	Samsung Electronics	Korea	44,188
3	PetroChina	China	43,512
4	Gazprom	Russia	42,731
5	Sinopec	China	35,696
6	Taiwan Semiconductor Mfg.	Taiwan	28,713
7	YUKOS	Russia	28,186
8	Anglo American	South Africa	22,903
9	PETROBRAS	Brazil	20,435
10	Teléfonos de México	Mexico	19,442
11	China Telecom	China	16,386
12	LUKOIL Holding	Russia	15,659
13	Oil & Natural Gas	India	14,478
14	Chunghwa Telecom	Taiwan	13,846
15	Teva Pharmaceutical	Israel	13,351
16	SK Telecom	Korea	13,343
17	Wal-Mart de Mexico	Mexico	12,589
18	BBVA Bancomer	Mexico	12,180
19	Surgutneftegaz	Russia	11,867
20	Sibneft	Russia	11,853
21	América Móvil	Mexico	11,804
22	CNOOC	China	11,481
23	Korea Telecom	Korea	11,321
24	Vale do Rio Doce	Brazil	11,210
25	Korea Electric Power	Korea	10,589
26	NR Huaneng Power	China	10,252
27	RAO Unified Energy System	Russia	9,782
28	United Microelectronics	Taiwan	9,722
29	Cathay Financial Holdings	Taiwan	9,696
30	Kookmin Bank	Korea	9,309
31	Reliance Industries	India	8,868
32	Malayan Banking	Malaysia	8,047
33	Sasol	South Africa	7,814
34	China Unicom	China	7,444
35	Banco Itaú	Brazil	7,378
36	Cemex	Mexico	7,375
37	Hindustan Lever	India	7,369
38	AmBev	Brazil	7,329
39	Pohang Iron & Steel (POSCO)	Korea	7,303
40	Tenaga Nasional	Malaysia	7,288
41	Anglo American Platinum	South Africa	7,263
42	Hon Hai Precision Industries	Taiwan	6,903
43	Fubon Financial Holding	Taiwan	6,475
44	Nan Ya Plastics	Taiwan	6,465
45	Telekom Malaysia	Malaysia	6,459
46	Anglogold	South Africa	6,315
47	COPEC	Chile	6,237
48	Jiangsu Expressway	China	6,049
49	Hyundai Motor	Korea	5,992
50	Formosa Plastics	Taiwan	5,946

SOURCE: *BUSINESSWEEK*, JULY 14, 2003

The World's Top 20 Electronics Companies

Rank	Company	Electronics Revenue ($ mil.)	Total Revenue ($ mil.)
1	IBM	81,186.0	81,186.0
2	Hewlett-Packard	63,083.0	63,083.0
3	Matsushita Electric Industrial	57,872.0	57,872.0
4	Siemens	46,165.4	82,438.2
5	NEC	39,183.5	39,183.5
6	Fujitsu	37,646.4	37,646.4
7	Sony	36,466.6	56,979.0
8	Dell Computer	35,404.0	35,404.0
9	Toshiba	34,533.7	41,111.6
10	Samsung Electronics	33,880.2	33,880.2
11	Nokia	31,465.8	31,465.8
12	Microsoft	30,785.0	30,785.0
13	Hitachi	30,739.3	60,273.1
14	Intel	26,764.0	26,764.0
15	Motorola	26,679.0	26,679.0
16	Canon	24,501.1	24,501.1
17	Philips Electronics	24,017.0	33,356.9
18	Ingram Micro	22,459.3	22,459.3
19	Electronic Data Systems	21,502.0	21,502.0
20	Cisco Systems	19,209.0	19,209.0

*For the four quarters ending closest to December 21, 2002

SOURCE: *ELECTRONIC BUSINESS*, AUGUST 1, 2003

The World's Top 20 Motor Vehicle and Parts Manufacturers

Rank	Company	Country	2002 Revenue ($ mil.)
1	General Motors	US	186,763
2	Ford Motor	US	163,871
3	DaimlerChrysler	Germany	141,421
4	Toyota Motor	Japan	131,754
5	Volkswagen	Germany	82,204
6	Honda Motor	Japan	65,420
7	Nissan Motor	Japan	56,041
8	Fiat	Italy	52,613
9	Peugeot	France	51,466
10	BMW	Germany	39,975
11	Hyundai Motor	South Korea	38,459
12	Renault	France	34,353
13	Robert Bosch	Germany	33,069
14	Mitsubishi Motors	Japan	31,882
15	Delphi	US	27,427
16	Johnson Controls	US	20,103
17	Mazda Motor	Japan	19,405
18	Volvo	Sweden	19,159
19	Denso	Japan	19,145
20	Visteon	US	18,395

SOURCE: *FORTUNE*, JULY 21, 2003

The World's Top 20 Telecommunications Companies

Rank	Company	Country	2002 Revenue ($ mil.)
1	Nippon Telegraph & Telephone	Japan	89,644
2	Verizon Communications	US	67,625
3	Deutsche Telekom	Germany	50,760
4	Vodafone	UK	46,987
5	AT&T	US	46,727
6	France Télécom	France	44,086
7	SBC Communications	US	43,138
8	Olivetti	Italy	29,694
9	BT	UK	29,301
10	Sprint	US	27,180
11	Telefónica	Spain	26,861
12	KDDI	Japan	22,859
13	BellSouth	US	22,440
14	China Mobile Communications	China	19,783
15	China Telecommunications	China	18,013
16	Alcatel	France	15,644
17	AT&T Wireless Services	US	15,632
18	Qwest Communications	US	15,487
19	KT	South Korea	13,102
20	BCE	Canada	13,021

SOURCE: *FORTUNE*, JULY 21, 2003

The World's Top 20 Advertising Organizations

Rank	Company	Headquarters	Revenue ($ mil.)
1	Omnicom Group	New York	$7,536.3
2	Interpublic Group of Cos.	New York	6,203.6
3	WPP Group	London	5,781.5
4	Publicis Groupe	Paris	2,711.9
5	Dentsu	Tokyo	2,060.9
6	Havas	Suresnes, France	1,841.6
7	Grey Global Group	New York	1,199.7
8	Hakuhodo	Tokyo	860.8
9	Cordiant Communications	London	788.5
10	Asatsu-DK	Tokyo	339.5
11	TMP Worldwide	New York	335.3
12	Carlson Marketing Group	Minneapolis	328.5
13	Incepta Group	London	240.9
14	Protocol Marketing Group	Deerfield, IL	225.0
15	Digitas	Boston	203.9
16	Daiko Advertising	Osaka	192.2
17	Tokyu Agency	Tokyo	180.4
18	Maxxcom	Toronto	169.5
19	Cheil Communications	Seoul	165.0
20	George P. Johnson Co.	Auburn Hills, MI	149.3

SOURCE: *ADVERTISING AGE*, APRIL 21, 2003

The World's Top 10 Aerospace and Defense Companies

Rank	Company	Country	2002 Revenue ($ mil.)
1	Boeing	US	54,069
2	EADS	Netherlands	28,270
3	United Technologies	US	28,212
4	Lockheed Martin	US	26,806
5	Honeywell International	US	22,274
6	Northrop Grumman	US	17,837
7	Raytheon	US	16,962
8	Bombardier	Canada	15,116
9	General Dynamics	US	13,863
10	BAE Systems	UK	12,135

SOURCE: *FORTUNE*, JULY 21, 2003

The World's Top 10 Petroleum Refining Companies

Rank	Company	Country	2002 Revenue ($ mil.)
1	Exxon Mobil	US	182,466
2	Royal Dutch/Shell Group	UK/Netherlands	179,431
3	BP	UK	178,721
4	Total	France	96,945
5	ChevronTexaco	US	92,043
6	ConocoPhillips	US	58,384
7	ENI	Italy	46,328
8	China National Petroleum	China	44,864
9	Sinopec	China	44,503
10	SK	South Korea	34,683

SOURCE: *FORTUNE*, JULY 21, 2003

The World's Top 10 Energy Companies

Rank	Company	Country	2002 Revenue ($ mil.)
1	Suez	France	43,575
2	RWE	Germany	41,114
3	Gazprom	Russia	19,552
4	American Electric Power	US	15,583
5	TXU	US	14,086
6	El Paso	US	12,503
7	Cinergy	US	11,990
8	Edison	Italy	11,950
9	Reliant Resources	US	11,558
10	Gasunie	Netherlands	10,282

SOURCE: *FORTUNE*, JULY 21, 2003

The World's Top 10 Electric and Gas Utilities

Rank	Company	Country	2002 Revenue ($ mil.)
1	Electricité De France	France	45,720
2	Tokyo Electric Power	Japan	40,370
3	Enel	Italy	28,341
4	Centrica	UK	21,510
5	Kansai Electric Power	Japan	21,462
6	Chubu Electric Power	Japan	17,859
7	Korea Electric Power	South Korea	17,075
8	Endesa	Spain	15,826
9	Duke Energy	US	15,663
10	Exelon	US	14,955

SOURCE: *FORTUNE*, JULY 21, 2003

The World's Top 10 Pharmaceutical Companies

Rank	Company	Country	2002 Revenue ($ mil.)
1	Merck	US	51,790
2	Johnson & Johnson	US	36,298
3	Pfizer	US	35,281
4	GlaxoSmithKline	UK	31,874
5	Novartis	Switzerland	20,823
6	Aventis	France	19,497
7	Roche Group	Switzerland	19,096
8	Bristol-Myers Squibb	US	18,119
9	AstraZeneca	UK	18,032
10	Abbott Laboratories	US	17,685

SOURCE: *FORTUNE*, JULY 21, 2003

Forbes' "Richest People in the World" by Net Worth

Rank	Name	Net Worth ($ bil.)	Country	What
1	Gates, William H. III	40.7	United States	Microsoft Corp.
2	Buffett, Warren E.	30.5	United States	Berkshire Hathaway
3	Albrecht, Karl & Theo	25.6	Germany	Retail
4	Allen, Paul G.	20.1	United States	Microsoft Corp.
5	Alsaud, Prince Alwaleed Bin Talal	17.7	Saudi Arabia	Investments
6	Ellison, Lawrence J.	16.6	United States	Oracle Corp.
7	Walton, Alice L.	16.5	United States	Wal-Mart Stores
7	Walton, Helen R.	16.5	United States	Wal-Mart Stores
7	Walton, Jim C.	16.5	United States	Wal-Mart Stores
7	Walton, John T.	16.5	United States	Wal-Mart Stores
7	Walton, S. Robson	16.5	United States	Wal-Mart Stores
12	Bettencourt, Liliane	14.5	France	L'Oréal
13	Thomson, Kenneth & family	14.0	Canada	Publishing
14	Kamprad, Ingvar	13.0	Sweden	IKEA
15	Rausing, Birgit & family	12.9	Sweden	Packaging
16	Ballmer, Steven A.	11.1	United States	Microsoft Corp.
17	Kluge, John W.	10.5	United States	Media
18	Anthony, Barbara Cox	10.3	United States	Media
18	Chambers, Anne Cox	10.3	United States	Media
18	Ortega, Amancio	10.3	Spain	Apparel
21	Mars, Forrest E. Jr.	10.0	United States	Candy
21	Mars, Jacqueline	10.0	United States	Candy
21	Mars, John F.	10.0	United States	Candy
24	Dell, Michael	9.8	United States	Dell Computer
25	Johnson, Abigail	8.2	United States	Mutual Funds
26	Khodorkovsky, Mikhail B.	8.0	Russia	Oil
26	Redstone, Sumner M.	8.0	United States	Viacom
28	Li Ka-shing	7.8	Hong Kong	Diversified
29	Newhouse, Donald E.	7.7	United States	Media
29	Newhouse, Samuel I. Jr.	7.7	United States	Media
29	Rausing, Hans	7.7	Sweden	Packaging
32	Pritzker, Robert A.	7.6	United States	Hotels
32	Pritzker, Thomas J.	7.6	United States	Hotels
34	Grosvenor, Gerald Cavendish	7.5	UK	Real Estate
35	Slim Helu, Carlos	7.4	Mexico	Telecom
36	Johnson, Samuel C.	7.3	United States	Floor wax
37	Saji, Nobutada & family	7.1	Japan	Beverages
38	Soros, George	7.0	United States	Hedge Funds
39	Olayan, Khaled, Hayat, Hutham, Lubna & Mary	6.9	Saudi Arabia	Investments
40	Arnault, Bernard	6.7	France	LVMH
40	Persson, Stefan	6.7	Sweden	Retail
42	Kwok, Walter, Thomas & Raymond	6.6	Hong Kong	Real Estate
43	Weston, Galen & family	6.2	Canada	Retail
44	Warner, H. Ty	6.0	United States	Toys
45	Berlusconi, Silvio	5.9	Italy	Media
45	Ergen, Charles	5.9	United States	Satellite TV
45	Premji, Azim	5.9	India	Software
48	Icahn, Carl	5.8	United States	Investments
49	Abramovich, Roman A.	5.7	Russia	Oil
49	Engelhorn, Curt	5.7	Germany	Drugs

SOURCE: FORBES, FEBRUARY 27, 2003

Hoover's Handbook of

World
Business

The Companies

ABB Ltd.

ABB is more than just a big business; it's a bunch of businesses (just not as many as before). Restructured into two major divisions, power technologies and automation technologies, the company serves a broad range of utility, industrial, and commercial customers. ABB's power technologies division supplies the power supply industry with products, systems, and services for transmission, distribution, and automation. It has the largest market share for generator circuit breakers for power plants. ABB's automation technologies unit provides products and services for control, motion, protection, and plant integration for process plants and utilities. ABB's oil, gas, and petrochemicals unit is up for sale.

To help cut down on more than $4 billion in debt, ABB has been selling some of its operations and cutting its workforce. The group has also consolidated its business area segments. Its new power technologies division combined its former power technology products and utilities divisions, and its automation technologies division combined its former automation technology products and industries divisions.

In the past few years ABB has been hit by controversial executive pension payments, a costly asbestos liability charge, underperforming operations, and a plummeting stock price. Almost in tandem with ABB's falling share price has been the rapid descent of Swiss financier Martin Ebner, who resigned from ABB's board in 2002. Ebner had been ABB's largest investor before Investor AB, the investment vehicle of Sweden's Wallenberg family, increased its stake from nearly 7% to almost 11%.

HISTORY

Asea Brown Boveri (ABB) was formed in 1988 when two giants, ASEA AB of Sweden and BBC Brown Boveri of Switzerland, combined their electrical engineering and equipment businesses. Percy Barnevik, head of ASEA, became CEO.

ASEA was born in Stockholm in 1883 when Ludwig Fredholm founded Electriska Aktiebolaget to manufacture an electric dynamo created by engineer Jonas Wenstrom. In 1890 the company merged with Wenstrom's brother's firm to form Allmanna Svenska Electriska Aktiebolaget (ASEA), a pioneer in industrial electrification. Early in the 1900s ASEA began its first railway electrification project. By the 1920s it was providing locomotives and other equipment to Sweden's national railway, and by the next decade ASEA was one of Sweden's largest electric equipment manufacturers. In 1962 it bought 20% of appliance maker Electrolux. ASEA created the nuclear power venture ASEA-ATOM with the Swedish government in 1968 and bought full control in 1982.

BBC Brown Boveri was formed in 1891 as the Brown, Boveri, and Company partnership between Charles Brown and Walter Boveri in Baden, Switzerland. It made power generation equipment and produced the first steam turbines in Europe in 1900. BBC entered Germany (1893), France (1894), and Italy (1903) and diversified into nuclear power equipment after WWII.

By 1988 BBC, the bigger company, had a West German network that ASEA, the more profitable company, coveted. Both had US joint ventures. In an unusual merger, ASEA (which became ABB AB) and BBC (later ABB AG) continued as separate entities sharing equal ownership of ABB. Barnevik crafted a unique decentralized management structure under which national subsidiaries were closely linked to their local customers and labor forces. In six years ABB took over more than 150 companies worldwide.

An ABB-led consortium built one of the world's largest hydroelectric plants in Iran in 1992, and in 1995 ABB merged its transportation segment into Adtranz (a joint venture with Daimler-Benz, now DaimlerChrysler) to form the world's #1 maker of trains.

Tragedy struck in 1996. Robert Donovan, CEO of ABB's US subsidiary, died in a plane crash along with Commerce Secretary Ron Brown and other executives on a trade mission. Donovan's death hastened the US unit's restructuring.

In 1997 Barnevik gave up the title of CEO, remaining as chairman, and was succeeded by Göran Lindahl, an engineer who had worked his way up the ranks at ASEA. (Barnevik remained chairman until 2001.) After 1997 profits dipped drastically, Lindahl scrapped Barnevik's vaunted regional matrix structure in favor of one organized by product areas.

In 1999 ABB acquired Elsag Bailey, a Dutch maker of industrial control systems, for about $1.5 billion, and sold its 50% stake in Adtranz to DaimlerChrysler. ABB and France's Alstom combined their power generation businesses to form the world's largest power plant equipment maker. That year ABB AB and ABB AG were at last united under a single stock.

ABB scaled back its power plant-related activities in 2000. The company sold its nuclear power business to BNFL and its 50% stake in ABB Alstom Power to ALSTOM for $1.2 billion. In 2001 Lindahl resigned and Jörgen Centerman, head of the company's automation business, replaced him.

Also in 2001 ABB acquired French company Entrelec, a supplier of industrial automation and control products. With economic slowdowns occurring in the company's key markets, ABB announced plans to cut 12,000 jobs, or about 8% of its workforce, over 18 months. Later that year, amid rising numbers of asbestos claims against US subsidiary Combustion Engineering, ABB took a $470 million fourth-quarter charge to cover asbestos liabilities. The claims charged asbestos exposures stemming from products supplied before the mid-1970s by Combustion Engineering, which ABB had acquired in 1990.

In early 2002 ABB found itself embroiled in controversy after revealing not only a record loss but also payments of large pensions to former chairman Barnevik and former chief executive Lindahl. The former executives agreed that year to return a part (about $82 million) of their pension payoffs to ABB. That year the company, which faced $4.4 billion in debts after industry slumps had affected its sales of power systems and equipment, industrial automation, and controls, agreed to sell part of its financial services unit to GE Commercial Finance for $2.3 billion.

The day after the company sold its structured finances unit, ABB's chief executive, Jörgen Centerman, resigned and was replaced by the chairman, Jürgen Dormann.

In 2003, as part of its settlement with asbestos plaintiffs, ABB placed Combustion Engineering into bankruptcy. Later that same year the company announced that it would sell its reinsurance business to the Bermuda-based White Mountains for a reported $425 million.

EXECUTIVES

Chairman and CEO: Jürgen Dormann, age 63
EVP and CFO: Peter Voser, age 45
EVP Human Resources: Gary Steel, age 51
EVP Power Technology Products: Peter Smits, age 52
EVP Automation Technologies: Dinesh C. Paliwal, age 45
Interim Head of Oil, Gas and Petrochemicals Business: Erik Fougner, age 45
SVP Corporate Communications: Björn Edlund
Manager Group Internal Audit: Markus Kistler
SVP Large Projects: Sune Karlsson
General Counsel: John G. Scriven, age 60
CTO: H. Markus Bayegan, age 57
CIO: Haider Rashid
Group Controlling: Hannu Kasi
Deputy CFO, Head, Group Function Corporate Finance and Taxes: Alfred Storck
Investor Relations: Michel Gerber, age 39
Finance Advisory: Enrico Viale
VP Risk Management and Insurance: Charles Salek
Mergers and Acquisitions and New Ventures: Eric Elzvik
SVP Sustainability Affairs: Christian Kornevall
President and CEO, ABB Lummus Global: Stephen M. Solomon
Corporate Communications: Thomas Schmidt
Auditors: KPMG Klynveld Peat Marwick Goerdeler SA; Ernst & Young AG

LOCATIONS

HQ: Affolternstrasse 44, CH-8050 Zurich, Switzerland
Phone: +41-43-317-7111   **Fax:** +41-43-317-7958
US HQ: 501 Merritt 7, Norwalk, CT 06856-5308
US Phone: 203-750-2200   **US Fax:** 203-750-2263
Web: www.abb.com

ABB operates in more than 100 countries worldwide.

2002 Sales

	$ mil.	% of total
Europe	10,265	56
The Americas	4,101	23
Asia	2,603	14
Middle East & Africa	1,326	7
Total	**18,295**	**100**

PRODUCTS/OPERATIONS

2002 Sales

	$ mil.	% of total
Automation technologies	5,035	27
Utilities	4,826	26
Industries	4,412	24
Power technologies	4,355	23
Adjustments	(333)	—
Total	**18,295**	**100**

COMPETITORS

Aker Kvaerner
ALSTOM
Bechtel
Emerson Electric
Endress+Hauser
Fluor
GE
Halliburton
Hitachi
Honeywell ACS
Invensys
JGC
McDermott
Samsung
Schneider
Siemens
Technip
Toshiba
VA Technologie

HISTORICAL FINANCIALS

Company Type: Public

Income Statement

FYE: December 31

	REVENUE ($ mil.)	NET INCOME ($ mil.)	NET PROFIT MARGIN	EMPLOYEES
12/02	18,295	(783)	—	139,051
12/01	23,726	(691)	—	156,865
12/00	22,967	1,443	6.3%	160,818
12/99	24,681	1,614	6.5%	164,154
12/98	30,872	1,305	4.2%	199,232
12/97	31,265	572	1.8%	213,057
12/96	33,767	1,233	3.7%	214,894
12/95	33,738	1,315	3.9%	209,637
12/94	29,718	760	2.6%	207,557
12/93	28,883	609	2.1%	206,490
Annual Growth	(4.9%)	—	—	(4.3%)

2002 Year-End Financials

Debt ratio: 530.7%
Return on equity: —
Cash ($ mil.): 2,478
Current ratio: 1.08
Long-term debt ($ mil.): 5,376

No. of shares (mil.): 1,113
Dividends
  Yield: 0.0%
  Payout: —
Market value ($ mil.): 3,195

Stock History

NYSE: ABB

	STOCK PRICE ($) FY Close	P/E High/Low	PER SHARE ($) Earnings	Dividends	Book Value
12/02	2.87	— —	(0.83)	0.00	0.91
12/01	9.41	— —	(0.61)	0.00	1.81
Annual Growth	(69.5%)	— —	—	—	(49.7%)

ABN AMRO Holding N.V.

When the tulip bed got a little too crowded, ABN AMRO Holding decided to cultivate more exotic acreage, concentrating on Asia, the US, and the rest of Europe for much of its growth. Holland's #1 purely banking company, ABN AMRO and its subsidiaries operate more than 800 offices at home and another 2,600 in 75 other countries. Other lines include investment banking services (corporate advisory, finance, and asset management), leasing, and growing operations in pan-European real estate development, financing, and management. In the US, where it is the largest foreign bank by assets, the company owns Chicago-based LaSalle Bank and Standard Federal Bank, one of Michigan's biggest.

ABN AMRO has a large presence in Brazil (through its ownership of Banco Real and Paraiban, plus its 2003 purchase of Banco Sudameris from IntesaBci) and Malaysia (where it has operated for more than 100 years) and has picked up operations in the Philippines, India, Singapore, Taiwan, and Thailand.

ABN AMRO divides its business along three lines: private clients and asset management, consumer and commercial clients, and wholesale clients (although the latter category has taken a backseat to the first two). Reacting to a slowing economy, the company is trimming staff at home and abroad. Slackening volume in its US institutional equity business compelled the company to sell its Prime Brokerage division, which mainly serves hedge fund clients, to UBS. ABN AMRO is also closing or converting about one-third of its 830 domestic branches. It plans to have about 570 bank shops (for more quotidian transactions) and 80 advisory branches (that offer financial planning and loans).

HISTORY

ABN AMRO comes by its initials honestly. It is the product of a 1991 merger between the Netherlands' #1 and #2 banks — Algemene Bank Nederland (ABN) and Amsterdam-Rotterdam Bank (AMRO), respectively — and a final amalgamation of what were the four top banks in the Netherlands.

The Netherlands Trading Society was founded in 1824 to finance business ventures in the Dutch colonies, operating from an office in what is now Jakarta, Indonesia. The company prospered, moving into agricultural financing and commercial banking and acquiring banks in the early 1900s. Although the firm weathered WWI and the Depression, WWII was catastrophic — Germany occupied the homeland and Japan took over the Dutch East Indies.

The Netherlands Trading Society never recovered, and in 1964 it merged with Twentsche Bank (founded in 1861 as an agricultural bank) to form Algemene Bank Nederland. ABN's chief rival was AMRO, product of the 1964 merger of Amsterdam Bank and Rotterdam Bank. Founded in 1863, Rotterdam Bank financed commercial activity in the colonies before refocusing on the shipping business through Rotterdam. Amsterdam Bank was founded in 1871 by several Dutch and German banks and was the largest Dutch bank when it merged with Incasso Bank in 1948. In 1964 the new entity added the operations of Hollandsche Bank – Unie.

ABN was smaller than AMRO until it bought merchant bank Mees & Hope (1975) followed by the purchase of Chicago-based LaSalle National Bank (1979). ABN had retreated so far from its colonial roots that it was largely unscathed by the mass default of Third World banks in 1987. Instead, AMRO financed oil and gas exploration and construction on the English Channel Tunnel.

ABN and AMRO merged in 1991, and the new company turned its attention to overseas markets like the American Midwest, where LaSalle National Bank was gobbling up competitors like Talman Home Federal Savings (1991). ABN AMRO also took control of European American Bank (EAB), which had sustained heavy losses on bad real estate and Third World loans. The company bought investment banks Chicago Corp. and Alfred Berg in 1995.

Expansion brought internal oversight problems during the next few years: in 1995 Swiss banking authorities asked ABN AMRO to better police its branches there after the bank lost as much as $124 million to embezzlement. In 1997 the firm closed its diamond office after losing about $100 million to fraud.

In 1998 ABN AMRO bought Brazil's Banco Real and Bandepe banks (and then closed their European and US offices). The next year it began buying minority interests in Italian banks. Also in 1999 the company elected to become a major force in European real estate with the acquisition of Bouwfonds Nederlandse Gemeenten, the Netherlands' #5 mortgage lender. As part of this effort, it expanded its mortgage servicing portfolio with the purchase of Pitney Bowes subsidiary Atlantic Mortgage and Investment Corp.

ABN AMRO cut 150 branches in its over-banked home market (and about 10% of its Dutch workforce) in 2000. It bought the energy-derivative business of Merrill Lynch, Barclays' Dial car-leasing unit, and Alleghany Corporation's asset management unit.

In 2001 ABN AMRO sold EAB to Citigroup and bought US-based Michigan National Corporation from National Australia Bank and merged it with another Michigan holding, Standard Federal Bancorporation, to form Standard Federal Bank, one of the largest banks in Michigan. It also bought the US brokerage and corporate finance operations of Dutch rival ING Groep in a quarter-billion dollar deal.

EXECUTIVES

Chairman, Supervisory Board: Jonkheer Aarnout A. Loudon, age 67
Vice Chairman: Maarten C. van Veen, age 68
Chairman, Managing Board: Rijkman W. J. Groenink, age 54
Chairman, Executive Committee, Consumer and Commercial Clients (Brazil and New Growth Markets) and Private Clients: Dolf Collee, age 51
Chairman, Executive Committee, Wholesale Clients and Asset Management: Wilco G. Jiskoot, age 53
Chairman, Executive Committee, Consumer & Commercial Clients (the Netherlands and North America): Joost Ch. L. Kuiper, age 56
Chairman, Executive Committee, Corporate Center and CFO: Tom de Swaan, age 57
COO: Hugh Y. Scott-Barrett, age 45
CEO, The Netherlands: Jan Peter Schmittmann
SEVP, Consumer and Commercial Clients and CEO, Brazil; President, Banco ABN AMRO Real: Fabio C. Barbosa
SEVP, Consumer and Commercial Clients and CEO, United States: Norman R. (Norm) Bobins, age 60
SEVP, Private Clients; CEO, New Growth Markets: Lex Kloosterman
SEVP, Asset Management: Tom Cross Brown
SEVP, Corporate Center/European Union Affairs: Gerard B.J. Hartsink
SEVP, Corporate Center/Group Legal and Compliance: Jaap J. Kamp
SEVP, Corporate Center/Finance: Eltjo H. Kok
SEVP, Corporate Center/Group Human Resources: Garmt J.A. Louw
SEVP, Corporate Center/Group Operations: Maurice B.G.M. Oostendorp
SEVP and COO, Wholesale Clients Support Services: Ron Teerlink
Head, Investor Relations: Richard Bruens, age 36
President, ABN AMRO Services: Sam Halim
Auditors: Ernst & Young

LOCATIONS

HQ: Gustav Mahlerlaan 10, 1082 PP Amsterdam, The Netherlands
Phone: +31-20-628-9393   **Fax:** +31-20-629-9111
US HQ: 135 S. La Salle St., Ste. 625, Chicago, IL 60603
US Phone: 312-904-2000   **US Fax:** 312-904-6521
Web: www.abnamro.com

ABN AMRO Holdings and its subsidiaries have some 3,500 offices, with operations in Africa, the Americas, Asia, Australia, and Europe.

PRODUCTS/OPERATIONS

2002 Sales

	$ mil.	% of total
Interest	28,747	75
Commissions	5,694	15
Financial transactions	1,551	4
Other	2,436	6
Total	**38,428**	**100**

Selected Subsidiaries

Global
ABN AMRO Bank N.V.
AAGUS Financial Services Group N.V. (67%)
AA Interfinance B.V.
ABN AMRO Bouwfonds N.V.
ABN AMRO Lease Holding N.V.
ABN AMRO Levensverzekering N.V.
ABN AMRO Participaties Holding B.V.
ABN AMRO Projectontwikkeling B.V.
ABN AMRO Schadeverzekeringen N.V.
ABN AMRO Trustcompany (Nederland) B.V.
ABN AMRO Verzekeringen B.V.
Consultas N.V.
Hollandsche Bank-Unie N.V.
IFN Group B.V.
Nachenius, Tjeenk & Co. N.V.

Africa
ABN AMRO Bank (Maroc) S.A. (99%, Morocco)
ABN AMRO Delta Asset Management (Egypt) (61%)
ABN AMRO Delta Securities (Egypt)
ABN AMRO Securities (South Africa) (Pty) Ltd. (76%)
Middle East Saudi Hollandi Bank (40%, Saudi Arabia)

Asia
ABN AMRO Asia Ltd. (Hong Kong)
ABN AMRO Asia Merchant Bank (Singapore) Ltd.
ABN AMRO Asia Securities Plc. (40%, Thailand)
ABN AMRO Asset Management (Japan) Ltd.
ABN AMRO Bank (Kazakstan) Ltd. (51%)
ABN AMRO Bank Berhad, (Malaysia)
ABN AMRO Bank N.B., Uzbekistan A.O. (50%)
ABN AMRO Savings Bank (Philippines)
ABN AMRO Securities (India) Private Ltd. (75%)
Bank of Asia (79%, Thailand)
PT ABN AMRO Finance Indonesia (85%)

Australia
ABN AMRO Australia Ltd.
ABN AMRO Capital Markets (Australia) Ltd.
ABN AMRO Equities Australia Ltd.

Europe
ABN AMRO (Magyar) Bank Rt. (Hungary)
ABN AMRO Bank (Deutschland) A.G. (Germany)
ABN AMRO Bank (Luxembourg) S.A.
ABN AMRO Bank (Moscow) (Russia)
ABN AMRO Bank (Polska) S.A. (Poland)
ABN AMRO Bank (Romania) S.A.
ABN AMRO Bank (Schweiz) A.G. (Switzerland)
ABN AMRO Corporate Finance (Ireland) Ltd.
ABN AMRO Corporate Finance Ltd. (UK)
ABN AMRO Investment Management S.A. (Luxembourg)
ABN AMRO Leasing (Hellas) S.A. (Greece)
ABN AMRO Portfolio Management S.A. (Czech Republic)
ABN AMRO Securities (France) S.A.
ABN AMRO Trust Company (Denmark) A/S
ABN AMRO Trust Company (Jersey) Ltd. (Channel Islands)
Alfred Berg Holding A/B (Sweden)
Banca di Roma (10%, Italy)

Latin America and the Caribbean
ABN AMRO (Chile) Seguros Generales S.A.
ABN AMRO Bank (Chile) S.A.
ABN AMRO Bank (Colombia) S.A.
ABN AMRO Bank Asset Management (Curaçao) N.V. (Netherlands Antilles)
ABN AMRO Securities (Argentina)
Banco ABN AMRO Real S.A. (Brazil)
Real Paraguaya de Seguros S.A. (Paraguay)
Real Segures S.A. (Colombia)
Real Uruguaya de Seguros S.A. (Uruguay)

North America
ABN AMRO Bank (Mexico) S.A.
ABN AMRO Bank Canada
ABN AMRO Inc. (US)
ABN AMRO North America Inc. (US)
Alleghany Asset Management Inc. (US)
LaSalle Bank N.A. (US)
Standard Federal Bank

COMPETITORS

BBVA
Bank Nederlandse Gemeenten
BANK ONE
Citigroup
Crédit Agricole
CCF
Credit Suisse
Deutsche Bank
Dresdner Bank
Harris Bankcorp
HSBC Holdings
ING
Mitsubishi Tokyo Financial
Mizuho Financial
Northern Trust
Rabobank
Société Générale

HISTORICAL FINANCIALS

Company Type: Public

Income Statement

FYE: December 31

	ASSETS ($ mil.)	NET INCOME ($ mil.)	INCOME AS % OF ASSETS	EMPLOYEES
12/02	583,986	2,318	0.4%	107,416
12/01	532,430	2,879	0.5%	112,206
12/00	511,557	2,353	0.5%	115,098
12/99	462,097	2,594	0.6%	108,689
12/98	503,896	2,132	0.4%	105,826
12/97	412,867	1,902	0.5%	74,935
12/96	346,741	1,911	0.6%	66,172
12/95	339,773	1,626	0.5%	63,694
Annual Growth	**8.0%**	**5.2%**	**—**	**7.8%**

2002 Year-End Financials

Equity as % of assets: 1.8%
Return on assets: 0.4%
Return on equity: 22.9%
Long-term debt ($ mil.): 115,703
No. of shares (mil.): 1,591

Dividends
Yield: 5.1%
Payout: 56.6%
Market value ($ mil.): 25,747
Sales ($ mil.): 38,428

Stock History

NYSE: ABN

	STOCK PRICE ($) FY Close	P/E High/Low		PER SHARE ($) Earnings	Dividends	Book Value
12/02	16.18	14	7	1.45	0.82	7.12
12/01	16.28	14	8	1.86	0.86	6.84
12/00	22.75	17	13	1.53	0.86	7.85
12/99	25.31	15	11	1.73	0.65	8.24
12/98	21.75	19	10	1.42	0.29	8.67
12/97	19.50	19	14	1.29	0.00	14.73
Annual Growth	**(3.7%)**	**—**	**—**	**2.4%**	**—**	**(13.5%)**

Accor

Accor est l'hospitalité. The company is one of the world's leading hotel operators, owning or managing almost 4,000 properties throughout the world in all price ranges. Hotel Sofitel is its primary entrant in the luxury market, but the company's strength lies in its moderate and budget brands, which include Etap Hotel, Ibis, and Formule 1, as well as US-based Motel 6 and Red Roof Inns. The firm is also a leading distributor of service vouchers, which provide prepaid access to restaurants, transportation, child care, medical care, and other services. Other lines of business include casino operations and catering. Accor owns 50% of Carlson Wagonlit Travel, one of the largest travel agencies in the world.

With a third of Accor's hotels located in North America, the company is expanding in underdeveloped markets, primarily in Asia, South America, and Africa. It also is growing its casino business in Africa, the Mediterranean, and Northern Europe. In 2002 Accor opened 261 new hotels, largely Ibis, Etap, and Mercure properties. Later that year the company acquired a 30% stake in Dorint AG, a German hotel group.

HISTORY

Until Gérard Pélisson and Paul Dubrule built their first hotel in 1967, French hotels were generally quaint old inns or expensive luxury hotels. Pélisson and Dubrule's Novotel introduced midpriced hotels based on the American model. The pair opened the Ibis Hotel in 1973 and bought the Mercure chain in 1975.

By 1979, when it opened its first US hotel in Minneapolis, Novotel was Europe's #1 hotel chain, operating 184 hotels on four continents.

Dubrule and Pélisson married their growing hotel business to Jacques Borel International, forming publicly traded Accor in 1983. Jacques Borel had started out with one restaurant in 1957 and was Europe's #1 restaurateur by 1975, when he took over Belgium's Sofitel chain of luxury hotels. Losses in the hotel game prompted Borel to sell Sofitel to Dubrule and Pélisson in 1980, making their company one of the world's top 10 hotel operators — a list traditionally dominated by US chains. They picked up the rest of Borel's empire in 1983, launching Accor into the restaurant business.

Accor began offering packaged vacations in 1984, after buying a majority stake in Africatours (Africa's largest tour operator), then expanded into the South Pacific, Asia, and the Americas by buying Islands in the Sun (1986), Asietours (1987), and Americatours (1987).

The company opened its first budget hotels (Formule 1) in France in 1985. Accor started marketing Paquet cruises in 1986 and formed the Hotelia and Parthenon chains (Brazilian residential hotels) the next year.

Faced with a mature European market and eager to take advantage of favorable exchange rates, Accor bought Dallas-based budget chain Motel 6 (along with its high debts and poor reputation, which Accor began remedying with an expensive renovation program) in 1990. The next year Accor bought US-based Regal Inns (now part of Motel 6).

Also in 1990 Accor joined Société Générale de Belgique to buy 26.7% of Belgium's Wagons-Lits, owner of about 300 hotels in Europe, Thailand, and Indonesia, as well as restaurants, caterers, and travel agencies in Europe. After a battle involving both Belgian and EC antitrust officials, Accor was allowed to buy a majority stake of Wagons-Lits.

This buy — along with Accor's attempt to increase its share of the luxury market, the continuing burden of its US purchases, and a recession in the travel business — took a financial toll. In response, it began selling assets in 1994, ridding itself of expensive hotel real estate. The company also sold some of its Wagons-Lits operations in the Netherlands.

In 1997 co-chairmen Dubrule and Pélisson retired from active management and were succeeded by Jean-Marc Espalioux, formerly of Générale des Eaux (now Vivendi Universal). As part of its strategy to continue to expand internationally, Accor reached an agreement that year with the Moroccan government to develop that country's hotel industry. In 1999 Accor continued hotel acquisitions with US chain Red Roof Inns and hotels in Finland, France, the Netherlands, Poland, and Sweden.

The following year the company opened a luxury Sofitel hotel in downtown Manhattan and began developing other Sofitels in Dallas, Chicago, and Washington, DC. It also sold its EuropCar stake to Volkswagen. In 2001 the company announced plans for a 370-room Sofitel in the high-tech center of Shenyang, China. Early in 2002 Accor bought a 22% stake in Compagnie Européenne de Casinos, an operator of 24 casinos mostly in France, in a bid to buy out the company. However, after a two-month bidding war with competitor Groupe Partouche, Accor sold its stake to Partouche. The bidding war had driven up Compagnie Européenne's stock dramatically, and Accor ended up pocketing some £12 million from the sale. The company also owns 60% of tour operator Go Voyages and has plans to buy the remaining shares.

EXECUTIVES

Co-Chairman: Paul Dubrule, age 69
Co-Chairman: Gérard Pélisson, age 71
Chairman Management Board and CEO: Jean-Marc Espalioux, age 51
Executive Vice Chairman Management Board: Benjamin Cohen, age 64
Senior Vice Chairman Management Board: John Du Monceau, age 65
Member Management Board: André Martinez
CFO: Jacques Stern
General Manager, Business and Leisure Hotel Operations: Claude Moschéni
Technologies, Reservations, Sales, Marketing, Partnerships, Purchasing and Technical Affairs: Serge Ragozin
Director Investor Relations and Financial Communications: Eliane Rouyer
Corporate Secretary: Pierre Todorov
Human Resources General Manager: Cathy Kopp
Auditors: Deloitte Touche Tohmatsu

LOCATIONS

HQ: 2, rue de la Mare Neuve, 91021 Évry, France
Phone: +33-1-69-36-80-80   **Fax:** +33-1-69-36-79-00
US HQ: 245 Park Ave., New York, NY 10167
US Phone: 212-949-5700   **US Fax:** 212-490-0499
Web: www.accor.com

PRODUCTS/OPERATIONS

Selected Hotel Chains

Atria	Motel 6 (US)
Coralia	Novotel
Etap Hotel	Red Roof Inns (US)
Formule 1	Sofitel
Ibis	Suitehotel
Mercure	

Selected Other Activities

Casinos (Accor Casinos)
Institutional catering (Gemeaz Cuzin, Lenôtre)
Railway onboard services (Wagons-Lits)
Restaurants (Courtepaille)
Service vouchers (Ticket Restaurant)
Tour operators (Accor Tour, Couleurs Locales, Frantour, Go Voyages, Tiempo Libre)
Travel agencies (50%, Carlson Wagonlit Travel)

COMPETITORS

American Express
Avis Europe
Cendant
Euro Disney
Ford
Four Seasons Hotels
Helmsley
Hilton Group
Hilton
Hyatt
Lufthansa
Marriott International
Ritz-Carlton
Sixt
Starwood Hotels & Resorts
Thomas Cook AG

HISTORICAL FINANCIALS

Company Type: Public

Income Statement

FYE: December 31

	REVENUE ($ mil.)	NET INCOME ($ mil.)	NET PROFIT MARGIN	EMPLOYEES
12/02	7,482	451	6.0%	157,412
12/01	6,458	420	6.5%	146,748
12/00	6,596	421	6.4%	145,347
12/99	6,145	354	5.8%	128,850
12/98	6,561	347	5.3%	126,908
12/97	5,298	251	4.7%	121,396
12/96	5,409	202	3.7%	124,378
12/95	6,317	188	3.0%	120,668
12/94	6,272	133	2.1%	146,931
12/93	5,546	53	1.0%	143,740
Annual Growth	**3.4%**	**26.8%**	**—**	**1.0%**

2002 Year-End Financials

Debt ratio: 82.7%
Return on equity: 11.6%
Cash ($ mil.): 188
Current ratio: 1.01
Long-term debt ($ mil.): 3,376

Net Income History

OTC: ACRFY

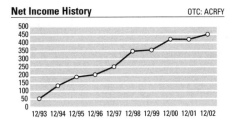

Acer Inc.

Acer's plan: divide and conquer. The company is a leading manufacturer of notebook and desktop computers. Other Acer products include motherboards, set-top boxes, storage drives, displays, keyboards, printers, scanners, and software. Products carrying its own moniker are offered through the company's Acer Branded Operations (ABO) unit. Its Design, Manufacturing and Services (DMS) unit, which it spun off and renamed Wistron, makes PCs and other hardware for companies such as Fujitsu and Hitachi. Acer's management is handled through its third unit, Holding & Investment Business (HIB).

Slumping sales in a weakening computer hardware market prompted Acer's restructuring efforts. In addition to clarifying the structure of Acer's sizable operations, the separation of ABO and Wistron serves to eliminate possible customer concerns about a conflict of interest between the two businesses. Acer also renamed its communications and multimedia unit (now BenQ). The company has eliminated jobs and cut back its retail business in North America, and will make China and other Asian markets the primary target for ABO.

HISTORY

Acer founder and chairman Stan Shih, respected enough for his business acumen to once be considered for the premiership of Taiwan, designed that country's first desktop calculator in the early 1970s. The company's precursor, Multitech International, was launched in 1976 with $25,000 by Shih and four others who called themselves the "Gardeners of Microprocessing." In 1980 Multitech introduced the Dragon Chinese-language terminal, which won Taiwan's top design award; in 1983 it introduced an Apple clone and its first IBM-compatible PC. Multitech set up AcerLand, Taiwan's first and largest franchised computer retail chain, in 1985.

The company changed its name to Acer (the Latin word for "sharp, acute, able, and facile") in 1987 and went public on the Taiwan exchange the next year. Acer got into the semiconductor market in 1989 when it entered into a joint venture with Texas Instruments (named TI-Acer) to design and develop memory chips in Taiwan. In 1990 Acer's US subsidiary, Acer America, paid $90 million for Altos Computer Systems, a US manufacturer of UNIX systems.

During the prosperous 1980s Acer increased its management layers and slowed the decision making process. In late 1990 the company restructured, trimming its workforce by 8% (about 400 employees), including two-thirds of headquarters. The layoff was unprecedented — being asked to resign from a job in Taiwan carries a social stigma. Shih wrote a letter to all those affected, explaining the plight of the company. The following year Acer began its decentralization plan to create a worldwide confederation of publicly owned companies.

Acer suffered its first loss in 1991 on revenues of almost $1 billion, partly because of increased marketing budgets in the US and Europe and continuing investment in TI-Acer. The company bounced back in 1993, with 80% of its profit coming from that joint venture.

The Aspire PC, available in shades of gray and green, was unveiled in 1995. In 1996 the company expanded into consumer electronics, introducing a host of new, inexpensive videodisc players, video telephones, and other devices in order to boost global market share. In 1997 Acer purchased TI's notebook computer business. A slowdown in memory chip sales, plus a financial slide at Acer America, cost the firm $141 million, but Acer finished the year in the black.

Shih stepped down as president in 1998 to focus on restructuring. The company ended its venture with TI, buying TI's 33% stake and renaming the unit Acer Semiconductor Manufacturing. The company also began making information appliances, introducing a device able to play CD-ROMs via TV sets and perform other task-specific functions. Continued losses due to a highly competitive US market caused a drop in profits for 1998.

In 1999 Acer sold a 30% stake in its struggling Acer Semiconductor Manufacturing affiliate to Taiwan Semiconductor Manufacturing Corp. (TSMC completed its purchase of the remaining 70% of the business, which was renamed TSMC-Acer Semiconductor Manufacturing, the following year.) The competitive heat and the rise of under-$1,000 PCs took a toll that year when Acer cut US jobs, streamlined operations, and withdrew from the US retail market. The company intensified its focus on providing online software, hardware, and support for users, launching a digital services business and a venture capital operation to invest in promising Internet startups.

The company suffered a financial blow in 2000 when large customer IBM cancelled an order for desktop computers. Late that year, after continued losses in a slowing PC market, the company announced it would cut more jobs in the US and Germany and close an unspecified number of plants worldwide.

In 2001 the company spun off its contract manufacturing and peripherals units, and renamed them Wistron and BenQ, respectively. Acer's restructuring efforts continued the following year, when it merged with its distribution unit, Acer Sertek. (Although Sertek was the surviving entity, the company immediately revived the Acer name to maintain its stronger brand.)

EXECUTIVES

Chairman and CEO: Stan Shih, age 58
President: J. T. Wang
SVP, Finance and Investment: Philip Peng
VP, Investor Relations: Howard Chan
Manager, Investor Relations: Andrew Chang
Chairman and CEO, Wistron: Simon Lin, age 50
President, Wistron: Dixon Cheng
CFO, Wistron: Frank F. C. Lin
VP, Account Management, Wistron: Emily Hong
Chief Information Officer, Business Process Improvement, Wistron: Frachard Lung
Associate VP, Administration and Human Resources, Wistron: Terry Lu
Associate VP, Service, Wistron: Andy Wang
President and COO, Acer America: Patrick S. N. Lin
CFO, Acer America: Ming Wang
General Manager, Canadian Operations, Acer America: Terry Tomecek
Senior Director, Customer Service, Acer America: Mark Groveunder
Senior Director, Human Resources and Administration, Acer America: Lenny Pollak
Director, Information Technology, Acer America: Alan Wang
Director, Product Management and Fulfillment, Acer America: David C. W. Lee
Auditors: KPMG Peat Marwick

LOCATIONS

HQ: 9F, 88 Hsin Tai Wu Rd., Sec 1,
Hsichih, Taipei 221, Taiwan
Phone: +886-2-696-1234   **Fax:** +886-2-696-3535
US HQ: 2641 Orchard Pkwy., San Jose, CA 95134
US Phone: 408-432-6200   **US Fax:** 408-922-2933
Web: www.acer.com

Acer sells its products in more than 100 countries.

PRODUCTS/OPERATIONS

Products

Computers
Desktop (home and business)
Notebook
Personal digital assistants (PDAs)
Servers
Displays
Digital projectors
Monitors (cathode-ray tube and liquid-crystal display)
Plasma displays
Imaging
Printers
Scanners
Storage
CD-ROM drives
CD-RW drives
DVD-ROM drives
Other
Keyboards (desktop and wireless)
Motherboards
Set-top boxes
Software

COMPETITORS

Apple Computer	Legend Group
Compal Electronics	Matsushita
Dell	NEC
eMachines	Samsung Electronics
Founder Holdings	Samsung
Fujitsu	Sharp Electronics
Fujitsu Siemens	Siemens
Computers	Sony
Gateway	Sun Microsystems
Hewlett-Packard	Tatung
Hitachi	Toshiba
IBM	TriGem

HISTORICAL FINANCIALS

Company Type: Public

Income Statement

FYE: December 31

	REVENUE ($ mil.)	NET INCOME ($ mil.)	NET PROFIT MARGIN	EMPLOYEES
12/02	3,070	247	8.1%	2,900
12/01	3,226	30	0.9%	4,480
12/00	4,764	205	4.3%	3,863
12/99	5,779	233	4.0%	33,912
12/98	5,269	77	1.5%	23,000
12/97	4,220	115	2.7%	4,401
12/96	4,191	111	2.7%	4,394
12/95	3,924	203	5.2%	—
12/94	2,397	120	5.0%	—
12/93	1,275	40	3.2%	—
Annual Growth	10.3%	22.4%	—	(6.7%)

2002 Year-End Financials

Debt ratio: 12.8%   Current ratio: 1.74
Return on equity: 0.1%   Long-term debt ($ mil.): 241
Cash ($ mil.): 650

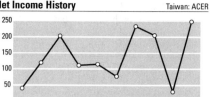

Net Income History   Taiwan: ACER

250	
200	
150	
100	
50	
0	

12/93 12/94 12/95 12/96 12/97 12/98 12/99 12/00 12/01 12/02

adidas-Salomon

Jesse Owens and Muhammad Ali broke barriers and records in their adidas athletic shoes. The heart of the adidas-Salomon product line is athletic shoes, including tennis, running, and basketball, but the three-stripe logo appears on apparel and other jock-type accoutrements. Bankruptcy once had adidas-Salomon on the ropes, but it made a comeback by shifting production to Asia and beefing up its marketing budget. The #2 maker of sporting goods worldwide, behind NIKE, adidas-Salomon owns sponsorship deals with popular US football and basketball stars, as well as the New York Yankees. Its purchase of Salomon, the French maker of ski and golf gear, steered the company into the equipment arena.

adidas-Salomon makes athletic clothing and gear such as Salomon skis, snowboards, and in-line skates; TaylorMade golf clubs; and Mavic bike components. (adidas products account for nearly 80% of sales.) adidas-Salomon is also repositioning its adidas brand, marketing its products as both performance and lifestyle wear. In January 2003, in an effort to strengthen the adidas brand in sportswear and uniforms, adidas partnered with Betlin, Inc., for the manufacturing and selling of custom and stock uniforms.

Although the purchase of Salomon was intended to create economies of scale and an advantage in emerging markets for trendy sports, integrating the company has been difficult. adidas-Salomon also has been hurt by soft demand for TaylorMade's golf products in Asia and the US. However, at the end of 2002, TaylorMade acquired the Maxfi brand of golf balls and accessories from the Dunlop Slazenger Group. The move was meant to bolster the company's golfing products portfolio.

In early 2003, adidas was delisted from the Paris Euronext exchange due to low trading volume. The company remains listed on the Frankfurt Stock Exchange. Later that year, a senior executive in the US division pleaded guilty to conspiracy to commit fraud. Top sales executive Timothy McCool admits to cooking the books for adidas by reporting to auditors that the company owed $2.2 million to footwear retailer Just For Feet, when the actual number was less than $50,000.

HISTORY

adidas grew out of an infamous rift between German brothers Adi and Rudi Dassler, who created athletic shoe giants adidas and Puma. As WWI was winding down, Adi scavenged for tires, rucksacks, and other refuse to create slippers, gymnastics shoes, and soccer cleats at home. His sister cut patterns out of canvas. By 1926 the shoes' success allowed the Dasslers to build a factory. At the 1928 Amsterdam Olympics, German athletes first showcased Dassler shoes to the world. In 1936 American Jesse Owens sprinted to Olympic gold in Dassler's double-striped shoes.

Business boomed until the Nazis commandeered the Dassler factory to make boots for soldiers. Whereas both Rudi and Adi were reportedly members of the Nazi party, only Rudi was called to service. Adi remained at home to run the factory. When Allied troops occupied the area, Adi made friends with American soldiers — even creating shoes for a soldier who wore them at the 1946 Olympics. Rudi came home from an American prison camp and joined his brother; together they scavenged the war-torn landscape for tank materials and tents to make shoes.

Soon a dispute between the brothers split the business. Rumors circulated that Rudi resented that Adi had failed to use his American connections to help spring him from prison camp. Rudi set up his own factory facing Adi across the River Aurach. The brothers never spoke to each other again, except in court. Rudi's company was named Puma, and Adi's became adidas. Adi added a third stripe to the Dassler's trademark shoe, while Rudi chose a cat's paw in motion. Thus began one of the most intense rivalries in Europe. The children of Puma and adidas employees attended separate elementary schools, and the employees even distinguished themselves by drinking different beers.

With Adi's innovations throughout the late 1940s and 1950s (such as the replaceable-cleat soccer shoe), adidas came to dominate the world's athletic shoe market. In the late 1950s it capitalized on the booming US market, overtaking the canvas sneakers made by P.F. Flyers and Keds. The company also initiated the practice of putting logos on sports bags and clothing.

In the 1960s and 1970s, adidas continued to expand globally to maintain its dominant position. However, a flood of new competitors following the 1972 Munich Olympics and the death of Adi in 1978 signaled the end of an era. As NIKE and Reebok captured the North American market during the 1980s, adidas made one of its biggest missteps — it turned down a sneaker endorsement offer from a young Michael Jordan in 1984.

French politician and entrepreneur Bernard Tapie bought the struggling company in 1989, but he stepped down in 1992 amid personal, political, and business scandals. The next year Robert Louis-Dreyfus became CEO. He shifted production to Asia, pumped up the advertising budget, and brought in former NIKE marketing geniuses to re-establish the company's identity.

adidas became adidas-Salomon in 1997 with its $1.4 billion purchase of Salomon, a French maker of skis and other sporting goods. The company also opened its first high-profile store in Portland, Oregon, that year. In a 1998 reorganization, Louis-Dreyfus sacked Jean-Francois Gautier as Salomon's president in the wake of disappointing sales, particularly from TaylorMade Golf, Salomon's golf subsidiary.

Amid a 10% slide in revenue, several key executives decided to leave the company in 2000, including adidas America CEO Steve Wynne. Citing poor health, Louis-Dreyfus soon followed (but remained as chairman); he was replaced by the new CEO of adidas America, Ross McMullin, who soon after was diagnosed with cancer.

In 2001 Louis-Dreyfus retired as chairman and in March COO Herbert Hainer became chief executive. That year adidas-Salomon opened adidas Orginals retail stores in Toyko and Berlin; that was followed with a New York City store in 2002. Despite slumping sales in the US amid deep discounting by competitors, adidas announced in 2003 that it would not offer discounts and still intends to capture 20% of the country's shoe market.

EXECUTIVES

Chairman and CEO: Herbert Hainer, age 49
Deputy Chairman and Chief Investment Officer: Fritz Kammerer, age 58
CFO: Robin Stalker, age 44
SVP of Global Marketing: Erich Stamminger, age 45
President and CEO, adidas America: Ross McMullin, age 43
Interim President and CEO, adidas America: Jim Stutts, age 43
Managing Director, adidas Japan: Rob Langstaff, age 42
Head of Global Business Development: Hermann Deininger
Head of Asia/Pacific Region: Christophe Bezu, age 46
Head of Corporate and Global Public Relaitions: Jan Runau
Head of Investor Relations: Natalie M. Knight
Director of Global Operations: Glenn Bennett, age 38
Director of Human Resources & Administration: Michel Perraudin, age 54
Director of Licensing and Business Development, adidas America: David Howitt
Sales Director Customer Service, Area Central, and Director: Hans Ruprecht, age 48
System Manager Footwear Quality, Global Operations and Director: Sabine Bauer, age 39
Legal and Environmental Affairs: Manfred Ihle, age 60
Auditors: KPMG Deutsche Treuhand-Gesellschaft AG

LOCATIONS

HQ: adidas-Salomon AG
Adi-Dassler-Strasse 1-2,
91074 Herzogenaurach, Germany
Phone: +49-9132-84-0   **Fax:** +49-9132-84-2241
US HQ: 5055 N. Greeley Ave., Portland, OR 97217
US Phone: 971-234-2300   **US Fax:** 971-234-2450
Web: www.adidas.com

2002 Sales

	% of total
Europe	47
North America	30
Asia	17
Latin America	3
Other	3
Total	**100**

PRODUCTS/OPERATIONS

2002 Sales

	% of total
adidas	78
Salomon	11
TaylorMade-adidas golf	11
Total	**100**

Selected Brands

adidas (footwear and apparel for basketball, cycling, running, soccer, and tennis)
Mavic (bicycle components)
Salomon (ski and snowboard equipment, in-line skates, and hiking boots)
TaylorMade (golf clubs, accessories)

COMPETITORS

Amer Group	K-Swiss
Benetton	Mizuno
Callaway Golf	New Balance
Converse	NIKE
Fila USA	PUMA
Fortune Brands	Reebok
Head	Rollerblade
Head-Tyrolia-Mares	SHC
Huffy	Skis Rossignol
K2	Trek

HISTORICAL FINANCIALS

Company Type: Public

Income Statement

FYE: December 31

	REVENUE ($ mil.)	NET INCOME ($ mil.)	NET PROFIT MARGIN	EMPLOYEES
12/02	6,837	240	3.5%	14,716
12/01	5,414	185	3.4%	13,941
12/00	5,494	171	3.1%	13,157
12/99	5,392	229	4.3%	12,433
12/98	5,911	239	4.0%	12,036
12/97	3,724	259	6.9%	7,993
12/96	3,055	204	6.7%	6,986
12/95	2,434	170	7.0%	5,730
12/94	2,063	76	3.7%	5,087
12/93	1,539	8	0.5%	5,096
Annual Growth	18.0%	45.7%	—	12.5%

2002 Year-End Financials

Debt ratio: 145.6%
Return on equity: 23.6%
Cash ($ mil.): 80
Current ratio: 2.05
Long-term debt ($ mil.): 1,650

Net Income History

OTC: ADDDY

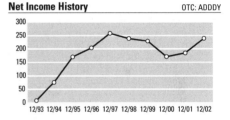

AEGON N.V.

Not only has AEGON expanded across Europe, it has also spread Transamerica. The Dutch life insurance giant is using its expertise in acquisition (the largest one being US rival Transamerica) and consolidation to build a transnational collection of financial services businesses. Its subsidiaries offer personal and commercial life and accident insurance, as well as retirement and savings advice and management services. Its US operations also offer life, nonmedical health, and long-term-care insurance and sell annuities and other retirement products.

Expanding in Asia and the Pacific, life insurance accounts for some 85% of revenues. Vereniging AEGON, an independent trust, owns about 15% of AEGON.

Further improving its position in the US, AEGON bought the direct marketing and life insurance services of retailer J.C. Penney. Focusing on life insurance and pensions, the company sold its Transamerica Finance subsidiary (which had been on the market since 1999) to GE Commercial Finance and First American.

HISTORY

AEGON traces its roots to 1844, when former civil servant and funeral society agent J. Oosterhoff founded Algemeene Friesche, a burial society for low-income workers. The next year a similar organization, Groot-Noordhollandsche, was founded. These companies later became insurers and expanded nationwide. Meanwhile Olveh, a civil servants' aid group, was founded in 1877. The three companies merged in 1968 to form AGO Holding.

AEGON's other operations came from different traditions. Vennootschap Nederland was founded in 1858 as a tontine (essentially a death pool, with the survivors taking the pot) by Count A. Langrand-Dumonceau, an ex-French Foreign Legionnaire from Belgium. In 1913 the company merged with Eerste Nederlandsche, whose accident and health division had been previously spun off as Nieuwe Eerste Nederlandsche.

A year after Vennootschap was founded, C. F. W. Wiggers van Kerchem founded a similar scheme, Nillmij, in the Dutch East Indies. The government promoted Nillmij to colonial civil servants and military people, and for a while the company enjoyed a monopoly in the colony. Nillmij's Indonesian operations were nationalized after independence in 1957, but its Dutch subsidiaries continued to operate. All insurers were hit by fast-growing postwar government social programs. As a result, industry consolidation came early to the Netherlands. In 1969 Eerste Nederlandsche, Nieuwe Eerste Nederlandsche, and Nillmij merged to form Ennia.

The shrinking Dutch insurance market forced companies to look overseas. AGO moved into the US in 1979 by buying Life Investors; by 1982 half of its sales came from outside the Netherlands. Ennia, meanwhile, expanded in Europe (it entered Spain in 1980) and the US (buying Arkansas-based National Old Line Insurance in 1981).

AGO and Ennia merged in 1983 to form AEGON. The company made more purchases at home and abroad and spent much of the rest of the decade assimilating operations.

AEGON's US units accounted for about 40% of sales in the mid-1980s, and the firm increased that figure with acquisitions. In 1986 it bought Baltimore-based Monumental Corp. (life and health insurance) and expanded the company's US penetration.

This left AEGON underrepresented in Europe, as deregulation paved the way for economic union and social service cutbacks spurred opportunities in private financial planning in the region. So in the 1990s AEGON began buying European companies, including Regency Life (UK, 1991) and Allami Biztosito (Hungary, 1992). It formed an alliance with Mexico's Grupo Financiero Banamex in 1994. This reduced its reliance on US sales. It continued buying specialty operations in the US, particularly asset management lines.

In 1997 AEGON began to concentrate on life insurance and financial services and shed its other operations. It bought the insurance business of Providian and sold noncore lines such as auto coverage. The next year it sold FGH Bank (mortgages) to Germany's Bayerische Vereinsbank (now Bayerische Hypotheken und Vereinsbank) and in 1999 sold auto insurer Worldwide Insurance.

That year AEGON expanded further in the US with the $9.7 billion purchase of Transamerica and bought the life and pensions businesses of the UK's Guardian Royal Exchange. In 2000 the company sold Labouchere N.V., a Dutch banking subsidiary, to Dexia. Also in 2000 AEGON acquired UK-based third-party administrator HS Administrative Services.

EXECUTIVES

Chairman, Executive Board and AEGON USA: Donald J. Shepard, age 56
Member of the Executive Board and CFO: Joseph B.M. Streppel, age 54
Member of the Executive Board and CEO, AEGON Netherlands: Johan G. van der Werf
Member of the Executive Board: Alexander R. Wynaendts
EVP, Group Business Development: Marc van Weede, age 37
EVP, Group Treasury and Investor Relations: Robert J. McGraw
SVP, Group Communications: Gerard van Dongen
SVP, Group Finance and Information: Ruurd A. van den Berg
SVP, Group Legal: Erik Lagendijk
SVP, Group Tax: Adri D.J. Verzijl
SVP, Group Treasury and Treasurer: C. Michiel van Katwijk
VP, Group Corporate Responsibility: Charles Henderson, age 43
Company Secretary: Peter Tuit
Auditors: Ernst & Young

LOCATIONS

HQ: AEGONplein 50,
2501 CE The Hague, The Netherlands
Phone: +31-70-344-8344   **Fax:** +31-70-344-8445
US HQ: 1111 N. Charles St., Baltimore, MD 21201-5574
US Phone: 410-576-4571   **US Fax:** 410-347-8685
Web: www.aegon.com

AEGON operates worldwide, but primarily in the Netherlands, the UK, and the US.

2002 Sales

	% of total
US	56
Netherlands	30
UK	11
Other	3
Total	**100**

PRODUCTS/OPERATIONS

2002 Sales

	% of total
Life insurance	84
Accident & health	13
General insurance	3
Total	**100**

Selected Subsidiaries

The Americas
AEGON USA, Inc.
AUSA Life Insurance Company, Inc.
Bankers United Life Assurance Company
Commonwealth General Corporation
First AUSA Life Insurance Company
Life Investors Insurance Company of America
Monumental Life Insurance Company
Peoples Benefit Life Insurance Company
PFL Life Insurance Company
Transamerica Corporation
Transamerica Insurance Corp. of California
Transamerica Life Insurance and Annuity Company
Transamerica Life Insurance Company of Canada
Transamerica Occidental Life Insurance Company
Veterans Life Insurance Company
Western Reserve Life Assurance Co. of Ohio

The Netherlands
AEGON Bank N.V.
AEGON Financiele Diensten B.V.
AEGON International N.V.
AEGON Levensverzekering N.V.
AEGON Nederland N.V.
AEGON Schadeverzekering N.V.
AEGON Spaarkas N.V.
AEGON Vastgoed Holding B.V.
AMVEST Vastgoed B.V. (50%)
AXENT/AEGON Leven N.V.
AXENT/AEGON Schade N.V.
Nederlandse Verzekeringsgroep Leven N.V.
Nederlandse Verzekeringsgroep Schade N.V.
Spaarbeleg Kas N.V.
Van Nierop Assuradeuren N.V.

The UK
AEGON Asset Management UK plc
AEGON UK plc
Guardian Assurance plc
Guardian Linked Life Assurance Limited
Guardian Pensions Management Limited
Scottish Equitable International Holdings plc
Scottish Equitable plc

Rest of the world
AB-AEGON Altalanos Biztosito Rt. (Hungary)
AEGON Lebensversicherungs-AG (Germany)
AEGON Union Aseguradora S.A. de Seguros y Reaseguros (Spain)

COMPETITORS

Allianz	MetLife
AIG	New York Life
AXA	Prudential
CIGNA	Prudential plc
Citigroup	Royal & Sun Alliance
Fortis	Insurance
The Hartford	Swiss Life
ING	Winterthur
Legal & General Group	Zurich Financial Services
Merrill Lynch	

HISTORICAL FINANCIALS

Company Type: Public

Income Statement

FYE: December 31

	ASSETS ($ mil.)	NET INCOME ($ mil.)	INCOME AS % OF ASSETS	EMPLOYEES
12/02	250,188	1,625	0.6%	26,659
12/01	235,358	2,136	0.9%	25,663
12/00	230,003	1,946	0.8%	28,928
12/99	230,913	1,584	0.7%	24,316
12/98	153,070	1,385	0.9%	20,723
12/97	134,623	1,089	0.8%	23,429
12/96	105,027	929	0.9%	19,346
12/95	93,660	823	0.9%	19,806
12/94	79,032	632	0.8%	19,713
12/93	66,002	517	0.8%	19,393
Annual Growth	**16.0%**	**13.6%**	**—**	**3.6%**

2002 Year-End Financials

Equity as % of assets: 6.0%
Return on assets: 0.7%
Return on equity: 11.4%
Long-term debt ($ mil.): 2,756
No. of shares (mil.): 1,445

Dividends
Yield: 5.9%
Payout: 67.3%
Market value ($ mil.): 18,534
Sales ($ mil.): 32,764

Stock History

NYSE: AEG

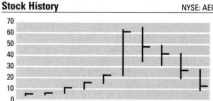

	STOCK PRICE ($) FY Close	P/E High/Low		PER SHARE ($) Earnings	Dividends	Book Value
12/02	12.83	24	8	1.13	0.76	10.35
12/01	26.77	27	13	1.56	0.72	9.58
12/00	41.44	34	22	1.46	0.60	8.96
12/99	47.75	50	27	1.30	0.54	10.22
12/98	61.13	50	18	1.26	0.69	7.94
12/97	22.41	24	16	0.96	0.00	7.72
12/96	15.81	19	13	0.82	0.37	6.10
12/95	11.00	15	8	0.76	0.20	4.85
12/94	6.35	10	8	0.63	0.20	4.43
12/93	5.43	12	8	0.50	0.18	4.42
Annual Growth	10.0%	—	—	9.5%	17.4%	9.9%

Agrium Inc.

It's no bull that Agrium is a top producer and marketer of fertilizers in North America. A leader in the production of nitrogen (it has about 3% of the world market), the company has 14 plants in North America and Argentina that produce mostly nitrogen products, but also phosphate, potash, sulfate, and micronutrients used primarily in fertilizers. In addition to wholesale sales, Agrium operates about 225 fertilizer retail outlets in the US and nearly 20 in Argentina. The company also has a 50%-owned joint venture with Spain's Repsol-YPF that runs Argentina's largest nitrogen plant (Profertil).

As with most every chemical company worldwide, escalating prices for natural gas (a raw material in nitrogen fertilizer) along with low-selling prices for phosphate have dogged Agrium. However, the company hopes to boost profits with the onset of production at its Profertil nitrogen plant.

HISTORY

Agrium was formed in 1992 to facilitate the reorganization of Cominco's fertilizer division and to acquire the fertilizer business of the Alberta Energy Company (1993). Cominco was founded in 1896 as the Smelting and Refining Company when Fritz Heinze fired up his first smelter at Trail Creek Landing, British Columbia. Using the ores of the nearby Rossland mines, the company soon diversified into other products (such as fertilizers) and new metallurgical technologies. In 1906 the Smelting and Refining Company, the Rossland mines, and the nearby St. Eugene Mine merged to form the Consolidated Mining and Smelting Company of Canada Limited.

During WWI the Canadian government conscripted all the company's lead, zinc, and chemical production and instructed the company to make explosive-grade ammonium nitrate at its fertilizer plants. Cominco became the company's official name in 1966.

Alberta Energy was formed in 1973 to lessen Alberta's dependence on foreign oil, in response to the OPEC oil embargo. In 1989 its petrochemical division established fertilizer (ammonium nitrate) subsidiaries in the US.

Agrium was established to compete in the rapidly consolidating fertilizer market (the number of North American ammonia producers fell from 55 in 1980 to 26 at the end of 1996). The phos-

phate and potash industries also consolidated, albeit on a smaller scale.

Between 1993 and 1996 the company expanded its US operations by acquiring Crop Protection Services and Western Farm Service (both retail operations), AG-BIO (the phosphate-based fertilizer business of Imperial Oil), and Nu-West Industries. Agrium expanded into South America in 1995 by opening retail sales units for selling fertilizer, agricultural chemicals, and other services in the farming regions of Argentina.

In 1996 Agrium acquired Viridian, a Canadian fertilizer producer with nitrogen- and phosphate-based fertilizer plants in Alberta. Expanding its supply base, the company bought a phosphate mine in Alberta in 1997. The company also bought back 10% of its shares in 1998.

Agrium opened a phosphate rock mine in Ontario in 1999 to replace its reliance on phosphate rock imported from West Africa. In 2000 Agrium bought Unocal's nitrogen-based fertilizer operations for around $325 million. That year Agrium's Profertil nitrogen plant, a joint venture with Spain's industrial giant Repsol-YPF, began production in Argentina, but the plant was shut down by a government agency following an accidental discharge of ammonia. The plant was reopened later in 2000. Agrium also increased its nitrogen production capacity some 60% with the acquisition of Unocal's agricultural products division.

EXECUTIVES

Chairman: Frank W. Proto, age 60
Vice Chairman and CEO: John M. Van Brunt
President and COO: Michael M. (Mike) Wilson
SVP, Finance and CFO: Bruce G. Waterman
SVP, Marketing and Distribution: John D. Yokley
SVP, North America Retail: Richard L. Gearheard
VP and Controller: Garnet K. Amundson
VP and Treasurer: Patrick J. Freeman
VP, General Counsel, and Corporate Secretary: Leslie A. O'Donoghue
VP, Human Resources: James M. Grossett
VP, Operations: William C. McClung
VP, South America: Robert J. Rennie
VP, Strategic Development and Planning: Dorothy E. A. Bower
VP, Supply Management: Christopher W. (Chris) Tworek
Director, Investor Relations: Jim Pendergast
Director of Technology: Ron Wilkinson
Sales Manager, Canada: Kevin Helash
Sales Manager, US: J. Muse
Manager, Agronomic and New Products: Dale Marantz
Auditors: KPMG LLP

LOCATIONS

HQ: 13131 Lake Fraser Dr. SE, Calgary, Alberta T2J 7E8, Canada
Phone: 403-225-7000 **Fax:** 403-225-7609
US HQ: 4582 S. Ulster St., Ste. 1700, Denver, CO 80237
US Phone: 303-804-4400 **US Fax:** 303-804-4478
Web: www.agrium.com

Agrium has plants in Argentina, Canada, and the US.

2002 Sales

	$ mil.	% of total
North America		
Wholesale	1,172	54
Retail	849	39
South America		
Wholesale	64	3
Retail	80	4
Adjustments	(82)	—
Total	**2,083**	**100**

PRODUCTS/OPERATIONS

2002 Sales

	$ mil.	% of total
Wholesale	1,236	57
Retail	929	43
Adjustments	(82)	—
Total	**2,083**	**100**

2002 Sales

	$ mil.	% of total
Wholesale		
Nitrogen	773	36
Phosphate	239	11
Potash	158	7
Sulfate and other	66	3
Retail		
Fertilizers	419	19
Chemicals	361	17
Other	149	7
Adjustments	(82)	—
Total	**2,083**	**100**

Subsidiaries and Affiliates

Agrium Nitrogen Company (US)
Agrium Partnership
Agrium U.S. Inc.
Agroservicios Pampeanos SA (Argentina)
Canpotex Limited (International, 33%)
Crop Production Services, Inc. (US)
Nu-West Industries, Inc. (US)
Profertil SA (50%, Argentina)
Viridian Fertilizers Ltd.
Viridian Inc.
Western Farm Service, Inc. (US)

COMPETITORS

CF Industries
Farmland Industries
IMC Global
Koch
Mississippi Chemical
PCS
SQM
Terra Industries
Terra Nitrogen

HISTORICAL FINANCIALS

Company Type: Public

Income Statement
FYE: December 31

	REVENUE ($ mil.)	NET INCOME ($ mil.)	NET PROFIT MARGIN	EMPLOYEES
12/02	2,083	0	—	4,829
12/01	2,063	(45)	—	4,988
12/00	1,873	82	4.4%	4,958
12/99	1,716	64	3.7%	4,536
12/98	1,805	121	6.7%	4,530
12/97	1,938	185	9.5%	4,432
12/96	1,814	151	8.3%	4,520
12/95	1,171	112	9.6%	3,481
12/94	763	62	8.1%	2,008
12/93	396	20	4.9%	2,070
Annual Growth	20.3%	—	—	9.9%

2002 Year-End Financials

Debt ratio: 135.5%
Return on equity: —
Cash ($ mil.): 109
Current ratio: 1.87
Long-term debt ($ mil.): 736

No. of shares (mil.): 126
Dividends
  Yield: 1.0%
  Payout: —
Market value ($ mil.): 1,425

Stock History
NYSE: AGU

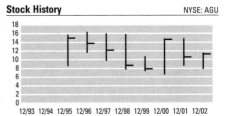

12/93 12/94 12/95 12/96 12/97 12/98 12/99 12/00 12/01 12/02

	STOCK PRICE ($) FY Close	P/E High/Low		PER SHARE ($) Earnings	Dividends	Book Value
12/02	11.31	—	—	(0.08)	0.11	6.06
12/01	10.60	—	—	(0.49)	0.11	6.46
12/00	14.63	23	11	0.63	0.11	7.55
12/99	7.88	22	15	0.49	0.11	6.82
12/98	8.69	17	8	0.94	0.11	6.29
12/97	12.19	11	7	1.40	0.11	5.00
12/96	13.75	15	11	1.07	0.07	4.99
12/95	14.99	10	5	1.59	0.02	6.17
Annual Growth	(3.9%)	—	—	—	27.6%	(0.3%)

Air France

It's clear skies ahead for Air France. Europe's #3 airline (after British Airways and Lufthansa) serves more than 200 destinations in 90 countries. Though still 54% owned by the state, the carrier has been partially privatized and has been enjoying growth with an increasing number of flights to major destinations in Asia, South America, and the US. Air France Cargo is a world-leading air cargo carrier. Aided in part by expansions at its Charles de Gaulle hub in Paris, Air France has also benefited from its SkyTeam alliance with Delta, AeroMéxico, and Korean Air Lines. Also, the carrier has agreed to acquire Dutch carrier KLM.

The deal would surpass British Airways as Europe's leading airline. It also allows the French government, which had been looking for ways to privatize its flag carrier, an opportunity to reduce its stake in Air France from 54% to 44%. Air France and KLM would continue to operate under their own names.

In an industry increasingly defined by global marketing alliances, the addition of KLM will help Air France's Skyteam better compete with Oneworld (anchored by British Airways and American Airlines) and Star (anchored by United Airlines and Lufthansa).

At a time when other airlines are abandoning transatlantic routes, Air France has increased the frequency of popular routes to places such as Los Angeles, Montreal, New York, and Tokyo. Air France has also acquired regional carriers that have helped bolster the airline's domestic and European presence. The airline also owns a 23% interest in the computer reservation system Amadeus.

HISTORY

Société Air France was founded in 1933, the product of consolidation during the adolescence of French aviation. The government that year forced a four-way merger of France's competing airlines: Air Union, Air Orient, Société Générale de Transport Aérien, and Compagnie Internationale de Navigation Aérienne.

Air France expanded during the 1930s to become one of the world's leading airlines, but its ascent was interrupted by WWII and the German occupation, during which the carrier shuttered operations.

Air France resumed flight after the war, and as the French state began nationalizing some industries to quickly rebuild the postwar economy,

it took control of the airline in 1948. Renamed Compagnie Nationale Air France, the carrier enjoyed government-backed financing that allowed it to launch its expansion.

With the era of big jets dawning, Air France began adding Boeing 707s to its fleet in 1960. Then France and the UK agreed in 1962 to jointly develop a supersonic transport — the Concorde. The next year French authorities realigned France's airline industry: International flights to Africa, Australia, and the Pacific were granted to a private carrier, Union de Transports Aériens (UTA); Air France controlled the remaining international routes. The domestic market was closed to both.

Air France added more jets to its fleet in the early 1970s and launched its cargo transport services. The company began flying the Concorde in 1976. Though spiraling development costs had made the Mach 2 jetliner a debatable investment, the supersonic transport served as a symbol of national pride.

In 1987 Air France joined in creating the Amadeus computer reservation system (launched 1989). The late 1980s were boom times in the industry, with Air France scoring healthy profits. But its attempt to take control of the domestic market by buying Air Inter was challenged by UTA, which increased its Air Inter stake in opposition. The battle was resolved in 1990: Air France bought control of both airlines.

But this French consolidation came just as the Gulf War, high oil prices, and an economic downturn began to wreak havoc on airlines. Air France fell into a money-losing streak just as deregulation in Europe was about to unleash new levels of competition. The government slapped down chairman Christian Blanc's attempt to cut wages and jobs in 1993 in the face of massive strikes. The airline eventually slimmed down and achieved net profits in 1997; Blanc, however, resigned in 1997 as the state dragged its feet on privatization.

With the 1998 signing of a US-France open skies agreement, Air France boosted flights to the US and struck code-sharing deals with Delta and Continental. The government finally launched a public offering of Air France in 1999 (keeping 63%, later reduced to 54%).

To better compete with members of the Star and Oneworld global airline marketing alliances, Air France joined Delta Air Lines, AeroMéxico, and Korean Air Lines to form the SkyTeam alliance in 2000. Also that year Air France further consolidated the domestic market by acquiring or upping stakes in regional carriers Proteus Airlines, Flandre Air, and Regional Airlines.

An Air France Concorde jet crashed shortly after takeoff from Paris in 2000, killing all 109 people on board and four more on the ground. Concorde flights were grounded after the crash, but resumed the following year.

Air France fared better than most airlines in the wake of September 2001 terrorist attacks on the US. The airline curbed its expansion plans and streamlined its fleet, but did not cut back on routes or resort to layoffs to stay aloft.

EXECUTIVES

Chairman and CEO: Jean-Cyril Spinetta, age 60
President and COO: Pierre-Henri Gourgeon
Deputy COO General Coordination: Auguste Gayte
CFO: Philippe Calavia
EVP Information Systems — Telecom: Jean-Paul Hamon
EVP Air France Cargo: Marc Boudier
SVP Commercial France: Christian Boireau

SVP Flight Operations: Gilbert Rovetto
SVP Ground Operations: Pascal de Izaguirre
SVP International Commercial Affairs: Patrick Alexandre
SVP Industrial Logistics: Alain Bassil
SVP Marketing and Development: Marc Lamidey
SVP Network Management: Bruno Matheu
SVP Social Policy: Jacques Pichot
VP Inspector General: Alain Vidalon
Auditors: Constantin Associés; Deloitte Touche Tohmatsu

LOCATIONS

HQ: 45, rue de Paris, 95747 Roissy, France
Phone: +33-1-41-56-78-00   **Fax:** +33-1-41-56-56-00
US HQ: 125 W. 55th St., 2nd Fl., New York, NY 10019
US Phone: 212-830-4000   **US Fax:** 212-830-4244
Web: www.airfrance.com

2003 Sales

	% of total
Europe	
France	20
Other	26
North America	18
Asia	12
Africa & Middle East	11
Caribbean & Indian Ocean	10
Latin America	5
Total	**100**

PRODUCTS/OPERATIONS

2003 Sales

	% of total
Passenger	47
Maintenance	31
Cargo	22
Total	**100**

COMPETITORS

Alitalia
AMR
British Airways
Iberia
KLM
Lufthansa
SAS
Brussels Airlines
UAL
Virgin Atlantic Airways

HISTORICAL FINANCIALS

Company Type: Public

Income Statement

FYE: March 31

	REVENUE ($ mil.)	NET INCOME ($ mil.)	NET PROFIT MARGIN	EMPLOYEES
3/03	13,696	130	0.9%	71,525
3/02	10,899	133	1.2%	70,156
3/01	10,790	370	3.4%	64,717
3/00	9,861	338	3.4%	59,190
3/99	9,766	268	2.7%	55,199
3/98	9,810	303	3.1%	46,385
3/97	7,693	66	0.9%	44,874
3/96	8,269	(436)	—	45,084
3/95	13,558	(722)	—	47,343
3/94	10,335	(1,588)	—	—
Annual Growth	**3.2%**	**—**		**5.3%**

2003 Year-End Financials

Debt ratio: 93.4%
Return on equity: 3.3%
Cash ($ mil.): 208
Current ratio: 2.00
Long-term debt ($ mil.): 4,027

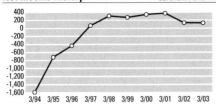

Net Income History Euronext Paris: AF

Airbus S.A.S.

Can you imagine 550 people all tucked into one airplane? Airbus, which is neck-and-neck with Boeing as the world's #1 commercial aircraft maker, is betting that airlines will go bonkers for its A380 (due out in 2006), which carries 555 passengers. Airbus — which has fewer planes in service, but boasts a larger order backlog than Boeing — also makes single-aisle (A318, A319, A320, A321) and wide-body (A300, A310, A330, A340) jets with capacities ranging from about 110 to 400 passengers. European Aeronautic Defence & Space Company (EADS) owns 80% of Airbus; UK-based BAE SYSTEMS owns the other 20%.

EADS consists of DaimlerChrysler Aerospace (Germany), Aerospatiale Matra (France), and CASA (Spain). Each company oversees part of the production; for example, aircraft wings hail from the UK, cockpits are from France, and interiors come from Germany. Airbus plants in France and Germany assemble the parts.

The company is banking on its jumbo A380 (which received brisk orders even before it was formally approved — so much so that Boeing scrapped plans for a competing plane), a steady increase in passenger air travel and air cargo transport, new flight routes, and the need for more midsized, long-range aircraft for future success.

HISTORY

In the 1970s three US companies, Boeing, Lockheed, and McDonnell Douglas, dominated the commercial aircraft market. France and the UK had been discussing an alliance to build competing jets since 1965, but political infighting stalled the talks. Finally, in 1969 France and West Germany committed to building the Airbus A300. Airbus Industrie was born in 1970 as a *groupement d'intérêt économique* (grouping of economic interest, a structure used by allied French vineyards). Seed money came from partners Aerospatiale Matra and Deutsche Airbus. CASA joined in 1971.

The A300 entered service with Air France in 1974, but Airbus had trouble selling it outside member countries. The following year the firm hired former American Airlines president George Warde to help market the A300 in the US. His efforts paid off when Eastern Air Lines decided to buy the A300. Also in 1975 Airbus launched the A310, a smaller, more fuel-efficient version of the A300. The UK joined the consortium in 1979.

By 1980 Airbus trailed only Boeing among the world's commercial jet makers. The A320 was introduced in 1984 — it featured a groundbreaking "fly-by-wire" system that allowed pilots to adjust the aircraft's control surfaces via a computer, helping to make it the fastest-

selling jetliner in history. The firm launched the A330 and A340, larger planes designed for medium- and long-range flights, in 1987. Two years later Airbus introduced the A321, an elongated version of the A320, and received a $6 billion order from Federal Express.

The German government sold its 20% stake in Deutsche Airbus to Daimler-Benz (now DaimlerChrysler) in 1992, giving Daimler-Benz 100% ownership of the German partner (now about 38%).

In 1993 Airbus sold only 38 planes, about one-sixth as many as Boeing. Sales rebounded in 1995, and the next year the firm won a contract worth about $5 billion to provide planes to USAir (now US Airways). The four Airbus partners agreed in 1997 to restructure the consortium as a limited liability company, possibly as a first step toward taking it public.

In 1998 Airbus won orders from Iberia Airlines and three Latin American carriers, then landed orders from longtime Boeing customers British Airways and UPS, narrowing the gap with its chief rival.

Seeking more customers in Asia, Airbus signed parts contracts with Japanese suppliers in 1999 and launched production of its A318, a 107-seat short-haul passenger jet designed to compete with Boeing's 717. Also that year Airbus won a contract worth $946 million to provide British Airways with up to 24 of its A318s. For the first time ever, the company recorded more plane orders than Boeing.

In 2000 the UK government pledged $836 million in loans to back consortium partner BAE SYSTEMS' participation in the A3XX project, an ambitious plane that would seat more than 550 passengers. That year the German government announced plans to purchase up to 75 Airbus A400M transports valued at around $9.8 billion. In June the company announced that it had finally inked a deal to turn Airbus into a corporation, to be known as Airbus Integrated Company. Not surprisingly, it also committed to producing the superjumbo A3XX and soon received 17 firm orders from Air France and Emirates Airlines. Around the same time, the European Aeronautic Defence & Space Company, which owns 80% of Airbus, launched its own IPO.

Airbus officially launched the A3XX — and renamed it the A380 — late in 2000. Early in 2001 Airbus announced that it would become a stand-alone corporation (rather than a consortium) before the end of the year. The company also announced that it was setting up a subsidiary in Japan — where Boeing traditionally dominates. In July Airbus Industrie was incorporated in France as Airbus S.A.S. The next month Airbus announced that it would create 4,000 new jobs over two years, primarily to support the development and production of the A380.

Faced with the drastic downturn in the commercial aviation market due to the September 11 attacks, in 2002 the company announced that it would cut full-time equivalent work hours by around 13% (equal to about 6,000 jobs) through voluntary retirement, reduction in part-time work, and cancellation of temporary contracts. In March Airbus won a contract from South African Airways for about 40 aircraft — worth around $3.5 billion, to be spread out over 10 years.

EXECUTIVES

Chairman, Supervisory Board: Manfred Bischoff
President and CEO: Noël Forgeard, age 57
COO: Gustav Humbert, age 53
CFO: Andreas Sperl
EVP and Customer Affairs: John J. Leahy
EVP, Programs: Gérard Blanc
EVP, Human Resources: Erik Pillet
EVP, Procurement: Ray Wilson
EVP, Government Relations, Communications, and External Affairs: Philippe Delmas, age 49
SVP, Training and Flight Operations: Jean-Michel Roy
General Manager, Airbus España: Francisco Fernández Sáinz
Special Advisor to the CEO: Jürgen Thomas
EVP, Quality and Integration: Bill Black, age 47
EVP, Engineering: Alain Garcia, age 60
EVP, Customer Services: Patrick Gavin
EVP, Manufacturing: Karl-Heinz Hartmann, age 52

LOCATIONS

HQ: 1, Rond point Maurice Bellonte, 31707 Blagnac, France
Phone: +33-5-61-93-33-87   **Fax:** +33-5-61-93-49-55
US HQ: 198 Van Buren St., Ste. 300, Herndon, VA 20170
US Phone: 703-834-3400   **US Fax:** 703-834-3548
Web: www.airbus.com

Airbus S.A.S. has offices in China, North America, and Singapore, and it manufactures airplanes in factories throughout Europe, with final assembly carried out in France and Germany.

PRODUCTS/OPERATIONS

Selected Aircraft

Single-aisle twin-engine jets
A318
A319
A320
A321

Superjumbo four-engine jets
A380 (previously known as the A3XX)

Wide-body twin-engine jets
A300-310
A300-600F

Wide-body two- and four-engine jets
A330 (two-engine)
A340 (four-engine)
A340-500
A340-600

Selected Customers

Aer Lingus	Japan Air System
Air Canada	Korean Airlines
Air France	Lufthansa
Alitalia	Northwest
America West	SilkAir (Singapore Airlines)
American Airlines	
China Southern	United
Delta	US Airways
Federal Express	Virgin Atlantic Airways
Iberia	

COMPETITORS

Boeing Commercial Airplanes
Boeing
Bombardier
Embraer
Gulfstream Aerospace
Sextant Avionique

HISTORICAL FINANCIALS

Company Type: Joint venture

Income Statement

FYE: December 31

	REVENUE ($ mil.)	NET INCOME ($ mil.)	NET PROFIT MARGIN	EMPLOYEES
12/02	20,333	—	—	46,000
12/01	18,159	—	—	45,000
12/00	17,200	—	—	45,000
12/99	16,817	—	—	45,000
12/98	13,300	—	—	2,700
12/97	11,600	—	—	2,289
12/96	8,800	—	—	2,207
12/95	9,600	—	—	2,182
12/94	8,500	—	—	1,367
12/93	8,700	—	—	2,700
Annual Growth	**9.9%**	—	—	**37.0%**

Revenue History

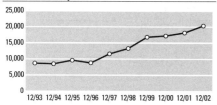

Akzo Nobel N.V.

Akzo Nobel is the world's largest paint maker, but it can do more than paint a pretty picture. The company is among the world's largest chemical manufacturers and also is a major salt producer. Akzo Nobel is organized along three business lines. The company's coatings group makes paints, automotive finishes, and industrial coatings. Its chemical unit produces pulp and paper chemicals, functional chemicals (including flame retardants and animal feed additives), surfactants (used in detergents and personal care products), polymers, and catalysts. A third unit, pharmaceuticals, produces contraceptives, fertility treatments, antidepressants, antipsychotics, over-the-counter drugs, and veterinary medicines.

In May 2003 Hans Wijers, the former Dutch economics affairs minister, took over from Cees van Lede as CEO and promised to fix Akzo Nobel's pharmaceuticals business and to initiate a $500 million divestment program. The program will include slicing $120 million in costs from pharmaceuticals and cutting 800 jobs from the division by year's end. Wijers also suggested that the company is considering a possible break up of its businesses. All options are open, including selling off the entire pharmaceuticals unit.

By the end of the third quarter the company had cut more than 3,400 jobs. About half of those job cuts came from Akzo Nobel's coatings division, which lost almost 1,000 jobs with the sale of subsidiary Casco Impregnate Papers earlier in the year.

In September 2003 Wijers announced that the company would sell three of its chemicals divisions: catalysts, coating resins, and phosphorous

chemicals. The divestment represents more than $1 billion in annual sales.

Akzo Nobel has operations in 80 countries; about half its sales are in Europe.

HISTORY

The Akzo side of Akzo Nobel traces its roots to two companies — German rayon and coatings maker Vereinigte Glanzstoff-Fabriken (founded in 1899) and Dutch rayon maker Nederlandsche Kunstzijdebariek (founded in 1911 and known as NK or Enka). In 1928 NK built a plant near Asheville, North Carolina, in what later became the town of Enka. The two companies merged in 1929 to create Algemene Kunstzijde-Unie (AKU).

In 1967 two Dutch companies merged to form Koninklijke Zout-Organon (KZO). In 1969 KZO bought US-based International Salt and merged with AKU to form Akzo. In the 1980s Akzo focused on building its chemicals, coatings, and pharmaceuticals businesses. Akzo sold its paper and pulp business to Nobel in 1993. A few months later the company reclaimed that business when it bought Nobel.

Best remembered for the prizes that bear his name (which were first awarded in 1901 through a bequest in his will), Alfred Nobel invented the blasting cap in 1863, making it possible to control the detonation of nitroglycerin. He then persuaded Stockholm merchant J. W. Smitt to help him finance Nitroglycerin Ltd. to make and sell the volatile fluid (1864). Nobel's quest to improve nitroglycerin led to his invention of dynamite in 1867.

After Nobel's death in 1896, Nitroglycerin Ltd. remained an explosives maker, and in 1965 it changed its name to Nitro Nobel. In 1978 Swedish industrialist Marcus Wallenberg bought Nitro Nobel for his KemaNord chemical group, known afterward as KemaNobel. Within six years industrialist Erik Penser controlled both armaments maker Bofors and KemaNobel, and he merged them in 1984 as Nobel Industries.

Risky investments led Penser to ruin in 1991. His holdings, including Nobel, were taken over by a government-owned bank and conveyed into Securum, a government-owned holding company (which still owns 18% of Akzo Nobel). In 1992 Nobel spun off its consumer-goods segment.

Akzo bought Nobel in 1994. Although the company had good financial results in 1995, it faced pressure from rising costs for raw materials and a difficult foreign-exchange environment. Akzo announced major closings and layoffs — it sold its polyethylene packaging resin business and moved some clothing-grade rayon operations to Poland.

The merger between Akzo and Nobel was legally completed in 1996. That year the company introduced Puregon, a fertility drug, and Remeron, touted as a replacement for Prozac, in the US and other countries. In 1997 Akzo Nobel put most of its worst-performing segment, fibers, into a joint venture with Turkish conglomerate Sabanci. It also sold its North American salt unit to Cargill.

Akzo Nobel acquired Courtaulds (coatings, sealants, and fibers) in 1998 and changed the firm's name to Akzo Nobel UK. Akzo Nobel also bought BASF deco, the European decorative-coatings business of BASF Coatings. Akzo Nobel combined its fiber business with Akzo Nobel UK to form a new division, Acordis. Akzo Nobel then sold Acordis to investment firm CVC Capital Partners in 1999 for $859 million (Akzo Nobel retains a minority share). Also in 1999 Akzo

Nobel bought Hoechst's animal-health unit, Hoechst Roussel Vet, for $712 million. The next year the company bought Dexter Corporation's aircraft coatings business.

In 2001 Akzo Nobel sold its medical diagnostics division to French drugmaker bioMérieux-Pierre Fabre. Later that year the company picked up the vehicle refinishes business of MAC Specialty Coatings of the US. In November Akzo Nobel agreed to sell its printing inks business to a private equity firm.

EXECUTIVES

Chairman, Supervisory Board:
Jonkheer Aarnout A. Loudon, age 67
Deputy Chairman, Supervisory Board:
Frits H. Fentener van Vlissingen, age 69
Chairman, Board of Management and CEO:
G. J. (Hans) Wijers, age 52
Deputy Chairman, Board of Management and CFO:
Fritz W. Fröhlich, $796,954 pay
Member, Board of Management, Chemicals:
Dag Strömqvist, $651,772 pay
Member, Board of Management, Coatings:
R. M. J. (Rudy) van der Meer, $734,329 pay
Member, Board of Management, Pharma:
A. T. M. (Toon) Wilderbeek, age 51
SVP, Finance: Frits H. Hensel
SVP, Human Resources: Paul L. Matson, age 54
General Counsel: A. Jan A. J. Eijsbouts
Secretary: G.H. (Han) Jalink
Senior Group Director, Chemicals; President and Treasurer, Akzo Nobel, Inc.: Conrad S. Kent
Senior Group Director, Coatings:
M. (Rinus) Rooseboom
Group Director Technology, Pharmaceuticals:
Jan H. Dopper
Corporate Information Officer: Bill Stubbins, age 50
Director, Corporate Social Responsibility and Health, Safety, and Environment: André Veneman, age 45
Director, Internal Auditing: Paul Grimmelikhuizen, age 51
Manager, Surfactants Americas: Frank Sherman, age 49
Auditors: KPMG Accountants N.V.

LOCATIONS

HQ: Velperweg 76, 6824 BM Arnhem, The Netherlands
Phone: +31-26-366-4433   **Fax:** +31-26-366-3250
US HQ: Akzo Nobel Inc., 525 W. Van Buren St., Chicago, IL 60607
US Phone: 312-544-7000
Web: www.akzonobel.com

Akzo Nobel has operations in roughly 80 countries.

2002 Sales

	% of total
Europe	
Germany	8
UK	7
The Netherlands	6
Sweden	4
Other countries	27
US & Canada	27
Asia	11
Other regions	10
Total	**100**

PRODUCTS/OPERATIONS

2002 Sales

	$ mil.	% of total
Coatings	5,799	39
Chemicals	4,829	33
Pharmaceuticals	4,209	28
Adjustments	(131)	—
Total	**14,706**	**100**

Selected Products

Coatings
Car refinishes
Decorative coatings
Industrial finishes
Industrial products
Marine and protective coatings
Powder coatings

Chemicals
Base Chemicals
Catalysts
Energy
Functional Chemicals
Polymer Chemicals
Pulp and Paper Chemicals
Resins
Salt
Surface Chemistry

Pharmaceuticals
Drugs for human healthcare (including oral
    contraceptives, antidepressants, and infertility
    treatments)
Pharmaceutical ingredients
Veterinary medicines (including antibiotics, vaccines,
    and anti-infectives)

COMPETITORS

Abbott Labs	ICI American
Alfa	ICI
BASF AG	Johnson & Johnson
Bayer AG	Merck
Borden Chemical	Novartis
Bristol-Myers Squibb	Novo Nordisk
Degussa	PPG
Dow Chemical	Roche
DuPont	Rohm and Haas
Eli Lilly	RPM
Engelhard	Sherwin-Williams
Ferro	Solutia
FPC	Solvay
GlaxoSmithKline	TOTAL
Sabanci Holding	Wattyl
H.B. Fuller	Wyeth
Hercules	

HISTORICAL FINANCIALS

Company Type: Public

Income Statement

FYE: December 31

	REVENUE ($ mil.)	NET INCOME ($ mil.)	NET PROFIT MARGIN	EMPLOYEES
12/02	14,706	859	5.8%	67,900
12/01	12,576	598	4.8%	66,300
12/00	13,188	909	6.9%	68,400
12/99	14,565	206	1.4%	68,000
12/98	14,557	711	4.9%	85,900
12/97	11,872	797	6.7%	68,900
12/96	12,882	757	5.9%	70,700
12/95	13,363	817	6.1%	69,800
12/94	12,794	680	5.3%	70,400
12/93	8,499	283	3.3%	73,400
Annual Growth	6.3%	13.1%	—	(0.9%)

2002 Year-End Financials

Debt ratio: 98.3%
Return on equity: 37.8%
Cash ($ mil.): 546
Current ratio: 1.19
Long-term debt ($ mil.): 2,167

No. of shares (mil.): 286
Dividends
    Yield: 3.4%
    Payout: 36.0%
Market value ($ mil.): 9,125

Stock History

NASDAQ: AKZOY

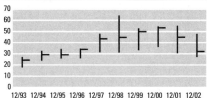

	STOCK PRICE ($) FY Close	P/E High/Low		PER SHARE ($) Earnings	Dividends	Book Value
12/02	31.89	16	9	3.00	1.08	7.70
12/01	44.85	19	11	2.10	1.10	8.17
12/00	53.25	17	12	3.19	0.93	8.06
12/99	49.75	19	13	0.71	2.11	6.57
12/98	44.63	26	13	2.49	1.06	7.44
12/97	43.44	17	11	2.80	0.78	31.28
12/96	33.75	13	10	2.66	0.90	31.07
12/95	29.00	12	9	2.88	0.83	28.89
12/94	29.06	13	10	2.31	0.76	25.36
12/93	24.19	18	12	1.50	0.75	29.34
Annual Growth	3.1%	—	—	8.0%	4.1%	(13.8%)

Alcan Inc.

Alcan's can-do attitude has helped make it the world's second-largest aluminum producer, behind the US's Alcoa. The company controls 18% of the world's aluminum production capacity. It mines bauxite (aluminum ore) and makes and recycles aluminum sheet, foil, wire and cable, and extrusions (doors, windows, auto parts). Alcan also generates hydroelectric power and makes aluminum-related specialty chemicals and packaging products. The company sells mainly to customers in the packaging, transportation, and construction industries. Former Algroup shareholders own about 34% of Alcan (Alcan bought Algroup in 2000).

Alcan's Global Automotive Products unit coordinates supplying aluminum parts to automakers worldwide. Alcan also generates hydroelectric power and is one of the world's largest aluminum recyclers. The company operates in more than 38 countries.

After reorganizing its operations into six divisions (Bauxite, Alumina and Specialty Chemicals; Primary Metal; Rolled Products Americas and Asia; Rolled Products Europe; Engineered Products; and Packaging), Alcan has continued to streamline through divestitures, mostly in the company's fabrication segment. In the midst of declining aluminum prices, Alcan cut its workforce by about 9% from the prior year. With the weakening demand for glass, Alcan has sold a majority of its glass operations.

Alcan's plan for growth during tough market times is to grow selectively through acquisitions. Opportunities in the packaging, engineered products, and primary metals sectors are of interest to the company. Alcan went one step further by purchasing VAW Flexible Packaging from Norsk Hydro ASA, which appreciably bolsters Alcan's packaging sector.

Alcan is still in hot pursuit for French competitor Pechiney. The company had launched a hostile bid offering of about $3.9 billion in cash

and stock. Unfortunately for Alcan, Pechiney's board members steadfastly rejected the offer. Alcan tried again and offered $4.3 billion, but Pechiney rejected the bid, stating it was still too low. The third time was the charm for Alcan. The company upped the ante to around $4.7 billion, which around 92% of Pechiney's shareholders tendered. Alcan has reopened the offer to Pechiney's shareholders who have not tendered their shares. If Alcan acquires more than 95% of the shares it would consider taking Pechiney private.

HISTORY

In 1886 American chemist Charles Hall and a French chemist simultaneously discovered an inexpensive process for aluminum production. Two years later Hall, with an investor group led by Captain Alfred Hunt, formed the Pittsburgh Reduction Company. It became the Aluminum Company of America (Alcoa) in 1907.

As mandated by a US antitrust divestment order, in 1928 Alcoa organized its Canadian and other foreign operations as a separate company, Aluminium Limited. Aluminium (British spelling for aluminum) Limited retained close ties with Alcoa and appointed Edward Davis, brother of former Alcoa chairman Arthur Davis, as its first chief executive.

After narrowly surviving the Depression, Aluminium Limited expanded globally, building plants in Asia and Europe. Aluminum demand during WWII made it the world's largest smelter by war's end.

US courts in 1950 ordered the Mellon and Davis families to end their joint ownership of Alcoa and Aluminium Limited. Both families opted to stay with Alcoa.

In 1961 the company began fabricating its own products in Oswego, New York. Aluminium Limited changed its name to Alcan in 1966. Alcan had to readjust its strategy when Guyana nationalized its raw resources in 1971. Six years later Jamaica (a major bauxite producer) acquired 70% of Alcan's assets, and the two formed joint venture Jamalcan.

David Culver became the company's CEO (the first non-Davis family member to hold the position) in 1979 and led Alcan through an early 1980s recession with a massive cost-cutting campaign. In 1989 Alcan built the world's largest aluminum beverage-can recycling plant in Berea, Kentucky.

The entrance of former Soviet republics and other Eastern Bloc countries into the international aluminum market in 1991 caused a drastic drop in aluminum prices worldwide. That year Alcan shut down 8% of its smelting capacity and began selling off less-profitable operations. By 1994 increased global demand for aluminum and cutbacks in production spurred industrywide recovery, and Alcan's operations returned to the black for the first time in four years. In 1998 Alcan signed a 10-year pact to supply aluminum to General Motors. As market conditions in Asia soured, Alcan reduced its ownership of Nippon Light Metal Company from 45% to about 11%.

In 1999 the company also announced the sale of its alumina refinery in Ireland to Glencore International AG and agreed to acquire Pechiney and Alusuisse Lonza Group (Algroup) in a three-way merger to create Alcan-Pechiney-Algroup.

In 2000 the European Commission approved a proposed merger between Alcan and Algroup, but Alcan's plan to include Pechiney in a three-way merger had to be withdrawn because of antitrust concerns. Pechiney pulled out of the deal entirely after Alcan voted against selling its 50% stake in a German aluminum plant (Norf). In the meantime, Alcan and Taihan Electric Wire agreed to acquire 66% and 30%, respectively, of Aluminum of Korea (Koralu) from Hyundai. The same year Alcan acquired Algroup in a $5.3 billion deal.

Company president and CEO Jacques Bougie resigned in 2001 and was replaced by former ITT Industries' CEO Travis Engen. To reflect its broader array of products, the company changed its name from Alcan Aluminium to Alcan Inc. that year.

Alcan acquired VAW Flexible Packaging from Norsk Hydro for around $545 million in 2003. Mid-year Alcan launched a hostile bid for French competitor Pechiney for roughly $3.9 billion in cash and stock. Pechiney's board members unanimously rejected Alcan's takeover bid indicating the offer was undervalued. Alcan raised its offer to $4.3 billion but Pechiney rejected that offer as well. The company relentlessly counter offered a third time with a proposal of roughly $4.7 billion, which about 92% of Pechiney's shareholders accepted.

Also in 2003 independent ratings agency GovernanceMetrics International gave Alcan the highest possible rating for its corporate governance practices.

EXECUTIVES

Chairman: L. Yves Fortier, age 67
President, CEO, and Director: Travis Engen, age 58, $2,830,000 pay
EVP (Office of the President), Primary Metal, Bauxite, Alumina and Specialty Chemicals, and Engineered Products; President, Alcan Global Fabrication Group: Richard B. (Dick) Evans, age 56, $872,500 pay
EVP (Office of the President), Rolled Products Americas and Asia, Rolled Products Europe, and Packaging; President, Aluminum Fabrication, Americas and Asia: Brian W. Sturgell, age 52, $1,170,000 pay
EVP and CFO: Geoffery Merszei, $975,000 pay
EVP; President, Alcan Engineered Products Group: Kurt Wolfensberger
SVP, Corporate and External Affairs: Daniel Gagnier
SVP, Human Resources: Gaston Ouellet
SVP, Mergers and Acquisitions and Chief Legal Officer: David McAusland
SVP; President, Alcan Bauxite, Alumina and Specialty Chemicals Group: Michael Hanley
SVP; President, Alcan Packaging: Armin Weinhold
SVP; President and CEO, Alcan Engineered Products: Michel Jacques
SVP; President and CEO, Alcan Packaging: Christel Bories, age 38
SVP; President and CEO, Alcan Primary Metal Group: Cynthia Carroll, $1,176,433 pay
SVP; President and CEO, Rolled Products Americas and Asia: Martha Finn Brooks
SVP; President and CEO, Alcan Rolled Products Europe: Christopher Bark-Jones
VP and Controller: Thomas J. Harrington
VP and Treasurer: Glenn R. Lucas
Auditors: PricewaterhouseCoopers LLP

LOCATIONS

HQ: 1188 Sherbrooke St. West,
   Montreal, Quebec H3A 3G2, Canada
Phone: 514-848-8000   **Fax:** 514-848-8115
US HQ: 6060 Parkland Blvd., Cleveland, OH 44124-4185
US Phone: 440-423-6600   **US Fax:** 440-423-6667
Web: www.alcan.com

Alcan operates bauxite mines in Australia, Brazil, and Ghana; alumina plants in Australia, Brazil, Canada, and the UK; and manufacturing plants or sales offices in more than 38 countries in Africa, Asia, Australia, Europe, and the Americas.

2002 Sales

	$ mil.	% of total
Europe		
Germany	1,431	11
UK	1,030	8
Switzerland	202	2
Other countries	2,329	19
US	4,574	37
Asia	1,648	13
Canada	708	5
Brazil	395	3
Australia	103	1
Other regions	120	1
Total	**12,540**	**100**

PRODUCTS/OPERATIONS

Selected Products and Services

Fabrication Group
Castings (automobile engine components, aluminum alloys)
Extrusions (automobile components, doors, and windows; extrusion ingots)
Flat-rolled products (foil and sheet)
Flexible packaging
Recycling
Wire and cable (electrical wire and cable, screen wire, cable coverings)

Primary Metal Group
Alumina refining
Aluminum activities
Bauxite mining
Power generation

COMPETITORS

Alcoa
Alumina
Aluminum Corporation of China
Grupo Carso
Commercial Metals
Corus Group
SEPI
Graenges
Hydro Aluminium
Imsa
Industria Espanola Del Aluminio
Kaiser Aluminum
MAXXAM
SMI
Nissho Iwai-Nichimen
Noranda
Ormet
Pechiney
Quanex
Rio Tinto
Ryerson Tull
Silgan
Southwire
Trans-World Metals
Vale do Rio Doce
VAW aluminium

HISTORICAL FINANCIALS

Company Type: Public

Income Statement

FYE: December 31

	REVENUE ($ mil.)	NET INCOME ($ mil.)	NET PROFIT MARGIN	EMPLOYEES
12/02	12,540	374	3.0%	48,000
12/01	12,626	5	0.0%	52,000
12/00	9,148	618	6.8%	37,000
12/99	7,324	460	6.3%	36,000
12/98	7,789	399	5.1%	36,000
12/97	7,777	485	6.2%	33,000
12/96	7,614	410	5.4%	34,000
12/95	9,287	263	2.8%	39,000
12/94	8,216	96	1.2%	43,900
12/93	7,232	(104)	—	43,900
Annual Growth	**6.3%**	**—**	**—**	**1.0%**

2002 Year-End Financials

Debt ratio: 37.6%
Return on equity: 4.4%
Cash ($ mil.): 110
Current ratio: 1.31
Long-term debt ($ mil.): 3,187
No. of shares (mil.): 321
Dividends
  Yield: 1.8%
  Payout: 47.4%
Market value ($ mil.): 9,490

Stock History

NYSE: AL

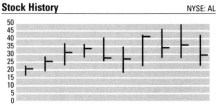

12/93 12/94 12/95 12/96 12/97 12/98 12/99 12/00 12/01 12/02

	STOCK PRICE ($) FY Close	P/E High/Low		PER SHARE ($) Earnings	Dividends	Book Value
12/02	29.52	37	20	1.14	0.54	26.83
12/01	35.93	—	—	(0.01)	0.60	27.39
12/00	34.19	19	12	2.45	0.60	28.38
12/99	41.38	20	11	2.06	0.60	25.38
12/98	27.06	20	11	1.71	0.60	24.42
12/97	27.63	20	13	2.09	0.60	22.32
12/96	33.63	21	16	1.74	0.60	21.46
12/95	31.13	35	22	1.06	0.45	21.40
12/94	25.38	83	58	0.34	0.30	20.74
12/93	20.75	—	—	(0.54)	0.30	19.86
Annual Growth	**4.0%**	**—**	**—**	**—**	**6.7%**	**3.4%**

Alcatel

Alcatel found its calling. One of France's largest industrial companies, Alcatel is a leading global supplier of high-tech equipment for telecommunications. Core network switching and transmission systems for wireline and wireless networks for carriers and enterprises account for most of its sales. The company also manufactures cell phones, communications cable, and satellite equipment and provides such network services as consulting, integration, design, planning, operation, and maintenance. Alcatel's clients include top European telecom service providers Orange and Deutsche Telekom.

Chairman and CEO Serge Tchuruk (pronounced "cha-RUK") has honed a once lumbering Alcatel with broad industrial interests into a focused telecom heavyweight. He has overseen an extensive restructuring that included the sale of noncore businesses such as engineering, nuclear power, and defense electronics. Restructuring continues in the form of layoffs; the company plans to reach an employee count of 60,000 by late 2003.

Despite slacking revenues, Alcatel has performed better than other leading global equipment makers like Nortel and Lucent. Alcatel is a global leader in the market for DSL infrastructure equipment, but trails its competitors in sales of wireless equipment; the company continues to put money into R&D for fiber-optic products.

Alcatel is building its presence in the US through acquisitions and pursuing contracts in the burgeoning market of China. Alcatel has hinted that it might sell its optoelectronics unit, Alcatel Optronics, to offset declining sales.

HISTORY

In 1898 Pierre Azaria combined his electric generating company with three others to form Compagnie Générale d'Électricité (CGE). As one of Europe's pioneer electric power and manufacturing companies, CGE expanded operations in France and abroad through acquisitions. After the French government nationalized electric utilities in 1946, CGE diversified into the production of telecommunications equipment, consumer appliances, and electronics.

In 1970 CGE bought Alcatel, a French communications pioneer founded in 1879 that had introduced digital switching exchanges. CGE combined its telecom division with Alcatel to form CIT Alcatel.

The Mitterrand government nationalized CGE in 1982. The next year the company traded its electronics units for Thomson's communications businesses, making CGE the world's fifth-largest telephone equipment maker. Later, CGE combined Alcatel with ITT's phone equipment operations to form Alcatel NV, a Brussels-based company that started off as the world's second-largest telecom enterprise, after AT&T.

In 1987 the government sold CGE to the public. Two years later CGE and UK-based The General Electric Company, plc (GEC, now known as Marconi plc) combined their power systems and engineering businesses to create GEC Alsthom NV. The company adopted the Alcatel Alsthom name in 1991 (shortened to Alcatel in 1998) and purchased the transmission equipment unit of US-based Rockwell International (now Rockwell Automation).

Turnaround specialist Serge Tchuruk, the former head of French oil giant TOTAL, was chosen to lead the company in 1995. Deregulation and intense competition in the European telecom market, along with massive writeoffs of bad investments dating back to the 1980s, led to a $5 billion loss in 1995, Alcatel's first loss and one of the largest to date by a French company. As a result Alcatel divested nonstrategic assets and cut its workforce by more than 12,500 employees. The company bounced back with a profit in 1996.

Following the recommendation of the French government, in 1998 Alcatel, Dassault Industries, and Aerospatiale joined forces to buy part of the state's stake in defense electronics group Thomson-CSF (now Thales). Intensifying its telecommunications focus, Alcatel sold its main engineering unit (Cegelec) to GEC Alsthom in 1998 and then spun off the venture as ALSTOM. That year Alcatel bought networking specialists

Packet Engines and DSC Communications to further push into the US market.

In 1999 Alcatel acquired several more US-based data network equipment makers, including Xylan and Assured Access. The next year it swapped all but 10% of its stake in nuclear power company Framatome for an additional 10% of Thomson-CSF. The company pressed further into the US that year with the purchases of Genesys Telecommunications (computer-telephony software) and Canadian equipment maker Newbridge Networks.

Alcatel changed the name of its power and communication cables business, one of the world's largest cable manufacturing operations, to Nexans in 2000. The company also sold 20% of its optical components unit to create the first European tracking stock.

In 2001 Genesys acquired IBM's CallPath computer-telephony software unit. Alcatel also took control of its satellite communications joint venture with Thales. A market slowdown that year led Alcatel to announce staff cuts of about 10%. In mid-2001 Alcatel spun off Nexans to the public, sold its remaining stake in ALSTOM, and bought a controlling stake in its joint venture in China with Shanghai Bell. The company beefed up its line of fiber-optic products when it bought passive component maker Kymata that year.

In 2002 Alcatel sold its enterprise distribution and services operations in Europe to Platinum Equity. The company also sold several of its European manufacturing facilities to contractor Sanmina-SCI; items produced at these locations included point-to-point microwave systems and wireline network access systems.

The company added to its optical transport products for metro networks with the acquisition of startup Astral Point that year, and it announced that it would acquire privately held Telera, a US-based provider of software for making Web content accessible by phone, in order to strengthen Genesys' contact center software business. That year it sold its semiconductor business, Alcatel Microelectronics, to STMicroelectronics for about $345 million; the two companies will jointly develop chipsets for DSL networking equipment.

EXECUTIVES

Chairman and CEO: Serge Tchuruk, age 65, $1,600,321 pay
President and COO: Philippe Germond, age 46
CFO: Jean-Pascal Beaufret, age 51
CTO: Niel Ransom, age 49
EVP; President, Alcatel Europe and South: Jacques Dunogué, age 52
EVP; President, Mobile Communications Group: Etienne Fouques, age 54
EVP; President, Private Communications Group: Olivier Houssin, age 50
EVP; CEO, Alcatel USA: Mike Quigley, age 49
EVP: Christian Reinaudo, age 48
EVP; President, Asia-Pacific: Ronald (Ron) Spithill, age 61
SVP, Fixed Networking: Mike Dobbs
SVP, Corporate Human Resources: Thomas Edig, age 41
SVP, Corporate Communications: Caroline Mille
SVP, Corporate Operations: Christian Tournier, age 60
SVP, Product Strategy, Marketing, and Development, Optical Networks: Romano Valussi
President, e-Business Networking: Patrick Liot
President, Mobile Phone: Jacques Combet
President, Wireless Transmission: Gianni Jones
President, Fixed Solutions: Alan Mottram
President, Operations: André Navarri, age 54
President, Fixed Networks: Michel Rahier
President, Integration and Services: Frederic Rose
President, Optical Networks: Jean-Marie Vansteenkiste

Senior Director Communications, Americas: Mark Burnworth
Director, Investor Relations, North America: Peter Campbell
Director, Shareholder Relations: Michel Faul
General Counsel: Pascal Durand-Barthez
Auditors: Barbier Frinault & Autres; Deloitte Touche Tohmatsu

LOCATIONS

HQ: 54, rue La Boétie, 75008 Paris, France
Phone: +33-1-40-76-10-10 **Fax:** +33-1-40-76-14-05
US HQ: 1000 Coit Rd., Plano, TX 75075
US Phone: 972-477-2555 **US Fax:** 972-519-3999
Web: www.alcatel.com

Alcatel has operations in more than 130 countries.

PRODUCTS/OPERATIONS

Selected Operations

Access systems
Core optical transmission equipment
Data switching and routing equipment
Enterprise networking systems
Metro optical transmission equipment
Mobile network transmission and switching equipment and software
Modems (ADSL, SHDSL)
Optical components
Optical fiber, cable, and connectivity hardware
Professional services
  Consulting
  Deployment
  Design
  Integration
  Maintenance
  Operation
  Planning
Satellite systems
Software
  Call center
  Messaging and billing
  Network management
  Operation support systems
  Service creation
Submarine systems
Telephones
Transport automation equipment
Video delivery products
Voice and multimedia switching equipment
Wireless access and transmission systems

Selected Subsidiaries and Affiliates

Alcatel USA Inc.
Nexans (20%)
Thales (16%)

COMPETITORS

3Com	Marconi
ADC Telecommunications	Motorola
Avaya	NEC
Cisco Systems	Nokia
Corning	Nortel Networks
ECI Telecom	Oki Electric
Ericsson	Panasonic Mobile
Fujitsu	Communications
Harris Corp	Sagem
Hitachi	Siemens
Hughes Electronics	Tellabs
Juniper Networks	Toshiba
Lucent	

HISTORICAL FINANCIALS

Company Type: Public

Income Statement

FYE: December 31

	REVENUE ($ mil.)	NET INCOME ($ mil.)	NET PROFIT MARGIN	EMPLOYEES
12/02	17,379	(4,984)	—	75,940
12/01	22,597	(4,424)	—	99,314
12/00	29,580	1,247	4.2%	131,598
12/99	23,235	650	2.8%	115,712
12/98	24,906	2,741	11.0%	118,000
12/97	30,854	774	2.5%	189,500
12/96	31,269	526	1.7%	190,600
12/95	32,709	(5,216)	—	191,830
12/94	31,400	678	2.2%	203,000
12/93	26,456	1,195	4.5%	196,500
Annual Growth	(4.6%)	—	—	(10.0%)

2002 Year-End Financials

Debt ratio: 93.6%	No. of shares (mil.): 1,265
Return on equity: —	Dividends
Cash ($ mil.): 5,664	Yield: 3.2%
Current ratio: 1.58	Payout: —
Long-term debt ($ mil.): 4,923	Market value ($ mil.): 5,615

Stock History

NYSE: ALA

12/93 12/94 12/95 12/96 12/97 12/98 12/99 12/00 12/01 12/02

	STOCK PRICE ($) FY Close	P/E High/Low	PER SHARE ($) Earnings	Dividends	Book Value
12/02	4.44	— —	(4.39)	0.14	4.16
12/01	16.55	— —	(3.86)	0.43	6.92
12/00	55.94	76 33	1.13	0.39	11.76
12/99	45.00	67 30	0.69	0.00	62.70
12/98	24.44	15 5	3.08	0.39	62.99
12/97	25.31	29 16	0.97	0.00	44.71
12/96	16.00	27 20	0.70	0.31	48.30
12/95	17.50	— —	(0.65)	0.61	46.32
12/94	17.00	31 16	0.98	0.41	76.41
12/93	28.63	18 13	1.68	0.00	68.28
Annual Growth	(18.7%)	— —	—	—	(26.7%)

Alitalia

Airline deregulation has touched down in Alitalia's territory. Once a monopoly, Alitalia – Linee Aeree Italiane now competes for the 25 million passengers that it carries each year. It flies to about 130 destinations in more than 60 countries from its hubs in Rome and Milan. Subsidiaries offer low-fare and regional airline services. Dutch airline KLM, however, terminated its passenger and cargo partnership with Alitalia because of problems with operations at a new Milan airport and the Italian government's delays in selling its ownership in the airline, which has since increased to 62%.

A European court found KLM's reason for abandoning the deal insufficient and ordered the Dutch carrier to pay Alitalia 150 million euros. The KLM deal would have combined passenger and cargo operations of the two airlines under a single management.

Alitalia has retained its code-sharing agreements with Continental and British Midland. It has added Air France and Delta Air Lines, which head up the SkyTeam global marketing alliance, as code-sharing partners and has joined their alliance. As European competition grows, Alitalia has launched low-fare carrier Alitalia Team and regional Alitalia Express. The carrier has also strengthened its foothold in Asia, inking a code-share deal with China Airlines.

HISTORY

Alitalia got off the ground in 1946 as Alitalia Aerolinee Italiane Internazionali. The airline was 40%-owned by BEA (British European Airways, later part of British Airways) and 60%-owned by the Italian government. Alitalia was intended to be an international carrier; TWA and the Italian state set up Linee Aeree Italiane (LAI) for domestic flights.

Alitalia began flying in 1947 with a Turin-Rome-Catania route, and service to Africa and Brazil was launched from Rome in 1948. To better compete with other European carriers, Alitalia and LAI merged in 1957 and took the name Alitalia – Linee Aeree Italiane. The government bought the shares held by BEA and TWA and assigned Alitalia to IRI, the Italian state holding company. The new airline's fleet boasted 37 aircraft.

By 1960 Alitalia carried a million passengers and had introduced its first jets. By 1968 it had an all-jet fleet. The stylized "A" tailfin logo appeared a year later, and in 1970 Alitalia adopted use of the Boeing 747.

But Alitalia began losing money in the 1970s. Facing rising fuel prices, inflation, and labor strikes, it responded by cutting underused routes and buying fuel-efficient Boeing 727s.

In the early 1980s Alitalia diversified by creating Sigma (travel-related information systems) and Italiatour (tour operator). Diversification came, however, at the expense of the airline's expansion, and it began losing market share to rivals Air France and Lufthansa. In 1988 Alitalia brought in Carlo Verri from the private sector to deal with labor and structural problems. He secured labor contracts and developed aircraft financing, but his auspicious start ended with a fatal car crash in 1989. Alitalia limped through the early 1990s with losses, aging equipment, and a reputation for poor service.

IRI hired former IBM executive Renato Riverso as chairman in 1994. With deregulation fast approaching, Alitalia penned code-sharing partnerships with Continental (1994) and Canadian Airlines (1995). In 1995 several labor strikes flared up amid talk of restructuring and cost-cutting measures. After receiving little government support, Riverso resigned in 1996. His short-lived reign laid a foundation: Labor tensions were eased with the promise of an employee-owned share in the company.

Europe's air transportation market was opened to competition in 1996 (after a long process that began in 1983). Alitalia began low-fare carrier Alitalia Team, signed on Italian regional airline Azzurra as a code-share partner the next year, and set up its own regional carrier, Alitalia Express. In 1997 it also achieved its first annual profit since 1988.

IRI reduced its stake in Alitalia to 53% in 1998, and employees got their 20% stake. Alitalia began an alliance with Dutch carrier KLM, and in 1999

Alitalia and KLM completed a "virtual merger" that unified their management structures for passenger and cargo joint ventures and allowed them to share profits. KLM ditched the partnership in 2000, however, and demanded Alitalia repay $91 million it had spent to upgrade an Italian airport. Alitalia protested KLM's termination of the alliance, and the dispute between the carriers wound up in arbitration proceedings.

IRI was liquidated in 2000, and the state holding company's stake in Alitalia was transferred to the Treasury Ministry. Another chance at an alliance hatched when Alitalia signed partnership agreements with Delta and Air France, which led to full membership in the SkyTeam alliance near the end of 2001.

Also in 2001 Alitalia said it would unload noncore assets, including its leisure division. The next year the company sold its reservation services unit, Sigma. That year the Italian government raised its stake in the airline from 53% to 62%.

EXECUTIVES

Chairman: Fausto Cereti
Managing Director: Michele Cicia
Managing Director: Francesco Mengozzi
Managing Director: Carlo Tamburi
Secretary: Carlo Angelici
Director Finance: Giovanni Lionetti
Auditors: Deloitte & Touche S.p.A.

LOCATIONS

HQ: Alitalia – Linee Aeree Italiane S.p.A.
Viale A. Marchetti 111, 00148 Rome, Italy
Phone: +39-06-6562-2151   **Fax:** +39-06-6562-4733
US HQ: 666 Fifth Ave., 6th Fl., New York, NY 10103
US Phone: 212-903-3300   **US Fax:** 212-903-3535
Web: www.alitalia.it

Alitalia – Linee Aeree Italiane serves about 130 destinations in Africa, Asia, Australia, Europe, the Middle East, and North America.

PRODUCTS/OPERATIONS

Selected Subsidiaries

Alitalia Express (regional airline)
Alitalia Team (low-fare airline)
Atitech (maintenance)
Eurofly (domestic charter flights)
Italiatour (tour promotion)
Racom Teledata (information technology services)

Selected Code-Sharing Partnerships

AeroMexico
Air France
Czech Airlines
Delta Air Lines
Korean Air

COMPETITORS

Aer Lingus
Air France
AMR
British Airways
easyJet
Iberia
Lufthansa
Ryanair
SAS
Brussels Airlines
UAL
US Airways
Virgin Atlantic Airways

HISTORICAL FINANCIALS

Company Type: Public

Income Statement

FYE: December 31

	REVENUE ($ mil.)	NET INCOME ($ mil.)	NET PROFIT MARGIN	EMPLOYEES
12/02	5,290	98	1.8%	22,536
12/01	4,875	(803)	—	22,948
12/00	5,330	(241)	—	23,478
12/99	5,104	6	0.1%	20,497
12/98	5,513	247	4.5%	19,600
12/97	4,949	252	5.1%	15,740
12/96	5,309	(797)	—	16,507
12/95	4,936	(57)	—	17,982
12/94	4,939	(194)	—	—
12/93	4,254	(200)	—	—
Annual Growth	2.5%	—	—	3.3%

2002 Year-End Financials

Debt ratio: 87.4%
Return on equity: 7.5%
Cash ($ mil.): 122

Current ratio: 1.44
Long-term debt ($ mil.): 1,620

Net Income History

Italian: AZA

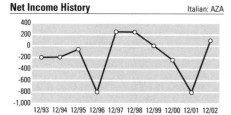

All Nippon Airways Co., Ltd.

Nippin' at the heels of Japan Airlines, All Nippon Airways (ANA) is Japan's second-largest airline overall (Japan Airlines is #1) and its leading domestic passenger carrier. With a fleet of more than 165 airliners (mostly Boeings), ANA serves 35 Japanese destinations and 25 international destinations in 12 countries. Having already suffered through Japan's chronic recession, ANA has had to trim routes in response to a worldwide slump in air travel in 2003 due to the SARS outbreak. The company also is involved in related businesses, including maintenance and ground support and an international hotel chain.

The company's ANA Hotels division owns hotels in Europe and the Asia/Pacific region, as well as in Japan.

Seeking strength in numbers, ANA is also a member of the global Star Alliance, which includes such ANA code-sharing partners as UAL's United Airlines, Lufthansa, and Brazil's VARIG. Alliance partners collectively serve about 730 cities in 125 countries.

ANA has been doubly challenged by Japan's lingering recession and the sweeping deregulation that has led to greater domestic and international competition. To reduce costs, the airline has resorted to streamlining management and modifying its route structure.

ANA also faces increased competition with Japan Airlines, which is merging with Japan's #3 carrier, Japan Air System (JAS). JAS has a strong domestic foothold and a growing presence in China.

HISTORY

Two domestic Japanese air carriers that started in 1952 — Nippon Helicopter and Aeroplane Transport and Far East Airlines — consolidated operations in 1957 as All Nippon Airways (ANA).

Throughout the 1960s ANA developed a domestic route network linking Japan's largest cities — Tokyo, Osaka, Fukuoka, and Sapporo — and its leading provincial centers, including Nagoya, Nagasaki, Matsuyama, and Hakodate. During this period domestic traffic grew at an annual rate of 30% to 60%.

In 1970 the Japanese cabinet formulated routes for its major airlines, giving ANA scheduled domestic service and unscheduled international flights. That year Tokuji Wakasa became ANA's chairman, and the company began a program of diversification that led to the establishment of ANA Trading, international charter service (starting with Hong Kong), and a hotel subsidiary. Air Nippon, a regional domestic airline, was started in 1974.

The company established Nippon Cargo Airlines, a charter service set up jointly with four steamship lines, in 1978. ANA carried 19.5 million passengers that year, but its growth slowed between 1978 and 1980. High jet fuel prices caused a $45.6 million loss in 1979, but ANA rebounded a year later. In 1982 ANA opened international charter service to Guam. The company founded ANA Sports in 1984 to manage the company soccer team.

Japan deregulated air routes in 1985, allowing ANA to offer scheduled international flights. The airline offered its first regular flight from Tokyo to Guam in 1986 and soon added service to Los Angeles and Washington, DC. Flights to China, Hong Kong, and Sydney began a year later.

Between 1988 and 1990 ANA added flights to Bangkok, London, Moscow, Saipan, Seoul, Stockholm, and Vienna. In 1988 ANA bought a minority stake in Austrian Airlines and set up the domestic computer reservation system (CRS). The company's international CRS, INFINI (a joint venture with CRS co-op ABACUS), went online in 1990.

ANA started World Air Network Charter (WAC) in 1991 to serve travelers from Japan's smaller cities. That year ANA opened its first European hotel (in Vienna), was listed on the London Stock Exchange, and opened a flight school in the US for its pilots.

In 1992 ANA premiered a hotel in Beijing. In 1995 the airline announced that it would increase its international traffic by more than 30%. As part of this strategy ANA and Air Canada began a code-sharing service in 1996 between Osaka and Vancouver, and a year later ANA became the first Japanese airline to operate a Boeing 777 on an international route (between Tokyo and Beijing).

As the Asian financial crisis sent Japanese airlines to the brink, a pilot strike in 1998 dashed ANA's hopes for a 15% pay cut. To cope, ANA formed alliances with UAL's United Airlines, Lufthansa, and Brazil's VARIG. ANA extended those partnerships in 1999 by joining the global Star Alliance. To shore up its financial strength,

ANA reorganized domestic routes, dropping some unprofitable ones and shifting others to its Air Nippon unit; it also announced plans to launch low-cost air service for international routes in Asia. Competition intensified when Japan fully deregulated domestic fares in 2000, sparking a fare war.

The following year ANA avoided a potentially costly strike and began working toward expanding through partnerships. However, terrorist attacks on the US caused a slump in worldwide air travel, and ANA was forced to cut back on its flights.

EXECUTIVES

Chairman: Kichisaburo Nomura
President and CEO: Yoji Ohashi
EVP; President, Air Nippon: Isamu Komatsu
EVP Airport Operations and Services, Haneda Airport: Kenichiro Hamada
EVP and General Manager, Tokyo: Shin Nagase
EVP Corporate Planning, Cargo Marketing, and Services: Koichiro Ono
EVP Engineering and Maintenance; Chairman, Environment Committee: Suguru Omae
EVP Facilities and Information Technology: Hiromichi Toya
EVP Finance and Accounting, Purchasing, and Investor Relations: Yasushi Morohashi
EVP Flight Operations: Masahiko Takada
EVP International and Regulatory Affairs: Katsuhiko Kitabayashi
EVP Marketing and Sales: Masao Nakano
EVP Personnel, Employee Relations, and Business Support: Mineo Yamamoto
SVP Administration and Legal Affairs: Koshichiro Kubo
SVP Cargo Marketing and Services: Kenkichi Honbo
SVP Finance and Accounting: Tomohiro Hidema
SVP Flight Operations: Hideo Koyanagi
SVP Inflight Services: Hitoshi Nakajima
SVP Marketing: Shinichiro Ito
SVP Operations and Airport Services: Tomoyuki Fujita
Auditors: Shin Nihon & Co.

LOCATIONS

HQ: Zen Nippon Kuyu Kabushiki Kaisha
Shiodome City Center, 1-5-2 Higashi-Shimbashi,
Minato-ku, Tokyo 105-7133, Japan
Phone: +81-3-6735-1030   **Fax:** +81-3-5756-1125
US HQ: 1251 Avenue of the Americas, Ste. 820,
New York, NY 10020
US Phone: 212-840-3700   **US Fax:** 212-840-3704
Web: www.ana.co.jp

All Nippon Airways flies to more than 35 cities in Japan and serves 27 international destinations in 13 countries.

PRODUCTS/OPERATIONS

2003 Sales

	% of total
Domestic passenger	49
International passenger	13
International cargo	3
Domestic cargo	2
Other	33
Total	**100**

2003 Fleet

Aircraft	No.
Boeing 767	53
Boeing 747	33
Boeing 737	27
Airbus A320	25
Boeing 777	21
Airbus A321	7
Total	**166**

COMPETITORS

Accor	Evergreen Marine
Air France	FlightSafety
AMR	Hyatt
British Airways	Japan Airlines
Carlson	Kinki Nippon Railway
Cathay Pacific	KLM
Central Japan Railway	Northwest Airlines
China Airlines	Qantas
Continental Airlines	Singapore Airlines
Delta	Virgin Atlantic Airways
East Japan Railway	

HISTORICAL FINANCIALS

Company Type: Public

Income Statement

FYE: March 31

	REVENUE ($ mil.)	NET INCOME ($ mil.)	NET PROFIT MARGIN	EMPLOYEES
3/03	10,146	(236)	—	29,001
3/02	9,081	(71)	—	29,095
3/01	10,130	(319)	—	29,831
3/00	11,465	(144)	—	14,919
3/99	8,990	(40)	—	15,273
3/98	8,120	(41)	—	15,200
3/97	8,254	35	0.4%	15,996
3/96	9,019	(80)	—	14,649
3/95	10,563	(86)	—	14,416
3/94	8,342	(91)	—	14,994
Annual Growth	2.2%	—	—	7.6%

2003 Year-End Financials

Debt ratio: 706.4%	Current ratio: 1.12
Return on equity: —	Long-term debt ($ mil.): 7,188
Cash ($ mil.): 1,292	

Net Income History

OTC: ALNPY

Allianz AG

Allianz is hoping its alliances will take it to the top. Allianz, one of the world's biggest insurers, joined forces with Dresdner Bank, creating the world's fourth-largest financial group (Citigroup is #1). Allianz offers a range of insurance products and services through some 100 subsidiaries and affiliates, including life, health, and property & casualty. Other businesses include risk consulting and public investment funds. Making its mark in the high-profile world of asset management, the company's Allianz Dresdner Asset Management manages private and institutional funds.

Allianz is part of a web of interlocking German corporate ownership. It holds stakes in the country's top corporations (including Deutsche Bank and Lufthansa), as well as 22% of the world's largest reinsurer, Munich Re (which has an equal stake in Allianz).

Allianz paid out claims of some $1.3 billion relating to the terrorist attacks on the World Trade Center. The company is setting up a terrorism

insurance unit, offering coverage primarily for companies within the European Union.

Although it remains profitable, Dresdner Bank's corporate and markets division has been hurt by falling equity markets and the company has announced job cuts totaling some 10,000 employees. After a year of record losses (primarily due to investment losses and Dresdner's struggles), former CEO Henning Schulte-Noelle stepped down and assumed the chair post in 2003.

Allianz plans to raise some $5 billion to improve its capital base. The company is also considering selling parts of investment bank Dresdner Kleinwort Wasserstein to raise additional cash. Allianz' stock lost more than 75% of its value in 2002.

HISTORY

Carl Thieme founded Allianz in Germany in 1890. That year the company took part in the creation of the Calamity Association of Accident Insurance Companies, a consortium of German, Austrian, Swiss, and Russian firms, to insure international commerce.

By 1898 Thieme had established offices in the UK, Switzerland, and the Netherlands. His successor, Paul von der Nahmer, expanded Allianz into the Balkans, France, Italy, Scandinavia, and the US. After a hiatus during WWI, Allianz returned to foreign markets.

In WWII, Allianz insured Auschwitz, Dachau, and other death camps. Company documents show Allianz wasn't worried about risk at the SS troop-guarded camps. After the German defeat, the victors seized Allianz's foreign holdings, except for a stake in Spain's Plus Ultra. In the 1950s Allianz repurchased confiscated holdings in Italian and Austrian companies.

Allianz saturated the German market and began a full-scale international drive in the late 1950s and 1960s. It became Europe's largest insurer through a series of acquisitions beginning in 1973. Allianz formed Los Angeles-based Allianz Insurance in 1977.

In 1981 Allianz launched a takeover (which turned hostile) of the UK's Eagle Star insurance company. After a 1983 bidding joust with Britain's B.A.T Industries (now part of Zurich Financial Services), Allianz withdrew.

The firm consoled itself by shopping. In 1984 it won control of Riunione Adriatica di Sicurtà (RAS), Italy's second-largest insurance company. Two years later the firm bought Cornhill in the UK (on its third try). As the Iron Curtain crumbled, Allianz in 1989 acquired 49% of Hungaria Biztosito. Its *drang nach Osten* continued the next year after national reunification, when it gained control of Deutsche Versicherungs AG, East Germany's insurance monopoly. Allianz that year became the first German insurer licensed in Japan; it also bought the US's Fireman's Fund Insurance.

Natural disasters led to large claims and set the company back in 1992, the first time in 20 years it lost money from its German operations. Allianz restructured operations that year; profits surged in 1993, mostly from international business.

Allianz expanded in Mexico in 1995, forming a life and health insurance joint venture with Grupo Financiero BanCrecer (now owned by Grupo Financiero Banorte). The company set up an asset management arm in Hong Kong in 1996 with an eye to further Asian expansion, getting a license in China the next year. In 1997 after Holocaust survivors sued Allianz and other insurers for fail-

ing to pay on life policies after WWII, Allianz agreed to participate in a repayment fund.

In 1998 Allianz bought control of Assurances Générales de France; it was the white knight that prevented Assicurazioni Generali from taking the company. In 1999 Allianz said it would restructure some of its insurance operations, including spinning off its marine and aviation lines, to better compete in the multinational market. That year US subsidiary Allianz Life bought Life USA Holding. In 2000 Allianz bought 70% of PIMCO Advisors Holdings to strengthen its asset management operations. That year the company continued its push into Asia, buying a 12% stake in Hana Bank of South Korea and planning to boost its ownership of Malaysia British Assurance Life. Also in 2000, Allianz acquired Dutch insurer Zwolsche Algemeene.

Allianz remained acquisitive in 2001, buying US investment manager Nicholas-Applegate, and took a majority stake in ROSNO, one of Russia's largest insurers.

EXECUTIVES

Chairman of the Supervisory Board:
Henning Schulte-Noelle, age 60
Chairman of the Management Board:
Michael Diekmann, age 48
Member of the Management Board (Finance):
Paul Achleitner, age 47
Member of the Management Board (Europe II and Reinsurance): Detlev Bremkamp, age 59
Member of the Management Board (Asset Management): Joachim Faber, age 53
Member of the Management Board (Europe I):
Reiner Hagemann, age 56
Member of the Management Board (Group Financial Risk Management): Horst Müller, age 65
Member of the Management Board (Group Controlling, Accounting, Taxes, Compliance): Helmut Perlet, age 56
Member of the Management Board (Group Information Technology): Gerhard Rupprecht, age 55
Member of the Management Board (Allianz Dresdner Banking); Chairman, Dresdner Bank: Herbert Walter, age 50
Member of the Management Board (Growth Markets):
Werner Zedelius, age 46
Auditors: KPMG Deutsche Treuhand-Gesellschaft AG

LOCATIONS

HQ: Königinstrasse 28, D-80802 Munich, Germany
Phone: +49-89-38-00-00 **Fax:** +49-89-34-99-41
US HQ: Allianz Insurance Company, 2350 Empire Ave., Burbank, CA 91504
US Phone: 818-260-7500 **US Fax:** 818-260-7202
Web: www.allianz.com

Allianz operates in more than 70 countries in Africa, Asia, Europe, North and South America, and the Pacific Rim.

2002 Sales

	% of total
Europe	
Germany	45
France	12
Italy	12
Rest of Europe	12
North & South America	13
Asia/Pacific & Africa	6
Total	**100**

PRODUCTS/OPERATIONS

2002 Assets

	$ mil.	% of total
Cash	22,065	2
Stocks	131,122	15
Bonds	338,555	38
Loans	288,733	32
Other	114,439	13
Total	**894,914**	**100**

2002 Sales

	$ mil.	% of total
Premiums	57,906	51
Interest	29,629	26
Investment income	14,445	13
Fees and commission income	6,409	6
Other	4,847	4
Total	**113,236**	**100**

COMPETITORS

AEGON
Allstate
AMB Generali
AIG
Generali
Aviva
AXA
Citigroup
ERGO
Fortis
ING
Legal & General Group
MetLife
Millea Holdings
Mitsui Sumitomo
  Insurance
Munich Re
New York Life
Nippon Life Insurance
Prudential
Prudential plc
Royal & Sun Alliance
  Insurance
Sompo Japan Insurance
State Farm
Winterthur
Zurich Financial Services

HISTORICAL FINANCIALS

Company Type: Public

Income Statement

FYE: December 31

	ASSETS ($ mil.)	NET INCOME ($ mil.)	INCOME AS % OF ASSETS	EMPLOYEES
12/02	894,914	(1,226)	—	—
12/01	840,429	1,447	0.2%	179,146
12/00	414,387	3,259	0.8%	119,683
12/99	385,486	2,249	0.6%	113,584
12/98	399,865	2,123	0.5%	105,676
12/97	212,165	1,133	0.5%	73,290
12/96	200,554	1,062	0.5%	65,836
12/95	199,835	1,133	0.6%	69,236
12/94	162,848	620	0.4%	67,785
12/93	136,104	554	0.4%	69,859
Annual Growth	**23.3%**	**—**	**—**	**12.5%**

2002 Year-End Financials

Equity as % of assets: 2.6%
Return on assets: —
Return on equity: —
Long-term debt ($ mil.): 144,240
No. of shares (mil.): 2,418
Dividends
  Yield: 1.4%
  Payout: —
Market value ($ mil.): 23,093
Sales ($ mil.): 113,236

Stock History   NYSE: AZ

	STOCK PRICE ($) FY Close	P/E High/Low	PER SHARE ($) Earnings	Dividends	Book Value
12/02	9.55	— —	(0.51)	0.13	9.46
12/01	23.60	64 31	0.59	0.14	11.70
12/00	37.50	28 25	1.33	0.00	13.64
Annual Growth	**(49.5%)**	**— —**	**—**	**—**	**(16.7%)**

Allied Domecq

The combination of doughnuts, ice cream, and Kahlua may be a little sweet for most tastes, but Allied Domecq banks on it. The company is the world's #2 distiller, after Diageo. Its spirits and wines unit produces a number of brands at or near the top of their respective categories, including Ballantine's scotch, Beefeater gin, Kahlua liqueur, Sauza tequila, Canadian Club whiskey, and Courvoisier cognac. The firm has distilleries in Europe and North America. Allied Domecq's retail operations include the Baskin-Robbins, Dunkin' Donuts, and Togo's Eateries franchises.

Allied Domecq also distributes spirits and offers a variety of specialty spirits and wines such as brandy, cordials, liqueurs, and sherry. It has introduced several new products, including WET, which extends the Beefeater brand.

The spirits industry has been consolidating since 1997, and plenty of suitable matches (via joint venture or acquisition) have been suggested for Allied Domecq. The company has been receptive to potential pairings. To make itself more attractive, it sold its UK pubs business. With that business gone, nearly 90% of the company's sales pour in from spirits and wines.

The rest of Allied Domecq's sales come from its quick-service restaurant franchises. Together, Dunkin' Donuts and Baskin-Robbins have about 10,000 locations worldwide (nearly 60% in the US). The Togo's Eateries sandwich chain has about 300 restaurants. Allied Domecq plans to open 1,000 new quick-service restaurants in 2004. Suntory Limited and Barclays each own about 3% of the company.

HISTORY

The "allied" in Allied Domecq dates back to the 1961 merger of three regional English breweries: Ind Coope, Tetley, and Ansell. The new entity, Ind Coope Tetley Ansell Limited, took the name Allied Breweries in 1963. Five years later the greatly fortified brewing operation purchased Showerings, Vine Products and Whiteways (SVPW), a wine and spirits company also formed through a 1961 triple merger. (SVPW also owned Harvey's of Bristol.)

In 1978 Allied bought its first food company, J. Lyons and Company, which owned the Baskin-Robbins ice-cream chain (founded in Glendale, California, in 1945) and several food brands. The company changed its name to Allied-Lyons three years later.

The firm acquired Hiram Walker's liquor division in 1987. It bought Dunkin' Donuts in 1989 and Mister Donut the next year.

The 1990 acquisition of Whitbread's liquor business brought the company a long-sought-after premium white liquor brand, Beefeater gin. Allied-Lyons shifted its brewing business into an ill-fated brewing and wholesaling joint venture with Carlsberg, under the name Carlsberg-Tetley, two years later. (It coincided with a downturn in the brewing industry, and Allied-Lyons sold its 50% in 1996.) In 1993 the company bought a chain of 550 Augustus Barnett liquor stores from Bass.

As part of its focus on core operations, Allied-Lyons paid more than $1 billion for the remaining 68% of Spanish distiller Pedro Domecq in 1994. The deal created the #2 distiller in the world, and the company changed its name to Allied Domecq. In 1994 and 1995 it sold nearly all its food operations, including its Tetley tea interests.

In 1997 Allied Domecq acquired the California sandwich franchise chain Togo's Eateries. In 1998 it merged its Victoria Wine chain of UK off-license (liquor store) interests with the Thresher stores of Whitbread to form First Quench Retailing.

Allied Domecq sold its Irish drinks unit, Cantrell & Cochrane, to investment firm BC Partners in 1999, and Allied Domecq finance director Philip Bowman succeeded CEO Tony Hales. After a bidding war with Whitbread late in the year, pub operator Punch Taverns spent $4.4 billion for Allied Domecq's 3,600 pubs as well as its stake in First Quench Retailing.

In 2000 Allied Domecq obtained Seagram's rights to Captain Morgan Old Spiced rum from the Puerto Rican distiller, Destileria Serralles. However, the deal was disputed both by Seagram's and Diageo, who together with Pernod Ricard successfully bid for Seagram's drinks unit. Later Allied Domecq gained the US distribution rights to Stolichnaya vodka. The company also purchased two French champagne houses — G. H. Mumm, the third-largest in the world and producer of the Cordon Rouge brand, and Champagne Perrier-Jouët, maker of Belle Epoque (Fleur de Champagne in the US) — for about $500 million from investment firm Hicks, Muse, Tate & Furst.

In 2001 Allied Domecq won a see-saw battle with Lion Nathan for control (70%) of New Zealand's top winemaker and distributor, Montana Group. In September 2001 the company acquired Kuemmerling, Germany's fourth-largest spirits brand and second-largest bitters brand. That year Allied Domecq also bought one of Spain's largest wine producers, Bodegas y Bebidas, for about $256 million.

In February 2002 the company bought Malibu rum from Diageo for about $796 million and dropped its lawsuit involving Captain Morgan, cementing Diageo's claim on that brand. It also picked up Mumm Cuvée Napa, a sparkling wine brand, in the deal.

Allied Domecq announced in November 2003 that is had licensed the Kahlua and Courvoisier brands to Vita Foods, which plans a line of sauces and flavored concentrates based on the two names.

EXECUTIVES

Chairman: Gerry Robinson
CEO: Philip Bowman, age 50, $2,635,680 pay
CFO: Graham C. Hetherington, age 44, $1,305,437 pay
CEO, Quick Service Restaurants: Jon L. Luther, age 58
President, Allied Domecq Spirits North America:
  Jim Clerkin
President, Allied Domecq Wines USA:
  William A. (Bill) Newlands Jr.
President, Asia Pacific: Ken Burnett
President, Europe: Neil Everitt
President, Global Operations: Richard G. Turner, age 54,
  $1,145,746 pay
President, Latin America and Mexico: Antonio Ariza
President, Wines: David Scotland, age 55,
  $1,387,608 pay
COO, Allied Domecq Wines USA: Jim DeBonis
EVP, Marketing, North America: Simon Cunningham
SVP, Marketing, Allied Domecq Wines USA:
  Chris Lynch
Executive Winemaker: Nick Goldschmidt, age 41
General Counsel and Corporate Secretary:
  Leonard A. Quaranto
Chief Marketing Officer: Kim Manley, age 37
**Director of Corporate Communications, Allied Domecq
  Wines USA:** George Rose
Investor Relations: Peter Durman
Auditors: KPMG Audit Plc

LOCATIONS

HQ: Allied Domecq PLC
  The Pavilions, Bridgwater Rd., Bedminster Down,
  Bristol BS13 8AR, United Kingdom
Phone: +44-117-978-5000   **Fax:** +44-117-978-5300
US HQ: 355 Riverside Ave., Westport, CT 06880-4810
US Phone: 203-221-5400   **US Fax:** 203-221-5444
Web: www.allieddomecq.co.uk

Allied Domecq has subsidiaries in more than 50
countries. The company owns 100% of what it calls its
principal subsidiaries in Canada, England, Luxembourg,
the Netherlands, and the US.

2003 Sales

	% of total
Europe	32
North America	22
Latin America	11
Asia/Pacific	11
Premium wine	15
Quick service restaurants	8
Other	1
Total	**100**

PRODUCTS/OPERATIONS

Selected Products and Brands

Quick-Service Restaurants
Baskin-Robbins
Dunkin' Donuts
Togo's Eateries

Spirits
American Rye Whiskey (Hiram Walker's)
Bourbon (Maker's Mark)
Brandy (Carlos I, Carlos III, Centenario, Don Pedro,
  Fundador, Presidente)
Canadian Rye Whiskey (Royal Reserve)
Canadian Whiskey (Canadian Club)
Cognac (Courvoisier, Courvoisier 3 star, JACoBI '1880'
  VSOP, Imperial, Initiale Extra, Napoleon, VS, VSOP,
  XO)
Gin (Beefeater, Crown Jewel, Oliphant, Wiser's)
Liqueurs (Frangelico, Hiram Walker's, Kahlua, Tia
  Maria, Tuaca)
Rum (Lamb's, Malibu)
Schnapps (Hiram Walker's)
Scotch (Ballantine's, Glendronach, Laphroaig, Long
  John, Teacher's)
Tequila (Sauza)
Vodka (Borzoi, Grand Duke, Oliphant, Hiram Walker's,
  Stolichnaya in the US)
Whiskey (Whisky DYC, Wiser's)

Wine
Atlas Peak (US)
Belle Epoque champagne (France)
Callaway (US)
Clos du Bois (US)
Cordon Rouge champagne (France)
Fleur de Champagne (US)
Marques de Arienzo (Spain)
Mumm Cuvée Napa (US)
Port (Cockburn's)
Sherry (Harveys Bristol Cream, La Ina)
William Hill Winery (US)

COMPETITORS

Bacardi	Jose Cuervo
Ben & Jerry's	Kendall-Jackson
Brown-Forman	Krispy Kreme
Constellation Brands	LVMH
CoolBrands	Mrs. Fields
Diageo	Pernod Ricard
Gallo	Rémy Cointreau
Fortune Brands	Robert Mondavi
Foster's	Skyy
Friendly Ice Cream	Sonic
Future Brands	V&S
Heaven Hill Distilleries	Wendy's
Dairy Queen	Winchell's
Jim Beam Brands	

HISTORICAL FINANCIALS

Company Type: Public

Income Statement

FYE: August 31

	REVENUE ($ mil.)	NET INCOME ($ mil.)	NET PROFIT MARGIN	EMPLOYEES
8/03	5,372	535	10.0%	12,549
8/02	5,163	606	11.7%	12,113
8/01	4,192	501	12.0%	9,785
8/00	3,823	463	12.1%	10,932
8/99	5,577	131	2.4%	40,495
8/98	7,203	458	6.4%	49,709
8/97	7,177	645	9.0%	50,871
8/96	8,393	66	0.8%	54,000
8/95	9,471	369	3.9%	—
8/94	8,710	553	6.3%	—
Annual Growth	(5.2%)	(0.4%)	—	(18.8%)

2003 Year-End Financials

Debt ratio: 197.7%
Return on equity: 42.1%
Cash ($ mil.): 276
Current ratio: 1.34
Long-term debt ($ mil.): 2,859
No. of shares (mil.): 277
Dividends
  Yield: 3.7%
  Payout: 45.2%
Market value ($ mil.): 6,780

Stock History

NYSE: AED

	STOCK PRICE ($) FY Close	P/E High	P/E Low	PER SHARE ($) Earnings	PER SHARE ($) Dividends	PER SHARE ($) Book Value
8/03	24.50	13	8	1.99	0.90	5.22
8/02	25.85	13	11	2.27	0.00	3.95
Annual Growth	(5.2%)	—	—	(12.3%)	—	32.3%

Allied Irish Banks, p.l.c.

Allied Irish Banks (AIB), one of Ireland's largest banks and private employers, is looking beyond the Emerald Isle for its proverbial pot o' gold. The company offers retail and commercial accounts and loans; life insurance; and financing, leasing, pension, and trust services through more than 350 branches in Ireland and Northern Ireland, where it operates First Trust Bank. In England and Scotland AIB focuses on commercial clients through about 40 locations. The company's capital markets division offers commercial treasury services, corporate banking, asset management, and stock brokerage. In 2003 AIB sold troubled Maryland-based bank Allfirst Financial to M&T Bank Corporation.

As part of the deal, AIB assumed ownership of more than 20% of M&T, becoming the company's largest shareholder. Under AIB's direction Allfirst grew into a major regional player with about 250 branches in Maryland, Virginia, Pennsylvania, and Washington, DC. However, the company lost nearly $700 million from 1996 to 2002, apparently from bogus foreign exchange transactions made by rogue trader John Rusnak, who pleaded guilty to bank fraud.

The small Irish market and its inevitable ties to the UK's economy have made AIB look overseas to remain competitive. (Its home turf also faces intruders — namely European banks free to do business in the EU-opened Irish market.) The firm has positioned itself as an international bank with a presence in Eastern Europe where it owns a majority stake in Poland-based Bank Zachodni. About 40% of AIB's shareholders, assets, and pre-tax profits now come from outside of the country.

HISTORY

Allied Irish Banks was formed in 1966 by the "trinity" of Provincial Bank (founded 1825), The Royal Bank (founded 1836), and Munster and Leinster (founded 1885 but with origins back to the late 1600s). Both AIB and its then-larger rival, Bank of Ireland, had to consolidate in order to compete with North American banks entering Ireland. From its start, AIB sought to expand overseas, and by 1968 it had an alliance with Canada's Toronto-Dominion Bank.

In the 1970s AIB expanded its branch network to England and Scotland. The 1980s saw AIB boost its presence in the US market (it had already debuted AIB branches) with the acquisition of First Maryland Bancorp.

The Irish Parliament's Finance Act of 1986 instituted a withholding tax known as the Deposit Interest Retention Tax (DIRT) for Irish residents. Consequently (with a wink and a nod) AIB and other banks let customers create bogus nonresident accounts to avoid paying DIRT. An investigation indicated that, at one point, AIB's branch in Tralee had 14,700 non-resident accounts on its rolls — more than half the local population. After tax authorities began probing, many of the accounts in question were reclassified as "resident," and customers had to pay the taxes on them. In 1991 AIB was reprimanded, but neither the bank nor its customers have paid the remaining $100 million tax bill.

Tom Mulcahy, who integrated AIB's treasury,

investment, and international banking activities, became Chief Executive in 1994. Mulcahy, a respected leader, envisioned AIB as an international, Ireland-based bank.

In 1995 AIB bought UK-based investment fund manager John Govett from London Pacific Group. Mulcahy moved AIB the same year into Eastern Europe with a stake in Poland-based Wielkopolski Bank Kredytowy (or WBK, of which it now owns 60%).

AIB was busy in 1999. It gained a toehold in Asia by entering a cross-marketing agreement with Singapore's Keppet TatLee bank, a survivor of the region's financial crisis. Liberalized Singapore banking laws allowed AIB the right to buy one-quarter of the bank by 2001. AIB also bought an 80% stake of Bank Zachodni in Poland in 1999.

That year AIB merged First Maryland Bancorp and its other US holdings into the renamed Allfirst Financial, a sizable mid-Atlantic states bank.

In 2001 AIB merged Wielkopolski Bank Kredytowy and Bank Zachodni into Bank Zachodni WBK in Poland to consolidate its power in Eastern Europe. That year Mulcahy retired but then was appointed by the Irish government to take over as chairman of troubled airline Aer Lingus.

EXECUTIVES

Chairman: Dermot Gleeson, age 54
Group Chief Executive: Michael D. Buckley, age 58
Group Director, Finance and Enterprise Technology: Gary E. Kennedy, age 45
Group Chief Risk Officer: Shom Bhattacharya, age 51
Group Internal Auditor: Paul Shantz
Managing Director, AIB Poland Division: Gerry Byrne, age 46
Managing Director, AIB Capital Markets: Colm Doherty, age 44
Managing Director, AIB Bank, Republic of Ireland: Donal Forde, age 42
Managing Director, AIB Bank, Great Britain and Northern Ireland: Aidan McKeon
Head of Corporate Relations: Catherine Burke
Head of Group Investor Relations: Alan Kelly
Head of Strategic Human Resources: Michael Lewis, age 51
CFO: Declan McSweeney, age 49
Auditors: KPMG

LOCATIONS

HQ: Bankcentre, Ballsbridge, Dublin 4, Ireland
Phone: +353-1-660-0311   **Fax:** +353-1-660-9137
US HQ: 405 Park Ave., New York, NY 10022
US Phone: 212-339-8000   **US Fax:** 212-339-8008
Web: www.aibgroup.com

Allied Irish Banks has operations in Ireland, Poland, the US, and the UK.

PRODUCTS/OPERATIONS

2002 Sales

	% of total
Interest	
Loans & advances	57
Securities	15
Finance leasing & installment credit	3
Noninterest	
Fees & commissions receivable	21
Other	4
Total	**100**

Selected Domestic Subsidiaries

AIB Capital Markets plc (banking and financial services)
AIB Corporate Finance Limited Corporate (finance)
AIB Finance Limited (industrial banking)
AIB Fund Management Limited Unit (trust management)
AIB International Financial Services Limited International (financial services)
AIB Investment Managers Limited (investment management)
AIB Leasing Limited Leasing
Ark Life Assurance Company (insurance and pensions business)
Goodbody Holdings Limited Stockbroking (corporate finance)

Selected Foreign Subsidiaries

AIB Asset Management Holdings Limited (UK, funds management)
AIB Bank (CI) Limited (St. Helier, Jersey, banking services)
AIB Bank (Isle of Man) Limited (Isle of Man, banking services)
AIB Group d/b/a First Trust Bank p.l.c. (Northern Ireland, banking and financial services)
Allied Irish Bank (GB) in Great Britain
Bank Zachodni S.A. (Poland, banking and financial services)

COMPETITORS

Anglo Irish Bank
Bank of America
Bank of Ireland
Barclays
Citigroup
HSBC Holdings
Lloyds TSB
Riggs National
Royal Bank of Scotland
SunTrust
Wachovia

HISTORICAL FINANCIALS

Company Type: Public

Income Statement

FYE: December 31

	ASSETS ($ mil.)	NET INCOME ($ mil.)	INCOME AS % OF ASSETS	EMPLOYEES
12/02	90,377	1,079	1.2%	31,300
12/01	79,180	476	0.6%	32,397
12/00	75,050	736	1.0%	31,778
12/99	67,687	784	1.2%	26,264
12/98	62,929	796	1.3%	23,749
12/97	53,724	543	1.0%	23,921
12/96	43,231	449	1.0%	15,882
12/95	38,201	396	1.0%	15,274
12/94	32,518	328	1.0%	15,250
12/93	29,639	203	0.7%	15,492
Annual Growth	**13.2%**	**20.4%**	**—**	**8.1%**

2002 Year-End Financials

Equity as % of assets: 5.4%
Return on assets: 1.3%
Return on equity: 21.8%
Long-term debt ($ mil.): 16,327
No. of shares (mil.): 449
Dividends
Yield: 3.1%
Payout: 34.0%
Market value ($ mil.): 12,061
Sales ($ mil.): 6,810

Stock History

NYSE: AIB

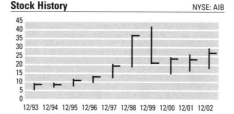

	12/93	12/94	12/95	12/96	12/97	12/98	12/99	12/00	12/01	12/02

	STOCK PRICE ($) FY Close	P/E High/Low		PER SHARE ($) Earnings	Dividends	Book Value
12/02	26.88	12	7	2.44	0.83	10.87
12/01	23.10	26	17	1.00	0.73	11.31
12/00	23.50	15	9	1.66	0.68	9.77
12/99	21.13	23	12	1.78	0.70	9.08
12/98	36.75	21	11	1.75	0.58	2.76
12/97	19.31	15	9	1.37	0.63	2.71
12/96	13.07	10	8	1.27	0.49	2.25
12/95	10.86	11	7	1.09	0.37	2.01
12/94	8.41	10	8	0.94	0.30	1.90
12/93	8.49	15	10	0.57	0.24	1.63
Annual Growth	**13.7%**	**—**	**—**	**17.5%**	**14.8%**	**23.5%**

AMP Limited

AMP is on top — down under. Formerly known as Australian Mutual Provident Society, the company is Australia's largest life insurer and financial services group. The company demutualized to gain cash and stock to use in making itself more competitive on the world stage. AMP's 5,000 or so representatives sell AMP's insurance and financial products, including life insurance; retirement products such as financial planning and advice, asset management and superannuation products (professionally managed retirement investment funds); banking and trust services; unit trusts; and property services.

To focus on investment and protection products, AMP got out of the general insurance market. Local rival Suncorp-Metway bought its domestic unit, and Churchill Insurance (a subsidiary of Credit Suisse) acquired its UK operations. Despite ridding itself of these more costly operations, the firm continues to feel a drag on earnings, this time from the UK. AMP's struggles forced CEO Paul Batchelor and chairman Stan Wallis to step down. The company is considering splitting itself into an Australian-based firm (to be called AMP) and a UK-based one (to be called Henderson). The move to divide its business divisions along geographic lines is an attempt to restore value to the firm, which lost almost half a billion US dollars in 2002. J.P. Morgan owns 8% of AMP; fellow Aussie bank WestPac owns nearly 6%.

HISTORY

AMP was conceived in Sydney in 1848 by W. S. Walsh (a clergyman), Thomas Mort (a businessman), and Thomas Holt (a wool trader), who convened with two others to discuss forming a mutual life insurance company in Australia. (Many of the UK's and US's largest mutuals were also founded about this time.) The next year Australian Mutual Provident Society was born; it opened for business with a staff of two: secretary William Perry and a small boy. In its first year the company sold only 42 policies. Luckily, no one died in the first three years of operations and the company was able to build up some reserves. The company grew slowly over the next decade, appointing just two agents — in Auckland, New Zealand, and Hobart, Australia.

Sales took off with the 1860 appointment of the company's first full-time agent, Benjamin Short, who had the novel idea of actively recruiting customers and actually *selling* policies. The company opened an office in New Zealand in 1871; it opened a branch in the UK in 1908.

In the next few decades, the company helped build the Australian economy through investment of its reserves. It funded industry and infrastructure, including farming communities as part of the South Australian Land Development Scheme. The company grew free of foreign competition, protected by regulations severely restricting the activities of foreign companies in the banking and financial industries in Australia. In 1958 the company formed AMP Fire and General Insurance (changed to AMP General in 1990).

In 1988 AMP moved abroad with the acquisition of London Life Assurance. The following year it made history with its acquisition of funds management group Pearl Assurance, then the largest takeover of a British financial firm by a foreign company.

The company founded AMP Asset Management in 1991 to manage its overseas assets. In 1995 the company expanded its international presence through a joint venture with the financial services arm of UK-based Virgin Group. The company also began offering mortgage and banking products in Australia through a new unit, Priority One.

After a careful inquiry, in 1996 AMP's board recommended demutualization; policyholders approved in 1997, and the conversion was completed the next year with the company taking the name AMP Limited. Trading got off to a rocky start, however, as the company imposed an unusual pricing mechanism by which the official initial stock price was linked to pricing activity over the first five days of trading. This was done to protect individual policyholders from typical opening day stock gyrations, but institutional investors were unable to value their investments for several days (a technical breach of accounting rules).

AMP has since expanded aggressively. It launched AMP Banking in Australia and bought Citibank's New Zealand retail banking business and UK fund manager Henderson in 1998. The next year AMP battled to buy general insurer GIO Australia Holdings, picking up 57% after resistance to its original low-ball offer; it also bought UK mutual insurer National Provident Institution (NPI).

The company streamlined all of its investment-management operations into a single unit in 1999 and expanded Asian operations with offices in Beijing and Tokyo. In 2000 the problems arising from the GIO takeover resulted in a board shakeup; chairman Ian Burgess resigned.

EXECUTIVES

CEO: Andrew Mohl, age 46, $691,635 pay
CFO: Paul Leaming
Managing Director, AMP Asia: Gavin Pearce, age 44
Managing Director, AMP UK Contemporary Financial Services: John Drabble
Managing Director, AMP UK Life Services: Ian Laughlin
Managing Director, Henderson Global Investors: Roger Yates, age 44
General Manager, AMP Australian Financial Services: Craig Dunn, age 38
General Manager, Corporate and Public Affairs: Matthew Percival, age 50
General Manager, Human Resources: Peter Hodgett
General Manager, Office of the CEO: Christine McLoughlin, age 39
General Manager, Strategy & Development: Marc de Cure, age 43
General Counsel: David Cohen
Auditors: Ernst & Young

LOCATIONS

HQ: 33 Alfred St., Sydney 2000, Australia
Phone: +61-2-9257-5000   **Fax:** +61-2-9257-7886
Web: www.ampgroup.com

AMP Limited operates in about 15 countries worldwide, primarily in Australia, New Zealand, and the UK.

PRODUCTS/OPERATIONS

2002 Sales

	% of sales
Corporate assets	31
Australian Financial Services	24
Asset Sales	16
UK Financial Services	15
Asset Management	14
Total	**100**

Selected Companies and Brands

AMP Financial Planning
AMPGID
AMP Henderson Global Investors
Arrive Wealth Management
Henderson Global Investors
Hillross Financial Services
MAGNIFY Financial Planners
NPI Limited (IFA sales and Corporate Pensions)
PremierOne
Towry Law and AMPLE
Virgin Money (joint venture with Virgin Group)

COMPETITORS

AIG
Australia and New Zealand
 Banking
Aviva
AXA Asia Pacific
Commonwealth Bank of
 Australia
Fortis
ING
National Australia Bank
Royal & Sun Alliance
 Insurance
Winterthur
Zurich Financial Services

HISTORICAL FINANCIALS

Company Type: Public

Income Statement

FYE: December 31

	ASSETS ($ mil.)	NET INCOME ($ mil.)	INCOME AS % OF ASSETS	EMPLOYEES
12/02	89,190	(506)	—	11,403
12/01	88,624	353	0.4%	15,000
12/00	99,061	2,508	2.5%	22,000
12/99	86,133	2,187	2.5%	22,400
12/98	68,895	(394)	—	12,000
Annual Growth	**6.7%**	**—**	**—**	**(1.3%)**

2002 Year-End Financials

Equity as % of assets: 11.3%
Return on assets: —
Return on equity: —
Long-term debt ($ mil.): 7,273
Sales ($ mil.): 14,344

Net Income History

Australian: AMP

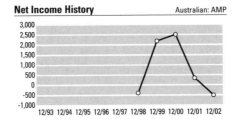

Anglo American

Anglo American's name might be a little misleading — it's never been American. The UK-based company owns stakes in leading global producers of gold (51%, AngloGold, #3 worldwide), platinum (70%, Anglo American Platinum), and diamonds (45%, De Beers Consolidated). It also is one of the world's largest independent coal miners. Additional Anglo American interests include forest products, ferrous and base metals, and industrial minerals. The company controls assets around the world. Descendants of the founding Oppenheimer family no longer control Anglo American, although Nicky Oppenheimer, who chairs De Beers, sits on the company's board.

The company, formerly Anglo American Corporation of South Africa, moved to the UK and began trading on the London Stock Exchange in an effort to reach international investors. When it was based in South Africa, Anglo American was unable to send its money overseas (the result of boycotts connected to that country's apartheid policies), so it bulked up on South African interests. It has sold many of those interests, particularly those in financial and industrial sectors.

Anglo American now depends on product and geographic diversity to weather global economic turmoil. The company completed a $1.3 billion deal in 2002 for Chilean copper assets (two mines and a smelter) formerly owned by Exxon Mobil.

HISTORY

In 1905 the Oppenheimers, a German family with a major interest in the Premier Diamond Mining Company of South Africa, began buying some of the region's richest gold-bearing land. The family formed Anglo American Corporation of South Africa in 1917 to raise money from J. P. Morgan and other US investors. The name was chosen to disguise the company's German background during WWI.

Under Ernest Oppenheimer the company bought diamond fields in German Southwest Africa (now Namibia) in 1920, breaking the De Beers hegemony in diamond production. Oppenheimer's 1928 negotiations with Hans Merensky, the person credited with the discovery of South Africa's "platinum arc," led to Anglo American's interest in platinum.

The diamond monopoly resurfaced in 1929 when Anglo American won control of De Beers, formed by Cecil Rhodes in 1888 with the help of England's powerful Rothschild family.

Anglo American and De Beers had become the largest gold producers in South Africa by the 1950s. They were also major world producers of coal, uranium, and copper. In the 1960s and 1970s, Anglo American expanded through mergers and cross holdings in industrial and financial companies. It set up Luxembourg-based Minorco to own holdings outside South Africa and help the company avoid sanctions placed on firms doing business in the apartheid country.

Minorco sold its interest in Consolidated Gold Fields in 1989, and in 1990 it bought Freeport-McMoRan Gold Company (US). In 1993 Minorco bought Anglo American's and De Beers' South American, European, and Australian operations as part of a swap that put all of Anglo American's non-African assets, except diamonds, in Minorco's hands. Some analysts claimed the company had moved the assets to protect them from possible nationalization by the new, black-controlled South African government. The company spun off insurer African Life to a group of black investors in 1994.

Anglo American bought a stake in UK-based conglomerate Lonrho (now Lonmin) in 1996. In 1997 Anglo American made mining acquisitions in Zambia, Colombia, and Tanzania and began reorganizing its gold and diamond operations. In 1998 the company's First National and Southern Life financial units merged with Rand Merchant Bank's Momentum Life Assurers to form FirstRand. (Anglo American has divested most of its interest in FirstRand.)

The company left its homeland for London in 1999, changed its name to Anglo American plc, and wrapped up the acquisitions of many of its minority interests including Amcoal, Amgold, Amic, and Minorco.

In 2000 the company bought UK building materials company Tarmac plc and later sold Tarmac America to Greece-based Titan Cement for $636 million. That year De Beers paid $590 million for Anglovaal Mining's stake in De Beers' flagship Venetia diamond mine and $900 million for Royal Dutch/Shell's Australian coal mining business. On the disposal side, Anglo American sold its 68% stake in LTA and its 14% stake in Li & Fung, a Hong Kong trading company. Harry Oppenheimer died that year at the age of 92.

In a surprising move, in early 2001 Anglo American announced that it had formed a consortium with Central Holding (Oppenheimer family) and Debswana Diamond to acquire De Beers (actually interlinked sister companies De Beers Centenary and De Beers Consolidated Mines). In February De Beers agreed to be acquired in a deal worth about $17.6 billion. The deal — giving Anglo American and Central Holding 45% each and Debswana a 10% stake — was completed in June 2001. Also that year the company took charges of around $513 million related to its base metals operations.

In 2002 Anglo American and Japan-based conglomerate Mitsui pooled their Australian coal resources; Anglo American owns 51% of the joint venture.

EXECUTIVES

Chairman: Sir Mark Moody-Stuart, age 63
CEO and Executive Director: Anthony J. (Tony) Trahar, age 53, $1,230,469 pay
Director, Finance and Executive Director: Anthony W. (Tony) Lea, age 54, $673,928 pay
Group Technical Director and Executive Director: William A. (Bill) Nairn, age 58, $504,136 pay
Executive Director; Executive Chairman, Anglo American Platinum Corp.: Barry E. Davison, age 57, $548,156 pay
Chief Executive, Base Metals: Simon Thompson
Chief Executive, Coal: Tony Redman
Auditors: Deloitte & Touche

LOCATIONS

HQ: Anglo American plc
20 Carlton House Terrace,
London SW1Y 5AN, United Kingdom
Phone: +44-20-7698-8888   **Fax:** +44-20-7698-8500
Web: www.angloamerican.co.uk

Anglo American's operations include subsidiaries in Australia, Austria, Brazil, Canada, Chile, the Czech Republic, France, Germany, Namibia, Peru, Poland, South Africa, Spain, the UK, and Venezuela.

2002 Sales by Origin

	$ mil.	% of total
Africa		
South Africa	5,863	39
Other countries	67	1
Europe	6,545	43
Australia & Asia	1,128	7
South America	908	6
North America	634	4
Total	**15,145**	**100**

2002 Sales by Destination

	$ mil.	% of total
Europe	8,295	55
Africa		
South Africa	2,566	17
Other countries	302	2
Australia & Asia	2,402	16
North America	1,144	8
South America	436	2
Total	**15,145**	**100**

PRODUCTS/OPERATIONS

2002 Sales

	$ mil.	% of total
Forest products	4,529	30
Industrial minerals	2,811	19
Platinum	1,964	13
Coal	1,463	10
Gold	1,450	10
Industries	1,241	8
Base metals	907	6
Ferrous metals	780	4
Total	**15,145**	**100**

COMPETITORS

ASARCO	Noranda
Barrick Gold	Peñoles
BHP Billiton Ltd	Phelps Dodge
Brascan	Placer Dome
Centromin	Rio Tinto
Freeport-McMoRan	Sasol
Copper & Gold	Shell Transport and
Grupo México	Trading
Harmony Gold	Stora Enso Oyj
Impala Platinum	Umicore
Inco Limited	UPM-Kymmene
International Paper	Vale do Rio Doce
Mitsubishi Materials	Weyerhaeuser
Newmont Mining	WMC Resources

HISTORICAL FINANCIALS

Company Type: Public

Income Statement

FYE: December 31

	REVENUE ($ mil.)	NET INCOME ($ mil.)	NET PROFIT MARGIN	EMPLOYEES
12/02	15,145	1,563	10.3%	177,000
12/01	14,786	3,176	21.5%	204,000
12/00	14,824	1,957	13.2%	249,000
12/99	11,578	1,552	13.4%	113,000
12/98*	6,907	789	11.4%	—
3/98	10,269	1,169	11.4%	—
3/97	3,207	1,607	50.1%	—
3/96	2,633	1,101	41.8%	—
3/95	1,577	761	48.3%	—
3/94	1,367	641	46.9%	—
Annual Growth	**30.6%**	**10.4%**	**—**	**16.1%**

*Fiscal year change

2002 Year-End Financials

Debt ratio: 35.9%	No. of shares (mil.): 1,469
Return on equity: 10.5%	Dividends
Cash ($ mil.): 1,070	Yield: 3.7%
Current ratio: 1.18	Payout: 49.1%
Long-term debt ($ mil.): 5,840	Market value ($ mil.): 21,450

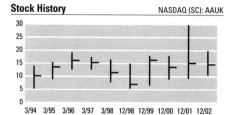

Stock History

NASDAQ (SC): AAUK

	STOCK PRICE ($) FY Close	P/E High/Low		Earnings	Dividends	Book Value
12/02	14.60	18	10	1.10	0.54	11.07
12/01	15.11	14	4	2.13	0.53	9.15
12/00	13.56	14	7	1.23	0.44	9.53
12/99	16.28	18	7	1.00	0.34	10.50
12/98*	7.00	18	7	0.83	0.27	9.69
3/98	11.47	13	6	1.25	0.38	9.83
3/97	15.31	10	7	1.72	0.33	8.32
3/96	16.09	16	11	1.18	0.32	6.88
3/95	13.56	15	9	1.03	0.23	7.47
3/94	10.13	16	6	0.87	1.12	6.23
Annual Growth	**4.1%**	**—**	**—**	**2.6%**	**(7.8%)**	**6.6%**

*Fiscal year change

Ansell Limited

It's not a stretch to say that Ansell (formerly Pacific Dunlop) makes its living from rubber products. The company's primary business unit is Ansell Healthcare, a leading manufacturer of industrial and medical gloves, condoms (brands include LifeStyles), and other latex products. Besides medical professionals, leading markets for Ansell's gloves include semiconductor and electronics manufacturers and companies that pack, process, prepare, and serve food. Ansell also owns a stake in South Pacific Tyres, a maker of Dunlop and Goodyear tires. About half of the company's sales come from the Americas.

Formerly a sprawling conglomerate, Ansell has divested noncore units in order to focus on its health care products businesses. The company is working to expand its sales of gloves designed to protect workers in automotive and durable goods manufacturing operations.

HISTORY

Ansell Limited's history begins with a veterinarian, a tricycle, and a bumpy road. In 1887 John Boyd Dunlop, a veterinarian in Belfast, Northern Ireland, gave his son a tricycle for his birthday. When his son complained about the jolting ride on rough country roads, Dunlop came up with an air-filled tire. Dunlop sold the rights to his tire to a pair of businessmen who founded the Pneumatic Tyre Company in 1889. By 1892 it had expanded into continental Europe and North America, and the next year it created a branch office of Dunlop UK to make bike tires in Australia.

The company went public in 1899 as Dunlop Pneumatic Tyre Company of Australia. In 1903 it moved into a new, growing market: automobile tires. The company, which was incorporated as Dunlop Rubber Company of Australia in 1920, merged with Sydney-based Perdriau Rubber Company in 1929.

Dunlop concentrated on rubber-based products until the 1960s, when it began to diversify by adding clothing, textiles, and footwear. In 1969 it acquired glove maker Ansell Rubber. During the 1970s Dunlop expanded outside Australia.

By 1980 the company had acquired its archrival, tire maker Olympic Consolidated Industries. Founded in 1922, Olympic began producing auto tires in 1934. The acquisition also netted Olympic's cable business.

Led by John Gough, Dunlop continued to expand during the 1980s. In 1985 it acquired the North American operations of UK-based battery maker Chloride. Dunlop entered its South Pacific Tyres joint venture with Goodyear in 1986 to sell tires in Australia and New Zealand. That year it changed its name to Pacific Dunlop Limited.

In 1987 Pacific Dunlop expanded its battery operations when it bought a stake in GNB Holdings, maker of Champion batteries. It moved into the health care business in 1988 with the acquisition of Nucleus (now Cochlear) and its US pacemaker unit Telectronics, a group of high-technology medical product makers.

Food was added to the company's business mix with the 1991 acquisition of Australia's Petersville Sleigh. The purchase of meat products maker Plumrose in 1993 expanded those operations.

Telectronics recalled three models of pacemaker parts in 1994 after failures led to the deaths of several patients, and a year later the FDA suspended US manufacturing of the parts. Pacific Dunlop took losses related to the Telectronics problems totaling $241.5 million that year. It also began disposing of businesses, selling most of its food operations, part of its industrial products unit, and a footwear company. The firm spun off its Cochlear hearing device business in 1995 and sold Telectronics in 1996, the year Rod Chadwick became managing director. Gough retired as chairman in 1997 in the midst of another pacemaker lawsuit filed against the company.

Faced with harsh competition in the non-energized US battery market, Pacific Dunlop agreed in 1998 to unload its GNB operations to metal recycler Quexco for a cut-rate $783 million, but the deal fell apart the next year. The company did manage to unload its cable business in 1999, however.

As part of a fundamental restructuring, Pacific Dunlop divested two major businesses in 2000: Its distribution business in New Zealand and Australia (sold to the Hagemeyer Group for $343 million); and GNB Technologies, a maker of auto and industrial batteries (sold to US-based battery giant Exide for $333 million). The company also acquired the worldwide medical glove business of Johnson & Johnson that year, a purchase that made Ansell the global market leader in that field.

In 2001 the company sold its Pacific Brands consumer goods unit (for about $730 million) to a private group led by CVC Asia Pacific. Pacific Dunlop changed its name to Ansell Limited in 2002.

EXECUTIVES

CEO: Harry Boon
CFO: Rustom Jilla, age 41
SVP and CIO: Peter Soszyn
SVP and General Counsel: Bill Reilly
SVP, Human Resources: Phil Corke
SVP and Regional Director, Americas: Bill Reed
SVP and Regional Director, Asia Pacific: Neil O'Donnell
SVP and Regional Director, Europe: Werner Heintz

SVP: Gwynne Woodward
VP, Global Supply: Scott Pappier
VP and Global Controller: Jim Smith
Head of Global Marketing and Program Director:
 Duane Dickson
Head of Global Manufacturing: Rainer Wolf
Company Secretary and General Manager, Corporate:
 Rob Bartlett
General Manager, Finance and Accounting:
 David Graham
Auditors: KPMG

LOCATIONS

HQ: Level 3, 678 Victoria St.,
 Richmond, Victoria 3121, Australia
Phone: +61-3-9270-7270   **Fax:** +61-3-9270-7300
US HQ: 200 Schulz Drive, Red Bank, NJ 07701
US Phone: 732-345-5400   **US Fax:** 732-219-5114
Web: www.ansell.com

PRODUCTS/OPERATIONS

Major Operations

Ansell Healthcare
South Pacific Tyres

COMPETITORS

Bandag
Bridgestone
Church & Dwight
Continental AG
Cooper Tire & Rubber
Kimberly-Clark
Maxxim Medical
MedPointe
Michelin
Playtex
Sime Darby
SSL International
Toyo Tire & Rubber

HISTORICAL FINANCIALS

Company Type: Public

Income Statement				FYE: June 30
	REVENUE ($ mil.)	**NET INCOME** ($ mil.)	**NET PROFIT MARGIN**	**EMPLOYEES**
6/03	880	33	3.8%	12,013
6/02	1,252	(65)	—	12,160
6/01	2,120	(71)	—	28,761
6/00	3,424	(52)	—	37,836
6/99	4,037	69	1.7%	38,438
6/98	3,700	15	0.4%	37,619
6/97	4,311	133	3.1%	38,148
6/96	5,538	(104)	—	40,671
6/95	6,033	67	1.1%	48,234
6/94	5,077	221	4.4%	49,449
Annual Growth	(17.7%)	(19.0%)	—	(14.5%)

2003 Year-End Financials

Debt ratio: 43.0%
Return on equity: 6.4%
Cash ($ mil.): 200
Current ratio: 2.07
Long-term debt ($ mil.): 242

Net Income History   NASDAQ: ANSL

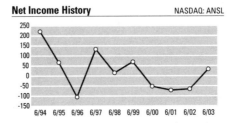

A.P. Møller – Mærsk A/S

Danish maritime giant A.P. Møller – Mærsk (formerly A.P. Møller) has been on a roll since its start as a steamship company in 1904. Now Denmark's largest industrial group, A.P. Møller – Mærsk owns one of the world's top container shipping lines, Mærsk Sealand. The group's fleet includes container carriers, bulk carriers, supply and specialty ships, and tankers. A.P. Møller – Mærsk also drills for oil and gas (primarily in the North Sea), and it owns a stake in one of Denmark's largest grocery and general merchandise chains. In addition, it builds ships and shipping containers, operates domestic airline Mærsk Air, and provides information technology services.

The former A.P. Møller was a group made up of two separately listed companies: Aktieselskabet Dampskibsselskabet Svendborg and Dampskibsselskabet af 1912, Aktieselskab. The group reorganized in 2003 and wound up with a single publicly traded company — A.P. Møller – Mærsk A/S — at its head. A.P. Møller – Mærsk owns direct and indirect interests in other group companies.

Mærsk Sealand's fleet includes more than 250 container carriers and about 800,000 containers. The shipping line has operations in more than 100 countries.

Among the group's major oil and gas assets is a 39% stake in the Dansk Undergrunds Consortium (DUC), which is engaged in exploration and production in the Danish sector of the North Sea.

A.P. Møller – Mærsk's retail segment includes a stake in Dansk Supermarked, Denmark's #2 supermarket chain (behind FDB). Dansk Supermarked operates stores under names such as Føtex, Bilka, and Netto in Denmark, Germany, Poland, Sweden and the UK.

HISTORY

Arnold Peter Møller and his father, sea captain Peter Mærsk Møller, founded Aktieselskabet Dampskibsselskabet Svendborg (Steamship Company Svendborg) in 1904 in Svendborg, Denmark. Their first ship, a second-hand steamer, bore on its funnel a white seven-pointed star on a blue background, which had been on Peter's first ship. Later known as the Mærsk star, the logo adorned all subsequent ships of the company, as well as ships of a second company formed eight years later — Dampskibsselskabet af 1912, Aktieselskab (Steamship Company of 1912). At that point, six ships were in the Mærsk fleet.

In 1917 the company began building its own ships after establishing the Odense Steel Shipyard. It launched regular liner service between the US and the Far East in 1928, calling the operation the Mærsk Line. With the addition of its first tankers that year, Mærsk owned 35 ships.

Mærsk Mc-Kinney Møller, A.P.'s son, became a partner in the company in 1940. That year, with Germany occupying Denmark, he fled to the US with his bride on one of the last ships out. Refusing to take orders from the Nazis, A.P. transferred control of the company to the US, where the 26-year-old Mærsk had established operations. Most of the Mærsk fleet flew under British or US flags during the war, which took the life of 148 Mærsk seamen and claimed 25 ships. Mærsk Mc-Kinney Møller returned to Denmark in 1947.

A.P. Møller formed the Mærsk Company in 1951 in London as a shipbroker, which became one of the world's largest shipowners. The early 1960s saw A.P. Møller diversifying as it moved into oil and gas exploration and production in Denmark in 1962 and established supermarket chain Dansk Supermarked in 1964. A.P. died the next year, having run the company for more than 60 years. Prior to his death, he had created three foundations to hold most of the company's shares. His son Mærsk took command of A.P. Møller and the Mærsk fleet, which contained 88 ships. Under his leadership the company expanded even further and became more international; his business savvy became apparent when he sold some of the company's tanker fleet in the 1970s, just prior to prices going down.

In 1970 A.P. Møller established domestic carrier Mærsk Air. A.P. Møller began seeing its first oil production in the North Sea in 1972. The next year the company acquired its first container vessel, the *Svendborg Mærsk*.

Mærsk Container Industri was formed in 1991 to produce intermodal containers. That year Mærsk and rival Sea-Land entered into a transpacific vessel-sharing agreement, which was expanded into a global alliance in 1995. In 1999, just months after buying South Africa's Safmarine Container Lines, Mærsk bought Sea-Land's international liner services and 18 terminals. The Mærsk Line and Sea-Land operations were merged to form Mærsk Sealand.

In 2000 A.P. Møller planned to extend its Bilka grocery chain into southern Sweden. That year Mærsk Sealand decided to shift its transshipment hub in Singapore to a Malaysian port. In 2001 Mærsk Air and Scandinavian Airlines System (SAS) were together fined $45 million by the European Commission for infringing on the EC's competition rules by entering a secret deal to monopolize certain air routes in Scandinavia. As a result, Mærsk Air's chairman and managing director stepped down and were replaced.

With the shipping industry in a slump, A.P. Møller in 2003 sold Mærsk Medical, a maker of catheters and continence products.

EXECUTIVES

Senior Partner and Chairman:
 Mærsk Mc-Kinney Møller, age 90
Chairman: Michael Pram Rasmussen
Partner and CEO: Jess Søderberg
Partner; CEO, Mærsk Sealand: Knud E. Stubkjaer
Partner; EVP, Mærsk Olie og Gas: Kjeld Fjeldgaard
Partner: Tommy Thomsen
EVP Industrial Companies: Bent Erik Carlsen, age 57
EVP: Lars-Erik Brenøe
EVP: Jørn Steen Nielsen, age 49
EVP: Søren Skou, age 39
SVP: Carsten Plougmann Andersen, age 45
SVP: Lars Bo Grønsedt
SVP: Claus V. Hemmingsen
SVP; CFO, Mærsk Sealand: Henning L. Knust
VP: Jette Clausen
VP: Sigurd Erlendsson
VP: Ivan Seistrup
VP: Palle Munk Weidlich
President, Mærsk Air: Flemming Ipsen

LOCATIONS

HQ: Esplanaden 50, DK-1098 Copenhagen K, Denmark
Phone: +45-3363-3363   **Fax:** +45-3363-4108
Web: www.apmoller.com

PRODUCTS/OPERATIONS

Selected Subsidiaries

A.P. Møller Finance S.A., Switzerland (holding company)
A.P. Møller Singapore Pte. Ltd. (shipping)
A/S Em. Z. Svitzer Group (salvage and towing)
A/S Roulunds Fabriker Group (automotive parts)
Danbor Service A/S Group (service, transport, production)
Dansk Industri Syndikat A/S (industrial air purification equipment)
Dansk Supermarked Group (supermarkets, hypermarkets, general merchandise)
Mærsk Air A/S Group (airline services)
Mærsk A/S Group (agency activities, drilling operations)
Mærsk Company Canada Ltd. (anchor-handling, platform supply vessels)
Mærsk Company Limited, UK (shipping, floating production)
Mærsk Data A/S Group (electronic data processing)
Mærsk Gulf Ltd. (agency activities, container repair, terminal operations, trucking; Central America and the Caribbean)
Mærsk Hong Kong Ltd. (agency activities)
Mærsk Inc. Group (agency activities, container terminals, land transport, distribution centers, liner-related businesses)
Mærsk Olie og Gas AS Group (oil and gas production)
Mærsk Sealand (container shipping services)
Mærsk Singapore Pte. Ltd (agency activities, feeder services, logistics and terminal operations)
Mærsk South America A/S (agency activities, container terminals, land transport, container-related activities)
Norfolkline B.V., The Netherlands (door-to-door transport and ferry services, rail freight)
Odense Staalskibsvaerft A/S Group (shipbuilding)
Rosti A/S Group (plastics)

COMPETITORS

Amerada Hess	ICA
Bolloré	Mitsui O.S.K. Lines
BP	Neptune Orient
COSCO Group	NYK Line
CP Ships	Norsk Hydro
Evergreen Marine	P&O
FDB	SAS
Hanjin Shipping	Statoil

HISTORICAL FINANCIALS

Company Type: Public

Income Statement

FYE: December 31

	REVENUE ($ mil.)	NET INCOME ($ mil.)	NET PROFIT MARGIN	EMPLOYEES
12/02	21,388	1,701	8.0%	60,000
12/01	17,865	1,003	5.6%	—
12/00	10,630	662	6.2%	—
12/99	6,632	279	4.2%	—
12/98	6,725	462	6.9%	—
12/97	6,028	367	6.1%	—
12/96	5,605	383	6.8%	—
12/95	5,123	333	6.5%	—
12/94	4,898	273	5.6%	—
12/93	4,098	294	7.2%	—
Annual Growth	20.2%	21.6%	—	—

2002 Year-End Financials

Debt ratio: 53.3%   Current ratio: 1.29
Return on equity: 18.0%   Long-term debt ($ mil.): 5,858
Cash ($ mil.): 1,881

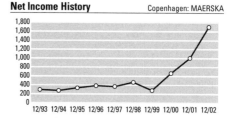

Net Income History   Copenhagen: MAERSKA

Asahi Shimbun

The Asahi Shimbun Company helps the Japanese wake up informed. The company's flagship *Asahi Shimbun* is the #2 newspaper in Japan (behind *Yomiuri Shimbun*). With a circulation of 12 million, it is noted for its in-depth political coverage and investigative reporting. Asahi Shimbun also publishes weekly Shukan *Asahi*, books, and several magazines. The firm's English-language *Asahi Evening News* has been replaced by the *International Herald Times / The Asahi Shimbun*, published in cooperation with the *International Herald Tribune*. The founding Murayama and Ueno families control Asahi Shimbun.

In addition to publishing, Asahi Shimbun operates in television broadcasting (as the largest shareholder of Asahi National Broadcasting) and advertising (through a 25% stake in Daiko Advertising). The company also publishes content on the Internet.

HISTORY

Ryohei Murayama, the son of a wealthy merchant in Osaka, published the first issue of *Asahi Shimbun* in 1879. The four-page paper was intended to provide news in an easy-to-read format for the general public. Riichi Ueno later joined Murayama, and together in 1881 they purchased the paper outright from their backers. By 1883 it was the most widely read newspaper in Japan. It expanded to Tokyo in 1888 and became the first Japanese newspaper publisher to have foreign correspondents in Europe and the US.

A sharp critic of the government and the military, Asahi Shimbun defied the government censorship during the Rice Riots of 1918 (when housewives plundered the warehouses of rice merchants who were speculating on rice prices). The company successfully launched two weeklies in the 1920s, *Shukan Asahi* (1922) and *Asahi Graph* (1923). Its criticism of the armed forces led to a military boycott of *Asahi Shimbun* in the 1930s, culminating in an assault on its Tokyo office by army officers in 1936. Military censorship stifled the newspaper's reporting during WWII, and following the war the company's executives admitted their complicity in publishing misleading information and resigned.

Regaining its standing as the "people's organ," the company launched its English-language *Asahi Evening News* and the English-language review, *Japan Quarterly*, in the 1950s. Asahi Shimbun became the first publisher in the world to use facsimile and offset printing to publish daily newspapers in 1959.

Major investigative pieces became the hallmark of *Asahi Shimbun* in the 1970s and 1980s. The paper exposed collusion between government, big business, and the civil service, such as the Lockheed scandal involving under-the-table payments to Japanese politicians. In 1988 *Asahi Shimbun* broke the "Recruit Affair," another bribery scandal that led to the resignation of then Prime Minister Noboru Takeshita and other top politicians. Its journalistic drive continued into the 1990s, breaking the 1992 story of ¥500 million in kickbacks to Japanese political kingmaker Shin Kanemaru in connection to scandals centering on parcel delivery service Tokyo Sagawa Kyubin. (The news touched off a nationwide political reform movement.)

In 1995 Asahi Shimbun scored an exclusive when it was the first to beam images of the Sakhalin (Russia) earthquake around the world. SOFTBANK and News Corp. sold their shares of Asahi National Broadcasting (TV Asahi) to Asahi Shimbun in 1997 to promote future cooperation of Japanese TV programming for Japan Sky Broadcasting (JSkyB), a satellite broadcasting network started by the two heavyweights. Asahi Shimbun president Muneyuki Matsushita passed away in 1999 and was replaced by Shinichi Hakoshima, the company's senior managing director. The next year TV Asahi went public to finance its conversion to digital broadcasting standards. In 2001 the firm joined the *International Herald Tribune* to publish a new English-language paper to replace the *Asahi Evening News*.

EXECUTIVES

President: Shinichi Hakoshima
Managing Director Finance: Mitsuru Gondo
President, Asahi America: Masato Tamura

LOCATIONS

HQ: The Asahi Shimbun Company
5-3-2 Tsukiji, Chuo-ku, Tokyo 104-11, Japan
Phone: +81-3-3545-0131   **Fax:** +81-3-3545-8450
US HQ: 845 3rd Ave., 11th Fl., New York, NY 10022
US Phone: 212-317-3030   **US Fax:** 212-317-3039
Web: www.asahi.com

PRODUCTS/OPERATIONS

Selected Operations
Book publishing
Magazines
  AERA (news)
  Ronza (business)
  Shukan Asahi (news)
Newspapers
  Asahi Shimbun
  International Herald Times/The Asahi Shimbun
  Shukan Asahi
Other investments
  Asahi National Broadcasting (TV Asahi)
  Daiko Advertising

COMPETITORS

Dow Jones
Fuji Television
International Herald
  Tribune
Kodansha
Nihon Keizai Shimbun
Nippon Television
Tokyo Broadcasting
  System
Yomiuri Shimbun

HISTORICAL FINANCIALS
Company Type: Private

Income Statement

	REVENUE ($ mil.)	NET INCOME ($ mil.)	NET PROFIT MARGIN	EMPLOYEES
3/01	5,716	—	—	10,733
3/00	3,954	—	—	7,543
3/99	3,187	—	—	7,470
3/98	3,135	—	—	7,543
3/97	3,376	—	—	7,580
3/96	3,785	—	—	7,698
3/95	4,651	—	—	7,832
Annual Growth	3.5%	—	—	5.4%

FYE: March 31

Revenue History

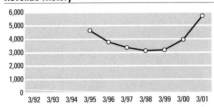

Assicurazioni Generali S.p.A.

Italy's largest insurance company, Assicurazioni Generali writes insurance for risks as varied as space launches and corporate package policies. It controls more than 600 companies, about 100 of which are involved in insurance (including life, accident, health, motor, fire, marine/aviation, and other lines of insurance, as well as reinsurance), financial services, and real estate. Besides its corporate and individual clients (the company targets individuals and small to medium-sized businesses), Generali has been insuring satellite and space missions since 1964.

Italy and Germany are Generali's largest markets; its home country accounts for 35% of Generali's premiums, Germany for about 25%. The insurer is further establishing itself in Germany, having acquired a controlling interest in one of the country's largest insurers, AMB Generali (formerly Aachener und Munchener), and establishing an alliance with Commerzbank, of which Generali owns nearly 10%. Generali also holds a much coveted license to do business in China. In 2002 Generali acquired Continent Holding from Toro Assicurazioni, upping its position in France's insurance market. Generali shareholders include Italy's secretive and powerful MEDIOBANCA (13%), as well as Banca d'Italia (4%), and Gruppo Unicredito (3%).

HISTORY

Assicurazioni Generali was founded as Assicurazioni Generali Austro-Italiche in 1831 by a group of merchants led by Giuseppe Morpurgo in the Austro-Hungarian port of Trieste. Formed to provide insurance to the city's bustling trade industry, the company offered life, marine, fire,

flood, and shipping coverage. That year Morpurgo established what he intended to be Generali's headquarters in Venice. (While the company maintained offices in both cities, Trieste ultimately won out.)

By 1835 Generali had opened 25 offices in Central and Western Europe; it had also expelled Morpurgo. The firm moved into Africa and Asia in the 1880s. In 1900 Generali began selling injury and theft insurance. In 1907 Generali's Prague office provided the young, experimental writer Franz Kafka his first job. (He found it disagreeable and quit after a few months.)

During WWI, the firm's Venice office pledged allegiance to Italy, while the office in Trieste (still part of Austria-Hungary) stayed loyal to the Hapsburgs. After the war Trieste was absorbed by the new Italian republic. Under Edgardo Morpurgo, Generali expanded further in the 1920s, managing 30 subsidiaries and operating in 17 countries. As fascist Italy aligned itself with Germany in the 1930s, adoption of anti-Semitic laws caused Morpurgo and a number of other high-ranking Jewish employees to flee the country. In 1938 Generali moved its headquarters to Rome (but moved them back to Trieste after WWII).

The firm maintained steady business both before and during Nazi occupation in WWII; in 1945, however, the Soviets seized all Italian properties in Eastern Europe, including 14 Generali subsidiaries. In 1950 Generali invaded the US market, offering shipping and fire insurance and reinsurance. Generali established a cooperative agreement with Aetna Life and Casualty (now Aetna Inc.) in 1966, further cementing its US connections.

In 1988 Generali tried to acquire French insurer Compagnie du Midi. Foreshadowing Generali's later dealings with Istituto Nazionale delle Assicurazioni (INA), Midi escaped Generali's grasp through a merger with AXA. As the Iron Curtain frayed in 1989, Generali formed AB Generali Budapest through a joint venture with a Hungarian insurer. In 1990 the firm opened an office in Tokyo through an agreement with Taisho Marine and Fire Insurance (which became Mitsui Marine & Fire Insurance and is now Mitsui Sumitomo Insurance). By 1993 Generali had become Italy's largest insurer.

In 1997 the firm was accused, along with other major European insurers, of not paying on policies of Holocaust victims. (It moved to settle claims in 1999.)

The company focused on the German and Swiss markets in 1998, acquiring controlling interests in insurer AMB Aachener und Munchener (now AMB Generali) and in Banca della Svizzera Italiana. Also that year Generali and Commerzbank established an alliance that gave the companies more access to each other's markets.

In 1999 Generali succeeded in a hostile takeover of INA, its largest domestic competitor. The move pre-empted INA's proposed merger with San Paolo IMI, which would have knocked Generali to second place among the country's insurers.

Avoiding violation of the EU's antitrust laws in connection with the INA acquisition, the company sold four subsidiaries (including Italian insurers Aurora and Navale) in 2000.

In 2002 Generali rolled together three securities investments firms, Banca Generali, Altinia, Ina Sim, and Prime Consult Sim, into Banca Generali.

EXECUTIVES

Chairman: Antoine Bernheim
Deputy Chairman: Gabriele Galateri di Genola
Vice Chairman: Francesco Cingano
General Manager: Giovanni Perissinotto
General Manager: Sergio Balbinot
General Manager: Giampaolo Brugnoli
Deputy General Manager: Luigi Boglioni
Deputy General Manager: Aldo Minucci
Deputy General Manager: Raffaele Agrusti
Director, Executive Committee: Tito Bastianello
Director, Executive Committee: Paolo Biasi
Director, Executive Committee: Gerardo Broggini
Director, Executive Committee: Piergaetano Marchetti
Secretary, Deputy General Manager: Vittorio Rispoli
Auditors: PricewaterhouseCoopers SpA

LOCATIONS

HQ: Piazza Duca degli Abruzzi, 2, 34132 Trieste, Italy
Phone: +39-040-6711 **Fax:** +39-040-671600
US HQ: 1 Liberty Plaza, 29th Fl., New York, NY 10006
US Phone: 212-602-7600 **US Fax:** 212-587-9537
Web: www.generali.com

2002 Sales

	% of total
Italy	35
Germany	26
France	17
Spain	5
Austria	4
Switzerland	3
Israel	3
North America	1
Latin America	1
Other regions	5
Total	**100**

PRODUCTS/OPERATIONS

2002 Sales

	% of total
Premiums	
Life	49
Non-life	27
Investments	13
Sale of assets	2
Other	9
Total	**100**

COMPETITORS

Allianz	Eureko
AGF	Fortis
AXA	ING
AXA Konzern	Swiss Re
ERGO	Zurich Financial Services

HISTORICAL FINANCIALS

Company Type: Public

Income Statement

FYE: December 31

	ASSETS ($ mil.)	NET INCOME ($ mil.)	INCOME AS % OF ASSETS	EMPLOYEES
12/02	246,014	(791)	—	59,753
12/01	203,417	974	0.5%	58,445
12/00	206,202	1,342	0.7%	57,443
12/99	176,747	1,596	0.9%	56,593
12/98	34,491	773	2.2%	54,598
12/97	29,481	585	2.0%	41,417
12/96	88,551	947	1.1%	40,003
12/95	79,598	438	0.6%	38,236
12/94	63,746	395	0.6%	37,917
12/93	51,036	355	0.7%	34,381
Annual Growth	**19.1%**	**—**	**—**	**6.3%**

Equity as % of assets: 4.1%   Long-term debt ($ mil.): —
Return on assets: —   Sales ($ mil.): 62,102
Return on equity: —

Net Income History   Italian: G

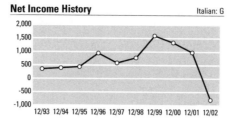

AstraZeneca PLC

AstraZeneca's products run the gamut from A (breast cancer drug Arimidex) to Z (migraine treatment Zomig). One of the world's top pharmaceutical firms, AstraZeneca specializes in drugs for gastrointestinal, cardiovascular, and oncology therapeutic areas. The firm's biggest seller is ulcer treatment Prilosec (Losec outside the US). For matters of the heart, AstraZeneca makes hypertension drugs Zestril and Atacand. The company's oncology drugs include Nolvadex (breast cancer) and Zoladex (prostate cancer), and lung cancer growth-inhibitor Iressa. The company also makes drugs for respiratory and central nervous system illnesses, and pain control.

AstraZeneca is dealing with numerous expired patents. Patent protection for Prilosec, which accounts for over a quarter of the company's sales, expired in 2002. Other expired patents include cancer drug Nolvadex and hypertension medication Zestril.

The company's cholesterol-killer Crestor will go up against Pfizer's Lipitor if approved. AstraZeneca also has high hopes for newly launched breast cancer drug Faslodex and Prilosec-follow-up Nexium has garnered a respectable share of the ulcer market and continues to grow.

Plans to become the world's top oncology drugmaker hit a snag when lung cancer drug Iressa failed in several test cases when used along with chemotherapy. Despite this, AstraZeneca persisted and gained FDA approval in May 2003.

Other units operate US cancer treatment centers (Salick Health Care); make such medical devices as urinary catheters and dental implant systems (Astra Tech); and make high-protein meat alternatives sold under the Quorn brand in Europe (Marlow Foods). Unlike other pharma rivals, AstraZeneca appears to be steering clear of biotechnology: It sold its Cellmark Diagnostics genetic testing division in early 2001.

HISTORY

AstraZeneca forerunner Imperial Chemical Industries (ICI) was created from the 1926 merger of four British chemical companies — Nobel Industries; Brunner, Mond and Company; United Alkali; and British Dyestuffs — in reaction to the German amalgamation that created I. G. Farben. ICI plunged into research, recruiting chemists, engineers, and managers and forming alliances with universities. Between 1933 and

1935, at least 87 new products were created, including polyethylene.

Fortunes declined as competition increased after WWII. In 1980 ICI posted losses and cut its dividend for the first time. In 1982 turnaround artist John Harvey-Jones shifted ICI from bulk chemicals to high-margin specialty chemicals such as pharmaceuticals and pesticides. That business became Zeneca, which ICI spun off in 1993.

The takeover specter loomed large over the company during its first year. Zeneca had several drugs in its pipeline, but it also had expiring patents on others, making them fair game for competitors. Bankrolled by its agrochemical business, Zeneca forged alliances with other pharmaceutical firms. In 1994 it entered a marketing alliance with Amersham International (now Amersham) to sell Metastron, a nuclear-medicine cancer agent. The next year Zeneca formed a joint venture with Chinese companies Advanced Chemicals and Tianli to make textile-coating chemicals.

In 1995 Glaxo was forced to sell a migraine drug candidate to complete its merger with Wellcome. Zeneca's gamble in buying the then-unproven drug (Zomig) paid off when the product gained US FDA approval two years later.

By 1997 Zeneca completed its gradual acquisition of Salick Health Care, formed to create more humane cancer treatment programs. The purchase followed a trend of large drug firms moving into managed care, which raised concerns that centers might be pressured to use their parent companies' drugs, but Zeneca maintained that Salick would remain independent except to the extent that it offered an opportunity to evaluate treatments.

In 1998 Zeneca got the FDA's OK to sell its brand of tamoxifen (Nolvadex) to women at high risk of contracting breast cancer. In 1999 it sued Eli Lilly to protect Nolvadex against Lilly's marketing claim that its osteoporosis treatment Evista reduced breast cancer risk, a use for which it was not approved.

In 1999 Zeneca completed its purchase of Sweden's Astra to form AstraZeneca. That year the firm sold its specialty chemicals unit, Zeneca Specialties, to Cinven Group and Investcorp. With its agricultural business stagnated due to crippled markets in Asia and Europe, AstraZeneca announced plans to merge the unit with the agrochemicals business of Novartis and spin it off as Syngenta. In 2000 Sweden approved Nexium, an ulcer drug the firm hopes will be its next blockbuster, as well as Symbicort Turbuhaler, an asthma inhaler slated to become another major product.

In 2001 AstraZeneca sold its genetic diversity testing services subsidiary, Cellmark Diagnostics, to Orchid BioSciences (with whom the company also announced a multi-year collaborative research agreement). Hoping to avoid US government price controls, the company joined with six fellow druggernauts in 2002 to offer Together Rx, a drug discount card for low-income senior citizens.

EXECUTIVES

Chairman: Percy N. Barnevik, age 62, $373,000 pay
Executive Deputy Chairman: Håkan Mogren, age 59, $1,692,000 pay
CEO and Executive Director: Tom McKillop, age 59, $2,093,000 pay
CFO and Executive Director: Jonathan Symonds, age 43, $1,224,000 pay
EVP, Development: Martin Nicklasson

EVP, Discovery Research: Jan Lundberg
EVP, Human Resources: Tony Bloxham
EVP, Europe, Japan, and Asia Pacific: Bruno Angelici
EVP, North America; President and CEO, AstraZeneca
  LP: David Brennan
EVP, Operations: Barrie Thorpe
EVP, Product Strategy, Licensing, and Business
  Development: John Patterson
VP, External Scientific Affairs: Catherine Bonuccelli
VP, Oncology Therapy: Brent Vose
Group Secretary and Solicitor: Graeme Musker
Group Treasurer: Adrian Marsh
Auditors: KPMG Audit Plc

LOCATIONS

HQ: 15 Stanhope Gate,
  London W1Y 1LN, United Kingdom
Phone: +44-20-7304-5000   **Fax:** +44-20-7304-5183
US HQ: 1800 Concord Pike,
  Wilmington, DE 19850-5438
US Phone: 302-886-3000   **US Fax:** 302-886-2972
Web: www.astrazeneca.com

AstraZeneca's corporate headquarters are in London and
its R&D headquarters are in Södertältje, Sweden.

2002 Sales

	$ mil.	% of total
Europe		
UK	3,964	17
France	1,111	5
Germany	682	3
Italy	676	3
Sweden	619	3
Spain	461	2
The Netherlands	226	1
Other countries &		
intra-group sales	2,899	13
The Americas		
US	9,325	41
Canada	570	2
Brazil	97	1
Other countries &		
intra-group sales	472	2
Asia, Africa, & Australasia		
Japan	960	4
Other countries &		
intra-group sales	782	3
Adjustments	(5,003)	—
Total	**17,841**	**100**

PRODUCTS/OPERATIONS

Selected Products

Gastrointestinal
Entocort (anti-inflammatory for inflammatory bowel
  disease)
Losec/Prilosec/Omepral (acid reflux disease)
Nexium (acid reflux disease)

Cardiovascular
Atacand (hypertension)
Crestor (cholesterol-lowering drug)
Seloken ZOK/Toprol-XL (beta-blocker)
Zestril (ACE inhibitor)

Oncology
Arimidex (breast cancer)
Casodex (prostate cancer)
Faslodex (breast cancer)
Iressa (anti-tumor)
Nolvadex (breast cancer)
Zoladex (prostate and breast cancer)

Respiratory and Inflammation
Accolate (asthma)
Oxis (asthma)
Pulmicort (anti-inflammatory)
Rhinocort (topical nasal anti-inflammatory)
Symbicort (anti-inflammatory and bronchodilator in one
  inhaler)

Central Nervous System
Seroquel (schizophrenia)
Zomig (migraines)

Pain Control and Anesthesia
Diprivan (general anesthetic)
Naropin (local anesthetic)
Xylocaine (local anesthetic)

Infection
Merrem/Meronem (antibiotic)

COMPETITORS

Abbott Labs
Aventis
Bayer AG
Bristol-Myers Squibb
Elan Corporation
Eli Lilly
GlaxoSmithKline
Hoffmann-La Roche
Johnson & Johnson
Memorial Sloan-Kettering
Merck
Novartis
Pfizer
Roche
Sanofi-Synthélabo
Schering
Schering-Plough
Wyeth

HISTORICAL FINANCIALS

Company Type: Public

Income Statement

FYE: December 31

	REVENUE ($ mil.)	NET INCOME ($ mil.)	NET PROFIT MARGIN	EMPLOYEES
12/02	17,841	2,836	15.9%	—
12/01	16,480	2,967	18.0%	54,600
12/00	15,804	2,538	16.1%	55,000
12/99	17,791	1,143	6.4%	58,000
12/98	9,144	1,185	13.0%	34,000
12/97	8,579	1,205	14.0%	31,400
12/96	9,184	1,101	12.0%	31,100
12/95	7,597	521	6.9%	30,800
12/94	7,011	539	7.7%	30,800
12/93	6,569	651	9.9%	32,300
Annual Growth	**11.7%**	**17.8%**	**—**	**6.8%**

2002 Year-End Financials

Debt ratio: 2.9%
Return on equity: 27.1%
Cash ($ mil.): 726
Current ratio: 1.48
Long-term debt ($ mil.): 328

No. of shares (mil.): 1,719
Dividends
  Yield: 2.2%
  Payout: 47.6%
Market value ($ mil.): 60,320

Stock History

NYSE: AZN

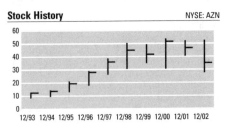

	STOCK PRICE ($) FY Close	P/E High/Low		PER SHARE ($) Earnings	Dividends	Book Value
12/02	35.09	28	15	1.64	0.78	6.50
12/01	46.60	29	23	1.69	0.26	5.61
12/00	51.50	30	18	1.44	0.78	5.39
12/99	41.75	30	22	0.64	0.76	5.80
12/98	44.88	40	25	1.25	0.28	4.38
12/97	35.96	10	7	3.82	0.00	1.21
12/96	27.97	25	16	1.16	0.56	1.22
12/95	19.44	38	24	0.55	0.49	1.02
12/94	13.69	19	14	0.61	0.44	0.93
12/93	12.40	16	12	0.76	0.17	0.93
Annual Growth	**12.3%**	**—**	**—**	**8.9%**	**18.4%**	**24.1%**

Atos Origin S.A.

Atos Origin has a firm toehold on Europe's information technology (IT) services mountain. The company provides services such as facilities management, e-commerce consulting, and systems design, implementation, and integration. Atos Origin also offers data and transaction processing services, Web site hosting, and outsourcing services for functions such as customer relationship management and enterprise resource planning. Philips Electronics, which owns nearly half of the company, took a 921 million write-off on its stake in Atos Origin in late 2002. The company has agreed to acquire the IT services arm of Schlumberger for about $1.5 billion, a purchase that would significantly increase its annual revenues.

Formed from the 2000 combination of Atos and Origin (the computer services division of Philips Electronics), Atos Origin targets clients in the financial services, automotive, manufacturing, and telecommunications industries. The company, which derives about 90% of its sales from customers in Europe, the Middle East, and Africa, has acquired KPMG International's British and Dutch operations, moving the company into high-end consulting and the realm of Cap Gemini Ernst & Young and IBM. Atos Origin is looking to expand further through acquisitions in Germany.

Customers include Vivendi Universal, BNP Paribas, and Unilever.

HISTORY

Atos Origin's lineage is a story of mergers. The company's predecessor, Groupe Sligos, was itself the product of a merger — the 1973 union of Sliga (Crédit Lyonnais' data processing services subsidiary) with Cegos Informatique, a management systems development and consulting company started in 1962.

In 1981 Sligos debuted the first bank/retailer network switching system. It acquired Soliac, France's largest credit card maker, in 1983. Sligos went public in 1986 and two years later acquired a majority stake in CMG (acquired by rival Logica plc to form LogicaCMG in 2002), one of France's leading computer engineering companies.

During the early 1990s Sligos focused on international growth, gaining majority interests in banking systems companies. It bought a controlling interest in Marben Group, a systems integration and networking firm, in 1993.

In 1996 Sligos joined with CyberCash, a (now defunct) US-based transaction processing company, to develop a secure Internet payment method for the European market. It sold CMG (by then a PC retailing subsidiary) to Infopoint and its Soliac magnetic strip and smart card unit to Schlumberger.

In late 1997 Sligos merged with French IT services company Axime. (Axime was created by the 1991 merger of IT service providers FITB, Segin, and Sodinforg. Bernard Bourigeaud joined Axime that year and became its chairman and CEO in 1992.)

Following the Sligos-Axime merger the company changed its name to Atos, with Axime's Bourigeaud assuming the role of chairman. Atos spent the last half of 1997 (and the first half of 1998) reorganizing its operations around four key areas: systems integration, outsourcing, multimedia, and services.

In 1998 Atos pared off its networking services and direct marketing subsidiaries. That year the company doubled the size of its Italian operation by acquiring IT services firm Sesam from Fiat and Digital Equipment (later acquired by Compaq), and it bought French customer relationship management specialist Statilogie. Atos in 1999 bought a controlling interest in France-based Odyssée, a consulting specialist in the financial services market. The next year the company developed a joint venture with ParisBourse to offer online stock trading and electronic banking.

In 2000 the company merged with Origin, the computer services arm of Philips Electronics. Bourigeaud became chairman and CEO of the new company, named Atos Origin. In 2002 the company acquired KPMG's British and Dutch operations for $617 million.

EXECUTIVES

Chairman, Supervisory Board: Henri Pascaud
Chairman and CEO: Bernard Bourigeaud, age 59
CFO: Eric Guilhou
Country Leader, Asia/Pacific, North America, Middle East, Nordic Region; Process Industries Sector: Timothy G. (Tim) Lomax
Country Leader, Central Europe; Human Resources, Communication, and Public Affairs; Discrete Manufacturing Sector: Jans Tielman
Country Leader, France, Italy, Iberia/Latin America; Consumer Packaged Goods and Retail Sector: Dominique Illien
Country Leader, Netherlands, Belgium, Luxembourg, UK; Telecom/Utilities/Media Sector: Wilbert Kieboom
Country Leader, the UK; Financial Services and Public Sectors: Jeremy Anderson
Head, Client Management, Atos Origin UK: Paul Bingham
Head, Corporate Operations, Atos Origin UK: Alan Downey
Managing Director, Consulting Division: Keith Rowling
Managing Director, Service Activities: Christian Huguet
Head of Applications Maintenance Services: Patrice Dannenberg
Commercial Director and General Counsel, Atos Origin UK: Rowan Vevers
Director, Communication and Public Relations: Marie-Tatiana Collombert
Finance Director, Atos Origin Germany: Heiner Diefenbach
Finance Director, Atos Origin UK: John Campbell
Director, Managed Services: Gerhard Fercho
Manager, Public Relations: Anne de Beaumont
Coordinator, Public Relations: Emilie Moreau
Auditors: Deloitte Touche Tohmatsu; Amyot Exco

LOCATIONS

HQ: Immeuble Ile-de-France, 3, place de la Pyramide, 92067 Paris, France
Phone: +33-1-49-00-90-00   **Fax:** +33-1-47-73-07-63
US HQ: 430 Mountain Ave., New Providence, NJ 07974-2761
US Phone: 908-771-3000   **US Fax:** 908-771-3200
Web: www.atosorigin.com

Atos Origin has offices in more than 30 countries.

2002 Sales

	$ mil.	% of total
France	1,198	37
Netherlands	953	30
Americas	146	5
Asia/Pacific	69	2
Other regions	823	26
Total	**3,189**	**100**

PRODUCTS/OPERATIONS

2002 Sales

	$ mil.	% of total
Consulting & systems integration	1,397	44
Managed services	1,384	43
Online services	408	13
Total	**3,189**	**100**

Management Consulting
Business transformation
Performance management
Program and change management

Systems Integration
Applications management
Network design, installation, and upgrading
Systems installation
Systems integration
Training

Managed Services
Applications maintenance and upgrading
Data center management
Enterprise resource planning
Facilities management
Remote management
Securities management
Stock market platforms
System design and installation

Online Services
Data warehousing
Enterprise application integration
Knowledge management

COMPETITORS

Altran Technologies	GFI Informatique
ARES	HP Services
Aubay	IBM Global Services
BT	LogicaCMG
Bull	Morse
Cap Gemini	Parity
CBGI	Siemens Business Services
Computacenter	Sopra
Computer Sciences	Steria
CS Communication	TEAMLOG
Devoteam	Transiciel
Diagonal	Triple P
DiData	Umanis
EDS	Unilog
Finsiel	Unisys
Fujitsu Services	Xansa
Getronics	

HISTORICAL FINANCIALS

Company Type: Public

Income Statement

FYE: December 31

	REVENUE ($ mil.)	NET INCOME ($ mil.)	NET PROFIT MARGIN	EMPLOYEES
12/02	3,189	74	2.3%	28,602
12/01	2,691	109	4.1%	26,278
12/00*	1,802	46	2.5%	26,916
9/99	1,154	51	4.4%	9,983
9/98	1,120	43	3.8%	9,400
9/97	968	30	3.1%	8,742
9/96	408	26	6.4%	2,702
9/95	415	26	6.2%	2,593
9/94	347	16	4.6%	2,444
9/93	333	6	1.7%	2,568
Annual Growth	**28.5%**	**33.3%**	**—**	**30.7%**

2002 Year-End Financials

Debt ratio: 98.2%   Current ratio: 3.26
Return on equity: 12.3%   Long-term debt ($ mil.): 762
Cash ($ mil.): 442

Net Income History   Euronext Paris: SAX

Aventis

Aventis helps docs treat their sneezy patients without making them sleepy, grumpy, or dopey. Aventis' core operations include prescription drugs, human vaccines, and therapeutic proteins. Its extensive product roster includes leading names Allegra (allergies, also available as non-drowsy Allegra-D), Taxotere (cancer), Lovenox (thrombosis), and Amaryl (diabetes). Subsidiary Aventis Pasteur makes the company's vaccines for hepatitis, influenza, measles, tetanus, and other diseases. Aventis also operates Merial, an animal health joint venture with Merck.

Aventis Pharma, the company's flagship unit, accounts for about 85% of sales. Aventis continues to target the lucrative North American market, where it makes almost 40% of its sales.

Hoping to be lean and mean in a world in which drug development speed can make or break a drug company, the firm has exited the crop sciences business to focus on pharmaceuticals. It sold its stake in Aventis CropScience, jointly owned with Schering, to Bayer, but won't be bidding adieu to its problems with genetically modified corn seed StarLink.

Aventis has initiated a wave of other divestitures as a part of its commitment to concentrate on pharmaceuticals. It has sold its Aventis Animal Nutrition business to CVC Capital Partners and also divested its Messer Griesham (industrial gases) subsidiary. The firm has spun off part of its clinical research arm into a joint venture (it owns 40%) with 3i Group. The company is also considering selling its Aventis Behring, its Wacker-Chemie (semiconductors) subsidiary, and its 25% stake in French chemicals group Rhodia.

The firm's pipeline includes drugs for asthma, cancer, and diabetes, and vaccines for meningitis and a combination vaccine for pediatric diseases such as polio, diphtheria, and Hib disease.

In a bid to stave off US government price controls, Aventis has teamed up with six other pharmaceutical firms to offer Together Rx, a drug discount card for low-income US seniors.

HISTORY

Aventis dates back to pharmacist Étienne Poulenc's purchase of a Parisian apothecary in 1858. The Établissements Poulenc Frères, established in Paris in 1900, developed such synthetic drugs as arsenobenzol, used to treat previously incurable syphilis. Poulenc branched into vaccines and veterinary products after WWI.

Société Chimique des Usines du Rhône began producing dyes in Lyons in 1895. In 1919 it moved into perfumes and specialty chemicals before merging with Poulenc in 1928. Post-WWII drug and chemical company buys helped

Rhône-Poulenc dominate the French chemical industry and rank third in Europe by 1970.

In the 1970s lower tariffs exposed Rhône-Poulenc to international competition. It failed to capitalize on the success of Thorazine when it licensed the US marketing rights to SmithKline. Rhône-Poulenc lost more than $500 million between 1980 and 1982, when it was nationalized by the Mitterrand government, which installed 39-year-old Loïk Le Floch-Prigent at the helm. He eliminated poorly performing units, cut the payroll, and returned Rhône-Poulenc to profitability.

In 1986 Jean-René Fourtou took over from Le Floch-Prigent. He sold 20 businesses and bought more than 30, including Union Carbide's agricultural chemical operations (1986) and Stauffer's industrial chemical business (1987).

In 1990 the French government transferred 35% of Roussel Uclaf, France's #3 drugmaker, to Rhône-Poulenc, which that year merged its drug business with US pharma firm Rorer (a 90-year-old US company that developed Maalox in the 1950s), to form Rhône-Poulenc Rorer, or RPR. The firm teamed with Merck & Co. in 1991 to develop vaccines for children. It also opened plastics and chemical factories in Asia.

Rhône-Poulenc was privatized in 1993 and expanded into biotechnology, buying 37% of Applied Immune Sciences. In 1994 the firm took over France's #2 OTC drug distributor, and the next year bought Fisons, a UK maker of asthma/allergy treatments. In 1996 the FDA cleared the company's Taxotere (derived from the yew tree) to treat advanced breast cancer.

In 1997 Rhône-Poulenc and Merck merged their animal health units to form Merial. Rhône-Poulenc in 1998 sold its lawn-and-garden operations to US-based Scotts, paving the way for a merger of its drug, agrochemical, and veterinary medicine businesses with those of Germany's chemical giant-cum-drug maven Hoechst. Rhône-Poulenc became Aventis in 1999, absorbing Hoechst. The predecessors' US subsidiaries, Hoechst Marion Roussel and Rhône-Poulenc Rorer Pharmaceuticals, merged into Aventis Pharmaceuticals.

In 2000 controversial "abortion pill" RU-486, made by Roussel Uclaf, was approved by the FDA. That year Aventis agreed to pay 22 US states in a vitamin price-fixing lawsuit settlement involving the likes of Roche and Takeda Chemical Industries.

Also in 2000 the firm agreed to sell a French R&D unit to DuPont Pharma. The company continued to streamline its operations in 2002, selling non-core businesses Aventis CropScience and its animal nutrition division.

EXECUTIVES

Vice Chairman of the Supervisory Board: Jean-René Fourtou, age 64

Chairman of the Supervisory Board: Jürgen Dormann, age 63

Chairman of the Management Board: Igor Landau, age 59

Vice Chairman of the Management Board and COO; CEO, Aventis Pharma: Richard J. Markham, age 53

Vice Chairman of the Management Board and CFO; Chairman and CEO, Aventis Agriculture: Patrick Langlois, age 58

Member of the Management Board and EVP, Commercial Operations: Thierry Soursac, age 46

Member of the Management Board and EVP, Drug Innovation and Approval: Frank L. Douglas, age 60

Member of the Management Board and EVP, Human Resources: Heinz-Werner Meier, age 51

Member of the Management Board, EVP, and General Counsel: Dirk Oldenburg, age 46

President, Commercial Operations, Aventis Japan: Jim Mitchum

Chairman and Deputy CEO, Aventis Pasteur: Jean-Jacques Bertrand

Communications: Gilles Brisson

Investor Relations: Arvind Sood

Media Relations: Carsten Tilger

Private Shareholder Relations: Jacques Mazard

Auditors: PricewaterhouseCoopers

LOCATIONS

HQ: Espace Européen de l'Entreprise,
16, Avenue de l'Europe, F-67917 Strasbourg, France
Phone: +33-3-88-99-11-00   **Fax:** +33-3-88-99-11-01
US HQ: 300 Somerset Corporate Blvd.,
Bridgewater, NJ 08807-2854
US Phone: 908-231-4000   **US Fax:** 908-231-3614
Web: www.aventis.com

PRODUCTS/OPERATIONS

Selected Pharmaceutical Products

Actonel (osteoporosis)
Allegra/Telfast (allergies)
Amaryl (diabetes)
Arava (rheumatoid arthritis)
Campto (colorectal cancer)
Copaxone (multiple sclerosis)
Delix/Tritace (cardiovascular conditions)
Insuman (insulin for diabetes mellitus)
Ketek (antibiotic)
Lantus (long-acting insulin)
Lovenox/Clexane (cardiovascular conditions)
Nasacort (nasal congestion relief)
Refludan (cardiovascular conditions)
Rilutek (Parkinson's disease)
Synercid (life-threatening infections)
Targocid (anti-infective)
Tavanic (anti-infective)
Taxotere (breast and ovarian cancer)

COMPETITORS

Abbott Labs	Merck
Baxter	Novartis
Bayer AG	Pfizer
Bristol-Myers Squibb	Roche
Dow Chemical	Schering-Plough
GlaxoSmithKline	Syngenta

HISTORICAL FINANCIALS

Company Type: Public

Income Statement

FYE: December 31

	REVENUE ($ mil.)	NET INCOME ($ mil.)	NET PROFIT MARGIN	EMPLOYEES
12/02	21,659	2,285	10.5%	—
12/01	20,447	1,455	7.1%	91,729
12/00	21,006	(27)	—	92,446
12/99	12,714	(859)	—	95,799
12/98	15,502	921	5.9%	65,180
12/97	14,933	(646)	—	68,377
12/96	16,535	528	3.2%	75,250
12/95	17,273	435	2.5%	82,556
12/94	16,171	359	2.2%	81,582
12/93	13,607	163	1.2%	81,678
Annual Growth	5.3%	34.1%	—	1.5%

2002 Year-End Financials

Debt ratio: 16.3%
Return on equity: 20.8%
Cash ($ mil.): 636
Current ratio: 0.92
Long-term debt ($ mil.): 1,877
No. of shares (mil.): 799
Dividends
 Yield: 0.9%
 Payout: 18.4%
Market value ($ mil.): 43,323

Stock History

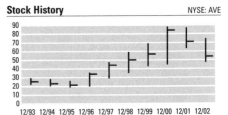

NYSE: AVE

12/93 12/94 12/95 12/96 12/97 12/98 12/99 12/00 12/01 12/02

	STOCK PRICE ($) FY Close	P/E High/Low		Earnings	Dividends	Book Value
12/02	54.19	27	17	2.77	0.51	14.89
12/01	71.00	51	38	1.68	0.44	13.47
12/00	84.25	—	—	(0.18)	0.41	12.98
12/99	56.88	—	—	(2.51)	0.64	13.84
12/98	50.25	29	18	2.02	0.00	24.41
12/97	44.19	—	—	(2.47)	0.61	19.52
12/96	33.88	—	—	1.63	0.87	29.59
12/95	21.38	—	—	1.37	0.61	28.85
12/94	23.13	—	—	0.93	0.52	29.60
12/93	25.38	—	—	0.71	0.41	27.65
Annual Growth	8.8%	—	—	16.3%	2.5%	(6.6%)

Aviva plc

In a consolidating European insurance industry, no acronym can last for long. Originally a merger of insurer CGU and nonlife specialist Norwich Union (which created CGNU), the company has reinvented itself as Aviva. A leading insurance firm throughout Europe, Aviva offers both life and general insurance. Its life and savings segments focus on life insurance, pensions, unit trusts, and other investment products; its general insurance segment includes home, auto, and fire coverage. Financial services include investment management, stock brokerage, and trustee services.

Strategically exiting unprofitable insurance markets, Aviva has sold its US general insurance operations to White Mountains Insurance Group. Focusing on smaller acquisitions in emerging markets, Aviva bought insurers in Holland, Belgium, and Hungary. The company also purchased Fortis' Australian operations, making it one of the country's top five insurance players. Extending its distribution channels, Aviva has teamed up with banks all across Europe (including a joint venture with Royal Bank of Scotland).

Aviva is primarily focused on growing its long-term savings business, including the launch of online wealth management services in the UK and expansion into central and eastern Europe (the company is the second-largest fund manager in the UK).

HISTORY

When insurers hiked premiums after the 1861 Great Tooley Street Fire of London, merchants formed Commercial Union Fire Insurance (CU). It opened offices throughout the UK and in foreign ports and soon added life (1862) and marine (1863) coverage.

Over the next 20 years, CU's foreign business thrived. The firm had offices across the US by the 1880s. In the 1890s CU entered Australia, India, and Southeast Asia. Foreign business eventually accounted for some 75% of CU's sales.

CU went shopping in the 20th century, adding accident insurer Palatine Insurance Co. of Manchester in 1900 and rescuing two companies ruined by San Francisco's 1906 earthquake and fire. CU recovered from the Depression with the help of a booming auto insurance market, and spent most of the 1930s and WWII consolidating operations to cut costs.

Profits suffered in the 1950s as CU faced increased competition in the US. To boost sales, it merged both with multiline rival North British and Mercantile and life insurer Northern and Employers Assurance in the early 1960s. While US business continued to lag in the 1970s, the company's European business grew.

From 1982 to 1992, CU cut its operations in the US, entered new markets (Poland, 1992; South Africa and Vietnam, 1996), and sold its New Zealand subsidiaries (1995). As competition in the UK increased, the company in 1997 reorganized and merged with General Accident in 1998.

General Accident & Employers Liability Assurance Association (GA) was formed in 1885 in Perth, Scotland, to sell workers' compensation insurance. Within a few years, GA had branches in London and Scotland. It diversified into insurance for train accidents (1887), autos (1896), and fire (1899); in 1906 its name changed to General Accident Fire and Life Assurance.

GA expanded into Australia, Europe, and Africa at the turn of the century. After WWI, the company's auto insurance grew along with car ownership. During the 1930s the company entered the US auto insurance market. WWII put a stop to GA's growth.

The company expanded after the war, forming Pennsylvania General Fire Insurance Association (1963) and acquiring the UK's Yorkshire Insurance Co. (1967). By the 1980s about one-third of its sales came from the US.

After 1986 GA acquired some 500 real estate brokerage agencies to cross-sell its home and life insurance. To increase presence in Asia and the Pacific, the company in 1988 acquired NZI Corp., a New Zealand banking and insurance company whose failing operations cost GA millions. At the same time, new US government regulations and a series of damaging storms hammered the company.

In response GA cut costs, posting a profit by 1993. As the industry consolidated, the company bought nonstandard auto insurer Sabre (1995), life insurer Provident Mutual (1996), and General Insurance Group Ltd. in Canada (1997). Unable to compete on its own, GA merged with Commercial Union to form CGU in 1998.

After the merger, CGU added personal pension plans and entered alliances to sell insurance in Italy and India. Merger costs and exceptional losses for 1998 hit operating profits hard. In 1999 CGU upped its stake in French bank Société Générale to about 7% to help it fend off a hostile takeover attempt by Banque Nationale de Paris (now BNP Paribas).

In 2000 the company merged with rival Norwich Union to form CGNU and made plans to exit the Canadian life and the US general insurance businesses. In 2001 CGNU sold its US property/casualty operations to White Mountains Insurance.

In an attempt to strengthen its brand name, the company changed its name to Aviva in 2002.

EXECUTIVES

Chairman: Pehr G. Gyllenhammar, age 68
Deputy Chairman: George Paul, age 63
Group Chief Executive: Richard Harvey, age 52
Group Finance Director: Mike Biggs, age 50
Group Executive Director, UK Life and Long-Term Savings: Philip Scott, age 49
Group Executive Director, UK General Insurance: Patrick Snowball, age 52
Group Executive Director, International and Fund Management Operations: Philip Twyman, age 58
Group Executive Director, Continental Europe and Ireland: Tony Wyand, age 59
Auditors: Ernst & Young

LOCATIONS

HQ: St. Helen's, 1 Undershaft,
   London EC3P 3DQ, United Kingdom
Phone: +44-20-7283-2000   **Fax:** +44-20-7662-2753
Web: www.aviva.com

Aviva has offices in more than 50 countries in Africa, the Asia/Pacific region, Europe, the Middle East, and North and South America.

PRODUCTS/OPERATIONS

2002 Sales

	% of total
Life premiums	65
General insurance	28
Investment sales	4
Health premiums	3
Total	**100**

Selected Subsidiaries and Affiliates

Belves Investments Limited (New Zealand)
Berlinische Lebensversicherung Aktiengesellschaft (99.5%, Germany)
CGU Bonus Limited
CGU Companhia de Seguros (99.9%, Brazil)
CGU Corporation (US)
CGU Holdings Canada Limited
CGU Insurance Australia Limited
CGU Insurance plc
CGU International Insurance plc
CGU Life Assurance Limited
CGU Participations SA (99.9%, France)
CGU SA NV (99.9%, Belgium)
CGU Underwriting Limited
Commercial Union Assurance (Malaysia) Berhad (60%)
Commercial Union Assurance Company (Thailand) Limited (49%)
Commercial Union Finance BV (the Netherlands)
Commercial Union Hayat Sigorta AS (90%, Turkey)
Commercial Union International Life SA (Luxembourg)
Commercial Union Italia SpA (Italy)
Commercial Union Life Assurance Company Limited
Commercial Union Polska Towarzystwo Ubezpieczen na Zycie SA (90%, Poland)
Commercial Union Polska Towarzystwo Ubezpieczen Ogolnych SA (90%, Poland)
Commercial Union Powszechne Towarzystwo Emerytalne BPH CU WBK SA (75%, Poland)
Commercial Union Sigorta AS (55%, Turkey)
Commercial Union zivotni pojist'ovna AS (Czech Republic)
Curepool Limited (Bermuda)
Delta Lloyd Nuts Ohra NV (the Netherlands)
GA Insurance Berhad (49%, Malaysia)
General Accident Lebensversicherung-Aktiengesellschaft (Germany)
General Accident plc
Hibernian Group plc (Ireland)
Hibernian Life & Pensions Limited (Ireland)
London & Edinburgh Insurance Group Limited
Morley Fund Management Limited
Morley Pooled Pensions Limited
Morley Properties Limited
The Northern Assurance Company Limited
Norwich Union Annuity Ltd.
Norwich Union General Insurance (Ireland) Ltd.
Norwich Union Healthcare Ltd.

Norwich Union Holdings Ltd.
Norwich Union Insurance Ltd.
Norwich Union Investment Management Ltd.
Norwich Union Life & Pensions Ltd.
Norwich Union Linked Life Assurance Ltd.
Norwich Union Portfolio Services Ltd.
Norwich Union Trust Managers Ltd.
Norwich Union Wealth Management Ltd.
Ogolnych SA (90%, Poland)
Pilot Insurance Company (Canada)
Plus Ultra Compañía Anónima de Seguros y Reaseguros (Spain)
Plus Ultra Vida Sociedad Anónima de Seguros y Reaseguros (Spain)
Quilter & Co Ltd. (74%)
Sabre Insurance Company Limited
Scottish General Insurance Company Limited
State Insurance Ltd. (New Zealand)
your-move.co.uk Limited

COMPETITORS

Abbey National	Lloyd's of London
Allianz	Millea Holdings
AXA UK	Prudential plc
Chubb	QBE
Cox Insurance Holdings	Royal & Sun Alliance
Guardian Royal Exchange	Insurance
plc	Standard Life
Highway Insurance	Zurich Financial Services
Legal & General Group	

HISTORICAL FINANCIALS

Company Type: Public

Income Statement

FYE: December 31

	ASSETS ($ mil.)	NET INCOME ($ mil.)	INCOME AS % OF ASSETS	EMPLOYEES
12/02	296,598	(857)	—	59,000
12/01	273,128	1,634	0.6%	68,107
12/00	288,566	(2,582)	—	72,749
12/99	296,117	1,621	0.5%	68,250
12/98	175,597	826	0.5%	51,965
12/97	151	2,494	1,652.9%	51,756
Annual Growth	355.7%	—	—	2.7%

2002 Year-End Financials

Equity as % of assets: 6.3%   Long-term debt ($ mil.): 174,241
Return on assets: —   Sales ($ mil.): 51,128
Return on equity: —

Net Income History   London: AV

AXA

The insurance world revolves around this AXA. AXA, which started as a sleepy collection of mutual insurance companies, is today the world's #2 insurance company (behind ING) and a financial management powerhouse. In the US, AXA owns AXA Financial, which owns a majority of investment manager Alliance Capital Management. The company also has major subsidiaries in the UK (AXA UK — formerly Sun Life and Provincial Holdings), Australia (National Mutual), and Belgium (Royale Belge). The companies offer life insurance, personal and commercial property/casualty insurance, reinsurance, financial services, and real estate investment services.

Mutuelles AXA (a group of eight mutuals) controls AXA through its 20% stake.

Rather than trying to run a cross-border organization, AXA instead builds businesses in each country, rebranding them under the AXA name. It has also established an Internet portal that it hopes will prevent the need for further acquisitions. Chairman Claude Bébéar brought a North American style to the once-genteel practice of business in France. The company wielded its power in the bank takeover struggle that resulted in the formation of BNP Paribas.

AXA has discontinued its slumping US-based reinsurance operations (Axa Corporate Solutions Reinsurance and Axa Corporate Solutions Life Reinsurance); the company will still be selling reinsurance in the US through Paris-based AXA Re.

In 2002 premium rate increases helped offset some of the company's losses, caused by ailing global stock markets.

In an attempt to strengthen its US retail insurance and annuity business, AXA, through subsidiary AXA Financial, has announced it is buying MONY Group for some $1.5 billion. The deal is expected to close in the first quarter of 2004.

HISTORY

AXA dates to the 1817 formation of regional fire insurer Compagnie d'Assurances Mutuelles contre l'incendie in Rouen, France (northwest of Paris). In 1881 France's first mutual life insurer was founded: Mutuelle Vie.

In 1946 these two operations and the younger Anciennes Mutuelles Accidents (founded 1922) were brought together by Sahut d'Izarn (general manager of Compagnie d'Assurances) as the Groupe Ancienne Mutuelle. Later members included Ancienne Mutuelle of Calvados (1946), Ancienne Mutuelle of Orleans (1950), Mutualité Générale (1953), and Participation (1954).

A long-term thinker, d'Izarn named not only his successor, Lucien Aubert, but also Aubert's successor, Claude Bébéar, a 23-year-old friend of d'Izarn's son. Never having held a job, Bébéar found the whole thing amusing and decided to try it.

Groupe Ancienne Mutuelle prospered during the 1960s, thanks to d'Izarn's disciplined management, but his technophobia kept the company from entering the computer age.

D'Izarn died in 1972. Aubert capitulated to worker demands during a series of strikes in the early 1970s; Bébéar ended a 1974 strike by threatening to use force against an employee sit-in, then ousted Aubert.

Bébéar spent the rest of the 1970s upgrading the firm's technology. During this period the company became known as Mutuelles Unies.

Bébéar then began building the firm through a series of spectacular acquisitions. In 1982 Mutuelles Unies gained control of crisis-ridden stock insurer Drouot. Two years later the company's name became AXA (which has no meaning and was chosen because it is pronounced the same in most Western languages). When another old-line insurer, Providence, went on the market, AXA went after it. Providence's management was entertaining another offer when AXA bought

tiny, inactive Bayas Tudjus, which held the right to a seat on the Providence board. Bébéar capitalized on small stockholders' dissatisfaction to spark a bidding war and used a new issue of Drouot stock in 1986 to buy Providence — France's first hostile takeover.

AXA bought lackluster US firm Equitable (now AXA Financial) in 1991, infusing $1 billion into the firm in return for the right to own up to 50% of its stock upon demutualization in 1992. AXA moved into Asia with the purchase of Australia's National Mutual in 1995.

Bébéar consolidated the operations into a global organization. In 1996 AXA bought the ailing Union des Assurances de Paris, which had done poorly since its 1994 privatization. It bought the 52% of Belgian insurer Royale Belge SA it didn't already own, as well as Belgian savings bank Anhyp in 1998.

Bébéar raised hackles when he supported the Société Générale-Paribas bank merger, then supported BNP's hostile takeover attempt of both (which garnered only Paribas). In 1999 AXA bought Guardian Royal Exchange, then sold the life and pensions business to Dutch insurer AEGON; Bébéar announced his retirement in 1999. In 2000 he stepped down from the management board but took over as Chairman of the Supervisory Board.

That year AXA took control of Japan's Nippon Dantai Life Insurance. It bought the remaining shares of AXA Financial and the 44% of AXA UK (formerly Sun Life and Provincial Holdings) it didn't already own. The next year AXA unloaded its debt-heavy subsidiary Banque Worms to Deutsche Bank.

EXECUTIVES

Chairman of the Supervisory Board: Claude Bébéar, age 68
Chairman of the Management Board and CEO: Henri de Castries, age 49
Member of the Management Board and Finance Director: Denis Duverne, age 49
Member of the Management Board; CEO and President, AXA Financial: Christopher M. (Kip) Condron, age 55
Member of the Management Board; CEO, AXA France Assurance: François Pierson
Member of the Management Board; EVP, Operations, Human Resources, and Transversal Projects: Claude Brunet
SEVP, Asia/Pacific Region: Michel Pinault
EVP, Information Systems and e-Business: Claude Cargou
EVP; Vice Chairman and CFO, AXA Financial and Equitable Life: Stanley B. Tulin, age 53
Head of Brand and Communications: Claire Dorland-Clauzel
Chairman and CEO, AXA Corporate Solutions: Philippe Donnet
Chairman and CEO, Colonia Konzern: Claus-Michael Dill
CEO, AXA Asia Pacific Holdings: Les Owen
CEO, AXA Investment Managers: Nicolas Moreau
CEO, AXA Re: Hans-Peter Gerhardt, age 47
CEO, AXA Royale Belge: Alfred J. Bouckaert, age 56
Group CEO, AXA UK: Dennis Holt, age 54
Auditors: Befec-Price Waterhouse

LOCATIONS

HQ: 25 Avenue Matignon, 75008 Paris, France
Phone: +33-1-40-75-57-00 **Fax:** +33-1-40-75-46-96
US HQ: 1290 Avenue of the Americas, 13th Fl., New York, NY 10104
US Phone: 212-554-1234 **US Fax:** 212-707-1746
Web: www.axa.com

AXA has operations in more than 60 countries in the Asia/Pacific region, Europe, and North and South America.

PRODUCTS/OPERATIONS

2002 Assets

	$ mil.	% of total
Cash	18,477	4
Bonds	155,182	33
Stocks	60,036	13
Net loans	19,184	4
Real estate	13,354	3
Goodwill	15,132	3
Assets in separate account	95,008	20
Receivables	26,646	6
Other	64,004	14
Total	**467,023**	**10**

2002 Sales

	$ mil.	% of total
Premiums	64,017	93
Bank revenues	1,038	2
Fees, commissions & other	3,902	5
Total	**68,957**	**100**

2002 Sales

	% of total
Life & savings	61
Property & casualty	24
International insurance	8
Asset management	6
Other financial services	1
Total	**100**

COMPETITORS

AEGON	ING
Allianz	Merrill Lynch
AIG	MetLife
AGF	Nationwide
CIGNA	New York Life
Citigroup	Nippon Life Insurance
Dai-ichi Mutual Life	Prudential
The Hartford	Sumitomo Life
Highway Insurance	

HISTORICAL FINANCIALS

Company Type: Public

Income Statement				FYE: December 31
	ASSETS ($ mil.)	NET INCOME ($ mil.)	INCOME AS % OF ASSETS	EMPLOYEES
12/02	467,023	997	0.2%	90,500
12/01	432,814	463	0.1%	90,151
12/00	446,993	3,677	0.8%	90,357
12/99	512,149	2,040	0.4%	92,008
12/98	450,849	1,794	0.4%	78,943
12/97	400,723	1,315	0.3%	80,613
12/96	216,438	793	0.4%	36,695
12/95	192,205	568	0.3%	36,625
12/94	149,525	425	0.3%	35,000
12/93	141,166	229	0.2%	43,340
Annual Growth	**14.2%**	**17.7%**	**—**	**8.5%**

2002 Year-End Financials

Equity as % of assets: 5.3%	Dividends
Return on assets: 0.2%	Yield: 3.7%
Return on equity: 4.2%	Payout: 86.2%
Long-term debt ($ mil.): 13,988	Market value ($ mil.): 23,702
No. of shares (mil.): 1,762	Sales ($ mil.): 68,957

Stock History

NYSE: AXA

12/93 12/94 12/95 12/96 12/97 12/98 12/99 12/00 12/01 12/02

	STOCK PRICE ($) FY Close	P/E High/Low		PER SHARE ($) Earnings	Dividends	Book Value
12/02	13.45	40	16	0.58	0.50	14.13
12/01	21.02	131	53	0.29	0.50	12.74
12/00	35.91	18	13	2.29	1.08	27.52
12/99	35.50	30	20	1.36	0.00	23.16
12/98	36.13	29	14	1.25	0.00	22.64
12/97	19.50	21	15	0.95	0.00	19.71
12/96	15.75	17	13	0.96	0.00	—
Annual Growth	(2.6%)	—	—	(8.1%)	—	(6.4%)

Axel Springer Verlag AG

The paper trail has been a path to success for Axel Springer Verlag. One of Europe's leading publishers, the company owns hundreds of newspapers and magazines throughout the continent, including *Bild* (Germany's #1 newspaper), *Die Welt,* and *Hamburger Abendblatt.* Its magazine portfolio boasts titles such as *Bild der Frau* (women's monthly), *Hörzu* (television guide), and *Sport Bild.* Axel Springer is also one of Germany's leading book publishers, owns 15 commercial printing plants (for company and third-party use), and has investments in online bookseller Booxtra and TV production company Schwartzkopff TV. The family of the late founder owns about 55% of the firm.

Axel Springer has been making several investments in new print titles and online publishing ventures, including the youth-targeted *Yam!* (launched in 2000) and an online site for *Hamburger Abendblatt.* It is also creating a new Web portal around its *Bild* banner with Deutsche Telekom's T-Online. In addition, the company is creating online marketing firm Interactive Media through a joint venture with T-Online. However, Axel Springer's investments have reduced the bottom line at a time when advertising revenue is under pressure, causing some consternation in the boardroom.

In early 2003 it agreed to sell the paperback unit of its Ullstein Heyne List book group to Random House.

The company has also sold off several of its stakes in TV production companies as it seeks to focus on its main publishing unit.

HISTORY

Hinrich Springer, whose newspaper business had been closed by the Nazi government in 1941, and his son Axel launched Axel Springer Verlag in 1946 with the magazine *Nordwestdeutsche Hefte.* In 1948 the company unveiled *Hamburger Abendblatt,* which became Hamburg's best-selling newspaper by 1950. Axel Springer eventually took over the business and introduced the tabloid *Bild Zeitung* (later renamed *Bild*) in 1952. The success of the paper helped fund the company's expansion.

Axel Springer bought the daily *Die Welt* in 1953 and *Berliner Morgenpost* in 1959. The company moved its headquarters to Berlin in 1966. Fiercely supportive of the reunification of Germany, Springer built the company's headquarters immediately next to the Berlin Wall. In the 1970s the company expanded into the regional newsletter and magazine market. Axel Springer's growing control over German media did not go unnoticed, however, and opposition to the company's power was demonstrated when its Hamburg office was bombed in 1972 (the company was the target of arson again in 1998). Springer considered selling the entire company, but opted to sell several individual publications instead.

The company expanded beyond print media in 1984, investing in satellite consortium SAT.1 Satelliten Fernsehen. In 1985 it acquired stakes in cable TV and bought two Munich radio stations. After taking the company public that year, founder Axel Springer passed away. In 1989 German media firm KirchGruppe (since renamed TaurusGroup) began buying shares in Axel Springer Verlag.

In 1996 Axel Springer entered the Czech and Slovak newspaper markets with the purchase of a 49% stake in Dutch firm Ringier-Taurus. The company formed a joint venture in 1998 with Infoseek (later absorbed by Walt Disney Internet Group) and other partners to launch a German-language Web search service. It also bought 95% of German book publisher ECON + LIST Verlagsgesellschaft. August Fischer, former chief executive of News Corp.'s News International, was appointed chairman and CEO that year. A 1998 bid to buy UK-based media firm Mirror Group (now Trinity Mirror) proved unsuccessful.

In 1999 Axel Springer acquired stakes in several TV production companies, including a 90% interest in Schwartzkopff TV-Productions. The following year the company merged its 41%-owned TV station SAT.1 with German TV station operator Pro Sieben Media to create ProSiebenSAT.1 Media, Germany's largest commercial TV group. (Axel Springer retained an 11% stake, which it sold to TaurusGroup.) Fischer retired at the end of 2001 was replaced by Mathias Döpfner. The company began investing in new online ventures, including a portal built around *Bild.* Döpfner took over for Fischer in 2002. TaurusGroup sold its shares in the company in 2003 to Deutsche Bank.

EXECUTIVES

Chairman of the Supervisory Board: Bernhard Servatius
Chairman of the Management Board and CEO of the Newspaper Division: Mathias Döpfner
Deputy Chairman of the Management Board and Head of Printing and Logistics Division: Rudolf Knepper
COO and CFO: Steffen Naumann
Head of Magazines and International Affairs Division: Andreas Wiele
Head of Electronic Media and Books Divisions: Hubertus Meyer-Burckhardt
Director of Finance and Accounting and Corporate Controlling: Fred Wilsdorf
Head of Investor Relations: Diana Grigoriev
Auditors: PwC Deutsche Revision AG

LOCATIONS

HQ: Axel-Springer-Platz 1, D-20350 Hamburg, Germany
Phone: +49-40-3-47-2-23-70   **Fax:** +49-40-3-47-2-90-37
Web: www.asv.de

PRODUCTS/OPERATIONS

Selected Magazines

Allegra	*HAMMER*
Auto Bild	*Hörzu*
Bild der Frau	*Journal für die Frau*
Bildwoche	*musikexpress*
Computer Bild	*Popcorn*
Familie & Co	*Sport Bild*
Finanzen	*TVneu*
Funk Uhr	*Yam!*

Selected Newspapers

Berliner Morgenpost
Bild
Bild am Sonntag
B.Z.
Die Welt
Euro am Sonntag
Hamburger Abendblatt
Welt am Sonntag

Selected Electronic Media Investments

Booxtra (25%, online bookseller)
CompuTel (audiotext provider)
Schwartzkopff TV (90%, TV production)

COMPETITORS

Bertelsmann
Dow Jones
Edipresse
Emap
Financial Times
Hachette Filipacchi Médias
IPC Media
Modern Times Group
News Corp.
Pearson
Reed Elsevier Group
Reuters
Schibsted
Time
Verlagsgruppe Georg von Holtzbrinck
Vivendi Universal Publishing
VNU

HISTORICAL FINANCIALS

Company Type: Public

Income Statement

FYE: December 31

	REVENUE ($ mil.)	NET INCOME ($ mil.)	NET PROFIT MARGIN	EMPLOYEES
12/02	2,910	64	2.2%	13,203
12/01	2,537	(175)	—	13,500
12/00	2,732	92	3.4%	13,590
12/99	2,683	152	5.7%	11,687
12/98	2,870	165	5.7%	13,331
12/97	2,566	118	4.6%	12,195
12/96	2,845	105	3.7%	12,346
12/95	2,875	99	3.4%	12,646
12/94	2,556	77	3.0%	13,331
12/93	2,209	42	1.9%	12,187
Annual Growth	3.1%	4.8%	—	0.9%

2002 Year-End Financials

Debt ratio: 18.5%   Current ratio: 2.00
Return on equity: 16.7%   Long-term debt ($ mil.): 81
Cash ($ mil.): 80

Net Income History

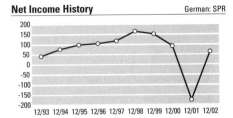

German: SPR

Bacardi Limited

You want proof? The folks at Bacardi Limited will pour it for you — from a bottle. One of the world's leading wine and spirits groups, Bacardi produces a dozen varieties of its rum, selling more than 200 million bottles per year in nearly 200 countries. It also owns Martini & Rossi vermouth, Dewar's Scotch whisky, DiSaronno Amaretto, Bombay gin, and B&B and Benedictine liqueurs. Other drinks by Bacardi include vodka, tequila, cognac, sparkling wine, and Hatuey beer. About 600 descendants of founder Facundo Bacardi y Maso own Bacardi.

Steeped in liquor lore, Bacardi claims the first Cuba Libre (rum and cola) was made with its product in 1898. Thanks to the popularity of the concoction, The Coca-Cola Company and Bacardi are working on a fountain machine that premixes the cocktail straight from the bar tap. Its bottles feature Bacardi's trademark bat logo, said to have been inspired by bats (an omen of good luck) that lived in the first distillery. To round out its white liquor portfolio, the distiller has been expanding its line of premium liquors through acquisitions, including one of Mexico's leading premium tequilas, Tequila Cazadores. It also holds distribution rights in Mexico to Brown-Forman's Jack Daniel's, Southern Comfort, and other popular brands.

Though a well-known family operation, Bacardi may go public. Shareholders have approved the creation of two classes of company stock — one for family members and one for the public. While family members would maintain a controlling interest in the company, the company needs outside investment to grow its business. It has yet to actually issue any new stock.

HISTORY

Facundo Bacardi y Maso immigrated to Cuba from Spain in 1830. He started in the liquor business as a rum salesman for John Nunes, an Englishman who owned a small distillery in Santiago, Cuba. In 1862 Facundo, his brother José, and a French wine merchant bought Nunes' distillery and began producing a smoother rum from a formula created by Facundo after years of trial and error. The more mixable quality of Bacardi's rum proved to be a key to its success. In 1877 Facundo passed company leadership to his sons; the eldest, Emilio, took over running the company (and spent some of his spare time in jail for his anti-Spanish activities).

Bacardi Limited struggled during the 1890s as Cuba's economy foundered. The business was thrown into even greater turmoil when revolutionary leader José Marti began what would be the final fight for Cuban independence. One of Marti's biggest supporters was Emilio, who earned another stay in jail and then exile for his sympathies. After Cuba gained its independence in 1902, Bacardi grew rapidly, getting a further boost from Prohibition as Havana became "the unofficial US saloon." (Prohibition did, however, end a venture in the US.)

The company moved into brewing in the 1920s and expanded its rum operations in the 1930s, opening a distillery in Mexico (1931) and another in Puerto Rico (1935). In 1944 it opened Bacardi Imports in the US and built up its overseas operations during the 1950s.

Amid all its success, Bacardi again became embroiled in Cuban politics during the late 1950s. Although some company leaders showed open opposition to Cuban leader Fulgencio Batista and support for Fidel Castro, others opposed Castro. As a result of the 1959 revolution, the Bacardi family was forced into exile, fleeing to the US and Europe. Castro seized Bacardi's assets in 1960. However, the expropriation was not a fatal blow since both the Mexican and Puerto Rican operations had been outearning the Cuban operations since the 1940s. Bacardi continued to enjoy explosive growth during the 1960s and 1970s. In 1977 some family members sold about 12% of the Bacardi empire to Hiram Walker.

By 1980 Bacardi was the #1 liquor brand in the US, but family squabbles and bad decisions threatened the company. Bacardi Capital, set up to manage the empire's money, lost $50 million in 1986. That year the empire's leadership started to buy up shares in Bacardi companies, including those sold to Hiram Walker and the 10% of Bacardi Corporation that had been sold to the public in 1962.

In an effort to diversify and to increase its European markets, the company bought a majority stake in Martini & Rossi in 1993. Two years later it launched Bacardi Limon, a citrus-flavored rum, and Hatuey (pronounced "ah-tway") beer. In 1996 family lawyer George Reid became president and CEO, the first nonfamily member to head the company.

Bacardi acquired the rights to the Havana Club trademark in 1997 from the Arechabala family. The move exacerbated a dispute with France's Pernod Ricard, which had partnered with the Cuban government to use the Havana Club name. Bacardi bought the Dewar's Scotch whisky and Bombay gin brands from Diageo in 1998.

In 2000 Reid resigned and Ruben Rodriguez was named president and CEO. Rodriguez added chairman to his titles when Manuel Jorge Cutillas retired later in the year. In 2000 Bacardi (along with partner Brown-Forman) also lost the bidding war for Seagram's alcoholic drinks business (Glenlivet, Sterling Vineyards, Martell Cognac) to rival bidding duo Diageo and Pernod Ricard.

In 2002 Bacardi acquired Tequila Cazadores, a leader in Mexico's Agave Reposado segment.

EXECUTIVES

Chairman: Ruben Rodriguez
CEO: Javier Ferran
CFO: Ralph Morera
VP, Communications: Patricia Neal
Human Resources: Alana Rogers

LOCATIONS

HQ: 65 Pitts Bay Rd., Pembroke HM 08, Bermuda
Phone: 441-295-4345   **Fax:** 441-292-0562
Web: www.bacardi.com

Bacardi Limited has production facilities in the Bahamas, Brazil, Canada, Martinique, Mexico, Panama, Puerto Rico, Spain, and Trinidad.

PRODUCTS/OPERATIONS

Selected Brands

Rum
Bacardi (8, 151, 1873 Solera, Anejo, Black, Carta Blanca, Exclusiv, Gold, Light, Limón, Select, Solera, Spice)
Castillo (Anejo, Gold, White)
Estelar Suave
Ron Bacardi Anejo

Other Spirits and Beverages
Alcohol-based aperitif (Pastis Casanis, Pastis Duval)
Amaretto (DiSaronno Amaretto)
Beer (Hatuey)
Brandy (Gran Reserva Especial, Vergel, Viejo Vergel)
Champagne (Charles Volner, Veuve Amiot)
Cognac (Exshaw, Gaston de la Grange, Otard)
Gin (Bombay, Bombay Sapphire, Bosford, Martini)
Liqueur (B&B, Benedictine, China Martini, Nassau Royale)
Low-alcohol beverage (Bacardi Breezer, Bacardi & Cola, Caribbean Classics, Martini Brand Jigger)
Scotch whisky (Dewar's, Glen Deveron, William Lawson's Finest Blend, William Lawson's Scottish Gold)
Sparkling wine (Grande Auguri, Martini & Rossi Asti Spumante, Montelera Riserva, Martini Brand Asti, Martini Brand Riesling)
Tequila (Camino Real, Tequila Cazadores)
Vodka (Eristoff, Martini, Natasha, Russian Prince)
Wine-based spirits (Martini & Rossi Bianco, Extra Dry, and Rosso; Martini Brand Bianco, Extra Dry, Rose, Rosso, and Vermouth; Noilly Prat; St. Raphael)

COMPETITORS

Allied Domecq
Brown-Forman
Constellation Brands
Diageo
Gallo
Fortune Brands
Heaven Hill Distilleries
Highland Distillers
Jim Beam Brands
Jose Cuervo
LVMH
Pernod Ricard
Rémy Cointreau
Robert Mondavi
Sebastiani Vineyards
Suntory

HISTORICAL FINANCIALS

Company Type: Private

Income Statement

FYE: March 31

	REVENUE ($ mil.)	NET INCOME ($ mil.)	NET PROFIT MARGIN	EMPLOYEES
3/03	3,000	—	—	6,300
3/02	2,900	—	—	6,300
3/01	2,700	—	—	6,200
3/00	2,600	—	—	6,000
3/99	2,464	—	—	6,200
3/98	2,400	—	—	6,200
Annual Growth	**4.6%**	**—**	**—**	**0.3%**

Revenue History

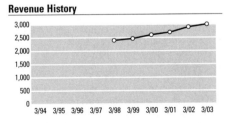

BAE SYSTEMS

It's fitting that BAE SYSTEMS (formerly British Aerospace), which helped win the Battle of Britain with its Mosquito and Spitfire fighters, is Europe's largest defense contractor. BAE's offerings include avionics, military and regional jet aircraft, air-defense systems, missiles, artillery locators, communications and navigation systems, radar, ships, space systems, and aerospace electronics. BAE's fighter aircraft include the Harrier, Hawk, Tornado, and the next-generation Eurofighter Typhoon. BAE also owns 20% of Airbus, Boeing's only competitor for large commercial aircraft.

The company's commercial aerospace unit will be making the Avro jet aircraft for regional markets for only a short while longer (this unit is being phased out — there are only four left to be completed). The closure of the regional jet business essentially makes BAE a pure defense contractor with a 20% stake in Airbus.

As such, BAE is continuing to concentrate on its core activities. BAE also wants to concentrate on leveraging its airborne technology know-how in its land and naval systems and has beefed up its defense electronics operations by buying units from Lockheed Martin. The company, which wants to expand its North American operations, made a bid for the defense and space assets of US aerospace and car parts maker TRW before that company agreed to be acquired by Northrop Grumman. Even so, BAE remains on the lookout for acquisition opportunities. Back in the UK, BAE has been selected as the prime contractor for the next-generation UK aircraft carrier program.

HISTORY

Post-Wright brothers and pre-WWII, a host of aviation companies sprang up to serve the British Empire — too many to survive after the war when the empire contracted. Parliament took steps in 1960 to save the industry by merging companies to form larger, stronger entities — Hawker-Siddeley Aviation and British Aircraft Corporation (BAC).

Hawker-Siddeley, made up of aircraft and missiles divisions, was created by combining A.V. Roe, Gloster Aircraft, Hawker Aircraft, Armstrong Whitworth, and Folland Aircraft. It attained fame in the 1960s for developing the Harrier "jump jet."

BAC was formed from the merger of Bristol Aeroplane, English Electric, and Vickers-Armstrong. In 1962 it joined France's Aerospatiale to build the supersonic Concorde and became a partner in ventures to develop the Tornado and Jaguar fighters. The cost of these ventures, plus the commercial failure of the Concorde, was more than the company could bear. Realizing British aviation was again in trouble, the British government nationalized BAC and Hawker-Siddeley in 1976 and merged them in 1977 with Scottish Aviation to form British Aerospace (BAe).

BAe joined the Airbus consortium in 1979. A partial privatization of the company began in 1981 when the government sold 52% to the public (the remaining stake sold in 1985). Also in 1981 BAe announced a joint venture with Comsat General and announced that it would be the prime contractor for L-SAT-1, the European Space Agency's telecommunications satellite.

In 1987 BAe bought Steinheil Optronik (optical equipment) and Ballast Nedam Groep (civil and marine engineering). In 1990 BAe formed Ballast Nedam Construction.

BAe began to restructure its troubled regional aircraft division in 1992 by laying off thousands of workers and closing a major plant. The company sold Ballast Nedam and its corporate jet business to Raytheon and won a $7.5 billion contract from Saudi Arabia for Tornado jets in 1993. BAe sold its satellite business in 1994.

Matra BAe Dynamics, the world's third-largest maker of tactical missiles, was formed in a 1996 merger between BAe and Lagardère subsidiary Matra Hachette. BAe joined Lockheed Martin in a competition to build fighter jets for the UK and the US.

BAe's emphasis on large jetliners led to the 1998 breakup of Aero International, its two-year-old regional-aircraft joint venture with Aerospatiale (France) and Alenia (Italy). Shortly thereafter, BAe spent $454 million for a 35% stake in Swedish military jet maker Saab AB. Also in 1998 BAe bought Siemens' UK- and Australia-based defense electronics operations. In 1999 BAe bought the electronic systems defense unit of Marconi Electronic Systems (MES) for $12.7 billion (including US-based Tracor). The company changed its name to BAE SYSTEMS to remove the British influence from its name.

In 2000 the UK government agreed to loan BAE about $836 million to support the Airbus A3XX superjumbo airliner project. The same year BAE acquired Lockheed Martin's control-systems unit for about $510 million. The prime contractor for the UK's new Type 45 destroyer, BAE was named to build two of the first three Type 45s. Late in the year BAE spent about $1.67 billion for a group of Lockheed Martin's defense electronics businesses, including its Sanders airborne electronics unit. BAE also sold its power and controls business (actuation equipment and starter motors) to Cobham.

Early in 2001 the company sold its 54% stake in BAE SYSTEMS CANADA (now known as CMC Electronics) to Oncap, a Toronto-based investment fund, as part of $398 million management buyout of the affiliate. The same year the Airbus Industrie consortium finally became Airbus S.A.S., a corporation. In November BAE announced that it would phase out its regional-aircraft business.

In June of 2002 BAE announced that it had entered talks to acquire US-based aerospace and car parts maker TRW, but TRW soon agreed to be acquired by US aerospace giant Northrop Grumman in a $7.8 billion stock deal. The same year BAE sold its defensive-countermeasures business to Esterline Technologies. BAE was selected as the prime contractor for the UK's next aircraft carrier in 2003.

EXECUTIVES

Chairman: Sir Richard (Dick) Evans, age 60, $957,528 pay
Vice Chairman: Sir Charles Masefield, age 63, $795,534 pay
CEO: Michael John (Mike) Turner, age 54, $1,109,898 pay
COO: Chris Geoghegan, age 48, $328,799 pay (partial-year salary)
COO, BAE Systems Programs: Steve Mogford, age 46, $689,677 pay
COO and President, BAE Systems, North America: Mark Ronald, age 61, $708,923 pay
Chief of Staff: George Mayhew
Director of Audit: Grenville Hodge

Group Communications Director: Hugh Colver
Group Finance Director: George Rose, age 50, $768,268 pay
Group Marketing Director: Mike Rouse
Group Legal Director: Michael Lester, age 62, $560,000 pay
Group Strategy Director: David Singleton
Group Managing Director, Network Enabled Capability: Alison Wood
Group Managing Director, Air Systems: Nigel Whitehead
Group Managing Director, Command/Control, Communications, Computing, Intelligence, Surveillance and Reconnaissance: Phill Blundell
Group Managing Director, Customer Solutions and Support: Ian King
Group Managing Director, International Partnerships: Stephen Henwood
Group Managing Director, Sea Systems: Brian Phillipson
Group HR Director; Group Managing Director, Shared Services: Alastair Imrie
Auditors: KPMG Audit Plc

LOCATIONS

HQ: Warwick House, PO Box 87, Farnborough, Hampshire GU14 6YU, United Kingdom
Phone: +44-1252-373232   **Fax:** +44-1252-383000
US HQ: 1601 Research Blvd., Rockville, MD 20850
US Phone: 301-738-4000   **US Fax:** 301-738-4643
Web: www.baesystems.com

BAE SYSTEMS has operations in Africa, Asia, Australia, Europe, and North America.

PRODUCTS/OPERATIONS

Selected Products and Services

North America
Advanced aerospace systems
Electronic warfare systems
Engine and flight controls
Imagery exploitation
Intelligent electronic systems
Technical services

Customer Solutions and Support
Military services and support

Programmes
Astute class submarine
Eurofighter Typhoon
Hawk
Nimrod
Type 45 destroyers

Avionics
Airborne electronic systems
Flight control systems

Commercial Aerospace
Airbus commercial jets
Avro RJ series (regional jets — these are being phased out)

International Partnerships
Air-to-air missiles
Combat and radar systems
Naval sonar

COMPETITORS

A.B.Dick
Astronautics
Boeing
Bombardier
Colt's
SEPI
EADS
Beretta

Glock
Honeywell International
Lockheed Martin
Lockheed Martin Missiles
Northrop Grumman
Thales
Ultra Electronics

HISTORICAL FINANCIALS

Company Type: Public

Income Statement

FYE: December 31

	REVENUE ($ mil.)	NET INCOME ($ mil.)	NET PROFIT MARGIN	EMPLOYEES
12/02	12,953	(1,100)	—	68,100
12/01	13,119	(194)	—	70,100
12/00	14,399	(19)	—	85,000
12/99	14,434	524	3.6%	83,400
12/98	14,283	1,148	8.0%	47,900
12/97	14,098	266	1.9%	43,400
12/96	10,982	525	4.8%	47,000
12/95	8,896	214	2.4%	45,400
12/94	11,193	219	2.0%	47,900
12/93	15,898	(316)	—	88,800
Annual Growth	(2.3%)	—	—	(2.9%)

2002 Year-End Financials

Debt ratio: 33.7%
Return on equity: —
Cash ($ mil.): 2,736

Current ratio: 0.91
Long-term debt ($ mil.): 3,068

Net Income History

OTC: BAESY

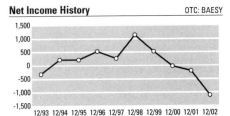

Bank of Montreal

Bank of Montreal, Canada's oldest and fifth-largest bank, has about 1,100 branches serving individuals, government agencies, institutions, and businesses large and small at home and abroad. The company, which also goes by BMO Financial Group, provides mortgages, insurance, asset management services, and mutual funds. In the US, it owns Chicago's Harris Bankcorp, which provides retail and corporate banking in the midwestern US. Subsidiaries BMO Nesbitt Burns (in Canada) and Harris Nesbitt (US) offer brokerage, merger and acquisition advice, and investment and merchant banking services.

After reorganizing along operational lines (Personal and Commercial Client Group, Private Client Group, and Investment Banking Group), the company is focused on building its business through acquisitions and organic growth. With about a third of its revenue coming from south of the border, it would like to repeat its successful Harris Bank acquisition experience in other stateside markets, including Texas, California, and Georgia. The bank has already made modest forays into Florida and Arizona, and bought online brokerage CSFBdirect, which it integrated into the Harris InvestorLine unit to form Harrisdirect. Harrisdirect is also acquiring the self-directed online client base of Morgan Stanley.

Continuing its southward push, Bank of Montreal bought New York-based investment bank Gerard Klauer Mattison and renamed it Harris Nesbitt Gerard.

HISTORY

Montreal was a key port for fur and agriculture trade by the early 1800s. To finance these activities, the Montreal Bank (Canada's first) opened in 1817. Chartered in 1822, the bank officially became Bank of Montreal. Its ties with the US were strong, and nearly 50% of its original capital came from Yanks.

When the fur trade shifted northward to Hudson Bay in the 1820s, the bank diversified. In 1832 Bank of Montreal financed Canada's first railroad, the Champlain & St. Lawrence. The bank also grew through acquisitions, including the Bank of Canada (1831) and the Bank of the People (1840). It opened a branch in New York in 1859.

Canada united in confederacy in 1867, and Bank of Montreal expanded west. During the 1860s, it became Canada's de facto central bank until the 1935 creation of the Bank of Canada. By 1914 Bank of Montreal was the nation's largest bank. It bought the British Bank of North America (1918), Merchants Bank of Canada (1922), and Molsons Bank (1925). During the Depression, however, its growth ground to a halt.

WWII pumped up Canada's economy and the company's finances. Bank of Montreal enjoyed even greater growth during the postwar boom. It began expanding internationally, particularly in Latin America. But the bank failed to capitalize on the growth of consumer and small-business lending during the 1960s and was the last major Canadian bank to issue a credit card (in 1972). In 1975 Bank of Montreal hired William Mullholland, a Morgan Stanley veteran, to run the company. Mullholland closed unprofitable branches and modernized operations.

The bank bought Chicago-based Harris Bankcorp in 1984. As Canada's banking industry deregulated, Bank of Montreal moved into investment banking, acquiring one of Canada's largest brokerage firms, Nesbitt Thomson, in 1987.

The Latin American debt crisis and the recession of the late 1980s and early 1990s hit Bank of Montreal hard. It tumbled into the red in 1989, partly because of loan defaults. The next year Matthew Barrett replaced Mullholland as chairman and began overhauling operations, focusing on consumer and middle-market business banking and on cutting costs.

By 1994 nonperforming assets were down, and Bank of Montreal began growing again. It bought brokerage Burns Fry and merged it with Nesbitt Thomson to form Nesbitt Burns, thus increasing its presence in merchant and investment banking and securities. It added to its Harris Bank network with the purchase of Suburban Bancorp. The next year Bank of Montreal expanded its private banking business for wealthy individuals; it also began targeting aboriginal Canadians.

Eyeing international growth, Bank of Montreal bought an interest in Mexico's Grupo Financiero Bancomer in 1996 (now called BBVA Bancomer) and opened branches in Beijing (1996) and Dublin, Ireland (1997). It agreed in 1998 to merge with Royal Bank of Canada, but Canada's finance minister rejected the merger.

Barrett stepped down as CEO and chairman in 1999; the firm named F. Anthony Comper its new CEO. The bank realigned its operations to focus on retail and commercial banking, investment banking, and wealth management and cut some 2,450 jobs. Eyeing growth in the US, in 2000 Bank of Montreal agreed to buy Florida's Village Banc of Naples, as well as Seattle brokerage Freeman Welwood. Also that year subsidiary Harris Bank began offering wireless banking.

In 2001 Bank of Montreal took its southern expansion one step further when it announced it would buy the 18-branch First National Bank of Joliet (Illinois) and merge it into Harris Bank. Later, Bank of Montreal sold its stake in BBVA Bancomer to Banco Bilbao Vizcaya Argentaria. The next year Bank of Montreal picked up online brokerage CSFBdirect.

EXECUTIVES

Chairman and CEO: F. Anthony (Tony) Comper, age 56, $1,340,850 pay
Deputy Chairman, Enterprise Risk and Portfolio Management Group: Ronald G. Rogers, age 55, $809,618 pay
Deputy Chairman and Head of Investment Banking Group; CEO, BMO Nesbitt Burns: William A. Downe, $2,800,000 pay
Chairman, Harris Bankcorp: Alan G. McNally, age 58, $782,000 pay
Chairman, BMO Nesbitt Burns; President, BMO Financial Group, Québec: L. Jacques Ménard, age 57
President and COO, BMO Nesbitt Burns: Yvan J.P. Bourdeau, $1,468,550 pay
President and CEO, Technology and Solutions and Head of E-Business: Lloyd F. Darlington, age 58
President, Personal Banking and Head of Personal & Commercial Client Group Products: Maurice A. D. Hudon
President and CEO, Private Client Group: Gilles G. Ouellette, $638,500 pay
President, Personal and Commercial Client Group: Robert W. (Rob) Pearce
President and CEO, Harrisdirect; CEO, BMO InvestorLine: Bruce S. Schwenger
President and CEO, Harris Bankcorp: Frank Techar, age 45
EVP and CFO: Karen E. Maidment
EVP and Head of Corporate Risk Management Group: Michel G. (Mike) Maila
EVP, Commercial Banking: Robert (Bob) McGlashan
EVP and Chief Economist: Timothy J. (Tim) O'Neill
EVP, Human Resources and Head of Office of Strategic Management: Rose M. Patten
EVP, Taxation and General Counsel: Ronald B. Sirkis
EVP and Treasurer: Penelope F. (Penny) Somerville
SVP, Corporate Communications: Angela Ferrante
Head of Mutual Fund Investments; Chairman and CEO, Jones Heward: Barry M. Cooper
Auditors: KPMG LLP

LOCATIONS

HQ: 1 First Canadian Place, 100 King St. West, Toronto, Ontario M5X 1A1, Canada
Phone: 416-867-5000   **Fax:** 416-867-6793
US HQ: 111 W. Monroe St., Fl. 21E, Chicago, IL 60690
US Phone: 312-461-2121   **US Fax:** 312-461-3869
Web: www.bmo.com

PRODUCTS/OPERATIONS

Selected Subsidiaries

Bank of Montreal Assessoria e Serviços Ltda. (Brazil)
Bank of Montreal Capital Markets (Holdings) Limited (UK)
  BMO Nesbitt Burns Limited (UK)
Bank of Montreal Global Capital Solutions Ltd.
Bank of Montreal Holding Inc.
  Bank of Montreal Insurance (Barbados) Limited
  Bank of Montreal Securities Canada Limited
    BMO Nesbitt Burns Corporation Limited
  BMO Holding Finance, LLC (US)
  BMO Investments Limited (Bermuda)
  BMO Nesbitt Burns Trading Corp. S.A. (Luxembourg)
  BMO Service Inc.
Bank of Montreal Ireland plc
Bank of Montreal Mortgage Corporation
Bankmont Financial Corp. (US)
BMO Financial, Inc. (US)
BMO Global Capital Solutions, Inc. (US)
BMO Managed Investments Corp. (US)
BMO Nesbitt Burns Corp. (US)
BMO Nesbitt Burns Equity Group (U.S.), Inc.
BMO Nesbitt Burns Financing, Inc. (US)
EFS (U.S.), Inc.
Harris Bancorp Insurance Services, Inc. (US)
Harris Bankcorp, Inc. (US)
Harris Investor Services, LLC (US)
Harris InvestorLine, Inc. (US)
Harris Trust Company (US)
Harris Trust/Bank of Montreal (US)
BMO Capital Corporation
BMO Investments Inc.
BMO InvestorLine Inc.
BMO Ireland Finance Company
BMO Life Insurance Company
BMO Nesbitt Burns Equity Partners Inc.
BMO (N.S.) Holdings Co.
  BMO (U.S.) Finance, LLC
dealerAccess Inc. (US)
  dealerAccess Canada Inc.
Guardian Group of Funds Ltd.
Lakeshore Funding Company, LLC
MyChoice Inc.
The Trust Company of Bank of Montreal

COMPETITORS

Bank of America
Scotiabank
BANK ONE
CIBC
Citigroup
Laurentian Bank
Northern Trust
RBC Financial Group
TD Bank
Wells Fargo

HISTORICAL FINANCIALS

Company Type: Public

Income Statement

FYE: October 31

	ASSETS ($ mil.)	NET INCOME ($ mil.)	INCOME AS % OF ASSETS	EMPLOYEES
10/02	162,339	910	0.6%	33,000
10/01	150,852	927	0.6%	33,000
10/00	153,248	1,219	0.8%	33,200
10/99	156,749	939	0.6%	32,844
10/98	144,216	875	0.6%	33,400
10/97	147,586	927	0.6%	34,286
10/96	126,949	873	0.7%	33,468
10/95	113,435	737	0.6%	33,341
10/94	102,153	610	0.6%	34,769
10/93	88,490	537	0.6%	32,067
Annual Growth	7.0%	6.0%	—	0.3%

2002 Year-End Financials

Equity as % of assets: 4.1%	Dividends
Return on assets: 0.6%	Yield: 3.1%
Return on equity: 14.3%	Payout: 43.6%
Long-term debt ($ mil.): 2,436	Market value ($ mil.): 12,111
No. of shares (mil.): 493	Sales ($ mil.): 8,384

Stock History

NYSE: BMO

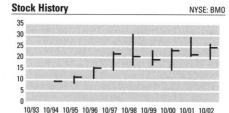

10/93 10/94 10/95 10/96 10/97 10/98 10/99 10/00 10/01 10/02

	STOCK PRICE ($) FY Close	P/E High/Low		PER SHARE ($) Earnings	Dividends	Book Value
10/02	24.59	15	11	1.72	0.75	15.50
10/01	21.37	17	12	1.71	0.71	13.76
10/00	23.19	11	7	2.16	0.67	15.00
10/99	19.03	14	10	1.61	0.62	13.98
10/98	20.44	20	11	1.51	0.61	13.00
10/97	21.56	14	9	1.64	0.59	12.09
10/96	15.19	10	7	1.55	0.52	10.91
10/95	11.13	9	7	1.27	0.47	9.96
10/94	9.25	8	8	1.10	0.00	9.10
Annual Growth	13.0%	—	—	5.7%	—	6.9%

Barclays PLC

An old hand at banking in Britain, Barclays PLC, which traces its origins to the 17th century, sports more than 2,000 branches in the UK and more than 500 branches in some 60 other countries. The company's offerings include personal financial services (savings, checking, and consumer loans); corporate banking; asset management for wealthy individuals; mortgage lender Woolwich; and Barclaycard, a leading credit card issuer in Europe. US-based Barclays Global Investors is one of the world's largest institutional fund managers, while Barclays Capital handles foreign exchange, derivatives, and fixed-income business. Barclays also operates one of the UK's largest online banks, with nearly 4 million registered users.

Barclays has an alliance with London-based Legal & General Group to market the insurance company's life insurance and pension products. It merged its Caribbean banking business with that of Canadian Imperial Bank of Commerce to create FirstCaribbean International Bank, an 85-branch regional bank.

HISTORY

Barclays first spread its wings in 1736 when James Barclay united family goldsmithing and banking businesses. As other family members joined the London enterprise, it became known as Barclays, Bevan & Tritton (1782).

Banking first became regulated in the 19th century. To ward off takeovers, 20 banks combined with Barclays in 1896. The new firm, Barclay & Co., began preying on other banks. Within 20 years it bought 17, including the Colonial Bank, chartered in 1836 to serve the West Indies

and British Guiana (now Guyana). The company, renamed Barclays Bank Ltd. in 1917, weathered the Depression as the UK's #2 bank.

Barclays began expanding again after WWII, and by the late 1950s it had become the UK's top bank. It had a computer network by 1959, and in 1966 it introduced the Barclaycard in conjunction with Bank of America's BankAmericard (now Visa).

In 1968 the UK's Monopolies Commission barred Barclays' merger with two other big London banks, but had no objections to a two-way merger, so Barclays bought competitor Martins.

Barclays moved into the US consumer finance market in 1980 when it bought American Credit, 138 former Beneficial Finance offices, and Bankers Trust's branch network.

During the 1980s, London banks faced competition from invading overseas banks, local building societies, and other financial firms. Banking reform in 1984 led to formation of a holding company for Barclays Bank PLC.

To prepare for British financial deregulation in 1986, Barclays formed Barclays de Zoete Wedd (BZW) by merging its merchant bank with two other London financial firms. Faced with sagging profits, Barclays sold its California bank in 1988 and its US consumer finance business in 1989.

In 1990 Barclays bought private German bank Merck, Finck & Co. and Paris bank L'Européenne de Banque. The company countered 1992's bad-loan-induced losses by accelerating a cost-cutting program begun in 1989. To appease stockholders, chairman and CEO Andrew Buxton (a descendant of one of the bank's founding families) gave up his CEO title, hiring Martin Taylor (previously CEO of textile firm Courtaulds) for the post.

The company sold its Australian retail banking business in 1994, then began trimming other operations, including French corporate banking and US mortgage operations. However, it bought the Wells Fargo Nikko Investment Company to boost Pacific Rim operations.

Barclays' piecemeal sale of BZW signaled its failure to become a global investment banking powerhouse. In 1997 it sold BZW's European investment banking business to Credit Suisse First Boston, retaining the fixed-income and foreign exchange business. (Credit Suisse bought Barclays' Asian investment banking operations in 1998.)

Losses in Russia and a $250 million bailout of US hedge fund Long-Term Capital Management hit Barclays Capital in 1998. Taylor resigned that year in part because of his radical plans for the bank. Sir Peter Middleton stepped in as acting CEO; Barclays later tapped Canadian banker Matthew Barrett for the post. (Middleton also became chairman upon Buxton's retirement.)

Barclays in 1999 started a move toward online banking at the expense of traditional branches. The company announced free lifetime Internet access for new bank customers.

In 2000 the bank ruffled feathers when it announced the closure of about 170 mostly rural UK branches. Also in 2000 the company agreed to sell its Dial auto leasing unit to ABN AMRO and bought Woolwich plc. The following year Barclay's announced that it would close its own life insurance division, opting instead to sell the life insurance and pension products of London-based Legal & General Group.

EXECUTIVES

Chairman, Barclays PLC and Barclays Bank: Sir Peter Middleton, $822,801 pay
Group Chief Executive: Matthew W. Barrett, $2,431,512 pay
Group Executive Director: Chris J. Lendrum, $882,145 pay
Group Finance Director: John S. Varley, $659,000 pay
Group Chief Administration Officer: Gary S. Dibb
Group Risk Director: Robert Nimmo
Chief Executive, Barclays Capital: Robert E. (Bob) Diamond Jr.
Chief Executive, Business Banking: Roger Davis
Chief Executive, Barclaycard: Gary Hoffman
Chief Executive, Barclays Private Clients: Naguib Kheraj
Chief Executive, Personal Financial Services: David Roberts
Chairman and CEO, Asia Pacific: Robert Morrice
CIO: David Weymouth
Group Secretary: Lawrence Dickinson
Group Treasurer: Peter Gallant
Group Marketing Director: Simon Gulliford
Group Taxation Director: Ian Menzies-Conacher
Group Human Resources Director: Valerie Scoular
Auditors: PricewaterhouseCoopers

LOCATIONS

HQ: 54 Lombard St., London EC3P 3AH, United Kingdom
Phone: +44-20-7699-5000   **Fax:** +44-20-7283-5055
US HQ: 200 Park Ave., New York, NY 10166
US Phone: 212-412-4000
Web: www.barclays.com

PRODUCTS/OPERATIONS

2002 Sales

	% of total
Interest	70
Fees & commissions	23
Dealing profits	5
Other	2
Total	**100**

COMPETITORS

Bank of New York	Lloyds TSB
CIBC	Mizuho Financial
Citigroup	RBC Financial Group
Credit Suisse	Royal Bank of Scotland
Deutsche Bank	Standard Chartered
HBOS	UBS
HSBC Holdings	Vanguard Group
J.P. Morgan Chase	

HISTORICAL FINANCIALS

Company Type: Public

Income Statement   FYE: December 31

	ASSETS ($ mil.)	NET INCOME ($ mil.)	INCOME AS % OF ASSETS	EMPLOYEES
12/02	649,541	3,594	0.6%	—
12/01	519,352	3,590	0.7%	78,400
12/00	472,767	3,698	0.8%	75,300
12/99	411,695	2,842	0.7%	74,300
12/98	364,250	2,222	0.6%	78,600
12/97	387,583	1,866	0.5%	83,200
12/96	318,528	2,807	0.9%	87,400
12/95	262,187	2,118	0.8%	89,300
12/94	254,161	1,845	0.7%	—
12/93	245,609	463	0.2%	—
Annual Growth	**11.4%**	**25.6%**	**—**	**(2.1%)**

2002 Year-End Financials

Equity as % of assets: 3.8%	Dividends
Return on assets: 0.6%	Yield: 4.6%
Return on equity: 15.8%	Payout: 52.6%
Long-term debt ($ mil.): 92,536	Market value ($ mil.): 40,607
No. of shares (mil.): 1,644	Sales ($ mil.): 27,663

Stock History   NYSE: BCS

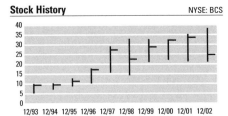

	STOCK PRICE ($) FY Close	P/E High/Low		PER SHARE ($) Earnings	Dividends	Book Value
12/02	24.70	18	10	2.15	1.13	14.90
12/01	33.64	16	10	2.14	0.98	12.67
12/00	32.19	13	9	2.42	0.90	11.86
12/99	28.78	17	11	1.87	0.56	9.17
12/98	22.50	22	10	1.47	0.92	6.58
12/97	27.30	24	13	1.22	0.79	6.30
12/96	17.19	10	6	1.79	0.83	6.23
12/95	11.31	11	8	1.18	0.45	6.69
12/94	9.56	9	7	1.13	0.40	5.94
12/93	9.44	34	19	0.29	0.20	4.84
Annual Growth	**11.3%**	**—**	**—**	**24.9%**	**21.2%**	**13.3%**

BASF

The world is BASF's ester. BASF is the world's largest chemical company, just ahead of Bayer and Dow. BASF has more than 100 major manufacturing facilities and does business worldwide through five business segments: plastics (including polyolefins and polystyrene), performance products (value-added chemicals, coatings, and dyes), basic chemicals (plasticizers, catalysts, solvents), oil and gas exploration and production (through subsidiary Wintershall AG), and agricultural products and nutrition (additives, herbicides, and fertilizers). BASF sold its fibers unit in 2003 to focus on core chemical operations, which it added to with the acquisition of the chemical division of Mine Safety Appliance (MSA) in September.

BASF uses what it calls "Verbund strategy" throughout its facilities — plants are both customers and suppliers of each other. The company continues to expand overseas, particularly in Asia, but Europe still accounts for about 55% of sales.

In 2003 BASF bought a portion of Bayer's agchem businesses. European antitrust regulators required the $1.3 billion deal as part of Bayer's acquisition of Aventis CropScience. BASF also acquired Honeywell International Specialty Materials' engineering plastics business in exchange for its fibers division. The company announced the deal for MSA's Callery Chemical Division in July and completed the acquisition in September. Callery strengthens BASF's line of inorganics, with a focus on providing to the pharmaceutical industry.

Chairman Jürgen Hambrecht announced that the company will push forward with a restructuring of its North American business. The focus

of the plan is to save more than $250 million over the next three years, and among the steps will be cutting workforce by more than 1,000 jobs by the end of 2003.

HISTORY

Originally named Badische Anilin & Soda-Fabrik, BASF AG was founded in Mannheim, Germany, by jeweler Frederick Englehorn in 1861. Unable to find enough land for expansion in Mannheim, BASF moved to nearby Ludwigshafen in 1865. The company was a pioneer in coal tar dyes, and it developed a synthetic indigo in 1897. Its synthetic dyes rapidly replaced more expensive organic dyes.

BASF scientist Fritz Haber synthesized ammonia in 1909, giving BASF access to the market for nitrogenous fertilizer (1913). Haber received a Nobel Prize in 1919 but was later charged with war crimes for his work with poison gases. Managed by Carl Bosch, another Nobel Prize winner, BASF joined the I.G. Farben cartel with Bayer, Hoechst, and others in 1925 to create a German chemical colossus. Within the cartel BASF developed polystyrene, PVC, and magnetic tape. Part of the Nazi war machine, I.G. Farben made synthetic rubber and used labor from the Auschwitz concentration camp during WWII.

After the war I.G. Farben was dismantled. BASF regained its independence in 1952 and rebuilt its war-ravaged factories. Strong postwar domestic demand for basic chemicals aided its recovery, and in 1958 BASF launched a US joint venture with Dow Chemical (BASF bought out Dow's half in 1978). The company moved into petrochemicals and became a leading manufacturer of plastic and synthetic fiber.

In the US the company purchased Wyandotte Chemicals (1969), Chemetron (1979), and Inmont (1985), among others. To expand its natural gas business in Europe, in 1991 the company signed deals with Russia's Gazprom and France's Elf Aquitaine. BASF bought Mobil's polystyrene-resin business and gained almost 10% of the US market.

BASF bought Imperial Chemical's polypropylene business in 1994 and became Europe's second-largest producer of the plastic. The next year the company paid $1.4 billion for the pharmaceutical arm of UK retailer Boots.

In 1997 BASF formed a joint venture with PetroFina (now TOTAL S.A.); in 2001 the venture opened the world's largest liquid steam cracker, in Port Arthur, Texas.

BASF made seven major acquisitions in 1998, including the complexing business of Ciba Specialty Chemicals. It also made six divestitures, which included its European buildings-paints operations, sold to Nobel N.V.

In 1999 the US fined the company $225 million for its part in a worldwide vitamin price-fixing cartel (in 2001 the European Commission fined it another $260 million, bringing the total expected cost of fines, out-of-court settlements, and legal expenses to about $800 million); BASF also faced a class-action suit as a result of the scheme. That year the company moved into oil and gas exploration in Russia through a partnership agreement with Russia's Gazprom. BASF also merged its textile operations into Bayer and Hoechst's DyStar joint venture, forming a $1 billion company that is a world leading dye maker.

BASF completed its acquisition of Rohm & Haas' industrial coatings business in 2000 and bought the Cyanamid division (herbicides, fungicides, and pesticides) of American Home Products (now Wyeth). That year BASF expanded its superabsorbents business by paying $656 million for US-based Amcol International's Chemdal International unit.

Rather than attempt to compete in the rapidly consolidating pharmaceutical industry, in 2001 BASF sold its mid-sized Knoll Pharmaceutical unit to Abbott Laboratories for about $6.9 billion. It also announced that it was closing 10 plants and cutting about 4,000 jobs (4% of its workforce).

EXECUTIVES

Honorary Chairman, Supervisory Board:
Berthold Leibinger, age 71
Chairman, Board of Executive Directors:
Jürgen Hambrecht, age 57
Vice Chairman, Board of Executive Directors:
Eggert Voscherau, age 60
Member, Board of Executive Directors and CFO:
Kurt W. Bock, age 45
Member, Board of Executive Directors: Peter Oakley, age 50
Member, Board of Executive Directors; CEO, BASF Corp.: Klaus Peter Löbbe, age 57
Member, Board of Executive Directors:
Andreas Kreimeyer, age 48
Member, Board of Executive Directors: John Feldman, age 54
Member, Board of Executive Directors:
Stefan Marcinowski, age 50
Head of Human Resources: Hans-Carsten Hansen, age 49
Head of Corporate Communications: Christian Schubert
Auditors: Deloitte & Touche GmbH

LOCATIONS

HQ: BASF Aktiengesellschaft, Carl-Bosch St. 38, 67056 Ludwigshafen, Germany
Phone: +49-621-60-0   **Fax:** +49-621-60-42525
US HQ: 3000 Continental Dr. North, Mount Olive, NJ 07828-1234
US Phone: 973-426-2600   **US Fax:** 973-426-2610
Web: www.basf.com

BASF AG has operations in more than 100 countries.

2002 Sales

	$ mil.	% of total
Europe		
Germany	7,362	22
Other countries	11,400	33
North America	8,278	24
Asia/Pacific & Africa	5,355	16
South America	1,760	5
Total	**34,155**	**100**

PRODUCTS/OPERATIONS

2002 Sales

	$ mil.	% of total
Plastics & fibers	8,987	26
Performance products	8,496	25
Chemicals	5,637	17
Agricultural products & nutrition	5,221	15
Oil & gas	4,452	13
Other	1,362	4
Total	**34,155**	**100**

Selected Products

Plastics
Engineering plastics
Foams
Polyurethane
Polyamide and intermediates
Styrenics

Performance Products
Automotive coatings
Automotive fluids
Decorative paints
Industrial coatings
Pigments
Printing systems
Superabsorbants
Textile chemicals

Chemicals
Inorganics (ammonia, formaldehyde, melamine, resins, and sulfuric acid)
Intermediates
Petrochemicals (feedstocks, industrial gases, and plasticizers)
Specialty chemicals

Ag Products and Nutrition
Agricultural products (fungicides, herbicides, and insecticides)
Fine chemicals (fragrances, pharmaceutical ingredients, UV absorbers, vitamins)

Oil and Gas
Crude oil and natural gas exploration
Natural gas distribution and trading

COMPETITORS

Air Products	GlaxoSmithKline
Akzo Nobel	Henkel
Ashland	Hercules
Bayer AG	Hoffmann-La Roche
BP	Honeywell International
Bristol-Myers Squibb	Honeywell Specialty
Cognis	Materials
Degussa	Huntsman International
Dow Chemical	LG Group
DSM	Mitsubishi Chemical
Dynea	Monsanto
Eastman Chemical	PPG
DuPont	Roche
Eli Lilly	Royal Dutch/Shell Group
Eni	Sony
Exxon Mobil	Syngenta
ExxonMobil Chemical	Teknor Apex
FMC	TOTAL
FPC	Wyeth

HISTORICAL FINANCIALS

Company Type: Public

Income Statement

FYE: December 31

	REVENUE ($ mil.)	NET INCOME ($ mil.)	NET PROFIT MARGIN	EMPLOYEES
12/02	34,155	1,580	4.6%	89,398
12/01	29,206	5,221	17.9%	92,545
12/00	33,989	1,164	3.4%	103,273
12/99	31,539	1,246	3.9%	104,628
12/98	32,255	1,983	6.1%	105,945
12/97	31,125	1,806	5.8%	104,979
12/96	31,642	1,842	5.8%	103,406
12/95	32,153	1,718	5.3%	106,565
12/94	30,052	829	2.8%	106,266
12/93	24,802	494	2.0%	112,020
Annual Growth	3.6%	13.8%	—	(2.5%)

2002 Year-End Financials

Debt ratio: 10.4%
Return on equity: 9.7%
Cash ($ mil.): 242
Current ratio: 1.61
Long-term debt ($ mil.): 1,803
No. of shares (mil.): 570
Dividends
  Yield: 3.0%
  Payout: 41.8%
Market value ($ mil.): 21,797

Stock History

NYSE: BF

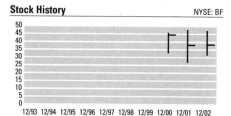

	STOCK PRICE ($) FY Close	P/E High/Low	PER SHARE ($) Earnings	Dividends	Book Value
12/02	38.22	17 12	2.73	1.14	30.47
12/01	37.91	6 3	8.66	1.21	26.22
12/00	44.44	24 18	1.90	0.00	21.35
Annual Growth	(7.3%)	— —	19.9%	—	19.5%

Bayer AG

You could get a headache trying to name all of Bayer AG's products. The company, which created aspirin in 1897, ranks behind BASF and ahead of Dow as the world's second-biggest chemical manufacturer. Bayer makes health care products (diagnostic equipment and pharmaceuticals), agricultural products (crop protection and animal health), chemicals (basic and fine chemicals), and polymers (plastics, synthetic rubber). The company operates in the US through Bayer Corporation. Bayer has reorganized, spinning off its divisions and becoming a management holding company. It's also announced that Bayer will separate its chemicals subgroup, which will be spun off as a publicly traded company under a new name by 2005.

Besides its line of Bayer aspirins, the company's best-known brands include Alka-Seltzer and One-A-Day vitamins. Bayer spends about 10% of revenues on R&D, with much of that money going to fuel advances in its health care unit. The success of drugs such as Cipro and Avalox (used to treat infectious diseases) has prompted the company to expand its biotechnology and genetic research efforts. In mid-2003 the company, along with partner GlaxoSmithKline, launched Levitra, its rival to Pfizer's $1 billion-earning Viagra. Bayer is going full-tilt on its promotional campaign to launch the erectile dysfunction medication; it has signed on as a sponsor for the NFL and hired former coach Mike Ditka as a spokesman.

In a bid to bolster its agrochemical business, Bayer acquired Aventis CropScience in 2002 for about $5 billion plus about $2 billion in debt. The company was combined with Bayer Crop Protection to form Bayer CropScience.

Bayer followed the creation of its crop science subsidiary with the launch of independent companies Bayer HealthCare, Bayer Chemicals, and Bayer Technology Services in September 2003. It later did the same with Bayer Polymers, Bayer Business Services, and Bayer Industry Services. In November Bayer announced that it planned to separate the chemicals business (combined with parts of Bayer Polymers) and spin it off as a public company, with the provisional name NewCo, by 2005.

HISTORY

Friedrich Bayer founded Bayer in Germany in 1863 to make synthetic dyes. Research led to such discoveries as Antinonin (synthetic pesticide, 1892), aspirin (1897), and synthetic rubber (1915).

Under Carl Duisberg, Bayer allegedly made the first poison gas used by Germany in WWI. During the war the US seized Bayer's US operations and trademark rights and sold them to Sterling Drug.

In 1925 Bayer, BASF, Hoechst, and other German chemical concerns merged to form I.G. Farben Trust. Their photography businesses, combined as Agfa, also joined the trust. Between wars Bayer developed polyurethanes and the first sulfa drug, Prontosil (1935).

During WWII the trust took over chemical plants of Nazi-occupied countries, used slave labor, and helped make Zyklon B gas used to kill people at Auschwitz. At war's end Bayer lost its 50% of Winthrop Laboratories (US) and Bayer of Canada (to Sterling Drug). The 1945 Potsdam Agreement called for the breakup of I.G. Farben, and Bayer AG emerged in 1951 as an independent company with many of its original operations, including Agfa.

After rebuilding in West Germany, Bayer AG and Monsanto formed a joint venture (Mobay, 1954); Bayer AG later bought Monsanto's share (1967). In the 1960s the company offered more dyes, plastics, and polyurethanes, and added factories worldwide. Agfa merged with Gevaert (photography, Belgium) in 1964; Bayer AG retained 60%. Over the next decades it acquired Miles Labs (Alka-Seltzer, US, 1978), the rest of Agfa-Gevaert (1981), Compugraphic (electronic imaging, US, 1989), and Nova's Polysar (rubber, Canada, 1990).

Bayer AG integrated its US holdings under the name Miles in 1992 (renamed Bayer Corporation in 1995). The next year it introduced its first genetically engineered product, Kogenate hemophilia treatment. It regained US rights to the Bayer brand and logo in 1994 by paying SmithKline Beecham $1 billion for the North American business of Sterling Winthrop.

Bayer AG formed a joint venture with Swiss rival Roche Holding in 1996 to market over-the-counter Roche drugs in the US. In 1997 Bayer, Baxter International, Rhône-Poulenc Rorer, and Green Cross agreed to a $670 million settlement over blood products that infected thousands of hemophiliacs with HIV during the 1980s.

In 1998 the company sold the food-ingredients arm of its Haarmann & Reimer unit to Tate & Lyle. Bayer bought US-based Chiron's diagnostics operations for $1.1 billion, created a North American joint venture with Crompton & Knowles' seed-treatment unit, and formed a research alliance with Millennium Pharmaceuticals (giving Bayer a 14% stake in Millennium).

Bayer, Hoechst, and BASF merged their textile activities in 1999 to form the world's largest dyemaking company. The next year Bayer boosted its polyurethane business by paying $2.5 billion for US-based Lyondell Chemical's polyols unit. The company also formed a joint venture with Exelixis Pharmaceuticals to develop gene-based insecticides and announced it would develop an anti-impotence drug to rival Pfizer's Viagra.

In 2001 Bayer agreed to invest as much as $874 million on two drug-development deals with US genomics company CuraGen (Bayer will take a 7% stake in the company).

The company's 2001 was marred by the one-two punch of sharply lower profits and the recall of Baycol (known as Lipobay in Europe), its popular cholesterol-lowering drug that has been linked to more than 100 deaths worldwide. Days after the recall Bayer announced that it would consider a pharmaceuticals deal in which its drug unit was the junior partner. Bayer announced in September of 2001 that it was separating its health care and agrochemical operations from its chemicals and polymers businesses, but that it was keeping its pharmaceuticals business. Bayer did indicate an interest in forming a majority-owned joint venture, preferably with a European partner for the pharmaceutical unit.

Bayer sold its household insecticide business, to S.C. Johnson & Son in October 2002. The company finally decided against forming a joint venture with its pharmaceutical business in late 2003 after failing to make a deal advantageous enough.

EXECUTIVES

Chairman, Supervisory Board: Manfred Schneider, age 64
Vice Chairman, Supervisory Board; Chairman, Group and Central Works Councils: Erhard Gipperich, age 61
Chairman, Management Board: Werner Wenning, age 57, $1,409,720 pay
Member, Management Board, Finance: Klaus Kühn, age 51, $620,470 pay
Member, Management Board; President and CEO, Bayer Corporation: Attila Molnar, age 55
Member, Management Board, Human Resources: Richard Pott, age 48, $620,470 pay
Member, Management Board, Technology and Environment: Udo Oels, age 59, $892,438 pay
Managing Director, Bayer Faser GmbH: Michael Radermacher, age 46
EVP and Chief Administrative and Financial Officer, Bayer Corporation: Joseph A. Akers
CEO, Bayer HealthCare: Rolf A. Classon, age 58
Head, HealthCare Diagnostic Division: Wolfgang Hartwig
Auditors: PwC Deutsche Revision AG

LOCATIONS

HQ: 51368 Leverkusen, Germany
Phone: +49-214-30-1   **Fax:** +49-214-30-66328
US HQ: 100 Bayer Rd., Pittsburgh, PA 15205-9741
US Phone: 412-777-2000   **US Fax:** 412-777-2034
Web: www.bayer.com

Bayer AG operates primarily in Canada, France, Germany, Japan, the UK, and the US.

2002 Sales

	% of total
Europe	46
North America	30
Asia/Pacific	13
Other regions	9
Discontinued operations	2
Total	**100**

PRODUCTS/OPERATIONS

Selected Operations and Products

Polymers
Coatings
Colorants
Fibers
Plastics
Polyurethanes
Rubber

Health Care
Diagnostics (laboratory products)

Pharmaceuticals
Pharmaceutical research and development
Consumer care products (over-the-counter drugs)

Chemicals
Basic and fine chemicals
Cellulose products (Wolff Walsrode)
Dyes and pigments
Flavors and fragrances (Haarmann & Reimer)
Specialty metals (H. C. Starck)
Specialty products

CropScience
BioScience (biotechnology and seeds)
Crop protection (insecticides and herbicides)
Environmental Science (lawn care and non-agricultural pesticides)

Selected Brands

Adalat (cardiovascular medication)
Alka-Seltzer (analgesic and antacid)
Aspirin (analgesic)
Cipro (antibiotic)
Dorlastan (spandex fabric)
Dralon (acrylic staple fiber)
Glucometer (blood sugar monitor)
Makrolon (polycarbonate resin)
One-A-Day (vitamins)

COMPETITORS

3M
Abbott Labs
Akzo Nobel
ATOFINA
BASF AG
Baxter
Bristol-Myers Squibb
Dow Chemical
Eastman Chemical
DuPont
Eli Lilly
Eni
GlaxoSmithKline
Hercules
Huntsman International
ICI American
IFF
ITOCHU
Johnson & Johnson
Lyondell Chemical
Merck
Norsk Hydro
Novartis
Perrigo
Pfizer
Roche
Schering-Plough
Wyeth
Zeon

HISTORICAL FINANCIALS

Company Type: Public

Income Statement

FYE: December 31

	REVENUE ($ mil.)	NET INCOME ($ mil.)	NET PROFIT MARGIN	EMPLOYEES
12/02	30,415	1,113	3.7%	122,600
12/01	25,792	860	3.3%	116,900
12/00	27,764	1,564	5.6%	122,100
12/99	27,511	2,016	7.3%	120,400
12/98	32,744	1,884	5.8%	145,100
12/97	30,580	1,635	5.3%	144,600
12/96	31,533	1,768	5.6%	142,200
12/95	31,006	1,665	5.4%	142,900
12/94	28,022	1,271	4.5%	148,248
12/93	23,585	763	3.2%	153,866
Annual Growth	**2.9%**	**4.3%**	**—**	**(2.5%)**

2002 Year-End Financials

Debt ratio: 47.7%
Return on equity: 7.1%
Cash ($ mil.): 806
Current ratio: 1.73
Long-term debt ($ mil.): 7,686
No. of shares (mil.): 730
Dividends
  Yield: 3.6%
  Payout: 52.0%
Market value ($ mil.): 15,812

	STOCK PRICE ($) FY Close	P/E High/Low	PER SHARE ($) Earnings	Dividends	Book Value
12/02	21.65	24 11	1.52	0.79	22.05

HVB Group

Other banks can set their sights on the world; Bayerische Hypo- und Vereinsbank (HVB Group for short) has its eyes on its neighbors. Germany's second-largest bank, after Deutsche Bank, HVB operates more than 2,000 branches in about 30 countries and is expanding eastward through such acquisitions as Bank Austria in 2001. In addition to offering lending and deposit services, it underwrites securities and provides investment services, capital management, and retail services for private clients. One of Europe's largest residential and commercial real estate lenders, the company also owns HVB Real Estate Bank.

HVB was formed in the 1998 merger of Bayerische Vereinsbank and Bayerische Hypotheken- und Wechsel-Bank. While Deutsche Bank aspires to international dominance, however, HVB is content to be a central European superregional. Under its own brand and subsidiaries, the company mainly operates in Germany, Austria, Poland, Switzerland, and Croatia, but is pulling out of the economic powderkeg Brazil. HVB is focusing its growth efforts inward and shifting realigning units for more efficiency within its central European scope.

A loss of nearly $1 billion in 2002 (caused in part by investment losses and Germany's languid economy) compelled the company to cancel its dividend for the first time since WWII. HVB overhauled its management and is paring some 2,000 positions in addition to approximately 9,000 jobs already cut, mainly in Germany and in its Polish subsidiaries, such as BPH-PBK Bank. To raise capital, HVB may also spin off part of Bank Austria or HVB Real Estate Bank, which plans to change its name to Hypo Real Estate Bank upon the completion of a pending merger with German mortgage lender Westfaelische Hypothekenbank.

Über-insurer Allianz owns almost a fifth of HVB Group.

HISTORY

King Ludwig I formed Bayerische Hypotheken- und Wechsel-Bank (BHWB) in 1835 as Bavaria's national bank to provide real estate loans, offer insurance, and issue currency (until German unification in 1871). The bank had become Germany's largest mortgage lender by 1908.

Bayerische Vereinsbank was created by Bavarian investors in 1869 with the permission of Ludwig's more eccentric grandson Ludwig II. Formed as a commercial bank to stimulate the Bavarian economy, it began writing mortgage loans within two years.

By the end of WWI, both Vereinsbank and BHWB had formed agreements with other regional lenders to guard against larger banks. Due partly to these agreements, Vereinsbank slipped through the Great Depression relatively unscathed. As paper currency value sank daily, the bank began issuing gold-backed loans in 1924.

Germany's defeat in WWII was crucial to Vereinsbank and BHWB's ascent: As punishment for having financed Nazi rampages, national banks were broken up and regionals filled the void. By 1946 Vereinsbank and BHWB had emerged as each other's main competitors; they considered, but nixed, a merger.

Both banks expanded throughout West Germany and overseas in the 1950s. In 1958, however, the national banks regrouped, and within 10 years, Germany's former Big Three (Deutsche Bank, Dresdner Bank, and Commerzbank) were back on top. Vereinsbank and BHWB again flirted with merger in 1969, but Bavaria intervened, insisting on the inclusion of state bank Bayerische Staatsbank in any merger. Ultimately Vereinsbank bought only Staatsbank in 1971.

Over the next decade, both banks expanded. As the Soviet Union faltered in 1989, Vereinsbank formed the Bank of Moscow through a joint venture with Credit Lyonnais and other European banks. After reunification, BHWB made the most real estate loans in the former East (and was thus the most exposed to failed loans.)

In 1994 BHWB formed Direkt Anlage Bank, Germany's first discount brokerage. In 1996 Vereinsbank formed online bank Advance Bank (sold to Dresdner after the HypoVereinsbank merger, when Direkt Anlage became the merged bank's online unit).

Throughout the 1990s, the Big Three overran the regional markets vital to BHWB and Vereinsbank; to stay alive, the banks finally merged in 1998, creating Europe's largest mortgage lender and Germany's first US-style superregional bank. HypoVereinsbank stayed regionally focused as Deutsche and Dresdner carved up foreign markets.

In 1999 HypoVereinsbank began talks with competitors about merging retail units; the bank decided to take its Direkt Anlage (now operating under the name DAB Bank AG) unit public that year. The following year the bank made plans to acquire Bank Austria to strengthen its presence in Eastern Europe and Austria (the deal was completed in 2001). Its Activest fund management unit began selling third-party funds, which made the business of UK asset manager subsidiary Foreign & Colonial redundant. Accordingly, HypoVereinsbank sold Foreign & Colonial to Eureko B.V., the pan-European insurance consortium.

In an effort to bolster flagging profits in mortgage lending, HypoVereinsbank announced plans to roll its real estate financing businesses together into a new bank by 2002. In 2001 the bank announced about 8,000 layoffs and the closure of up to 15% of its branches. The move underscores HypoVereinsbank's hopes to corral more customers into using its online and telephone banking services.

HypoVereinsbank also sold a 50% stake in mortgage-lender Westfälische Hypothekenbank to Düsseldorf-based WGZ Bank. HypoVereins-

bank's remaining 25% share was sold to German insurer Signal Iduna. In a bid to become more universally recognized, the bank took on the name HVB Group.

EXECUTIVES

Board Spokesman and CEO: Dieter Rampl, age 56
Managing Director, Corporates and Markets: Stephan W. Bub, age 44
Managing Director, Germany: Stefan Jentzsch, age 43
Managing Director and COO, Austria and Central and Eastern Europe: Gerhard Randa, age 59
Managing Director and Chief Risk Officer: MIchael Mendel, age 46
Managing Director and CFO: Wolfgang Sprissler, age 58
First Executive, Executive Office/Corporate Communication: Gunter Ernst
First Executive, Legal Department: Andreas Früh
First Executive, Operations: Wolfgang Haller
First Executive, Human Resource Management: Heinz Laber
First Executive, Accounting: Karl Limmer
Auditors: KPMG Deutsche Treuhand-Gesellschaft AG

LOCATIONS

HQ: Bayerische Hypo- und Vereinsbank Aktiengesellschaft. Am Tucherpark 16, 80538 Munich, Germany
Phone: +49-89-378-0   **Fax:** +49-89-378-27784
Web: www.hvbgroup.com

PRODUCTS/OPERATIONS

2002 Sales

	% of total
Interest & similar income	89
Fee & commission income	9
Other	2
Total	**100**

2002 Assets

	% of total
Cash & equivalents	1
Trading account	12
Placements with, and loans to, other banks	11
Investments	15
Net loans	57
Other	4
Total	**100**

Selected Subsidiaries

Activest Investmentgesellschaft Luxembourg S.A., Luxembourg
Activest Investmentgesellschaft mbH, Unterföhring
Allfonds Bayerische Kapitalanlagegesellschaft mbH, München
Allfonds BKG Asset Management GmbH, München
A/S Vereinsbank Riga (Latvia)
Asset Management GmbH, Wien (Austria)
Banco Inversión (Spain)
Bank Austria AG, Wien
Bank Austria Creditanstalt (Croatia)
Bank Przemyslowo-Handlowy S.A., Krakau (Poland)
Bank von Ernst & Cie. AG, Bern (Switzerland)
Bankhaus Gebrüder Bethmann, Frankfurt/Main
Bankhaus Maffei & Co. KgaA, München
BANKPRIVAT AG, Wien (Austria)
Bayerische Hypo- und Vereinsbank AG (Hongkong)
Bayerische Hypo- und Vereinsbank AG, München
Bayerische Hypo- und Vereinsbank AG, Singapur (Singapore)
Bayerische Hypo- und Vereinsbank AG, Tokyo (Japan)
Blue Capital, München
BPH (Bank Przemyslowo-Handlowy), Krakow (Poland)
Creditanstalt AG, Wien (Austria)
Direkt Anlage Bank AG, München
FGH Bank N.V., Utrecht (the Netherlands)
Hanseatische Leasing GmbH, Hamburg
H.F.S. HYPO-Fondsbeteiligungen für Sachwerte GmbH, München

HVB Americas, New York (USA)
HVB Asia, Hongkong
HVB Bank Yugoslavia
HVB Brazil
HVB Bulgaria
HVB Capital Asia Limited, Tokyo (Japan)
HVB Capital Management, Inc. (US)
HVB China
HVB Croatia
HVB Czech Republic
HVB France
HVB Greece
HVB Hungary
HVB India
HVB International Real Estate, München
HVB Iran
HVB Ireland
HVB Italy
HVB Korea
HVB Luxembourg
HVB Mexico
HVB Real Estate Bank AG, München
HVB Real Estate Capital Ltd., London
HVB Risk Management Products Inc., New York (US)
HVB Romania
HVB Slovak Republic
HVB South Africa
HVB Vietnam
HypoVereinsbank Australia AG
HypoVereinsbank Brazil
HypoVereinsbank London (UK)
HypoVereinsbank Singapore
INDEXCHANGE Investment AG, München
International Moscow Bank, Moscow (Russia)
JSCB Bank Austria Creditanstalt Ukraine
norisbank AG, Nürnberg (Germany)
Pfandbrief Bank International (Luxembourg)
Planethome AG, München
Powszechny Bank Kredytowy S.A. (Poland)
SKWB Schoellerbank Aktiengesellschaft, Wien (Austria)
Vereins- und Westbank AG Tallin, Tallinn (Estonia)
Vereins- und Westbank AG Vilnius, Vilnius (Lithuania)
Württembergische Hypothekenbank AG, Stuttgart

COMPETITORS

Bayerische Landesbank
Citigroup
Commerzbank AG
DePfa Bank
Deutsche Bank
Dresdner Bank
KfW
Landesbank Baden-Württemberg
WestLB

HISTORICAL FINANCIALS

Company Type: Public

Income Statement

FYE: December 31

	ASSETS ($ mil.)	NET INCOME ($ mil.)	INCOME AS % OF ASSETS	EMPLOYEES
12/02	724,402	(899)	—	65,926
12/01	645,013	857	0.1%	69,520
12/00	674,670	429	0.1%	72,867
12/99	506,748	362	0.1%	46,170
12/98	537,608	1,098	0.2%	36,900
12/97	244,890	472	0.2%	22,000
12/96	253,855	522	0.2%	21,825
12/95	243,401	418	0.2%	22,188
12/94	203,233	338	0.2%	22,029
12/93	164,479	306	0.2%	21,546
Annual Growth	17.9%	—	—	13.2%

2002 Year-End Financials

Equity as % of assets: 2.1%
Return on assets: —
Return on equity: —
Long-term debt ($ mil.): 284,623
Sales ($ mil.): 39,793

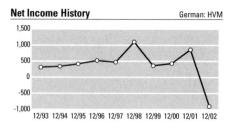

Net Income History　　　German: HVM

Bayerische Motoren Werke

Bayerische Motoren Werke (better known as BMW) is one of Europe's top automakers. BMW models include the 325 series coupe, sedan, and convertible; the 525 series coupe and sport wagon; the M3 coupe and convertible; the X5 sport utility; and the Z4 roadster. In addition to its BMW automobiles, the company's operations include motorcycles (K 1200 GT, R 1200 CL, and R 1150 GS models, among others), the MINI automotive brand, Rolls-Royce Motor Cars, and software (softlab GmbH). BMW's motorcycle division also offers a line of motorcycling apparel such as leather suits, gloves, and boots.

Despite worldwide economic doldrums, BMW turned in another record year in 2002. The company's line of cars and motorcycles outperformed the overall market at every turn. The introduction of the Mini in the US has been a hit; the model is featured in at least one 2003 Hollywood summer blockbuster. BMW has also successfully re-launched the Rolls-Royce brand after taking over control of the nameplate from Volkswagen. Germany's Quandt family controls almost half of the company.

HISTORY

BMW's logo speaks to its origin: a propeller in blue and white, the colors of Bavaria. In 1913 Karl Rapp opened an aircraft-engine design shop near Munich. He named it Bayerische Motoren Werke (BMW) in 1917. The end of WWI brought German aircraft production to a halt, and BMW shifted to making railway brakes until the 1930s. BMW debuted its first motorcycle, the R32, in 1923, and the company began making automobiles in 1928 after buying small-car company Fahrzeugwerke Eisenach.

In 1933 BMW launched a line of larger cars. The company built aircraft engines for Hitler's Luftwaffe in the 1930s and stopped all auto and motorcycle production in 1941. BMW chief Josef Popp resisted and was ousted. Under the Nazis, the company operated in occupied countries, built rockets, and developed the world's first production jet engine.

With its factories dismantled after WWII, BMW survived by making kitchen and garden equipment. In 1948 it introduced a one-cylinder motorcycle, which sold well as cheap transportation in postwar Germany. BMW autos in the 1950s were large and expensive and sold poorly. When motorcycle sales dropped, the company escaped

demise in the mid-1950s by launching the Isetta, a seven-foot, three-wheeled "bubble car."

Herbert Quandt saved the enterprise in 1959 by buying control for $1 million. Quandt's BMW focused on sports sedans and released the first of the "New Range" of BMWs in 1961. Success of the niche enabled BMW to buy automaker Hans Glas in 1966.

In the 1970s BMW's European exports soared, and the company set up a distribution subsidiary in the US. The company also produced larger cars that put BMW on par with Mercedes-Benz.

Rapid export growth in the US, Asia, and Australia continued in the 1980s, but Japanese bikes and poor demand hurt motorcycle sales. The launch of the company's luxury vehicles in 1986 heated up the BMW-Mercedes rivalry. US sales peaked that year and fell 45% by 1991. However, in 1992 BMW outsold Mercedes in Europe for the first time and became the first European carmaker to operate a US plant since Volkswagen pulled out in 1988.

BMW teamed with the UK's Rolls-Royce aerospace firm in 1990 to make jet engines for planes that included executive business-travel jets such as the Gulfstream V.

The company bought UK carmaker Rover from British Aerospace and Honda in 1994 and introduced a cheaper vehicle, the four-wheel-drive Discovery. It launched Highlander Land Rover in 1996 to meet a growing demand for 4x4 utility vehicles.

BMW offered to buy the luxury Rolls-Royce auto unit (including the Bentley) from UK-based Vickers in 1998, but lost out when Volkswagen (VW) countered with a higher offer. The company fared better, however, when aircraft engine maker Rolls-Royce sold the Rolls brand name and logo to BMW for $66 million. (VW got to use the name until 2003.) Also in 1998 BMW was hit by a class-action lawsuit brought by Holocaust survivors seeking compensation for their work as slave laborers during WWII.

In mid-1998 BMW began cutting jobs at its money-losing Rover unit. As Rover's plants continued their downward trend in 1999, BMW's board forced out chairman Brend Pischetsrieder, who spearheaded the Rover acquisition in 1994. The UK later pledged to help pay for renovations at Rover's Longbridge plant to save about 14,000 jobs and prevent it from moving operations to Hungary.

The company in 2000 sold its Land Rover SUV operations to Ford in a deal worth about $2.7 billion. Also that year BMW handed over its Rover Cars operations and MG brand to the Phoenix Consortium, a UK-based group led by former Rover CEO John Towers, for a lesser sum — about $15.

In 2001 BMW launched its MINI brand in the UK; other European markets soon followed. BMW brought the MINI Cooper to US shores in 2002. The following year BMW took control of the Rolls-Royce brand from Volkswagen, and began making Rolls-Royce Phantoms in Goodwood in the south of England.

EXECUTIVES

Chairman of the Board of Management: Helmut Panke
Member, Management Board, Finance: Stefan Krause
Member, Management Board, Development:
 Burkhard Göschel
Member, Management Board, Human Resources and Industrial Relations Director: Ernst Baumann
Member, Management Board, Production:
 Norbert Reithofer
Member, Management Board, Sales and Marketing:
 Michael Ganal
Executive Director, Management Board: Hagen Lüderitz
General Counsel: Dieter Löchelt
Chairman and CEO, BMW Financial Services:
 John Christman
Chairman and CEO, BMW of North America:
 Tom Purves
Auditors: KPMG Deutsche Treuhand-Gesellschaft AG

LOCATIONS

HQ: Bayerische Motoren Werke AG
 Petuelring 130, D-80788 Munich, Germany
Phone: +49-89-382-0 **Fax:** +49-89-382-2-44-18
US HQ: BMW of North America, LLC,
 300 Chestnut Ridge Rd.,
 Woodcliff Lake, NJ 07677
US Phone: 201-307-4000 **US Fax:** 201-307-4095
Web: www.bmw.com

The BMW Group operates globally, with 23 production and assembly plants in 14 countries.

2002 Sales

	$ mil.	% of total
Europe		
Germany	10,841	24
Other countries	13,748	31
US	14,189	32
Africa, Asia, Oceania	5,538	13
Total	**44,316**	**100**

PRODUCTS/OPERATIONS

Selected Products

Automobiles
BMW models
 3 Series (convertible, coupe, sedan, touring)
 5 Series (sedan, touring)
 7 Series (luxury sedan)
 M Models (coupe, roadster, sedan)
 X5 (sport utility vehicle)
 Z4 (sports car)
MINI
 MINI Cooper
 MINI Cooper S

Motorcycles

F Series	R Series
F 650 CS	R 1100 RS
F 650 GS	R 1100 S
K Series	R 1150 GS Adventure
K 1200 GT	R 1150 GS
K 1200 LT	R 1150 R
K 1200 RSA	R 1150 RT
	R 1200 CL

COMPETITORS

DaimlerChrysler	Peugeot Motors of
Ducati	America, Inc.
Fiat	Renault
Ford	Saab Automobile
General Motors	Suzuki Motor
Harley-Davidson	Toyota
Honda	Ultra Motorcycle
Kawasaki Heavy Industries	Volkswagen
Mazda	Yamaha
Nissan	

HISTORICAL FINANCIALS

Company Type: Public

Income Statement

FYE: December 31

	REVENUE ($ mil.)	NET INCOME ($ mil.)	NET PROFIT MARGIN	EMPLOYEES
12/02	44,316	2,117	4.8%	101,395
12/01	34,071	1,653	4.9%	97,275
12/00	33,291	966	2.9%	93,624
12/99	34,643	(2,504)	—	114,874
12/98	37,666	539	1.4%	115,927
12/97	33,556	695	2.1%	109,600
12/96	33,648	523	1.6%	116,112
12/95	32,094	478	1.5%	115,763
12/94	27,186	447	1.6%	109,362
12/93	16,688	301	1.8%	71,201
Annual Growth	**11.5%**	**24.2%**	**—**	**4.0%**

2002 Year-End Financials

Debt ratio: 92.0% Current ratio: 1.98
Return on equity: 17.6% Long-term debt ($ mil.): 13,370
Cash ($ mil.): 3,603

Net Income History

German: BMW

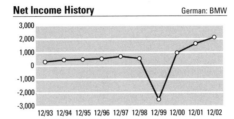

BCE Inc.

The ABCs for BCE are three Cs: content, connectivity, and commerce. Canada's biggest telecom company owns Bell Canada, which provides long-distance and local access (in Ontario and Quebec) and owns stakes in local phone companies across the nation. Bell Mobility provides wireless services. Other BCE services include Internet access, data and e-commerce services, and satellite communications. The company owns 70% of Bell Globemedia, which includes broadcaster CTV, Internet portal Sympatico, and *The Globe and Mail* newspaper. BCE is dismantling its 62%-owned Bell Canada International unit, which held interests in telecom companies in Latin America.

BCE (for Bell Canada Enterprises) has sold its Bell Canada directories business to Kohlberg Kravis Roberts & Co. and a unit of the Ontario Teachers' Pension Plan. In the deal, valued at C$3 billion, BCE kept a 10% stake in the new company. BCE has used the proceeds from this sale to buy back the 16% of Bell Canada owned by Texas-based SBC Communications and for other Bell Canada financial needs. Bell Canada has heard the call of the Web, too. Its Bell Nexxia unit operates an Internet protocol network that stretches across Canada.

Reaching for the sky, units Telesat and TMI Communications provide satellite services. Bell ExpressVu has more than 1.3 million direct-to-home satellite TV customers. BCE took full ownership of Internet portal Sympatico in 2002, acquiring the 29% formerly held by Lycos. Bell

Canada and ExpressVu have teamed up with Microsoft to develop Internet protocol TV (IPTV).

The company's Ventures division handles investments in other telecom and media firms, including troubled Bell Canada International, which held interests in telecom and cable TV providers in Latin America. BCE sold US-based long-distance operator Excel Communications to VarTec Telecom in 2002.

A lack of demand for its broadband services forced BCE to reconsider the value of its Teleglobe unit. In 2002 BCE discontinued long-term funding for Teleglobe, which began working to restructure its debt under bankruptcy protection. As 2002 ended Teleglobe was sold to a unit of Ernst & Young, the court-appointed creditors' monitor.

HISTORY

Alexander Graham Bell experimented with the telephone in his native Canada before moving to the US in the mid-1870s. His father sold his Canadian patent rights to National Bell Telephone (now AT&T), which combined with Canada's Hamilton District Telegraph to form Bell Telephone Company of Canada. Known as Bell Canada, it received a charter in 1880 and settled in Montreal. By 1882 it had 40 exchanges. AT&T owned 48% of the company in 1890, but by 1925 Canadians owned 95% of Bell Canada. (AT&T severed all ties in 1975.)

As telecommunications needs grew, the company began buying smaller exchanges (1954). It acquired a 90% stake in telecom equipment maker Northern Electric in 1957 and the rest in 1964. After Bell Canada reduced the stake in 1973, Northern became Northern Telecom in 1976 (now Nortel Networks). Bell Canada also invested in a satellite joint venture (Telesat, 1970) and formed Bell Canada International (BCI) to provide international telecom consulting (1976).

In 1983, responding to proposed legislation that would have calculated manufacturing profits in phone rate formulas, Bell created Bell Canada Enterprises (renamed BCE in 1988) as a holding company to separate unregulated businesses from phone carriers. BCE branched out with stakes in gas pipelines (1983) and real estate (1985) but dropped out of the ventures to focus on its core telecom business (1989). It began providing wireless phone service in 1985.

As deregulation rolled into Canada in the 1990s, Bell Canada had to maintain high long-distance rates to subsidize its regulated local service. In 1993 it was denied a rate increase and took a large loss. That year it bought stakes in cable operator Jones Intercable and the UK's Cable & Wireless (C&W). In 1994 regulators allowed local rate increases. The next year BCE announced 10,000 jobs cuts and began offering Internet access.

BCE took a loss in 1997, writing down assets in preparation for full competition. Also that year it floated part of BCI, following contracts for cellular systems in Brazil and India. BCE began staging a comeback in 1998 when it sold its shares in Jones Intercable and C&W. It made new investments, including 100% of Telesat Canada, a part of fONOROLA's fiber network, and more than 40% of computer consulting firm CGI Group. Insider Jean Monty (who had steered Nortel's turnaround) became CEO.

Through an alliance with MCI WorldCom (now WorldCom), the company gained access to a global network in 1999. Also that year Ameritech (now part of SBC Communications) bought a 20% stake in Bell Canada, which snapped up the 35% of its wireless subsidiary that it didn't already own and a 20% stake in Manitoba Telecom Services.

In 2000 Bell Canada spun off nearly all of its 40% Nortel stake to shareholders. That year it bought broadcaster CTV, and went on to buy global broadband services provider Teleglobe in a $5 billion stock deal. BCE combined its broadcasting and Internet portal assets with Thomson's *The Globe and Mail* newspaper to form a new company, Bell Globemedia, in 2001 (Thomson sold its stake in 2003).

EXECUTIVES

Chairman: Richard J. (Dick) Currie, age 65
President, CEO, and Director; CEO, Bell Canada; Chairman, BCE Emergis: Michael J. Sabia, $590,863 pay
Group President, National Markets: Stephen G. Wetmore, age 50, $468,313 pay
EVP Communications; BCE and Bell Canada: Peter Daniel
EVP Regulatory Affairs and Public Policy Issues: Lawson Hunter
SVP and Corporate Treasurer: Michael T. Boychuk
SVP Taxation: Barry W. Pickford
SVP; President, BCE Corporate Services Inc.: Alain Bilodeau
CFO: Siim A. Vanaselja
Chief Legal Officer: Martine Turcotte
Executive Counsel, BCE and Bell Canada: Bernard Courtois
Chief Talent Officer: Léo W. Houle
President and CEO, Bell Globemedia; CEO, CTV Inc.: Ivan Fecan, $754,698 pay
President, Bell Mobility: Michael A. Neuman
President, Bell Distribution Inc./Bell World: Garry M. Wood
President, Bell ExpressVu: Timothy (Tim) McGee, age 44
President, Bell West: Randall J. Reynolds
President, BCE Ventures: William D. Anderson
President, Customer Operations, Bell Canada: Terry Mosey
President, Enterprise Market, Bell Canada: Isabelle Courville
President, Network Operations, Bell Canada: David A. Southwell
President, Small and Medium Business, Bell Canada: Karen H. Sheriff
Group President, Consumer Markets, Bell Canada: Pierre J. Blouin, $405,333 pay
Group President, Bell Systems and Technology, Bell Canada: Eugene Roman
Auditors: Deloitte & Touche LLP

LOCATIONS

HQ: 1000, rue de La Gauchetière Ouest, Ste. 3700, Montreal, Quebec H3B 4Y7, Canada
Phone: 514-870-8777   **Fax:** 514-870-4385
Web: www.bce.ca

2002 Sales

	$ mil.	% of total
Canada	11,933	95
US	502	4
Other countries	126	1
Total	**12,561**	**100**

PRODUCTS/OPERATIONS

2002 Sales

	$ mil.	% of total
Bell Canada		
Local & Access	3,894	31
Data	2,387	19
Long-distance	1,633	13
Wireless	1,382	11
DTH satellite	502	4
Other revenues	1,256	10
Bell Globemedia	754	6
BCE Ventures	502	4
BCE Emergis	251	2
Total	**12,561**	**100**

Selected Subsidiaries and Affiliates

Bell Canada Holdings Inc.
Aliant (53%, local phone service, Atlantic Canada)
Bell Canada (telecommunications services)
Bell Distribution Inc. (retail outlets)
Bell ExpressVu L.P. (direct-to-home satellite TV)
Bell Mobility Inc. (wireless phone and paging)
Bell Nexxia Inc. (data services for businesses)
Bell West Inc. (60%, competitive local-exchange carrier)
Manitoba Telecom Services Inc. (22%, local phone service)
NorthernTel L.P. (63%, local phone service, Ontario)
Northwestel Inc. (local phone service, northwestern Canada)
Sympatico Inc. (Internet portal)
Télébec Itée (63%, local phone service, Quebec)

BCE Ventures
Bell Canada International (BCI, 62%, telecom investments outside Canada)
CGI Group Inc. (30%, IT (information technology) services)
Telesat Canada (satellite communications)
Bell Globemedia (70%, broadcast, print, and Internet services)
CTV Inc. (broadcast TV)
The Globe and Mail (newspaper)
BCE Emergis (65%, e-commerce)

COMPETITORS

Allstream	Persona (Canada)
Call-Net Enterprises	Quebecor
Canada Payphone	Rogers Communications
Cancom	Shaw Communications
CanWest Global Communications	Sprint
	TELUS
COGECO Inc.	Time Warner
GT	WorldCom
Microcell Telecommunications	

HISTORICAL FINANCIALS

Company Type: Public

Income Statement

FYE: December 31

	REVENUE ($ mil.)	NET INCOME ($ mil.)	NET PROFIT MARGIN	EMPLOYEES
12/02	12,561	1,573	12.5%	66,266
12/01	13,639	329	2.4%	75,000
12/00	12,065	3,242	26.9%	56,608
12/99	9,825	3,773	38.4%	55,000
12/98	17,735	2,970	16.7%	58,000
12/97	23,217	(1,074)	—	122,000
12/96	20,554	841	4.1%	118,450
12/95	18,059	574	3.2%	121,000
12/94	15,449	840	5.4%	116,000
12/93	14,977	(496)	—	118,000
Annual Growth	**(1.9%)**	**—**	**—**	**(6.2%)**

2002 Year-End Financials

Debt ratio: 117.9%
Return on equity: 18.4%
Cash ($ mil.): 194
Current ratio: 0.61
Long-term debt ($ mil.): 8,511

No. of shares (mil.): 916
Dividends
Yield: 4.2%
Payout: 44.2%
Market value ($ mil.): 16,495

Stock History

NYSE: BCE

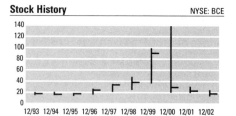

	STOCK PRICE ($) FY Close	P/E High/Low		PER SHARE ($) Earnings	Dividends	Book Value
12/02	18.01	13	8	1.72	0.76	8.93
12/01	22.80	82	57	0.36	1.20	13.20
12/00	28.94	28	4	4.95	1.18	14.38
12/99	90.19	17	6	5.77	1.25	19.21
12/98	37.94	10	6	4.57	1.36	13.77
12/97	33.31	—	—	(1.77)	1.36	10.79
12/96	23.88	20	14	1.24	1.00	13.74
12/95	17.25	21	18	0.82	0.99	13.19
12/94	16.06	16	13	1.25	0.99	13.08
12/93	17.44	—	—	(0.92)	1.03	13.39
Annual Growth	**0.4%**	**—**	**—**	**—**	**(3.3%)**	**(4.4%)**

Benetton Group

If Benetton had a theme song, it could be "We Are the World." The Benetton Group pushes a global attitude in its ads while dressing customers in 120 countries through more than 5,000 franchised Benetton stores, department stores, and megastores. Benetton's clothing — primarily casual knitwear and sportswear for men, women, and children — bears labels such as United Colors of Benetton and Sisley. Not content with selling sunglasses, watches, clothes, and shoes, Benetton once branched out into sporting goods, but withdrew to hone in on its clothing division. The Benetton family, through Edizione Holding, owns about 70% of Benetton.

The company's controversial ads, a mix of provocative images and political stances (bloody soldiers, death-row inmates, a priest and a nun kissing), have won a following as well as a fair share of critics. Benetton has since parted ways with the agency responsible for the shocking campaign.

The group's multimedia enterprises fall under the Fabrica umbrella, which Benetton describes as a "communication research and development center." Fabrica produces films, funds avant-garde music projects, and publishes the magazine "Colors."

In early 2003, the company pared down its branches and returned to its fashion roots by selling off its Nordica and Rollerblade subsidiaries. Tennis racket and sportswear maker Prince was sold off soon thereafter. Europe accounts for about 80% of Benetton's sales.

HISTORY

Luciano Benetton began selling men's clothing while still in his teens in post-WWII Treviso, Italy. His younger, artistic sister, Giuliana, knitted colorful and striking sweaters for a small, local clientele. In 1955 the two pooled their skills. Giuliana sold Luciano's accordion and a younger brother's bicycle, raising enough money to purchase a knitting machine. Luciano then marketed her moderately priced sweaters.

Demand for their clothes grew, and the pair did so well that 10 years later they built a factory in Ponzano, near Treviso. Siblings Gilberto and bicycleless Carlo joined the business, and the first Benetton store opened in Belluno, in the Alps, in 1968. By 1975 Benetton had 200 stores in Italy and had set up headquarters in a 17th-century villa. In 1979 the company opened five stores in the US.

Through the early to mid-1980s, the company averaged one store opening a day; Benetton was the first Western retailer to enter Eastern Europe. The company's controversial advertising program began in 1984 with ads depicting such provocative images as then-president Ronald Reagan with AIDS lesions.

When it went public in 1986, Benetton had almost 600 stores in the US. That year it established a factory in the US. In the late 1980s Edizione Holding, the family's investment firm, also bought a hotel chain and ski equipment maker Nordica.

Benetton began losing US market share in the late 1980s. Competition from The Gap and The Limited hurt and overexpansion brought complaints from franchisees that the stores were cannibalizing each other's sales. (In New York City there were seven stores on Fifth Avenue alone.) In the early 1990s The Gap established stores in the already-mature European market, and Benetton began looking for new markets.

Edizione increased its investments in those years, acquiring 80% of Prince Manufacturing, a US maker of tennis equipment, and purchased a 50% interest in the TWR group, a racecar manufacturer. The company formed Benetton Legs in 1991 to produce and sell pantyhose in Europe.

In 1995 Benetton won its second lawsuit against German retailers who refused to pay for merchandise because they said sales had been hurt by the company's shock advertising. The next year it opened a United Colors of Benetton megastore on Fifth Avenue in New York City, the first to combine Edizione's clothing, sporting goods, and accessories under one roof.

Benetton bought Edizione's sports equipment and apparel collection, Benetton Sportsystem, and renamed the division Playlife in 1998. Benetton began selling the sporting goods through specialty sports stores and a new chain of Playlife megastores.

Trying to win back US consumers, Benetton in 1998 cut a deal to sell Benetton USA-brand clothing in Sears, Roebuck & Co. stores. In early 2000, however, Sears yanked the Italian goods from its store after customers complained about Benetton's anti-death penalty ad campaign. Soon after, Benetton and controversial ad man Oliviero Toscani parted ways. Benetton's ads are now produced by an ad agency Toscani founded.

In 2001 Benetton announced plans to recapture the US market share it once held by opening megastore formats (starting with three new stores in Manhattan). Later, Carlo Gilardi stepped down as Joint Managing Director and

Luigi de Puppi (former CEO of Electrolux Zanussi) was named his successor.

Just weeks before its 2003 shareholders meeting, the company announced that Luigi de Puppi would step down since his mandate to clear out of Benetton's ailing sports divisions was completed with sales of Rollerblade, Nordica, and Prince. In late 2003 Benetton reorganized its internal operations — production and logistics are handled by Benind, trademarks and commercial activities by Bencom, and IT services and systems by United Web (under the name Bentec).

EXECUTIVES

Chairman: Luciano Benetton, age 68
Deputy Chairman: Carlo Benetton, age 59
Benneton Group Managing Director: Silvano Cassano, age 47
Tax, Legal, and Corporate Affairs Officer: Pierluigi Bortolussi, age 57
Investor Relations Manager: Mara Di Giorgio
CFO: Pier Francesco Facchini
Benetton Group Marketing and Strategy Director: Maximo Ibarra
Sales Director: Ariodante Valeri
Product Manager, United Colors of Benetton and The Hip Site Lines: Vincenzo Scognamiglio
Accounting and Financial Control Officer: Biagio Chiarolanza, age 41
Art Director, United Colors of Benetton: Joel Berg
Chairman and Editorial Director, Colors Magazine: Kurt Andersen
Auditors: Deloitte & Touche S.p.A.

LOCATIONS

HQ: Benetton Group S.p.A.
Villa Minelli, 31050 Ponzano Veneto, Treviso, Italy
Phone: +39-0422-519111   **Fax:** +39-0422-969501
US HQ: 597 5th Ave., 11th Fl., New York, NY 10017
US Phone: 212-593-0290   **US Fax:** 212-371-1438
Web: www.benetton.com

Benetton Group sells its products in more than 120 countries.

2002 Sales

	% of total
Italy	45
Rest of Europe	34
The Americas	10
Other	11
Total	**100**

PRODUCTS/OPERATIONS

2002 Sales

	% of total
Casual wear, accessories, & footwear	80
Fabrics & yarns	6
In-line skates & skateboards	4
Racquets	3
Ski boots	3
Sportswear	2
Skis & snowboards	1
Sports footwear	1
Total	**100**

Selected Brands

Casual wear
Sisley (higher-fashion men's and women's clothing)
United Colors of Benetton

Sportswear
Killer Loop (snowboarding clothing)
Playlife (sporty leisure wear)

Selected Products

Baby products	Perfume	Sunglasses
Dresses	Shirts	Underwear
Handbags	Shoes	Watches
Hats	Socks	
Knitwear	Sportswear	

COMPETITORS

Abercrombie & Fitch	Vendex
adidas-Salomon	Lands' End
Aeropostale	Levi Strauss
Amer Group	Limited Brands
American Eagle Outfitters	Liz Claiborne
AnnTaylor	Marks & Spencer
Burberry	Mossimo
Calvin Klein	Nautica Enterprises
C&A	NIKE
Columbia Sportswear	Polo Ralph Lauren
Cortefiel	Quiksilver
Inditex	SHC
Esprit Holdings	Skis Rossignol
French Connection	Swatch
Gap	Tommy Hilfiger
H&M	Variflex
Head-Tyrolia-Mares	Warnaco Group
J. Crew	Wet Seal
K2	

HISTORICAL FINANCIALS

Company Type: Public

Income Statement

FYE: December 31

	REVENUE ($ mil.)	NET INCOME ($ mil.)	NET PROFIT MARGIN	EMPLOYEES
12/02	2,092	(10)	—	7,162
12/01	1,870	132	7.1%	7,666
12/00	1,899	229	12.1%	6,672
12/99	1,996	168	8.4%	6,585
12/98	2,318	177	7.6%	7,235
12/97	2,055	164	8.0%	7,421
12/96	1,890	162	8.6%	5,973
12/95	1,866	139	7.4%	6,018
12/94	1,717	130	7.5%	6,300
12/93	1,602	121	7.6%	5,900
Annual Growth	**3.0%**	**—**	**—**	**2.2%**

2002 Year-End Financials

Debt ratio: 72.7%	No. of shares (mil.): 91
Return on equity: —	Dividends
Cash ($ mil.): 200	Yield: 4.0%
Current ratio: 3.00	Payout: —
Long-term debt ($ mil.): 871	Market value ($ mil.): 1,625

Stock History

NYSE: BNG

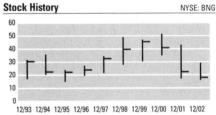

	STOCK PRICE ($) FY Close	P/E High/Low		Earnings	PER SHARE ($) Dividends	Book Value
12/02	17.90	—	—	(0.11)	0.71	13.20
12/01	22.30	29	12	1.46	0.81	12.18
12/00	40.75	20	14	2.52	2.00	1.22
12/99	45.44	25	17	1.85	2.21	1.24
12/98	39.75	25	14	1.96	0.00	14.78
12/97	32.63	22	14	1.52	0.00	12.64
12/96	23.93	13	10	2.10	0.52	13.21
12/95	22.25	14	9	1.65	0.32	11.53
12/94	22.49	22	13	1.62	0.33	10.21
12/93	30.54	19	11	1.61	0.31	7.28
Annual Growth	**(5.8%)**	**—**	**—**	**—**	**9.6%**	**6.8%**

Bertelsmann AG

Bertelsmann is so big, it needs space in the bookcase, CD rack, and magazine stand. One of the world's top media firms, Bertelsmann has operations in nearly 60 countries engaged in publishing, music distribution, and broadcasting. It owns #1 trade publisher Random House and music company BMG. It also has a 75% stake in publisher Gruner + Jahr (*Stern, Family Circle*), owns 90% of RTL Group, Europe's #1 over-the-air broadcaster, and owns media services firm arvato. In addition, Bertelsmann owns several book and music clubs, and online retail channels. Carl Bertelsmann founded the company in 1835. His descendants, the Mohn family, and Bertelsmann executives control the company. Groupe Bruxelles Lambert owns a 25% stake.

Bruxelles bought its stake in the company in 2001 with the understanding that it would eventually float its interest to the public, bringing an end to Bertelsmann's longtime status as a private company. (The Mohns own 17% and the Bertelsmann Foundation owns 57%.) The company's plans for an IPO and a massive expansion onto the Internet were the brainchild of former CEO Thomas Middelhoff. In mid-2002 the board unexpectedly fired Middelhoff citing differences of opinion in the company's direction. He was replaced by arvato's chairman Gunter Thielen. Speculation has it that the board was unhappy with Middelhoff's Web plans in light of other media companies' inability to meld old and new media successfully.

Thielen has implemented an e-commerce asset selloff at the company. The firm has agreed to sell some assets such as its 36% stake in barnesandnoble.com and the BOL.com book retailing service, but has also cut deals in which other companies operate the site for it in exchange for a profit percentage (such as Amazon.com's takeover of CDnow).

Bertelsmann had agreed to buy defunct Internet music company Napster, which it wanted to use as a subscription music service. However, a bankruptcy court refused to approve the deal, which hammered the last nail in the original Napster's coffin. The music service has since reemerged with help from Roxio as a paid music site, but the damage had already been done and music publishers have brought suit against Bertelsmann on the grounds that its initial funding of the Internet company contributed to copyright violations.

But Bertelsmann has bigger fish to fry in the music world than Napster. It hopes to bring new life into the doldrums of the industry with an agreement to combine BMG with Sony Music into a joint venture named Sony BMG. Bertelsmann and Sony Corp. would each own 50% of the new company.

Bertelsmann also sold BertelsmannSpringer, its science and trade publishing subsidiary, to UK investment firms Cinven Group and Candover Investments for an estimated $1.2 billion.

HISTORY

Carl Bertelsmann founded his publishing company C. Bertelsmann Verlag in Gütersloh, Germany, in 1835. The company primarily published hymnals and religious materials, expanding into newspapers during the 1860s. Heinrich Mohn, a fourth-generation descendant, took over the company in 1921 and expanded its op-

erations to include popular fiction, which helped Bertelsmann expand to more than 400 employees by 1939.

During WWII the company published books and propaganda material for the German army, but was closed by the Nazi government in 1944 as it was not considered important to the war effort. (The company had maintained for decades it was closed because it produced religious materials, but contrary evidence was uncovered in 2000 by historians working at the behest of the company.) After WWII Mohn's son, Reinhard (who had been captured by the Allies and interned in a Kansas POW camp), returned to Germany determined to rebuild the company.

Bertelsmann boosted book sales by launching book clubs in Germany during the 1950s and bought Germany's UFA (TV and film production) in 1964. It took a minority interest in publisher Gruner + Jahr in 1969, taking a controlling stake in 1973. In the US, Bertelsmann bought 51% of Bantam Books in 1977 (and the rest in 1981) and Arista Records in 1979. In 1986 it took control of Doubleday Publishing and bought RCA Records (forming Bertelsmann Music Group the next year). Mohn transferred substantial nonvoting shares in the company to the Bertelsmann Foundation in 1993.

The company teamed up with America Online in 1995 to form AOL Europe, and with Luxembourg broadcaster CLT it launched CLT-Ufa in 1997. Bertelsmann acquired book publisher Random House the next year. The company also took a 50% stake in online bookseller barnesandnoble.com (retaining nearly 40% after an IPO in 1999). In addition, Thomas Middelhoff became chairman and CEO in 1998. The next year Bertelsmann acquired some 85% of scientific publisher Springer Verlag. Also in 1999 Reinhard Mohn transferred his controlling shares in the company to Bertelsmann Verwaltungsgesellschaft, a firm controlled by Bertelsmann executives and the Mohn family.

In 2000 Bertelsmann announced that it would sell its half-interest in AOL Europe back to AOL (now part of Time Warner) by mid-2002; it also spun off Lycos Europe (retaining 27%, now about 20%). It later merged CLT-Ufa with Pearson TV to form RTL Group. (Bertelsmann got a 37% stake.) That year Bertelsmann bought online music retailer CDnow and began negotiating a merger between BMG and EMI Group. (Those talks fell apart in 2001.) Late in 2000 the company formed an alliance with online music service Napster, loaning the company start-up cash and allowing it to use the BMG music catalog to develop a subscription-based service. Bertelsmann bought Groupe Bruxelles Lambert's 30% stake in RTL Group in 2001. As part of the deal Bruxelles gained a 25% stake in Bertelsmann with the understanding that it would be able to float its interest to the public in four years. Bertelsmann combined RTL's Ufa Sports unit with French sports-rights company Jean-Claude Darmon in exchange for a 40% stake in the combined company, now called Sportfive. Later that year it sold its stake in online music venture GetMusic to Universal Music Group. Also that year, it bought Pearson's 22% stake in RTL Group.

The company's board fired Middelhoff in 2002 citing disagreements over the direction of company. He was replaced by Gunter Thielen, chairman of Bertelsmann's Arvato subsidiary. The following year Bertelsmann sold its science publishing subsidiary, BertelsmannSpringer.

EXECUTIVES

Chairman Emeritus; Founder, Bertelsmann Foundation: Reinhard Mohn, age 82
Chairman and CEO: Gunter Thielen, age 61
Deputy Chairman and CFO: Siegfried Luther, age 59
Chief Creative Officer; Chairman and CEO, BMG Entertainment: Rolf Schmidt-Holtz, age 55
SVP Media Relations and Chief Press Officer: Oliver Herrgesell
VP Media Relations: Markus Payer, age 38
Auditing: Klaus-Peter Blobel
Corporate Center New York: Rob Sorrentino
Corporate Controlling: Günther Grüger
Corporate Communications: Bernd Bauer, age 47
Financial Reporting, Accounting, and Taxes: Wolfgang Wiedermann
Human Resources: Detlef Hunsdiek
Legal Department: Urlich Koch
Treasury and Finance: Verena Volport
Chairman, arvato: Harmut Ostrowski, age 45
Chairman, RTL Group: Juan Abelló
Chairman, President, and CEO, Gruner + Jahr: Bernd Kundrun, age 46
Chairman and CEO, Bertelsmann Capital: Arnold Bahlmann, age 51
Chairman and CEO, Random House: Peter W. Olson, age 53
CEO, Digital World Services: Arni Sigurdsson
CEO, DirectGroup Bertelsmann: Ewald Walgenbach, age 44
CEO, RTL Group: Gerhard Zeiler
Auditors: KPMG Deutsche Treuhand-Gesellschaft AG

LOCATIONS

HQ: Carl-Bertelsmann-Strasse 270, D-33311 Gütersloh, Germany
Phone: +49-5241-80-0   **Fax:** +49-5241-80-9662
US HQ: 1540 Broadway #24, New York, NY 10036-4098
US Phone: 212-782-1000   **US Fax:** 212-782-7600
Web: www.bertelsmann.de

Bertelsmann has operations in nearly 60 countries.

PRODUCTS/OPERATIONS

2002 Sales

	$ mil.	% of total
RTL Group	4,572	23
arvato	3,845	19
Gruner + Jahr	2,934	15
BMG	2,845	15
DirectGroup	2,837	14
Random House	2,091	11
BertelsmannSpringer	766	3
Other	52	—
Adjustments	(749)	—
Total	**19,193**	**100**

Selected Operations

arvato (media services)
   arvato logistic services (direct marketing and supply chain management)
   arvato printing (commercial printing)
   arvato storage media
   arvato systems (supply chain and customer relationship management)
   AZ Direct (direct marketing)
   Bertelsmann Financial Group (credit reports and risk management)
   empolis (content management)
   Forms Facility Services (direct marketing)
   handy.de (wireless services)
   TJ-Net (wireless services)

BMG Entertainment (music publishing)
   Ariola (record label)
   Arista Records (record label)
   BMG Classics (record label)
   BMG Distribution
   BMG Music Publishing
   BMG Online
   Jive Records (record label)
   Private Music (record label)
   RCA Music Group (record label)
   Windham Hill (record label)
   Zomba Records (record label)
DirectGroup Bertelsmann (book and music clubs,
   e-commerce)
   Media Communities
   Online Shops
Gruner + Jahr (75%, magazine and newspaper
   publishing)
   Magazines
      Brigitte
      Capital
      Eltern
      Geo
      Family Circle
      Fast Company
      Inc.
      Muy Interesante
      Parents
      Stern
      YM
   Newspapers
      Blic
      Evenimentul Zilei
      Financial Times Deutschland
      Nový Cas
      Sächsische Zeitung
Random House (book publishing)
RTL Group (90%, broadcasting)
   Internet
   Radio
   SPORTFIVE (46%, sports rights and marketing)
   Television
      Antena 3 (17.2%, Spain)
      Club RTL (66%, Belgium)
      Channel 5 (64.6%, UK)
      FreemantleMedia (television programming
         production and distribution)
      M6 (47%, France)
      n-tv (47.4%, Germany)
      RTL II (35.9%, Germany)
      RTL 4 (the Netherlands)
      RTL 5 (the Netherlands)
      RTL 9 (35%, France)
      RTL KLUB (49%, Hungary)
      RTL SHOP (Germany)
      RTL Télé Lëtzbuerg (Luxembourg)
      RTL Television (Germany)
      RTL TVI (66%, Belgium)
      SUPER RTL (50%, Germany)
      Tele Monte Carlo (23.8%, France)
      Veronica (the Netherlands)
      VOX (99.7%, Germany)
      Yorin (the Netherlands)

COMPETITORS

Advance Publications	Sony
Amazon.com	TaurusHoldings
Axel Springer	Time Warner
Columbia House	Universal Music Group
Hachette Filipacchi Médias	Verlagsgruppe Georg von
Hearst	Holtzbrinck
Instant Web	Viacom
Lagardère	Virgin Group
McGraw-Hill	Vivendi Universal
News Corp.	Publishing
Pearson	VNU
PRIMEDIA	Walt Disney
Reed Elsevier Group	Wolters Kluwer
Schibsted	

HISTORICAL FINANCIALS
Company Type: Private

Income Statement

FYE: December 31

	REVENUE ($ mil.)	NET INCOME ($ mil.)	NET PROFIT MARGIN	EMPLOYEES
12/02*	19,193	973	5.1%	80,632
6/01	17,011	824	4.8%	82,162
6/00	15,785	641	4.1%	76,257
6/99	13,721	480	3.5%	64,937
6/98	12,700	621	4.9%	57,807
6/97	12,860	585	4.5%	57,173
6/96	14,126	594	4.2%	57,996
6/95	14,889	592	4.0%	57,397
6/94	11,589	478	4.1%	51,767
6/93	10,050	388	3.9%	50,437
Annual Growth	**7.5%**	**10.8%**	**—**	**5.4%**

Net Income History

BHP Billiton Limited

Two heads — or headquarters — are better than one. Aussie mining and oil company BHP Limited acquired UK miner Billiton plc in 2001. The result is a two-headquartered, dual-listed company run as a single entity with the same board of directors and management. The Melbourne side is BHP Billiton Limited; the London-based side is BHP Billiton plc; collectively they're known as BHP Billiton. The company ranks among the world's top producers of iron ore and coal (thermal and metallurgical) and is a major producer of petroleum products such as crude oil and natural gas. Other units produce aluminum, copper, nickel, lead, zinc, gold, and silver. BHP Billiton has operations on six continents.

The company says it will invest up to $4 billion over five years to boost its oil and gas interests, including a billion-plus investment on the Atlantis oil and gas field in the Gulf of Mexico. (Atlantis is estimated to be the third-largest such field identified in the Gulf of Mexico.) BHP Billiton will also boost its diamond production by 40% into 2004, primarily from its 80% stake in Canada's Ekati diamond mine and an exploration venture in India. In addition, the company has begun buying metals from other companies to trade on the open market.

In 2002 BHP Billiton spun off its steel business as BHP Steel.

HISTORY

In 1883 Charles Rasp, a boundary rider for the Mt. Gipps sheep station, believed valuable ore lay in the Broken Hill outcrop in New South Wales, Australia. He gathered a few young speculators, and The Broken Hill Proprietary Company (BHP) was incorporated in 1885. BHP immediately found a massive lode of silver, lead, and zinc. None of the founders knew how to run a mine, so they recruited US engineers William Patton and Herman Schlapp. From the beginning, labor and management clashed. The founding directors set up the head office in Melbourne, far from the mine, and gambled with gold sovereigns in the boardroom. But the miners worked in dangerous conditions. An 1892 labor strike was the first of BHP's bitter strikes.

In 1902 the new general manager, Guillaume Delprat, invented a flotation process that recovered valuable metals from iron ore waste. Delprat also foresaw a future in steel, although Australia had no steel industry. BHP commissioned the Newcastle steelworks in 1915 and soon became the country's largest steel producer. BHP's 1935 purchase of Australian Iron and Steel, its only competitor, gave it a virtual steel monopoly, while high tariffs protected it from outside competition. Its exhausted Broken Hill mine was closed that year.

In the 1960s BHP got into oil when it partnered with Esso Standard, the Australian subsidiary of Standard Oil of New Jersey, for offshore exploration. In 1967 the partners found oil in the Bass Strait, which soon supplied 70% of Australia's petroleum. In the 1960s and 1970s, BHP began expanding its iron ore, manganese, and coal interests. Meanwhile, public opposition mounted to BHP's market power and labor practices, and in 1972 the government took steps to limit BHP's power, removing some subsidies and tax breaks.

The weak steel market of the 1970s and 1980s caused BHP to lay off almost a third of its steelworkers in 1983, but with government intervention, BHP radically improved its steel productivity. In 1984 BHP bought Utah International's mining assets from General Electric (including Chile's rich Escondida copper mine). In 1986 corporate raider Robert Holmes à Court took a run at BHP; BHP decided to become an international mining company to prevent further raids. Its acquisitions in the late 1980s included ERG Inc. and Monsanto Oil (combined into BHP Americas), Aquila Steel, and Pacific Refining in Hawaii.

A peace deal with Holmes à Court gave BHP about 37% of Foster's Brewing, but in 1992 BHP took a $700 million write-down after Foster's stock declined. BHP also bought Arizona-based Magma Copper in 1996, but plunging world copper prices forced a $420 million write-down.

With new worries over Asia's economic troubles, BHP soon was struggling. In 1997 BHP sold most of its stake in Foster's, and three senior executives resigned. In 1998 the company unloaded Pacific Refining, which was acquired by Tesoro Petroleum for about $275 million.

As BHP's woes continued, CEO John Prescott resigned; Paul Anderson was recruited from Duke Energy to succeed Prescott. In 1999 D. R. Argus took over as chairman, replacing Jeremy Ellis. In a restructuring move, the company sold its engineering, power, insurance and information technology businesses in 1999 and 2000. BHP began to sell $2 billion worth of steel operations (including its long product unit, OneSteel). In

2000 the company shortened its official name to BHP Limited.

BHP acquired Billiton in 2001, forming BHP Billiton Ltd. and BHP Billiton plc. The combined BHP Billiton had sales of almost $20 billion and a market capitalization approaching $30 billion. In addition, BHP paid $436 million for Dia Met Minerals, which owned 29% of Canada's only producing diamond mine, Ekati.

Also in 2001 BHP Billiton and Alcoa combined their North American metals distribution businesses as joint venture Integris Metals. In order to focus on its minerals and oil and gas operations, in 2002 BHP Billiton spun off its steel business as BHP Steel.

EXECUTIVES

Chairman: Don R. Argus, age 66
Chief Executive and Director:
Charles W. (Chip) Goodyear, age 45, $2,041,373 pay
CFO: Christopher J. Lynch, age 49, $1,074,855 pay
Chief Legal Counsel: John Fast, age 53
Chief Commercial Officer: Marius Kloppers, age 41, $865,457 pay
President and CEO, Petroleum: Philip S. Aiken, age 54, $1,233,256 pay
President, Base Metals: Bradford A. (Brad) Mills, age 48, $990,665 pay
President, Carbon Steel Materials: Robert (Bob) Kirkby, age 56
President, Diamonds and Specialty Products: Marcus Randolph, age 47
President, Energy Coal: Mike Oppenheimer, age 49
President, Stainless Steel Materials: Chris Pointon, age 55
Director and President and CEO, Minerals:
Miklos (Mike) Salamon, age 48, $1,705,328 pay
VP, Human Resources: Ian Fraser, age 42, $1,162,446 pay
VP, Investor Relations and Communications: Mark Lidiard
VP, Investor and Media Relations: Michael Campbell
VP, Investor Relations (US): Francis McAllister
Manager, Communications: Ariane Gentil
Manager, Investor Relations: Andrew Nairn
Manager, Investor Relations: Tracey Whitehead
Company Secretary: Karen J. Wood, age 47
Auditors: KPMG

LOCATIONS

HQ: 180 Lonsdale St., Melbourne 3000, Australia
Phone: +61-3-9609-3333   **Fax:** +61-3-9609-3015
US HQ: BHP Tower, 1360 Post Oak Blvd., Ste. 150, Houston, TX 77056-3020
US Phone: 713-961-8500   **US Fax:** 713-961-8400
Web: www.bhpbilliton.com

BHP Billiton has operations worldwide. It maintains corporate offices in Houston, Johannesburg, London, and Melbourne.

2003 Sales

	$ mil.	% of total
Asia		
Japan	2,269	15
South Korea	1,149	7
Other Asia	2,165	14
Europe	5,136	33
Australia	1,769	11
North America	1,452	9
South Africa	918	6
Other regions	750	5
Total	**15,608**	**100**

PRODUCTS/OPERATIONS

2003 Sales

	$ mil.	% of total
Carbon steel materials	3,444	22
Aluminum	3,386	21
Petroleum	3,260	21
Energy coal	1,885	12
Base metals	1,522	10
Stainless steel materials	1,093	7
Diamond & specialty products	469	3
Other	549	4
Total	**15,608**	**100**

Business Divisions

Minerals	
Alumina/aluminum	Manganese (ores, alloys)
Chrome and	Molybdenum
ferrochrome	Nickel
Coal (metallurgical,	Silver
thermal)	Zinc
Copper	Petroleum
Diamonds	Crude oil
Gold	Ethane
Iron ore	Liquefied petroleum gas
Lead	Natural gas

COMPETITORS

Alcoa	Lonmin
Anglo American	MAXXAM
ASARCO	Norilsk Nickel
BP	Nippon Steel
Century Aluminum	Noranda
ChevronTexaco	Norsk Hydro
Codelco	Ormet
Corus Group	Pechiney
Eni	PDVSA
Eramet	Phelps Dodge
SEPI	RAG
Exxon Mobil	Rio Tinto
Falconbridge	Royal Dutch/Shell Group
Freeport-McMoRan	ThyssenKrupp
Copper & Gold	TOTAL
Hydro Aluminium	Trans-World Metals
Inco Limited	Trelleborg
Kaiser Aluminum	Vale do Rio Doce
Koch	WMC Resources

HISTORICAL FINANCIALS

Company Type: Public

Income Statement

FYE: June 30

	REVENUE ($ mil.)	NET INCOME ($ mil.)	NET PROFIT MARGIN	EMPLOYEES
6/03	15,608	1,900	12.2%	34,801
6/02	15,896	1,648	10.4%	50,224
6/01	10,558	1,024	9.7%	58,953
6/00*	12,841	971	7.6%	69,491
5/99	12,553	(1,509)	—	50,000
5/98	13,264	(923)	—	55,000
5/97	15,983	313	2.0%	61,000
5/96	15,271	835	5.5%	60,000
5/95	13,270	873	6.6%	49,000
5/94	12,201	947	7.8%	48,000
Annual Growth	**2.8%**	**8.0%**	**—**	**(3.5%)**

*Fiscal year change

2003 Year-End Financials

Debt ratio: 1.5%
Return on equity: 14.9%
Cash ($ mil.): 1,552
Current ratio: 1.00
Long-term debt ($ mil.): 195
No. of shares (mil.): 3,105
Dividends
Yield: 2.3%
Payout: 45.0%
Market value ($ mil.): 35,987

Stock History

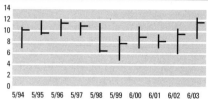

NYSE: BHP

	STOCK PRICE ($) FY Close	P/E High/Low		Earnings	PER SHARE ($) Dividends	Book Value
6/03	11.59	21	15	0.60	0.27	4.11
6/02	9.50	19	11	0.55	0.26	4.24
6/01	8.21	16	12	0.59	0.26	3.03
6/00*	8.97	21	14	0.51	0.30	3.24
5/99	7.83	—	—	(0.81)	0.30	3.04
5/98	6.49	—	—	(0.51)	0.17	3.99
5/97	10.90	67	55	0.17	0.38	5.44
5/96	11.40	25	19	0.49	0.18	5.64
5/95	9.63	22	18	0.53	0.32	5.04
5/94	10.15	16	10	0.67	0.26	4.16
Annual Growth	**1.5%**	**—**	**—**	**(1.2%)**	**0.4%**	**(0.1%)**

*Fiscal year change

BNP Paribas

No Napoleon complex here. One of Europe's largest banks, BNP Paribas operates some 2,200 retail branches in France and has operations in more than 85 other countries. The company provides corporate, retail, and investment banking services. Other activities include specialized financing, private banking, asset management, and insurance. In the US, it owns BancWest (the parent of Bank of the West and First Hawaiian Bank), and it has bought United California Bank from UFJ Holdings. BNP Paribas also controls consumer lender Cetelem and Belgian investment firm Cobepa.

BNP Paribas bought German online discount brokerage ConSors from SchmidtBank and merged the new addition with existing online unit Cortal to form CortalConSors. It is growing its asset-financing business with such purchases as US-based Capstar Partners.

BNP Paribas has been pulling back from a three-decade-old joint venture with Germany's Dresdner Bank (now owned by German insurance giant Allianz), citing differences in the banks' respective strategies. In China, BNP Paribas has won permission to start a joint venture with Wuhan-based Changjiang Securities. On a larger scale, BNP Paribas could be in the market for a merger partner, particularly if the partner is European. The company bought more than 10% of Crédit Lyonnais from the French government and purchased more than 5% on the open market soon after, leading to rumors that BNP Paribas might acquire its rival; however, Crédit Lyonnais agreed to be bought by Crédit Agricole. BNP Paribas is also looking to expand on the US West Coast.

HISTORY

BNP Paribas Group's predecessor Banque Nationale de Paris (BNP) is the progeny of two state banks with parallel histories; each was set up to jump-start the economy after a revolution in 1848.

For a century, Paris-based Comptoir National d'Escompte de Paris (CNEP) bounced between private and public status, depending on government whim. It was the #3 bank in France from the late 19th century through the 1950s.

Banque National pour le Commerce et l'Industrie (BNCI) started in Alsace, a region that was part of Germany from the Franco-Prussian War until WWI. BNCI served as an economic bridge between Germany and France, which had to give the bank governmental resuscitation during the Depression. By the 1960s BNCI had passed CNEP in size.

French leader Charles de Gaulle expected banking to drive post-WWII reconstruction, and in 1945 CNEP and BNCI were nationalized. In 1966 France's finance minister merged them and they became BNP. That year the company started an association with Dresdner Bank of Germany, under which the two still operate joint ventures, primarily in Eastern Europe.

By 1993 privatization was again in vogue, and BNP was cut loose by the government. It expanded outside France to ameliorate the influences of the French economy and government. Even before it was privatized, BNP was involved in such politically charged actions as the bailout of OPEC money repository Banque Arabe and the extension of credit to Algeria's state oil company Sonatrach.

The privatized BNP looked overseas in the late 1990s. In 1997 alone, it won the right to operate in New Zealand, bought Laurentian Bank and Trust of the Bahamas, took control of its joint venture with Egypt's Banque du Caire, and opened a subsidiary in Brazil.

BNP bought failed Peregrine Investment's Chinese operations in 1998. That year the bank also expanded in Peru, opened an office in Algeria, opened a representative office in Uzbekistan, set up an investment banking subsidiary in India, and bought Australian stock brokerage operations from Prudential.

After a decade of globe-trotting, BNP brought it on home in 1999 and set off a year of tumult in French banking. As France's other two large banks (Société Générale and Paribas) made plans to merge, BNP decided it would absorb both banks as a means to get a bigger chunk of the to-be-privatized Crédit Lyonnais and to protect France from Euro-megabank penetration by creating the globe's largest bank.

Executives at Société Générale (SG) had other ideas, forming a cartel called "Action Against the BNP Raid." Meanwhile, BNP tried to boost its controlling stakes its holdings in the two banks. (In Europe's cross-ownership tradition, the target banks also owned part of BNP.) France's central bank tried unsuccessfully to negotiate a deal (the government supported the triumvirate merger). A war of words was played out in the media, and finally shareholders had to vote on the proposals. In the end, BNP won control of Paribas, but not SG. As BNP prepared to integrate a reluctant Paribas into its operations, regulators ordered BNP to relinquish its stake in SG. The newly merged company was dubbed BNP Paribas Group.

In 2000 BNP Paribas and Avis Group launched a fleet-management joint venture. BNP also bought 150 shopping centers from French retailer Carrefour and the 40% of merchant bank Cobepa that it didn't already own. In 2001 BNP Paribas took full control of US-based BancWest.

EXECUTIVES

Chairman: Michel Pébereau, age 61
Vice Chairman: Michel François-Poncet, age 68
President and CEO: Baudouin Prot, age 52
COO: Georges Chodron de Courcel, age 53
COO: Jean Clamon
COO: Dominique Hoenn, age 63
Head of Corporate and Investment Banking:
Philippe Blavier
Head of Group Finance: Philipe Bordenave
Head of Group Information Systems: Hervé Gouëzel
Head of Group Human Resources: Bernard Lemée
Head of Asset Management and Services:
Vivien Lévy-Garboua
Head of BNP Paribas Capital: Amaury-Daniel de Seze
Head of French Retail Banking: Jean-Laurent Bonnafé
Head of International Banking and Financial Services:
Pierre Mariani, age 46
Head of Group Development: Laurent Tréca
Facilities Manager: Michel Clair
Advisor to the Chairman: Jacques de Larosière
Auditors: Barbier Frinault & Autres; Mazars & Guérard;
PricewaterhouseCoopers Audit

LOCATIONS

HQ: 16, boulevard des Italiens, 75009 Paris, France
Phone: +33-1-40-14-45-46   **Fax:** +33-1-40-14-69-73
US HQ: 787 7th Ave., New York, NY 10019
US Phone: 212-841-2000   **US Fax:** 212-841-2146
Web: www.bnpparibas.com

PRODUCTS/OPERATIONS

2002 Sales

	$ mil.	% of total
Interest	33,126.3	69
Commissions	6,456.3	13
Net gains on trading account securities	4,912.4	10
Other banking income	1,188.6	3
Other	2,432.6	5
Total	**48,116.2**	**100**

2002 Assets

	% of total
Cash & equivalents	34
Bonds & other fixed income instruments	6
Insurance company investments	8
Net loans	32
Other investments	5
Other	15
Total	**100**

COMPETITORS

ABN AMRO
BBVA
Banco Comercial
Português
Banco Popular
Bank of America
Barclays
Generale de Belgique
Citigroup
Crédit Agricole
CCF
Deutsche Bank
HSBC Holdings
J.P. Morgan Chase
Caisse d'Epargne
Mizuho Financial
Natexis
Société Générale
UBS
Wells Fargo

HISTORICAL FINANCIALS

Company Type: Public

Income Statement

FYE: December 31

	ASSETS ($ mil.)	NET INCOME ($ mil.)	INCOME AS % OF ASSETS	EMPLOYEES
12/02	744,485	3,454	0.5%	87,700
12/01	731,047	3,559	0.5%	85,000
12/00	653,505	3,883	0.6%	80,464
12/99	703,515	1,494	0.2%	77,472
12/98	379,047	1,362	0.4%	56,286
12/97	339,213	994	0.3%	52,702
12/96	355,647	737	0.2%	52,762
12/95	324,653	363	0.1%	53,600
12/94	272,093	310	0.1%	54,469
12/93	249,364	172	0.1%	56,141
Annual Growth	**12.9%**	**39.6%**	**—**	**5.1%**

2002 Year-End Financials

Equity as % of assets: 3.7%   Long-term debt ($ mil.): 101,891
Return on assets: 0.5%   Sales ($ mil.): 48,116
Return on equity: 13.9%

Net Income History

Euronext Paris: BNP

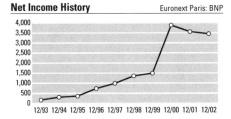

Bombardier Inc.

Bombardier makes the goods to get people moving. Its Bombardier Aerospace subsidiary is the world's #3 maker of civil aircraft behind Boeing and Airbus; the #1 regional aircraft maker (Canadair, de Havilland), ahead of Embraer and Fairchild Dornier; and one of the two largest makers of business jets (Challenger, Learjet), along with Gulfstream. Its Bombardier Transportation division — which added DaimlerChrysler's Adtranz rail systems unit in 2001 — is the world's largest railway equipment maker. Other Bombardier subsidiaries produce Ski-Doo and Lynx snowmobiles, all-terrain vehicles, and Sea-Doo personal watercraft, though the company is selling those operations. The Bombardier family controls the company.

Bombardier plans to sell units that can't generate the revenues needed to meet its target of 30% growth earnings per share. Notably, Bombardier has announced plans to divest its Recreational Products group, which accounts for about 11% of sales; the unit is expected to fetch more than $1.5 billion.

With the coming divestiture of the Recreation group, the company is turning all of its attention to its Aviation operations, which account for nearly 50% of sales (down from 65% in 2001), and its Transportation operations, which account for about 40% of sales. Bombardier's rail operations became the largest producer of railway equipment in the world — ahead of ALSTOM and Siemens AG — when the company acquired DaimlerChrysler's Adtranz rail systems unit.

On the Aviation group front, Bombardier cut

67

thousands of jobs and temporarily suspended production of business jets in response to the plunge in commercial aircraft demand. In August 2003 the company agreed to sell a substantial portion of its business aircraft market portfolio to a unit of GE Commercial Finance for $339 million. The business sold to GE is made up primarily of loans and leases relating to business aircraft financing.

Meanwhile, the company is pursuing international growth outside of North America and Western Europe. The Bombardier family owns more than 50% of the company.

HISTORY

Bombardier got its start in the 1920s when mechanic Joseph-Armand Bombardier began converting old cars into snowmobiles. He founded L'Auto-Neige Bombardier Limited in 1942 to make commercial snow vehicles. In 1959 Bombardier introduced the first personal snowmobile, the Ski-Doo.

At age 27, Laurent Beaudoin became the company's president in 1966. Bombardier went public in 1969. When the bottom dropped out of the snowmobile business due to the energy crisis in 1973, Beaudoin diversified, and in 1974 Bombardier won its first mass-transit contract to build Montreal subway cars. Expanding further into mass transportation, Bombardier merged with MLW-Worthington Limited, a builder of diesel engines and diesel-electric locomotives. In 1978 the company became Bombardier Inc.

During the 1980s Bombardier continued to diversify. It expanded into military vehicles and became the leading supplier to the North American rail transit industry. The company entered the European railcar market in 1986, the same year it acquired Canadair, Canada's largest aerospace company, from the national government.

Founded in 1920 as the aircraft division of Canadian Vickers, Canadair became a separate company producing military and civilian aircraft in 1944. Acquired by Electric Boat (which became part of General Dynamics) in 1947, it was nationalized by the Canadian government in 1976. In 1978 Canadair introduced its Challenger 600 business jet, which became a major seller.

Bombardier began development of a commuter aircraft, the Canadian Regional Jet (a 50-seat derivative of the Challenger), in 1989.

In 1990 the company bought US-based Learjet and its service centers, and two years later it acquired a stake in de Havilland, a regional aircraft maker, which it jointly owns with the Province of Ontario. The company bought German railroad-equipment maker Waggonfabrik Talbot in 1995.

In 1996 Amtrak selected an international consortium headed by Bombardier to produce high-speed trains, electric locomotives, and train-maintenance facilities. Also that year the Global Express business jet made its first flight.

Bombardier doubled the size of its European operations in 1998 by buying German railcar maker Deutsche Waggonbau. In 1999 Bombardier announced the launch of its all-new business jet, the eight-passenger Continental.

The company sold its 50% stake in Shorts Missile Systems to Thomson in 2000. Also that year Bombardier landed a $817 million contract to supply Spanish carrier Air Nostrum with 44 planes. It also inked a $2 billion deal to make 94 regional jets for Delta Air Lines; the Delta order includes options for an additional 406 aircraft through 2010.

To start off 2001, Bombardier signed a deal with SkyWest worth about $1.4 billion for 64 Canadair regional jets. It was also selected by a bankruptcy court as winning bidder for Outboard Marine's Evinrude and Johnson outboard marine engine assets. Completing an agreement made the year before, Bombardier acquired DaimlerChrysler's Adtranz rail systems unit for about $725 million, making it part of its Bombardier Transportation division. In September the company announced that it would take a charge of about $600 million and lay off about 10% of its aerospace workforce (it also said that it would cut another 7% of that workforce if demand did not grow).

In 2002 Bombardier sought about $870 million in damages from DaimlerChrysler over the Adtranz deal, claiming the level of equity in Adtranz was overstated and that the costs related to third-party contracts were higher than stated at the time of the deal. Late in 2002 Bombardier temporarily suspended business jet production. The next year Bombardier announced that it would divest its Recreational Products unit.

EXECUTIVES

Chairman: Laurent Beaudoin, $1,000,000 pay (prior to title change)
Vice Chairman: J.R. André Bombardier
Vice Chairman: Jean-Louis Fontaine, $917,062 pay
President and CEO: Paul M. Tellier, age 64
SVP and CFO: Pierre Alary
SVP: Carroll L'Italien
SVP, Public Affairs: Yvon Turcot
SVP, Strategy: Michael Denham
VP and Special Advisor to the President and CEO: Michel Lord
VP and Treasurer: François Lemarchand
VP, Corporate Audit and Risk Assessment: Carole Lamarche
VP, Investor Relations: Réjean Bourque
VP, Legal Services and Assistant Secretary: Daniel Desjardins
VP, Leadership and Organizational Development (HR): Jean Levert
VP: Richard C. Bradeen
Corporate Secretary: Roger Carle
Chairman, Bombardier Transportation: Jean-Yves Leblanc
SVP Public Affairs: William J. Fox
Auditors: Ernst & Young LLP

LOCATIONS

HQ: 800 René-Lévesque Blvd. West, Montreal, Quebec H3B 1Y8, Canada
Phone: 514-861-9481   **Fax:** 514-861-7053
US HQ: 1 Learjet Way, Wichita, KS 67209
US Phone: 316-946-2000   **US Fax:** 316-946-2163
Web: www.bombardier.com

Bombardier's principal production facilities are located in Canada, the UK, and the US.

2003 Sales

	$ mil.	% of total
The Americas		
US	7,264	47
Canada	1,201	8
Europe		
Germany	1,684	11
UK	1,528	10
Sweden	497	3
Switzerland	422	3
Italy	331	2
France	295	2
Spain	253	1
Portugal	160	1
Netherlands	141	1
Austria	132	1
Asia		
Japan	179	1
China	141	1
Other regions	1,254	8
Total	**15,482**	**100**

PRODUCTS/OPERATIONS

Selected Divisions, Products, and Services

Aerospace
Amphibious aircraft
  Canadair-415 turboprop
Business aircraft
  Canadair SE
  Challenger 604
  Continental
  Global Express
  Learjet 31A, 45, 60
Defense services
  Flying training
Military aircraft technical service
Special defense products (Unmanned Aerial Vehicle)
Regional aircraft
  CRJ 200
  CRJ 700
  CRJ 900
  Q100
  Q200
  Q300
  Q400

Transportation Equipment
Freight cars
Locomotives for passenger trains
Monorails
Rapid-transit cars
Single-level and bi-level railcars
Subway cars
Trams
Tram-trains
Turbotrains
Vehicles with tilting systems

Recreational Products
Bombardier all-terrain vehicles
Evinrude engines
Johnson engines
Lynx and Ski-Doo snowmobiles
Sea-Doo sport boats
Sea-Doo watercraft
Utility vehicles

Bombardier Capital
Aircraft and industrial equipment financing and leasing
Consumer financing
Inventory financing
Mortgage financing
Ski industry financing

COMPETITORS

Airbus
ALSTOM
Arctic Cat
BMW
Boeing
Brunswick
Cessna
Cirrus Design
Embraer
Fairchild Dornier
Fiat
Gulfstream Aerospace

Lockheed Martin
NetJets
Northrop Grumman
Polaris Industries
Raytheon
Safire
Siemens
Suzuki Motor
Textron
Trinity Industries
Yamaha

HISTORICAL FINANCIALS

Company Type: Public

Income Statement

FYE: January 31

	REVENUE ($ mil.)	NET INCOME ($ mil.)	NET PROFIT MARGIN	EMPLOYEES
1/03	15,482	(403)	—	70,411
1/02	13,614	246	1.8%	74,879
1/01	10,705	649	6.1%	58,000
1/00	9,419	497	5.3%	56,000
1/99	7,607	367	4.8%	53,000
1/98	5,853	289	4.9%	47,778
1/97	5,917	301	5.1%	41,150
1/96	5,170	112	2.2%	40,000
1/95	4,224	172	4.1%	37,000
1/94	3,586	132	3.7%	36,500
Annual Growth	17.6%	—	—	7.6%

2003 Year-End Financials

Debt ratio: 321.6%
Return on equity: —
Cash ($ mil.): 682

Current ratio: 1.10
Long-term debt ($ mil.): 5,767

Net Income History

Toronto: BBD.B

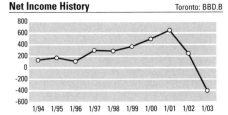

Bouygues SA

Bouygues (pronounced "bweeg") is très beeg in both construction (buildings and civic works, roads, and property development) and services (media, public utilities management, and telecommunications). The group runs more than 40 subsidiaries and affiliates in 80 countries, including Colas (road construction) and Saur (utilities management). The company is increasing its stake in Bouygues Telecom (France's #3 mobile phone carrier) to more than 80% and is buying more, and it also owns about 40% of TF1 (France's #1 TV channel). Brothers Martin and Olivier Bouygues together control more than 22% of Bouygues.

Although Bouygues has felt the squeeze of the global economic slowdown, its diversified international holdings have kept the company in the black. One of Europe's largest industrial groups, Bouygue separates its global network of sub-

sidiaries and affiliates into two main business sectors: construction and services.

Construction services generate about 65% of Bouygues' total sales. Spun off from the main group, Bouygues Construction is composed of building and civil works firms. Its Colas subsidiary provides road construction and maintenance internationally; it also produces emulsions. Other construction subsidiaries include ETDE (power and data transmission networks construction) and Bouygues Immobilier (property management). The construction division has been expanding in Western Europe, especially the UK and the Netherlands, while slowing down in the Asia/Pacific region.

On the services side of the business, utilities management firm Saur designs, constructs, and manages water and sewage systems, and it provides solid waste management services. The group's media holdings include its stake in Société Télévision Française 1 (TF1), France's oldest and leading TV channel. TF1 owns 66% of TPS, France's second-largest satellite operator. Bouygues also has been steadily upping its stake in Bouygues Telecom, hoping to grab more than 80% of the mobile operator.

Chairman Martin Bouygues and his brother Olivier, sons of the company's founder, together own the controlling stake in Bouygues through holding company SCDM.

HISTORY

With $1,700 in borrowed money, Francis Bouygues, son of a Paris engineer, started Entreprise Francis Bouygues in 1952 as an industrial works and construction firm in the Paris region of France. Within four years his firm had expanded into property development.

By the mid-1960s Bouygues had entered the civil engineering and public works sectors and developed regional construction units across France. In 1970 it was listed on the Paris stock exchange. Four years later the company established Bouygues Offshore to build oil platforms.

In 1978 the firm built Terminal 2 of Paris' Charles de Gaulle airport. Three years later it won the contract to construct the University of Riyadh in Saudi Arabia (then the world's largest building project at 3.2 million sq. ft.), which was completed in 1984. That year Bouygues acquired France's #3 water supply company, Saur, and power transmission and supply firm ETDE.

Expansion continued in 1986 with the chase of the Screg Group, which included Colas, France's top highway contractor. The next year the company led a consortium to buy 50% of newly privatized network Société Télévision Française 1 (TF1), France's leading TV channel. Bouygues became the largest shareholder with a 25% stake (increased to 40% by 1999). In 1988 the company began building the Channel Tunnel (completed in 1994) and moved into ultramodern headquarters, dubbed Challenger, in Saint-Quentin-En-Yvelines, outside Paris.

After rumors of failing health, Francis Bouygues resigned as chairman in 1989. His youngest son, Martin, took over as chairman and CEO, although the patriarch, called France's "Emperor of Concrete," remained on the board until his death in 1993.

Despite fears that the group would suffer without its founder's leadership, Bouygues continued to grow with the 1989 acquisition of a majority interest in Grands Moulins de Paris, France's largest flour milling firm (sold in 1998). In 1990 it purchased Swiss construction group Losinger.

The company entered the telecom industry in 1993 with a national paging network and added a mobile phone license a year later. In 1996 the group listed 40% of Bouygues Offshore's shares on the New York and Paris stock exchanges. Also that year it launched mobile phone operator Bouygues Telecom and entered a partnership with Telecom Italia.

By 1999 Bouygues Telecom had reached 2 million customers, and Bouygues bought back a 20% share held by the UK's Cable and Wireless to increase its stake to nearly 54%. That year Bouygues Offshore bought Norwegian engineering firm Kvaerner, and the group spun off its construction sector, creating Bouygues Construction.

After word circulated that Deutsche Telekom wanted to acquire the group's telecom unit, Bouygues became the target of takeover rumors. Francois Pinault, France's richest businessman, became Bouygues' largest non-family shareholder when he increased his stake to 14%. Then Pinault's biggest rival, Bernard Arnault, upped his stake to more than 9% of the group, fueling speculation of a battle over control of the board.

In 2001 the company pulled out of France's auction for a third-generation wireless license and remained the only European incumbent mobile carrier without a major domestic investment in 3G technology. The next year the company agreed to buy Telecom Italia's stake in Bouygues Telecom, increasing Bouygues' ownership in the mobile operator from 54% to more than 65%. In 2002 the company sold its 51% stake in oil services unit Bouygues Offshore to Italian oil services group Saipem, which announced plans to bid for the remaining shares.

However, talks with German utility giant E.ON over the sale of Bouygues' Saur subsidiary failed that year, after E.ON decided to focus instead on its electricity and gas operations.

EXECUTIVES

Chairman and CEO: Martin Bouygues, age 51, $2,017,194 pay
Vice Chairman, Deputy CEO, and COO: Michel Derbesse, age 68, $2,176,776 pay
Deputy CEO and CFO: Olivier Poupart-Lafarge, age 61, $1,828,162 pay
Deputy CEO, Utilities Management; Chairman, Saur: Olivier Bouygues, age 53, $1,956,942 pay
EVP Information Systems and New Technologies: Alain Pouyat, age 59, $1,110,200 pay
EVP: Pierre Daurès, age 63
SVP Group Human Resources and Administration: Jean-Claude Tostivin
SVP and Treasurer: Lionel Verdouck
Chairman and CEO, Bouygues Construction: Yves Gabriel, age 53, $1,024,710 pay
Chairman and CEO, Bouygues Immobilier: François Bertière, age 52
Chairman and CEO, Colas: Alain Dupont, age 63
Chairman and CEO, TF1: Patrick Le Lay, age 61, $1,847,231 pay
Chairman, Bouygues Telecom: Philippe Montagner, age 59
CEO, Bouygues Telecom: Gilles Pélisson
CEO, Saur: Hervé Le Bouc
Director Group Corporate Communications: Blandine Delafon
Press Department: Anne-Sophie Creton
Press Department: Hubert Engelmann
Investor Relations: Michel Madesclaire
Investor Relations: Anthony Mellor
Auditors: Mazars & Guérard; Salustro Fournet & Associés

LOCATIONS

HQ: 1, avenue Eugène Freyssinet,
  78061 Saint-Quentin-en-Yvelines, France
Phone: +33-1-30-60-23-11   **Fax:** +33-1-30-60-48-61
Web: www.bouygues.fr

2002 Sales

	% of total
Western Europe	
France	54
Other countries	9
Africa	22
Eastern Europe	6
North America	4
Asia/Pacific	4
Other regions	1
Total	**100**

PRODUCTS/OPERATIONS

2002 Sales

	% of total
Construction	64
Telecoms & media	25
Services (Saur)	11
Total	**100**

Selected Subsidiaries and Affiliates

Construction
Bouygues Bâtiment SA (99.9%)
Bouygues Construction SA (99.9%)
Bouygues TP SA (99.9%)
Colas SA (96%)
ETDE SA (99.9%)
O.F. Construction (formerly SB Ballestrero SA)
O.F. Equipement (formerly Olin-Lanctuit SA)
Parcofrance SA (99.9%)

Telecoms and Media
BDT SA (79%)
Bouygues Telecom SA (83%)
Télévision Française 1 SA (TF1, 42%)
Télévision Par Satellite SNC (TPS, 27%)

Services
Coved SA
Saur SA
Saur UK Ltd

COMPETITORS

AMEC
Autostrade
AWG
Balfour Beatty
Bechtel
Bilfinger Berger
Bovis Lend Lease
CANAL+
CSCEC
Dragados
Eiffage
Fluor
FCC
France Telecom
Cegetel
Halliburton
HOCHTIEF
HBG
Hyundai Engineering and
 Construction
MWH Global
Philipp Holzmann
Severn Trent
Skanska
Suez
Technip
Telesystem International
 Wireless
VINCI

HISTORICAL FINANCIALS

Company Type: Public

Income Statement

FYE: December 31

	REVENUE ($ mil.)	NET INCOME ($ mil.)	NET PROFIT MARGIN	EMPLOYEES
12/02	23,317	698	3.0%	121,604
12/01	18,135	305	1.7%	125,034
12/00	17,942	396	2.2%	118,645
12/99	16,916	62	0.4%	109,588
12/98	17,957	248	1.4%	103,350
12/97	15,320	126	0.8%	94,400
12/96	14,021	125	0.9%	94,895
12/95	15,042	(593)	—	93,857
12/94	13,568	107	0.8%	91,796
12/93	10,333	79	0.8%	86,998
Annual Growth	**9.5%**	**27.4%**	**—**	**3.8%**

2002 Year-End Financials

Debt ratio: 64.3%
Return on equity: 12.8%
Cash ($ mil.): 551

Current ratio: 1.05
Long-term debt ($ mil.): 4,298

Net Income History

Euronext Paris: EN

BP p.l.c.

BP, formerly BP Amoco, is the world's #3 integrated oil company, behind Royal Dutch/Shell and Exxon Mobil. The company, which was formed in 1998 from the merger of British Petroleum and Amoco, grew by buying Atlantic Richfield Company (ARCO). BP has proved reserves of 17.6 billion barrels of oil equivalent, including large holdings in Alaska. The largest US oil and gas producer, it is also a top refiner (3.5 million barrels of oil per day capacity) and petrochemicals and specialty chemicals manufacturer. BP operates 29,200 gas stations worldwide. In 2003 — in a major strategic move — BP, the Alfa Group, and Access-Renova combined their Russian oil assets to create TNK-BP, Russia's third-largest oil company.

Outside of the US, BP has significant production activities in Canada, the Gulf of Mexico, the North Sea, and Trinidad.

BP has swapped control of its stake in German natural gas supplier Ruhrgas, with E.ON, in return for ownership of Veba Oel, which operates Germany's largest gas station chain. To recoup some of BP's investment, Veba Oel's exploration and production operations were sold to Petro-Canada.

In 2003 BP agreed to sell some of its mature oil and gas assets in the US and the North Sea (including its Forties field, where oil was discovered in 1970) to Apache for $1.3 billion, as part of a strategy to focus on more profitable production assets. It has also sold its Boqueron field and Desarrollo Zulia Occidental assets, both located in Venezuela, to Europe's Perenco.

HISTORY

Today's BP (formerly BP Amoco) was born on two sides of the Atlantic. In the US, Amoco emerged from Standard Oil Trust, organized by John D. Rockefeller in 1882. In 1886 he bought Lima (Ohio) oil, a high-sulfur crude, anticipating the discovery of a sulfur-removing process. Such a process was, indeed, patented in 1887, and in 1889 Standard organized Standard Oil of Indiana, which later established such innovations as company-owned service stations and a research lab at the refinery.

Overseas, British Petroleum (BP) was a twinkle in the eye of English adventurer William D'Arcy, who began oil exploration of Persia in 1901. In 1908, bankrolled by Burmah Oil, D'Arcy's firm was the first to strike oil in the Middle East. D'Arcy and Burmah Oil formed Anglo-Persian Oil in 1909, and the British government took a 51% stake in 1914.

Back in the US, Standard was broken up into 33 independent oil companies in 1911. Standard Oil of Indiana kept its oil refining and US marketing operations. In 1925 it added a few Mexican and Venezuelan firms, including Pan American Petroleum and Transport, which held half of American Oil Co., known for Amoco antiknock gasoline. It began Amoco Chemicals in 1945.

Anglo-Persian took the BP name in 1954 and bought its own Standard Oil: After making a strike in Alaska in 1969, BP swapped Alaskan reserves for a 25% interest (later upped to 55%) in Standard Oil of Ohio (SOHIO). BP also struck North Sea oil in 1970. But falling oil and copper prices in the mid-1980s and a dry hole in the Beaufort Sea hurt earnings. Under Robert Horton, SOHIO sold off units. BP also bought livestock feed producer Purina Mills (1986, sold 1998) and the rest of SOHIO (1987).

Standard Oil of Indiana had its own problems, including being kicked out of Iran after the Islamic revolution and causing a major oil spill off the French coast in 1978. The firm, which became Amoco in 1985, bought Canada's Dome Petroleum in 1988, making it the largest private owner of North American gas reserves, but the big purchase proved hard to swallow.

In 1992 Amoco hurled itself into overseas oil exploration. It was the first foreign oil company to explore the Chinese mainland. But by 1995 production was down. That year John Browne, often compared to Rockefeller, became BP's CEO. In 1996 BP and Mobil merged their European fuel and lubricants operations, and the British government sold its remaining stake in BP.

As oil prices tumbled in 1998, BP merged with Amoco in a $52 billion deal that formed BP Amoco. The new oil major agreed the next year to buy US-based Atlantic Richfield (the deal closed in 2000). BP Amoco sold ARCO's Alaskan properties to Phillips (later ConocoPhillips) for $7 billion to win regulatory approval for the purchase.

Its stake in Siberian oil fields was nearly taken away in a controversial 1999 bankruptcy sale before BP Amoco and Russia's Tyumen Oil agreed to cooperate. In 2000 BP Amoco and Shell Oil sold their stakes in Altura Energy to Occidental Petroleum for $3.6 billion. Also that year BP Amoco bought motor-oil maker Burmah Castrol for $4.7 billion. It paid $1.5 billion for the 18% of former ARCO exploration and production unit Vastar Resources that it didn't already own.

The company adopted BP as its main worldwide brand in 2000, and it officially shortened its name the next year.

In 2001 BP agreed to swap control of its stake in German natural gas supplier Ruhrgas, plus $1.6 billion in cash and $950 million in assumed debt, to German utility giant E.ON for a majority interest in Veba Oel, owner of Germany's largest gas station chain. Regulators moved to keep E.ON from acquiring the Ruhrgas stake, but BP agreed to make up the difference in cash if necessary, and the deal proceeded. The agreement allowed BP to take full ownership of Veba Oel in 2002. To recoup some of its investment, BP (with E.ON's consent) sold Veba Oel's exploration and production operations to Petro-Canada.

That year BP increased it stake in Russian oil and gas producer Sidanco from 10% to 25%.

In 2003 BP sold its Boqueron field and Desarrollo Zulia Occidental assets, both located in Venezuela, to Europe's Perenco.

EXECUTIVES

Chairman: Peter D. Sutherland, age 57
Deputy Chairman: Sir Ian Prosser, age 60
Group Chief Executive and Director:
Lord John Browne, age 55, $4,469,000 pay
Deputy Chief Executive and Director:
Richard L. (Dick) Olver, age 56, $1,664,000 pay
CFO and Director: Byron E. Grote, age 54,
$1,569,000 pay
EVP and Group General Counsel: B. Peter Bevan, age 58
EVP, Group Chief of Staff, and Managing Director:
David C. Allen, age 48
**EVP; Chief Executive, Refining and Marketing, and
Managing Director:** John A. Manzoni, age 43
**Chief Executive Exploration and Production, and
Managing Director:** Anthony B. Hayward, age 45
Chief Executive, Gas, Power, and Renewables:
Ralph C. Alexander, age 47
Chief Executive, Chemicals: Iain C. Conn, age 40
Group VP and CIO: John Leggate
VP and CTO: Phiroz P. (Daru) Darukhanavala, age 55
Secretary: Judith C. Hanratty, age 58
COO, Global Supply Optimization and Trading:
Tony Fountain
Manager US Accounting and Reporting: Melinda Brown
Manager Investor Relations: Sean A. Daley
Auditors: Ernst & Young

LOCATIONS

HQ: 1 St. James's Square,
London SW1Y 4PD, United Kingdom
Phone: +44-20-7496-4000 **Fax:** +44-20-7496-4630
US HQ: 28100 Torch Pkwy., Warrenville, IL 60555
US Phone: 630-420-5111
Web: www.bp.com

2002 Sales

	$ mil.	% of total
US	78,282	44
UK	34,075	19
Other European countries	38,538	22
Other countries	27,826	15
Total	**178,721**	**100**

PRODUCTS/OPERATIONS

2002 Sales

	$ mil.	% of total
Refining & marketing	122,470	69
Gas, power & renewables	36,037	20
Chemicals	12,507	7
Exploration & production	7,197	4
Other	510	—
Total	**178,721**	**100**

Major Operations

Refining and Marketing
Marketing
Refining
Supply and trading
Transportation and shipping

Gas and Power
Natural gas marketing and trading
Natural gas liquids

Exploration and Production
Field development
Gas processing and marketing
Oil and gas exploration
Pipelines and transportation
  Alyeska Pipeline Service Co. (47%)
    Trans Alaska Pipeline System
    Valdez terminal

Chemicals
Chemical intermediates
Feedstock
Performance products
Polymers

Other
Coal mining
Solar power

Selected Subsidiaries

Amoco Canada Petroleum Company
Amoco Energy Company of Trinidad and Tobago (90%, US)
Atlantic Richfield Co
BP America Inc. (US)
The Standard Oil Company (US)
BP Amoco Company (US)
BP Amoco Corporation (US)
BP Australia
BP Chemicals Ltd.
BP Exploration Company Limited
BP España
BP France
BP International Ltd.
BP Middle East
BP Nederland
BP Oil International Limited
BP Oil New Zealand
BP Shipping
BP Singapore Pte
BP Solar
BP Southern Africa
Burmah Castrol
Deutsche BP AG
Gelsenberg AG (Germany)
TNK-BP (50%)
Veba Oel

COMPETITORS

Amerada Hess	ICI American
Apache	Imperial Oil
Ashland	Kerr-McGee
BASF AG	Koch
Bayer AG	Lyondell Chemical
BG Group	Norsk Hydro
BHP Billiton Ltd	Occidental Petroleum
Cargill	PETROBRAS
ChevronTexaco	PDVSA
Dow Chemical	PEMEX
DuPont	Royal Dutch/Shell Group
Eni	Sinclair Oil
Exxon Mobil	Sunoco
Hercules	TOTAL
Huntsman International	

HISTORICAL FINANCIALS

Company Type: Public

Income Statement

FYE: December 31

	REVENUE ($ mil.)	NET INCOME ($ mil.)	NET PROFIT MARGIN	EMPLOYEES
12/02	178,721	6,845	3.8%	115,250
12/01	174,218	8,010	4.6%	110,150
12/00	148,062	11,870	8.0%	107,200
12/99	83,566	4,686	5.6%	80,400
12/98	68,304	3,260	4.8%	96,650
12/97	71,783	4,080	5.7%	56,450
12/96	76,602	4,370	5.7%	53,150
12/95	56,000	1,740	3.1%	56,650
12/94	51,827	2,468	4.8%	60,000
12/93	51,709	910	1.8%	84,000
Annual Growth	**14.8%**	**25.1%**	**—**	**3.6%**

2002 Year-End Financials

Debt ratio: 17.2%
Return on equity: 9.5%
Cash ($ mil.): 1,520
Current ratio: 0.97
Long-term debt ($ mil.): 11,922
No. of shares (mil.): 3,730
Dividends
  Yield: 3.9%
  Payout: 86.3%
Market value ($ mil.): 151,615

Stock History

NYSE: BP

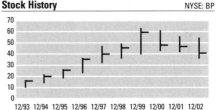

12/93 12/94 12/95 12/96 12/97 12/98 12/99 12/00 12/01 12/02

	STOCK PRICE ($) FY Close	P/E High/Low	Earnings	Dividends	Book Value
12/02	40.65	30 20	1.82	1.57	18.61
12/01	46.51	26 20	2.13	1.43	19.89
12/00	47.88	22 16	2.72	1.35	19.55
12/99	59.31	41 26	1.44	1.38	13.33
12/98	45.38	48 36	1.02	0.00	12.95
12/97	39.84	22 15	2.13	0.00	6.07
12/96	35.34	15 10	2.34	0.66	5.82
12/95	25.53	28 20	0.94	0.68	4.93
12/94	19.97	16 11	1.36	0.44	4.72
12/93	16.00	32 21	0.51	0.42	3.97
Annual Growth	**10.9%**	**— —**	**15.2%**	**15.8%**	**18.7%**

Bridgestone Corporation

Bridgestone's fortunes are in a skid due to tire recalls, but the company has worked hard to regain control. Bridgestone is the world's largest tire maker, but in addition to supplying tires to most major car manufacturers, the company also makes tires for heavy equipment (off-road mining vehicles) and aircraft. Non-tire products include building materials (roof tiles), sporting goods (golf balls), industrial rubber products (conveyor belts and automotive hoses), marine components (oil booms, fish-breeding reservoirs, and marine fenders), and switches.

Bridgestone has begun to bounce back after profits for 2000 plummeted as a result of a massive tire recall — primarily involving Ford Explorers — by US subsidiary Bridgestone Americas Holding. The fallout and ensuing blame-game (improper inflation guidelines/unstable vehicle vs. faulty tires) virtually ended its 95-year relationship with Ford (Bridgestone still does business with Ford outside the Americas).

While trying to re-establish consumer confidence in its Firestone brand in North America, Bridgestone is propping itself up with healthy market shares in Asia and Europe. The company has entered a development deal with Continental AG and Yokohama Rubber to adapt run-flat technology to conventional wheel systems. Bridgestone has also bought a 19% stake in Finnish tire maker Nokian Renkaat.

HISTORY

In 1906 Shojiro Ishibashi and his brother Tokujiro assumed control of the family's clothing business. They focused on making *tabi*, traditional Japanese footwear, and in 1923 began working with rubber for soles. In 1931 Shojiro formed Bridgestone (Ishibashi means "stone bridge" in Japanese) to make tires, and during that decade the company began producing auto tires, airplane tires, and golf balls. Bridgestone followed the Japanese military to occupied territories, where it built plants. The company's headquarters moved to Tokyo in 1937.

Although Bridgestone lost all of its overseas factories during WWII, its Japanese plants escaped damage. The company began making bicycles in 1946 and signed a technical assistance pact with Goodyear five years later, enabling Bridgestone to import badly needed technology. In the 1950s and 1960s, Bridgestone started making nylon tires and radials and again set up facilities overseas, mostly elsewhere in Asia. The company benefited from the rapid growth in Japanese auto sales in the 1970s. Shojiro died at age 87 in 1976.

In 1983 Bridgestone bought a plant in LaVergne, Tennessee, from tire maker Firestone. Five years later Bridgestone topped Italian tire maker Pirelli's bid and bought the rest of Firestone for $2.6 billion, valuing the tire manufacturer at a lofty 26 times its earnings. Bridgestone/Firestone (now Bridgestone Americas Holding) became Bridgestone's largest subsidiary. Harvey Firestone had founded his tire business in 1900 and expanded with the auto industry in the US. In the 1920s he leased one million acres in Liberia for rubber plantations and established a chain of auto supply and service outlets. After WWII Firestone started making synthetic rubber and automotive components, expanded overseas, and acquired US tire producers Dayton Tire & Rubber and Seiberling.

At the time of Firestone's purchase, General Motors (GM) dropped it as a supplier. Bridgestone/Firestone compensated for this loss in volume by selling more tires through mass-market retailers. It began selling tires to GM's Saturn Corporation in 1990.

The following year new Bridgestone/Firestone chairman Yoichiro Kaizaki moved to cut production costs, alienating union workers. He became company head in 1993. During the early 1990s Bridgestone bought Colonial Rubber Works, a US roofing material manufacturer, and America Off The Road Company, which makes tires for heavy equipment. To improve its distribution, in 1992 Bridgestone renamed its 1,550 North American MasterCare auto service centers "Tire Zone at Firestone" and took the

unheard-of step of selling rival Michelin's tires. It expanded operations in Brazil, Indonesia, Mexico, Thailand, and the US the next year.

Bridgestone's US operations have been plagued with problems, such as disputes with the United Rubber Workers (URW) union. Tensions rose in 1995 when the company hired 2,300 permanent replacement workers during a plant strike. In 1996, after URW members had become part of United Steelworkers of America, the two sides approved a new contract.

In 1997 Bridgestone built a South Carolina plant to help reduce Japanese imports. Expanding its markets, Bridgestone opened a retail outlet in Moscow in 1999 and acquired a radial tire plant in China from South Korea's Kumho Industrial Company in 2000. That year the company recalled approximately 6.5 million Firestone ATX, ATX II, and Wilderness AT tires after dozens of incidents where the tires came apart at road speeds. The affected tires had been used on light trucks and SUVs since 1990, many of them as original equipment on the Ford Explorer. Not long after the recall, Bridgestone/Firestone chairman and CEO Masatoshi Ono retired and was replaced by John Lampe.

In 2001 Bridgestone replaced president Yoichiro Kaizaki with senior vice president Shigeo Watanabe. Public bickering between Ford and Bridgestone over the cause of the multiple Firestone/Ford Explorer accidents continued unabated into the spring of 2001. Finally, in May, Bridgestone announced that it was ending its relationship with Ford Motor, which accounted for about 2% of sales. The two companies' founders — Henry Ford and Harvey Firestone — had been friends in the early days of mass automobile production. Then, in June, while revealing that it would face its first loss since listing 30 years ago, Bridgestone announced that it would close the Decatur, Illinois, plant at which many of the recalled tires were made. The plant employed about 1,500 workers. Later in the year the company announced that it would recall an additional 3.5 million tires at a cost of nearly $30 million.

Near the end of 2001 Bridgestone announced that it would inflate beleaguered subsidiary Bridgestone/Firestone with $1.3 billion in cash. The company also announced the restructuring of its Bridgestone/Firestone operations.

Bridgestone and Continental AG entered into an agreement in early 2002 whereby the two companies will adapt run-flat technology to conventional wheel systems (conventional systems utilize special wheels). In early 2003 the company's US subsidiary changed its name from Bridgestone/Firestone Americas Holding to Bridgestone Americas Holding.

EXECUTIVES

Chairman, President, and CEO: Shigeo Watanabe
EVP, Original Equipment and International Operations: Keisuke Suzuki
EVP, Diversified Products: Akira Sonoda
EVP, Technology and Production: Isao Togashi
EVP, CFO, and Chief Compliance Officer: Hiroshi Kanai
SVP; Chairman, CEO, and President, Bridgestone/Firestone Europe NV/SA: Shoshi Arakawa
VP, Original Equipment Sales: Tatsuya Okajima
VP, Replacement Tire Sales: Giichi Miyakawa
VP; Director, Chemical and Industrial Products Production Division: Hiroshi Kawakami
VP; Director, Bridgestone/Firestone Americas Holding, Inc.: Yasuyoshi Kawaguchi
VP, Overseas Operations and Director, International Tire Administration Division: Hiromichi Odagiri

VP, Brand Management and Product Planning: Minekazu (Mike) Fujimura
VP, Off-The-Road, Aircraft, and Motorsports Tire Sales: Hideki Inose
VP, Research and Development and Intellectual Property: Shigehisa Sano
VP, Quality, Safety, and Environment and Director, Quality Assurance Division: Osamu Inoue
VP, Human Resources and General Affairs: Tomuyuki Izumisawa
VP, Finance, IT, and Network: Shoji Mizuochi
VP, Steel Cord Manufacturing and Plant Manager, Kuroiso Plant: Kaoru Fujioka
VP, Industrial Products and Building Materials and Equipment and Director, Industrial Products Division: Yasuo Asami
Chairman, President, and CEO, Bridgestone/Firestone Americas Holding Inc.; Chairman and CEO, Bridgestone/Firestone North American Tire, LLC: John T. Lampe, age 54
Auditors: Deloitte Touche Tohmatsu; Tohmatsu & Co.

LOCATIONS

HQ: 10-1, Kyobashi 1-chome, Chuo-ku, Tokyo 104-8340, Japan
Phone: +81-3-3567-0111   **Fax:** +81-3-3535-2553
US HQ: 50 Century Blvd., Nashville, TN 37214
US Phone: 615-872-5000   **US Fax:** 615-872-1599
Web: www.bridgestone.co.jp

Bridgestone operates tire factories and diversified products plants in 24 countries.

2002 Sales

	$ mil.	% of total
The Americas	8,275	43
Japan	6,982	37
Europe	2,018	11
Other regions	1,687	9
Total	**18,962**	**100**

PRODUCTS/OPERATIONS

2002 Sales

	$ mil.	% of total
Tires	15,164	80
Other products	3,798	20
Total	**18,962**	**100**

Selected Products

Tires and Tubes

Agricultural machinery	Monorails
Aircraft	Motorcycles
Buses	Race cars
Cars	Scooters
Commercial vehicles	Subways
Construction and mining vehicles	Trucks

Industrial Rubber Products
Belts
Hoses
Inflatable rubber dams
Marine products
Multi-rubber bearings
Rubber tracks
Vibration-isolating and noise-insulating materials
Waterproofing materials

Chemical Products
Building materials
Ceramic foam
Flexible polyurethane foam products
Office equipment components
Thermal insulating polyurethane foam

Sporting Goods

Bicycles	Tennis balls
Golf balls	Tennis rackets
Golf clubs	Tennis shoes

COMPETITORS

3M
Acushnet
Ansell
Armstrong Holdings
Avon Rubber
Brunswick
Callaway Golf
Continental AG
Cooper Tire & Rubber
Goodyear
Huffy
K2
Michelin
Newell Rubbermaid
Sime Darby
TBC
Wingate Partners

HISTORICAL FINANCIALS

Company Type: Public

Income Statement

FYE: December 31

	REVENUE ($ mil.)	NET INCOME ($ mil.)	NET PROFIT MARGIN	EMPLOYEES
12/02	18,962	383	2.0%	106,846
12/01	16,270	133	0.8%	104,700
12/00	17,532	155	0.9%	102,165
12/99	20,403	868	4.3%	101,489
12/98	19,689	921	4.7%	97,767
12/97	16,624	300	1.8%	96,204
12/96	16,923	608	3.6%	92,458
12/95	16,294	523	3.2%	89,418
12/94	16,018	320	2.0%	89,711
12/93	14,297	254	1.8%	87,332
Annual Growth	3.2%	4.7%	—	2.3%

2002 Year-End Financials

Debt ratio: 36.3%
Return on equity: 5.9%
Cash ($ mil.): 1,742

Current ratio: 1.68
Long-term debt ($ mil.): 2,435

Net Income History

OTC: BRDCY

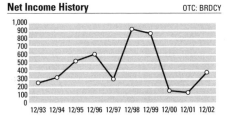

British Airways

A member of the royal family of European airlines, British Airways (BA) has no plans to relinquish its throne. From its hubs in London's Heathrow and Gatwick airports, the airline flies about 320 aircraft to nearly 220 destinations in some 94 countries. It owns minority stakes in Australia-based Qantas and Spain's Iberia. BA and AMR's American Airlines have formed the Oneworld global marketing alliance, which also includes Cathay Pacific Airways, Finnair, Qantas, and Iberia, among others. The threat of hoof-and-mouth disease in the UK and the September 11, 2001, terrorist attacks have reduced tourism, and BA is working to win back passengers.

BA has built a global network through partnerships. It owns 19% of Qantas Airways and 9% of Iberia. It has also signed a codeshare agreement with Swiss.

The airline moved into the red in 2000, the first time since being privatized. It responded by cutting unprofitable routes and focusing on business-class customers, and it has sold its interests in low-fare airline Go and French carrier Air Liberté. The efforts paid off and helped navigate the airline into the black.

BA is beefing up its local coverage by moving to an all-jet fleet for its regional routes under its British Airways CitiExpress banner. The regional arm of BA carries more than 5 million passengers a year to 26 destinations in the UK. The move is an effort to better compete with up-and-coming low-fare carriers which have been undercutting BA's sales through more simplified routes and pricing structures.

Britain's flag carrier has also been pushing hard to get regulatory approval to expand its codesharing agreement with American Airlines, for which the airlines have received tentative approval from US regulatory authorities.

HISTORY

British Airways has a jet trail winding back to 1916 and its biplane-flying ancestor, Aircraft Transport and Travel, which in 1919 launched the world's first daily international air service (between London and Paris). Concerned about subsidized foreign competition, British authorities in 1924 merged Aircraft Transport and Travel successor Daimler Airways with other fledgling British carriers — British Air Marine Navigation, Handley Page, and Instone Air Line — to form Imperial Airways.

Imperial pioneered routes from London to India (1929), Singapore (1933), and — in partnership with Qantas Empire Airways — Australia (1934). Competition on European routes emerged in the 1930s from upstart British Airways; in 1939 the government, troubled by the threat to Imperial, nationalized and merged the two airlines to form British Overseas Airways Corporation (BOAC).

After WWII, BOAC continued as the UK's international airline, but state-owned British European Airways (BEA) took over domestic and European routes. In 1972 the government combined the duo to form British Airways (BA).

BA and Air France jointly introduced supersonic passenger service in 1976 with the Concorde — a PR victory that contributed to years of losses. Colin Marshall became CEO in 1983 and reduced manpower and routes.

In 1987 the government sold BA to the public, and the airline bought chief UK rival British Caledonian. Hoping to become a globe-spanning carrier, in 1992 BA tried to gain a 44% stake in USAir (which became US Airways). American Airlines, United, and Delta strongly objected, demanding equal access to UK markets. BA settled for a 25% stake, the maximum foreign ownership allowed by US law, in 1993. It also bought 25% of Qantas.

That year BA settled a libel suit brought by UK competitor Virgin Atlantic Airways, which accused BA of waging a smear campaign against it. The settlement cost BA about $5 million, and Virgin Atlantic followed with a $1 billion antitrust suit in the US (dismissed in 1999). In 1994 BA paid out $4 million to settle yet another Virgin Atlantic suit, this one claiming BA had done

sloppy maintenance on Virgin aircraft. BA also sold British Caledonian.

In 1996 Marshall turned over the CEO job to Bob Ayling, who had joined BA in 1985. BA and American Airlines agreed to coordinate prices and schedules and to share market data for their transatlantic routes. Though the deal met regulatory obstacles from the start, in 1997 BA sold its stake in US Airways. BA and American also took the lead in forming the Oneworld global alliance (which took effect in 1999).

The next year BA launched low-fare European carrier Go. In 1999 BA and American all but abandoned plans for their comprehensive transatlantic linkup after US regulators denied antitrust immunity. Meanwhile, as fuel prices rose and passenger numbers fell, BA announced it would cut unprofitable routes and use smaller planes.

Ayling resigned in 2000, and Marshall stepped in as temporary CEO before Rod Eddington, a veteran of Cathay Pacific and Ansett, was appointed. Also that year BA took a 9% stake in Iberia and sold its interest in France's Air Liberté.

BA grounded its Concordes in 2000 (flights resumed in 2001), three weeks after the crash of an Air France Concorde outside Paris in which 113 people were killed. The airline put its no-frills carrier Go up for sale that year, and in 2001 sold the airline to venture capital firm, 3i Group. Also in 2001 BA and American announced plans to once again seek regulatory approval for a code-sharing partnership.

That year BA laid off 5,200 employees as a result of decreased demand for air travel after the terrorist attacks in New York and Washington, DC. The layoffs were on top of 1,800 job cuts the airline made earlier in the year, reducing BA's workforce by 10%.

BA's long-negotiated transatlantic alliance with American Airlines received tentative approval from the US Department of Transportation in 2002. But the airlines chose to abandon the deal rather than accept regulators' terms, which called for BA and American to give up more landing slots at London's Heathrow airport than they were willing to relinquish.

2003 saw the retirement of the BA's Concorde fleet, a longtime symbol of the airline's transatlantic dominance. The carrier also acquired four additional slots at London's Heathrow Airport that same year from rival United Airline, which has been reorganizing under bankruptcy protection.

EXECUTIVES

Chairman: Lord Colin Marshall
Chief Executive and Director: Roderick Eddington, age 53, $788,357 pay
CFO: John Rishton, age 45, $256,000 pay
CIO: Paul Coby, age 47
Director Customer Service, Operations and Director: Mike Street, age 55, $467,596 pay
Director Engineering: Alan McDonald, age 52
Director Flight Operations: Lloyd Cromwell Griffiths, age 58
Director Investments and Alliances: Roger Maynard, age 60
Director Marketing and Commercial Development: Martin George, age 41
Director People: Neil Robertson, age 50
Director Worldwide Sales: Dale Moss, age 54
Secretary: Alan Buchanan, age 44
General Counsel: Robert Webb, age 55
Auditors: Ernst & Young

LOCATIONS

HQ: British Airways Plc
Waterside, Harmondsworth,
London UB7 0GB, United Kingdom
Phone: +44-20-8562-4444   **Fax:** +44-20-8759-4314
US HQ: 75-20 Astoria Blvd., Jackson Heights, NY 11370
US Phone: 347-418-4000
Web: www.british-airways.com

British Airways serves about 220 destinations in some 94 countries.

2002 Sales

	% of total
Europe	
UK	47
Continental Europe	17
The Americas	19
Africa, Middle East & India	10
Far East & Australia	7
Total	**100**

PRODUCTS/OPERATIONS

2002 Aircraft

	No.
Boeing 737	58
Boeing 747	56
Boeing 777	43
Airbus A319	33
Embraer	28
Turboprops	28
Airbus A320	24
Boeing 767	21
Avro RJ100	16
Boeing 757	13
British Aerospace 146	5
Concorde	5
Total	**330**

Major Subsidiaries and Affiliates
British Airways Capital Ltd. (airline finance)
British Airways Finance B.V. (airline finance, the
  Netherlands)
British Airways Holidays Ltd. (package holidays)
Comair Ltd. (18%, South Africa)
Deutsche BA Luftfahrtgesellschaft mbH (German airline)
Iberia Lineas Aéreas de España SA (9%, Spain)
Qantas Airways Ltd. (19%, Australia)

COMPETITORS

Air France	Northwest Airlines
All Nippon Airways	Ryanair
Delta	SAS
easyJet	Singapore Airlines
Japan Airlines	Brussels Airlines
KLM	UAL
Lufthansa	Virgin Atlantic Airways

HISTORICAL FINANCIALS

Company Type: Public

Income Statement

FYE: March 31

	REVENUE ($ mil.)	NET INCOME ($ mil.)	NET PROFIT MARGIN	EMPLOYEES
3/03	12,150	114	0.9%	57,014
3/02	11,887	(202)	—	61,460
3/01	13,151	162	1.2%	62,175
3/00	14,245	(33)	—	65,157
3/99	14,367	332	2.3%	64,051
3/98	14,447	769	5.3%	60,770
3/97	13,705	907	6.6%	58,210
3/96	11,843	722	6.1%	55,296
3/95	11,634	405	3.5%	53,060
3/94	9,360	425	4.5%	48,628
Annual Growth	**2.9%**	**(13.6%)**	**—**	**1.8%**

2003 Year-End Financials

Debt ratio: 304.1%	No. of shares (mil.): 151
Return on equity: 3.7%	Dividends
Cash ($ mil.): 351	Yield: 0.0%
Current ratio: 0.94	Payout: 0.0%
Long-term debt ($ mil.): 9,890	Market value ($ mil.): 2,541

Stock History

NYSE: BAB

	STOCK PRICE ($) FY Close	P/E High/Low		PER SHARE ($) Earnings	Dividends	Book Value
3/03	16.85	34	13	1.06	0.00	21.56
3/02	35.10	—	—	(1.88)	2.02	26.53
3/01	45.75	46	26	1.49	2.90	42.10
3/00	53.75	—	—	(0.32)	6.28	46.36
3/99	68.63	37	17	3.09	0.00	50.38
3/98	104.06	18	12	7.02	2.20	53.44
3/97	104.75	13	9	8.32	2.73	48.80
3/96	82.00	12	9	6.75	1.75	39.63
3/95	65.75	17	14	3.97	1.88	35.45
3/94	60.00	18	10	4.10	1.80	28.44
Annual Growth	**(13.2%)**	**—**	**—**	**(14.0%)**	**—**	**(3.0%)**

British American Tobacco p.l.c.

When people pick up smoking, British American Tobacco (BAT) picks up steam. Spun off in the reorganization of B.A.T Industries, BAT is the world's #2 tobacco firm (behind Altria Group) with about 15% of the market. It sells nearly 780 billion cigarettes in about 180 countries. BAT's international cigarette brands include Dunhill, Kent, Lucky Strike, and Pall Mall; it also makes loose tobacco and regional cigarette brands. Its US unit, Brown & Williamson (Kool and GPC cigarettes), is merging with the US tobacco business of R.J. Reynolds Tobacco (RJRT). Companies controlled by South African billionaire Anton Rupert own about 28% of BAT.

BAT will own 42% of the new company created by the Brown & Williamson/RJRT merger, which will be called Reynolds American.

BAT has been looking to emerging markets in Korea, Vietnam, and Nigeria for growth. It also has announced plans to buy Italy's state tobacco company, Ente Tabacchi Italiani, which sold more than 26 billion cigarettes in 2002.

After winning a tentative government approval to build a factory in China, the world's top tobacco market, BAT is moving its Asian headquarters to Hong Kong. Meanwhile, it's scaling back in the UK and Canada. By the end of 2004 it will close a manufacturing plant in Darlington, UK, cutting about 500 jobs. Its subsidiary, Imperial Tobacco Canada (not affiliated with the

UK's Imperial Tobacco), will cut almost 850 jobs when it closes a Montreal plant and other Canadian facilities at the end of 2003. Imperial Tobacco says it controls about 60% of the Canadian cigarette market.

HISTORY

After a year of vicious price-cutting between Imperial Tobacco (UK) and James Buchanan Duke's American Tobacco in the UK, Imperial counterattacked in the US. To end the cigarette price war in the UK, the firms created British American Tobacco (BAT) in 1902. The truce granted Imperial the British market, American the US market, and they jointly owned BAT in the rest of the world.

With Duke in control, BAT expanded into new markets. In China it was selling 25 billion cigarettes a year by 1920. When the Communist revolution ended BAT's operations in China, the company lost more than 25% of its sales (although China later reemerged as a major export market for the company's cigarettes).

A 1911 US antitrust action forced American to sell its interest in BAT and opened the US market to the company. BAT purchased US cigarette manufacturer Brown & Williamson in 1927 and continued to grow through geographical expansion until the 1960s. In 1973 BAT and Imperial each regained control of its own brands in the UK and Continental Europe. Imperial sold the last of its stake in BAT in 1980.

Fearing that mounting public concern over smoking would limit the cigarette market, BAT acquired nontobacco businesses; it changed its name to B.A.T Industries in 1976. The acquisitions of retailers Saks (1973), Argos (UK, 1979), Marshall Field (1982), and later, insurance firms, diversified the company's sales base. After a 1989 hostile takeover bid from Sir James Goldsmith, it sold its retail operations and retained its tobacco and financial services.

In 1994 B.A.T acquired the former American Tobacco for $1 billion. In 1997 the company acquired Cigarrera de Moderna (with 50% of Mexico's cigarette sales) and formed a joint venture with the Turkish tobacco state enterprise, Tekel.

B.A.T's tobacco operations were spun off in 1998 as British American Tobacco (BAT). The financial services operations were merged with Zurich Insurance in a transaction that created two holding companies: Allied Zurich (UK) and Zurich Allied (Switzerland). With the changes, Martin Broughton became chairman of BAT. In late 1998 BAT and its rivals reached a settlement covering 46 states for about $206 billion. (Four states already had settled for $40 billion.)

The company in 1999 paid $8.2 billion to buy Dutch cigarette company Rothmans International (Rothmans, Dunhill) from Switzerland's Compagnie Financiere Richemont and South Africa's Rembrandt Group — both controlled by Anton Rupert. With the purchase, BAT received a controlling stake in Canada's Rothmans, Benson & Hedges (RBH). Also that year the US government filed a massive lawsuit against Big Tobacco to recover health care costs and profits allegedly derived from fraud.

In early 2000 BAT bought the 58% of Canada's Imasco it didn't already own. Imasco sold off its financial services and BAT received Imasco's Imperial Tobacco unit (not related to the UK's Imperial Tobacco Group) in the deal. (Formerly called Imperial Tobacco Company of Canada, Imasco was created in 1908 with help from BAT.) BAT also unloaded its share of RBH via public offering.

In 2001 BAT bought the 40.5% of its BAT Australasia subsidiary (formed in 1999 through the Rothmans merger) it didn't already own. Broughton announced that year that the Chinese government had approved development plans that would allow the company to build a factory in China. The company also announced it would build the first foreign-owned cigarette factory in South Korea, the world's #8 tobacco market.

Increasing its Latin American regional presence, BAT purchased a controlling stake in Peru's top tobacco company, Tabacalera Nacional, and several of its suppliers. However, two months later BAT said it would not make a planned $25 million investment in the company. The announcement came soon after Peru raised taxes on cigarettes to 37.5%.

EXECUTIVES

Chairman: Martin F. Broughton, age 56, $2,266,310 pay
Deputy Chairman: Rt. Hon. Kenneth H. Clarke, age 62, $200,487 pay
Managing Director: Paul Adams, age 50, $797,250 pay
Director, Finance: Paul Rayner, age 48
Director, Operations: Peter Taylor, age 50
Regional Director, America-Pacific: Nick Brookes, age 52
Regional Director, Asia Pacific: Tony Jones, age 55
Regional Director, Africa and Middle East: Jacques Kruger, age 52
President and CEO, Brown and Williamson: Susan M. Ivey
Head, Dunhill Brand Group: Bart Alkemade
Head, Kent Brand Group: Arun Chogle
Head, Investor Relations: Ralph Edmondson
Corporate and Regulatory Affairs Director: Michael Prideaux, age 52
Marketing Director: Jimmi Rembiszewski, age 52
Development Director: Ben Stevens, age 43
Legal Director and General Counsel: Neil Withington, age 46
Regional Director, Latin America and Caribbean: Antonio Monteiro de Castro, age 58
Manager, Supply Chain Integration: Geoff Wells
Human Resources Director: Tessa Raeburn, age 52
Secretary: Aileen McDonald
Auditors: PricewaterhouseCoopers LLP

LOCATIONS

HQ: Globe House, 4 Temple Place, London WC2R 2PG, United Kingdom
Phone: +44-20-7845-1000   **Fax:** +44-20-7240-0555
US HQ: 200 Brown & Williamson Tower, 401 S. 4th St., Louisville, KY 40202-5090
US Phone: 502-568-7000   **US Fax:** 502-568-7494
Web: www.bat.com

2002 Sales

	% of total
America-Pacific	35
Europe	27
Asia/Pacific	16
Latin America	12
Africa and Middle East	10
Total	**100**

PRODUCTS/OPERATIONS

Selected International Cigarette Brands

Barclay	Lucky Strike
Benson & Hedges	Misty
Capri	Pall Mall
Carlton	Peter Stuyvesant
Dunhill	Player's
GPC	Rothmans
John Player Gold Leaf	State Express 555
Kent	Viceroy
Kool	Winfield

Selected Regions and Brands

Argentina (Jockey Club)	Latin America (Belmont, Derby, Free, Hollywood)
Asia-Pacific (Holiday)	
Australia (Stradbroke)	Mexico (Boots)
Canada (du Maurier)	Peru (Hamilton)
Europe (Golden American)	Poland (Jan III Sobieski)
Finland (North State)	Russia (Yava Gold)
Germany (HB)	South Africa (Courtleigh)
Hungary (Sopianae)	Switzerland (Parisienne)
India (Wills)	US (GPC)
Indonesia (Ardath)	Uzbekistan (Xon)
Ireland (Carrolls)	

Selected Other Products and Brands

Cigars (Dunhill, Mercator, Schimmelpenninck)
Fine cut tobaccos (Ajja, Belgam, Javaanse Jongens, Samson, Schwarzer Krauser)
Pipe tobaccos (Captain Black, Clan, Dunhill, Erinmore)

COMPETITORS

Altadis
Carolina Group
Gallaher
Imperial Tobacco
Japan Tobacco
Philip Morris International
Reemtsma
R.J. Reynolds Tobacco
Santa Fe Natural Tobacco
Swedish Match
Swisher International
Tiedemanns
Vector

HISTORICAL FINANCIALS

Company Type: Public

Income Statement

FYE: December 31

	REVENUE ($ mil.)	NET INCOME ($ mil.)	NET PROFIT MARGIN	EMPLOYEES
12/02	37,596	1,856	4.9%	85,819
12/01	35,627	1,471	4.1%	81,425
12/00	35,254	1,002	2.8%	86,805
12/99	30,374	898	3.0%	107,620
12/98	24,202	574	2.4%	101,081
12/97	11,766	852	7.2%	117,339
Annual Growth	26.2%	16.8%	—	(6.1%)

2002 Year-End Financials

Debt ratio: 89.1%	No. of shares (mil.): 1,091
Return on equity: 24.3%	Dividends
Cash ($ mil.): 2,856	Yield: 5.5%
Current ratio: 1.40	Payout: 67.7%
Long-term debt ($ mil.): 7,442	Market value ($ mil.): 21,489

Stock History

AMEX: BTI

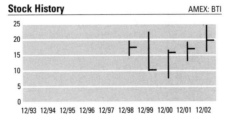

12/93 12/94 12/95 12/96 12/97 12/98 12/99 12/00 12/01 12/02

	STOCK PRICE ($) FY Close	P/E High/Low		PER SHARE ($) Earnings	Dividends	Book Value
12/02	19.70	15	10	1.61	1.09	7.66
12/01	17.00	15	10	1.28	0.95	6.35
12/00	15.81	19	9	0.86	0.86	7.11
12/99	10.25	26	12	0.87	1.05	7.16
12/98	17.50	27	21	0.73	0.00	0.14
Annual Growth	3.0%	—	—	21.9%	—	174.4%

British Broadcasting Corporation

The dominant broadcaster in the UK, British Broadcasting Corporation (BBC) operates two public TV channels, a 24-hour cable news channel, digital channels, five national radio networks, and an online news service. The BBC World Service broadcasts radio programming in more than 40 languages and is the sole source of news in some parts of the world. Subsidiaries BBC Worldwide and BBC Broadcast Limited offer international TV channels (BBC Prime, BBC America) and broadcast station management services, respectively. In addition, the company (often called The Beeb) owns 91% of beeb Ventures, which handles the company's e-commerce site and Internet access business and publishes books, magazines, and videos.

Established by royal charter, the BBC (once fondly referred to by Brits as "Auntie" for its prudish image) is governed by a 12-member board appointed by the Queen. It derives 75% of its sales from annual mandatory license fees paid by TV set owners in the UK. The BBC's growing involvement in commercial ventures under new director general Greg Dyke has prompted public grumbling that the broadcaster is straying from its public service role. It increased license fees to fund a move into digital television, which also is drawing fire. The BBC has launched a new digital TV service called "Freeview."

The company's BBC Technology Holdings Limited unit offers technology services designed specifically for media clients.

HISTORY

Established as the British Broadcasting Company Limited in 1922, the BBC was founded by a group of radio manufacturers aiming to block any single manufacturer from grabbing a broadcasting monopoly. Under general manager John Reith, BBC radio programming grew to include news, cultural events, sports, and weather. A burgeoning social and cultural presence led to its re-establishment in 1927 under a new royal charter. The organization was renamed the British Broadcasting Corporation, and the charter ensured it would remain outside the control of the British Parliament.

By 1935 BBC radio had reached about 95% of the British population. TV broadcasting debuted the next year, but the cost of TV sets limited audience numbers to about 20,000. Those who could afford a TV got to see the coronation of King George VI and Wimbledon. TV broadcasting would be short-lived, however: Beginning in 1939 and throughout WWII, the signal was blacked out when the transmitter proved a good aircraft direction finder.

Although TV screens went dark, BBC radio served a vital role during WWII. Its broadcasts to occupied territories and the airing of Prime Minister Winston Churchill's wartime speeches elevated the BBC's reputation as a news broadcaster.

BBC TV transmission resumed in 1946. The 1953 broadcast of the coronation of Queen Elizabeth II helped launch the television age of the

1950s. In 1955 commercial broadcaster Independent Television Network became the BBC's first rival for viewers. The BBC introduced its second public TV channel (BBC Two) in 1964. By 1969 both BBC One and BBC Two were broadcasting in color.

The corporate culture of the BBC during the 1970s and 1980s was dominated by financial upheaval. Budget cuts combined with growing competition prompted the formation of a committee to review the BBC's financing alternatives. Although the committee's 1986 report did not permit commercial advertising on the BBC, it did lead to more flexibility in funding.

Sir John Birt was appointed the BBC's director general in 1992, and the reorganization and cost-cutting program he instituted fueled the debate over the company's move toward commercialization. Through BBC Worldwide, the BBC inched away from its public service roots. In 1997 the BBC privatized its domestic TV and radio transmission business and launched a 24-hour cable news channel. UKTV (a commercial TV joint venture with Flextech) also went on the air that year. In 1998 the BBC began digital broadcasts. It teamed with Discovery Communications to launch BBC America, a US cable channel, and teamed with Scottish Power to provide free Internet access.

In 1999 Greg Dyke, who had been chief executive of Pearson Television, was named to succeed Birt, who left in January 2000. Shortly after Dyke took the reins, he announced a massive restructuring of the organization designed to cut costs (eliminating hundreds of jobs), foment more partnerships with private entities, and increase the amount spent on programming. In 2001 the BBC received approval for five digital radio and four digital TV channels. Dyke announced that he would explore privatizing parts of the company, such as its magazine and book operations.

In 2002 the company started commercial subsidiary BBC Broadcast, which offers channel management services.

EXECUTIVES

Chairman: Gavyn Davies, age 51
Director General: Greg Dyke, age 56
Chief Executive, BBC Ventures: Roger Flynn
Chief Executive, BBC Worldwide Limited: Rupert Gavin
Director, BBC News: Richard Sambrook
Director, BBC World Service and Global News:
  Mark Byford
Director, Drama, Entertainment, and Children:
  Alan Yentob, age56
Director, Finance, Property, and Business Affairs:
  John Smith, age 45
Director, Human Resources & International Communications: Stephen Dando, age 39
Director, Marketing & Communications: Andy Duncan
Director, Nations and Regions: Pat Loughrey
Director, New Media: Ashley Highfield, age 34
Director, Public Policy and Legal: Caroline Thomson
Director, Radio & Music: Jenny Abramsky, age 57
Director, Sport: Peter Salmon
Director, Strategy and Distribution: Carolyn Fairbairn
Director, Television: Jana Bennett
Joint Director, Factual and Learning: Glenwyn Benson
Director, Play-out and Media Services, BBC Broadcast Limited: Margaret Kelley
Auditors: KPMG

LOCATIONS

HQ: Broadcasting House, Portland Place,
  London W1A 1AA, United Kingdom
Phone: +44-20-7580-4468   **Fax:** +44-20-7765-1181
US HQ: 7475 Wisconsin Ave., Ste. 110,
  Bethesda, MD 20814
US Phone: 301-347-2233   **US Fax:** 301-656-8591
Web: www.bbc.co.uk

PRODUCTS/OPERATIONS

Selected Television Channels

BBC America (US cable channel)
BBC Four (digital channel focusing on culture and the arts)
BBC Knowledge (digital channel)
BBC News 24 (24-hour news programming)
BBC One (news and entertainment programming)
BBC Parliament (unedited coverage of the Parliament)
BBC Prime (international entertainment programming)
BBC Three (digital channel featuring youth-oriented programming)
BBC Two (entertainment and informational programming)
BBC World (international news programming)
CBBC (children's digital channel)
CBeebies (children's digital channel)

Selected Radio Networks

1Xtra from the BBC (digital channel aimed at hip-hop audiences)
6 Music from the BBC (digital channel aimed at popular music)
Five Live Sports Extra (digital channel focusing on live sports events)
Radio 1 (news and music programming)
Radio 2 (news and music programming)
Radio 3 (classical music programming)
Radio 4 (news, educational, dramatic, and documentary programming)
Radio 5 Live (sports radio programming)

Selected BBC Worldwide Magazines

BBC History
BBC Wildlife
eve
Good Homes
Radio Times
Robot Wars
star: the celebrity magazine
Top Gear

Selected Affiliations

Discovery Communications (US Cable TV)
Flextech (UK channel partnership)
FOXTEL (Australian TV venture)
Pearson Television (Australian TV venture)

Selected Subsidiaries and Units

BBC Broadcast Limited (channel management services)
BBC Resources (broadcast facilities)
BBC Online (Internet site)
BBC Technology Holdings (tech support)
BBC Worldwide (oversees BBC commercial interests)
beeb Ventures (91%, oversees BBC commercial Internet interests)

COMPETITORS

BSkyB	GWR Group
Capital Radio	Liberty Media
Carlton Communications	International
Channel 4	Pearson
Chrysalis Group	RTL Group
Daily Mail and General Trust	Scottish Radio
	SMG
Emap	Telewest
Flextech	Time Warner
Future Network	Yorkshire-Tyne Tees
Granada	Television Holdings

HISTORICAL FINANCIALS

Company Type: Government-owned

Income Statement

FYE: March 31

	REVENUE ($ mil.)	NET INCOME ($ mil.)	NET PROFIT MARGIN	EMPLOYEES
3/03	5,559	(495)	—	27,148
3/02	4,823	(23)	—	25,568
3/01	4,482	11	0.2%	24,219
3/00	4,781	(19)	—	23,640
3/99	4,593	—	—	23,119
3/98	4,159	—	—	21,023
3/97	3,825	—	—	19,517
3/96	2,776	—	—	19,000
3/95	2,826	—	—	
Annual Growth	**8.8%**	**—**	**—**	**5.2%**

2003 Year-End Financials

Debt ratio: 187.1%   Current ratio: 1.49
Return on equity: —   Long-term debt ($ mil.): 251
Cash ($ mil.): 109

Net Income History

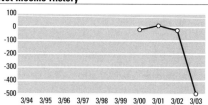

British Sky Broadcasting Group plc

The lofty British Sky Broadcasting Group (BSkyB) is the UK's #1 pay-TV provider. BSkyB distributes entertainment, news, and sports programming to 10.2 million subscribers in the UK and Ireland, including 6 million who subscribe to its digital direct-to-home (DTH) satellite service. The company terminated its analog satellite service in 2001. BSkyB also offers interactive TV services, holds broadcast rights to the leading football (soccer) leagues in England and Scotland, and has minority stakes in several clubs. Rupert Murdoch's News Corp. owns 36% of BSkyB.

Besides scoring big points with broadcasting rights to the leading football (soccer) leagues, BSkyB owns sport-related Web site operator Sports Internet. BSkyB also has acquired British Interactive Broadcasting, which operates the Open interactive TV service. In addition, the company resells fixed-line and mobile phone services.

However, BSkyB is moving away from telephone-only services and focusing more on its betting services offered through its interactive TV division. The company has also inked a deal with AOL which will allow BSkyB customers to use AOL's instant messaging and email services on their televisions.

To boost brand awareness, BSkyB broadcasts three channels — Sky News, Sky Sports News, and Sky Travel — over a free-to-air network run by the BBC and Crown Castle. With 15 million untapped homes in the UK, the company is hoping increased brand awareness will bring in more subscriber revenue, which currently accounts for 80% of BSkyB's revenues. Advertising and interactive services account for 7% and 9%, respectively.

HISTORY

Australian-born media czar Rupert Murdoch, after taking control of several British newspapers, moved into satellite TV service in the UK in 1989 when his News Corp. holding company started Sky Network Television. Broadcasting SkyTV's four channels via satellites owned by the Luxembourg-based Astra group allowed Murdoch to avoid restrictions of the British Broadcasting Act, which prohibited owners of national newspapers from owning more than 20% of a TV company.

In 1990 a consortium of companies, including Chargeurs, Granada, and Pearson, set up rival service British Satellite Broadcasting. The rivals faced a consumer market slow to adapt to new technology and a shrinking advertising base caused by an economic recession; both companies posted huge losses (SkyTV's weekly losses grew to more than $20 million in 1990). In the wake of such financial hemorrhaging, the firms merged that year and became British Sky Broadcasting (BSkyB), a slimmer operation with five channels. The small stake held by Chargeurs was later transferred to its Pathé communications unit.

In 1993 BSkyB teamed up with US media group Viacom to produce a Nickelodeon channel (children's programming) for the UK market. Then the firm allied with home shopping channel QVC to launch QVC UK. By year's end, more than 3 million UK homes were receiving BSkyB's programs.

BSkyB sold about 20% of itself to the public in 1994, dropping News Corp.'s stake from 50% to 40%. That year it reinforced its position as the top UK sports broadcaster by launching Sky Sports 2. BSkyB teamed with rival BBC in 1995 to acquire more sports programming. It also formed an alliance with international news agency Reuters in an effort to strengthen its Sky News Channel.

In 1996 BSkyB announced a joint venture with Kirch Gruppe (now TaurusHolding) to sell digital TV in Germany, but the deal later fell through. In 1997 BSkyB began developing digital satellite TV and interactive services in the UK through British Interactive Broadcasting, a joint venture with British Telecommunications (now BT Group), HSBC Holdings, and Matsushita Electric Industrial. (The service, Sky Digital, was launched in 1998 and offers subscribers about 150 channels.)

Managing director Sam Chisholm and his deputy, David Chance, resigned in 1997, opening the door for Murdoch's 29-year-old daughter, Elisabeth, to take a greater role at BSkyB. (She left the company in 2000.) Mark Booth (formerly with Murdoch's Japanese Sky Broadcasting) became CEO. BSkyB launched digital pay-per-view TV in the UK in 1997.

In 1999 the government blew the whistle on BSkyB's plan to buy UK soccer team Manchester United for $1 billion, saying it would have reduced competition in soccer broadcasting. (BSkyB retained its minority stake in the team.) Fox/Liberty Networks CEO Tony Ball replaced Booth as CEO in 1999 after Booth was named to head a News Corp.-backed new media company.

French conglomerate Vivendi (now Vivendi Universal) bought Pathé's stake in BSkyB, along with those of Granada and Pearson, and Rupert Murdoch took over as chairman of BSkyB, replacing Pathé's Jerome Seydoux. Vivendi announced in 2000 that it would sell its BSkyB stake to clear regulatory hurdles in its bid to acquire Canada's Seagram and take over the Universal entertainment group. That year BSkyB paid $1 billion for a 24% stake (later reduced to 22%) in Germany's KirchPayTV.

News Corp. in 2000 spun off its satellite holdings, including BSkyB, to form a new company, Sky Global Networks, in large part to accommodate Murdoch's acquisition of US-based DIRECTV. A planned IPO was postponed in 2001 after Murdoch pulled out of the bidding for the market-leading satellite operator. That year BSkyB completed the transition to an all-digital network and discontinued analog service.

EXECUTIVES

Chairman: K. Rupert Murdoch, age 72
Chief Executive: Anthony (Tony) Ball, age 46, $3,054,709 pay
COO: Richard Freudenstein, age 37
CFO: Martin Stewart, age 39, $1,046,752 pay
Managing Director Sky Interactive: Jon Florsheim
Managing Director Sky Networks: Dawn Airey, age 41
Managing Director Sky Sports: Vic Wakeling, age 59
Group Director Engineering and Platform Technology: Alun Webber, age 36
Director Broadcasting and Production: Mark Sharman, age 52
Director Corporate Communications: Julian Eccles
Director Group IT and Strategy: Simon Post, age 37
Director Sales: Peter Shea, age 44
Head of Legal and Business Affairs: Deanna Bates
Head of New Music Channels: Lester Mordue
Company Secretary: David (Dave) Gormley
Auditors: Deloitte & Touche

LOCATIONS

HQ: 6 Centaurs Business Park, Grant Way, Isleworth, London TW7 5QD, United Kingdom
Phone: +44-20-7705-3000   **Fax:** +44-20-7705-3060
Web: www.sky.com

British Sky Broadcasting provides cable and satellite TV services throughout the UK and Ireland.

PRODUCTS/OPERATIONS

Selected Services

Sky Box Office (pay-per-view movies)
Sky Cinema (classic cinema programming)
Sky MovieMax (action, comedy, and adventure movies)
Sky News (five news channels)
Sky One (key general entertainment channel)
Sky Pictures (original film production)
Sky Productions (original non-film production)
Sky Premier (premium movie channel)
Sky Sports (five sports channels plus MUTV)

Selected Subsidiaries and Affiliates

Adventure One (50%, adventure programming)
attheraces (33%, broadcast horse racing)
Australian News Channel Pty Limited (33%, 24-hour news)
British Interactive Broadcasting Holdings Limited (interactive TV services)
British Sky Broadcasting Limited (satellite TV services)
British Sky Broadcasting SA (satellite transponder leasing, Luxembourg)
Granada Sky Broadcasting Limited (80%, general entertainment channels)
The History Channel (UK) (50%, history programming)
MUTV (33%, Manchester United football channel)
National Geographic Channel UK (50%, natural history channel)

Nickelodeon UK (50%, children's programming)
Paramount Comedy Channel (25%, comedy programming)
QVC (UK) (20%, home shopping channel)
Sky In-Home Service Limited (supply, installation, and maintenance of satellite TV equipment)
Sky Subscribers Services Limited (support services)
Sky Television Limited (investment holding company)
Sky Travel (travel programming)
Sky Ventures Limited (joint ventures holding company)

COMPETITORS

Groupe AB	NTL
BBC	RTL Group
CanWest Global	SMG
Communications	Telewest
Carlton Communications	UGC Europe
Channel 4	UnitedGlobalCom
Flextech	Yorkshire-Tyne Tees
Granada	Television Holdings
Metromedia International	

HISTORICAL FINANCIALS
Company Type: Public

Income Statement
FYE: June 30

	REVENUE ($ mil.)	NET INCOME ($ mil.)	NET PROFIT MARGIN	EMPLOYEES
6/03	5,253	314	6.0%	9,132
6/02	4,251	(2,117)	—	9,083
6/01	3,260	(761)	—	9,948
6/00	2,801	(412)	—	10,730
6/99	2,439	(450)	—	8,271
6/98	2,390	415	17.4%	4,634
6/97	2,114	480	22.7%	4,580
6/96	1,563	362	23.2%	4,025
6/95	1,240	218	17.6%	3,054
6/94	850	143	16.9%	2,403
Annual Growth	**22.4%**	**9.1%**	**—**	**16.0%**

2003 Year-End Financials

Debt ratio: —
Return on equity: —
Cash ($ mil.): 76
Current ratio: 1.08
Long-term debt ($ mil.): 1,899

Net Income History
NYSE: BSY

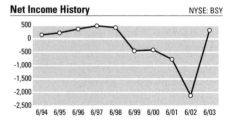

BT Group plc

Once upon a time, BT Group rivals could have fit into one of the company's signature red phone booths. Though competition has taken its toll, BT Group still wears the crown as the UK's leading telecommunications carrier. Formerly known as British Telecommunications, the BT Group offers local and long-distance phone service with more than 29 million access lines and provides Internet and other data services. In a major reorganization, BT Group has turned itself into a holding company. Ordered to upgrade and open its domestic networks, it has split its UK fixed-line network operations into separate wholesale and retail businesses.

BT Group has countered increasing competition and mounting debt woes through restructuring that includes the sale of its Yellow Pages unit, Yell, to two buyout firms, Hicks, Muse, Tate & Furst and Apax Partners. And in a further effort to cut debt, it sold much of its property holdings and unloaded interests in the Pacific Rim.

To complete its restructuring, the company has spun off its domestic and international wireless businesses, combined under the mmO2 brand (formerly BT Wireless), which includes BT Cellnet, a leading UK mobile phone operator. The decision leaves BT Group as the only top-tier European telecom firm without a wireless network. The company also has agreed to sell a 77% stake in Brightstar, its technology incubator that is a unit of its BTexact Technologies division, to private equity investment firm Coller in a deal valued at $77 million. BT Group will hold on to the remaining 23% stake.

BT also has dismantled Concert, its failed business telecom services joint venture with AT&T that combined most of the companies' international operations. In addition, it has sold its 26% stake in France's Cegetel to Vivendi Universal and has unloaded other noncore assets, including its 21% stake in the Hong Kong wireless carrier SmarTone Telecommunications.

BT is refocusing its other international holdings to concentrate on Europe. It has teamed up with Microsoft to deliver broadband applications using the MSN 8 Web browser and the company has created separate units for its broadband Internet protocol business and its consumer ISP (BTopenworld). Data transmission makes up more and more of BT's network traffic. The group has also announced plans to reduce its workforce by about 17% by 2005.

BT Group operates primarily in the UK, but the BT Group empire stretches into other parts of Western Europe and across the pond to North America. The company has introduced a new corporate identity, its first change since 1991, which, the company said, better reflects the range of activities that BT Group now encompasses. The company also has announced an expansion of its information communications technology services offered to multi-site corporations in the US at the same time it announced a $7.4 million expansion of its multi-protocol label switching (MPLS) capacity in North America.

HISTORY

In 1879 the British Post Office (now known as Royal Mail Group and formerly Consignia) got the exclusive right to operate telegraph systems. When private firms tried to offer phone service, the government objected, arguing in court that its telegraph monopoly was imperiled. The courts agreed, and the Post Office was empowered to license private phone companies, collect a 10% royalty, and operate its own systems.

The private National Telephone Company emerged as the leading phone outfit, competing with the Post Office. When National's license expired in 1911, the Post Office took over and became the monopoly phone company. In 1936 the phone system introduced its familiar red public call offices (phone booths), designed for King George V's jubilee.

Under a 1981 law, telecommunications were split from the Post Office and placed under the newly created British Telecommunications (BT). The government also allowed competitor Mer-

cury Communications (now One 2 One) to compete. The Thatcher government soon called for BT's privatization.

After the Telecommunications Act of 1984, BT went public in one of the largest UK stock offerings in history. The act set up the regulatory Office of Telecommunications (OFTEL). The next year Cellnet, BT's joint venture with Securicor, launched its mobile phone network. To become a multinational concern, BT bought control of Canadian phone equipment maker Mitel (1986, sold in 1992) and 20% of firm McCaw Cellular (1989, sold to AT&T in 1994).

In 1990 the British government opened the UK to more phone competition and BT responded with improvements to its network and a workforce reduction. The government sold almost all of its remaining shares in BT in 1993. The next year the company bought a 20% stake in MCI, the #2 US long-distance carrier, and the two formed Concert, a joint venture to compete in the international arena. BT's 1996 attempt to buy Cable and Wireless failed when the company asked for more than BT was willing to pay.

In 1996 BT announced a plan to buy out MCI, but as losses mounted from MCI's expansion into the US local market, BT in 1997 lowered its bid and lost MCI to upstart WorldCom. In 1998 BT bought the remaining 25% stake in Concert and found a new US partner in AT&T; the two agreed in 1999 to merge most of their international operations in a $10 billion global joint venture that took the Concert name (but after repeated losses the two parent companies dismantled the venture in 2002).

Also in 1999 BT expanded in continental Europe, Latin America (a 20% stake in IMPSAT), Asia (with AT&T, a 30% stake in Japan Telecom), and the US, where it bought systems integration firm Control Data Systems and Yellow Book USA. At home BT bought out Securicor's stake in Cellnet. UK regulators also ordered the company to upgrade its UK phone network and open it to rivals by 2001.

BT bought Ireland's Esat Telecom in 2000. That year the government sold its remaining stake in BT and the company bought Telenor's stake in VIAG Interkom; early the next year the company took full ownership of the German mobile phone company. Also in early 2001, BT sold its stakes in Japan Telecom and J-Phone Communications to Vodafone, which later that year bought BT's Airtel Móvil interest.

EXECUTIVES

Chairman: Sir Christopher Bland, age 65, $729,907 pay
Deputy Chairman: Sir Anthony Greener, age 63, $128,304 pay
Chief Executive: Bernardus J. (Ben) Verwaayen, age 50, $3,099,254 pay
Group Finance Director: Ian Livingston, age 37, $1,590,970 pay
Group Strategy Director and Regional Director, London: Clive R. Ansell
Managing Director, BT Openworld: Duncan Ingram
Managing Director, ICT (Information and Communications Technology) Services: Bill Halbert
Managing Director, Products and Enterprises: Steve Andrews
Managing Director-select, Consumer and Ventures Division: Gavin Patterson, age 36
Senior Director, BT Retail: Carol Borghesi

Chief Executive, BT Exact: Stewart Davies
Chief Executive, BT Global Services: Andy Green, age 46, $1,084,882 pay
Chief Executive, BT Mobile: Steven Evans, age 48
Chief Executive, BT Retail: Pierre Danon, age 47, $1,181,823 pay
Chief Executive, BT Wholesale: Paul Reynolds, age 45, $1,043,539 pay
Chief Executive, Syntegra: Tim Smart
CTO: Matthew W. Bross, age 42
Director New Services and Strategy: John Butler
Company Secretary: Larry Stone
Auditors: PricewaterhouseCoopers

LOCATIONS

HQ: BT Centre, 81 Newgate St.,
    London EC1A 7AJ, United Kingdom
Phone: +44-20-7356-5000   **Fax:** +44-20-7356-5520
US HQ: 40 E. 52nd St., New York, NY 10022
US Phone: 212-418-7787
Web: www.btplc.com

BT Group operates primarily in the UK, but it owns or has stakes in operations in the Americas, the Asia/Pacific region, and Western Europe.

2003 Sales

	% of total
Europe	
UK	87
Other countries	11
Asia/Pacific	2
America	—
Total	**100**

PRODUCTS/OPERATIONS

2003 Sales

	$ mil.	% of total
BT Retail	18,246	45
BT Wholesale	15,408	38
BT Global Services	6,893	17
Other revenues	53	—
Adjustments	(11,004)	—
Total	**29,596**	**100**

Selected Operating Units

BT Exact (research and development)
BT Global Services (formerly BT Ignite, international data and IP (Internet protocol) services)
    Syntegra (business transformation and change management services)
BT Retail (consumer communications services and products)
    BT Broadband (high-speed Internet access)
    BT Openworld (Internet access and portal services)
BT Wholesale (carrier-level network and communications services and products)

COMPETITORS

Accenture
Cable & Wireless
Centrica
 Telecommunications
COLT Telecom
Deutsche Telekom
Energis
France Telecom
Freeserve
NTL
KPN
T-Com
Telecom Italia
Telefónica
Verizon
Vodafone
WorldCom

HISTORICAL FINANCIALS

Company Type: Public

Income Statement

FYE: March 31

	REVENUE ($ mil.)	NET INCOME ($ mil.)	NET PROFIT MARGIN	EMPLOYEES
3/03	29,596	4,245	14.3%	104,700
3/02	26,293	1,418	5.4%	108,600
3/01	28,953	(2,565)	—	137,000
3/00	29,820	3,275	11.0%	136,800
3/99	27,322	4,808	17.6%	124,700
3/98	26,145	2,852	10.9%	129,200
3/97	24,486	3,405	13.9%	127,500
3/96	22,048	3,031	13.7%	130,700
3/95	22,521	2,806	12.5%	—
3/94	20,307	2,624	12.9%	—
Annual Growth	4.3%	5.5%	—	(3.1%)

2003 Year-End Financials

Debt ratio: 509.4%
Return on equity: 231.7%
Cash ($ mil.): 144
Current ratio: 1.19
Long-term debt ($ mil.): 21,266
No. of shares (mil.): 867
Dividends
  Yield: 2.8%
  Payout: 14.5%
Market value ($ mil.): 22,059

Stock History

NYSE: BTY

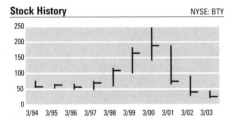

| | 3/94 | 3/95 | 3/96 | 3/97 | 3/98 | 3/99 | 3/00 | 3/01 | 3/02 | 3/03 |

	STOCK PRICE ($) FY Close	P/E High/Low		PER SHARE ($) Earnings	Dividends	Book Value
3/03	25.44	19	10	4.90	0.71	4.81
3/02	40.18	11	4	1.70	0.00	(0.59)
3/01	74.30	—	—	(3.93)	3.55	30.28
3/00	188.13	50	29	4.92	3.54	38.68
3/99	164.19	33	19	7.30	5.46	37.22
3/98	109.38	26	14	4.46	0.00	28.12
3/97	70.00	14	9	5.38	1.85	28.68
3/96	56.63	14	11	4.82	2.97	30.75
3/95	63.25	14	12	4.51	2.84	31.19
3/94	57.50	18	13	4.23	2.54	31.14
Annual Growth	(8.7%)	—	—	1.6%	(13.2%)	(18.7%)

Bull

This Bull is having a tough time at the IT rodeo. The company has sold much of its Integris unit, retaining operations in France, Italy, and Greece under the Bull Services division. Bull Services offers outsourcing, consulting, network integration, and other information technology (IT) services. The company's Bull Infrastructure and Systems unit sells PCs, servers, storage, and other hardware. Bull's Evidian subsidiary offers Internet security and network management software. The company has sold its smart card operation and split its hardware and service units into independent entities. The European Union is putting legal pressure on the French government to make Bull repay a 2002 loan from the government.

The company's board of directors opted in late 2003 to seek a capital infusion of 44 million, three-quarters of which would be guaranteed by some of its largest shareholders.

Japanese computer maker NEC, Motorola, and state-owned France Telecom each owns around 17% of Bull. The French government owns about 16% of the company.

Bull's clients come primarily from Europe in the government, finance, telecommunications, and manufacturing markets.

HISTORY

Bull is named for Norwegian engineer Fredrik Bull, who in 1921 invented a punch card machine. Georges Vieillard, a French bank employee, bought the patents for Bull's machine in 1931. Vieillard, who wanted to develop a better adding machine, persuaded the owners of a punch card supplier to finance his venture, and Compagnie des Machines Bull was incorporated in Paris in 1933.

The company started competing with IBM in 1935, after unveiling a tabulator capable of printing up to 150 lines a minute. Bull went on to confound its American rival by pioneering the use of germanium diodes (instead of electron tubes) in its first mainframe computer (1952). But the battle of one-upmanship was costly. Bull defaulted on a $4 million loan payment in 1964 and, faced with financial ruin, jumped at the chance when General Electric (US) offered to buy a 50% stake (later increased to 66%). The company (renamed Bull-GE) continued to lose money until 1969. It became Compagnie Honeywell Bull in 1970 when GE sold its computer businesses to Honeywell.

Meanwhile, in 1966 the French government had formed Compagnie Internationale pour l'Informatique (CII) to ensure the survival of the French computer industry. CII merged with Honeywell Bull in 1975 to form CII-Honeywell Bull (CII-HB). Initially Honeywell owned a 47% stake in the company, but in 1982 it accepted a gradual buyout offer from the French government. CII-HB then merged with three other French computer companies (Transac, Sems, and R2E) to form Groupe Bull in 1983.

In 1987 the company entered a US-based three-way mainframe computer partnership (Honeywell Bull) with Honeywell and NEC. Originally owning 42.5% of the venture, Bull upped its share to 72% and renamed it Bull HN Information Systems. In 1989 Bull bought Zenith's ZDS, a leading US laptop and PC maker.

In 1991 the company acquired the rest of Bull HN. The next year the European Commission approved a state injection of $1.3 billion into debt-laden Bull. In 1993 the firm bought a 19.9% stake in Packard Bell and teamed it with Zenith Data Systems to jointly develop desktop PCs.

Jean-Marie Descarpentries was named CEO in 1993 (the company's third CEO in as many years). He reduced Bull's Paris offices from 25 to five and reorganized the sprawling conglomerate. In 1995 Bull recorded a small profit, its first since 1988.

To improve Packard Bell's cash flow, in 1996 Bull and NEC provided a $650 million infusion — partly in cash and partly through Packard Bell's acquisition of Zenith.

In 1997 Descarpentries stepped down as chairman. He was succeeded by former Lyonnaise des Eaux (now Suez) executive Guy de Panafieu, who moved to expand its core strengths in servers, services, and software technology. In 1998 the company shortened its name to Bull and bought NBS Technology's European smart card operations.

In 1999 Packard Bell NEC's operations were folded into NEC, and the Packard Bell brand name was eliminated. Bull said it would take up to about a $230 million charge related to the closing. In 2000 Bull formed its Evidian subsidiary to boost its e-business security software line and acquired Arcanet, Italy's leading telecom applications company.

The company continued its reorganization in 2001, cutting jobs and streamlining its hardware and services businesses into two autonomous units: Bull Infrastructure and Systems (hardware and infrastructure) and Integris (IT services). Bull also sold its smart card business to Schlumberger for about $325 million. Late that year Panafieu stepped down and was replaced by Pierre Bonelli.

Bonelli, who disagreed with Panafieu's planned sale of Integris to Groupe Steria, finally agreed to a revised acquisition at the end of 2001. Bull retained its Integris operations (under the division name Bull Services) in France, Italy, and Greece, but sold the rest of its European services business to Groupe Steria.

In 2002 the French government bailed out the struggling company with a $305 million cash injection. Bull announced that it would cut an additional 1,500 jobs in order to reduce costs.

EXECUTIVES

Chairman and CEO: Pierre S. E. Bonelli
Deputy COO and Director, Finance and Administration: Gervais Pellissier
Chairman, Bull International: Antonio Barrera de Irimo
CEO, Bull Services France: André Felix
CEO, Bull Western Europe and South America: Lucio Rispo
COO, Bull Technologies: Noël Saille
VP and General Manager, Bull Services, Public Sector Business Unit: Mike Berman
Director, Bull Asia, Africa, Eastern Europe: Luc Saint-Jeannet
Director, Central Marketing: Danielle Asheuer
Director, Corporate and Financial Communications: Marie-Claude Bessis
Director, Group Strategy: Geraldine Capdeboscq
Director, Human Resources: Patrick Semtob, age 52
Director, Organisation and Special Projects: Jean Bréchon
Director, Research and Development: Michel Guillemet
General Manager, Bull-NEC Strategy Partnership Office: Sadakazu Matsuba
Open Source Strategist: Jean-Pierre Laisne
Scientific Advisor to Executive Management: Gérard Roucairol
Auditors: Deloitte Touche Tohmatsu

LOCATIONS

HQ: 68, route de Versailles, 78430 Louveciennes, France
Phone: +33-1-39-66-60-60   **Fax:** +33-1-39-66-60-62
US HQ: 300 Concord Rd., Billerica, MA 01821
US Phone: 978-294-6000   **US Fax:** 978-294-3635
Web: www.bull.com

Bull has offices in more than 50 countries.

2002 Sales

	% of total
France	49
Other European countries	35
North America	7
Africa/Asia	6
South America	3
Total	**100**

PRODUCTS/OPERATIONS

Products and Services

Bull Services (Integris)
Consulting
Desktop support
Network integration
Outsourcing
Systems and maintenance

Bull Infrastructure and Systems
Computer systems
   Communications products (France Telecom,
     Motorola, 3COM)
   PCs (NEC)
   Servers (GCOS, Intel, UNIX)
   Storage products (EMC and Epoch)
Smart cards, terminals, and related equipment

Other
Security, networking, and Web applications software
  (Evidian subsidiary)

COMPETITORS

Accenture	Hewlett-Packard
Acer	Hitachi
Altran Technologies	HP Services
ARES	IBM Global Services
Atos Origin	LogicaCMG
Aubay	NEC
Ausy	SAP Systems Integration
Cap Gemini	Satyam
CBGI	Siemens
Computer Associates	Sopra
Computer Sciences	Steria
CS Communication	Sun Microsystems
Dell	Team Partners Group
EDS	TEAMLOG
Finsiel	Toshiba
Groupe Focal	Transiciel
Fujitsu Services	Unilog
Gateway	Unisys
Getronics	Valtech
GFI Informatique	

HISTORICAL FINANCIALS

Company Type: Public

Income Statement

FYE: December 31

	REVENUE ($ mil.)	NET INCOME ($ mil.)	NET PROFIT MARGIN	EMPLOYEES
12/02	1,587	(574)	—	8,351
12/01	2,254	(224)	—	12,731
12/00	3,055	(229)	—	17,209
12/99	3,795	(290)	—	18,358
12/98	4,435	4	0.1%	20,646
12/97	4,103	101	2.5%	21,267
12/96	4,596	72	1.6%	21,700
12/95	5,430	62	1.1%	24,000
12/94	5,605	(367)	—	27,902
12/93	4,771	(856)	—	31,735
Annual Growth	(11.5%)	—	—	(13.8%)

2002 Year-End Financials

Debt ratio: —
Return on equity: —
Cash ($ mil.): 123

Current ratio: 0.85
Long-term debt ($ mil.): 211

Net Income History

Euronext Paris: BUL

Cable and Wireless plc

Telegraph cables and short-wave radio have given way to webs of optical fiber, but Cable and Wireless nonetheless promotes its famous name like never before. The company has been rerouting its corporate strategy and is taking on the business world's data needs, focusing on the demand for business data and Internet services. But falling revenues and decreasing demand for services has forced the unit to close some operations and led to the sale of its US operations. Cable & Wireless has reorganized geographically with a customer focus and has discontinued the Global and Regional division distinctions. The company has tried to sharpen its focus through acquisitions and divestitures.

In its buying and selling spree, Cable and Wireless intended to rid itself of noncore holdings and to invest in the development of IP (Internet protocol) networks and Web hosting facilities. But overcapacity in the market has forced the company to withdraw from many fronts and it is refocusing on its UK operations and those in the Caribbean.

The company has sold its controlling interest in Cable & Wireless Optus, and in 2001 Optus agreed to be acquired by Singapore Telecommunications. Also that year Cable and Wireless bought US-based Digital Island and in 2002 it completed its acquisition of assets from bankrupt Exodus Communications. But the Exodus purchase has proved unwise and the company is cutting 30% of its work force, 3,500 jobs, from C&W Global, its Internet unit. The division is now focusing on multinational clients and is supported by the company's international connections and fiber-optic networks. The company also has said it is cutting as much as 65% of its work force in continental Europe, or about 800 jobs. It is selling some operations in Europe, including businesses offering domestic-only services in Belgium, the Netherlands, Russia, Sweden, and Switzerland. The company also has sold its 14% stake in Hong Kong operator PCCW.

In the US, the company has agreed to sell its operations, including Cable & Wireless Internet Services and Cable & Wireless USA, to private investment firm Gores Technology. The deal, valued at $125 million, is conditioned on US operations entering Chapter 11 bankruptcy.

Also Cable and Wireless purchased bankrupt PSINet's Japan unit in 2002 and announced plans to build a fiber-optic network in Japan. It also has teamed up with Alcatel to lay a new transatlantic cable for Internet traffic.

Claiming that few acquisition targets remained, the company then announced plans to return $2.5 billion to shareholders through a stock buy-back plan and special dividend. However, company executives faced heated scrutiny by shareholders when an unexpected tax liability of more than $2 billion surfaced.

Cable and Wireless offers both wireless and fixed-line voice and services in the Caribbean, Panama, Macao, the Middle East, and in Southeast Asia.

HISTORY

British cable and telegraph veteran John Pender began Eastern Telegraph in 1872. When he died in 1896, Eastern and associated companies owned one of every three miles of telegraph cable on the planet.

As the new century began, telecommunications expanded to include the wireless radio communications promoted by inventor Guglielmo Marconi, head of the UK's Marconi Wireless Telegraph. After WWI, the industry grew in importance, and, partly to counter a threat from a new US company called ITT, UK companies, including Marconi Wireless and Eastern Telegraph, joined in 1929 to form Cable and Wireless (C&W).

C&W began providing telegraph and telephone services in the UK's far-flung colonies, from Hong Kong to the Philippines to the Cayman Islands. It was nationalized in 1947, and in the 1950s C&W began losing franchises in former colonies or had local governments strip it of its monopolies.

The Thatcher government returned C&W to private ownership in 1985. C&W began building a network of undersea fiber-optic cables and satellites to link the Caribbean, Hong Kong, Japan, the UK, and the US. To complete the task, C&W assembled the world's largest commercial fleet of cable ships.

C&W joined British Petroleum (BP) and Barclays Merchant Bank in 1982 to form Mercury Communications as a rival to giant British Telecommunications (BT, now BT Group). C&W bought out BP and Barclays in 1984. The next year Mercury won the right to interconnect with BT.

As the 1990s began, C&W was adrift. In 1993 C&W and U S WEST's cable unit (later MediaOne) launched a digital cellular service — One 2 One — in the UK, but overall C&W wasn't making much headway in Europe. In 1996 merger talks with BT to build the world's largest telecom company failed. At this low point, Dick Brown, an American, was named C&W's CEO. Under Brown's direction C&W disposed of underperforming assets and created Cable & Wireless Communications (CWC) by combining Mercury with cable firms NYNEX CableComms, Bell Cablemedia, and Videotron.

When the UK handed over Hong Kong to China in 1997, C&W — in a bid to get access to the mainland market — sold a stake in Hong Kong Telecom to China Telecom. When MCI agreed to merge with WorldCom in 1998, C&W bought MCI's Internet business (later selling the US dial-up operation to Prodigy), a major step toward its emerging data-centric strategy.

Hong Kong Telecom became Cable & Wireless HKT in 1999. Brown left that year and was succeeded by Graham Wallace, former boss of CWC. C&W won a bidding war with NTT for Japan's International Digital Communications (now Cable & Wireless IDC). But selling was generally the order of the day: C&W sold its Global Marine undersea-cable operations to Global Crossing and struck a deal (which closed in 2000) to sell its UK consumer phone and cable TV business to rival NTL. It also sold One 2 One for about $11 billion to Deutsche Telekom.

In 2000 C&W announced plans to build a fiber-optic network in Japan. It took an 11% stake in Japanese ISP Garnet Connections and continued to acquire European ISPs. That year the company completed the sale of Cable & Wireless HKT, Hong Kong's dominant telecom carrier, to Pacific Century CyberWorks (now called PCCW).

EXECUTIVES

Chairman: Richard D. Lapthorne, age 60
Executive Deputy Chairman: Robert O. (Rob) Rowley, age 53
Deputy Chairman-select: Lord George Robertson
CEO: Francesco Caio, age 45
COO: Kevin Loosemore, age 44
Group CFO: Charles Herlinger
Group Director, Mobile: Barbara Poggiali
CEO Cable & Wireless USA: Simon Cunningham
CEO Cable & Wireless Japan/Asia: Phil Green
Company Secretary: Ken Claydon, age 59
VP, Investor Relations: Virginia Porter
Auditors: KPMG Audit Plc

LOCATIONS

HQ: 124 Theobalds Rd.,
    London WC1X 8RX, United Kingdom
Phone: +44-20-7315-4000   **Fax:** +44-20-7315-5198
US HQ: 8219 Leesburg Pike, Vienna, VA 22182
US Phone: 703-790-5300   **US Fax:** 571-203-3993
Web: www.cwplc.com

Cable and Wireless has operations in the Asia/Pacific region, the Caribbean basin, Europe, the Indian Ocean, the Middle East, Panama, and the US.

2003 Sales

	$ mil.	% of total
Cable & Wireless Global		
Europe		
UK	2,707	39
Other European countries	480	7
US	833	12
Japan	511	7
Cable & Wireless Regional		
Caribbean	1,666	24
Asia	243	4
Other regions	308	4
Other revenues	192	3
Total	**6,940**	**100**

PRODUCTS/OPERATIONS

Selected Subsidiaries and Affiliates

Cable & Wireless (Barbados) Limited (81%)
Cable & Wireless (Cayman Islands) Limited
Cable & Wireless Global Limited (formerly Cable & Wireless Global Markets Limited)
Cable & Wireless IDC Inc. (98%, Japan)
Cable & Wireless Internet Services Inc. (US)
Cable & Wireless Jamaica Limited (82%)
Cable & Wireless Panama SA (49%)
Cable & Wireless UK (formerly Cable & Wireless Communications Mercury)
Cable & Wireless USA, Inc.
Cable & Wireless (West Indies) Limited
Companhia de Telecomunicaçes de Macau S.A.R.L. (51%)
Dhivehi Raajjeyge Gulhun Private Limited (45%)
Yemen International Telecommunications Company LLC (51%)

COMPETITORS

AT&T
BT
Deutsche Telekom
Equant
France Telecom
Global Crossing
Infonet
Level 3 Communications
NTT
Sprint FON
WorldCom

HISTORICAL FINANCIALS

Company Type: Public

Income Statement
FYE: March 31

	REVENUE ($ mil.)	NET INCOME ($ mil.)	NET PROFIT MARGIN	EMPLOYEES
3/03	6,940	(10,383)	—	23,152
3/02	8,425	(7,302)	—	35,561
3/01	11,480	3,731	32.5%	47,904
3/00	14,661	12,905	88.0%	54,919
3/99	12,803	1,463	11.4%	50,671
3/98	11,704	2,153	18.4%	46,550
3/97	9,919	1,110	11.2%	37,488
3/96	8,420	926	11.0%	39,636
3/95	8,320	409	4.9%	—
3/94	6,978	764	10.9%	—
Annual Growth	**(0.1%)**	**—**	**—**	**(7.4%)**

2003 Year-End Financials

Debt ratio: 33.6%
Return on equity: —
Cash ($ mil.): 4,985
Current ratio: 1.55
Long-term debt ($ mil.): 1,140
No. of shares (mil.): 794
Dividends
  Yield: 7.9%
  Payout: —
Market value ($ mil.): 2,629

Stock History
NYSE: CWP

	STOCK PRICE ($) FY Close	P/E High	P/E Low	PER SHARE ($) Earnings	PER SHARE ($) Dividends	PER SHARE ($) Book Value
3/03	3.31	—	—	(13.29)	0.26	4.28
3/02	9.84	—	—	(8.01)	0.68	16.20
3/01	20.60	—	—	4.10	1.35	23.34
3/00	56.00	10	4	7.21	0.68	15.86
3/99	36.94	31	16	1.82	0.20	9.70
3/98	37.75	14	8	2.86	0.00	6.82
3/97	23.75	17	12	1.49	0.61	6.74
3/96	24.25	16	12	1.57	0.49	6.72
3/95	18.88	40	29	0.56	0.42	7.40
3/94	20.25	24	15	1.05	0.36	6.68
Annual Growth	**(18.2%)**	**—**	**—**	**—**	**(3.6%)**	**(4.8%)**

Cadbury Schweppes plc

Drop a melted Cadbury chocolate bar on your favorite white shirt? Not to worry, Schweppes club soda will get it right out. A leading global confectioner, Cadbury Schweppes is also the world's #3 soft-drink producer, after The Coca-Cola Company and PepsiCo. Its beverage brands are sold mainly in North America and Western Europe and include 7 UP (US only), A&W Root Beer, Canada Dry, Dr Pepper, and Hawaiian Punch. It also makes Mott's apple products and Clamato juice. The company's confections are the market leaders in the UK. Along with the famous Cadbury Créme Egg, its candy brands include Trebor and

Bassett. Cadbury Schweppes' gum brands include Bubbas, Trident, and Dentyne.

Cadbury Schweppes' US candy brands — which include Cadbury, Peter Paul, and York — are licensed to Hershey Foods. In other countries, the firm markets its powerful Cadbury name with regional brands.

Through subsidiary Cadbury Schweppes Americas, Cadbury Schweppes has about 15% of the US market for soft drinks. It owns about 40% of Dr Pepper/Seven Up Bottling Group. Snapple, Mistic, Stewart's, and Yoo-Hoo belong to its Snapple Beverage Group. The purchase of Spain's La Casera and France's Orangina has strengthened the company's European drinks business. It also owns juice company Nantucket Allserve.

Cadbury's 2003 purchase of Pfizer's consumer brands brought with it Halls. Cadbury plans a makeover for the cough drop brand in 2004 that will bring new flavors like watermelon and tropical fruit.

The company has realized the need for cost cutting, announcing a four-year plan to cut its work force by 10% and reduce its 133 production sites by 20%.

HISTORY

Cadbury Schweppes is the product of a merger between two venerable British firms: Schweppes, the world's first soft-drink maker, and Cadbury, a candy confectionery. Schweppes began in 1783 in London, where Swiss national Jacob Schweppe first sold his artificial mineral water. The company introduced a lemonade in 1835 and tonic water and ginger ale in the 1870s. Beginning in the 1880s Schweppes expanded worldwide. In the 1960s it diversified into food products.

John Cadbury opened a coffee and tea shop in Birmingham, England, in 1824. He sold cocoa for drinking, which proved so popular that in 1831 he began making cocoa and was producing 15 varieties of chocolates by 1841.

The companies merged in 1969. Under Dominic Cadbury (great-grandson of founder John), Cadbury Schweppes acquired Peter Paul (Mounds, Almond Joy) in 1978 while increasing beverage sales in Europe and Asia. In 1982 it acquired applesauce and juice maker Duffy-Mott.

The company sold its non-candy and non-beverage businesses in 1986. It then acquired Canada Dry, the rights to Sunkist soda, and 34% of Dr Pepper (reduced to 18% when Dr Pepper merged with Seven Up in 1988).

Fatigued by Mars' and Hershey Foods' US dominance, Cadbury Schweppes signed a licensing agreement with Hershey in 1988, ending its direct involvement in the US candy market. The company added the Orange Crush and Hires brands in 1989, and it acquired candy makers Trebor and Bassett and the non-cola soft-drink operations of Source Perrier in 1990.

The Camelot Group, a UK consortium that includes Cadbury Schweppes, was picked in 1994 to operate the UK's National Lottery. Cadbury Schweppes bought the rest of Dr Pepper/Seven Up for $2.5 billion in 1995, and became the world's #3 soft-drink company. John Sunderland was appointed CEO of Cadbury Schweppes in 1996 and named executive chairman in 2003.

Cadbury Schweppes and The Carlyle Group investment firm created American Bottling through acquisitions in 1998. In 1999 Cadbury Schweppes and Carlyle bought the Dr Pepper Bottling Company of Texas for $691 million, combining it with American Bottling to form Dr Pepper/Seven Up Bottling Group.

In 1999 Cadbury Schweppes sold its beverage operations in more than 160 countries (excluding Australia, Continental Europe, and the US) to The Coca-Cola Company for $973 million.

In 2000 the company acquired Snapple Beverage Group from Triarc Companies in a deal worth about $1.45 billion. Deciding to continue soft-drink operations in Australia, that month Cadbury Schweppes also bought Pepsi Cola Bottlers Australia (a joint venture between Lion Nathan and Pepsi Cola). It also bought France's largest chewing gum maker, Hollywood, for $170 million, making it the world's #4 confectioner.

In June 2001 the company sold Royal Crown Cola's international division to Canada's Cott Corporation for $94 million. (It retained the RC business in the US, Canada, Puerto Rico, and Mexico.) Expanding further into soft drinks, the firm agreed to buy Pernod Ricard's soft-drink businesses (including the Orangina and Yoo-Hoo brands) in Continental Europe, North America, and Australia in September for about $640 million.

In February 2002 Cadbury Schweppes acquired Squirt, a leading carbonated soft drink brand in Mexico. In May the company bought Nantucket Allserve (Nantucket Nectars) from Ocean Spray Cranberries and folded Nantucket's brands into its Snapple group in order to bolster its noncarbonated drinks business. In September of same year it also purchased Denmark's Dandy chewing gum company, further bolstering its global status as the world's #4 gum company. Later in 2002 Cadbury and Nestlé made a joint $10.5 billion bid for Hershey Foods but Hershey subsequently called the sale off.

In February 2003 Cadbury Schweppes revised its organizational structure by reducing its number of reporting units from 10 to five. The units included Americas Beverages, Americas Confectionery, EMEA Confectionery (Europe, Middle East, and Africa), Europe Beverages, and Asia Pacific. In March 2003 Cadbury Schweppes completed its purchase of Pfizer Inc.'s Adams confectionery business for $4.2 billion.

The company announced in December 2003 that it would cut 480 jobs from its UK chocolate division as part of its worldwide effort to cut its workforce by 10%.

EXECUTIVES

Executive Chairman: John M. Sunderland, age 57, $2,306,408 pay
CEO: H. Todd Stitzer, age 50, $1,268,685 pay
CFO: David J. Kappler, age 55, $1,307,179 pay
Chief Executive, Bebidas de Espana: Patrick Falgas
President and CEO, Americas Confectionery: Matt Shattock, age 40
President, Americas Confectionery-USA: Brad Irwin
President and CEO, Asia Pacific: Rajiv Wahi
President and CEO, Cadbury Schweppes Americas Beverages: Gil Cassagne, age 46
President and CEO, Europe Beverages: Marie-Bernard Trannoy, age 55
President and CEO, Europe, Middle East, and Africa Confectionery: Andy Cosslett, age 47
President and CEO, Snapple Beverage Group and Mott's: Jack Belsito
President, Dr Pepper/Seven Up: Michael S. (Mike) McGrath
President, Global Commercial: Nick Fell
President, Global Supply Chain: Matthew Litobarski

CFO, Snapple Beverage Group and Mott's: Dave Gerics
Chief Human Resources Officer: Robert J. (Bob) Stack, age 52, $1,077,821 pay
Chief Marketing and Operations Officer, Snapple Beverage Group and Mott's: Michael Sands
Group Secretary and Chief Legal Officer: Mike A. C. Clark, age 55
Corporate Communications Director: Sally Jones
Head of Group Public Relations: Dora McCabe
Auditors: Arthur Andersen & Co.

LOCATIONS

HQ: 25 Berkeley Sq., London W1J 6HB, United Kingdom
Phone: +44-20-7409-1313   **Fax:** +44-20-7830-5200
US HQ: 5301 Legacy Dr., Plano, TX 75024
US Phone: 972-673-7000   **US Fax:** 972-673-7980
Web: www.cadburyschweppes.com

Cadbury Schweppes' confections are made in 25 countries and sold in more than 170. Cadbury Schweppes sells beverages in 10 countries and licenses the sale of its beverages in about 20 other countries.

2002 Sales

	% of total
US	34
UK	18
Australia	10
France	10
Rest of world	28
Total	**100**

PRODUCTS/OPERATIONS

2002 Sales

	% of total
North American beverage	34
European confectionery	29
European beverage	14
Asia/Pacific	12
Africa, India & Middle East	6
Americas confectionery	5
Total	**100**

Selected Brand Names

Confections
Allan (Canada, US)
Barratt (UK)
Bassett
Beldent
Bim Bim (Egypt)
Bouquet d'Or (France)
Butterkist (UK)
Cadbury
Cadbury Dairy Milk
Cadbury Caramel
Cadbury Creme Egg
Cadbury Crunchie
Cadbury Dream
Cadbury Flake
Cadbury Miniature Heroes
Cadbury Roses
Cadbury TimeOut
Carambar (France)
Choclairs
Dulciora (Spain)
Elegan
Fry's
Fuzzy Peach
Halls

Jelibon (Turkey)
La Pie Qui Chante (France)
MacRobertson (Australia)
Mantecol (Argentina)
Maynards (UK)
Miss
Olips (Turkey)
Pascall
Peter Paul
Piasten (Germany)
Picnic
Poulain (France)
Red Tulip (Australia)
Relax (Turkey)
Sharps (UK)
Sportlife (China)
Sour Patch Kids
Stani (Argentina)
Swedish Fish
Trebor
Turbo (Turkey)
Wedel (Poland)
York

Chewing Gum
Bazooka
Bubbas
Dentyne
Relax (Kent)
Sportlife
Trident
V6

Beverages
7 UP (US and Puerto Rico)
A&W Root Beer
Canada Dry
Clamato
Cottee's (Australia)
Country Time (licensed, US)
Crush
Crystal Light (licensed, US)
Dr Pepper (Australia, Canada, Europe, Mexico, US)
Diet Rite
Gini (Europe)
Hawaiian Punch
La Casera
Mauna La'i
Mistic (fruity beverages)
Mott's
Nantucket Nectars
Nehi
Oasis
Orangina (France)
RC Cola
Schweppes
Solo (Australia)
Snapple
Spring Valley (Australia)
Squirt
Stewart's (sodas)
Sunkist (licensed)
Sun Valley Squeeze
Trinaranjus (Europe)
Wave (Australia)
Welch's (licensed, US)
YooHoo

COMPETITORS

Archibald Candy	Nestlé
Campbell Soup	Ocean Spray
Lindt & Sprüngli	PepsiAmericas
Coca-Cola	PepsiCo
Cott	Pernod Ricard
CSM	Russell Stover
Ferolito, Vultaggio	See's Candies
Hershey	Thorntons
Jelly Belly Candy	Tootsie Roll
Kraft Foods International	Virgin Group
Mars	Wrigley
National Beverage	
National Grape Cooperative	

HISTORICAL FINANCIALS

Company Type: Public

Income Statement

FYE: Saturday nearest December 31

	REVENUE ($ mil.)	NET INCOME ($ mil.)	NET PROFIT MARGIN	EMPLOYEES
12/02	8,538	883	10.3%	42,848
12/01	8,037	789	9.8%	38,489
12/00	6,841	742	10.8%	36,460
12/99	6,950	1,037	14.9%	37,425
12/98	6,814	589	8.6%	38,656
12/97	6,893	1,143	16.6%	41,320
12/96	8,759	591	6.7%	42,911
12/95	7,417	480	6.5%	—
12/94	6,306	422	6.7%	—
12/93	5,511	360	6.5%	—
Annual Growth	**5.0%**	**10.5%**	**—**	**(0.0%)**

2002 Year-End Financials

Debt ratio: 50.6%
Return on equity: 19.5%
Cash ($ mil.): 282
Current ratio: 0.79
Long-term debt ($ mil.): 2,462
No. of shares (mil.): 514
Dividends
   Yield: 2.9%
   Payout: 41.7%
Market value ($ mil.): 13,170

12/93 12/94 12/95 12/96 12/97 12/98 12/99 12/00 12/01 12/02

	STOCK PRICE ($) FY Close	P/E High/Low		PER SHARE ($) Earnings	Dividends	Book Value
12/02	25.61	18	14	1.75	0.73	9.46
12/01	25.72	19	15	1.56	0.68	8.20
12/00	29.00	20	14	1.47	0.71	7.74
12/99	24.19	17	11	2.02	0.66	7.16
12/98	34.56	30	17	1.16	0.46	6.01
12/97	20.69	6	4	3.52	0.27	5.46
12/96	17.06	15	12	1.17	1.08	4.41
12/95	16.63	18	13	0.97	1.22	4.12
12/94	13.50	16	13	0.99	0.61	5.65
12/93	15.00	17	14	0.91	0.66	4.87
Annual Growth	6.1%	—	—	7.5%	1.1%	7.7%

Canadian Imperial Bank of Commerce

Canadian Imperial Bank of Commerce (CIBC) is both Canadian and imperial when it comes to growing its business. CIBC's approximately 1,150 branches offer a range of consumer and business services, including deposit accounts, loans, brokerage, mutual funds, and trust services. It operates in five segments: retail products (credit cards and mortgages); retail markets (consumer and small business banking); wealth management; Amicus, its electronic banking operations; and broker-dealer CIBC World Markets, which boasts expertise in securities underwriting, mergers and acquisitions advice, and debt, equity, and foreign exchange trading services.

Operating units within CIBC's business lines include trust and custody services provider CIBC Mellon, a joint venture with Mellon Financial; CIBC Wood Gundy, the asset management arm of CIBC World Markets; and institutional fund manager TAL Global Asset Management.

CIBC tried to grow through megamergers and diversification, but both moves were nixed by the government for fear of excessive industry consolidation. Now CIBC faces the prospect of good, old-fashioned organic growth with a piecemeal acquisition here and there.

To build its customer base, the bank is focusing on its core banking operations, targeting small businesses in Canada and retail banking customers in growing cities in the US. The company snagged US-based Merrill Lynch's Canadian retail brokerage, asset management, and securities operations and merged its Caribbean banking business with that of UK-based Barclays to create First Caribbean Bank.

HISTORY

In 1858 Bank of Canada was chartered; Toronto financier William McMaster bought the charter in 1866 when investors failed to raise enough money to open it and changed the name to Canadian Bank of Commerce.

Canadian Bank of Commerce opened in 1867, bought the Gore Bank of Hamilton (1870), and expanded within seven years to 24 branches in Ontario, as well as Montreal and New York. Led by Edmund Walker, the bank spread west of the Great Lakes with the opening of a Winnipeg, Manitoba, branch in 1893 and joined the Gold Rush with branches in Dawson City, Yukon Territory, and Skagway, Alaska, in 1898.

As the new century began, the bank's purchases spanned the breadth of Canada, from the Bank of British Columbia (1901) to Halifax Banking (1903) and the Merchants Bank of Prince Edward Island (1906). More buys followed in the 1920s; the bank's assets peaked in 1929 and then plunged during the Depression. It recovered during WWII.

In 1961 Canadian Bank of Commerce merged with Imperial Bank of Canada to become Canadian Imperial Bank of Commerce. Imperial Bank was founded in 1875 by Henry Howland; it went west to Calgary and Edmonton and became known as "The Mining Bank." It bought Barclays Bank (Canada) in 1956.

As the energy and agriculture sectors declined in the early 1980s, two of CIBC's largest borrowers, Dome Petroleum and tractor maker Massey-Ferguson, defaulted on their loans. Donald Fullerton became the bank's CEO in 1984 and slashed costs, increasing profits to record levels. Earnings were hit again in 1987 when Brazil, a big CIBC creditor, suspended payment on its foreign debts.

Deregulation opened investment banking to CIBC, which in 1988 bought a majority share of Wood Gundy, one of Canada's largest investment dealers; CIBC also purchased Merrill Lynch Canada's retail brokerage business.

In 1992 CIBC added substantially to its loss reserves (resulting in an earnings drop of 98%) to cover real estate losses from developer Olympia & York and others. This launched more cost-cutting as the company reorganized by operating segments.

Deregulation allowed CIBC to begin selling insurance in 1993; the company built a collection of life, credit, personal property/casualty, and nonmedical health companies.

In 1996 the bank formed Intria, a processing and technical support subsidiary. The next year CIBC Wood Gundy became CIBC World Markets, and CIBC bought securities firm Oppenheimer & Co. and added its stock underwriting and brokerage abilities to CIBC World Markets.

In 1998, increasing foreign competition prompted CIBC and Toronto-Dominion to plan a merger (as did Royal Bank of Canada and Bank of Montreal); the government halted both plans citing Canada's already highly concentrated banking industry.

Spurned, the bank overhauled its operations to spark growth in the late 1990s. To cut costs it eliminated some 4,000 jobs and sold its more than $1 billion real estate portfolio. It teamed with the Winn-Dixie (1999) and Safeway (2000) supermarket chains to operate electronic branches in the US. The firm scaled back its disappointing international operations and began selling its insurance units.

In 2000 CIBC created Amicus as a holding company for CIBC World Markets' retail electronic banking business. The following year the bank sold its merchant card services business to US-based Global Payments Inc. and bought the Canadian securities and private client businesses of Merrill Lynch. In 2002 it began pulling back from its US supermarket operations.

EXECUTIVES

Chairman and CEO: John S. Hunkin, $574,650 pay
Vice Chairman, Retail Markets: G. H. Jill Denham
Vice Chairman and Chief Risk Officer: Wayne C. Fox, $510,800 pay
Vice Chairman; Chairman and CEO, CIBC World Markets: David J. Kassie, age 48, $319,250 pay
Vice Chairman, Wealth Management: Gerald T. McCaughey, $446,950 pay
SEVP and Chief Administrative Officer: Ron A. Lalonde, $430,987 pay
SEVP, Corporate Development: Richard E. Venn, age 52
SEVP and CIO: Mike D. Woeller, $446,949 pay
SEVP and Chief Accountant: Barbara E. MacDonald
SEVP and Ombudsman: Lachlan W. (Lach) MacLachlan
EVP and CFO: Tom D. Woods
EVP, Global Private Banking and Investment Management Services: Sonia A. Baxendale
EVP and General Counsel: Michael Capatides
EVP and Treasurer: Michael G. Horrocks
EVP, Human Resources: Joyce D. Phillips
SVP and Controller: Douglas Chornoboy
SVP, Investor Relations: Kathryn A. Humber
SVP, Corporate Communications and Public Affairs: R. E. (Bob) Waite
VP and Corporate Secretary: Paul T. Fisher
Auditors: Deloitte & Touche LLP; PricewaterhouseCoopers LLP

LOCATIONS

HQ: Commerce Court, Toronto, Ontario M5L 1A2, Canada
Phone: 416-980-2211   **Fax:** 416-980-5026
US HQ: 425 Lexington Ave., New York, NY 10017
US Phone: 212-856-4000   **US Fax:** 212-667-4776
Web: www.cibc.com

PRODUCTS/OPERATIONS

Selected Subsidiaries

Amicus Bank
CIBC Asia Ltd. (Singapore)
CIBC Australia Holdings Limited
   CIBC Australia Limited
CIBC BA Limited
CIBC Delaware Holdings Inc. (US)
   Amicus Holdings Inc. (US)
      Amicus FSB (US)
      CIBC National Bank (US)
   Canadian Imperial Holdings Inc. (US)
      CIBC INC. (US)
      CIBC Trading (Delaware Corp.) (US)
   CIBC World Markets Corp. (US)
   Juniper Financial Corp. (90%, US)
CIBC Financial Planning Inc.
CIBC Holdings (Cayman) Limited (Cayman Islands)
   CIBC Bank and Trust Company Limited (Cayman Islands)
   CIBC Investments (Cayman) Limited (Cayman Islands)
   CIBC Offshore Services Inc. (Barbados)
      CIBC Reinsurance Company Limited (Barbados)
   CIBC Trust Company (Bahamas) Limited
   CIBC World Markets (International) Arbitrage Corp. (Barbados)
CIBC Investor Services Inc.
CIBC Life Insurance Company Limited
CIBC Mortgages Inc.
   3877337 Canada Inc. (Home Loans Canada)
CIBC Offshore Banking Services Corporation (Barbados)
CIBC Offshore Finance (Ireland) Limited
   CIBC World Markets Ireland Limited
      CIBC World Markets Securities Ireland Limited
CIBC Securities Inc.
CIBC Trust Corporation

CIBC World Markets Inc.
   CIBC World Markets (Japan) Inc.
   CIBC World Markets Asset Securitization Pty
     Limited (Australia)
   CIBC World Markets Securities Australia Limited
CIBC World Markets plc (UK)
CM Investment Management Inc.
EDULINX Canada Corporation
INTRIA Corporation
   INTRIA-HP Corporation
   INTRIA Items Inc.
Services Hypothecaires CIBC Inc.
   TAL Global Asset Management Inc.
     T.A.L. Asset Management (Cayman) Limited
      (Cayman Islands)
     TAL CEF Global Holding Limited (British Virgin
      Islands)
     TAL CEF Asset Management Holding Limited
      (British Virgin Islands)
     TAL CEF Global Asset Management Limited (Hong
      Kong)
     TAL CEF Global Asset Management (Bermuda)
      Limited
     TAL Global Asset Management (Cayman) Limited
      (Cayman Islands)
   T.A.L. Asset Management (Guernsey) Limited (UK)
   TAL Private Management Ltd.
   Talvest Fund Management Inc.
     Talvest (LSVC) Inc.

COMPETITORS

Bank of America
Bank of Montreal
Bank of New York
Scotiabank
Barclays
Bear Stearns
Citigroup Global Markets
Citigroup
Credit Suisse
Deutsche Bank
Goldman Sachs
HSBC Holdings
J.P. Morgan Chase
Lehman Brothers
Merrill Lynch
Mizuho Financial
Morgan Stanley
National Bank of Canada
RBC Financial Group
State Farm
TD Bank
UBS Financial Services

HISTORICAL FINANCIALS

Company Type: Public

Income Statement

FYE: October 31

	ASSETS ($ mil.)	NET INCOME ($ mil.)	INCOME AS % OF ASSETS	EMPLOYEES
10/02	175,454	419	0.2%	42,552
10/01	181,137	1,062	0.6%	41,000
10/00	175,773	1,353	0.8%	44,215
10/99	170,150	699	0.4%	45,998
10/98	182,339	684	0.4%	47,171
10/97	168,996	1,101	0.7%	42,446
10/96	148,688	1,020	0.7%	41,606
10/95	133,336	755	0.6%	39,329
10/94	111,608	658	0.6%	40,807
10/93	106,988	553	0.5%	41,511
Annual Growth	5.7%	(3.0%)	—	0.3%

2002 Year-End Financials

Equity as % of assets: 3.4%
Return on assets: 0.2%
Return on equity: 7.0%
Long-term debt ($ mil.): 2,329
No. of shares (mil.): 359
Dividends
  Yield: 4.0%
  Payout: 117.2%
Market value ($ mil.): 9,109
Sales ($ mil.): 10,949

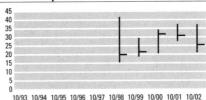

Stock History   NYSE: BCM

	STOCK PRICE ($) FY Close	P/E High/Low		PER SHARE ($) Earnings	Dividends	Book Value
10/02	25.37	42	25	0.87	1.02	22.05
10/01	30.82	14	11	2.56	0.94	20.65
10/00	31.75	11	7	3.18	0.98	19.79
10/99	21.50	19	13	1.51	0.80	18.68
10/98	19.94	28	11	1.46	0.82	17.36
Annual Growth	6.2%	—	—	(12.1%)	5.6%	6.2%

Canon Inc.

Canon is still banging away at the document reproduction market. The company makes printers and other computer peripherals for home and office use. Its other well-known lines include copiers, fax machines, and scanners. Canon's optical segment features products used in such diverse applications as semiconductor manufacturing equipment, television broadcast lenses, and devices used for eye examinations. Canon still operates its original camera business, which makes digital cameras, camcorders, liquid-crystal display projectors, lenses, and binoculars.

Perhaps still best known for its cameras, Canon has seen its photographic business drop to about 15% of revenues. However, the company has seen significant growth in its digital camera sales. Canon's peripheral products continue to lead copiers as the largest sales group amid falling PC prices, which have opened up consumer spending on printers and scanners. Faced with strong competition and falling sales of business machines, the company is focusing on digital technology and making its products network-compatible.

Canon adheres to the *kyosei* philosophy (living and working together for the common good), which stresses respect for local cultures and customs and more local control of subsidiaries. The company, which generates about three-quarters of its revenues outside of Japan, continues to emphasize its product development and marketing efforts in Europe and the US.

HISTORY

Takeshi Mitarai and a friend, Saburo Uchida, formed Seiki Kogaku Kenkyusho (Precision Optical Research Laboratory) in Tokyo in 1933 to make Japan's first 35mm camera. In 1935 the camera was introduced under the brand name Kwanon (the Buddhist goddess of mercy) — but later renamed Canon. In response to a pre-World War II military buildup, the company made X-ray machines for the Japanese.

In 1947 the company became Canon Camera Company as the brand name gained popularity. Canon opened its first overseas branch — in New York — in 1955. It diversified into business equipment by introducing the first 10-key electronic calculator (1964) and a plain-paper photocopier (1968) independent of Xerox's patented technology. Canon dropped "Camera Company" from its name in 1969.

The company invented the "liquid dry" copying system, which uses plain paper and liquid developer, in 1972. It failed to produce new cameras and was surpassed by Minolta as Japan's top camera exporter. Sales were sluggish in the early 1970s, and in 1975 Canon suspended dividends for the first time since World War II.

At that time Ryuzaburo Kaku, Canon's managing director, convinced Mitarai that the company's problems stemmed from indecisive leadership and weak marketing. Kaku turned Canon around, unleashing the electronic AE-1 in a media blitz that in 1976 included the first-ever TV commercials for a 35mm camera. With automated features, the AE-1 appealed to the clumsiest photographers. Its success catapulted Canon past Minolta as the world's #1 camera maker.

In 1979 Canon introduced the first copier to use a dry developer. As the copier market matured in the early 1980s, Canon shifted to making other automated office equipment, including laser printers and fax machines.

Mitarai died in 1984. Minolta the next year again displaced Canon as the world's #1 camera maker, when it introduced a fully automated model. But Canon came back in 1987 with the electronic optical system (EOS) auto-focus camera, which returned the company to preeminence in 1990. That year the company initiated an ink cartridge recycling program. Canon teamed up with IBM in 1992 to produce portable PCs. In 1993 Takeshi Mitarai's son Hajime, who had joined Canon in 1974, was named president and began expanding product development.

In 1995 Canon introduced the world's first color ferroelectric liquid-crystal display designed to replace cathode-ray tubes in computer and TV screens as the industry standard. When Hajime died that year, cousin Fujio Mitarai, a 34-year Canon employee who served as the head of Canon U.S.A. in the 1980s, was named president and CEO. In 1996 the company made Canon Latin America a direct subsidiary of Canon U.S.A., with the *kyosei* idea that regionalized control would make the subsidiary more efficient.

Canon stopped making PCs in 1997. The next year the company unveiled its Hyper Photo System, which combines a scanner, PC server, and printer to produce photo prints, and expanded its copier remanufacturing operations. In 1999, after 16 years of production, Canon stopped making optical memory cards. The company also opened a research and development facility in the US.

In 2000 Canon and Toshiba began working together to develop technology for flat-panel displays. Canon expanded its line of digital cameras in 2001; the company's sales in that segment almost doubled that year.

The next year the company announced that it would merge two of its office equipment subsidiaries, Copyer and Canon Aptex, in an effort to improve operating efficiency.

EXECUTIVES

President and CEO; Chairman, Management Strategy Committee and New Business Development Committee: Fujio Mitarai, age 68
Senior Managing Director; Group Executive, Technology Management: Ichiro Endo, age 62

Senior Managing Director; Chief, Global Marketing
Promotion Committee; Group Executive, Human
Resources Management and Organization:
Yukio Yamashita, age 64

Senior Managing Director; Group Executive, Finance
and Accounting: Toshizo Tanaka, age 63

Managing Director; Group Executive, Internet
Business Promotion; EVP, Research and
Development, Canon Europe Ltd.: Takashi Saito,
age 62

Managing Director; Group Executive, Global
Environment Promotion and Production Management:
Yusuke Emura, age 59

Managing Director; President, Canon U.S.A.:
Kinya Uchida, age 65

Managing Director; Chief Executive, Optical Products
Operations: Akira Tajima, age 63

Managing Director; Chief, Global Legal Affairs
Coordination Committee; Group Executive, Corporate
Intellectual Property and Legal; Senior General
Manager, Legal Affairs Coordination:
Nobuyoshi Tanaka, age 57

Managing Director; Chief Executive, Image
Communication Products Operations: Tsuneji Uchida,
age 62

Managing Director; Chief Executive, Peripheral
Products Operations: Junji Ichikawa, age 60

Managing Director; President, Canon Europa N.V.;
Managing Director, Canon Europe, Ltd.:
Hajime Tsuruoka, age 60

Director; EVP and CTO, Canon U.S.A.: Toru Takahashi,
age 61

Auditors: KPMG

LOCATIONS

HQ: 30-2, Shimomaruko 3-chome, Ohta-ku,
 Tokyo 146-8501, Japan
Phone: +81-3-3758-2111   Fax: +81-3-5482-5135
US HQ: 1 Canon Plaza, Lake Success, NY 11042
US Phone: 516-328-5000   US Fax: 516-328-5069
Web: www.canon.com

Canon has manufacturing operations in China, France,
Germany, Japan, Malaysia, Mexico, Singapore, South
Korea, Taiwan, Thailand, and the US.

2002 Sales

	$ mil.	% of total
Americas	8,418	34
Europe	7,143	29
Japan	6,105	25
Other regions	2,835	12
Total	**24,501**	**100**

PRODUCTS/OPERATIONS

2002 Sales

	$ mil.	% of total
Business machines		
Computer peripherals	8,487	35
Copying machines	7,820	32
Business systems	2,245	9
Cameras	4,048	16
Optical & other	1,901	8
Total	**24,501**	**100**

Selected Products

Business Machines

Computer peripherals	Business systems
Consumables	Document scanners
Printers	Fax machines
Scanners	Handy terminals
Copiers	
Consumables	
Office	
Personal	

Cameras

Compact	Single-lens reflex (SLR)
Digital	Video camcorders
Lenses	
Liquid-crystal	
display projectors	

Optical
Broadcasting equipment
Digital radiography
Medical equipment
Semiconductor production equipment

COMPETITORS

Agfa	Nikon Corporation
ASML	Océ
Eastman Kodak	Oki Electric
Fuji Photo	Olympus
Fuji Xerox	Pentax
Fujitsu	Philips Electronics
Hewlett-Packard	Polaroid
Hitachi	Ricoh
Imagistics	SANYO
IBM	Seiko Epson
Konica Minolta	Sharp
Kyocera	Sony
Lexmark International	Toshiba
Matsushita	Victor Company of Japan
NEC	Xerox

HISTORICAL FINANCIALS

Company Type: Public

Income Statement				FYE: December 31
	REVENUE ($ mil.)	NET INCOME ($ mil.)	NET PROFIT MARGIN	EMPLOYEES
12/02	24,501	1,590	6.5%	97,802
12/01	22,027	1,269	5.8%	93,620
12/00	24,272	1,170	4.8%	86,673
12/99	25,709	689	2.7%	81,009
12/98	24,364	945	3.9%	79,799
12/97	21,239	914	4.3%	78,767
12/96	22,054	812	3.7%	75,628
12/95	21,026	534	2.5%	72,280
12/94	19,410	312	1.6%	67,672
12/93	16,452	189	1.1%	64,535
Annual Growth	**4.5%**	**26.7%**	**—**	**4.7%**

2002 Year-End Financials

Debt ratio: 5.1%
Return on equity: 13.1%
Cash ($ mil.): 4,344
Current ratio: 2.13
Long-term debt ($ mil.): 678
No. of shares (mil.): 878
Dividends
 Yield: 0.6%
 Payout: 11.7%
Market value ($ mil.): 32,346

Stock History

NYSE: CAJ

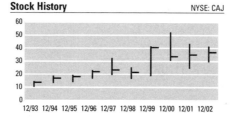

12/93 12/94 12/95 12/96 12/97 12/98 12/99 12/00 12/01 12/02

	STOCK PRICE ($) FY Close	P/E High/Low		PER SHARE ($) Earnings	Dividends	Book Value
12/02	36.85	23	17	1.79	0.21	15.11
12/01	35.06	31	18	1.43	0.18	12.61
12/00	33.69	39	23	1.32	0.16	12.95
12/99	40.56	52	25	0.78	0.14	13.52
12/98	21.50	23	16	1.07	0.15	2.27
12/97	23.35	31	19	1.04	0.14	1.95
12/96	22.00	25	19	0.92	0.11	1.98
12/95	18.28	31	24	0.61	0.12	1.97
12/94	17.00	51	38	0.36	0.11	1.89
12/93	13.75	59	45	0.24	0.10	1.62
Annual Growth	**11.6%**	**—**	**—**	**25.0%**	**8.6%**	**28.1%**

Cap Gemini Ernst & Young

Cap Gemini Ernst & Young's global reach will not exceed its grasp of information technology (IT) services. Europe's leading provider of IT consulting and services, the company offers its clients a wealth of strategy and management consulting, systems integration, software development, and outsourcing services. It specializes in developing and implementing enterprise systems for customer relationship management (CRM), enterprise resource planning (ERP), and wireless networking systems. Its outsourcing services cover network operations, desktop management, and business processes. The firm has operations in more than 30 countries and is in talks to acquire consulting firm Transiciel for about $435 million.

Cap Gemini cemented its presence in the US in 2000 when it acquired the consulting business of accounting giant Ernst & Young. Business in North America now accounts for about a third of Cap Gemini's revenue.

The slowdown in the IT market, however, precipitated major managerial restructuring and workforce reductions, prompting the company to launch in 2002 a reorganization plan known as the LEAP program. LEAP divided the company's management into four disciplines (consulting, outsourcing, technology, and local professional services) and national units. The second phase of the plan is creating three geographical divisions — North Europe, South Europe, and North America.

Cap Gemini's Sogety division focuses in local professional services and is responsible for 6% of the group's revenues. It operates mainly in France, the Netherlands, Scandinavia, and the US.

The Telecom & Media subsidiary is a joint-venture with Cisco and has clients such as Time Warner, Comcast, Deutsche Telekom, France Telecom, and Nextel.

French investment company Wendel Investissement owns 11% of Cap Gemini; founder and chairman Serge Kampf owns 6%.

HISTORY

Serge Kampf founded software house Sogeti in 1967 in Grenoble, France. He had an economics degree and had held a variety of jobs — from selling bakery ovens and computers to working for the French national telephone company. Frustrated as an executive with French computer company Groupe Bull, he resigned and started Sogeti.

Believing the future of information technology (IT) would be in support rather than hardware, Kampf focused on providing computer services to companies outside Paris that were being overlooked by his larger competitors. He was immediately successful, and three years later opened a Paris branch. In 1973 Kampf changed the focus of the company, abandoning the more specialized activities of data processing for general consulting, software, and technical assistance.

Cap Gemini Sogeti was created two years later by merging Sogeti with two French software service companies, C.A.P. (Computerized Applications Programming, started in 1962) and Gemini (1969). At first it operated as a "body shop," a loose organization of freelance programmers offering temporary help to computer users. It set up a consulting team in the US in 1978 and began a series of US acquisitions that led to the formation of Cap Gemini America (1981).

The company acquired a 42% stake in French competitor Sesa in 1982; six years later it bought the rest as part of a new strategy to become a global operator with a range of services. Cap Gemini Sogeti's 1990 purchase of Hoskyns Group, the UK's largest computer services company, was just one of a string of acquisitions aimed at fulfilling that goal. (Over a five-year period, it bought 22 European and American companies for $1.1 billion.) To raise money for his international expansion plans, Kampf sold 34% of the company to German carmaker Daimler-Benz (now DaimlerChrysler) in 1991.

As Cap Gemini Sogeti expanded around the world, its decentralized network of operations rarely shared business or expertise. In 1993, on the heels of its first loss, the company launched a restructuring program that set up seven strategic business areas with dual regional and segment roles and modified product lines. Cap Gemini Sogeti returned to profitability in 1995.

The mid-1990s brought more than a dozen partnerships, including deals with French chemical conglomerate Rhône-Poulenc (now Aventis, 1995) and British Steel (now Corus Group, 1996). Also in 1996 the company launched its year 2000 date fixing software. It completed the reorganization, creating holding company Cap Gemini, and moved its corporate headquarters to Paris.

In 1997 Daimler-Benz sold its stake (then 24%) in Cap Gemini to Compagnie Générale d'Industrie et de Participations (CGIP, now controlled by Wendel Investissement). The next year Cap Gemini bought the UK finance and commerce arm of AT&T. The company sold its UK training unit in 1999 to focus its UK operations on IT services. Expanding further into the US that year, the company bought telecommunications specialist Beechwood.

In 2000 Cap Gemini solidified its US presence (and changed its name) with the $11 billion purchase of the consulting business of Ernst & Young. Geoff Unwin took over as CEO that year; Kampf remained as chairman.

Stung by a slowdown in IT spending (primarily in the US), in 2001 the company announced it was cutting 5,400 jobs. Later that year Unwin announced his retirement as CEO, and was succeeded by COO Paul Hermelin. In 2002 another 5,500 jobs (about 10% of its workforce) were cut, mainly in its telecom and financial services units. The appointment of Alexandre Haeffner as COO launched major managerial restructuring.

EXECUTIVES

Executive Chairman: Serge Kampf, age 69
Vice Chairman: Ernest-Antoine Sellière
CEO: Paul Hermelin, age 49
CFO: William H. Bitan
COO: Alexandre Haeffner
EVP, Outsourcing: Hubert Giraud
Group Leader, Business Solutions and Technology: Chell Smith
Group Leader, Consumer Products, Retail and Distribution: Fred Crawford
Group Leader, Energy, Utilities and Chemicals: Colette Lewiner
Group Leader, Financial Services: Jim Greene
Group Leader, High Technology and Automotive: Kevin Mahanay
Group Leader, Life Sciences: Stephen Phillips
Group Leader, Outsourcing: Duncan Aitchinson
Group Leader, Strategy and Technology Consulting: Tom Manning
Consulting: Terrence (Terry) Ozan

CEO, North America: John W. McCain, age 44
CTO: Jean-Paul Figer
Director, Communications: Florence Mairal
General Secretary: Jean-Pierre Durant des Aulnois
Manager, Investor Relations: Lawrence Chalmet
Auditors: Coopers & Lybrand Audit

LOCATIONS

HQ: 6-8, rue Duret, 75017 Paris, France
Phone: +33-1-53-644444   **Fax:** +33-1-53-644445
US HQ: 5 Times Sq., New York, NY 10036
US Phone: 917-934-8000   **US Fax:** 917-934-8001
Web: www.cgey.com

Cap Gemini Ernst & Young has offices in more than 30 countries.

2002 Sales

	% of total
North America	32
France	18
UK	17
Benelux	13
Nordic	7
Germany & Central Europe	6
Southern Europe	5
Asia/Pacific	2
Total	**100**

PRODUCTS/OPERATIONS

2002 Sales

	% of total
Technology	42
Outsourcing	27
Consulting	25
Local Professional Services	6
Total	**100**

Services

Application management
Customer relationship management
Enterprise resource planning
Finance and employee transformation
Information technology consulting
Knowledge management
Management consulting
Outsourcing
Program management
Software development
Strategy consulting
Supply chain management
Systems integration
Training

COMPETITORS

Accenture
Affiliated Computer
 Services
A.T. Kearney
Atos Origin
Bain & Company
BearingPoint
Booz Allen
Bull
Capita
Computer Sciences
Deloitte Consulting
DiData
EDS
Fujitsu Services
Getronics
Hewlett-Packard
IBM
Keane
LogicaCMG
McKinsey & Company
Perot Systems
Siemens
T-Systems International
Unisys

HISTORICAL FINANCIALS

Company Type: Public

Income Statement   FYE: December 31

	REVENUE ($ mil.)	NET INCOME ($ mil.)	NET PROFIT MARGIN	EMPLOYEES
12/02	7,386	(539)	—	52,683
12/01	7,455	135	1.8%	57,760
12/00	6,526	406	6.2%	59,549
12/99	3,098	117	3.8%	39,626
12/98	4,615	219	4.8%	34,606
12/97	3,364	127	3.8%	31,094
12/96	2,832	54	1.9%	25,950
12/95	2,308	11	0.5%	22,079
12/94	1,907	(18)	—	19,823
12/93	1,863	(73)	—	20,559
Annual Growth	**16.5%**	**—**	**—**	**11.0%**

2002 Year-End Financials

Debt ratio: 4.4%   Current ratio: 1.54
Return on equity: —   Long-term debt ($ mil.): 162
Cash ($ mil.): 903

Net Income History   Euronext Paris: CAP

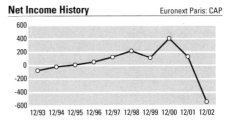

Carlsberg A/S

If any company has thirst quenching down to a science, it's Carlsberg A/S, the majority owner of Carlsberg Breweries. In addition to the worldwide brewing operations of its central subsidiary, Carlsberg A/S also operates the Carlsberg Research Center, which houses 80 beer brewing laboratories. The company is controlled by the Carlsberg Foundation, established in 1876 by founder J.C. Jacobsen.

Carlsberg A/S receives more than 90% of its revenue from the sales of beer and other beverages. While most of this comes from the sale of Carlsberg beers, the group also owns the Tuborg brand. Soft drink production centers around licenses to produce drinks from Coca-Cola, Pepsi, and Schweppes, but the company also produces regional beverages. In Denmark, Norway, and Sweden, Carlsberg produces leading brands of mineral water.

HISTORY

Carlsberg stems from the amalgamation of two proud Danish brewing concerns. Captain J. C. Jacobsen founded the first of these in Copenhagen; his father had worked as a brewery hand before acquiring his own small brewery in 1826. Studious and technically minded, J. C. inherited the brewery in 1835. He opened the Carlsberg Brewery (named for his son Carl) in 1847 and exported his first beer (to the UK) in 1868. J. C. established the Carlsberg Foundation in 1876 to conduct scientific research and oversee brewery operations.

Carl, who conflicted with his father over brewery operations, opened a new facility (New Carlsberg) adjacent to his dad's in 1881. Both men bestowed gifts upon their city, such as a church, an art museum, a royal castle renovation, and Copenhagen Harbor's famous Little Mermaid statue. Father and son willed their breweries to the foundation, which united them in 1906.

Tuborgs Fabrikker was founded in 1873 by a group of Danish businessmen who wanted to establish a major industrial project (including a brewery) at Tuborg Harbor. Philip Heyman headed the group and in 1880 spun off all operations but the brewery.

Carlsberg and Tuborg became Denmark's two leading brewers. After WWII, both began marketing their beers outside the country. Between 1958 and 1972 they tripled exports and established breweries in Europe and Asia. Both brewers' desire to grow internationally influenced their decision to merge, which they did in 1969 as United Breweries.

During the 1980s the firm diversified, forming Carlsberg Biotechnology in 1983 to extend its research to other areas. It strengthened its position in North America through licenses with Anheuser-Busch (1985) and John Labatt (1988). United Breweries reverted to the old Carlsberg name in 1987.

Carlsberg and Allied-Lyons (now Allied Domecq) combined their UK brewing, distribution, and wholesaling operations under the name Carlsberg-Tetley in 1992, creating the UK's third-largest brewer (behind Bass and Courage).

The firm teamed up with India's United Breweries in 1995 to distribute Carlsberg beer on the subcontinent. Bass acquired Allied's 50% of Carlsberg-Tetley in 1996 but sold its stake to Carlsberg in 1997 upon orders from regulators. Also in 1997 Carlsberg and Coca-Cola set up Coca-Cola Nordic Beverages to bottle and distribute soft drinks in Nordic countries. That year Poul Svanholm retired after 25 years as CEO; he was replaced by Jørn Jensen.

Carlsberg acquired a 60% stake in Finnish brewer Sinebrychoff in 1998. Carlsberg then sold a 60% stake in Vingaarden to Finland's Oy Rettig (1999), sold its remaining 43% share of the Tivoli amusement park to Danish tobacco group Skandinavisk Tobakskompagni (2000), and reduced its 64% holding in Royal Scandinavia to 28% (2000). Carlsberg bought the beverage operations of Swedish firm Feldschlösschen Hürlimann in 2000 and agreed to combine brewing businesses with Norway-based Orkla in a deal worth $1.5 billion; Carlsberg Breweries was formed in February 2001 after both agreed to divest several brands and distribution rights to gain regulatory approval.

Carlsberg stopped production at Coca-Cola Nordic Beverages (the company still exists but has no operations) in 2001 because of conflicts with Orkla's Pepsi bottling contracts in Sweden and Norway; Carlsberg and Coca-Cola continued to produce and sell Coke in Denmark and Finland. In 2002 Carlsberg sold 32% of its Lithuanian brewery to Russia's Baltic Beverage Holding, a joint venture between Carlsberg and Scottish & Newcastle. That year Carlsberg also signed an agreement giving Carib Brewery Ltd., part of the ANSA McAl Group, the rights to brew and distribute Carlsberg Beer in selected areas of the Caribbean.

In January 2003 Carlsberg Breweries acquired an additional 27.5% stake in Pirinsko Pivo, a Bulgarian brewery, bringing its overall owner-

ship to 94.5%. That same month it purchased the Chinese brewer Kunming in southeast China. Carlsberg bought a second Chinese brewer, Dali, in June 2003.

EXECUTIVES

Chairman: Povl Krogsgaard-Larsen, age 70
Deputy Chairman: Jens Bigum
CEO: Jørn P. Jensen, age 39
CFO: Per Brøndum Andersen
EVP, Research: Klaus Bock
VP, Trust Administration: Finn Terkelsen
Secretariat: Hans Henrik Schmidt
Property Department: Orla Kristensen
Corporate Communications and Public Affairs Director: Margrethe Skov
Investor Relations Manager: Mikael Bo Larsen
Auditors: KPMG; PricewaterhouseCoopers

LOCATIONS

HQ: 1, Valby Langgade, DK-2500 Valby, Denmark
Phone: +45-33272727   **Fax:** +45-33274850
Web: www.carlsberg.com

COMPETITORS

BBAG	Interbrew
Heineken	SABMiller
Holsten-Brauerei	Scottish & Newcastle

HISTORICAL FINANCIALS

Company Type: Public

Income Statement   FYE: December 31

	REVENUE ($ mil.)	NET INCOME ($ mil.)	NET PROFIT MARGIN	EMPLOYEES
12/02	5,015	143	2.8%	28,466
12/01	4,082	142	3.5%	27,368
Annual Growth	22.9%	0.8%	—	4.0%

Net Income History   Copenhagen: CARC

160									
140									
120									
100									
80									
60									
40									
20									
0									

12/93 12/94 12/95 12/96 12/97 12/98 12/99 12/00 12/01 12/02

Carrefour SA

At the junction of groceries, merchandise, and services, you'll find Carrefour (which means "crossroads"). The world's second-largest retailer (behind Wal-Mart), Carrefour operates more than 9,500 stores under some two dozen names, including hypermarkets (Carrefour), supermarkets (Champion), convenience stores (Shopi, Marché Plus), discount stores (Dia, Ed), and cash-and-carry stores (Promocash) in 30 countries in Europe, Latin America, and Asia. France accounts for more than half of the retailer's sales. Carrefour secured its spot as the #1 European retailer when it merged with food retailer Promodès early in 2000 and raised its banner over those stores.

Carrefour is an originator of hypermarkets — huge department store and supermarket combinations that sell food, clothing, electronics, and household appliances, among other items, at a discount. It is consolidating many of its store names under the Carrefour name for hypermarkets and Champion for supermarkets.

The French retail giant is in the express lane toward growth. Unable to build new stores in its homeland due to regulations protecting smaller stores, Carrefour expands through acquisitions at home and abroad. It has about 700 hypermarkets, supermarkets, and discount stores in Latin America (including the 140-plus store Norte grocery chain in Argentina, and about 200 outlets in Brazil where is continues to expand), and about 125 hypermarkets in eight Asian countries, including China, Japan, and South Korea. Carrefour, which has more than 40 stores in about 20 cities in China, has been rapidly expanding there. The retailer opened about 15 new hypermarkets in China in 2003, including Dia discount stores in Shanghai and Beijing. The company has met with less success in Japan. Still, it has opened three new stores there, for a total of seven stores in the world's second-largest retail market. Carrefour is investing $800 million in South Korea over the next four years to shore up its competitive position there.

Closer to home Carrefour is in the midst of an expansion drive in Italy. Carrefour already has more than 35 hypermarkets there, two of which opened in 2003, and 12 supermarkets under construction. Worldwide, the retailer opened more than 800 new outlets, including 60 hypermarkets, in 2003.

HISTORY

Although its predecessor was actually a supermarket opened by Marcel Fournier and Louis Defforey in a Fournier's department store basement in Annecy, France, the first Carrefour supermarket was founded in 1963 at the intersection of five roads (Carrefour means "crossroads"). That year Carrefour opened a vast store, dubbed a hypermarket by the media, in Sainte-Genevieve-des-Bois, outside Paris.

The company opened outlets in France and moved into other countries, including Belgium (1969), Switzerland (1970 — the year it went public), Italy and the UK (1972), and Spain (1973). Carrefour stepped up international expansion during the mid-1970s after French legislation limited its growth within the country.

Carrefour imported its French-style hypermarkets to the US (Philadelphia) in 1988. Scant advertising, limited selection, and a union strike led Carrefour to close it US operations in 1993. Carrefour opened its first hypermarket in Taiwan in 1989. The next year it formed Carma, a 50-50 joint venture with Groupama, to sell insurance. Carrefour paid over $1 billion for two rival chains (the bankrupt Montlaur chain and Euromarche) in 1991.

Daniel Bernard replaced Michel Bon, the hard-charging expansion architect, in 1992 after a 50% drop in first-half profits. A year later Carrefour partnered with Mexican retailer Gigante to open a chain of hypermarkets in Mexico. (In 1998 Carrefour bought Gigante's share of the joint venture.) In 1996 the company bought a 41% stake in rival GMB (Cora hypermarket chain) and sold its 11% stake in US warehouse retailer Costco (it now owns 20% of Costco UK). The next year Carrefour allowed 16 hypermarkets owned by Guyenne et Gascogne, Coop

Atlantique, and Chareton to operate under the Carrefour name. It expanded into Poland in 1997 and the Czech Republic in 1998.

Its biggest acquisition up to that time came in 1998 when Carrefour acquired French supermarket operator Comptoirs Modernes (with about 800 stores under the Stoc, Comod, and Marché Plus flags).

In August 1999 Carrefour announced a deal even bigger than the one for Comptoirs Modernes — a $16.3 billion merger with fellow French grocer Promodès, which operated more than 6,000 hypermarkets, supermarkets, convenience stores, and discount stores in Europe. Paul-Auguste Halley and Leonor Duval Lemonnier founded Promodès in Normandy, France, in 1961. Initially a wholesale food distributor, Promodès opened its first supermarket in 1962. This was followed by a cash-and-carry wholesale outlet (1964), a hypermarket (1970), and convenience stores (Shopi and 8 à Huit, during the 1970s). To gain regulatory approval for the acquisition, Carrefour divested its stake in the Cora chain and sold nearly 40 other stores in France and Spain. The Promodès acquisition was completed in 2000.

The company partnered with US retailer Sears and software maker Oracle, among others, to form Internet-based supply exchange GlobalNetXchange in early 2000. Also that year Carrefour bought Belgian retailer GB (about 500 stores).

In 2001 Carrefour sold its 74%-stake in Picard Surgelés (frozen food stores). Carrefour also opened its first Japanese grocery store near Tokyo that year.

The grocer sold its 10% stake in PETsMART in a public offering in July 2002. That December Carrefour acquired the remaining 20% of the shares of Centro Comerciales Carrefour, its Spanish subsidiary, it didn't already own in a public tender offer.

In February 2003, Carrefour acquired two hypermarkets in Italy from Hyparlo. In October, it entered the Scandinavian market through a franchise partnership and supply agreement with Norwegian grocer NorgesGruppen. Soon after, Carrefour Poland acquired two hypermarkets there from troubled Dutch retailer Royal Ahold.

EXECUTIVES

Chairman and CEO: Daniel Bernard, age 57
COO and Director: Joël Saveuse, age 50
Chief Financial Officer: José-Luis Duran
Managing Director, DIA International: Javier Campo
Director, Americas: Philippe Jarry
Director, Asia: René Brillet
Director, Brazil: Eric Uzan
Director, France: Bernard Dunand
Director, Human Resources: Jacques Beauchet
Director, Korea: Philippe Broianigo
Director, Merchandise: Jean-François Domont
Director, Other European Countries: Guy Yraeta
Director, Supermarkets: Philippe Pauze
General Counsel and Secretary: Etienne van Dyck
Investor Relations: Vincent Barucq
Media Relations: Christian d'Oléon
Auditors: Barbier Frinault & Autres; KPMG Audit

LOCATIONS

HQ: 6, avenue Raymond Poincaré, BP 419.16,
75016 Paris, France
Phone: +33-1-53-70-19-00   **Fax:** +33-1-53-70-86-16
Web: www.carrefour.com

Carrefour has operations in 30 countries, including Argentina, Belgium, Brazil, Chile, China, Colombia, the Czech Republic, France, Greece, Indonesia, Italy, Japan, Malaysia, Mexico, Poland, Portugal, Singapore, South Korea, Spain, Switzerland, Taiwan, Thailand, and Turkey.

PRODUCTS/OPERATIONS

Selected Operations and Banners

Hypermarkets	Ed
Carrefour	Minipreco
Supermarkets	**Other Stores**
Champion	Cash-and-carry stores
GB	Docks Market
Globi	Promocash
GS	Puntocash
Marinopoulos	
Norte	**Convenience Stores**
Super GB	8 à Huit
Super GS	Di per Di
Unic	GB Express
	Marché Plus
Hard Discount Stores	Proxi
Dia	Shopi

Other Operations

Carfuel (petroleum products)
Comptoirs Modernes (supermarkets)
Costco UK (20%, warehouse club)
Erteco (hard-discount stores)
Financiera Pryca (46%, consumer credit, Spain)
Fourcar B.V. (investments, the Netherlands)
GlobalNetXchange (Internet-based supply exchange joint venture)
Immobiliere Carrefour (real estate)
Ooshop (online shopping)
Prodirest (catering)
Providange (auto centers)
S2P (60%, consumer credit)

COMPETITORS

AEON
ALDI
Auchan
Brasileira de Distribuição
Casino Guichard
Comerci
Dairy Farm International
Delhaize
Disco
Distribución y Servicio
E.Leclerc
Edeka Zentrale
Eroski
Falabella
Migros
Galeries Lafayette
Globex Utilidades
ITM Entreprises
Ito-Yokado
Rinascente
Lidl & Schwarz Stiftung
Marui
METRO AG
Pinault-Printemps-Redoute
Primisteres Reynoird
Rallye
REWE-Zentral
Royal Ahold
SHV Holdings
Generale Supermercati
Tengelmann
Tesco
Wal-Mart

HISTORICAL FINANCIALS

Company Type: Public

Income Statement

FYE: December 31

	REVENUE ($ mil.)	NET INCOME ($ mil.)	NET PROFIT MARGIN	EMPLOYEES
12/02	72,035	1,440	2.0%	396,662
12/01	61,551	1,121	1.8%	382,821
12/00	61,018	1,004	1.6%	330,247
12/99	37,626	761	2.0%	297,290
12/98	31,985	755	2.4%	132,875
12/97	28,217	597	2.1%	113,289
12/96	29,602	597	2.0%	103,600
12/95	29,459	720	2.4%	102,900
12/94	25,539	398	1.6%	95,900
12/93	20,808	508	2.4%	81,500
Annual Growth	14.8%	12.3%	—	19.2%

2002 Year-End Financials

Debt ratio: 135.2%
Return on equity: 21.0%
Cash ($ mil.): 3,174
Current ratio: 0.65
Long-term debt ($ mil.): 8,731

Net Income History   Euronext Paris: CA

Casino Guichard-Perrachon S.A.

You won't hit the jackpot at Casino Guichard-Perrachon, but odds are you'll go home with the groceries. The company owns and operates about 8,400 hypermarkets (mostly Géant), supermarkets (Casino, Franprix, Leader Price, and Monoprix, to name a few), restaurants (Casino Cafétéria), convenience stores, and discount stores. Casino is the #1 convenience store operator in France (primarily Petit Casino, but other banners include Vival and Spar). Most of its stores are in France, but it has more than 1,900 outlets in 14 countries worldwide, including Argentina, Mexico, Poland, Taiwan, and the US (where Casino owns about 60% of the Smart & Final warehouse grocery chain). France's Rallye SA owns about 50% of Casino.

About 75% of Casino's sales are made at home in France. The company's 117 Géant hypermarkets (warehouse-style stores that sell groceries and other merchandise) contribute about 40% of revenues, with supermarkets and convenience stores a close second (about 37% of sales in 2002). Casino is France's fifth-largest supermarket company. Casino Cafétéria operates about 240 eating places in varying size and cuisines, including Poncholito (Tex-Mex) and La Pastaria (Italian). Casino is also active in e-commerce (Caly-online).

Casino has an option until the end of 2008 to increase to 51% the 38% stake it purchased in 2002 in Dutch supermarket operator Laurus.

HISTORY

Frenchman Geoffroy Guichard married Antonia Perrachon, a grocer's daughter, in 1889 in Saint-Etienne, France. Three years later Geoffroy took over his father-in-law's general store (a converted "casino" or musical hall). In 1898 the company became Société des Magasins du Casino. By 1900, when it became a joint stock company, Casino had 50 stores; it opened its 100th store in 1904. That year the company introduced its first private-label product: canned sardines. In 1917 Guichard named his two sons, Mario and Jean, as managers.

By WWI there were about 215 branches, more than 50 in Saint-Etienne. From 1919 to the early 1920s the company opened several factories to manufacture goods such as food, soap, and perfumes. In 1925 the elder Guichard retired, leaving the day-to-day operations of Casino to his two sons. (Geoffroy died in 1940.) WWII took a heavy toll on the company: About 70 Casino stores were leveled and another 450 were damaged.

The company began opening cafeterias in 1967, and in 1976 it formed Casino USA to run them. Casino USA bought an interest in the California-based Thriftimart volume retailer in 1983, renaming the company after Thriftimart's Smart & Final warehouse stores.

Casino grew by acquiring companies across France, including CEDIS (16 hypermarkets, 116 supermarkets, and 722 smaller stores in eastern France; 1985) and La Ruche Meridionale (18 hypermarkets and 112 supermarkets in southern France, 1990). Casino bought nearly 300 hypermarkets and supermarkets from Rallye SA in 1992, giving Rallye about 30% of the company. The company opened its first hypermarket in Warsaw, Poland, in 1996.

Rival Promodès made a roughly $4.5 billion hostile takeover bid for Casino in 1997. Guichard family members voted against the Promodès offer, instead backing a $3.9 billion friendly offer from Rallye (increasing their stake to nearly 50%). Casino also launched a massive counterattack — buying more than 600 Franprix and Leader Price supermarket stores from food manufacturer TLC Beatrice and acquiring a 21% stake in hypermarket chain Monoprix. Promodès withdrew its bid four months later.

Casino expanded internationally in the late 1990s, acquiring stakes in food retailers in Argentina (Libertad), Uruguay (Disco), Colombia (Exito), Brazil (Companhia Brasileira de Distribuicao), and Thailand (Big C, the country's largest retailer). It also opened its first hypermarket in Taichung, Taiwan.

Expansion in France included a joint venture (called Opera), formed in 1999 with retailer Cora SA to buy food and nonfood goods for the Casino and Cora stores, and the acquisition of 100 convenience stores (converted to the Petit Casino banner) in southwest France from retailer Guyenne et Gascogne.

Casino acquired 100 Proxi convenience stores in southeast France in 2000 from Montagne (most became Vival franchises) and more than 400 convenience stores (Eco Service and others) from Auchan. Casino also bought 51% of French online retailer CDiscount.com (CDs, videos, CD-ROMs, and DVDs), and it upped its ownership in several of its international supermarket operations, including gaining 100%

ownership of Libertad. It also increased its ownership of Monoprix to 49%.

In July 2002, Casino bought a 38% stake in Laurus NV, its financially troubled Dutch rival. Laurus operates nearly 2,000 supermarkets in Netherlands, Spain, and Belgium. (Soon after, Casino sold Laurus's unprofitable stores in Spain and Belgium.) Also in 2002, the company sold its wine division, Les Chais Beaucairois, to wine and spirits company Marie Brizard for $22 million.

EXECUTIVES

Chairman, Supervisory Board: Antoine Guichard, age 77
Chairman, Management Board: Christian P. Couvreux, age 53
CEO: Pierre B. Bouchut, age 48
Deputy Managing Director, European Hypermarkets (France and Poland): Daniel Sicard
Deputy Managing Director, European Supermarkets (France and the Netherlands): Jean-Brice Hernu
Deputy Managing Director, Purchasing, Marketing, Logistics and Information Systems: Jacques-Edouard Charret
Director, Asian and Indian Ocean region (Thailand, Taiwan, Vietnam, Reunion Island, Madagascar, Mauritius and Mayotte): André Mercier
Director, Business Development and Real Estate: Daniel Pain
Director, Corporate Communication: Jean-Pierre Berger
Director, Human Resources: Thierry Bourgeron
Director, Latin American region (Argentina, Uruguay, Venezuela, Brazil and Colombia): Francis Mauger
President and COO, Smart & Final: Etienne Snollaerts, age 47
Director, Real Estate: Jacques Ehrmann
Auditors: Bernard Roussel; Ernst & Young Audit

LOCATIONS

HQ: 24, rue de la Montat, 42008 Saint-Etienne, France
Phone: +33-4-77-45-31-31   **Fax:** +33-4-77-45-38-38
Web: www.casino.fr

Casino Guichard-Perrachon has operations in France and 14 other countries (Argentina, Brazil, Colombia, Madagascar, Mauritius, Mexico, Netherlands, Poland, Taiwan, Thailand, Uruguay, the US, Venezuela, and Vietnam).

2002 Sales

	% of total
France	77
North America	10
Asia	6
Poland	4
Latin America	3
Indian Ocean	—
Total	**100**

2002 Stores

	No.
France	6,428
Netherlands	771
Brazil	500
US	186
Poland	122
Colombia	88
Mexico	54
Venezuela	52
Argentina	48
Uruguay	45
Thailand	37
Indian Ocean	33
Taiwan	13
Total	**8,377**

PRODUCTS/OPERATIONS

Selected Operations

Banque du Groupe Casino (financial services)
Big C (68%, Thailand)
Caly-online (40%, online services)
  Cdiscount (51%, discount-priced books, CDs, DVDs, CD-ROMs, videos online)
  C-mesCourses (40%, Internet grocery shopping)
  C-online (40%, shopping hub for stores and services)
Casino (supermarkets)
Casino Cafétéria (restaurants, cafeterias, catering)
Casino Enterprise (non-food operations)
Casino USA (99.7%, with a 60% stake in Smart & Final)
Cativen (58%)
  Cada (supermarkets in Venezuela)
  Super Maxy's (hypermarkets in Venezuela)
Companhia Brasileira de Distribuicao (25%)
  Barateiro (discount stores in Brazil)
  Eletro (specialty shops in Brazil)
  Extra (hypermarkets in Brazil)
  Pão de Açúcar (supermarkets in Brazil)
Disco (50%, supermarkets in Uruguay)
Devoto (48%, supermarkets in Uruguay)
Eco Service (convenience stores)
Exito (27%, supermarkets in Colombia)
Franprix (70%, supermarkets)
Géant (hypermarkets)
Imagica (photo and digital imaging processing)
Komogo (multimedia specialist in PCs, software and video games, telephony, books)
Leader Price (70%, supermarkets)
Les Chais Beaucairos (wine production, bottling, and sales)
Libertad (hypermarkets in Argentina)
Monoprix (49%, supermarkets)
Opera (50%, joint-purchasing venture with Cora SA)
Petit Casino (convenience stores)
Spar (convenience stores)
Vival (convenience stores)

COMPETITORS

ALDI	ITM Entreprises
A.P. Møller — Mærsk	Kingfisher
Auchan	METRO AG
Carrefour	Pinault-Printemps-Redoute
Costco Wholesale	
E.Leclerc	Primisteres Reynoird
Migros	Royal Ahold
Groupe Flo	Tesco
Guyenne et Gascogne	Wal-Mart
IGA	

HISTORICAL FINANCIALS

Company Type: Public

Income Statement

FYE: December 31

	REVENUE ($ mil.)	NET INCOME ($ mil.)	NET PROFIT MARGIN	EMPLOYEES
12/02	23,957	467	1.9%	115,757
12/01	19,473	336	1.7%	106,736
12/00	17,959	344	1.9%	101,061
12/99	15,748	297	1.9%	82,548
12/98	16,519	252	1.5%	70,418
12/97	12,694	185	1.5%	58,626
12/96	12,774	160	1.3%	54,856
12/95	13,064	129	1.0%	52,482
12/94	11,711	92	0.8%	52,045
12/93	10,642	77	0.7%	45,326
Annual Growth	9.4%	22.2%	—	11.0%

2002 Year-End Financials

Debt ratio: 160.8%
Return on equity: 14.0%
Cash ($ mil.): 2,834

Current ratio: 0.96
Long-term debt ($ mil.): 5,062

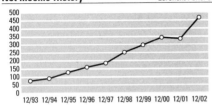

CASIO COMPUTER

CASIO COMPUTER wants a watch on every arm and a handheld in every pocket. The company makes a wide range of consumer electronics products, including calculators, digital cameras, watches, and musical keyboards. CASIO COMPUTER also manufactures visual and communications devices (PDAs, handheld PCs, cellular phones), mobile networking hardware, and electronic components. The company seeks superlatives in all its products: the G-Shock watch (1983) boasts that it's the toughest (able to survive a fall from a three-story building), and the EXILIM camera (2002) claims to be the world's thinnest (roughly the size of a credit card). The three younger brothers of late founder Tadao Kashio continue to run CASIO COMPUTER.

CASIO COMPUTER generates about a third of sales from consumer electronic products (calculators, digital cameras, and electronic dictionaries), about 20% of sales come from mobile network solutions (cellular phones, PDAs, and pocket computers) and approximately 15% of revenue comes from timepieces (digital watches, analog watches, and clocks). To combat sluggish consumer electronics sales, the company is focusing on three product categories: digital cameras, electronic dictionaries, and thin-film transistor LCD panel displays. The company plans a joint venture with Hitachi to develop mobile phone handsets.

HISTORY

In 1942 Tadao Kashio started a Tokyo-based machine shop, Kashio Manufacturing. His brother, Toshio, later joined him. After reading about a 1946 computing contest in which an abacus bested an electric calculator, Toshio, an inventor, wrote a note to himself: "Abacus is human ability; calculator is technology." In 1950 he began developing a calculator. The other Kashio brothers — Yukio, a mechanical engineer, and Kazuo, who took over sales — joined the company in the 1950s.

The brothers incorporated in 1957 as CASIO COMPUTER, an anglicization of the family name. That year the company launched its first product, an electric calculator featuring an innovative floating decimal point display; it was the first Japanese-built electric calculator. CASIO COMPUTER took advantage of new transistor technology to create electronic calculators, and in 1965 it introduced the first electronic desktop calculator with memory. The company began exports to the US in 1970.

In the 1970s only CASIO COMPUTER and Sharp emerged as significant Japanese survivors of the fierce "calculator war." CASIO COMPUTER's strategy of putting lots of new functions on a proliferation of small models and selling them at rock-bottom prices worked not only with calculators but with digital watches as well. The company introduced its first digital watch in 1974 and went on to dominate that market.

CASIO COMPUTER expanded its product line into electronic music synthesizers (1980), pocket TVs (1983), and thin-card calculators (1983). Determined to break away from the production of delicate timepieces, CASIO COMPUTER introduced shock-resistant (G-Shock) digital watches in 1983. In the mid-1980s sales were hurt by a rising yen and stiff price competition from developing Asian nations. The company responded by releasing sophisticated calculators for such specialized users as architects and insurance agents. To offset the effects of the yen's heightened value in the late 1980s, CASIO COMPUTER moved manufacturing to Taiwan, Hong Kong, South Korea, California, and Mexico. Kazuo Kashio was named president in 1988.

In 1990 CASIO COMPUTER established CASIO COMPUTER Electronic Devices to sell LCDs and chip-on-film components. In 1991 the company acquired a capital interest in Asahi, a producer of communications equipment and light electrical appliances. CASIO COMPUTER moved much of its production overseas in 1994, primarily to Thailand and Malaysia, after the high yen contributed to a nearly 28% drop in exports.

The company introduced its first digital camera in 1995. The next year CASIO COMPUTER launched its CASSIOPEIA handheld PC, and in 1997 it entered the US pager market. In 1998 the company formed subsidiary CASIO Soft to develop Microsoft-based software for handheld PCs and other mobile devices.

In 2000 the company restructured its management system, and cut expenses (particularly research and development). The following year it instituted a three-year plan designed to strengthen its digital imaging, mobile networking, and electronic components businesses. It has also reduced manufacturing costs by moving production overseas.

EXECUTIVES

Chairman: Toshio Kashio
President and CEO: Kazuo Kashio
EVP: Yukio Kashio
VP: Kiyotaka Hachiya
VP: Chikafusa Miyamoto
VP: Fumitune Murakami
VP: Tateki Oishi
VP: Naomitsu Satoh
VP: Eiichi Takeuchi
VP: Tomimoto Umeda
VP: Shinji Yamamoto
President, Casio Micronics: Noriyuki Kakihisa
Managing Director: Masayuki Hakata
Managing Director: Yoshio Ono
Managing Director: Yozo Suzuki
Managing Director: Akinori Takagi
Director: Masami Chikauchi
Director: Akira Kashio
Director: Atsushi Mawatari
Director: Tadashi Takasu
Director: Koichi Takeichi
Auditors: Asahi & Co.

LOCATIONS

HQ: Casio Keisanki Kabushiki Kaisha (CASIO COMPUTER CO., LTD.)
6-2, Hon-machi 1-chome, Shibuya-ku, Tokyo 151-8543, Japan
Phone: +81-3-5334-4111   **Fax:** +81-3-5334-4921
US HQ: 570 Mount Pleasant Ave., Dover, NJ 07801
US Phone: 973-361-5400   **US Fax:** 973-361-3819
Web: world.casio.com

CASIO COMPUTER has subsidiaries in Canada, China, France, Germany, Hong Kong, India, Japan, Malaysia, Mexico, Singapore, South Korea, Taiwan, Thailand, the UK, and the US.

2003 Sales

	$ mil.	% of total
Japan	3,422.8	70
Asia (excluding Japan)	748.7	15
Europe	414.4	8
North America	348.1	7
Adjustments	(1,277.9)	—
Total	**3,676.1**	**100**

PRODUCTS/OPERATIONS

2003 Sales

	$ mil.	% of total
Consumer electronics	1,188.9	32
Mobile network solutions	732.8	20
Timepieces	571.6	15
Electronic components	505.3	14
System equipment	428.4	12
Other	249.1	7
Total	**3,676.1**	**100**

Selected Products

Consumer electronics
Digital cameras
Electronic calculators
Electronic dictionaries
Electronic musical instruments
Label printers

Mobile network solutions
Cellular phones
PDAs
Pocket computers

Timepieces
Analog watches
Clocks
Digital watches

System equipment
Electronic cash registers (including POS)
Office computers
Page printers

Electronic components
Bump processing consignments
Carrier tape
LCDs
TCP assembly and processing consignments

Other
Factory automation
Molds
Toys

COMPETITORS

Canon	Ricoh
Fujitsu	Roland
Hewlett-Packard	Samsung
Hitachi	SANYO
IBM	Seiko
Matsushita	Sharp
Motorola	Sony
NEC	Timex
Nikon Corporation	Toshiba
palmOne	Yamaha
Philips Electronics	

HISTORICAL FINANCIALS

Company Type: Public

Income Statement

FYE: March 31

	REVENUE ($ mil.)	NET INCOME ($ mil.)	NET PROFIT MARGIN	EMPLOYEES
3/03	3,676	47	1.3%	11,481
3/02	2,881	(188)	—	14,670
3/01	3,514	52	1.5%	18,119
3/00	3,889	59	1.5%	19,325
3/99	3,788	(72)	—	17,783
3/98	3,773	88	2.3%	18,668
3/97	3,709	30	0.8%	18,725
3/96	3,841	7	0.2%	18,797
3/95	4,641	58	1.3%	18,407
3/94	3,735	52	1.4%	17,285
Annual Growth	(0.2%)	(1.1%)	—	(4.4%)

2003 Year-End Financials

Debt ratio: 110.7%
Return on equity: 4.5%
Cash ($ mil.): 644

Current ratio: 1.86
Long-term debt ($ mil.): 1,219

Net Income History

Pink Sheets: CSIOY

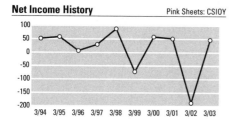

Centrica plc

Centrica is not as centered on natural gas supply as it once was. Still the UK's largest gas supplier, Centrica provides gas to 12.8 million households under the British Gas, Scottish Gas, and Nwy Prydain brands. The company also serves 5.8 million residential electricity customers, and it supplies electricity and gas to nearly 1 million businesses. Other operations include gas production, wholesale energy marketing, retail energy marketing in North America, telecommunications services, and gas heating and cooking equipment sales. Under the Goldfish name, the company offers financial services and issues credit cards. Centrica's Automobile Association provides home and motor insurance and roadside services.

The company has gained about 4.4 million retail power and gas supply customers through its aggressive acquisition strategy in North America, including more than 800,000 in the purchase of two Texas retail electric providers from American Electric Power. Centrica has also acquired Electricity Direct, a UK commercial retail supplier serving nearly 1 million customers. The company has entered continental Europe by investing in Belgium energy supplier Luminus. It has purchased several power plant interests in the UK to support its supply business, and it plans to buy plants in North America as well.

Centrica has expanded its financial services division by forming a joint venture with UK banking company Lloyds TSB. Other operations include the installation of heating and air-

conditioning and security systems. Centrica's natural gas production interests — the company has proven and probable reserves of 2.8 trillion cu. ft. — account for about 25% of its supply.

HISTORY

William Murdock invented gas lighting in 1792. In 1812 the Gas Light and Coke Company of London was formed as the world's first gas supplier to the public, and by 1829 the UK had 200 gas companies.

In the second half of the 19th century, the gas industry began looking for new uses for the fuel. Gas stoves were introduced in 1851, the geyser water heater was invented in 1868, and in 1880 the first gas units to heat individual rooms were developed.

Gas companies countered the emerging electricity industry by renting gas stoves at low prices and installing gas fittings (stove, pipe, and lights) in poor homes with no installation charges or deposits. By 1914 the UK had 1,500 gas suppliers.

The electricity industry soon made major strikes against the gas industry's dominance. In 1926 the government began reorganizing the fragmented electricity supply industry, building a national power grid and establishing the Central Electricity Generating Board to oversee it.

The gas industry was nationalized in 1949, and 1,050 gas suppliers were brought under the control of the British Gas Council. Still, the gas industry was losing. Supplying gas was more expensive than generating electricity: Gas was seen as a power supply of the past. The Gas Council sought to change that image through an aggressive marketing campaign in the 1960s, touting gas as a modern, clean fuel. Other factors played a part in its re-emergence: The Clean Air Act of 1956 steadily reduced the use of coal for home heating, liquefied natural gas was discovered in the North Sea, and OPEC raised oil prices in the 1970s. When natural gas was introduced, most of the old gasworks were demolished, and the British Gas Council (which became the British Gas Corp. in 1973) set about converting, free of charge, every gas appliance in the UK to natural gas.

As Margaret Thatcher's government began privatizing state industries, the British Gas Corp. was taken public in 1986. Freed from government control, British Gas expanded its international exploration and production activities. When the US gas industry began deregulating, British Gas formed joint venture Accord Energy in 1994 with US gas trader Natural Gas Clearinghouse (now NGC) to sell gas on the wholesale market.

With the opening of the UK gas-supply market (which began regionally in 1996 and went nationwide in 1998), British Gas split into two public companies to avoid a conflict of interest between its supply business and its monopoly transportation business. In 1997 it spun off Centrica, the retail operations, and BG (now BG Group), which received the transportation business and the international exploration and production operations.

The UK electricity supply market began opening up to competition in 1998, and Centrica won 750,000 UK electricity customers, most of them also gas customers. In 1999 it bought the Automobile Association, which provides roadside service to motorists and sells insurance, from AA members. In 2000 Centrica began offering telecom services in the UK.

Centrica moved into North America in 2000 by

purchasing two Canadian companies: natural gas retailer Direct Energy Marketing and gas production company Avalanche Energy. It gained a 28% stake in US marketing firm Energy America through the Direct Energy transaction and purchased the remaining 72% from US firm Sempra Energy the next year. Continuing its non-domestic strategy, Centrica bought a 50% interest in Belgium energy supplier Luminus.

The firm purchased 60% of the 1,260-MW Humber Power station in 2001, its first domestic power plant interest. It also acquired the UK operations of Australia's One.Tel, and it bought Enron's European retail supply business, Enron Direct, for $137 million.

In 2002 Centrica purchased the retail energy services business of Canadian pipeline company Enbridge for $637 million; it also agreed to acquire another Enron-controlled company, US retail energy supplier NewPower Holdings, for $130 million. But Centrica withdrew its offer to buy NewPower a month after the deal was announced because of concerns about NewPower's potential Enron-related liabilities. Later that year Centrica acquired 200,000 retail customer accounts in Ohio and Pennsylvania from NewPower.

EXECUTIVES

Chairman: Sir Michael Perry, age 69
Chief Executive: Roy A. Gardner, age 57, $1,690,510 pay
Deputy Chief Executive; Managing Director, British Gas: Mark S. Clare, age 46, $960,736 pay
Group Finance Director: Phillip K. Bentley, age 44, $1,012,061 pay
Group General Counsel and Company Secretary: Grant Dawson
Group Director Human Resources: Anne Minto
Group Director Marketing; Deputy Managing Director, British Gas: Simon Waugh
Director Corporate Affairs: Charles Naylor
Managing Director, Automobile Association: Roger N. B. Wood, age 60, $935,074 pay
Managing Director, Centrica Business Services: Chris Weston
Managing Director, Centrica Energy Management Group: Jake Ulrich
Managing Director, Europe: Simon Lewis
Managing Director, Goldfish: Ian Peters
Managing Director, One.Tel: Ian El-Mokadem
CEO, North America: Deryk I. King
Auditors: PricewaterhouseCoopers

LOCATIONS

HQ: Millstream, Maidenhead Road, Windsor SL4 5GD, United Kingdom
Phone: +44-1753-494-000   **Fax:** +44-1753-494-001
Web: www.centrica.co.uk

Centrica has operations in Belgium, Canada, the UK, and the US.

PRODUCTS/OPERATIONS

2002 Sales

	% of total
Retail energy supply	
British Gas residential	42
Business services	7
Energy production & wholesale sales	36
Centrica North America	8
Automobile Association	5
One.Tel	1
Goldfish	1
Other	—
Total	**100**

Selected Subsidiaries and Affiliates

Accord Energy Limited (wholesale energy trading)
AccuRead Limited (49%, meter reading)
Automobile Association Developments Limited (roadside and financial services)
Automobile Association Insurance Services Limited (financial services)
British Gas Services Limited (installation and servicing of gas heating systems)
British Gas Telecommunications (local phone service, mobile phone service, and Internet access)
British Gas Trading Limited (energy supply)
Centrica Business Services (commercial energy marketing)
Centrica Insurance Company Limited (insurance services)
Centrica Resources Limited (gas production)
CPL Retail Energy LP (retail energy marketing, US)
Direct Energy Marketing Limited (energy sales, Canada)
Energy America (energy sales, US)
Goldfish Bank Limited (75%, financial services, Goldfish credit cards)
Hydrocarbon Resources Limited (gas production)
Luminus N.V. (50%, energy supply, Belgium)
One.Tel (local phone service and Internet access)
WTU Retail Energy LP (retail energy marketing, US)

COMPETITORS

AGL Resources
British Energy
Calor
Community Energy
Gasunie
Gaz de France
Green Mountain Energy
Innogy
Powergen
Ruhrgas
Scottish and Southern Energy
Scottish Power
TNP Enterprises
United Utilities
Viridian Group
Western Power Distribution

HISTORICAL FINANCIALS

Company Type: Public

Income Statement

	REVENUE ($ mil.)	NET INCOME ($ mil.)	NET PROFIT MARGIN	EMPLOYEES
12/02	22,960	767	3.3%	38,051
12/01	18,299	469	2.6%	31,550
12/00	14,827	491	3.3%	28,305
12/99	11,666	294	2.5%	19,600
12/98	12,409	148	1.2%	16,427
12/97	12,936	(1,305)	—	15,423
12/96	13,804	(1,801)	—	19,702
Annual Growth	8.8%	—	—	11.6%

FYE: December 31

2002 Year-End Financials

Debt ratio: 34.9%
Return on equity: 26.5%
Cash ($ mil.): 45
Current ratio: 0.97
Long-term debt ($ mil.): 1,257

Net Income History

London: CNA

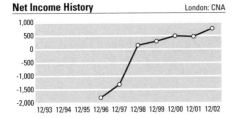

12/93 12/94 12/95 12/96 12/97 12/98 12/99 12/00 12/01 12/02

Société Nationale des Chemins de Fer Français

France's state-owned railway company, Société Nationale des Chemins de Fer Français (SNCF), is still blazing a trail as the nation's primary provider of local and long-distance passenger and freight service. The company carries about 900 million passengers annually, primarily in the region surrounding Paris. SNCF's Eurostar joint venture shuttles passengers between Paris and London via the Channel Tunnel, and Thalys links Paris with other European capitals. SNCF's high-speed TGV passenger trains travel at up to 250 mph. In addition, the company carries more than 125 million metric tons of freight annually. SNCF owns stakes in dozens of other passenger and freight transportation companies.

Holdings managed by the rail company's main investment arm, SNCF Participations, include stakes in Keolis, a French bus operator that also has operations in Canada and Germany; Géodis, one of France's largest transport and logistics groups; and Seafrance, a ferry operator.

To be a major player in Europe's increasingly deregulated road and rail transport network, SNCF is forging cross-border alliances; transnational ventures have included working with Deutsche Bahn to design a European high-speed rail system, operating a bus and rail joint venture with UK-based Go-Ahead Group, and joining the UK's FirstGroup in bidding for a UK rail franchise.

HISTORY

France's first railway line, opened in 1827, was used to haul coal from Saint-Etienne to the port of Andrezieux. Four years later the first steam locomotives and passenger service were introduced between Saint-Etienne and Lyon. Paris opened its first rail line in 1837. Although the early railway companies were under private ownership, the state controlled the network of rail lines through licensing. Under Napoleon III's Second Empire (1852-1870), the government encouraged an expansion of railway lines that linked Paris to every major town and city in France. By 1870 the main routes of France's modern railway system had been laid; in 1914 the network system had grown to nearly 40,000 km.

Following the devastation of WWI, railway companies invested heavily in rebuilding. Burdened by debt, the rail network was forced to seek government intervention for its survival. In 1938 the government set up Société Nationale des Chemins de Fer Français to unify the five largest railway systems: Compagnie de l'Est, Compagnie du Midi, Compagnie du Nord, Compagnie du Paris-Lyon-Méditerranée, and Compagnie du Paris-Orléans.

Although WWII destroyed the French railway system for a second time, the massive rebuilding enabled postwar French governments to adopt modern innovations. In 1950 SNCF began a systemwide electrification of its tracks; a decade later 7,600 km of its major lines were powered by electricity.

SNCF also pioneered the development of fast trains. Following an overhaul of SNCF in the early 1970s, the company continued to develop high-speed trains to stay competitive with airlines. In 1981 the company's TGV (*train à grande vitesse*) hit a record speed of 380 kph (236 mph). TGVs entered commercial service that year. By 1987 some 43 cities were connected to Paris by TGVs.

To add to its European logistics and freight services, SNCF acquired 20% of Spanish trucking firm TRANSFESA in 1993. In 1995 it launched Eurostar, a London-Paris service using the newly opened Channel Tunnel. Partners in the joint venture were Belgian National Railroads (Société Nationale des Chemins de Fer Belges) and European Passenger Services, the British Rail unit later spun off as Eurostar (UK). That year SNCF saw its operations disrupted by a nationwide rail strike that lasted three weeks. In 1995 SNCF also created road transport and logistics group Géodis, which it privatized a year later.

Diversifying further, SNCF also entered telecommunications in 1996 and set up a communications network to lease spare capacity. That year the company's chairman resigned following charges of corruption related to his tenure at an oil company. SNCF, also plagued by debts and strikes, decided to get back on track. It began restructuring and appointed former Aerospatiale chief Louis Gallois to head the company. In 1997 it shifted most of its debt load to Réseau Ferré de France, which was created to manage France's rail infrastructure.

In 1999 SNCF acquired Via-GTI, France's largest privately owned public transport company, which was in a joint venture with UK transport group Go-Ahead to operate the Thameslink train franchise. That year SNCF acquired Swiss rolling stock group Ermewa; it also sold its hotel interests to Accor but formed an alliance with the hotelier to offer discount lodging.

SNCF and German railway Deutsche Bahn agreed in 2000 to collaborate on developing a new generation of high-speed trains.

EXECUTIVES

Chairman: Louis Gallois, age 59
CEO: Guillaume Pepy
Deputy Managing Director, Operations: Jacques Couvert
Deputy Managing Director, Freight: Marc Véron
Director, Communications: Bernard Emsellem
Director, Economy and Finance: Claire Dreyfus-Cloarec
Director, Human Resources: Pierre Izard
Director, Production Operations: Claude Solard
Director, Voyages France Europe: Mireille Faugère
Chairman, Geodis: Pierre Blayau
Chairman, Keolis: Olivier Marembaud
Chairman, SNCF-Participations: Armand Toubol
Secretary General: Paul Mingasson
Auditors: Ernst & Young Audit; Mazars & Guérard

LOCATIONS

HQ: 34 rue du Commandant Mouchotte, 75699 Paris, France
Phone: +33-1-53-25-60-00   **Fax:** +33-1-53-25-61-08
Web: www.sncf.fr

PRODUCTS/OPERATIONS

2002 Sales

	% of total
Passengers	49
Freight	29
Infrastructure management & other services	22
Total	**100**

COMPETITORS

Air France
Arriva
British Airways
FirstGroup
National Express Group
P&O
Stagecoach
Veolia Environnement
Virgin Group

HISTORICAL FINANCIALS

Company Type: Government-owned

Income Statement

FYE: December 31

	REVENUE ($ mil.)	NET INCOME ($ mil.)	NET PROFIT MARGIN	EMPLOYEES
12/02	23,243	66	0.3%	182,815
12/01	17,830	(124)	—	220,700
12/00	18,680	167	0.9%	216,605
12/99	16,413	52	0.3%	210,911
12/98	21,619	(96)	—	210,437
12/97	20,496	(110)	—	210,437
12/96	15,442	—	—	209,746
12/95	13,785	—	—	215,787
12/94	14,322	—	—	192,089
Annual Growth	6.2%	—	—	(0.6%)

2002 Year-End Financials

Debt ratio: 441.4%
Return on equity: 1.6%
Cash ($ mil.): 2,432

Current ratio: 2.51
Long-term debt ($ mil.): 19,800

Net Income History

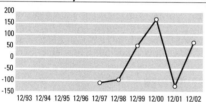

Club Méditerranée

Hobbled by a reputation that has become passe, Club Méditerranée (popularly known as Club Med) is struggling to revamp its 1970s "sea, sex, and sun" image and overcome recent losses. With more than 1.5 million guests annually, the company has 150 leisure operations in more than 40 countries, including about 120 resort villages, 12 villas, a cruise ship operation, and a French tour operator. Nearly three-quarters of its visitors come from Europe. Former chairman Philippe Bourguignon, who breathed life into Euro Disney, returned Club Med to profitability and tried new concepts such as Club Med World recreational centers.

The company closed 17 of its resorts (12 just for the winter) following September 11, 2001, to help cut costs in a diminished market for tourism. Amid losses for a second consecutive year, Bourguignon resigned in 2002.

Exor, owned by the Agnelli family of Italy, owns 24% of Club Med.

HISTORY

Belgian diamond cutter Gérard Blitz dreamed up the Club Méditerranée concept as an escape from the post-WWII doldrums in Europe. In 1950 he convened a gathering of charter members on the island of Majorca, where the group slept in tents, cooked their own food, and had a great deal of fun. The Club Med philosophy was born — vacation villages in exotic locations, combining low prices and simple amenities with community spirit and entertainment.

Frenchman Gilbert Trigano, who provided the tents for that first gathering, came on board as managing director of the company in 1954 and launched a major expansion drive. Polynesian-style huts replaced the tents at the newly opened location in Greece in 1954, and in 1956 the company set up its first ski resort in Leysin, Switzerland. Club Méditerranée was incorporated the following year.

The Rothschild Group was the company's main shareholder from 1961 until 1988, providing the capital for much of Club Méditerranée's expansion. The company went public in 1966.

Club Méditerranée expanded into the cruise line business during the late 1960s, but surly crews and the outbreak of the Arab-Israeli War in 1967 scuttled plans. In the late 1960s Club Méditerranée gained a foothold in the US, opening an office in New York and a hotel in Northern California. In the 1970s the company became one of the biggest leisure groups in France through a series of mergers and acquisitions. The 1970s and 1980s also saw the company hone its freewheeling, anything-goes image.

Club Med, Inc., was set up in New York in 1984 to handle the company's business in the Americas and Asia. Trigano relaunched the cruise line concept in 1990. Club Méditerranée's expansion came to a crashing halt in 1991 as the company suffered its first-ever loss. Political unrest in its prime tourist locations plagued operations, leading in 1993 to a major loss and Trigano's resignation (though he remained as a director). His son Serge took over as chairman that year and set about cutting costs. Lawsuits plagued the company in 1996 — one involving the fatal crash of a Club Med plane, the other involving a blackface minstrel show.

Board members looking to turn around losses created a new position for Serge Trigano in 1997 and replaced him as chairman with Philippe Bourguignon, who had helped revive Euro Disney. To boost profits, the company sold its *Club Med 1* cruise ship, as well as other assets that were outside the scope of its core resort business. It also phased out its lower-priced Club Aquarius resorts as part of its efforts to refocus on a single brand. But Club Med suffered record losses in 1997, and Trigano and his father later resigned.

With its restructuring plan in full swing in 1998, Club Med made its way back into the black. The company began renovating its village resorts and consolidating and centralizing its administrative offices. Club Med also implemented a new advertising campaign in 1998 and announced plans to open new ski resorts in the US and Canada, as well as Club Med at Paris Bercy, a recreational center in Paris. In 1999 Club Med bought French travel company Jet Tours Holding.

In 2000 it branched into e-commerce through its creation of Internet subsidiary Club Med On Line. It also purchased its third US village in 2000 in Crested Butte in Colorado. Club Med branched into the body building business in 2001 when it purchased Gymnase Club, a chain of 200 fitness clubs since renamed Club Med Gym.

In 2002 the company struck a licensing deal with Coty Inc. to begin selling beauty products.

EXECUTIVES

Chairman: Pascal Lebard
Vice Chairman, Supervisory Board: Willy Stricker
CEO: Henri Giscard d'Estaing, age 47
Auditors: Cogerco-Flipo; Ernst & Young Audit

LOCATIONS

HQ: Club Méditerranée S.A.
11 rue de Cambrai, 75957 Paris, France
Phone: +33-1-53-35-35-53   **Fax:** +33-1-53-35-32-73
Web: www.clubmed.com

Club Méditerranée has operations in about 40 countries.

Selected Club Med Resort Locations

Australia	Mauritius
Bahamas	Mexico
Croatia	Montenegro
Cuba	Morocco
Dominican Republic	New Caledonia
Egypt	Portugal
France	Saint Lucia
French West Indies	Saint Martin
Greece	Senegal
Haiti	Spain
Indonesia	Switzerland
Israel	Thailand
Italy	Tunisia
Ivory Coast	Turkey
Japan	Turks and Caicos
Malaysia	US
Maldives	

PRODUCTS/OPERATIONS

Selected Brands

Club Med
Club Med Business
Club Med Cruises
Club Med Discovery
Club Med Gym
Club Med Voyages
Club Med World
Jet Tours

COMPETITORS

Accor
Carlson
Carnival
ClubCorp
Hilton
Hyatt
Kerzner International
Société du Louvre
Marriott International
Rank
Royal Caribbean Cruises
Royal Olympic
Sandals Resorts
Sol Meliá
Starwood Hotels & Resorts
TUI
Vail Resorts
Walt Disney

HISTORICAL FINANCIALS

Company Type: Public

Income Statement   FYE: October 31

	REVENUE ($ mil.)	NET INCOME ($ mil.)	NET PROFIT MARGIN	EMPLOYEES
10/02	1,758	(61)	—	22,518
10/01	1,829	(63)	—	25,150
10/00	1,636	50	3.0%	23,700
10/99	1,586	41	2.6%	24,200
10/98	1,513	31	2.0%	23,100
10/97	1,423	(224)	—	19,400
10/96	1,562	(145)	—	20,000
10/95	1,734	35	2.0%	—
10/94	1,704	18	1.1%	—
10/93	1,378	(50)	—	—
Annual Growth	2.7%	—	—	2.0%

2002 Year-End Financials

Debt ratio: 73.0%   Current ratio: 1.95
Return on equity: —   Long-term debt ($ mil.): 445
Cash ($ mil.): 80

Net Income History

OTC: CLMDY

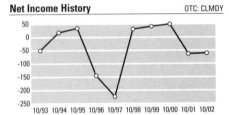

Coles Myer Ltd.

Coles Myer is the top dingo of Australian retailers. The company is Australia's largest retailer with more than 1,900 stores throughout Australia and New Zealand. Accounting for about 60% of sales is the food and liquor group, which includes about 675 Bi-Lo and Coles supermarkets, some 620 Liquorland outlets, and 150 Coles Express convenience stores. Coles Myer also sells apparel and general merchandise through its struggling department store chain Myer Grace Bros, and the discount chains Target and Kmart. (Coles Myer holds the rights from Kmart and Target Corporation to use the Kmart and Target names in Australia and New Zealand.) The retailer also sells online via e.colesmyer.

CEO John Fletcher is leading a radical five-year restructuring plan to improve the performance of Cole's nonfood operations, which includes the sale of some of the struggling divisions, but met resistance from dissident board member and former executive chairman Solomon Lew. Following a messy public brawl over the future direction of the company Lew, Coles Myer's largest shareholder, was voted off the board in November 2002. (Fletcher had threatened to quit if Lew was re-elected.) Lew's boardroom ally, Mark Leibler, was re-elected. In a bid to revive business at Myer Grace Bros, Coles is upgrading five key stores and closing two others in New South Wales. The department store chain has gone upscale and is busy luring fashion labels — including JAG, Ocean Pacific, Sean Jean, and Tommy Hilfiger — to its aisles.

Coles Myer is expanding throughout Australia

by acquiring supermarket (Franklins), liquor (Theo's Liquor), and hotel operators, and converting the outlets to its own banners. The company plans to add about 200 stores by 2007 and to refurbish all of its Kmart stores by 2006.

To better compete with rival Woolworths, which sells gasoline at its supermarkets to drive business, Coles Myer forged a discount fuel alliance with Royal Dutch/Shell Group to become the operator of Shell's network of 584 service stations in Australia by mid-2004. The Shell deal has sparked a fuel price war with archrival Woolworths. However, competition authorities are giving the Coles-Shell tie-up another look, and could scuttle the deal.

Coles Myer became Australia's #1 online seller of groceries in 2003 when it acquired ShopFast. It also operates about 70 Officeworks stores.

HISTORY

After studying US and UK chain-store retailing, including the five-and-dime stores of S. S. Kresge, George James Coles opened his first "3d, 6d, and 1/-" discount variety store in 1914 in a working-class neighborhood of Collingwood, Australia. Coles expanded to a larger store five years later. With the formation of G. J. Coles & Coy in 1921, Coles spent the 1920s and 1930s opening stores in other Australian cities. The company went public in 1927.

Following WWII the firm embarked on a major acquisition binge. Coles & Coy bought Selfridges (Australasia — New South Wales, 1950), F&G Stores (Victoria, 1951), and Penneys (Queensland, 1956). The company expanded into food retailing in 1958 with the purchase of the 54-store John Connell Dickins chain. A year later it acquired Beilby's of South Australia and, in 1960, the Matthews Thompson group of 265 outlets in New South Wales.

Coles & Coy opened its first major discount store, Colmart, in 1968 and opened its first Kmart the following year through a joint venture with S. S. Kresge. In 1978 it bought out the renamed Kmart Corporation's interest in return for stock.

The company bought several liquor store chains in 1981, including Liquorland and Mac the Slasher (converted to the Liquorland banner). Coles & Coy began opening Super K food and general merchandise stores in 1982. Two years later it bought Katies, a women's apparel chain with 117 stores.

Coles & Coy became Coles Myer in 1986 when it merged with the Myer Emporium chain of Melbourne. Founded in 1900 by Sidney Myer, the company went public in 1925 and began opening Target stores in 1970. At the time of the merger, Myer was Australia's #3 retailer and largest department store chain, with 56 department stores, 68 Target stores, 122 Fosseys variety stores, 45 Country Road stores (spun off in 1987), and a number of Red Rooster fast-food outlets.

In 1987 Coles Myer entered discount food retailing with the acquisition of 25 Bi-Lo supermarkets. The next year it moved outside Australia when it opened a Kmart in New Zealand. In 1993 the company introduced World 4 Kids toy and recreation stores and a chain of office supply stores, Officeworks. That year Coles Myer repurchased the 21.5% stake owned by Kmart while continuing to use the Kmart name in Australia and New Zealand.

When finance director Philip Bowman was fired in 1995, he sued the company for wrongful dismissal. Bowman claimed he was investigating

a 1990 transaction that cost the company $18 million while indirectly benefiting chairman Solomon Lew by the same amount. The "Yannon" deal resulted in Lew's ouster as chairman, though he stayed on the board of directors. Bowman's suit was settled for $1.1 million. In 1997 former chairman and CEO Brian Quinn was found guilty of conspiring to defraud Coles Myer of $3.5 million (used to pay for renovations to his Melbourne home) and sentenced to four years in prison.

In 1997 and 1998 Coles Myer started a dozen concept stores, including Myer Megamart (furniture and electronics), Target Home (home furnishings), and Essentially Me (health and beauty items). The trend continued in 1999 with let's eat (a combination restaurant and grocery).

In 2000 Coles Myer created an e-commerce unit, e.colesmyer, under which it consolidated all of its online businesses. John Fletcher became CEO in September 2001 following the retirement of Dennis Eck.

Under Fletcher, Coles Myer began in 2002 its biggest restructuring in more than a decade. Changes include the sale of its fast-food restaurant chain Red Rooster in May 2002, the sale and leaseback of properties, a flatter management structure, and the discontinuation of the company's popular shareholder discount plan, which gave investors discounts in some Coles Myer stores. Stan Wallis' five-year stint as chairman came to an end prematurely in October when he was replaced by director Rick Allert.

Coles Myer bought the Australian operations of Office Depot in January 2003. In March of that year it sold its Sydney Central Plaza shopping center to Westfield Trust as part of its five-year restructuring plan. In June, the company acquired Australia's biggest online food retailer ShopFast. Overall, in 2003 Coles Myer opened 182 new stores including 42 new supermarkets.

EXECUTIVES

Chairman: Richard H. (Rick) Allert, age 60
Managing Director, Chief Executive Officer, and Director: John E. Fletcher, age 52, $2,044,636 pay
CFO: Fraser MacKenzie
Chief Officer, Corporate and Property Services: Tim Hammon, $812,853 pay
Managing Director, BiLo: Peter Merritt
Managing Director, Coles Express: Joe Barberis
Managing Director, Coles Supermarkets: Gerry Masters
Managing Director, Food, Liquor, and Fuel: Steven Cain, age 38
Managing Director, Kmart: Hani Zayadi, age 50
Managing Director, Liquor: Craig Watkins
Managing Director, Myer Grace Bros.: Dawn Robertson, $1,125,315 pay
Managing Director, Target: Larry Davis, $886,529 pay
CIO: Peter Mahler
General Manager, Corporate Affairs: Pamela Catty
General Manager, Human Resources: Ian Clubb
General Manager, Supply Chain: Andrew Potter
Auditors: PricewaterhouseCoopers

LOCATIONS

HQ: 800 Toorak Rd., Tooronga, Victoria 3146, Australia
Phone: +61-3-9829-3111   **Fax:** +61-3-9829-6787
Web: www.colesmyer.com

Coles Myer operates more than 1,900 retail stores throughout Australia and New Zealand.

PRODUCTS/OPERATIONS

2003 Sales

	% of total
Food & Liquor Group	61
Kmart & Officeworks	16
MGB and Megamart	12
Target	10
Emerging businesses (e.colesmyer)	1
Total	**100**

2003 Stores

	No.
Supermarkets (Bi-Lo, Coles)	677
Liquorland	618
Kmart & Officeworks	340
Target	260
Myer Grace Bros.	69
Total	**1,964**

COMPETITORS

ALDI
Barbeques Galore
Body Shop
David Jones
Esprit Holdings
Harris Scarfe Holdings
Harvey Norman Holdings
InterTAN
Metcash Trading
Metro Cash and Carry
Woolworths

HISTORICAL FINANCIALS

Company Type: Public

Income Statement

FYE: Last Sunday in July

	REVENUE ($ mil.)	NET INCOME ($ mil.)	NET PROFIT MARGIN	EMPLOYEES
7/03	17,496	278	1.6%	165,000
7/02	13,946	192	1.4%	164,000
7/01	12,100	77	0.6%	155,000
7/00	14,414	174	1.2%	157,000
7/99	14,614	255	1.7%	151,284
7/98	12,499	215	1.7%	148,346
7/97	14,298	290	2.0%	148,000
7/96	14,583	217	1.5%	152,744
7/95	12,396	293	2.4%	143,281
7/94	11,782	314	2.7%	135,365
Annual Growth	**4.5%**	**(1.3%)**	**—**	**2.2%**

2003 Year-End Financials

Debt ratio: 36.9%
Return on equity: 16.2%
Cash ($ mil.): 586
Current ratio: 1.35
Long-term debt ($ mil.): 740

No. of shares (mil.): 152
Dividends
  Yield: 3.1%
  Payout: 68.6%
Market value ($ mil.): 5,751

Stock History

NYSE: CM

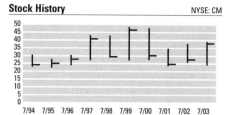

	STOCK PRICE ($) FY Close	P/E High/Low		PER SHARE ($) Earnings	Dividends	Book Value
7/03	37.95	23	14	1.72	1.18	16.14
7/02	27.50	31	22	1.19	1.05	12.13
7/01	24.70	69	48	0.50	1.52	11.22
7/00	30.19	39	23	1.20	1.32	11.08
7/99	46.50	27	15	1.77	1.23	12.63
7/98	29.50	28	20	1.51	0.73	11.48
7/97	40.75	21	14	2.02	1.39	13.08
7/96	27.75	20	16	1.49	0.72	14.00
7/95	25.00	19	16	1.45	1.21	14.08
7/94	24.01	17	13	1.78	1.08	15.16
Annual Growth	**5.2%**	**—**	**—**	**(0.4%)**	**1.0%**	**0.7%**

Compass Group

This is one compass that's really attracted to medals. Compass Group, the world's largest food service company with operations in more than 90 countries, managed nearly all of the food serving operations at the 2002 Winter Olympics in Salt Lake City. It provides contract catering and concession services at airports, hospitals, rest areas, and schools. Compass also operates about 5,000 eateries, including Upper Crust and Caffè Ritazza, and franchises a number of Burger King, Pizza Hut, and Krispy Kreme outlets. In addition, the company provides corporate food services for clients such as American Express, IBM, and ChevronTexaco.

Compass Group was a large player in the hotel business through its Forte Hotel Group, which included about 400 hotels operating under the Le Méridien brand. As part of its plan to focus solely on catering, Compass sold that division to Japanese investment bank Nomura International in 2001. Compass sold its Travelodge budget motel business and Little Chef roadside eateries to London-based private equity firm Permira in 2003.

Despite its size and reach, Compass continues to grow through strategic acquisitions, especially in the fertile US market. In late 2000/2001 the company bought the 280-unit Boston-based Au Bon Pain bakery-café chain, vending machine company Vendepac, and health care services company Crothall Services. Its Olympic contract, estimated to be worth between $25 million and $40 million, marked only the second time since 1968 that Philadelphia-based rival ARAMARK did not supply food service operations at the Olympic Village. Compass enjoys contracts in the UK at the Liverpool Football Club and the Sydney Football Stadium. It is penetrating deeper into the Asian market with its buy of Seiyo Food Systems, Japan's #2 food services group.

Compass' success derives from the global scope of its operations and its standardized sup-

port structure, which allow it to leverage its strengths in gaining major contracts. Adding to that strength, the company merged in 2000 with UK hospitality and media giant Granada Group. In conjunction with the merger plans, Granada spun off its media assets as a separate company, Granada Media. However, in 2001 the new Granada Compass demerged and made Compass Group a public company again. That year Compass purchased Morrison Management Specialists.

HISTORY

Compass Group was formed in 1987 when management bought out the catering business of London-based food and spirits giant Grand Metropolitan (now Diageo) for $260 million. The company went public the next year, listing on the London Stock Exchange. Gerry Robinson, CEO at the time, left in 1991 to take a position with British TV programming giant Granada Group, where he helped that company diversify into food service operations. Finance director Francis Mackay took over as CEO.

Believing that real growth in the catering industry could come from size and economies of scale, Mackay orchestrated a $2.5 billion acquisition plan over the next five years. In 1992 Compass bought Traveller's Fare (now Upper Crust), a railway caterer, from British Rail. The company expanded into airports the following year with the acquisition of Scandinavian Airlines System's catering operations. Then in 1994 Compass bought Canteen Corporation, the US's third-largest vending and food service company.

Compass achieved its goal of becoming the world's largest caterer in 1995 with the acquisition of France's Eurest International, putting it ahead of Sodexho and Granada. Mackay calmed London investors nervous about the pace of Compass' acquisitions by selling off its hospital management operations and paying lip service to focusing on organic growth. Later that year Compass was awarded the world's largest food service contract, a $250-million, five-year deal with IBM.

By 1996 the company seemed to have forgotten all about organic growth, buying Service America, and then Daka International and France's SHRM in 1997. French subsidiary Eurest later snatched a $40 million contract from rival Sodexho to supply the staff restaurants at Euro Disney, one of France's top three catering contracts. The next year Compass solidified its position in the airport markets with a five-year licensing deal for use of the TGI Friday's brand, joining Taco Bell, Pizza Hut, Burger King, and Harry Ramsden's fish and chip shops in Compass' quiver of branded airport outlets.

In 1999 CEO Mackay became group chairman, leaving the reins to Compass' chief of North American operations, Michael Bailey. The company's US acquisitions quickly paid off that year with a contract to serve 90% of the food venues at the 2002 Winter Olympics in Salt Lake City. In 2000 the company merged with UK hospitality giant Granada Group (the combined firm became Granada Compass), which then spun off its media operations as a separate company, Granada Media. Late that year it bought Boston-based bakery/café chain Au Bon Pain.

The new company got a quick divorce in 2001 when Granada Compass decided to demerge and make Compass Group public again. Compass Group later sold the Le Méridien hotel operations it gained from the Granada merger to Nomura International for nearly $3 billion. (The firm kept the Travelodge chain but sold it in 2003.) The company then began making purchases, including Morrison Management Specialists for $563 million, the 66% it didn't already own in Selecta Group, UK vending machine company Vendepac, and health care services management company Crothall Services. Compass lost seven operating sites during the September 11 terrorist attacks on the World Trade Center. Late in 2001 Compass strengthened its presence in Japan with the $277 million acquisition of Seiyo Food Systems, that country's #2 food services group.

In 2002 Compass signed arguably the industry's largest contract ever, a $200 million a year deal to feed ChevronTexaco employees around the world. In February 2003 the company sold its Travelodge motel business and Little Chef diners to private equity firm Permira for $1.14 billion, a 5% discount to the asking price.

EXECUTIVES

Chairman: Francis H. Mackay, age 58, $621,733 pay
Group Chief Executive: Michael J. Bailey, age 54, $367,188 pay
Group Finance Director: Andrew P. Lynch, age 45, $329,153 pay
Group Human Resources Director: Clive W. P. Grundy, age 51
Group Strategy & Development Director: Mark Boyle
Group Company Secretary: Ronald M. Morley, age 49
CEO, Bon Appetit: Fedele Bauccio
CEO, Commercial Services: Chris D. Bucknall, age 52
CEO, Western Europe: Antoine E. A. Cau, age 54
CEO, UK and Ireland: Don A. Davenport, age 59
CEO, Global Business: Alain F. Dupuis, age 57, $382,470 pay
CEO, North America: Gary R. Green, age 45
CEO, Northern Europe and Central Europe: Marcel Jacobs, age 57
CEO, Canteen Vending Services, Compass Group North America: Mike Kiser
CEO, Restaurant Associates: Nick Valenti
CEO, Southern Europe, South America, and Asia Pacific: Miguel Ramis, age 45
CEO, Foodbuy LLC: Tony Shearer
Senior Director Corporate Communications, Compass Group North America: Cheryl Webster Queen
Corporate Communications Director: Cathi Lawrence
Treasurer: Justin Besley
Public Relations: Paul Kelly
Auditors: Deloitte & Touche LLP

LOCATIONS

HQ: Compass Group PLC
Compass House, Guildford St.,
Chertsey, Surrey KT16 9BQ, United Kingdom
Phone: +44-1932-573-000   **Fax:** +44-1932-569-956
US HQ: 2400 Yorkmont Rd., Charlotte, NC 28217
US Phone: 704-329-4000   **US Fax:** 704-329-4160
Web: www.compass-group.com

Compass Group's food catering and concession service operates in more than 90 countries.

2002 Sales

	$ mil.	% of total
Continental Europe & other regions	5,856	35
North America	5,785	35
UK	4,933	30
Total	**16,574**	**100**

PRODUCTS/OPERATIONS

Selected Operating Units

Canteen Vending (vending machines)
Chartwells (education food services)
Eurest (workplace food service contracts)
Eurest Sutcliffe (UK workplace food service contracts)
FLIK (upscale food services)
Letheby & Christopher (sporting and leisure events)
Levy Restaurants (sporting and leisure events)
Medirest (health care services)
Morrison Management Specialists (health care food service)
Patina (sporting and leisure events)
Restaurant Associates (sporting and leisure events)
Roux Fine Dining (executive hospitality)
Scolarest (education food services)
Select Service Partner (airport food service)
Selecta (vending machines)

COMPETITORS

Albert Abela	Pret A Manger
ARAMARK	Rentokil Initial
Autogrill	Sodexho Alliance
Delaware North	Sodexho
HDS Services	
Morrison Management Specialists	

HISTORICAL FINANCIALS

Company Type: Public

Income Statement

FYE: September 30

	REVENUE ($ mil.)	NET INCOME ($ mil.)	NET PROFIT MARGIN	EMPLOYEES
9/02	16,574	347	2.1%	392,352
9/01	12,839	657	5.1%	344,830
9/00	7,968	180	2.3%	211,127
9/99	7,924	226	2.8%	191,407
9/98	7,156	194	2.7%	154,758
9/97	5,974	161	2.7%	130,548
9/96	4,144	155	3.7%	107,843
Annual Growth	**26.0%**	**14.3%**	**—**	**24.0%**

2002 Year-End Financials

Debt ratio: 65.3%
Return on equity: 8.1%
Cash ($ mil.): 638

Current ratio: 0.57
Long-term debt ($ mil.): 2,885

Net Income History

London: CPG

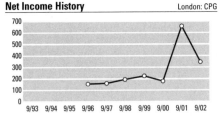

COMPETITORS (continued / Computacenter section)

Computacenter

Computacenter has learned that the key to success is not so much what you sell, but rather how you serve. The UK's largest PC distributor provides hardware and software from such leading vendors as IBM, Sun Microsystems, and Microsoft. The company also offers a wide range of information technology (IT) services, including outsourcing, systems integration, and network

support and management. In addition, Computacenter has a 50% stake in electronic procurement software firm Biomni, a joint venture with sister company Dealogic (formerly Computasoft).

The company has maintained steady growth by focusing its geographic scope and expanding the range of its services. The company has acquired several continental business units from GE Capital IT Solutions. (This after selling its own German operations to GE in 2001.) Its customers include Royal Mail Group (formerly Consignia), Elior, Royal & Sun Alliance Insurance Group, and Safeway.

Co-founders Peter Ogden and Philip Hulme each owns about 22% of the company. Schroder Investment Management has reduced its equity stake to less than 10%.

HISTORY

Computacenter's story is nothing if not about timing. It began at the dawn of the PC revolution, and blossomed because the company's two founders were already awake. Management consultant Philip Hulme and ex-Morgan Stanley executive Peter Ogden formed Computacenter in 1981. The UK entrepreneurs, who met while seeking MBAs at Harvard University in the early 1970s, started their computer distribution business after perceiving a need among large corporations for computer systems more adaptable than the wall-sized, expensive mainframes then in vogue.

By 1983, thanks mainly to the birth of IBM's PC, Computacenter was generating sales of £1.5 million. The next year Computacenter created a sibling company called Computasoft to specialize in financial-sector applications. By 1984 Computacenter had six branch stores. In 1989 it joined the International Computer Group, a joint venture formed that year to cater to international organizations with global service concerns.

In 1990 Investcorp, a development capital firm for a consortium of rich Arab investors, bought 30% of Computacenter. (Investcorp sold its stake in 1995 at a strong profit.) The company continued to ride the corporate networked PC trend and in 1993 logged $526 million in sales and cemented its reputation as the UK's #1 desktop services firm.

Michael Norris, who began at Computacenter as a junior salesman in 1984, was named CEO in 1994. Using his background as one of the company's star sellers, Norris intensified Computacenter's organic growth. The company also reengineered its maintenance business that year. Computacenter suffered a bit of infamy in 1994 after four people were murdered during a robbery on a yacht in the Caribbean. The yacht, named for the company, was owned by Odgen.

In 1995 Computacenter won the largest desktop contract in Europe, signing an agreement with British Telecommunications. That year the company bought French firm Networx SA and made it a majority-owned Computacenter subsidiary. The company in 1996 beefed up its technical acumen to include consulting and major networking support. Sales that year exceeded $1.3 billion.

Sales reached the $1.8 billion mark in 1997, and the company bought German firm BITService and revamped it into a German subsidiary. Computacenter went public in 1998 in the midst of a high-tech stock frenzy that made 30 of its employees millionaires overnight. The already wealthy Hulme and Ogden donated most of their money to individual charitable trusts.

Also in 1998, in a continuing effort to expand its services, Computacenter forged an alliance with Microsoft to supply planning and support services to Windows NT customers. That year the company founded its e-commerce division, iGroup, which develops Internet commerce strategies and provides Web site monitoring and hosting services.

In 1999 Computacenter signed a three-year contract renewal with British Telecommunications (now BT Group) to provide the telecom giant with systems maintenance and e-commerce implementation services. Later that year Computacenter launched Biomni, a 50-50 joint venture with Computasoft (now Dealogic), to develop business-to-business software for electronic trading networks.

Citing reasons of unprofitability, Computacenter discontinued operations in Germany in 2001, selling its German arm to GE Capital IT Solutions. (It acquired GE's IT business units in the UK and France as part of the deal.) The company also closed its UK-based iGroup business that year.

EXECUTIVES

Chairman: Ron Sandler, age 51
CEO: Michael J. (Mike) Norris, age 41
COO: Chris Webb
Group Director, Finance: Tony Conophy, age 45
Secretary: Alan Pottinger
Director, Client Services and Financial Services Sector: Simon Walsh
Director, Commercial Sector: Mark Kenealy
Director, Commercial Sector: Julie O'Hara
Director, Corporate Planning and Strategy: Cherry Freeman
Director, Direct Businesses: Mike Jones
Director, Government Sector: Colin Brown
Director, Human Resources and Customer Satisfaction: Tim Way
Director, Information Systems: Mark Slaven
Director, International Operations: Mohammed (Mo) Siddiqi
Director, Maintenance: Ian Roberts
Director, Marketing: Adam Austin
Director, Remote Services: Neil Meddick
Director, Scotland: Andy Purvis
Director, Services: John Joslin
Director, Strategic Partners Sector: Sarah Long
Manager, Public Relations: Tessa Freeman
Auditors: Ernst & Young LLP

LOCATIONS

HQ: Computacenter plc
Hatfield Ave., Hatfield,
Hertfordshire AL10 9TW, United Kingdom
Phone: +44-17-0763-1000   **Fax:** +44-17-0763-9966
Web: www.computacenter.co.uk

Computacenter has offices in Austria, Belgium, France, Germany, Luxembourg, and the UK.

2002 Sales

	$ mil.	% of total
UK	2,562	83
France	508	16
Belgium & Luxembourg	20	1
Total	**3,090**	**100**

PRODUCTS/OPERATIONS

Services

Disaster recovery
E-commerce consulting
Management outsourcing
Procurement
Systems planning and implementation
Technical support
Training

COMPETITORS

Atos Origin	ITC Infotech
Azlan	LogicaCMG
Bull	Misys
Cap Gemini	MoreDirect
Dell	Morse
Diagonal	NIIT
DiData	Patni Computer Systems
EDS	Resilien
Fujitsu Services	Satyam
GE Access	Silverline Technologies
Getronics	Tata Consultancy
HCL Technologies	Triple P
Hewlett-Packard	Unisys
Infosys Tech	Wipro
IBM	

HISTORICAL FINANCIALS

Company Type: Public

Income Statement

FYE: December 31

	REVENUE ($ mil.)	NET INCOME ($ mil.)	NET PROFIT MARGIN	EMPLOYEES
12/02	3,090	59	1.9%	5,974
12/01	3,038	28	0.9%	5,894
12/00	2,968	59	2.0%	5,703
12/99	2,846	86	3.0%	5,618
12/98	2,631	65	2.5%	3,939
12/97	1,870	51	2.7%	2,844
Annual Growth	**10.6%**	**3.0%**	**—**	**16.0%**

2002 Year-End Financials

Debt ratio: 0.1%
Return on equity: 16.5%
Cash ($ mil.): 148

Current ratio: 1.44
Long-term debt ($ mil.): 1

Net Income History

London: CCC

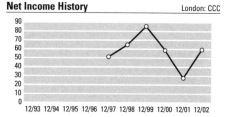

Corus Group plc

Keeping a stiff upper lip is mandatory for Corus Group (formerly British Steel), one of the world's largest steel companies. The company was formed when the UK privatized its major steelworks in 1988. It then changed its name to Corus Group after acquiring most of Dutch rival Koninklijke Hoogovens. Corus makes coated and uncoated strip products, sections and plates, wire rod, engineering steels, and semi-finished carbon steel products. It also manufactures alu-

minum, including rolled and extrusion products. Customers include the automotive, construction, and packaging industries.

Corus has implemented a strategic plan that includes cutting more than 12,000 jobs (about 10,000 in the UK). As part of that same plan the company is looking for a buyer for its aluminum and stainless steel units to concentrate solely on its carbon-steel business. As a consequence, the company sold its stainless steel interests in AvestaPolarit to Outokumpu, cutting its interest in the stainless steel market.

Corus was looking into taking a giant leap forward by purchasing Brazilian-based steelmaker Companhia Siderúrgica Nacional (CSN) but the deal fell through because of CSN's large debt and the ailing Brazilian currency.

French aluminum producer Pechiney had agreed to buy Corus Group's aluminum assets but Corus' supervisory board denied the sale, which was then upheld by an Amsterdam court. The deal, worth about $815 million, would have cut debt and helped offset losses at the company's UK steel operations.

HISTORY

It took decades of aggressive government regulation of the UK steel industry to hammer out Corus Group. The process began with price-control measures in the 1930s and in 1950 the Labour government followed up by nationalizing steel producers on the grounds that they represented an unduly powerful oligopoly. A Conservative government took over in 1951 and sold most of the nationalized firms, primarily to their former shareholders. In place of nationalization, an Iron Steel Board — with the power to set maximum steel prices and with the final say on large investments — was formed.

The presence of price controls and an ever-present chance of renationalization discouraged capital investment. Even so, technological innovations such as continuous casting and oxygen-based production enabled UK steelmakers to double production between 1945 and 1960. Meanwhile, competition from European producers stiffened, as did competition from a rebuilt Japan. To add to the UK steel industry's woes, demand began slacking off in the 1960s.

In 1964 the Labour Party, which was committed to renationalizing steel, returned to power. It passed the Iron and Steel Act of 1967, nationalizing about 90% of the UK's steel-making capacity under a new holding company, British Steel Corporation (BSC). However, specialized, nonintegrated companies and rerolling companies remained freestanding, allowing them to benefit from price controls on BSC steel. BSC consisted of 14 crude steel companies' assets with a 475,000 ton annual capacity. The government compensated shareholders based on stock market values, paying much more than the companies were worth. To make matters worse, the companies' return on capital was a meager 3.7%.

BSC began consolidating its small, outdated facilities into larger works with advanced equipment. In the midst of a huge investment program, the mid-1970s' energy crisis hit and steel demand fell; the company began closing its outdated mills. A 1980 strike cost BSC a large chunk of its market share and showed that steel requirements could be met through imports. That year the European Commission (EC) established production limits to reduce the steel glut. It also decided to regulate the amount of state aid steel producers could receive. By the end of 1980, BSC's workforce had been reduced to about 130,000 people — half its size when the companies were nationalized in 1967. During the 1980s BSC disposed of about $1 billion in noncore assets to focus on efficient steelmaking. State aid to European steel producers was largely prohibited in 1985 and the EC's quota system ended in 1988.

The British Steel Act of 1988 privatized BSC, and British Steel was born. The company recorded big profits in 1990, but then a recession hit, and British Steel suffered two years of losses before returning to profitability in 1994. The next year the company announced plans to expand its operations in emerging markets such as Asia, Central Europe, and Latin America. In 1996 British Steel sold about 6,000 tons of rails to Latin America. The next year it built a steel plant in Alabama — its first outside the UK — and sold its British Steel Forgings unit, which made components for the aerospace and automobile industries.

In 1998 British Steel joined other steelmakers in asking the EC to investigate Asian steel dumping. Stiff competition and a strong domestic currency caused the company to suffer a loss for fiscal 1999. That year British Steel paid $2.4 billion for Dutch steelmaker Koninklijke Hoogovens. At the same time, British Steel became Corus, a name chosen because it has no significant meaning in any language. Amid losses, joint chief executives John Bryant and Fokko van Duyne were forced out in 2000.

In 2001 the company announced that it was cutting more than 6,000 jobs in an effort to return to profitability. In 2002 Corus agreed to sell its stainless steel operations to Outokumpu Oyj (Finnish metal producer) for approximately $525 million. That same year, Corus came close to buying Brazil's largest steelmaker, Companhia Siderúrgica Nacional (CSN), but its debt of about $2.6 billion and the weakening Brazilian currency put a stop to the deal.

In 2003 president Anthony Pedder resigned after a tumultuous financial year and a court decision, which reigned in the sale of its aluminum business to French aluminum maker Pechiney.

EXECUTIVES

Chairman: Jim Leng, age 56
Chief Executives: Philippe Varin, age 50
Executive Director and COO: Stuart I. Pettifor, age 57, $513,248 pay
Executive Director, Finance and Board Member: David M. Lloyd, age 39, $513,248 pay
Executive Director and Board Member: Franswillem C.W. Briët, age 53, $377,260 pay
Executive Director and Board Member: Henk A.M. Vrins, age 58, $513,248 pay
Executive Director, Long Products: Paul Lormor, age 53
Executive Director, Technology: Jeffrey W. Edington, age 62
Executive Director: Chris Hollick, age 54
Executive Director: Allan J. Johnston, age 53
President, Corus Group (U.S.): Thomas Kinley
Secretary: Richard Reeves, age 57
Investor Relations: Anthony Hamilton
Auditors: PricewaterhouseCoopers

LOCATIONS

HQ: 30 Millbank, London SW1P 4WY, United Kingdom
Phone: +44-20-7717-4444   **Fax:** +44-20-7717-4455
US HQ: 475 N. Martingale Rd., Schaumburg, IL 60173-2405
US Phone: 847-619-0400   **US Fax:** 847-619-0468
Web: www.corusgroup.com

Corus has sales and service centers in about 40 countries throughout Europe and North America; it manufactures steel in more than 15 countries.

2002 Sales

	$ mil.	% of total
EU (excluding UK)	5,554	48
UK	2,803	24
Other European countries	3,226	28
Total	**11,583**	**100**

PRODUCTS/OPERATIONS

2002 Sales

	$ mil.	% of total
Carbon steel	10,041	87
Aluminum	1,542	13
Total	**11,583**	**100**

Selected Products and Operations

Aluminum products
Channels
Columns
Electrical steels
Engineering billet and bar
Joists
Light-gauge steel for packing and non-packing
Processing
Railway products
Semi-finished steel
Special strip
Stainless steel
Steel plate products
Strip products
Tube products
Universal beams
Wire rod

Selected Subsidiaries

Corus LP (60%, Canada)
European Electrical Steels Limited (75%)
Norsk Stål AS (50%, Norway)
Norsk Stål Tynnplater AS (50%, Norway)
Orb Electrical Steels Limited (75%)
Thomas Steel Strip Corp. (US)
Tuscaloosa Steel Corporation (US)

COMPETITORS

Acesita
Allegheny Technologies
Arcelor
BHP Steel
BÖHLER-UDDEHOLM
Carpenter Technology
Cockerill Sambre
Gerdau AmeriSteel
International Steel Group
Kobe Steel
Nippon Steel
Nucor
POSCO
Salzgitter
Sumitomo Metal Industries
ThyssenKrupp
United States Steel

HISTORICAL FINANCIALS

Company Type: Public

Income Statement

FYE: December 31

	REVENUE ($ mil.)	NET INCOME ($ mil.)	NET PROFIT MARGIN	EMPLOYEES
12/02	11,583	(738)	—	50,900
12/01	11,211	(610)	—	55,600
12/00*	17,491	(2,017)	—	64,900
3/99	10,087	(131)	—	46,500
3/98	11,613	378	3.3%	50,000
3/97	11,844	508	4.3%	52,900
3/96	10,757	1,186	11.0%	50,100
3/95	7,755	759	9.8%	—
3/94	6,224	103	1.6%	—
3/93	6,510	(197)	—	—
Annual Growth	**6.6%**	**—**	**—**	**0.3%**

*Fiscal year change

2002 Year-End Financials

Debt ratio: 52.5%
Return on equity: —
Cash ($ mil.): 371
Current ratio: 2.02
Long-term debt ($ mil.): 2,301
No. of shares (mil.): 313
Dividends
　Yield: 0.0%
　Payout: —
Market value ($ mil.): 1,305

Stock History

NYSE: CGA

	STOCK PRICE ($) FY Close	P/E High/Low		PER SHARE ($) Earnings	Dividends	Book Value
12/02	4.17	—	—	(2.36)	0.00	14.01
12/01	10.43	—	—	(1.95)	0.00	14.25
12/00*	10.00	—	—	(6.49)	0.16	16.48
3/99	20.19	—	—	(0.66)	0.62	35.35
3/98	24.25	16	11	1.91	2.06	35.96
3/97	26.63	12	9	2.50	1.97	38.28
3/96	29.50	5	4	5.84	1.59	35.41
3/95	26.25	7	5	3.76	0.58	32.82
3/94	20.38	43	23	0.51	0.23	27.86
3/93	13.38	—	—	(0.98)	0.33	28.14
Annual Growth	**(12.1%)**	**—**	**—**	**—**	**—**	**(7.5%)**

*Fiscal year change

Creative Technology Ltd.

Creative Technology wants PC audiophiles to get creative. The company is a leading maker of digital entertainment products, including PC sound cards (Sound Blaster), graphics accelerator cards (the 3D Blaster family), MP3 players (Nomad), and PC multimedia upgrade kits. Creative also makes modems and CD and DVD drives for PCs. Subsidiaries include Cambridge Soundworks (PC speakers), Creative Labs, and E-MU/ENSONIQ (audio chips and electronic musical instruments). Creative's top customers include computer manufacturers Dell, Gateway, and

Hewlett-Packard. Co-founder and CEO Sim Wong Hoo owns about 33% of Creative.

The company generates about a third of its sales from PC audio products. Nearly half of Creative's sales are to customers in the Americas.

After sales of its PC sound products had softened, Creative turned to a variety of online initiatives during the Internet boom. The subsequent dot-com bust and a general downturn in worldwide electronics markets led the company to write off losses on its Internet investments and to refocus on its core audio products — PC cards and chipsets, speakers, and the Nomad line of MP3 players.

Creative has entered the market for graphics chips with its acquisition of 3Dlabs, and has launched its first mass market graphics card (Graphics Blaster) for digital camera and computer gaming applications. The company is also targeting the game development market with its Sound Blaster Audigy sound cards and software tools for multi-channel interactive content development. Creative has announced it will emphasize sales of personal digital entertainment products such as MP3 players and digital cameras by selling directly to retail consumers through warehouse sales and sales outlets in the US.

HISTORY

In 1981 Sim Wong Hoo (chairman and CEO) and Ng Kai Wa (later joined by Chay Kwong Soon) used a $6,000 stake to found Creative Technology as an engineering services company. It began making Apple II clones for the Chinese market in 1984; two years later it started producing PC clones. From 1983 to 1988 most of Creative's revenues came from PCs.

With stiff competition in the PC market, Sim shifted Creative's focus to sound cards and other PC enhancements. The company introduced its first Sound Blaster audio card in 1989; Sound Blaster soon became the industry standard. That year Creative launched PJS, an artificial intelligence-based Chinese-language operating system, and Views, a complementary word processor and desktop publisher with a more than 70,000-character alphabet. Also in 1989 Tandy (now RadioShack) ordered a large supply of Game Blasters — a sound card targeted at gamers — for its 8,000 Radio Shack stores, giving Creative a strong foothold in the US.

In 1991 Creative launched the first of its market-dominating upgrade kits, the Sound Blaster Multimedia Upgrade Kit, a software package bundled with a high-performance CD-ROM drive and a set of software applications. The company went public in 1992.

The growing popularity of multimedia products was music to Creative's ears. More computers were selling with sound cards and multimedia capabilities pre-installed, so the company signed deals to supply manufacturers including Compaq and Dell. Creative also diversified: In 1993 it acquired ShareVision Technology (videoconferencing products) and E-MU Systems (digital sound production systems).

The company also tried its hand at communication products. In 1994 it acquired modem maker Digicom (now Broadxent). The next year it released Phone Blaster, which combined voice mail, e-mail, and fax transmission functions.

Cracks began to show in Creative's progress in 1995. The slowing of the sound board market caused a steep drop in profits and prompted the company to restructure and refocus on sound products. Ng resigned that year, and Chay left in

1996. Creative introduced Graphics Blaster add-on graphics accelerator cards and signed a deal for Samsung to build its CD-ROM drive products that year.

Opting to add new technology quickly through acquisitions, in 1997 Creative bought speaker maker Cambridge Soundworks; ENSONIQ, maker of audio chips and electronic musical instruments (now part of E-MU/ENSONIQ); and the NetMedia Group of core logic chipset maker OPTi. In 1998 the company acquired Silicon Engineering, a maker of communications, multimedia, and storage integrated circuits. In 1999 Creative debuted the Nomad MP3 player, which plays digitally encoded music downloaded from PCs.

Sharp declines in Creative's Internet investments and the broader electronics market led the company to restructure its operations in 2001. Creative closed a factory, cut its staff by one-tenth, wrote off substantial losses in its investment portfolio, and recentered its operations on its core lines of digital audio products.

In 2002 the company acquired graphics chip maker 3Dlabs in a deal worth about $105 million.

EXECUTIVES

Chairman and CEO: Sim Wong Hoo, age 48
CFO: Ng Keh Long, age 44
President, Creative Labs: Craig McHugh
SVP and CTO; President, 3Dlabs: C. Hock Leow, age 52
Director of Corporate Communications:
 Phil O'Shaughnessy
Manager of Investor Relations: Lisa Laymon
Brand Manager, NOMAD Products: Lisa O'Malley
Public Relations Specialist: Jennifer Ellard
Public Relations Specialist: Karen Hoskins
Auditors: PricewaterhouseCoopers

LOCATIONS

HQ: 31 International Business Park, Creative Resource, 609921, Singapore
Phone: +65-6895-4000   **Fax:** +65-6895-4999
US HQ: 1901 McCarthy Blvd., Milpitas, CA 95035
US Phone: 408-428-6600   **US Fax:** 408-428-6611
Web: www.creative.com

Creative Technology has production facilities in Ireland, Malaysia, Singapore, and the US.

2003 Sales

	$ mil.	% of total
Americas	344.0	49
Europe	262.1	37
Asia/Pacific	95.7	14
Total	**701.8**	**100**

PRODUCTS/OPERATIONS

2003 Sales

	% of total
Audio products	33
Speakers	23
Personal digital entertainment	18
Graphics & video products	12
Communications & other products	13
Multimedia upgrade kits	1
Total	**100**

Selected Products

Audio
Digital sampling systems
Electronic musical instruments
Sound cards and chipsets (Sound Blaster)
Speakers (Cambridge Soundworks)
Personal digital entertainment
MP3 players (Nomad family)

Graphics and video
2-D/3-D graphic accelerator cards (3D Blaster line)
Desktop digital camera (Video Blaster WebCam)
PC digital video disk (DVD) players (Encore)
Multimedia upgrade kits (sound card, drive, speakers, software)

Communications
Bridging and routing devices
Modems (internal and external)
Wireless modems

Other
Rewritable CD drives (Blaster CD-RW)

Selected Subsidiaries

Broadxent, Inc. (formerly Digicom Systems; modems, US)
Cambridge Soundworks (speakers, US)
Creative Advanced Technology Center (US)
Creative Future Computer Co., Ltd. (China)
Creative Labs (Portugal)
Creative Labs A/S (Denmark)
Creative Labs GmbH (Germany)
Creative Labs (HK) Limited (Hong Kong)
Creative Labs, Inc. (Canada)
Creative Labs, Inc. (US)
Creative Labs (Ireland) Ltd.
Creative Labs NV (Belgium)
Creative Labs Pty Ltd. (Australia)
Creative Labs (Pty) Ltd. (South Africa)
Creative Labs SA (France)
Creative Labs Sdn Bhd (Malaysia)
Creative Labs SL (Spain)
Creative Labs Srl (Italy)
Creative Labs Taiwan Co., Ltd
Creative Media KK (Japan)
Creative Technologies Scandinavia AB (Sweden)
Cubic Electronics Sdn Bhd (Malaysia)
Data Stream KK (Japan)
E-MU Systems, Inc. (digital sound production systems, US)
hifi.com (online audio and video equipment shopping, US)

COMPETITORS

Acer	Iomega
Altec Lansing	Logitech
Technologies	Matrox Electronic Systems
ATI Technologies	Matsushita
Bose	Mitsumi Electric
Boston Acoustics	NVIDIA
D-Link	Philips Electronics
Eastman Kodak	Sony
ESS Technology	Toshiba
Guillemot	U.S. Robotics
Harman International	Viking Components
Hewlett-Packard	Yamaha
Intel	Zoom Technologies

HISTORICAL FINANCIALS

Company Type: Public

Income Statement

FYE: June 30

	REVENUE ($ mil.)	NET INCOME ($ mil.)	NET PROFIT MARGIN	EMPLOYEES
6/03	702	23	3.3%	3,900
6/02	806	(20)	—	4,300
6/01	1,229	(130)	—	5,000
6/00	1,344	161	12.0%	5,000
6/99	1,297	115	8.9%	4,000
6/98	1,234	135	10.9%	5,000
6/97	1,233	167	13.5%	3,489
6/96	1,308	(38)	—	4,170
6/95	1,202	27	2.2%	4,185
6/94	658	98	14.9%	4,100
Annual Growth	**0.7%**	**(14.7%)**	**—**	**(0.6%)**

2003 Year-End Financials

Debt ratio: 9.1%
Return on equity: 5.5%
Cash ($ mil.): 232
Current ratio: 2.19
Long-term debt ($ mil.): 39

No. of shares (mil.): 80
Dividends
  Yield: 3.2%
  Payout: 86.2%
Market value ($ mil.): 631

Stock History

NASDAQ: CREAF

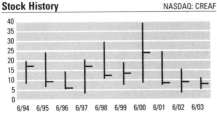

	STOCK PRICE ($)	P/E		PER SHARE ($)		
	FY Close	High/Low		Earnings	Dividends	Book Value
6/03	7.91	37	19	0.29	0.25	5.38
6/02	8.98	—	—	(0.27)	0.25	5.38
6/01	8.46	—	—	(1.65)	0.50	5.16
6/00	23.88	21	5	1.86	0.25	9.69
6/99	13.44	15	6	1.25	0.50	6.67
6/98	12.38	21	8	1.42	0.00	6.70
6/97	17.00	11	2	1.84	0.00	5.88
6/96	6.00	—	—	(0.43)	0.00	3.04
6/95	9.38	80	23	0.30	0.00	3.45
6/94	17.25	18	8	1.11	0.00	3.09
Annual Growth	(8.3%)	—	—	(13.9%)	—	6.4%

Crédit Agricole

The name suggests a country farmer's credit union, but Crédit Agricole's scope is much greater. France's largest bank, it offers lending and deposit services at more than 7,200 locations in France. The company is active in wholesale banking and capital markets in some 60 countries (primarily through subsidiary Crédit Agricole Indosuez), property/casualty and life insurance, and asset management. The Crédit Agricole group operates in some 60 countries; it is particularly active in the Middle East and Southeast Asia. The company added considerable bulk to its balance sheet and retail branch network when it won a bidding war and acquired large French bank Crédit Lyonnais.

Founded as the lending institution to farmers, Crédit Agricole is expanding its services and its geographic reach, particularly in central and southern Europe. Its acquisition of Polish leasing company Europejski Fundusz Leasingowy boosted its presence in Eastern Europe. When the going gets tough, Crédit Agricole gets going. Or so it has in Argentina, where the financial meltdown saw the bank leave three local subsidiaries (Banco Bisel, Banco Suquia and Banco de Entre Rios) behind. The Argentine government, through Banco de la Nación Argentina, took control of them.

Crédit Agricole is organized in a three-tiered structure of local banks (almost 2,700), regional banks (about 45 of them, which own more than 70% of the company and are in turn owned by the local banks), and a national bank. Once organized as a mutual company, the bank sold a small percentage of its shares and went public in order to remain independent.

HISTORY

In the mid-1800s France's farmers were suffering from crop failures and a lack of credit. The government tried to meet the credit crunch without much success until in 1894 it created an agricultural credit company, Crédit Agricole, that was tax-exempt and provided state-subsidized farm loans (a monopoly it enjoyed until 1989). Five years later the government established the regional banks as intermediaries between it and the local banks. By the turn of the century, Crédit Agricole's three-tiered structure was in place.

The first 30 years of the 20th century were a time of growth for the bank. The government allowed Crédit Agricole to expand its lending to include long-term personal loans to encourage the growth of rural farming (1910) and loans to businesses involved in other industries (1919). The bank survived WWI and the drop in farm production largely through government support. After the war Crédit Agricole funded rural electrification and other infrastructure.

After WWII the bank grew as it issued loans to finance the modernization of France's farms. In 1959 the government allowed Crédit Agricole to begin writing mortgages; expansion of the bank's operations continued in the 1960s as it was permitted to broaden its lending scope and create subsidiaries, including one to finance individual investments (Union d'Etudes et d'Investisements). In 1967 it began keeping deposits (before it had transferred them to the French Treasury) and used the assets to fuel its national growth.

The early 1970s saw the bank continue to expand its lending operations. Its diversification came under fire from both the government, which wanted the bank to focus on agriculture, and rival banks, which resented their tax-exempt competitor. Crédit Agricole expanded beyond France in the mid-1970s, offering mainly agricultural loans and funds to export firms. It opened its first international office in Chicago in 1979.

In the early 1980s the government continued to allow Crédit Agricole to broaden its lending scope but at a price: The bank lost its tax-exempt status. It continued diversifying; it established such subsidiaries as Predica (life insurance, 1986) and bought stakes in two brokerage firms (1988). As the 1980s closed, Crédit Agricole became a mutual company when the government sold 90% of the bank to the regional banks.

In 1991 the last restrictions on Crédit Agricole's lending were removed, and the bank began transforming itself into a financial services firm. It expanded its lending operations around the world and added subsidiaries offering a variety of financial services. In 1996 it bought Banque Indosuez (now Crédit Agricole Indosuez), fueling its growth in international wholesale banking. In the late 1990s the bank sought partnerships to expand its operations.

Its expansion was slowed by financial turmoil in Russia and Asia, and the bank closed its emerging markets business. The next year Crédit Agricole teamed with Spain's Banco Bilbao Vizcaya Argentaria and Commercial Bank of Greece as part of its plans to expand its presence in the Mediterranean and southern Europe; it already owned sizable stakes in Italy's Banca Intesa (now IntesaBci) and major banks in Lebanon, Morocco, and Portugal.

In 2000 the bank signaled its intention to shed its mutual status and list on an exchange in the near future. The next year the bank bought a majority share in Poland-based Europejski Fundusz Leasingowy, and declined an offer to become the controlling shareholder of fellow French bank Crédit Lyonnais, which it eventually subsumed in 2003. At the end of 2001, Crédit Agricole went public on the Euronext Paris Exchange.

EXECUTIVES

Chairman: Rene Carron, age 60
CEO: Jean Laurent
First Deputy CEO: Dominique Ferrero
Deputy CEO: Georges Pauget
Director, International Retail Banking and Private Banking: Marc-Antoine Autheman
Director, Crédit Lyonnais' Retail Banking Business: Jacques Baudouin
Director, Group Human Resources: Jérôme Brunel
Director, Asset Management: Thierry Coste
Director, Group Finance: Gilles de Margerie
Director, Operations and Logisitics: Patrice Durand
Director, Group Risk Management; Senior General Manager, Crédit Agricole Indosuez: Yves Perrier
Director, Specialized Financial Services; Chairman and CEO, Sofinco: Patrick Valroff
Deputy Director, Operations and Logisitics: Bernard Michel
Bank Operations and IT Manager: Aline Bec
Head, Strategy and Development Division: Jérôme Grivet
General Secretary: Gilles Guitton
Auditors: Barbier Frinault & Autres; Ernst & Young

LOCATIONS

HQ: Crédit Agricole S.A.
  91-93 Boulevard Pasteur, 75 015 Paris, France
Phone: +33-1-43-23-52-02   **Fax:** +33-1-43-23-34-48
Web: www.credit-agricole.fr

PRODUCTS/OPERATIONS

2002 Sales

	% of total
Interest receivable and similar income	88
Trading transactions	6
Gross margin on insurance activities	5
Other	1
Total	**100**

2002 Assets

	% of total
Cash, money market & interbank items	21
Internal transactions	30
Securities	10
Customer-related items	12
Lease financing	1
Insurance companies' investments	17
Other	9
Total	**100**

COMPETITORS

ABN AMRO
Bank of America
Generale de Belgique
BNP
Commerzbank AG
CCF
Credit Suisse
Deutsche Bank
Dresdner Bank
HSBC Holdings
HTV Group
Caisse d'Epargne
Société Générale
UBS

HISTORICAL FINANCIALS

Company Type: Public

Income Statement

FYE: December 31

	ASSETS ($ mil.)	NET INCOME ($ mil.)	INCOME AS % OF ASSETS	EMPLOYEES
12/02	530,043	1,115	0.2%	96,500
12/01	438,530	945	0.2%	96,000
12/00	504,217	2,600	0.5%	91,033
12/99	442,523	2,389	0.5%	93,244
12/98	456,229	2,194	0.5%	86,100
12/97	419,763	1,646	0.4%	85,250
12/96	481,657	1,451	0.3%	85,240
12/95	385,678	1,326	0.3%	72,607
12/94	328,704	1,086	0.3%	73,590
12/93	281,692	902	0.3%	73,250
Annual Growth	7.3%	2.4%	—	3.1%

2002 Year-End Financials

Equity as % of assets: 3.1%
Return on assets: 0.2%
Return on equity: 7.6%
Long-term debt ($ mil.): 73,779
Sales ($ mil.): 5,585

Net Income History

Euronext Paris: ACA

Credit Suisse

Credit Suisse Group is the second-largest financial services firm in Switzerland, behind rival UBS. The firm provides conventional consumer and business banking services within its home market, where it has some 250 locations, but most of its business is done outside the nation. Bulge-bracket investment bank subsidiary Credit Suisse First Boston (CSFB), one of the top IPO underwriters in the world, provides corporate and investment banking services throughout the world. But the unit, which also includes Credit Suisse First Boston (USA), has hit rough waters as it faces a sluggish market and pays off fines levied due to questionable IPO allocation practices.

Credit Suisse offers insurance through its Winterthur subsidiary, the heart of its retail bancassurance (banking and insurance) operations in Europe. Its Credit Suisse Private Banking unit serves a global clientele of wealthy individuals through about 50 offices in Switzerland and 35 around the world. Credit Suisse Asset Management administers investment portfolios for institutional clients.

Eschewing European merger-mania, Credit Suisse has expressed a desire to remain independent and grow internally. Under chairman and CEO Lukas Mühlemann, the company expanded CSFB when it bought US investment firm Donaldson, Lufkin & Jenrette, now CSFB (USA), in 2000. Shareholders critical of Credit Suisse's profitability after such an ambitious

growth strategy pressured Mühlemann out of his job. His CEO duties have been split between John Mack and Oswald Grübel, with Walter Kielholz, former CEO of Swiss Re, as chairman.

HISTORY

In 1856, shortly after the creation of the Swiss federation, Alfred Escher opened Credit Suisse (CS) in Zurich. Primarily a venture capital firm, CS helped fund Swiss railroads and other industries. It later opened offices in Italy and helped establish the Swiss Bank Corporation.

CS shifted its focus to commercial banking in 1867 and sold most of its stock holdings. By 1871 it was Switzerland's largest bank, buoyed by the nation's swift industrialization. In 1895 CS helped create the predecessor of Swiss utility Electrowatt. Foreign activity grew in the 1920s. A run on banks in the Depression forced CS to sell assets at a loss and dip into reserves of unreported retained profits.

Trade declined in WWII, but neutrality left Switzerland's institutions intact and made it a major banking center, partly due to CS's role as a conduit for the Nazi's plundered gold. Foreign exchange and gold trading became important activities for CS after WWII. Mortgage and consumer credit acquisitions fueled domestic growth in the 1970s.

In 1978 the bank took a stake in US investment bank First Boston and, with it, formed London-based Credit Suisse-First Boston (CSFB). CS created 44%-owned holding company Credit Suisse First Boston to own First Boston, CSFB, and Tokyo-based CS First Boston Pacific.

The stock market crash of 1987 led a damaged First Boston to merge with CSFB the next year. In 1990 CS (renamed CS Holding) injected $300 million into CSFB and shifted $470 million in bad loans from its books, becoming the first foreign owner of a major Wall Street investment bank.

In the early 1990s, CS Holding strengthened its insurance business with a Winterthur Insurance alliance. In 1993 and 1994 acquisitions helped it gain share in its overbanked home market.

In 1996 CS Holding reorganized as Credit Suisse Group and grew internationally, including further merging the daredevil US investment banking operations into Credit Suisse's more staid and relationship-oriented corporate banking. It bought Winterthur (Switzerland's #2 insurer) in 1997, as well as Barclays' European investment banking business.

In 1996, Credit Suisse and other Swiss banks came under fire for refusing to relinquish assets from Jews' bank accounts from the Holocaust era and for gold trading with the Nazi regime. In 1997 the banks agreed to establish a humanitarian fund for Holocaust victims. A stream of lawsuits by American heirs and boycott threats from US states and cities led in 1998 to a tentative $1.25 billion settlement (unpopular in Switzerland); Credit Suisse is to pay one-third.

CS in 1998 expanded its investment banking by buying Brazil's Banco de Investimentos Garantia; it also moved to expand US money management operations by allying with New York-based Warburg Pincus Asset Management. By 1999 that joint venture — which was to give the investment firm access to CS's mutual fund distribution channels in Europe and Asia — had morphed into CS's $650 million purchase of Warburg Pincus Asset Management.

Japan revoked the license of the company's financial products unit for obstructing an investi-

gation (the harshest penalty ever given to a foreign firm); it also accused the company of helping 60 others hide losses and cover up evidence.

In 2000 the company started a mortgage and home-buying Web site and decided to allow searches of Holocaust-era accounts. The next year, as a part of its European expansion, Credit Suisse acquired Spanish broker and asset manager General de Valores y Cambios. The collapse of Credit Suisse's share price, along with what proved to be an over-ambitious acquisition strategy, brought about the downfall of chairman and CEO Lukas Mühlemann, who stepped down in 2002.

EXECUTIVES

Chairman: Walter B. Kielholz, age 52
Vice Chairman and Co-CEO; CEO, Credit Suisse First Boston: John J. Mack, age 58
Co-CEO; CEO, Credit Suisse Financial Services: Oswald J. Grübel
CFO: Phillip K. Ryan
Chief Risk Officer: Richard E. Thornburgh
Group Chief Financial Reporting Officer: Peter W. Bachmann
Group Chief Accounting Officer: Rudolph A. Bless
Group Chief Auditor: Heinz Leibendgut
Chief of Staff: Philip Hess
Chief Group Communications Officer: Karin R. Hug
Chief Strategic Officer: Christopher Lawrence
Head of Investor Relations: Gerhard Beindorff
Head of Group Treasury: Kim Fox-Moertl
Head of Human Resources: Timothy S. Gardner
Head of Group Corporate Development: Stefan Goetz
Head of Group Risk Management: Tobias Guldimann
Head of Security Services: Jean-Pierre Huwyler
Head of Credit Risk Management: Ann F. Lopez
Head of Tax: Fritz Müller
Head of Public Affairs: Ulrich Pfister
General Counsel: David P. Frick
Special Advisory: Alfred Gremli
Chairman, Japan: Yuji Suzuki
Auditors: KPMG Klynveld Peat Marwick Goerdeler SA

LOCATIONS

HQ: Credit Suisse Group
   Paradeplatz 8, 8070 Zurich, Switzerland
Phone: +41-1-212-1616   **Fax:** +41-1-333-2587
US HQ: 11 Madison Ave., New York, NY 10010
US Phone: 212-325-2000   **US Fax:** 212-325-8249
Web: www.credit-suisse.com

PRODUCTS/OPERATIONS

2002 Sales

	% of total
Premium income	42
Interest & discount income	22
Commission income	20
Trading portfolios	12
Financial investments	3
Other	1
Total	**100**

2002 Assets

	% of total
Cash & equivalents	23
Securities & precious metals trading portfolios	18
Investments from the insurance business	14
Mortgages	10
Other investments	4
Due from customers	19
Other	12
Total	**100**

COMPETITORS

ABN AMRO	HSBC Holdings
Barclays	Merrill Lynch
Bear Stearns	Mitsubishi Tokyo Financial
Citigroup Global Markets	Mizuho Financial
Citigroup	Nomura Securities
Deutsche Bank	UBS
Goldman Sachs	UBS Financial Services

HISTORICAL FINANCIALS

Company Type: Public

Income Statement

FYE: December 31

	ASSETS ($ mil.)	NET INCOME ($ mil.)	INCOME AS % OF ASSETS	EMPLOYEES
12/02	691,991	(2,396)	—	78,457
12/01	617,087	958	0.2%	79,699
12/00	655,199	2,780	0.4%	80,538
12/99	454,246	3,356	0.7%	63,963
12/98	473,147	2,225	0.5%	62,300
12/97	473,457	273	0.1%	62,242
12/96	388,503	(1,919)	—	34,821
12/95	357,554	1,214	0.3%	33,527
12/94	299,032	1,017	0.3%	53,243
12/93	232,774	1,148	0.5%	56,804
Annual Growth	12.9%	—	—	3.7%

2002 Year-End Financials

Equity as % of assets: 3.0%	Dividends
Return on assets: —	Yield: 6.4%
Return on equity: —	Payout: —
Long-term debt ($ mil.): 285,657	Market value ($ mil.): 23,750
No. of shares (mil.): 1,116	Sales ($ mil.): 65,804

Stock History

NYSE: CSR

12/93 12/94 12/95 12/96 12/97 12/98 12/99 12/00 12/01 12/02

	STOCK PRICE ($) FY Close	P/E High/Low	PER SHARE ($) Earnings	Dividends	Book Value
12/02	21.28	— —	(2.01)	1.36	18.50
12/01	42.65	54 39	0.80	0.00	18.06
Annual Growth	(50.1%)	— —	—	—	2.5%

Dai Nippon Printing Co.

Dai Nippon Printing has used the power of the press to become one of the world's top commercial printing companies. At its 33 Japanese and eight overseas plants, Dai Nippon produces promotional materials, direct mail pieces, books, magazines, business forms, CD-ROMs, catalogs, smart cards, and packaging for consumer products. It also offers electronics, including photomasks used in the manufacture of integrated circuits (ICs) and color filters for liquid crystal displays, as well as artificial wood panels for walls,

floors, and kitchen cabinets. In addition, the company owns 58% of Hokkaido Coca-Cola Bottling.

Dai Nippon is implementing strategies to respond to changing global needs. The company is positioning itself as a complete provider of information communications, offering clients marketing and promotional support, communications software, and cross-media services. It also is emphasizing its environmentally friendly products and has reorganized its production systems and undertaken a number of cost-cutting measures to survive a slowdown caused by a recession in Japan.

HISTORY

In 1876 Shueisha, the predecessor to Dai Nippon Printing (DNP), was established in central Tokyo. As the only modern printing firm in Japan, it was well-positioned to attract the business of the emerging newspaper and book industries. The company originally used a movable-type hand printer, but became the first private industry to use steam power in Japan when it updated its presses in 1884.

Following Japanese victories over China and Russia at the turn of the century, Japan embarked on a period of military and economic expansion. This was matched by a growing demand for printing. In 1927 Japan published 20,000 book titles and 40 million magazines. The country's first four-color gravure printing system was inaugurated the following year. In 1935 Shueisha changed its name to Dai Nippon Printing following its merger with Nisshin Printing.

The 1930s and 1940s were lean times for printers; Japan's repressive military government suppressed publishers and banned books. WWII devastated the publishing industry, along with the rest of the Japanese economy, but the publishing industry recovered soon after the end of the war. DNP was assisted in its recovery by government contracts; in 1946 it was designated by the Ministry of Finance to print 100-yen notes. In 1949 the company entered the securities printing business, and in 1951 it expanded into packaging and decorative interiors production. DNP reemerged in 1958 as Japan's largest printing firm.

In 1963 DNP followed Toppan in setting up an office in Hong Kong. Both Hong Kong and Singapore had become havens for Shanghai printing entrepreneurs who had emigrated in the face of the Communist takeover of China in 1949. These cities became centers for low-cost, high-quality color printing for British and American book publishers. In 1973 DNP overtook R. R. Donnelley as the world's largest printer. The next year the company set up a subsidiary in the US, DNP (America), Inc.

DNP moved into the information processing business in the 1980s, developing a credit card-sized calculator in 1985, a digital color printer system in 1986, and a Japanese-language word processor in 1987. The company launched Hi-Vision Static Pictures in 1989 to market a process that converted data into a form used by high-definition TV. In 1990 DNP bought a controlling stake in Tien Wah Press, the #1 printer in Singapore.

The next year DNP completed the first construction stage of its Okayama plant, dedicated to information media supplies (mainly transfer ribbons for color printers). The second stage, specializing in interior decorative materials, was completed in 1993.

In 1994 the company launched its Let's Go to

an Amusement Park! virtual reality software system. Two years later DNP produced an integrated circuit card for about a tenth of current costs, giving it a major competitive edge in the magnetic card market.

In 1999 the company began selling CD-ROMs online through subsidiary TransArt. The following year Dai Nippon formed partnerships or joint ventures with Toshiba (to develop printed circuit boards), Microsoft (to develop Windows-based smart cards), and Numerical Technologies (to develop advanced phase-shifted photomasks). In 2002 the company joined with Toshiba and Takara to develop and promote a lightweight educational computer called an Ex-Pad.

EXECUTIVES

Chairman, President, and CEO: Yoshitoshi Kitajima
Senior Managing Director: Ryozo Kitami
Senior Managing Director: Kenichi Nakamura
Senior Managing Director: Satoshi Saruwatari
Senior Managing Director: Minoru Suzuki
Senior Managing Director: Taira Takahashi
Senior Managing Director: Koichi Takanami
Senior Managing Director and CFO: Masayoshi Yamada
Managing Director: Mitsuhiko Hakii
Managing Director: Kuniaki Kamei
Managing Director: Noriaki Nakamura
Managing Director: Masakazu Sato
Managing Director: Teruomi Yoshino
Human Resources, DNP America: Tina Kent
Auditors: Meiji Audit Corporation

LOCATIONS

HQ: Dai Nippon Insatsu Kabushiki Kaisha (Dai Nippon Printing Co., Ltd.)
1-1, Ichigaya Kagacho 1-chome, Shinjuku-ku, Tokyo 162-8001, Japan
Phone: +81-3-3266-2111   **Fax:** +81-3-5225-8239
US HQ: 335 Madison Ave., 3rd Fl., New York, NY 10017
US Phone: 212-503-1060   **US Fax:** 212-286-1501
Web: www.dnp.co.jp

PRODUCTS/OPERATIONS

Selected Products and Services

Electronic Components & Information Media Supplies
Color filters
Photomasks
Ribbons (fax machines)
Shadowmasks

Information Media
Bank notes
Books
Business forms
Catalogs
CD-ROMs and DVDs
Direct mail
Magazines
Plastic cards
Promotional publications

Lifestyle Products
Decorative materials
Packaging

COMPETITORS

DuPont Photomasks
International Imaging Materials
Japan Times
Kodansha
Nihon Keizai Shimbun
Photronics
Quad/Graphics
Quebecor World
R. R. Donnelley
Times Publishing
Toppan Printing

HISTORICAL FINANCIALS

Company Type: Public

Income Statement

FYE: March 31

	REVENUE ($ mil.)	NET INCOME ($ mil.)	NET PROFIT MARGIN	EMPLOYEES
3/03	10,922	240	2.2%	35,182
3/02	9,891	118	1.2%	34,868
3/01	10,624	265	2.5%	34,094
3/00	12,195	370	3.0%	35,347
3/99	10,659	256	2.4%	11,836
3/98	10,044	425	4.2%	14,309
3/97	10,583	454	4.3%	14,427
3/96	11,611	494	4.3%	14,514
3/95	13,782	569	4.1%	14,498
3/94	11,149	397	3.6%	14,308
Annual Growth	(0.2%)	(5.4%)	—	10.5%

2003 Year-End Financials

Debt ratio: 0.9%
Return on equity: 3.2%
Cash ($ mil.): 1,993

Current ratio: 1.71
Long-term debt ($ mil.): 73

Net Income History

OTC: DNPCY

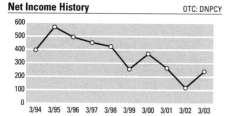

The Daiei, Inc.

Japan's economic woes put The Daiei on a diet. One of Japan's largest and most troubled retailers, Daiei operates about 2,000 stores through its subsidiaries and franchisees. Its retail businesses include supermarkets, discount stores, department stores, and specialty shops. Other businesses include restaurants, hotels, and real estate services. Domestic sales make up more than 90% of its revenues. Daiei diversified haphazardly during the 1980s loading up on debt and failing to keep up with new, more efficient competitors. The company has been on life support for years, courtesy of its banks and the Japanese government, which have extended Daiei credit despite the ongoing deterioration of its businesses.

Most recently the government-owned Japan Development Bank extended Daiei (pronounced die-ay) another $480 million. After rejecting help from the Industrial Revitalization Corporation of Japan — an agency formed to turn around struggling Japanese companies — The Daiei is asking its main banks to forgive an additional $185 million of debt related to its professional baseball team, the Fukuoka Hawks.

Daiei has been trying to reduce its nearly $14 billion in debt by selling stakes in its subsidiaries, including Japan's second-largest convenience store chain, Lawson, and its department store subsidiary Printemps Ginza. It also has been closing stores and trimming its workforce as part of a three-year restructuring plan. The company is getting out of the electronics business, which it once led, and will rent the empty space in its stores to other discounters. It is also cleaning its plate of two restaurant units including Wenco Japan, which operates 82 Wendy's restaurants, and its stake in the Big Boy franchise. It has agreed to sell its hotel and ballpark operations in Fukuoka to US investment firm Colony Capital LLC. However, for now, Daiei is holding on to its baseball team. Daiei is closing 60 unprofitable stores and refurbishing others in the hope of engineering a turnaround. The company also plans to liquidate its wholly owned finance unit, Asahi Finance Service, by late 2003.

In a partnership with an affiliated food retailer Maruetsu, Daiei has announced a new business plan that focuses on its supermarket operations and extending store hours. Daiei plans to open two new supermarkets by February 2004 — the company's first store openings in three years.

HISTORY

Daiei founder Isao Nakauchi narrowly escaped death and the law before launching his first Daiei corner drugstore. As a Japanese soldier serving in the Philippines in WWII, he came under heavy fire but survived. He later thanked sloppy American engineering (the bombs that fell near him did not explode) for his survival. After the war he and his brother made a fortune selling penicillin above the legal price; his brother was arrested for his part in the dealings.

Nakauchi launched his Housewives' Store Daiei in Osaka in 1957 at the depth of the post-Korean War depression. The low prices of a discount drugstore appealed to hard-pressed consumers, and the success of the first store prompted Nakauchi to open others in the Osaka area. He also took advantage of the depression at the wholesale level, buying up surplus goods from cash-strapped manufacturers.

In 1958 the company opened in Sannomiya and introduced the concept of the discount store chain to Japan. Over the next three decades, Daiei diversified its offerings while staying focused on its "for the customers" philosophy, i.e., very low prices.

The company expanded into Tokyo in 1964 with the purchase of Ittoku and opened its first suburban store in 1968 near Osaka. By 1972 Daiei was not only a nationwide chain, it was also Japan's #1 supermarket operator (with 75 stores) and #2 retailer. In 1974 the company overtook Mitsukoshi to become Japan's top retailer. A year later Daiei opened its first convenience store, Lawson.

Showing an increasing interest in sourcing from international businesses, Daiei teamed up with J. C. Penney (1976) and Marks and Spencer (1978) for retailing and Wendy's and Victoria Station (both in 1979) for restaurants. The retailer entered the US market with the 1980 purchase of Holiday Mart, a three-store discount chain in Hawaii, where it also set up its first purchasing office.

Daiei entered the hotel business in 1988 by winning the contract for a $2.2 billion recreation center in Fukuoka. In 1992 the company opened the first American-style membership warehouse in Japan (Kobe), Kou'S Wholesale Membership Club. That year Daiei acquired 42% of major retailer Chujitsuya. The company launched private-label products in 1994. Also that year Daiei merged with retail affiliates Chujitsuya, Uneed Daiei, and Dainaha, establishing Japan's first nationwide network of stores.

When Japan lifted a 50-year ban on holding companies in 1997, Daiei was the first to take advantage of the relaxed laws, forming K.K. Daiei Holding Corporation to oversee its non-retail businesses. The company was hit hard in 1997 and 1998 as Japan's consumer spending slowed just as many of its stores were undergoing renovation. In response, in 1998 Daiei began selling real estate assets, restructuring operations, and closing unprofitable stores.

In 1999 Tasdasu Toba became president, replacing founder Nakauchi, who remained chairman of Daiei. In early 2000 trading company Mitsubishi Corp. purchased a 20% stake in convenience store chain Lawson (Daiei and subsidiaries would retain about 75% of the company).

Amid allegations of an insider trading scandal, Toba resigned as president and Nakauchi resigned as chairman and CEO in 2000. Hiroshige Sasaki, a former managing director, became acting president and Kunio Takagi was named to replace him as the head of Daiei in 2001. Daiei further reduced its stake in Lawson to about 21%. It sold an additional 8% stake in the chain to Mitsubishi, which already held 20%.

In early 2002 Daiei was rescued by a bank-led bailout and the company announced a three-year restructuring plan that includes 60 store closures, and reducing its work force by about 5,000 employees. The retailer closed all four of its members-only "Kou'S" stores in August 2002. The state-run Development Bank of Japan announced a new $480 million funding plan in October 2002 to aid Daiei in its restructuring.

EXECUTIVES

Chairman: Jiro Amagai
Vice Chairman: Heihachiro Yoshino
President and CEO: Kunio Takagi
Senior Managing Director: Takao Endoh
Executive Managing Director, and Board Member: Toshio Hasumi
Executive Managing Director: Shinji Kiyono
Executive Managing Director: Tadahiko Tsuchiya
Finance Director: Kazuya Uezuka
Director: Mitsuru Hazeyama
Director: Osamu Satoh
Director: Kazuhiko Iwata
Director: Mikio Kinohara
Director: Hiroyuki Ogawa
Director: Kazuo Takahashi
Corporate Auditor: Satoru Kita
Auditors: Deloitte Touche Tohmatsu

LOCATIONS

HQ: 4-1-1, Minatojima Nakamachi, Chuo-ku, Kobe 650-0046, Japan
Phone: +81-78-302-5001   **Fax:** +81-78-302-5572
US HQ: 801 Kaheka St., Honolulu, HI 96814
US Phone: 808-973-6600   **US Fax:** 808-941-6457
Web: www.daiei.co.jp

The Daiei operates retail locations throughout Japan and maintains purchasing offices in China, the Philippines, and the US.

PRODUCTS/OPERATIONS

2002 Sales

	% of total
Retail	82
Financing	4
Real estate	2
Other	12
Total	**100**

COMPETITORS

HISTORICAL FINANCIALS

Company Type: Public

Income Statement

FYE: Last day in February

	REVENUE ($ mil.)	NET INCOME ($ mil.)	NET PROFIT MARGIN	EMPLOYEES
2/03	18,692	1,152	6.2%	26,589
2/02	18,714	2,490	13.3%	28,697
2/01	25,082	395	1.6%	34,841
2/00	25,883	(200)	—	—
2/99	25,267	(344)	—	—
2/98	24,868	10	0.0%	—
2/97	26,023	(99)	—	—
2/96	30,095	49	0.2%	—
2/95	33,236	(522)	—	—
2/94	25,517	52	0.2%	—
Annual Growth	(3.4%)	41.0%	—	(12.6%)

2003 Year-End Financials

Debt ratio: 314.9%
Return on equity: 82.6%
Cash ($ mil.): 1,280

Current ratio: 0.43
Long-term debt ($ mil.): 1,771

Net Income History

NASDAQ (SC): DAIEY

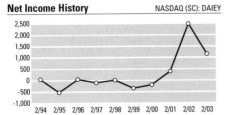

DaimlerChrysler

It's a luxury sedan, it's a minivan, it's, it's . . . DaimlerChrysler, the world's #3 carmaker in sales (behind General Motors and Ford). Formed by the $37 billion acquisition of Chrysler by Germany's Daimler-Benz in 1998, the company makes about 4.7 million vehicles a year. Chrysler's brands include Dodge, Jeep, and, of course, Chrysler vehicles (Plymouth has been discontinued); the Mercedes brand is limited to luxury sedans, commercial vehicles, and SUVs. Also, DaimlerChrysler's Freightliner unit is the US's #1 heavy-truck maker. The carmaker also has a 10% stake in Hyundai Motor, a 37% stake in Mitsubishi Motors, and a 33% stake in EADS, the European aerospace and defense consortium.

DaimlerChrysler is looking to increase its presence in the Pacific Rim through mergers and acquisitions. To that end it took stakes in Hyundai Motor and Mitsubishi Motors. Eager to get a bigger slice of the Asian commercial truck market (more than 40% of all commercial vehicles are sold in Asia), DaimlerChrysler has pur-

chased a 43% stake in Mitsubishi Fuso Truck and Bus, a new company formed early in 2003. Mitsubishi Motors controls a 42% stake in the truck venture while several other Mitsubishi group companies hold the remaining 15%. DaimlerChrysler has also agreed to exercise its option to take a 50% stake in Hyundai Motor's commercial vehicle business.

Deutsche Bank and the government of Kuwait, both shareholders of former Daimler-Benz, own 12% and 7% of DaimlerChrysler, respectively.

HISTORY

Former Buick president and GM VP Walter Chrysler was hired to get Maxwell Motor Car Company out of receivership in 1920. He became president in 1923 and introduced the Chrysler car the next year. He renamed the company for himself in 1925. The company acquired Dodge (1928) and introduced the low-priced Plymouth and the more luxurious DeSoto. Chrysler retired in 1935.

While other carmakers made style modifications, Chrysler kept the same models from 1942 until 1953. It lost market share and for several decades misjudged customer demands in the 1960s by introducing small cars before their time and in the 1970s by holding on to large-car production.

Facing bankruptcy, Chrysler negotiated $1.5 billion in loan guarantees from the US government and brought in former Ford president Lee Iacocca as CEO in 1978. By 1983 it had repaid its loans, seven years ahead of schedule. The company introduced the first minivan in 1984.

Iacocca was replaced by GM's head of European operations, Robert Eaton, in 1992. Chrysler sold most of its aerospace and defense holdings in 1996 and sold off Pentastar Electronics and the Dollar Thrifty Group the next year.

Chrysler's acquirer, Daimler-Benz, was formed by the merger of two German motor companies — Daimler and Benz — in 1926. Daimler-Benz bought Auto Union (Audi) in 1958 (sold to Volkswagen in 1966). The company's Mercedes cars gained notoriety and sales expanded worldwide in the 1970s.

Daimler-Benz diversified in the 1980s, buying aerospace, heavy truck (Freightliner), and consumer and industrial electrical companies. Although diversification continued, sales slowed. Losses at its aerospace unit forced Daimler-Benz into the red in 1995. Also that year the company and ABB Asea Brown Boveri formed joint venture Adtranz, the #1 train maker in the world, and Jürgen Schrempp became chairman.

In 1998 Daimler-Benz acquired Chrysler and introduced a subcompact car, the smart, in Europe. DaimlerChrysler rolled both companies' financial services units into DaimlerChrysler Interservices (DEBIS) and acquired the remaining shares of Adtranz in 1999.

North American influence in the company began to fade in 2000 with the exit of US management, including co-chairman Robert Eaton. Prior to his retirement, Eaton announced DaimlerChrysler's goal to become the world's #1 carmaker through partnerships or acquisitions.

In 2000 DaimlerChrysler agreed to buy a controlling $2.1 billion stake (34%) in Mitsubishi Motors (later upped to 37% when it acquired 3.3% from Volvo), with a condition that allowed GM to fully acquire the company. It took a minority stake in South Korea-based Hyundai Motor, and the two bid jointly on Daewoo Motor (now named GM Daewoo Auto & Technology; South Korea), but

Ford was named exclusive bidder (although it later withdrew). DaimlerChrysler bought Canada-based truck maker Western Star Holdings for $456 million and paid about $473 million for the 79% of Detroit Diesel (heavy-duty truck engines) that it didn't already own. The company also agreed to sell its rail systems unit, Adtranz, to Bombardier (completed in 2001 for about $1.1 billion).

Also in 2000, in an effort to turn things around at its money-losing Chrysler division, James Holden was replaced with Dieter Zetsche, who immediately began making personnel changes. Days after Zetsche was installed, billionaire investor Kirk Kerkorian filed a $8 billion lawsuit seeking to undo the 1998 Daimler-Benz/Chrysler merger on grounds that portraying the deal as a "merger of equals" was misrepresentative.

Zetsche announced early in 2001 that Chrysler would eliminate almost 26,000 North American jobs over three years (largely through retirement and attrition) and make wholesale changes in the group's senior management positions overseeing the Chrysler and Mercedes divisions. DaimlerChrysler agreed to sell Temic GmbH, its auto-electronics business, to Continental. The deal calls for Continental to first take a 60% stake, then acquire the rest by 2005. In June DaimlerChrysler announced that it was seeking a buyer for its 45% stake in Debis Air-Finance, a major aircraft-leasing business.

EXECUTIVES

Chairman of the Supervisory Board: Hilmar Kopper, age 68
Deputy Chairman of the Supervisory Board: Erich Klemm, age 48
Chairman of the Management Board: Jürgen E. Schrempp, age 58
Member of the Board of Management, Advisor for Global Procurement and Supply: Gary C. Valade, age 59
Member of the Board of Management, Aerospace and Industrial Business: Manfred Bischoff, age 61
Member of the Board of Management and Executive Advisor to the Chairman, Central and Eastern Europe and Central Asia: Klaus J. Mangold, age 60
Member of the Board of Management; President and CEO, Chrysler Group: Dieter Zetsche, age 49
Member of the Board of Management, Commercial Vehicles: Eckhard Cordes, age 53
Member of the Board of Management, Finance and Controlling: Manfred Gentz, age 61
Member of the Board of Management, Human Resources and Labor Relations Director: Günther Fleig, age 54
Member of the Board of Management, Mercedes Car Group: Jürgen Hubbert, age 64
Member of the Board of Management, Global Procurement and Supply: Thomas W. Sidlik, age 54
Member of the Board of Management; COO, Chrysler Group: Wolfgang Bernhard, age 42
Member of the Board of Management, Corporate Development: Rüdiger Grube, age 51
Deputy Member of the Board of Management, DaimlerChrysler Services: Bodo Uebber, age 43
Deputy Member of the Board of Management, Research and Technology: Thomas Weber, age 48
President and CEO, DaimlerChrysler Services North America LLC: Juergen H. Walker
EVP Global Sales and Marketing, Chrysler Group: Joe Eberhardt, age 39
SVP and General Counsel, Chrysler Group: William O. O'Brien
SVP Human Resources, Chrysler Group: Nancy A. Rae
Auditors: KPMG Deutsche Treuhand-Gesellschaft AG

LOCATIONS

HQ: DaimlerChrysler AG
Epplestrasse 225, 70546 Stuttgart, Germany
Phone: +49-711-17-0   **Fax:** +49-711-17-94022
US HQ: 1000 Chrysler Dr., Auburn Hills, MI 48326-2766
US Phone: 248-576-5741   **US Fax:** 248-576-4742
Web: www.daimlerchrysler.com

DaimlerChrysler has manufacturing facilities in 37 countries and sells its products in 200 countries around the world.

2002 Sales

	$ mil.	% of total
Americas		
US	81,594	52
Other countries	12,713	8
European Union		
Germany	24,284	15
Other countries	24,603	16
Asia	6,600	4
Other regions	7,313	5
Total	**157,107**	**100**

PRODUCTS/OPERATIONS

2002 Sales

	$ mil.	% of total
Chrysler Group	62,720	40
Mercedes Group	49,150	31
Commercial vehicles	28,258	18
Services	14,457	9
Other	2,522	2
Total	**157,107**	**100**

Selected Divisions and Models

Chrysler Group

Chrysler
 300 M
 Concorde
 Crossfire
 Pacifica
 PT Cruiser
 Sebring convertible
 Sebring coupe
 Sebring sedan
 Town & Country
 Voyager
Dodge
 Caravan
 Cargo van
 Conversion van

Dakota
Durango
Grand Caravan
Intrepid
Neon
Ram Pickup
Sprinter (van)
SRT-4
Stratus coupe
Stratus sedan
Viper
Jeep
 Grand Cherokee
 Liberty
 Wrangler

Mercedes Car Group

Maybach
Mercedes-Benz
C-Class
CL-Class
CLK-Class
E-Class

G-Class
M-Class
S-Class
SL-Class
SLK-Class

smart

Commercial Vehicles Division
Freightliner
Mercedez-Benz
Setra
Sterling Trucks
Western Star Trucks

COMPETITORS

ALSTOM	Nissan
AM General	PACCAR
BMW	Peugeot
Boeing	Renault
Fiat	Saab Automobile
Ford	Saturn
Fuji Heavy Industries	Scania
General Motors	Siemens
Honda	Suzuki Motor
Isuzu	Toyota
MAN	Volkswagen
Mazda	Volvo
Navistar	

HISTORICAL FINANCIALS

Company Type: Public

Income Statement

FYE: December 31

	REVENUE ($ mil.)	NET INCOME ($ mil.)	NET PROFIT MARGIN	EMPLOYEES
12/02	157,107	4,955	3.2%	365,571
12/01	136,256	(590)	—	372,470
12/00	152,446	7,411	4.9%	416,501
12/99	151,035	5,785	3.8%	466,938
12/98	154,615	5,656	3.7%	441,500
Annual Growth	**0.4%**	**(3.3%)**	**—**	**(4.6%)**

2002 Year-End Financials

Debt ratio: 139.7%
Return on equity: 13.9%
Cash ($ mil.): 9,589
Current ratio: 1.52
Long-term debt ($ mil.): 51,238

No. of shares (mil.): 1,013
Dividends
 Yield: 3.3%
 Payout: 20.4%
Market value ($ mil.): 31,042

Stock History

NYSE: DCX

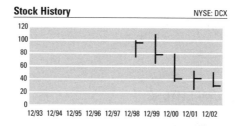

	STOCK PRICE ($) FY Close	P/E High/Low		PER SHARE ($) Earnings	Dividends	Book Value
12/02	30.65	10	6	4.90	1.00	36.21
12/01	41.67	—	—	(0.59)	2.08	34.65
12/00	41.20	34	16	7.31	2.22	39.68
12/99	78.00	21	13	5.73	2.50	36.19
12/98	96.06	17	13	5.75	0.00	35.57
Annual Growth	**(24.8%)**	**—**	**—**	**(3.9%)**	**—**	**0.4%**

Danka Business Systems PLC

From sales to service, Danka is print proficient. Danka Business Systems is a leading independent distributor of photocopiers, network printers, multifunction devices, and other automated office equipment, parts, and supplies. The company primarily sells products manufactured by Canon, Heidelberger Druckmaschinen, Konica, Ricoh, and Toshiba. It also generates revenue

from equipment rentals, and services that include maintenance and supply contracts, training, and technical support. Equity firm Cypress Associates owns about a quarter of the company.

Supplies, rentals, and services account for about 60% of Danka's sales. It generates about 55% of its revenues in the US. The company, which has racked up debt in the midst of product transitions and restructuring efforts, continues to shift its emphasis from analog to digital products. Its streamlining measures have included job cuts and the sale of some of its business units and properties. Among its divestitures was the sale of its Danka Services International (DSI) unit to Pitney Bowes.

FMR owns about 7% of Danka. All officers and directors, as a group, own about 27%.

HISTORY

Daniel Doyle saw an opportunity in 1977 to enlarge his prospects by selling Japanese copiers. Doyle and a partner, Frank McPeak, started Danka that year by relocating in the hot-growth Tampa region and buying local office equipment specialist Gulf Coast Business Machines. The company was named from letters in the partners' first names.

In its first 10 years Danka's revenues grew at a compounded annual rate of more than 50%. The prosperity resulted from Doyle's aggressive, larger-than-life grit. He sold rabbits at age 10 and grew up reading books on how to become wealthy. As a 26-year-old sales manager at Litton Industries in 1967, Doyle made his copier quota for the year in one day when he chartered a helicopter to fly area executives to a downtown Cleveland hotel for a sales pitch.

Danka continued developing relationships with the copier dealers who sold Japanese models from Canon, Ricoh, and others. In 1986 McPeak retired and Doyle, searching for ways to boost expansion, sold Danka to a UK firm for tax purposes. The new corporate parent, Danka Business Systems PLC, began trading on the London Stock Exchange in 1986.

By 1988 the company had 28 sales and services offices around the US. That year it added fax machines to its product line. In 1992 Danka started trading American Depositary Receipts (ADRs) on the Nasdaq so US investors could more easily buy shares. It raised $86 million in a 1994 ADR offering.

Between 1993 and 1996, driven by Doyle's sales zeal, Danka bought more than 100 copier dealers in an acquisition tear, including Saint Group (1994), which sharpened its image in Europe, and two Australian companies (1996). Strong sales of copier supplies and service contracts pushed revenues over $1 billion for the first time in 1996.

The intense pace culminated in a financial paper jam when Danka bought Eastman Kodak's money-losing copier business and its document management outsourcing operations in 1996. The $588 million purchase doubled Danka's size and gave it instant global credibility in large corporations. But efforts to transmute Kodak's buttoned-down sales atmosphere into Danka's no-holds-barred brand of doing business caused fights over pay and perks. Many Kodak representatives quit; the two sales forces at one point competed with each other, and clients complained about receiving house calls from two ends of the same company. This failure to integrate the teams left sales and shares lowered.

The company reduced its workforce by some

1,200 employees through layoffs and attrition during 1997. That December, after Doyle announced that sales would be off for the quarter, Danka lost $1 billion of its $1.76 billion market value in a day. Shareholders began filing lawsuits accusing Danka of securities fraud (all were dismissed in 2000).

The company cut another 5% of its workforce in 1998, shuffled management, and drastically trimmed operations. Doyle chose Brian Merriman, a veteran respected for turning around Toshiba's office equipment unit, to lead operations. Later that year Doyle and chairman Mark Vaughn-Lee resigned under pressure. CFO Larry Switzer, a former executive with Fruit of the Loom, was named CEO.

In 1999, in the shadow of heavy losses for the fiscal year, Danka restructured, selling its fax business, Omnifax, to rival Xerox and terminating 1,400 more jobs. Also that year Danka established distribution deals with Canon and Kodak, and it received an investment from Cypress Group giving that company 23% of Danka's voting power. Switzer resigned in 2000, amidst company warnings of earnings shortfalls; director Michael Gifford was named interim CEO.

In early 2001, chairman David Kendall retired, and interim CEO Gifford was named to his position. Former Anacomp executive P. Lang Lowrey was brought in as CEO. The company also announced a plan for cutting and refinancing its debt, part of which included the sale of its outsourcing division — Danka Services International — to Pitney Bowes for approximately $290 million in cash. Layoffs and attrition caused a workforce reduction of about 5,000 employees during fiscal 2002. Early in 2002 Lowrey took over the chairman post from Gifford, who remained on the board of directors; also that year Merriman retired as president and COO, shifting his responsibilities to three regional division heads for Europe, the US, and the rest of the world.

EXECUTIVES

Chairman and CEO: P. Lang Lowrey III, age 50, $1,402,235 pay
EVP and CFO: F. Mark Wolfinger, age 48, $913,971 pay
EVP and Chief Strategy and Marketing Officer: Donald W. Thurman, age 57
SVP of Finance and Controller: Jeffrey H. Foster
SVP, Chief Administrative Officer, and General Counsel: Keith J. Nelsen, age 40, $353,309 pay
SVP, Professional Services: Michael (Mike) Howard, age 48
President and COO, Danka Europe: Peter Williams, age 51, $335,238 pay
President and COO, Danka International Group: Michael D. (Mike) Popielec, age 41
President and COO, Danka US: Todd L. Mavis, age 42, $709,764 pay
President and General Manager, Canada, International Operating Group: Paul Natale
President, Latin America, International Operating Group: James McClenahan
EVP, US Human Resources: Ricardo A. (Rick) Davis, age 55
EVP, US Operations: Michael C. Wedge
EVP, US Sales: Wayne Frahn
EVP, US Technical Services: Manos Menayas
SVP, Finance, Danka Americas: Kevin J. Dean, age 54, $206,955 pay
CIO: Gene Hatcher
Secretary: Paul G. Dumond, age 48
Auditors: Ernst & Young LLP

LOCATIONS

HQ: Masters House, 107 Hammersmith Rd., London W14 0QH, United Kingdom
Phone: +44-207-605-0150   **Fax:** +44-207-603-8448
US HQ: 11201 Danka Circle North, St. Petersburg, FL 33716-3712
US Phone: 727-576-6003
Web: www.danka.com

Danka Business Systems markets its products and services to retailers in 25 countries.

2003 Sales

	$ mil.	% of total
US	748	53
Europe	532	38
Other regions	120	9
Total	**1,400**	**100**

PRODUCTS/OPERATIONS

Services
Leasing
Maintenance
Supply contracts
Support
Training

Distributed Products
Color printers
Digital copiers
High-volume copiers
Multifunction devices (integrated printer, copier, fax, and scanner machines)
Software
Toner, developer, and other supplies
Workgroup copiers and printers

Distributed Brands
Canon
Heidelberger Druckmaschinen
Konica
Ricoh
Toshiba

COMPETITORS

A.B.Dick	Lexmark International
Best Buy	Océ
Canon USA	Office Depot
Circuit City Stores	Olivetti
CompUSA	Ricoh
Costco Wholesale	SAM'S CLUB
Global Imaging Systems	Seiko Epson
Hewlett-Packard	Sharp
IKON	Target
Imagistics	Xerox
Lanier Worldwide	

HISTORICAL FINANCIALS

Company Type: Public

Income Statement

FYE: March 31

	REVENUE ($ mil.)	NET INCOME ($ mil.)	NET PROFIT MARGIN	EMPLOYEES
3/03	1,400	10	0.7%	8,700
3/02	1,555	138	8.8%	9,500
3/01	2,063	(221)	—	14,500
3/00	2,496	10	0.4%	17,000
3/99	2,897	(295)	—	18,000
3/98	3,349	52	1.6%	20,000
3/97	2,101	42	2.0%	21,800
3/96	1,240	45	3.6%	10,500
3/95	802	39	4.9%	7,080
3/94	789	39	5.0%	5,350
Annual Growth	**6.6%**	**(14.4%)**	**—**	**5.6%**

2003 Year-End Financials

Debt ratio: 265.4%
Return on equity: 17.1%
Cash ($ mil.): 82
Current ratio: 1.09
Long-term debt ($ mil.): 174
No. of shares (mil.): 62
Dividends
Yield: 0.0%
Payout: —
Market value ($ mil.): 221

Stock History

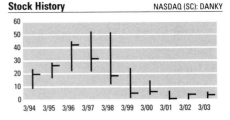

NASDAQ (SC): DANKY

	STOCK PRICE ($) FY Close	P/E High/Low		PER SHARE ($) Earnings	Dividends	Book Value
3/03	3.54	—	—	(0.13)	0.00	1.05
3/02	3.84	3	0	1.95	0.00	0.77
3/01	0.64	—	—	(3.91)	0.00	(1.17)
3/00	6.13	141	42	0.10	0.00	6.56
3/99	5.00	—	—	(5.18)	0.13	3.00
3/98	18.38	57	14	0.90	0.24	8.44
3/97	31.44	72	31	0.72	0.19	8.21
3/96	42.25	51	26	0.88	0.12	8.07
3/95	26.25	35	21	0.80	0.10	4.31
3/94	19.63	39	16	0.59	0.08	5.38
Annual Growth	**(17.3%)**	**—**	**—**	**—**	**—**	**(16.6%)**

Groupe Danone

You say Danone, I say Dannon; let's call the whole thing one of the largest food producers in the world. Groupe Danone is the global leader in cultured dairy products (including yogurt, cheese, and dairy desserts) and second-largest producer of biscuits (after Kraft's Nabisco) with Jacob's and LU cookies and crackers. Its Evian and other brands make it #2 in bottled water (behind Nestlé). Danone has dozens of regional and international brands, including Dannon yogurt (US), and HP and Lea & Perrins sauces. It owns almost 45% of BSN Emballage, a maker of glass containers.

Danone discovered that increased worldwide sales through billions of dollars in acquisitions didn't mean a similar gain in profits. Hence, it has divested a sack full of beer operations and grocery products businesses.

But acquisitions are still part of the company's growth plan. Danone has vigorously snapped up leading home and office water delivery companies around the globe.

HISTORY

In 1965 Antoine Riboud replaced his uncle as chairman of family-run Souchon-Neuvesel, a Lyons, France-based maker of glass bottles. Antoine quickly made a mark in this field — he merged the firm with Boussois, a major French flat-glass manufacturer, creating BSN in 1966.

Antoine enlarged BSN's glass business and filled the company's bottles by acquiring well-established beverage and food concerns. In 1970 BSN purchased Brasseries Kronenbourg (France's largest brewer), Société Européenne de Brasseries (another French brewer), and Evian (mineral water, France). The 1972 acquisition of Glaverbel (Belgium) gave BSN 50% of Europe's flat-glass market. The next year BSN merged with France's Gervais Danone (yogurt, cheese, Panzani pasta; founded in 1919 and named after founder Isaac Carasso's son Daniel). This moved the company into pan-European brand-name foods.

As increasing energy costs depressed flat-glass earnings, BSN began divesting its flat-glass businesses. In the late 1970s it acquired interests in brewers in Belgium, Spain, and Italy.

BSN bought Dannon, the leading US yogurt maker (co-founded by Daniel Carasso, who had continued making Danone yogurt in France until WWII), in 1982. It established a strong presence in the Italian pasta market by buying stakes in Ponte (1985) and Agnesi (1986). BSN also purchased Generale Biscuit, the world's #3 biscuit maker (1986), and RJR Nabisco's European cookie and snack-food business (1989).

In a series of acquisitions starting in 1986, BSN took over Italy and Spain's largest mineral water companies and several European pasta makers and other food companies. Adopting the name of its leading international brand, BSN became Groupe Danone in 1994.

Antoine's son, Franck, succeeded him as chairman in 1996 and restructured the company to focus on three core businesses: dairy, beverages (specifically water and beer), and biscuits.

By 1997 Danone had begun shedding non-core grocery products. The company simultaneously stepped up acquisitions of dairy, beer, biscuit, and water companies in developing markets. The 1998 purchase of AquaPenn Spring Water for $112 million doubled its US water-bottling production capacity. Danone in 1999 completed a merger and subsequent sale of part of its BSN Emballage glass-packaging unit to UK buyout firm CVC Capital Partners for $1.23 billion; Danone retained 44% ownership.

Thirsty for the #2 spot in US bottled water sales, Danone gulped down McKesson Water (the #3 bottled water firm in the US after Nestlé and Suntory) for $1.1 billion in 2000. Also that year Danone's joint venture Finalrealm (which includes several European equity firms), with Burlington Biscuits (Nabisco and Hicks, Muse, Tate & Furst), acquired 87% of leading UK biscuit maker United Biscuits. Danone then bought Naya (bottled water, Canada) and sold its brewing operations (#2 in Europe) to Scottish & Newcastle for more than $2.6 billion.

During 2001 Danone announced restructuring would shutter two LU biscuit plants and eliminate about 1,800 jobs; the move met with strikes and legal battles. That same year, having been bumped to the #2 spot in the US yogurt market (after General Mills' Yoplait brand), Danone acquired 40% of Stonyfield Farm, the #4 yogurt brand in the US.

The company launched 2002 with a series of beverage acquisitions including Frucor (New Zealand), and Zywiec Zdroj (the top brand of water in Poland). It then struck a deal handing Coca-Cola the distribution and marketing of Evian in North America, and formed a joint venture with Coke to distribute its lower-end water brands. Antoine Ribaud died that same year, at the age of 83.

Danone continued divesting non-core companies during 2002, including the sale of its Italian meat and cheese business, Galbani, and its Kro Beer Brands (Kronenbourg, 1664 brands) to Scottish & Newcastle. Then, typical of its consolidation strategy, later in 2002 Danone ac-

quired the home and office water delivery companies Chateaud'eau (France), Patrimoine des Eaux du Quebec (Canada), and Sparkling Spring Water (Canada).

EXECUTIVES

Chairman and CEO: Franck Riboud, age 47
Vice Chairman and CEO: Jacques Vincent, age 57
EVP, Finance, Strategy, Information Systems: Emmanuel Faber, age 39
Group Secretary General: Jean-René Buisson, age 55
EVP, Human Resources: Franck Mougin, age 44
EVP, Dairy Products Worldwide: Bernard Hours, age 46
EVP, Biscuits Worldwide: Jean-Louis Gourbin, age 55
EVP, Water Worldwide: Pierre E. Cohade, age 41
EVP, Asia-Pacific: Simon Israel, age 49
EVP, International Strategy: Georges Casala, age 61
Auditors: PricewaterhouseCoopers

LOCATIONS

HQ: 7, rue de Téhéran, 75008 Paris, France
Phone: +33-1-44-35-20-20   **Fax:** +33-1-42-25-67-16
US HQ: 120 White Plains Rd., Tarrytown, NY 10591-5536
US Phone: 914-366-9700   **US Fax:** 914-366-2805
Web: www.danonegroup.com

2002 Sales

	% of total
Europe	
France	26
Other countries	33
Other regions	41
Total	**100**

PRODUCTS/OPERATIONS

2002 Sales

	% of total
Fresh dairy products	46
Beverages	27
Biscuits	24
Other	3
Total	**100**

Selected Products and Brands

Biscuits
Argentina (Bagley)
Asia/Pacific (Griffins)
Colombia (Noel)
Czech Republic, Slovakia (Opavia)
France (Heudebert)
Greece (Papadopolous)
International (Britannia, Danone, LU, Jacob's, Vitalinea)
Italy (Saiwa)
Poland (Wedel)
Russia (Bolshevik)

Bottled Water
Asia/Pacific (Aqua)
Argentina (San Francisco, Villa del Sur, Villavicencio)
Canada (Crystal Springs, Labrador, Naya)
China (Wahaha)
France (Badoit, Salvetat, Brumisateur, Arvie)
International (Evian, Volvic)
Italy (Boario, Ferrarelle)
Mexico (Bonafont)
Spain (Fonter, Font Vella, Lanjarón)
Turkey (Hayat)
US (Alhambra, Crystal, Dannon, Naya, Sparkletts)

Fresh Dairy
Africa (Clover)
Argentina (La Serenissima, Ser)
Canada (Delisle)
France (Danone, Blédina)
International (Actimel, Danone)
Italy (Bel Paese, Casa Romagnoli, Dolcelatte, Santa Lucia)
Latin America (Corpus, La Serenisima, Mastellone)
US (Dannon)

Grocery
Amoy (Asian foods)
Danone (baby foods, biscuits)
HP (sauces)
Lea & Perrins (sauces)

COMPETITORS

Arla
Bahlsen
Biscuits Gardeil
Coca-Cola
Culligan
Dairy Crest
Fonterra
Friesland Coberco
General Mills
Glanbia
Kellogg Snacks
Kerry Group
Kraft Foods
Lactalis
Leche Pascual
Nestlé
Nestlé Waters North America
Owens-Illinois
Parmalat
Pepsi-Cola North America
Saint-Gobain
SODIAAL
Suntory
United Biscuits Finance

HISTORICAL FINANCIALS

Company Type: Public

Income Statement

FYE: December 31

	REVENUE ($ mil.)	NET INCOME ($ mil.)	NET PROFIT MARGIN	EMPLOYEES
12/02	14,237	1,348	9.5%	92,209
12/01	12,897	118	0.9%	100,560
12/00	13,455	679	5.0%	86,657
12/99	13,415	688	5.1%	75,965
12/98	15,154	701	4.6%	78,945
12/97	14,687	608	4.1%	80,631
12/96	16,041	646	4.0%	81,579
12/95	16,185	435	2.7%	73,823
12/94	14,394	661	4.6%	68,181
12/93	11,841	578	4.9%	56,419
Annual Growth	**2.1%**	**9.9%**	**—**	**5.6%**

2002 Year-End Financials

Debt ratio: 80.4%
Return on equity: 25.3%
Cash ($ mil.): 597
Current ratio: 1.22
Long-term debt ($ mil.): 4,298

No. of shares (mil.): 646
Dividends
Yield: 1.4%
Payout: 18.7%
Market value ($ mil.): 17,260

Stock History

NYSE: DA

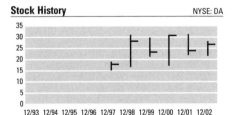

12/93 12/94 12/95 12/96 12/97 12/98 12/99 12/00 12/01 12/02

	STOCK PRICE ($) FY Close	P/E High/Low		PER SHARE ($) Earnings	Dividends	Book Value
12/02	26.70	14	11	1.98	0.37	8.27
12/01	23.95	182	131	0.17	0.00	7.87
12/00	30.70	32	18	0.96	0.00	9.61
12/99	23.28	31	23	0.95	0.00	9.18
12/98	28.13	32	18	0.96	0.00	10.32
12/97	17.88	23	19	0.83	0.00	9.70
Annual Growth	**8.3%**	**—**	**—**	**19.0%**	**—**	**(3.2%)**

Deloitte Touche Tohmatsu

This company is "deloitted" to make your acquaintance, particularly if you're a big business in need of accounting services. Deloitte Touche Tohmatsu (which now does business simply as Deloitte) is one of accounting's Big Four, along with Ernst & Young, KPMG, and PricewaterhouseCoopers. Deloitte offers traditional audit and fiscal-oversight services to a multinational clientele. It also provides human resources and tax consulting services, as well as services to governments and international lending agencies working in emerging markets. Units include Deloitte & Touche (the US accounting arm) and Deloitte Consulting.

Deloitte spent the 1980s and 1990s pursuing a strategy of using accountants and consultants in concert to provide seamless service in auditing, accounting, strategic planning, information technology, financial management, and productivity. Deloitte Consulting became Deloitte's fastest-growing line, offering strategic and management consulting, in addition to information technology and human resources consulting services.

Increasingly, though, Deloitte and its peers were coming under fire for their combined accounting/consulting operations; regulators and observers wondered whether accountants could maintain objectivity when they were auditing clients for whom they also provided consulting services. Criticism mounted after Enron's collapse capsized Arthur Andersen and put the entire accounting industry under scrutiny. (Deloitte picked up new business and members in Andersen's wake.)

Deloitte in 2002 announced it would spin off its consulting business, becoming the last of the big accountants to do so; a year later it called off the split, citing a weakened market for consulting, among other woes.

HISTORY

In 1845 William Deloitte opened an accounting office in London, at first soliciting business from bankrupts. The growth of joint stock companies and the development of stock markets in the mid-19th century created a need for standardized financial reporting and fueled the rise of auditing, and Deloitte moved into the new field. The Great Western Railway appointed him as its independent auditor (the first anywhere) in 1849.

In 1890 John Griffiths, who had become a partner in 1869, opened the company's first US office in New York City. Four decades later branches had opened throughout the US. In 1952 the firm partnered with Haskins & Sells, which operated 34 US offices.

Deloitte aimed to be "the Cadillac, not the Ford" of accounting. The firm, which became Deloitte Haskins & Sells in 1978, began shedding its conservatism as competition heated up; it was the first of the major accountancy firms to use aggressive ads.

Deloitte Haskins & Sells tried to merge with Price Waterhouse in 1984, but the deal was dropped after Price Waterhouse's UK partners objected. In 1989 Deloitte Haskins & Sells joined the flamboyant Touche Ross (founded 1899) to become Deloitte & Touche. Touche Ross's Japanese affiliate, Ross Tohmatsu (founded 1968)

rounded out the current name. The merger was engineered by Deloitte's Michael Cook and Touche's Edward Kangas, in part to unite the former firm's US and European strengths with the latter's Asian presence. Cook continued to oversee US operations, with Kangas presiding over international operations. Many affiliates, particularly in the UK, rejected the merger and defected to competing firms.

As auditors were increasingly held accountable for the financial results of their clients, legal action soared. In the 1990s Deloitte was sued because of its actions relating to Drexel Burnham Lambert junk bond king Michael Milken, the failure of several savings and loans, and clients' bankruptcies.

Nevertheless, in 1995 the SEC chose Michael Sutton, the firm's national director of auditing and accounting practice, as its chief accountant. That year Deloitte formed Deloitte & Touche Consulting to consolidate its US and UK consulting operations; its Asian consulting operations were later added to facilitate regional expansion.

In 1996 the firm formed a corporate fraud unit (with special emphasis on the Internet) and bought PHH Fantus, the leading corporate relocation consulting company. The next year Deloitte and Thurston Group (a Chicago-based merchant bank) teamed up to form NetDox, a system for delivering legal, financial, and insurance documents via the Internet. In 1997, amid a new round of industry mergers, rumors swirled that a Deloitte and Ernst & Young union had been scrapped because the firms could not agree on ownership issues. Deloitte disavowed plans to merge and launched an ad campaign directly targeted against its rivals.

The Asian economic crisis hurt overseas expansion in 1998, but provided a boost in restructuring consulting. In 1999 the firm sold its accounting staffing service unit (Resources Connection) to its managers and Evercore Partners, citing possible conflicts of interest with its core audit business. Also that year Deloitte Consulting decided to sell its computer programming subsidiary to CGI Group, and Kangas stepped down as CEO to be succeeded by James Copeland; the following year Kangas ceded the chairman's seat to Piet Hoogendoorn.

In 2001 the SEC forced Deloitte & Touche to restate the financial results of Pre-Paid Legal Services. In an unusual move, Deloitte & Touche publicly disagreed with the SEC's findings.

The accountancy put some old trouble to bed in 2003 when it agreed to pay $23 million to settle claims it had been negligent in its auditing of failed Kentucky Life Insurance, a client in the 1980s. Later that year the UK's High Court found Deloitte negligent in audits related to the failed Barings Bank; however, the ruling was considered something of a victory for the accountancy because it essentially cleared Deloitte of the majority of charges against it and effectively limited its financial liability in the matter. Copeland retired from the global CEO's office that year and handed the reins over to Bill Parrett, who had formerly served as managing director for the US and the Americas.

EXECUTIVES

Chairman: Piet Hoogendoorn
CEO; Senior Partner, US: William G. (Bill) Parrett, age 57
CFO and Managing Partner, Global Office: William A. Fowler
CIO: Wolfgang Richter

Global Managing Partner, Reputation, Excellence, and Practice Protection; Managing Partner, Netherlands: Willy A. Biewinga
Global Managing Partner, Innovation and Investment; Managing Partner, Germany and Regional Managing Partner, Europe/Middle East/Africa: Wolfgang Grewe
Global Managing Partner, Client Service Excellence; Tohmatsu Representative to DTT, and Regional Managing Partner, Japan: Shuichiro Sekine
Global Managing Partner, Brand and Eminence; Chief Executive and Managing Partner, Canada and Regional Managing Partner, North America: Colin Taylor
Global Managing Partner, Intellectual Capital, Inclusion, and Development; Chief Executive, France: Philippe Vassor
Global Managing Partner, Financial Advisory Services: Ralph G. Adams
Global Managing Partner, Audit: Stephen Almond
Global Managing Partner, Regulation and Risk: Jeffrey K. (Jeff) Willemain
CEO, Deloitte Consulting: Paul Robinson, age 50
Chairman, Deloitte & Touche LLP: Sharon L. Allen, age 51
CEO, Deloitte & Touche LLP: James H. (Jim) Quigley, age 50
Global Managing Partner, Clients & Markets: Jerry Leamon
Chief Executive, Southern Africa and Deputy to the Regional Partner for Europe/Middle East/Africa: Vassi Naidoo
Global Managing Partner, Tax & Legal Services: Alan Schneier
Global Managing Partner, Human Resources: Conrad Venter
Managing Director, Finance and Administration: S. Ashish Bali
General Counsel: Joseph J. Lambert

LOCATIONS

HQ: 1633 Broadway, New York, NY 10019
Phone: 212-489-1600   **Fax:** 212-492-4154
Web: www.deloitte.com

Deloitte Touche Tohmatsu operates through about 700 offices in nearly 150 countries.

PRODUCTS/OPERATIONS

Selected Services

Accounting and auditing
Corporate finance
Emerging markets consulting
Forensic services
Human resources, actuarial, insurance, and managed care consulting
Legal services
Management consulting
Outsourcing
Reorganization services
Risk management
Tax advice and planning
Transaction services

Selected Industry Specializations

Aviation and transport services
Banking and securities
Consumer products
Consumer services
Gas and oil
Insurance
Investment management
Manufacturing
Mining
Retail/wholesale and distribution
Technology, media, and telecommunications
Utilities

Accenture
BDO International
Booz Allen
Boston Consulting
Cap Gemini
EDS
Ernst & Young
Grant Thornton
  International

H&R Block
KPMG
Marsh & McLennan
McKinsey & Company
PricewaterhouseCoopers
Towers Perrin
Watson Wyatt

HISTORICAL FINANCIALS

Company Type: Partnership

Income Statement

FYE: May 31

	REVENUE ($ mil.)	NET INCOME ($ mil.)	NET PROFIT MARGIN	EMPLOYEES
5/03	15,100	—	—	119,237
5/02	12,500	—	—	98,000
5/01	12,400	—	—	95,000
5/00*	11,200	—	—	90,000
8/99	10,600	—	—	90,000
8/98	9,000	—	—	82,000
8/97	7,400	—	—	65,000
8/96	6,500	—	—	63,440
8/95	5,950	—	—	59,000
8/94	5,200	—	—	56,600
Annual Growth	12.6%	—	—	8.6%

*Fiscal year change

Revenue History

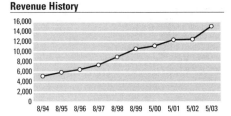

Dentsu Inc.

Unlike Godzilla, Dentsu is one monster that doesn't leave Japan in ruins. One of the largest advertising conglomerates in the world, Dentsu is the #1 ad firm in Japan. Its numerous agencies operate in 27 countries and provide creative services for more than 6,000 clients, although sales outside Japan only account for a small percentage of revenue. Dentsu also offers a host of other services, including public relations, media and event planning, and market research. The company has expanded its operations in Asia through a partnership with US-based Young & Rubicam and owns a 15% stake in ad conglomerate Publicis Groupe. The company completed its IPO on the Tokyo Stock Exchange in late 2001.

As Japan's largest ad conglomerate Dentsu controls more than 30% of Japan's advertising market. While Dentsu has outdistanced its closest domestic rivals, Hakuhodo and Asatsu-DK, the company has designs on becoming a global powerhouse on par with ad conglomerates such as WPP Group and Omnicom, but currently less than 10% of Dentsu's revenues are generated outside of Japan.

Dentsu's strategy for international expansion has been varied and somewhat unfocused; in ad-

dition to its partnership with Young & Rubicam, the company purchased US ad firm Oasis International Group in 2001, and owns a 15% stake in Publicis (as a result of its investment in Bcom3). Dentsu's future growth plans include expanding its operations in Asia using the Dentsu brand and maintaining a grip in the US and Europe through its partnership with Publicis.

Dentsu has organized itself along four business lines representing the company's current position and the lines it would like to grow. Advertising services comprise the bulk of Dentsu's operations, while specialized marketing services, e-solutions services, and overseas operations represent Dentsu's growth objectives.

HISTORY

Seeing a need for a Japanese wire service, Sino-Japanese war correspondent Hoshiro Mitsunaga founded Telegraphic Service Co. in 1901. Mitsunaga let newspapers pay their wire service bills with advertising space, which his advertising agency, Japan Advertising (also founded in 1901) resold. He merged the two companies as Nihon Denpo-Tsushin Sha (Japan Telegraphic Communication Company) in 1907. Known as Dentsu for short (the name was officially changed in 1955), the company gained Japanese rights to the United Press wire in 1908 and began extracting even more favorable advertising rates from its clients.

With its mix of content and advertising, Dentsu became a leading Japanese communications business. But in 1936 Japan's government consolidated all news services into its propaganda machine, Domei, taking half of Dentsu's stock. During WWII, all of Japan's advertising agencies were combined into 12 entities. Following the war, US occupation forces dismantled Domei, and its 50% holding in Dentsu stock was transferred to two new press agencies, Kyodo and Jiji.

Hideo Yoshida, who became president of Dentsu in 1947, began the task of rebuilding the company, currying favor by employing the sons of politicians and business leaders. He also helped build the television industry in Japan by investing in start-up broadcasters. Their gratitude translated into preferential treatment for Dentsu, leading to its decades-long domination of Japanese TV advertising.

By 1973 Dentsu had become the world's largest advertising agency, but the company's growth stalled with the slowing Japanese economy. Slow to expand overseas (it formed a joint venture with Young & Rubicam in 1981), foreign billings accounted for just 7% of revenues in 1986. The next year Saatchi & Saatchi passed Dentsu as the world's #1 advertising group. Young & Rubicam/Dentsu later joined with Havas' Eurocom to form HDM Worldwide (named after Havas, Dentsu, and Y&R's Marsteller).

Dentsu rebounded with Japan's economic boom in the late 1980s, but the company continued to struggle abroad. Eurocom pulled out of HDM Worldwide in 1990, and the newly named Dentsu, Young & Rubicam Partnerships reorganized to focus on North America, Asia, and Australia. Dentsu joined with Collett Dickenson Pearce to maintain its presence in Europe after HDM's demise. Restructuring in 1996 created several new units, including one to focus on the Olympics, and in 1997 the company set up the Interactive Solution Center to focus on digital media.

The company agreed to buy UK ad agency

Harari Page in 1998 and announced plans for its own public offering. Dentsu took a 20% stake in Bcom3 (formerly BDM) in 2000, the new advertising holding company formed by the merger of The Leo Group and MacManus Group. It also formed a Japanese Internet services joint venture with US consulting company marchFIRST. After marchFIRST's demise Dentsu gained full ownership of the company and renamed it DentsuFUSE.

The following year Dentsu reorganized its US and European units and purchased US ad firm Oasis International Group and became a publicly listed company in late 2001.

EXECUTIVES

Chairman and CEO: Yutaka Narita, age 74
President and COO: Tateo Mataki
EVP and CFO: Hitoshi Hanatsuka
EVP: Tetsu Nakamura
EVP: Fumio Oshima, age 66
Senior Managing Director and CIO: Hideaki Furukawa
Senior Managing Director: Ko Matsumoto
Senior Managing Director: Tatsuyoshi Takashima
Managing Director: Isao Maruyama
Managing Director and Chief Creative Officer:
  Toshiaki Nozue
Managing Director: Takehiko Kimura
Managing Director: Hiromori Hayashi
Executive Director: Jun Sakakibara
Executive Director: Toyohiko Yamonouchi
Auditors: KPMG

LOCATIONS

HQ: 1-8-1, Higashi-shimbashi, Minato-ku,
  Tokyo 105-7001, Japan
Phone: +81-3-6216-5111   **Fax:** +81-3-5551-2013
US HQ: 488 Madison Ave., 23rd Fl., New York, NY 10022
US Phone: 212-829-5120   **US Fax:** 212-829-0009
Web: www.dentsu.com

Dentsu has offices in 31 cities in Japan and 41 cities in 27 countries.

2003 Sales

	% of total
Japan	93
Other countries	7
Total	**100**

PRODUCTS/OPERATIONS

2003 Sales

	% of total
Advertising	79
Specialized marketing services	7
e-Solutions	6
Overseas operations	6
Other services	2
Total	**100**

Selected Operations

Creative Associates
DentsuFUSE (Internet services)
Dentsu Kosan Service (management services)
Dentsu Management Services
Dentsu Music Publishing
Dentsu Public Relations
Dentsu Research
Dentsu TEC
Dentsu Young & Rubicam (50%, advertising)

COMPETITORS

Asatsu-DK
Grey Global
Hakuhodo
Havas

Interpublic Group
Omnicom
Publicis
WPP Group

HISTORICAL FINANCIALS

Company Type: Public

Income Statement

FYE: March 31

	REVENUE ($ mil.)	NET INCOME ($ mil.)	NET PROFIT MARGIN	EMPLOYEES
3/03	2,359	(39)	—	13,623
3/02	2,216	204	9.2%	12,167
3/01	2,390	380	15.9%	11,037
3/00	2,462	196	8.0%	10,841
3/99	2,003	37	1.8%	—
3/98	1,812	68	3.8%	—
3/97	1,818	110	6.0%	—
3/96	1,903	131	6.9%	—
3/95	2,026	72	3.6%	—
3/94	1,622	24	1.5%	—
Annual Growth	4.2%	—	—	7.9%

2003 Year-End Financials

Debt ratio: 35.5%
Return on equity: —
Cash ($ mil.): 556

Current ratio: 1.17
Long-term debt ($ mil.): 1,161

Net Income History

Exchange: Tokyo

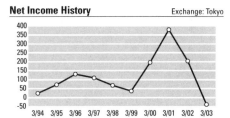

Deutsche Bahn

Deutsche Bahn gets you from Punkt A to Punkt B. The railway's main divisions, DB Regio (local passenger transport) and DB Reise & Touristik (long-distance passenger transport), carry more than 1.8 billion passengers yearly throughout Germany and to neighboring countries. The company's freight transport division, which moves about 78 billion ton-kilometers of freight annually, has been strengthened with the acquisition of logistics provider Stinnes. Deutsche Bahn's DB Stations & Services division manages the company's train stations, and its DB Netz division provides track infrastructure services. The company, owned by the German government, is one of Europe's largest transportation providers.

To encourage more use of the rails, Deutsche Bahn has doubled its train capacity on more popular routes, particularly the Frankfurt to Berlin route. It has opened a new line from Cologne to Rhein/Main. Deustche Bahn also hopes to increase passenger transport through DB Regio by expanding its bus services. The company expects its new Stinnes unit to drive an increase in freight traffic.

The government had planned to take Deutsche Bahn public by 2003, but financial losses stalled plans for an IPO. CEO Hartmut Mehdorn is working to reduce costs in preparation for privatization, but the company's powerful unions are expected to block any job cuts.

HISTORY

In 1989 the Federal Cabinet of West Germany adopted a resolution to set up an independent government railway commission. That year the wall between East Germany and West Germany came down, and the two nations became united into one Germany, known as the Federal Republic of Germany, in 1990.

In 1993 the Cabinet approved the legal package on railway reform submitted by the federal minister of transport. Later that year the legislation won the two-thirds majority of the German Parliament and the Federal Council it needed to pass. Deutsche Bahn was then established in 1994 to unify Germany's western (Deutsche Bundesbahn) and eastern (Deutsche Reichsban) railway systems as a public company. The Federal Republic of Germany was sole shareholder.

The next year Deutsche Bahn created a subsidiary, DBKom, to offer telecom services in competition with Deutsche Telekom. In 1996 a consortium led by German conglomerate Mannesmann bought a 50% stake in DBKom. By 1997 Deutsche Bahn had been transformed from a government department into a registered company and split into four operating units: tracks, freight, local passenger services, and intercity passenger services. That year Deutsche Bahn also bought Lufthansa's 33% stake in tour operator Deutsches Reisebüro (DER), giving it full ownership of the company as well as DER's 20% stake in tour group TUI.

Trouble came in 1998: Deutsche Bahn sent its 59 first-generation high-speed InterCityExpress (ICE) trains for inspections after one of the trains crashed and killed 98 passengers. Investigators believed a broken wheel caused the crash.

Deutsche Bahn and French state-owned railway SNCF announced plans in 1999 to develop a high-speed train capable of traveling up to 320 km (198 miles) per hour. Also that year Hartmut Mehdorn, credited with turning around printing equipment manufacturer Heidelberger Druck and DaimlerChrysler's aerospace unit, became Deutsche Bahn's new CEO. Tasked with improving the railway's punctuality, Mehdorn pledged to make Deutsche Bahn more efficient by cutting losses and raising productivity. That year the company sold its stake in TUI to conglomerate Preussag and its DER unit to supermarket giant Rewe.

In 2000 the company's DB Cargo unit and Dutch rail freight company N.S. Cargo formed a new group, Railion (joined by Danish State Railways' freight unit DSB Gods in 2001). Also in 2000, Germany's transport minister indefinitely postponed plans to float Deutsche Bahn after it posted losses for the first time since 1994.

Hoping to take advantage of Deutsche Bahn's financial troubles, Connex, then a subsidiary of French conglomerate Vivendi, offered in 2001 to acquire Deutsche Bahn's long-distance express passenger trains. But Mehdorn refused the offer, stating the company did not want to give up its long-distance traffic. Deutsche Bahn did agree in 2001 to form a railway telematics (communications system) joint venture with Mannesmann Arcor, a company controlled by Vodafone. The agreement called for Deutsche Bahn to keep its 18% stake in Arcor but lose its minority veto rights — which Deutsche Bahn had used earlier that year to block an Arcor IPO.

In 2002 the company bought the 65% stake in logistics provider Stinnes held by E.ON. Deutsche Bahn took full ownership of Stinnes the next year.

EXECUTIVES

Honorary Chairman of the Supervisory Board:
Günther Sassmannshausen
Chairman of the Supervisory Board: Michael Frenzel, age 56
Deputy Chairman of the Supervisory Board:
Norbert Hansen
Executive Chairman and CEO; Chairman of the Supervisory Board, Stinnes: Hartmut Mehdorn
CFO: Diethelm Sack
Director, Freight Transport; Chairman and CEO, DB Cargo; Chairman of the Board of Management, Stinnes: Bernd Malmström, age 62
Director, Marketing: Klaus Daubertshäuser
Director, Passenger Transport; Chairman and CEO, DB Regio and DB Reise & Touristik: Christoph Franz
Director, Personnel: Norbert Bensel
Director, Technology: Karl-Freidrich Rausch
Director, Track Infrastructure and Integrated Operations; Chairman and CEO, DB Netz:
Roland Heinisch
Auditors: PwC Deutsche Revision AG

LOCATIONS

HQ: Deutsche Bahn AG, Potsdamer Platz 2, D-10785 Berlin, Germany
Phone: +49-30-2-97-6-11-33   **Fax:** +49-30-2-97-6-19-19
Web: www.bahn.de

PRODUCTS/OPERATIONS

2002 Sales

	% of total
Passenger transport	
Local & regional	50
Long-distance	21
Freight transport	24
Passenger stations	1
Track infrastructure	1
Other	3
Total	**100**

Major Subsidiaries

Passenger Transport
DB Regio AG (local passenger transport)
DB Reise & Touristik AG (long-distance passenger transport)

Freight Transport
DB Cargo AG
Railion GmbH (92%, freight transport joint venture)
Stinnes AG (logistics)

Passenger Stations
DB Station & Service AG

Track Infrastructure
DB Netz AG

COMPETITORS

Air France
A.P. Møller — Mærsk
Bombardier
British Airways
SNCF
Deutsche Telekom
Hamburger Hochbahn
KLM
Lufthansa
National Express Group
TUI
Veolia Environnement

HISTORICAL FINANCIALS

Company Type: Government-owned

Income Statement

FYE: December 31

	REVENUE ($ mil.)	NET INCOME ($ mil.)	NET PROFIT MARGIN	EMPLOYEES
12/02	21,905	(475)	—	250,690
12/01	15,533	(360)	—	214,371
12/00	16,259	80	0.5%	222,656
12/99	17,644	88	0.5%	241,638
12/98	18,011	200	1.1%	252,468
12/97	16,938	217	1.3%	268,273
12/96	19,457	727	3.7%	288,768
12/95	20,806	184	0.9%	349,627
12/94	18,662	117	0.6%	—
Annual Growth	2.0%	—	—	(4.6%)

2002 Year-End Financials

Debt ratio: 317.8%
Return on equity: —
Cash ($ mil.): 284

Current ratio: 0.91
Long-term debt ($ mil.): 18,678

Net Income History

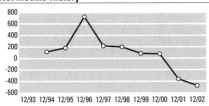

Deutsche Bank

Deutsche Bank has two primary divisions but one central goal: global domination. The bank's two primary operating segments are Corporate and Investment Banking and Private Clients and Asset Management. One of the largest banks in the world, Deutsche Bank offers retail services primarily in Germany, but operates its investment banking and asset management businesses across the globe, primarily in Europe with additional markets in Asia, the Pacific Rim, and the Americas. The bank's global ambitions have caused some boardroom clashes between tradition-minded executives and their faster-paced cohorts.

The times keep a-changin', but not quickly enough for chairman Josef Ackermann, who has pushed for the reorganization of the bank's management structure away from the consensus-based German model to a more individualistic Anglo-American model. Ackermann believes such a change will allow for more rapid decision-making. Conservative board members, chafing from the influence Deutsche Bank's London and New York investment bankers wield, have resisted Ackermann's makeover as an Anglo-American-styled bank.

Deutsche Bank is reorganizing and retooling to help it reclaim a top spot in world banking. The company is looking to shore up its flagging retail banking operations and expand its investment banking reach, as well as consolidating its private clients and business operations. The company sold more than 75% of insurance company Versicherungsholding der Deutschen Bank to Zurich Financial Services and tossed in its Italian, Portuguese, and Spanish insurance holdings to boot. In return it picked up US-based asset manager Scudder Investments. Zurich Financial and Deutsche Bank have signaled their intention to collaborate in the marketing of asset management, banking, and insurance.

The bank has entered an alliance with US-based asset manager INVESCO in the hopes of further boosting its product offerings in that market. Along with the Scudder acquisition, this move positions Deutsche Bank to become the "Wal-Mart of asset management" in the US. To shore up its flagging financial position, the bank has shed numerous non-core holdings, such as its securities custody business, which was bought by State Street, and its passive asset management operations, sold to Northern Trust. Deutsche Bank is also dismantling its Deutsche Financial Services division, selling its commercial inventory financing business to GE Commercial Finance and arranging to sell its consumer finance operations to E*TRADE. Deutsche Bank sold off its corporate real estate holdings and plans to divest some of its private-equity portfolio as well.

Mortgage bank subsidiary Eurohypo merged with Commerzbank's RheinHyp and Dresdner Bank's Deutsche Hypothekenbank to form a gigantic mortgage-banking firm, capable of rivaling Germany-based HVB Group's HVB Real Estate. The new, turbo-charged Eurohypo specializes in commercial property across Europe and in the US. Deutsche Bank holds 35%, Commerzbank 35%, and Dresdner 30%. Deutsche Bank is also building its already-massive real estate investment and management business through acquisitions (such as RREEF) and restructuring.

Deutsche Bank and insurer Allianz are at the core of a tangled web of cross-ownership among German corporations. Deutsche Bank is seeking to unravel the situation: It is selling big chunks of Allianz and reorganizing internally. Responding to the slowing pace of world banking, Deutsche Bank has announced almost 15,000 job cuts in most areas of the company.

HISTORY

Georg von Siemens opened Deutsche Bank in Berlin in 1870. Three years later the firm opened an office in London and was soon buying other German banks. In the late 1800s Deutsche Bank helped finance Germany's electrification (carried out by Siemens AG) and railroad construction in the US and the Ottoman Empire. Von Siemens ran the bank until his death in 1901.

The bank survived post-WWI financial chaos by merging with Disconto-Gesellschaft and later helped finance the Nazi war machine. After the war, the Allies split the company into 10 banks; it became extinct in Soviet-controlled East Germany.

The bank was reassembled in 1957 and primarily engaged in commercial banking, often taking direct interests in its customers. It added retail services in the 1960s. In 1975, to prevent the Shah of Iran from gaining a stake in Daimler-Benz (now DaimlerChrysler), the bank bought 29% of that company.

The firm opened an investment banking office in the US in 1971 and a branch office in 1978. In the 1980s it expanded geographically, buying Bank of America's Italian subsidiary (1986) and UK merchant bank Morgan Grenfell (1989); it also moved into insurance, creating life insurer DB Leben (1989).

Terrorists killed chairman Alfred Herrhausen, a symbol of German big business, in 1989. After German reunification in 1990, successor Hilmar Kopper oversaw the bank's re-establishment in eastern Germany.

In 1994 Deutsche Bank bought most of ITT's commercial finance unit. That year the company suffered scandal when real estate developer Jurgen Schneider borrowed more than DM1 billion and disappeared; he was later found and returned to Germany.

The company grew its global investment banking operations in 1995 under its Morgan Grenfell subsidiary. Deutsche Bank's global aspirations suffered a setback in 1998 when losses on investments in Russia trimmed its bottom line. Still trying to put WWII behind it, the bank accepted responsibility for its wartime dealing in gold seized from Jews but has rejected liability to compensate victims of Nazi forced labor who toiled in industrial companies in which it holds stakes.

In 1999 the bank acquired Bankers Trust. Despite a decision to divest its industrial portfolio, in 1999 the company bought Tele Columbus, the #2 cable network in Germany, and Piaggio, the Italian maker of the famed Vespa motor scooter. On the banking front, Deutsche Bank bought Chase Manhattan's Dutch auction business and sought a foothold in Japan through alliances with Nippon Life Insurance and Sakura Bank (now part of Sumitomo Mitsui Banking).

In 2000 the company agreed to merge with Dresdner Bank (after which they would spin off their retail banking businesses), but the merger collapsed, in part over the fate of investment banking subsidiary Dresdner Kleinwort Benson. German mega-insurer Allianz bought Dresdner in 2001. Deutsche Bank's reorganization plans the same year saw the bank eliminate 2,600 jobs worldwide and realign its businesses into two divisions. Deutsche Bank also bought Banque Worms from French insurer AXA.

Looking for a steady supply of cash, in 2001 Deutsche Bank's Morgan Grenfall Private Equity bought 3,000 English pubs owned by UK-based conglomerate Whitbread plc. In 2002 more shuffling of the executive board members allowed Deutsche Bank to grow in the international Anglo-American style, rather than as a domestic player.

EXECUTIVES

Spokesman of the Board of Managing Directors and Chairman of the Group Executive Committee: Josef Ackermann, age 55, $4,494,034 pay

Chairman of the Supervisory Committee: Rolf E. Breuer, age 65

CFO and Chief Risk Officer: Clemens Börsig, age 54, $2,162,754 pay

Chief Administrative Officer: Tessen von Heydebreck, age 57, $2,162,754 pay

COO: Hermann-Josef Lamberti, age 46, $2,162,754 pay

Head of Global Corporate Finance: Michael Cohrs

Head of Global Transaction Banking, Global Banking Division, and Global Relationship Management Germany: Jürgen Fitschen

Head of Asset Management: Thomas (Tom) Hughes

Head of Global Markets: Anshu Jain

Head of Private and Business Clients: Rainer Neske

Head of Global Equities: Kevin Parker

Head of Private Wealth Management: Pierre de Weck, age 53

Auditors: KPMG Deutsche Treuhand-Gesellschaft AG

LOCATIONS

HQ: Deutsche Bank AG
Taunusanlage 12,
60325 Frankfurt-am-Main, Germany
Phone: +49-69-910-00   **Fax:** +49-69-910-34227
US HQ: 31 W. 52nd St., New York, NY 10101-6160
US Phone: 212-469-8000   **US Fax:** 212-469-3210
Web: www.deutsche-bank.de

PRODUCTS/OPERATIONS

2002 Assets

	$ mil.	% of total
Cash & equivalents	36,414	5
Central bank funds sold & securities purchased under resale agreements	123,608	15
Securities borrowed	39,459	5
Trading assets	312,002	39
Net loans	175,717	22
Other	109,296	14
Total	**796,495**	**100**

COMPETITORS

ABN AMRO	Goldman Sachs
BANK ONE	HSBC Holdings
Bankgesellschaft Berlin	Intuit
Barclays	J.P. Morgan Chase
HVB Group	KfW
BNP	Lehman Brothers
Charles Schwab	Merrill Lynch
Citigroup Global Markets	Mizuho Financial
Citigroup	Morgan Stanley
Commerzbank AG	National Australia Bank
cortalconsors	Rabobank
Credit Suisse	SCH
Dresdner Bank	Société Générale
DZ BANK	TD Bank
E*TRADE Financial	UBS

HISTORICAL FINANCIALS

Company Type: Public

Income Statement
FYE: December 31

	ASSETS ($ mil.)	NET INCOME ($ mil.)	INCOME AS % OF ASSETS	EMPLOYEES
12/02	796,495	416	0.1%	77,442
12/01	818,411	149	0.0%	94,782
12/00	874,927	12,727	1.5%	98,311
12/99	845,744	2,589	0.3%	93,232
12/98	731,151	2,014	0.3%	95,847
12/97	581,974	569	0.1%	76,141
12/96	570,465	1,428	0.3%	74,356
12/95	501,923	1,475	0.3%	74,119
12/94	382,468	1,107	0.3%	73,450
12/93	320,145	1,247	0.4%	73,176
Annual Growth	10.7%	(11.5%)	—	0.6%

2002 Year-End Financials

Equity as % of assets: 4.0%
Return on assets: 0.1%
Return on equity: 1.3%
Long-term debt ($ mil.): 109,060
Sales ($ mil.): 57,913

Net Income History
NYSE: DB

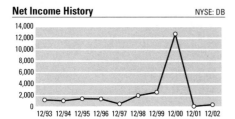

Deutsche Post

Europe's largest postal service provider, Deutsche Post is a bundle about to burst. The company is adding locations, services, and products to compete with private courier services and online delivery. Also known as the "Yellow Giant," it provides traditional and same-day letter delivery, online bulk mail management, and mail process outsourcing. Besides its mail services, the company offers financial services through Deutsche Postbank, and express delivery and logistics services through DHL. The German government owns about 70% of Deutsche Post.

Through a series of acquisitions, Deutsche Post has gained control of express delivery and logistics operations across Europe and in the US. In 2003 Deutsche Post (through DHL) paid about $1 billion in cash for the ground delivery network of US-based Airborne.

To eliminate overlaps in its operations, Deutsche Post has united its parcel and express delivery services (DHL and Euro Express) and logistics services (Danzas) under the DHL brand. The new DHL consists of four divisions: DHL Express, DHL Freight, DHL Danzas Air & Ocean, and DHL Solutions.

In addition, Deutsche Post is moving to cut costs by centralizing processes such as purchasing and by using ground transportation rather than airplanes for mail in some regions.

The company has announced plans to sell a minority stake in Deutsche Postbank in an IPO. Some of the proceeds are likely to be used for acquisitions of postal and logistics operations in Europe.

HISTORY

The German postal system was established in the 1490s when German emperor Maximilian I ordered a reliable and regular messenger service to be set up between Austria (Innsbruck, where the emperor had his court) and the further reaches of his Holy Roman Empire: the Netherlands, France, and Rome. The Tassis (later renamed Taxis) family of Italy was responsible for running the network. Members of the von Taxis family settled in major cities across Europe to expand the postal business.

Although the family operated what was officially an exclusively royal mail service, by the early 1500s the company was also delivering messages for private patrons. In 1600 a Tassis family member who served as general postmaster was authorized to collect fees for private mail deliveries. By the early 19th century, Thurn und Taxis, as the company was then called, was the leading postal service in the Holy Roman Empire, serving more than 11 million people.

The dissolution of the Holy Roman Empire, prompted by Napoleon's military adventures, led to creation of a federation of 39 independent German states. Thurn und Taxis had to make agreements with members of the separate states, including Austria and Prussia. Following Austria's defeat in 1866 by Prussia, the confederation was dissolved and all Thurn und Taxis postal systems were absorbed by Prussia. When Bismarck's Prussian-led German Reich was established in 1870, the new postal administration (Reichspostverwaltung) began issuing postage stamps valid across Germany.

Following Germany's defeat in WWII and the formation of two separate Germanies in 1949,

two postal systems were established: Deutsche Post (East Germany) and Deutsche Bundespost (West Germany). The fall of the Berlin Wall in 1989 preceded a reunion of the two German states in 1990. That year Deutsche Post, led by chairman Klaus Zumwinkel, was integrated into Deutsche Bundespost. The merger resulted in losses and a huge backlog of undelivered mail. Zumwinkel initiated the company's first steps to recovery by cutting 140,000 jobs.

The heavy costs of East German reunification (it was 1994 before Deutsche Bundespost posted a profit again) prompted the German government to set the postal system on a course toward full privatization. In 1995 the postal system was restructured as Deutsche Post AG and placed under the management of executives from the private sector.

In 1998 a new postal law reaffirmed Deutsche Post's monopoly on traditional letter delivery until 2002. However, other special mail delivery options (such as same-day delivery of letters) were granted to private companies. That year Deutsche Post acquired shares in parcel delivery companies in Europe and the US, including a 50% stake in the distribution unit of the UK's Securicor and nearly 25% of DHL. In 1999 it acquired Deutsche Postbank, the former retail banking arm of Deutsche Bundespost, as part of a strategy to make it more attractive for an IPO. The company also began offering new products, such as office and stationery goods as well as Internet and in-house services.

Continuing its buying spree, Deutsche Post grabbed Swiss-based logistics giant Danzas Holding, Swedish freight forwarder ASG, and the distribution and logistics unit of Dutch transport group Royal Nedlloyd. Undeterred by a European Commission probe into whether it received improper state subsidies, Deutsche Post added more units in 2000, including US-based airfreight forwarder Air Express International, which was integrated into Danzas. It also acquired New York-based QuickMAIL. The German government sold a minority stake in Deutsche Post to the public in 2000.

The German government in 2001 extended Deutsche Post's monopoly over letter delivery until 2007. The next year the postal service took full ownership of DHL.

EXECUTIVES

Chairman of the Supervisory Board: Josef Hattig
Chairman of the Board of Management and CEO:
Klaus Zumwinkel
Director Corporate Services: Frank Appel
Director Euro Express: Peter Kruse
Director Finance: Edgar Ernst
Director Financial Services: Wulf von Schimmelmann, age 55
Director Mail: Hans-Dieter Petram
Director Personnel: Walter Scheurle
Director Worldwide Express: Uwe R. Dörken
President and CEO, Deutsche Post World Net USA:
Wolfgang Pordzik
Auditors: PwC Deutsche Revision AG

LOCATIONS

HQ: Deutsche Post AG
    Charles-de-Gaulle-Str. 20, 53113 Bonn, Germany
Phone: +49-228-182-0   **Fax:** +49-228-182-7099
Web: www.dpwn.de

2002 Sales

	% of total
Europe	
Germany	59
Other countries	26
Americas	9
Other regions	6
Total	**100**

PRODUCTS/OPERATIONS

2002 Sales

	% of total
Express	29
Mail	28
Logistics	22
Financial services	21
Total	**100**

COMPETITORS

CNF
Exel
FedEx
Hays
KLM
Royal Mail
SAS
Stinnes
TPG
UPS
U.S. Postal Service

HISTORICAL FINANCIALS

Company Type: Public

Income Statement   FYE: December 31

	REVENUE ($ mil.)	NET INCOME ($ mil.)	NET PROFIT MARGIN	EMPLOYEES
12/02	44,295	691	1.6%	371,912
12/01	30,963	1,402	4.5%	321,369
12/00	30,798	1,424	4.6%	324,203
12/99	23,697	1,120	4.7%	301,229
12/98	18,295	190	1.0%	258,491
12/97	16,231	(214)	—	266,823
12/96	18,878	217	1.2%	284,889
12/95	17,486	—	—	307,388
12/94	15,809	—	—	—
12/93	13,646	—	—	—
Annual Growth	**14.0%**	**21.3%**	**—**	**2.8%**

2002 Year-End Financials

Debt ratio: 18.0%   Current ratio: 199.00
Return on equity: 13.7%   Long-term debt ($ mil.): 962
Cash ($ mil.): 2,766

Net Income History   Exchange: German

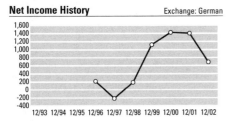

Deutsche Telekom AG

Deutsche Telekom is leading the charge as the former state-owned telecommunications monopolies in Europe confront competition. It is the #1 telecom company in Europe and one of the largest in the world, behind NTT and AT&T. Deutsche Telekom is still Germany's #1 fixed-line phone operator, with about 57 million access lines. The company's T-Com unit provides network access services; its T-Mobile International division serves wireless phone customers; the company's majority-owned T-Online subsidiary, with 10.7 million customers, is Europe's leading ISP; and the company's T-Systems division specializes in IT services. The German government owns about 43% of Deutsche Telekom.

Deutsche Telekom's T-Mobile Germany unit is that country's leading wireless telecom provider (along with Vodafone's German network). The company's T-Mobile International unit moved into the US mobile phone market in 2001 with the acquisitions of VoiceStream Wireless and Powertel, now known as T-Mobile USA. The German government's stake in Deutsche Telekom decreased by 17% largely to accommodate US regulators for the VoiceStream and Powertel acquisitions. Counting customers from its other European holdings (including One 2 One in the UK), T-Mobile serves 66.9 million customers overall.

Its T-Com division also provides traditional telecom access to residential customers and small to midsized businesses, as well as data services, telecom equipment sales, and international carrier services.

Until 2003 Deutsche Telekom was also Germany's #1 cable provider through the company's six regional cable TV operations, which it sold for $1.87 billion to a group of US investors that includes Apax Partners, the Goldman Sachs Group, and Providence Equity Partners. The deal represents a substantial discount from a 2001 agreement to sell the cable networks to US-based Liberty Media for about $5 billion. But German regulatory authorities blocked that sale. (Deutsche Telekom had previously sold controlling stakes in three other regional networks.)

With competition flourishing in Germany, Deutsche Telekom is working hard to lose its bureaucratic image and reposition itself as a slimmer, customer-friendly organization. To cut costs and eliminate debt the company plans to reduce its workforce by 22,000 jobs, or 9%, over the next two years. The company has sold a minority stake in T-Online to the public but has postponed plans for an IPO of T-Mobile because of market conditions. As the company's share price slumped amid the general telecom industry downturn, CEO Ron Sommer was forced to resign in July 2002. That year the company announced plans to sell its phone directory unit (DeTeMedien), saying it hoped to raise 1 billion, but reversed that decision a year later after making progress at reducing its debt burden. Also in 2003 the company announced plans to acquire the 51% of Polish wireless operator Polska Telefonia Cyfrowa that

it does not yet own from Vivendi Universal and Elektrim. But the company pulled out of the deal, which was valued at $1.26 billion, after Elektrim officials sought a higher price.

HISTORY

Deutsche Telekom was formed by the 1989 separation of West Germany's telecommunications services from the nation's postal system. Dating back to the 15th century (when the Thurn und Taxis private postal system was created for German principalities), the service covered Austria, France, the Netherlands, and most of Germany by the 1850s. After the 1866 Austro-Prussian War, it became part of the North German Postal Confederation. When the German Empire was formed in 1871, the postal operation became the Deutsche Reichspost (later the Bundespost). Shortly thereafter, the newly invented telephone was introduced in Germany.

Post-WWI inflation shook the Bundespost, and the government allowed it to try new organizational structures. A 1924 law allowed the state-run service to operate as a quasi-commercial company.

Hitler came to power in 1933, and the German postal service became an instrument of Nazi surveillance. After WWII occupation forces began rebuilding Germany's badly damaged infrastructure. In 1947 the American-British zone returned postal authority to the Germans, and in 1949 the USSR established the state of East Germany.

Only by the 1960s did West Germany's postal and phone services meet modern standards. Privatization of the Bundespost became a political cause when many complained about the monopoly's cost and inefficiency. Efforts to privatize the agency (named Deutsche Telekom in 1989) intensified with the 1990 German reunification. Faced with updating the antiquated phone system of the former East Germany, political opposition to taking Deutsche Telekom public faded.

The company began operating T-D1, its mobile phone network, in 1992, and the next year it launched T-Online, now Germany's largest online service provider. In 1996 Deutsche Telekom finally went public and raised more than $13 billion in Europe's largest IPO. It also launched Global One with France Telecom and Sprint; as part of the partnership, Deutsche Telekom took a 10% stake in Sprint.

In 1998 European Union (EU) member countries opened their phone markets to competition, and Deutsche Telekom's long-distance market share quickly eroded. Under EU pressure, in 1999 Deutsche Telekom said it would sell its cable network, which it divided into nine regional units.

Deutsche Telekom's plan to merge with Telecom Italia in 1999 blew up in its face: Olivetti butted in and took over Telecom Italia, while an angry France Telecom filed a lawsuit claiming that Deutsche Telekom's merger plan had violated their agreements. (The case was settled in 2000.)

Undaunted, Deutsche Telekom forged ahead with its international expansion plans, buying French fixed-line carrier SIRIS and UK wireless provider One 2 One. In 2000 the company sold its stake in Global One to France Telecom, as did Sprint. (In the fallout from the unwinding of the Global One partnership, Deutsche Telekom in 2001 sold its stake in Sprint PCS and sold its interest in France Telecom the next year.)

Later in 2000 Deutsche Telekom agreed to pay $5.3 billion for a controlling stake in DaimlerChrysler's Debis Systemhaus information technology services unit. It also launched an IPO of its Internet subsidiary, T-Online.

EXECUTIVES

Chairman, Supervisory Board: Klaus Zumwinkel
Chairman, Management Board, and CEO: Kai-Uwe Ricke, age 42
Deputy CEO, Finance, and Controlling (CFO): Karl-Gerhard Eick
Head of Group Strategy and Policy: Arndt Rautenberg, age 36
Head of the Human Resources Division: Heinz Klinkhammer
Chairman and CEO of T-Com: Josef Brauner
Head of T-Mobile International: René Obermann, age 40
Head of T-Online: Thomas Holtrop
Head of T-Systems: Konrad F. Reiss
Auditors: PwC Deutsche Revision AG

LOCATIONS

HQ: Friedrich-Ebert-Allee 140, 53113 Bonn, Germany
Phone: +49-228-181-0   **Fax:** +49-228-181-8872
US HQ: 280 Park Ave., 26th Fl., New York, NY 10017
US Phone: 212-424-2900   **US Fax:** 212-424-2989
Web: www.telekom.de

Deutsche Telekom operates primarily in Germany, but it holds interests in operations worldwide.

2002 Sales

	% of total
Germany	87
Other countries	13
Total	**100**

PRODUCTS/OPERATIONS

2002 Sales

	$ mil.	% of total
T-Com	26,503	47
T-Mobile	19,173	34
T-Systems	8,459	15
T-Online	1,692	3
Other revenues	563	1
Total	**56,390**	**100**

Operating Divisions

T-Com (fixed-line network voice and data services)
T-Mobile (mobile communications services and equipment sales)
T-Systems (data communications and systems services for large business customers)
T-Online (consumer Internet services)

COMPETITORS

America Online	Metromedia
AT&T	mobilcom
Belgacom	NTT
BT	KPN
Cable & Wireless	Siemens
COLT Telecom	Swisscom
EDS	TDC
France Telecom	Telecom Italia
Hungarian Telephone and Cable	Telefónica
	TeliaSonera
IBM	Vodafone
Lagardère	WorldCom

HISTORICAL FINANCIALS

Company Type: Public

Income Statement

FYE: December 31

	REVENUE ($ mil.)	NET INCOME ($ mil.)	NET PROFIT MARGIN	EMPLOYEES
12/02	56,390	(25,824)	—	256,000
12/01	43,058	(3,079)	—	257,058
12/00	38,556	5,581	14.5%	227,015
12/99	35,796	1,265	3.5%	170,000
12/98	41,868	2,630	6.3%	186,000
12/97	37,559	1,837	4.9%	191,000
12/96	40,917	1,140	2.8%	201,060
12/95	45,997	3,667	8.0%	213,467
12/94	41,184	2,320	5.6%	229,474
12/93	33,927	1,199	3.5%	232,964
Annual Growth	**5.8%**	**—**	**—**	**1.1%**

2002 Year-End Financials

Debt ratio: 169.2%
Return on equity: —
Cash ($ mil.): 2,001
Current ratio: 0.73
Long-term debt ($ mil.): 55,842
No. of shares (mil.): 4,195
Dividends
Yield: 2.6%
Payout: —
Market value ($ mil.): 53,278

Stock History

NYSE: DT

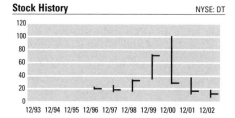

	STOCK PRICE ($) FY Close	P/E High/Low		PER SHARE ($) Earnings	Dividends	Book Value
12/02	12.70	—	—	(6.15)	0.33	7.87
12/01	16.90	—	—	(0.83)	0.56	12.95
12/00	29.25	54	16	1.85	0.57	11.94
12/99	71.00	167	83	0.43	0.65	11.56
12/98	32.75	35	18	0.96	0.67	10.38
12/97	18.63	37	24	0.67	0.35	9.46
12/96	20.38	41	37	0.54	0.00	10.74
Annual Growth	**(7.6%)**	—	—	—	—	**(5.0%)**

Diageo plc

Diageo's holiday parties must be the talk of the town. Formed by the 1997 merger of alcoholic beverage giant Guinness with food and spirits company Grand Metropolitan, Diageo is the world's largest producer of alcoholic drinks. Its beers and distilled spirits include Guinness Stout, Harp Lager, Johnnie Walker Scotch, Tanqueray gin, and Smirnoff vodka. Diageo helps stock bars and shelves in 200 countries around the globe. The company gained the Captain Morgan, Crown Royal, and VO Canadian brands through its purchase of Seagram's drinks business from Vivendi Universal. Diageo has sold The Pillsbury Company to General Mills. It also sold its Burger King business.

Diageo also owns 34% of Moët Hennessy. In a rebranding move to emphasize the Diageo name, the company scrapped its Guinness/UDV unit

and folded those operations into its new premium drinks division. In 2003 Diageo cut 150 jobs from its Guinness operation amid declining sales of the well-known stout.

HISTORY

Diageo — from the Latin word for "day" and the Greek word for "world" — was born from Guinness and GrandMet's 1997 merger to fight flat liquor sales and spirited competitors.

Guinness began business in 1759, when Arthur Guinness leased a small brewery in Dublin, Ireland. Guinness began specializing in porters in 1799. Managed by the third generation of Guinnesses, the company went public as a London-based firm in 1886.

In the 1950s managing director Hugh Beaver was credited with conceiving the *Guinness Book of World Records*. During the 1970s Guinness bought more than 200 companies, with disappointing results. Guinness refocused on brewing and distilling operations in the late 1980s by selling noncore businesses and acquiring firms such as Schenley (Dewar's). In 1988 and 1989 it bought 24% of LVMH Moët Hennessy Louis Vuitton (later exchanged for 34% of LVMH's wine and spirits business). More acquisitions followed in the 1990s, capped by Guinness' 1997 announcement of its $19 billion merger with Grand Metropolitan.

GrandMet was established by Maxwell Joseph. In 1931 he began acquiring properties for resale, but WWII slowed his progress. He started buying hotels in 1946, and by 1961 GrandMet had gone public.

Diversification began in 1970 with the purchases of catering firms, restaurants, and betting shops. In the early 1970s, in what was the largest British takeover up to that time, GrandMet bought brewer Truman Hanburg, followed by Watney Mann, which owned International Distillers & Vintners, makers of Bailey's, Bombay Gin, and J&B.

GrandMet looked overseas through the 1970s, taking over the Liggett Group, a US cigarette maker (sold in 1986) whose Paddington unit was the US distributor of J&B Scotch. In 1987 it bought Heublein (Smirnoff, Lancers, José Cuervo). Two years later it bought The Pillsbury Company (Burger King and Green Giant) in a hostile takeover.

When Diageo was created, the companies and brands were divided among four divisions: The Pillsbury Company, Burger King, Guinness, and United Distillers & Vintners.

In 2000 COO Paul Walsh, a former Pillsbury CEO, took over as CEO of both Diageo and its newly combined alcoholic beverage division, Guinness/UDV. Also that year Diageo, along with fellow wine and spirits producer Pernod Ricard, agreed to pay $8.2 billion to Vivendi Universal for the Seagram's drinks business that holds several brands, including Crown Royal, VO Canadian whiskies, and Sterling Vineyards.

In 2001 Diageo sold its Guinness World Records business to media company Gullane Entertainment for $63 million. That year the company also completed its sale of Pillsbury to General Mills. After months of wrangling with the FTC, Diageo finally won regulatory approval for the Seagram's drinks purchase in late 2001.

In May 2002 Diageo completed the sale of its Malibu rum brand to Allied Domecq for about $796 million; the deal also sealed Diageo's ownership of the Captain Morgan rum brand, as Allied Domecq agreed to drop its lawsuit involving

Captain Morgan. Later in 2002 Diageo discontinued marketing its Captain Morgan Gold rum drink in the US because of disappointing sales.

Also in 2002 Diageo sold Burger King for $1.5 billion to a group composed of Texas Pacific Group, Bain Capital, and Goldman Sachs Capital Partners. Diageo's decision to sell its Pillsbury unit and its Burger King business (the #2 burger chain, after McDonald's) was part of the company's new focus on its spirits, wine, and beer businesses. The Pillsbury divestiture gave the company a 33% stake in General Mills. That same year Diageo and Pernod Ricard, which together own rights to the Seagram's brand, sold Seagram's line of nonalcoholic mixers to The Coca-Cola Company.

In March 2003 Diageo and Jose Cuervo said they would jointly sell Don Julio and Tres Magueyes tequilas. Diageo also joined with Heineken to purchase 30% of Interbrew's Nambia Breweries in southern Africa. The brewery will make Heineken and Beck's beer.

Diageo said in September 2003 that it would launch a low-alcohol version of its highly popular Baileys Irish Cream. Known as Baileys Glide, the drink still is made with Irish whiskey, but Diageo said it would be manufactured in Germany. Also in September Diageo reopened the George Dickel distillery in Tullahoma, Tennessee.

EXECUTIVES

Chairman: Lord Blyth, age 63
CEO: Paul S. Walsh, age 49
CFO: Nicholas C. (Nick) Rose, age 46
CIO; President, Venture Markets: Andrew Morgan, age 47
President and CEO, North America: Paul Clinton, age 45
President, Key Markets: Stuart Fletcher, age 46
President, Global Marketing, Sales, and Innovation: Robert M. Malcolm, age 51
President, European Major Markets and Global Supply: Ian Meakins, age 47
COO, North America: Ivan Menezes, age 44
Group Investor Relations Director: Catherine James
Strategy Director: James (Jim) Grover, age 44
Director, Marketing, Diageo Korea: Frank Fenn
General Counsel: Timothy D. (Tim) Proctor, age 53
Company Secretary: Roger H. Myddelton, age 60
Human Resources Director: Gareth Williams, age 50
Auditors: KPMG Audit Plc

LOCATIONS

HQ: 8 Henrietta Place,
London W1G OMD, United Kingdom
Phone: +44-20-7927-5200   **Fax:** +44-20-7927-5056
Web: www.diageo.co.uk

Diageo has operations in more than 50 countries and sells its products in more than 200. Production takes place in Canada, Ireland, Italy, the UK, and the US.

2003 Sales

	% of total
Europe	43
North America	33
Asia/Pacific	11
Latin America	5
Other regions	8
Total	**100**

PRODUCTS/OPERATIONS

2003 Sales

	% of total
Premium drinks	95
Quick-serve restaurants	5
Total	**100**

Selected Divisions and Brands

Beer
Dragon stout
Guinness (Draught, Draught Bitter, Draught Extra Cold, Extra Stout, Foreign Extra)
Harp lager
Kilkenny Irish beer
Malta (nonalcoholic)
Red Stripe lager
Satzenbrau lager
Smithwick's ale

Wine and Spirits
American whiskey (Seagram's 7)
Canadian whiskey (Crown Royal, Seagram's VO)
Champagne (Moët & Chandon)
Cognac (Hennessy)
Gin (Gilbey's, Gordon's, Tanqueray)
Liqueur (Baileys Original Irish Cream, Baileys Glide)
Rum (Bundaberg, Cacique in Venezuela and Spain, Captain Morgan, Myers in the US)
Schnapps (Archers)
Scotch whisky (Bell's 8 Year Old, Buchanans Deluxe, Cardhu, Dimple, J&B, Johnnie Walker, Old Parr, Vat 69, White Horse, Windsor Premier in Korea)
Single malt whiskies (Cragganmore, Dalwhinnie, Glenkinchie, Lagavulin, Oban, Talisker)
Specialty spirits (Pimms)
Tequila (Don Julio, José Cuervo outside Mexico, Tres Magueyes)
Vodka (Gordon's, Popov, Smirnoff)
Wine (Blossom Hill, Beaulieu Vineyard, MG Vallejo, Le Piat d'Or, Seagram Chateau & Estates wine, Sterling Vineyards)

Selected Affiliates, Properties, and Subsidiaries

Gleneagles Hotels PLC (golf resort)
José Cuervo (45%, Mexico)
Moët Hennessy (34%, France)

COMPETITORS

Adolph Coors	Heineken
Allied Domecq	Highland Distillers
Anheuser-Busch	Interbrew
Bacardi	Jim Beam Brands
BBAG	Labatt
Boston Beer	Lion Nathan
Brown-Forman	Martini & Rossi
Campari	Maxxium
Carlsberg	Miller Brewing
Constellation Brands	Molson
Yuengling & Son	Pernod Ricard
Gallo	Rémy Cointreau
Edrington	SABMiller
Fortune Brands	Scottish & Newcastle
Foster's	Skyy
Future Brands	Sleeman Breweries
Gambrinus	V&S
Heaven Hill Distilleries	

HISTORICAL FINANCIALS

Company Type: Public

Income Statement

FYE: June 30

	REVENUE ($ mil.)	NET INCOME ($ mil.)	NET PROFIT MARGIN	EMPLOYEES
6/02	17,276	2,476	14.3%	62,124
6/01	18,124	1,733	9.6%	71,523
6/00	17,998	1,480	8.2%	72,474
6/99	18,618	1,487	8.0%	72,000
6/98	29,497	2,230	7.6%	77,029
6/97	8,107	1,174	14.5%	20,555
6/96	7,253	922	12.7%	21,533
6/95	7,339	1,003	13.7%	23,774
6/94	6,890	640	9.3%	23,264
6/93	6,590	792	12.0%	24,032
Annual Growth	**11.3%**	**13.5%**	**—**	**11.1%**

2002 Year-End Financials

Debt ratio: 62.2%	No. of shares (mil.): 804
Return on equity: 30.0%	Dividends
Cash ($ mil.): 2,444	Yield: 2.8%
Current ratio: 1.00	Payout: 49.0%
Long-term debt ($ mil.): 5,717	Market value ($ mil.): 41,514

Stock History

NYSE: DEO

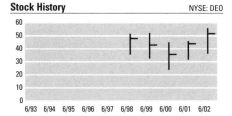

	STOCK PRICE ($) FY Close	P/E High/Low		PER SHARE ($) Earnings	Dividends	Book Value
6/02	51.65	21	14	2.98	1.46	11.43
6/01	43.95	19	13	2.05	1.38	8.60
6/00	35.56	20	11	1.74	1.43	8.35
6/99	43.00	31	20	1.67	1.30	7.42
6/98	48.00	22	16	2.30	5.45	8.59
Annual Growth	**1.8%**	**—**	**—**	**6.7%**	**(28.1%)**	**7.4%**

Electricité de France

While France has been slow to open its own doors to competition in the utilities industry, state-owned Electricité de France (EDF) has been quick to expand globally. One of the world's top electric utilities (as well as one of the last major state-owned energy monopolies in Europe), EDF has a generating capacity of more than 100,000 MW and provides power to 32 million French customers. Internationally, the company has interests in electric and gas utilities that serve 15 million customers, and it operates power plants that generate 20,000 MW of capacity in Europe, Africa, the Americas, Asia, and the Middle East.

Nuclear plants provide more than 60% of EDF's domestic power supply; other sources include hydroelectric and fossil-fueled plants. The company is also developing renewable energy facilities. Making use of its extensive experience, especially in developing nuclear power, EDF builds power plants and provides plant management and consulting services worldwide.

Subsidiary EDF Trading markets electricity, natural gas, coal, and oil throughout Europe. EDF's 34%-owned Dalkia unit (Veolia Environnement — formerly Vivendi Environnement — owns 66%) offers energy management and industrial services.

EDF is investing aggressively abroad, including in the liberalized markets of its European neighbors, which has spurred criticism for the company since it has been relatively intransigent in opening its own market. Currently only 30% of the French market has been opened, just more than the percentage required by European Union (EU) rulings. Deregulation of 70% of the market is scheduled for July 2004, with full competition taking effect in 2007. EDF is auctioning off capacity rights to some of its domestic generation facilities to comply with EU regulations.

The French government plans to spin off part of EDF to the public; the IPO is slated for 2004.

HISTORY

The French government nationalized hundreds of regional private firms to form Electricité de France in 1946 as part of an effort to rebuild the nation's badly shaken post-war economy. This was a marked difference from the notoriously complex and inefficient pre-war electrical industry.

By the 1950s EDF had taken advantage of the centralized control and developed massive hydroelectric projects. Hydroelectric power would account for more than 70% of EDF's power.

But in France as elsewhere, hydro wasn't enough to keep up with the growing demand for electricity, and fossil fuels became an increasingly important power source. Then came the oil shortages of the 1970s, and France — with limited domestic supplies of oil and gas — began searching for alternatives to fossil-fueled plants. Nuclear power was determined to be the answer.

The government moved to invest billions of dollars in developing its relatively small nuclear power production facilities. Muddled with Malthusian predictions of power shortages and a preoccupation with having enough energy to be self-reliant, France found its nuclear operations left the government with more energy than it could use and more debt than it wanted. The company began to build a cable connecting the Continent to the UK in 1981. With the power grids of the two countries connected finally in 1986, EDF was finally able to start exporting its power to the Brits.

The 1990s brought with them deregulation. EDF fought to keep the UK-France grid closed to other energy sellers. After the government forbade the utility from diversifying into areas other than electricity in 1995, the company turned its attention to foreign investment, especially in Latin America.

The company faced increasing deregulatory pressures from without in the late 1990s. The newly formed European Union required open competition from member states. Begrudgingly and behind schedule, EDF opened about 30% of its market to competition in 2000.

Other members of the EU complained that EDF was trying to play it both ways: It was making aggressive acquisitions in the UK liberalized market (it bought London Electricity in 1999) while resisting a competition-enabling breakup or even allowing a foreign competitor to buy a stake in the French market.

EDF in 2001 expanded its stake in Italy's Montedison, a conglomerate with substantial energy holdings, by forming a consortium (Italenergia) with Italian automaker Fiat and some Italian banks to wrest control of Montedison from Italian bank MEDIOBANCA. Although the consortium owns 94% of Montedison, EDF has only 2% of voting rights. (Montedison changed its name to Edison in 2002.)

EDF also purchased a 35% interest in German utility Energie Baden-Württemberg in 2001, and it merged its energy services unit with Dalkia, a unit of Vivendi Environnement (now Veolia Environnement), taking a 34% stake in Dalkia (which will eventually be increased to 50%). EDF subsidiary London Electricity agreed to buy $2.4 billion in UK assets from TXU Europe that year, including a 2,000 MW power plant, TXU's Eastern Electricity distribution unit, and its interest in TXU/EDF joint venture 24seven; the deals were completed in 2001 and 2002.

In 2002 EDF increased its stake in Brazilian utility Light Serviços de Eletricidade to 88% by swapping Light's interest in Sao Paulo utility Eletropaulo for AES's 24% interest in Light. Later that year EDF purchased UK electric and gas utility SEEBOARD (1.9 million customers) from US utility AEP in a $2.2 billion deal.

EXECUTIVES

Chairman and CEO: François Roussely, age 57
SEVP and COO, Operations: Gérard Creuzet, age 49
SEVP and COO, Finance: Daniel Camus, age 50
SEVP and COO, Human Resources: Yann Laroche, age 57
SEVP, Corporate Communications and Public Affairs: Philippe Méchet
EVP, Development Branch: Gérard Menjon
EVP, Distribution Branch (EDF-GDF Services): Robert Durdilly
EVP, Energy Branch: Bruno Lescoeur, age 48
EVP, Local Development Project Branch: Pierre Bart, age 53
EVP, Supply Branch: Jean Pierre Benqué, age 54
EVP, Transmission Branch; CEO, R.T.E.: André Merlin, age 60
EVP, Americas Branch: Fernando Ponasso, age 50
EVP, Asia/Pacific Branch: Hervé Machenaud, age 52
EVP, Central European Branch: Marc Boudier, age 47
EVP, Western Europe, Mediterranean, and Africa Branch: Michel Cremieux, age 53
COO, Dalkia: Olivier Barbaroux, age 47
Head of Gas Project Division: Dominique Venet, age 46
Corporate Secretary: Marie-Hélène Poinssot
Auditors: Deloitte Touche Tohmatsu; Ernst & Young Audit; Mazars & Guérard

LOCATIONS

HQ: 22-30, avenue de Wagram, 75382 Paris, France
Phone: +33-1-4042-5430   **Fax:** +33-1-4042-7940
Web: www.edf.fr

2002 Sales

	% of total
Europe	
France	72
UK	9
Germany	7
Italy	1
Latin America	4
Other regions	7
Total	**100**

PRODUCTS/OPERATIONS

2002 Sales

	% of total
Domestic utility	58
Other	42
Total	**100**

2002 Sales

	% of total
Generation & supply	68
Distribution	20
Transmission	6
Other	6
Total	**100**

Selected Subsidiaries and Affiliates

Dalkia Holding (34%, energy services)
Edemsa (51%, electric utility, Argentina)
Edenor (90%, electric utility, Argentina)
EDF Trading (energy marketing and trading)
Electricite de Strasbourg (75%, electric utility)
Energie Baden-Württemberg Aktiengesellschaft (EnBW, 35%, electric utility, Germany)
Hidroeléctrica Del Cantábrico, S.A. (35%, electric and gas utility, Spain)
Italenergia (18%, Italy)
Edison (formerly Montedison, 94%, conglomerate, Italy)
Light Serviços de Eletricidade S.A. (Light Energy, 95%, electric utility, Brazil)
London Electricity (electric and gas utility, UK)
Shandong Zhonghua Power Company (20%, power generation, China)

COMPETITORS

AEP
Eletrobras
Duke Energy
Edison International
Electricidade de Portugal
Endesa
Enel
E.ON
Gaz de France
Hydro-Québec
Iberdrola
International Power
RWE
Suez
Unified Energy System
Unión Fenosa
Vattenfall
Veolia Environnement

HISTORICAL FINANCIALS

Company Type: Government-owned

Income Statement

FYE: December 31

	REVENUE ($ mil.)	NET INCOME ($ mil.)	NET PROFIT MARGIN	EMPLOYEES
12/02	50,685	504	1.0%	171,995
12/01	36,066	745	2.1%	162,491
12/00	32,403	716	2.2%	117,249
12/99	32,278	720	2.2%	132,550
12/98	34,419	790	2.3%	114,380
12/97	31,664	690	2.2%	116,462
12/96	36,538	1,147	3.1%	116,919
Annual Growth	**5.6%**	**(12.8%)**	**—**	**6.6%**

Net Income History

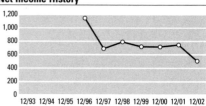

AB Electrolux

AB Electrolux has a hunting license for dust bunnies. The world's #1 producer of household appliances cranks out washing machines, dishwashers, refrigerators, and freezers under the Frigidaire, Electrolux, Zanussi, and AEG names. Electrolux is also the world's #1 maker of vacuum cleaners, including the Eureka (US) and Electrolux (outside North America) brands; it has bought the right to use the Electrolux name in North America (from long-unaffiliated vacuum maker Electrolux LLC) beginning in 2004. Electrolux also makes food and beverage machines for the food service industry, commercial laundry equipment, and lawn and garden equipment (Husqvarna chainsaws, Weed Eater trimmers).

Household appliances account for about 80% of Electrolux's sales. As part of a restructuring effort to combat the effects of diminishing consumer demand and higher material costs, Electrolux intends on cutting nearly 6,000 jobs (about 5.9% of its workforce) by 2004 and consolidating its operations in China and India. The firm is also facing pending asbestos allegations and has made a provision of under $9 million for litigation.

Through Investor AB — which also has stakes in Saab and other multinational companies — the Wallenberg family controls more than 20% of Electrolux's voting power.

HISTORY

Swedish salesman Axel Wenner-Gren saw an American-made vacuum cleaner in a Vienna, Austria, store window in 1910 and envisioned selling the cleaners door-to-door, a technique he had learned in the US. Two years later he worked with fledgling Swedish vacuum cleaner makers AB Lux and Elektromekaniska to improve their existing designs. The two companies merged to form AB Electrolux in 1919. When the board of the new company balked at Wenner-Gren's suggestion to mass-produce vacuum cleaners, he guaranteed Electrolux's sales through his own sales company.

In the 1920s the company used the "Every home — an Electrolux home" slogan as Wenner-Gren drove his sales force on and launched new sales companies in Europe and North and South America. He scored a publicity coup by securing the blessing of Pope Pius XI to vacuum the Vatican, gratis, for a year. By the end of the 1920s, Electrolux had purchased most of Wenner-Gren's sales companies (excluding Electrolux US) and had gambled on refrigerator technology and won. By buying vacuum cleaner maker Volta (Sweden, 1934), it gained retail distribution.

Despite the loss of Eastern European subsidiaries during WWII, the company did well until the 1960s, when it backed an unpopular refrigeration technology. Swedish electrical equipment giant ASEA, controlled by Marcus Wallenberg, bought a large stake in Electrolux in 1964, and in 1967 he installed Hans Werthén as chairman. Werthén slashed overhead and sold the company's minority stake in Electrolux US to Consolidated Foods. (The US Electrolux business was taken private in 1987.)

Since 1970 Electrolux has bought more than 300 companies (many of them troubled appliance makers), updated their plants, and gained global component manufacturing efficiencies. Acquisitions included National Union Electric (Eureka vacuum cleaners, US, 1974), Tappan (appliances, US, 1979), Zanussi (appliances, industrial products; Italy; 1984), White Consolidated Industries (appliances, industrial products; US; 1986), and Lehel (refrigerators, Hungary, 1991). By 1996 the company had acquired a 41% interest in Refrigeração Paraná, Brazil's #2 manufacturer of appliances. (Electrolux owned it all by 1998.)

To better focus on its "white goods" (washers, refrigerators, etc.), in 1996 Electrolux began selling noncore businesses. In 1997, under new CEO Michael "Mike the Knife" Treschow, the company launched a restructuring plan involving the closing of about 25 plants and the elimination of more than 12,000 jobs, mostly in Europe. The plan worked: Electrolux's profits more than quadrupled in 1998. Also that year the company formed a joint venture in India with Voltas Limited, forming that country's largest refrigerator manufacturer.

Electrolux acquired the European operations of chainsaw maker McCulloch, North America, in 1999. To strengthen its Asian presence, Electrolux teamed up with Toshiba for future collaboration on household appliances. Also that year the company said it would sell its vending machine unit and professional refrigeration business. In 2000 the company agreed to buy the Electrolux brand name in North America from long-unaffiliated US company Electrolux LLC (which will remain independent). That year AB Electrolux agreed to buy the major appliance business of Email Ltd., Australia's top household appliance maker.

In January 2002 it finalized the sale of its leisure appliance operations — mostly refrigerators for recreational vehicles — to private equity firm EQT Northern Europe. In April 2002 Electrolux CEO Michael Treschow resigned; board member Hans Sträberg replaced him. The firm acquired Diamant Boart International, a world-leading manufacturer and distributor of diamond tools and related equipment, in June 2002.

EXECUTIVES

Chairman: Rune Andersson
Deputy Chairman: Jacob Wallenberg, age 47
President and CEO: Hans Sträberg
Head of Floor Care Products and Small Appliances: Magnus Yngen, age 43
Head of Group Staff Communication and Public Affairs: Lars Göran Johansson
Head of Group Staff Controlling, Accounting, Taxes, Auditing, and IT: Fredrik Rystedt
Head of Group Staff Legal: Cecilia Vieweg
Head of Group Staff Organizational Development and Management Resources: Lilian Fossum
Head of Group Staff Treasury: Nina Linander
Head of Outdoor Products: Bengt Andersson
Head of Professional Indoor Products: Detlef Münchow
Head of White Goods Europe: Wolfgang König
Head of White Goods North America and Outdoor Products North America: Robert E. (Bob) Cook
Head of White Goods Outside Europe and North America: Johan Bygge
EVP and Head of White Goods North America: Keith R. McLoughlin, age 47
VP, Investor Relations and Financial Information: Asa Stenqvist
President, Electrolux Home Products International: Andrew Bentley
President, The Eureka Company: Daniel G. Clifford
EVP, Manufacturing and Engineering, The Eureka Company: Cennert Steffen
VP, Human Resources and Corporate Services: Koustuv Mitra
Auditors: KPMG

LOCATIONS

HQ: St Göransgatan 143, Stockholm, Sweden
Phone: +46-8-738-6400   **Fax:** +46-8-656-4478
Web: www.electrolux.com

AB Electrolux sells its goods in about 150 nations.

2002 Sales

	$ mil.	% of total
Europe	7,106.2	46
North America	6,113.8	40
Other regions	2,132.0	14
Total	**15,352.0**	**100**

PRODUCTS/OPERATIONS

2002 Sales

	$ mil.	% of total
Consumer products	12,858.1	84
Professional products		
Indoor	1,255.3	8
Outdoor	1,221.8	8
Other	16.8	—
Total	**15,352.0**	**100**

Selected Products

Consumer
Cookers
Dishwashers
Freezers
Garden equipment (lawn mowers, trimmers, leafblowers)
Light-duty chainsaws
Refrigerators
Room air conditioners
Vacuums
Washing machines

Professional Indoor
Absorption refrigerators
Components (compressors, motors)
Food service equipment
Laundry equipment

Professional Outdoor
Chainsaws
Clearing saws
Landscape maintenance equipment
Power cutters
Turf-care equipment

COMPETITORS

Aga Foodservice
American Household
BISSELL
Black & Decker
Brasmotor
BSH Bosch und Siemens Hausgeräte
Candy
Coast Distribution
Daewoo Electronics
Deere
Dover
Emak
Enodis
GE Consumer Products
Goodman Manufacturing
Haier Group
Hitachi
HMI Industries
Holmes Group
Hussmann International
Ingersoll-Rand Climate Control
Kirby Company
Lennox
LG Electronics
Matsushita
Maytag
Merloni
Middleby
Royal Appliance
SANYO
SEB
Sharp
Sub-Zero
Tatung
Toro
Toshiba
U.S. Home & Garden
Vorwerk
Whirlpool

HISTORICAL FINANCIALS

Company Type: Public

Income Statement

FYE: December 31

	REVENUE ($ mil.)	NET INCOME ($ mil.)	NET PROFIT MARGIN	EMPLOYEES
12/02	15,352	587	3.8%	83,347
12/01	12,956	369	2.8%	85,749
12/00	13,209	473	3.6%	87,128
12/99	14,023	490	3.5%	92,926
12/98	14,503	491	3.4%	99,322
12/97	14,295	45	0.3%	105,950
12/96	15,983	269	1.7%	112,140
12/95	17,312	411	2.4%	112,300
12/94	14,527	650	4.5%	114,100
12/93	12,015	70	0.6%	109,400
Annual Growth	2.8%	26.6%	—	(3.0%)

2002 Year-End Financials

Debt ratio: 49.8%
Return on equity: 19.8%
Cash ($ mil.): 690
Current ratio: 1.93
Long-term debt ($ mil.): 1,586
No. of shares (mil.): 169
Dividends
Yield: 2.7%
Payout: 23.9%
Market value ($ mil.): 5,362

Stock History

NASDAQ: ELUX

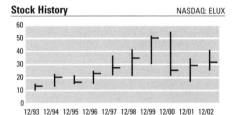

12/93 12/94 12/95 12/96 12/97 12/98 12/99 12/00 12/01 12/02

	STOCK PRICE ($) FY Close	P/E High/Low		PER SHARE ($) Earnings	Dividends	Book Value
12/02	31.66	11	7	3.60	0.86	18.81
12/01	29.32	16	8	2.17	0.77	15.04
12/00	25.63	21	8	2.63	0.77	15.26
12/99	50.25	19	12	2.67	0.72	16.52
12/98	34.88	15	8	2.68	0.00	16.50
12/97	27.60	151	93	0.24	0.00	28.42
12/96	23.10	17	11	1.47	0.70	35.60
12/95	16.55	19	14	1.14	0.55	34.79
12/94	20.35	5	3	4.15	0.28	30.07
12/93	13.60	39	28	0.38	0.28	22.09
Annual Growth	9.8%	—	—	28.4%	13.3%	(1.8%)

EMI Group plc

Depending on how you look at it, EMI Group is either the smallest major record company or the biggest independent label. The company ranks last in US sales among the five major music labels and is #3 in worldwide sales. EMI distributes albums through more than 70 labels, including Blue Note, Capitol, and Virgin. It also owns EMI Music Publishing, the world's largest music publishing arm, with rights to more than a million songs. The only major record company not tied to a media conglomerate, EMI saw acquisition deals with both Time Warner and Bertelsmann nixed by European regulators.

Being unaffiliated with a larger media company, EMI has struggled in its efforts to market new albums and artists. EMI also suffered from a 3% industry downturn in US record sales in 2001 (the most in a decade). Its ill-fated five-record contract with pop diva Mariah Carey was a huge embarrassment for the firm. After Carey's first EMI album, *Glitter*, sold a meager 500,000 copies, the company bought out Carey's deal for $28 million. It subsequently laid off about 20% of its workforce, cut 400 acts from its roster, and took a $340 million charge for the year.

To improve its reach to audiences and reduce costs, the company has turned to EMI Music Publishing, its licensing division, which has struck a number of deals with online distribution companies. It also joined with Warner Music, BMG, and RealNetworks to form MusicNet in 2001. In addition, EMI is taking steps to further develop its South East Asian business with plans to expand into China. The company has also sold its stake in retail joint venture HMV Media Group.

HISTORY

Electric & Musical Industries (EMI) was established in 1931 as a successor to a 19th-century gramophone producer. It gradually expanded operations to produce everything from radar systems during WWII to the first television system for the BBC. In 1955 the company bought Los Angeles-based Capitol Records (founded in 1942), which featured such artists as Frank Sinatra and Nat "King" Cole. EMI became a major force in the entertainment industry over the next decades, topping off a string of acquisitions with the purchase of Associated British Picture Corporation in 1969.

EMI suffered through the 1970s with money-losing films and the PR sting of signing the outrageous punk group The Sex Pistols in 1976. (The company canceled its contract with the band in 1978.) In 1979 the struggling firm was bought by appliance and electronics giant Thorn Electrical Industries (founded by Jules Thorn as the Electrical Lamp Service Company in 1928) for $356 million. Renamed THORN EMI in 1980, the conglomerate lacked strategic focus and continued to suffer losses. Colin Southgate was tapped as CEO in 1985 and streamlined its operations to four business sectors. The company acquired 50% of Chrysalis Records in 1989, and the next year it added Filmtrax music publishing (UK). Also in 1990 the company's HMV stores unit opened its first US superstore in New York City.

In 1992 the company acquired Virgin Records from founder Richard Branson for $960 million. The purchase boosted EMI's US market share and made it one of the world's top music companies. THORN EMI sold its lighting division the next year, and in 1995 it bought UK bookstore business Dillons (later merged with and rebranded Waterstone's).

In 1996 EMI and Thorn split into separately traded companies to maximize the value of its disparate assets; however, share prices plunged when profits failed to materialize. The next year EMI paid $132 million for 50% of Berry Gordy's Jobete companies and its 15,000-song Motown catalog. The Spice Girls, five women brought together by a newspaper ad, became one of Virgin's biggest moneymakers that year.

To focus more on music and less on retail, EMI transferred its HMV and Dillons chains to HMV Media Group, a joint venture with Advent International, in 1998. That year EMI Music head James Fifield resigned with a healthy buyout package after Southgate scotched a succession plan that would have made Fifield CEO. The following year Eric Nicoli, former CEO of United Biscuits, was tapped as Southgate's replacement.

Seeking a bigger presence on the Internet, the company bought an equity stake in music Web site Musicmaker.com in 1999. It also bought music publisher Windswept Pacific for $200 million. The following year the company sold its stake in Musicmaker.com for a hefty profit and later agreed to merge its music operations into a joint venture with Time Warner's Warner Music Group. Its deal with Warner was scrapped, however, to appease European regulators examining the merger of Time Warner and AOL. EMI opened negotiations with Bertelsmann, but the talks broke off in 2001 (again due to pressure from regulators). That year it formed online distribution venture MusicNet with Warner Music, BMG, and RealNetworks. Ken Berry, CEO of the EMI Recorded Music division, left the company in 2001 and was replaced by Alain Levy, a former PolyGram executive. In 2002 the company acquired Mute, a leading European independent record company, for $33.5 million. Also that year it sold off its remaining stake in HMV.

EXECUTIVES

Chairman: Eric L. Nicoli, age 52, $977,249 pay
CFO: Roger Faxon, age 53, $140,706 pay
Vice Chairman, EMI Recorded Music; Chairman and CEO, EMI Recorded Music North America: David Munns
Chairman and CEO, EMI Music Publishing: Martin N. Bandier, age 60, $5,248,774 pay
Chairman and CEO, EMI Recorded Music: Alain Levy, age 56
CFO, EMI Recorded Music: Stuart Ells, age 40
Chairman and CEO, Virgin Records America: Matt Serletic
President and CEO, Capitol Records: Andrew (Andy) Slater
President and CEO, Capitol Nashville: Mike Dungan
President and COO, Virgin Records: Roy Lott
President, EMI Music Canada: Deane Cameron
Managing Director, Parlophone, EMI UK & Ireland: Keith Wozencroft
COO, EMI Recorded Music North America: Ivan Gavin
COO, Virgin Records America: Charlie Dimont
EVP: John Rose
SVP and Financial Controller: Prescott Price
SVP Human Resources: Avery Duff
VP Legal Affairs: David Widd
VP Marketing: Leonor Villanueva
VP Sales: Al Andruchow
Secretary and Group General Counsel: Charles P. Ashcroft
Auditors: Ernst & Young

LOCATIONS

HQ: 4 Tenterden St., Hanover Square, London W1A 2AY, United Kingdom
Phone: +44-20-7355-4848 **Fax:** +44-20-7495-1307
US HQ: 2751 Centerville Rd., Ste. 205, Wilmington, DE 19808
US Phone: 302-994-4100 **US Fax:** 302-994-4299
Web: www.emigroup.com

PRODUCTS/OPERATIONS

Selected Labels

Astralwerks	Forefront Records
Blue Note Records	Hemisphere Records
Capitol Records	Java Records
Capitol Records Nashville	Mosaic Records
Caroline Records	Mute
Chrysalis	Scamp Records
EMI Classics	Sparrow Label Group
EMI Electrola	Virgin Records America
EMI Records UK	Virgin Records Nashville
EMI-Medley	Virgin Records UK
Food Records	

Selected Artists

The Beatles	Pink Floyd
Coldplay	Radiohead
Daft Punk	Ringo Shiina
Everclear	Robbie Williams
Garth Brooks	Smashing Pumpkins
Ice Cube	Spice Girls
Janet Jackson	UB40
Lenny Kravitz	Utada Hikaru

COMPETITORS

BMG Entertainment	Universal Music Group
edel music	Warner Music
KOCH Entertainment	Zomba Records
Sony Music Entertainment	

HISTORICAL FINANCIALS

Company Type: Public

Income Statement

FYE: March 31

	REVENUE ($ mil.)	NET INCOME ($ mil.)	NET PROFIT MARGIN	EMPLOYEES
3/03	3,424	362	10.6%	8,088
3/02	3,487	(284)	—	9,270
3/01	3,785	137	3.6%	9,996
3/00	3,799	281	7.4%	10,802
3/99	3,829	235	6.1%	10,292
3/98	5,548	383	6.9%	10,452
3/97	6,535	254	3.9%	—
Annual Growth	(10.2%)	6.1%	—	(5.0%)

2003 Year-End Financials

Debt ratio: —
Return on equity: 191.4%
Cash ($ mil.): 158

Current ratio: 0.79
Long-term debt ($ mil.): 1,451

Net Income History

London: EMI

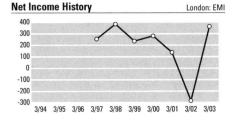

Enel S.p.A.

Arrivederci monopolio! Italy's largest electric utility, Enel, has given up its monopoly status and is racing into the deregulating power marketplace. Enel distributes electricity to nearly 29 million Italian customers and has about 42,000 MW of primarily fossil-fueled and hydro-electric generating capacity in the country. The company's Wind Telecomunicazioni unit provides fixed-line and wireless telecom services. Enel also owns gas and water distribution businesses in Italy, and it has renewable and international power generation assets. Other operations include information technology, real estate, and engineering and construction services. The Italian government owns a 61% stake in the company.

Italy's Bersani Decree, passed in 1999, required Enel to divest 25% of its capacity and turn over a portion of its municipal distribution networks to local governments to enhance com-

petition in the country's power market. Enel has completed the required generation asset sales, reducing its capacity by 15,000 MW. Enel sold its final generation divestment company, Interpower (2,600 MW), to a consortium of utilities (including Belgian utility Electrabel and Italian utility ACEA) for about $880 million in 2003. Enel has also reduced its customer count by approximately 1 million through municipal distribution asset sales, and it has transferred management and control of the national transmission grid to an independent operator.

Besides the required asset divestitures, Enel is also facing a 17% rate cut (to be phased in over three years). Italian regulators have passed a decree requiring Enel to divest most of its power transmission assets, held by subsidiary Terna; regulators are also trying to force Enel to sell additional power generation assets. The Italian government, which floated 32% of the utility in 1999, began the second round of Enel's privatization process in 2003 by selling a 7% stake to Morgan Stanley for more than $2.3 billion.

Enel hasn't just been sipping cappuccino while competitors rush in: The company has moved to become a multi-utility. It has combined its two telecom units: Infostrada, one of Italy's top fixed-line operators, has been merged into Wind. Enel purchased France Telecom's 27% stake in Wind for $1.4 billion in 2003, making the unit a wholly owned subsidiary; Enel plans to eventually sell shares in Wind in an IPO.

Enel has also acquired several Italian water and gas distribution companies; it has grown to became Italy's second-largest gas distributor (after Italgas) with 1.7 million customers.

Internationally, Enel is building and buying independent power plants, primarily in Europe and the Americas; in 2002 it purchased Spanish power giant Endesa's Viesgo unit, which generates 2,400 MW of capacity and distributes power to 500,000 customers.

HISTORY

Italy's energy consumption doubled in the 1950s as the country experienced a period of rapid industrialization and urbanization. A tight-knit oligopoly controlled the electric power industry and included Edison, SADE, La Centale, SME, and Finelettrica. The economic boom pushed into the 1960s, and the Italian government created Enel (Ente Nazionale per l'Energia Elettrica) in 1962 to nationalize the power industry. In 1963 Enel began gradually buying some 1,250 electric utilities. About 160 municipal utilities and the larger independents, such as Edison, were left out of the takeover.

The company spent the late 1960s and early 1970s connecting Italy's unwieldy transmission network and building new power plants, including the La Spezia thermoelectric plant (600 MW). Construction costs, coupled with the high prices Enel was required to pay for its takeover targets, caused the utility to become steeped in debt. The Arab oil embargoes of the early 1970s made matters worse, and the Italian government helped Enel with an endowment in 1973.

The energy crisis also prompted Enel to build its first nuclear power plant, Caorso, which came on line in 1980. However, nuclear power was short-lived in Italy: After the 1986 Chernobyl accident, a national referendum forced Enel to deactivate its nukes in 1987. The firm also stepped up its development of renewable energy sources in the 1980s.

Meanwhile, Enel opened its Centro Nazionale

de Controllo (CNC) in Rome in 1985 to supervise Italy's power grid. The next year the company turned its first profit.

To begin disassembling Enel's monopoly, the Italian government in 1992 opened the power generation market to outside producers and converted Enel into a joint stock company (with the state holding all of the shares). Following the European Union's 1997 directive to deregulate Europe's power industry, Enel unbundled its utility activities and began trimming its staff. Italy's Bersani Decree (passed in 1999) outlined the restructuring process: Enel was ordered to divest 15,000 MW of its generating capacity, a state-controlled operator was set up to oversee Italy's grid, and large users were allowed to choose their own suppliers.

In response, Enel began to diversify in 1998. It started Wind Telecomunicazioni, a joint venture with France Telecom and Deutsche Telekom. (Deutsche Telekom sold its stake to the other partners in 2000.) Wind began offering fixed-line and mobile telecom services to corporations in 1998 and extended the services to residential users the next year. Enel also began building water infrastructure to serve local distributors and purchased three water operations in southern Italy.

Also in 1999 the government floated 32% of Enel in one of the world's largest IPOs at the time. The next year the company bought Colombo Gas, a northern Italian gas distributor with about 75,000 customers. It also transferred control of its transmission network to an independent government-owned operator (Gestore della Rete di Trasmissione Nazionale), while retaining ownership of the assets.

Enel bought fixed-line telephone company Infostrada from Vodafone in 2001, acquired two more Italian gas distributors, and sold its 5,400-MW Elettrogen generation unit to Spain's Endesa for $2.3 billion. Enel also put its 7,000-MW Eurogen generation unit on the auction block in 2001. The high bidder, with a $2.6 billion offer, was a consortium backed by Fiat and Electricité de France; the sale was completed in 2002.

Also in 2002 Enel purchased Camuzzi Gazometri's gas distribution business (Italy's second-largest) for $870 million from Mill Hill Investments, and it bought Endesa's Viesgo unit (power generation and distribution) for about $1.8 billion.

EXECUTIVES

Chairman: Piero Gnudi
CEO, General Manager, Director, and Interim Head of Generation and Energy Management: Paolo Scaroni, age 56
CFO: Fulvio Conti, age 55
Head of Corporate Affairs and Secretary: Claudio Sartorelli, age 58
Head of Accounting: Luciana Tarozzi, age 59
Head of Auditing: Antonio Cardani, age 53
Head of E-Business Development: Alessandro Bufacchi
Head of Human Resources: Angelo Delfino, age 63
Head of Legal Affairs: Salvatore Cardillo, age 53
Head of Press and Communications: Gianluca Comin
Head of Public and International Affairs: Massimo Romano, age 44
Head of Regulatory Relations: Alfredo Macchiati, age 51
Head of Sales, Infrastructures, and Networks: Vincenzo Cannatelli, age 50
Head of Telecommunications: Tommaso Pompei, age 61
Investor Relations Manager: Luca Torchia
Media Relations Manager: Gerardo Orsini
Retail Investors Manager: Fabio Bonomo
International Press Officer: Ralph Traviato
Press Officer: Chiara Raiola
Auditors: KPMG S.p.A.

LOCATIONS

HQ: Viale Regina Margherita, 137, 00198 Rome, Italy
Phone: +39-06-8509-1   **Fax:** +39-06-8509-3771
Web: www.enel.it

Enel provides utility services in Italy, has independent power production and distribution operations in other European countries and in the Americas, and has other operations in Africa and the Middle East.

PRODUCTS/OPERATIONS

2002 Sales

	% of total
Sales, infrastructure & networks	49
Generation & energy management	28
Telecommunications	9
Parent company	5
Electricity transmission	2
Services & other activities	7
Total	**100**

Selected Subsidiaries and Affiliates

Sales, Infrastructure, and Networks
Camuzzi (gas distribution)
Electra de Viesgo Distribucion SL (electricity distribution, Spain)
Enel Distribuzione SpA (electricity distribution)
Enel Distribuzione Gas SpA (gas distribution)
Enel Energia SpA (formerly Enel Trade, electricity sales)
Enel.si SpA (energy services)
So.l.e. — Società luce elettrica SpA (public lighting)

Generation and Energy Management
Conphoebus Scrl (renewable energy-related services)
Elettroambiente SpA (70%, waste-to-energy operations)
Enel Green Power SpA (electricity from renewable resources)
Enel North America (formerly CHI Energy, renewable electricity generation, US)
Enel Produzione SpA (electricity generation)
Enel Trade SpA (formerly Enel.FTL, fuel trading and logistics)
Enel Logistica Combustibili SpA (energy logistics services)
Energia Global International, LLC (EGI, renewable electricity generation, Latin America)
Viesgo Generaciòn SL (electricity generation, Spain)

Telecommunications
Wind Telecomunicazioni SpA (fixed-line, mobile, and data services)

Services and Other Activities
CESI SpA Centro Elettrotecnico Sperimentale Italiano (51%, research)
Enel Hydro SpA (water distribution)
Enel.it SpA (information technology)
Enelpower SpA (power-related engineering and construction)
Enel Real Estate SpA (commercial properties ownership and management)

COMPETITORS

ABB	ERG S.p.A.
ACEA	Hidrocántabrico
Acque Potabili	Iberdrola
AEM	International Power
Autostrade	Italgas
Edison International	Risanamento di Napoli
Edison	RWE
Electricité de France	Telecom Italia
Endesa	Tractebel
Eni	Unión Fenosa
E.ON	Vodafone Omnitel

HISTORICAL FINANCIALS

Company Type: Public

Income Statement

FYE: December 31

	REVENUE ($ mil.)	NET INCOME ($ mil.)	NET PROFIT MARGIN	EMPLOYEES
12/02	31,431	2,105	6.7%	71,204
12/01	25,653	3,767	14.7%	72,660
12/00	24,000	2,000	8.3%	72,647
12/99	21,107	2,362	11.2%	78,511
12/98	22,918	2,598	11.3%	84,938
12/97	21,452	1,889	8.8%	88,957
12/96	23,833	—	—	95,464
12/95	22,225	—	—	—
12/94	21,840	—	—	—
12/93	21,160	—	—	—
Annual Growth	**4.5%**	**2.2%**	**—**	**(4.8%)**

2002 Year-End Financials

Debt ratio: 82.7%
Return on equity: 10.4%
Cash ($ mil.): 419
Current ratio: 0.66
Long-term debt ($ mil.): 18,005
No. of shares (mil.): 1,213
Dividends
  Yield: 6.6%
  Payout: 96.6%
Market value ($ mil.): 31,104

Stock History

NYSE: EN

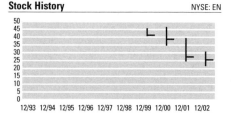

	STOCK PRICE ($) FY Close	P/E High/Low		Earnings	PER SHARE ($) Dividends	Book Value
12/02	25.65	17	13	1.75	1.69	17.96
12/01	27.45	14	9	2.72	1.10	15.41
12/00	38.65	32	25	1.43	1.11	7.01
12/99	41.25	24	22	1.90	0.00	7.30
Annual Growth	**(14.6%)**	**—**	**—**	**(2.7%)**	**—**	**35.0%**

Eni S.p.A.

It's not teeny, it's Eni — and it's huge. One of Italy's largest companies, Eni operates in the oil and natural gas, petrochemicals, and oil field services industries and has expanded into power generation. Its main subsidiaries are EniPower (power generation), Snamprogetti (contracting, engineering), Saipem (oil field services), and Italgas (natural gas transmission); it also owns a controlling stake in pipeline operator Snam Rete Gas. As one of the world's leading oil enterprises, Eni has proved reserves of more than 7 billion barrels of oil equivalent, most of it in Italy and in Africa. The Italian government owns about 30% of Eni but is considering selling the holding.

The company's oil and gas holdings and exploration and production efforts extend into more than 30 countries on five continents. Eni has expanded outside its traditional bases of Africa and Italy, with ventures in the Americas, the Asia/Pacific region, Europe, and the Middle East.

In response to the opening up of Italy's energy markets, Eni is increasing its natural gas hold-

ings and adding electricity generating power units. In 2002 Eni agreed to buy Fortum's Norwegian oil and gas business (Fortum Petroleum) for $420 million.

In 2003 the company boosted its stake in Italgas from 44% to 98%.

HISTORY

Although the Italian parliament formed Ente Nazionale Idrocarburi (National Hydrocarbon Agency) in 1953, Enrico Mattei is the true father of Eni. In 1945 Mattei, a partisan leader during WWII, was appointed northern commissioner of Agip, a state-owned petroleum company founded in 1926 by Mussolini, and ordered to liquidate the company. Mattei instead ordered the exploration of the Po Valley, where workers found methane gas deposits in 1946

When Eni was created in 1953, Mattei was named president. His job was to find energy resources for an oil-poor country. He initiated a series of joint ventures with several Middle Eastern and African nations, offering better deals than his large oil company rivals, which he dubbed the Seven Sisters.

Mattei didn't stick to energy: By the time he died in a mysterious plane crash in 1962, Eni had acquired machinery manufacturer Pignone, finance company Sofid, Milan newspaper *Il Giorno*, and textile company Lane Rossi. Eni grew during the 1960s, partly because of a deal made for Soviet crude in 1958 and a joint venture with Esso in 1963. It also expanded its chemical activities.

By the early 1970s losses in Eni's chemical and textile operations, the oil crisis, and the Italian government's dumping of unprofitable companies on Eni hurt its bottom line. Former finance minister Franco Reviglio took over in 1983 and began cutting inefficient operations.

EniChem merged with Montedison, Italy's largest private chemical company, in 1988, but clashes between the public agency and the private company made Montedison sell back its stake in 1990. Eni became a joint stock company in 1992, but the government retained a majority stake.

Franco Bernabe took over Eni following a 1993 bribery scandal and began cutting noncore businesses. The Italian government began selling Eni stock in 1995. In 1996 Eni signed on to develop Libyan gas resources and build a pipeline to Italy. A year later the company merged its Agipa exploration and production subsidiary into its main operations. Eni also took a 35% stake in Italian telecom company Albacom.

The government cut its stake in Eni from 51% to 38% in 1998. That year Vittorio Mincato, a company veteran, succeeded Bernabe as CEO. In 1999 Eni and Russia's RAO Gazprom, the world's largest natural gas production firm, agreed to build a controversial $3 billion natural gas pipeline stretching from Russia to Turkey. Eni agreed to invest $5.5 billion to develop oil and gas reserves in Libya; it also sold interests in Saipem and Nuovo Pignone, as well as some of its Italian service stations.

Chairman Renato Ruggiero resigned in 1999, amid disagreements with CEO Mincato, after only four months on the job. The Italian government, which began liberalizing the country's natural gas industry in 2000, appointed Gian Maria Gros-Pietro as Ruggiero's replacement.

In 2000 Eni paid about $910 million for a 33% stake in Galp, a Portuguese oil and gas company that also has natural gas utility operations. Also that year Eni bought British-Borneo Oil &

Gas in a $1.2 billion deal, and in 2001 it paid $4 billion for UK independent exploration and production company LASMO, topping a bid by US-based Amerada Hess.

The Italian government sold off another 5% of Eni in 2001, reducing its stake to about 30%, and announced that it was considering selling its entire investment. In an effort to reduce noncore holdings, the company sold property management subsidiary Immobiliare Metanopoli to Goldman Sachs. Also that year Eni sold a minority stake in its gas pipeline unit, Snam Rete Gas, to the public.

In 2002 Eni entered discussions to acquire Enterprise Oil, but lost out to a rival bid from Royal Dutch/Shell. Later that year Eni's oil field services unit Saipem gained control of Bouygues Offshore.

EXECUTIVES

Chairman: Roberto Poli, age 65
Managing Director and CEO: Vittorio Mincato, age 67
Group SVP Finance and CFO: Marco Mangiagalli, age 54
Group SVP Administration: Roberto Jaquinto, age 61
Group SVP Legal Affairs: Carlo Grande, age 62
Group SVP Human Resources: Renato Roffi, age 56
Group SVP Supply Operations: Vittorio Giacomelli, age 62
Group SVP Public Affairs and Communication: Eugenio Palmieri, age 56
Group SVP Strategies and International Relations: Leonardo Maugeri, age 39
CTO; Chairman, Snamprogetti: Luigi Patron, age 63
Chairman, Saipem: Pietro Franco Tali
Chairman, Snam Rete Gas: Salvatore Russo
Chairman, Stoccaggi Gas Italia: Giorgio Ruffoni
Chairman and Managing Director, EniPower: Giovanni Locanto
Managing Director, Saipem: Hugh O'Donnell
Auditors: PricewaterhouseCoopers SpA

LOCATIONS

HQ: Piazzale Enrico Mattei 1, 00144 Rome, Italy
Phone: +39-065-982-1   **Fax:** +39-065-982-2631
US HQ: 666 Fifth Ave., New York, NY 10103
US Phone: 212-887-0330   **US Fax:** 212-246-0009
Web: www.eni.it

Eni's subsidiaries have operations in more than 70 countries in Africa, Asia, Europe, the Middle East, and North and South America.

2002 Sales

	% of total
Europe	
Italy	49
Other EU countries	18
Other countries	10
The Americas	11
Asia	7
Africa	5
Total	**100**

PRODUCTS/OPERATIONS

2002 Sales

	% of total
Refining & marketing	43
Gas & power	31
Exploration & production	9
Petrochemicals	9
Oil field services & engineering	8
Total	**100**

Major Subsidiairies

EniPower SpA (power generation)
Italgas SpA (natural gas supply)
Saipem SpA (oil field services)
Snam Rete Gas SpA (gas pipeline)
Snamprogetti SpA (contracting and engineering)

COMPETITORS

AEM
Amerada Hess
Anonima Petroli Italiana
Ashland
BASF AG
Bayer AG
BG Group
BP
ChevronTexaco
Chiyoda Corp.
ConocoPhillips
Dow Chemical
DuPont
E.ON
ERG S.p.A.
Exxon Mobil
Koch
Lyondell Chemical
Marathon Oil
Norsk Hydro
Occidental Petroleum
PETROBRAS
PDVSA
PEMEX
Royal Dutch/Shell Group
Sunoco
TOTAL
Unocal

HISTORICAL FINANCIALS

Company Type: Public

Income Statement

FYE: December 31

	REVENUE ($ mil.)	NET INCOME ($ mil.)	NET PROFIT MARGIN	EMPLOYEES
12/02	50,332	4,824	9.6%	80,655
12/01	43,607	6,908	15.8%	70,948
12/00	46,000	5,435	11.8%	69,969
12/99	31,225	2,877	9.2%	72,023
12/98	33,177	2,725	8.2%	78,906
12/97	34,323	2,893	8.4%	75,729
12/96	37,973	2,930	7.7%	83,424
12/95	35,915	2,732	7.6%	86,422
12/94	31,277	2,006	6.4%	100,000
12/93	31,343	141	0.5%	106,391
Annual Growth	**5.4%**	**48.0%**	**—**	**(3.0%)**

2002 Year-End Financials

Debt ratio: 24.9%
Return on equity: 18.5%
Cash ($ mil.): 3,429
Current ratio: 1.01
Long-term debt ($ mil.): 6,879
No. of shares (mil.): 800
Dividends
Yield: 4.1%
Payout: 51.3%
Market value ($ mil.): 62,820

Stock History

NYSE: E

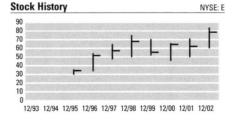

	STOCK PRICE ($) FY Close	P/E High/Low		PER SHARE ($) Earnings	Dividends	Book Value
12/02	78.49	13	10	6.30	3.23	34.46
12/01	61.96	8	6	8.83	1.89	30.61
12/00	64.31	10	7	6.80	1.61	13.18
12/99	55.13	19	15	3.59	1.59	11.58
12/98	67.75	22	15	3.41	1.57	11.82
12/97	57.06	18	13	3.62	1.42	10.48
12/96	51.63	15	9	3.66	1.36	10.42
12/95	34.25	10	9	3.41	0.00	9.09
Annual Growth	**12.6%**	—	—	**9.2%**	—	**21.0%**

E.ON AG

E.ON is transforming itself from a conglomerate into a multi-utility. Subsidiary E.ON Energie is one of Germany's top two power companies (running neck and neck with RWE's utility unit) and one of the largest utilities in continental Europe, with some 27 million electricity, natural gas, and water customers and over 34,000 MW of electric generating capacity. E.ON also owns Powergen, a leading UK energy provider, and US utility LG&E Energy. The company has completed its controversial acquisition of Ruhrgas, Germany's #1 natural gas supplier. Other E.ON operations include chemicals manufacturing, real estate, and telecommunications.

E.ON's 2003 acquisition of Ruhrgas was thwarted by numerous regulatory objections, as well as a lawsuit filed by competitors that was eventually settled out of court. Both E.ON and Ruhrgas agreed to sell several utility and gas assets in order for the $11.2 billion deal to receive ministerial approval.

The company is selling noncore operations to focus on its utility businesses. To raise cash for acquisitions, and to comply with US regulations on ownership of utilities, E.ON has sold off some high-profile businesses. It has sold its Veba Oel subsidiary, which explores for and produces oil and gas and operates the Aral service station chain (Germany's largest), to UK-based BP. The company has also sold its stakes in aluminum manufacturer VAW, metals distributor Klöckner, silicon wafer manufacturer MEMC, and logistics provider Stinnes. E.ON has sold its majority stake in chemical maker Degussa (and plans to further decrease its interest in the firm). The company has sold a 6% stake in Bouygues Telecom to Bouygues S.A., and it has agreed to sell its remaining 10% interest in the telecom firm to Bouygues by the end of 2003.

E.ON was formed in 2000 from the merger of Germany's VEBA and VIAG conglomerates.

HISTORY

VEBA (originally Vereinigte Elektrizitats-und Bergwerks AG) was formed in 1929 in Berlin to consolidate Germany's state-owned electricity and mining interests. These operations included PreussenElektra, an electric utility formed by the German government in 1927; Hibernia, a coal mining firm founded in 1873; and Preussag, a mining and smelting company founded in 1923.

In the 1930s VEBA produced synthetic gasoline (essential to the German war machine) from coal at its Hibernia plant. In 1938 the company and chemical cartel I. G. Farben set up Chemische Werke Hüls to make synthetic rubber. After WWII, VEBA's assets in western Germany were transferred to the government, and several executives were arrested. Preussag was spun off in 1959.

In 1965 the government spun off VEBA to the public. That year the company entered trading and transportation by buying Stinnes, one of West Germany's largest industrial companies. In 1969 VEBA transferred its coal mining interests to Ruhrkohle and a few years later moved into oil exploration and development. The company shortened its name to VEBA in 1970.

The West German government sold its remaining stake in VEBA in 1987. In a changed regulatory environment, large investors were able to accumulate big portions of stock, and their dissatisfaction with the company's lackluster results made it a takeover target. In response, new chairman Ulrich Hartmann began cutting noncore businesses and reducing staff.

In 1990 VEBA began accumulating mobile communications, networking, and cable TV companies. It allied with the UK's Cable and Wireless (C&W) in 1995 to develop a European mobile phone business, but in 1997 C&W sold its interest to VEBA (as part of the deal, VEBA gained a 10% stake in C&W, which it sold in 1999). In anticipation of the 1998 deregulation of the German telecom market, VEBA and RWE merged their German telecom businesses in 1997.

VEBA acquired a 36% stake in Degussa, a specialty chemicals company, in 1997; two years later Degussa merged with Hüls to form a separately traded chemical company called Degussa-Hüls, in which VEBA took a 62% stake. VEBA sold a 30% stake in Stinnes to the public in 1999. The company's telecom venture sold its fixed-line telephone business, its cable TV unit, and its stake in mobile phone operator E-Plus.

These moves, however, were just the prelude to a bigger deal: a $14 billion merger agreement between VEBA and fellow German conglomerate VIAG. The partners announced plans to dump noncore businesses and beef up their energy and chemicals holdings. VEBA and VIAG completed their merger in 2000, and the combined company adopted the name E.ON. The companies' utilities businesses were combined into E.ON Energie, and their chemicals units were brought together as Degussa.

To gain regulatory approval to form E.ON, VEBA and VIAG agreed to sell their stakes in German electric utilities Bewag and VEAG and coal producer LAUBAG. E.ON sold its VEAG and LAUBAG interests, along with semiconductor and electronics distribution units, in 2000 and sold Bewag in 2001.

That year E.ON agreed to buy UK electricity generator Powergen, and it announced plans to sell off nonutility operations, including Degussa and Veba Oel. Later that year E.ON agreed to swap a 51% stake in Veba Oel for BP's 26% stake in German natural gas supplier Ruhrgas. E.ON also sold Klöckner to UK steel trader Balli and sold its stake in silicon wafer maker MEMC to buyout firm Texas Pacific Group.

In 2002 E.ON sold its VAW Aluminum unit to Norwegian conglomerate Norsk Hydro in a $2.8 billion deal. Regulators moved to prevent E.ON from acquiring BP's stake in Ruhrgas in 2002, but BP agreed to pay for the Veba Oel stake in cash if necessary, and the swap was completed later that year. E.ON also acquired Vodafone and ThyssenKrupp's stakes in Ruhrgas in 2002, and it sold its remaining stake in Veba Oel to BP.

Also in 2002 E.ON completed its purchase of Powergen for about $8 billion, and it sold its 65% stake in logistics company Stinnes to German railroad operator Deutsche Bahn. In late 2002 E.ON acquired the UK energy supply and generation businesses of TXU Europe in a $2.5 billion deal.

The following year E.ON swapped its majority stake in chemical maker Degussa with coal group RAG for RAG's 18% interest in Ruhrgas. It completed its acquisition of Ruhrgas by purchasing the combined 40% stake held by Royal Dutch/Shell, Exxon Mobil, and TUI (formerly Preussag). It also sold subsidiary Viterra's energy services unit (gas and water meters) to CVC Capital Partners.

EXECUTIVES

Chairman of the Supervisory Board: Ulrich Hartmann, age 65
Deputy Chairman of the Supervisory Board: Hubertus Schmoldt, age 58
Chairman of the Board of Management and CEO; Chairman, Powergen: Wulf H. Bernotat, age 55
Member of the Board of Management, Finance, Accounting, Taxes, and Information Technology and CFO: Erhard Schipporeit, age 54
Member of the Board of Management, Controlling and Corporate Planning, Mergers and Acquisitions, and Legal Affairs: Hans Michael Gaul, age 61
Member of the Board of Management, Gas Business; Chairman of the Management Board, Ruhrgas: Burckhard Bergmann, age 60
Member of the Board of Management, Human Resources, Personnel, Infrastructure and Services, Procurement, and Organization: Manfred Krüper, age 62
EVP Corporate Communications: Peter Blau
EVP Investor Relations: Kiran Bhojani
EVP: Gert von der Groeben
EVP: Ulrich Hüppe
EVP: Heinrich Montag
EVP: Rolf Pohlig
EVP: Hans Gisbert Ulmke
Chairman of the Board of Management, E.ON Energie: Johannes Teyssen, age 44
Manager Investor Relations: Peter Blankenhorn
Auditors: PwC Deutsche Revision AG

LOCATIONS

HQ: E.ON-Platz 1, 40479 Düsseldorf, Germany
Phone: +49-211-4579-0   **Fax:** +49-211-4579-501
US HQ: 405 Lexington Ave., New York, NY 10174
US Phone: 212-922-2700   **US Fax:** 212-557-5189
Web: www.eon.com

2002 Sales

	$ mil.	% of total
Europe		
Germany	21,595	56
Other European Union countries	3,353	9
Other European countries	7,035	18
US	4,092	10
Other countries	2,781	7
Total	**38,856**	**100**

PRODUCTS/OPERATIONS

2002 Sales

	$ mil.	% of total
E.ON Energie	20,464	53
Chemicals	12,336	32
Powergen	4,693	12
Real estate	1,285	3
Other	78	—
Total	**38,856**	**100**

Selected Subsidiaries and Affiliates

Bouygues Telecom (10%, mobile phone services)
Degussa AG (47%, chemicals)
E.ON Energie AG (electric, gas, heat, and water utility)
E.ON Telecom GmbH
LG&E Energy (natural gas and electric utility, US)
Powergen (electric utility and independent power producer, UK)
RAG Aktiengesellschaft (39%, coal production, energy and technology conglomerate)
Ruhrgas (natural gas supply)
VIAG Telecom Beteiligungs GmbH
Viterra (real estate)

COMPETITORS

AGIV	Eni
Akzo Nobel	EVN
BASF AG	France Telecom
Bayer AG	Nuon
Deutsche Telekom	RWE
Dow Chemical	Suez
DuPont	Unión Fenosa
Electricité de France	Vattenfall
Endesa	Vodafone
Enel	WorldCom
EnBW	

HISTORICAL FINANCIALS

Company Type: Public

Income Statement

FYE: December 31

	REVENUE ($ mil.)	NET INCOME ($ mil.)	NET PROFIT MARGIN	EMPLOYEES
12/02	38,856	2,912	7.5%	107,856
12/01	70,909	1,846	2.6%	151,953
12/00	77,904	3,352	4.3%	186,788
12/99	53,392	2,693	5.0%	131,602
12/98	50,200	1,404	2.8%	132,337
12/97	46,212	1,570	3.4%	126,734
12/96	47,990	1,583	3.3%	123,727
12/95	50,335	1,470	2.9%	125,158
12/94	46,010	982	2.1%	126,875
12/93	38,160	692	1.8%	128,348
Annual Growth	**0.2%**	**17.3%**	**—**	**(1.9%)**

2002 Year-End Financials

Debt ratio: 96.9%
Return on equity: 12.0%
Cash ($ mil.): 8,792
Current ratio: 0.84
Long-term debt ($ mil.): 26,055
No. of shares (mil.): 652
Dividends
Yield: 3.4%
Payout: 31.5%
Market value ($ mil.): 26,687

Stock History

NYSE: EON

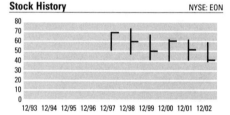

	STOCK PRICE ($) FY Close	P/E High/Low		PER SHARE ($) Earnings	Dividends	Book Value
12/02	40.91	14	10	4.47	1.41	41.23
12/01	51.51	18	12	3.44	1.39	31.68
12/00	60.38	11	7	5.40	0.00	36.92
12/99	50.06	11	7	6.00	0.00	28.87
12/98	59.88	26	17	2.80	0.00	27.46
12/97	69.00	22	16	3.12	0.00	24.89
Annual Growth	**(9.9%)**	**—**	**—**	**7.5%**	**—**	**10.6%**

LM Ericsson

Ericsson has a way without wires. The company is the world's leading maker of wireless telecom infrastructure equipment. Network operators and service providers use Ericsson's antennas, transmitters, and other wireless infrastructure gear to build and expand networks. Ericsson's other products include corporate networking gear, cable, defense electronics, and software for mobile messaging and commerce. The company is also a top seller of cell phones through a joint venture with Sony. The company is controlled by two groups, the Wallenberg family and Industrivärden, which wield 38% and 28% of the voting power respectively.

To offset the impact of plummeting sales caused by the depressed global telecom market, Ericsson has reorganized its product and geographic divisions, shedding more than 40,000 employees since 2000 in the process. The company plans to continue making layoffs (to the tune of about 14,000) through 2003. Ericsson is expanding its professional services business to pick up the slack in equipment sales.

Ericsson, which builds products around all the major wireless standards, continues to focus on upgrading carrier networks to the third generation (3G) primarily in Western Europe, Latin America, and the US. To that end, it has increased shipments of products based on interim GPRS technology (an enhancement of the leading GSM standard) to bridge the gap between existing 2G and emerging 3G networks. The company is also working to increase its shipments of equipment based on the competing CDMA standard.

Ericsson has combined its mobile phone handset business with that of consumer product expert Sony into a 50%-owned joint venture called Sony Ericsson Mobile Communications. The pair hopes that together they will gain ground on industry leaders Nokia, Motorola, Samsung, and Siemens for a larger share of the cell phone market.

HISTORY

Lars Magnus Ericsson opened a telegraph repair shop in Stockholm in 1876, the same year Alexander Graham Bell applied for a US patent on the telephone. Within two years Ericsson was making telephones. His company grew rapidly, supplying equipment first to Swedish phone companies and later to other European companies. In 1885 Ericsson crafted a combination receiver-speaker in one handset.

In 1911 Ericsson and SAT, the Stockholm telephone company, merged under the Ericsson banner. The company adopted its present name in 1926. In 1930 international financier Ivar "The Match King" Kreuger, owner of the Swedish Match Co., won control of Ericsson. His triumph was short-lived. Krueger committed suicide in 1932 and one of his creditors, Sosthenes Behn's ITT, took over.

ITT in 1960 sold its interest in Ericsson to the top Swedish industrialist family, the Wallenbergs. In 1975 Ericsson introduced its computer-controlled exchange, called AXE. Buoyed by AXE's success, the company unveiled the "office of the future" in the early 1980s, diversifying into computers and office furniture.

However, Ericsson's timing was off: The demand for office automation never materialized and profits plunged. Electrolux chairman Hans Werthen was recruited to split his time between the two companies and rescue Ericsson. The company sold its computer business to Nokia in 1988 and refocused on telephone equipment. It dusted off its aging AXE system for the burgeoning cellular market and quickly won key contracts.

The company and aircraft maker Saab merged their military aviation electronics operations as Ericsson Saab Avionics in 1996. (It was dissolved

in 1998.) In 1998 manager Sven-Christer Nilsson was appointed CEO. He reorganized the company and laid off 14,000 workers.

After Ericsson fought bitterly with rival QUALCOMM over wireless standards and patents, the companies settled in 1999, agreeing to push for the standardization of third-generation technology based on QUALCOMM's code-division multiple access technology. As a part of the deal, Ericsson purchased QUALCOMM's infrastructure business. To expand its Internet offerings, Ericsson bought Internet router maker Torrent and Internet telephony company Touchwave.

By mid-1999 Nilsson was pushed out for moving too slowly on restructuring plans and was replaced as CEO by chairman Lars Ramqvist, who put many of the duties on president Kurt Hellström. Hellström immediately set out to simplify the company's managerial and accounting structure, trim its workforce and slow-growth businesses, and push new phone models to market.

The next year Ericsson sold noncore businesses including its private radio systems, power supply, and equipment shelter operations. The company also agreed to develop a standard for secure wireless transactions with Nokia and Motorola and formed a joint venture with Web router maker Juniper to sell routers for mobile Internet applications.

Fierce competition, an industrywide slowdown in handset sales, and manufacturing glitches led Ericsson to outsource the manufacture of its phones to Flextronics and form a joint venture (Sony Ericsson Mobile Communications) with Sony to link the development and marketing of their handsets in 2001. Ericsson also sold its direct enterprise sales and service unit, outsourced IT operations in Europe to EDS, and cut more than 20,000 jobs that year. Hellström became CEO in 2001.

Chairman Ramqvist became honorary chairman in 2002; Electrolux CEO Michael Treschow was named as the acting chairman. Ericsson announced 20,000 more layoffs in 2002. That year the company sold its semiconductor unit to Infineon for about $380 million. Ericsson sold its optoelectronic components business in early 2003.

EXECUTIVES

Honorary Chairman: Lars Ramqvist, age 65
Chairman: Michael Treschow, age 59
President and CEO: Carl-Henric Svanberg
EVP and COO: Per-Arne Sandström, age 55
EVP and CFO: Karl-Henrik Sundström
EVP, Asia Pacific: Ragnar Bäck, age 58
EVP, Europe, Middle East, and Africa: Mats Dahlin, age 48
EVP, Americas: Gerhard Weise, age 55
SVP, Legal Affairs: Carl Olof Blomqvist, age 52
SVP, People and Culture: Marita Hellberg
SVP, Marketing and Strategic Business Development: Torbjörn Nilsson, age 50
SVP, Corporate Communications: Henry Sténson
SVP and CTO: Jan Uddenfelt, age 52
VP; General Manager, Research and Development: Hakan Eriksson
VP, Investor Relations: Gary Pinkham
President, Mobile Platforms Division: Sandeep Chennakeshu
President, Ericsson Enterprise: Lars E. Svensson
CIO: Björn Olsson
Director, Media Relations: Ase Lindskog
Auditors: PricewaterhouseCoopers AB

LOCATIONS

HQ: Telefonaktiebolaget LM Ericsson
   Telefonvägen 30, SE-126 25 Stockholm, Sweden
Phone: +46-8-719-0000   **Fax:** +46-8-18-40-85
US HQ: 6300 Legacy Dr., Plano, TX 75024
US Phone: 972-583-0000   **US Fax:** 972-669-8860
Web: www.ericsson.com

Ericsson operates in more than 140 countries worldwide.

2002 Sales

	$ mil.	% of total
Europe	8,519	50
Asia/Pacific	4,144	25
North America	2,648	16
Latin America	1,497	9
Total	**16,808**	**100**

PRODUCTS/OPERATIONS

Selected Operations

Mobile systems
Antennas
Complete network service hardware platforms
Fixed cellular terminals
Microwave and high-speed electronics
Circuit board
Interconnect products
Passive components
Semiconductor devices
Point-to-point and point-to-multipoint microwave
   systems
Radio base station controllers
Routers
Wireless broadband systems

Multi-service networks
ATM and IP routers
Circuit switching hardware platforms (AXE)
IP switching hardware platforms (ANS)
Services
Consulting
Customer management
Network design, integration, management, and
   migration
Product support
Staff training and education
Software
Billing
Customer management
Network and transmission management
Service provisioning

Other
Defense electronics
Modular airborne computers
RADAR systems
Secure wireless communications systems
Enterprise products
Business communication and call center software
Network access routers
PBX systems (BusinessPhone, MD110, WebSwitch)
Telephones and terminals
Wireless LAN systems

COMPETITORS

ADC Telecommunications
Alcatel
Andrew Corporation
CIENA
Cisco Systems
Fujitsu
Harris Corp
Hitachi
Kyocera
Lucent
Marconi
Mitsubishi Electric
Motorola
Nokia

Nortel Networks
Oki Electric
Panasonic Mobile
   Communications
Philips Electronics
QUALCOMM
Sagem
Samsung Electronics
SANYO
Scientific-Atlanta
Siemens
Tellabs
Toshiba

HISTORICAL FINANCIALS

Company Type: Public

Income Statement

FYE: December 31

	REVENUE ($ mil.)	NET INCOME ($ mil.)	NET PROFIT MARGIN	EMPLOYEES
12/02	16,808	(2,192)	—	64,621
12/01	22,117	(2,029)	—	85,000
12/00	29,026	2,230	7.7%	105,129
12/99	25,267	1,423	5.6%	103,290
12/98	22,760	1,609	7.1%	103,667
12/97	21,219	1,511	7.1%	100,774
12/96	18,291	1,033	5.6%	93,949
12/95	14,902	813	5.5%	84,513
12/94	11,342	531	4.7%	76,144
12/93	7,622	340	4.5%	69,597
Annual Growth	9.2%	—	—	(0.8%)

2002 Year-End Financials

Debt ratio: 49.1%	No. of shares (mil.): 1,582
Return on equity: —	Dividends
Cash ($ mil.): 2,071	Yield: 0.0%
Current ratio: 2.27	Payout: —
Long-term debt ($ mil.): 4,164	Market value ($ mil.): 10,663

Stock History

NASDAQ: ERICY

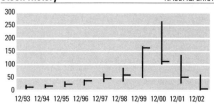

12/93 12/94 12/95 12/96 12/97 12/98 12/99 12/00 12/01 12/02

	STOCK PRICE ($) FY Close	P/E High/Low	PER SHARE ($) Earnings	Dividends	Book Value
12/02	6.74	— —	(1.74)	0.00	5.36
12/01	52.20	— —	(2.57)	0.50	81.12
12/00	111.88	94 37	2.80	0.60	122.98
12/99	164.22	93 28	1.80	0.60	103.65
12/98	59.84	40 18	2.10	0.00	99.78
12/97	46.64	29 16	2.20	0.00	85.39
12/96	37.74	31 17	1.30	0.30	76.44
12/95	24.38	30 15	1.10	0.20	66.86
12/94	17.23	22 14	0.90	0.30	45.09
12/93	12.62	38 15	0.50	0.00	36.78
Annual Growth	(6.7%)	— —	—	—	(19.3%)

Ernst & Young International

Accounting may actually be the *second*-oldest profession, and Ernst & Young is one of the oldest practitioners. Ernst & Young is also one of the world's largest accounting firms, offering auditing and accounting services around the globe. The firm also provides legal services and services relating to emerging growth companies, human resources issues, and corporate transactions (mergers and acquisitions, IPOs, and the like). Ernst & Young has one of the world's largest tax practices, serving multinational clients that have to comply with multiple local tax laws.

After spending decades building them, the big accountancies have all moved toward shedding their consultancies, because of internal and regulatory pressures, as well as the perceived conflict of interest in providing auditing and consulting services to the same clients. Ernst & Young was the first to split off its consultancy, selling it in 2000 to what is now Cap Gemini Ernst & Young.

Ernst & Young, which gained an impressive amount of weight in former rival Andersen's diaspora, has also boosted its legal services, assembling some 2,000 lawyers in dozens of countries.

Ernst & Young has faced Andersen-style trouble of its own. Federal regulators in 2002 sued the firm for its alleged role in the failure of Superior Bank FSB, and threatened civil charges for purported fraud relating to Cendant. In the UK, insurer Equitable Life in 2003 sued the accountancy for professional negligence related to work performed when Ernst & Young was its auditor. More problems followed with clients Healthsouth and America Online.

Rick Bobrow retired as the firm's global CEO after a year on the job; the departure was presumed to have been related to the airing of previously unpublicized Ernst & Young financial information during Bobrow's divorce proceedings.

HISTORY

In 1494 Luca Pacioli's *Summa di Arithmetica* became the first published text on double-entry bookkeeping, but it was almost 400 years before accounting became a profession.

In 1849 Frederick Whinney joined the UK firm of Harding & Pullein. His ledgers were so clear that he was advised to take up accounting, which was a growth field as stock companies proliferated. Whinney became a name partner in 1859 and his sons followed him into the business. The firm became Whinney, Smith & Whinney (WS&W) in 1894.

After WWII, WS&W formed an alliance with Ernst & Ernst (founded in Cleveland in 1903 by brothers Alwin and Theodore Ernst), with each firm operating on the other's behalf across the Atlantic. Whinney merged with Brown, Fleming & Murray in 1965 to become Whinney Murray. In 1979 Whinney Murray, Turquands Barton Mayhew (also a UK firm), and Ernst & Ernst merged to form Ernst & Whinney.

But Ernst & Whinney wasn't done merging. Ten years later, when it was the fourth-largest accounting firm, it merged with #5 Arthur Young, which had been founded by Scotsman Arthur Young in 1895 in Kansas City. Long known as "old reliable," Arthur Young fell on hard times in the 1980s because its audit relationships with failed S&Ls led to expensive litigation (settled in 1992 for $400 million).

Thus the new firm of Ernst & Young faced a rocky start. In 1990 it fended off rumors of collapse. The next year it slashed payroll, even thinning its partner roster. Exhausted by the S&L wars, in 1994 the firm replaced its pugnacious general counsel, Carl Riggio, with the more cost-conscious Kathryn Oberly.

In the mid-1990s Ernst & Young concentrated on consulting, particularly in software applications, and grew through acquisitions. In 1996 the firm bought Houston-based Wright Killen & Co., a petroleum and petrochemicals consulting firm, to form Ernst & Young Wright Killen. It also entered new alliances that year, including ones with Washington-based ISD/Shaw, which provided banking industry consulting, and India's Tata Consulting.

In 1997 Ernst & Young was sued for a record $4 billion for its alleged failure to effectively handle the 1993 restructuring of the defunct Merry-Go-Round Enterprises retail chain (it settled for $185 million in 1999). On the heels of a merger deal between Coopers & Lybrand and Price Waterhouse, Ernst & Young agreed in 1997 to merge with KPMG International. But Ernst & Young called off the negotiations in 1998, citing the uncertain regulatory process they faced.

In 1999 the firm reached a settlement in lawsuits regarding accounting errors at Informix and Cendant and sold its UK and Southern African trust and fiduciary businesses to Royal Bank of Canada (now RBC Financial Group).

In 2000 Ernst & Young became the first of the (then) Big Five firms to sell its consultancy, dealing it to France's Cap Gemini Group for about $11 billion. The following year the UK accountancy watchdog group announced it would investigate Ernst & Young for its handling of the accounts of UK-based The Equitable Life Assurance Society. The insurer was forced to close to new business in 2000 because of massive financial difficulties.

E&Y made headlines and gave competitors plenty to talk about in 2002 when financial records that had been closely held were made public during a divorce case involving executive Rick Bobrow (who in 2003 abruptly retired as global CEO after just a year on the job). The firm in 2002 also formed an alliance with former New York City mayor Rudy Giuliani to help launch a business consultancy and an investment firm bearing the Giuliani name.

EXECUTIVES

Global Chairman and CEO; Chairman for the Americas: James S. (Jim) Turley
CFO and Global Managing Partner — Finance and Infrastructure: Norbert R. Becker
COO: Paul J. Ostling
Global Managing Partner — Quality & Risk Management: Michael N.M. Boyd
Global Managing Partner — Markets: Mike Cullen
Global Managing Partner — People: Timothy T. (Tim) Griffy
Global Managing Partner — Practice Integration: Jean-Charles Raufast
Deputy Global Managing Partner — Infrastructure; VC of Knowledge & Technology, Ernst & Young LLP: John G. Peetz Jr.
Global Director — Business Risk Services: Thomas Bussa
Vice Chairman — Strategy: Beth A. Brooke
Vice Chairman — Assurance and Advisory Business Services: James A. Hassett
Vice Chairman — Global Financial Services: Robert W. Stein
Vice Chairman — Tax: Karl Johansson
Vice Chairman — Technology, Communications and Entertainment: Stephen E. Almassy
Vice Chairman — Law: Patrick Bignon
Vice Chairman — Emerging Growth Markets Accounts: Roger F. Dunbar
Vice Chairman — Sales: Patrick J.P. Flochel
Vice Chairman — Corporate Finance: Francis Small
Director, Entrepreneur of the Year Program: Nancy Clark

LOCATIONS

HQ: 5 Times Square, New York, NY 10036
Phone: 212-773-3000   **Fax:** 212-773-6350
Web: www.eyi.com

Ernst & Young International has approximately 670 offices in more than 140 countries.

PRODUCTS/OPERATIONS

2003 Sales

	$ mil.	% of total
Assurance & advisory business services	7,736	59
Tax & law services	4,165	32
Transaction advisory services	960	7
Other	275	2
Total	**13,136**	**100**

Industry Specializations

Chemicals
Communications
Construction
Energy
Entertainment
Financial services
Health sciences
Hospitality
Industrial products
Real estate
Retail and consumer products
Technology
Utilities

Selected Services

Assurance and Advisory
Actuarial services
Audits
Accounting advisory
Business risk services
Internal audit
Real estate advisory services
Technology and security risk services
Transaction support services

Corporate and M&A
Employment
Finance
Information technology services
Intellectual property
International trade and anti-trust
Litigation and arbitration
Real estate

Emerging Growth Companies
Corporate finance services
IPO services
Mergers and acquisitions advisory
Operational consulting
Strategic advisory

Human Capital
Compensation and benefits consulting
Cost optimization and risk management
Transaction support services
Law

Tax
Customs and international trade
Electronic VAT assurance
International tax
Partial exemption evaluation process
Tax outsourcing

Transactions
Capital management
Due diligence and transaction support
Financial and business modeling
M&A advisory
Post-deal advisory
Strategic finance
Valuation

COMPETITORS

AMS
Bain & Company
BDO International
Deloitte Touche Tohmatsu
Grant Thornton
  International
IBM
KPMG
PricewaterhouseCoopers

HISTORICAL FINANCIALS

Company Type: Partnership

Income Statement

FYE: June 30

	REVENUE ($ mil.)	NET INCOME ($ mil.)	NET PROFIT MARGIN	EMPLOYEES
6/03	13,136	—	—	103,000
6/02	10,124	—	—	87,206
6/01	9,900	—	—	82,000
6/00*	9,500	—	—	88,625
9/99	12,500	—	—	97,800
9/98	10,900	—	—	85,000
9/97	9,100	—	—	79,750
9/96	7,800	—	—	72,000
9/95	6,867	—	—	68,452
9/94	6,020	—	—	61,287
Annual Growth	9.1%	—	—	5.9%

*Fiscal year change

Revenue History

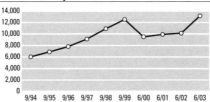

Espírito Santo Financial Group

Espírito Santo Financial Group (ESFG) wields its earthly powers via two main entities: Banco Espírito Santo and Companhia de Seguros Tranquilidade, one of Portugal's top insurance firms. Its Banco Internacional de Crédito offers mortgage lending and private banking. Although most of its operations are in Portugal, ESFG has banking, insurance, and financial services interests in other European countries, Brazil, the Caribbean, and the US, where it owns Espírito Santo Bank of Florida. Entities associated with the founding Espírito Santo family are ESFG's major shareholders.

ESFG's other holdings include stockbroker Espírito Santo Dealer (formerly ESER) and investment bank Banco Espírito Santo de Investimento. ESFG sells the lion's share of Tranquilidade's insurance, pension, and investment products through approximately 400 bank offices, which also provide consumer and business banking services.

Willing to do what it takes to stay strong in a unifying European economy, ESFG is growing by adding bank branches and new products. The company has benefited from Portugal's position in the EU (the country has been a major recipient of financial aid) and from the privatization of the country's formerly state-controlled economy.

HISTORY

The Espírito Santo financial empire traces its roots to a bank founded by José Maria de Espírito Santo Silva in Lisbon in 1884. After WWI, Portugal underwent a major banking expansion, and in 1920 the Espírito Santo family established Banco Espírito Santo, which grew rapidly thanks to postwar expansion and speculation.

After José Maria's oldest son, José, fled the bank and the country in scandal, his brother, Ricardo, led the massive growth of both the bank and the family's fortune. During the 1930s the Espírito Santos acquired a major interest in insurance company Tranquilidade, and in 1937 Banco Espírito Santo merged with Banco Comercial de Lisboa (founded 1875) to create Banco Espírito Santo e Comercial de Lisboa.

The family's fortunes were aided by dictator Antonio de Oliveira Salazar, who came to power in 1933. During WWII, Salazar declared Portugal neutral, and the country became a sanctuary for many of Europe's elite, who brought the Espírito Santos business and contacts.

The Espírito Santo empire was fostered by Salazar's postwar protectionist policies. Banco Espírito Santo became one of Portugal's largest banks and Tranquilidade one of its largest insurance companies. The family also acquired large coffee, sugar, and palm-oil plantations in Portugal's colonies Angola and Mozambique. At their peak, the Espírito Santo holdings were valued at $4 billion.

But the family's fortunes turned with political upheaval in Portugal during the 1970s. In 1974 the military overthrew Salazar's successor, Marcelo Caetano. A year later the leftist government nationalized Portugal's major corporations, including Banco Espírito Santo and Tranquilidade.

The family fled to London and pooled their savings to create a new company in Luxembourg, Espírito Santo Financial Holding (ESFH). In the late 1970s they got a banking license in Brazil and later set up a fund management company in Switzerland and banks in Miami and Paris. The family's name attracted business and investors.

The Portuguese government in 1986 reprivatized financial services organizations. That year ESFH and France's Crédit Agricole opened Banco Internacional de Crédito in Portugal. After raising money on the Eurobond market, ESFH bought back control of Tranquilidade in 1990. A year later the company and a group of investors, including Crédit Agricole, reacquired control of Banco Espírito Santo.

In 1993 ESFH reduced its interest in Banco Internacional de Crédito to 47% (it regained 100% control in 1997). Since then the company has concentrated on Portugal. In the early 1990s recession rocked the economy — and the company. But in the mid-1990s, despite poor commercial demand, consumer-related services rebounded.

ESFH expanded its commercial banking network in 1995 and 1996. In 1997 the company and Brazil's Monteiro Aranha bought more than 60% of that country's Banco Boavista. The company also dropped "Holding" in favor of "Group," and the next year ESFG, in a vote of confidence in Brazil, moved to raise its holdings in Banco Boavista.

In 1999, amid a flurry of speculation about Spanish/Portuguese banking mergers, the company agreed to buy a majority interest in Spanish brokerage Benito y Monjardin. The company also moved to bolster its asset management operations by inking a deal to buy Portugal-based fund manager Gescapital.

In 2000 ESFG bought the majority stake of French credit institution Via Banque from BNP Paribas (it acquired the rest of Via Banque in 2001). The next year ESFG, in conjunction with Portugal Telecom, launched Banco Electrónico de Serviço Total (Banco Best) as a technologically integrated banking, investment, and brokerage service.

EXECUTIVES

Chairman and President:
 Ricardo Espírito Santo Silva Salgado
Vice Chairman: José Manuel
 Pinheiro Espírito Santo Silva
Director: Manuel de Magalhães Villas-Boas
SVP: Mário A. Fernandes Cardoso
SVP: Erich Dähler
SVP: Jean-Luc Schneider
Secretary: Teresa de Souza
Auditors: PricewaterhouseCoopers S.a.r.l.

LOCATIONS

HQ: Espírito Santo Financial Group S.A.
 231 Val des Bons Malades,
 L-2121 Luxembourg-Kirchberg, Luxembourg
Phone: +352-434-945   **Fax:** +352-434-9454
US HQ: 320 Park Avenue, 29th Fl., New York, NY 10022
US Phone: 212-702-3410   **US Fax:** 212-750-3888
Web: www.esfg.com

Espírito Santo Financial Group has operations in Angola, Austria, Belgium, Brazil, the British Virgin Islands, the Cayman Islands, France, Ireland, Luxembourg, Macao, Portugal, Spain, Switzerland, the UK, and the US.

2002 Sales

	% of total
Portugal	83
Spain	4
British Virgin Islands	3
France	2
UK	2
US	1
Total	**100**

PRODUCTS/OPERATIONS

Selected Subsidiaries

Banco Boavista-InterAtlantico (BBIA, Brazil)
Banco Espírito Santo de Investimento SA (Portugal)
Banco Espírito Santo do Oriente SARL (BES-ORIENTE, Macao)
Banco Espírito Santo e Comercial de Lisboa SA (BES, Portugal)
Banco Internacional de Crédito SA (BIC, Portugal)
Cia. de Seguros Tranquilidade SA (insurance, Portugal)
Compagnie Financière Espírito Santo SA (asset management, Switzerland)
Espírito Santo Activos Financeiros SGPS SA (holding company, Portugal)
Espirito Santo Bank Ltd. (US)
Espirito Santo Dealer
Via Banque SA (France)

COMPETITORS

BBVA	Crédit Agricole
Chemical	Credit Suisse
Banco Comercial	Deutsche Bank
Português	Itaúsa
Banco de Comercio e	J.P. Morgan Chase
Industria	Merrill Lynch
Banco Portugues do	SCH
Atlantico	Société Générale
BNP	UBS
Citigroup	Zurich Financial Services

HISTORICAL FINANCIALS

Company Type: Public

Income Statement

FYE: December 31

	ASSETS ($ mil.)	NET INCOME ($ mil.)	INCOME AS % OF ASSETS	EMPLOYEES
12/02	47,882	(47)	—	10,127
12/01	38,102	10	0.0%	10,969
12/00	35,207	100	0.3%	11,000
12/99	32,821	84	0.3%	11,000
12/98	33,169	71	0.2%	1,076
12/97	25,646	51	0.2%	1,083
12/96	24,838	39	0.2%	1,119
12/95	21,827	30	0.1%	1,112
12/94	—	25	—	1,156
12/93	13,451	42	0.3%	8,215
Annual Growth	**15.2%**	**—**	**—**	**2.4%**

2002 Year-End Financials

Equity as % of assets: 0.1%
Return on assets: —
Return on equity: —
Long-term debt ($ mil.): 11,858
No. of shares (mil.): 48

Dividends
 Yield: 2.4%
 Payout: —
Market value ($ mil.): 802
Sales ($ mil.): 3,882

Stock History

NYSE: ESF

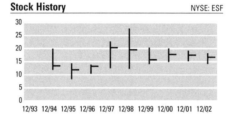

	STOCK PRICE ($) FY Close	P/E High/Low		PER SHARE ($) Earnings	Dividends	Book Value
12/02	16.74	—	—	(1.09)	0.40	0.88
12/01	17.51	86	70	0.22	0.63	1.87
12/00	17.75	9	7	2.28	0.64	3.33
12/99	15.75	11	8	1.86	0.65	9.28
12/98	19.56	18	8	1.53	0.00	10.59
12/97	20.31	14	8	1.57	0.00	8.73
12/96	13.25	11	9	1.25	0.55	12.22
12/95	11.88	14	9	0.98	1.08	12.58
12/94	13.38	19	12	1.02	0.65	—
Annual Growth	**2.8%**	**—**	**—**	**—**	**(5.9%)**	**(31.6%)**

EADS N.V.

It's flying alphabet soup! DaimlerChrysler Aerospace (DASA, Germany), Aerospatiale Matra (France), and Construcciones Aeronauticas SA (CASA, Spain) have combined to form the European Aeronautic Defence and Space Company (EADS). EADS is Europe's largest aerospace firm; worldwide it trails only Boeing. Among EADS's major operations are an 80% stake in Airbus (BAE SYSTEMS owns the other 20%), helicopters (Eurocopter), jet fighters (EADS owns about 40% of Eurofighter), satellites (Astrium), missiles (it owns about 40% of MBDA), and commercial satellite launchers (Arianespace).

Airbus, which accounts for about 63% of EADS's sales, and its new super-jumbo A380 jet, are key to EADS's success. With the A380, Airbus hopes to wrest customers away from Boeing, which has enjoyed a monopoly on jumbo jets and

is Airbus' only competition in long-range passenger aircraft. Scheduled to be flying as early as 2005, the A380 will carry up to 600 people in a double-decker configuration. However, the downturn in the civil airline market after the terrorist attacks of September 11 has led the company to plan to invest more in its military business.

After years of negotiations and countless dead ends, a group of Western European aerospace companies finally closed a deal. The drama is far from over, however, as everyone waits anxiously to see how well they get along under the same management structure — if not under the same roof. As with its Airbus operations, EADS's production will be in multiple countries and the company's complex ownership and management structure (German and French co-CEOs!) is designed to maintain parity between French and German stakes.

DaimlerChrysler owns about 30% of EADS; the French government (SOGEPA), France-based Lagardère, BNP Paribas, and AXA together own about 30%; Spain's state-owned SEPI owns about 5.5%.

HISTORY

The short life of the European Aeronautic Defence and Space Company — EADS — is overshadowed by the long history of its components and by the obstacles overcome to cement the deal: The French and the Germans historically aren't overly fond of each other, so how did it come to pass that Germany's DaimlerChrysler Aerospace (DASA) and France's Aerospatiale Matra put aside their differences to band together with Spain's Construcciones Aeronáuticas SA (CASA)?

The US aerospace sector in the 1990s saw many companies consolidate, scrambling to make their way in the post-Cold War era. Boeing, the largest aerospace company in the world, got that way by acquiring a slew of operations, including Rockwell International's aerospace and defense operations (1995) and most importantly, McDonnell Douglas in a $16 billion deal (1997). Lockheed, the world's #2, merged with Martin Marietta (1995) and acquired Loral (1997). These US companies had it relatively easy — they all paid taxes to Uncle Sam, but acquisition deals in Europe were stymied by concerns over national security and privatization because much of Europe's defense industry was government-owned.

Spurred into action by their US rivals, in 1997 DASA and British Aerospace (now BAE SYSTEMS) — partners in Airbus — began merger talks. Fearful of being left out in the cold, France's government-owned Aerospatiale — another Airbus partner — began talks to merge with Matra, a French defense company controlled by Lagardère. Weeks after the Aerospatiale-Matra deal was announced in 1998, the chairman of DASA's parent company, Jürgen Schrempp, met with Lagardère's CEO, Jean-Luc Lagardère, and proposed a three-way deal. It never occurred and in 1999 the BAE SYSTEMS and DASA deal fell through as well.

Later that year Schrempp and Lagardère met again and laid the groundwork for a merger between DASA and Aerospatiale Matra. Less than three weeks after the Aerospatiale-Matra merger was completed, Lagardère found himself pitching the DASA/Aerospatiale Matra merger idea to a stunned French government (which still held a 48% stake in Aerospatiale Matra). Marathon negotiations ensued. Late in the year

Spain's Construcciones Aeronáuticas SA (CASA) agreed to become part of EADS.

In 2000 EADS went public and Airbus announced that it would abandon its consortium structure in favor of incorporation. The next year EADS began pushing for a consolidation of army and naval equipment manufacturing among EU countries similar to the aerospace consolidation that created EADs. For Airbus, the long-sought switch from consortium to corporation finally occurred in July 2001 when Airbus S.A.S. was incorporated.

Early in 2003 EADS bought out BAE SYSTEMS' 25% share in their Astrium joint venture.

EXECUTIVES

Co-Chairman: Manfred Bischoff, age 61
Co-Chairman: Arnaud Lagardère, age 42
Co-CEO and Director: Phillippe Camus, age 56
Co-CEO and Director: Rainer Hertrich, age 54
CFO: Hans-Peter Ring, age 52
EVP, Strategic Coordination: Jean-Luis Gergorin, age 57
Director; President and CEO, Airbus: Noël Forgeard, age 57
COO, Airbus: Gustav Humbert, age 53
Head, Aeronautics Division: Dietrich Russell, age 62
Head, Defence and Civil Systems Division: Thomas Enders, age 44
Head, Marketing: Jean-Paul Gut, age 42
Head, Military Transport Aircraft: Francisco Fernández Sáinz
Head, Space Systems Division: François Auque, age 47
Senior Military Advisor: Jeremy Blackham
Group VP, Human Resources: Jussi Itävuori
Chairman and CEO, EADS North America: Ralph D. Crosby Jr., age 56
CFO and VP, Investor Relations, EADS North America: Christopher Emerson
VP, Communications and Public Relations, EADS North America: Diane Murphy
General Counsel, EADS North America: Pierre Cardin

LOCATIONS

HQ: European Aeronautic Defence and Space Company EADS N.V.
37, boulevard de Montmorency,
75016 Paris, France
Phone: +33-1-42-24-24-24
Web: www.eads-nv.com

European Aeronautic Defence and Space Company EADS has operations in Canada, France, French Guiana, Morocco, the Netherlands, Spain, the UK, and the US.

PRODUCTS/OPERATIONS

Selected Operations and Interests

Aircraft and aerospace design, manufacture, and maintenance (Construcciones Aeronáuticas SA)
Aviation, aerospace, and telecommunications technology (58%-owned Donier GmbH)
Commercial airplanes (Airbus, 80%)
Commercial satellite launchers (Arianespace)
Helicopters (Eurocopter SAS, 100%)
Industrial aeronautics (ATR)
Jet fighters (Eurofighter, 43%)
Light aircraft (Socata)
Missile systems (Matra BAe Dynamics, 37.5%)
Satellites (Astrium, 75%)

COMPETITORS

BAE SYSTEMS
Boeing
Bombardier
LMCSS
Lockheed Martin
Northrop Grumman
Orbital Sciences
Raytheon
Textron

HISTORICAL FINANCIALS

Company Type: Public

Income Statement

FYE: December 31

	REVENUE ($ mil.)	NET INCOME ($ mil.)	NET PROFIT MARGIN	EMPLOYEES
12/02	31,339	(313)	—	103,967
12/01	27,281	1,215	4.5%	102,967
12/00	18,293	(850)	—	88,879
12/99	22,711	(1,016)	—	91,940
12/98	24,020	1,387	5.8%	—
Annual Growth	**6.9%**	**—**	**—**	**4.2%**

2002 Year-End Financials

Debt ratio: 29.7%
Return on equity: —
Cash ($ mil.): 6,498
Current ratio: 1.11
Long-term debt ($ mil.): 3,973

Net Income History

Euronext Paris: EAD

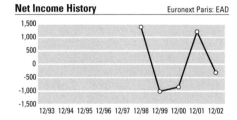

1,500									
1,000									
500									
0									
-500									
-1,000									
-1,500									
12/93	12/94	12/95	12/96	12/97	12/98	12/99	12/00	12/01	12/02

Fiat S.p.A.

The country that gave us Sophia Loren and Leonardo da Vinci also gave us century-old Fiat and its plethora of auto offerings, which range from compacts and sedans such as the Fiat Seicento to its Alfa Romeo, Ferrari, and Maserati sports cars. Having sold some noncore businesses, Fiat's refined focus is on cars, CNH Global agricultural and construction equipment, and Iveco commercial vehicles. It also operates insurance and publishing subsidiaries. Fiat wants to expand its auto business outside Western Europe. The founding Agnelli family owns about 30% of Fiat.

Thanks to Fiat's automotive unit, the entire enterprise is in trouble, but the company ironed out an agreement with the Italian government aimed at putting the ailing company back on the road to profitability. The plan called for as many as 5,600 layoffs in order to trim costs for 2003 by one billion Euros. However, this scheme could not work fast enough. The company has sold its entire 5.1% stake in GM to an unnamed investment bank for nearly $1.2 billion in order to obtain much needed cash (GM took a 20% stake in Fiat Auto in 2000). Fiat then announced it would cut another 12,300 jobs (6.9% of its worldwide workforce) over a three-year period and close 12 factories in hopes of being profitable by 2006. Most of the cuts will be at CNH Global, Iveco, and Fiat Auto. The company is also selling its Fiat Avio aviation division to raise cash.

A provision of the 2000 deal that gave GM 20% of Fiat also gave the Italian automaker the option to force GM to buy the remaining 80% as early as 2004 (or as late as 2009). This "put option" has been backed off by Fiat to 2005 (or as late as

2010). The move has been interpreted as a sign that GM will never own Fiat Auto outright, an idea that comes as no small comfort for many GM investors.

HISTORY

Ex-cavalry officer Giovanni Agnelli founded Fabbrica Italiana di Automobili Torino (Fiat) in 1899. Between 1903 and 1918 the automaker expanded into trucks, rail cars, aviation, and tractors. Protected by tariffs, Fiat became Italy's dominant auto company.

WWII boosted Fiat's fortunes, but bombs damaged many of its plants. With US support, Fiat rebuilt and survived by exporting and by building plants abroad. As growth in Italy resumed, Fiat began making steel and construction equipment.

After the European Community forced Italy to lower tariffs in 1961, Fiat lost market share, although foreign sales helped offset its woes. Giovanni Agnelli II (the founder's grandson) became chairman in 1966. Fiat then bought high-end Italian carmakers Lancia and Ferrari in 1969.

The company formed Fiat Auto S.p.A. in 1979, bringing together the Fiat, Lancia, Autobianchi, Abarth, and Ferrari lines. The next year Cesare Romiti became managing director and cut 23,000 jobs and broke union influence at Fiat. The company closed its unprofitable US car operations in 1983. Fiat and British Ford combined their truck operations in 1986, and Fiat also bought Alfa Romeo that year.

In 1989 Fiat purchased 49% of luxury carmaker Maserati (it bought the rest in 1993). Fiat and Ford merged their farm and construction equipment divisions in 1991 to form Fiat subsidiary New Holland (renamed CNH Global in 1999). After posting its biggest loss in 1993, Fiat restructured.

Slow car sales in Italy prompted Fiat to temporarily lay off about 74,000 workers in 1996, and chairman Agnelli stepped down. In 1997 Agnelli's successor, Romiti, and financial director Paolo Mattioli were convicted of falsifying records and illegally financing political parties. They were barred from employment at Fiat.

Paolo Fresco, former vice chairman of General Electric, replaced Romiti as head of Fiat in 1998. Challenged with slumping car sales in Italy and South America, the company sold its chemicals and telecom businesses. Car-price wars in Europe contributed to a stark downward shift in 1998 profits.

Deals abounded in 1999. Fiat's New Holland subsidiary bought agricultural and construction equipment maker Case Corporation for around $4.3 billion and changed its name to CNH Global. Also, Fiat began making light commercial trucks in China with Yuejin Motor. Fiat's truck-making division agreed in 1999 to buy vehicle-leasing company Fraikin for $596 million.

Other deals in 1999 included Fiat's Comau robotics unit's purchase of a 51% stake in France-based Renault Automation; the two began a bus-making joint venture and combined their foundry operations under Fiat subsidiary Teksid. Also, Fiat bought Progressive Tool & Industries (automated welding equipment, US) for $350 million.

To expand its auto business outside Europe, Fiat agreed in 2000 to trade a 20% stake in its car unit for a 5.1% stake in GM. That year ALSTOM agreed to buy a 51% stake in Fiat's rail unit (Fiat Ferrovia). Also in 2000 Fiat began selling off the divisions of Magneti Marelli. These included heating and cooling (to Denso of Japan), rearview mirrors (to Ficosa of Spain), and lubricants (to Doughty Hanson & Co. Ltd. of the UK). Fiat agreed to sell Magneti Marelli's shock absorber and suspension systems units to ThyssenKrupp Automotive in 2000. The company's bid (with a consortium including Electricite de France) of about $5.5 billion for control of agro-energy group Montedison was accepted in July.

Toward the end of 2001, Fiat announced that it would postpone selling off any more of Magneti Marelli due to the economic downturn. The company added that the deal to sell its shocks and suspensions unit to ThyssenKrupp Automotive would be renegotiated. Fiat then announced it would reorganize Fiat Auto into four business units (Fiat/Lancia, Alfa Romeo, International Development, and Services) in order to fully take advantage of brand valuation.

In 2002 Fiat sold the aluminum components division of its Teksid casting subsidiary to a group of funds including JP Morgan Partners, Questor Management Company, and Italy's Private Equity Partners.

As 2002 came to a close, Fiat announced it would lay off as many as 5,600 workers, and it sold its entire stake in GM to an unnamed investment bank for nearly $1.2 billion. Gianni Agnelli, Fiat's honorary chairman and grandson of the company's founder, died at the age of 81 in early 2003.

Later that year Fiat agreed to sell its Fiat Avio aviation unit to Carlyle (a private equity firm) and Italian defense group Finmeccanica for about $1.8 billion.

EXECUTIVES

Chairman: Umberto Agnelli
Vice Chairman: Alessandro Barberis
CEO: Giuseppe Morchio
CEO, Fiat Auto: Herbert Demel

LOCATIONS

HQ: 250 Via Nizza, 10126 Turin, Italy
Phone: +39-011-686-1111 **Fax:** +39-011-686-3798
Web: www.fiatgroup.com/e-index.htm

Fiat operates 242 production facilities in 61 countries.

2002 Sales

	$ mil.	% of total
Europe		
Italy	22,060	36
Other countries	23,103	38
North America	8,126	13
Mercosur	3,583	6
Other regions	4,142	7
Total	**61,014**	**100**

PRODUCTS/OPERATIONS

2002 Sales

	$ mil.	% of total
Automobiles (Fiat Auto Holdings)	24,282	38
Agricultural & construction equipment	11,527	18
Commercial vehicles	10,017	15
Insurance	5,390	8
Auto components	3,605	5
Production systems	2,544	4
Services	2,154	3
Metallurgical products	1,687	3
Aviation	1,682	3
Ferarri	1,324	2
Publishing & communications	395	1
Adjustments	(3,593)	—
Total	**61,014**	**100**

Selected Brand Names

Automobiles
Alfa Romeo
Ferrari
Fiat
Lancia
Maserati

Agricultural and Construction Equipment
Case
Case IH
New Holland
Steyr

Commercial Vehicles
Iveco (buses, diesel engines, trucks)

Components
Magneti Marelli

COMPETITORS

AGCO	Mazda
AUDI	Navistar
BMW	Nissan
Caterpillar	Oshkosh Truck
DaimlerChrysler	PACCAR
Deere	Peugeot
FMC	Porsche
Ford	Renault
Halliburton	Saab Automobile
Honda	Suzuki Motor
Ingersoll-Rand	Toyota
Isuzu	Volkswagen
JLG Industries	Volvo
Kia Motors	

HISTORICAL FINANCIALS

Company Type: Public

Income Statement

FYE: December 31

	REVENUE ($ mil.)	NET INCOME ($ mil.)	NET PROFIT MARGIN	EMPLOYEES
12/02	61,014	(4,147)	—	186,492
12/01	54,661	(397)	—	198,764
12/00	57,679	625	1.1%	223,953
12/99	48,741	356	0.7%	220,000
12/98	56,535	728	1.3%	234,454
12/97	53,480	1,368	2.6%	239,457
12/96	50,993	1,561	3.1%	237,865
12/95	51,382	1,355	2.6%	237,426
12/94	43,046	623	1.4%	248,200
12/93	33,325	(1,040)	—	260,951
Annual Growth	**7.0%**	**—**	**—**	**(3.7%)**

2002 Year-End Financials

Debt ratio: 247.5%
Return on equity: —
Cash ($ mil.): 3,665
Current ratio: 1.81
Long-term debt ($ mil.): 19,858

No. of shares (mil.): 433
Dividends
  Yield: 5.3%
  Payout: —
Market value ($ mil.): 3,444

Stock History

NYSE: FIA

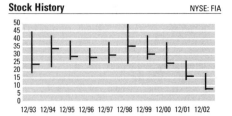

	STOCK PRICE ($) FY Close	P/E High/Low		PER SHARE ($) Earnings	Dividends	Book Value
12/02	7.95	—	—	(6.99)	0.42	18.52
12/01	16.00	—	—	(1.08)	0.55	29.52
12/00	24.25	33	19	1.12	0.56	34.15
12/99	30.13	67	44	0.62	0.64	35.29
12/98	35.25	37	19	1.31	0.00	8.29
12/97	29.50	9	6	4.24	0.60	7.88
12/96	27.95	8	6	4.24	0.58	9.19
12/95	28.63	77	54	0.50	0.18	5.54
12/94	33.63	36	19	1.16	0.00	5.00
12/93	23.63	—	—	(2.42)	13.18	4.88
Annual Growth	**(11.4%)**	**—**	**—**	**—**	**(31.8%)**	**16.0%**

Formosa Plastics Corporation

Formosa Plastics Corporation (FPC) is foremost in its industry. Taiwan's top petrochemical company and among the world's largest producers of polyvinyl chloride (PVC), FPC is a member of industrial giant Formosa Plastics Group. The company makes acrylic fiber and yarn, polyethylene, caustic soda, chlorine, calcium carbonate, and acrylic acid. FPC subsidiaries include Formosa Plastics Corporation, U.S.A., which produces PVC in the US and is involved in chemical manufacturing (products like caustic soda). Joint ventures include Formosa Komatsu Silicon (with Komatsu Electronic Metals), a maker of silicon wafers, and Formosa Asahi Spandex with Asahi Chemical Industry.

The Taiwanese government fears the country's industry might become too dependent on its business in China and regulates the issue closely. Despite this fact, Formosa Plastics, along with FPG's other units, have developed a thermal plant in China's Fujian province. The company is planning further Chinese investment, including a PVC plant. Founder and chairman Yung-Ching Wang is one of Taiwan's wealthiest industrialists.

HISTORY

In 1932 Yung-Ching Wang borrowed $200 from his father, a Taiwanese tea merchant, to buy a rice mill near the town of Jiayi. The mill was destroyed by Allied bombs in 1944, but Wang went on to make a fortune in timber and founded Formosa Plastics, a small polyvinyl chloride (PVC) plant, in 1954. He bought the technology from the Japanese, later joking that he didn't even know then what the "P" in PVC stood for.

At first Wang had trouble finding buyers for his PVC resins. In 1958 he set up his own resin processor, Nan Ya Plastics, and later formed Formosa Chemicals & Fibre to make rayon backing for PVC leather (1965). For the next 15 years, the company grew into the Formosa Plastics Group (FPG), an exclusively Taiwanese enterprise.

Between 1980 and 1988 Wang bought 14 US PVC manufacturers, including Imperial Chemical's vinyl chloride monomer plant (1981), Stauffer Chemical's PVC plant (1981), and Manville Corporation's PVC businesses (1983). He started building a Texas PVC plant in 1981 and cut construction costs up to 40% by importing equipment from Taiwan. When the PVC market became saturated in the mid-1980s, Wang diversified, building plants to make semiconductor chemicals.

Wang bought several Texas-based oil and gas properties in 1988, including 218 producing wells, a gas-processing plant, and a pipeline firm. Faced with stricter pollution controls in Taiwan, Wang began building an ethylene plant in Point Comfort, Texas, in 1988.

In 1992 Wang wanted to build an ethylene complex in mainland China, where there were no pollution controls. Taiwan balked at the proposal, suggesting that FPG build at home. Attempting to circumvent a Taiwanese law against direct investment in the mainland, Wang sought Chinese approval through subsidiary Formosa Plastics Corporation, U.S.A. In 1993 Chinese authorities rejected a plan that would require them to finance up to two-thirds of a $7 billion petrochemical complex.

Formosa Plastics bought bankrupt US computer maker Everex Systems in 1993. Meanwhile, the group's focus again turned to mainland China when Nan Ya Plastics made plans in 1994 to build three plants along China's Long River.

The 1995 death of Wang's mother (at age 108) set off a power struggle between family factions. The company won licenses in 1996 to build power plants, which would make FPG Taiwan's first private-sector power supplier and end a 50-year government utility monopoly. That year, in defiance of Taiwan's policy of limiting investment in China, FPG announced it would build a power plant there. Pressure from the Taiwanese government put the project on hold in 1997.

FPG upped its investment in a new Taiwanese petrochemical complex in 1998. It formed ventures with Asahi Chemical to make spandex fiber and with France's Renault to make hybrid (gasoline/electric) cars. Also that year the group admitted to combining mercury-laden waste with cement and sneaking the toxic mixture to Cambodia disguised as 3,000 tons of cement block. FPG apologized after villagers living near the dump became ill.

Undaunted by a history of animosity between the two countries, Formosa Plastics and FPG's other flagship companies in 1999 invested a 60% stake in the production of power plants in the Chinese province of Fujian.

EXECUTIVES

Chairman: Yung-Ching Wang
President: C. T. Lee
CFO: W. H. Hung
EVP, Formosa Plastics Corporation U.S.A.: C.L. Tseng

LOCATIONS

HQ: 201 Tung Hwa North Rd., Taipei, Taiwan
Phone: +886-22-712-2211   **Fax:** +886-22-712-9211
US HQ: 9 Peach Tree Hill Rd.,
    Livingston, NJ 07039-5702
US Phone: 201-992-2090   **US Fax:** 201-992-9627
Web: www.fpc.com.tw

Formosa Plastics has manufacturing operations in Asia and the US.

PRODUCTS/OPERATIONS

Selected Products

Acrylic acid
Acrylic staple fiber
Calcium carbide
Calcium carbonate
Carbon fiber
Esters
Flake caustic soda
Hydrochloric acid
Hydrochlorofluorocarbons
Liquid caustic soda
Petrochemical production
Plastic modifiers
Polyvinyl chloride (PVC) resins
Polypropylene
Vinyl chloride monomer

Selected Affiliates and Subsidiaries

Formosa Asahi Spandex Co., Ltd.
Formosa Daikin Advanced Chemicals Co., Ltd.
Formosa Heavy Industries Corp.
Formosa Komatsu Silicon Corporation
Formosa Petrochemical Corp.
Formosa Plastics Corporation, America (US)
Mailiao Harbor Administration Corp.
Mailiao Power Corp.
Yungchia Chemical Industries Corp.

COMPETITORS

BASF AG	Jilin Chemical
Bayer AG	LG Group
BP	Lyondell Chemical
Dow Chemical	Norsk Hydro
Eastman Chemical	Occidental Petroleum
DuPont	PVC Container
Hercules	PW Eagle
Huntsman International	Sinopec Shanghai
ICC Industries	Petrochemical
ICI	Yizheng Chemical
IBM	

HISTORICAL FINANCIALS

Company Type: Public

Income Statement

FYE: December 31

	REVENUE ($ mil.)	NET INCOME ($ mil.)	NET PROFIT MARGIN	EMPLOYEES
12/02	1,879	—	—	4,471
12/01	1,705	—	—	4,591
12/00	1,566	—	—	4,703
12/99	1,310	—	—	4,577
12/98	1,112	—	—	4,274
12/97	1,472	—	—	4,897
12/96	1,598	—	—	3,891
12/95	1,603	—	—	3,585
12/94	1,523	—	—	3,449
12/93	1,019	—	—	3,345
Annual Growth	7.0%	—	—	3.3%

Revenue History

Exchange: Taiwan

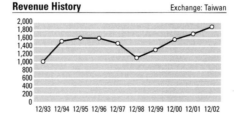

Fortis

Fortis earns the "Muscles from Brussels" moniker for its insurance and banking machismo, not for any bad action flicks. Its insurance arm offers life and non-life insurance, such as health, auto, and fire lines, as well as employee benefits packages. Its products are sold through independent agents and brokers, financial planners, and through the company's Fortis Bank branches. In addition to bancassurance, Fortis Bank offers consumer and commercial banking, asset management, private banking, investment banking, access to financial markets, and other financial services.

The company's insurance operations accounts for almost half of sales.

After 10 years as a joint venture between Fortis (B) and Fortis (NL), the parent companies merged their stock listings into Fortis in 2001. The acquisitive Benelux group has been strengthening its niche operations; the company has bought CORE, provider of employee absence management. Fortis is expanding its employee benefits segment in the US. Cutting costs, Fortis plans to reduce its bank branches in Belgium from about 2,200 to 1,200 and let some 4,000 employees go by 2003.

Taking advantage of China's entry into the World Trade Organization, Fortis is partnering with life insurer China Insurance Group and securities specialist Haitong.

HISTORY

Fortis can trace its roots back to Let op Uw Einde, one of many burial funds set up in the Netherlands in the 19th century. Formed by W. P. Ingenegeren and D. Stolwerk in 1847, the fund allowed impoverished households to prepay funeral expenses and avoid paupers' graves. By 1871 the company had become the country's largest burial fund. More than 10 years later, Let op Uw Einde took advantage of changes in Dutch law to form a life insurance firm, Ultrecht Life, which eventually absorbed the original burial fund.

In the late 19th and early 20th centuries, Ultrecht set up subsidiaries across Europe and became a land developer. It saw investment income shrink during WWI, and the Depression forced it to set aside a reserve that helped it weather WWII. Between the wars, the firm set up holding company N.V. Algemeene Maatschappij tot Exploitatie van Verzekeringsmaatschappijen (AMEV, which became its name in 1968), and afterwards it used its streamlined structure to expand insurance operations primarily at home through purchases in the 1960s and 1970s.

By the late 1970s the Dutch insurance market was saturated, so AMEV focused on expanding in Europe, the US, and Asia. In 1978 it joined with rivals in the UK and West Germany to form the AREA Benefits Network to provide services to multinational corporations in some 40 countries; within 10 years half of AMEV's new business came from this channel. In the 1980s it continued its geographic expansion with such deals as its majority stake in Spain's Bilbao Insurance Group and its purchase of two life insurers and two mutual fund firms from The St. Paul Companies in the US. AMEV, however, was forced to pull out of Australia and New Zealand by poor market conditions and changes in local tax laws. It ended the decade on two high notes:

it gradually bought Dutch savings bank Verenigde Spaarbank Groep (VSB) and joined with Belgian life insurer Compagnies Assurances Générales sur la Vie, les Fonds Doutaux et les Survivances (better known as AG 1824) in a 50-50 joint venture to form Fortis.

Windstorms in Europe took their toll on Fortis' first year results, but it quickly announced plans to expand its presence in Spain; in 1992 the firm joined with Caja de Ahorros y Pensiones de Barcelona (La Caixa) to form a bancassurance joint venture. The next year, however, the company again took a tumble when its Belgian and Dutch home markets soured, but it fought back by diversifying: Fortis bought half of Algemene Spaar en Lijfrente Kas/Caisse Generale d'apargne et de Retraite (ASLK/CGER), the Belgian state-owned bank the government was privatizing. In 1995 its parents, which had taken the names Fortis (NL) and Fortis (B), became listed on the London and Luxembourg exchanges.

In 1996 Fortis moved further into its transition from insurer to financial services provider when it bought merchant banking firm MeesPierson from ABN Amro. Two years later the company bought Belgium's Generale de Banque, merging it with its ASLK/CGER, VSB, and MeesPierson operations under the Fortis Bank brand (although MeesPierson kept its name for private banking services). On the insurance side, it bought American Bankers Insurance in the US, Northern Star in the UK, and the Netherlands' ASR Verzekeringsgroep (making it the top Benelux insurer).

In 2000 Fortis' parents began steps to merge their dual structure. The next year Fortis sold Fortis Financial Group, its US life insurance subsidiary, to Hartford Financial. British insurer Aviva (formerly CGNU) bought the company's Australian general insurance subsidiary. Also in 2001, the company merged insurers ASR and AMEV Nederland to create AMEV Stad Rotterdam Verzekeringsgroep.

EXECUTIVES

Co-Chairman: Maurice Lippens
Co-Chairman: J.R. (Jaap) Glasz
Vice Chairman: Viscount Étienne F. Davignon, age 70
Vice Chairman: Jan J. (Jan) Slechte
CEO and Director; Chairman, Fortis Bank, Fortis Insurance, and Fortis, Inc.: Anton van Rossum, age 57
Deputy CEO; Chairman of the Executive Committee, Fortis Bank: Herman Verwilst, age 55
CFO: Gilbert Mittler, age 53
Managing Director, Insurance Belgium and International: Jozef De Mey, age 59
Managing Director, Insurance Netherlands: Jacques van Ek, age 52
Managing Director, Merchant Banking: Filip Dierckx, age 47
Managing Director, Network Banking: Karel De Boeck, age 53
Managing Director, Private Banking and Asset Management: Joop Feilzer, age 53
President and CEO, Fortis, Inc. (US): J. Kerry Clayton, age 57
General Secretary: Michel van Pée, age 60
Human Resources Director: Michel Deboeck
Auditors: KPMG Accountants N.V.

LOCATIONS

HQ: Rue Royale 20, 1000 Brussels, Belgium
Phone: +32-2-510-52-11   **Fax:** +32-2-510-56-26
US HQ: 1 Chase Manhattan Plaza, New York, NY 10005
US Phone: 212-859-7000   **US Fax:** 212-859-7034
Web: www.fortis.com

Fortis has operations in Asia and the Pacific Rim, Europe, and North America.

2002 Premiums

	% of total
US	39
Netherlands	24
Belgium	21
Luxembourg	2
Rest of the world	14
Total	**100**

PRODUCTS/OPERATIONS

Selected Subsidiaries

American Memorial Life Insurance Company (US)
AMEV Stad Rotterdam Verzekeringsgroep (the Netherlands)
Assurant Group (US)
Bank van De Post (50%)
Banque General du Luxembourg
Belgolaise
DEFAM (the Netherlands)
Dental Health Alliance (US)
Fortis AG
Fortis Assurances (France)
Fortis Australia
Fortis Bank
Fortis Bank (the Netherlands)
Fortis Bank Luxembourg
Fortis Benefits (US)
Fortis Commercial Finance (the Netherlands)
Fortis Family (US)
Fortis Investment Management (the Netherlands)
Fortis Lease
Fortis Lease (the Netherlands)
Fortis Vastgoed (the Netherlands)
Fortis, Inc. (US)
Groeivermogen (the Netherlands)
Krediet aan de Nilverheld
MeesPierson (the Netherlands)
Seguros Bilbao (Spain)
Theodoor Gilissen Bankiers N.V. (the Netherlands)
TOP Lease Belgium N.V.

COMPETITORS

ABN AMRO	Credit Suisse First Boston
AEGON	Deutsche Bank
Allianz	Dexia Group
Almanij	Eureko
AMP Limited	Goldman Sachs
Generali	ING
AGF	Merrill Lynch
AXA	New York Life
Bear Stearns	Nippon Life Insurance
Citigroup Global Markets	Rabobank
Citigroup	

HISTORICAL FINANCIALS

Company Type: Public

Income Statement

FYE: December 31

	ASSETS ($ mil.)	NET INCOME ($ mil.)	INCOME AS % OF ASSETS	EMPLOYEES
12/02	509,131	557	0.1%	69,000
12/01	427,815	2,302	0.5%	66,210
12/00	412,499	2,606	0.6%	62,881
12/99	408,952	2,332	0.6%	61,109
12/98	394,336	2,084	0.5%	59,481
12/97	166,395	1,002	0.6%	35,229
12/96	177,311	917	0.5%	34,403
12/95	160,064	805	0.5%	30,388
12/94	126,887	673	0.5%	30,538
12/93	108,585	530	0.5%	21,683
Annual Growth	18.7%	0.6%	—	13.7%

2002 Year-End Financials

Equity as % of assets: 2.7%
Return on assets: 0.1%
Return on equity: 4.3%
Long-term debt ($ mil.): 65,185
Sales ($ mil.): 48,332

Net Income History   Euronext Brussels: FOR

3,000
2,500
2,000
1,500
1,000
500
0
12/93 12/94 12/95 12/96 12/97 12/98 12/99 12/00 12/01 12/02

Foster's Group

Foster's Group may boast that "Foster's is Australian for beer," but it's wine that now brings in the greater share of revenues. Foster's distributes its beers and wines in about 150 countries. Its Carlton and United Breweries (CUB) is Australia's #1 brewer, producing beers such as Foster's Lager and Victoria Bitter. Its Beringer Blass Wine Estates division makes the Mildara Blass wine brands (Wolf Blass, Yellowglen, Rothbury). Beringer Blass also produces the Beringer, Stag's Leap, Meridian, and other wine brands.

In addition to beer, Foster's sells pre-mixed cocktails, bourbon, cider, scotch, and vodka.

In the US, where Foster's Lager is the #7 import, the company sells beer through its 50%-owned Foster's USA unit.

HISTORY

Upon finding that Australia's only beers were English-styled ales served at room temperature, American emigrants W. M. and R. R. Foster built a lager brewery near Melbourne in 1888 and gave customers ice to chill their Foster's Lager. The brothers began exporting in 1901 when Australians left to serve in the Boer War in South Africa. Carlton and United Breweries Proprietary (CUB) was formed in 1907 when the brothers merged their operations with five other breweries, including Victoria and Carlton.

Over the years CUB acquired stakes in trading company Elder Smith Goldsbrough Mort and Henry Jones (IXL), a diversified food company owned by John Elliott. Faced with a takeover, in 1981 Elder Smith was merged into Henry Jones, forming Elders IXL. CUB became that firm's largest stockholder, with 49%, in 1983. Elders bought the rest of CUB in 1984.

Elders expanded internationally with it purchases of UK's Courage Breweries (1986) and Canada's Carling O'Keefe Breweries (1987). In 1989 Carling O'Keefe and Molson formed a joint venture, Molson Breweries. To fight possible takeover attempts, that year Harlin Holdings (led by Elliott) offered to buy a 17% stake of Elders from two companies, but regulators forced the firm to extend its offer to all shareholders. As a result, Harlin ended up with more than 55% of Elders. The deal saddled Elders with debt, and in 1990 the company began selling its non-brewing assets. Also that year Elliott resigned as chairman and CEO, and Elders changed its name to Foster's Brewing Group.

Foster's purchased the brewing interests of Grand Metropolitan (now Diageo) in 1991. Elliott's investment firm went bankrupt in 1992 and Australian conglomerate Broken Hill Proprietary (BHP), which also owned 19% of Elders, assumed control of its shares. (BHP sold its stake in 1997.) Also in 1992 Molson Breweries chief Ted Kunkel became CEO. He wrote off over $2 billion in non-brewing assets that were still on the books and sold 10% of the brewer's interest in Molson.

In 1995 Foster's sold its UK brewing operations to Scottish & Newcastle. The next year it entered the wine business, buying Mildara Blass and Rothbury Wines, and in 1997 it entered the Australian wine club business with the purchase of Cellarmaster Wines. The next year Foster's bought wine clubs Bourse du Vin International (the Netherlands) and 51% of Germany's Heinrich Maximilian Pallhuber (later acquiring the rest).

Also in 1998 Foster's sold its Canadian brewing interests — 50% of Molson Breweries and 25% of Coors Canada — to The Molson Companies (but retained a 25% interest in Molson USA). In July 1998 Foster's acquired the Austotel Trust hotel chain from Brierly Investments, making it the largest operator of hotels in Australia.

Subsidiary Mildara Blass acquired the US direct wine marketer Windsor Vineyards in 2000; also subsidiary Cellarmaster Wines bought a 25% interest in online wine retailer Wine Planet (increased in mid-2001 to about 90%). Foster's bought Beringer Wine Estates, a leading California winery, for about $1.2 billion. Wine profits for Foster's doubled in the year following the company's 2000 purchase of Beringer.

In 2001 Foster's renamed its wine division Beringer Blass Wine Estates, merging the Beringer and Mildara Blass wine businesses. That year the company dropped "Brewing" from its official name, becoming Foster's Group Limited. In 2002 Beringer Blass Wine Estates agreed to buy the Carmenet brand from Napa-based Chalone Wine Group. In 2002 sales of wine surpassed those of the company's beers for the first time.

Foster's spun off its Australian Leisure and Hospitality group in November 2003, which included pubs, liquor shops, and interests in hotels and real estate development. That division became a separate company known as the Australian Leisure & Hospitality Group Ltd.

EXECUTIVES

Chairman: Frank J. Swan, age 62, $126,787 pay
President, CEO, and Board Member:
 Edward T. (Ted) Kunkel, age 60, $848,051 pay
CFO: Peter F. Scott, age 52, $485,163 pay
SVP, Commercial Affairs: Peter A. Bobeff, $441,696 pay
SVP, Corporate Affairs: Graeme Willersdorf
SVP, Global Strategy and Business Development:
 Neville Fielke
SVP, Human Resources: Ben Lawrence
VP, Investor Relations: Robert Porter
Managing Director, Beringer Blass Wine Estates:
 Walter Klenz, $533,747 pay
Managing Director, Carlton and United Breweries:
 Trevor O'Hoy, $453,226 pay
Managing Director, Foster's Brewing International:
 Richard W. Scully, $674,302 pay
Managing Director, Lensworth Group: John O'Grady,
 $329,379 pay
Auditors: PricewaterhouseCoopers

LOCATIONS

HQ: Foster's Group Limited
 77 Southbank Blvd., Southbank,
 Victoria 3006, Australia
Phone: +61-3-9633-2000   **Fax:** +61-3-9633-2002
US HQ: 11921 Freedom Dr., Ste. 550, Reston, VA 20190
US Phone: 703-904-4321   **US Fax:** 703-904-4336
Web: www.fostersgroup.com

Foster's Brewing Group distributes beer in more than 150 countries from breweries in Australia, Canada, China, France, Germany, India, Ireland, Portugal, the UK, and Vietnam. It has wineries in Australia, Chile, Italy, New Zealand, and the US.

2003 Sales

	% of total
Australia	57
Americas	35
Europe	5
Asia/Pacific	3
Total	**100**

PRODUCTS/OPERATIONS

2003 Sales

	% of total
Wine	39
Beer	
Australia	35
International	4
Leisure & hospitality	18
Property	4
Total	**100**

Selected Products and Brands

Beer
Carlton (Cold Filtered Bitter, D-Ale, Diamond Draft, Draught, Lager, Light, Light Bitter, Midstrength, Sterling)
Carlton and United Premium Dry
Cascade (Bitter, Diet, Draught, Four Seasons, Lager, Light Bitter, Pale Ale, Premium, Premium Light, Stout, Tiger Head)
Crown Lager
Foster's (Extra Lager, Ice, Lager, Light, LightIce, Special Bitter)
Matilda Bay (Bitter, Draught, Pilsner, Premium)
Melbourne Bitter
Powers (Bitter, Gold, Ice, Light)
Redback (Hefeweitzen, Light, Original)
Reschs (Dinner Ale, Draught, Pilsner, Real Bitter, Smooth Black Ale)
sub zero (non-beer alcoholic soda)
Victoria Bitter

Imported Beer

Asahi	Kronenbourg — 1664
Corona Extra	Leffe (Blonde, Radieus,
Guinness	Vieille Cuvee)
Harp Lager	Miller Genuine Draft
Heineken Lager	Moosehead
Hoegaarden (Forbidden	Negra Modelo
Fruit, White)	Shanghai
Kilkenny Ale	Stella Artois

Wines

Australian	Chilean
Wolf Blass	Dallas-Conte, Vina
Yellowglen	Tarapaca
Jamiesons Run	Italian
Saltram	Catello di Gabbiano
Greg Norman Estates	New Zealand
The Rothbury Estate	Matua Valley
California	
Beringer	
Chateau St. Jean	
Chateau Sourverain	
Etude	
Meridian Vineyards	
Stags' Leap	
St. Clement	

Spirits
Black Douglas
Cougar
Karloff

COMPETITORS

Accor	Interbrew
Adolph Coors	Kendall-Jackson
Allied Domecq	Kirin
Anheuser-Busch	Lion Nathan
Asahi Breweries	Marriott International
Asia Pacific Breweries	Pabst
Boston Beer	Peerless Importers
Carlsberg	Ravenswood Winery
Diageo	Robert Mondavi
Gallo	San Miguel
FEMSA	Scottish & Newcastle
Gambrinus	Starwood Hotels & Resorts
Geerlings & Wade	Terlato Wine
Heineken	Tsingtao

HISTORICAL FINANCIALS

Company Type: Public

Income Statement

FYE: June 30

	REVENUE ($ mil.)	NET INCOME ($ mil.)	NET PROFIT MARGIN	EMPLOYEES
6/03	3,155	309	9.8%	13,400
6/02	2,576	319	12.4%	12,950
6/01	2,130	239	11.2%	13,700
6/00	2,035	255	12.6%	14,000
6/99	2,066	255	12.3%	12,718
6/98	3,060	253	8.3%	8,207
6/97	1,960	187	9.5%	10,379
6/96	1,850	231	12.5%	10,436
6/95	3,106	204	6.6%	14,024
6/94	3,052	205	6.7%	—
Annual Growth	**0.4%**	**4.6%**	**—**	**(0.6%)**

2003 Year-End Financials

Debt ratio: 54.5%   Current ratio: 1.32
Return on equity: 11.6%   Long-term debt ($ mil.): 1,612
Cash ($ mil.): 238

Net Income History

Pink Sheets: FBRWY

France Telecom

Adieu, monopole; bonjour, competition. Former monopoly France Telecom provides fixed-line and wireless voice, data, and Internet services, as well as cable TV and corporate and wholesale telecom services. The company's 99% owned Orange mobile phone unit (it plans to buy the rest) has 19 million subscribers in France and another 27 million in other European countries with nearly 50 million subscribers worldwide (more than the 49.5 million fixed-line customers). France Telecom also owns 54% of data network operator Equant, as well as 73% of Groupe Wanadoo, a European directory publisher and ISP. The French government, which is mandated by law to be France Telecom's majority owner, owns 56.5% of the company.

France Telecom has brought together its mobile phone operations under the umbrella of its

Orange unit, which is France's #1 mobile phone company (and Orange is #2 behind Vodafone in the UK market). The wireless subsidiary also has minority stakes in wireless phone operators throughout Europe and in the Middle East. France Telecom raised about 10 billion in 2001 when it sold a minority stake in Orange to the public but it has announced plans to buy back the 14% it does not own.

The company also has gained control of data network operator Equant in a two-part deal in which Equant acquired France Telecom's Global One unit and France Telecom acquired airline cooperative SITA's stake in Equant (also in 2001).

To reduce debt, France Telecom sold its Dutch cable unit, Casema, to a group led by US private equity firms Providence Equity Partners and Carlyle Group in a deal valued at 665 million. An earlier agreement for the sale of Casema to Liberty Media was dropped over regulatory concerns. France Telecom also has sold its TDF broadcast unit to a new business controlled by investment funds, retaining a 36% stake in the new entity. It also agreed to sell its 27% stake in Italian competitive telecom group Wind (held through Orange), as well as most of its holdings in Eutelsat and other noncore holdings.

As the company struggled to deal with its burdensome debt, including its stake in troubled MobilCom, in 2002 CEO Michel Bon resigned. Turnaround specialist Thierry Breton, who is credited with salvaging THOMSON multimedia, was named Bon's successor. The company then received a 9 billion loan from the French government and Breton's new management team sought to reduce its nearly 70 billion debt. It announced plans to reduce the number of workers by 22,000, or about 16% of the company's workforce, over three years, and sold its 5.4% stake in US mobile operator Sprint PCS in a deal valued at $330 million.

To refocus its attentions on operations in France and the UK, France Telecom agreed to sell its stakes held in Telecom Argentina (held through Nortel Inversora) and CTE Salvador in separate deals valued at $342 million.

HISTORY

Shortly before he abdicated, King Louis Philippe laid the groundwork for France's state-owned telegraphic service. Established in 1851, the operation became part of the French Post Office in the 1870s, about the time Alexander Graham Bell invented the telephone. The French government licensed three private companies to provide telegraph service, and during the 1880s they merged into the Société Générale de Téléphones (SGT). In 1883 the country's first exchange was initiated in Rheims. Four years later an international circuit was installed connecting Paris and Brussels. The government nationalized SGT in 1889.

By the turn of the century France had more than 60,000 phone lines, and in 1924 a standardized telephone was introduced. Long-distance service improved with underground cabling, and phone exchanges in Paris and other leading cities became automated during the 1930s.

WWII proved a major setback to the French government's telephone operations, Direction Générale des Télécommunications (DGT), because a large part of its equipment was destroyed or damaged. For the next two decades France lagged behind other nations in telephony infrastructure development. An exception to this technological stagnation was Centre National

d'Etudes des Télécommunications (CNET), the research laboratory formed in 1944 that eventually became France Telecom's research arm.

In 1962 DGT was a key player in the first intercontinental television broadcast, between the US and France, via a Telstar satellite. The company began to catch up with its peers when it developed a digital phone system in the mid-1970s. In 1974 CNET was instrumental in the launch of France's first experimental communications satellite. In another technological advance, DGT began replacing its paper directories with the innovative Minitel online terminals in 1980.

The French government created France Telecom in 1988. In 1993 France Telecom and Deutsche Telekom (DT) teamed up to form the Global One international telecommunications venture, and Sprint joined the next year. Global One was formally launched in 1996. Also that year France Telecom began providing Internet access, though Minitel still reigned as the country's top online service.

In 1997 the government sold about 20% of France Telecom to the public. With Europe's state telephone monopolies ending in 1998, France Telecom reorganized and brought prices in line with those of its competitors.

Tightening their alliance, DT and France Telecom in 1998 announced plans to construct a fiber-optic network linking 16 European countries. But the alliance came apart the next year when France Telecom sued DT over the German company's plan (since abandoned) to merge with Telecom Italia. The lawsuit was settled in 2000.

The next year France Telecom paid $4.3 billion to DT and Sprint to take full ownership of Global One, and it agreed to pay $3.6 billion for a 29% stake in Germany's MobilCom. Later in 2000 France Telecom snatched up UK mobile phone operator Orange in a $37.5 billion cash and stock deal after Vodafone was forced to divest the company before merging with Mannesmann.

France Telecom also invested $4.5 billion in UK cable operator NTL and sold its stake in Mexican telecom giant Telmex. In 2001 the company sold its 49.9% stake in Noos, France's #1 cable TV operator, and it made plans to sell its stake in Sprint, which it had acquired when Global One was formed. The next year it sold its nearly 11% stake in Greek mobile carrier Vodafone-Panafon to Vodafone Group for €311 million.

EXECUTIVES

Chairman and CEO: Thierry Breton, age 48
SEVP, Financial Balancing and Value Added Program: Frank E. Dangeard, age 45
SEVP, Large Business Division: Barbara Dalibard
SEVP, Fixed-Line Division and Distribution Division: Jean-Yves Gouiffés, age 55
SEVP, Network and Operators Division: Jean-Philippe Vanot, age 51
SEVP, Information Systems, and SEVP, International Division: Jean-Paul Cottet, age 49
SEVP; Chairman and CEO, Orange SA: Solomon D. Trujillo, age 51
SEVP; CEO, Groupe Wanadoo SA: Olivier Sichel, age 35
SEVP and CFO: Michel Combes, age 40
EVP, Human Resources: Bernard Bresson, age 54
SEVP, Animation and Management Networks Evaluation Group: Michel Davancens, age 56
SEVP, Secrétarit Général: Jacques Champeaux, age 55
SEVP, Technology and Innovation Group: Jean-Jacques Damlamian, age 61
SEVP, Corporate Communication: Marc Meyer, age 43
SEVP, Purchasing and Performance Improvement Group: Louis-Pierre Wenes, age 53
VP, Investor Relations: Sylvie Chevallier
Auditors: Ernst & Young Audit; RSM Salustro Reydel

LOCATIONS

HQ: France Telecom SA 6, Place d'Alleray, 75505 Paris, France
Phone: +33-1-44-44-22-22   **Fax:** +33-1-44-44-95-95
US HQ: 1270 Avenue of the Americas, 28th Fl., New York, NY 10020
US Phone: 212-332-2100   **US Fax:** 212-245-8605
Web: www.francetelecom.fr

France Telecom has investments and operations in more than 75 countries worldwide.

2002 Sales

	$ mil.	% of total
France	34,713	71
Other countries	14,179	29
Total	**48,892**	**100**

PRODUCTS/OPERATIONS

2002 Sales

	$ mil.	% of total
Fixed-line services		
Domestic	19,557	40
International	9,778	20
Orange	17,601	36
Wanadoo	1,956	4
Total	**48,892**	**100**

Selected Services

Calling cards
Data transmission (Equant)
Directories
Equipment sales and rentals
International calling
Internet access (Wanadoo)
Leased lines
Local telephone service
Long-distance
Mobile phone service (Orange)
Pay phones
Radiopaging

COMPETITORS

AT&T	Portugal Telecom
Belgacom	KPN
Bertelsmann	Swisscom
Bouygues	TDC
BT	Telecom Italia
Cable & Wireless	Telefónica
CANAL+	Telenor
Carrier1 International	TeliaSonera
COLT Telecom	UGC Europe
Deutsche Telekom	Vodafone
Global Crossing	WorldCom
Cegetel	

HISTORICAL FINANCIALS

Company Type: Public

Income Statement

FYE: December 31

	REVENUE ($ mil.)	NET INCOME ($ mil.)	NET PROFIT MARGIN	EMPLOYEES
12/02	48,892	(21,742)	—	243,573
12/01	38,349	(7,380)	—	206,000
12/00	31,714	3,447	10.9%	188,866
12/99	27,424	2,788	10.2%	174,262
12/98	28,938	2,700	9.3%	165,000
12/97	26,039	2,469	9.5%	159,335
12/96	29,144	406	1.4%	165,200
12/95	30,112	1,873	6.2%	167,660
12/94	26,716	1,857	7.0%	167,882
12/93	21,449	811	3.8%	154,548
Annual Growth	**9.6%**	**—**	**—**	**5.2%**

2002 Year-End Financials

Debt ratio: —
Return on equity: —
Cash ($ mil.): 2,956
Current ratio: 0.31
Long-term debt ($ mil.): 49,172

No. of shares (mil.): 1,190
Dividends
Yield: 5.1%
Payout: —
Market value ($ mil.): 21,149

Stock History

NYSE: FTE

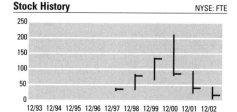

	STOCK PRICE ($)	P/E		PER SHARE ($)		
	FY Close	High/Low		Earnings	Dividends	Book Value
12/02	17.77	—	—	(20.04)	0.91	(8.77)
12/01	39.99	—	—	(6.69)	0.88	16.29
12/00	85.69	66	25	3.18	0.95	27.06
12/99	133.50	50	25	2.68	0.88	18.58
12/98	78.94	31	13	2.69	1.10	19.47
12/97	36.00	15	13	2.47	0.00	15.57
Annual Growth	(13.2%)	—	—	—	—	—

Fuji Photo Film

Fuji Photo Film Co. enjoys accentuating the negatives. As Japan's #1 photographic film and paper producer, Tokyo-based Fuji leads the film market on its home turf; it has hammered away at rival Eastman Kodak's lead (#1 US), and the two are now virtually tied in the global market. However, Fuji understands the changes wrought by digital technology. Today, film-related sales make up just 10% of total sales. The company makes a range of digital imaging products, floppy disks, medical imaging products, office automation systems, and industrial films and chemicals. Fuji has operations in Europe, Australia, Asia, and North and South America, although most of its sales come from Japan.

Like its rival Kodak, Fuji is choosing to invest more in digital technologies and less in traditional film. To meet increasing demand from consumers for digital images, Fuji has adopted what it calls hybrid imaging to combine its expertise in imaging with the latest electronics, such as flat-panel displays and camera-equipped cell phones. In fact, the company has designed lenses for use in cell phones.

Through a joint venture with Xerox, the company generates nearly 40% of its revenues from sales of printers and office copiers.

HISTORY

Mokichi Morita, president of Japan's leading celluloid maker (Dainippon Celluloid Company, founded 1919), decided to start making motion picture film in the early 1930s. Movies were becoming popular in Japan, but there was no domestic film supplier. Working with a grant from the government, Dainippon Celluloid established Fuji Photo Film Co., an independent company, in 1934 in Minami Ashigara Village, near Mount Fuji.

At first the company had trouble gaining acceptance in Japan as a quality film producer. However, German emulsion specialist Dr. Emill Mauerhoff helped Fuji overcome its product deficiencies, producing black-and-white photographic film (1936) and the first Japanese-made color film (1948). In the meantime Fuji added 35mm photographic film, 16mm motion picture film, and X-ray film to its product line. By the early 1940s the company was operating four factories and a research laboratory in Japan. Its first overseas office, opened in Brazil in 1955, was followed by offices in the US (1958) and Europe (1964).

Fuji continued to expand its product line, adding magnetic tape in 1960. Two years later it formed Fuji Xerox, a Japanese joint venture with Xerox, to sell copiers in Japan and the Pacific Rim. It operated as a private-label film supplier in the US and did not market its products under its own brand name until 1972.

International marketing VP Minoru Ohnishi became Fuji's youngest president in 1980 at age 55. To decrease dependence on Japanese film sales, he built sales in the US (agreeing to sponsor the 1984 Los Angeles Olympics, after Eastman Kodak refused to, was key) and pumped money into the production of videotapes, floppy disks, and medical diagnostic equipment. Fuji introduced Fujicolor Quicksnap, the world's first 35mm disposable camera, in 1986. It began establishing manufacturing operations in the US two years later.

The company created the FUJIFILM Microdevices subsidiary to produce image-processing semiconductors in 1990. In 1992 Fuji scientists completed a crude artificial "eye" (a possible forerunner of more efficient eyes for robots). The following year it launched the Pictrostat instant print system, which produces color prints in one minute from photos, slides, and objects.

Fuji was forced to temporarily raise US prices in 1994 after Kodak accused it of illegally dumping its photographic paper exported to the US. But Fuji skirted the problem in 1995 by making the paper at its US plant. That year Kodak asked for economic sanctions against Fuji and the Japanese government, saying that the government encouraged Fuji to use exclusive contracts to control film distribution, thus keeping Kodak from selling film in many stores. (The case was rejected by the World Trade Organization in 1997.)

The firm unveiled the Advanced Photo System (co-developed with Kodak and three other companies) in 1996, combining conventional photography with digital-image processing and printing technology. Also that year Fuji bought six off-site wholesale photofinishing plants from Wal-Mart (the largest US provider of photofinishing services) and won contracts to provide supplies to all of Wal-Mart's in-store one-hour photo labs.

In 1997 it chopped film prices in the US and began making film at its US plant. In 1999 Fuji introduced a high-quality image sensor for digital cameras (Super CCD) and Instax, an instant picture camera.

Fuji and Sony launched HiFD, a floppy disk with 140 times the storage capacity of traditional disks, in early 2000. Fuji later announced plans to develop more efficient, low-cost ink jet printers through an alliance with Xerox and Sharp Corp. In March 2001 Fuji acquired half of Xerox's 50% stake in the companies' Fuji Xerox joint venture.

EXECUTIVES

Chairman: Minoru Ohnishi
President and CEO: Shigetaka Komori
SEVP and Director: Yasuo Tanaka
EVP: Akikazu Mikawa
EVP: Kotaro Aso
EVP: Nobuyuki Hayashi
EVP: Takashi Matsushima
SVP: Goro Uehara
SVP: Hidenobu Fukunaga
SVP: Hirokuni Watanabe
SVP: Hisatoyo Kato
SVP: Keigo Shioya
SVP: Shigenori Moriuchi
SVP: Shigenori Moriuchi
SVP: Yoshiharu Ohgaki
SVP: Yousuke Uchida
President, Fuji Photo Film U.S.A.:
Yasuo (George) Tanaka
CFO and Treasurer, Fuji Photo Film U.S.A.:
Noboru Tanaka
VP Human Resources, Fuji Photo Film U.S.A.:
Joseph Convery
Auditors: Ernst & Young

LOCATIONS

HQ: Fuji Shashin Film Kabushiki Kaisha
(Fuji Photo Film Co., Ltd.)
26-30, Nishiazabu 2-chome, Minato-ku,
Tokyo 106-8620, Japan
Phone: +81-3-3406-2111   **Fax:** +81-3-3406-2173
US HQ: 555 Taxter Rd., Elmsford, NY 10523
US Phone: 914-789-8100   **US Fax:** 914-789-8295
Web: www.fujifilm.co.jp

Fuji Photo Film Co. has operations in Asia, Australia, Europe, and North and South America.

2003 Sales

	% of total
Japan	53
Americas	22
Europe	13
Asia & other regions	12
Total	**100**

PRODUCTS/OPERATIONS

2003 Sales

	% of total
Document solutions (printers, etc.)	38
Imaging solutions (cameras, photo labs, etc.)	33
Information solutions (data storage, graphics etc.)	29
Total	**100**

Selected Products

Information Solutions
Data storage media
  CD-Rs
  Data storage tapes
  Floppy disks
  Magnetic disks
  Zip disks
Graphic systems
  Chemicals
  Electronic imaging equipment
  Films
  Pre-sensitized plates
LCD materials
  Cellulose triacetate films
  Photosensitive color transfer films
  Wide View films
Medical imaging products
  Computed radiography systems
  DRI-CHEM analytical systems
  Endoscopes
  Medical X-ray imaging products
Miscellaneous industrial materials and equipment
  Bio-imaging analyzers
  Industrial chemicals
  Industrial X-ray imaging products
  Lenses and optical equipment

Office automation systems
  Carbonless copying papers
  Electronic filing systems
  Heat-sensitive papers
  Microfilming systems
Imaging Solutions
Electronic imaging systems
  Digital cameras
  Image scanners
  Photo players
  Photo-video imagers
General-use batteries
Magnetic products
  Audio tapes
  Professional videocassettes
  Videocassettes
Motion picture films
Optical products
  Compact cameras
  Instant cameras
  Professional cameras
Photographic films
  Amateur
  Instant
  One-time
  Professional

Document Solutions
Digital-imaging services
Digital color printers
Digital photo printers
Photographic papers, equipment, and chemicals
Processing and printing services

COMPETITORS

Agfa	Nikon Corporation
Canon	Olympus
Concord Camera	Pentax
Datapulse Technology	Philips Electronics
Eastman Kodak	PhotoWorks
EFI	Polaroid
GenTek	Ricoh
Hewlett-Packard	Scitex
Imation	Sharp
Iomega	Sony
Jazz Photo	TDK
Konica Minolta	Toshiba
Kyocera	Veutron
Matsushita	Xerox
Mitsubishi Paper Mills	

HISTORICAL FINANCIALS

Company Type: Public

Income Statement

FYE: March 31

	REVENUE ($ mil.)	NET INCOME ($ mil.)	NET PROFIT MARGIN	EMPLOYEES
3/03	20,881	405	1.9%	72,633
3/02	18,054	612	3.4%	72,569
3/01	11,476	938	8.2%	70,722
3/00	13,658	827	6.1%	37,151
3/99	11,883	591	5.0%	37,551
3/98	10,440	673	6.4%	36,580
3/97	10,098	688	6.8%	33,154
3/96	10,119	680	6.7%	29,903
3/95*	5,403	315	5.8%	27,565
10/94	11,009	658	6.0%	26,555
Annual Growth	7.4%	(5.3%)	—	11.8%

*Fiscal year change

2003 Year-End Financials

Debt ratio: 7.4%
Return on equity: 3.0%
Cash ($ mil.): 3,418
Current ratio: 2.01
Long-term debt ($ mil.): 1,037
No. of shares (mil.): 513
Dividends
  Yield: 0.7%
  Payout: 25.3%
Market value ($ mil.): 15,563

Stock History NASDAQ (SC): FUJIY

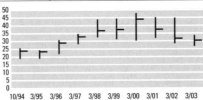

	STOCK PRICE ($) FY Close	P/E High/Low		PER SHARE ($) Earnings	Dividends	Book Value
3/03	30.32	42	34	0.79	0.20	27.28
3/02	31.60	37	24	1.19	0.19	24.81
3/01	37.56	24	18	1.83	0.21	25.16
3/00	44.00	30	19	1.61	0.19	28.45
3/99	37.38	38	27	1.15	0.08	23.33
3/98	36.75	33	25	1.31	0.09	21.06
3/97	32.75	26	21	1.34	0.25	21.08
3/96	28.88	25	18	1.23	0.07	11.35
3/95*	23.38	41	33	0.59	0.07	13.25
10/94	23.81	20	15	1.28	0.14	11.59
Annual Growth	2.7%	—	—	(5.2%)	4.0%	10.0%

*Fiscal year change

Fujitsu Limited

Don't judge Fujitsu Limited by its name — with operations worldwide and products ranging from air conditioners to telephony, its reach seems almost limitless. Its computer products include PCs (it competes with NEC for #1 in Japan), servers, peripherals, and software. The company's other lines include telecommunications network equipment, consumer electronics such as televisions and car audio components, semiconductors, and information technology services (consulting, systems integration, and support). Fujitsu also owns Japan's top Internet services provider, Nifty.

Computers and information technology (IT) services account for about three-quarters of Fujitsu's sales. Key IT subsidiaries include Fujitsu IT Holdings (formerly Amdahl) and Fujitsu Services (formerly International Computers Limited, ICL), a leading UK-based firm.

Fujitsu has targeted flash memory for devices such as cell phones and digital cameras and system-on-a-chip (SOC) circuits as growth areas; Fujitsu has formed a joint venture with AMD that manufactures flash memory (Fujitsu AMD Semiconductor), and an alliance with rival Toshiba will focus on SOC operations.

Fujitsu has also partnered with top tech companies for growth in other areas. Fujitsu and Germany's Siemens have combined most of their European computer operations (Fujitsu Siemens Computers). A company formed with Hitachi (Fujitsu Hitachi Plasma Display) aims to commercialize plasma display panels for televisions.

HISTORY

Siemens and Furukawa Electric created Fuji Electric in 1923 to produce electrical equipment. Fuji spun off Fujitsu, its communications division, in 1935. Originally a maker of telephone equipment, Fujitsu produced antiaircraft

---

weapons during WWII. After the war it became one of four major suppliers to state-owned monopoly Nippon Telegraph and Telephone (NTT) and continued to benefit from Japan's rapid economic recovery in the 1950s and 1960s.

With encouragement from Japan's Ministry of International Trade and Industry (MITI), Fujitsu developed the country's first commercial computer in 1954. MITI erected trade barriers to protect Japan's new computer industry and in the early 1960s sponsored the production of mainframe computers, directing Fujitsu to develop the central processing unit. The company expanded into semiconductor production and factory automation in the late 1960s. Its factory automation business was spun off as Fujitsu Fanuc in 1972.

Fujitsu gained badly needed technology when it bought 30% of IBM-plug-compatible manufacturer Amdahl in 1972. By 1979 Fujitsu had passed IBM to become Japan's #1 computer manufacturer. In Europe, Fujitsu entered into computer marketing ventures with Siemens (1978) and UK mainframe maker ICL (1981). In the US it teamed with TRW to sell point-of-sale systems (1980), assuming full control of the operation in 1983. Fujitsu released its first supercomputer in 1982.

Fujitsu bought 80% of ICL (from the UK's Standard Telephones & Cables) in 1990 for $1.3 billion. In 1993 it formed a joint venture with Advanced Micro Devices to make flash memory products.

The company doubled its share of Japan's PC market in 1995 to more than 18% and the next year expanded its PC business globally. In 1997 Fujitsu paid about $878 million for the 58% of Amdahl it didn't already own. The next year it bought the 10% of ICL it didn't own. Fujitsu's 1998 earnings suffered from a slump in the semiconductor market, Amdahl-related expenses, and a weak Asian economy.

Also in 1998 Naoyuki Akikusa, son of a former NTT president, became head of Fujitsu. He began trimming some operations while ramping up the company's Internet activities. Fujitsu in 1999 became full owner of online services provider Nifty Serve, making it Japan's largest Internet service provider. It merged Nifty with the operations of another ISP called InfoWeb. Also that year Siemens and Fujitsu combined their European computer operations in a 50-50 joint venture (Fujitsu-Siemens Computers) as one part of a larger global alliance. A restructuring of Fujitsu's semiconductor operations caused losses for 1999.

Akikusa's reorganization continued in 2000. Fujitsu overhauled its server business (subsidiary Amdahl ceased production of IBM-compatible mainframes) and accelerated production of flash memory. Responding to a global slump in its markets, in 2001 Fujitsu announced that it would cut more than 16,000 jobs — about 10% of its workforce — to control costs. Soon after it announced it would cut an additional 4,500 jobs.

In 2002 Fujitsu moved to outsource its semiconductor test and assembly operations when it agreed to sell a two-thirds stake in Kyushu Fujitsu Electronics to Amkor Technology; the deal included plans for Amkor to buy out Fujitsu's remaining stake after three years.

EXECUTIVES

Chairman: Naoyuki Akikusa
President: Hiroaki Kurokawa
EVP: Akira Takashima
EVP: Masamichi Ogura
EVP; President, Platforms Business Group:
  Junji Maeyama

**EVP; President, Software and Services Business
  Group:** Hiroya Madarame
SVP; President, Electronic Devices Business Group:
  Toshihiko Ono
EVP; President, Sales Group: Kuniaki Suzuki
Auditors: Shin Nihon & Co.

LOCATIONS

HQ: Shiodome City Center, 1-5-2,
  Higashi-Shimbashi, Minato-ku,
  Tokyo 105-7123, Japan
Phone: +81-3-6252-2175   **Fax:** +81-3-6252-2783
US HQ: 3055 Orchard Dr., San Jose, CA 95134-2022
US Phone: 408-432-1300   **US Fax:** 408-432-1318
Web: www.fujitsu.com

Fujitsu Limited has offices in more than 60 countries.

2003 Sales

	% of total
Japan	75
Europe	11
The Americas	5
Other regions	9
Total	**100**

PRODUCTS/OPERATIONS

2003 Sales

	% of total
Software & services	41
Platforms	36
Electronic devices	13
Financing	3
Other	7
Total	**100**

Selected Products

Information Technology and Computers
ATMs
Electronic components and input devices
Mainframes
PCs
Point-of-sale systems
Servers
Supercomputers
Workstations

Peripherals
Hard disk drives
Magneto-optical disk drives
Printers
Scanners
Storage systems

Semiconductor
ASICs
Compound semiconductors
Linear ICs
Logic devices
Memory

Software
Application server
Database
ERP systems
Financial systems
Groupware
Internet/intranet
System/network management
Translation

Specialty Products
Air conditioners
Car audio
LCD projectors
Plasma screen televisions

Telecommunications
IP telephony
Mobile and wireless systems
Optical networking
PBX systems
Routers
Submarine networks
Switches

COMPETITORS

Alcatel	Nokia
Canon	Nortel Networks
Cisco Systems	Oki Electric
Dell	Oracle
EDS	Philips Electronics
Ericsson	Ricoh
Fuji Photo	Samsung Electronics
Hewlett-Packard	SANYO
Hitachi	Seagate Technology
Infineon Technologies	Seiko Epson
Intel	Sharp
IBM	Siemens
Lucent	Sony
Matsushita	STMicroelectronics
Micron Technology	Sun Microsystems
Microsoft	Texas Instruments
Mitsubishi Electric	Toshiba
Motorola	Unisys
NEC	

HISTORICAL FINANCIALS

Company Type: Public

Income Statement

FYE: March 31

	REVENUE ($ mil.)	NET INCOME ($ mil.)	NET PROFIT MARGIN	EMPLOYEES
3/03	38,529	(1,019)	—	157,044
3/02	37,748	(2,884)	—	170,111
3/01	43,415	68	0.2%	187,399
3/00	49,808	405	0.8%	188,053
3/99	44,018	(115)	—	188,000
3/98	37,464	42	0.1%	180,000
3/97	36,379	373	1.0%	167,000
3/96	35,075	588	1.7%	164,800
3/95	37,640	520	1.4%	164,364
3/94	30,553	(367)	—	163,990
Annual Growth	**2.6%**	**—**	**—**	**(0.5%)**

2003 Year-End Financials

Debt ratio: —   Current ratio: 1.17
Return on equity: —   Long-term debt ($ mil.): 10,494
Cash ($ mil.): 2,370

Net Income History   OTC: FJTSY

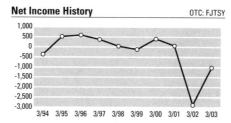

The Future Network plc

The future of this company is tied to the fortunes of the publishing world. The Future Network is one of Europe's leading consumer magazine publishers with more than 80 titles circulated worldwide. It is best-known for such gaming and computing titles as *PC Gamer* and *Official PlayStation Magazine*. In the US, its Future Network USA subsidiary produces *MacAddict* and *Maximum PC*. Future Network also publishes special interest titles such as *Cycling Plus* and

Total Guitar. The company also publishes content on about 30 Web sites and licenses nearly 40 magazine titles.

About 50% of the company's revenue comes from subscriptions and magazine sales; advertising accounts for more than 40%. Outside the UK, Future Network has publishing operations in France, Italy, and the US.

The company is back in the black again, following a restructuring and a successful launch of *Official Xbox Magazine*, which accompanied Microsoft's new video game system. Recent times had been particularly bleak: The dot-com collapse and a weak computer games market had forced Future Network to shutter about 20 titles and reduce headcount by about 650 in 2000. The next year, it also sold Future Network USA's flagship *Business 2.0* to Time Inc.'s FORTUNE Group for nearly $70 million. Founder Chris Anderson owns about 8% of the company.

HISTORY

Oxford-educated Chris Anderson left UK media giant Emap in 1985 to start his own publishing firm with one magazine and a $25,000 loan. His newly created Future Publishing put out the first issue of *Amstrad Action*, a 100-page tome targeting personal-computer users, in 1985. The magazine exploded in popularity after Anderson began including free software with each issue. In 1986 Future Publishing launched two new titles, *8000 Plus* and *PC Plus*. Sales that year exceeded $700,000. The company launched *Sega Power* in 1989 and split its *ST Amiga Format* (launched in 1988) into two titles: *ST Format* and *Amiga Format*. Sales soared and Future Publishing became the largest computer magazine publisher in the UK.

The company made its first big push beyond computer magazines in 1990 with *Classic CD*, which included a free music CD with each issue. It followed up the next year with *Needlecraft* and bought *Mountain Biking UK*. By 1992 the company had 21 titles and a staff of 300. The next year Future Publishing acquired US-based GP Publications and launched *PC Gamer*.

Anderson sold his majority stake in Future Publishing to UK media conglomerate Pearson in 1994 for $86 million. He retained 50% ownership of GP Publications, however, and moved to the US. (He bought the rest of GP Publications, which was renamed Imagine Media, in 1996.) Under Pearson's New Entertainment division, Future Publishing forged ahead, launching *.net* and *Total Guitar* in 1994. It also debuted its FutureNet Web site that year. The company joined PlayStation maker Sony to publish *Official UK PlayStation Magazine* the next year and acquired Music Maker Publications (*The Mix*) and Aspen Litharne (*Cross Stitch*) in 1996.

In 1998 Pearson sold Future Publishing for $236 million in a buyout led by Apax Partners, Anderson, and Future Publishing managing director Greg Ingham. Anderson became chairman and Ingham became chief executive of the newly minted Future Publishing Holdings. The deal also included Future Online and French publisher Edicorp. In 1999 Future Publishing bought its Italian affiliate Il Mio Castello Editore and later went public as The Future Network. Concurrent with its public offering, the company bought Anderson's Imagine Media.

Later that year Future Network acquired the official magazines of UK soccer teams Manchester United and Chelsea from Zone Publishing and won the right to publish a Sony PlayStation

2 magazine. It also expanded into the Netherlands. US-based Imagine Media spun off its Affiliation Networks, which later became Snowball.com (now IGN Entertainment, 45%-owned by Anderson). In 2000 Apax Partners sold its 12% stake in Future Network to the public. That year Future Network bought UK titles *Hi-Fi Choice* and *Home Entertainment* from Dennis Publishing (creator of *Maxim* magazine), while Imagine Media debuted a new US music magazine, *Revolution* (later shuttered).

In 2001 the company announced a reorganization that included shutting down about 20 titles and cutting about 650 jobs. It later sold *Business 2.0* to Time Inc.'s FORTUNE Group for about $70 million. That year Anderson was replaced by Roger Parry as chairman.

In 2002 Imagine Media changed its name to Future Network USA.

EXECUTIVES

Chairman: Roger G. Parry, age 49
Chief Executive and Executive Director: Greg Ingham, age 40, $326,475 pay
COO and Managing Director, Future Publishing UK: Colin Morrison, age 49, $452,712 pay
Group Finance Director and Board Member: John Bowman
Business Development: Dominic Beaver
President, Imagine Media: Jonathan Simpson-Bint
Managing Director, Future Media Italy: Bernardo Notarangelo
Managing Director, Future France: Sari Zaimi
Publisher, Computing, Future Media Italy: Costantino Cialfi
Publisher, Tech & Creative Magazines, Future Media Italy: Simonetta Notargiacomo
Publishing Director, Games, Future Media Italy: Andrea Minini Saldini
Publishing Director, Future France: Vincent Alexandre
Financial Director, Future Media Italy: Claudio Cuna
Finance Director, Future Publishing UK: Susannah Burton
Commercial Director, Future Publishing UK: Ian Linkins, age 46
Group Communications: Terri Davey
General Counsel, Imagine Media: Charles Schug
Human Resources: Sue Handford
Auditors: PricewaterhouseCoopers

LOCATIONS

HQ: Beauford Court, 30 Monmouth St., Bath BA1 2BW, United Kingdom
Phone: +44-1225-442-244   **Fax:** +44-1225-446-019
US HQ: 150 North Hill Dr., Brisbane, CA 94005
US Phone: 415-468-4684   **US Fax:** 415-468-4686
Web: www.thefuturenetwork.plc.uk

The Future Network has operations in France, Italy, the UK, and the US.

PRODUCTS/OPERATIONS

Selected Titles

Computing
Computer Arts (France, Italy)
Computer Magazine (Italy)
Home PC (France)
Il Mio Computer (Italy)
Linux Format
MacAddict (US)
Maximum PC (US)
PC Achat (France)
PC Answers (UK)
PC Guide (UK)
PC Max (France)
PC Plus (UK)
Windows News (France)

Games
Consoles Max (France)
Edge
GamesMaster (UK)
Giocchi per Il Mio Computer (Italy)
Jeux Video (France)
NGC
Official PlayStation 2
Official PlayStation Magazine
Official Xbox Magazine (France, Italy)
Online Gamer (France)
PC Format (UK)
PC Gamer (UK and US)
PC Jeux (France)
Play Power Station (Italy)
PlayStation Plus (Italy)
PSM (Italy and US)
PSM2 (France)
Ufficiale PlayStation 2 Magazine (Italy)
Ufficiale PlayStation Magazine (Italy)

Creative
3D World
Computer Arts (France, Italy, and the UK)
Crete Online

Entertainment
DVD Shopper
Home Entertainment
SFX
Total Film
What DVD?
What Mountain Bike?

Hobbies
Celebrations in Cross Stitch Hobbies
Cross Stitch Collection Hobbies
Cross Stitcher Hobbies
Good Woodworking Hobbies
Jane Greenhof's Cross Stitch Hobbies
Needlecraft Hobbies
Quick and Easy Cross Stitch Hobbies

Internet
.net (France, Italy, UK)
.netpro (France)
Internet Advisor
Internet Pratique (France)
Internet Works
Practical Web Pages

Music
Classic Rock
Computer Music
Future Music
Guitar Techniques
Guitarist
Metal Hammer
Rhythm
Total Guitar

Sports
Chelsea — The Official Magazine
Cycling Plus
Diesel Car
Glory Glory Manchester
Manchester United — The Official Magazine
Mountain Biking UK
Redline

COMPETITORS

Axel Springer
BBC
CNET Networks
Condé Nast
Emap
Gruner + Jahr
Hachette Filipacchi Médias
International Data Group
Penton Media
Terra Lycos
Time
Ziff Davis Media

HISTORICAL FINANCIALS

Company Type: Public

Income Statement
FYE: December 31

	REVENUE ($ mil.)	NET INCOME ($ mil.)	NET PROFIT MARGIN	EMPLOYEES
12/02	265	10	3.7%	934
12/01	253	(179)	—	1,403
12/00	379	(91)	—	1,828
12/99	281	(11)	—	1,338
12/98	133	(8)	—	1,200
Annual Growth	18.8%	—	—	(6.1%)

2002 Year-End Financials

Debt ratio: 2.2%
Return on equity: 5.9%
Cash ($ mil.): 20
Current ratio: 1.12
Long-term debt ($ mil.): 4

Net Income History
London: FNET

Gallaher Group

When the smoke finally settles over London, Gallaher Group helps kick it up again. The #2 UK cigarette company, Gallaher makes tobacco products and sells them in Asia, Continental Europe, Ireland, Russia and other former Soviet republics, and the UK. Its premium cigarettes include top UK brands Benson & Hedges and Silk Cut; mid-priced brands include Berkeley; and low-priced brands include Dorchester and Mayfair. Gallaher also makes Hamlet cigars, Amber Leaf hand-rolling tobacco, and Condor pipe tobacco.

Although most of its sales come from cigarettes, Gallaher also controls nearly half of the UK cigar market and a third of all UK sales of hand-rolling tobacco.

Gallaher was spun off in 1997 from Fortune Brands, the result of a flurry of tobacco-related lawsuits in the US. Gallaher and other firms are fighting the European Union's ban on tobacco advertising (scheduled to start in 2006). The company has a European joint venture with R.J. Reynolds and seeks new international markets for its products by also partnering with Indonesian tobacco maker Sampoerna International to sell the ST Dupont Paris luxury cigarette brand in Russia. Gallaher is one of several companies, including British American Tobacco, interested in expanding its share of Chinese smokers, who puff 1.7 trillion cigarettes every year.

The company is involved in some health-related lawsuits from smokers, but to date no court has ordered it to pay damages.

HISTORY

Tom Gallaher started his business making and selling pipe tobacco in Londonderry, Ireland, in 1857. By 1873 he had moved his business to Belfast. By 1888 Gallaher was making cigarettes (which had become popular) and flake tobacco. That year Gallaher opened its first London office. The firm was incorporated as Gallaher Limited in 1896. In 1908 it bought Ireland's entire tobacco crop. Gallaher died in 1927.

In 1955 Gallaher bought the UK and Ireland units of cigarette firm Benson & Hedges. Richard Benson and William Hedges launched their firm in England in 1873; they pioneered selling tobacco in sealed tins for freshness. In 1877 Queen Victoria endorsed Benson & Hedges with her Royal Warrant. As more women began smoking in the early 1900s, Benson & Hedges made specialized cigarettes for them, including some with floral designs.

Gallaher bought J. Wix and Sons (Kensitas cigarettes) from American Tobacco in 1962 for a Gallaher stake. American Tobacco had increased its stake to 67% by 1968; it renamed itself American Brands in 1970 as it added nontobacco products.

Diversifying in the 1970s, Gallaher bought Dollond & Aitchison Group (optical services/products, 1970), created retail franchise Marshell Group (tobacco and confectionery concessions, 1971), and bought TM Group (Vendepac and other cigarette and snack vending machines, 1973) and Forbuoys (tobacco, sweets, and newspapers stores; 1973). In 1974 it expanded to Italy through Dollond & Aitchison. American Brands controlled 100% of Gallaher by 1975.

The company continued its acquisitions in the 1980s, including NSS Newsagents in 1986 (550 stores, combined with the 450-store Forbuoys subsidiary). By 1987 Gallaher was the #1 UK tobacco manufacturer. In 1990 the firm acquired Scotland's Whyte & Mackay Distillers.

During the early 1990s Gallaher expanded to France, Spain, and Greece. In 1993 it cut 15% of its workforce, blaming cigarette taxes for lower sales. Gallaher had become Ireland's #1 tobacco firm by 1994.

When parent American Brands sold US subsidiary American Tobacco to British American Tobacco Industries (B.A.T) in 1994, Gallaher sold B.A.T its Silk Cut rights outside Europe in exchange for a manufacturing deal. To focus on tobacco and distilling, Gallaher sold Dollond & Aitchison that year and the next year sold its other noncore units (including Forbuoys and TM Group). It also closed several plants during this period.

Twelve people sued Gallaher and rival Imperial Tobacco in 1996, alleging the firms continued using tar in cigarettes after discovering its link to cancer; the suit was abandoned after the statute of limitations expired.

As US tobacco-related litigation skyrocketed, in 1997 American Brands renamed itself Fortune Brands and spun off Gallaher Group, which floated on the London Stock Exchange in May — the first time a UK firm de-merged from a US parent. In 1998 it began exporting to China.

In 1999 Gallaher bought the UK tobacco business of RJR Nabisco (the Dorchester and Dickens & Grant brands and distribution of Camel and More). In a sign of tobacco's fall from favor, the Royal Palace withdrew Queen Victoria's 122-year-old endorsement of Benson & Hedges.

Gallaher entered 2000 with new CEO Nigel Northridge. In August the company bought Russian cigarette maker and distributor Liggett-Ducat from Vector Group for about $400 million. In mid-2001 Gallaher bought 41% of Austria Tabak (90% domestic market share) for more than $700 million and increased its share to more than 99% by the end of the year.

In 2002 Gallaher made an agreement with the state-run China National Tobacco Corporation (CNTC) allowing it to become one of the first Western tobacco companies to have a brand distributed widely in China.

EXECUTIVES

Chairman: Peter M. Wilson, age 61
Deputy Chairman: Sir Graham J. Hearne, age 65
CEO and Board Member: Nigel Northridge, age 47
Group Operations Director and Board Member: Nigel Dunlop, age 46
Finance Director and Board Member: Mark Rolfe, age 44
Commerical Director, Continental Europe; Board Member: Nigel Simon, age 47
Commerical Director, UK and Republic of Ireland; Board Member: Neil England, age 48
Financial Controller: Jon Moxon, age 39
Managing Director, CIS: Stewart Hainsworth, age 34
Managing Director, UK Division: Barry Jenner
Director, Group Human Resources: Mike Griffiths, age 45
Director, Investor Relations: Claire Jenkins, age 40
Director, Group Marketing: Yann Tardif, age 42
Head of Business Development: Suhail Saad, age 48
Auditors: PricewaterhouseCoopers LLP

LOCATIONS

HQ: Gallaher Group Plc
Members Hill, Brooklands Rd., Weybridge, Surrey KT13 0QU, United Kingdom
Phone: +44-1932-859-777   **Fax:** +44-1932-832-792
Web: www.gallaher-group.com

Gallaher Group owns factories in Austria, Ireland, Kazakstan, Russia, the UK, and Ukraine.

2002 Sales

	% of total
Europe	
UK	47
Other countries	44
Former Soviet republics	4
Other regions	5
Total	**100**

PRODUCTS/OPERATIONS

Selected Products and Brands

Cigarettes	Silk Cut
Benson & Hedges	Sovereign
Berkeley	Sterling
Blend	St. George
Club	
Dorchester	**Cigars**
Level	Hamlet
Mayfair	
Memphis	**Tobacco**
Milde Sorte	Amber Leaf
Novost	Condor
	Old Holborn

COMPETITORS

Altadis
British American Tobacco
Carolina Group
Imperial Tobacco
Japan Tobacco
Philip Morris International
Swedish Match
Taiwan Tobacco & Wine
Tchibo Holding

HISTORICAL FINANCIALS

Company Type: Public

Income Statement

FYE: December 31

	REVENUE ($ mil.)	NET INCOME ($ mil.)	NET PROFIT MARGIN	EMPLOYEES
12/02	12,022	411	3.4%	9,602
12/01	7,944	342	4.3%	6,217
12/00	6,659	372	5.6%	3,519
12/99	7,017	390	5.6%	3,066
12/98	7,061	361	5.1%	—
12/97	7,264	396	5.5%	—
Annual Growth	**10.6%**	**0.7%**	**—**	**46.3%**

2002 Year-End Financials

Debt ratio: —
Return on equity: —
Cash ($ mil.): 119
Current ratio: 1.08
Long-term debt ($ mil.): 3,847
No. of shares (mil.): 163
Dividends
Yield: 4.4%
Payout: 67.9%
Market value ($ mil.): 6,386

Stock History

NYSE: GLH

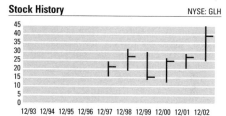

	STOCK PRICE ($) FY Close	P/E High/Low		PER SHARE ($) Earnings	Dividends	Book Value
12/02	39.20	18	10	2.52	1.71	(3.58)
12/01	26.95	13	10	2.17	1.54	(2.89)
12/00	24.63	11	5	2.34	1.54	(5.36)
12/99	15.38	13	6	2.32	1.49	(4.80)
12/98	27.19	15	9	2.09	0.79	(4.83)
12/97	21.31	10	7	2.31	0.77	(5.10)
Annual Growth	**13.0%**	**—**	**—**	**1.8%**	**17.3%**	**—**

OAO Gazprom

Gazprom, Russia's largest company, produces 94% of the country's natural gas and controls 25% of the world's reserves. It is also the world's largest gas producer. The company is engaged in gas exploration, processing, transport, and marketing. It operates Russia's domestic gas pipeline network and delivers gas to countries of the former Soviet Union and to some 25 European countries. Burdened by debt, Gazprom relies heavily on its Western exports and partnerships. It also holds stakes in Russian financial institutions and a polypropylene plant and has its own telecom network. The Russian government controls about 51% of Gazprom.

Gazprom, which evolved from the natural gas ministry of the former Soviet Union, accounts for about 25% of Russia's tax revenues.

The company expects to boost gas exports by 20% after completing two huge gas pipelines, Blue Stream and Yamal-Europe. Exports to Europe are critical to Gazprom, burdened by debt because of the insolvency of Russian consumers and hordes of nonpaying customers. Gazprom also holds strategic partnerships with Western energy companies, including Germany's Ruhrgas, which owns almost 4% of the company's shares. Other partners include Royal Dutch/Shell Group, Eni of Italy, and Finland's Fortum.

Gazprom owned a significant stake in Russian independent television channel NTV, which in 2002 it agreed to sell in order to focus on its core energy businesses. That year Gazprom announced plans to build a $3.5 billion natural gas pipeline from Iran to India via Pakistan.

HISTORY

Following the breakup of the Soviet Union in the early 1990s, one of the first priorities of the Russian government was to move some state monopolies toward a free-market economic system. A presidential decree in 1992 moved the company toward privatization by calling for the formation of a Russian joint-stock company to explore for and produce gas, gas condensates, and oil; provide for gas processing; operate gas wells; and build gas pipelines and storage facilities. By 1993 the government had converted its natural gas monopoly, Gazprom, into a joint-stock company.

The new Gazprom was 15%-owned by Gazprom workers and 28% by people living in Russia's gas-producing regions. The state retained about a 40% share (boosted to 51% in 2003). The company inherited all of the export contracts to Western and Central Europe of the Commonwealth of Independent States.

Thanks to the power of Viktor Chernomyrdin (Gazprom's former Soviet boss and gas industry minister, who became Russia's prime minister in 1992), the company was able to enjoy large tax breaks and maintain its role as a monopoly — even as other industries were being more deeply privatized. However, the privatization of Gazprom was later attacked as being manipulated to profit the company's top management, including Chernomyrdin. Top managers were rumored to have each received from 1% to 5% of shares — holdings potentially worth $1.2 billion to $10 billion each.

Needing to raise cash, in 1996 Gazprom offered 1% of its stock to foreigners, the first sale of stock to foreign investors. In 1997 Gazprom and Royal Dutch/Shell formally became partners. That year Gazprom began building its Blue Stream pipeline across the Black Sea to Turkey. Italian group Eni helped back the project and became a partner by 1999.

In 1998 Gazprom acquired a stake in Promostroibank, Russia's fourth-largest financial institution. German energy powerhouse Ruhrgas acquired a 3% stake in Gazprom in 1998, which it increased to nearly 4% in 1999. Also in 1999 Gazprom started building its Yamal-Europe pipeline, which was to stretch to Germany for exports to Europe.

The next year an attempt by Gazprom to muscle into Hungary's chemicals sector by offering cheaper raw materials was blocked by Hungary's TVK and Borsodchem and their allies. Also in 2000 Gazprom became embroiled in a politically controversial issue when it called for the country's leading private media holding group, Media-MOST, to sell shares to the gas giant in order to settle millions of dollars of debt. Because Media-MOST held NTV television, a major critic of Russian president Vladimir Putin, the deal was alleged to have been directed by the Kremlin. A government probe into the deal was later ordered.

The alignment of Gazprom's board changed in 2000 after the annual shareholder meeting. For the first time in Gazprom's history, company managers did not have a majority of seats. A new chairman, Dmitri Medvyedev, second in command to Putin, was elected to replace Chernomyrdin. In 2001 the board fired CEO Rem Vyakhirev and replaced him with deputy energy minister Alexei Miller, a Putin ally. Later that year Gazprom agreed to sell its stake in NTV and devote the proceeds to its core business.

EXECUTIVES

Chairman of the Board of Directors:
Dmitri A. Medvyedev
Deputy Chairman of the Board of Directors and Chairman of the Executive Board: Alexei B. Miller
Deputy Chairman Executive Board and Chief Accountant: Elena A. Vasilyeva
Deputy Chairman Executive Board:
Alexander G. Ananenkov
Deputy Chairman Executive Board: Yury A. Komarov
Deputy Chairman Executive Board: Sergei A. Lukash
Deputy Chairman Executive Board:
Alexander N. Ryazanov
Deputy Chairman Executive Board: Boris D. Yurlov
Head of Corporate Finance Department:
Andrei V. Kruglov
Head of Gas, Oil, and Gas Condensate Production Department: Boris A. Nikitin
Head of Gas Transportation, Underground Storage, and Processing Department: Bogdan V. Budzulyak
Head of Gazexport: Alexander Medvedev
Head of Investments and Capital Construction Department: Mikhail A. Axelrod
Head of Perspective Development, Science, and Ecology Department: Vladimir I. Rezunenko
Head of Property Management and Corporate Relations Department: Alexander V. Krasnenkov
General Director, Mezhregiongaz: Nikolai N. Gornovski
Advisor to the Chairman of the Executive Board:
Alexander N. Semenyaka
Auditors: ZAO PricewaterhouseCoopers Audit

LOCATIONS

HQ: 16 Nametkina, 117997 Moscow V-420, Russia
Phone: +7-95-719-3001   **Fax:** +7-95-719-8333
Web: www.gazprom.ru

OAO Gazprom operates Russia's extensive gas pipeline system and delivers natural gas to 25 countries in Western and Eastern Europe, the Commonwealth of Independent States, and the Baltic states.

PRODUCTS/OPERATIONS

Selected Subsidiaries

Gazprom Finance B.V.
OOO Astrakhangazprom
OOO Bashtransgaz
OOO Burgaz
OOO Ecological and Analytical Center of the Gas Industry
OOO Dagestangazprom
OOO Gazexport
OOO Gazflot
OOO Gazkomplektimpex
OOO Gaznadzor
OOO Gazobezopasnost
OOO Gazpromavia
OOO Gazprominvestholding
OOO Gazpromokhrana
OOO Gazpromrazvitiye
OOO Gaztorgpromstroy
OOO Gazsvyaz
OOO Informgaz
OOO IRTsGazprom
OOO Kavkaztransgaz
OOO Kubangazprom
OOO Lentransgaz
OOO Mezhregiongaz
OOO Mostransgaz
OOO Nadymgazprom
OOO Nadymstroygazdobycha
OOO NIIGazekonomika

OOO Novourengoy GCC
OOO Noyabrskgazdobycha
OOO Orenburggazprom
OOO Permtransgaz
OOO Podzemgazprom
OOO Samaratransgaz
OOO Servicegazprom
OOO Severgazprom
OOO Surgutgazprom
OOO Surgutstroygaz
OOO Szhizhenny gas
OOO Tattransgaz
OOO Tomsktransgaz
OOO TyumenNIIGiprogaz
OOO Tyumentransgaz
OOO Ulyanovskgazservice
OOO Uraltransgaz
OOO Urengoygazprom
OOO VNIIgaz
OOO Volgogradtransgaz
OOO Volgotransgaz
OOO Yamburggazdobycha
OOO Yugtransgaz
ZAO Yamalgazinvest

COMPETITORS

BP
Gasunie
ITERA
LUKOIL
Ruhrgas
Sibneft
Surgutneftegas
Tatneft
Yukos

HISTORICAL FINANCIALS

Company Type: Public

Income Statement

FYE: December 31

	REVENUE ($ mil.)	NET INCOME ($ mil.)	NET PROFIT MARGIN	EMPLOYEES
12/02	19,216	3,807	19.8%	295,487
12/01	19,287	3,290	17.1%	310,700
12/00	17,448	1,712	9.8%	300,000
12/99	12,113	(2,883)	—	298,000
12/98	6,732	1,105	16.4%	278,400
Annual Growth	30.0%	36.2%	—	1.5%

2002 Year-End Financials

Debt ratio: 15.0%   Current ratio: 1.55
Return on equity: —   Long-term debt ($ mil.): 8,266
Cash ($ mil.): 3,126

Net Income History

Exchange: Russian

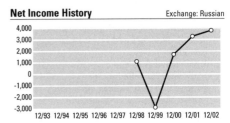

George Weston

George Weston Limited fuels Canadians through those long winters. About 80% of the company's sales come from its 61%-owned Loblaw Companies Limited, Canada's largest supermarket operator (with more than a dozen chains such as Loblaws, Provigo, and Zehrs) and the country's largest wholesale food distributor. The rest comes from its food-processing units, with operations in Canada and the US that focus on fresh-baked goods, frozen dough, and other bakery products. (Its Interbake Foods division is a major supplier of Girl Scout cookies in the US.) The units also have fish and dairy operations. Chairman and president Galen Weston owns more than 62% of the company, which was founded by his grandfather in 1882.

Already a strong food retailer in most Canadian provinces, Loblaw stepped up its efforts in the lucrative Quebec market when it bought food retailer/wholesaler Provigo. (Loblaw has about a 36% market share in Quebec and 30% market share in Canada.)

The food-processing segment is expanding its bakery and biscuit operations through acquisitions; its purchase of Bestfoods Baking has made it one of the top bakeries in the US. However, it has sold noncore operations, including its forest products business and canned seafood business (Conners). Weston's fisheries business is primarily engaged in hatching, growing, and processing fresh farmed salmon in North America and Chile.

HISTORY

A baker's apprentice, George Weston began delivering bread in Toronto with a single horse in 1882. He added the Model Bakery in 1896 and began making cookies and biscuits in 1908.

Upon George's death in 1924, his son Garfield took control of the company and took it public as George Weston Limited in 1928. Having popularized the premium English biscuit in Canada, Garfield acquired bakeries in the UK to make cheap biscuits (uncommon at the time). He grouped the bakeries as a separate public company called Allied Bakeries in 1935 (it later became Associated British Foods and is still controlled by the Weston family).

Expansion-minded Garfield led the company into the US with the purchase of Associated Biscuit in 1939. By the late 1930s George Weston was making cakes, breads, and almost 500 kinds of candy and biscuits.

During the 1940s the company made a number of acquisitions, including papermaker E.B. Eddy (1943; sold in 1998 to papermaker Domtar, giving it a 20% stake in Domtar); Southern Biscuit (1944); Western Grocers (1944, its first distribution company); and William Neilson (1948, chocolate and dairy products).

In 1953 it acquired a controlling interest in Loblaw Groceterias, Canada's largest grocery chain. George Weston continued its acquisitions during the 1950s and 1960s, adding grocer National Tea and diversifying into packaging (Somerville Industries, 1957) and fisheries (British Columbia Packers, 1962; Conners Bros., 1967).

By 1970, when Garfield's son Galen became president, the company's holdings were in disarray. Galen brought in new managers, consolidated the food distribution and sales operations

under Loblaw Companies Limited, and cut back on National Tea (which shrank from over 900 stores in 1972 to 82 in 1993). When Garfield died in 1978, Galen became chairman.

Ever since Galen, a polo-playing chum of Prince Charles, was the target of a failed kidnapping attempt by the Irish Republican Army in 1983, the family has kept a low public profile.

George Weston became the #1 chocolate maker in Canada with its purchase of Cadbury Schweppes' Canadian assets in 1987. The 1980s concluded with a five-year price war in St. Louis among its National Tea stores, Kroger, and a local grocer. This ultimately proved fruitless, and Loblaw sold its US supermarkets in 1995, ending its US retail presence. As part of its divestiture of underachieving subsidiaries, the company sold its Neilson confectionery business back to Cadbury Schweppes in 1996 and sold its chocolate products company in 1998.

In early 1998 Loblaw set its sights on Quebec, buying Montreal-based Provigo. Other George Weston acquisitions in the late 1990s included Oshawa Foods' 80-store Agora Foods franchise supermarket unit in eastern Canada and its Field-fresh Farms dairy business, the frozen-bagel business of Quaker Oats, Pennsylvania-based Maier's Bakery, and Bunge International's Australian meat processor, Don Smallgoods. It also sold its British Columbia Packers fisheries unit.

Early in 2001 George Weston surprised analysts when it won Unilever's Bestfoods Baking Company (Entenmann's, Oroweat) with a bid of $1.77 billion. The company reduced its stake in Loblaw by 2% and sold its Connors canned seafood business to fund the purchase, which was completed in July 2001. To help pay down debt, in early 2002 the company sold its Oroweat business in the western US to Mexican bread giant Grupo Bimbo for $610 million.

EXECUTIVES

Chairman and President: W. Galen Weston, age 62, $1,648,920 pay
CFO: Richard P. (Rick) Mavrinac, age 50
SVP, Labour Relations: Roy R. Conliffe, age 52
SVP, Secretary and General Counsel: Stewart E. Green, age 58
SVP, Finance: Louise M. Lacchin, age 45
SVP; President and CEO, President's Choice Bank: Donald G. (Don) Reid, age 53, $630,120 pay
SVP, Corporate Development: Robert G. Vaux, age 54
VP, Taxation: J. Bradley Holland, age 39
VP, Legal Counsel: Michael N. Kimber, age 47
VP, Community Affairs: Garfield R. Mitchell
VP, Industry and Investor Relations: Geoffrey H. (Geoff) Wilson, age 47
Treasurer: Lisa R. Swartzman, age 32
President, Weston Foods US: Gary Prince, age 51, $1,109,850 pay
President, Weston Foods Canada: Ralph A. Robinson, age 54, $409,604 pay
President, Loblaw Companies: John A. Lederer, age 47, $1,256,667 pay
President, Fisheries: Fraser J. Walsh
President, Interbake Foods: Raymond A. Baxter, age 58
President, Maplehurst Bakeries: Paul D. Durlacher, age 50
Human Resources, Fisheries: Gary V. Wadden, age 45
Auditors: KPMG LLP

LOCATIONS

HQ: George Weston Limited
22 St. Clair Ave. East, Toronto, Ontario
M4T 2S7, Canada
Phone: 416-922-2500   **Fax:** 416-922-4395
Web: www.weston.ca

George Weston Limited's Loblaw Companies operates in Canada, and its Weston Foods divisions operate in Canada and the US. George Weston also has fisheries operations in North America and Chile.

2002 Sales

	% of total
Canada	86
US	14
Total	**100**

PRODUCTS/OPERATIONS

Operating Divisions

Food Distribution Segment (Selected Loblaw Banners)
Atlantic Superstore
Extra Foods
Fortinos
Loblaws
Maxi
Maxi & Co.
no frills
Provigo
The Real Canadian Superstore
The Real Canadian Wholesale Club
SuperValu
valu-mart
Your Independent Grocer
Zehrs Markets

Food Processing Segment (Selected Units)
George Weston Bakeries Inc. (fresh-baked goods, US)
Heritage Salmon (fresh farmed salmon, Canada)
Interbake Foods Inc. (cookies and crackers, US)
Maplehurst Bakeries, Inc. (frozen bakery products, US)
Neilson Dairy (milk processor, Canada)
Ready Bake Foods Inc. (frozen bakery products, Canada)
Stroehmann Bakeries, LC (fresh-baked goods, US)
Weston Bakeries Limited (fresh-baked goods, Canada)
Weston Fruitcake Company

COMPETITORS

Bimbo	Interstate Bakeries
Bridgford Foods	Jim Pattison Group
Campbell Soup	Kellogg Snacks
Canada Safeway	Lanes Biscuits
Empire Company	Maple Leaf Foods
FlowersFoods	Metro
IGA	Otis Spunkmeyer
International Multifoods	Tasty Baking

HISTORICAL FINANCIALS

Company Type: Public

Income Statement

FYE: December 31

	REVENUE ($ mil.)	NET INCOME ($ mil.)	NET PROFIT MARGIN	EMPLOYEES
12/02	17,406	438	2.5%	142,850
12/01	15,499	366	2.4%	139,000
12/00	14,908	321	2.2%	126,000
12/99	14,414	243	1.7%	119,000
12/98	9,588	503	5.2%	124,000
12/97	9,722	170	1.8%	87,330
12/96	9,273	174	1.9%	81,030
12/95	9,502	139	1.5%	76,650
12/94	9,275	84	0.9%	77,100
12/93	9,002	43	0.5%	69,600
Annual Growth	7.6%	29.4%	—	8.3%

2002 Year-End Financials

Debt ratio: 123.0%
Return on equity: 17.3%
Cash ($ mil.): 986
Current ratio: 1.06
Long-term debt ($ mil.): 3,419

Net Income History

Toronto: WN

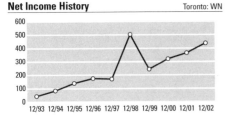

GlaxoSmithKline

GlaxoSmithKline calms your nerves and helps you breathe easier. One of the top five pharmaceutical firms in the world, GSK's top sellers include central nervous system therapies such as antidepressant Paxil, respiratory drugs including asthma medications Flonase and Serevent, and anti-infectives like Amoxil, Augmentin, and Valtrex. Other international bestsellers include Avandia for diabetes, migraine reliever Imitrex, cancer-related nausea drug Zofran, and ulcer drug Zantac. The company's OTC products include Tums for sour stomachs, Oxy for skin suffering the ravages of adolescence, and NicoDerm for smokers looking to kick the habit.

The firm gains more than half its revenues from the US, and maintaining US patent protection for its bestsellers can make or break its future. It has lost patent disputes that would have safeguarded Wellbutrin and Zyban (essentially the same drug but sold for different indications) and Augmentin. Flonase and Paxil patents expire in 2003 and 2006, respectively.

In the research lab, GSK is creating its next big hits and hoping the FDA doesn't think it's producing misses: The FDA dashed hopes of an easy approval for non-Hodgkin's therapy Bexxar (developed with Corixa) and also deemed the company's antibiotic candidate Factive unworthy in early 2002.

In an effort to stave off government price controls in the US, the company has joined with six other major drug companies to offer Together Rx, a discount prescription card for low-income seniors.

HISTORY

Englishman Joseph Nathan started an import-export business in New Zealand in 1873. He obtained the rights to a process for drying milk and began making powdered milk in New Zealand, selling it as baby food Glaxo.

Nathan's son Alec, dispatched to London to oversee baby food sales in Britain, increased Glaxo's name recognition by publishing the Glaxo Baby Book, a guide to child care. After WWI the company began distribution in India and South America.

In the 1920s Glaxo launched vitamin D-fortified formulations. It entered the pharmaceutical business with its 1927 introduction of Ostelin, a liquid vitamin D concentrate, and con-

tinued to grow globally in the 1930s, introducing Ostermilk (vitamin-fortified milk).

Glaxo began making penicillin and anesthetics during WWII; it went public in 1947. A steep drop in antibiotic prices in the mid-1950s led Glaxo to diversify; it bought veterinary, medical instrument, and drug distribution firms.

In the 1970s the British Monopolies Commission quashed both a hostile takeover attempt by Beecham and a proposed merger with retailer and drugmaker Boots. Glaxo launched US operations in 1978.

In the 1980s Glaxo shed nondrug operations to concentrate on pharmaceuticals. A 1981 marketing blitz launched antiulcer drug Zantac (to vie with SmithKline's Tagamet) in the US, where Glaxo's sales had been small. The company boosted outreach by contracting to use Hoffmann-La Roche's sales staff. The Zantac sales assault gave Glaxo leadership in US antiulcer drug sales.

Under CEO Sir Richard Sykes, Glaxo in 1995 made a surprise bid for UK rival Wellcome. Founded in 1880 by Americans Silas Burroughs and Henry Wellcome to sell McKesson-Robbins' products outside the US, Burroughs Wellcome and Co. began making its own products two years later. By the 1990s the company, which fostered Nobel Prize-winning researchers, led the world in antiviral medicines. Its primary drug products were Zovirax (launched 1981) and Retrovir (1987).

Though an earlier bid by Glaxo had been rejected, Sykes won the takeover by getting backing from Wellcome Trust, Wellcome's largest shareholder.

In 1997 the company formed a new genetics division, buying Spectra Biomedical and its gene variation technology. That year the company pulled diabetes drug Romozin (Rezulin in the US) from the UK market over concerns that it caused liver damage.

Glaxo in 1998 ended its joint venture with Warner-Lambert (begun in 1993), selling its former partner the Canadian and US marketing rights to acid blocker Zantac 75.

In 1999 Glaxo trimmed its product line, pulling hepatitis treatment Wellferon because of slow sales and selling the US rights to several anesthesia products. It also cut some 3,400 jobs (half from the UK). Also that year Glaxo threatened to leave the UK after the National Health Service opted not to cover antiflu inhalant Relenza, claiming the drug is not cost-effective.

The FDA in 2000 approved Glaxo's Lotronex for irritable bowel syndrome, but several hospitalizations linked to the drug prompted the FDA to ask the company to withdraw it from the US market. Later that year Glaxo completed its merger with former UK rival SmithKline Beecham to create GlaxoSmithKline (GSK); Jean-Pierre Garnier took over as CEO.

Although GSK has largely escaped the flurry of patent worries afflicting other druggernauts, in 2001 a US court declared invalid three patents protecting Augmentin from generics until 2017 and opened the door for cheaper rivals as early as 2002.

EXECUTIVES

Chairman: Sir Christopher A. Hogg, age 67, $404,183 pay
CEO and Director: Jean-Pierre Garnier, age 55, $3,721,048 pay
CFO and Director: John Coombe, age 57, $1,494,834 pay
CIO: Ford Calhoun

SVP and General Counsel: Rupert Bondy
SVP, Corporate Communications and Community Partnerships: Jennie Younger
SVP, Human Resources: Daniel (Dan) Phelan
SVP, Worldwide Development and Research and Development: Ronald Krall
Chairman, Research and Development: Tadataka (Tachi) Yamada, age 56
President and COO, Pharmaceutical Operations: David M. Stout, age 49
President, Consumer Healthcare: John B. (Jack) Ziegler, age 57
President, Global Manufacturing and Supply: David Pulman
President, Pharmaceuticals International: Russell Grieg
President, Pharmaceuticals Japan: Marc Dunoyer
President, Pharmaceuticals Europe: Andrew Witty
President, US Pharmaceuticals: Chris Viehbacher
Director, Investor Relations: Thomas Curry
Auditors: PricewaterhouseCoopers LLP

LOCATIONS

HQ: GlaxoSmithKline plc
  980 Great West Rd., Brentford,
  London TW8 9GS, United Kingdom
Phone: +44-20-8047-5000   **Fax:** +44-20-8047-7807
US HQ: 1 Franklin Plaza, Philadelphia, PA 19101
US Phone: 215-751-5000   **US Fax:** 215-751-3233
Web: www.gsk.com

PRODUCTS/OPERATIONS

Selected Pharmaceutical Products

Anti-Bacterials
Amoxil (antibiotic)
Augmentin (antibiotic)
Bactroban (skin infections)
Fortum/Fortaz (injectable antibiotic)
Malarone (malaria)
Zinnat/Ceftin (oral antibiotic)

Anti-Virals
Agenerase (protease inhibitor for HIV/AIDS)
Combivir/Biovir (reverse transcriptase inhibitor for HIV/AIDS)
Epivir/3TC (reverse transcriptase inhibitor for HIV/AIDS)
Retrovir/AZT (reverse transcriptase inhibitor for HIV/AIDS)
Trizivir (three reverse transcriptase inhibitors for HIV/AIDS)
Valtrex/Zelitrex (shingles and genital herpes)
Zeffix/Septavir/Heptodin/Epivir HBV (hepatitis B)
Ziagen (reverse transcriptase inhibitor for HIV/AIDS)
Zovirax (herpes infections, shingles, chicken pox, and cold sores)

Cardiovascular
Coreg (antihypertensive)
Flolan (blood clotting inhibitor)
Lacipil (antihypertensive)
Lanoxin (cardiac anti-arrhythmic)
Pritor (antihypertensive)

Central Nervous System Disorders
Imigran/Imitrex (migraines)
Lamictal (epilepsy)
Naramig/Amerge (migraines)
Requip (Parkinson's disease therapy)
Seroxat/Paxil (antidepressant)
Wellbutrin (depression)
Zyban (smoking cessation aid)

Metabolic and Gastrointestinal
Avandia (type 2 diabetes)
Zantac (stomach ulcers)

Oncology and Emesis
Hycamtin (anti-ovarian cancer agent)
Navelbine (lung and breast cancer)
Zofran (cancer therapy-induced nausea)

Respiratory
Beconase (allergies)
Becotide/Beclovent (asthma and bronchitis)
Flixonase/Flonase (allergies)
Flixotide/Flovent (asthma and bronchial conditions)
Seretide/Advair (asthma)
Serevent (asthma and bronchitis)
Ventolin (asthma and bronchitis)

Vaccines
Engerix-B (hepatitis B vaccine)
Havrix (hepatitis A vaccine)
Infanrix (diphtheria, tetanus, and whooping cough vaccine)
Twinrix (combined hepatitis A and hepatitis B vaccine)

Selected Consumer Products

Over-the-Counter Medicines
Abtei (vitamins and nutritional supplements)
Contac (respiratory product)
Nicabate/NicoDerm CQ/NiQuitin CQ (smoking cessation aid)
Nicorette (smoking cessation gum)
Oxy (dermatological products)
Panadol (analgesic)
Tagamet HB (gastrointestinal relief)
Tums (antacid)
Zantac Relief (gastrointestinal relief)

Oral Care
Aquafresh (toothpaste and toothbrushes)
Dr Best (toothbrushes)
Macleans (toothpaste)
Odol (toothpaste)
Polident (denture cleaner)
Poli-Grip (denture adhesive)
Sensodyne (toothpaste)

Nutritional Healthcare
Horlicks (milk-based malted food and chocolate drinks)
Lucozade (glucose energy drink)
Ribena (line of juice drinks rich in vitamin C)

COMPETITORS

Abbott Labs	Hoffmann-La Roche
Amgen	Johnson & Johnson
AstraZeneca	Merck
Aventis	Mylan Labs
Barr Labs	Novartis
Bayer AG	Novo Nordisk
Bristol-Myers Squibb	Pfizer
Chiron	Sanofi-Synthélabo
Elan Corporation	Schering-Plough
Eli Lilly	Wyeth
Genentech	

HISTORICAL FINANCIALS
Company Type: Public

Income Statement FYE: December 31

	REVENUE ($ mil.)	NET INCOME ($ mil.)	NET PROFIT MARGIN	EMPLOYEES
12/02	34,183	6,341	18.6%	106,166
12/01	29,836	4,504	15.1%	107,899
12/00	27,032	6,295	23.3%	108,201
12/99	13,718	2,926	21.3%	60,726
12/98	13,248	3,047	23.0%	54,350
12/97	13,181	3,056	23.2%	53,068
12/96	14,284	3,420	23.9%	53,808
12/95*	15,850	3,691	23.3%	65,702
6/95	10,320	1,655	16.0%	47,189
6/94	8,730	2,011	23.0%	
Annual Growth	16.4%	13.6%	—	10.7%

*Fiscal year change

2002 Year-End Financials

Debt ratio: 47.0%
Return on equity: 58.8%
Cash ($ mil.): 1,695
Current ratio: 1.22
Long-term debt ($ mil.): 4,983

No. of shares (mil.): 3,012
Dividends
 Yield: 3.4%
 Payout: 59.2%
Market value ($ mil.): 112,834

Stock History
NYSE: GSK

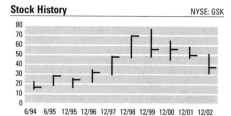

	STOCK PRICE ($) FY Close	P/E High/Low		PER SHARE ($) Earnings	Dividends	Book Value
12/02	37.46	24	15	2.13	1.26	3.52
12/01	49.82	27	22	1.47	1.31	3.55
12/00	56.00	32	22	2.02	1.29	3.70
12/99	55.87	47	30	1.61	1.29	2.79
12/98	69.49	41	28	1.70	0.00	2.47
12/97	47.87	28	17	1.72	0.00	1.70
12/96	31.74	18	12	1.93	0.98	1.18
12/95*	24.37	24	16	1.05	0.94	0.41
6/95	28.12	123	82	0.23	0.00	1.21
6/94	16.62	17	11	1.32	0.75	5.10
Annual Growth	9.4%	—	—	5.5%	5.9%	(4.0%)

*Fiscal year change

Granada plc

With operations in television broadcasting and production, pay and digital TV, and television leasing, Granada (formerly Granada Compass) has the channels covered. The company owns seven of the UK's Independent Television (ITV, a national network) stations, holding almost 15% of the UK's audience share. It produces some 9,000 hours of programming (*Coronation Street*, *Heartbeat*) for ITV, as well as other broadcasters. Granada's broadband division has stakes in pay TV channels and Internet ventures. The company also owns small stakes in several UK soccer clubs. An agreement for Granada and Carlton Communications to merge has gotten a green light from UK officials.

In 2000 the old Granada Group split its hospitality and media businesses into separate entities. To do that, the company acquired Compass Group and spun off its TV unit as Granada Media. (Granada Compass retained about 80% of the new media company.) However, the new firm didn't last very long. In early 2001 Granada Compass demerged by transferring its hospitality and catering assets back into Compass Group (which is public again), absorbing Granada Media, and changing its name to Granada plc.

After struggling unsuccessfully against rival British Sky Broadcasting, the company's ITV Digital (a joint venture with Carlton Communications) shut down in mid-2002.

HISTORY

Granada traces its roots to the Edmonton Empire, a north-London theater built by Alexander Bernstein in 1906. After Bernstein died in 1922, his sons Cecil and Sidney set up a chain of movie theaters during the 1920s and incorporated their business as Granada Theatres Ltd. in 1934. Granada went public the next year. Between 1936 and 1938, it opened a cinema every three months.

In 1955 Granada was granted a TV broadcasting license for the north of England. Changing its name to Granada Group Ltd. in 1957, the company began diversifying in the late 1950s. Granada first got into the TV rental business and later started Granada Motorway Services. By 1967 Granada was operating more than 200 TV rental showrooms nationwide and later expanded into North America. Sidney Bernstein resigned in 1979, and his nephew Alex took over as chairman.

During the 1980s, the company's TV production arm gained international acclaim with shows like *Brideshead Revisited* (1981) and *The Jewel in the Crown* (1984). In 1986 it fended off a hostile bid from rival leisure company The Rank Organisation (now The Rank Group). By the end of the 1980s, Granada had disposed of its theater operations and invested in startup British Satellite Broadcasting (later British Sky Broadcasting) in 1990. Overextended and facing a recession, Granada sold its bingo businesses in 1991.

That year chief executive Derek Lewis resigned, and Irish-born Gerry Robinson took over. The former chief of catering giant Compass Group, Robinson fired nearly all of the senior management during his first year. Under his acquisitive management, Granada bought the Sutcliffe Group, a major catering firm, from cruise operators P & O for $500 million in 1993 and the next year acquired London Weekend Television for $150 million.

Robinson replaced Bernstein as chairman in 1996, and Granada TV head Charles Allen was appointed as chief executive. Buying Forte for $6.1 billion that year added hotel operations and Little Chefs restaurants. The next year the company bought the 73% of Yorkshire Tyne Tees Television it did not already own in a deal valued at about $1.1 billion. In 1998 Granada's digital TV joint venture ON Digital (with Carlton Communications) began broadcasting. (The venture was later renamed ITV Digital and was shut down in 2002.)

In 1999 the company disposed of its stake in BSkyB and acquired fish and chips chain Harry Ramsden's. A proposed merger between rivals Carlton and United News & Media (now United Business Media) that year threatened Granada's dominance in UK television. In 2000 Granada proposed its own merger with either company, temporarily derailing the deal. (It was all moot anyway when Carlton and United canceled their deal after it raised too many competition concerns.) Later that year, the company purchased hospitality firm Compass Group, and spun off its media business as Granada Media. (Granada Compass retained about 83% of the new TV company.)

In early 2001 Allen took on the title of chairman and Steve Morrison took over as chief executive. Shortly after completing the deal, in 2001 the fickle company demerged by placing its hospitality assets back into Compass Group (which is a public firm again) and absorbing its stake in Granada Media. Granada Compass then changed its name to Granada plc. Morrison left as CEO in 2002.

EXECUTIVES

Chairman: Charles Lamb Allen, age 46, $2,041,919 pay
Finance Director: Henry Staunton, age 55
Commercial Director: Graham Parrot, age 53
Chief Executive, Granada Content: Simon Shaps
Chief Executive, Granada Broadcasting and Enterprises: Mick Desmond
Director of Entertainment and International Formats: Paul Jackson

President, Granada Entertainment USA: Antony Root
COO, Granada Sport and Interactive: Max Graesser
VP, Alternative Programming, Granada USA:
  Curt Northrup
Interactive and Online Sales Director, Granada
  Enterprises: John Doyle
Controller Interactive, Granada Sport and Interactive:
  Justin Judd
Client Marketing: John Creedon
Auditors: KPMG Audit Plc

LOCATIONS

HQ: London Television Centre, Upper Ground,
  London SE1 9LT, United Kingdom
Phone: +44-20-7620-1620   Fax: +44-20-7261-3520
Web: www.granadamedia.com

PRODUCTS/OPERATIONS

Selected Operations

Anglia Television (ITV franchise)
Border Television (ITV franchise)
Box Clever (50%, television rental retail chain)
Granada Enterprises (commercial TV sales)
Granada Learning (educational television, software, and
  other materials)
Granada Sky Broadcasting (50%, pay TV operations)
Granada TV (ITV franchise)
Independent Television News (20%, news service
  supplier)
London News Network (50%, regional news and weather
  programming)
London Weekend Television (ITV franchise)
Meridian Broadcasting (ITV franchise)
SMG (18%, television broadcasting in Scotland)
Tyne-Tees Television (ITV franchise)
Yorkshire Television (ITV franchise)

COMPETITORS

BBC	Flextech
BSkyB	HTV Group
Carlton Communications	NTL
Channel 4	RTL Group
Chrysalis Group	Telewest
Daily Mail and General	
Trust	

HISTORICAL FINANCIALS

Company Type: Public

Income Statement

FYE: September 30

	REVENUE ($ mil.)	NET INCOME ($ mil.)	NET PROFIT MARGIN	EMPLOYEES
9/02	2,228	(590)	—	4,696
9/01	3,602	(194)	—	30,797
9/00	7,968	180	2.3%	211,127
9/99	6,751	1,425	21.1%	191,407
9/98	6,845	946	13.8%	170,158
Annual Growth	(24.5%)	—	—	(59.2%)

2002 Year-End Financials

Debt ratio: 0.8%
Return on equity: —
Cash ($ mil.): 165
Current ratio: 1.09
Long-term debt ($ mil.): 20

Net Income History

London: GAA

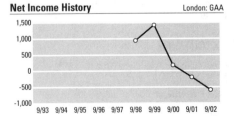

Gucci Group

Gucci Group, an Italian company that sells French fashion designed by Texas-born creative director Tom Ford, does quite well in Japan, too. Offerings include handbags and other leather goods (about 30% of sales), shoes, ready-to-wear clothing, ties, and watches. Gucci family squabbles and imprudent licensing once nearly doomed the firm. New management revived it with fresh product lines and stricter licensing and invested heavily in its Asian presence. Gucci has about 200 company-owned and franchised stores worldwide. French retailer Pinault-Printemps-Redoute (PPR) owns about 68% of Gucci.

The company almost doubled its size with the 1999 purchase of Sanofi Beauté (renamed YSL Beauté), which included most of French fashion house Yves Saint Laurent. Gucci has continued its quest for growth, adding such luxury brands as Boucheron, Alexander McQueen, Bedat & Co., and Bottega Veneta. More than 160 Gucci shops and about 40 YSL Beauté stores operate worldwide; about a third of Gucci's sales come from Asia.

PPR's stake increased when it bought luxury rival LVMH's stake for $806.5 million in October 2001. The company is continuing to open stores in Japan, China, and Australia.

HISTORY

Guccio Gucci began his leather goods business in Florence, Italy, in 1923, later fabricating a pedigree that said the family had been saddlemakers to Florence's aristocrats. In 1935 Gucci Group's leather supply was cut off when the League of Nations sanctioned Italy after Mussolini's invasion of Ethiopia. Gucci turned to making canvas bags trimmed with Italian leather.

By the 1950s such luminaries as Grace Kelly, Elizabeth Taylor, and Queen Elizabeth patronized Gucci shops. The first Gucci shop in the US opened in New York in 1953. With Guccio's death that year, the company's reins passed to son Aldo, who turned the Gucci name into a global fashion brand. Through licensing, Aldo put his family's name on thousands of items. In 1974 the company launched its men's and women's ready-to-wear lines.

By the mid-1980s Gucci was struggling. Family tensions had arisen when Aldo's son Paolo set out to sell products under the Paolo Gucci name. In 1983 Aldo's brother Rodolfo died, leaving his 50% stake in Gucci to son Maurizio, setting up a feud worthy of Italian opera. Paolo charged his father with tax evasion, and Aldo was forced out in 1984 and later sentenced to prison. Aldo and son Roberto accused Maurizio of forgery, but his one-year jail sentence on fraud charges was overturned.

The Aldo faction sold its half of Gucci in 1987 to Investcorp, which had backed the buyout of Tiffany & Co. Maurizio took Gucci's helm in 1989. To give Gucci goods more cachet, he reined in the rampant licensing of the Gucci name — it had appeared on everything from key chains to scotch — and reduced the number of outlets selling Gucci items. As a result, cash flow dwindled, and amid a global recession, Gucci lost money.

In 1993 Investcorp bought out Maurizio, the last remaining Gucci involved in the company. (Maurizio was murdered in 1995; his ex-wife and four others were convicted in the slaying.)

Investcorp named Gucci America chief

Domenico De Sole president in 1994. De Sole turned Gucci around with the help of Tom Ford, a Gucci designer since 1990. Ford's early 1995 collections struck runway gold as he combined Italian quality with an American-inspired look. Investcorp took Gucci public in 1995 and sold the rest of its stake in 1996.

Italian fashion house Prada revealed in 1998 that it had acquired a 9.5% stake in Gucci. Prada sold its stake to LVMH in 1999. Gucci issued millions of new shares, diluting LVMH's stake.

In 1999 French retailer Pinault-Printemps-Redoute (PPR) paid $2.9 billion for more than 40% of Gucci. (Gucci again issued new shares, diluting LVMH's stake.) In addition, Artemis — the company that controls PPR — bought the beauty business of French pharmaceuticals firm Sanofi Beauté and sold it to Gucci for about $960 million. It was renamed YSL Beauté. The deal included Yves Saint Laurent's (YSL) non-couture business and such fragrances as Oscar de la Renta. Gucci also bought 70% of Italian shoemaker Calzaturificio Sergio Rossi.

In 2000 Gucci appointed Ford creative director of YSL, replacing YSL co-founder Pierre Berge. Ford remained creative director for Gucci Group. Gucci also upped the ante in its rivalry with LVMH when it bought Swiss luxury firm Boucheron (jewelry, watches, and fragrances) for $144.8 million. The company also bought back its YSL licenses and the factory that makes its womenswear. As LVMH continued to fight PPR and Gucci in court, Gucci took the catfight to the catwalk and bought 51% of Alexander McQueen, the eponymous label of LVMH's Givenchy designer. Gucci then bought 85% of Swiss luxury watchmaker Bedat & Co.

In early 2001 it bought about 67% of Bottega Veneta, an Italian luxury leather goods company, and agreed to acquire Di Modolo, a watch production facility, and Di Modolo Associates, its design studio. Also in 2001 Gucci snagged Chloe designer Stella McCartney (daughter of Beatles co-founder Paul McCartney) from Richemont. PPR paid $806.5 million for LVMH's stake in Gucci in October, which resulted in PPR owning 53.2% of Gucci.

In November 2003 Gucci purchased a 70% stake in Italian footwear company Pigini SRL.

EXECUTIVES

Chairman: Adrian D. P. Bellamy, age 61
President, CEO, and Board Member:
  Domenico De Sole, age 59, $2,662,650 pay
Vice Chairman and Creative Director: Tom Ford,
  $6,363,000 pay
EVP and CFO: Robert Singer
EVP of Strategy and Acquisitions; President,
  Emerging Brands: James McArthur
EVP; President, Gucci Group Watches; President and
  CEO, Boucheron: Brian Blake
President, Gucci America: Patricia Malone
Director of Advertising: Alexandra Gillespie
Director of Internet Activities: Richard Swanson
Director of Investor Relations and Corporate
  Development: Cedric Magnelia
Director of Tax Planning and Treasury: Marco Biagioni
Worldwide Director of Communications: Lisa Schiek
Worldwide Director of Corporate Communications:
  Tomaso Galli
Worldwide Director of Human Resources: Renato Ricci
Group Controller: Emilio Foà
General Counsel: Allan Tuttle
CIO: Marco Forneris
Auditors: PricewaterhouseCoopers N.V.

LOCATIONS

HQ: Gucci Group N.V.
Rembrandt Tower, 1 Amstelplein, 1096 HA
Amsterdam, The Netherlands
Phone: +31-20-462-1700   **Fax:** +31-20-465-3569
US HQ: 50 Hartz Way, Secaucus, NJ 07094
US Phone: 201-867-8800   **US Fax:** 201-392-2679
Web: www.gucci.com

2002 Sales

	% of total
Europe	42
US	21
Japan	20
Rest of Asia	12
Other	5
Total	**100**

PRODUCTS/OPERATIONS

2002 Revenue

	% of total
Owned stores	50
Wholesale distribution	48
Royalties	2
Total	**100**

2002 Revenue

	% of total
Leather goods	32
Fragrances	16
Ready-to-wear	13
Shoes	12
Watches	9
Cosmetics	6
Jewelry	5
Royalties	2
Other	5
Total	**100**

Major Products

Eyewear	Ready-to-wear apparel
Gifts	Scarves
Jewelry	Shoes
Leather goods	Ties
Perfume	Watches

COMPETITORS

AnnTaylor
Bally
Bulgari
Calvin Klein
Chanel
Christian Dior
Donna Karan
Escada
Etienne Aigner
Gianni Versace
Armani
Hermès
Hugo Boss
Prada
Jil Sander
Jones Apparel
Kenneth Cole
Liz Claiborne
LVMH
Rolex
Oscar de la Renta
Phillips-Van Heusen
Polo Ralph Lauren
Richemont
Tiffany
Tommy Hilfiger
Vera Wang

HISTORICAL FINANCIALS

Company Type: Public

Income Statement

FYE: January 31

	REVENUE ($ mil.)	NET INCOME ($ mil.)	NET PROFIT MARGIN	EMPLOYEES
1/03	2,738	244	8.9%	10,684
1/02	2,285	278	12.2%	9,934
1/01	2,259	337	14.9%	9,223
1/00	1,236	330	26.7%	7,908
1/99	1,043	195	18.7%	2,806
1/98	975	176	18.0%	1,954
1/97	881	168	19.1%	1,504
1/96	500	83	16.6%	1,176
1/95	264	18	6.8%	1,157
1/94	203	(22)	—	—
Annual Growth	**33.5%**	**—**	**—**	**32.0%**

2003 Year-End Financials

Debt ratio: 25.7%
Return on equity: 5.4%
Cash ($ mil.): 3,158
Current ratio: 3.16
Long-term debt ($ mil.): 1,294
No. of shares (mil.): 100
Dividends
Yield: 0.5%
Payout: 21.0%
Market value ($ mil.): 9,418

Stock History

NYSE: GUC

	STOCK PRICE ($) FY Close	P/E High/Low		PER SHARE ($) Earnings	Dividends	Book Value
1/03	93.96	42	35	2.38	0.50	50.16
1/02	86.00	35	24	2.74	7.50	39.33
1/01	91.10	35	22	3.31	0.45	41.16
1/00	106.81	35	18	3.48	0.40	38.71
1/99	68.81	23	10	3.28	0.40	9.86
1/98	39.81	27	10	2.86	0.30	7.52
Annual Growth	**18.7%**	**—**	**—**	**(3.6%)**	**10.8%**	**46.2%**

Hanson PLC

Breaking rocks in the hot sun is no punishment for building materials company Hanson PLC. Its Hanson Building Materials America (nearly half of sales) provides North America with aggregates, cement, bricks, and concrete pipe. Hanson Building Materials Europe is one of the UK's top producers of aggregates and concrete products and a leading brickmaker on the Continent. Operations include quarries, marine dredging, and recycling. Hanson also has subsidiaries in Asia and Australia. The company is what's left of the Hanson Group — a huge industrial conglomerate that was broke up into four publicly traded enterprises involving tobacco, coal, chemicals, and building materials.

Hanson has been meeting the challenges of a flat demand in its key markets by selling noncore assets, cutting costs, and raising some prices. The company continues to look for acquisitions within the fragmented building products industry, especially in high-growth markets. It made

10 acquisitions in 2002, including US-based concrete pipe maker Choctaw Inc. In the UK, the British government's 10-year program to modernize the country's transportation infrastructure should benefit Hanson.

The company beefed up its Hanson Australia unit with the acquisition of Pioneer International and in late 2002 agreed to merge that unit with the Aussie operations of global rivals CSR Ltd. (Australia) and Holcim (Switzerland). Hanson will hold 25% of the new company, Australia's largest cement producer.

HISTORY

In the 1950s and 1960s James Hanson and Gordon White were British *bon vivants*. Hanson was once engaged to Audrey Hepburn, and White dated Joan Collins. However, they later became better known as sharp businessmen.

Through the Wiles Group, a fertilizer business they took over in 1964, Hanson and White sought poorly managed companies in mature industries at low prices. Within 10 years Hanson and White had collected 24 such businesses with sales in excess of $120 million.

Perceiving an antibusiness attitude in the UK, White formed a New York subsidiary, Hanson Industries, in 1973. He made his first American purchase in 1974, buying Seacoast (animal feed). Other purchases in hot dogs, shoes, and batteries followed, including conglomerate US Industries in 1984. That year the company acquired leading UK brick maker London Brick.

In bitterly fought hostile takeovers in 1986, Hanson acquired SCM (Smith-Corona office equipment, Glidden Paints, Durkee's Famous Foods, SCM Chemicals) and Imperial Group (cigarettes, beer, food, hotels, restaurants). It acquired US cement maker Kaiser Cement in 1987. The company changed its name to Hanson PLC that year.

Hanson acquired Peabody (coal) in 1990 and Beazer PLC, a UK construction firm with extensive US holdings, a year later. During 1992 the company sold a number of assets; the next year it bought Quantum Chemicals (propane distribution) for $3.4 billion. Hanson took Beazer Homes (home building materials, US) public in 1994, retaining 30%.

In 1995 the company spun off some of its US operations as U.S. Industries and sold its 62% stake in Suburban Propane, a major US propane distributor. It also reorganized Beazer's US operations as Cornerstone Construction & Materials. Hanson also merged its Butterley Brick and London Brick into one company, Hanson Brick. Also in 1995 founder White died.

The Hanson conglomerate in 1996 began to split up its operations, creating four separate public companies focused on chemicals (Millennium Chemicals), tobacco (Imperial Tobacco), energy (Energy Group PLC), and building materials and equipment (Hanson PLC). In 1997 Cornerstone Construction & Materials acquired Concrete Pipe and Products for about $125 million. James Hanson retired that year.

Joining the consolidation of the US building-materials sector, Hanson bought six US firms in 1998 — HG Fenton (aggregates and ready-mix concrete), Becker Minerals (aggregates), Condux (concrete pipe), Gifford-Hill American (aggregates), and Nelson & Sloan (aggregates and ready-mix concrete). Also that year the company paid $155 million to settle environmental liabilities inherited when it purchased Koppers Company in 1991.

In 1999 Hanson sold Grove Worldwide — a world-leading maker of cranes and materials-handling equipment — to Robert Bass' investment firm, Keystone, and also sold its 24% stake in Westralian Sands (titanium and zircon, Australia). Hanson bought the North American brick business of Canada-based Jannock, as well as San Francisco (Jones Sand) and North Carolina (Brewer Sand) sand businesses.

Hanson acquired Pioneer International, a giant Australian concrete and aggregate company, for about $2.5 billion in 2000. Smaller acquisitions during the year included US concrete pipe and products makers Joelson Taylor, Cincinnati Concrete Pipe, and Milan Concrete Products.

In late 2000 Hanson acquired Davon, another US-based (Ohio) concrete and aggregate company. In early 2001 the company sold its waste management division, part of Hanson Quarry Products Europe, to Waste Recycling Group. Hanson's 2001 acquisitions included Centennial Pipe and Products, a major Canadian pipe maker (from LaFarge), as well as businesses in Mexico, Spain, and the UK.

Early in 2002 Andrew Dougal retired as CEO and was replaced by Alan Murray. Hanson added to its US operations midyear with the purchase of Choctaw Inc. (concrete pipes, corrugated steel pipes, and precast concrete structures) from Amatek Holdings Ltd. for $135 million. That year it sold its 50% stake in North Texas Cement Co. In 2003 Hanson acquired US-based aggregates company Better Materials for $150 million.

EXECUTIVES

Chairman: Christopher D. Collins, age 63
CEO and Director; President and CEO, Hanson Building Materials America: Alan J. Murray, age 49
Finance Director and Director: Jonathan Nicholls, age 45
Legal Director and Director: Graham Dransfield, age 51
Chief Executive, Hanson Australia: Leslie (Les) Cadzow
Chief Executive, Hanson Building Materials Europe, and Director: Simon N. Vivian, age 45
Chief Executive, Hanson Pacific: Patrick O'Shea
EVP and CFO, Hanson Building Materials America: Michael J. Donahue
Managing Director, UK Aggregates: Mike Ogden
Chief Accountant: Kenneth Ludlam
Secretary: Paul Tunnacliffe
Group Treasurer: Karl Fenlon
Group Finance Manager: Nick Swift
Head, Corporate Development and Corporate Affairs: Justin Read
Head of Tax: Cecil Avery
Auditors: Ernst & Young

LOCATIONS

HQ: 1 Grosvenor Place,
London SW1X 7JH, United Kingdom
Phone: +44-20-7245-1245   **Fax:** +44-20-7235-3455
US HQ: 1333 Campus Pkwy., Neptune, NJ 07753
US Phone: 732-919-9777   **US Fax:** 732-919-1149
Web: www.hansonplc.com

Hanson has operations in Asia (China, Indonesia, Malaysia, Singapore, and Thailand), Australia, Europe (the UK, Belgium, the Czech Republic, France, Germany, the Netherlands, and Spain), Israel, and North America (Canada, Mexico, and the US).

2002 Sales

	% of total
North America	46
Europe	37
Australia	11
Asia	6
Total	**100**

PRODUCTS/OPERATIONS

Selected Products

Aggregates
Asphalt
Clay brick
Concrete and ready-mix concrete
Pipe
Roofing tiles

Selected Operations

Hanson Building Materials America
  Hanson Aggregates
  Hanson Brick and Tile
  Hanson Pipe & Products
Hanson Building Materials Europe
  Hanson Aggregates
  Hanson Aggregates Marine
  Hanson Building Products
Hanson Australia
  Australian Cement Holdings (joint venture with CSR)
  Metromix (joint venture with CSR)
  Pioneer Building Product
  Pioneer Construction Materials
  Pioneer Road Services (joint venture)
Hanson Pacific

COMPETITORS

Aggregate Industries	Italcementi
BayWa	Lafarge SA
Boral	Martin Marietta Materials
CEMEX	Readymix
CBR	RMC
CRH	Saint-Gobain
CSR Limited	Siam Cement
Dyckerhoff	Taiheiyo Cement
FLS Industries	Tarmac
FCC	Trinity Industries
Franz Haniel	Ube
HeidelbergCement	Vulcan Materials
Holcim	

HISTORICAL FINANCIALS

Company Type: Public

Income Statement

FYE: December 31

	REVENUE ($ mil.)	NET INCOME ($ mil.)	NET PROFIT MARGIN	EMPLOYEES
12/02	5,880	302	5.1%	25,600
12/01	5,568	406	7.3%	26,800
12/00	4,689	381	8.1%	24,700
12/99	3,103	540	17.4%	16,800
12/98	3,029	589	19.4%	16,000
12/97	4,993	1,286	25.8%	80,000
12/96	3,995	496	12.4%	76,000
12/95	17,673	1,604	9.1%	75,000
12/94	17,655	1,679	9.5%	74,000
12/93	14,467	1,098	7.6%	80,000
Annual Growth	**(9.5%)**	**(13.4%)**	**—**	**(11.9%)**

2002 Year-End Financials

Debt ratio: 36.6%
Return on equity: 7.3%
Cash ($ mil.): 2,209
Current ratio: 1.32
Long-term debt ($ mil.): 1,567
No. of shares (mil.): 147
Dividends
  Yield: 5.2%
  Payout: 56.1%
Market value ($ mil.): 3,269

Stock History

NYSE: HAN

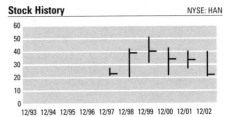

12/93 12/94 12/95 12/96 12/97 12/98 12/99 12/00 12/01 12/02

	STOCK PRICE ($) FY Close	P/E High/Low		PER SHARE ($) Earnings	Dividends	Book Value
12/02	22.18	19	10	2.05	1.15	29.08
12/01	33.62	15	10	2.75	1.10	26.92
12/00	34.25	18	9	2.67	1.22	24.58
12/99	40.31	16	10	4.11	2.59	22.89
12/98	39.00	15	7	4.51	0.42	19.60
12/97	23.00	6	5	9.88	0.00	11.11
Annual Growth	**(0.7%)**	**—**	**—**	**(27.0%)**	**—**	**21.2%**

Heineken N.V.

Smaller brewers might be green with envy. Heineken, a global brewing giant, sells beer in more than 170 nations. The company's global brands include Amstel and Murphy's as well as Heineken. The company's national and regional brands include Buckler (Europe), Quilmes (Argentina), Moretti (Italy), Tiger (Asia's leading regional brew), Zagorka (Bulgaria), and Bochkaryov (Russia). Heineken also distributes soft drinks and other nonalcoholic beverages. Heineken has interests in more than 110 breweries and continues to acquire more worldwide.

Heineken is the #2 imported beer in the US (behind Grupo Modelo's Corona, which tapped the #1 spot after nearly 65 years of Heineken dominance). About 75% of Heineken's sales are in Europe, where it has solidified its base by buying breweries in Central Europe, Italy, Spain, and Russia.

Heineken purchased Austrian brewer BBAG Österreichische Brau-Beteiligungs-AG for $1.7 billion in June 2003. It plans to combine its regional operations with BBAG, creating Brau Union AG. The company also plans to grow steadily in new markets such as Asia and South America; political unrest has impeded its growth in Africa. However, it joined with Diageo to purchase 30% of Interbrew's Namibia Breweries in southern Africa.

The company plans to trim costs by cutting 450 jobs in the Netherlands in the next two years.

The founding Heineken family owns 50% of Heineken Holding, which owns 50% of Heineken.

HISTORY

Every Sunday morning Gerard Heineken's mother was appalled by crowds of drunken Dutchmen who had consumed too much gin the night before. Heineken, who wanted his mother's financial backing, insisted that drunkenness would decrease if people drank beer instead of gin and pointed out that there were no good beers in Holland. His strategy worked. In 1863 Heineken's mother put up the money to buy De Hooiberg (The Haystack), a 271-year-old brewery in Amsterdam.

Gerard proved his aptitude for brewing and within 10 years had established a brewery in Rotterdam. He named his brewery Heineken in 1873 and launched the company's lucrative foreign trade by exporting beer first to France three years later. (By the 1950s half the beer brewed by the company was for export.) The company perfected the yeast strain (Heineken A-yeast) in 1886 that it still uses in its beer today.

In 1917 Gerard's son Dr. Henri Pierre Heineken inherited the firm and decided to expand operations to the US, making a voyage to that country himself. While at sea, Henri Pierre met Leo van Munching, a ship's bartender who displayed a remarkable knowledge of beer. Recognizing van Munching's talent, Henri Pierre hired him as Heineken's US importer. Prohibition killed the US operations, although the company entered new markets elsewhere; after repeal, Heineken was the first foreign beer to reenter the US market.

After WWII, Henri Pierre sent his son, Alfred, to learn the business under van Munching, who had created a national distribution system in the US. Alfred succeeded his father in 1953 and stepped down in 1989.

Heineken bought the Amstel Brewery in Holland (founded 1870) in 1968. Two years later it became a producer of stout through the acquisition of James J. Murphy in Cork, Ireland. Facing a consolidation of the European market, Heineken launched a campaign in the 1980s to expand its European beer operations, purchasing breweries in France, Greece, Ireland, Italy, and Spain.

In 1991 Heineken bought the van Munching US import business and a majority interest in Hungarian brewer Komaromi Sorgyar, its first Eastern European investment. Two years later Karel Vuursteen was appointed chairman.

The firm cut over 1,300 jobs in 1993 and sold its spirits and wine operations in 1994. In 1995 Heineken began a major spending spree, acquiring Interbrew Italia and 66% of Zlaty Bazant, the largest Slovakian brewery and maltworks (it acquired the rest in 1999). The company bought Birra Moretti, Italy's third-largest brewery, in 1996. It also purchased interests in two African breweries. All the acquisitions led to high integration costs and lower profits.

To boost its sales in Poland, in 1998 Heineken raised its stake in brewer Zaklady Piwowarskie W. Zywcu (Zywiec) to 75%, bought a minority stake in Brewpole, and merged the companies to create the largest Polish brewer. Also in 1998 Heineken bought about 25% of Pivara Skopje, the largest brewery in the former Yugoslav republic of Macedonia, through its Brewinvest joint venture. In 1999 the company bought about 18% of Israel's leading brewer, Tempo (Goldstar and Maccabee beers).

In 2000 Heineken bought 99% of Spanish brewer Cruzcampo, most of it from Diageo. Cruzcampo later merged with Heineken's Spanish brewer El Águila to create Heineken España. In February 2001 Heineken created BrauHolding International, a joint venture with Bayerische BrauHolding, to sell Paulaner Weiss beer and give Heineken access to two German beer makers.

In 2002 vice president Anthony Ruys replaced Vuursteen as CEO. Heineken also announced it would launch its premium Heineken beer in the U.K. in early 2003 and eventually withdraw its Heineken Cold Filtered and Heineken Export beers from that market. It also signed a deal allowing Belgium's Interbrew to brew and sell Murphy's Irish Stout in the U.K. Heineken also

gained EU approval that year to buy a stake in German brewer Karlsberg.

Also in 2002 Heineken agreed to buy stakes in two Central American breweries: Costa Rica's Florida Ice and Farm Company (FIFCO) and Nicaragua's Consorcio Cervecero Centroamericano S.A. (COCECA). With FIFCO and Coca-Cola bottler Panamerican Beverages, Heineken purchased Cervecerías Baru-Panamá, the country's second-largest brewer, for $138 million. The company later purchased Russian brewer Bravo International (which changed its name to Heineken Brewery in 2003). Heineken also bought a controlling stake in Egyptian brewer Al Ahram Beverages Co. in 2002, which produces Fayrouz, a nonalcoholic beer favored by Muslims. The brewer also agreed to increase its stake in Lebanese brewer Almaza S.A.L. from 10% to 79%.

In January 2003 Heineken sold all of its shares (15% of outstanding shares) in Quilmes to Beverage Associates Corp. (BAC); AmBev agreed to acquire 8.6% of the Quilmes shares from BAC.

EXECUTIVES

Chairman, Executive Board: Anthony Ruys, age 56
Member, Executive Board: Marc J. Bolland, age 44
Member, Executive Board: Jean François van Boxmeer, age 42
Member, Executive Board: René Hooft Graafland, age 48
Director, Corporate Finance: David R. Hazelwood
President and CEO, Heineken USA:
  Frans Van der Minne
Auditors: KPMG Accountants N.V.

LOCATIONS

HQ: Tweede Weteringplantsoen 21,
  1017 ZD Amsterdam, The Netherlands
Phone: +31-20-523-92-39   **Fax:** +31-20-626-35-03
US HQ: 360 Hamilton Ave., Ste. 1103,
  White Plains, NY 10601
US Phone: 914-681-4100   **US Fax:** 914-681-1900
Web: www.heinekeninternational.com

Heineken has more than 110 breweries in more than 60 countries.

2002 Sales

	% of total
Europe	74
Western Hemisphere	14
Africa/Middle East	8
Asia/Pacific	4
Total	**100**

PRODUCTS/OPERATIONS

Selected Beer Brands

33 Export	Maccabee
Aguila	Moretti
Amstel	Murphy's
Bochkaryov	Okhota
Buckler	Paulaner Weiss
Cruzcampo	Piton
Dreher	Primus
EB	Quilmes
Fayrouz (alcohol-free)	Star
Fischer	Tiger
Goldstar	Vos
Guinness (licensed)	Warka
Heineken	Wieckse Witte
Ichnusa	Zagorka
Kaiser	Zywiec
Loewenbrau (licensed)	

COMPETITORS

Adolph Coors	Gambrinus
Allied Domecq	Interbrew
Anheuser-Busch	Kirin
Asahi Breweries	Lion Nathan
Bavaria	Miller Brewing
AmBev	Grupo Modelo
Boston Beer	Molson
Carlsberg	Grolsch
Cervecerías Unidas	SABMiller
Constellation Brands	San Miguel
Diageo	Scottish & Newcastle
FEMSA	Taiwan Tobacco & Wine
Foster's	

HISTORICAL FINANCIALS
Company Type: Public

Income Statement

FYE: December 31

	REVENUE ($ mil.)	NET INCOME ($ mil.)	NET PROFIT MARGIN	EMPLOYEES
12/02	10,788	833	7.7%	48,237
12/01	8,515	679	8.0%	40,025
12/00	7,634	585	7.7%	37,857
12/99	7,198	548	7.6%	36,733
12/98	7,361	522	7.1%	33,511
12/97	6,668	376	5.6%	32,421
12/96	7,053	379	5.4%	31,682
12/95	6,492	413	6.4%	27,379
12/94	5,751	382	6.6%	26,197
12/93	4,647	267	5.7%	23,997
Annual Growth	9.8%	13.5%	—	8.1%

2002 Year-End Financials

Debt ratio: 47.8%   Current ratio: 1.20
Return on equity: 32.6%   Long-term debt ($ mil.): 1,273
Cash ($ mil.): 815

Net Income History

OTC: HINKY

Henkel KGaA

Henkel is focusing on home and hearth. The company sold its chemical operations (Cognis and joint venture Henkel-Ecolab) and its fertilizer and plant care business (Substral) to focus on its branded laundry, home care, cosmetics, toiletries, and adhesive products. Most of Henkel's operations are centered in Europe, where the company is a leading maker of toiletries, cosmetics, detergents, and cleansers. It also makes adhesives and surface care preparation products for industrial use through its Henkel Technologies division. Relatives of the founding Henkel family control the company.

Germany accounts for almost 25% of Henkel's sales, while the rest of Europe, along with Africa and the Middle East, brings in almost 50%. The company owns almost 29% of US bleach giant Clorox. Henkel has operations in more than 75 countries.

HISTORY

In 1876 Fritz Henkel, a chemical plant worker, started Henkel & Cie in Aachen to make a universal detergent. Henkel moved the company to Düsseldorf in 1878 and launched Henkel's Bleaching Soda, one of Germany's first brand-name products. In the 1880s the company began making water glass, an ingredient of its detergent, which differs from soap in the way it emulsifies dirt. Henkel debuted Persil, a detergent that eliminated the need for rubbing or bleaching clothes, in 1907. Persil became a leading detergent in Germany.

Henkel set up an Austrian subsidiary in 1913. In response to a postwar adhesives shortage, the company started making glue for its own packaging and soon became Europe's leading glue maker. Henkel began making cleansers with newly developed phosphates in the late 1920s.

When Fritz died in 1930, Henkel stock was divided among his three children. In the 1930s the company sponsored a whaling fleet that provided fats for its products, and by 1939 the firm had 16 plants in Europe.

During WWII Henkel lost most of its foreign plants and made unbranded soap in Germany. After the war the company retooled its plants, branched out into personal care products, and competed with Unilever, Procter & Gamble, and Colgate-Palmolive for control of the German detergent market. (By 1968 Henkel dominated, with a nearly 50% share.)

In 1960 Henkel bought its first US company, Standard Chemicals (renamed Henkel Corp. in 1971). Konrad Henkel, who took over in 1961, modernized the company's image by making changes in management structure and marketing techniques. Henkel patented a substitute for environmentally harmful phosphates, acquired 15% of Clorox in 1974, and bought General Mills' chemical business in 1977.

Henkel, owned at the time by 66 family members, went public with nonvoting shares in 1985. It bought US companies Nopco (specialty chemicals) and Parker Chemical (metal surface pretreatment) in 1987 and Emery, the #1 US oleochemicals maker, in 1989.

Henkel reorganized its product lines in 1991 by selling several noncore businesses. That year Henkel formed a partnership with Ecolab (of which it owned 24% — later expanded to 50%); acquired interests in Hungary, Poland, Russia, and Slovenia; and introduced Persil in Spain and Portugal. In 1994 Henkel expanded into China and bought 25% of a Brazilian detergent maker. The company's 1995 acquisition of Hans Schwarzkopf GmbH made Henkel the #1 hair-coloring manufacturer in Germany. The company bought Novamax Technologies, a US-based maker of metal-surface treatments, in 1996. The next year Henkel paid $1.3 billion for US adhesive giant Loctite, its biggest purchase to date. In 1998 it bought Ohio-based adhesives maker Manco to combine its US and Canadian consumer adhesives businesses (parts of Loctite and LePage, respectively) under Manco. Henkel pushed into the US toiletries market in 1998 by paying $93 million for DEP and creating a new subsidiary, Schwarzkopf & DEP Inc.

In 1999 Henkel created a new chemicals unit, Cognis, to focus primarily on palm kernel- and coconut oil-based products. To strengthen Cognis, Henkel bought Laboratoires Serobiologiques, a French producer of ingredients for the cosmetic and food industries, and divested specialty paper chemicals operations. Henkel also formed a joint venture with soap maker Dial (Dial/Henkel LLC); the joint venture later bought the Custom Cleaner home dry cleaning business from Creative Products Resource.

Henkel picked up Yamahatsu Sangyo, a Japanese maker of hair colorants, in 2000. The company sold its Substral unit (fertilizer and plant care) to Scotts Company. In 2001 Henkel bought ATOFINA's metal treatment chemicals business. Later in the year the company sold its Cognis specialty chemicals unit to private equity funds Schroeder Ventures and Goldman Sachs Capital Partners for about $2.2 billion. That year Henkel also said it would cut between 2,500 and 3,000 jobs (about 5% of its workforce) over the next two years. Also that year the company sold its stake in joint venture Henkel-Ecolab to Ecolab for about $430 million.

In March 2003 Henkel bought a 6.9% stake in German hair-care company Wella. Later that year, Henkel purchased a majority stake in La Luz S.A., a Central American manufacturer and marketer of detergents and household cleaners. Henkel entered the Latin American detergents market via Mexico in 2000.

Henkel strengthened its adhesives business in Russia and North, Central, and Eastern Europe when it acquired Makroflex from YIT Construction Ltd. in July 2003. Makroflex, located in Finland and Estonia, develops, makes, and sells sealants and insulation materials for the construction industry.

EXECUTIVES

Chairman: Albrecht Woeste, age 57
President and CEO: Ulrich Lehner, age 57
EVP, Consumer and Craftsman Adhesives: Alois Linder, age 56
EVP, Cosmetics and Toiletries: Uwe Specht, age 60
EVP, Laundry and Home Care: Klaus Morwind, age 60
EVP, Finance: Jochen Krautter, age 61
EVP, Henkel Technologies: Guido De Keersmaecker, age 61
EVP, Human Resources and Logistics: Knut Weinke, age 60
President and CEO, Henkel Corporation (US): John E. Knudson
Controller: Lothar Steineback, age 55
Manager, Corporate Development: Pierre Brusselmans
Manager, Information Systems: Peter Hinzman
Manager, Research and Development: Wolfgang Gawrisch
General Counsel: Franz-Josef Acher
Media Relations: Sven Jacobsen
Auditors: KPMG Deutsche Treuhand-Gesellschaft AG

LOCATIONS

HQ: Henkelstr. 67, D-40191 Düsseldorf, Germany
Phone: +49-211-797-0   **Fax:** +49-211-798-2484
US HQ: 2200 Renaissance Blvd., Ste. 200, Gulph Mills, PA 19406
US Phone: 610-270-8100   **US Fax:** 610-270-8104
Web: www.henkel.com

2002 Sales

	$ mil.	% of total
Germany	2,429	24
Asia/Pacific	1,316	13
North America	911	9
Latin America	607	6
Other Europe, Africa & Middle East	4,858	48
Total	**10,121**	**100**

PRODUCTS/OPERATIONS

2002 Sales

	$ mil.	% of total
Laundry & home care	3,239	32
Henkel Technologies	2,935	29
Cosmetics/toiletries	2,226	22
Consumer & craftsmen adhesives	1,417	14
Corporate	304	3
Total	**10,121**	**100**

Selected Products

Adhesives
Consumer and craftsmen adhesives
Engineering adhesives
Industrial and packaging adhesives

Detergents and Household Cleansers
Bath and toilet cleansers
Dishwashing products
Fabric softeners
Floor and carpet care products
Furniture and kitchen care products
Glass cleaners
Heavy-duty detergents
Household cleansers
Plant care products
Scouring agents
Shoe and laundry conditioning products
Specialty detergents

Cosmetics and Toiletries
Bath and shower products
Dental care and oral hygiene products
Deodorants
Hair colorants
Hair salon products
Hairstyling and permanent-wave products
Perfumes and fragrances
Shampoos and conditioners
Skin care products
Skin creams
Toilet soaps

Industrial and Institutional Hygiene and Surface Technologies

COMPETITORS

3M	Johnson & Johnson
Alticor	Kimberly-Clark
Avon	L'Oréal
Bayer AG	Playtex
Beiersdorf	Procter & Gamble
Church & Dwight	Reckitt Benckiser
Colgate-Palmolive	Sara Lee
Dial	Sara Lee Household
Dow Chemical	S.C. Johnson
Estée Lauder	Shiseido
Gillette	Unilever
H.B. Fuller	

HISTORICAL FINANCIALS

Company Type: Public

Income Statement

FYE: December 31

	REVENUE ($ mil.)	NET INCOME ($ mil.)	NET PROFIT MARGIN	EMPLOYEES
12/02	10,121	456	4.5%	48,638
12/01	11,569	445	3.8%	59,995
12/00	12,033	441	3.7%	60,475
12/99	11,441	407	3.6%	56,396
12/98	12,729	434	3.4%	56,291
12/97	11,196	629	5.6%	53,753
12/96	10,495	332	3.2%	46,665
12/95	9,875	339	3.4%	41,664
12/94	9,080	300	3.3%	40,590
12/93	7,976	221	2.8%	40,480
Annual Growth	**2.7%**	**8.4%**	**—**	**2.1%**

Debt ratio: 9.5%   Current ratio: 1.85
Return on equity: 13.9%   Long-term debt ($ mil.): 328
Cash ($ mil.): 237

Net Income History   German: HENKY

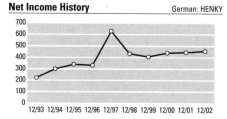

broke Group. It had 109 off-track betting shops in operation; by 1971 it had 660.

Stein pushed to diversify the company into real estate and casinos during the 1970s, and in 1973 Ladbroke bought three hotels. In the late 1970s the company suffered a major setback when its casino ventures in London were closed down and it was found guilty of violating gaming laws. The firm abandoned the casino business in 1979. In 1984 the company bought the Belgian Le Tierce betting shop chain and broke into the US market in 1985 with the acquisition of the Detroit Race Course (sold in 1998). In 1987 Ladbroke beat out competitors to buy the 91-hotel Hilton International chain from Allegis Corporation for more than $1 billion. The deal made Ladbroke one of the world's top hotel operators.

Stein retired as chairman in 1994 and was replaced by John Jackson. Peter George, who had been with the company since 1963, was appointed chief executive. That year the company re-entered the casino business, paying $75 million for three London casinos. Though Ladbroke's property and retail division suffered in the 1990s, the hotel chain continued to expand; by 1995 there were 160 in operation. In 1997 Ladbroke entered into a sales and marketing alliance with US-based Hilton Hotels to promote the Hilton brand throughout the world. The next year Ladbroke acquired #3 betting shop operator Coral from leisure group Bass (now split into Mitchells & Butlers and InterContinental Hotel Group). However, UK regulators later forced the company to sell the chain. (A venture capital company backed by Morgan Grenfell Private Equity bought it for about $655 million.)

With its $2 billion acquisition of Stakis in 1999, Ladbroke gained 55 hotels and 20 casinos in the UK and Ireland, as well as the LivingWell health club chain. Stakis' CEO David Michels became head of Hilton International. Ladbroke changed its name to Hilton Group that year. In 2000 Peter George resigned from the company and was replaced by Michels. That year Hilton Group sold its casino operations for $373 million to Gala Group Holdings. In 2001 the company bought the Scandic Hotel chain for about $885 million. Also that year, Jackson retired as chairman and was replaced by Ian Robinson.

EXECUTIVES

Chairman: Sir Ian Robinson, age 60
Group Chief Executive: David M. C. Michels, age 56
Deputy Group Chief Executive and Group Finance Director: Brian G. Wallace, age 49
Chief Executive, Ladbrokes Betting Worldwide: Christopher Bell, age 45
President, The Americas: Howard Friedman
President, Europe and Africa: Jurgen Fischer
President, Middle East and Asia Pacific: Koos Klein
President, UK and Ireland: Wolfgang M. Neumann
Managing Director, Ladbrokes: Alan Ross
Managing Director, Ladbrokes eGaming: John O'Reilly
Managing Director, LivingWell: Paul Harvey
SVP Real Estate, Hilton International: Desmond Taljaard
Director Corporate Affairs: Alex Pagett
Director Corporate Development: Roger Devlin
Director Human Resources and Legal Services: Brian Taker
Investor Relations: James Mason
Auditors: Ernst & Young

Hilton Group plc

Hilton Group knows how to cover its bets as well as its beds. The company is a major hotel operator through its Hilton International division and is the #1 operator of betting shops in the UK. Hilton Group's Ladbroke division operates more than 2,500 betting shops across Belgium, Ireland, and the UK. It also has a telephone betting operation and maintains two gambling Web sites. Its Hilton International unit owns the rights to the Hilton brand outside the US and operates some 400 hotels in more than 75 countries. The company also operates a centralized reservation system and rewards program with US-based Hilton Hotels. In addition, Hilton International owns the LivingWell chain of health clubs.

Hospitality accounts for about a third of Hilton's revenue while its gaming activities make up the remaining two-thirds. The Ladbroke division's Web operations offer online betting on a variety of events, including cricket, soccer, football, rugby, greyhound racing, and golf. Its online casino features roulette, blackjack, craps, video poker, and other games. The division also runs Vernons soccer betting pools.

Given that there are no real synergies between its two business lines, Hilton Group has had to adopt two different strategies to grow its overall business. The company is committed to expanding its hotel business through new construction and acquisitions, and in 2001 bought the Scandic chain, with more than 150 properties, for about $884 million. Meanwhile, it has streamlined its gaming business by selling off its Ladbroke Casinos in 2000. It is also looking for new gaming products to offer its patrons, including more online gambling opportunities.

HISTORY

The Hilton Group traces its roots to the village of Ladbroke in central England, where Arthur Bendir, a local racehorse trainer, set up a partnership in 1886 to take bets on horse races. Although off-track betting was illegal, betting on credit was allowed for wealthier members of society. The partnership, Ladbroke and Co., moved to London in 1900 and established itself as a quality credit betting shop in the city's plush West End. Bendir sold the business in 1957 to the Stein family. In 1960 the government legalized cash betting and Ladbroke began to expand. Cyril Stein became chairman in 1966 and took the company public the next year as the Lad-

LOCATIONS

HQ: Maple Court, Central Park, Reeds Crescent, Watford, Hertfordshire WD24 4QQ, United Kingdom
Phone: +44-20-7856-8000   **Fax:** +44-20-7856-8001
Web: www.hiltongroup.com

Hilton Group has nearly 400 hotels in more than 75 countries, as well as 100 health clubs in the UK. Its Ladbrokes unit operates more than 2,500 betting shops in Belgium, Ireland, and the UK.

PRODUCTS/OPERATIONS

Selected Operations

Hilton International
Hilton International Hotels (branded hotel chains)
LivingWell (health clubs)
Scandic (hotel chain)
Ladbroke Betting and Gaming
Ladbrokes (betting shops)
Vernons (soccer betting pools)

COMPETITORS

Camelot
Coral Eurobet
Four Seasons Hotels
Hyatt
Marriott International
Millennium & Copthorne Hotels
Rank
Stanley Leisure
Starwood Hotels & Resorts
Thistle Hotels
Whitbread
William Hill
Wyndham
Zetters

HISTORICAL FINANCIALS

Company Type: Public

Income Statement   FYE: December 31

	REVENUE ($ mil.)	NET INCOME ($ mil.)	NET PROFIT MARGIN	EMPLOYEES
12/02	8,788	156	1.8%	51,637
12/01	6,039	208	3.4%	55,413
12/00	5,898	208	3.5%	53,631
12/99	6,950	155	2.2%	53,483
12/98	7,764	354	4.6%	46,702
12/97	6,295	249	4.0%	71,000
12/96	6,399	35	0.5%	70,000
Annual Growth	5.4%	28.3%	—	(4.9%)

2002 Year-End Financials

Debt ratio: 56.9%   Current ratio: 0.79
Return on equity: 4.0%   Long-term debt ($ mil.): 2,254
Cash ($ mil.): 643

Net Income History   OTC: HLTGY

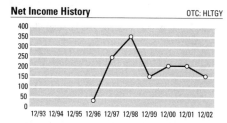

Hitachi, Ltd.

Hitachi, which means "risen sun," is looking for a new dawn of profits from its galaxy of businesses. The company is a world-leading maker of powerful, corporate transaction-oriented mainframes, as well as semiconductors, PCs, and other information system and telecommunications technologies. Hitachi also makes elevators and escalators, industrial robots and control systems, and power plant equipment. The company's power and industrial systems unit is its biggest revenue producer. Other products include metals, wire, and cable. Hitachi's consumer goods range from TVs to refrigerators and washing machines; the company also has operations in financial services, property management, and transportation.

Decreased demand for PC components and weakness in the telecom sector have hurt Hitachi, and the company is working to cut costs and reduce debt. It also hopes to combine packages of information services with more of its products. In 2002 Hitachi merged its system chip unit with that of Mitsubishi Electric to form a new company, Renesas Technology.

HISTORY

Namihei Odaira, an employee of Kuhara Mining in the Japanese coastal city of Hitachi, wanted to prove that Japan did not have to depend on foreigners for technology. In 1910 he began building electric motors in Kuhara's engineering and repair shop. Japanese power companies were forced to buy Odaira's generators when WWI made imports scarce. Impressed, they reordered, and in 1920 Hitachi (meaning "risen sun") became an independent company.

During the 1920s acquisitions and growth turned Hitachi into a major manufacturer of electrical equipment and machinery. In the 1930s and 1940s, Hitachi developed vacuum tubes and light bulbs and produced radar and sonar for the Japanese war effort. Postwar occupation forces removed Odaira and closed 19 Hitachi plants. Reeling from the plant closures, war damage, and labor strife, Hitachi was saved from bankruptcy by US military contracts during the Korean War.

In the 1950s Hitachi became a supplier to Nippon Telegraph and Telephone Corporation (NTT), the state-owned telecommunications monopoly. Japan's economic recovery led to strong demand for the company's communications and electrical equipment. Hitachi began mass-producing home appliances, radios, TVs, and transistors. The group spun off Hitachi Metals and Hitachi Cable in 1956 and Hitachi Chemical in 1963.

With the help of NTT, the Ministry of International Trade and Industry, and technology licensed from RCA (bought by General Electric in 1986), Hitachi produced its first computer in 1965. Hitachi built factories in Southeast Asia and started manufacturing integrated circuits.

Hitachi launched an IBM-compatible computer in 1974. The company sold its computers in the US through Itel until 1979, when Itel was bought by National Semiconductor, and afterward through National Semiconductor's NAS (National Advanced Systems) unit. In 1982 FBI agents caught Hitachi staff buying documents allegedly containing IBM software secrets. Settlement of a civil lawsuit required Hitachi to make payments to IBM for eight years as compensation for the use of IBM's software.

When in the late 1980s the rising Japanese yen hurt exports, Hitachi focused on its domestic market and invested heavily in factory automation. But a recession at home caused earnings to fall. In 1988 the company and Texas Instruments joined in the costly development and production of 16-megabyte DRAM semiconductor chips. In 1989 Hitachi bought 80% of NAS, giving it direct control of its US distribution.

Despite its rivalry with IBM, in 1991 Hitachi began to resell IBM notebook PCs under its own name in Japan. In a major move to combat sluggish consumer electronics sales, in 1994 Hitachi merged with its marketing subsidiary, Hitachi Sales Corp. Hitachi used joint ventures to beef up its international presence, including a 1995 agreement with India's Tata Group.

Tokyo police in 1997 began investigating Hitachi, charging that the company and others had paid off a corporate racketeer. A slump in microchip prices, coupled with the Asian economic turmoil, hurt Hitachi in 1998. Etsuhiko Shoyama became president in 1999, replacing Tsutomu Kanai, who became chairman. Hitachi posted its then-worst loss in history that fiscal year; the firm combined some subsidiaries and announced layoffs.

In 2000 Hitachi launched the Internet & Network Services Group to focus on Internet business development; the next year it joined NEC Corp. to develop semiconductors for LCD panels and cell phone displays.

The company teamed with Sun Microsystems in 2002 in a multibillion-dollar storage software distribution and cross-licensing agreement. Hitachi also formed a joint venture with IBM for Hitachi to acquire IBM's disk drive operations.

EXECUTIVES

Chairman: Tsutomu Kanai
President, CEO, and Director: Etsuhiko Shoyama
EVP and Director: Yoshiki Yagi
EVP and Director: Yoshiro Kuwata
EVP: Katsukuni Hisano
EVP: Kazuo Kumagai
SVP; General Manager, Research and Development Group: Michiharu Nakamura
VP; President and CEO, Information and Telecommunication Systems: Kazuo Furukawa
VP; President and CEO, Power and Industrial Systems: Shozo Saito
VP; President and CEO, Urban Planning and Development Services: Yoshito Tsunoda
VP; CEO, Platform and Network Systems Operation and Information and Telecommunications Systems: Manabu Shinomoto
VP; CEO, Social and Industrial Infrastructure Systems Operation and Industrial Systems: Takuya Tajima
VP; General Manager, Corporate Marketing: Tadahiko Ishigaki
VP; General Manager, Legal, Legal and Corporate Communications and Auditing: Takashi Hatchoji
General Manager, Finance: Takashi Miyoshi
General Manager, Human Capital: Iwao Hara
Auditors: KPMG

LOCATIONS

HQ: Hitachi Seisakusho Kabushiki Kaisha
6, Kanda-Surugadai 4-chome, Chiyoda-ku, Tokyo 101-8010, Japan
Phone: +81-3-3258-1111   **Fax:** +81-3-3258-2375
US HQ: 50 Prospect Ave., Tarrytown, NY 10591
US Phone: 914-332-5800   **US Fax:** 914-332-5555
Web: www.hitachi.com

2003 Sales

	% of total
Asia	
Japan	76
Other countries	10
North America	9
Europe	4
Other regions	1
Total	**100**

PRODUCTS/OPERATIONS

2003 Sales

	% of total
Power & industrial systems	22
Information & telecommunication systems	19
Electronic devices	15
High functional materials & components	12
Digital media & consumer products	12
Financial services	6
Logistics, services & other	14
Total	**100**

Selected Operations

Power and industrial systems
Air-conditioning equipment
Automotive equipment
Construction machinery
Elevators
Environmental control systems
Escalators
Hydroelectric power plants
Industrial machinery and plant construction
Nuclear power plants
Rolling stock
Thermal power plants

Information and telecommunication systems
Computer peripherals
Fiber-optic components
Mainframes
PCs
RAID storage systems
Servers
Software
Switches
Systems integration

Electronic devices
LCDs
Medical electronics equipment
Memories
Multi-purpose semiconductors
Semiconductor manufacturing equipment
System LSIs
Testing and measurement equipment

Logistics, services and other
General trading
Property management
Transportation

High-functional materials and components
Cables
Carbon products
Chemical products
Components
Copper products
Electrical insulating materials
Fine ceramics
Magnetic materials
Malleable cast-iron products
Printed circuit boards
Specialty steels
Synthetic resins
Wires

Digital media and consumer products
Batteries
Fluorescent lamps
Information storage media
Kitchen appliances
LCD projectors
Mobile phones
Optical storage drives
Refrigerators
Room air conditioners
TVs
VCRs
Videotapes
Washing machines

Financial services
Insurance services
Leasing
Loan guarantees

COMPETITORS

ALSTOM
Dell
Ericsson
Fluor
Fujitsu
GE
Hewlett-Packard
Intel
IBM
Matsushita
McDermott
Micron Technology
Mitsubishi Electric
Motorola
NEC
Nippon Steel
Nokia
Nortel Networks
Oki Electric
Philips Electronics
Samsung
SANYO
Sharp
Siemens
Sony
Texas Instruments
Toshiba
United Technologies
Whirlpool

HISTORICAL FINANCIALS

Company Type: Public

Income Statement

FYE: March 31

	REVENUE ($ mil.)	NET INCOME ($ mil.)	NET PROFIT MARGIN	EMPLOYEES
3/03	69,343	236	0.3%	320,528
3/02	60,104	(3,638)	—	306,989
3/01	67,879	842	1.2%	340,939
3/00	77,956	165	0.2%	337,911
3/99	65,929	(2,800)	—	328,351
3/98	63,764	26	0.0%	331,494
3/97	68,735	712	1.0%	330,152
3/96	75,771	1,322	1.7%	331,852
3/95	87,713	1,316	1.5%	331,673
3/94	72,174	637	0.9%	330,637
Annual Growth	(0.4%)	(10.4%)	—	(0.3%)

2003 Year-End Financials

Debt ratio: 81.6%
Return on equity: 1.4%
Cash ($ mil.): 7,010
Current ratio: 1.19
Long-term debt ($ mil.): 12,800

No. of shares (mil.): 337
Dividends
Yield: 0.0%
Payout: —
Market value ($ mil.): 11,839

Stock History

NYSE: HIT

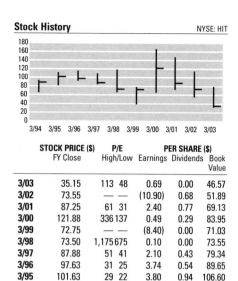

3/94 3/95 3/96 3/97 3/98 3/99 3/00 3/01 3/02 3/03

	STOCK PRICE ($) FY Close	P/E High/Low		Earnings	PER SHARE ($) Dividends	Book Value
3/03	35.15	113	48	0.69	0.00	46.57
3/02	73.55	—	—	(10.90)	0.68	51.89
3/01	87.25	61	31	2.40	0.77	69.13
3/00	121.88	336	137	0.49	0.29	83.95
3/99	72.75	—	—	(8.40)	0.00	71.03
3/98	73.50	1,175	675	0.10	0.00	73.55
3/97	87.88	51	41	2.10	0.43	79.34
3/96	97.63	31	25	3.74	0.54	89.65
3/95	101.63	29	22	3.80	0.94	106.60
3/94	88.88	47	34	1.88	0.86	87.94
Annual Growth	(9.8%)	—	—	(10.5%)	—	(6.8%)

Hollinger Inc.

Hollinger makes headlines as one of the largest newspaper groups in the world. It operates through a 32% ownership stake (72% voting interest) in Hollinger International, which publishes more than 150 daily, non-daily, trade, and specialty titles primarily in Israel, the UK, and the US. Hollinger International owns leading UK broadsheet *The Daily Telegraph, The Jerusalem Post* (Israeli English-language daily), and such US titles as the *Chicago Sun-Times*. Embattled leader Conrad Black controls about 78% of Hollinger through a private holding company.

Hollinger has been significantly paring down operations in recent years in an effort to focus on its larger newspapers. The company sold most of its Canadian newspapers in 2000, but kept a 50% stake in the *National Post* until 2002, when it sold out to partner CanWest. It also sold many of its US community papers. In addition, Hollinger has ceased investments in unrelated Internet companies, concentrating instead on Web sites for its newspapers and online partnerships related to editorial operations.

In 2003 its Hollinger International unit announced it was evaluating strategic alternatives and made a number of management changes including removing Black as CEO after the discovery of certain unauthorized payments to Black and other executives. (He remains at Hollinger International as non-executive chairman.)

HISTORY

A born entrepreneur, Conrad Black bought his first share of stock (in General Motors) at age eight. Some of his early childhood deals weren't quite so constructive: He was expelled from a private school at age 14 for selling exams and was kicked out of one law school after spending all his time playing the stock market.

Black entered publishing in 1969 when he and Peter White founded Sterling Newspapers and

bought the *Sherbrooke Record.* The two added to their flagship with a group of small daily papers in British Columbia, Quebec, and Prince Edward Island. In 1975 Black bought his father's 22% of the Ravelston Corporation, which owned Argus, a company formed in 1945 by E. P. Taylor to invest in breweries, malting and bottling operations, and a chemical business. Black took control of the company in the late 1970s by obtaining a loan through Sterling.

After assuming the leadership of Argus (through Ravelston), Black sold off chunks of the business to refine the company's holdings to key businesses. The company adopted the Hollinger name (left over from Argus's early investment in Hollinger Consolidated Gold Mines) in 1985 and gained control of struggling newspaper *The Daily Telegraph* (London), which it turned around by cutting staff and modernizing. In 1989 the firm purchased Jerusalem Post Publications.

Hollinger continued to acquire and restore struggling companies in the 1990s. It bought a stake in Southam in 1992 and acquired the Sun-Times Company, publisher of the *Chicago Sun-Times,* in 1994.

Hollinger purchased two daily and 12 non-daily papers in 1995 from Armadale, a closely held Canadian firm. Hollinger also bought 19 paid-circulation papers (12 dailies and seven weeklies) and several free publications from Canadian publisher Thomson Corporation. That year it sold its interests in the Telegraph Group, Southam, and John Fairfax (an Australian publisher) to subsidiary Hollinger International.

In 1996 Hollinger International assumed full control of the Telegraph Group, increased its stake in Southam to about 51%, and formed Hollinger Digital to coordinate new media businesses, especially on the Web. It sold most of its John Fairfax holdings to New Zealand-based Brierley Investments. In 1997 Hollinger International made an unsuccessful bid to buy the rest of Southam. It sold a stack of community newspapers to Leonard Green & Partners in 1998. Also that year, Southam launched Canada's *National Post,* its first national newspaper.

In 1999 Hollinger International finally bought all of Southam. Also that year Hollinger combined the smaller publications of Southam, Sterling Newspapers, and UniMedia into Hollinger Canadian Newspapers (in which it holds an 87% stake).

The company had a flurry of activity in 2000. The firm decided to sell off hundreds of its Canadian and American community newspapers and trade magazines in order to concentrate on its larger papers. It sold 13 of its larger Canadian daily newspapers, 136 community newspapers, and a 50% stake in the *National Post,* to CanWest Global Communications for $3.5 billion. (CanWest purchased the rest of the *National Post* in 2002.) It also sold off most of its US community papers. In late 2000 the company bought Copley's Fox Valley Press newspapers in Chicago. In 2001 the firm sold UniMédia Company, its Quebec-based French-language newspaper group, to Gesca Ltd. That year Black announced that Hollinger would join with a small group of investors to launch a new New York City daily paper in 2002 called the *New York Sun* aimed at a conservative audience. (The *Sun* debuted in April 2002.)

After a scandal involving unauthorized payments, Black stepped down as CEO of Hollinger International in 2003 but remained chairman.

EXECUTIVES

**Chairman and CEO; Non-executive Chairman,
  Hollinger International:** Lord
  Black (Conrad Moffat) of Crossharbour, age 58
**Vice Chairman and COO; Deputy Chairman and CEO,
  Telegraph Group:** Daniel W. Colson, age 54
EVP and Director: Peter Y. Atkinson, age 55
VP and Group Corporate Controller:
  Frederick A. Creasey, age 51
VP Editorial and Director: Barbara Amiel Black, age 62
VP and Secretary: Charles G. Cowan
Publisher, *The Jerusalem Post*: Tom Rose
Treasurer: Tatiana Samila
Auditors: KPMG LLP

LOCATIONS

HQ: 10 Toronto St., Toronto, Ontario M5C 2B7, Canada
Phone: 416-363-8721   **Fax:** 416-364-2088
US HQ: 401 N. Wabash Ave., Ste. 740, Chicago, IL 60611
US Phone: 312-321-2299   **US Fax:** 312-321-0629

Hollinger publishes newpapers in Israel, the US, and
the UK.

PRODUCTS/OPERATIONS

Selected Publications

Chicago Sun-Times (newspaper)
The Daily Telegraph (newspaper, London)
The Jerusalem Post (newspaper)
The Jerusalem Report (newsweekly)
The Spectator (magazine, UK)

Selected Subsidiaries

Hollinger International (72% voting power; newspapers;
  Israel, UK, US)
Chicago Group
Community Group (small US community newspaper)
Telegraph Group

COMPETITORS

Bell Globemedia
Daily Mail and General
  Trust
Dow Jones
Gannett
Hearst
Independent News
Knight-Ridder

New York Times
News Corp.
Northern & Shell
Torstar
Tribune
Trinity Mirror
Washington Post

HISTORICAL FINANCIALS

Company Type: Public

Income Statement

FYE: December 31

	REVENUE ($ mil.)	NET INCOME ($ mil.)	NET PROFIT MARGIN	EMPLOYEES
12/02	1,052	(56)	—	6,249
12/01	1,206	(83)	—	6,660
12/00	2,126	126	5.9%	9,600
12/99	2,254	107	4.7%	17,000
12/98	2,144	72	3.4%	16,500
12/97	2,180	120	5.5%	16,600
12/96	1,372	34	2.5%	12,500
12/95	1,109	8	0.7%	8,700
12/94	906	84	9.3%	8,700
12/93	873	25	2.9%	5,700
Annual Growth	2.1%	—	—	1.0%

2002 Year-End Financials

Debt ratio: —   Current ratio: 0.72
Return on equity: —   Long-term debt ($ mil.): 618
Cash ($ mil.): 120

Net Income History

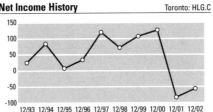

Toronto: HLG.C

Honda Motor Co., Ltd.

*Accord*ing to Honda, other carmakers can merge all they want — it's taking to the road alone. Honda is Japan's #3 automaker (after Toyota and Nissan) and the world's largest motorcycle producer. The company's car models include the Accord, CR-V, Civic, and Passport, as well as the luxury Acura and the Insight — a gasoline-electric hybrid. Honda's line of motorcycles includes everything from scooters to superbikes. The company's power products division makes commercial and residential-use machinery (lawn mowers, snowblowers), portable generators, and outboard motors.

While the rest of the automotive industry seems to be in the grips of acquisition/merger fever, Honda, the world leader in the manufacture of internal combustion engines (about 11 million per year), has stated publicly that it wants to remain on its own. The company's more than 110 factories in 31 countries give it the global reach and technological strength it needs to compete against the automotive giants. Honda plans to leverage its engine prowess through supply agreements with the likes of GM and through increased demand for gas-electric hybrids and the development of fuel cell-powered vehicles. North America accounts for nearly 50% of sales.

HISTORY

Soichiro Honda spent six years as an apprentice at Tokyo service station Art Shokai before opening his own branch of the repair shop in Hamamatsu in 1928. He also raced cars and in 1931 received a patent for metal spokes that replaced wood in wheels.

Honda started a piston ring company in 1937. During WWII the company produced metal propellers for Japanese bombers. When bombs and an earthquake destroyed most of his factory, Honda sold it to Toyota in 1945.

In 1946 Honda began motorizing bicycles with war-surplus engines. When this proved popular, Honda began making engines. The company was renamed Honda Motor Co. in 1948 and began producing motorcycles. In 1949 Soichiro Honda hired Takeo Fujisawa to manage the company so Honda could focus on engineering. Honda's innovative overhead valve design made its early 1950s Dream model a runaway success. In 1952 the smaller Cub, sold through bicycle dealers, accounted for 70% of Japan's motorcycle production.

Funded by a 1954 public offering and Mitsubishi Bank, Honda expanded capacity and began exporting. American Honda Motor Company was formed in Los Angeles in 1959, accompanied by the slogan, "You meet the nicest people on a Honda," in a campaign crafted to counter the stereotypical biker image. Honda added overseas factories in the 1960s and began producing lightweight trucks, sports cars, and minicars.

Honda began selling its tiny 600 model in the US in 1970, but it was the Civic, introduced in 1973, that first scored with the US car market. Three years later Honda introduced the Accord, which featured an innovative frame adaptable for many models. In 1982 Accord production started at the company's Ohio plant.

Ex-Honda engineer Nobuhiko Kawamoto was named president in 1990, a year before Soichiro Honda died. Kawamoto cut costs and continued to expand the company internationally. That year the Big Three US automakers (GM, Ford, and Chrysler), clamoring for trade sanctions against Japanese carmakers, threw Honda out of the US carmakers' trade association.

In 1997 Honda bought Peugeot's plant in Guangzhou, China, and boosted its US vehicle production by opening a plant to produce all-terrain vehicles (ATV) in South Carolina in 1998. American Honda agreed in 1998 to pay $330 million to settle a class-action lawsuit filed by 1,800 dealers who accused Honda of delivering popular models only to dealers who paid bribes (18 executives from American Honda were convicted). That year Hiroyuki Yoshino, an engineer with US management experience, succeeded Kawamoto as CEO.

In 1999 Honda and GM agreed to a deal in which Honda would supply low-emission V6 engines and automatic transmissions to GM, while Isuzu, a GM affiliate, would supply Honda with diesel engines. True to Honda's go-it-alone style, the deal has no equity component.

In 2000 Honda announced that its super low-emission engine (as called for by US regulators) would make its mass-market debut in 2001, well ahead of competitor versions. Also Honda recalled 500,000 cars in Japan due to problems with audio systems and engine oil seals.

Honda announced in 2001 that it would introduce diesel-powered vehicles in Europe by 2003. Later that year Honda's R&D unit set up a solar-powered hydrogen production station in California as part of its efforts to develop renewable-energy fuel cell vehicles by 2003.

EXECUTIVES

Chairman and Representative Director:
  Yoshihide Munekuni, age 65
President, CEO, and Representative Director:
  Takeo Fukui, age 59
**EVP and Representative Director; COO, Regional
  Operations (North America); Chairman and CEO,
  American Honda Motor Co., Inc.; President and
  Director, Honda North America, Inc.:** Koichi Amemiya,
  age 63
**Senior Managing and Representative Director; COO,
  Automotive Operations:** Michiyoshi Hagino, age 59
**Senior Managing and Representative Director; COO,
  Business Management Operations:** Satoshi Aoki,
  age 57
**Senior Managing and Representative Director; COO,
  Business Support Operations; Group Officer, Driving
  Safety Promotion for Business Support Operations:**
  Hiroshi Okubo, age 58
**Senior Managing and Representative Director; COO,
  Production Operations:** Motoatsu Shiraishi, age 57
**Senior Managing and Representative Director; COO,
  Regional Operations (Europe, the Middle and Near
  East, and Africa):** Minoru Harada, age 56

Managing Director; President and Director, Honda of America Manufacturing, Inc.: Koki Hirashima, age 57
Managing Director, President and Director of Honda R&D Co., Ltd.: Takanobu Ito, age 50
Managing Director; President, COO, and Director, American Honda Motor Co., Inc.: Koichi Kondo, age 56
Auditors: KPMG

LOCATIONS

HQ: Honda Giken Kogyo Kabushiki Kaisha
1-1, 2-chome, Minami-Aoyama, Minato-ku,
Tokyo 107-8556, Japan
Phone: +81-3-3423-1111   **Fax:** +81-3-5412-1515
US HQ: 540 Madison Ave., 32nd Fl.,
New York, NY 10022
US Phone: 212-355-9191   **US Fax:** 212-813-0260
Web: world.honda.com

Honda Motor Co. operates more than 110 production facilities in 31 countries.

2003 Sales

	$ mil.	% of total
North America	39,887	46
Japan	33,174	38
Europe	6,980	8
Other regions	6,674	8
Adjustments	(19,236)	—
Total	**67,479**	**100**

PRODUCTS/OPERATIONS

2003 Sales

	$ mil.	% of total
Automobiles	54,515	81
Motorcycles	8,280	12
Financial services	2,040	3
Other	2,762	4
Adjustments	(118)	—
Total	**67,479**	**100**

Selected Car and Truck Models

Accord (coupe and sedan)
Acura (CL, MDX, NSX, RL, RSX, TL, Type S)
Civic (coupe, sedan)
Civic Hybrid
Civic Si
CR-V (SUV)
Element
Insight (gasoline-electric hybrid)
Odyssey (minivan)
Pilot (SUV)
S2000 (roadster)

Selected Motorcycle Models

CBR1100XX
CBR600F4i
Elite 80 (scooter)
FourTrax (ATV)
Gold Wing
Gold Wing ABS
Interceptor
Magna
Nighthawk 750
Rebel
Shadow Spirit 750
Silver Wing (scooter)
Sportrax (ATV)
ST1100
ST1300
ST1300 ABS
Valkyrie

Selected Power Products

Commercial mowers
Engines
Lawn mowers
Marine motors
Portable generators
Pumps
Snowblowers
Tillers
Trimmers

COMPETITORS

BMW	Kia Motors
Black & Decker	Mazda
Briggs & Stratton	Nissan
Brunswick	Peugeot
Caterpillar	Renault
DaimlerChrysler	Saab Automobile
Deere	Suzuki Motor
Fiat	Textron
Ford	Toro
Fuji Heavy Industries	Toyota
General Motors	Triumph Motorcycles
Harley-Davidson	Volkswagen
Isuzu	Volvo
Kawasaki Heavy Industries	Yamaha

HISTORICAL FINANCIALS

Company Type: Public

Income Statement

FYE: March 31

	REVENUE ($ mil.)	NET INCOME ($ mil.)	NET PROFIT MARGIN	EMPLOYEES
3/03	67,479	3,612	5.4%	126,900
3/02	55,253	2,722	4.9%	120,600
3/01	52,170	1,874	3.6%	114,300
3/00	57,455	2,472	4.3%	112,400
3/99	51,688	2,530	4.9%	112,200
3/98	45,418	1,973	4.3%	109,400
3/97	42,654	1,782	4.2%	91,300
3/96	39,984	666	1.7%	96,800
3/95	45,821	711	1.6%	92,800
3/94	37,673	231	0.6%	91,300
Annual Growth	**6.7%**	**35.7%**	**—**	**3.7%**

2003 Year-End Financials

Debt ratio: 43.4%
Return on equity: 17.4%
Cash ($ mil.): 4,634
Current ratio: 1.05
Long-term debt ($ mil.): 9,652
No. of shares (mil.): 1,923
Dividends
  Yield: 0.7%
  Payout: 6.5%
Market value ($ mil.): 31,926

Stock History

NYSE: HMC

	STOCK PRICE ($) FY Close	P/E High/Low		PER SHARE ($) Earnings	Dividends	Book Value
3/03	16.60	13	9	1.86	0.12	11.57
3/02	21.17	16	10	1.40	0.10	2.48
3/01	20.53	24	17	0.96	0.11	2.31
3/00	20.31	19	13	1.27	0.09	2.33
3/99	22.28	18	10	1.30	0.00	1.88
3/98	17.75	19	14	1.01	0.00	1.56
3/97	14.63	18	11	0.92	0.03	1.44
3/96	10.75	34	20	0.34	0.03	1.38
3/95	8.22	26	20	0.37	0.06	1.51
3/94	8.09	71	48	0.12	0.06	1.21
Annual Growth	**8.3%**	**—**	**—**	**35.6%**	**8.0%**	**28.5%**

Hopewell Holdings

Hopewell Holdings springs eternal in the mind of its founder and chairman, Sir Gordon Wu. Undeterred by the collapse of several projects in the wake of the Asian economic crisis, Wu has good reason to be hopeful about the future of his real estate and infrastructure development company as the market stabilizes. Hopewell has extensive holdings in real estate in Hong Kong (including Hopewell Centre and Panda Hotel) and is a major infrastructure developer. The company builds toll roads and bridges, primarily in mainland China. After halting construction on a power plant in Indonesia and an elevated road and train project in Thailand, Hopewell has been relying on Chinese infrastructure projects to keep it afloat.

Although its property and hotel businesses are concentrated mainly in Hong Kong, where it gets 78% of its sales, Hopewell's infrastructure projects (toll roads and bridges) are primarily in China's fast-growing Guangdong province. Mainland toll roads have been one of Hopewell's primary operations, contributing heavily to its earnings. However, the group may spin off its mainland infrastructure projects to finance a controversial bridge that would link Hong Kong with Macao and Zhuhai on China's Pearl River delta.

One of the first companies outside of China to invest in that country's infrastructure projects, Hopewell has been involved in building in China since the 1970s. In addition to the Hopewell Centre and Panda Hotel, the group's Hong Kong holdings include the Hongkong International Trade and Exhibition Centre, Mega Tower Hotel, and Nova Taipa Gardens. The group also operates the China Hotel in Guangzhou, the capital of Guangdong. A downturn in the economy of Europe, Japan, and the US has caused a decrease in customers for the group's hotel operations, but Hopewell has seen a substantial growth in visitors from the mainland.

Asian economic instability, coupled with a few missteps in the region, has cost the company dearly. Hopewell had to halt construction on a 1,320-MW power plant in Indonesia after it was 80% complete. The company is hoping to sell the power station. In addition, the Thai government canceled an elevated road and train project in Bangkok after several delays, changes, and rising costs because of currency devaluation. (The Thai government is in negotiations with Hopewell to resolve the situation.)

HISTORY

Sir Gordon Wu's Hopewell Holdings empire grew from humble beginnings. His father started out as a Hong Kong taxi owner and driver and helped finance Gordon's first-class education — he received an engineering degree from Princeton University.

On his return to Hong Kong in 1962, Wu took a job in the government's land department. He later left to help his father develop a property business. When his father retired in 1969, custom forbade Wu Sr. from handing the company over to Gordon, the seventh of nine children. Instead, he liquidated the company and guaranteed a $2.5 million loan to his son to start a property company of his own.

By 1972 Wu's company was large enough to be listed on the Hong Kong Stock Exchange as Hopewell Holdings Limited. But his American-style "can-do" approach gained him some enemies. He took on the Hong Kong government after it banned him from building a towering headquarters in central Hong Kong — and won. The result was the 66-floor Hopewell Centre.

While visiting nearby Guangzhou in China to promote a hotel project in the early 1980s, Wu spotted opportunity in the region's frequent power outages. Realizing that the province would boom in the 1980s and 1990s, Wu dropped the hotel idea and persuaded China to let him build a power plant. By 1987 the 700-MW plant was on line.

Other major Chinese infrastructure projects followed, including contracts for two more power stations in Guangdong province and a contract to build China's first modern highway, a six-lane toll road linking the cities of Guangzhou and Hong Kong. Wu attributed his success in negotiating with the Chinese authorities to 11 years of lobbying and consuming gallons of *mao tai* (a very potent liquor served at formal dinners in China).

In 1990 Wu gained a contract with the Thai government for a mass transit system, the Bangkok Elevated Road and Train System (BERTS) project. But the project was soon delayed, first by political unrest and then by bureaucratic red tape.

Hopewell spun off 40% of its power subsidiary, Consolidated Electric Power Asia (CEPA), in 1993. The sale helped fund other projects, including the Guangdong toll road and a power plant in the Philippines. But the Philippines project ran into problems in 1995: Although the plant was completed, the local electric utility refused to take the power. That year Wu set the company up for another fall when he pledged $100 million to Princeton. (The Asian economic crisis forced him to postpone the pledge in 1999, by which time he had given only a third of the amount.)

By late 1995 Hopewell was hemorrhaging money. After failing to raise funds by spinning off several transport projects as a public company in 1996, Hopewell sold CEPA to US utility Southern Company.

The Asian financial contagion of 1997 and 1998 didn't help matters. In 1998 the elevated train project in Bangkok was halted by the Thai government, and Hopewell lost its $153 million stake in Peregrine Investment Holdings when the Hong Kong-based firm collapsed. Hopewell also stopped work on a major Indonesian power plant that it was building in a venture. The firm fell into the red in 1998.

That year, however, the company gained a contract to help build a toll road in southern China, and in 1999 it won another contract for a toll road in the Philippines. By the end of 1999 it had regained profitability, although it lost its listing on the Hong Kong index in 2000. In 2002 the company made plans to spin off its major toll road, the Guangzhou-Shenzhen Superhighway, and to rebid for the BERTS project. Also that year, Sir Gordon stepped down from his duties as managing director but remained chairman of the group.

EXECUTIVES

Honorary Chairman: James Man Hon Wu
Chairman: Sir Gordon Ying Sheung Wu
Managing Director: Eddie Ping Chang Ho
COO: Thomas Jefferson Wu
Deputy Managing Director: Josiah Chin Lai Kwok

Executive Director, Finance: Robert Van Jin Nien
Executive Director: Alan Chi Hung Chan
Executive Director: David Yau-gay Lui
Executive Director: Colin H. Weir
Company Secretary: Peter Yip Wah Lee
Group Personnel Manager: Vicki Wong
Auditors: Deloitte Touche Tohmatsu

LOCATIONS

HQ: Hopewell Holdings Limited
64th Fl., Hopewell Centre, 183 Queen's Rd. East, Hong Kong
Phone: +852-2528-4975   **Fax:** +852-2861-2068
Web: www.hopewellholdings.com

Hopewell Holdings operates primarily in Asia, including China, Hong Kong, Indonesia, the Philippines, and Thailand.

2002 Sales

	% of total
Hong Kong	78
Other regions in China	22
Total	**100**

PRODUCTS/OPERATIONS

Selected Subsidiaries

Goldhill Investments Limited (property investment)
Hopewell China Development (Superhighway) Limited (investment in superhighway project, 97.5%)
Hopewell Construction Company, Limited (construction, project management, and investments)
HH Finance Limited (loan financing)
Hopewell Food Industries Limited (restaurant operation)
Hopewell Guangzhou-Zhuhai Superhighway Development Limited (investment in superhighway project)
Hopewell Property Management Company Limited (building management)
International Trademart Company Limited (property investment and operation of trademart)
Kowloon Panda Hotel Limited (hotel owernship and operations)

COMPETITORS

ABB	Jardine Matheson
AES	Marriott International
ALSTOM	McDermott
Bechtel	Peter Kiewit Sons'
Fluor	Siemens
Foster Wheeler	Sime Darby
GE	Swire Pacific
Hutchison Whampoa	

HISTORICAL FINANCIALS

Company Type: Public

Income Statement

FYE: June 30

	REVENUE ($ mil.)	NET INCOME ($ mil.)	NET PROFIT MARGIN	EMPLOYEES
6/03	103	79	77.3%	1,100
6/02	145	44	30.0%	1,123
6/01	224	39	17.5%	1,009
6/00	202	22	10.8%	1,100
6/99	174	18	10.5%	2,000
6/98	191	(363)	—	4,000
6/97	368	28	7.5%	5,318
6/96	306	99	32.5%	7,095
6/95	281	272	96.5%	6,288
6/94	298	315	105.8%	7,983
Annual Growth	(11.2%)	(14.2%)	—	(19.8%)

2003 Year-End Financials

Debt ratio: 27.0%
Return on equity: 4.5%
Cash ($ mil.): 89
Current ratio: 0.57
Long-term debt ($ mil.): 473

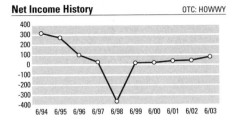

Net Income History   OTC: HOWWY

HSBC Holdings

HSBC would be a real alphabet soup if the company's name reflected its geographic diversity. HSBC Holdings is the UK's largest banking company; it also owns The Hongkong and Shanghai Banking Corporation, France's CCF, and 62% of Hong Kong's Hang Seng Bank. HSBC has more than 8,000 offices in about 80 countries, providing consumer and business banking services, asset management, investment banking, securities trading, insurance, and leasing. US operations, which include HSBC USA and joint venture Wells Fargo HSBC Trade Bank, got a boost with the purchase of consumer lender Household International. HSBC plans to buy offshore private Bank of Bermuda as well.

HSBC's banking and financial services subsidiaries extend into Central and South America, where it owns Banco Múltiplo in Brazil and bought Mexico's Grupo Financiero Bital in 2002. The purchase should allow HSBC to conduct NAFTA-related business with greater facility. The company also assumed 100% ownership of Merrill Lynch HSBC, a former joint venture that offers investment services via the Web to the mass affluent outside the US. HSBC also holds some 60% of HSBC Equator Bank (South Africa's Nedcor owns the rest), which provides banking services in sub-Saharan Africa.

HSBC is hoping that its North American purchases, a move into mainland China, and HSBC Asset Management (Taiwan) Limited (formerly China Securities Investment Trust) will jolt growth.

HISTORY

Scotsman Thomas Sutherland and other businessmen in 1865 opened the doors to Hongkong & Shanghai Bank, financing and promoting British imperial trade in opium, silk, and tea in East Asia. It soon established a London office and created an international branch network emphasizing China and East Asia. It claims to have been the first bank in Thailand (1888).

War repeatedly disrupted, but never demolished, the bank's operations. During WWII the headquarters were temporarily moved to London. The bank's chief prewar manager, Sir Vandeleur Grayborn, died in a Japanese POW camp. After the Communists took power in China in 1949, the bank gradually withdrew; by 1955 only its Shanghai office remained, and it was later closed. The bank played a key role in Hong Kong's postwar growth by financing industrialists who fled there from China.

In the late 1950s Hongkong & Shanghai Bank's acquisitions included the British Bank of the Middle East (founded in 1889, now the Saudi

British Bank) and Mercantile Bank (with offices in India and Southeast Asia). In 1965 the company bought 62% of Hang Seng, Hong Kong's #2 bank. It also added new subsidiaries, including Wayfoong (mortgage and small-business finance, 1960) and Wardley (investment banking, Hong Kong, 1972).

In the late 1970s and into the 1980s, China began opening to foreign business. The bank added operations in North America to capitalize on business between China and the US and Canada. Acquisitions included Marine Midland Bank (US, 1980), Hongkong Bank of Canada (1981), 51% of treasury securities dealer Carroll McEntee & McGinley (US, 1983), most of the assets and liabilities of the Bank of British Columbia (1986), and Lloyds Bank Canada (1990).

Following the 1984 agreement to return Hong Kong to China, Hongkong & Shanghai Bank began beefing up in the UK, buying London securities dealer James Capel & Co. (1986) and the UK's #3 bank, Midland (1992). In 1993 the company formed London-based HSBC Holdings and divested assets, most notably its interest in Hong Kong-based Cathay Pacific Airways.

The company then began expanding in Asia again, particularly Malaysia, where its Hongkong Bank Malaysia became the country's first locally incorporated foreign bank. HSBC returned to China with offices in Beijing and Guangzhou. It also added new European branches.

Latin American banks acquired in 1997 were among the non-Asian operations that cushioned HSBC from the worst of 1998's economic crises. Nonetheless, The Hong Kong Monetary Authority took a stake in the bank to shore up the stock exchange and foil short-sellers.

In 1999 China's government made HSBC a loan for mainland expansion. That year the company was foiled in its attempt to buy South Korea's government-owned Seoulbank, but did buy the late Edmond Safra's Republic New York Corporation and his international bank holding company, Safra Republic Holdings (it negotiated a $450 million discount on the $10 billion deal after a Japanese probe of Republic's securities division caused delays).

In 2000 the company unveiled several online initiatives, including Internet ventures with Cheung Kong (Holdings) and Merrill Lynch, and bought CCF (then called Crédit Commercial de France). However, HSBC's plans to buy a controlling stake in Bangkok Metropolitan Bank fell through before the year's end.

In 2001 HSBC agreed to pick up Barclays Bank's fund management operations in Greece. Later, in response to the slowing economy, it froze the salaries of 14,000 employees. Argentina's 2001 peso devaluation cost the company half a billion dollars in currency conversion losses alone. Total charges pertaining to Argentina equaled more than $1 billion that year.

EXECUTIVES

Group Chairman: Sir John R. H. Bond, age 61
Deputy Chairman: The Baroness Dunn, age 63
Deputy Chairman: Sir Brian Moffat, age 64
Group Chief Executive: Stephen K. Green, age 54
Group COO: Alan W. Jebson, age 53
Executive Director; CEO, HSBC Bank plc; Deputy Chairman, Merrill Lynch HSBC Limited:
William R. P. Dalton, age 59
Executive Director; Chairman and CEO, CCF:
Charles de Croisset, age 59
Executive Director; Chairman, and CEO, The Hongkong and Shanghai Banking Corporation:
David G. Eldon, age 57

Executive Director, Corporate and Investment Banking:
John J. Studzinski, age 47
Executive Director, Markets: Stuart T. Gulliver, age 44
Group Finance Director and Executive Director:
Douglas J. Flint, age 47
Group Company Secretary: R. G. Barber, age 52
Group General Manager, Legal and Compliance:
R. E. T. Bennett, age 51
Group General Manager and Global Head of Corporate and Institutional Banking: Charles-Henri Filippi, age 50
Group Chief Accounting Officer: R. C. Picot, age 45
Group General Manager, Human Resources:
J. C. S. Rankin, age 61
Group General Manager, Marketing: P. E. Stringham, age 53
Chairman, Global Investment Banking Dvision, HSBC Investment Bank plc: Krishna Patel, age 54
President and CEO, HSBC USA and HSBC Bank USA:
Youssef A. Nasr, age 48
Auditors: KPMG Audit Plc

LOCATIONS

HQ: HSBC Holdings plc
8 Canada Sq., London E14 5HQ, United Kingdom
Phone: +44-20-7991-8888   **Fax:** +44-20-7992-4880
US HQ: 452 5th Ave., New York, NY 10018
US Phone: 212-525-5000
Web: www.hsbc.com

2002 Sales

	% of total
Europe	46
Hong Kong	24
North America	19
Rest of Asia/Pacific	10
South America	1
Total	**100**

PRODUCTS/OPERATIONS

Selected Subsidiaries

Asia/Pacific
Hang Seng Bank Limited (62%)
The Hongkong and Shanghai Banking Corporation Limited
HSBC Asset Management (Taiwan) Ltd. (97%)
HSBC Bank Australia Limited
HSBC Bank Malaysia Berhad
HSBC Insurance (Asia-Pacific) Holding Limited
HSBC Insurance (Asia) Limited
HSBC Investment Bank Asia Limited

Europe
CCF S.A.
The Cyprus Popular Bank Limited (22%)
HSBC Asset Finance (UK) Limited
HSBC Bank Malta p.l.c. (70% owned)
HSBC Bank plc
HSBC Finance (Netherlands)
HSBC Guyerzeller Bank AG (98% owned)
HSBC Insurance Brokers Limited
HSBC Investment Bank plc
HSBC Life (UK) Limited
HSBC Republic Bank (Guernsey) Limited
HSBC Republic Bank (Suisse) S.A
HSBC Republic Bank (UK) Limited
HSBC Trinkaus & Burkhardt KGaA (73%)

Latin America
HSBC Bank Argentina S.A
HSBC Bank Brasil S.A. — Banco Múltiplo
HSBC La Buenos Aires Seguros SA
HSBC Seguros (Brasil) S.A.

Middle East and Africa
British Arab Commercial Bank Limited (46%)
HSBC Bank Egypt SAE (95%)
HSBC Bank Middle East
The Saudi British Bank (40%)

North America
HSBC Bank Canada
HSBC Bank USA
HSBC Securities (USA) Inc
HSBC USA Inc.
Wells Fargo HSBC Trade Bank, N.A. (20%)

COMPETITORS

Bank of America	J.P. Morgan Chase
Bank of China	Lloyds TSB
Barclays	Mizuho Financial
CIBC	RBC Financial Group
Citigroup	Standard Chartered
Credit Suisse First Boston	Sun Hung Kai
Deutsche Bank	UBS
Hutchison Whampoa	

HISTORICAL FINANCIALS

Company Type: Public

Income Statement

FYE: December 31

	ASSETS ($ mil.)	NET INCOME ($ mil.)	INCOME AS % OF ASSETS	EMPLOYEES
12/02	759,246	6,239	0.8%	192,000
12/01	695,877	5,406	0.8%	176,682
12/00	673,814	6,628	1.0%	169,858
12/99	569,139	5,408	1.0%	146,897
12/98	483,128	4,318	0.9%	144,521
12/97	472,431	5,534	1.2%	132,969
12/96	401,904	5,287	1.3%	109,298
12/95	351,466	3,815	1.1%	109,093
12/94	315,325	3,212	1.0%	—
12/93	304,439	2,668	0.9%	—
Annual Growth	**10.7%**	**9.9%**	**—**	**8.4%**

2002 Year-End Financials

Equity as % of assets: 6.9%
Return on assets: 0.9%
Return on equity: 12.7%
Long-term debt ($ mil.): 31,762
No. of shares (mil.): 1,896
Dividends
Yield: 5.0%
Payout: 83.3%
Market value ($ mil.): 104,251
Sales ($ mil.): 40,373

Stock History

NYSE: HBC

	STOCK PRICE ($) FY Close	P/E High/Low		PER SHARE ($) Earnings	Dividends	Book Value
12/02	54.98	20	15	3.30	2.75	27.64
12/01	59.71	138	75	0.58	3.21	24.57
12/00	73.60	20	14	3.75	1.98	24.58
12/99	71.38	22	16	3.25	0.57	19.75
Annual Growth	**(8.3%)**	**—**	**—**	**0.5%**	**69.0%**	**11.9%**

Hudson's Bay Company

Here's a company that's traveled a fur piece from its 17th-century roots. (The chain's coat of arms features two moose, four beavers, and a fox.) Hudson's Bay Company (HBC) is Canada's largest department store chain. Founded in 1670 as a fur trading enterprise, HBC is also Canada's oldest corporation. Its Zellers chain is Canada's #2 discount department store (behind Wal-Mart), with more than 300 stores. HBC also runs nearly 100

The Bay department stores, about 100 smaller Fields general merchandise and apparel stores in Western Canada, about 40 Home Outfitters, and Hbc.com, an e-Commerce site. Its department and discount store chains stretch from Newfoundland to British Columbia.

Mass merchandiser Zellers, which accounts for about 60% of company sales, is facing increasing pressure from discounters and specialty stores, such as Best Buy. Wal-Mart opened 14 new supercenters in Canada in 2002 and has plans to bring SAM'S CLUB to Canada, with four to six outlets opening in Ontario in 2003. As a countermeasure, HBC has been renovating and enlarging its Zellers stores and enlisting hot designers, including Mossimo, to promote the image of an upscale discounter (à la Target), along with introducing smaller Zellers Select stores in smaller markets and emphasizing private labels in all of its stores. Also in 2003 HBC signed a deal with Salton, whereby Westinghouse-branded products and a new line of home appliances will be offered across HBC's retail banners.

HBC's The Bay traditional department stores focus on more-upscale fashion merchandise and home furnishings, and its Home Outfitters superstores emphasize bedding and linens. Fast-growing Home Outfitters plans to open 11 stores in 2003.

HISTORY

In 1668 the British ketch *Nonsuch* reached the bay named for explorer Henry Hudson. The ship returned to Britain the following year laden with furs, attracting the attention of King Charles II, who in 1670 granted a royal trading charter to a party of 18 men. Hudson's Bay Company (HBC) built a series of fortifications and engaged in a seesaw battle with French warships for control of the bay that continued until 1713, when the Treaty of Utrecht placed the bay officially in British hands. From the company's base at York Factory, company explorers began to penetrate Canada's vast interior. In 1774 Samuel Hearne established the firm's first inland post on the Saskatchewan River.

During the late 18th century, the Montreal-based North West Company, a rival fur-trading concern, threatened HBC's dominance. After a period of violent clashes between the competing traders, the two competitors merged under the Hudson's Bay Company name in 1821, giving the company control over 173 posts throughout 3 million square miles of wilderness. It transferred possession of company-chartered land to the Canadian government in 1869.

By the turn of the century, HBC had transformed many posts into stores to serve growing Canadian cities. In 1929 the company formed Hudson's Bay Oil and Gas. It acquired the Henry Morgan department store chain in 1960 and five years later changed its store name to Bay. HBC moved its headquarters from London to Winnipeg in 1970 (and later to Toronto).

The company expanded its department store holdings in the late 1970s by purchasing Zellers, Fields, and Simpsons. Newspaper magnate Kenneth Thomson bought 75% of HBC in 1979 (the last of the family's interest was sold in 1997). Mired in debt during the 1980s from its prolific acquisitions, the company sold its oil and gas operations, its large fur houses, and 179 of its original stores in the far north.

During a steep recession in 1990, the company spun off its Markborough real estate subsidiary to shareholders and purchased the

Towers Bonimart chain of discount department stores (which it converted to the Zellers format). HBC later converted six of its Simpsons high-fashion stores into The Bay stores, selling the rest to Sears for $37 million.

HBC in 1995 opened the first of its Zellers Plus larger stores with expanded merchandise (almost twice as large as its average format) to compete with Wal-Mart. Profits dropped almost 80% in fiscal 1996 because of a Wal-Mart price war and depressed Christmas sales. In 1997 Bill Fields, former head of Blockbuster Entertainment, succeeded CEO George Kosich. Fields liquidated old inventory at Zellers, writing off more than $100 million. (The move, along with restructuring, created a loss for fiscal 1998.)

In 1998 the company bought Kmart Canada (112 discount stores) for $168 million. HBC then set about converting about 60 former Kmarts into Zellers stores; about 40 weaker stores were closed, and about a dozen were converted to specialty stores. Fields, who had touted the growth potential of the Kmart stores, resigned in 1999 and was replaced as president and CEO by George Heller, head of the Zellers chain. In 2000 the company launched its e-commerce site, hbc.com. The company also began opening Zeller Select stores, smaller concept stores that include grocery sections, and Home Outfitters, superstores carrying kitchen, bed, and bath décor. HBC opened 16 new Home Outfitters stores in 2001.

Home Outfitters continued to charge ahead, opening 16 new stores in 2002.

EXECUTIVES

Governor: L. Yves Fortier, age 67
President and CEO: George J. Heller, $1,195,670 pay
EVP and CFO: Michael S. (Mike) Rousseau
EVP; President and COO, The Bay: Marc R. Chouinard, $566,370 pay
EVP; President and COO, Zellers: Thomas Haig, $503,440 pay
EVP, HBC Managed Services: Peter A. Kenyon, $393,312 pay
SVP, Human Resources: Robert M. Kolida
SVP, Merchandising: Bruce Dinan
SVP, Procurement: Deborah A. Edwards
SVP, Real Estate and Development: Donald C. Rogers
VP and CIO: Gary B. Davenport
VP, Audit Services: J. Gregory Armstrong
VP, Tax and Risk Management: Harold J. Chmara
VP, Secretary and General Counsel: James A. Ingram
VP and Controller: Arthur N. (Art) Mitchell
VP, Corporate Communications: Robert R. (Rob) Moore
VP, Customer Relationship Management: Robert J. Shields
VP, Logistics: Michael J. Thomas
Auditors: KPMG LLP

LOCATIONS

HQ: 401 Bay St., Ste. 500, Toronto, Ontario M5H 2Y4, Canada
Phone: 416-861-6112   **Fax:** 416-861-4720
Web: www.hbc.com

2003 Sales

	% of total
Ontario	44
Western Canada	32
Quebec	17
Maritimes	7
Total	**100**

PRODUCTS/OPERATIONS

Stores

The Bay (department stores)
Fields (small general merchandise stores)
Home Outfitters (household furnishings superstores)
Zellers (discount stores)
Zeller Select (small concept stores with groceries)

COMPETITORS

American Eagle Outfitters	Men's Wearhouse
Best Buy	North West Company
The Brick	Reitmans
Canadian Tire	SAM'S CLUB
Costco Wholesale	Sears Canada
Gap	Toys "R" Us
Gendis	Wal-Mart
Le Château	

HISTORICAL FINANCIALS

Company Type: Public

Income Statement				FYE: January 31
	REVENUE ($ mil.)	NET INCOME ($ mil.)	NET PROFIT MARGIN	EMPLOYEES
1/03	4,831	73	1.5%	70,678
1/02	4,686	46	1.0%	71,730
1/01	4,999	83	1.7%	71,700
1/00	5,046	66	1.3%	70,000
1/99	4,680	26	0.6%	65,000
1/98	4,435	(62)	—	61,500
1/97	4,457	27	0.6%	60,000
1/96	4,343	25	0.6%	60,900
1/95	4,143	107	2.6%	63,700
1/94	4,093	111	2.7%	62,200
Annual Growth	**1.9%**	**(4.6%)**	**—**	**1.4%**

2003 Year-End Financials

Debt ratio: 16.2%   Current ratio: 1.91
Return on equity: 4.6%   Long-term debt ($ mil.): 254
Cash ($ mil.): 38

Net Income History   Toronto: HBC

Hutchison Whampoa

Hutchison Whampoa has a hand in just about everything in Hong Kong. The company, one of Hong Kong's oldest *hongs* (trading companies), has extensive holdings in retailing and manufacturing (A.S. Watson Group), ports, energy (Hongkong Electric, Husky Energy), telecommunications (fixed-line, mobile phone, and paging services), and infrastructure (power plants, toll roads, and construction materials). In addition, Hutchison Whampoa owns hotels and a sizable portfolio of Hong Kong properties. Outside

Hong Kong, the company has operations in China and elsewhere in the Asia/Pacific region, as well as in Europe and the Americas. Hutchison Whampoa is controlled by Li Ka-shing, one of the world's wealthiest men.

Hutchison Whampoa's retail and manufacturing segment, the A.S. Watson Group, accounts for more than a third of sales. Operations include supermarkets (PARKnSHOP), health and beauty stores (Watsons Your Personal Store, Kruidvat), soft drink and water bottling operations, and wine retailing (Watson's Wine Cellar). Overall, the company has more than 3,200 retail outlets in Europe and Asia.

In addition to owning a controlling interest in Hongkong International Terminals, which handles traffic passing through Hong Kong's container port, Hutchison Whampoa has large investments in terminal operations in southern China. The world's biggest port operator, Hutchison Whampoa operates in five of the seven busiest container ports in the world, including three key ports on Britain's East Coast and ports on both ends of the Panama Canal.

With an eye to the future, the company has invested heavily in next-generation wireless phone networks. It recently rolled out its 3G wireless service in several markets, including Austria, Denmark, Italy, Norway, Sweden, and the UK.

Hutchison Whampoa has strong connections to the Chinese government, thanks to its rags-to-riches chairman, Li, who has spent years building business relationships inside China. Li's Cheung Kong (Holdings) Limited owns 49.9% of Hutchison Whampoa. In turn, Hutchison Whampoa owns about 85% of Cheung Kong Infrastructure.

HISTORY

Hongkong and Whampoa Dock was the first registered company in Hong Kong. The enterprise was founded in 1861 when it bought dry docks in Whampoa (near Canton, China) after the kidnapping and disappearance of the docks' owner, John Couper, during the Second Opium War (1856-60). It bought docks in Hong Kong in 1865.

Founded in 1880 by John Hutchison, Hutchison International became a major Hong Kong consumer goods importer and wholesaler. It took control of Hongkong and Whampoa Dock and in A.S. Watson (drugstores, supermarkets, soft drinks) during an acquisition spree in the 1960s. The purchases entailed a complex web of deals that fell apart in the mid-1970s. To save Hutchison International, the Hongkong & Shanghai Bank took a large stake in the company and brought in Australian turnaround specialist Bill Wyllie. Wyllie slashed expenses, sold 103 companies in 1976, and bought the rest of Hongkong and Whampoa Dock in 1977. The company became Hutchison Whampoa that year.

In a surprise move, in 1979 Hongkong & Shanghai Bank sold its 23% stake in Hutchison to Cheung Kong Holdings: Cheung Kong founder Li Ka-shing, who began his career at age 14 by selling plastic flowers, became the first Chinese to control a British-style *hong*. Wyllie left in 1981.

In the 1980s Hutchison redeveloped its older dockyard sites, which had become prime real estate. The company's International Terminals unit grew with Hong Kong's container traffic into the world's largest privately owned container terminal operator. In the 1980s the firm diversified into energy (buying stakes in utility Hongkong Electric and Canada-based Husky Oil) and pre-

cious metals and mining. It also moved into telecommunications, buying Australian paging and UK mobile telephone units in 1989.

The following year the *hong* launched the AsiaSat I satellite in a venture with Cable & Wireless (C&W) and China International Trust & Investment. More acquisitions followed, including European mobile phone businesses and telecom equipment makers. In 1996 the firm reorganized its Hong Kong telecom operations into Hutchison Telecommunications and launched its European wireless operations as a new public company, Orange. In 1998 Hutchison Telecommunications made a move into the US when it bought a 20% stake in Western Wireless's digital PCS unit, VoiceStream.

In 1999 the company and C&W sold their stakes in AsiaSat. It also traded its stake in Orange to Mannesmann, acquiring 10% of the German conglomerate, which was later acquired by Vodafone. Hutchison Whampoa recorded a profit that year of more than $15 billion on its investment in Orange. Also in 1999 Hutchison Whampoa and Global Crossing formed a $1.2 billion telecom joint venture to build a fiber-optic network in China (in 2002, the company purchased the remaining 50% of the venture from the beleaguered telecommunications company and renamed it Hutchison Global Communications).

Hutchison Whampoa, Dutch phone company KPN, and Japanese mobile phone giant NTT DoCoMo (which had purchased a 19% stake in Hutchison Whampoa in 1999) formed an alliance in 2000 to bid on next-generation mobile phone licenses in Europe.

In 2001 Hutchison Whampoa sold its 18% stake in US-based mobile phone operator VoiceStream to Deutsche Telekom for $5.1 billion in cash and stocks and purchased a 15% stake in travel Web site priceline.com. The next year, its A.S. Watson Group bought the Netherlands-based health-and-beauty retail chain Kruidvat Group. Also in 2002 supermarket chain PARKnSHOP opened four large stores in southern China.

In April 2003 Hutchison Telecommunications backed out of a joint bid to invest $125 million in bankrupt Global Crossing, citing regulatory difficulties. In November the company sold $5 billion worth of bonds (a record global bond sale) to finance its heavy investment in high-speed mobile phone networks in Europe.

EXECUTIVES

Chairman: Li Ka-shing, age 74
Deputy Chairman and Executive Director: Victor T. K. Li
Group Managing Director and Executive Director: Canning K. N. Fok, age 51
Deputy Group Managing Director and Executive Director: Susan M. F. Chow Woo, age 49
Group Finance Director and Executive Director: Frank J. Sixt, age 51
Executive Director: Dominic K. M. Lai, age 49
Executive Director: George C. Magnus, age 67
Executive Director: Kam Hing Lam, age 56
Company Secretary: Edith Shih
General Manager, Human Resources: Mary Tung
Auditors: PricewaterhouseCoopers

LOCATIONS

HQ: Hutchison Whampoa Limited
Hutchison House, 22nd Fl., 10 Harcourt Rd.,
Hong Kong
Phone: +852-2128-1188   **Fax:** +852-2128-1705
Web: www.hutchison-whampoa.com

Hutchison Whampoa operates in Hong Kong and China. It has other diversified holdings in about 40 countries, including Australia, the Bahamas, Canada, Germany, Ghana, India, Indonesia, Israel, Japan, Macao, Myanmar, Panama, the Philippines, Singapore, Sri Lanka, Switzerland, Taiwan, Thailand, the UK, and the US.

2002 Sales

	% of total
Hong Kong	36
Americas & other	33
China	14
Europe	11
Asia & Australia	6
Total	**100**

PRODUCTS/OPERATIONS

Selected Subsidiaries and Affiliates

Retail and Manufacturing
A. S. Watson & Co., Limited
Kruidvat Holding B.V. (Netherlands)

Ports and Related Services
Hongkong International Terminals Limited (87%)
Hongkong United Dockyards Limited (50%)
Port of Felixstowe Limited (90%, UK)
Shanghai Container Terminals Limited (37%, China)
Yantian International Container Terminals Limited (48%, China)

Energy
Hongkong Electric Holdings Limited (33%, utility)
Husky Energy (35%, Canada)
Powercor Australia Limited (42%, electricity distribution)

Telecommunications and e-commerce
Hutchison 3G UK Ltd. (65%)
Hutchison Global Communications Limited
Hutchison Telecommunications (Hong Kong) Limited
Hutchison Telecommunications (Australia) Limited (58%)
TOM.COM Limited (29%, Internet portal)

Infrastructure
Cheung Kong Infrastructure Holdings Limited (85%)

Property and Hotels
Harbour Plaza Hotel Management (International) Limited (50%)
Hutchison Properties Limited

Finance and Investments
Hutchison Whampoa (Europe) Limited (consulting, UK)

COMPETITORS

AT&T
Boots Group
BT
Cable & Wireless
China Mobile (Hong Kong)
Deutsche Telekom
France Telecom
Hopewell Holdings
Jardine Matheson
Nextel
Orange
SBC Communications
Sime Darby
SkyTel Communications
Sprint PCS
Swire Pacific
TIM
Verizon
Wharf Holdings

HISTORICAL FINANCIALS

Company Type: Public

Income Statement

FYE: December 31

	REVENUE ($ mil.)	NET INCOME ($ mil.)	NET PROFIT MARGIN	EMPLOYEES
12/02	9,645	1,832	19.0%	117,843
12/01	7,879	1,550	19.7%	77,253
12/00	7,310	4,374	59.8%	49,570
12/99	7,135	15,102	211.7%	42,510
12/98	6,633	1,124	16.9%	39,860
12/97	5,755	1,635	28.4%	31,271
12/96	4,740	1,554	32.8%	27,733
12/95	4,530	1,237	27.3%	29,137
12/94	3,899	1,037	26.6%	26,855
12/93	3,205	816	25.5%	22,500
Annual Growth	13.0%	9.4%	—	20.2%

2002 Year-End Financials

Debt ratio: 62.6%
Return on equity: 6.4%
Cash ($ mil.): 5,494

Current ratio: 1.06
Long-term debt ($ mil.): 18,149

Net Income History

Pink Sheets: HUWHY

(Chart: Net income, $ mil., 12/93–12/02, with peak near 15,000 in 12/99)

Hyundai Motor Company

Hyundai Motor has been selling cars in the US since 1986, but it only started selling its heavy trucks stateside in 1998. South Korea's #1 carmaker, Hyundai produces about a dozen models of cars and minivans, as well as trucks, buses, and other commercial vehicles. The company reestablished itself as Korea's leading carmaker in 1998 by acquiring a 51% stake in Kia Motors (since reduced to about 46%). Hyundai's exports include the Accent and Sonata, while its Korean models include the Atos sub-compact. The company also manufactures machine tools for factory automation and material handling equipment.

Hyundai hopes to establish a US manufacturing presence. DaimlerChrysler has purchased a 9% stake in Hyundai as part of a plan to boost DaimlerChrysler's Asian market presence. The two companies plan to form a joint venture to develop small cars for the global market. In another deal, DaimlerChrysler chose to exercise its option to purchase 50% of Hyundai's spun-off heavy-truck business.

HISTORY

Hyundai Motor Company was established in 1967, and it initially began manufacturing cars and light trucks through a technology collaboration with Ford's UK operations. By the early 1970s Hyundai was ready to build cars under its own nameplate. The company debuted the sub-compact Hyundai Pony in 1974 at Italy's annual Turin Motor Show.

The Pony was an instant domestic success and soon propelled Hyundai to the top spot among Korea's carmakers. During the mid-1970s, the company began exporting the Pony to El Salvador and Guatemala.

By the 1980s Hyundai was ready to shift into high gear and begin high-volume production in anticipation of penetrating more overseas markets. The company began exporting to Canada in 1983.

Hyundai introduced the Hyundai Excel in 1985. That year the company established its US subsidiary, Hyundai Motor America. By 1986, Hyundai was exporting Excels for sale in the US. Sales of the Excel soared the next year, so Hyundai decided to build a factory in Bromont, Quebec.

But by the time the factory was finished in 1989, consumers were tiring of the aging compact car and the quality problems that came with it. Hyundai closed the plant after just four years in operation.

The company introduced its first sports car, the Scoupe, in 1990. The following year it developed the first Hyundai-designed engine, called the Alpha. Two years later Hyundai unveiled its second-generation proprietary engine, the Beta.

By 1998 Hyundai was beginning to feel the pinch of the Asian economic crisis as domestic demand dropped drastically. However, the decrease in Korean demand was largely offset by exports. That year Hyundai took a controlling stake in Korean competitor Kia Motors.

In hopes of increasing its share of the Asian automotive market, DaimlerChrysler took a 9% stake in Hyundai in 2000. The deal includes the establishment of a joint venture to manufacture commercial vehicles, as well as an agreement among Hyundai, DaimlerChrysler, and Mitsubishi Motors to develop small cars for the global market.

In 2001 Hyundai decreased its stake in Kia Motors to about 46%.

The following year DaimlerChrysler announced it would exercise its option to take a 50% stake in Hyundai's heavy-truck business.

EXECUTIVES

Chairman and CEO: Mong-koo Chung
President and Director: Kim Dong-Jin
VP: Chung Oue-Sun
President, Planning and General Affairs, Hyundai Motor and Kia Motors: Chung Soon-Won
Director of Global Public Relations: Oles Gadacz
Auditors: Anjin & Co.

LOCATIONS

HQ: Hyundai Jadongcha Chusik Hoesa
231, Yangjae-Dong, Seocho-Gu,
Seoul 137-938, South Korea
Phone: +82-2-3464-2545   **Fax:** +82-2-3463-3484
US HQ: 10550 Talbert Ave.
Fountain Valley, CA 92728-0850
US Phone: 714-965-3000   **US Fax:** 714-965-3001
Web: www.hyundai-motor.com

Hyundai Motor has manufacturing subsidiaries in India, Korea, and Turkey, and sells its vehicles worldwide.

PRODUCTS/OPERATIONS

Selected Models

Passenger Cars
Atos
Atos Prime
Centennial
Elantra
Hyundai XG
Sonata

Recreational Vehicles
Galloper
H-I Van
Matrix
Santa Fe
Terracan
Trajet

Commercial Vehicles
Aero buses
Aero Town
Cargo Truck
County
H-1 Truck
H 100 Minibus
H 100 Truck
HD65/HD72
Special vehicles
6KL steel tank lorry
Bulk cement truck & trailer
H100 home lorry
H900 tractor
HD120 passenger car transporter

COMPETITORS

DaimlerChrysler	Isuzu
Fiat	Mazda
Ford	NUMMI
General Motors	Nissan
GM Daewoo Auto & Technology	Peugeot
Honda	Renault
Ingersoll-Rand Industrial Solutions	Toyota
	Volkswagen

HISTORICAL FINANCIALS

Company Type: Public

Income Statement

FYE: December 31

	REVENUE ($ mil.)	NET INCOME ($ mil.)	NET PROFIT MARGIN	EMPLOYEES
12/02	40,111	1,196	3.0%	49,855
12/01	30,108	870	2.9%	50,000
12/00	25,667	476	1.9%	52,000
12/99	21,401	480	2.2%	48,000
12/98	—	—	—	46,300
12/97	—	—	—	46,412
12/96	—	—	—	47,166
12/95	—	—	—	45,444
12/94	—	—	—	44,154
Annual Growth	23.3%	35.5%	—	1.5%

2002 Year-End Financials

Debt ratio: 77.5%
Return on equity: 15.5%
Cash ($ mil.): 5,907

Current ratio: 0.73
Long-term debt ($ mil.): 6,677

Net Income History

Exchange: Korea

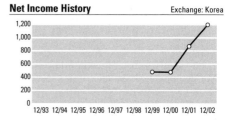

Ifi Istituto Finanziario Industriale

What are the chances of untangling the Agnelli web of holdings? Pretty Ifi. Controlled by the wealthy Agnelli family through parent firm Giovanni Agnelli and C., the holding company Ifi Istituto Finanziario Industriale owns stakes in a variety of companies. These holdings include a more than 50% stake in sister company Finanziaria di Partecipazioni (Ifil), as well as about 20% of automotive giant Fiat (which, combined with Ifil's 12% holding, gives the Agnelli family effective control of the automaker). Ifi also holds interests in companies involved in sports, retail, publishing, insurance, sugar, and other businesses.

Carmaker Fiat also makes Maserati, Alfa Romeo, and Ferrari sports cars. Ifi also owns Turin's top-ranked Juventus soccer club and has holdings in food production, hospitality, and insurance industries. In addition, Ifil has shares of companies involved in tourism (Alpitour) and retail (Gruppo Rinascente, co-owned with the French Auchan group).

Subsidiary EXOR Group extends Ifi's reach beyond Italy with international holdings in French real estate (Societé Foncière Lyonnaise), Portuguese banking (Espírito Santo Financial Holding), and American packaging (30% of Riverwood International). Other business sectors include wine and telecommunications.

Ifi plans to spin off about 35% of Juventus in an IPO.

HISTORY

Istituto Finanziario Industriale (Ifi) was formed by Giovanni Agnelli in 1927 as a family "safe" for his stakes of various industrial businesses. Automaker Fiat immediately became and remains the centerpiece of Ifi's holdings.

Fiat benefited from Mussolini's protectionist policies in the 1930s, but Agnelli remained a liberal. During WWII, when Axis defeat appeared imminent, Agnelli slowed war production and put Italian resistance members on his payroll. At the end of the war, Fiat executives — unable to wait for the Marshall Plan — traveled to the US to seek reconstruction loans.

Giovanni Agnelli died in 1945. Ownership of Ifi passed to his Agnelli and Nasi family heirs. In 1958 Ifi gained control of Finanziaria di Partecipazioni (Ifil), another industrial holding company.

Ten years later Ifi formed Infint (renamed EXOR Group in 1994) to manage Ifi's foreign shares. Also in 1968 Ifi stock was offered to the public to fund company expansion. The Agnelli and Nasi families' shares decreased throughout the 1970s and 1980s as more capital was sought.

The 1970s saw Ifi dispose of non-core holdings, such as Società Assicuratrice Industriale, in order to cut debt.

Ifi and Ifil bought back shares of Fiat in the 1980s while Ifil began to invest more widely. Parent company Giovanni Agnelli e C. S.a.p.az. (G.A. e. C.), controlled solely by the Agnelli and Nasi families, formed in 1987 and bought Ifi.

In 1997 Ifi and Ifil reacted to the privatization and competition rocking the once-static world of Italian financial holdings. The companies invested in Istituto Bancario San Paolo di Torino (now San Paolo IMI) and spun off cement maker Unicem.

In 1999 G.A. e C. and Ifi upped their stakes in EXOR Group; together they controlled about 85%. Two years later Ifi sold its stake in the Rockefeller Center to T. Speyer & Crown.

EXECUTIVES

Chairman: Giovanni Agnelli, age 82
Deputy Chairman: Gianluigi Gabetti, age 77
Deputy Chairman and Managing Director: Umberto Agnelli
General Manager: Virgilio Marrone
Secretary and Legal Consultant: Franzo Grande Stevens
Director Finance: Roberto Longo
Director Personnel: Luciana Bellandi

LOCATIONS

HQ: Ifi Istituto Finanziario Industriale S.p.A.
Corso Matteotti, 26, 10121 Turin, Italy
Phone: +39-011-509-0266   **Fax:** +39-011-535-600
Web: www.gruppoifi.com

Istituto Finanziario Industriale has holdings primarily in Italy and to a lesser degree France, Spain, and the US.

PRODUCTS/OPERATIONS

Selected Holdings

EXOR Group (23%)
Château Margaux (75%, wine, France)
Club Méditerranée (16%, resorts, France)
Distacom (7%, telecommunications, Hong Kong)
Espírito Santo Financial Holding (6%, banking, Portugal)
Riverwood International (30%, packaging, US)
Societé Foncière Lyonnaise (18%, real estate, France)

Fiat (30%, with Ifil's holding)
CNH Global (84%, agriculture and construction equipment)
COMAU (production systems)
Ferrari e Maserati (87%, sports cars)
Fiat Auto Holdings (80%)
Fiat Avio (aviation)
General Motors (6%)
Itedi (publishing and communications)
IVECO (commercial vehicles)
Magneti Marelli (auto components)
Teksid (66%, metallurgical products)
Toro Assicurazioni (99.5%, insurance)

Ifil (54%)
Alpitour (tourism)
Ciaoholding (Web portal)
Club Méditerranée (6%, resorts, France)
Gruppo Rinascente (52%, retail)
San Paolo IMI (5%, bank)
Sifalberghi (25%, hotels)
Worms et Cie (53%, sugar and paper, France)

Juventus F.C. S.p.A.

COMPETITORS

Edison
Investor
Italmobiliare
Wendel Investissement

HISTORICAL FINANCIALS

Company Type: Public

Income Statement

FYE: December 31

	REVENUE ($ mil.)	NET INCOME ($ mil.)	NET PROFIT MARGIN	EMPLOYEES
12/02	66,558	(842)	—	209,141
12/01	59,239	145	0.2%	198,764
12/00	63,129	205	0.3%	223,953
12/99	54,868	215	0.4%	244,385
Annual Growth	6.6%	—	—	(5.1%)

2002 Year-End Financials

Debt ratio: 151.2%   Current ratio: —
Return on equity: —   Long-term debt ($ mil.): 17,834
Cash ($ mil.): 3,913

Net Income History

Italian: IFP

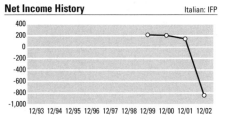

IKEA International

How Swede it is. One of the world's top furniture retailers, IKEA International sells Scandinavian-style home furnishings and other housewares in about 175 giant stores in more than 30 countries. To cut transportation costs, IKEA uses flat packaging; customers assemble the products at home. The company designs its own furniture, which is made by more than 2,000 suppliers in more than 50 countries. IKEA's stores feature playrooms for children and Swedish cuisine restaurants. It also sells by mail order. An acronym for founder Ingvar Kamprad and his boyhood home, Elmtaryd, Agunnaryd, IKEA began operating in Sweden in 1943. It is owned by Kamprad's Netherlands-based charitable foundation, Stichting Ingka.

If you're looking for fussy furniture in neutral tones, IKEA is not the place for you. Known for its use of bold colors and creative product names (a Ticka alarm clock, a Ringo stool), the company sells furniture and other household items, including dinnerware, pillows, lighting, and rugs.

The company plans to open more store locations in Europe, North America, and Asia. In 2002 IKEA announced a global partnership with Royal Philips Electronics, whereby Philips' consumer electronics products will be featured in IKEA's furniture displays, as well as being sold throughout its worldwide locations.

HISTORY

At the age of 17, Ingvar Kamprad formed his own company in Sweden in 1943, peddling fish, vegetable seeds, and magazines by bicycle. He called the company IKEA, an acronym for his name and the village in which he grew up (Elmtaryd, Agunnaryd). Four years later he added the newly invented ballpoint pen to his product assortment and started a mail-order catalog.

In 1950 Kamprad added furniture and housewares to his mail-order products, and in 1953 he bought a furniture factory and opened a small showroom. The showroom was a hit with price-conscious Swedes and was replaced by the first official IKEA store in 1958. The first store outside Sweden was established in 1963 in Norway. Two years later the company opened its flagship store in Stockholm, a 150,000-sq.-ft. marvel whose round design was inspired by the Guggenheim Museum in New York. The store featured a nursery, a restaurant, a bank, and parking spaces for 1,000 cars. By 1969 two more stores were opened in Sweden and another in Denmark.

A fire badly damaged the Stockholm store in 1973, but the subsequent fire sale pulled in more shoppers than the store's grand opening. That year IKEA expanded beyond Scandinavia, opening stores in Switzerland and Germany. In 1976 it opened its first store outside Europe, in Canada, and during the late 1970s and early 1980s, it entered Australia, the Canary Islands, Hong Kong, Iceland, Kuwait, Saudi Arabia, and Singapore. To avoid questions of succession after his death, Kamprad in 1980 transferred ownership of the company to a charitable foundation. IKEA opened its first US store, in Philadelphia, in 1985. Anders Moberg was named president of IKEA in 1986. By 1991 there were seven outlets in the US and 95 total in 23 countries. IKEA began its push into Eastern Europe two years later, but at the same time struggled with economic downturns in its major markets, Germany and Scandinavia.

Kamprad's reluctant announcement that he had associated with pro-Nazi groups in the 1940s and 1950s brought a torrent of bad press. The revelation prompted IKEA to reconsider opening a store in Israel, believing the Israeli government would not sanction the investment. Instead, Jewish groups claimed the company was deliberately avoiding the country. IKEA agreed in 1995 to open an Israeli store and finally granted a license for a franchise to Blue Square – Israel Ltd. in 1997.

That year IKEA announced plans to build about 20 plants over five years in the Baltics, Bulgaria, and Romania, a move designed to reduce its dependence on contract manufacturers and nearly double its own manufacturing capacity. Also in 1997 it began offering prefab housing in Sweden with construction firm Skanska.

IKEA opened its largest store (400,000 sq. ft.) outside Europe in Chicago in 1998 and announced plans to open more stores in Russia, China, and Eastern Europe. In 1999 Anders Dahlvig was named group president, replacing Moberg, who left to take a position with retailer Home Depot. In 2000 the company opened its first store in Moscow, with plans for more Russian locations.

In 2001 IKEA stated plans to open 60 to 70 more store locations in Europe, North America, and Asia over the next five years. Since June 2002 IKEA has run its own freight trains between depots in Sweden and Germany, and the company plans to extend its rail services to Italy and Poland and to double its rail transport of goods to 40% by 2006. In December 2002 IKEA Netherlands received a letter with a bomb threat and temporarily shut down ten of its retail locations. Explosives

were discovered in two stores in the Netherlands and detonated; two IKEA employees were minimally injured. Federal authorities confirmed that the motive behind the attacks was extortion.

EXECUTIVES

Honorary Chairman: Ingvar Kamprad, age 77
Group President and CEO: Anders Dahlvig, age 46
CFO: Hans Gydell
President, IKEA North America: Pernille Spiers-Lopez
Director of Human Resources: Lars Gejroth

LOCATIONS

HQ: IKEA International A/S
    Box 640, SE 25 106 Helsingborg, Sweden
Phone: +46-42-267-100   **Fax:** +46-42-132-805
US HQ: 496 W. Germantown Pike,
    Plymouth Meeting, PA 19462
US Phone: 610-834-0180   **US Fax:** 610-834-0872
Web: www.ikea.com

2002 Sales

	% of total
Europe	77
North America	19
Australia, Asia, Middle East	4
Total	**100**

PRODUCTS/OPERATIONS

Selected Products

Armchairs	Instruments for children
Bath accessories	Kitchen organizers
Bath suites	Kitchen units
Bean bags	Leather sofas
Bed linens	Lighting
Beds and bedroom suites	Mattresses
Bookcases	Mirrors
Boxes	Office chairs and suites
CD storage	Posters
Ceiling lamps	Rugs
Children's furniture	Sofas and sofa beds
Clocks	Spotlights
Coffee tables	Stools
Cookware	Table lamps
Cord management	Toy storage
Desk accessories	TV cabinets and stands
Dining tables and chairs	Utility storage
Dinnerware	Video storage
Entertainment units	Wall shelves and systems
Floor lamps	Wardrobe units
Frames	Window treatments

COMPETITORS

Bassett Furniture	Levitz Furniture
Bed Bath & Beyond	Linens 'n Things
Bombay Company	METRO AG
Coin	MFI Furniture
Euromarket Designs	Otto Versand
GUS	Pier 1 Imports
Harvey Norman Holdings	Pier Import Europe
Horten	Pinault-Printemps-
Hulsta-Werke Huls	Redoute
Jennifer Convertibles	Rooms To Go
John Lewis	Skandinavisk Holding
Rinascente	Williams-Sonoma

HISTORICAL FINANCIALS

Company Type: Private

Income Statement

FYE: August 31

	REVENUE ($ mil.)	NET INCOME ($ mil.)	NET PROFIT MARGIN	EMPLOYEES
8/02	11,779	—	—	75,500
8/01	10,355	—	—	70,000
8/00	8,500	—	—	58,000
8/99	8,076	—	—	49,400
8/98	7,027	—	—	36,400
8/97	5,885	—	—	36,400
8/96	6,149	—	—	33,400
8/95	5,487	—	—	26,600
8/94	4,810	—	—	26,600
8/93	4,294	—	—	—
Annual Growth	**11.9%**	—	—	**13.9%**

Revenue History

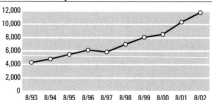

Imperial Chemical Industries PLC

Selling many of its commodities operations, Imperial Chemical Industries (ICI) has moved from the madding crowd of commodity chemical production to focus on specialty products and paints. Its specialty products group consists of National Starch and Chemical (industrial adhesives, starch), Quest (fragrance, food ingredients, flavors), and Uniqema (natural and synthetic lubricants and personal care products). Its paint offerings include the Alba, Dulux, and Glidden brands. ICI's regional and industrial chemicals segment (subsidiaries in Argentina, India, and Pakistan) makes explosives, soda ash, rubber chemicals, sulfur-related products, and fibers.

ICI began transforming itself from being a bulk chemicals company, vulnerable to cyclical pricing, when it bought Unilever's specialty chemicals business. It gained market share in specialty starches, industrial adhesives, fragrances, and flavors. To remedy heavy debt associated with the purchase, ICI has disposed of more than 50 companies — but that has not been enough. Threatened with its debt rating being reduced to junk bond status, the company raised about $1.15 billion in a share offering in order to reduce debt.

In May 2003 the company sold its 30% stake in Huntsman ICI Chemicals for nearly $500 million, which it will use to pay down more of its debt.

HISTORY

Imperial Chemical Industries (ICI) began in 1926 when four British chemical companies (Nobel Industries; Brunner, Mond and Company; United Alkali; and British Dyestuffs) merged to compete with German cartel I. G. Farben. The most-famed ICI predecessor, Nobel Industries, was created as the British arm of Alfred Nobel's explosives empire. Nobel mixed nitroglycerin with porous clay to make dynamite. In 1886 he created the London-based Nobel Dynamite Trust to embrace British and German interests. After Nobel's death in 1896, the empire unraveled, and WWI severed the German and UK components of the Nobel firm. The British arm became Nobel Industries (1920).

In 1929 ICI and American chemical company DuPont signed a patents-and-process agreement to share research information. Around the same time it focused on research and between 1933 and 1935 created some 87 new products, including polyethylene.

After WWII the cartel club began to disband. The US government won antitrust sanctions against the DuPont-ICI alliance in 1952, and ICI faced new competition from the sundered components of I. G. Farben (Bayer, BASF, Hoechst). ICI added foreign operations in the 1960s, but fortunes declined, and in 1980 it posted losses and cut its dividend for the first time.

The company recruited turnaround artist John Harvey-Jones in 1982. He cut layers of decision making, reorganized along product lines, and added non-UK directors to the board. ICI also shifted production from bulk chemicals such as soda and chlorine to high-margin specialty chemicals such as pharmaceuticals and pesticides.

Harvey-Jones bought 100 companies between 1982 and his retirement in 1987. ICI expanded in the US market by purchasing Beatrice's chemical operations (1985) and Glidden paints (1986).

ICI sold its nylon business to DuPont in 1992 and spun off its pharmaceutical and agricultural operations as Zeneca the next year. It opened its first plant in China, a paint factory, in 1994 and named 30-year Unilever veteran Charles Miller Smith its new CEO in 1995.

In 1997 ICI bought Unilever's specialty chemicals unit in a deal worth about $8 billion. The same year it picked up Canada-based St. Clair Paint & Wallpaper. ICI then sold its polyester resin and intermediates operations (1997) and film business (1998) to Dupont for around $2 billion. In 1998 ICI paid $560 million for specialty chemicals maker Acheson Industries. ICI's attempts to reduce debt from the Unilever purchase stumbled when W. R. Grace & Co. terminated its deal to buy ICI's Crosfield silicas and catalysts business and DuPont and NL Industries backed out of the $1 billion purchase of ICI's titanium dioxide business.

Still saddled with debt, ICI sold a rash of companies in 1999: its utilities and services division to Enron for about $500 million; its polyurethanes and titanium-dioxide businesses and some petrochemicals businesses to US-based Huntsman for about $2.8 billion (though it kept a 30% stake); its industrial coatings and auto refinish businesses in the Americas and Europe, and Germany-based coatings business to PPG Industries for $684 million; and its acrylics division (raw materials such as methylacrylates and value-added products such as Lucite and Perspex) to Belgium-based Ineos Acrylics for $833 million.

Continuing to divest in 2000, ICI sold paint distribution network Master Distribution to Lafarge SA. The next year ICI sold its giant plant in Runcorn, UK, to Ineos Chlor.

EXECUTIVES

Chairman: Lord (Alex) Trotman, age 69
Deputy Chairman: Peter B. Ellwood, age 59
Chief Executive and Director: John D. G. McAdam, age 55, $507,518 pay
CFO: Timothy A. (Tim) Scott, age 40
EVP, Mergers and Acquisitions, General Counsel, and Secretary: Michael H. C. Herlihy, age 50
EVP, Performance Specialties: Leonard J. Berlik, age 55
EVP, Regional and Industrial Businesses: Michael (Mike) Gardner, age 56
EVP, Human Resources: Rolf Deusinger
Chairman and CEO, ICI Paints: David Hamill, age 46
Chairman and COO, National Starch and Director: William H. Powell, age 57
Chairman and Chief Executive, Quest International: Charles F. Knott
Communications Director: Penny Prudholm
Chief Press Officer: John Edgar
Auditors: KPMG Audit Plc

LOCATIONS

HQ: 20 Manchester Sq.,
   London W1U 3AN, United Kingdom
Phone: +44-20-7009-5000   **Fax:** +44-20-7009-5703
US HQ: 10 Finderne Avenue,
   Bridgewater, NJ 08807-3300
US Phone: 908-685-5000   **US Fax:** 908-685-5005
Web: www.ici.com

Imperial Chemical Industries has more than 200 manufacturing facilities on six continents.

PRODUCTS/OPERATIONS

International Businesses

Paints
Packaging coatings (for food and drink cans)
Paints (Devoe, Dulux, Inca, Glidden)

National Starch
Adhesives
Electronic and engineering materials
Specialty starches
Specialty synthetic polymers

Performance Specialties
Natural and synthetic lubricants
Personal care products

Quest (flavor, fragrance, and food-ingredient products)

Regional and Industrial Chemicals

ICI Argentina
Sulfur-related chemicals
Wine chemicals

ICI India
Catalysts
Explosives
Adhesives
Rubber chemicals

ICI Pakistan
Fibers
Soda ash

COMPETITORS

Air Products
Akzo Nobel
BASF AG
Bayer AG
Ciba Specialty Chemicals
Clariant International
Degussa
Dow Chemical
Eastman Chemical
DuPont
Engelhard
E.ON
Ferro
FPC
H.B. Fuller
Hercules
Honeywell Specialty
   Materials
Huntsman International
IFF
Lyondell Chemical
mg technologies
Millennium Chemicals
Mitsubishi Chemical
Occidental Petroleum
PPG
Rohm and Haas
Royal Dutch/Shell Group
RPM
Sherwin-Williams
TOTAL
Wattyl

HISTORICAL FINANCIALS

Company Type: Public

Income Statement

FYE: December 31

	REVENUE ($ mil.)	NET INCOME ($ mil.)	NET PROFIT MARGIN	EMPLOYEES
12/02	9,870	288	2.9%	36,660
12/01	9,356	176	1.9%	38,600
12/00	11,565	(340)	—	45,930
12/99	11,616	407	3.5%	53,500
12/98	15,093	320	2.1%	58,700
12/97	14,395	428	3.0%	69,500
12/96	18,016	471	2.6%	64,000
12/95	15,927	830	5.2%	64,800
12/94	14,381	294	2.0%	67,500
12/93	15,730	204	1.3%	67,000
Annual Growth	(5.0%)	3.9%	—	(6.5%)

2002 Year-End Financials

Debt ratio: 273.1%
Return on equity: 146.9%
Cash ($ mil.): 430
Current ratio: 1.20
Long-term debt ($ mil.): 2,196

No. of shares (mil.): 298
Dividends
   Yield: 5.7%
   Payout: 78.8%
Market value ($ mil.): 4,285

Stock History

NYSE: ICI

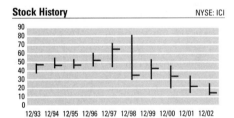

	STOCK PRICE ($) FY Close	P/E High/Low		PER SHARE ($) Earnings	Dividends	Book Value
12/02	14.39	18	9	1.04	0.82	2.70
12/01	21.85	16	7	0.98	1.64	(2.26)
12/00	33.69	—	—	(1.89)	2.22	(1.77)
12/99	42.56	19	11	2.26	2.19	2.16
12/98	34.94	26	10	1.77	2.10	1.36
12/97	64.94	9	6	2.35	2.42	1.33
12/96	52.00	18	14	3.33	2.18	34.08
12/95	46.75	11	9	4.58	2.06	33.59
12/94	46.50	33	27	1.63	1.77	32.30
12/93	47.25	42	33	1.14	2.94	33.15
Annual Growth	(12.4%)	—	—	(1.0%)	(13.2%)	(24.3%)

Imperial Oil

Imperial Oil, Canada's largest oil company, holds sway over a vast empire of oil and gas resources. It has proved reserves of 1.7 billion barrels of oil and natural gas liquids and 1.2 trillion cu. ft. of natural gas. Imperial is one of Canada's top natural gas producers, the #1 refiner and marketer of petroleum products, and a major supplier of petrochemicals. It sells petroleum products, including gasoline, heating oil, and diesel fuel, under the Esso name and other brand names. Most of the company's production comes from fields in Alberta and the Northwest Territories. Imperial also owns 25% of Syncrude Canada, which operates the world's largest oil sands development. Exxon Mobil owns about 70% of Imperial.

The oil company sells gasoline to motorists at 2,100 Esso service stations across Canada. At Cold Lake, Alberta, the company uses steam to recover very heavy crude and related products from oil sands deposits, through its participation in the Syncrude Project. Management is seeking to boost production from its plentiful oil sands holdings; its research laboratories in Ontario and Alberta are focused on developing technology for finding better ways to recover heavy oil.

Imperial's petroleum products and chemicals business operates four refineries and has an extensive network of wholesale outlets (in addition to its gas station chain) in every region of Canada. The company's chemicals segment operates a manufacturing plant in Sarnia, Ontario, and a number of distribution centers across Canada.

Imperial has reduced employment and closed service stations to stay competitive; it also is selling noncore assets and underperforming units (including refineries).

In 2002 Imperial worked out a deal to offer the popular Tim Hortons brand of soups and sandwiches at its Esso stations across Canada.

HISTORY

London, Ontario, boomed from the discovery of oil in the 1860s and 1870s, but when the market for Canadian kerosene became saturated in 1880, 16 refiners banded together to form the Imperial Oil Company.

The company refined sulfurous Canadian oil, nicknamed "skunk oil" for its powerful smell. Imperial faced tough competition from America's Standard Oil, which marketed kerosene made from lighter, less-odorous Pennsylvania crude. Guided by American expatriate Jacob Englehart, Imperial built a better refinery and hired a chemist to develop a process to clean sulfur from the crude.

By the mid-1890s Imperial had expanded from coast to Canadian coast. Cash-starved from its expansion, the company turned to old nemesis Standard Oil, which bought controlling interest in Imperial in 1898. That interest is today held by Exxon Mobil.

After the turn of the century, Imperial began producing gasoline to serve the new automobiles. The horseless carriages were spooking the workhorses at the warehouse where fuel was sold, so an Imperial manager in Vancouver opened the first Canadian service station in 1907. The company marketed its gas under the Esso banner borrowed from Standard Oil.

An Imperial crew discovered oil in 1920 at Nor- man Wells in the remote Northwest Territories. In 1924 a subsidiary sparked a new boom with a gas well discovery in the Turner Valley area northeast of Edmonton. But soon Imperial's luck ran as dry as the holes it was drilling; it came away empty from the next 133 consecutive wells. That string ended in 1947 when it struck oil in Alberta at the Leduc No. 1. To get the oil to market, Imperial invested in the Interprovincial Pipe Line from Alberta to Superior, Wisconsin.

In 1964 the company began research to extract bitumen from the oil sands in Cold Lake, Alberta. During the 1970s oil crisis, Imperial continued to search for oil in northern Canada. It found crude on land near the Beaufort Sea (1970) and in its icy waters (1972). The company formed its Esso Resources Canadian Ltd. subsidiary in 1978 to oversee natural resources production.

In 1989 Texaco (acquired by Chevron in 2001), still reeling from a court battle with Pennzoil, sold Texaco Canada to Imperial. To diminish debt and comply with regulators, Imperial agreed to sell some of Texaco Canada's refining and marketing assets in Atlantic Canada, its interests in Interhome Energy, and oil and gas properties in western Canada.

Imperial reorganized in 1992, centralizing several units, and in 1993 closed its refinery at Port Moody, British Columbia. It sold most of its fertilizer business in 1994; disposed of 339 unprofitable gas stations in 1995; and the next year closed down Canada's northernmost oil refinery at Norman Wells.

In 1997 Imperial announced an ambitious program to expand Syncrude's oil sands bitumen upgrading plant. In 1998 Exxon agreed to buy Mobil, which had substantial Canadian oil assets. In 1999 Canada pre-approved the potential merger of Imperial Oil and Mobil Canada. Later that year Exxon completed its purchase of Mobil to form Exxon Mobil.

In the face of public pressure for cleaner gasoline (Imperial had been implicated by government tests as Canada's "dirtiest" oil producer), Bob Peterson (who stepped down as CEO in 2002) told shareholders in 2000 that he did not agree with the theory of global warming.

EXECUTIVES

Chairman, President, and CEO:
Timothy J. (Tim) Hearn, age 59, $704,173 pay
SVP Finance and Administration, Controller, and Director: Paul A. Smith, age 50, $270,275 pay
SVP Products and Chemicals Division and Director: Brian J. Fischer, age 56, $457,258 pay
SVP Resources Division and Director; President and CEO, Imperial Oil Resources: K. C. Williams, age 53, $570,500 pay
VP and Treasurer: John F. Kyle, age 60, $455,000 pay
VP and General Counsel: Brian W. Livingston
Corporate Secretary: John Zych
Auditors: PricewaterhouseCoopers LLP

LOCATIONS

HQ: Imperial Oil Limited
    111 St. Clair Ave. W., Toronto, Ontario
    M5W 1K3, Canada
Phone: 416-968-5078   **Fax:** 416-968-5345
Web: www.imperialoil.ca

Imperial Oil's exploration and development are conducted primarily in Alberta and the Northwest Territories. It owns two refineries in Ontario, and one each in Alberta and Nova Scotia. It also operates a chemical plant in Ontario.

PRODUCTS/OPERATIONS

2002 Sales

	% of total
Petroleum products	79
Natural resources	15
Chemicals	6
Total	**100**

Selected Products and Operations

Petroleum Products
Marketing
Refining
Supply
Transportation

Natural Resources
Exploration and development
Land holdings
Petroleum and natural gas production

Chemicals
Benzene
Ethylene
Plasticizer intermediates
Resins
Solvents

COMPETITORS

Abraxas Petroleum	Murphy Oil
Ashland	Occidental Petroleum
BHP Billiton Ltd	Petro-Canada
BP	PETROBRAS
Canadian Natural	PDVSA
ConocoPhillips	PEMEX
Devon Energy	Pioneer Natural Resources
Dominion Resources	Royal Dutch/Shell Group
DuPont	Suncor
EnCana	Sunoco
Eni	Talisman Energy
Koch	TOTAL
Lyondell Chemical	Unocal
Marathon Oil	

HISTORICAL FINANCIALS

Company Type: Public

Income Statement

FYE: December 31

	REVENUE ($ mil.)	NET INCOME ($ mil.)	NET PROFIT MARGIN	EMPLOYEES
12/02	10,732	769	7.2%	6,460
12/01	10,776	781	7.2%	6,740
12/00	11,888	947	8.0%	6,704
12/99	7,091	402	5.7%	6,550
12/98	5,815	358	6.2%	6,689
12/97	7,463	593	7.9%	7,096
12/96	7,577	574	7.6%	7,483
12/95	6,810	377	5.5%	7,800
12/94	7,781	310	4.0%	8,252
12/93	6,725	211	3.1%	9,470
Annual Growth	5.3%	15.5%	—	(4.2%)

2002 Year-End Financials

Debt ratio: 50.9%
Return on equity: 25.2%
Cash ($ mil.): 487
Current ratio: 1.09
Long-term debt ($ mil.): 1,686

No. of shares (mil.): 379
Dividends
    Yield: 1.9%
    Payout: 26.6%
Market value ($ mil.): 10,873

	STOCK PRICE ($) FY Close	P/E High/Low		PER SHARE ($) Earnings	Dividends	Book Value
12/02	28.70	16	12	2.03	0.54	8.74
12/01	27.88	15	11	1.99	0.74	7.34
12/00	26.30	12	8	2.27	0.78	7.23
12/99	21.63	26	16	0.93	0.74	7.11
12/98	16.06	26	17	0.81	0.50	6.26
12/97	21.29	17	11	1.28	0.54	6.89
12/96	15.65	14	11	1.09	0.36	6.98
12/95	12.03	20	16	0.65	0.43	7.44
12/94	10.99	19	16	0.62	1.16	8.89
12/93	11.28	36	29	0.36	0.47	8.52
Annual Growth	10.9%	—	—	21.2%	1.6%	0.3%

Imperial Tobacco Group

The UK's #1 cigarette maker (ahead of Gallaher Group), Imperial Tobacco Group has traded up to an even bigger throne. The company's 2002 purchase of 90% of German tobacco firm Reemtsma (Davidoff and West cigarettes) nearly doubled its size and made it the world's #4 tobacco company. Imperial's brands include Lambert & Butler, the UK's #1 cigarette, as well as Castella cigars, and Amphora and St Bruno pipe tobacco. Its Drum brand is the #1 hand-rolling tobacco worldwide, and Rizla is a top cigarette paper. Acquisitions in Australia and New Zealand have assured Imperial's presence in emerging markets.

Imperial Tobacco also looks to open new markets in China, where it recently signed a 10-year deal to produce and sell cigarettes. Imperial also is expanding to new markets in Africa. Despite global expansion, the UK still rings up nearly 70% of its sales. Imperial controls 44% of the UK market.

Like rivals British American Tobacco and Gallaher, Imperial was spun off from a conglomerate eager to distance itself from increasingly problematic tobacco operations (it was part of Hanson until that group's 1996 four-way demerger). The company's purchase of 90% of Reemtsma nearly doubled Imperial's business without exposing it to the litigious US market.

HISTORY

Imperial Tobacco Group was formed in 1901 to fight American Tobacco's invasion of the UK. American Tobacco had become the dominant US tobacco company partly by using a large cash reserve to undercut competitors. When it bought UK tobacco and cigarette factory Ogden's that year, 13 UK tobacco firms responded by registering as The Imperial Tobacco Company. The firms (including Wills, Lambert & Butler, and John Player & Sons) continued to make and sell their products separately.

As expected, American Tobacco cut prices, and Imperial fought back, acquiring the Salmon & Cluckstein tobacco shop chain and offering bonuses to retailers that sold its products. When Imperial threatened US expansion in 1902, American Tobacco surrendered: It gave Ogden's to Imperial and halted its Ireland and Great Britain business in exchange for Imperial's pledge to stay out of the US (except for buying tobacco leaf). The two formed the British American Tobacco Company (BAT) to sell both firms' cigarettes overseas. But when American Tobacco split into four companies in 1911 and sold its BAT interest, the agreement was modified to let Imperial sell some of its brands in the US.

By the 1950s Imperial controlled more than 80% of the UK tobacco market, but its share decreased during the 1960s due to competition from Gallaher Group (Benson & Hedges). Imperial diversified, buying companies such as Golden Wonder Crisps snack food (1961) and the Courage & Barclay brewery (1972).

In 1973 BAT and Imperial agreed that each firm would control its own brands in the UK and Continental Europe. Imperial sold the last of its stake in BAT in 1980. Conglomerate Hanson Trust paid $4.3 billion for Imperial in a 1986 hostile takeover. Hanson reduced Imperial's tobacco brands from more than 100 to five brand families (a move that decreased its UK market share to 33% by 1990). It also sold Imperial's drinks unit, including Courage and John Smith beer, to Elders IXL (now Foster's Brewing). Between 1986 and 1993 Hanson cut Imperial's tobacco operations from five factories and 7,500 employees to three factories and 2,600 employees; it also sold Imperial's restaurant and food operations.

As UK cigarette consumption dropped, Imperial began expanding overseas in 1994. By 1996 exports had risen to 15% of sales. That year Gareth Davis became CEO of Imperial.

Facing further declining UK cigarette sales and a government tax hike, Imperial bought the world's #1 cigarette paper brand, Rizla (1997), and Sara Lee's cut-tobacco unit, Douwe Egberts Van Nelle (1998), which it renamed Van Nelle Tabak. That acquisition added Drum hand-rolling tobacco and Amphora pipe tobacco to Imperial's brands. In 1999 the company added a bevy of Australian and New Zealand brands (Horizon, Brandon, Flagship, Peter Stuyvesant) from BAT.

In 2000 Imperial acquired paper maker EFKA (Germany, Canada) and tobacco maker Baelen (Belgium). That year Imperial tripled its cigarette vending operations by acquiring Mayfield Vending (27,000 UK locations).

Imperial expanded operations in Africa in 2001 with the acquisition of 75% of Tobaccor. It also began distributing the Marlboro brand in the UK.

The company bought 90% of Reemtsma in 2002; the deal, valued at $5.1 billion, made Imperial the #4 tobacco company in the world.

EXECUTIVES

Chairman: Derek C. Bonham, age 60
Vice Chairman: Anthony Alexander, age 65
Chief Executive: Gareth Davis, age 53
Finance Director: Robert Dyrbus, age 51
Corporate Affairs Director and Board Member: Frank A. Rogerson, age 51
Manufacturing Director and Board Member: David Cresswell, age 58

Sales and Marketing Director and Board Member: Bruce Davidson, age 47
Secretary: Richard Hannaford, age 57
Group Financial Controller: Alison Cooper, age 37
Group Human Resources Director: Kathryn Brown, age 48
Group Media Relations Manager: Alex Parsons
Investor Relations Manager: Nicola Tate
Auditors: PricewaterhouseCoopers LLP

LOCATIONS

HQ: Imperial Tobacco Group PLC
Upton Road, Bristol BS99 7UJ, United Kingdom
Phone: +44-117-963-6636   **Fax:** +44-117-966-7405
Web: www.imperial-tobacco.com

Imperial Tobacco operates about 25 factories in Africa, Canada, Europe, New Zealand, and the UK.

2002 Sales

	% of total
UK	68
Western Europe	15
Germany	4
Other	13
Total	**100**

PRODUCTS/OPERATIONS

Selected Products and Brands

Cigarettes
Low-priced (Horizon, John Brandon, Lambert & Butler, Richmond)
Mid-priced (John Player, JPS/John Player Special, Peter Jackson, Route 66, Superkings)
Premium (Embassy, Fusion, Imperial, Peter Stuyvesant, Regal)

Other
Cigarette Paper (EFKA, Rizla)
Cigars (Carl Upmann, Castella Panatellas, Classic, King Edward Coronets, Panama, Small Classic)
Pipe Tobacco (Amphora, St Bruno Ready Rubbed)
Roll Your Own Tobacco (Blend 11, Brandaris, Champion, Dr Pat, Drum, Drum Milde, Five Star, Flagship, Golden Virginia, Greys, Horizon, Interval, Log Cabin, Pocket Edition, Roverstone, Rotterdam Shag, Stockman, Van Nelle, Virginia Gold)

COMPETITORS

Altadis	Rothmans
British American Tobacco	Skandinavisk
Gallaher	Tobakskompagni
General Cigar	Swedish Match
Gudang Garam	Swisher International
Japan Tobacco	Tiedemanns
JT International	UST
Philip Morris International	

HISTORICAL FINANCIALS

Company Type: Public

Income Statement   FYE: Saturday nearest September 30

	REVENUE ($ mil.)	NET INCOME ($ mil.)	NET PROFIT MARGIN	EMPLOYEES
9/02	3,478	426	12.2%	11,440
9/01	2,171	515	23.7%	6,360
9/00	1,917	476	24.8%	4,915
9/99	1,979	473	23.9%	4,306
9/98	1,611	392	24.4%	3,630
9/97	1,346	342	25.4%	3,296
9/96	1,219	542	44.5%	2,800
Annual Growth	19.1%	(3.9%)	—	26.4%

2002 Year-End Financials

Debt ratio: —	No. of shares (mil.): 365
Return on equity: —	Dividends
Cash ($ mil.): 489	Yield: 22.0%
Current ratio: 0.92	Payout: 546.9%
Long-term debt ($ mil.): 5,714	Market value ($ mil.): 11,576

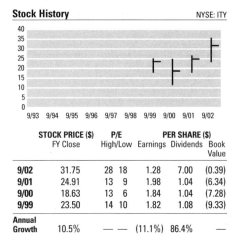

	STOCK PRICE ($) FY Close	P/E High/Low		PER SHARE ($) Earnings	Dividends	Book Value
9/02	31.75	28	18	1.28	7.00	(0.39)
9/01	24.91	13	9	1.98	1.04	(6.34)
9/00	18.63	13	6	1.84	1.04	(7.28)
9/99	23.50	14	10	1.82	1.08	(9.33)
Annual Growth	10.5%	—	—	(11.1%)	86.4%	—

Inco Limited

Inco turns nickel into gold. The company is the world's #2 producer of nickel (after Russian giant Norilsk Nickel), which is used primarily for manufacturing stainless steel and batteries. Inco also mines and processes cobalt, copper, gold, silver, and platinum. It manufactures nickel battery materials and nickel foams, flakes, and powders for use in catalysts, electronics, and paints. The company's primary mining and processing operations are in Asia, Europe, and North America. In 2002 Inco reached a deal that will allow it to develop the huge Voisey's Bay nickel deposit in Labrador and Newfoundland, Canada.

Digging its way in a challenging nickel market, Inco continues to reduce base costs (the company is a leader in using high-tech approaches to mining), develop new low-cost orebodies, and increase its value-added nickel products business.

HISTORY

In 1883 a Canadian Pacific Railway blacksmith discovered copper and nickel deposits in the Sudbury Basin. Two companies — the Orford Nickel and Copper Company and the Canadian Copper Company — tried to exploit the ore but couldn't separate the copper from the nickel. Nickel was all but worthless at the time. In 1890 Orford, led by Robert Thompson, patented a process to separate the two metals just as the US Navy was beginning to use a nickel-steel alloy for armaments.

Enter financier J. P. Morgan, architect of U.S. Steel. With Morgan's help Orford and Canadian Copper combined with five smaller companies in 1902 to form New Jersey-based International Nickel Company. In 1916 the company formed a Canadian subsidiary, International Nickel Company of Canada.

Sales plummeted after WWI, and in a 1928 restructuring, the Canadian subsidiary became the parent company. In 1929 International Nickel gained control of the world's nickel output when it bought Mond Nickel, a British metals refiner. By the 1950s the company accounted for 85% of noncommunist production.

Oil crises and inflation decreased demand for metals and battered International Nickel during the 1970s and early 1980s. In 1974 the company bought ESB Ray-O-Vac, the world's largest battery maker (sold in the early 1980s). Two years later the company shortened its name to Inco Limited.

Inco suffered from lack of demand for its metals until 1986. Then-CEO Donald Phillips cut employees and boosted productivity at Inco's mines and refineries. Demand for stainless steel rose in the late 1980s; Inco's sales more than doubled from 1987 to 1989.

Metal prices declined again in the early 1990s in response to a North American recession and the entry of former Iron Curtain countries into the metals markets. With a worldwide surplus, Inco cut nickel production. The company also reorganized. In 1991 it merged its gold interests with Consolidated TVX Mining (in 1993 it sold its 62% interest in TVX). These actions, however, could not stave off a loss in 1992.

As the US economy recovered and new Asian markets developed, exploration activities revved up with new ore discoveries in 1994 and 1995. In 1995 Inco bought a 25% share of the copper, cobalt, and nickel rights to rich deposits at Voisey's Bay in Newfoundland and Labrador; the following year it bought the remaining rights along with their holder, mining company Diamond Fields (the total cost was $3.2 billion).

Inco also unloaded some of its nonmining businesses. The company spun off Doncasters (aircraft components) in 1997. About 4,700 miners went on strike that year, cutting the company's nickel production by more than half. As rising worldwide nickel production drove prices down in 1998, the company reduced its work force by more than 1,400. It also sold Inco Alloys International to Special Metals.

In 1999 Inco entered into joint ventures with Dowa Mining of Japan to search for copper, zinc, silver, and gold in Indonesia and Turkey. That year the company shut down its Manitoba nickel production facility for several months over a contract dispute with labor. Inco also created Inco Special Products and commissioned a $14 million nickel processing plant in Wales to increase its sales of value-added nickel products.

Inco started building a nickel-cobalt mining and refining facility on the French island of New Caledonia in 2000 (production is scheduled for 2004). The company continued negotiations throughout 2001 with the governments of Canada, Labrador, and Newfoundland, and an agreement was reached in mid-2002.

EXECUTIVES

Chairman and CEO: Scott M. Hand, age 60, $862,000 pay
President, COO, and Director: Peter C. Jones, age 54, $530,000 pay
EVP and CFO: Farokh S. Hakimi, age 54
EVP, General Counsel, and Secretary: Stuart F. Feiner, age 55, $452,000 pay
EVP, Marketing: Peter J. Goudie, age 54
VP and CIO: Subi Bhandari, age 58
VP, Exploration: Robert A. Horn, age 59
VP, Human Resources: Mark J. Daniel, age 56
VP, Public and Government Affairs: Alan C. Stubbs, age 58
VP, Taxation: Gary G. Kaiway, age 54
VP, Technology and Engineering: William Gordon Bacon, age 58
VP and Treasurer: Donald T. Hurley, age 55
President, Canadian and UK Operations: Ronald C. Aelick, age 54
President, Inco Asia Limited and Inco Pacific Sales Limited: C.M. (James) Shih
President, Inco China: K.C. (David) Luo
President and Representative Director, Inco Limited, Japan: Shozo Kawaguchi

President, Inco United States: Richard L. Guido, age 58
President, International Nickel: David J. Anderson, age 55
President, Voisey's Bay Nickel Company Limited: A. Stewart Gendron, age 60
President and CEO, PT International Nickel Indonesia Tbk: Edward W. Hodkin
Auditors: PricewaterhouseCoopers LLP

LOCATIONS

HQ: 145 King St. West, Ste. 1500, Toronto, Ontario M5H 4B7, Canada
Phone: 416-361-7511   **Fax:** 416-361-7781
US HQ: Park 80 West-Plaza Two, Saddlebrook, NJ 07662
Web: www.inco.com

Inco Limited's core subsidiaries operate mines and facilities in Canada, China, Indonesia, Japan, New Caledonia (in the southwest Pacific), South Korea, Taiwan, and the UK. The company also operates in France, Guatemala, and the US and has exploration activities in Australia, Brazil, Canada, Peru, Turkey, and the US.

PRODUCTS/OPERATIONS

Selected Products

Cobalt
Copper
Nickel (including intermediates)
Precious metals
    Gold
    Iridium
    Palladium
    Platinum
    Rhodium
    Ruthenium
    Silver
Special products (foams, flakes, powders, oxides, and nickel-coated graphite and carbon fibers)
Other
    Liquid sulfur dioxide
    Sulfuric acid

Selected Subsidiaries and Affiliates

I.E.L. Holdings (UK)
Inco Asia Limited (Barbados)
Inco Europe Limited (UK)
International Nickel, Inc.
Inco S.A. (France)
Inco TNC Limited (67%, Japan)
Inco United States, Inc.
Goro Nickel S.A. (85 %, France)
Monticello Capital (Barbados)
P.T. International Nickel Indonesia Tbk (59%, Indonesia)
Voisey's Bay Nickel Company Limited (Newfoundland and Labrador)

COMPETITORS

Anglo American
ASARCO
BHP Billiton Ltd
Eramet
Falconbridge
Norilsk Nickel
Newmont Mining
Nippon Mining
Noranda
Outokumpu
Phelps Dodge
Rio Tinto
Southern Peru Copper
Special Metals
Stillwater Mining
Trelleborg
Umicore
WMC Resources

HISTORICAL FINANCIALS

Company Type: Public

Income Statement

FYE: December 31

	REVENUE ($ mil.)	NET INCOME ($ mil.)	NET PROFIT MARGIN	EMPLOYEES
12/02	2,161	(1,481)	—	10,534
12/01	2,066	305	14.8%	10,258
12/00	2,917	400	13.7%	10,143
12/99	2,113	17	0.8%	10,198
12/98	1,766	(76)	—	11,007
12/97	2,367	75	3.2%	14,278
12/96	3,105	179	5.8%	16,308
12/95	3,471	227	6.5%	15,818
12/94	2,484	22	0.9%	15,709
12/93	2,131	28	1.3%	16,087
Annual Growth	0.2%	—	—	(4.6%)

2002 Year-End Financials

Debt ratio: 46.4%
Return on equity: —
Cash ($ mil.): 1,087
Current ratio: 2.14
Long-term debt ($ mil.): 1,546

No. of shares (mil.): 183
Dividends
Yield: 0.0%
Payout: —
Market value ($ mil.): 3,888

Stock History

NYSE: N

12/93 12/94 12/95 12/96 12/97 12/98 12/99 12/00 12/01 12/02

	STOCK PRICE ($) FY Close	P/E High/Low		PER SHARE ($) Earnings	Dividends	Book Value
12/02	21.22	—	—	(8.27)	0.00	20.77
12/01	16.94	14	7	1.49	0.00	29.06
12/00	16.76	13	7	1.97	0.00	26.30
12/99	23.50	—	—	(0.05)	0.00	25.50
12/98	10.44	—	—	(0.63)	0.10	26.24
12/97	17.00	151	68	0.25	0.40	26.93
12/96	31.88	34	26	1.09	0.40	27.12
12/95	33.25	21	13	1.82	0.40	16.95
12/94	28.63	1,042 713		0.03	0.40	15.56
12/93	26.88	347 217		0.08	0.40	15.11
Annual Growth	(2.6%)	—	—	—	—	3.6%

ING Groep N.V.

Together ING stands — a hybrid of banking, insurance, and financial services. The world's largest insurer, Amsterdam-based ING Groep offers life, health, and disability products; personal insurance lines (auto and fire coverage); commercial property/casualty insurance; and reinsurance. ING's banking lines range from humble post office deposit accounts (the Postbanks) in the Netherlands to consumer and corporate banking throughout Europe. Other lines are corporate finance, securities, and investment and asset management services (through its ING banking network subsidiary) and auto, airplane, and other equipment leasing.

The company has struggled with investment banking arm ING Barings, which it bought after the Nick Leeson trading scandal but before the Asian and Russian economic crises. As a result, the company eliminated some 1,000 jobs from ING Barings. In a streamlining effort, ING has regrouped its ailing banking operations (including ING Barings and ING Bank) into one organization. ING sold its US investment banking services, including New York-based Furman Selz, to Dutch rival ABN AMRO.

Aiming to become a financial services player in all four corners of the world, ING has taken a majority stake in India's Vysya Bank and has set up new joint banking ventures in Australia and China.

Exposed to the collapse of Enron, ING lost about $200 million. Citing the slumping US economy, the company laid off about 15% of its US staff (some 1,600 people). ING also cut costs domestically by reorganizing its Dutch operations into four divisions (retail, wholesale, intermediary, and operations/IT).

Despite big investment losses in 2002, the company managed to grow net income from its insurance operations, thanks in part to lowered operating costs in the US. ING's banking operations posted lowered totals, mainly due to increased risk costs.

The company announced it is taking a $14 billion goodwill writedown on its underperforming US acquisitions (ReliaStar and health care insurer Aetna's financial services businesses) in 2003.

HISTORY

ING Groep's roots go back to 1845 when its earliest predecessor, the Netherlands Insurance Co., was founded. The firm began expanding geographically; in 1903 it added life insurance. In 1963 it merged with the century old Nationale Life Insurance Bank to form Nationale-Nederland (NN). Over the next three decades, the company grew primarily through acquisitions in Europe, North America, and Australia. In 1986 NN became the first European life insurance company to be licensed in Japan.

Another predecessor, the Rijkspostspaarbank, was founded in 1881 to provide Dutch citizens with simple post office savings accounts. In 1918 the Postcheque-en Girondienst (giro) system was established to allow people to use vouchers drawn on their savings accounts to pay bills. This system became the main method of settling accounts (instead of bank checking accounts).

Rijkspostspaarbank and Postcheque merged in 1986 to become Postbank. Postbank merged in 1989 with the Nederlandse Middenstandsbank (founded 1927) to become NMB Postbank. The vast amounts of cash tied up in the post office savings and giro systems fueled NMB's business.

In 1991, as the Europe economic union became a reality, and barriers between banking and insurance began to fall, NN merged with NMB Postbank to form Internationale Nederland Groep (ING). ING began cutting costs, shedding redundant offices and unprofitable operations in both its segments. In the US, where insurance and banking were legally divided, the company "debanked" itself in order to keep its more lucrative insurance operations (but retained the right to provide banking services to those operations).

In the 1990s ING sought to increase its investment banking and finance operations. In 1995 it took over UK-based Barings Bank (personal banker to the Queen of England) after Nicholas Leeson, a trader in Barings' Singapore office, lost huge sums of money in derivatives trading. The acquisition gave the firm a higher profile but cost more than anticipated and left it embroiled in lingering legal actions.

In 1996 ING bought Poland's Bank Slaski (the company had first entered Poland in 1994). The next year it expanded its securities business by acquiring investment bank Furman Selz, doubled its US life insurance operations by purchasing Equitable of Iowa, and listed on the NYSE. In 1998 ING's acquisition strategy again involved Europe and North America: It bought Belgium's Banque Bruxelles Lambert and Canadian life insurer Guardian Insurance Co. (from Guardian Royal Exchange now part of AXA UK).

In 1999 ING turned eastward, kicking off asset management operations in India and buying a minority stake in Korea's HC&B (formerly Housing & Commercial Bank). In 2000 the company bulked up its North American operations with the purchase of 40% of Savia SA, a Mexican insurance concern. It also bought US firm ReliaStar Financial in a $6 billion deal and Charterhouse Securities from CCF (then called Crédit Commercial de France).

Soon after, however, ING announced plans to unload ING Barings through sales and closures. ING also acquired US-based Aetna's financial services and international divisions. ING Barings axed 1,100 jobs in 2001, primarily in London.

EXECUTIVES

Chairman: Ewald Kist, age 58
Vice Chairman; Chairman, ING Europe: Michel Tilmant, age 50
CFO: Cees Maas, age 55
Chairman, ING Americas and ING Asia/Pacific: Fred Hubbell, age 51
Chairman, ING Asset Management: Alexander Rinnooy Kan, age 53
CEO, ING Asia/Pacific: Jacques Kemp
Head of Pensions: Jan Nijssen
Head of Private Banking Group: Philippe Damas
Head of UK region: Igno van Waesberghe
Chairman, Management Committee, Central Europe, ING Europe: Eli Leenaars
Chairman, Management Committee, Netherlands, ING Europe: Diederik Laman Trip
Chairman, Management Committee, Southwest-Europe, ING Europe: Luc Vandewalle
CEO, ING U.S. Financial Services: Thomas J. McInerney
CIO, ING Europe: Angelien Kemna
Financial Markets, ING Europe: Ted de Vries
Operations/IT, ING Europe: Erik Dralans
Wholesale Operations, ING Europe: Harry van Tooren
ING Direct and Retail Financial Services, ING Europe: Hans Verkoren
Auditors: Ernst & Young

LOCATIONS

HQ: Strawinskylaan 2631, 1077 ZZ Amsterdam, The Netherlands
Phone: +31-20-541-54-11   **Fax:** +31-20-541-54-51
US HQ: ING Americas, 5780 Powers Ferry Rd. NW, Atlanta, GA 30327-4390
US Phone: 770-980-3300   **US Fax:** 770-980-3301
Web: www.ing.com

ING Groep operates in some 65 countries in Africa, Asia, Europe, North America, the Pacific Rim, and South America.

2002 Sales

	% of total
Americas	52
Europe	35
Asia/Pacific	11
Other	2
Total	**100**

PRODUCTS/OPERATIONS

2002 Assets

	$ mil.	% of total
Cash	11,996	2
Investments	312,548	41
Loans	298,755	40
Other	129,104	17
Total	**752,403**	**100**

2002 Sales

	$ mil.	% of total
Insurance operations		
Premiums	66,630	68
Investments, commission & other	14,188	15
Banking		
Interest	9,815	10
Commission	4,658	5
Other	2,194	2
Total	**97,874**	**100**

Selected Companies

Insurance
Golden American Life Insurance Company (US)
ING America Insurance Holdings, Inc. (US)
ING Australia Pty. Ltd.
ING Insurance Company of Canada
ING Insurance N.V. (Belgium)
ING Life Insurance and Annuity Company (US)
ING Life Insurance Company Ltd. (Japan)
ING Re (Netherlands) N.V.
ING Seguros, S.A. de C.V. (Mexico)
ING Seguros de Vida S.A. (Chile)
ING Verzekeringen N.V. (Netherlands)
Nationale-Nederlanden Levensverzekering Maatschappij
 N.V. (Netherlands)
Postbank Levensverzekering N.V. (Netherlands)
ReliaStar Life Insurance Company (US)
United Life & Annuity Insurance Company (US)

Banking
Allgemeine Deutsche Direktbank (Germany; 70%)
Baring Asset Management Holdings Ltd. (UK)
Furman Selz Holding LLC (US)
ING Bank (Australia) Ltd.
ING Bank N.V. (Netherlands)
ING Baring Securities (Japan) Ltd.
ING Capital Markets (Hong Kong) Ltd.
ING Direct N.V. (Canada, Germany, Spain, Australia,
 France, USA, and Italy)
ING Vysya Bank Ltd. (India; 44%)
Postbank N.V. (Netherlands)

COMPETITORS

ABN AMRO	Deutsche Bundesbank
AEGON	Fortis
Allianz	General Re
Allstate	Goldman Sachs
AIG	HSBC Holdings
Generali	Legal & General Group
AGF	Lehman Brothers
AXA	Lloyd's of London
Barclays	Merrill Lynch
HVB Group	MetLife
Bear Stearns	Prudential
Chubb	Prudential plc
CIGNA	Swiss Life
Citigroup	UBS
CNP Assurances	Union des Assurances
Credit Suisse	Fédérales
Deutsche Bank	

HISTORICAL FINANCIALS

Company Type: Public

Income Statement

FYE: December 31

	ASSETS ($ mil.)	NET INCOME ($ mil.)	INCOME AS % OF ASSETS	EMPLOYEES
12/02	752,403	4,726	0.6%	113,060
12/01	628,473	4,079	0.6%	112,000
12/00	612,332	11,287	1.8%	108,965
12/99	497,349	4,967	1.0%	86,040
12/98	460,563	3,113	0.7%	82,750
12/97	306,232	2,026	0.7%	64,162
12/96	279,985	1,922	0.7%	58,106
12/95	246,356	1,647	0.7%	52,144
12/94	203,913	1,327	0.7%	51,176
12/93	174,034	1,042	0.6%	49,030
Annual Growth	**17.7%**	**18.3%**	**—**	**9.7%**

2002 Year-End Financials

Equity as % of assets: 2.5%	Dividends
Return on assets: 0.7%	Yield: 5.3%
Return on equity: 24.6%	Payout: 36.9%
Long-term debt ($ mil.): 96,687	Market value ($ mil.): 33,557
No. of shares (mil.): 1,993	Sales ($ mil.): 97,874

Stock History

NYSE: ING

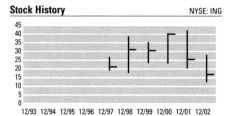

	STOCK PRICE ($) FY Close	P/E High/Low		PER SHARE ($) Earnings	Dividends	Book Value
12/02	16.84	11	5	2.44	0.90	10.75
12/01	25.45	20	10	2.09	1.06	10.76
12/00	40.06	7	4	5.91	0.85	13.24
12/99	30.50	14	9	2.55	1.17	18.29
12/98	31.09	24	11	1.63	0.32	16.41
12/97	21.16	20	15	1.30	0.00	12.32
Annual Growth	**(4.5%)**	**—**	**—**	**13.4%**	**—**	**(2.7%)**

Interbrew S.A.

A collection of global beers is bound to include a lot of Interbrew. Among the world's largest brewers (closely ranked with Heineken, which trails Anheuser-Busch and SABMiller), Interbrew has about 200 brands of lagers, premium beers, and specialty brews, which it sells in 120 countries. Among them are its flagship beers, Stella Artois and Bass Ale (#1 imported ale in the US), as well as popular brews Hoegaarden, Labatt Blue, Leffe, and Rolling Rock. Interbrew also owns Germany's Brauerei Beck & Co., maker of the well-known Beck's brand. A voting trust of Interbrew's founding families owns more than 60% of the company.

Flat demand in its core market of Belgium spurred Interbrew to expand internationally. In addition to the acquisition of Beck's, the company also recently negotiated with Diageo the rights to sell Bass ale in the US. Like other global brewers, the company also has been looking to emerging markets for growth. Interbrew owns a

portion of the Zhujiang brewery and a controlling interest in the KK Group, both of which brew popular beers in China. The company also has purchased German brewer Gabriel Sedlmayr Spaten-Franziskaner Braeu KGaA, the originator of Löwenbräu.

In addition to brewing beer, Interbrew also operates Belgian Beer Cafés around the world, expanding them to the Czech Republic, Hungary, and Romania in 2002. It owns 20% of the Toronto Blue Jays, having sold an 80% stake in the baseball team to cable firm Rogers Communications in December 2000.

HISTORY

Monks at the Leffe Abbey in Belgium were brewing beer as early as 1240, and surviving records from 1366 mention Belgium's Den Horen brewery. Belgian master brewer Sebastien Artois (best known for his Stella Artois lager) took over Den Horen in 1717. In 1853 the Piedboeuf family founded a brewery at Liege and established the Jupiler lager. Albert Van Damme assumed management of that brewery in 1920.

Over the years, the Artois and Piedboeuf families took over or established operations both in and outside Belgium. Direct descendants (the clans de Spoelberch, Van Damme, and de Mevius) of the two families were still managing the companies in 1987 when they decided the key to survival in the fragmented European beer market was to merge.

Artois-Piedboeuf-Interbrew acquired the Hoegaarden brewery in Belgium in 1989. The company changed its name to Interbrew three years later, acquired another Belgian brewery (Belle-Vue), and bought stakes in breweries in Bulgaria, Croatia, and Hungary. In 1995 Dommelsche Bierbrouwerij bought Allied Breweries Nederland, an Allied Domecq subsidiary, and Interbrew acquired the Oranjeboom breweries in the Netherlands.

The company purchased John Labatt Ltd. for $2 billion in 1995. As a result of the deal, Interbrew gained control of Latrobe Brewing (Rolling Rock beer, US), 22% of Mexico's FEMSA Cerveza (increased to 30% in 1998), the Toronto Argonauts football team, 90% of the Toronto Blue Jays, and various broadcast properties.

Interbrew sold many noncore assets, including Lehigh Valley Dairies (US) and John Labatt Retail (pubs, UK), in 1996. Also that year the company established joint ventures in the Dominican Republic and the US (to import Mexican beers through FEMSA).

In 1998 Interbrew paid $250 million for 50% of the Doosan Group's Oriental Brewery, South Korea's second-largest brewer, and bought a majority stake in Russian brewer Rosar. The next year Interbrew combined its Russian operations with Sun Brewing, forming Russian brewer Sun-Interbrew. It then bought Korea's Jinro-Coors Brewery for about $378 million. Hugo Powell was later named CEO of Interbrew.

Interbrew bought Britain's third-largest brewer, Whitbread Beer Company, in May 2000 for $590 million. Having gained a foothold in the UK market, the company then bought Bass Brewers from Bass PLC in August 2000 for more than $3 billion. Interbrew went public on the Euronext (Brussels) exchange in December 2000.

In 2001 Baron Paul De Keersmaeker retired as chairman and was replaced by Pierre Jean Everaert. That year the company took an 80% stake in Germany's tenth-largest brewer, Diebels. Interbrew also sold Carling, which controls about 18% of the UK beer market, to Coors for $1.7 billion, after being ordered to remedy unfair competition advantages related to the Bass Brewers purchase.

John Brock, former COO of Cadbury Schweppes, became CEO of Interbrew in February 2003. In April, Interbrew sold a minority stake of its Namibian Breweries in southern Africa to Diageo and Heineken.

EXECUTIVES

Chairman: Pierre Jean Everaert, age 63
CEO: John F. Brock, age 54
CFO: Francois Jaclot, age 54
EVP and CTO: Larry J. Macauley, age 53
SVP, Legal: Catherine Noirfalisse
Zone President, Asia-Pacific: Patrice J. Thys, age 48
Zone President, Canada: Stewart Gilliland, age 46
Zone President, Europe: Jerry Fowden, age 47
Zone President, US-Latin America:
Stéfan Descheemaeker, age 43
Regional President, Benefralux: Alain Beyens, age 42
Regional President, Canada and Cuba: Bruce Elliot, age 48
Regional President, Central Europe: Jaak De Witte, age 46
Regional President, USA: Steve Cahillane, age 38
EVP, Finance, Beck's North America: Tom O'Grady
CIO: Jacques Purnode, age 47
CTO: André Weckx
Chief Human Resources Officer: Peter Vrijsen, age 49
Chief Commercial Officer: Brent Willis
Chief Planning and Performance Officer:
Jo Van Biesbroeck, age 47
President and CEO, Beck's North America:
Thomas Cardella
Auditors: Klynveld Peat Marwick Goerdeler

LOCATIONS

HQ: Vaartstraat 94, B-3000 Leuven, Belgium
Phone: +32-16-24-71-11   **Fax:** +32-16-24-74-07
US HQ: 101 Merritt 7, Norwalk, CT 06856-5075
US Phone: 203-750-6600   **US Fax:** 203-750-6699
Web: www.interbrew.com

Interbrew has operations in 21 countries across Asia/Pacific, the Americas, and Europe.

2002 Sales

	% of total
Western Europe	49
Americas	29
Emerging Markets	20
Global Exports	2
Total	**100**

PRODUCTS/OPERATIONS

Selected Countries and Brands

International (Bass Ale, Beck's, Belle-Vue, Hoegaarden, Jupiler, Labatt, Leffe, Rolling Rock, Samuel Adams outside US, Stella Artois)
Belgium (Julius, Hougaardse Das, Piedboeuf, Safir, Vieux Temps)
Bulgaria (Astika, Kamenitza)
Canada (Alexander Keith's, Kokanee; licensed — Budweiser, Carlsberg, Guinness)
China (Best Ice, Jinling Dry, Yali Dry)
Croatia (Bozicno, Ozujsko Pivo, Tomislav Pivo)
Dominican Republic (Soberana)
France (La Bécasse)
Hungary (Borsodi Sor)
Mexico (Bohemia, Dos Equis, Sol, Tecaté)
Montenegro (Nik Gold, Niksico Pivo)
The Netherlands (Dommelsch, Hertog Jan, Oranjeboom)
Romania (Bergenbier, Hopfen Konig)
Russia (Klinskoye, Sibirskaya Korona, Tolstyak)
South Korea (Cafri, OB Lager)
UK (Boddingtons, Caffrey's, Murphy's, Wadworth 6X, Worthington Bitter)
Ukraine (Chernigivski Pivo, Gubernator, Taller Pils)
US (Löwenbräu)

COMPETITORS

Adolph Coors	Heineken
Anchor Brewing	Holsten-Brauerei
Anheuser-Busch	Kirin
Asahi Breweries	Labatt
Asia Pacific Breweries	Lion Nathan
BBAG	Miller Brewing
Yanjing	Grupo Modelo
Big Rock Brewery	Molson
Blaue Quellen Mineral	Pyramid Breweries
Boston Beer	Radeberger Gruppe
Brau und Brunnen	Redhook Ale
Carlsberg	Grolsch
CBR Brewing	SABMiller
Constellation Brands	San Miguel
Yuengling & Son	Sapporo
Diageo	Scottish & Newcastle
FEMSA	Suntory
Foster's	Tsingtao
Gambrinus	Vidrala

HISTORICAL FINANCIALS

Company Type: Public

Income Statement

FYE: December 31

	REVENUE ($ mil.)	NET INCOME ($ mil.)	NET PROFIT MARGIN	EMPLOYEES
12/02	7,328	490	6.7%	35,044
12/01	6,469	618	9.6%	37,617
12/00	7,690	(857)	—	34,203
12/99	4,532	232	5.1%	24,348
12/98	4,200	222	5.3%	16,727
12/97	2,886	144	5.0%	13,835
12/96*	3,016	127	4.2%	13,735
9/95	2,757	117	4.3%	13,237
9/94	1,526	84	5.5%	8,143
9/93	1,629	47	2.9%	9,778
Annual Growth	**18.2%**	**29.7%**	**—**	**15.2%**

*Fiscal year change

2002 Year-End Financials

Debt ratio: 30.5%
Return on equity: 10.7%
Cash ($ mil.): 259
Current ratio: 0.64
Long-term debt ($ mil.): 1,502

Net Income History   Euronext Brussels: INTB

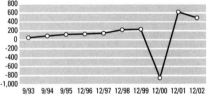

IntesaBci S.p.A.

The *gran che* of Italian banking, Milan-based IntesaBci (formerly Banca Intesa) is Italy's largest banking company. IntesaBci provides commercial and retail banking and other financial services through about 4,400 branches in Italy and 40 other countries. IntesaBci has also embraced telephone, wireless, and Internet banking. Other offerings include merchant banking services, mutual fund management, real estate lending, and leasing. Subsidiary Carivita sells life insurance. A syndicate headed by France's Crédit Agricole owns about 40% of IntesaBci.

Its acquisition and integration of Banca Com-

merciale Italiana (Comit) allowed it to surpass Sanpaolo IMI in size. Before the takeover, Banca Intesa itself was the product of a merger between the staid Cassa di Risparmio delle Provincie Lombarde (Cariplo) and the somewhat more colorful Banco Ambroveneto, whose history helped inspire the plot of *The Godfather, Part III*.

The company provides standard retail banking services as well as merchant banking, mutual fund and asset management, and real estate, factoring, leasing, and other financial services.

IntesaBci is restructuring along operational lines with Comit forming the core of its investment and corporate arm. This will create competition with MEDIOBANCA, the powerful and secretive investment bank with which IntesaBci has historically been linked. IntesaBci is putting itself in position to compete in the brave new world created by European economic unification, snapping up Eastern European banks as they become available. In addition to reorganizing, IntesaBci has embraced technology (computer, telephone, and wireless banking) and has launched online brokerage IntesaTrade. IntesaBci's component companies were formerly controlled by the Italian government and a private foundation.

HISTORY

Industrialization came slowly to Italy after its unification in the 1860s. It wasn't until the 1920s that it began building the infrastructure necessary for industrialization (the country remained largely agricultural until after WWII). In the 1920s specialized institutions were founded to finance utilities and transportation; one of them, La Centrale Societa per il Finanziamento di Imprese Elettriche e Telefoniche, was formed in 1925 to help finance Italy's energy and telecommunications industries. In 1965 this entity enlarged its focus and changed its name to La Centrale Finanziaria Generale.

La Centrale's interests in energy were transferred to ENEL, the state holding company in 1985, which left it with holdings in banking, finance, and insurance. That year the bank merged with Nuovo Banco Ambrosiano, formerly Banco Ambrosiano.

Banco Ambrosiano was founded in 1896 by Guiseppi Tovino, whose good works and sturdy faith made him a saint (he was beatified in 1998). Betraying his legacy, in 1981 chairman Roberto Calvi was found hanging under the Blackfriars Bridge in London. Calvi, called "God's Banker" for his connections to the Vatican, left behind a tangle of debt, phony holding companies, and fraud that implicated the Catholic Church, brought down an archbishop, and involved a secretive Masonic lodge. Banco Ambrosiano was taken over by a group of creditor banks and its name was changed to Nuovo Banco Ambrosiano.

In 1989, Nuovo Banco Ambrosiano merged with its subsidiary, Banco Cattolica del Veneto, and became known as Banco Ambroveneto. It bought Banco Centro-Sud from US-based Citicorp (now Citigroup) in 1991 and in 1997 bought La Cassa di Risparmio delle Provincie Lombarde (Cariplo), Italy's biggest savings bank.

Cariplo was founded by the Austro-Hungarian government in 1823, when the region was still recovering from Napoleon's depredations. Count Giovanni Pietro Porro wanted to allow artisans and day laborers to set aside money, and the company remained true to that mission throughout the *Risorgimento* and two world wars.

In the 1960s Cariplo's business began offering

medium and long-term credit; the next decade it expanded internationally, opening offices in London, New York, Hong Kong, and other banking centers. Banking reform allowed Cariplo to become a stock company in 1991.

Ambroveneto's purchase of Cariplo was a slap in the face to MEDIOBANCA, the powerful investment bank that wanted Cariplo's rich savings deposits for Banca Commerciale Italiana (Comit), in which it held an interest.

Banco Ambroveneto and Cariplo merged to form Banca Intesa in 1998. The next year MEDIOBANCA's wish was granted when the bank's offer for Comit was accepted over rival UniCredito Italiano's hostile bid. The acquisition of a majority of Comit has created Italy's largest bank, eclipsing Sanpaolo IMI. In 2001 Banca Intesa integrated Comit to form IntesaBci.

EXECUTIVES

CEO: Corrado Passera
Chairman: Giovanni Bazoli, age 68
Deputy Chairman: Jean Laurent
Deputy Chairman: Sandro Molinari
Deputy Chairman: Alfonso Desiata
General Manager and COO: Christian Merle

LOCATIONS

HQ: Piazza Paolo Ferrari, 10, 20121 Milan, Italy
Phone: +39-02-8844-1   **Fax:** +39-02-8844-3638
Web: www.bancaintesa.it

IntesaBci and its subsidiaries operate about 4,400 branches in Italy and 40 other countries.

PRODUCTS/OPERATIONS

Selected subsidiaries

Banca Carime — Cosenza
Banca Commerciale Italiana — Milano
Banca Intesa (France)
Banca Intesa International (Luxembourg)
Banca Popolare FriulAdria
Banco Ambrosiano Veneto
Caboto Holding Sim
Caboto International
Cariparma & Piacenza (formerly Cassa di Risparmio di Parma e Piacenza)
CARIPLO
Fundsworld Financial Services
Intesa Asset Management
Intesa Bank Overseas (formerly Ambroveneto International Bank) (Cayman Islands)
Intesa e-Lab (formerly Banca Proxima)
Intesa Fiduciaria Sim (formerly Ambrofid -Gestioni fiduciarie)
Intesa Formazione
Intesa Gestione Crediti (formerly Cassa di Risparmio Salernitana)
Intesa Ireland
Intesa Italia Sim (formerly Ambro Italia Sim)
Intesa Leasing
Intesa Preferred Capital Company LLC (US)
Intesa Preferred Capital Company LLC II (US)
Intesa Riscossione Tributi
Intesa Sec — Milano Intesa Sistemi e Servizi
Italfid
La Centrale Consulenza
Mediocredito Lombardo
Mediofactoring
Setefi

COMPETITORS

Monte dei Paschi di Siena
Banca Nazionale del
 Lavoro
Banca Popolare di Milano
BBVA
Banco di Napoli
Banca Popolare di Verona
Capitalia
DePfa Bank
Dexia Group
Mediobanca
Sanpaolo IMI
UniCredito Italiano

HISTORICAL FINANCIALS

Company Type: Public

Income Statement

FYE: December 31

	ASSETS ($ mil.)	NET INCOME ($ mil.)	INCOME AS % OF ASSETS	EMPLOYEES
12/02	294,236	210	0.1%	72,683
12/01	278,936	822	0.3%	70,182
12/00	312,863	1,376	0.4%	75,894
12/99	305,211	855	0.3%	77,774
12/98	179,635	685	0.4%	35,681
12/97	158,377	399	0.3%	34,592
Annual Growth	13.2%	(12.1%)	—	16.0%

2002 Year-End Financials

Equity as % of assets: 5.0%
Return on assets: 0.1%
Return on equity: —
Long-term debt ($ mil.): —
Sales ($ mil.): 26,159

Net Income

Italian: BIN

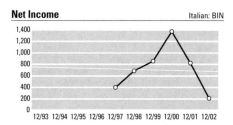

Invensys plc

Having slimmed down and sold off non-core assets, Invensys is betting on efficiency. Invensys now has only two primary divisions: Production Management focuses on optimizing customers' supply and production processes using Invensys' control, production, and automation systems; Rail Systems makes signalling, communication, and control systems for railroads and subways. Invensys also has a Development division, which makes appliance controls, home control systems, wind power gears, power supplies, and process management systems for food, beverage, and health care products, but those operations are in the process of being divested.

Formed by the 1999 purchase of BTR by Siebe, Invensys has fallen on hard times of late. Faced with a faltering economy — and mostly steadily declining sales and profits since 1999 — Invensys has cut jobs and costs and divested more than $1 billion in noncore businesses. Among the things to go: its energy storage, sensor systems, and flow control businesses. The company, which has also agreed to sell its metering business, wants to focus on "the management of customers' production assets and energy resources." It's also notable that its Rail Systems division has been elevated to one of the two main divisions.

The company announced in 2003 that it intended to sell — either as a group or piecemeal — the businesses in its Development division. Previously those businesses were in a wait-and-see-what-happens mode.

HISTORY

Immigrant Austrian artillery officer Augustus Siebe founded Siebe in London in 1819. A lifelong inventor, Siebe's creations included breech-loading rifles, carbon arc lamps, the world's first diving suit, and early ice-making machines.

From the 1890s to the early 1970s, Siebe made a name for itself in marine engineering and as a maker of breathing apparatuses, developing products such as submarine escape and diving equipment for Britain's Royal Navy. General Dynamics veteran Barrie Stephens took over management of the struggling Siebe in 1963. Stephens cut costs, restructured, terminated half the workforce, and in the late 1960s, started making acquisitions.

With its 1972 purchase of European safety equipment specialist James North & Sons, Siebe began transforming from a marine-based engineer to a controls and engineering company. It expanded into continental Europe and in 1982 moved into North America with the purchase of Tecalemit (garage equipment).

Included in the Tecalemit buy were two healthy electronic controls businesses, which Stephens tried, but failed, to sell. When Siebe acquired CompAir (compressed air) in 1985 (sold 2002), the deal included three pneumatic controls companies. Without trying, Siebe had established a controls presence. That segment was strengthened further in 1986 when it bought Robertshaw (appliance controls, US). The following year's additions of US concerns Ranco and Barber-Colman added automotive, industrial, and commercial building controls.

In 1990 Siebe hit the jackpot with the $650 million acquisition of Foxboro, which had developed a UNIX-based system capable of controlling entire oil refineries and automobile plants. With Foxboro, Siebe's control business began to seriously challenge Honeywell.

Mid- to late- 1990s acquisitions included AVP (food and drinks industry equipment), Wonderware (factory application software), Eurotherm (temperature controls), and Electronic Measurement (industrial power supply). To offset costs associated with these acquisitions, Siebe began restructuring in 1998 and sold its North Safety Products Business (personal safety and life support products) to Norcross Safety Products.

In 1999 Siebe acquired engineering rival BTR plc in a $6 billion deal that nearly tripled Siebe's size; the combined company changed its name to BTR Siebe and later to Invensys. Also that year the company sold more than a dozen businesses, including its automotive and aerospace operations. It also sold 90% of its Paper Technology Group to investment firm Apax Partners in a deal valued at about $800 million. Invensys' 1999 acquisitions included Best Power (uninterruptible power supplies), purchased from industrial products maker SPX for around $240 million.

Invensys formed a pact with Microsoft in early 2000 to develop standards for connecting home appliances to the Internet. Later that year the company gained control of Netherlands-based Baan Company, a near-bankrupt maker of software that allows manufacturers to manage their internal operations, in a $709 million deal.

Early in 2002 Invensys sold its energy storage business for $425 million. In May of 2002 the company reorganized and sold its flow control business to US-based Flowserve Corporation for $535 million. Invensys also sold its Invensys Sensor Systems business to Honeywell for $415 million in cash. Late in 2003 Invensys agreed to sell its metering business for about $650 million.

EXECUTIVES

Chairman: Lord Colin Marshall, age 69
CEO: Richard Haythornthwaite, age 46, $660,000 pay
SVP, Finance and CFO: Adrian Hennah, age 45
SVP and General Counsel: Victoria Hull
SVP, Group Development: Rod Powell
SVP, Group Marketing and Communications:
 Victoria Scarth
SVP, Human Resources and Group Services:
 Regina Hitchery
SVP, Project Management and Customer Development:
 Jim Siler
SVP, Supply Chain Management: Shelley Stewart
SVP, Service Delivery: Ed Mulvey
CIO: Stephen C. (Steve) Hassell
CTO: Phil Whalen
COO, Development Division: John H. Duerden, age 61
COO, Production Management: Leo Quinn
Change Management Director: Alex Tregellas
Auditors: Ernst & Young LLP

LOCATIONS

HQ: Invensys House, Carlisle Place,
 London SW1P 1BX, United Kingdom
Phone: +44-20-7834-3848   **Fax:** +44-20-7834-3879
US HQ: 33 Commercial St., Foxboro, MA 02035
US Phone: 508-543-2700   **US Fax:** 508-543-2735
Web: www.invensys.com

Invensys has major subsidiaries in Australia, Brazil, Denmark, Japan, Luxembourg, the Netherlands, Spain, the UK, and the US.

2003 Sales

	$ mil.	% of total
North America	3,256.4	41
Europe		
UK	708.3	9
Other countries	1,561.3	20
Asia/Pacific	925.5	12
South America	157.4	2
Other countries	92.7	1
Discontinued operations	1,196.2	15
Total	**7,897.8**	**100**

PRODUCTS/OPERATIONS

2003 Sales

	$ mil.	% of total
Energy management	3,232.8	41
Production management	2,280.6	29
Development	1,188.3	15
Discontinued operations	1,196.1	15
Total	**7,897.8**	**100**

Selected Products (after reorganization)

Development
Climate controls
Metering systems
Power Components (switching and power supply products)
Wind Power (gear units for turbines)

Production Management
Enterprise software
Process engineering and automation systems
Temperature and process controllers

Rail Systems
Communication systems
Control systems
Signalling systems

COMPETITORS

ABB	Rockwell Automation
A. O. Smith	Schlumberger
Dee Van Enterprise	Siemens
Emerson Electric	Siemens Dematic
Endress+Hauser	SPX
GE Industrial Systems	Texas Instruments
GE Power Systems	Tomkins
Honeywell International	Trippe Manufacturing
Magnetek	Vicor
PECO II	

HISTORICAL FINANCIALS

Company Type: Public

Income Statement

FYE: March 31

	REVENUE ($ mil.)	NET INCOME ($ mil.)	NET PROFIT MARGIN	EMPLOYEES
3/03	7,898	(2,270)	—	48,867
3/02	9,939	(1,239)	—	73,005
3/01	11,136	111	1.0%	89,922
3/00	14,380	(379)	—	96,260
3/99	15,185	(169)	—	129,504
3/98	6,153	519	8.4%	148,355
3/97	4,925	416	8.4%	—
Annual Growth	8.2%	—	—	(19.9%)

2003 Year-End Financials

Debt ratio: —
Return on equity: —
Cash ($ mil.): 623
Current ratio: 1.52
Long-term debt ($ mil.): 2,809

Net Income History

OTC: IVNSY

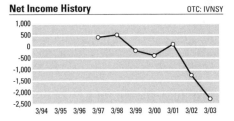

1,000	
500	
0	
-500	
-1,000	
-1,500	
-2,000	
-2,500	

3/94 3/95 3/96 3/97 3/98 3/99 3/00 3/01 3/02 3/03

Ispat International

After gobbling up failing state-owned steel mills around the world, Ispat (Sanskrit for "steel") has moved inland. The company's 1998 purchase of Inland Steel Industries' US operations (renamed Ispat Inland) made it one of the world's leading steelmakers. In addition to Ispat Inland, Ispat operates other subsidiaries, including Ispat Mexicana, Caribbean Ispat (Trinidad), Ispat Sibdec (Canada), Ispat Germany, and Ispat Unimétal (France). The company produces flat (sheet, slab) and long (wire rod, bars, pipes) steel products using direct-reduced iron, which is cheaper than using iron ore or scrap iron.

Ispat is part of founder and CEO Lakshmi Mittal's LNM Group, which also makes steel in Indonesia (Ispat Indo) and Kazakhstan (Ispat Karmet). The company operates through subsidiaries in Europe and the Americas. It entered the US with its much heralded purchase of Inland Steel Industries' steel-making operations

(renamed Ispat Inland). Roughly one-half of Ispat Inland's sales are derived from automotive customers such as Ford Motor, DaimlerChysler, and General Motors. Ispat Inland also provides a majority of steel obligations to Maytag and about 70% to Whirlpool.

The company ships its products to over eighty-five countries worldwide, with its largest markets coming from Europe and North America.

Indian entrepreneur Mittal (fittingly pronounced "metal") has long marked the US steelmaking market as a target for infiltration. Ispat has a history of snatching up steel mills on the cheap and turning them around to become profitable.

The company plans to pursue its debt reduction plan by applying all surplus cash to reducing its heavy debt load. It is also part of a joint venture with Commerce One to link metals buyers and sellers online.

HISTORY

Ispat International is the product of decades of steelmaking by India's Mittal family. In 1967 patriarch Mohan Mittal unsuccessfully tried to open a steel mill in Egypt. He and his four younger brothers then set up a steel company in India, but squabbles pushed Mohan to chart his own course, eventually giving rise to the Ispat empire. Mohan's son Lakshmi began working part-time at the family steel mill while in school; he started full-time at 21, after graduating in 1971.

Mohan set up an operation in Indonesia in 1975 (Ispat Indo) and put Lakshmi in charge. The next year, fueled by ambitions and held back by government regulations in India, Lakshmi formed Ispat International in Jakarta, Indonesia, to focus on expansion through acquisitions. He spent the next decade strengthening the Indonesian operations and perfecting the minimill process using direct-reduced iron (DRI).

Ispat took advantage of the recessionary late 1980s and early 1990s by making a string of acquisitions. In 1988 it took over the management of Trinidad and Tobago's state steel companies (bought 1994; renamed Caribbean Ispat).

In 1992 Ispat bought Mexico's third-largest (albeit bankrupt) steel and DRI producer. Two years later it acquired Canada's Sidbec-Dosco steelmaker. Also that year Lakshmi took exclusive control of international operations, leaving his brothers Pramod and Vinod to control the Indian divisions.

The mid-1990s brought more acquisitions: In 1995 Ispat bought Germany's Hamburger Stahlwerks and a mill in Kazakhstan. The next year it purchased Ireland's only steelmaker, Irish Steel. Lakshmi moved to London in 1996 and purchased a home on Bishops Avenue, known as "millionaire's row." (Saudi Arabia's King Fahd is a neighbor.)

In 1997 the company bought the long-product (wire rod) division of Germany's Thyssen AG (renamed Ispat Stahlwerk Ruhrort and Ispat Walzdraht Hochfeld). It also completed a $776 million IPO — the steel industry's biggest, outside of privatizations.

Ispat acquired Chicago-based Inland Steel in 1998 (now Ispat Inland), including the steel-finishing operations of I/N Tek (60% Inland-owned joint venture with Nippon Steel) and I/N Kote (50% Inland-owned joint venture with NSC).

In 1999 Ispat formed a joint venture with Mexican steelmaker Grupo Imsa to make flat-rolled steel to sell throughout most of the Americas. It also paid $96 million for France-based Usinor's

Unimétal, Tréfileurope, and Société Métallurgique de Révigny subsidiaries, which specialize in carbon long products. That year the company's Ispat Inland subsidiary became the target of a US federal criminal grand jury investigation and a related civil lawsuit for allegedly defrauding the Louisiana Highway Department. (The case has since been settled for $30 million, with the cost split between Ispat-Inland and Contech Construction Products Inc. of Ohio.)

In 2000 the company responded to a downturn in the steel industry by starting a Web-based joint venture with Commerce One to connect buyers and sellers in the worldwide metals market. It also offered to buy VSZ, Slovakia's #1 steelworks, but was outbid by U.S. Steel.

After struggling with heavy debt, high labor and energy costs, new environmental regulations, and EU steel quotas in 2001, Ispat closed down its subsidiary, Irish Ispat, which accounted for about 2% of the parent company's steel production.

In 2002, the company's 51% owned pipe making subsidiary, Productura Mexicana de Tuberia, sold largely all of its production assets.

EXECUTIVES

Chairman and CEO: Lakshmi N. Mittal, age 52
President, COO, and Director: Malay Mukherjee, age 55
CFO and Board Member: Bhikam C. Agarwal
President and CEO, Ispat Inland: Louis Schorsch
President and CEO, Ispat Sidbec:
  Richard Jean-Pierre LeBlanc
President and COO, Ispat Europe, and Board Member:
  Gerhard Renz
CEO, Ispat Unimétal: Alain Grenaut
CEO, Trefileurope: Bernard Laupretre
EVP and COO, Ispat Sidbec: Denis Fraser
CFO, Ispat Europe S.A.: Augustine Kochuparampil
Managing Director, Caribbean Ispat: John Kuriyan
Managing Director, Imexsa: Kumar Arun Prasad Singh
Managing Director, Ispat Hamburger Stahlwerke
  GmbH: Gregor Munstermann
Managing Director, Ispat Mexicana: Vijay K Bhatnagar
Director, Human Resources: Inder Walia
Director, Technology: Greg Ludkovsky
General Counsel: Simon Evans
Secretary: Vijay K. Goyal
Head of Communications: Annanya Sarin
Auditors: Deloitte & Touche

LOCATIONS

HQ: Ispat International N.V.
  Hofplein 20, 15th Fl.,
  3032 Rotterdam, The Netherlands
Phone: +31-10-282-9465   **Fax:** +31-10-282-9468
US HQ: 3210 Watling St., East Chicago, IN 46312
US Phone: 219-399-1200   **US Fax:** 219-399-5544
Web: www.ispat.com

Based in the Netherlands and run from its London headquarters, Ispat International has steelmaking operations in Canada, France, Germany, Ireland, Mexico, Trinidad and Tobago, and the US.

2002 Sales

	$ mil.	% of total
US	2,388	49
France	618	13
Germany	609	12
Mexico	588	12
Canada	557	11
Trinidad	129	3
Total	**4,889**	**100**

PRODUCTS/OPERATIONS

Selected Products

Direct reduced iron (DRI)
Flat steel
Cold-rolled sheet and slab
Hot-rolled sheet and slab
Long steel
Bars
Pipes
Structural
Wire (products and rod)

Selected Subsidiaries

Caribbean Ispat Limited (Trinidad and Tobago)
Consorcio Minero Benito Juárez Peña Colorada SA de CV
  (50%, mining and pelletizing, Mexico)
Delta Tube (40%, Canada)
Empire Iron Mining Partnership (40%, taconite pellets)
I/N Kote (50%, galvanizing)
I/N Tek (60%, cold rolling)
Ispat Hamburger Stahlwerke GmbH (Germany)
Ispat Inland Inc. (US)
Ispat Mexicana, SA de CV (Mexico)
Ispat Sidbec Inc. (Canada)
Ispat Stahlwerk Ruhrort GmbH (Germany)
Ispat Unimétal (France)
Ispat Walzdraht Hochfeld GmbH (Germany)
PCI Associates (50%, pulverized coal)
Servicios Siderúrgicos Integrados, SA de CV (50%;
  port operations, lime, industrial gases, and
  engineering; Mexico)
Sorevco (50%, galvanizing plant, Canada)

COMPETITORS

AK Steel Holding	Nippon Steel
Corporation	Nucor
Algoma Steel	Oregon Steel Mills
BHP Steel	Rouge Industries
Chaparral Steel	Stelco
Corus Group	ThyssenKrupp
Dofasco	United States Steel
Geneva Steel	Vallourec
Gerdau AmeriSteel	Weirton Steel
Highveld Steel and	Worthington Industries
Vanadium	

HISTORICAL FINANCIALS

Company Type: Public

Income Statement

FYE: December 31

	REVENUE ($ mil.)	NET INCOME ($ mil.)	NET PROFIT MARGIN	EMPLOYEES
12/02	4,889	49	1.0%	15,400
12/01	4,486	(312)	—	16,300
12/00	5,097	99	1.9%	17,800
12/99	4,680	85	1.8%	15,000
12/98	3,492	237	6.8%	15,000
12/97	2,190	289	13.2%	7,550
12/96	1,774	613	34.6%	5,839
12/95	1,828	556	30.4%	5,358
12/94	735	246	33.5%	—
12/93	396	280	70.7%	—
Annual Growth	**32.2%**	**(17.6%)**	**—**	**16.3%**

2002 Year-End Financials

Debt ratio: 1,579.7%
Return on equity: 21.0%
Cash ($ mil.): 77
Current ratio: 1.27
Long-term debt ($ mil.): 2,022
No. of shares (mil.): 124
Dividends
  Yield: 0.0%
  Payout: —
Market value ($ mil.): 273

Stock History

NYSE: IST

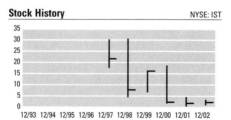

	STOCK PRICE ($) FY Close	P/E High/Low		PER SHARE ($) Earnings	Dividends	Book Value
12/02	2.20	8	3	0.40	0.00	1.03
12/01	1.75	—	—	(2.58)	0.00	2.66
12/00	2.25	22	2	0.82	0.15	7.37
12/99	16.13	23	10	0.71	0.15	6.72
12/98	7.75	16	2	1.93	0.15	6.31
12/97	21.63	12	7	2.46	0.00	23.39
Annual Growth	**(36.7%)**	**—**	**—**	**(30.5%)**	**—**	**(46.4%)**

Isuzu Motors

After years of traveling the backroads to financial losses, Isuzu Motors is plotting a shortcut to profitability. In addition to producing its line of SUVs (including the Axiom and the Rodeo), Tokyo-based Isuzu is one of the world's top makers of light-, medium-, and heavy-duty trucks (C&E Series, N Series, and F Series, respectively). It also makes pickups, diesel engines, and buses. Isuzu introduced its latest SUV offering, the seven-passenger Ascender, in 2003. After a recapitalization scheme, General Motor's stake in the company was reduced from 49% to 12%.

In the summer of 2002 Isuzu announced a revised three-year business plan. To avoid bankruptcy, Isuzu asked its creditor banks to forgive 100 billion yen (about $750 million) in debt in exchange for stakes in the company. As part of the plan, GM wrote off its entire stake in Isuzu, and re-infused the ailing carmaker with $84 million. The deal resulted in a recapitalized Isuzu and reduced GM's stake to 12%. As part of the scheme GM boosted its stake in US-based joint venture DMAX Ltd., and took a stake in Isuzu's wholly owned Polish unit. To reduce its workforce, Isuzu offered voluntary retirement to about 3,700 workers.

HISTORY

After collaborating on car and truck production for 21 years, Tokyo Ishikawajima Shipbuilding and Engineering and Tokyo Gas and Electric Industrial formed Tokyo Motors, Inc., in 1937. The partners began producing the A truck (1918) and the A9 car (1922) under licenses from Wolseley (UK).

Tokyo Motors made its first truck under the Isuzu nameplate in 1938. It spun off Hino Heavy Industries in 1942. By 1943 the company was selling trucks powered by its own diesel engines, mostly to the Japanese military.

By 1948 the company was Japan's premier maker of diesel engines. It was renamed Isuzu (Japanese for "50 bells") in 1949. With generous public- and private-sector financing and truck orders from the US Army during the Korean War, Isuzu survived and refined its engine- and truck-making prowess. A pact with the Rootes Group (UK) enabled Isuzu to enter automaking. Beginning in 1953, Isuzu built Rootes' Hillman Minx in Japan.

Despite its strong reputation as a truck builder, Isuzu suffered financially, and by the late 1960s its bankers were shopping the company around to more stable competitors. GM, after witnessing rapid Japanese progress in US and Asian auto markets, bought about 34% of Isuzu in 1971. During the 1970s Isuzu launched the popular Gemini car and gained rapid entry to the US through GM, exporting such vehicles as the Chevy Luv truck and the Buick Opel.

As exports to GM waned, Isuzu set up its own dealer network in the US in 1981. That year GM CEO Roger Smith told stunned Isuzu chairman Toshio Okamoto that Isuzu lacked the global scale GM sought. Smith asked Okamoto for help in buying a piece of Honda. After Honda declined and GM settled for 5% of Suzuki, Isuzu extended its GM ties, building the Geo Storm and establishing joint production facilities in the UK and Australia.

Despite a high-profile advertising campaign featuring Joe Isuzu, the company suffered in the 1980s in its efforts to gain any kind of significant share of the US passenger car market. Post-1985 yen appreciation hurt exports. Subaru-Isuzu Automotive, a joint venture with Fuji Heavy Industries, initiated production of Rodeos in Lafayette, Indiana, in 1989.

After Isuzu lost nearly $500 million in 1991 and 1992, it called on GM for help. GM responded by sending Donald Sullivan, a strategic business planning expert, to become Isuzu's #2 operations executive.

Isuzu signed a joint venture with Jiangxi Automobile Factory and ITOCHU in 1993 to build light-duty trucks in China. In 1994 Nissan and Isuzu agreed to cross-supply vehicles.

Isuzu weathered a public relations storm in 1996 when *Consumer Reports* magazine claimed that the top-selling Trooper sport utility vehicle was prone to tip over at relatively low speeds. Isuzu dismissed the report as unscientific, and the National Highway Traffic Safety Administration sided with the automaker. In 1997 the company sued the magazine for defamation. (Isuzu lost the case in 2000.) Also in 1997 Isuzu agreed to develop GM's diesel engines and began constructing a plant in Poland to supply engines to GM's Germany-based subsidiary Opel AG.

The next year GM and Isuzu announced a joint venture to make diesel engines in the US. Also in 1998 Isuzu announced restructuring plans that included cutting 4,000 jobs and reducing the number of its domestic marketing subsidiaries. In 1999 the plant in Poland opened, and GM boosted its stake in Isuzu to 49%. Isuzu also agreed to form a joint venture with Toyota to manufacture buses.

Amid mounting losses and pressure from GM, Isuzu announced a management shake-up in 2001 that included naming GM chairman John Smith Jr. as special advisor and installing Randall Schwarz (GM truck group) as vice president. Days later Isuzu announced its "Isuzu V plan," its sweeping cost-savings scheme that includes job cuts and the closure of one factory.

The Isuzu V plan was revised in 2002 when the company announced GM would write off its entire stake while infusing Isuzu with about $84 million. Near the close of 2002 Isuzu agreed to sell its 49% stake in carmaking joint venture Subaru-Isuzu Automotive Inc. to Fuji Heavy Industries (FHI). When the deal was completed in January 2003, FHI renamed the company Subaru of Indiana Automotive Inc.

EXECUTIVES

President and Representative Director: Yoshinori Ida
EVP and Representative Director: Basil N. Drossos
EVP and Director: Kozo Sakaino
EVP and Director: Randall J. Schwarz
EVP and Director: Shigeki Toma
Senior Executive Officer: Minoru Matsushima
Senior Executive Officer: Goro Miyazaki
Senior Executive Officer: Ryuuichi Ohgi
Senior Executive Officer: Jun Utsumi
Executive Director: Yoshito Mochizuki
Executive Director: Hiromasa Tsutsui
Executive Officer: Fujio Anzai
Executive Officer: Hiroo Majima
Executive Officer: Yasushi Mase
Executive Officer: Tadaharu Matsuo
Executive Officer: Chikao Mitsuzaki
Executive Officer: Shunichi Satomi
Executive Officer: Akira Shinohara
Executive Officer: Takashi Urata
Executive Officer: Makoto Ushiyama
Auditors: Shin Nihon & Co.

LOCATIONS

HQ: Isuzu Jidosha Kabushiki Kaisha
   (Isuzu Motors Limited)
   26-1, Minami-oi 6-chome, Shinagawa-ku,
   Tokyo 140-8722, Japan
Phone: +81-3-5471-1141   **Fax:** +81-3-5471-1043
US HQ: 13340 183rd Street, Cerritos, CA 90702-6007
US Phone: 562-229-5000   **US Fax:** 562-229-5463
Web: www.isuzu.co.jp

2003 Sales

	$ mil.	% of total
Japan	6,784	60
North America	2,933	26
Other regions	1,543	14
Total	**11,260**	**100**

PRODUCTS/OPERATIONS

2003 Sales

	$ mil.	% of total
Automobiles	11,156	99
Finance	37	—
Other	67	1
Total	**11,260**	**100**

Selected Vehicles and Brands

Buses
Erga heavy-duty bus
Erga Mio medium-duty bus

Commercial Vehicles
Heavy-duty trucks (C&E Series)
Light-duty trucks (N Series)
Medium-duty trucks (F Series)

Pickups
Crew Cab
D-MAX
Single Cab
Space Cab

Sport Utility Vehicles
Ascender
Axiom
Rodeo

Selected Subsidiaries and Affiliates

American Isuzu Motors Inc. (US)
Anadolu Isuzu Otomotiv Sanayi Ve Ticaret AS (Turkey)
Automotive Foundry Co., Ltd.
DMAX Ltd. (US)
IFCO Inc.
Isuzu Bus Manufacturing Ltd.
Isuzu (China) Holding Co., Ltd.
Isuzu Estate Co., Ltd.
Isuzu LINEX Corporation
Isuzu Motors America, Inc. (US)
Isuzu Motors Asia Ltd. (Singapore)
Isuzu Motors Europe Ltd. (UK)
Isuzu Motors Germany GmbH
Isuzu Motors Kinki Co., Ltd.
Isuzu Motors Polska Sp. zo. o. (Poland)
Isuzu Philippines Corporation
Isuzu Truck (UK) Ltd.
Isuzu-General Motors Australia Ltd.
IT Forging (Thailand) Co., Ltd.
Jidosha Buhin Kogyo Co., Ltd.
Kanagawa Isuzu Motors Co., Ltd.
P.T. Mesin Isuzu Indonesia
Qingling Motors Co., Ltd. (China)
Taiwan Isuzu Motors Co., Ltd.
TDF Corporation
Tokyo Isuzu Motors Ltd.
Tri Petch Isuzu Sales Co., Ltd. (Thailand)

COMPETITORS

BMW	Nissan
Caterpillar	Oshkosh Truck
Cummins	PACCAR
DaimlerChrysler	Penske
Fiat	Peugeot
Ford	Renault
General Motors	Scania
Honda	Suzuki Motor
Kubota	Toyota
Mazda	Volkswagen
Navistar	Volvo

HISTORICAL FINANCIALS

Company Type: Public

Income Statement

FYE: March 31

	REVENUE ($ mil.)	NET INCOME ($ mil.)	NET PROFIT MARGIN	EMPLOYEES
3/03	11,260	(1,204)	—	20,690
3/02	12,045	(324)	—	26,234
3/01	12,422	(529)	—	30,232
3/00	14,280	(988)	—	12,963
3/99	13,593	52	0.4%	13,035
3/98	13,524	45	0.3%	13,520
3/97	15,536	77	0.5%	13,877
3/96	15,681	350	2.2%	14,317
3/95	8,763	75	0.9%	13,500
3/94	15,546	29	0.2%	13,500
Annual Growth	**(3.5%)**	**—**	**—**	**4.9%**

2003 Year-End Financials

Debt ratio: 766.3%
Return on equity: —
Cash ($ mil.): 529
Current ratio: 0.66
Long-term debt ($ mil.): 1,690

Net Income History

OTC: ISUZF

ITOCHU Corporation

Trading giant ITOCHU is nothing to sneeze at. With more than 150 offices in about 80 countries, ITOCHU is a leading Japanese *sogo shosha* (general trading company), along with Mitsui and Mitsubishi. The company has seven major business groups: aerospace, electronics, and multimedia; chemicals, forest products, and general merchandise; energy, metals, and minerals; finance, realty, insurance, and logistics services; food; plant, automobile and industrial machinery; and textiles. ITOCHU's food businesses account for more than 20% of the company's revenue.

The weakness of the Japanese economy has forced the company to scale back in many areas. Divesting unprofitable operations, the company is focusing on expected moneymakers — multimedia, consumer and retail, financial services, and natural resource development. It also is working to expand its presence in North America and in Asian nations other than Japan.

HISTORY

Chubei Itoh was only 18 when he organized his own wholesale linen business, C. Itoh & Co., in 1858. As Japan opened to foreign trade in the 1860s, the company prospered and was one of Osaka's largest textile wholesalers by the 1870s. C. Itoh established a trade office in San Francisco in 1889.

By 1919 C. Itoh had trading offices in New York, Calcutta, Manila, and four cities in China. Although it was not one of the *zaibatsu* (industrial groups) that flourished in Japan during the period between the world wars, C. Itoh benefited from the general increase in trade.

In 1941 C. Itoh was merged with two other trading companies, Marubeni and Kishimoto, into a new company, Sanko Kabushiki Kaisha. In 1949 C. Itoh and Marubeni were separated. C. Itoh supplied UN troops with provisions during the Korean War; profits were used to diversify into petroleum, machinery, aircraft, and automobiles.

After the oil crisis of 1973 demonstrated Japan's vulnerability to oil import disruptions, C. Itoh actively participated in the development of petroleum production technology. To prevent the failure of Japan's 10th-largest trading company, Ataka, the Japanese government arranged a merger in 1977, making C. Itoh the third-largest *sogo shosha*.

The company established Japan Communications Satellite (JCSAT) with Mitsui and Hughes Communications in 1985. JCSAT launched its first two satellites in 1989 and 1990. The following year C. Itoh and Toshiba joined Time Warner in a limited partnership, Time Warner Entertainment Company, to produce and distribute movies and television programs and to operate cable TV systems in the US. C. Itoh, Time Warner, and Toshiba formed another joint venture to distribute Warner Bros. films and develop amusement parks in Japan.

C. Itoh changed its name to ITOCHU, a transliteration of its Japanese name, in 1992. After sales dropped the next year, ITOCHU began selling poorly performing subsidiaries, reducing its investment portfolio by more than one-third.

In 1996 the company formed an alliance with US oil company Atlantic Richfield to buy Coastal Corp.'s western US coal operations, and it took a stake in a massive project led by Amoco and British Petroleum to develop oil and gas deposits in the Caspian Sea. That year PerfecTV! (a joint venture with Sumitomo and other Japanese companies) began satellite broadcasting. Also in 1996 ITOCHU bought stakes in the Asia Broadcasting and Communications Network, a satellite communications company.

To help cover its losses from the Asian currency crisis, the company sold 40% of its stake in Time Warner in 1998; in 1999 ITOCHU sold its remaining stake. ITOCHU also sold low-performing real estate investments and laid plans to divest about one-third of its subsidiaries.

Two of ITOCHU's agricultural subsidiaries were liquidated in 2000. The company also sought out partnerships in order to offset costs incurred in new ventures: it joined with Japan's other top trading companies and Brazil's Petrobras to develop oil fields in South America. And in response to the rapid consolidation of Japan's steel industry, ITOCHU and Marubeni agreed to integrate their steel operations in 2001 to better compete.

In 2002 ITOCHU formed a partnership with Bally International to expand the European fashion brand's presence in Japan.

EXECUTIVES

Chairman: Minoru Murofushi
President and CEO: Uichiro Niwa
EVP; President, Energy, Metals, and Minerals: Hiroshi Sumie
EVP; President, Textile: Makoto Kato
EVP, CFO, and Chief Compliance Officer: Sumitaka Fujita
EVP; President, Plant, Automobile, and Industrial Machinery: Akira Yokota
Managing Director; President, Aerospace, Electronics, and Multimedia: Yoichi Okuda
Managing Director; President, Finance, Realty, Insurance, and Logistics Services: Hiroshi Ueda
Managing Director; President, Food: Kouhei Watanabe
Managing Director, Corporate Planning, Affiliate Administration, General Affairs, and Legal, and CIO: Eizo Kobayashi
Managing Director; President, Chemicals, Forest Products, and General Merchandise: Toshihito Tamba
Auditors: KPMG

LOCATIONS

HQ: Itochu Shoji Kabushiki Kaisha
5-1, Kita-Aoyama 2-chome, Minato-ku, Tokyo 107-8077, Japan
Phone: +81-3-3497-2121   **Fax:** +81-3-3497-4141
US HQ: 335 Madison Ave., New York, NY 10017
US Phone: 212-818-8000   **US Fax:** 212-818-8543
Web: www.itochu.co.jp

2003 Transactions

	% of total
Asia	
Japan	79
Other countries	13
North America	5
Europe	1
Other regions	2
Total	**100**

PRODUCTS/OPERATIONS

2003 Sales

	% of total
Food	23
Aerospace, electronics & multimedia	18
Textile	16
Chemicals, forest products & general merchandise	15
Plant, automobile & industrial machinery	9
Finance, realty, insurance & logistics	6
Energy, metals & minerals	6
Other	7
Total	**100**

COMPETITORS

Altria	Mitsubishi Corporation
ADM	Mitsui
Balli	Nestlé
Dow Chemical	Nippon Steel
SEPI	NTT
Exxon Mobil	Nippon Television
Fluor	Nissho Iwai-Nichimen
Hutchison Whampoa	Samsung
Kanematsu	Sharp
Klöckner	Sumitomo
LG Group	Tokyo Broadcasting
Lockheed Martin	System
Marubeni	TOMEN
Matsushita	TOTAL
MAXXAM	Unilever

HISTORICAL FINANCIALS

Company Type: Public

Income Statement

FYE: March 31

	REVENUE ($ mil.)	NET INCOME ($ mil.)	NET PROFIT MARGIN	EMPLOYEES
3/03	4,723	168	3.5%	4,355
3/02	4,364	228	5.2%	4,580
3/01	4,841	558	11.5%	5,012
3/00	5,804	(837)	—	5,306
3/99	5,388	(286)	—	5,775
3/98	4,484	(714)	—	6,675
Annual Growth	**1.0%**	**—**	**—**	**(8.2%)**

2003 Year-End Financials

Debt ratio: 384.3%   Current ratio: 1.06
Return on equity: 5.1%   Long-term debt ($ mil.): 13,667
Cash ($ mil.): 4,457

Net Income History

OTC: ITOCY

Ito-Yokado Co.

From morning coffee-and-paper pit stops to late night runs for diapers and milk, Ito-Yokado Co. is eclectic and convenient. The firm operates more than 9,700 Seven-Eleven stores in Japan (the country's largest retailer) and about 1,000 other stores (department stores, restaurants, specialty shops, supermarkets, and superstores). The retailer's York Mart supermarket chain operates about 50 grocery stores in the Tokyo metro area. It owns about 73% of 7-Eleven, Inc., which franchises the 7-Eleven name worldwide and runs more than 5,800 stores in North America. The company is the Japanese franchisee for Oshman's sporting goods stores, Robinson's department stores, and Denny's restaurants in Japan.

In addition to its nearly 575 Denny's restaurants, Ito-Yokado runs about 330 Famil restaurants in Japan. The company's banking subsidiary, IYBank, maintains more than 5,200 ATMs (no branches) in its Ito-Yokado stores, principally Seven-Eleven convenience store locations. Ito-Yokado also operates several superstores in China through a joint venture, a meal delivery service, and a publishing company. Stores in North America account for about 25% of the company's sales.

Ito-Yokado has begun a new clothing line, L&B, and is expanding its other private-label clothing line, IY Basics (IYB). On the high-tech front, consumers may order products online through 7dream.com and pick them up at a nearby 7-Eleven, and the convenience store chain has launched a credit card that allows users to receive points toward purchases and provides the company with customer data.

HISTORY

After fighting in WWII, 21-year-old Masatoshi Ito joined his mother and brother in running a small family clothing shop (founded 1913) in Tokyo that grew into a department store. Ito took over the store when his brother died in 1956. Two years later the company was incorporated as Kabushiki Kaisha Yokado.

Ito visited the US in 1961, meeting with officials of National Cash Register (who wanted to sell cash registers to Japanese retailers still using abacuses) and retailers such as Sears and Safeway. Confident that US-style self-service retailing could work in Japan, Ito opened two hypermarkets (food, clothing, and household products) in Tokyo. By 1965, the year he changed the operation's name to Ito-Yokado Co., he had opened six more stores.

Famil, a chain of family-style restaurants, was launched in 1972, as were several Denny's restaurant franchises in Japan. Ito returned to the US that year to meet with Dallas-based Southland, owner of the 7-Eleven convenience store chain, and in 1974 he opened Japan's first 7-Eleven. The 7-Elevens quickly stole much of the market from the family-owned shops that dominated Japanese retailing. (The 7-Elevens were small enough to avoid triggering Japan's Large-Scale Retail Store Law, a law designed to protect small family stores by establishing rigid controls over store sizes and hours.) Ito co-opted his fallen competitors by recruiting them to become 7-Eleven franchisees. In 1975 Ito-Yokado established its York Mart subsidiary to open supermarkets in areas that could not support hypermarkets.

In the 1980s Ito acquired Japanese rights to Robinson's department stores (from the May Company) and Oshman's sporting goods stores. The company bought 58 7-Elevens in Hawaii in 1989 and the next year acquired 70% of the bankrupt Southland for $430 million.

Ito, along with several other heads of major corporations, was found in 1992 to have paid protection money to local mobsters, known as *sokaiya*, to prevent disruption of the company's annual meeting. Ito resigned, remaining a director and honorary chairman, and was replaced by Toshifumi Suzuki.

Earnings remained flat as sales rose slowly in the early 1990s, reflecting consumer uncertainty. In 1996 Ito-Yokado signed a joint venture agreement to develop superstores in China. The company opened its first store in Sichuan (1997), followed by a second superstore in Beijing (1998). With the Asian markets weak, and after years of cutting the store count in the US, Southland began expanding again in 1997.

Southland changed its name to 7-Eleven, Inc., in 1999. Seven-Eleven Japan Co. joined with SOFTBANK and two other companies in

1999 to form an online bookselling joint venture, e-Shopping! Books.

Seven-Eleven Japan Co. launched the Web site 7dream.com in 2000. In 2001 the company established an Internet bank accessible through Web kiosks in its retail stores. It launched a credit card company, IY Card Service, in October 2001. As part of a restructuring plan, the company sold its 88.4% stake in the Daikuma discount store chain to Yamada Denki in May 2002.

EXECUTIVES

Honorary Chairman, Ito-Yokado, Seven-Eleven Japan, and Denny's Japan: Masatoshi Ito, age 79
Chairman and CEO; Chairman of Seven-Eleven Japan; Chairman of 7-Eleven, Inc.: Toshifumi Suzuki, age 71
Vice Chairman; Chairman of York-Benimaru; Director of Denny's Japan; Director of 7-Eleven, Inc.: Nobutake Sato, age 65
President and COO: Sakae Isaka, age 61
Senior Managing Director, and Director of China Division: Akihiko Hanawa, age 61
Senior Managing Director; Chief Administrative Officer, and CFO: Noritoshi Murata, age 59
Senior Managing Director: Atsushi Kamei, age 59
Senior Managing Director: Akira Hinosawa, age 57
Managing Director and Director of Corporate Communications Department and Office of Social and Cultural Affairs: Sakue Mizukoshi, age 62
Managing Director and Chief of General Affairs Division: Minoru Inaoka, age 58
Managing Director and Chief of Personnel Division: Yoshiaki Ota, age 57
Managing Director: Shigeru Takemoto, age 54
Director of Public Relations Department: Yoshinobu Naito, age 57
Director of Household Goods Division: Shigeo Kawa, age 57
Senior Merchandiser in charge of Household Commodities and Cosmetics & Drugs: Akira Sakamoto, age 55
Director of Information System Division: Yoji Okamura, age 55
Director of Food Division: Tsutomu Omori, age 53
President IYBank: Takashi Anzai
Auditors: PricewaterhouseCoopers

LOCATIONS

HQ: Ito-Yokado Co., Ltd.
1-4, Shibakoen 4-chome, Minato-ku, Tokyo 105-8571, Japan
Phone: +81-3-3459-2111　**Fax:** +81-3-3459-6873
US HQ: 1 Union Sq., 600 University St., Ste. 1916, Seattle, WA 98101
US Phone: 206-667-8973　**US Fax:** 206-667-8971
Web: www.itoyokado.iyg.co.jp

2003 Sales

	% of total
Japan	75
US	24
Other	1
Total	**100**

PRODUCTS/OPERATIONS

2003 Sales

	% of total
Convenience stores	50
Superstores	46
Restaurants	4
Other	—
Total	**100**

Principal Retail and Restaurant Operations

Convenience Stores
7-Eleven, Inc. (73%, US)
Seven-Eleven Japan Co., Ltd. (51%)

Superstores and Other Retail Operations
Ito-Yokado superstores
Mary Ann womenswear boutiques
Oshman's sporting goods stores (Japan)
Robinson's department stores (Japan)
York Benimaru supermarkets
York Mart supermarkets

Restaurants
Denny's Japan
Famil

Other
IY Bank
IY Card Service

COMPETITORS

AEON	Mycal Corporation
Carrefour	Seiyu
Casey's General Stores	Takashimaya
Daiei	Tokyu Department Store
Daimaru	Co.
FamilyMart	Uny
Isetan	Wal-Mart
Marui	Yamazaki Baking
Matsuzakaya Co.	

HISTORICAL FINANCIALS

Company Type: Public

Income Statement

FYE: Last day in February

	REVENUE ($ mil.)	NET INCOME ($ mil.)	NET PROFIT MARGIN	EMPLOYEES
2/03	28,436	179	0.6%	125,400
2/02	22,352	390	1.7%	106,911
2/01	26,440	417	1.6%	109,077
2/00	29,308	433	1.5%	116,636
2/99	27,225	555	2.0%	113,921
2/98	24,642	555	2.3%	39,245
2/97	24,949	614	2.5%	38,149
2/96	27,543	730	2.7%	36,932
2/95	29,771	737	2.5%	34,597
2/94	27,735	565	2.0%	33,629
Annual Growth	**0.3%**	**(12.0%)**	**—**	**15.7%**

2003 Year-End Financials

Debt ratio: 34.1%　　　Current ratio: 1.61
Return on equity: 2.0%　Long-term debt ($ mil.): 3,141
Cash ($ mil.): 5,180

Net Income History　　　　Exchange: Tokyo

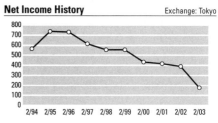

J Sainsbury plc

J Sainsbury is having trouble getting its grocery trolley back on track. The UK's third-largest retailer (after Tesco and ASDA) operates the long-struggling Sainsbury's Supermarkets chain — some 500 stores in the UK (accounting for about 83% of sales). The supermarkets get about 40% of their sales from private-label products. In addition to supermarkets, the company operates

55-plus Sainsbury's Local convenience stores and Savacentre hypermarkets. Sainsbury also owns 55% of Sainsbury's Bank (in a joint venture with Scottish bank HBOS) and a property development company. In the US it runs about 185 Shaw's Supermarkets and Star Markets in New England. The Sainsbury family controls 38% of the company's shares.

Stiff competition from price-chopping rivals Tesco and Wal-Mart-owned ASDA Group has eroded Sainsbury's market share to about 16% of the UK grocery market. Sainsbury lost its #1 title to Tesco in 1995, and was kicked out of second place by ASDA in mid-2003. A decision by UK competition authorities in September 2003 clearing the way for fifth-ranked Wm Morrison Supermarkets to bid for Safeway plc, could create another strong competitor to challenge Sainsbury. However, in a bid to thwart the takeover, Sainsbury is in talks with Safeway to buy a large parcel of its medium-sized supermarkets, up from the 24 sites allowed under the original commission ruling.

Nevertheless, the company is adding Savacentre hypermarkets (50,000-85,000 sq. ft.) in northern England and the Midlands, where ASDA and Tesco are strong. The food retailer is also making a big push into the growing UK convenience store market with plans to open 100 stores at Shell filling stations over the next several years. To that end, Sainsbury tried to acquire 171 convenience stores from its smaller rival Somerfield, but abandoned the plan after it was referred to UK competition authorities.

Sainsbury's online division, Sainsbury's To You, covers about 75% of the UK population and is in second place behind Tesco.com.

Concentrating on its struggling grocery business, the company sold its 280-outlet UK-based Homebase home and garden supply superstores. In the US, Shaw's Supermarkets acquired 18 stores in New England from bankrupt discounter Ames Department Stores, strengthening its position as the second-largest food retailer in the region.

Amid falling sales, Sainsbury cut 200 jobs in June 2003 and said it may cut another 500 this year in a recovery program — to be completed in March 2004 — that could eliminate as many as 1,000 positions overall at the company. To bolster its non-food offerings, the grocery retailer has launched its own line of houseware and cookware products.

Justin King, formerly head of food at Marks & Spencer, will join Sainsbury as its CEO in March 2004, succeeding Sir Peter Davis.

HISTORY

Newlyweds John James and Mary Ann Sainsbury established a small dairy shop in their London home in 1869. Customers flocked to the clean and efficient store, a far cry from most cluttered and dirty London shops. They opened a second store in 1876. By 1914, 115 stores had been opened, and the couple's sons had entered the business.

During WWI the company's stores established grocery departments to meet demand for preserved products, such as meat and jams, which were sold under the Sainsbury's label.

Mary Ann died in 1927 and John James the next year. Son John Benjamin, wholly devoted to the family business, took charge. (He is reported to have said on his deathbed, "Keep the stores well lit.") In the 1930s he engineered the company's first acquisition, the Thoroughgood stores.

Sales dropped by 50% during WWII, and some shops were destroyed by German bombing. Under third-generation leader Alan John Sainsbury, the company opened its first self-service store in 1950 in Croydon. The 75,000-sq.-ft. store opened in 1955 in Lewisham was considered to be the largest supermarket in Europe.

J Sainsbury went public in 1973. It established a joint venture with British Home Stores in 1975, forming the Savacentre hypermarkets (the company bought out its partner in 1989).

Sainsbury partnered with Grand Bazaar Innovation Bon Marche, of Belgium, in 1979 to establish Homebase, a do-it-yourself chain. (It bought the remaining 25% in 1996 and then sold the company in 2001, retaining only 18%.)

By 1983 most of Sainsbury's 229 stores were clustered in the south of England. A mature market and stiff competition forced the company to look elsewhere — both overseas and close to home. It began buying out US-based Shaw's Supermarkets in New England and in 1984 opened its first Scottish hypermarket. By 1987 the grocer owned 100% of Shaw's, which had 60 stores in Massachusetts, Maine, and New Hampshire.

In 1991 Sainsbury came under competitive pressure from Tesco and the Argyll Group (later renamed Safeway plc), which also began building superstores. It responded with an expansion drive of its own, including opening its first Scottish supermarket (in Glasgow) the next year.

In 1994 the company purchased a $325 million stake in Maryland-based Giant Food. Sainsbury bought home improvement retailer Texas Homecare from UK leisure concern Ladbroke in 1995 and integrated it into its Homebase unit. The following year it bought 12 supermarkets in Connecticut from Dutch retailer Royal Ahold (the purchase lowered its profits for the year) and entered Northern Ireland.

A year later the company opened Sainsbury's Bank. Royal Ahold bought Giant Food, including Sainsbury's 20% stake, in 1998. David Sainsbury — a great-grandson of the founders — retired as chairman in 1998 to pursue politics, marking the first time a Sainsbury had not headed up the company in its more-than-a-century history.

As a cost-cutting effort in 1999, Sainsbury cut 2,200 jobs, more than half in management. It also launched its convenience store concept, called Sainsbury's Local. Also that year Sainsbury bought the 53-store Star Markets chain of Massachusetts, merging it into its Shaw's operations. In March 2000 Sir Peter Davis took over as CEO of Sainsbury's Supermarkets, replacing David Bremner.

In 2001 Sainsbury acquired 19 Grand Union stores in the US (17 of which were converted to the Shaw's banner), and opened 25 new stores in the UK. The company also exited the Egyptian market, and sold its home-and-garden chain Homebase to private equity firm Permira in March 2001.

In 2002 Shaw's Supermarkets bought control of 18 stores in New England from bankrupt discounter Ames.

In November 2003, Sainsbury reached a £2 million out-of-court settlement with designer Jeff Banks over termination of his contract to revamp its clothing line in a bid to emulate rival ASDA's success with its George line of apparel.

EXECUTIVES

Chairman: Sir George Bull, age 66, $356,400 pay
Group Chief Executive and Board Member: Sir Peter Davis, age 61, $1,722,125 pay
CEO: Justin King, age 42 (Effective March 2004)

Group Finance Director, and Board Member: Roger Matthews, age 48, $855,360 pay
Group Human Resources and Information Systems Director, and Board Member: John E. Adshead, age 58, $721,354 pay
Managing Director, Sainsbury's Supermarkets, and Board Member: Stuart Mitchell, age 42, $756,994 pay
Managing Director, Sainsbury's To You: Toby Anderson
Deputy Managing Director, Sainsbury's Supermarkets, and Board Member: Sara Weller, age 41, $737,035 pay
President and CEO, Shaw's Supermarkets: Paul T. Gannon
Customer Marketing Director: Stephen Vowles
Format Director: Ian Jones
Human Resources Director, Sainsbury's Supermarkets: Imelda Walsh
IT Director: Maggie Miller
Product Development Director: Jean-Paul Barat
Property Director, Sainsbury's Supermarkets: Desmond Taljaard
Regional Operations Director, Eastern England: Stuart Machin
Retail Director: Adam Fowle
Group Legal Adviser: David Thurston
Head of Investor Relations: Lynda Ashton
Head of Public Affairs: Erica Zimmer
Auditors: PricewaterhouseCoopers LLP

LOCATIONS

HQ: 33 Holborn, London EC1N 2HT, United Kingdom
Phone: +44-20-7695-6000   **Fax:** +44-20-7695-7610
US HQ: 750 W. Center St., West Bridgewater, MA 02379
US Phone: 508-313-4000   **US Fax:** 508-313-3112
Web: www.j-sainsbury.co.uk

2003 Sales

	% of total
UK	85
US	15
Total	**100**

PRODUCTS/OPERATIONS

2003 Sales

	% of total
Sainsbury's Supermarkets	83
Shaw's Supermarkets	15
Sainsbury's Bank	1
JS Developments	1
Total	**100**

2003 Stores

	No.
Sainsbury's Supermarkets	256
Shaw's Supermarkets	185
Sainsbury's Local	57
Total	**498**

Store Formats

Community Stores (small town grocery stores averaging 10,000-20,000 sq. ft. and 10,000 product lines, including fresh foods)
Sainsbury's Central (convenience stores averaging 10,000 sq. ft. and 6,500 product lines)
Sainsbury's Local (convenience stores averaging 3,000 sq. ft. and 2,500 product lines)
Sainsbury's Supermarkets (full-service supermarkets averaging 20,000-30,000 sq. ft. and 17,000 product lines)
Savacentre (hypermarkets averaging 50,000-85,000 sq. ft. and 30,000 product lines)
Superstores (full-service supermarkets averaging 30,000-50,000 sq. ft. and 26,000 product lines, plus amenities such as restaurants, dry cleaners, gasoline stations)

Other Operations

Sainsbury's Bank plc (55%, banking)
J Sainsbury Developments Ltd (100%, property development)

COMPETITORS

ALDI
ASDA
Big Food
Boots Group
Budgens
Cooperative Group
CVS
DeMoulas Super Markets
First Quench
Hannaford Bros.

John Lewis
Marks & Spencer
METRO AG
Safeway plc
Somerfield
Stop & Shop
Tesco
Wal-Mart
Wm Morrison
 Supermarkets

HISTORICAL FINANCIALS

Company Type: Public

Income Statement

FYE: March 30

	REVENUE ($ mil.)	NET INCOME ($ mil.)	NET PROFIT MARGIN	EMPLOYEES
3/03	27,433	715	2.6%	174,500
3/02	24,466	519	2.1%	174,700
3/01	24,423	371	1.5%	185,200
3/00*	25,900	556	2.1%	189,227
2/99	26,283	956	3.6%	178,000
2/98	23,874	802	3.4%	175,551
2/97	21,794	656	3.0%	165,992
2/96	20,670	747	3.6%	160,435
Annual Growth	4.1%	(0.6%)	—	1.2%

*Fiscal year change

2003 Year-End Financials

Debt ratio: 37.7%
Return on equity: 9.7%
Cash ($ mil.): 1,037

Current ratio: 0.87
Long-term debt ($ mil.): 2,967

Net Income History

OTC: JSNSY

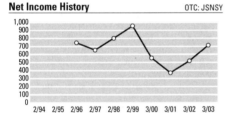

Japan Airlines

Japan Airlines System is going back to its roots. The holding company for Japan's #1 airline, Japan Airlines (JAL), was created as a result of the merger of JAL and Japan Air Systems (Japan's #3 airline) to boost domestic coverage. Combined the airlines serve more than 170 cities in 30 countries and operate a fleet of more than 285 mostly jet aircraft. The group also carries air cargo, operates a low-fare domestic airline, provides maintenance and ground-support services, and owns the international chain of Nikko hotels. Both carriers will continue to operate separately until 2004, when their operations will be fully integrated.

Competition has been growing, with the deregulation wave making its way to Japan's shores. However, the merger of the two airlines gives the group a better grasp on domestic routes, which have been dominated by rival All Nippon Airways. The merger has also expanded the group's presence in China, a rapidly growing new market.

Although it has been courted by Oneworld (led by American and British Airways), Japan Airlines has so far refused to join a global marketing alliance. Instead it has signed code-sharing agreements with 19 carriers, including American Airlines, Air France, and Iberia.

Reduced demand in international air traffic resulting from the September 11 terrorist attacks on the US has sent the airline back into the red after only three years of profitability since Japan's chronic recession and Asia's economic crisis.

The two airlines have already begun to eliminate route redundancies.

HISTORY

After WWII Japan was not allowed to form its own airline until the end of US occupation in 1951. That year a group of bankers led by Seijiro Yanagito founded Japanese Air Lines (JAL). JAL was essentially a revival of the prewar Nihon Koku Kabushiki Kaisha (Japan Air Transport Company), the national airline created by the Japanese government in 1928 and dissolved by the Allies in 1945. Since the Allied Peace Treaty forbade the airline to use Japanese flight crews, it leased both pilots and equipment from Northwest. In 1953 the airline was reorganized as Japan Airlines, with the government and the public owning equal shares.

Under Yanagito, who ran the airline until 1961, JAL expanded quickly, opening a transpacific route from Tokyo to San Francisco in 1954 and extending regional service to Hong Kong in 1955, Bangkok in 1956, and Singapore in 1958. A polar route from Tokyo to London and Paris gave the airline a foothold in Europe in 1961. Service to Moscow began in 1967, and that year JAL formed Southwest Airlines (now Japan TransOcean Air) to serve the islands of Japan.

In 1974 JAL suspended flights to Taipei, the mainstay of Chinese nationalists, in favor of new service to Beijing and Shanghai. Japan Asia Airways, a new subsidiary, resumed flights to Taipei the next year.

JAL ran into problems in the early 1980s: in 1982 a mentally unstable pilot crashed a plane into Tokyo Bay, killing 24; and in 1985 a JAL 747 crashed into a mountainside, killing all but four of the 524 on board. The worst single-plane accident in history, the disaster led to the resignation of most of JAL's top executives.

Facing a strong US currency in 1985, JAL signed an 11-year, $3 billion aircraft contract with Boeing, set at a fixed exchange rate of 184 yen per dollar. But the contract would haunt the airline in the 1990s, denying JAL the benefit of a weakened dollar that would fall below 100 yen.

The government sold its stake in JAL to the public in 1987. With air transport no longer nationalized, overseas routes were opened to the company's longtime domestic rival, All Nippon Airways (ANA).

In 1992 JAL reported its first loss ($100 million) since privatization, the result of high labor costs and the expansion of its fleet and facilities. With Japan sliding into recession, the company announced a five-year, $4.8 billion belt-tightening program.

Falling short of those cost-cutting goals, in 1993 JAL announced it would close half its North American offices, suspend recruitment, and freeze salaries. It also signed an agreement with ANA to share some aircraft maintenance costs. Traffic increased in 1994, but JAL was forced to cut prices to meet lower competing fares.

In 1995 JAL hooked up with American Airlines to connect computer reservation systems and act as agents for each other's cargo businesses. But JAL's losses continued, and chairman Susumu Yamaji and president Akira Kondo resigned in 1998. That year the airline announced job cuts, restructured routes, and launched low-cost domestic carrier JAL Express.

JAL finally posted a profit again in 1999. It also added Alitalia and Iberia Airlines as code-sharing partners and reduced its stake in delivery giant DHL from 26% to 6%. JAL came under renewed pressure in 2000, when government deregulation of domestic fares sparked a price war.

The next year demand for international travel slumped in the wake of the September 11 terrorist attacks on the US. In response, JAL had to modify its route structure, which included reducing several flights and modifying its code-sharing agreement with American Airlines.

In 2002 JAL merged with Japan's #3 carrier Japan Air Systems and created a new holding company called Japan Airlines System to operate the two airlines.

EXECUTIVES

President and CEO: Isao Kaneko
Senior Managing Director: Takenori Matsumoto
Senior Manging Director; SVP Human Resources and Purchasing: Hidekazu Nishizuka
Managing Director: Fumitaka Kurihara
Managing Director: Gentaro Maruyama
EVP; SVP Associated Business Corporate Affairs: Toshiyuki Shinmachi
SVP Corporate Compliance: Susumu Miyoshi
SVP Finance and Investor Relations: Nobuyoshi Sera
SVP: Juntaro Shimizu
SVP: Katsuo Haneda
SVP: Ken Moroi
SVP: Takashi Masuko
SVP: Toshiki Okazaki
SVP: Shunji Kono
Auditors: Showa Ota & Co.; Shin Nihon & Co.

LOCATIONS

HQ: Nippon Koku Shisutemu Kabushiki Kaisha (Japan Airlines System Corporation) Shingawa Intercity Tower-A, 2-15-1 Konan, Minato-ku, Tokyo 108-6024, Japan
Phone: +81-3-5769-6097 **Fax:** +81-3-5460-5929
US HQ: 655 Fifth Ave., New York, NY 10022
US Phone: 212-310-1454 **US Fax:** 212-310-1230
Web: www.jal.co.jp

Japan Airlines flies to about 170 cities in 30 countries.

PRODUCTS/OPERATIONS

2003 Sales

	% of total
Air transporation	70
Transportation services	19
Hotel and resort	2
Other	9
Total	**100**

2003 Fleet

Aircraft	No.
Boeing 747	71
Airbus A300	46
Boeing 767	28
Boeing 737	23
Boeing 777	20
Douglas MD-81	18
Douglas MD-90	16
Douglas DC-10	15
Saab 340	14
YS-11	11
Douglas MD-87	8
Douglas MD-11	6
CRJ 200	5
JS31	3
Dash8-400	2
Total	**286**

Selected Subsidiaries

Airport Ground Service Co., Ltd. (99%)
AXESS International Network Inc. (75%, computer reservation system)
JAL Express Co., Ltd. (domestic regional carrier)
JAL Hotels Co., Ltd. (91%, hotel management)
JAL Logistics Inc. (cargo services)
JAL Royal Catering Co., Ltd. (51%, in-flight catering)
JALPAK Co., Ltd. (78%, package tours)
JALways (low-fare carrier)
Japan Asia Airways Co., Ltd. (91%, regional services)
Japan TransOcean Air Co., Ltd. (51%, air transport)

COMPETITORS

Accor
Air Canada
Air France
All Nippon Airways
British Airways
Carlson
Central Japan Railway
China Airlines
China Eastern Airlines
Continental Airlines
Delta
East Japan Railway
Evergreen Marine
Garuda
Hyatt
Kinki Nippon Railway
KLM
Korean Air
Lufthansa
Northwest Airlines
Singapore Airlines
Skymark
Thai Airways
UAL
Virgin Atlantic Airways
West Japan Railway

HISTORICAL FINANCIALS

Company Type: Public

Income Statement

FYE: March 31

	REVENUE ($ mil.)	NET INCOME ($ mil.)	NET PROFIT MARGIN	EMPLOYEES
3/03	17,385	97	0.6%	54,885
3/02	12,095	(276)	—	46,075
3/01	13,740	331	2.4%	45,319
3/00	15,080	186	1.2%	18,535
3/99	13,051	223	1.7%	16,325
3/98	11,982	(477)	—	17,863
3/97	12,638	(117)	—	19,046
3/96	13,670	(86)	—	20,030
3/95	15,578	(169)	—	21,396
3/94	9,581	(247)	—	21,396
Annual Growth	**6.8%**	**—**	**—**	**11.0%**

2003 Year-End Financials

Debt ratio: 430.4%
Return on equity: 5.1%
Cash ($ mil.): 1,111
Current ratio: 0.86
Long-term debt ($ mil.): 9,131

Net Income History

Exchange: Tokyo

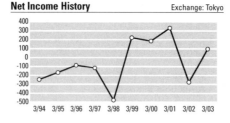

Japan Tobacco

Japan Tobacco has plenty to puff about. It controls more than 70% of the cigarette market in a country where half the men smoke and warning labels suggest, "There's a risk of damage to your health, so let's be careful not to smoke too much." A state monopoly until 1985, Japan Tobacco is two-thirds owned by the Japanese Finance Ministry. It's the world's #3 tobacco company, after Altria and British American Tobacco. Its JT International unit (acquired from R.J. Reynolds) sells Camel, Salem, and Winston brands outside the US. The company also operates in foods, pharmaceuticals, agribusiness, engineering, and real estate.

In a country with the highest rate of smokers among developed nations, Japan Tobacco makes nine of the nation's top 10 brands, including Mild Seven, Caster, Seven Stars, and (for Philip Morris) Marlboros. Two new brands, Icene Super Cooling Menthol and LUCIA Citrus Fresh Menthol are said to have less odor and smoke than conventional brands. Japan Tobacco has expanded into 70 markets worldwide through its JT International unit. The company also is expected to bid for a government-run tobacco firm in Turkey.

But there are clouds on the horizon for Japan Tobacco. The company intends to close 13 of its 25 manufacturing plants and six of its 30 sales branches by March 2006. Japan Tobacco says in April 2005 it will end its agreement with Philip Morris to make and sell Marlboro cigarettes. These reductions will slash as many as 4,000 jobs from company payrolls, as demand for cigarettes, partly depressed by higher taxes, continues to decline. Japan Tobacco says it will fill the gap left by Marlboro with its own line of premium smokes.

In January 2004 the company will unveil six new brands: Mild Seven One Menthol Box, Bitter Valley, Fuji Renaissance, Fuji Renaissance 100's, Hi-Lite Menthol, and BB Slugger. An added brand, Hope Menthol, currently being tested in the marketplace, also will see expanded availability.

HISTORY

In 1898, roughly 325 years after tobacco was introduced in Japan, the nation's Ministry of Finance formed a bureau to monopolize the production of the crop. The purpose of the monopoly was to fund military and industrial expansion. In 1905 the bureau also became responsible for a salt monopoly.

During WWII, Japan's tobacco leaf import supply from North and South America grew scarce and led to cigarette rationing. In 1949 the government began operating the tobacco production bureau as a business: the Japan Tobacco and Salt Public Corporation.

The company launched Hope, the first Japanese-made filter cigarette, in 1957, and it became the world's top seller a decade later. In 1972 it began printing mild packaging "warnings": "Be careful not to smoke excessively for your health."

Japan Tobacco and Salt began selling Marlboro cigarettes licensed from Philip Morris in 1973. The Mild Seven brand (its current bestseller) went on sale in 1977; it became the world's #1 cigarette in 1981 but dropped to #2 (behind Marlboro) in 1993.

When its tobacco monopoly ended in 1985, the government established the firm as Japan Tobacco (a government-owned joint stock company). As competition from foreign imports increased, the firm came up with new means of making yen. It formed Japan Tobacco International (cigarette exports mainly to the US and Southeast Asia), moved into agribusiness and real estate operations, and, in 1986, created JT Pharmaceutical. In 1987 cigarette import tariffs ended, and importers lowered prices to match the company's; its sales and market share declined. During the late 1980s it introduced HALF TIME beverages and its first low-tar cigarettes (Mild Seven Lights is now the world's #1 light cigarette).

In 1992 Japan Tobacco bought its first overseas production facility, Manchester Tobacco (closed in 2001). Former Ministry of Finance official Masaru Mizuno became CEO that year — and soon took up smoking. Also in 1992 the company and Agouron Pharmaceuticals agreed to jointly develop immune system drugs; in 1994 they added antiviral drugs. The government sold about 20% of the firm's stock to the public in 1994 and 13% in 1996. The firm began operating Burger King restaurants in Japan in 1996. Japan Tobacco bought Pillsbury Japan in 1998.

Japan Tobacco in 1999 paid nearly $8 billion for R.J. Reynolds International, the international tobacco unit of RJR Nabisco. The company then renamed the unit, which has operations in 70 countries worldwide, JT International. It also bought the food products division of Asahi Chemical, Torii Pharmaceutical from Asahi Breweries, and the Unimat vending machine company.

Slowing sales prompted Japan Tobacco to announce in 2000 that it would reduce its workforce by 6,100 by 2005. Company exec Katsuhiko Honda became CEO that year (Mizuno remained as chairman) and said he'd push the government to sell its stake. In February 2001 the company announced plans to sell parts of its OTC drugs and health care businesses to Nichiiko Pharmaceutical to concentrate on prescription drugs. It also intends to sell all 25 of its Burger King outlets. In May Mizuno stepped down as chairman and was replaced by Takashi Ogawa.

In December 2001 Japan's Ministry of Finance recommended that it cut its holdings in the company from 66% to 50%; it would also allow the company to sell additional shares, which could further dilute the government's stake to as little as 33%.

In 2002 Japan Tobacco completed the sale of its 25 Burger King outlets and its OTC drug business.

EXECUTIVES

Chairman: Tadashi Ogawa

President and CEO: Katsuhiko Honda, age 58
Executive Deputy President; President, Tobacco Headquarters, Printing Business Division, and Vending Machinery Division: Masakazu Kakei
Executive Deputy President, Finance, Corporate Communications, and Real Estate Management: Takao Hotta
Executive Deputy President, Compliance, General Administration and Corporate Regulatory, Legal, and Operational Review and Business Assurance: Minoru Umeno
Executive Deputy President, Planning, Human Resources, and Agribusiness: Kazuei Obata
EVP; President, Pharmaceutical Division: Takashi Kato
EVP; President, Food and Soft Drink Business: Tetsuji Kanamori
EVP; R&D, General Division, and Corporate, Scientific and Regulatory Affairs, Tobacco: Ichiro Kumakura
EVP and Deputy President, Tobacco: Eiji Ito
EVP and Chief Communications Officer: Hideo Katsuura
EVP and Chief Scientifc Officer, Pharmaceuticals: Tsumoru Miyamoto
EVP and Head, Central Pharmaceutical Research Institute: Shigeo Ishiguro
EVP, Domestic Leaf Tobacco General Division: Mutsumi Makinoda
EVP, Manufacturing General Division: Seigo Nishizawa
EVP, Product Group: Yasumasa Matsunaga
SVP, Legal: Ryuichi Shimomura
SVP, Finance: Shinichi Totani
SVP, Human Resources: Mitsuomi Koizumi
Auditors: Deloitte Touche Tohmatsu

LOCATIONS

HQ: Nihon Tabako Sangyo (Japan Tobacco Inc.)
2-1, Toranomon 2-chome, Minato-ku,
Tokyo 105-8422, Japan
Phone: +81-3-3582-3111   **Fax:** +81-3-5572-1441
US HQ: 375 Park Ave., Ste. 1307,
New York, NY 10152-0133
US Phone: 212-319-8990   **US Fax:** 212-319-8993
Web: www.jti.co.jp/JTI/Welcome_c.html

Japan Tobacco operates 25 tobacco factories in Japan.

PRODUCTS/OPERATIONS

2003 Sales

	% of total
Tobacco	92
Foods	5
Pharmaceuticals	1
Other	2
Total	**100**

Selected Cigarette Brands

BB Slugger (January 2004)
Bitter Valley (January 2004)
Cabin and Cabin Mild
Camel (outside the US)
Caster and Caster Mild
Frontier
Fuji Renaissance (January 2004)
Hi-Lite Menthol (January 2004)
Hope Menthol
Marlboro Light Menthol (licensed, Philip Morris)
Mild Seven (regular, Lights, Super Lights)
Salem (outside the US)
Seven Stars
Winston (outside the US)

Selected Divisions and Operations

Agribusiness
Beverage business
Engineering
Food business
Pharmaceuticals
Real estate
Tobacco

COMPETITORS

Ajinomoto
Altadis
Asahi Breweries
British American Tobacco
Coca-Cola
Gallaher
Imperial Tobacco
Kraft Foods International
Mitsubishi Chemical
Nestlé
Nisshin Seifun Group
Philip Morris International
Reemtsma
Suntory
Unilever
Vector

HISTORICAL FINANCIALS

Company Type: Public

Income Statement

FYE: March 31

	REVENUE ($ mil.)	NET INCOME ($ mil.)	NET PROFIT MARGIN	EMPLOYEES
3/03	37,483	628	1.7%	38,628
3/02	34,259	278	0.8%	39,387
3/01	35,636	346	1.0%	40,237
3/00	41,431	481	1.2%	41,703
3/99	16,107	627	3.9%	—
3/98	13,030	436	3.3%	28,326
3/97	14,605	648	4.4%	22,160
3/96	16,116	634	3.9%	22,625
3/95	19,467	803	4.1%	23,208
Annual Growth	**8.5%**	**(3.0%)**	**—**	**6.6%**

2003 Year-End Financials

Debt ratio: 21.5%
Return on equity: 4.9%
Cash ($ mil.): 5,028

Current ratio: 2.26
Long-term debt ($ mil.): 2,904

Net Income History

Exchange: Tokyo

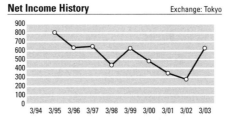

Jardine Matheson Holdings

The British no longer govern Hong Kong, but don't tell Jardine Matheson Holdings. The firm is the oldest of the Hong Kong *hongs* (diversified trading companies) and one of the few still in British hands. Jardine Matheson owns large tracts of prime real estate in Hong Kong and is active in a variety of retail ventures, including fast food, convenience stores, auto dealerships, and supermarkets (Dairy Farm). Other businesses include financial services, hotels (Mandarin Oriental), construction, and shipping. It has numerous

investments in China and throughout Asia. Members of the Keswick family, descendants of co-founder William Jardine, control the firm through a complex ownership structure.

Jardine Matheson has diversified geographically, but the Asia/Pacific region is where the money is — about 70% of the company's revenues come from that part of the world. To maintain its footing in the region's uncertain economic times, Jardine Matheson is working to control costs. The company is also moving to buy up additional shares in its affiliates, and focusing on buildings its businesses in Southeast Asia.

Farther afield Jardine Matheson is expanding its Mandarin Oriental hotel business, with new properties under development in New York, Tokyo, and Washington.

HISTORY

Scotsmen William Jardine and James Matheson met in Bombay in 1820. In 1832 they founded Jardine, Matheson in Canton, the only Chinese city then open to foreigners. The company started shipping tea from China to Europe and smuggling opium from India to China. In 1839 Chinese authorities tried to stop the drug trade, seizing 20,000 chests of opium, 7,000 of them Jardine's. Jardine persuaded Britain to send gunboats to China, precipitating the First Opium War. China lost the war and ceded Hong Kong to Britain in 1842.

Jardine moved to Hong Kong and resumed trading opium. The Second Opium War (1856-60) resulted in the opening of 11 more ports and the legalization of opium imports. Jardine flourished and later branched into the more legitimate fields of brewing, textiles, banking, insurance, and sugar. It formed Hongkong Land (HKL), a real estate company; introduced steamships to China; and built the country's first railroad line (1876). The company earned the sobriquet "the Princely *Hong*" because of its high-society officers with free-spending habits.

The Sino-Japanese War and WWII shut the company down. In 1945, with China gripped by civil war, Jardine reopened in Hong Kong. Attempts to re-establish operations in China ended in 1954 after the Communist takeover. The company went public in 1961.

The cost incurred in an acquisition program begun in the 1970s made Jardine a takeover target by 1980. *Taipan* (big boss) David Newbigging defended the company by erecting a bulwark of crossholdings of it and HKL stock. The resulting debt pushed Jardine to the brink of bankruptcy, forcing it to sell assets.

Simon Keswick — Henry's younger brother — succeeded Newbigging in 1984 and reorganized the company, making investments in Mercedes-Benz distributorships and fast-food franchises that helped turn Jardine around. As the UK and China negotiated the transfer of Hong Kong to Chinese control, Keswick moved Jardine's legal home to Bermuda. Jardine continued to be plagued by takeover attempts, however, particularly by Li Ka-shing, who was assisted by China's investment organization, CITIC. In a 1986 anti-takeover transaction, the company created Jardine Strategic Holdings to hold interests in HKL and its spinoffs. When the Chinese army put down student demonstrations in Beijing two years later, Keswick called the Chinese government "a thuggish, oppressive regime."

To increase its holdings outside of Hong Kong, Jardine bought 26% of Trafalgar House in 1993 but sold its stake in the troubled British conglomerate in 1996, which contributed to lower profits. Jardine delisted five of its companies from the Hong Kong stock exchange in 1994. Continuing to expand geographically, the company acquired 20% of India's Tata Industries and bought London's Hyde Park Hotel in 1996.

Hong Kong was returned to China in 1997, and in a display of public fence-mending, Chinese Vice Premier Zhu Rongji welcomed Jardine's participation in mainland ventures. But Jardine's stormy relationship with China continued even as Jardine's profits dropped during the Asian economic crisis. In 1999 China closed down Jardine's Beijing and Guangzhou brokerage offices (and banned the two chief China officers from the business for life), claiming that Jardine was engaging in unauthorized activities.

In 2000 Jardine sold its minority holdings in UK-based investment firm Robert Fleming Group. That year and again in 2001 the Keswicks turned back attempts by US-based Brandes Investment Partners, which owns about 10% of Jardine, to seize control of the company.

In 2002 Jardine increased its stake in Singapore-based Cycle & Carriage from 29% to more than 50%. Also that year, Dairy Farm sold its New Zealand business in June to focus on its Asian retail network. (Dairy Farm exited the Australian market in 2001.)

EXECUTIVES

Chairman, Jardine Matheson Holdings, Matheson & Co., and Jardine Strategic: Henry Keswick
Managing Director, Jardine Matheson Holdings, Dairy Farm, Hongkong Land, Jardine Strategic, and Mandarin Oriental; Chairman and Managing Director, Jardine Matheson Ltd.: Percy Weatherall
Group Strategy Director: Brian Richard Keelan
Group Finance Director: Norman Lyle
Chairman, Cycle & Carriage, Jardine Motors Group, Jardine Pacific, and MCL Land: Anthony J. L. Nightingale
Group General Counsel: James Watkins
Chairman, Dairy Farm, Hongkong Land, and Mandarin Oriental: Simon Keswick, age 60
Deputy Chairman, Jardine Lloyd Thompson: C. G. R. Leach
Group Head of Human Resources, Jardine Matheson Limited: Ritchie Bent
Group Taxation Manager, Jardine Matheson Limited: Betty Chan
Group Treasurer, Jardine Matheson Limited: Simon Mawson
Group Financial Controller, Jardine Matheson Limited: P. M. Kam
Group Corporate Secretary; Director, Group Corporate Affairs, Jardine Matheson Limited: Neil M. McNamara
Group Audit Controller, Jardine Matheson Limited: Colin Terry
Group Legal Manager, Jardine Matheson Limited: Jonathan Collins
Auditors: PricewaterhouseCoopers

LOCATIONS

HQ: Jardine Matheson Holdings Limited
48th Fl., Jardine House, Hong Kong
Phone: +852-2843-8288 **Fax:** +852-2845-9005
Web: www.jardines.com

PRODUCTS/OPERATIONS

Major Subsidiaries and Affiliates

Cycle & Carriage Ltd (50%, motor and property group, Singapore)
Dairy Farm International Holdings Ltd (69%; supermarkets, restaurants)
Hongkong Land Holdings Ltd (41%, real estate)
Jardine Lloyd Thompson (32%, insurance and brokerage, UK)

Jardine Motors Group (100%, auto distribution)
Jardine Pacific Holdings Ltd. (100%, engineering and construction, property, restaurants, shipping and financial services, trading and distribution)
Jardine Strategic Holdings Ltd. (79%, holding)
Mandarin Oriental International Ltd. (72%, hotels)

COMPETITORS

Accor	ITOCHU
Carrefour	Kumagai Gumi
Cheung Kong Holdings	Marriott International
China Resources	Marubeni
Enterprise	McDonald's
Daiei	Royal Ahold
Hopewell Holdings	Samsung
HSBC Holdings	Seiyu
Hutchison Whampoa	Sime Darby
Hyatt	Swire Pacific

HISTORICAL FINANCIALS
Company Type: Public

Income Statement
FYE: December 31

	REVENUE ($ mil.)	NET INCOME ($ mil.)	NET PROFIT MARGIN	EMPLOYEES
12/02	7,398	352	4.8%	110,000
12/01	9,413	115	1.2%	130,000
12/00	10,362	931	9.0%	150,000
12/99	10,675	207	1.9%	150,000
12/98	11,230	117	1.0%	160,000
12/97	11,522	476	4.1%	175,000
12/96	11,605	536	4.6%	200,000
12/95	10,636	420	3.9%	200,000
12/94	9,558	453	4.7%	220,000
12/93	8,425	424	5.0%	200,000
Annual Growth	(1.4%)	(2.0%)	—	(6.4%)

2002 Year-End Financials

Debt ratio: 104.8%
Return on equity: 16.7%
Cash ($ mil.): 1,273
Current ratio: 1.32
Long-term debt ($ mil.): 2,282

Net Income History
Pink Sheets: JARLY

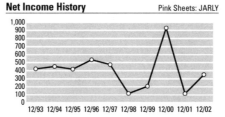

Kao Corporation

More than a century after Kao affixed a lunar logo to its name, Japanese consumers still think the company's products hang the moon. Kao (pronounced "cow") is Japan's #1 maker of personal care, laundry, and cleaning products. Its brands include Attack (laundry detergent), Family Power Gel (dishwashing detergent), Laurier (sanitary napkins), Feather (shampoo), Bioré (skin care), Super Merries (disposable diapers) and Prestige (cosmetics). The company also makes cooking oils and fatty chemicals (mainly surfi-cants), printer and copier toner products, and plastics used in products such as sneaker soles.

Although popular in Japan (its Attack detergent is #1 in Japan), Kao is striving to attain the international scope of rivals like Procter & Gamble (P&G) and Unilever. Subsidiaries Goldwell and Guhl Ikebana make hair care products in Europe, and its Andrew Jergens subsidiary makes skin care products in North America. To bring new products to market, Kao invests heavily in research and development.

Declining sales in Japan have spurred Kao to concentrate on acquistions in China as well as the US. (In 2001 it lost out on its offer for Clairol to P&G.) In 2002 Kao agreed to acquire John Frieda Professional Hair Care through subsidiary Andrew Jergens.

Kao brought its fat-reducing Healthy Econa cooking oil to the US in early 2003. Introduced in Japan in 1999, Econa will ease into the US market through a venture with Archer Daniels Midland Co.

Kao stands apart from the traditionally stuffy Japanese management style with a non-hierarchical structure that encourages debate among employees.

HISTORY

Tomiro Nagase founded the Kao Soap Company in 1887; shortly afterward, he began selling bars under the motto, "A Clean Nation Prospers." Kao's longtime rivalry with Procter & Gamble (P&G) was foreshadowed when it adopted a moon trademark in 1890 strikingly similar to the one chosen by P&G eight years earlier.

Kao moved into detergents in the 1940s. In the 1960s the company struck upon an idea that would vertically integrate it and set it apart from other consumer products manufacturers: It set up a network of wholesale distributors ("hansha") who only sell Kao products. The hansha system improved distribution time and cut costs by eliminating middlemen.

Yoshio Maruta, one of several chemical engineers to run Kao, took over as president in 1971. Maruta presented himself as more Buddhist scholar than corporate honcho; during his 19 years at the top, he gave the company a wider vision through his emphasis on creativity and his insistence on an active learning environment. To encourage sharing of ideas, the company used open conference rooms for meetings and anyone interested could attend and participate in any meeting.

Under Maruta, Kao launched a string of successful products in new areas in the 1980s. In 1982 the company introduced its Sofina cosmetics line, emphasizing the line's scientifc basis in a break from traditional beauty products marketing. The next year its Super Merries diapers (with a new design that reduced diaper rash) trounced P&G's Pampers in Japan. Its popular Attack laundry detergent (the first concentrated laundry soap) led the market within six months of its 1987 debut.

Seeking a way to enter the US market, Kao bought the Andrew Jergens skin care company — based in Cincinnati, as is P&G — in 1988. (It also purchased a chemical company to supply the materials to make Jergens' products.) P&G and Unilever braced themselves for the new competition, but Kao didn't deliver, releasing products like fizzy bath tablets that didn't sell well in a nation of shower-takers. In 1989 it bought a 75% interest in Goldwell, a German maker of hair care and beauty products sold through hair stylists. (By 1994 Kao owned all of Goldwell.)

In the mid-1980s Kao built a name for itself in the floppy disk market and became the top producer of 3 1/2-in. floppy disks in North America by 1990. However, competition crowded the field and drove the price of disks down. In 1997 the company stopped production of floppy disks in the US.

Chemical engineer Takuya Goto took over as president that year. Kao looked to other Asian markets and the US for potential consumers and found a willing audience in the US for its Bioré face strips. In 1998 Kao purchased Bausch & Lomb's skin care business, gaining the Curel and Soft Sense lotion brands.

In 2000 Kao established a joint venture with Novartis to make baby foods and over-the-counter drugs such as stomach medicines and other pain relief drugs. In 2001 it formed a joint venture with Archer Daniels Midland to produce an anti-obesity diacylglycerol oil (used in margarine, cooking oil, salad dressing, and mayonnaise) and in 2002 began marketing it in the US under the brand name Enova. Also in 2002 Kao dissolved its OTC-medicine-manufacturing joint venture with Novartis and renamed its Sofina cosmetics brand Prestige Cosmetics.

EXECUTIVES

President and CEO: Takuya Goto
President, Cleanliness and Sanitation: Toshio Hirasaka
President, Global Feminine and Baby: Hiroshi Kanda
President, Global Health Care: Tetsuya Imamura
President, Global Prestige Cosmetics: Toshio Takayama
SEVP, President, International Consumer Products: Toshio Hoshino
EVP, and President, Kao Hanabi Company: Takahiko Kagawa
EVP, Global Production and Engineering: Yasuo Idemitsu
EVP, Global Purchasing: Akio Tsuruoka
Executive Officer and President, Global Chemicals: Kuniaki Watanabe
Executive Officer and President, Global Fabric and Home Care: Motoki Ozaki
Executive Officer and President, Global Personal Care: Shozo Tanaka
Executive Officer and President, Greater China: Nobuatsu Higuchi
Executive Officer and EVP, Global R&D: Naotake Takaishi
Executive Officer, Legal and Compliance, Global: Shunichi Nakagawa
Global Communications: Masatoshi Kitahara
Global Human Capital Development: Norihiko Takagi
Global Marketing Service: Masateru Kanazawa
Auditors: Deloitte Touche Tohmatsu

LOCATIONS

HQ: 14-10 Nihonbashi Kayabacho, 1-chome, Chuo-ku, Tokyo 103-8210, Japan
Phone: +81-3-3660-7111   **Fax:** +81-3-3660-8978
Web: www.kao.co.jp

Kao sells its products primarily in Asia but also in Australia, Europe, North America, and South Africa.

2003 Sales

	% of total
Japan	73
Asia & Oceania	11
North America	8
Europe	8
Total	**100**

PRODUCTS/OPERATIONS

2003 Sales

	% of total
Consumer products	75
Chemical products	16
Prestige cosmetics	9
Total	**100**

Selected Products

Fatty chemicals and edible oils (fatty acids, fatty alcohols, fatty amines, glycerine)
Hygiene and bath products (sanitary napkins, disposable diapers, bath additives)
Laundry and cleaning products (laundry detergents, laundry finishers, kitchen and other household detergents, fabric softeners)
Personal care products and cosmetics (soap, body cleansers, shampoos, conditioners, hair care products, cosmetics and skin care products, toothpastes, toothbrushes)

Selected Brand Names

Attack (laundry detergent)
Ban (deodorant)
Biore (skin care)
Bub Shower (shower gel)
Emal (laundry detergent)
Family Power Gel (dishwashing detergent)
Goldwell (hair care)
Guhl Ikebana (hair care)
Healthy Econa (cooking oil)
Jergens (skin care)
Laurier (sanitary napkins)
Quickle Wiper (electrostatic duster)
Prestige (cosmetics)
Super Merries (disposable diapers)

COMPETITORS

Alticor	Nisshin Oillio
Colgate-Palmolive	Pfizer
Johnson & Johnson	Procter & Gamble
Kanebo	Shiseido
Kimberly-Clark	Unicharm
Lion Corporation	Unilever

HISTORICAL FINANCIALS

Company Type: Public

Income Statement

FYE: March 31

	REVENUE ($ mil.)	NET INCOME ($ mil.)	NET PROFIT MARGIN	EMPLOYEES
3/03	7,220	521	7.2%	19,807
3/02	6,325	454	7.2%	19,923
3/01	6,504	470	7.2%	19,068
3/00	8,027	494	6.2%	16,088
3/99	7,763	291	3.8%	15,900
3/98	6,818	184	2.7%	17,100
3/97	7,281	231	3.2%	18,700
3/96	7,791	229	2.9%	18,900
3/95	9,205	274	3.0%	18,500
3/94	7,532	216	2.9%	17,600
Annual Growth	(0.5%)	10.3%	—	1.3%

2003 Year-End Financials

Debt ratio: 8.5%
Return on equity: 15.0%
Cash ($ mil.): 705
Current ratio: 1.37
Long-term debt ($ mil.): 297

Net Income History

Exchange: Tokyo

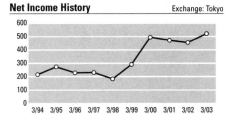

Karstadt Quelle

Seems like unification has caught on in Germany. Karstadt Quelle is the product of a merger between Germany's biggest department store group, Karstadt, and #1 mail-order firm, Quelle. It operates about 190 department stores (Karstadt, Hertie, Wertheim, Alsterhaus, and KaDeWe) and about 295 specialty stores, including Runners Point and Golf House (sports apparel), SinnLeffers and Wehmeyer (apparel), Schaulandt/Schürmann and WOM World of Music (multimedia), and LeBuffet (restaurants). Karstadt Quelle is a leader in travel services and has expanded into real estate and financial services. Schickedanz-Holding, owned by the Riedel and Herl families, has a 36% stake in Karstadt Quelle.

Karstadt Quelle has reshaped itself for a new Germany. The group has reorganized into four principal business segments: retail stores, mail order, services, and real estate.

With a whopping 50% of the department store market, Karstadt Quelle is prevalent in Germany.

Under the Quelle and Neckermann brands, the company mails out 618 million catalogs per year all over Europe. Those are supplemented by nearly 180 specialty catalogs, which cover women's fashion, baby products, kitchenware, and children's clothing, among other things.

The service companies of Karstadt Quelle provide consulting, information, financial, and travel services. With airline operator Deutsche Lufthansa, Karstadt Quelle shares a 50/50 joint venture in Thomas Cook AG, making it the #3 travel services company in the world (behind American Express and Carlson Wagonlit) and the second-largest in Europe (after TUI).

The real estate unit was set up to handle the group's numerous property locations and to develop shopping centers throughout Germany.

HISTORY

In 1881 Rudolph Karstadt opened a store in Mecklenburg, Germany, selling candy, apparel, and fabric. His store was one of Germany's first department stores; it offered separate departments for merchandise and offered low, fixed prices and cash-only sales. In 1885 Theodor Althoff took control of his mother's haberdashery, wool, and linen shop in Westfalen, Germany. He adopted the same business model as Karstadt.

Rudolph Karstadt AG was founded in 1920 and soon merged with Althoff's business. Six years later Karstadt founded EPA Einheitspreis, an American-style discount store. The company grew rapidly, reaching 89 outlets in 1929. But overexpansion and a worldwide depression hurt Karstadt, and it found itself in financial trouble by 1931. With the help of a bank consortium, the company restructured that year.

Karstadt operated 67 stores in 1939, but by the end of WWII, only 45 remained in West Germany and most were heavily damaged. (The company lost the remainder to East Germany and the Iron Curtain.) Postwar economic reform and reconstruction boosted personal incomes; as a result, Karstadt's sales rose too. In 1948 the retailer was accepted into "Interkontinentale Warenhausgruppe" (the "Intercontinental Department Store Group").

In 1971 Karstadt and mail-order firm Quelle founded travel firm TransEuropa-Reisen, which became KS-Touristik-Beteiligungs in 1972. (Karstadt sold its share in 1976.) In 1976

Karstadt became a major shareholder in Germany's third-largest mail-order company, Neckermann Versand, which was restructured into a public limited company. The next year Karstadt upped its stake to 51% of Neckermann Versand, and it controlled virtually all of the company by 1984. (Neckermann Versand travel subsidiary NUR Neckermann+Reisen became NUR Touristik in 1982.) Karstadt also founded Runners Point in 1984.

The company in 1988 opened a distribution center in Unna, Germany. When the wall came down, bringing trade barriers with it, Karstadt established cooperation agreements with 10 Centrum and four Magnet department stores in the former East Germany. The same sort of agreement was set up with GUM department store in Moscow in 1992.

Karstadt opened Optic Point Warenhandelsgesellschaft in 1993 and acquired Hertie Waren- und Kaufhaus in 1994, making it by far Germany's largest department store group. In 1995 the company extended its travel empire with the acquisition of 51% of business travel chain Euro Lloyd Reiseburo from Lufthansa. Euro Lloyd went online the next year.

Retail group Schickedanz bought 20% of Karstadt in 1997. A year later Karstadt formed travel group C&N Touristic with Lufthansa (regulations forced the companies to sell Euro Lloyd, which was picked up by Swiss-based Kuoni). Karstadt also transferred its NUR Touristik operations to C&N Touristic.

In 1999 the company purchased mail-order company Quelle from Schickedanz-Holding and became Karstadt Quelle, one of Europe's largest retailers. Amidst European travel industry consolidation in 2000, C&N Touristic bought Thomas Cook from rival Preussag AG (now TUI) and took on the Thomas Cook name. The move made it the second-largest travel company in Europe and #3 in the world.

In 2001 Karstadt Quelle's major restructuring plan included almost 4,000 job cuts.

In September 2002, the company reorganized into four subholding companies for each of its four business segments: retail stores, mail order, real estate, and services.

EXECUTIVES

Chairman: Hans Meinhardt
Chairman, Management Board: Wolfgang Urban, age 57
Chairman, Neckermann Versand and Quelle AG: Christoph Achenbach, age 45
Chairman, Services, New Media, Tourism: Peter Gerard, age 56
Group Secretary: Sylvia Ehlert
Director, Foreign Offices, Logistics, Personnel, Environment and Corporate Policy, and Synergies: Prof Helmut Merkel, age 54
Director, Corporate Communications: Thomas Diehl
Director, Investor Relations: Detlef Neveling
Manager, Investor Relations: Jürgen Koch
Director, Finance and Control, Neckermann Versand and Quelle AG: Arwed Fischer
Director, Logistics and IT, Neckermann Versand and Quelle AG: Ulrich Wiggers
Director, Marketing and Sales, Neckermann Versand and Quelle AG: Gebhard Stammler
Director, Sales and Marketing: Thomas Freude
Director, Specialty Mail Order, Neckermann Versand and Quelle AG: Leo Günther Kraftsik
Director, Technology and Consumer Durables, Neckermann Versand and Quelle AG: Michael Badke
Director, Textile, Neckermann Versand and Quelle AG: Helmut Klier
Manager, New Media: Annette Noll-Decke
Auditors: BDO Deutsche Warentreuhand AG

LOCATIONS

HQ: Karstadt Quelle AG
Theodor-Althoff-Strasse 2, D-45133 Essen, Germany
Phone: +49-20-17271   **Fax:** +49-20-1727-5216
Web: www.karstadtquelle.com

Karstadt Quelle has operations in Austria, Belgium, Eastern Europe, France, Germany, the Netherlands, Scandinavia, Spain, and Switzerland.

PRODUCTS/OPERATIONS

2002 Sales

	% of total
Mail order	47
Retail stores	42
Services	8
Real estate	3
Total	**100**

Selected Operations

Mail Order
Neckermann
Quelle

Department Stores
Alsterhaus
Hertie
Karstadt
KaDeWe
Wertheim

Specialty Retail
Runners Point and Golf House (sports)
SinnLeffers and Wehmeyer (fashion)
Schaulandt/Schürmann and WOM World of Music (multimedia)
LeBuffet (restaurants)

Services
INTELLIUM (information technology)
KarstadtQuelle Bank (financial services)
Quelle Versicherungen (insurance)
Thomas Cook Tourism Group (50% joint venture)

Real Estate
KARSTADT Immobilien

COMPETITORS

American Express	H&M
AVA AG	Lidl & Schwarz Stiftung
C&A	METRO AG
Carlson Wagonlit	Otto Versand
Carrefour	TUI
Douglas Holding	Wal-Mart
Edeka Zentrale	

HISTORICAL FINANCIALS

Company Type: Public

Income Statement

FYE: December 31

	REVENUE ($ mil.)	NET INCOME ($ mil.)	NET PROFIT MARGIN	EMPLOYEES
12/02	16,575	81	0.5%	104,536
12/01	14,232	208	1.5%	112,141
12/00	14,350	234	1.6%	113,120
12/99	14,948	73	0.5%	113,490
12/98	10,884	119	1.1%	89,399
12/97	13,272	92	0.7%	94,463
12/96	15,482	38	0.2%	99,991
12/95	16,756	76	0.5%	105,129
12/94	15,606	27	0.2%	108,286
12/93	10,763	130	1.2%	75,951
Annual Growth	**4.9%**	**(5.2%)**	**—**	**3.6%**

2002 Year-End Financials

Debt ratio: 95.1%
Return on equity: 4.8%
Cash ($ mil.): 178

Current ratio: 1.16
Long-term debt ($ mil.): 1,672

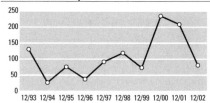

Net Income History   German: KAR

250
200
150
100
50
0
12/93 12/94 12/95 12/96 12/97 12/98 12/99 12/00 12/01 12/02

Kingfisher plc

Home improvement is netting the big catch in retail these days, and Kingfisher is angling for it. Kingfisher operates a network of some 550 home improvement stores in seven countries, mostly in Europe, where it is the largest DIY retailer. The company's do-it-yourself (DIY) portfolio includes France's Castorama-Dubois, which merged with Kingfisher's B&Q chain. Kingfisher's other DIY stores include Brico Dépôt in France and Koçtas in Turkey. Kingfisher sold its chain of about 700 Superdrug stores (even though it was the UK's #2 drugstore chain, behind Boots The Chemists) in early 2001, and it spun off its Woolworths and other general merchandise stores in a public offering in August 2001.

Kingfisher also owns 21.2% of Hornbach Holding, the parent company of Germany's Hornbach-Baumarkt chain.

Kingfisher will create some 1,500 new jobs by the end of 2004 through the expansion of its B&Q operations.

HISTORY

The beginning of Kingfisher is directly tied to the former US Woolworth chain (now Foot Locker). With the success of F.W. Woolworth general merchandise stores in the US, founder Frank Woolworth expanded overseas, first to Canada, then in 1909 to Liverpool, England. By 1914 Woolworth's UK subsidiaries had 31 stores.

Growing quickly, the company went public in 1931, with its US parent retaining a 53% stake. The company spent most of the postwar years rebuilding bombed stores and had 762 stores by 1950.

In 1967 the company opened its first Woolco Department Store, modeled after the US Woolco stores of its parent. However, other retailers had cut into sales, and by 1968 it lost its place as Britain's leading retailer to Marks and Spencer. In 1973 it opened Shoppers World, a catalog showroom. It made its first takeover in 1980, buying B&Q, a chain of 40 do-it-yourself stores.

An investment group acquired Woolworth in 1982 using the vehicle Paternoster Stores. (The US parent sold its stake in Woolworth.) The company, renamed Woolworth Holdings, closed unprofitable Woolworth stores and sold its Shoppers World stores in 1983 and its Ireland Woolworth stores in 1984. It also acquired Comet, a UK home electronics chain, and continued to expand B&Q.

Two years later all of its F.W. Woolworth stores were renamed Woolworths, and food and clothing lines were abandoned. Also in 1986 the company sold its Woolco stores and bought record and tape distributor Record Merchandisers (later renamed

Entertainment UK). The next year Woolworth Holdings acquired Superdrug, a chain of 297 discount drugstores. Adding to its Superdrug chain, in 1988 the company acquired and integrated two UK pharmacy chains: 110-store Tip Top Drugstores and 145-store Share Drug.

To reflect its growing diversity of businesses, the company was renamed Kingfisher in 1989. Also that year it bought drug retailer Medicare, with 86 stores. Expanding further into electronics, in 1993 Kingfisher acquired Darty, with 130 stores. Adding music retail to music distribution, that year the firm founded Music and Video Club (MVC).

In 1998 Kingfisher increased its presence in France by taking control of electronics chain BUT. It also merged its B&Q chain with the do-it-yourself stores of France's Castorama in 1998 and gained a 55% stake in the new group (though as part of the deal Kingfisher received only 50% of the group's voting rights).

Following the lead of rival Dixons, in 1999 Kingfisher launched its own free Internet access service in France called Libertysurf. Soon thereafter, Libertysurf acquired 70% of Objectif Net and its Web site, Nomade.fr. Kingfisher's planned purchase of food retailer ASDA Group collapsed in June 1999 after being outbid by Wal-Mart Stores.

Kingfisher sold its 35% stake in Libertysurf to Italian ISP Tiscali in 2001, and it sold its Superdrug chain to Kruidvat, a Dutch health and beauty group. Kingfisher demerged Woolworths Group the same year in a public offering. With Woolies went electronic entertainment companies EUK, MVC, VCI, and Streets Online. Also in 2001 Kingfisher bought 25% plus one share of the unlisted ordinary voting shares of Germany's Hornbach Holding, a family-owned group that owns 80% of one of Germany's leading DIY chains, Hornbach-Baumarkt.

In 2002 Kingfisher acquired the remainder of Castorama and bought 17.4% of Hornbach's listed non-voting preference shares (which with the 2001 purchase represents a 21.2% stake in Hornbach). Kingfisher additionally bought 5.5% of the ordinary shares of Hornbach-Baumarkt.

CEO Geoffrey Mulcahy stepped down in 2002 and was replaced by Gerry Murphy, formerly Carlton's CEO, in 2003. Kingfisher sold its 20 retail parks for $1.1 billion to a consortium that includes real estate firms Pillar Property and Capital & Regional Properties the same year. Also in 2003 Kingfisher sold ProMarkt, with about 190 stores in Germany, to its former owners, Michael and Matthias Wegert.

To focus on DIY, Kingfisher floated its electrical businesses as a new company, Kesa Electricals, in 2003. Kesa Electricals includes Darty, France's leading electrical retailer with more than 180 stores and Comet, with some 260 stores in the UK. Kingfisher sold two home improvement chains that year. Réno-Dépôt, which operates about 20 home-improvement stores in Canada, was sold to RONA. NOMI, with about 40 stores in Poland, was acquired by Enterprise Investors.

In 2003 Kingfisher opened its 14th B&Q in Beijing, China, in line with plans to operate 70 stores in that country within five years. At 250,000 sq. ft., the store in Beijing is B&Q's largest to date. Also that year Kingfisher sold Dubois Materiaux, a French building materials dealer, to Saint-Gobain Building Distribution.

EXECUTIVES

Chairman: Francis Mackay, age 58
Deputy Chairman: John Nelson, age 55
CEO: Gerry Murphy, age 47
Chief Executive, International and Development: Ian Cheshire, $517,598 pay (prior to promotion)
Group Finance Director: Helen Weir, age 41, $494,970 pay
Group Finance Director: Duncan Tatton-Brown
Group Human Resources Director: Tony Stanworth
CEO, B&Q: William (Bill) Whiting, age 55, $523,254 pay
CEO, B&Q: Rob Cissell
Chief Executive, Castorama France: Philippe Tible
Secretary: Helen Jones
Commercial Director: George Adams
Director, Communications: Ian Harding
Head, External Communications: Nigel Cope
Head, Investor Relations: Loraine Woodhouse
Auditors: PricewaterhouseCoopers LLP

LOCATIONS

HQ: 3 Sheldon Square, Paddington, London W2 6PX, United Kingdom
Phone: +44-20-7372-8008   **Fax:** +44-20-7644-1001
Web: www.kingfisher.co.uk

Kingfisher operates stores mostly in the UK, but also in China, France, Ireland, Italy, Taiwan, and Turkey.

2003 Sales

	% of total
UK & Ireland	55
France	30
Other	15
Total	**100**

PRODUCTS/OPERATIONS

2003 Sales

	% of total
Home improvement	63
Electrical and furniture	36
Financial services	.5
Property	.5
General merchandise	—
Total	**100**

Selected Operations

Castorama-Dubois Investissements (do-it-yourself stores)
B&Q (UK)
Brico Dépôt (France)
Castorama (France)
Koçtas (Turkey)

COMPETITORS

Focus Wickes
Homebase
METRO AG
Saint-Gobain Building Distribution
Tengelmann
Travis Perkins
Wolseley

HISTORICAL FINANCIALS

Company Type: Public

Income Statement
FYE: January 31

	REVENUE ($ mil.)	NET INCOME ($ mil.)	NET PROFIT MARGIN	EMPLOYEES
1/03	17,735	281	1.6%	99,879
1/02	15,893	(352)	—	119,002
1/01	17,744	608	3.4%	134,061
1/00	17,484	677	3.9%	118,416
1/99	12,282	720	5.9%	78,133
1/98	10,458	631	6.0%	83,364
1/97	9,310	445	4.8%	77,254
1/96	7,958	347	4.4%	75,501
Annual Growth	**12.1%**	**(3.0%)**	**—**	**4.1%**

2003 Year-End Financials

Debt ratio: 31.9%   Current ratio: 1.02
Return on equity: 5.2%   Long-term debt ($ mil.): 2,354
Cash ($ mil.): 163

Net Income History
London: KGF

Kirin Brewery Company

A mythical eastern unicorn called a *kirin* — a symbol of good fortune — brands the Kirin beer bottle. But Tokyo-based Kirin Brewery Company, one of Japan's — and the world's — largest brewers, may need more than luck in its battle with archrival Asahi Breweries, Japan's top brewer by a razor-thin margin. Kirin makes several leading brews in Japan, including Kirin Lager and Ichiban Shibori. Kirin Tanrei is Japan's leading happo-shu (low-malt) beer. Other beverages include chuhai (a fruity cocktail), canned coffee and tea, fruit juices, and soft drinks. Also active in floriculture and pharmaceuticals, Kirin is part of the Mitsubishi *keiretsu*.

Kirin also sells beer in Europe and owns more than 45% of Lion Nathan, through which it is expanding beer operations in China. In reciprocal deals with Anheuser-Busch, Kirin brews Budweiser beer in Japan while Anheuser-Busch makes Kirin brands in the US. Kirin has negotiated exclusive rights with Pernod Ricard and Diageo to distribute Chivas Regal in Japan.

In addition, Kirin Beverage offers Tropicana fruit juices. Facing declining beer sales, it has high hopes for its chuhai fruit-flavored cocktail drink. Kirin also is looking for growth from the "shochu" distilled liquor market with its Pure Blue brand.

Kirin has a number of other businesses, including a joint venture with Danone and Mitsubishi to sell mineral water as well as flower growing and food processing operations. Its pharmaceuticals unit has developed two popular blood treatments. Kirin plans to expand its medical sales force and more than double revenues from its pharmaceutical business by 2010.

Other businesses include dairy, dietary supplements, tomato-based foods, and processed meats. It also owns 15% of Philippine food and beverage firm, San Miguel Corporation.

HISTORY

American William Copeland went to Yokohama, Japan, in 1864 and five years later established the Spring Valley Brewery, the first in Japan, to provide beer for foreign nationals. Lacking funds to continue the brewery, Copeland closed it in 1884. The next year a group of foreign and Japanese businessmen reopened it as Japan Brewery. The business created the Kirin label in 1888 and was soon profitable.

The operation was run primarily by Americans and Europeans at first, but by 1907 Japanese workers had filled the ranks and adopted the Kirin Brewery Company name. Sales plummeted during WWII when the government limited brewing output. After the war, the US occupation forces inadvertently assisted Kirin when they split Dai Nippon Brewery (Kirin's main competitor) into two companies (Asahi and Sapporo Breweries) while leaving Kirin intact. The company became Japan's leading brewer during the 1950s.

During the 1970s the company introduced several soft drinks and in 1972 branched into hard liquor through a joint venture with Seagram (Kirin-Seagram).

The firm bought several Coca-Cola bottling operations in New England and Japan in the 1980s. Kirin also entered the pharmaceuticals business, in part through a joint venture with US-based Amgen. In 1988 the brewer signed an agreement with Molson to produce Kirin beer for the North American market. In 1989 Kirin bought Napa Valley's Raymond Vineyards.

In 1991 Kirin formed a partnership to market Tropicana drinks in Japan. It also entered an alliance with Sankyo (Japan's #2 drug company) in 1991 to market Kirin's medication for anemia, which it had developed with Amgen. Chairman Hideyo Motoyama resigned in 1993 after four company executives were arrested for allegedly paying a group of racketeers who had threatened to disrupt Kirin's annual meeting. Joint venture Kirin-Amgen won the rights to make thrombopoietin (TPO), a blood platelet growth stimulator in 1995.

Yasuhiro Satoh became president of Kirin in 1996. The brewer moved into China that year through an agreement with China Resources (Shenyang) Snowflake Brewery. To brew its beers in the US, the company formed Kirin Brewery of America, also in 1996.

In response to losing market share to Asahi, Kirin cut its workforce in 1998 and introduced Tanrei, a cheaper, low-malt beer that quickly captured half its market. Building on its presence in China, Kirin bought 45% of brewer Lion Nathan (based in Australia and New Zealand) for $742.5 million that year. It became a licensed brewer of Anheuser-Busch in 1999.

Like other Japanese brewers, Kirin struggled against dwindling demand for its most expensive brews in 2000. In December 2001 Kirin announced that it would form a joint venture with Japan's largest drugmaker, Takeda Chemicals, to create food seasonings, before fully acquiring Takeda.

In 2002 Kirin bought 15% of Philippine food and drink giant San Miguel for about $530 million as part of its plan to overcome slow growth domestically through expanded global interests. It also boosted ties with beverage giant Pernod Ricard by purchasing 32% of SIFA, a French food services firm, for an estimated $155 million. (The deal gives Kirin a 3% indirect interest in Pernod Ricard.) In 2002 Kirin also formed Flower Season Ltd., a joint venture with Dole Food Company to sell flowers to Japanese retailers. Also in 2002 Kirin launched its new Pure Blue brand of "shochu" distilled liquor.

Kirin said it will begin selling Four Roses Kentucky Straight Bourbon in the US with the help of Southern Wine & Spirits of America. The brand had been sold exclusively as an export since 1959. Kirin purchased the Four Roses brand from Diageo.

EXECUTIVES

Chairman: Yasuhiro Satoh
President: Koichiro Aramaki
Senior Executive Officer: Kunpei Kitamura
Senior Executive Officer: Yoshiyuki Morioka
Managing Executive Officer: Shozo Sawada
Managing Executive Officer: Takeshi Shigenaga
Managing Executive Officer: Yoshikazu Arai
Director and General Manager, Logistics Division: Kiyoaki Nakazawa
Director and General Manager, Production Division: Akira Negami
Director and General Manager, Sales and Marketing Division: Kazuyasu Kato
President, Agribio Business Division: Yoshiyuki Matsushima
President, International Beer Division: Hitoshi Oshima
President, Nutrient Food and Feed Division: Yoshihiko Kitamura
President, Pharmaceutical Division: Katsuhiko Asano
General Manager, Corporate Communications Department: Hideo Mori
General Manager, Finance and Accounting: Kazuhiro Sato
General Manager, Research and Development Department: Kazuo Yoshioka
Auditors: Asahi & Co.

LOCATIONS

HQ: Kirin Brewery Company Limited
10-1 Shinkawa 2-chome, Chuo-ku,
Tokyo 104-8288, Japan
Phone: +81-3-5540-3411 **Fax:** +81-3-5540-3547
US HQ: 2400 Broadway, Ste. 240,
Santa Monica, CA 90404
US Phone: 310-829-2400 **US Fax:** 310-829-0424
Web: www.kirin.co.jp

Kirin Brewery Company owns 11 breweries, one hop center, a pharmaceutical plant, seven laboratories and 10 regional sales offices in Japan. The company has subsidiaries and affiliates in Asia, Australia, Europe, and the US.

PRODUCTS/OPERATIONS

2002 Sales

	% of total
Alcoholic beverages	55
Soft drinks	30
Other	15
Total	**100**

Selected Products and Brands

Beverages
Beer (Beer Shokunin, Gokunama, Kirin Chu-hi Hyoketsu, Kirin Ichiban Shibori, Kirin Europe, Kirin Ichiban, Kirin Lager, Lager Special Light, Kirin Tanrei, Tanrei Green Label)

Liquors and Wines (Absolut, Boston Club, Chivas Regal, Evermore, Four Roses, Franzia, Kirin Hyoketsu, Martell, Myers's, Perrier-Jouet, Kirin Mugi Shochu Pure Blue, Robert Brown)
Soft Drinks (Alkaline-ion no Mizu, Cadi, Fire, Gogono-kocha, Ho Oh Oolong Tea, Namacha, Issen, Jive Coffee, Kirin Lemon, Kiriri, Naturals, Supli, Tropicana 100% Juice)

Other
Agribio (Kirin carnation, mum, and petunia; kalanchoe)
Pharmaceuticals (ESPO glycoprotein, GRAN white-blood cell stimulant)
Restaurants and Food (Giraffe, Kirin City, Koiwai Pure Butter, Makiba Milk, Tavola Baccano, Tsubu-Tsubu Yasai Ketchup)
Yeast-related (Brewer's yeast, GBF, high-moleculated chitosan, Kirin Chloerlla 5.5, mushroom-growing medium, RNA, yeast extract)

COMPETITORS

Adolph Coors	Mercian
Allied Domecq	Miller Brewing
Anheuser-Busch	Nippon Beet Sugar
Asahi Breweries	Novartis
Asia Pacific Breweries	Pabst
Yanjing	Pepsi Bottling
Carlsberg	Red Bull
Chugai	SABMiller
Diageo	San Miguel
Gallo	Sapporo
FEMSA	Snow Brand Milk Products
Foster's	Suntory
Heineken	Taiwan Tobacco & Wine
Interbrew	Takara Holdings
ITOCHU	Tsingtao
Kokubu & Co.	YUM!
LVMH	

HISTORICAL FINANCIALS

Company Type: Public

Income Statement

FYE: December 31

	REVENUE ($ mil.)	NET INCOME ($ mil.)	NET PROFIT MARGIN	EMPLOYEES
12/02	9,486	271	2.9%	23,070
12/01	11,837	175	1.5%	—
12/00	9,353	287	3.1%	—
12/99	8,860	325	3.7%	—
12/98	7,735	234	3.0%	—
12/97	6,649	195	2.9%	—
12/96	13,750	296	2.2%	—
12/95	15,865	389	2.5%	—
12/94	17,054	524	3.1%	—
12/93	14,111	385	2.7%	—
Annual Growth	**(4.3%)**	**(3.8%)**	**—**	**—**

2002 Year-End Financials

Debt ratio: 30.6%
Return on equity: 4.4%
Cash ($ mil.): 902
Current ratio: 1.14
Long-term debt ($ mil.): 1,961
No. of shares (mil.): 985
Dividends
Yield: 1.5%
Payout: 33.3%
Market value ($ mil.): 5,917

Stock History

NASDAQ (SC): KNBWY

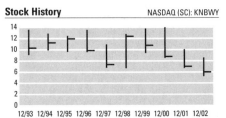

| | 12/93 | 12/94 | 12/95 | 12/96 | 12/97 | 12/98 | 12/99 | 12/00 | 12/01 | 12/02 |

STOCK PRICE ($) FY Close	P/E High/Low	PER SHARE ($) Earnings	PER SHARE ($) Dividends	PER SHARE ($) Book Value
12/02	6.01	31 20	0.27	0.09	6.52
12/01	7.00	498 342	0.02	0.10	0.60
12/00	8.78	463 288	0.03	0.11	0.65
12/99	10.78	43 30	0.32	0.10	0.69
12/98	12.38	58 31	0.22	0.05	0.62
12/97	7.34	57 36	0.19	0.05	0.55
12/96	9.85	48 35	0.28	0.09	0.61
12/95	11.95	33 26	0.37	0.13	0.67
12/94	11.23	26 20	0.50	0.08	0.66
12/93	10.30	37 25	0.36	0.07	0.56
Annual Growth	(5.8%)	— —	(3.1%)	2.8%	31.5%

KLM Royal Dutch Airlines

Venerable KLM Royal Dutch Airlines is the world's oldest international airline and soon may be part of Europe's largest. Through its partnerships (including a long-time codeshare agreement with Northwest), the airline provides passenger and cargo services to some 350 destinations in almost 75 countries. With its primary hub located in Amsterdam, the airline carries nearly 16 million passengers and about 490,000 tons of cargo annually. KLM operates a fleet of more than 210 aircraft, mostly Boeings. KLM also operates regional carrier KLM cityhopper, but sold its buzz unit in an effort to boost lagging revenues. Hope may be on the horizon as KLM has agreed to merge with European competitor Air France.

Part of KLM's woes have been rooted in its inability to find a European partner — until Air France came along.

In 2003 the two airlines agreed to merge to form a joint holding company in a deal that would create Europe's largest airline. For the new holding company's first three years of existence, KLM will be 51% controlled by Dutch interests which will include the Dutch government. The airlines will also continue to operate independently, even on competing routes, for the time being.

The new deal did not come in time to prevent the airline from seeking to cut some 3,000 jobs (about 10% of its workforce) in 2003.

Before it found its European partner, the company had been relying on KLM cityhopper to cover smaller markets and low-fare carrier, buzz, based at London's Stansted airport to give it a better foothold in Europe. However, the carrier was unable to turn a profit with buzz and chose instead to sell the low-fare carrier to Ryanair.

HISTORY

Flight lieutenant Albert Plesman founded Koninklijke Luchtvaart Maatschappij voor Nederland en Kolonien (Royal Airline Company for the Netherlands and Colonies) in The Hague in 1919. Queen Wilhelmina granted the honorary title of *koninklijke* (or royal), and Dutch businessmen financed the venture. Early passengers — who flew in an open cockpit with the pilot — were issued leather jackets, goggles, gloves, and parachutes.

Under Plesman's leadership KLM established service between Amsterdam and London, Copenhagen, Brussels, and Paris in the early 1920s. The airline initiated the longest air route in the world, from Amsterdam to Indonesia, in 1928 and extended its European network in the years before WWII. Hitler's occupation of Holland shut down KLM's European operations in 1940; the Germans imprisoned Plesman from 1940 to 1942, bombing or confiscating two-thirds of KLM's planes.

After the war Plesman quickly re-established commercial service, using 47 US military surplus airplanes, and in 1946 KLM became the first continental European airline to offer scheduled service from Europe to the US. Plesman died in 1953, and KLM began trading on the NYSE in 1957.

KLM established NLM Dutch Airlines in 1966 (renamed cityhopper in 1976) to provide commuter flights within the Netherlands. The airline addressed overcapacity problems in the 1970s by converting the rear portions of its 747s to cargo space.

In 1988 KLM bought 40% of Dutch charter airline Transavia (increased to 80% in 1991) and began looking for partners to help it compete in key markets. It bought 10% of Covia Partnership, owner and operator of United Airlines' Apollo computer reservation system (1988), and invested in Wings Holdings, a company formed to buy Northwest Airlines (1989). In 1991 KLM bought 35% of Air Littoral, a French regional airline, and 40% of ALM Antillean Airlines.

Airline deregulation in Europe spawned numerous efforts to develop strategic relationships. A deal giving KLM and British Airways 20% each of Belgium's national airline, Sabena, fell apart in 1990, and KLM-British Airways merger talks collapsed in early 1992. In 1994, when Northwest recovered from four straight losses, KLM bought brewer Foster's 6% stake in the airline.

American Airlines and British Airways invited KLM in 1996 to join a proposed alliance, which would combine transatlantic flights and marketing. However, the plan would have required KLM to sell its Northwest stake. That year KLM executed a buyback of about 13% of KLM stock from the Dutch government; it also took a 25% stake in Kenya Airways.

In 1998 KLM sold back its 19% stake in Northwest Airlines for about $1.1 billion, while forming a strategic partnership with the carrier. The deal resolved a feud stemming from KLM's attempt to increase its Northwest stake to 25%.

Meanwhile, in 1997 KLM and Italian carrier Alitalia announced a partnership that would later evolve into the integration of their fleets. Although it remained an independent company, KLM contributed its fleet and personnel to the operation, as did Alitalia.

In 2000 KLM's low-fare European service, buzz, began service from its hub at London's Stansted airport. Also that year KLM terminated its passenger and cargo joint operations with Alitalia, citing problems with the operations of a new airport near Milan and a delay in the sale of the Italian government's stake in Alitalia. KLM's potential merger with British Airways was called off as well.

The airline cut back its flights in the wake of the September 11, 2001, terrorist attacks on the US in anticipation of reduced demand for transatlantic service.

EXECUTIVES

Chairman: Floris A. Maljers, age 70
Vice Chairman: Arie Maas, age 69
President and CEO: Leo M. van Wijk, age 57
Managing Director and COO: Peter F. Hartman, age 54
Managing Director and CFO: Rob Ruijter, age 52
Managing Director and Chief Human Resources Officer: Cees van Woudenberg, age 55
General Secretary: Hans Eric Kuipéri, age 44
Auditors: KPMG Accountants N.V.

LOCATIONS

HQ: Koninklijke Luchtvaart Maatschappij N.V.
Amsterdamseweg 55,
1182GP Amstelveen, The Netherlands
Phone: +31-20-649-9123   **Fax:** +31-20-649-2324
Web: www.klm.nl

2003 Sales

	% of total
Asia/Pacific	33
North Atlantic	25
Central & South Atlantic	13
Africa	11
Europe	10
Middle East & South Asia	8
Total	**100**

PRODUCTS/OPERATIONS

2003 Sales

	% of total
Passenger	68
Cargo	17
Charter	9
Engineering & Maintenance	5
Other	1
Total	**100**

Selected Subsidiaries and Affiliates

Kenya Airways Ltd. (26%)
KLM cityhopper bv (regional airline)
Martinair Holland nv (50%, international cargo and passenger airline)
Transavia Airlines bv (80%, charters and scheduled holiday service)
BASIQ AIR (low-fare airline)

COMPETITORS

Air Canada	Iberia
Air France	Lufthansa
All Nippon Airways	SAS
AMR	Singapore Airlines
BAX Global	Brussels Airlines
British Airways	UAL
Delta	UPS
DHL	US Airways
FedEx	Virgin Atlantic Airways
Finnair	Virgin Group

HISTORICAL FINANCIALS

Company Type: Public

Income Statement

FYE: March 31

	REVENUE ($ mil.)	NET INCOME ($ mil.)	NET PROFIT MARGIN	EMPLOYEES
3/03	7,066	(454)	—	33,038
3/02	5,688	(136)	—	33,265
3/01	6,100	67	1.1%	33,763
3/00	6,018	322	5.4%	30,159
3/99	5,718	223	3.9%	28,374
3/98	5,666	1,059	18.7%	26,811
3/97	5,516	126	2.3%	26,385
3/96	5,769	330	5.7%	25,003
3/95	5,969	305	5.1%	29,047
3/94	4,619	55	1.2%	24,610
Annual Growth	**4.8%**	**—**		**3.3%**

2003 Year-End Financials

Debt ratio: 268.9%   No. of shares (mil.): 47
Return on equity: —   Dividends
Cash ($ mil.): 662   Yield: 3.1%
Current ratio: 0.83   Payout: —
Long-term debt ($ mil.): 4,327   Market value ($ mil.): 290

Stock History

NYSE: KLM

	STOCK PRICE ($) FY Close	P/E High/Low		PER SHARE ($) Earnings	Dividends	Book Value
3/03	6.20	—	—	(10.09)	0.19	34.37
3/02	14.48	—	—	(2.93)	0.52	37.06
3/01	18.40	21	11	1.41	0.00	38.58
3/00	21.00	1,137	426	6.85	0.95	41.23
3/99	36.99	14	6	4.79	0.00	50.45
3/98	54.15	11	7	5.19	0.07	46.47
3/97	38.16	23	15	2.13	1.32	33.01
3/96	46.32	11	8	4.72	1.27	39.35
3/95	39.82	10	7	4.40	0.00	38.27
3/94	32.99	50	25	0.72	0.00	29.78
Annual Growth	(17.0%)	—	—	—	—	1.6%

Koç Holding

In Turkey, Koç (pronounced "coach") class equals first class. Led by its automotive businesses, Koç Holding is Turkey's top industrial conglomerate. The company's Tofas unit, a joint venture with Fiat, is Turkey's leading carmaker; Koç's joint venture with Ford Motor sells imported Ford models. Other businesses include supermarkets (Migros), large household appliances (Arçelik), and energy (distribution of liquefied petroleum gas). Subsidiaries engage in food production, construction, international trading, and hospitality and tourism. Koç also operates banking, securities brokerage, and insurance businesses. The Koç family, Turkey's wealthiest dynasty, controls the company.

Koç is looking to accelerate growth in its retail financial services businesses in Russia, the Balkans, Europe, Central Asia and the Caucasus. It is also expanding its information technology-related businesses in Turkey.

HISTORY

In 1917, 16-year-old Vehbi Koç and his father opened a small grocery store in Ankara, Turkey. With the fall of the Ottoman Empire after WWI, Turkey's capital was moved to Ankara, which was then only a village. The Koçs recognized an opportunity and expanded into construction and building supplies, winning a contract to repair the roof of the Turkish parliament building. By age 26, Koç was a millionaire.

Ford Motor made Koç its Turkish agent in 1928. In 1931 Mobil Oil and Koç entered an exclusive agreement to search for oil in Turkey. The company incorporated in 1938 as Koç Ticaret Corpo-

ration, the first Turkish joint stock company with an employee stock-ownership program.

Despite Turkey's neutrality in WWII, the fighting disrupted Koç's business. The nation became isolationist after the war and restricted foreign concerns to selling through local agents; Koç benefited by importing foreign products.

General Electric and Koç entered a joint venture in 1946 to build Turkey's first lightbulb factory. In 1955 Koç set up Arçelik, the first Turkish producer of refrigerators, washing machines, and water heaters; Türk Demir Döküm, the first Turkish producer of radiators and, later, auto castings; and Turkay, the country's first private producer of matches. In 1959 Koç constructed Turkey's first truck assembly plant (Otosan).

Other firsts followed in the 1960s as the company leveraged its size and government influence to attract more ventures. These included a tire factory (with Uniroyal), a cable factory (with Siemens), production of electric motors and compressors (with GE), and the production of Anadol, the first car to be made entirely in Turkey (by Otosan, under license from Ford). In 1974 Koç expanded into retailing with the purchase of Migros, Turkey's largest chain of supermarkets.

The Turkish military imposed martial law in 1980 and restricted foreign exchange payments, forcing Koç to limit its operations. In 1986, a year after foreign companies were allowed to export products directly to Turkey, Koç and American Express started Koç-Amerikan Bank (which Koç bought out and renamed Koçbank in 1992). In the late 1980s Vehbi's only son, Rahmi, took over the company's leadership. Vehbi Koç died in 1996.

Auto sales fell sharply in 1996 as buyers awaited the country's entry into the European Union's customs union. In an effort to offset market risks, Koç forged a number of alliances in 1997. It participated in a British-Canadian-Turkish consortium that was building a large power plant in central Turkey.

Reflecting a greater willingness to open the company to foreign investors, Koç announced plans to offer $250 million in shares in a public offering in 1998, but it soon canceled the offering because of market volatility. A year later, the company completed an auto plant in Samarkand, Uzbekistan, to build Otoyol-Iveco buses and trucks.

In 2001 the company announced plans to open supermarkets in Iran and Syria. Koç entered into a joint venture — Koç Finansal Hizmetler — with Unicredito Italiano in 2002 in an effort to further consolidate its financial holdings.

EXECUTIVES

Honorary Chairman: Rahmi M. Koç
Chairman: Mustafa V. Koç
Vice Chairman: Ternel Atay
Vice Chairman: Suna Kiraç, age 62
CEO: F. Bülend Özaydinli
President, Auditing and Financial Control Group: Nadir Özsahin
President, Corporate Communications and Foreign Relations Group: Hasan Bengü, age 54
President, Durable Goods Group: Cengiz Solakoğlu, age 60
President, Energy Group: Ömer Koç, age 41
President, Fiat Group: Aydin I. Cubukcu
President, Financial Group: Rüsdü Saraçoğlu
President, Food and Retailing Group: Hasan Yilmaz
President, Koç Information Technology Group: Ali Y. Koç, age 36
President, Strategic Planning Group: Mehmet Ali Berkman

President, Supplies and Other Automotive Group: Selçuk Gezdur
President, Tourism and Construction Group: Bülent Bulgurlu
Group President, Executive Board Member Energy Group Companies: Erol Memioğlu, age 49
Secretary General: Tahsin Saltik
Accounting Manager: Emine Alangoya
Human Resources Coordinator: Serife Füsun Ömür
Legal Affairs: Kemal Erol
Auditors: PricewaterhouseCoopers

LOCATIONS

HQ: Koç Holding A.S.
    Nakkastepe, Azizbey Sok. No. 1, Kuzguncuk, 34674 Istanbul, Turkey
Phone: +90-216-531-00-00   Fax: +90-216-531-00-99
Web: www.koc.com.tr

Koç Holding has operations in Algeria, Austria, Bahrain, Bulgaria, France, Germany, Hong Kong, Iraq, Italy, Kazakhstan, the Netherlands, Poland, Russia, Spain, Switzerland, Tunisia, Turkmenistan, the UK, Ukraine, the US, and Uzbekistan.

PRODUCTS/OPERATIONS

2002 Sales

	% of total
Durable goods	20
Automotive	18
Food & retailing	16
Financial services	16
Energy	16
Other	14
Total	**100**

Core Businesses

Automotive
Construction and mining
Durable goods
Energy
Financial services
Food and retailing
International trade
New business development
Tourism and services

COMPETITORS

Opel
Caterpillar
Electrolux AB
Sabanci Holding
Honda
International Power
Renault
Robert Bosch
Siemens

HISTORICAL FINANCIALS

Company Type: Public

Net Income Statement

FYE: December 31

	REVENUE ($ mil.)	NET INCOME ($ mil.)	NET PROFIT MARGIN	EMPLOYEES
12/01	4,901	(214)	—	39,866
12/00	6,580	101	1.5%	45,626
12/99	5,424	24	0.4%	35,531
12/98	5,794	169	2.9%	37,178
12/97	9,585	157	1.6%	39,931
12/96	9,192	438	4.8%	41,750
12/95	11,504	425	3.7%	36,280
12/94	8,212	330	4.0%	32,721
12/93	14,406	536	3.7%	41,437
12/92	11,458	320	2.8%	39,725
Annual Growth	(9.0%)	—	—	0.0%

2001 Year-End Financials

Debt ratio: —
Return on equity: —
Cash ($ mil.): 560

Current ratio: 1.41
Long-term debt ($ mil.): 442

Net Income History   Istanbul: KCHOL

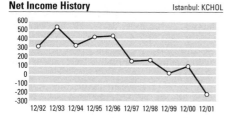

Komatsu Ltd.

Like a sumo wrestler, Komatsu can throw a lot of weight around. The diversified company is the world's #2 construction equipment maker, behind Caterpillar. Komatsu makes building and mining equipment ranging from bulldozers and wheel loaders to dump trucks and debris crushers. Komatsu also makes industrial machinery such as laser-cutting machines and sheet-metal presses. Its electronics division produces LCD manufacturing equipment and silicon wafers; a civil engineering and construction division makes prefabricated structures and offers contracting and real-estate sales and leasing services. Other products include generators, armored vehicles, diesel engines, and computer software.

Komatsu means "little pine tree" in Japanese. Its largest segment, building and mining equipment, generates about 70% of the company's sales.

In response to weak demand for construction equipment in Japan, Komatsu has been consolidating, reducing inventory, and closing plants to cut costs. The company, which recorded its first loss in fiscal 1999, has since focused on its construction and mining equipment businesses in the US and Europe. Battered by the weak economy, the company is cutting jobs and reducing costs.

Komatsu agreed to acquire KONE Corporation's Partek Forest AB and Partek Forest Holdings, LLC, subsidiaries (collectively known as Partek Forest) in 2003.

HISTORY

Komatsu's roots reach back to the Takeuchi Mining Company, founded in Japan in 1894. The company grew during WWI, and in 1917 it created an in-house ironworks to make machine tools and mining equipment. The ironworks was separated in 1921 to create Komatsu Manufacturing.

The firm grew into one of Japan's major makers of machine tools and pumps by adding new products to its line. Komatsu introduced its first metal press in 1924 and in 1931 made Japan's first crawler-type farm tractor. Komatsu began making high-grade casting and specialty steel materials in 1935.

During WWII Komatsu made munitions and bulldozers for the Japanese Navy. After the war it began making construction machinery and industrial vehicles as Japan rebuilt its infrastructure. The company began building diesel engines

in 1948. Komatsu continued to expand during the 1950s. In 1952 it began producing motor graders, which became its first construction equipment to be exported (to Argentina) in 1955.

During the 1960s Komatsu entered joint ventures with US manufacturers, including Cummins Engine (1961), Bucyrus Erie (1963), and International Harvester (now Navistar, 1965). Komatsu established its first overseas subsidiary, Komatsu Europe, in Belgium in 1967 and introduced the world's first radio-controlled bulldozer.

The company changed its name to Komatsu Limited in 1970. International expansion continued as subsidiaries were established in the US, Brazil, and Germany (1970), Singapore (1971), and Panama (1972). Komatsu began making bulldozers in Mexico (1976) and opened an Australian subsidiary (1978).

In the 1980s Komatsu pushed further into the US market, going head-to-head with Caterpillar. A strong dollar helped Komatsu undercut Caterpillar's prices by as much as 30%. In 1986 the company opened its first US factory in Chattanooga, Tennessee. In 1988 it merged American construction equipment-making operations with those of Dresser Industries', creating Komatsu Dresser.

Komatsu partnered with semiconductor giant Applied Materials in 1993 and entered the LAN market the next year with a print server and two types of hubs. The company expanded its construction equipment operations outside Japan in the mid 1990s, when it formed a joint venture in Vietnam and opened plants in China. Demand for construction equipment in Japan plunged soon after.

In 1997 Komatsu set up a joint venture with India's Larsen & Toubro to make hydraulic excavators. A semiconductor industry downturn prompted Komatsu to close some of its US silicon wafer operations in 1998.

Hammered by low demand for construction equipment in Japan (down nearly 80% over three years), Komatsu recorded its first loss in fiscal 1999 and closed plants. The company backed out of its joint venture with Applied Materials, selling its stake back to Applied Materials for $87 million in cash. Company president Satoru Anzaki hired former GM manager Keith Sheldon to overhaul the company's ailing global finances and prepare the company for stock listing on the New York Stock Exchange. In March 2000 the company sold its machine vision systems business to Cognex Corporation. Komatsu reached profitability in fiscal 2001 thanks to a new growth strategy focused on its construction and mining equipment businesses. Later the same year — as the economy swooned — Komatsu announced that it expected losses and was cutting about 2,200 jobs in Japan.

Komatsu's reorganization plans launched during the last quarter of 2001 carried over through 2002 and 2003. The company implemented its new growth strategy for the construction and mining equipment business, reduced fixed costs, and restructured its electronics business. In 2003 the company showed an increase of 5.2% in consolidated net sales over the previous year. That year the company decided to dissolve its Komatsu Metal Ltd. subsidiary.

EXECUTIVES

Chairman: Toshitaka Hagiwara
President and CEO: Masahiro Sakane
Senior Executive Officer; President, Construction and Mining Equipment Marketing Division, Regional Director of Japan, Asia and Pacific and China: Kunio Noji
Senior Executive Officer; President, Defense Systems Division: Shigeki Fujimori
Senior Executive Officer; President, Development Division and President, Engines and Hydraulics Business Division, Supervising Research and Development Operations: Kunihiko Komiyama
Senior Executive Officer; President, Procurement Division; President, Production Division; Supervising Quality Assurance Operations: Susumu Isoda
Senior Executive Officer; VP, Construction and Mining Equipment Marketing Division; General Manager, Customer Support: Teruo Nagayasu
Senior Executive Officer; General Manager, Corporate Planning, Supervising External Corporate Affairs, Regional Director of Americas and Europe: Kazuhiro Aoyagi
Senior Executive Officer; Deputy General Manager, Corporate Planning; Supervising Structural Reorganization and Human Resources: Masahiro Yoneyama
Senior Executive Officer, Supervising Compliance, Defense Systems and Environment and Safety: Naomi Anesaki
Senior Executive Officer, Supervising General Affairs, Corporate Communications and Investor Relations: Munenori Nakao
Chairman and CEO, Komatsu America: David W. (Dave) Grzelak
Auditors: KPMG

LOCATIONS

HQ: 2-3-6 Akasaka, Minato-ku, Tokyo 107-8414, Japan
Phone: +81-3-5561-2687   **Fax:** +81-3-3505-9662
US HQ: 440 N. Fairway Dr., Vernon Hills, IL 60061-8112
US Phone: 847-970-4100   **US Fax:** 847-970-4187
Web: www.komatsu.com

Komatsu has subsidiaries and affiliates in Australia, Belgium, Brazil, Canada, China, Egypt, France, Germany, Ghana, Hong Kong, India, Indonesia, Iran, Italy, Kenya, Malaysia, Mexico, Mongolia, Myanmar, the Netherlands, Norway, Pakistan, the Philippines, Poland, Russia, Saudi Arabia, Singapore, South Africa, Spain, Taiwan, Thailand, Turkey, United Arab Emirates, the UK, the US, and Vietnam.

2003 Sales

	$ mil.	% of total
Asia/Oceania		
Japan	3,821	42
Other Asia/Oceania	1,470	16
Americas	2,097	23
Europe	1,214	13
Middle East/Africa	491	6
Total	**9,093**	**100**

PRODUCTS/OPERATIONS

2003 Sales

	$ mil.	% of sales
Construction & mining equipment	6,407	70
Electronics	711	8
Others	1,975	22
Total	**9,093**	**100**

Products and Services

Construction and Mining Equipment
Articulated-type dump trucks
Backhoe loaders
Bulldozers
Crawler carriers
Hydraulic excavators
Mini excavators
Mini wheel loaders
Motor graders
Rigid-type dump trucks

Shield Machines
Skid steer loaders
Small-diameter pipe jacking machines (Iron Moles)
Tunnel-boring machines
Vibratory rollers
Wheel loaders

Electronics
Excimer laser
LAN peripheral equipment
Mobile tracking and communication terminals
Monosilane gas
Network information terminals
Polycrystalline silicon
Semiconductor manufacturing-related thermoelectric
  devices
Silicon wafers
Thermoelectric modules
Vehicle controllers

Industrial Machinery, Vehicles and Others
Crankshaft millers
Defense systems (ammunition and armored personnel
  carriers)
Fine plasma cutting machines
Forging presses
Forklift trucks
Large presses
Laser cutting machines
Outdoor power equipment
Packing and transport
Prefabricated office structures
Press brakes
Shears
Small- and medium-sized presses
Recycling plants

COMPETITORS

Caterpillar	Mitsubishi Heavy
CNH Global	Industries
Deere	Mitsubishi Materials
Ingersoll-Rand	RAG
Infrastructure	

HISTORICAL FINANCIALS

Company Type: Public

Income Statement FYE: March 31

	REVENUE ($ mil.)	NET INCOME ($ mil.)	NET PROFIT MARGIN	EMPLOYEES
3/03	9,093	25	0.3%	30,666
3/02	7,810	(608)	—	30,760
3/01	8,679	55	0.6%	32,002
3/00	10,006	127	1.3%	28,522
3/99	8,913	(104)	—	31,785
3/98	8,297	145	1.7%	26,871
3/97	8,877	147	1.7%	27,007
3/96	9,317	133	1.4%	27,917
3/95	10,617	118	1.1%	28,040
3/94	8,232	13	0.2%	28,446
Annual Growth	1.1%	7.9%	—	0.8%

2003 Year-End Financials

Debt ratio: 78.6%
Return on equity: 0.8%
Cash ($ mil.): 640
Current ratio: 1.46
Long-term debt ($ mil.): 2,593

Net Income History OTC: KMTUY

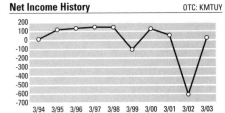

Koor Industries

Once a socialist vision, now a model of capitalism, Koor Industries is Israel's leading holding company. Koor's core businesses are agrochemicals (Makhteshim-Agan), defense electronics (Elisra Electronics Systems), and telecommunications equipment (ECI Telecom, Telrad Networks, Nortel Networks Israel). The company's venture capital arm has invested in enterprises including Chiaro Networks and Mysticom. Koor also has operations in tourism, real estate, and trade. Claridge Israel, a unit of Canadian billionaire Charles Bronfman's investment firm, owns 30% of Koor. The company was founded to provide employment for Jewish refugees during WWII.

Koor's general strategy for its agrochemical business is based upon timing the commercial release of the generic equivalent products that it develops to coincide with the expiration of patents for similar existing products.

While Koor's bread and butter is its chemical business, the company is attempting to build up its export-based businesses, which include its telecom equipment and defense electronics units. To this end, the company's investment arm has distributed venture capital primarily to communications-oriented hardware and software developers.

The company has reorganized the operations of ECI Telecom in part by divesting its wireless networking equipment unit in 2002 so that ECI could focus more closely on core wireline products.

HISTORY

Koor Industries is an offshoot of Solel Boneh, a construction company formed in 1924 in British Palestine by the Histadrut Labour Federation. Solel Boneh founded Koor in 1944 to build factories to provide employment for Jewish refugees arriving during WWII.

An Arab attack quickly followed Israel's creation in 1948. Israel prevailed, but the threat of future conflicts spurred development of its defense industry. In 1952 Koor teamed with a Finnish firm to create Soltam, an Israeli artillery manufacturer. The previous year, it had diversified into telecommunications equipment with Telrad.

Koor continued to expand and diversify through joint ventures, creating a steel company in 1954 and Alliance Tire & Rubber in 1955 (it bought full control of Alliance in 1983). Koor and the Israeli government founded Tadiran (defense electronics, 1962), and Koor acquired chemical maker Makhteshim (1963) and food processor Hamashbir Lata (1970). The Sinai campaign (1956), Six-Day War (1967), and Yom Kippur War (1973) continued to spur Israeli defense spending. However, with Histadrut's emphasis on socialist aims, Koor never became very profitable. Successful subsidiaries were offset by money-losers.

The company was hurt in the 1980s by a government program that cut subsidies and lowered trade barriers. Inflation damaged Koor's global competitiveness. With the help of junk bond guru Michael Milken, Koor raised $105 million in a 1986 debt issue. That year, however, Koor posted its first loss in 20 years, and losses widened in 1987. Benjamin Gaon became CEO in 1988 and began restructuring the heavily indebted company, which by then had about 130 units. He kept closing plants, but the company incurred a loss

in 1988 and a record $369 million deficit in 1989. Gaon negotiated a new arrangement with creditors in 1991.

By 1992 Gaon's cost cutting had begun to pay off, and the company returned to profitability. Histadrut sold out in 1995, severing a link to Koor's socialist past. That year the company raised nearly $120 million in an international IPO, and Northern Telecom (now Nortel Networks) acquired 20% of Telrad (sold back to Koor in 2000).

Koor continued divesting assets to focus on its core businesses. ITT Sheraton International took a 50% stake in Koor Tourism in a 1996 alliance to manage hotels in Israel, and Henkel bought 50% of Koor's detergent operations. Discontinued operations included Beep-A-Call (wireless paging, 1995), Gamda Trade (food retail, 1996), and TAMI (food industry, 1997).

In 1995 Gaon sowed the seeds for his departure by selling a controlling stake in Koor to the Shamrock Group, a Disney family investment firm. Disagreements with Gaon over Koor's strategy led Shamrock to sell its stake in 1997 to Claridge Israel, an investment fund controlled by Canadian billionaire Charles Bronfman. Jonathan Kolber, then CEO of Claridge Israel, replaced Gaon in 1998.

Kolber made plans to increase exports and focus on Koor's telecom equipment, defense electronics, and agrochemicals segments, while scaling back in construction materials. In 1998 Koor bought a stake in Israel's ECI Telecom, which merged with Tadiran Telecom in 1999. Koor also dumped several noncore assets (including cable TV, energy, and software services units), raising more than $360 million. It then sold its 50% stake in cement group Mashav.

In 2000 Koor and Nortel Networks launched Nortel Networks Israel to deliver high-performance Internet products to carrier and enterprise customers. The restructuring of the Elisra Group (formerly the Elisra-Tadiran Group) was completed in 2001. The next year Koor sold a 30% stake in Elisra Electronics Systems to government-owned Israel Aircraft Industries.

EXECUTIVES

Chairman: Charles F. Bronfman, age 72
Vice Chairman and CEO: Jonathan Kolber, age 41
President: Danny Biran, age 60
SVP and CFO: Yuval Yanai, age 51
VP: Aron Zuker, age 57
Managing Director, Koor Corporate Venture Capital: Jackie Goren
General Counsel and Corporate Secretary: Shlomo Heller, age 60
Auditors: Somekh Chaikin

LOCATIONS

HQ: Koor Industries Inc.
  14 Hamelacha St., Rosh Ha'ayin 48091, Israel
Phone: +972-3-623-8333 **Fax:** +972-3-623-8334
Web: www.koor.com

PRODUCTS/OPERATIONS

2002 Sales

	% of total
Agrochemicals	58
Defense electronics	24
Telecommunications	12
Other	6
Total	**100**

Selected Subsidiaries and Affiliates

Agrochemicals
Makhteshim-Agan Industries Ltd. (53%)
Defense Electronics
Elisra Electronics Systems (70%)
BVR Systems (46%)
Spectralink
Tadiran Electronic Systems

Telecommunications Equipment
ECI Telecom Ltd. (30%)
Nortel Networks Israel (28%)
Telrad Networks

Venture Capital Investments
Koor Corporate Venture Capital

Other
Knafaim-Arkia Holdings (28%, flight and tourism operator)
Koor Trade
Sheraton-Moriah Israel (hotels, 55%)

COMPETITORS

Alcatel	The Israel Corporation
Ampal-American Israel	Lucent
Clal Industries	NEC
DuPont	Oryx Technology
Elron	Philips Electronics
GE	Raytheon
Gilat Satellite	Rockwell Automation
Harris Corp	Siemens
Hughes Electronics	Toshiba

HISTORICAL FINANCIALS

Company Type: Public

Income Statement

FYE: December 31

	REVENUE ($ mil.)	NET INCOME ($ mil.)	NET PROFIT MARGIN	EMPLOYEES
12/02	1,528	(165)	—	6,899
12/01	1,618	(575)	—	7,297
12/00	2,049	66	3.2%	8,680
12/99	2,571	132	5.1%	8,680
12/98	3,034	11	0.4%	15,035
12/97	3,565	138	3.9%	21,500
12/96	3,525	181	5.1%	21,000
12/95	3,256	156	4.8%	20,600
12/94	2,804	129	4.6%	20,700
12/93	2,360	126	5.4%	17,184
Annual Growth	(4.7%)	—	—	(9.6%)

2002 Year-End Financials

Debt ratio: 120.0%
Return on equity: —
Cash ($ mil.): 5
Current ratio: 1.07
Long-term debt ($ mil.): 446
No. of shares (mil.): 76
Dividends
Yield: 0.0%
Payout: —
Market value ($ mil.): 159

Stock History

NYSE: KOR

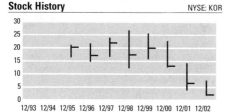

12/93 12/94 12/95 12/96 12/97 12/98 12/99 12/00 12/01 12/02

	STOCK PRICE ($) FY Close	P/E High/Low	PER SHARE ($) Earnings	Dividends	Book Value
12/02	2.10	— —	(0.44)	0.00	4.90
12/01	6.51	— —	(7.56)	0.00	6.27
12/00	13.13	21 12	1.08	0.70	10.32
12/99	20.00	15 10	1.66	0.42	13.42
12/98	17.44	177 83	0.15	0.62	12.30
12/97	21.94	14 10	1.74	0.00	14.65
12/96	17.13	9 7	2.27	0.24	13.96
12/95	20.25	10 8	2.09	0.00	11.40
Annual Growth	(27.7%)	— —	—	—	(11.4%)

KPMG International

Businesses all over the world count on KPMG for accounting. The firm is the most geographically dispersed of accounting's Big Four, which also includes Deloitte Touche Tohmatsu, Ernst & Young, and PricewaterhouseCoopers. KPMG has reorganized its operations, transforming itself from a confederation of accounting firms into three more closely linked regional units: the Americas, Europe/Middle East/Africa, and Asia/Pacific. The firm's offerings include assurance, tax, and financial advisory services. KPMG is discontinuing its KLegal International network, which includes some 3,000 lawyers around the world.

After much regulatory pressure, KPMG separated its accounting and consulting operations; it sold a chunk of the consulting business to networking equipment maker Cisco Systems, then took it public and sold off its shares in 2002. The consulting unit, which in 2002 changed its name to BearingPoint, is buying KPMG's Austrian, German, and Swiss consulting businesses.

In 2003 the SEC charged the firm and four partners with fraud in relation to alleged profit inflation at former client Xerox in the late 1990s.

HISTORY

Peat Marwick was founded in 1911, when William Peat, a London accountant, met James Marwick during an Atlantic crossing. University of Glasgow alumni Marwick and Roger Mitchell had formed Marwick, Mitchell & Company in New York in 1897. Peat and Marwick agreed to ally their firms temporarily, and in 1925 they merged as Peat, Marwick, Mitchell, & Copartners.

In 1947 William Black became senior partner, a position he held until 1965. He guided the firm's 1950 merger with Barrow, Wade, Guthrie, one of the US's oldest firms, and built its consulting practice. Peat Marwick restructured its international practice as PMM&Co. (International) in 1972 (renamed Peat Marwick International in 1978).

The next year several European accounting firms led by Klynveld Kraayenhoff (the Netherlands) and Deutsche Treuhand (Germany) began forming an international accounting federation. Needing an American member, the European firms encouraged the merger of two American firms founded around the turn of the

century, Main Lafrentz and Hurdman Cranstoun. Main Hurdman & Cranstoun joined the Europeans to form Klynveld Main Goerdeler (KMG), named after two of the member firms and the chairman of Deutsche Treuhand, Reinhard Goerdeler. Other members were C. Jespersen (Denmark), Thorne Riddel (Canada), Thomson McLintok (UK), and Fides Revision (Switzerland).

Peat Marwick merged with KMG in 1987 to form Klynveld Peat Marwick Goerdeler (KPMG). KPMG lost 10% of its business as competing client companies departed. Professional staff departures followed in 1990 when, as part of a consolidation, the firm trimmed its partnership rolls.

In the 1990s the then-Big Six accounting firms all faced lawsuits arising from an evolving standard holding auditors responsible for the substance, rather than merely the form, of clients' accounts. KPMG was hit by suits stemming from its audits of defunct S&Ls and litigation relating to the bankruptcy of Orange County, California (settled for $75 million in 1998). Nevertheless KPMG kept growing; it expanded its consulting division with the acquisition of banking consultancy Barefoot, Marrinan & Associates in 1996.

In 1997, after Price Waterhouse and Coopers & Lybrand announced their merger, KPMG and Ernst & Young announced one of their own. But they called it quits the next year, fearing that regulatory approval of the deal would be too onerous.

The creation of PricewaterhouseCoopers (PwC) and increasing competition in the consulting sides of all of the Big Five brought a realignment of loyalties in their national practices. KPMG Consulting's Belgian group moved to PwC and its French group to Computer Sciences Corporation. Andersen nearly wooed away KPMG's Canadian consulting group, but the plan was foiled by the ever-sullen Andersen Consulting group (now Accenture) and by KPMG's promises of more money. Against this background, KPMG sold 20% of its consulting operations to Cisco Systems for $1 billion. In addition to the cash infusion, the deal allowed KPMG to provide installation and system management to Cisco's customers.

Even while KPMG worked on the IPO of its consulting group (which took place in 2001), it continued to rail against the SEC as it called for relationships between consulting and auditing organizations to be severed. In 2002 KPMG sold its British and Dutch consultancy units to France's Atos Origin.

EXECUTIVES

Chairman, KPMG International and KPMG UK: Michael (Mike) Rake, age 55
VC and Managing Partner, Global Markets: Hiroaki Yoshihara
CEO: Robert W. Alspaugh, age 56
COO: Colin Holland
CFO: Joseph E. Heintz
Chairman and CEO, KPMG LLP: Eugene D. O'Kelly, age 51
Chairman, Corporate Finance: David M. Beever, age 62
Chairman, Asian Anchor Practice: Marvin K.T. Cheung
Deputy Chairman, KPMG LLP: Jeffrey M. Stein, age 49
Vice Chairman, Assurance & Advisory Services, KPMG LLP: Timothy P. Flynn
Vice Chairman, Human Resources, KPMG LLP: Kathy H. Hannan
Vice Chairman, Marketing & Communications, KPMG LLP: Timothy R. Pearson
Vice Chairman, Tax Services, KPMG LLP: Richard Smith
CEO, KLegal International: Robert Glennie
National Partner in Charge, State and Local Tax Practice (SALT), KPMG LLP: Michael H. (Mike) Lippman

Partner in Charge, NY Financial Services, KPMG LLP:
 Robert F. Arning
Partner in Charge, Corporate Finance: Stephen Barrett
Managing Partner, Legal Services: Hartwich Lübmann
Managing Partner, Assurance: Rolf Nonnenmacher
General Counsel, KPMG LLP: Claudia L. Taft

LOCATIONS

HQ: Burgemeester Rijnderslaan 10,
 1185 MC Amstelveen, The Netherlands
Phone: +31-20-656-7890   **Fax:** +31-20-656-7700
US HQ: 345 Park Ave., New York, NY 10154
US Phone: 212-758-9700   **US Fax:** 212-758-9819
Web: www.kpmg.com

KPMG International has offices in more than 150 countries.

PRODUCTS/OPERATIONS

Selected Services

Assurance
Financial statement audits
Information risk management
Management assurance services

Corporate Finance Advisory
Insolvency services
Investigations
Restructuring and turnaround

Forensic Services
Dispute resolution
Intellectual property
Litigation services
Risk advisory

Tax and Legal
Global transfer pricing services
Indirect tax services
International corporate tax services
International executive services
Mergers and acquisitions
Trade and customs services

Transaction Services
Stock exchange reporting
Strategic and commercial intelligence
Transaction evaluation
Transaction structuring
Vendor assistance

COMPETITORS

Aon	H&R Block
Bain & Company	Hewitt Associates
Baker Tilly International	Marsh & McLennan
BDO International	McKinsey & Company
Booz Allen	PricewaterhouseCoopers
Deloitte Touche Tohmatsu	Towers Perrin
Ernst & Young	Watson Wyatt
Grant Thornton	
International	

HISTORICAL FINANCIALS

Company Type: Partnership

Income Statement

FYE: September 30

	REVENUE ($ mil.)	NET INCOME ($ mil.)	NET PROFIT MARGIN	EMPLOYEES
9/02	10,720	—	—	98,000
9/01	11,700	—	—	103,000
9/00	10,700	—	—	108,000
9/99	12,200	—	—	102,000
9/98	10,600	—	—	85,300
9/97	9,200	—	—	83,500
9/96	8,100	—	—	77,000
9/95	7,500	—	—	72,000
9/94	6,600	—	—	76,200
9/93	6,000	—	—	76,200
Annual Growth	**6.7%**	**—**	**—**	**2.8%**

Revenue History

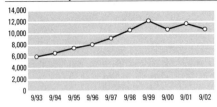

Kubota Corporation

Kubota is an old hand when it comes to turning Japanese soil. The Osaka-based company, which dates to 1890, is Japan's top maker of tractors and farm equipment such as rice transplanters and combine harvesters. It also leads the nation in the production of iron ductile pipe used in water-supply systems. Kubota, a diversified enterprise, makes industrial castings (ductile tunnel segments), PVC pipe, building materials (siding, cement roofing, and prefabricated houses), waste-recycling plants, and agricultural and industrial engines. In addition, the company builds water- and sewage-treatment plants, and it makes vending machines for cigarettes and beverages.

Kubota, which has suffered from the Japanese economic downturn (about 80% of its sales are in Japan), has reorganized its businesses, cut thousands of jobs, and reduced costs throughout the company in an effort to streamline its operations and return to profitability. Cost reduction and improved efficiency remain top goals for the company as it expects conditions to remain bleak. That said, Kubota believes its overseas tractor business has good room for growth. The company is less optimistic about its environmental engineering businesses because Japan has reduced its public works expenditures.

HISTORY

The son of a poor farmer and coppersmith, Gonshiro Oode left home in 1885 at age 14 and moved to Osaka to find work. He began as an apprentice at the Kuro Casting Shop, where he learned about metal casting. He saved his money and in 1890 opened Oode Casting.

Oode's shop grew rapidly, thanks to the industrialization of the Japanese economy and the expansion of the iron and steel industries. One of Oode's customers, Toshiro Kubota, took a liking to the hardworking young man, and in 1897 Kubota adopted him. Oode changed his own name to Kubota and also changed the name of his company to Kubota Iron Works.

Kubota made a number of technological breakthroughs in the early 1900s, including a new method of producing cast-iron pipe (developed in 1900). The company became the first to make the pipe in Japan, and it continued to grow as the country modernized its infrastructure.

Kubota began making steam engines, machine tools, and agricultural engines in 1917, and it also began exporting products to countries in

Southeast Asia. In 1930 Kubota restructured and incorporated. It continued to add product lines, including agricultural and industrial motors.

Although WWII brought massive destruction to Japan, the peacetime that followed created plenty of work for Kubota's farm equipment and pipe operations as the country rebuilt. By 1960 the company was Japan's largest maker of farm equipment, ductile iron pipe, and cement roofing materials. That year Kubota introduced the first small agricultural tractor in Japan.

Over the next three decades, Kubota expanded its products and its geographic reach. The company created subsidiaries in Taiwan (1961), the US (1972), Iran (1973), France (1974), and Thailand (1977). It also made a major push into the US high-tech industry during the 1980s with the 44% purchase of supercomputer graphics company Ardent (1985). Two years later Kubota bought disk company Akashic Memories, and in 1989 it formed a joint venture with disk drive maker Maxtor to build optical storage products.

While loading up on high-tech operations, Kubota also expanded its lower-tech core businesses in the US. The company opened its first US manufacturing plant in 1989 in Georgia to make front-end loader attachments, and in 1990 it bought a 5% interest in Cummins Engine.

The next year Kubota took over the operations of struggling Stardent Computers; however, Kubota was unable to revive the graphic workstation business and dissolved its Kubota Graphics subsidiary in California in 1994.

In 1995 Kubota formed subsidiary Kubota Biotech to develop and sell biotechnological products such as biological insecticides. The next year Kubota launched a rice-cultivation machine for use in large fields.

Kubota gave its unprofitable computer hard disk business the boot in 1997 with the sale of Akashic Memories and the management buyout of subsidiary Maxoptix (computer memory storage drives). In 1998 the company formed a joint venture in China to make cast-steel products, and the following year it established a subsidiary there to make combine harvesters.

With its sales decreasing in response to Japan's economic slowdown, in 2000 Kubota implemented a three-year cost-cutting strategy. It began cutting its workforce by about 13% and jettisoning unprofitable businesses. The company's net sales increased in 2001, the result in part of its introduction of sub-compact tractors to the US the previous year. Kubota continued slimming down in 2002, exiting its Kubota Concrete (concrete piles) and Kubota House (pre-manufactured housing) businesses.

EXECUTIVES

President and Representative Director:
 Daisuke Hatakake
EVP and Representative Director: Mikio Kinoshita
EVP and Representative Director: Tomomi Soh
Executive Managing Director: Tsuyoshi Hayashi
Executive Managing Director: Tadahiko Kinoshita
Managing Director: Yoshihiro Fujio
Managing Director: Moriya Hayashi
Managing Director: Masaru Ishiguro
Managing Director: Akio Nishino
Managing Director: Akira Seike
Managing Director: Toshiyuki Yotsumoto
Director: Toshihiro Fukuda
Director: Nobuo Izawa
Director: Junichi Maeda

Director: Yasuo Masumoto
Director: Yoshiharu Nishiguchi
Director: Eisaku Shinohara
Director: Teisuke Sono
Director: Tadahiko Urabe
Director: Masateru Yoshikawa
Auditors: Deloitte Touche Tohmatsu

LOCATIONS

HQ: 2-47, Shikitsuhigashi 1-chome, Naniwa-ku, Osaka
 556-8601, Japan
Phone: +81-6-6648-2111   **Fax:** +81-6-6648-3862
US HQ: 2715 Ramsey Rd., Gainesville, GA 30501
US Phone: 770-532-0038   **US Fax:** 770-532-9057
Web: www.kubota.co.jp

Kubota has primary manufacturing facilities in Japan, and it has subsidiaries and affiliates in the Americas, Asia, Australia, Europe, and the Pacific Rim region.

2003 Sales

	$ mil.	% of total
Japan	6,976	79
North America	1,337	15
Other regions	470	6
Adjustments	(1,066)	—
Total	**7,717**	**100**

PRODUCTS/OPERATIONS

2003 Sales

	$ mil.	% of total
Internal combustion engine & machinery	3,701	48
Pipes, valves & industrial castings	1,477	19
Environmental engineering	1,137	15
Building materials & housing	536	7
Other	866	11
Total	**7,717**	**100**

Selected Products

Internal Combustion Engine & Machinery
Ancillary tools & implements for agriculture
Construction machinery
 Carriers
 Mini-excavators
 Welders
 Wheel loaders
Engines
 Gasoline & diesel engines for farming & industrial
  purposes
Farm facilities
 Cleaning & vending machines for rice
 Cooperative facilities for rice seedlings
 Dairy & stock raising facilities
 Farm facilities
 Gardening facilities
 Multipurpose warehouse
 Rice driers
 Rice mill plants
Farm machinery
 Combine harvesters
 Harvesters
 Power tillers
 Reaper binders
 Rice transplanters
 Tillers
 Tractors
Outdoor power equipment
Lawn & garden equipment

Pipes, Valves & Industrial Castings
Castings
Cargo oil pipes
Cast steel products
Castings for engines
Castings for machinery
Cast-iron soil pipes
Ductile tunnel segments
G-columns
G-piles
Reformer tubes
Rolls for steel mills
Suction roll shells for paper industry

Pipes
Ductile iron pipes
Filament winding pipes
Plastic valves
Polyethylene pipes
Polyvinyl chloride pipes & fittings
Spiral welded steel pipes

Environmental Engineering
Amusement fountains

Building Materials and Housing
Cement siding materials
Colored cement roofing materials
Condominiums
Photovoltaic shingles
Septic tanks

COMPETITORS

AGCO	Isuzu
Caterpillar	Komatsu
CNH Global	Lafarge SA
Deere	Nippon Steel
Fiat	Sekisui House
Fuji Electric	

HISTORICAL FINANCIALS

Company Type: Public

Income Statement

FYE: March 31

	REVENUE ($ mil.)	NET INCOME ($ mil.)	NET PROFIT MARGIN	EMPLOYEES
3/03	7,718	(67)	—	22,834
3/02	7,339	72	1.0%	23,064
3/01	8,020	79	1.0%	25,369
3/00	9,314	155	1.7%	24,334
3/99	8,072	125	1.5%	24,900
3/98	7,799	165	2.1%	20,000
3/97	9,206	233	2.5%	18,500
3/96	10,110	243	2.4%	21,000
3/95	11,393	226	2.0%	16,046
3/94	9,510	80	0.8%	16,046
Annual Growth	**(2.3%)**	**—**	**—**	**4.0%**

2003 Year-End Financials

Debt ratio: 49.4%
Return on equity: —
Cash ($ mil.): 561
Current ratio: 1.44
Long-term debt ($ mil.): 1,300
No. of shares (mil.): 269
Dividends
 Yield: 1.9%
 Payout: —
Market value ($ mil.): 3,485

Stock History

NYSE: KUB

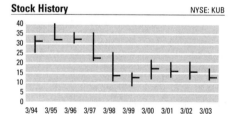

	STOCK PRICE ($) FY Close	P/E High	P/E Low	PER SHARE ($) Earnings	PER SHARE ($) Dividends	PER SHARE ($) Book Value
3/03	12.95	—	—	(0.24)	0.24	9.77
3/02	15.75	83	49	0.25	0.24	2.64
3/01	16.06	—	—	(0.40)	0.27	3.11
3/00	17.38	42	24	0.52	0.25	3.76
3/99	12.81	36	21	0.42	0.11	3.11
3/98	13.81	47	21	0.54	0.00	2.36
3/97	22.75	47	28	0.76	0.12	2.54
3/96	32.25	46	39	0.78	0.13	2.75
3/95	32.00	51	41	0.78	0.26	3.20
3/94	31.25	121	92	0.28	0.24	2.68
Annual Growth	**(9.3%)**	**—**	**—**	**—**	**0.0%**	**15.5%**

Kyocera Corporation

Don't confuse Kyocera's ceramics with pots and planters. The company makes a wide range of components and fine ceramic products primarily for the electronics industry, including capacitors, fiber-optic connectors, and semiconductor components. It is the world's largest maker of integrated ceramic packages for computers. Kyocera also makes ceramic products for other applications, such as cutting tools, dental products, jewelry, and solar panels. In addition to components, the company makes a number of finished electronics products, including cellular handsets, copiers, fax machines, and cameras.

Kyocera has been hit hard by weak demand for electronics and telecommunications gear, as more than 80% of the company's business comes from customers in the information technology and telecom markets. In response, the company is looking to diversify its customer base by developing products for new markets, such as components for the automotive industry.

Kyocera is also expanding its manufacturing operations in China and consolidating operations elsewhere to cut costs. The company has operations in the Americas, Asia, and Europe; Japan accounts for almost 40% of sales.

HISTORY

Born to a poor Japanese family in 1932, Kazuo Inamori never quite fit the mold. He went to work for Shofu Industries (ceramic insulators) in the mid-1950s, but quit three years later and started Kyoto Ceramic with seven colleagues in 1959. Their first product was a ceramic insulator for cathode-ray tubes. In the late 1960s the company developed the ceramic package for integrated circuits (ICs) that has made it a world-class supplier.

Kyoto Ceramic started manufacturing in the US in 1971. A few years later the company began to diversify its interests when it ventured into artificial gemstones (Crescent Vert, 1977) and dental implants (New Medical, 1978). In 1979 Inamori bought control of failing Cybernet Electronics (Japanese citizens-band radio maker), using it to move Kyoto Ceramic into the production of copiers and stereos.

The company merged five subsidiaries in 1982, forming Kyocera Corporation. The 1983 acquisition of Yashica moved it into the production of cameras and other optical equipment. That year Kyocera ran into trouble. At the time Nippon Telegraph and Telephone (NTT) was the only legal supplier of phones in Japan, and when Kyocera started marketing cordless phones without the required approval, the government forced it to recall the phones.

The government abolished NTT's monopoly in 1984, and Kyocera joined 24 other companies to form Daini-Denden ("second phone company") — now KDDI. In 1988 Inamori set up Kyocera regional offices in Asia, Europe, and the US. The company bought Elco (electronic connectors, US) in 1989 and AVX (multilayer ceramic capacitors, US) in 1990.

In order to diversify further, Kyocera entered into a series of alliances in the 1990s that included partnerships with Canon to produce video and electronic optical equipment, with

Carl Zeiss (Germany) to make cameras and lenses, and with Cirrus Logic to make chips for a cordless phone project.

The company's Guangdong-based optical instrument joint venture began making cameras and lenses for the Chinese market in 1996. The next year Inamori went into partial retirement. Kyocera's bottom line suffered in 1997 and 1998, largely because of the worldwide semiconductor slump and a troubled Asian economy. In 1998 the company took over failed copier maker Mita Industrial, which had been a major buyer of Kyocera's electronic components.

In 1999 Kyocera acquired Golden Genesis (solar electric systems, US) and changed the company's name to Kyocera Solar, Inc. In the same year Kyocera's product line grew even more diverse as it entered the health food market and began selling mushroom products in Japan. Kyocera purchased the wireless phone business of QUALCOMM in early 2000.

Also in early in 2000 the company's acquisition of failed copier maker Mita Industrial (which changed its name to Kyocera Mita Corporation) was approved. The deal included the forgiveness (by Mita's creditors) of most of Mita's debt and a cash infusion in Kyocera Mita by Kyocera. As economic conditions worsened during 2001, the company was forced to begin cutting its workforce and consolidate some operations.

EXECUTIVES

Chairman Emeritus: Kazuo Inamori, age 71
Chairman: Kensuke Itoh, age 65
President; Chairman, Kyocera Communication Systems: Yasuo Nishiguchi, age 60
EVP and General Manager, Corporate Development Division: Masahiro Umemura, age 60
EVP and General Manager, Corporate General Affairs Division: Michihisa Yamamoto, age 61
President, Kyocera ELCO: Yuzo Yamamura, age 62
President, Kyocera Communication Systems: Naoyuki Morita, age 61
President, Kyocera Mita: Koji Seki, age 66
EVP, Kyocera Chemical: Noboru Nakamura, age 59
Senior Managing Director: Isao Kishimoto, age 60
EVP, Kyocera Tianjin Sales and Trading: Hisao Hisaki, age 57
President, Kyocera International: Rodney N. Lanthorne, age 58
Managing Director; President and CEO, AVX Corporation: John S. Gilbertson, age 60
General Manager, Corporate Solar Energy Division: Isao Yukawa
Deputy General Manager, Corporate General Affairs Division: Hisashi Sakumi
General Manager, Corporate Business Systems Administration Division: Hideki Ishida
Auditors: PricewaterhouseCoopers

LOCATIONS

HQ: 6 Takeda Tobadono-cho, Fushimi-ku, Kyoto 612-8501, Japan
Phone: +81-75-604-3500   **Fax:** +81-75-604-3501
US HQ: 8611 Balboa Ave., San Diego, CA 92123
US Phone: 858-576-2600   **US Fax:** 858-492-1456
Web: www.kyocera.co.jp

Kyocera has operations throughout the Americas, Asia, and Europe.

2003 Sales

	$ mil.	% of total
Asia		
Japan	3,586	39
Other countries	1,512	17
US	2,244	25
Europe	1,223	13
Other regions	501	6
Total	**9,066**	**100**

PRODUCTS/OPERATIONS

2003 Sales

	$ mil.	% of total
Electronic equipment	4,490	49
Fine ceramics	2,024	22
Electronic devices	1,932	21
Other	731	8
Adjustments	(111)	—
Total	**9,066**	**100**

Selected Products

Electronic Equipment
Information equipment
  Copy machines
  Facsimile machines
  Page printers (Ecosys)
Optical instruments
  Compact zoom cameras
  Digital cameras
  SLR cameras and lenses
Telecommunications equipment
  Cellular handsets
  Personal Handyphone System (PHS) products (base stations handsets)
  Wireless local loop systems

Electronic Devices
Capacitors
High-frequency modules
Thin-film products
Timing devices (TCXOs, VCOs)

Fine Ceramics
Consumer-related products
  Cutting tools (Ceratip)
  Dental and orthopedic implants (Bioceram)
  Jewelry and applied ceramic products (Crescent Vert)
  Solar energy products
Fine ceramic parts
  Ceramic substrates
  Fiber-optic network components
  OA equipment components
  Parts for semiconductor fabrication equipment
Semiconductor parts
  Ceramic dual-in-line packages (Cerdips)
  Metalized products
  Multilayer packages
  Organic packages

Other Products and Services
Credit finance
Hotel operations
Leasing
Office renting

COMPETITORS

Canon	NGK INSULATORS
Ericsson	NTT
Fuji Photo	Nokia
Fujitsu	Oki Electric
Hewlett-Packard	Philips Electronics
Hitachi	Ricoh
IBIDEN	Samsung
IBM	SANYO
Lexmark International	Seiko
LG Electronics	Sharp
Lucent	Sony
Matsushita	TDK
Motorola	Toshiba
Murata Manufacturing	Xerox
NEC	

HISTORICAL FINANCIALS

Company Type: Public

Income Statement

FYE: March 31

	REVENUE ($ mil.)	NET INCOME ($ mil.)	NET PROFIT MARGIN	EMPLOYEES
3/03	9,066	349	3.8%	49,420
3/02	7,779	240	3.1%	44,235
3/01	10,199	1,742	17.1%	51,113
3/00	7,779	489	6.3%	—
3/99	6,007	239	4.0%	—
3/98	5,454	354	6.5%	—
3/97	5,764	368	6.4%	13,270
3/96	6,048	771	12.8%	13,162
3/95	5,760	500	8.7%	13,300
3/94	4,177	359	8.6%	13,470
Annual Growth	**9.0%**	**(0.3%)**	**—**	**15.5%**

2003 Year-End Financials

Debt ratio: 6.1%
Return on equity: 4.3%
Cash ($ mil.): 2,528
Current ratio: 2.13
Long-term debt ($ mil.): 515
No. of shares (mil.): 185
Dividends
  Yield: 1.0%
  Payout: 26.2%
Market value ($ mil.): 9,117

Stock History

NYSE: KYO

	STOCK PRICE ($) FY Close	P/E High/Low		PER SHARE ($) Earnings	Dividends	Book Value
3/03	49.29	41	24	1.87	0.49	45.98
3/02	70.00	79	40	1.27	0.48	41.19
3/01	92.50	20	8	9.19	0.55	42.62
3/00	166.00	109	20	2.58	0.50	41.00
3/99	52.63	47	32	1.26	0.22	34.26
3/98	53.63	46	23	1.86	0.45	30.42
3/97	56.88	40	27	1.96	0.27	30.62
3/96	67.25	22	15	4.10	0.24	33.35
3/95	72.75	29	23	2.66	0.43	35.74
3/94	62.50	35	21	1.92	0.39	28.30
Annual Growth	**(2.6%)**	**—**	**—**	**(0.3%)**	**2.6%**	**5.5%**

Lagardère SCA

Lagardère is flying high with its mix of media, missiles, and motor vehicles. The company's primary holdings include publisher Hachette Filipacchi Médias (*Elle, Premier,* and *Car & Driver*) and a 15% stake in #3 aerospace firm European Aeronautic Defence and Space Company, which produces defense and weapon systems, military aircraft, satellites and space systems, and commercial aircraft. The firm's other media holdings include book publishing (Hachette Livre), Internet content (Lagardère Active), and satellite television (34%-owned CanalSatellite). Lagardère is also involved in the automotive industry through its Matra Automobile unit. The conglomerate's media operations account for more than 60% of its revenue.

Eager to continue the growth of its media operations, Lagardère has been studying a number of possible acquisitions. The company is buying the assets of Vivendi Universal Publishing, (VUP) with the exception of the Houghton Mifflin educational subsidiary, from troubled media giant Vivendi Universal. (Vivendi Universal has sold VUP to investment bank Investima 10, from which Lagardère will then buy the company.)

The company is also beginning to leverage its established print brands across other mediums such as television and the Internet through Lagardère Active. Lagardère has expanded its retailing business through its purchase of 16 French Virgin Megastores from Richard Branson's Virgin Group. General partner and co-CEO Arnaud Lagardère owns about 5% of the company through Lagardère Capital & Management.

HISTORY

Jean-Luc Lagardère began his rise to industrial titan when he joined French aerospace contractor Dassault as an engineer in the 1950s. He was tapped to be president and CEO of military equipment manufacturer Mécanique Aviation TRAction (Matra) in 1963, where he pushed the firm to branch out into electronics, space systems, and automobiles during the 1970s. Lagardère turned his focus to the media world in 1981 when he joined with Filipacchi Médias to acquire control of venerable French publishing firm Hachette.

Started by schoolteacher Louis Hachette in 1826, the publishing firm first catered to the textbook market and later began producing general trade books and travel guides. It became involved in the newspaper business in the 1920s and launched fashion magazine *Elle* in 1945. A diversification strategy in the 1970s proved disastrous, however, leading to Lagardère's takeover.

The engineer-turned-entrepreneur launched international spinoffs of Hachette's magazines, including a successful US *Elle* in 1985 in partnership with media maven Rupert Murdoch. In the late 1980s Hachette invested in radio broadcasting, bought US magazine distributor Curtis Circulation, and acquired Spanish encyclopedia publisher Salvat. Meanwhile, Matra launched its Espace minivan in 1983 (marketed by Renault). In 1988 Hachette acquired encyclopedia publisher Grolier for $1.1 billion and later bought out Murdoch's share of *Elle*.

In 1990 Hachette bought a 25% stake in money-losing French TV network La Cinq. The station collapsed a year later, leaving Hachette with a $643 million write-off. To cover the huge debt, Lagardère merged Matra with Hachette in 1993 under the holding company that now bears his name. Its Matra division acquired British Aerospace's satellite division the next year and Hachette expanded its North American distribution business in 1995. Two years later Filipacchi Médias and Hachette Filipacchi Press merged to form Hachette Filipacchi Médias.

With French industry decreasing its reliance on defense business, Lagardère merged its Matra unit with France's state-owned aerospace firm, Aerospatiale, in 1999. Not long after, the new Aerospatiale Matra agreed to merge with Germany's DaimlerChrysler Aerospace and Spain's Construcciones Aeronauticas to form European Aeronautic Defence and Space Company (EADS). Completed the following year, the merger created the world's #3 aerospace company. (Lagardère retained a minority stake in the venture.)

Later in 2000 Lagardère sold Grolier to Scholastic Corp. for about $400 million and bought the rest of Hachette Filipacchi Médias from its minority shareholders. The same year Jean-Luc Lagardère escaped a 1988 fraud charge when a judge ruled that the time limit for prosecution had expired. To begin leveraging its media assets, the company created multimedia unit Lagardère Active in 2001.

Jean-Luc Lagardère died in 2003 of a rare neurological disease.

EXECUTIVES

General Partner and CEO, Lagardère Media; Chairman and CEO, Lagardère Active; Co-Chairman, EADS: Arnaud Lagardère, age 42
General Partner and Co-CEO, EADS: Phillippe Camus, age 56
EVP Human Relations and Communications: Thierry Funck-Brentano
EVP Legal and Administrative: Pierre Leroy
EVP and CFO: Dominique D'Hinnin
COO, Lagardère Media: Jean-Luc Allavena
VP Strategy and Development, Lagardère Media: Frèdèrique Bredin
Director Corporate Executive Office, Committee Secretary: Patrick Dechin
Management Committee Director, International: Jean-Paul Gut
Management Committee Director, Strategy: Jean-Louis Gergorin
Chairman and CEO, Matra Automobile: Philippe Guédon
Chairman and CEO, Hachette Distribution Services: Jean-Louis Nachury
Chairman and CEO, Hachette Filipacchi Médias: Gérald de Roquemaurel
Chairman and CEO, Hachette Livre: Arnaud Nourry
Co-Chairman, EADS: Manfred Bischoff, age 61
Co-CEO, EADS: Rainer Hertrich, age 54
CEO, Lagardère Newspapers: Ghislain Leleu
Auditors: Barbier Frinault & Autres; Mazars & Guérard; Alain Ghez

LOCATIONS

HQ: 4 rue de Presbourg, 75016 Paris, France
Phone: +33-1-40-69-1600   **Fax:** +33-1-40-69-2131
US HQ: 1633 Broadway, 45th Fl., New York, NY 10019
US Phone: 212-767-6753   **US Fax:** 212-767-5635
Web: www.lagardere.fr

2002 Sales

	$ mil.	% of total
Europe		
France	4,591	33
Other EU countries	3,691	27
Other countries	1,082	7
North America	3,425	26
Asia/Pacific	559	4
Middle East	199	1
Other regions	304	2
Ajustments	623	—
Total	**14,474**	**100**

PRODUCTS/OPERATIONS

2002 Sales

	$ mil.	% of total
Lagardère Media	8,485	62
High technology	4,548	32
Automobile	819	6
Adjustment	622	—
Total	**14,474**	**100**

COMPETITORS

Advance Publications	News Corp.
Axel Springer	Northrop Grumman
BAE SYSTEMS	NRJ
Bertelsmann	Pearson
Boeing	PRIMEDIA
Bombardier	Raytheon
Dawson Holdings	Siemens
Emap	Textron
Hearst	Time Warner
Lockheed Martin	Viacom
Meredith	Vivendi Universal
Modern Times Group	Walt Disney

HISTORICAL FINANCIALS

Company Type: Public

Income Statement

FYE: December 31

	REVENUE ($ mil.)	NET INCOME ($ mil.)	NET PROFIT MARGIN	EMPLOYEES
12/02	14,474	(305)	—	45,826
12/01	11,777	546	4.6%	46,337
12/00	12,173	547	4.5%	43,902
12/99	12,865	243	1.9%	49,285
12/98	1,967	50	2.5%	49,961
12/97	10,986	230	2.1%	46,230
12/96	10,778	198	1.8%	47,172
12/95	10,711	128	1.2%	43,622
12/94	9,934	115	1.2%	40,326
12/93	9,117	26	0.3%	41,394
Annual Growth	**5.3%**	**—**	**—**	**1.1%**

2002 Year-End Financials

Debt ratio: 74.1%   Current ratio: 1.77
Return on equity: —   Long-term debt ($ mil.): 2,860
Cash ($ mil.): 919

Net Income History

Euronext Paris: MMB

LEGO Company

At the LEGO Company, toy blocks are the building blocks of success. Since 1949 the Danish firm has sold more than 320 billion of its interlocking plastic toys, keeping little hands and imaginations busy around the globe. In a nod to kids' high-tech skills, it also offers LEGO kits to build PC-programmable robots (including Spybotics and Mindstorms), and its BIONICLE line features an evolving story line on the Internet and a variety of merchandising opportunities. The company also owns LEGO theme parks (in California, Denmark, Germany, and the UK), as well as LEGO retail outlets in the US and Europe. With operations in about 30 countries, LEGO is owned by the founding Kristiansen family.

The word LEGO is derived from the Danish words for "play well," and children have been playing well with the company's familiar building blocks for years. In fact, LEGO toys were named the Toy of the Century by *Fortune* magazine in 1999. In an effort to incorporate its blocks into the business world, LEGO has introduced a tool called Serious Play, which is designed to assist business managers by combining creative play with corporate strategizing. The company has been working to improve its recent disappointing sales performance with other product additions such as the widely successful Harry Potter and Bob the Builder lines, as well as forming alliances with the NHL, the NBA, and NIKE.

LEGO has entered into the arts and crafts market with the introduction of CLIKITS: a fashion design system made up of a variety of kits allowing girls (ages 6 and up) to design room decor, picture frames, jewelry, and fashion and hair accessories. The new product line targets the 'tween market (girls ages 7-14) and includes an initial marketing partnership with Limited Too (a fashion retailer with over 500 stores nationwide).

In addition to its toys and LEGOLAND theme parks (which feature LEGO sculptures, rides, and exhibits), the company produces television shows, educational materials, and merchandise such as books, video games, and computer game software. In late 2003 LEGO and Miramax Film Corp. debuted (on DVD and video) *BIONICLE: Mask of Light* — a 3-D animated film based on the BIONICLE toy line.

HISTORY

Ole Kirk Christiansen opened a carpentry shop in 1916 in Denmark and began making carved wooden toys in 1932. Two years later Ole held a contest among his employees to name the company, from which came LEGO (a combination of two Danish words, "leg" and "godt," meaning "play well"). A fire destroyed the LEGO factory in 1942, but the company quickly resumed manufacturing.

The availability of quality plastic following WWII prompted the company to add plastic toys to its line. The predecessor to the common LEGO block was invented in 1949; called Automatic Binding Bricks, they fit on top of each other but did not snap together.

After hearing criticism that no company made a comprehensive toy system, in 1954 Ole's son Godtfred assembled a list of 10 product criteria for LEGO's toys, including that they have lots of compatible components. Deciding that the Automatic Binding Bricks had the most potential, the firm launched the first LEGO playset in 1955. It introduced the "stud and tube" snap-together building block in 1958. LEGOs were soon one of the most popular toys in Europe. When a second fire in 1960 destroyed its warehouse for wooden toys, the company ceased production of wooden toys in favor of plastics.

Luggage-maker Samsonite began manufacturing and distributing LEGOs in the US in 1961 under license. LEGO's first LEGOLAND park, built from 42 million LEGO blocks, opened in Billund, Denmark, in 1968. (A UK park followed in 1996, a California park in 1999, and one in Germany in 2002.) By 1973, after relatively lackluster US sales, Samsonite opted not to renew its license, and The LEGO Company set up a sales and production facility in Connecticut. US sales increased tenfold by 1975.

Aiming for the preteen market, the company introduced the more-complex LEGO Technic model sets in 1977 and the popular LEGOLAND Space playset two years later. However, LEGO hit a bump when its patent for the LEGO brick expired in 1981 and a slew of knockoffs flooded the market.

The first LEGO Imagination Center opened in Minneapolis in 1992, and the second followed in Walt Disney World five years later. Two years later Godtfred died; his son, Kjeld, who changed the spelling of Christiansen to Kristiansen, succeeded him.

In the 1990s growth of the video game industry far outpaced the growth of the construction toys market, and LEGO suffered. With profits shrinking, in 1998 the company reversed its tradition of avoiding commercial tie-ins; it snapped together an agreement to produce building kits and figures based on the popular *Star Wars* movies and Walt Disney's Winnie the Pooh. However, those events came too late to prevent LEGO from suffering its first loss since the 1930s. The company began cutting up to 10% of its workers in 1999.

As part of its efforts to build up its interactive, electronic, and educational toy development, LEGO bought smart toys developer Zowie Intertainment in 2000, marking the first time the company purchased another toy maker. In 2001 LEGO inked a deal to create children's online games and activities for software giant Microsoft Corporation. After suffering its biggest annual loss since 1954, LEGO announced in 2001 it would cut 500 jobs and discontinue some non-core products.

EXECUTIVES

President and CEO: Kjeld Kirk Kristiansen, age 54
EVP and COO: Poul Plougmann, age 53
SVP, Brand Retail: Dominic Galvin, age 35
SVP, Global Brand Communications: Francesco Ciccolella
Interim President, LEGO Systems, US: Stig Toftgaard
President, LEGO Systems, US: Torp Laursen
Director of Communications: Peter Kjelstrup
Director of Global Business Support: Soeren Pedersen
Director of Human Resources: Christian Iversen
Director, Human Resources, LEGO Systems, US: Chrisa Connors
Brand Manager, CLIKITS: Joanna Gale

LOCATIONS

HQ: LEGO Center, DK-7190 Billund, Denmark
Phone: +45-79-50-60-70   **Fax:** +45-75-35-33-60
US HQ: 555 Taylor Rd., Enfield, CT 06083-1600
US Phone: 860-763-3211   **US Fax:** 860-763-6680
Web: www.lego.com

Selected Countries of Operation

Australia	The Netherlands
Austria	New Zealand
Belgium	Norway
Canada	Poland
China	Portugal
Czech Republic	Russia
Denmark	Singapore
Finland	South Africa
France	South Korea
Germany	Spain
Hong Kong	Sweden
Hungary	Switzerland
Italy	Taiwan
Japan	UK
Mexico	US

PRODUCTS/OPERATIONS

Selected Products

Action Wheelers
Animals
Baby Mickey
Basic sets
BIONICLE
CLIKITS (fashion design system for girls)
Galidor
Harry Potter
LEGO BABY toys
LEGO Belville toys (for girls)
LEGO Bob the Builder
LEGO Creator sets
LEGO EXPLORE toys(formerly LEGO DUPLO)
LEGO Life on Mars
LEGO Mindstorms toys
LEGO Mosaic (for adults)
LEGO MyBot
LEGO Scala toys (for girls)
LEGO SERIOUS PLAY (adult learning tool)
LEGO System toys
LEGO Technic
Little Forest Friends
RoboRiders
Rock Raiders
Speed Slammers
Star Wars
Town
Trains
Winnie The Pooh

Other Operations

LEGO Educational Division (materials for students and teachers in science and technology, biology, mathematics, geography, environmental studies, and history)
LEGO Imagination Center (retail stores)
LEGO Learning Institute (research into play, learning, and creativity)
LEGO Lifestyle (licensing agreements for children's clothes, watches, bags, books)
LEGO Media products (television production)
LEGOLAND Parks (theme parks)
LEGO Software

COMPETITORS

Bandai
Discovery Toys
Playmobil
Hasbro
Hershey Entertainment
JAKKS Pacific
Mattel
Mega Bloks
Strombecker
Toy Quest
VTech Holdings
Walt Disney
Zindart

HISTORICAL FINANCIALS

Company Type: Private

Income Statement

FYE: December 31

	REVENUE ($ mil.)	NET INCOME ($ mil.)	NET PROFIT MARGIN	EMPLOYEES
12/02	1,612	60	3.7%	8,297
12/01	1,266	51	4.0%	7,247
12/00	1,194	(105)	—	7,669
12/99	1,327	37	2.8%	7,821
12/98	1,200	(30)	—	8,670
12/97	1,115	9	0.8%	9,867
12/96	1,267	79	6.2%	9,450
12/95	1,230	77	6.3%	9,660
12/94	1,016	—	—	—
Annual Growth	5.9%	(3.5%)	—	(2.1%)

Net Income History

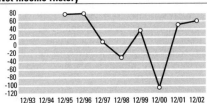

LG Group

LG Group used to be Lucky, but Asia's economic woes have brought hard times to this leading South Korean *chaebol* (family-run industrial group). Formerly Lucky Goldstar, the group consists of more than 50 affiliated companies that operate through more than 300 offices in more than 120 countries. Its major operations are divided into four business sectors: Chemicals & Energy (LG Chem, LG Petrochemical, and LG-Caltex), Electronics & Telecommunications (LG Electronics and Dacom), Finance (LG Investment & Securities), and Services (LG International and LG Engineering and Construction).

LG Group plans to simplify its ownership and management organization by reorganizing its operations into a traditional holding company structure. Korea's government has ordered the country's *chaebol* to streamline their operations and let member companies stand or fall on their own. The plan includes a reorganization of its subsidiaries into two holding companies led by its flagship companies, LG Electronics and LG Chemical. Following the restructuring, both companies will have separate ownership and management.

The company plans to expand its LG Electronics and LG Chemical groups by financing research and development activities centered around the enhancement of digital TV's, LCD's, bio-engineering, higher-end chemical goods, and other electronics and construction materials. In an effort to focus on its core operations, LG Group has divested its interest in subsidiaries DACOM IN, LG Cable, LG Caltex Gas, LG Nikko Copper, and Kukdong City Gas.

HISTORY

During WWII Koo In-Hwoi made tooth powder for Koreans to use in place of salt, then the common dentifrice. Koo founded the Lucky Chemical Company in 1947 to make facial creams and, later, detergent, shampoo, and Lucky Toothpaste. The enterprise soon became Korea's only plastics maker. Koo established a trading company in 1953.

Emulating Japanese exporters, Koo formed Goldstar Company in 1958 to make fans. The company became the first company in South Korea to make radios (1959), refrigerators (1965), TVs (1966), elevators and escalators (1968), and washing machines and air conditioners (1969). In 1967 Lucky collaborated with Caltex to build the Honam Oil Refinery, the first privately owned refinery in Korea. Both Lucky and Goldstar benefited from the *chaebol's* cozy relationship with President Park Chung Hee's government (1962-79) and used plentiful loans from Korean banks to diversify into everything from energy and semiconductors to insurance. Lucky began petrochemical production in 1977 and later built the world's largest single-unit petrochemical plant in Saudi Arabia (1986).

During the 1970s and 1980s, Goldstar expanded rapidly as it took advantage of cheap Korean labor to export private-label electronics items to its large retail customers abroad. In the late 1970s the group began investing heavily in semiconductor production, in part to fulfill its own chip requirements. Goldstar companies teamed with more technically accomplished partners, including AT&T, NEC, Hitachi, and Siemens, and set out to capture office-automation and higher-end consumer electronics markets with Goldstar-brand goods.

In 1983 the *chaebol* became Lucky Goldstar. Although electronics sales grew rapidly, Lucky Goldstar's inefficient organizational structure slowed progress, and in 1984 archrival Samsung finally outdid it. In the late 1980s Lucky Goldstar suffered from rising wage rates, labor unrest, and Korean currency appreciation. In 1989 the group created Goldstar Electron (LG Semicon Co.) and in 1990 business rebounded. Lucky Goldstar acquired 5% of US television maker Zenith in 1991.

In 1994 Lucky Goldstar signed an agreement with the government of the Sakha region in Russia to develop the Elga, the world's largest coal field. Lucky Goldstar became the LG Group in 1995, marking its new thrust: globalization. That year it acquired a controlling interest in troubled Zenith, by then the last TV manufacturer in the US.

The Asian contagion hit in 1997. LG Group announced that it would pull out of 90 business areas, but in 1998 it was one of several *chaebol* caught funneling money to ailing subsidiaries (the *chaebol* were collectively fined $93 million). LG Group members went abroad in 1998 looking for new partners: Among other deals, LG Chemicals allied with top drugmakers such as SmithKline Beecham (now GlaxoSmithKline), Warner-Lambert (now Pfizer), and Merck; and British Telecommunications (now BT Group) bought a nearly 25% stake in LG Telecom.

Under government pressure to consolidate scattered businesses with those of other *chaebol*, LG Group in 1999 agreed to sell LG Semicon and began restructuring its operations. After lengthy negotiations, the Hyundai Group took control of the unit, which became Hyundai MicroElectronics. Electronics giant Philips paid $1.6 billion for a 50% stake in LG Electronics' LCD unit. Meanwhile, LG Group acquired control of Dacom, one of Korea's top long-distance carriers and a leading ISP. In 2000 Dacom opened a high-speed Internet line linking Hong Kong, Japan, and Australia.

Looking for new markets, in 2001 LG's personal care products (detergents and diapers) unit LG Household & Healthcare Ltd., launched operations in India. In 2002, LG started its investment in research and development activities for its chemical and electronics business sectors. In 2003 LG sold its DACOM IN, LG Cable, LG Caltex Gas, LG Nikko Copper, and Kukdong City Gas subsidiaries in an effort to divest its non-core operations.

EXECUTIVES

Chairman; Chairman and CEO, LGCI and LGEI:
Koo Bon-Moo, age 58
Chairman and CEO, LG Electronics: John C. H. Koo, age 57
President and CEO, LG International: Lee Soo-Ho, age 59
CEO, Bumin Mutual Savings Bank: Koo Hyung-Woo
CEO, LG Engineering and Construction; EVP and
CEO, LG Cable: Han Dong-Kyu
CEO, LG-Caltex Oil: Hur Dong-Soo, age 60
CEO, LG Chem: No Ki-Ho, age 56
CEO, LG Economic Research Institute: Lee Youn-Ho
CEO, LG Electronics Investment and LG.Phillips LCD:
Koo (BJ) Bon-Joon, age 51
CEO, LG Energy and LG Power: Cho Bang-Rae
CEO, LG Futures: Sohn Bok-Jo
CEO, LG Investment and Securites: Suh Kyung-Suk
CEO, LG Investment Trust Management:
Park Kee-Hwan

CEO, LG Life Sciences: Yang Heung-Joon
CEO, LG Micron: Cho Young-Hwan
CEO, LG Petrochemical: Peter B. S. Kim, age 54
CEO, LG Siltron: Cheung Doo-Hoo, age 59
Auditors: Samil Accounting Corporation

LOCATIONS

HQ: LG Twin Towers, 20 Yoido-dong, Youngdungpo-gu, Seoul 150-721, South Korea
Phone: +82-2-3773-1114   **Fax:** +82-2-3773-7813
US HQ: 1000 Sylvan Ave., Englewood Cliffs, NJ 07632
US Phone: 201-816-3090   **US Fax:** 201-816-3094
Web: www.lg.co.kr

LG Group's companies operate in more than 120 countries.

PRODUCTS/OPERATIONS

Selected Subsidiaries and Affiliates

Chemicals and Energy
LG Chem Investment Ltd.
LG Chem Ltd.
LG Energy Corp.
LG Household & Healthcare Ltd.
LG MMA Corp. (joint venture, organic chemicals)
LG Petrochemical Co., Ltd.
LG Power Co., Ltd.
LG Siltron Inc. (silicon wafers)
LG-Caltex Gas Co., Ltd. (joint venture)
LG-Caltex Oil Corp. (joint venture)

Electronics and Telecommunications
Dacom Corp.
Hanaro Telecom, Inc.
LG Electronics Inc.
LG Industrial Systems Co., Ltd.
LG Micron Ltd.
LG Philips LCD Co. Ltd
LG TeleCom Ltd.

Finance
Bumin Mutual Savings & Finance Corp.
LG Capital Services Corp.
LG Futures Co., Ltd.
LG Investment & Securities Co., Ltd.
LG Investment Trust Management Co., Ltd.

Service (Trading)
LG Ad Inc.
LG Department Store Co., Ltd.
LG Engineering & Construction Co., Ltd.
LG Home Shopping Inc.
LG International Corp. (general trading)
LG Mart Co., Ltd. (specialty markets)

COMPETITORS

AMD
Akzo Nobel
BASF AG
Bayer AG
Dow Chemical
DuPont
FPC
Fujitsu
GE
Hewlett-Packard
Hitachi
IBM
ITOCHU
Marubeni
Matsushita
Motorola
NEC
Nokia
Nortel Networks
Philips Electronics
Samsung
SANYO
Sharp
SK Group
Sony
Ssangyong
Texas Instruments
Toshiba

HISTORICAL FINANCIALS

Company Type: Group

Income Statement FYE: December 31

	REVENUE ($ mil.)	NET INCOME ($ mil.)	NET PROFIT MARGIN	EMPLOYEES
12/02	52,478	1,423	2.7%	140,000
12/01	48,279	696	1.4%	130,000
12/00	72,616	—	—	100,000
12/99	66,523	—	—	100,000
12/98	50,000	—	—	126,000
12/97	46,707	—	—	126,000
12/96	70,015	—	—	130,000
12/95	64,263	—	—	—
12/94	38,967	—	—	—
Annual Growth	3.8%	4.7%	—	1.2%

Net Income History

Lloyd's of London

After a lot of R&R (reconstruction and renewal), Lloyd's of London is back at work as the world's leading insurance exchange. Not an insurance company, it regulates syndicates of wealthy individuals (called Names, their number has been dropping steadily since the 1980s and is down to some 2,500) and corporate underwriters that transact insurance business worth billions in premiums each year. Lloyd's is a top conduit for aviation and marine insurance, as well as specialty insurance, such as policies covering art and jewelry or protecting against acts of terrorism.

Despite its overhaul, Lloyd's tradition of specialty lines has hampered its ability to compete against global insurance firms offering more comprehensive service. Encouraged by Lloyd's to consolidate, some syndicates, infused with capital from corporate-owned managing agencies that enables them to completely underwrite a contract, are turning into full-service insurance companies. Corporate underwriters, such as ACE Limited and Berkshire Hathaway's GeneralCologne Re now account for most of Lloyd's capital backing, where Names once dominated.

Lloyd's is catching up to its rivals, particularly bargain-rate insurers who entered the offshore markets in the early 1990s. Catastrophic losses in recent years have forced them to raise their prices, making Lloyd's competitive again. But Lloyd's corporation remains in debt and is taking drastic cost-cutting steps — such as outsourcing operations ranging from data processing and catering to facilities management. The company was hit hard by the attacks on the World Trade

Center, resulting in £3.1 billion in losses. For the first time in its 300-year history, the insurer issued an annual report to publicly document the heavy losses.

In another attempt to renew itself, Lloyd's has unveiled plans to replace its current accounting system and stop accepting capital from traditional Names. The company is lobbying for changes in the regulatory practices of the Names, most significantly the shift to a franchise system. Lord Peter Levene, the former of Mayor of London, has assumed the chairman's post. Despite Levene's inexperience in the insurance industry, critics feel his government experience is the change needed to jumpstart the ailing insurer.

HISTORY

In 1688 Edward Lloyd opened Lloyd's Coffee House near London's docks. Maritime insurance brokers and underwriters met at Lloyd's, which offered a comfortable venue for exchanging shipping information. The loose association of brokers began publishing shipping newspaper *Lloyd's List* in 1734 (sold 1996).

The coffeehouse attracted people who used insurance as a cover for gambling — members who "insured" the gender of the transvestite Chevalier d'Eon, began Lloyd's tradition of specialty insurance.

In 1871 Parliament enacted the Lloyd's Act, which formed Lloyd's Corporation to oversee the activities of the underwriting syndicates (made up of Names with unlimited personal liability). In the 1880s the market began covering nonmarine risks.

By 1900 Lloyd's members wrote 50% of the world's nonlife insurance. Prompt claims payment after the 1906 San Francisco earthquake boosted the market's image in the US. After WWI, Lloyd's members began writing automotive, credit, and aviation insurance.

In 1981 and 1982 a syndicate managed by Richard Outhwaite wrote contracts on the future liabilities of old insurance contracts with claims (many with environmental exposure) still pending.

That decade Lloyd's attracted new Names: the merely well-off — highly paid people without great wealth — who pledged assets often overvalued in the 1980s boom. Exercising little oversight, Lloyd's let syndicates close their books on pending claims by reinsuring them repeatedly through new syndicates financed by neophyte Names.

The boom's end coincided with a rise in US environmental claims covered by insurance contracts such as those written by Outhwaite. When Names with reduced net worth balked at paying claims, Lloyd's faced disaster. From 1991 to 1994, the number of syndicates fell by half and premium rates increased. In 1993, with billions in claims and many Names refusing to pay or suing their syndicates for not disclosing the risks, Lloyd's imposed new underwriting and reporting rules, took control of most syndicates' back-office functions, and brought in capital by finally admitting corporate members (mostly foreign insurers).

Lloyd's reached a multibillion-pound settlement with its most of its Names in 1996. It also required its active investors to help finance a new insurance company, Equitas, to cover old liabilities (billions in claims are still outstanding). In 1997 Lloyd's sought to increase the number of broker members. The next year, amid regulatory disagreements with Singapore's gov-

ernment and a faltering Asian economy, it called off plans to open an exchange branch there. In 1999 Lloyd's began cutting its operating costs. It also began bolstering its Central Fund with insurance rather than cash (providers include Swiss Re and The Chubb Corporation) and admitted the captive insurer of pharmaceuticals powerhouse SmithKline Beecham (now GlaxoSmithKline) into its marketplace.

In 2000, as litigation dragged on over whether a recalcitrant group of Names owed Lloyd's more than £50 million for claims, the corporation continued to trim costs by selling property. That year the US became Lloyd's single largest market for the first time in the company's 300-year history.

EXECUTIVES

Chairman: Lord Peter Levene
Deputy Chairman: John Coldman, age 55
Deputy Chairman: Bronek Masojada
CEO and Chairman, Lloyd's Market Board:
Nicholas E. T. Prettejohn, age 42
Director, Commercial: Roger Sellek
Director, Communications: David Peel, age 42
Director, Finance, Risk Management, and Operations:
Andrew Moss
Director, Franchise Performance: Rolf Tolle, age 54
Director, Human Resources: Geoff Morgan
Director, Worldwide Markets: Julian James
Director and General Counsel: Sean McGovern
Compliance Officer: John Baker
Special Counsel, September 11: Jeremy Pinchin, age 43
Auditors: Ernst & Young

LOCATIONS

HQ: 1 Lime St., London EC3M 7HA, United Kingdom
Phone: +44-20-7327-1000   **Fax:** +44-20-7327-5599
US HQ: 590 5th Avenue, 17th Fl., New York, NY 10036
US Phone: 212-382-4060   **US Fax:** 212-382-4070
Web: www.lloyds.com

Lloyd's of London's syndicates operate in more than 100 countries.

PRODUCTS/OPERATIONS

2002 Assets

	% of total
Cash and investments	50
Reinsurers' share of technical provisions	28
Other assets	22
Total	**100**

Selected Subsidiaries

Additional Securities Ltd. (overseas insurance reserves)
Centrewrite Limited (reinsurance)
Equitas (reinsurance)
Lioncover Insurance Co. Ltd.
Lloyd's America, Inc. (liaison with US producers)
lloyds.com Limited
LPSO Limited (services to the Lloyd's market)

COMPETITORS

Allianz	General Re
AIG	ING
Aon	Markel
AGF	Marsh & McLennan
Aviva	Millea Holdings
AXA	Munich Re
Chubb	Swiss Re
Citigroup	Zurich Financial Services

HISTORICAL FINANCIALS

Company Type: Insurance society

Income Statement

FYE: December 31

	REVENUE ($ mil.)	NET INCOME ($ mil.)	NET PROFIT MARGIN	EMPLOYEES
12/02	207	(7)	—	589
12/01	208	85	41.0%	825
12/00	218	177	81.1%	1,176
12/99	266	124	46.8%	1,645
12/98	311	40	13.0%	1,833
12/97	327	57	17.6%	—
Annual Growth	(8.7%)	—	—	(24.7%)

2002 Year-End Financials

Debt ratio: 4.9%
Return on equity: —
Cash ($ mil.): 51

Current ratio: 1.79
Long-term debt ($ mil.): 7

Net Income History

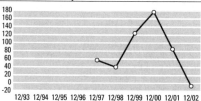

Logitech International

While many companies want to improve the proverbial mousetrap, Logitech International is more concerned about making a better mouse. The company is a leading maker of mice — it competes with Microsoft for leadership in this market — and other devices for controlling computers, including joysticks, trackballs, and cordless keyboards and mice. The company also offers PC speakers. Logitech sells its products directly to manufacturers — most of the world's largest PC makers are customers — as well as through distributors and retailers worldwide. Logitech performs its high-volume manufacturing in China.

Logitech's growth strategy includes enhancing functionality — especially Internet-related features — for its PC devices and expanding its product line beyond the PC platform. It continues to roll out new products like the WingMan Force Feedback Mouse, which lets video game players feel things like the recoil from weapons, and lets less violent users "feel" the difference between dragging a 1 GB and a 1 KB file across the desktop. The company expanded its product lines, particularly its computer speaker offerings, when it acquired Labtec in 2001.

HISTORY

Italian Pierluigi Zappacosta and Swiss Daniel Borel met while studying computer engineering at Stanford University in the 1970s. The two wanted to bring the entrepreneurial spirit of California's Silicon Valley to Europe and start a high-tech company. At the time, though, there was little venture capital in Europe, and no European bank would lend them enough money.

In 1981 Zappacosta and Borel obtained the rights to sell a Swiss-designed mouse in the US and, with Swiss backers, started Logitech in California and Switzerland. The co-founders originally intended Logitech to be a software company in the mold of Microsoft, but this vision changed quickly as the importance of the mouse and other peripherals became apparent. The company improved its manufacturing process and soon developed a cordless mouse.

Hewlett-Packard was Logitech's first big client, quickly followed by others including Olivetti and AT&T. Logitech made its first foray into the US retail market in 1986, with limited success. Since its brand was not recognized and the company had a small advertising budget, it bypassed the regular retail route and offered its mouse at a discount through specialty computer magazines. Consumers, and later dealers and distributors, took notice; Logitech was soon supplying mice to Apple. With a new Taiwan manufacturing plant on line and increased capacity, it reached an agreement in 1988 to supply IBM. That year Logitech went public.

In 1991 Logitech formed a joint venture in China that involved funding from China National Aerotechnology Import and Export Corporation and the International Resources Technology Association of Hong Kong. That year the company also purchased 51% of Gazelle Graphics Systems, developer of single-board digitizers and cordless digitizing pens (Gazelle had developed the first trackball for Apple's PowerBook laptops). Logitech purchased the rest of Gazelle in 1993.

Logitech announced a new design for its stationary desktop mouse for Macintosh (TrackMan) in 1993. The next year Logitech eliminated 500 jobs. At that time Zappacosta announced that the company would shift its focus from mice to input devices such as cameras and scanners.

With stiff competition and pricing pressures eroding profits, Logitech struggled through 1995, closing factories and consolidating plants. After taking a $20 million restructuring charge, Logitech returned to profitability in 1996.

Logitech sold its scanner business in late 1997 to Storm Technology (which later went bankrupt). In 1998 Guerrino De Luca, a former executive at Apple Computer and Claris, joined the company as president and CEO, replacing Borel, who remained chairman. (Zappacosta stepped down as vice chairman; he chairs fingerprint recognition systems maker DigitalPersona.) That year also saw Logitech buy the digital camera business of Connectix.

In 1999, the 30th anniversary of the mouse's invention, Logitech sold its 200 millionth digital rodent. Also that year it spun off SpotLife, which allows users to share video content through its Web site. In 2000 Logitech announced an agreement with Compaq (now part of Hewlett-Packard) to bundle its QuickCam cameras with Compaq Presario PCs, and one with Motorola to develop cordless PC peripherals based on the Bluetooth wireless protocol.

In 2001 the company bought audio device and peripherals provider Labtec in a deal valued at about $125 million. The next year the company posted its best-ever profits for fiscal 2002, and it repurchased the shares of SpotLife it had spun off in 1999.

EXECUTIVES

Chairman: Daniel V. Borel, age 53
President and CEO: Guerrino De Luca, age 50
SVP; General Manager, Control Devices: David J. Henry, age 46
SVP, Audio and Interactive Entertainment: Robert Wick, age 40
SVP, Finance and CFO: Kristen Onken, age 53
SVP, Operations; General Manager, Far East: Erh-Hsun Chang, age 54
SVP, Video: Junien Labrousse, age 45
SVP, Worldwide Sales and Marketing: Marcel Stolk, age 36
VP and Associate Legal Counsel: Margaret Wynne
VP; General Manager, Logicool Japan: Matthew Aoyagi
VP, Business Development: Bernard Gander
VP, Engineering, Control Devices: Aldo Bussien
VP, Legal and General Counsel: Catherine L. Valentine
VP, Marketing: Robin Selden
VP, Worldwide Human Resources: Roberta Linsky
VP, Worldwide IT and CIO: Dan Poulin
VP, Worldwide OEM Sales: Vladimir Langer
Auditors: PricewaterhouseCoopers SA

LOCATIONS

HQ: Logitech International S.A.
Moulin du Choc, CH-1122 Romanel-sur-Morges, Vaud, Switzerland
Phone: +41-21-863-51-11   **Fax:** +41-21-863-53-11
US HQ: 6505 Kaiser Dr., Fremont, CA 94555
US Phone: 510-795-8500   **US Fax:** 510-792-8901
Web: www.logitech.com

Logitech International has subsidiaries in China, Switzerland, Taiwan, and the US, and it has sales offices in 20 countries.

2003 Sales

	$ mil.	% of total
Europe	488	44
North America	435	40
Asia/Pacific	177	16
Total	**1,100**	**100**

PRODUCTS/OPERATIONS

Selected Products

Cameras
Digital pens
Game controllers
Headsets (mobile phone, PC)
Keyboards (handheld computer, PC)
Mice
PC microphones
Speakers
Trackballs

COMPETITORS

Altec Lansing Technologies
Creative Technology
Eastman Kodak
Interlink Electronics
Mad Catz Interactive
Microsoft
Mitsumi Electric
Philips Electronics
Plantronics
Sharp
Sony
Telex Communications

HISTORICAL FINANCIALS

Company Type: Public

Income Statement
FYE: March 31

	REVENUE ($ mil.)	NET INCOME ($ mil.)	NET PROFIT MARGIN	EMPLOYEES
3/03	1,100	99	9.0%	4,936
3/02	944	75	7.9%	4,404
3/01	761	45	5.9%	4,794
3/00	616	30	4.9%	4,350
3/99	448	7	1.6%	4,170
3/98	390	16	4.0%	2,669
3/97	414	21	5.1%	2,995
3/96	355	8	2.3%	2,322
3/95	303	(17)	—	2,112
3/94	326	19	5.8%	2,489
Annual Growth	14.5%	20.1%	—	7.9%

2003 Year-End Financials

Debt ratio: 36.0%
Return on equity: 28.7%
Cash ($ mil.): 219
Current ratio: 2.37
Long-term debt ($ mil.): 132

No. of shares (mil.): 48
Dividends
  Yield: 0.0%
  Payout: —
Market value ($ mil.): 1,425

Stock History
NASDAQ: LOGI

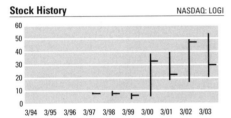

	STOCK PRICE ($) FY Close	P/E High/Low		PER SHARE ($) Earnings	Dividends	Book Value
3/03	29.74	27	11	1.97	0.00	7.63
3/02	47.20	33	11	1.50	0.00	67.43
3/01	22.38	41	19	0.96	0.00	57.65
3/00	32.75	55	9	0.69	0.00	43.24
3/99	6.44	44	23	0.18	0.00	34.92
3/98	7.94	24	17	0.39	0.00	32.70
3/97	8.13	14	13	0.60	0.00	30.70
Annual Growth	24.1%	—	—	21.9%	—	(20.7%)

Lonmin Plc

At Lonmin, all that glitters is not gold — platinum is more precious these days. The company, formerly Lonrho, is the world's #3 platinum producer (after Anglo Platinum and Impala Platinum). Its Lonmin Platinum, or Lonplats, unit mines both platinum group metals (PGMs, including platinum, palladium, rhodium, and iridium) and gold through two South African companies: Western Platinum and Eastern Platinum. Lonmin also owns a 28% interest in Ashanti Goldfields in Ghana and has interests in two Australian PMG producers. Applications for platinum include catalytic converters for vehicles and jewelry.

Lonmin has decided to concentrate primarily on its PGM operations and says it intends to expand its platinum production more than 40% by 2007 — from 630,000 ounces to more than 800,000 ounces per year. To that end, the company has added smelter capacity and sunk new shafts in South Africa. In addition to its Australian investments, Lonmin has exploration activities in North America and Tanzania.

The company has been selling off its non-platinum assets, including its gold assets in politically troubled Zimbabwe. It has also divested its holdings in coal-mining, hotel, and insurance businesses.

HISTORY

Founded in 1909 as the London & Rhodesian Mining & Land Company to acquire mining rights in Zambia and Zimbabwe, the company later expanded into real estate, ranching, and agriculture. In 1961 Roland "Tiny" Rowland traded his Rhodesian assets for a 48% interest in the company and managing directorship.

Rowland then bought the Beira oil pipeline (southern Rhodesia to Mozambique) in 1961, changed its name to Lonrho in 1963, and shut down the pipeline in 1965 when economic sanctions were imposed against Rhodesia after white settlers declared independence. Rowland also bought a major interest in the Ashanti gold fields of Ghana in 1968.

In 1973 a group of directors tried to oust Rowland, claiming he had bribed African leaders and violated Rhodesian sanctions. A British inquiry cleared him but found that he had made questionable payments. Lonrho bought Volkswagen and Audi distributors in the UK in 1975, Princess Hotels in 1979, and the *Observer* newspaper in 1981. His attempt to buy retailer House of Fraser (owner of Harrod's) was frustrated by the British Mergers and Monopolies Commission in 1985.

Back in Africa, where Tanzania had nationalized Lonrho's operations (1978), Rowland continued his politically incorrect dealings through the 1980s. He helped the Marxist government of Mozambique manage its agricultural resources and increased Lonrho's South African holdings despite sanctions against the government's policy of apartheid.

Weakened by debt and low commodity prices, Lonrho began shedding assets in the late 1980s. In 1992 Rowland sold a third of the Metropole Hotel chain to Libya and accepted a loan from Colonel Gadhafi. Lonrho's stock plummeted, attracting the attention of German financier Dieter Bock, who bought about 18% of the company.

Bock and Rowland were co-CEOs for about a year until Bock won control of the board. Rowland was forced out of management in 1994. Rowland, angered by Bock's plan to dismember the company, sold his 6% of the firm in 1995 but remained a frequent critic of its new management. In 1996 EU regulators rejected Bock's plan to spin off Lonrho's mining operations.

Bock resigned as CEO in 1996 and sold his 18% interest in Lonrho to South African titan Anglo American. Nicholas Morrell assumed the CEO position that year. Lonrho sold its Metropole Hotel chain to Stakis (UK) for $533 million that year, as well, and sold its Lonrho Sugar operations in 1997. Sir John Craven took the helm as chairman as the company continued to restructure. Anglo sold its 26% stake in Lonrho to JCI in 1997. The next year the deal was restructured so that Anglo kept a 7% stake in Lonrho.

In 1998 Lonrho bought Tavistock (a JCI coal operation) and divested its Lonrho Africa division, Hondo Oil & Gas, and Princess Hotels.

The company changed its name to Lonmin in 1999 and made a failed attempt to increase its interests in the Ashanti gold mines. Having decided to focus on platinum production that year,

Lonmin sold its Duiker and Tweefontein coal operations for $209 million to Switzerland-based commodity house Glencore International in 2000. The company sold its interests in its hotel and insurance businesses that year, as well. With restructuring completed, Nick Morrell stepped down as CEO to become director of Cardew & Co., a London PR firm, and Edward Haslam, a lifelong mining executive, took his place.

Lonmin was able to bounce back from a major smelting furnace fire in early 2003 by recommissioning a stand-by facility.

EXECUTIVES

Chairman: Sir John A. Craven, age 62
Deputy Chairman: J. Roger B. Phillimore, age 53
Chief Executive: G. Edward Haslam, age 58, $655,662 pay
Executive Director: Sam Esson Jonah, age 53, $78,055 pay
Finance Director: John N. Robinson, age 48, $426,180 pay
Director Corporate Development and Marketing: Ian P. Farmer, age 40, $377,006 pay
Group Financial Controller: Amanda Bradshaw
Associate Director and Group Secretary (HR): Michael J. Pearce
Group IT Manager: Gary Twinn
Group Technical Director: Chris Davies
Investor Relations Manager and Assistant Secretary: Teresa Heritage
Consulting Geologist: Tom Evans
Divisional Director, Business Development: Albert Jamieson
Division Director, Marketing: Fraser King
Divisional Director, Mining Services: Eddie Facculyn-Ghose
Divisional Director, Smelting and Refining: Alan Keeley
Managing Director, Platinum: Peter J. Ledger, age 53
Corporate Affairs, Platinum: Tony Reilly
Finance Director, Platinum: Brian Abbott
Mining Director, Platinum: Stompie Shiels
Strategic Services, Platinum: Geoff Fenner
Auditors: KPMG Audit Plc

LOCATIONS

HQ: 4 Grosvenor Place, London SW1X 7YL, United Kingdom
Phone: +44-20-7201-6000   **Fax:** +44-20-7201-6100
Web: www.lonmin.com

Lonmin has mining and exploration activities in Australia, Ghana, North America, Tanzania, and South Africa.

2002 Sales by Destination

	% of total
The Americas	31
Asia	29
Africa	
South Africa	13
Zimbabwe	9
Europe	18
Total	**100**

PRODUCTS/OPERATIONS

Selected Mining and Refining Operations

Ashanti Goldfields Co. Ltd. (28%, gold, Ghana)
Eastern Platinum Ltd. (PGMs and gold, South Africa)
Lonmin Platinum (Lonplats, 73%)
Munni Munni Project (11%, PGMs, Australia)
Panton Sill Project (44%, PGMs, Australia)
Western Platinum Ltd. (PGMs and gold, South Africa)

COMPETITORS

Anglo American	North American Palladium
AngloGold	Placer Dome
Barrick Gold	Rio Tinto
Inco Limited	Stillwater Mining

HISTORICAL FINANCIALS

Company Type: Public

Income Statement

FYE: September 30

	REVENUE ($ mil.)	NET INCOME ($ mil.)	NET PROFIT MARGIN	EMPLOYEES
9/02	1,088	289	26.5%	24,071
9/01	1,276	404	31.6%	26,829
9/00	891	215	24.1%	31,051
9/99	896	130	14.5%	32,027
9/98	1,705	66	3.9%	55,382
Annual Growth	(10.6%)	44.5%	—	(18.8%)

2002 Year-End Financials

Debt ratio: —
Return on equity: —
Cash ($ mil.): 53
Current ratio: 0.97
Long-term debt ($ mil.): 203

Net Income History

Pink Sheets: LNMIY

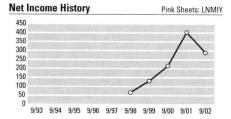

L'Oréal SA

L'Oréal's success is built on a strong foundation — as well as other cosmetic creations. The world's largest beauty products company, it creates makeup, perfume, and hair and skin care products. L'Oréal's brands for women and men include L'Oréal and Maybelline (mass-market products), Lancôme (upscale products), and Redken and SoftSheen/Carson for retail and salon hair care. L'Oréal also conducts cosmetology and dermatology research. Liliane Bettencourt, daughter of the company's founder, and her family indirectly control L'Oréal. Swiss food giant Nestlé also owns a large stake.

L'Oréal's cosmetics, which generate nearly all of the company's revenue, generally fall under four divisions: Professional (salon hair care), Consumer (hair and skin care, makeup), Luxury (beauty products, fragrances), and Active Cosmetics (dermo-cosmetic products). Consumer brands such as GARNIER, L'Oréal, Maybelline, and Softsheen/Carson make up 54% of the company's cosmetic sales. However, well-known Luxury brands, including Lancôme, Ralph Lauren, and Giorgio Armani, continue to gain popularity. Sales outside of Europe account for about half of the company's cosmetic business.

L'Oréal derives some sales from its dermatology subsidiaries, including Galderma and Sanofi-Synthélabo, a French pharmaceuticals group. The company also has formed The Laboratoires Inneov with Nestlé to develop diet supplements for skin care, hair care, and nail care.

Looking to compete further in the domestic shampoo and conditioner market, in early 2003 L'Oréal introduced its Fructis line in the US via the biggest product launch in the company's history. (The brand has been sold in Europe for several years.)

L'Oréal funds more than 2,800 scientists on three continents who file about 500 patents a year. Of note is the company's creation of UV absorbing makeup and test models of human skin. Liliane Bettencourt is L'Oréal's primary stockholder. She and her family own 51% of Gesparal, the holding company that owns 54% of L'Oréal. (Nestlé owns the remaining shares of Gesparal.)

HISTORY

Parisian Eugène Schueller, a chemist by trade, invented the first synthetic hair dye in 1907. Schueller quickly found a market for his products with local hairdressers and in 1909 established L'Oréal to pursue his growing hair products operation. The company's name came from its first hair color, Auréole (French for "aura of light").

L'Oréal expanded to include shampoos and soaps, all under the watchful direction of the energetic Schueller, who was known to taste hair creams to ensure that they were made up of the exact chemical composition that he required. In the 1920s the company began advertising on the radio (before its French competitors).

Demand for L'Oréal's products intensified after WWII. In 1953 the company formed licensee Cosmair to distribute its hair products to US beauty salons, and Cosmair soon offered L'Oréal's makeup and perfume as well. (Cosmair became L'Oréal USA in 2000.) When Schueller died in 1957, control of L'Oréal passed to right-hand man François Dalle. Dalle carried L'Oréal's hair care products into the consumer market and overseas and sold its soap units in 1961.

The company went public in 1963; Schueller's daughter, Liliane Bettencourt, retained a majority interest. Diversification came in 1965 with the acquisition of upscale French cosmetics maker Lancôme. L'Oréal entered the pharmaceuticals business in 1973 by purchasing Synthélabo. Bettencourt traded nearly half of her L'Oréal stock for a 3% stake in Swiss food producer Nestlé in 1974. L'Oréal purchased a minority stake in the publisher of French fashion magazine Marie Claire three years later.

During the 1980s L'Oréal vaulted from relative obscurity to become the world's #1 cosmetics company, largely through acquisitions. These included Warner Communications' cosmetics operations (Ralph Lauren and Gloria Vanderbilt brands, 1984), Helena Rubinstein (US beauty products, 1988), Laboratoires Pharmaeutiques Goupil (1988), and its first major investment in Lanvin (1989). Englishman Lindsay Owen-Jones became CEO in 1988.

Chairman Jacques Correze died in 1991 during an investigation into his Nazi war activities. (He had served five years in prison.) In 1994 the company purchased control of Cosmair from Nestlé and Bettencourt. It acquired two generic drug companies in 1995: Lichtenstein Pharmazeutica in Germany and Irex in France. That year L'Oréal became the #2 US cosmetics maker (behind Procter & Gamble, maker of Cover Girl and Max Factor, by buying #3 Maybelline for $508 million.

L'Oréal then added subsidiaries in Japan and China (1996) and in Romania and Slovenia (1997). It also acquired sun protection brand Ombrelle (#2 in Canada) in 1997 and ethnic hair care products maker Soft Sheen Products in 1998. Also in 1998 L'Oréal's 57%-owned Synthélabo subsidiary merged with Elf Aquitaine's pharmaceuticals unit, Sanofi. L'Oréal retained a 19.5% stake in the newly formed pharmaceuticals group, Sanofi-Synthélabo.

In 2000 L'Oréal acquired Carson (an ethnic beauty products maker, now Soft Sheen/Carson Products), family-owned prestige cosmetics company Kiehl's Since 1851, and salon products maker Matrix Essentials (from Bristol-Myers Squibb).

In 2001 L'Oréal sold its stake in Marie Claire. That same year the company bought Colorama, a Brazilian makeup and hair care brand, from Revlon. It also acquired CosMedic Concepts' 60 BioMedic products, which are distributed to dermatologists in 60 countries.

Expanding its leadership in the professional hair salon products market, L'Oréal subsidiary, L'Oréal USA, acquired Artec Systems Group in 2002. Brand names involved in the takeover included Artec Color Deposit System, Kiwi, Purehair, and Textureline.

EXECUTIVES

Chairman and CEO: Lindsay Owen-Jones, age 56
Vice Chairman: Jean-Pierre Meyers, age 55
President, Professional Products: Jean-Jacques Lebel
President, Consumer Products: Patrick Rabain
President, Luxury Products: Gilles Weil
EVP, Strategic Business Development:
Béatrice Dautresme
EVP, Corporate Communications and External Affairs:
Giorgio Galli
EVP, Research and Development: Jean-François Grollier
EVP, Production and Technology: Marcel Lafforgue
EVP Administration and Finance: Christian Mulliez,
age 41
EVP, Human Resources: François Vachey
Auditors: Étienne Jacquemin

LOCATIONS

HQ: 41, rue Martre, 92117 Clichy, France
Phone: +33-1-47-56-82-65   **Fax:** +33-1-47-56-86-42
US HQ: 575 5th Ave., New York, NY 10017
US Phone: 212-818-1500   **US Fax:** 212-984-4538
Web: www.loreal.com

2002 Sales

	$ mil.	% of total
Western Europe	7,383	50
North America	4,652	30
Other	2,940	20
Total	**14,975**	**100**

PRODUCTS/OPERATIONS

2002 Sales by Category

	$ mil.	% of total
Cosmetics		
Consumer	7,967	53
Luxury	3,817	26
Professional	1,989	13
Active	728	5
Mail order	122	1
Dermatology	336	2
Other	16	—
Total	**14,975**	**100**

Selected Operations

Cosmetics
Active Cosmetics
La Roche-Posay
Vichy

Consumer Products
Gemey
Laboratoires GARNIER
L'Oréal
Maybelline
SoftSheen/Carson

Luxury Products
Biotherm
Cacharel (fragrances only)
Giorgio Armani (fragrances only)
Guy Laroche (fragrances only)
Helena Rubinstein
Kiehl's
Lancôme
Lanvin (fragrances only)
Paloma Picasso (fragrances only)
Ralph Lauren (fragrances only)
Shu Uemura

Professional Products
Artec
Inne
Kérastase
L'Oréal Professionnel
Matrix
Redken

Dermatology, Luxury Goods, and Pharmaceuticals
Innéov Firmness
Tri-Luma
RozexMetvix

COMPETITORS

Alberto-Culver	Mary Kay
Alticor	Merle Norman
Avon	Novartis
Bath & Body Works	Nu Skin
BeautiControl Cosmetics	Perrigo
Body Shop	Procter & Gamble
Chanel	Puig Beauty & Fashion
Clarins	Revlon
Estée Lauder	Shiseido
Hoffmann-La Roche	Unilever
Intimate Brands	Wella
Johnson & Johnson	Yves Saint-Laurent Groupe
LVMH	

HISTORICAL FINANCIALS

Company Type: Public

Income Statement				FYE: December 31
	REVENUE ($ mil.)	NET INCOME ($ mil.)	NET PROFIT MARGIN	EMPLOYEES
12/02	14,975	1,526	10.2%	50,491
12/01	12,171	1,089	8.9%	49,150
12/00	11,931	968	8.1%	48,222
12/99	10,825	702	6.5%	42,164
12/98	13,417	839	6.3%	49,665
12/97	11,522	664	5.8%	47,242
12/96	11,532	668	5.8%	43,158
12/95	10,872	641	5.9%	39,929
12/94	8,923	585	6.6%	38,972
12/93	6,783	437	6.4%	32,261
Annual Growth	9.2%	14.9%	—	5.1%

2002 Year-End Financials

Debt ratio: 11.1%
Return on equity: 21.6%
Cash ($ mil.): 2,323
Current ratio: 1.32
Long-term debt ($ mil.): 865

Net Income History   OTC: LORLY

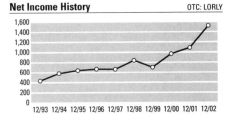

Deutsche Lufthansa AG

Germany's Deutsche Lufthansa is Europe's #3 passenger airline (behind #1 British Airways and #2 Air France); it also the world's #2 cargo airline behind FedEx. Including code-sharing agreements, Lufthansa serves about 330 destinations in nearly 90 countries. It flies about 370 aircraft. With hubs in Frankfurt and Munich, the carrier is part of the Star Alliance that includes United Air Lines, Air Canada, and All Nippon Airways. Lufthansa also has interests in travel-related businesses, including ground services, catering, and leisure travel services. Lufthansa owns a stake in Amadeus, one of the world's largest computerized airline reservation systems.

European airline deregulation, rising fuel prices, and air traffic constraints have applied pressure to Lufthansa's bottom line, but the carrier has still managed to turn a profit. It's even expanding its catering, ground services, and information technology operations.

The company is also riding high on the wings of the Star Alliance, the global marketing and code-sharing alliance that includes such major carriers as UAL's United, Air Canada, and All Nippon Airways. Member airlines share revenues on some routes, operate joint ticketing offices, and offer joint frequent-flier programs.

Lufthansa is facing fierce competition from Air France, which has acquired Dutch carrier KLM, and British Airways, which is looking for another European partner and has begun courting Iberia.

In the cargo game, Lufthansa has sold its 24% stake in delivery firm DHL to Deutsche Post.

HISTORY

The Weimar government created Deutsche Luft Hansa (DLH) in 1926 by merging private German airlines Deutscher Aero Lloyd (founded 1919) and Junkers Luftverkehr (formed in 1921 by aircraft manufacturer Junkers Flugzeugwerke). DLH built what would become Europe's most comprehensive air route network by 1931. It served the USSR through Deruluft (formed 1921; dissolved 1941), an airline jointly owned by DLH and the Soviet government. In 1930 DLH and the Chinese government formed Eurasia Aviation Corporation to develop air transport in China.

DLH established the world's first transatlantic airmail service from Berlin to Buenos Aires in 1934 and went on to develop air transport throughout South America. The outbreak of WWII ended operations in Europe, and the Chinese government seized Eurasia Aviation in 1941. Klaus Bonhoeffer, head of DLH's legal department, led an unsuccessful coup against the Nazi leadership and was executed in 1945. Soon afterward all DLH operations ceased.

In 1954 the Allies allowed the recapitalization of Deutsche Lufthansa. The airline started with domestic routes, returned to London and Paris (1955), and then re-entered South America (1956). In 1958 it made its first nonstop flight between Germany and New York and initiated service to Tokyo and Cairo. Meanwhile, it started a charter airline with several partners in 1955. Lufthansa bought out its partners in 1959 and renamed the unit Condor two years later.

The carrier resumed service behind the Iron Curtain in 1966 with flights to Prague. The stable West German economy helped Lufthansa maintain profitability through most of the 1970s.

The reunification of Germany in 1990 ended Allied control over Berlin airspace, allowing Lufthansa, which had bought Pan Am's Berlin routes, to fly there under its own colors for the first time since the end of WWII. The company began seeking international partners in 1991, but that year European air travel suffered its first-ever slowdown, forcing Lufthansa into the red for the first time since 1973.

The company restructured in 1994 into a group of new business units: Lufthansa Technik, Lufthansa Cargo, and Lufthansa Systems. In 1995 the carrier began to face increased domestic competition from Deutsche BA, a British Airways affiliate.

The airline formed a code-sharing agreement with Air Canada in 1996. In 1997 the Star Alliance was formed, and Lufthansa signed a pact with Singapore Airlines. That year the German government sold its remaining 38% stake in Lufthansa. In 1998 Lufthansa and All Nippon Airways formed a code-sharing alliance, and Condor was combined with Karstadt's tour company NUR Touristic to form C&N Touristic. (After buying UK-based travel operator Thomas Cook in 2000, C&N Touristic changed its name to Thomas Cook in 2001.)

In a plan to gain more access to London's Heathrow Airport, Lufthansa took a 20% stake in British Midland, which was admitted into the Star Alliance in 2000 along with Mexicana Airlines. In 2001 the airline bought the 52% of Texas-based Sky Chefs it did not already own and formed a new unit, LSG Sky Chefs International, to hold its catering operations.

EXECUTIVES

Chairman and CEO: Jürgen Weber, age 62
Deputy Chairman; CEO, Passenger Airlines: Wolfgang Mayrhuber
Member of the Executive Board and CFO: Karl-Ludwig Kley
Member of the Executive Board and Chief Officer Human Resources: Stefan Lauer
Auditors: PwC Deutsche Revision AG

LOCATIONS

HQ: Von-Gablenz-Strasse 2-6,
D-50679 Cologne 21, Germany
Phone: +49-69-696-0   **Fax:** +49-69-696-6818
US HQ: 1640 Hempstead Tpke., East Meadow, NY 11554
US Phone: 516-296-9200   **US Fax:** 516-296-9660
Web: www.lufthansa.com

Deutsche Lufthansa serves about 330 destinations in nearly 90 countries, including cities served through code-sharing partnerships. The company has hubs in Frankfurt and Munich, Germany.

2002 Sales

	% of total
Europe	52
North America	20
Asia/Pacific	20
Africa	3
South America	3
Middle East	2
Total	**100**

PRODUCTS/OPERATIONS

2002 Sales

	% of total
Lufthansa Passenger Airline	54
LSG Sky Chefs	16
Lufthansa Technik	14
Lufthansa Cargo	12
Lufthansa Systems	3
Other	1
Total	**100**

Selected Operations

Delvag Luftfahrt-Versicherungs-AG (insurance)
GlobeGround GmbH (airport ground services)
LSG Sky Chefs International AG (catering)
Lufthansa Cargo AG (cargo services)
Lufthansa CityLine GmbH (passenger airline)
Lufthansa Commercial Holding GmbH (holding company)
Lufthansa Flight Training GmbH (LFT)
Lufthansa Systems GmbH (support services, information technology services)
Lufthansa Technik AG (technical services)
Thomas Cook AG (50%, leisure travel services)

COMPETITORS

Accor	Finnair
Aer Lingus	Iberia
Air France	Japan Airlines
Air Inter	KLM
AMR	Liberty Travel
BAX Global	Northwest Airlines
British Airways	Otto Versand
Carlson	Qantas
CNF	Sabre
Continental Airlines	Brussels Airlines
Cuisine Solutions	Swire Pacific
Delta	TUI
Deutsche Bahn	US Airways
DHL	Virgin Atlantic Airways
FedEx	

HISTORICAL FINANCIALS

Company Type: Public

Income Statement

FYE: December 31

	REVENUE ($ mil.)	NET INCOME ($ mil.)	NET PROFIT MARGIN	EMPLOYEES
12/02	17,788	751	4.2%	94,135
12/01	14,784	(561)	—	87,975
12/00	14,313	649	4.5%	69,523
12/99	12,885	635	4.9%	66,207
12/98	13,515	854	6.3%	54,867
12/97	12,917	466	3.6%	58,250
12/96	13,431	357	2.7%	57,999
12/95	13,841	1,020	7.4%	57,586
12/94	12,156	189	1.6%	58,044
12/93	10,198	(58)	—	46,818
Annual Growth	**6.4%**	**—**	**—**	**8.1%**

2002 Year-End Financials

Debt ratio: 114.3%
Return on equity: 20.2%
Cash ($ mil.): 3,201
Current ratio: 3.58
Long-term debt ($ mil.): 4,940

Net Income History

OTC: DLAKY

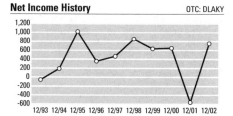

1,200
1,000
800
600
400
200
0
-200
-400
-600

12/93 12/94 12/95 12/96 12/97 12/98 12/99 12/00 12/01 12/02

LUKOIL

Most Russians look to LUKOIL for their oil and gas needs. Russia's #1 integrated oil company produces, refines, and sells oil and oil products; it accounts for 24% of Russia's crude oil production. LUKOIL has proved reserves of 19.3 billion barrels of oil equivalent, more than half of which are located in western Siberia. The company has operations in 58 regions in Russia and 25 countries and owns eight refineries and more than 4,000 service stations. LUKOIL moved into the US retail market by buying Getty Petroleum Marketing. LUKOIL has formed separate businesses for its exploration and production and refining and marketing activities. Managers and employees own some 20% of LUKOIL, the Russian government, 8%.

LUKOIL, Russia's second-largest company behind natural gas monopoly Gazprom, is trying to transform itself from a top-heavy, bureaucratic enterprise into a decentralized, entrepreneurial company with hopes of competing in free markets.

The company explores for oil and gas in Azerbaijan, Egypt, Iraq, Kazakhstan, and other areas in the Middle East and central Asia. It operates four refineries in Russia, one in the Ukraine, one in Bulgaria, and one in Romania, and owns a gas stations network in Russia, the Baltic States, Central and Eastern Europe, and the US.

With an appetite for expansion, the company is upping its production with refinery acquisitions, and is investing heavily in new oil patches, such as the Caspian Sea.

HISTORY

LUKOIL was formed from the combination of three major state-owned oil and gas exploration companies — Langepasneftegaz, Uraineftegaz, and Kogalymneftegaz — that traced their origins to the discovery of oil in western Siberia in 1964. More than 25 years later, after the Soviet Union broke up, the oil and gas sector was one of the first industries marked for privatization.

In 1992 the government called for Langepasneftegaz, Uraineftegaz, and Kogalymneftegaz to merge, and LUKOIL was created the next year. (The LUK of LUKOIL comes from the initials of the three companies.) Russian president Boris Yeltsin appointed Siberian oil veteran Vagit Alekperov as the company's first president. The Russian government also formed several other large integrated oil companies, including Yukos, Surgutneftegaz, Sidanco, and Sibneft.

LUKOIL went public on the fledgling Russian Trading System in 1994. The next year the company absorbed nine other enterprises, including oil exploration companies Astrakhanneft, Kaliningradmorneftegaz, and Permneft. That year LUKOIL became the first Russian oil company to set up an exploration and production trading arm. In 1996 LUKOIL acquired a 41% stake in *Izvestia*, Russia's major independent newspaper.

Chevron and LUKOIL, with seven other oil and gas companies and three governments, agreed in 1996 to build a 1,500-kilometer pipeline to link the Kazakhstan oil fields to world markets.

In 1997 LUKOIL became the first Russian corporation to sell bonds to international investors, and the government announced plans to sell 15% of its stake in the company. That year LUKOIL's 50%-owned Nexus Fuels unit opened its first gas stations located in the parking lots of US grocery stores (the partnership dissolved and Nexus went bankrupt in 2000).

LUKOIL began a partnership with Conoco (later ConocoPhillips) in 1998 to develop oil and natural gas reserves in Russia's northern territories. LUKOIL also acquired 51% of Romania's Petrorel refinery. In 1999 it acquired control of refineries in Bulgaria and Ukraine and in a petrochemical firm in Saratov. It also acquired oil company KomiTEK in one of Russia's largest mergers.

The government sold a 9% stake in LUKOIL to a Cyprus-based unit, Reforma Investments, held in part by LUKOIL's "boss of bosses," Vagit Alekperov (gained at the bargain price of $200 million). Critics cited the sale as Yeltsin's bid to gain Alekperov's political support.

The company announced the first major oil find in the Russian part of the Caspian Sea in 2000, and formed a joint venture (Caspian Oil Company) with fellow Russian energy giants Gazprom and Yukos to exploit resources in the Caspian. The next year LUKOIL acquired more than 1,300 gas stations on the East Coast of the US when it bought Getty Petroleum Marketing.

That year LUKOIL also acquired Bitech, a Canadian oil exploration and production firm with operations in the Republic of Komi in the Russian Federation. In 2002 the company announced plans to sell its oil service business, a move that would cut its overall workforce by some 20,000, and result in savings of $500 million annually.

EXECUTIVES

Chairman: Valery Graifer
President: Vagit Y. Alekperov
First VP Finance and Planning: Sergei P. Kukura
First VP Production: Ravil U. Maganov
VP and Head of Corporate Finances and Investments: Alexander K. Matytsin
VP and Head of Development and Securities: Leonid A. Fedun
VP and Senior Accountant: Lyubov Khoba
VP and Head of General Affairs, Personnel, and Transport: Anatoly A. Barkov
VP and Head of Geology and Exploration: Anatoly Novikov
VP and Head of Planning and Marketing: Anatoly G. Kozyrev
VP and Head Oil and Gas Production: Dzhevan K. Cheloyants
VP and Head of Oil and Gas Supplies and Export of Products: Yury Storozhev
Head of Oil Refining and Petrochemicals: Vladimir Rakitsky
Head of Legal Services: Ivan Maslyaev
Head of Internal Audit: Vagit S. Sharifov
VP; General Director, OOO Torgovy Dom LUKOIL: Alexander S. Smirnov
VP; General Director, LUKOIL Western Siberia: Vladimir I. Nekrasov
Director of Strategic Planning: Richard Karplus
Auditors: ZAO KPMG

LOCATIONS

HQ: OAO LUKOIL
   11 Sretenski Blvd., 101000 Moscow, Russia
Phone: +7-95-927-4444   **Fax:** +7-95-928-9841
Web: www.lukoil.com

LUKOIL operates in 58 regions within Russia and in 25 other countries.

PRODUCTS/OPERATIONS

Selected Subsidiaries

Refining, Supplies, Marketing, and Transportation
Getty Petroleum Marketing
OAO LUKOIL Ukhtaneftepererabotka (refining)
OOO LUKOIL Adygheya (marketing)
OOO LUKOIL Astrakhannefteprodukt (marketing)
OOO LUKOIL Chelyabnefteprodukt (marketing)
OOO LUKOIL Kirovnefteprodukt (marketing)
OOO LUKOIL Permnefteorgsintez (refining)
OOO LUKOIL Permnefteprodukt (marketing)
OOO LUKOIL Volgogradneftepererabotka (refining)
OOO LUKOIL Volgogradnefteprodukt (marketing)
OOO LUKOIL Vologdanefteprodukt (marketing)

Exploration and Production
OAO KomiTEK
OOO LUKOIL Astrakhanmorneft
OOO LUKOIL Kaliningradmorneft
OOO LUKOIL Nizhnevolzhskneft
OOO LUKOIL Permneft
OOO LUKOIL Western Siberia
ZAO LUKOIL Perm

Other
LUKOIL International GmbH
OAO LUKOIL Arktik Tanker (shipping)
ZAO LUKOIL Neftekhim (petrochemicals)

COMPETITORS

Ashland	Rosneft
BP	Royal Dutch/Shell Group
Exxon Mobil	Sibneft
Imperial Oil	Surgutneftegas
Norsk Hydro	Tatneft
Occidental Petroleum	TOTAL
PETROBRAS	Unocal
PDVSA	Yukos
PEMEX	

HISTORICAL FINANCIALS

Company Type: Public

Income Statement
FYE: December 31

	REVENUE ($ mil.)	NET INCOME ($ mil.)	NET PROFIT MARGIN	EMPLOYEES
12/02	15,449	1,843	11.9%	130,000
12/01	13,562	2,109	15.6%	130,000
12/00	13,240	3,312	25.0%	120,000
12/99	9,752	1,120	11.5%	120,000
12/98	3,960	6	0.1%	90,000
12/97	9,003	303	3.4%	107,000
12/96	8,787	767	8.7%	94,236
12/95	6,711	546	8.1%	119,824
12/94	5,002	1,041	20.8%	82,900
12/93	5,341	2,165	40.5%	86,900
Annual Growth	12.5%	(1.8%)	—	4.6%

2002 Year-End Financials
Debt ratio: 11.9%
Return on equity: 14.0%
Cash ($ mil.): 1,252
Current ratio: 1.35
Long-term debt ($ mil.): 1,666

Net Income History
OTC: LUKOY

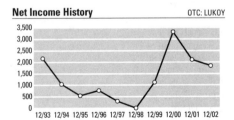

LVMH Moët Hennessy Louis Vuitton SA

LVMH Moët Hennessy Louis Vuitton is the world's largest luxury goods company, with brands that are bywords for the good life. LVMH makes wines and spirits (Dom Pérignon, Moët & Chandon, Veuve Clicquot, Hennessy, and Hine), perfumes (Christian Dior, Guerlain, and Givenchy), cosmetics (Bliss, Fresh, and BeneFit), fashion and leather goods (Christian Lacroix, Donna Karan, Givenchy, Kenzo, and Louis Vuitton), and watches and jewelry (TAG Heuer, Ebel, Chaumet, and Fred). LVMH's retail division includes Sephora cosmetics stores, Le Bon Marché Paris department stores, and 61% of DFS Group (duty-free shops). Chairman Bernard Arnault and his family own 48% of LVMH.

The company has been focusing on controlling as much of its distribution as possible. LVMH has more than 1,500 retail outlets, including 280-plus Vuitton stores, some 150 DFS Group duty-free shops, Le Bon Marché, and hundreds of designer boutiques. Its Sephora self-serve cosmetics and fragrance chain boasts nearly 500 stores worldwide.

Though the company denies rumors that it wants to unload DFS and Sephora, it has sold its teen-targeted Hard Candy and Urban Decay cosmetics brands. LVMH shed several of the less productive of its 50 brands in 2003, including auction house Phillips, de Pury & Luxemborg and fashion brand Michael Kors.

HISTORY

Woodworker Louis Vuitton started his Paris career packing dresses for French Empress Eugenie. He later designed new types of luggage, and in 1854 he opened a store to sell his designs. In 1896 Vuitton introduced the LV monogram fabric that the company still uses. By 1900 Louis Vuitton had stores in the US and England, and by WWI Louis' son, Georges, had the world's largest retail store for travel goods.

Henry Racamier, a former steel executive who had married into the Vuitton family, took charge in 1977, repositioning the company's goods from esoteric status symbols to designer must-haves. Sales soared from $20 million to nearly $2.5 billion within a decade. Concerned about being a takeover target, Racamier merged Louis Vuitton in 1987 with Moët Hennessy (which made wines, spirits, and fragrances) and adopted the name LVMH Moët Hennessy Louis Vuitton.

Moët Hennessy had been formed through the 1971 merger of Moët et Chandon (the world's #1 champagne maker) and the Hennessy Cognac company (founded by Irish mercenary Richard Hennessy in 1765). Moët Hennessy acquired rights to Christian Dior fragrances in 1971.

Racamier tried to reverse the merger when disagreements with chairman Alain Chevalier arose. Racamier invited outside investor Bernard Arnault to increase his interest in the company. Arnault gained control of 43% of LVMH and became chairman in 1989. Chevalier stepped down, but Racamier fought for control

for another 18 months and then set up Orcofi, a partner of cosmetics rival L'Oréal.

LVMH increased its fashion holdings with the purchases of the Givenchy Couture Group (1988), Christian Lacroix (1993), and Kenzo (1993). The company also acquired 55% of French media firm Desfosses International (1993), Celine fashions (1996), the Château d'Yquem winery (1996), and duty-free retailer DFS Group (1996). Next LVMH bought perfume chains Sephora (1997) and Marie-Jeanne Godard (1998). In 1998 LVMH integrated the Paris department store Le Bon Marché, which was controlled by Arnault.

LVMH accumulated a 34% stake in Italian luxury goods maker Gucci in early 1999 and planned to buy all of it. Fellow French conglomerate Pinault-Printemps-Redoute (PPR) later thwarted LVMH by purchasing 42% of Gucci.

Through its LV Capital unit, in 1999 LVMH began acquiring stakes in a host of luxury companies, including a joint venture with fashion company Prada to buy 51% of design house Fendi (LVMH bought Prada's 25.5% stake for $265 million in November 2001). It has since upped its Fendi stake to about 70%. LVMH later added the Ebel, Chaumet, and TAG Heuer brands to its new watch division.

In early 2000 LVMH bought Miami Cruiseline Services, which operates duty-free shops on cruise ships, auction house L'Etude Tajan, and 67% of Italian fashion house Emilio Pucci. The company later purchased 35% of French video game retailer Micromania and 51% of department store Samaritaine. In late 2000 LVMH acquired Gabrielle Studio, which owns all Donna Karan licenses. In 2001 the company bought Donna Karan International.

LVMH bought in 2001 the Newton and MountAdam vineyards for about $45 million. It then began marketing De Beers diamond jewelry in a 50-50 joint venture with the diamond powerhouse. In March LVMH prompted the investigation of a Dutch court into the PPR-Gucci alliance. The company sold its stake in Gucci to PPR for $806.5 million in October.

In October 2002 LVMH ceased trading on the Brussels and Nasdaq exchanges to concentrate on its Euronext investors. In October 2003 the company sold Canard-Duchene to the Alain Thienot Group.

EXECUTIVES

Chairman and CEO: Bernard Arnault
Group Managing Director: Antonio (Toni) Belloni
Adviser to the Chairman: Pierre Godé
Adviser to the Chairman, Group EVP of Synergies, and Group Delegate for Italy: Concetta Lanciaux
Development and Acquisitions, Managing Director, Groupe Arnault: Nicolas Bazire
EVP, Sales Development, Moet Hennessy LVMH Wines & Spirits Business Group: Gilles Hennesy
Executive Committee, Finance: Patrick Houël
Executive Committee, Fashion & Leather Goods: Yves Carcelle
Executive Committee, Perfumes & Cosmetics: Patrick Choël
Executive Committee, LV Capital: Daniel Piette, age 57
Executive Committee, Operations: Bernard Rolley
Executive Committee, Travel Retail: Edward Brennan
Executive Committee, Watches and Jewelry: Philippe Pascal
Executive Committee, Wines and Spirits Group: Christophe Navarre
Executive Committee, Selective Retailing: Pierre Letzelter
President, Fendi USA: François Cress
President, German Operations: Heinz Buchmann

President, LVMH Fashion Group, Asia Pacific:
Hugues Witvoet
President, LVMH Fashion Group, Europe:
Bernardo Sanchez Incera
Director, Human Resources: Sophie Guieysse
Auditors: Cogerco-Flipo; Ernst & Young Audit

LOCATIONS

HQ: 22 avenue Montaigne, 75008 Paris, France
Phone: +33-1-44-13-22-22   **Fax:** +33-1-44-13-21-19
US HQ: 19 E. 57th St., New York, NY 10022
US Phone: 212-931-2000   **US Fax:** 212-931-2903
Web: www.lvmh.com

2002 Sales

	% of total
Europe	
France	17
Other countries	20
Asia	
Japan	15
Other countries	15
US	27
Other regions	6
Total	**100**

PRODUCTS/OPERATIONS

Selected Brands and Operations

Fashion and Leather Goods
Berluti
Celine
Christian Lacroix
Donna Karan
Emilio Pucci
Fendi
Gabrielle Studio (Donna Karan label)
Givenchy
Kenzo
Loewe
Louis Vuitton
Marc Jacobs
Thomas Pink

Retailing
DFS Group
La Samaritaine
Le Bon Marché
Miami Cruiseline Services (duty-free shops)
Sephora

Fragrances and Cosmetics
Aqua di Parma
BeneFit
Bliss
Fresh
Guerlain
Kenzo Parfums
Make Up For Ever
Marc Jacobs Fragrances
Parfums Christian Dior
Parfums Givenchy

Spirits and Wines
Canard-Duchêne
Chandon Estates
Château d'Yquem
Dom Pérignon
Hennessy
Hine
Krug
Mercier
Moët & Chandon
MountAdam
Newton
Ruinart
Veuve Clicquot

Watches and Jewelry
Chaumet
De Beers
Ebel
Fred
Omas
TAG Heuer
Zenith

D.I. Group
Investor
La Tribune
Radio Classique
System TV

COMPETITORS

Allied Domecq	Prada
Avon	Kirin
Bacardi	L'Oréal
Brown-Forman	MacAndrews & Forbes
Calvin Klein	Oscar de la Renta
Chanel	Pinault-Printemps-
Inditex	Redoute
Douglas Holding	Polo Ralph Lauren
Gallo	Puig Beauty & Fashion
Eckes	Rémy Cointreau
Escada	Richemont
Estée Lauder	Shiseido
Galeries Lafayette	Swatch
Gianni Versace	Taittinger
Armani	Tiffany
Gucci	Unilever
GUS	Vera Wang
Hermès	Yves Saint-Laurent Groupe
Hugo Boss	

HISTORICAL FINANCIALS

Company Type: Public

Income Statement

FYE: December 31

	REVENUE ($ mil.)	NET INCOME ($ mil.)	NET PROFIT MARGIN	EMPLOYEES
12/02	13,304	583	4.4%	56,591
12/01	10,900	9	0.1%	53,795
12/00	10,909	680	6.2%	51,127
12/99	8,589	696	8.1%	41,235
12/98	8,126	313	3.9%	33,057
12/97	7,974	752	9.4%	32,348
12/96	6,007	711	11.8%	20,644
12/95	6,071	825	13.6%	19,517
12/94	5,238	1,203	23.0%	15,826
12/93	4,031	605	15.0%	14,874
Annual Growth	**14.2%**	**(0.4%)**	**—**	**16.0%**

2002 Year-End Financials

Debt ratio: 64.4%   Current ratio: 1.20
Return on equity: 8.6%   Long-term debt ($ mil.): 4,773
Cash ($ mil.): 914

Net Income History

Euronext Paris: MC

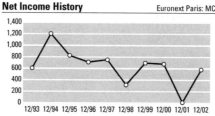

MAN

This venerable old MAN still shows considerable strength. MAN Aktiengesellschaft (founded in 1845) and its subsidiaries manufacture a variety of heavy equipment that range from commercial vehicles to diesel engines for ships. MAN is one of Europe's largest truck makers as well as a leading supplier of equipment for newspaper printing presses and industrial compressors and

turbines. The company also makes components for rocket launchers and space transport systems, and it provides trading and industrial services. Additionally, MAN is a top manufacturer of equipment used to process plastics and metals.

Although its sales are global, European customers account for more than two-thirds of MAN's sales.

The MAN Group has discovered what it has termed as "serious balance-sheet fraud" at ERF, the British truck subsidiary acquired in 2000. As a result of the accounting errors, the MAN Group will seek legal actions against ERF's previous owner and redesign its acquisition procedures. Poised for an estimated decline in truck sales, the group will reorganize and reduce its workforce.

HISTORY

MAN grew out of a company started by Carl August Reichenbach and Carl Buz, who leased an engineering plant in Augsburg, Germany, in 1844. Reichenbach, whose uncle had invented the flatbed printing press, began producing printing presses in 1845. On the same premises, Buz began manufacturing steam engines and industrial drive systems, and he soon added rotary printing presses, water turbines, pumps, and diesel engines. In 1898 the company took the name MAN (Maschinenfabrik Augsburg-Nurnberg) after merging with a German engineering company of the same name.

Another German heavy-industry company, Gutehoffnungshutte Aktienverein AG (GHH, with roots stretching to 1758), bought a majority interest in MAN in 1921. Through acquisitions and internal growth MAN emerged from the world wars as one of Germany's major heavy-industry companies, with added interests in commercial vehicles, shipbuilding, and plant construction. By 1955 MAN's commercial vehicles were a major division destined to dominate the company's sales; MAN moved the division's headquarters to Munich that year.

During the 1970s an overseas recession caused the sales of some operations to slump, although MAN's commercial vehicles and printing-equipment businesses held steady. When economic hardship reached Europe in the 1980s, MAN sought markets outside its home region, especially targeting Asia, the Middle East, and the US. Late in the decade the company dropped its less-profitable products (lifts, pumps, heavy cranes) and began licensing more of its technology and subcontracting out more work. MAN moved its corporate headquarters to Munich in 1985 and merged with GHH in 1986.

After a fast start in the 1990s, Europe's economy again faltered, taking a toll on the company's sales. MAN's profits slumped in fiscal 1994. It laid off about 10% of its workforce between 1993 and 1995. As the economy recovered, so did MAN, and by fiscal 1998, its stagnant profits had rebounded.

Early in 2000 MAN purchased truckmakers ERF Holdings (UK) and STAR (Poland). Later that year MAN picked up Alstom's diesel engine business. MAN acquired the Neoplan busmaking business of Gottlob Auwarter GmbH in 2001, as well as the turbomachinery business of Sulzer AG of Switzerland. After discovering accounting irregularities that year, the company suspended the CEO (John Bryant) and CFO (Klaus Wagner) of the newly acquired ERF. In 2002 the company began implementing its Truck Generation A (TG-A) technology into all of its commercial vehicles.

EXECUTIVES

Chairman, Supervisory Board: Volker Jung, age 64
Deputy Chairman of the Supervisory Board:
 Gerlinde Strauss-Wieczorek
Chairman of the Executive Board: Rudolf Rupprecht
Member of the Executive Board; Chairman, Ferrostaal:
 Klaus von Menges
Member of the Executive Board; Chairman, MAN B&W
 Diesel: Hans-Jürgen Schulte
Member of the Executive Board, Controlling:
 Philipp J. Zahn
Member of the Executive Board, Finances:
 Ferdinand Graf Von Ballestrem
Chairman, MAN Roland Druckmaschinen:
 Gerd Finkbeiner
Chairman, MAN Technologie: Wolfgang Brunn
Chairman, Schwaebische Huettenwerke:
 Manfred Heinritz
Speaker of the Executive Board, RENK:
 Manfred M. Hirt
Auditors: BDO Deutsche Warentreuhand AG

LOCATIONS

HQ: MAN Aktiengesellschaft
 Ungererstrasse 69, D-80805 Munich, Germany
Phone: +49-89-3-60-98-0   **Fax:** +49-89-3-60-98-2-50
Web: www.man.de

MAN Aktiengesellschaft has manufacturing facilities in
Austria, Germany, Poland, South Africa, Turkey, and
the UK.

PRODUCTS/OPERATIONS

2002 Sales

	% of total
Commercial vehicles	52
Industrial services	25
Printing machines	12
Diesel engines	11
Total	**100**

Selected Subsidiaries and Products

Deggendorfer Werft und Eisenbau
Autoclaves
Condensers
Dump barges
Floating dredgers
Gas coolers
Heat exchangers
Pilot reactors
Pressure vessels
Tube reactors
Salt bath-cooled reactors

Ferrostaal
Facility construction and contracting
Industrial equipment and systems
Steel trading and logistics

MAN B&W Diesel
Diesel engines for locomotives, marine propulsion, and
 power plants
Exhaust gas turbochargers
Power turbines

MAN Nutzfarzeuge
Buses and coaches
Components
Axles
Cabs
Cast parts
Pressed parts
Tools
Transfer cases
Diesel engines for automobiles, boats, and power
 generation
Gas Motors
Transport logistics and fleet management
Trucks (6 to 50 tons gross weight)

MAN Roland Druckmaschinen
Digital-based printing systems
Sheet-fed offset printing presses
Web-fed offset printing presses

MAN Technologie
Space transport propulsion components and systems

MAN Turbomaschinen GHH BORSIG
Industrial compressors
Industrial turbines

RENK
Automatic transmissions for tracked vehicles
Bearings
Couplings
Industrial gear units

Schwäbische Hüttenwerke
Brake discs
Castings
Chilled cast iron rolls
Industrial pumps
Sintered parts

SMS
Plant and rolling-mill equipment
Plastics-processing equipment
Pressing and forging equipment

COMPETITORS

ALSTOM	J.M. Voith
ArvinMeritor, Inc.	Kawasaki Heavy Industries
Baldwin Technology	Koenig & Bauer
Cummins	mg technologies
DaimlerChrysler	Mitsubishi Heavy
Dana	Industries
DEUTZ	Navistar
Federal-Mogul	PACCAR
Fiat	Renault
GE Power Systems	Scania
Goss International	Sumitomo Heavy
HHIC	Industries
Heidelberg	TUI
ITT Industries	Volvo

HISTORICAL FINANCIALS
Company Type: Public

Income Statement
FYE: December 31

	REVENUE ($ mil.)	NET INCOME ($ mil.)	NET PROFIT MARGIN	EMPLOYEES
12/02	16,812	142	0.8%	75,054
12/01	14,439	134	0.9%	77,606
12/00*	7,085	151	2.1%	76,604
6/00	13,881	404	2.9%	71,239
6/99	13,687	355	2.6%	66,838
6/98	13,716	316	2.3%	64,054
6/97	12,251	184	1.5%	62,564
6/96	13,279	198	1.5%	57,826
6/95	13,475	186	1.4%	56,503
6/94	11,425	95	0.8%	58,527
Annual Growth	**4.4%**	**4.6%**	**—**	**2.8%**

*Fiscal year change

2002 Year-End Financials

Debt ratio: 41.2%   Current ratio: 2.39
Return on equity: 5.3%   Long-term debt ($ mil.): 1,136
Cash ($ mil.): 1,338

Net Income History
German: MAN

Marks and Spencer Group

The sun now sets on Marks and Spencer (M&S). The department stores sell mid-priced clothing, food, and household items under the company's famous private label, the "very British" St. Michael brand (found on items ranging from tweed jackets to marmalade). The UK's largest seller of clothing, it has sold off most overseas operations in order to salvage its 330 M&S stores in the UK. The company got rid of more than 220 Brooks Brothers clothing stores in the US and Asia (to Retail Brand Alliance, 2001) and its 18 M&S stores in France (to Galeries Lafayette, 2001). New York grocer Gristede's offered to pay $120 million for M&S's Kings Super Markets chain, but in 2003 the company announced it does not plan to sell.

A previous deal to sell the New Jersey-based supermarket chain to Gristede's rival D'Agostino failed, as did an earlier offer made by Gristede's in 2002.

M&S (Marks & Sparks in Cockney rhyming slang) also sells prepared foods, such as its popular (and high-margin) ready-to-go meals. The company is building Simply Food outlets around the UK (it plans to have 150 by 2006, including a pilot program to put Simply Food stores in railway stations), and it is rebranding 26 of its existing food stores as Marks & Spencer Food (seven are due to open by March 2004) over the next two years. M&S Food stores are larger than the Simply Food outlets and designate a small amount of floor space to general merchandise. In addition, M&S offers credit cards, life insurance, and pension funds. M&S is closing its catalog operations.

In 2002 the company pinched rival Selfridges PLC's chief executive Vittorio Radice to head up its housewares business, which is set to expand across the UK as a stand-alone store (Marks&Spencer Lifestore); M&S Lifestore is slated to open its first outlet in the spring of 2004.

Launched in the fall of 2003, M&S is diversifying its clothing offerings with a new "smart casual" menswear line — called SP — aimed at middle-aged men. The clothing retailer is also working on a new underwear collection for men and women.

HISTORY

Fleeing anti-Semitic persecution in Russian Poland, 19-year-old Michael Marks immigrated to England in 1882. Eventually settling in Leeds, Marks eked out a meager existence as a traveling peddler until he opened a small stall at the town market in 1884. Because he spoke little English, Marks laid out all of his merchandise and hung a sign that read, "Don't Ask the Price, It's a Penny," unaware at the time that self-service would eventually become the retailing standard. His methods were so successful that he had penny bazaars in five cities by 1890.

Finding himself unable to run the growing operation alone, Marks established an equal partnership with Englishman Tom Spencer, a cashier for a local distributor, forming Marks and Spencer in 1894. By the turn of the century, the company had 36 branches. Following the deaths of Spencer (1905) and Marks (1907), management of the company did not return to family hands until 1916, when Marks' 28-year-old son Simon became chairman.

Marks and Spencer broke with time-honored British retailing tradition in 1924 by eliminating wholesalers and establishing direct links with manufacturers. In 1926 the firm went public, and two years later it launched its now famous St Michael brand. The company turned its attention to pruning unprofitable departments to concentrate on goods that had a rapid turnover. In 1931 the Marks & Spencer stores (M&S) introduced a food department that sold produce and canned goods.

The company sustained severe losses during WWII, when bombing damaged approximately half of its stores. Marks and Spencer rebuilt, and in 1964 Simon's brother-in-law Israel Sieff became chairman. The company expanded to North America a decade later by buying three Canadian chains: Peoples (general merchandise, sold 1992), D'Allaird's (women's clothing, sold 1996), and Walker's (clothing shops, converted to M&S). Sieff's son Marcus Sieff became chairman in 1972. It opened its first store in Paris in 1975.

Derek Rayner replaced Marcus Sieff as chairman in 1984, becoming the first chairman hired from outside the Marks family since 1916. Under Rayner, Marks and Spencer moved into financial services by launching a charge card in 1985. The company purchased US-based Kings Super Markets and Brooks Brothers (upscale clothing stores) in 1988. Rayner retired in 1991, and CEO Richard Greenbury became chairman. During the 1990s M&S opened new stores in Germany, Hong Kong, Hungary, Spain, and Turkey.

In 1997 it paid Littlewoods $323 million for 19 UK stores, which it converted to M&S. Greenbury, facing criticism that the company was too slow to expand and embrace new ideas, in 1999 was succeeded as CEO by handpicked heir Peter Salsbury. That year, continued poor sales led Marks and Spencer to cut 700 jobs, close its 38 M&S stores in Canada, and part ways with its clothing supplier of 30 years, William Baird. In early 2000 Marks and Spencer dodged a takeover attempt by investor Philip Green. Chairman Luc Vandevelde took over as CEO, in September, when Salsbury resigned.

In spring 2001 Marks and Spencer announced a recovery plan to salvage its struggling M&S chain by selling off many of its global operations, including its profitable US businesses (Brooks Brothers and Kings Super Markets). Unhappy with the company's direction and its departure from older values, Marks and Spencer board members Sir David Sieff (the last remaining founder member), Sir Ralph Robins, and Sir Michael Perry left the board in July 2001. Marks and Spencer sold Brooks Brothers to Retail Brand Alliance for $225 million (a loss from the $750 million the company paid for it in 1988) in November 2001 and nearly managed to sell its Kings Super Markets business to New York supermarket operator D'Agostino in July 2002, but the deal fell through later in the year due to a lack of financing.

Also in July 2002 Vandevelde — who is credited with masterminding the M&S turnaround — announced he would give up his role as CEO and hand the reins to managing director Roger Holmes. Vandevelde became the company's part-time chairman on January 1, 2003.

EXECUTIVES

Part-time Chairman: Luc Vandevelde, age 52, $1,777,723 pay
CEO and Director: Roger Holmes, age 43, $1,466,943 pay
CFO and Board Member: Alison Reed, age 46, $913,810 pay
Executive Director, Clothing, Outlets and International: David Norgrove, age 55, $819,720 pay
Executive Director, Home Division: Vittorio Radice, age 45, $463,320 pay (partial-year salary)
Director, Communications: Flic Howard-Allen, age 42
Director, Human Resources: Jean Tomlin, age 47
Director, IT: Stuart Senior, age 54
Director, Marketing and E-Commerce: Alice Avis, age 40
Director, Retail: Barry Stevenson, age 41
Director, Strategic Marketing: Nick Penny
Director, Supply Chain and Technology: Vince McGinlay, age 51
Business Unit Director, Menswear: Maurice Halfgott, age 35
Business Unit Director, Womenswear: Steve Longdon, age 50
Creative Director, Clothing: Yasmin Yusuf, age 43
Business Unit Director, Beauty and Lingerie: Jack Paterson, age 41
Chief Executive of Marks & Spencer Financial Services, and Board Member: Laurel Powers-Freeling, age 45, $305,078 pay (partial-year salary)
Group Secretary and Head of Corporate Governance: Graham Oakley, age 46
Financial Controller: Ian Moss, age 43
Auditors: PricewaterhouseCoopers LLP

LOCATIONS

HQ: Marks and Spencer Group p.l.c.
Michael House, Baker St.,
London W1U 8EP, United Kingdom
Phone: +44-20-7935-4422   **Fax:** +44-20-7487-2679
Web: www.marksandspencer.com

2003 Sales

	% of total
UK retail	88
International retail	8
Financial services	4
Total	**100**

PRODUCTS/OPERATIONS

2003 Sales

	% of total
Retailing	96
Financial services	4
Total	**100**

COMPETITORS

Allders
Arcadia
ASDA
Benetton
Burberry
Carrefour
Debenhams
Fortnum & Mason
Gap
GUS
Harrods
Harvey Nichols
House of Fraser
J Sainsbury
John Lewis
Kingfisher
Littlewoods
Mothercare
New Look
NEXT plc
Pret A Manger
Safeway plc
Somerfield
Syms
Tesco

HISTORICAL FINANCIALS

Company Type: Public

Income Statement

FYE: March 31

	REVENUE ($ mil.)	NET INCOME ($ mil.)	NET PROFIT MARGIN	EMPLOYEES
3/03	12,713	756	5.9%	67,133
3/02	11,598	218	1.9%	69,899
3/01	11,438	2	0.0%	76,491
3/00	13,046	412	3.2%	75,657
3/99	13,265	600	4.5%	75,492
3/98	13,820	1,390	10.1%	71,297
3/97	12,850	1,237	9.6%	68,208
3/96	11,000	996	9.0%	65,498
3/95	—	—	—	63,331
Annual Growth	**2.1%**	**(3.8%)**	**—**	**0.7%**

2003 Year-End Financials

Debt ratio: 59.6%
Return on equity: 17.2%
Cash ($ mil.): 264
Current ratio: 1.96
Long-term debt ($ mil.): 2,849

Net Income History

Pink Sheets: MAKSY

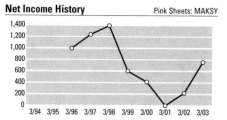

Marubeni Corporation

Marubeni's name combines the Japanese words for "circle" and "red," and Marubeni hopes the comprehensive range of products manufactured and traded by its circle of operating units will keep the company out of the red. One of Japan's largest *sogo shosha* (general trading companies), Marubeni has 12 business divisions: Agri-Marine Products; Chemicals; Development and Construction; Energy; Finance and Logistics; Forest Products and General Merchandise; IT; Metals and Mineral Resources; Plant and Ship; Textiles; Transportation and Industrial Machinery; and Utility and Infrastructure.

The company has hundreds of subsidiaries in more than 70 countries, but it has been particularly active in Asia, where its diversity has enabled it to develop local industries and to help build utility and industrial infrastructures such as telephone systems, power plants, and water systems. Marubeni has championed international expansion since the mid-1990s, but Japan's credit crunch and the Asian economic crisis have hurt the company's production and processing operations across Southeast Asia. Marubeni is trying to reduce debt and control operating costs.

HISTORY

Marubeni's origins are closely linked to those of another leading Japanese trading company. ITOCHU founder Chubei Itoh set up Marubeni Shoten K. K. in 1858 as an outlet in Osaka for his textile trading business (originally C. Itoh & Co.). The symbol for the store was a circle (*maru*) drawn around the Japanese word for red (*beni*). As C. Itoh's global operations expanded, the Marubeni store served as headquarters.

Marubeni was split off from C. Itoh in 1921 to trade textiles, although it soon expanded its operations to include industrial and consumer goods. To mobilize for WWII, the Japanese government reunited Marubeni and C. Itoh in 1941, merging them with another trading company, Kishimoto, into a new entity, Sanko Kabushiki Kaisha. In 1944 Sanko, Daido Boeki, and Kureha Spinning were ordered to consolidate into a larger entity to be called the Daiken Co., but the war ended before all operations were fully integrated.

Spun off from Daiken in 1949, Marubeni began trading internationally. It opened a New York office in 1951 and diversified into food, metals, and machinery. During the Korean War, Marubeni benefited from the UN's use of Japan as a supply base.

In 1955 Marubeni merged with Iida & Company and changed its name to Marubeni-Iida. It received a government concession to supply silicon steel and iron sheets critical to the growing Japanese auto and appliance industries. The company expanded into engineering — building factories, aircraft, and a nuclear reactor for the Japan Atomic Energy Research Institute — and into petrochemicals, fertilizers, and rubber products.

Marubeni-Iida was behind the Fuyo *keiretsu* formed in the early 1960s. Fuyo (another word for Mt. Fuji) is a powerful assemblage of some 150 companies, including Canon, Hitachi, and Nissan, that form joint ventures and develop think tanks.

The firm became Marubeni Corp. in 1972, and a year later it bought Nanyo Bussan, another trading company. In 1973 Marubeni's image was tarnished by allegations that it had hoarded rice for sale on the Japanese black market.

In the 1990s Marubeni won several major construction contracts. Among them, Marubeni formed a venture in 1998 with John Laing and Turkey's Alarko Alsim to rebuild three airports in Uzbekistan.

Marubeni had begun offering Internet access in 1995, and two years later it launched an Internet-based long-distance telephone service. In 1999 the trading house formed two ventures with US firm Global Crossing, one to start operating Pacific Crossing One (the Japan-US cable) and another to lay a cable network in Japan.

That year Marubeni tied up with fellow trading company ITOCHU to integrate their steel processing subsidiaries in China to try to keep their Chinese businesses afloat.

In 2000 ITOCHU and Marubeni formed an on-line steel trading joint venture with US-based e-commerce company MetalSite. The two companies also integrated their entire steel divisions in 2001, forming the Marubeni-Itochu Steel joint venture, among the largest steel companies in Japan.

Taking responsibility for the sharp downturn in Marubeni's financial performance, chairman Iwao Toriumi announced in 2001 that he would step down. The company launched a major restructuring effort the next year that was designed to give more autonomy to the managers of individual business units.

EXECUTIVES

Chairman: Tohru Tsuji
President and CEO: Nobuo Katsumata
Executive Deputy President: Katsuo Koh
Executive Deputy President: Shigeki Kuwahara
EVP and CIO: Toshio Nakagawa
EVP: Yuji Kato
EVP; General Manager for the Americas; President and CEO, Marubeni America: Kazuhiko Sakamoto
SVP: Akira Matsuda
SVP: Makoto Isogai
SVP: Kazuo Ogawa
SVP: Tomoyuki Nakayama
SVP: Susumu Watanabe
SVP; Chief Executive for Europe and Africa; Managing Director and CEO, Marubeni Europe: Kiyoshi Yoshimitsu
SVP; Chief Representative in Indonesia; President and CEO, Marubeni Indonesia: Masakatsu Takita
Auditors: Ernst & Young

LOCATIONS

HQ: 4-2, Ohtemachi 1-chome, Chiyoda-ku, Tokyo 100-8088, Japan
Phone: +81-3-3282-2111   **Fax:** +81-3-3282-4241
US HQ: 450 Lexington Ave., New York, NY 10017
US Phone: 212-450-0100   **US Fax:** 212-450-0708
Web: www.marubeni.co.jp

PRODUCTS/OPERATIONS

2003 Sales

	% of total
Overseas units	17
Agri-marine products	14
Transportation & industrial machinery	13
Forest products & general merchandise	10
Development & construction	8
IT	8
Energy	7
Chemicals	7
Textile	6
Metals & mineral resources	3
Plant & ship	3
Utility & infrastructure	2
Finance & logistics	1
Domestic units	1
Total	**100**

COMPETITORS

ITOCHU	Nissho Iwai-Nichimen
Jardine Matheson	Samsung
LG Group	Sime Darby
Mitsubishi Corporation	Sumitomo
Mitsui	TOMEN

HISTORICAL FINANCIALS

Company Type: Public

Income Statement

FYE: March 31

	REVENUE ($ mil.)	NET INCOME ($ mil.)	NET PROFIT MARGIN	EMPLOYEES
3/03	3,543	253	7.1%	3,914
3/02	3,293	(878)	—	4,234
3/01	3,798	119	3.1%	7,073
3/00	4,298	20	0.5%	5,344
3/99	4,386	(988)	—	8,618
3/98	4,017	130	3.2%	9,041
3/97	4,011	163	4.1%	9,282
Annual Growth	**(2.0%)**	**7.7%**	**—**	**(13.4%)**

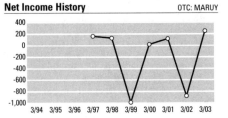

2003 Year-End Financials

Debt ratio: 731.5%   Current ratio: 1.05
Return on equity: 12.2%   Long-term debt ($ mil.): 15,873
Cash ($ mil.): 3,893

Net Income History   OTC: MARUY

Matsushita Electric Industrial Co.

Matsushita Electric Industrial, the world's #2 consumer electronics maker (behind Sony), may have an unfamiliar name, but its brands are recognizable: Panasonic, Quasar, Technics, and JVC, to name a few. Its AVC Networks sector produces TVs, VCRs, CD and DVD players, PCs, cellular phones, and other communications equipment. Matsushita also sells components (batteries, semiconductors, electric motors), home appliances (washing machines, vacuum cleaners), and industrial equipment (welding and vending machines, medical equipment). The Matsushita group includes more than 380 consolidated companies around the globe; its products are sold worldwide.

Matsushita (whose founder's name means "lucky man under the pine tree") also makes products sold around the world under the National and Victor brands. The company plans to change the brand name for all home appliance products in non-Japanese markets to Panasonic from National; the National brand will continue to be used (along with Panasonic) in Japan.

Matsushita has created a new division for automotive electronics, which focuses on car audio and navigation systems; it also plans to merge two German car electronics divisions into a new unit, Panasonic Automotive Systems Europe.

Matsushita has announced that it will work with Sony to develop software that uses the Linux operating system to run home electronics. Matsushita also launched joint ventures with Toshiba (CRT development and manufacturing), NEC (mobile handset development), and Nokia (data exchange technology development).

The fast-growing flat-screen television market has become a new focus for Matsushita; with its plasma display panel (PDP) and liquid crystal display (LCD) products, the company hopes to double its share of that market by 2005. Matsushita is also accelerating its chip-making operations, viewing semiconductors as a key ingredient in product innovation.

Matsushita wrote the book on long-range planning: In 1932 founder Konosuke Matsushita created a 250-year business plan for the company.

HISTORY

Grade school dropout Konosuke Matsushita took $50 in 1918 and went into business making electric plugs (with his brother-in-law, Toshio Iue, founder of SANYO). His mission, to help people by making high-quality, low-priced conveniences while providing his employees with good working conditions, earned him the sobriquet, "god of business management." Matsushita Electric Industrial grew by developing inexpensive lamps, batteries, radios, and motors in the 1920s and 1930s.

During WWII the Japanese government ordered the firm to build wood-laminate products for the military. Postwar occupation forces prevented Matsushita from working at his firm for four years. Thanks to unions' efforts, he rejoined his namesake company shortly before it entered a joint venture with Dutch manufacturer Philips in 1952. The following year it moved into consumer goods, making televisions, refrigerators, and washing machines and later expanding into high-performance audio products. Matsushita bought a majority stake in Victor Company of Japan (JVC, originally established by RCA Victor) in 1954. Its 1959 New York subsidiary opening began Matsushita's drive overseas.

Sold under the National, Panasonic, and Technics names, the firm's products were usually not cutting edge but were attractively priced. Under Masaharu Matsushita, the founder's son-in-law who became president in 1961, the company became Japan's largest home appliance maker, introducing air conditioners, microwave ovens, stereo components, and VCRs in the 1960s and 1970s. JVC developed the VHS format for VCRs, which beat out Sony's Betamax format.

Matsushita built much of its sales growth on new industrial and commercial customers in the 1980s. The company expanded its semiconductor, office and factory automation, auto electronics, audiovisual, housing, and air-conditioning product offerings that decade. Konosuke died in 1989.

The next year Matsushita joined the Japanese stampede for US acquisitions, buying Universal Studios owner MCA (Universal Studios is now named Vivendi UNIVERSAL Entertainment). In 1993 Yoichi Morishita was named president and the company acquired Philips' stake in the two firms' joint venture. Two years later, when cultural incompatibility depressed MCA's performance, Matsushita sold 80% of the company (now Universal) to liquor mogul Seagram, resulting in a fiscal 1996 loss. That same year Matsushita introduced the first DVD player.

A lagging market led Matsushita to close its North American semiconductor operations in late 1998. Also that year the company bought a stake in Mobile Broadcasting (a digital satellite broadcasting venture of nine companies) and introduced digital TVs.

Matsushita in 1999 bought a 9% stake in Symbian, a venture created by the makers of 85% of the world's mobile phones (including Motorola and Nokia). In 2000 Yoichi Morishita became chairman and Kunio Nakamura took the reigns as president of Matsushita. The next year the company began making chips for cell phones, digital cameras, and digital TVs.

In early 2002 Matsushita announced plans to turn its financial slump around by cutting 13,000 local jobs (through early retirement) and trimming directors' salaries. The company also reclassified its former consumer, industrial, and components categories into four new divisions:

AVC networks, home appliances, industrial equipment, and components and devices.

In April 2002 Matsushita buddied up with Chinese home appliance manufacturer, TCL Holdings; by combining efforts in sales and product development, Matsushita intends to increase its presence in China's growing consumer electronic market. That month the firm established a joint venture with Toshiba for the manufacture and sale of liquid crystal display (LCD) panels and next-generation display devices.

Matsushita combined its Home Appliance and Housing Electronics division with its Air-Conditioner division to form the Matsushita Home Appliances Company in April 2003.

EXECUTIVES

Honorary Chairman: Masaharu Matsushita, age 91
Chairman: Yoichi Morishita, age 69
Vice Chairman: Masayuki Matsushita, age 58
President: Kunio Nakamura, age 64
EVP, Corporate Marketing for Panasonic and National Brands, Corporate Sales Strategy: Kazuo Toda, age 62
EVP, Overseas Operations: Yukio Shohtoku, age 64
EVP, Public and Private Institutions, Recycling Business Promotion, and Panasonic Center: Osamu Tanaka, age 63
Senior Managing Director, Storage Device Business; President, Panasonic AVC Networks Company: Fumio Ohtsubo, age 58
Senior Managing Director, Technology, Device Technology, and Environmental Technology, Production Engineering, Intellectual Property, Overseas Research Laboratories, and Camera Module Business; President, Semiconductor Company: Susumo Koike, age 58
Senior Managing Director; President, Panasonic Automotive Systems Company: Takami Sano, age 60
Managing Director, Appliance Business, Packaged Air-Conditioner Company, and Healthcare Business Company; President, Matsushita Home Appliances Company: Yoshitaka Hayashi, age 57
Managing Director, Corporate Facility Management; President, Display Devices Company: Hidetsugu Otsuru, age 60
Managing Director, Corporate Legal Affairs Division: Haruo Ueno, age 63
Managing Director, Finance and Accounting: Tetsuya Kawakami, age 62
Managing Director, Multimedia Technology, Software Technology, and Digital Network Strategic Planning: Yoshiaki Kushiki, age 57
Director, Personnel, General Affairs, and Social Relations: Shinichi Fukushima, age 55
Auditors: KPMG

LOCATIONS

HQ: Matsushita Denki Sangyo Kabushiki Kaisha
(Matsushita Electric Industrial Co., Ltd.)
1006, Kadoma, Kadoma City,
Osaka 571-8501, Japan
Phone: +81-6-6908-1121   **Fax:** +81-6-6908-2351
US HQ: 1 Panasonic Way, Secaucus, NJ 07094
US Phone: 201-348-7000   **US Fax:** 201-392-6007
Web: matsushita.co.jp

2003 Sales

	$ mil.	% of total
Asia		
Japan	28,782.2	47
Other	12,724.5	21
Americas	11,841.2	19
Europe	8,333.0	13
Total	**61,680.9**	**100**

PRODUCTS/OPERATIONS

2003 Sales

	$ mil.	% of total
AVC Networks		
Information and communications equipment	19,132.6	31
Video and audio equipment	17,499.3	28
Components and devices	12,582.8	21
Home appliances	10,091.3	16
Industrial equipment	2,374.9	4
Total	**61,680.9**	**100**

Selected Products

Information and Communications Equipment
Audio-visual systems (business and broadcast)
Cable TV systems
Car audio and navigation equipment
CD-ROM drives
Cellular phones
Copiers
Cordless phones
DVD-ROM drives
Fax machines
HDDs
Large-screen displays
PCs
Printers

Video and Audio Equipment
Camcorders
Digital still cameras
CD players
DVD players and receivers
Electronic musical instruments
Mini Disc players
Stereo equipment
Tape recorders
TVs (CRT, flat-screen, LCD, plasma display)
VCRs

Components
Batteries
Compressors
Display devices
Electric motors
General electronic components
Semiconductors

Home Appliances and Household Equipment
Air conditioners and purifiers
Bicycles
Dishwashers
Dryers
Electric lamps
Fans
Irons
Microwave ovens
Refrigerators
Rice cookers
Vacuum cleaners
Washing machines
Water heaters

Industrial Equipment
Factory automation equipment
Medical equipment
Power distribution equipment
Vending machines
Ventilating and air-conditioning equipment
Welding equipment

COMPETITORS

3M	Maytag
Bose	Mitsubishi Electric
Canon	Mitsumi Electric
Daewoo Electronics	Motorola
Dell	NEC
Eastman Kodak	Nokia
Electrolux AB	Oki Electric
E-MU / ENSONIQ	Philips Electronics
Evercel	Pioneer
Fuji Electric	Samsung
Fujitsu	SANYO
GE	Sharp
Hewlett-Packard	Siemens
Hitachi	Sony
IDT International	Tatung
Intel	TDK
IBM	THOMSON
ITOCHU	Toshiba
LG Group	Whirlpool
Mabuchi Motor	Xerox

HISTORICAL FINANCIALS

Company Type: Public

Income Statement

FYE: March 31

	REVENUE ($ mil.)	NET INCOME ($ mil.)	NET PROFIT MARGIN	EMPLOYEES
3/03	61,681	(162)	—	288,324
3/02	51,830	(3,248)	—	297,196
3/01	61,199	331	0.5%	292,790
3/00	71,118	971	1.4%	290,448
3/99	63,668	113	0.2%	282,000
3/98	59,259	703	1.2%	—
3/97	61,903	1,112	1.8%	—
3/96	64,102	(537)	—	—
3/95	78,069	1,017	1.3%	—
3/94	64,307	238	0.4%	—
Annual Growth	(0.5%)	—	—	0.6%

2003 Year-End Financials

Debt ratio: 18.5%
Return on equity: —
Cash ($ mil.): 9,729
Current ratio: 1.55
Long-term debt ($ mil.): 4,902

No. of shares (mil.): 2,359
Dividends
Yield: 0.9%
Payout: —
Market value ($ mil.): 20,125

Stock History

NYSE: MC

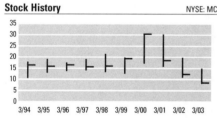

	STOCK PRICE ($) FY Close	P/E High/Low	PER SHARE ($) Earnings	Dividends	Book Value
3/03	8.53	— —	(0.07)	0.08	11.23
3/02	12.35	— —	(1.57)	0.10	11.78
3/01	18.45	332 178	0.09	0.12	7.23
3/00	30.30	67 39	0.45	0.12	1.64
3/99	19.34	390 256	0.05	0.05	1.43
3/98	15.99	68 44	0.31	0.05	1.34
3/97	15.63	38 29	0.49	0.05	1.41
3/96	16.50	— —	(0.25)	0.06	1.53
3/95	15.80	40 28	0.47	0.12	1.74
3/94	16.40	160 98	0.11	0.10	1.52
Annual Growth	(7.0%)	— —	—	(2.4%)	24.8%

Mazda Motor Corporation

Mazda Motor Corporation, Japan's fifth-largest automaker — behind Toyota, Nissan, Honda, and Mitsubishi — has been steering for a better position. Mazda makes cars, minivans, pickup trucks, and commercial vehicles. Models sold by Mazda in the US include sedans (Protegé, Mazda 6), minivans (MPV), sports cars (Miata, RX-8), and pickup trucks (B-Series). Operating from two Japanese and 17 international manufacturing plants, Mazda sells some 330,000 vehicles annually in Japan, and more than 630,000 abroad. Ford Motor owns a controlling 33% of Mazda.

Mazda's recovery could be credited to Ford. After raising its stake in Mazda, Ford installed its own management and sought to improve cash flow and reduce debt by closing sales outlets and selling hundreds of millions of dollars worth of holdings in other companies. Ford also consolidated businesses in the US, cut jobs, and tightened control over subsidiaries' operations and budgets.

The changes seem to have paid off. Mazda hopes to keep its momentum going by building a single brand image for Mazda models and by sharing platforms and technology with Ford.

HISTORY

Ingiro Matsuda founded cork producer Toyo Cork Kogyo in Hiroshima in 1920. The company changed its name to Toyo Kogyo in 1927 and began making machine tools. Impressed by Ford trucks used in 1923 earthquake-relief efforts, Matsuda had the company make a three-wheel motorcycle/truck hybrid in 1931.

The second Sino-Japanese War forced Toyo Kogyo to make rifles and cut back on its truck production. Although the company built a prototype passenger car in 1940, the outbreak of WWII refocused it on weapons. The August 1945 bombing of Hiroshima killed more than 400 Toyo Kogyo workers, but the company persevered, producing 10 trucks that December. By 1949 it was turning out 800 per month.

The company launched the first Mazda, a two-seat minicar, in 1960. The next year Toyo Kogyo licensed Audi's new rotary engine technology. After releasing a string of models, the company became Japan's #3 automaker in 1964. Toyo Kogyo introduced the first Mazda powered by a rotary engine, Cosmo/110S, in 1967, followed by the Familia in 1968.

The company grew rapidly and began exporting to the US in 1970. However, recession, high gas prices, and concern over the inefficiency of rotary engines halted growth in the mid-1970s. Sumitomo Bank bailed out Toyo Kogyo. The company shifted emphasis back to piston engines but managed to launch the rotary engine RX-7 in 1978.

Ford's need for small-car expertise and Sumitomo's desire for a large partner for its client led to Ford's purchase of 25% of Toyo Kogyo in 1979. The company's early 1980s GLC/323 and 626 models were sold as Fords in Asia, Latin America, and the Middle East.

Toyo Kogyo changed its name to Mazda Motor Corporation in 1984. ("Mazda" is loosely derived from Matsuda's name, but the carmaker has never discouraged an association with the Zoroastrian god of light, Ahura Mazda.) The company opened a US plant in 1985, but a strong yen, expensive increases in production capacity, and a growing number of models led to increased overhead, soaring debt, and shrinking margins. By 1988 Mazda had begun to focus on sporty niche cars; it launched the hot-selling Miata in 1989.

The company faced more problems with the early 1990s' recession. In 1992 Mazda introduced a new 626 model. That year Mazda also sold half its interest in its Flat Rock, Michigan, plant to Ford. As the yen, development costs, and prices for its cars in the US all rose, sales in the US fell. In 1993 Mazda reorganized subsidiary Mazda of America by cutting staff.

Ford sank $481 million into Mazda in 1996, increasing its stake to 33%. That year the Ford-appointed former EVP of Mazda, Henry Wallace, became Mazda's president, making history as the first non-Japanese to head a major Japanese corporation. In 1997 Wallace resigned to become CFO of Ford's European operations, and former Ford executive James Miller replaced him. That year Mazda consolidated four US operations into Mazda North American Operations.

Restructuring continued in 1998 as Mazda consolidated some European operations and closed a plant in Thailand. In 1999 Mazda sold its credit division to Ford and its Naldec auto parts unit to Ford's Visteon unit. It announced plans to sell its stake in South Korean carmaker Kia Motors. Later in the year, another American, Ford's Mark Fields, took over as president.

In 2000 Mazda recalled 30,000 MPV minivans (year 2000) to fix a powertrain control module and asked owners of all year 2000 MPVs to bring in their vehicles for front-bumper reinforcement. Mazda also announced plans to close about 40% of its North American dealership outlets over the next three years.

In 2001 Mazda completed a program to assume direct control over distribution in some European markets including France, Italy, Spain, and the UK.

EXECUTIVES

Representative Director and Chairman: Kazuhide Watanabe
President and CEO: Hisakazu Imaki
Senior Managing Executive Officer, CFO, and Representative Director: Gideon Wolthers
Senior Managing Executive Officer, China and Overseas Sales: Tsuneo Matsubara
Senior Managing Executive Officer, IT Solution, e-Business, General Affairs, Legal Affairs, Risk Management, and Osaka Branch; Assistant to the CFO: Ryoichi Hasegawa
Senior Managing Executive Officer, Marketing, Sales, and Customer Service: Stephen T. Odell
Senior Managing Executive Officer, Purchasing: Mutsumi Fujiwara
Senior Managing Executive Officer, Secretariat, Personnel and Human Development, Internal Auditing and Mazda Hospital: Takashi Yamanouchi
Managing Executive Officer, Corporate Planning and Cost Planning; General Manager, Corporate Planning Division: M. Greg Gollaher
Managing Executive Officer, Design, Product Development, and Strategic Cost Innovation: Joseph Bakaj
Managing Executive Officer, Domestic Marketing, Domestic Sales, and Domestic Customer Service: Masao Furuta
Managing Executive Officer, Financial Services and Domestic Dealer Financial Administration; General Manager, Financial Services Division: Kiyoshi Ozaki
Executive Officer; President and CEO, Mazda Motor of America (Mazda North American Operations): James J. O'Sullivan

Executive Officer, Corporate Communications and Liaison; General Manager, Corporate Communications and Liaison Division: Masazumi Wakayama
Executive Officer; General Manager, Personnel and Human Development Division: Masaki Kanda
Auditors: Asahi & Co.

LOCATIONS

HQ: Matsuda Jidosha Kabushiki Kaisha
3-1, Shinchi, Fuchu-cho, Aki-gun,
Hiroshima 730-8670, Japan
Phone: +81-82-282-1111   **Fax:** +81-82-287-5190
US HQ: 7755 Irvine Center Dr., Irvine, CA 92623
US Phone: 949-727-1990   **US Fax:** 949-727-6101
Web: www.mazda.co.jp

Mazda Motor Corporation has production facilities in 15 countries. Its sales and service network includes about 1,300 sales outlets in Japan and more than 4,800 in other countries.

PRODUCTS/OPERATIONS

Selected Models

Bongo (van)
B-Series (pickup)
Demio (compact wagon)
Familia (compact wagon)
Miata (sports car)
MPV (van)
Protegé (compact sedan)
RX-8 (sports car)

Selected Subsidiaries and Affiliates

AutoAlliance International, Inc. (US)
Malox Co., Ltd.
Mazda Australia Pty. Ltd.
Mazda Motor Logistics Europe NV (Belgium)
Mazda Motor of America, Inc. (US)
Toyo Advanced Technologies Co., Ltd.

COMPETITORS

BMW	Kia Motors
DaimlerChrysler	Nissan
Fiat	Peugeot
Ford	Renault
Fuji Heavy Industries	Saab Automobile
General Motors	Suzuki Motor
Honda	Toyota
Isuzu	Volkswagen

HISTORICAL FINANCIALS

Company Type: Public

Income Statement

FYE: March 31

	REVENUE ($ mil.)	NET INCOME ($ mil.)	NET PROFIT MARGIN	EMPLOYEES
3/03	19,730	201	1.0%	36,184
3/02	15,794	67	0.4%	37,824
3/01	15,957	(1,229)	—	39,601
3/00	20,487	248	1.2%	43,818
3/99	17,271	325	1.9%	31,851
3/98	15,341	(51)	—	31,665
3/97	15,301	(142)	—	32,919
3/96	17,182	(111)	—	33,705
3/95	25,467	(476)	—	35,361
3/94	21,296	(477)	—	33,118
Annual Growth	(0.8%)	—	—	1.0%

2003 Year-End Financials

Debt ratio: 184.0%
Return on equity: 13.8%
Cash ($ mil.): 2,320
Current ratio: 0.82
Long-term debt ($ mil.): 2,980

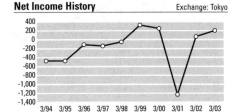

Net Income History   Exchange: Tokyo

METRO AG

A ride on METRO could be a shopper's delight. The company, Germany's largest retailer, owns and operates more than 2,300 wholesale stores, supermarkets, hypermarkets, department stores, and specialty retailers (home improvement, consumer electronics), mainly in Germany and the rest of Europe. Its store banners include Metro, Makro, and Galeria Kaufhof. METRO also owns a 49% stake in Divaco, a holding company for noncore interests that were once a part of the company. METRO runs restaurants in its department stores and hypermarkets. It offers advertising and insurance to its retail chains. Nearly 60% of METRO is owned by founder Otto Beisheim, Franz Haniel & Cie, and the Schmidt-Ruthenbeck family.

Germany's über-retailer, METRO reaps about 45% of its sales outside its home country. Beyond Europe, the retailer has stores in China, India, Morocco, Russia, Turkey, Ukraine, and Vietnam, giving the retailer a presence in 28 countries worldwide. METRO plans to open three Metro Cash & Carry hypermarkets in Beijing by 2006, with the first slated to open in August 2004.

Nearly half of the firm's revenues (about 47%) are earned from its Metro and Makro wholesale outlets, which sell food and other grocery and non-grocery items to businesses and institutional customers. More than 765 hypermarkets (Real) and supermarkets (Extra), located primarily in Germany, complete its food retailing operations. METRO also runs consumer electronics chains (Media Markt, Saturn), home improvement centers (nearly 350 Praktiker stores), and department stores (Galeria Kaufhof). METRO is seeking buyers for its Praktiker stores after the chain missed financial targets.

The company has scrapped plans to sell its extensive real estate portfolio, which was estimated as worth $3.5 billion. METRO had been hoping to sell off the assets, which include some 350 supermarket and other retail properties across Europe, and lease them back in order to focus on its core retail business.

HISTORY

In 1964 Otto Beisheim founded METRO SB-Grossmarkte in the German town of Mulheim. A wholesale business serving commercial customers, it operated under the name METRO Cash & Carry. Three years later Beisheim received backing from the owners of Franz Haniel & Cie (an industrial company founded in 1756) and members of the Schmidt-Ruthenbeck family (also in wholesaling). This allowed METRO to expand rapidly in Germany and, in 1968, into the Netherlands under the name Makro Cash & Carry via a part-

nership with Steenkolen Handelsvereeniging (SHV). During the 1970s the company expanded its wholesaling operations within Europe and moved into retailing.

METRO's foray into retailing was aided during the next decade by the acquisition of department store chain Kaufhof AG. By the 1980s the rise of specialty stores had many department stores on the defensive, and Kaufhof's owners sold it to METRO and its investment partner, Union Bank of Switzerland.

As METRO's ownership interest in Kaufhof rose above 50%, the chain began converting some of its stores from department stores into fashion and sporting goods sellers. Kaufhof began acquiring a stake in computer manufacturer and retailer Vobis in 1989. In 1993 METRO, now operating as METRO Holding AG, acquired a majority interest in supermarket company Asko Deutsche Kaufhaus, which owned the Praktiker building materials chain. The reclusive Beisheim retired from active management the following year.

To cut costs and prepare for expansion into Asia, in 1996 METRO Holding merged its German retail holdings — Kaufhof; Asko; another grocery operation, Deutsche SB Kauf; and its German cash-and-carry operations — into one holding company, METRO AG. The new subsidiary purchased 58 Wirichs home improvement centers in Germany that year to complement its Praktiker chain.

In 1998 METRO bought the 196-store Makro self-service wholesale chain from Dutch-based SHV. METRO also added to its German food operations by acquiring the 94-store German Allkauf hypermarket chain and then by purchasing the 20-store Kriegbaum hypermarket chain.

Later that year METRO transferred its interests in noncore businesses, including office supply stores, footwear stores, discount stores, computer operations (including Vobis), and 25 unprofitable Kaufhof department stores to its Divaco (formerly Divag) unit. Divaco then sold 165 German Tip discount stores to Tengelmann Group.

Hans-Joachim Korber became METRO's CEO in 1999. In 2000 the company transferred 290 hypermarkets and department stores in Germany, Greece, Hungary, Luxembourg, and Turkey to a joint venture company (51% owned by Westdeutsche Landesbank) to raise cash for the expansion and remodeling of its wholesale outlets. Expanding on the Internet, METRO acquired control of German e-commerce business Primus Online.

In 2001 METRO redistributed all of its shares held by METRO Holding AG to its top three shareholders for tax purposes. At the end of the year, the first two Cash & Carry stores in Russia and one in Croatia opened.

In August 2002 METRO sold its entire stake in Primus Online to Beisheim Holding Schweiz AG. Overall in 2002 METRO opened 61 stores — 53 of which were Metro Cash & Carry outlets — including new stores in China, Bulgaria, and Russia (one each), and Vietnam (two outlets). In April 2003 the company opened its first store in St. Petersburg (its fourth in Russia). In July, a third Metro Cash and Carry store opened in Vietnam. The German retailer opened a global sourcing headquarters in Hong Kong in September that covers all markets outside the European Union.

As part of its international expansion plan, in October 2003 METRO opened the first of two cash and carry distribution centers in Bangalore, India.

EXECUTIVES

Chairman Supervisory Board: Jan von Haeften
Vice Chairman Supervisory Board: Klaus Bruns
Chairman and CEO Management Board: Hans-Joachim Körber, age 54
CFO: Thomas Unger
COO, Asia-Pacific: Heinrich Birr
Director of Purchasing/Imports, Advertising, and Catering: Stefan Feuerstein
Director of Industrial Relations, Human Resources and Social Affairs, Information Technology, Logistics, e-Business, and Real Estate: Zygmunt Meirdorf
Managing Director and Country Manager, India: Harsh Bahadur
General Director, Metro Cash & Carry, Russia: Herbert Zlabinger
General Director, Metro Cash and Carry, Vietnam: James Scott
Project Director, Russia and Eastern Europe: Franz Muller
Head of Quality Assurance: Hans-Jürgen Matern
Auditors: Fasselt-Mette & Partner GmbH

LOCATIONS

HQ: Metro-Strasse 1, 40235 Düsseldorf, Germany
Phone: +49-211-6886-0   **Fax:** +49-211-6886-2178
Web: www.metro.de

METRO AG operates approximately 2,300 stores in more than 25 countries, primarily in Europe, but also in China, Morocco, Turkey, and Vietnam.

2002 Sales

	% of total
Germany	54
Other countries	46
Total	**100**

PRODUCTS/OPERATIONS

Retail Operations

Cash and Carry
Makro
Metro

Food Retail
Extra
Real

Nonfood Specialty Stores
Media Markt (consumer electronics)
Praktiker (home improvement)
Saturn (consumer electronics)

Department Store
Galeria Kaufhof

Other Operations

Dinea-Gastronomie (restaurants/catering)
Divaco (investment group)
METRO MGE Einkauf (purchasing)
METRO MGI Informatik (IT services)
METRO Real Estate Management (construction services)
METRO Werbegesellschaft (advertising)
METRO Online AG (Internet retailer)
MGB METRO Buying Group Hong Kong Ltd. (purchasing, Asia and Non-European Union countries)

COMPETITORS

ALDI
AVA AG
Carrefour
Casino Guichard
Edeka Zentrale
Karstadt
Vendex
Lidl & Schwarz Stiftung
REWE-Zentral
Royal Ahold
Tengelmann
Wal-Mart

HISTORICAL FINANCIALS

Company Type: Public

Income Statement

FYE: December 31

	REVENUE ($ mil.)	NET INCOME ($ mil.)	NET PROFIT MARGIN	EMPLOYEES
12/02	54,004	464	0.9%	235,283
12/01	43,867	296	0.7%	230,848
12/00	44,189	398	0.9%	234,351
12/99	44,114	367	0.8%	216,457
12/98	54,711	439	0.8%	181,300
12/97	31,717	309	1.0%	134,019
12/96	35,431	393	1.1%	130,019
Annual Growth	**7.3%**	**2.8%**	**—**	**10.4%**

2002 Year-End Financials

Debt ratio: 114.9%
Return on equity: 11.5%
Cash ($ mil.): 1,387
Current ratio: 0.85
Long-term debt ($ mil.): 4,985

Net Income History

German: MEO

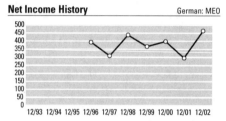

Michelin

The Michelin Man (whose name, by the way, is Bibendum) produces more than 840,000 tires a day — pity the Michelin Woman. Compagnie Générale des Établissements Michelin sells about 36,000 products, including tires, wheels, and inner tubes used on passenger cars and trucks, aircraft, bicycles, and agricultural vehicles. Michelin's tire brands include BF Goodrich, Uniroyal, and Siamtyre. Other company products include travel publications such as road maps and travel guides. A vertically integrated corporation, Michelin owns rubber plantations and factories around the globe.

In response to the massive tire recall by Bridgestone/Firestone, Michelin stepped up production in the US to meet demand. The company is also revamping its operations in Asia, including a new joint venture in China with Shanghai Tyre & Rubber. Edouard Michelin, youngest son of patriarch François Michelin and the fourth generation of Michelins in the business, has been tapped to lead the company. Edouard and his father, along with partner René Zingraff, control the company.

HISTORY

After toying with making rubber balls, Edouard Daubrée and Aristide Barbier formed a partnership in Clermont-Ferrand, France, in 1863 and entered the rubber business in earnest. Both men soon died, but Barbier in-law André Michelin, a successful businessman, took over the company in 1886. André recruited his brother, Edouard, a Parisian artist, to run the company, and in 1889 it was renamed Compagnie Générale des Établissements Michelin.

That year Edouard found that air-filled tires made bicycling more comfortable. But pneumatic tires were experimental and, because they were glued to the rims, required hours to change. In 1891 Edouard made a detachable bicycle tire that took only 15 minutes to change.

The Michelins promoted their tires by persuading cyclists to use them in long-distance races where punctures were likely. They demonstrated the applicability of such tires for cars in an auto race in 1895. In 1898 André commented that a stack of tires would look like a man if it had arms, a notion that led to the creation of Bibendum, the Michelin Man. André launched the *Michelin Guide* for auto tourists in 1900.

Expansion followed as Michelin opened a London office (1905) and began production in Italy (1906) and the US (in New Jersey in 1908). Innovations included detachable rims and spare tires (1906), tubeless tires (1930), treads (1934), and modern low-profile tires (1937). During the Depression, Michelin closed its US plant and accepted a stake in Citroën, later converted into a minority stake in Peugeot, in lieu of payment for tires.

Michelin patented radial tires in 1946. Expansion was largely confined to Europe in the 1950s but, thanks to radials, increased worldwide in the 1960s. Sears began selling Michelin radials in 1966. Radials took hold during the 1970s, and Michelin returned to manufacturing in the US, opening a plant in South Carolina in 1975.

Expanding aggressively (Michelin opened or bought a plant every nine months from 1960 to 1990), the company went into the red when economic conditions dipped in the early 1980s and in 1990 and 1991. The company's $1.5 billion purchase of Uniroyal Goodrich in 1990 contributed to the latter losses but improved Michelin's position in the US, the world's largest auto market.

In response to the losses, Michelin attacked its bloated infrastructure and reinvented itself along nine product lines (according to tire/vehicle type plus travel, suspension, and primary product manufacturing). It also consolidated facilities and cut about 30,000 jobs. The company continued to focus on R&D, bringing out new high-performance tires such as its "green" tire designed to help cars save fuel.

Michelin bought a majority interest in a Polish tire maker in 1995, and the next year it bought 90% of Taurus, a Hungarian firm that produces most of that country's rubber. Michelin joined German competitor Continental in 1996 to make private-label tires for independent distributors. The next year Michelin introduced a run-flat tire capable of traveling 50 miles after a puncture for the automotive aftermarket. The company acquired Icollantas, a Colombian tire group with two factories in Bogotá and Cali, in 1998.

After leading the company for more than 40 years, patriarch François Michelin stepped down in 1999, leaving his youngest son, Edouard, in charge. Almost immediately, Edouard announced a restructuring that would cut 7,500 jobs in Europe, including almost 2,000 in France. The company benefited somewhat from Firestone's recall woes in 2000, but Michelin still faced rising material costs and difficult market conditions.

The European Commission fined Michelin nearly $20 million in 2001, claiming the company engaged in anticompetitive behavior by abusing its dominant position in Europe. In 2003 Michelin and TRW Automotive created EnTire Solutions, a joint venture, to develop a tire pressure monitoring system.

EXECUTIVES

Chairman of the Supervisory Board:
Eric Bourdais de Charbonnière
Co-Managing Partner and General Partner:
Edouard Michelin
Co-Managing Partner and General Partner:
René Zingraff
Member of the Executive Board, Earthmovers, South America: René Fontès
Member of the Executive Board, Europe, Euromaster:
Thierry Coudurier
Member of the Executive Board, Finances, Agriculture:
Michel Rollier
Member of the Executive Board, North America, TCI:
Jim Micali
Member of the Executive Board, Europe:
Christian Tschann
Member of the Executive Board, Passenger Car and Light Truck: Hervé Coyco
Member of the Executive Board, Personnel:
Jean Moreau
Member of the Executive Board, Quality, Aircraft, 2 Wheels: Michel Caron
Member of the Executive Board, Technology Center:
Didier Miraton
Member of the Executive Board, Specialty Product Lines, Agricultural, Aircraft, 2-Wheel, Earthmover, Wheels, Components, South America:
Bernard Vasdeboncoeur
Investor Relations: Eric Le Corre
Shareholders Relations: Jacques-Henri Thonier
Auditors: Compagnie Régionale de Paris

LOCATIONS

HQ: Compagnie Générale des Établissements Michelin
12, cours Sablon, 63000 Clermont-Ferrand, France
Phone: +33-4-73-98-59-00   **Fax:** +33-4-73-98-59-04
US HQ: 1 Parkway South, Greenville, SC 29615
US Phone: 864-458-5000   **US Fax:** 864-458-6359
Web: www.michelin.com

Michelin has more than 80 manufacturing facilities in 19 countries; six rubber plantations in Brazil and Nigeria; and offices in more than 170 countries.

PRODUCTS/OPERATIONS

Selected Products and Services

Agricultural tires
Aircraft tires
Earthmover tires
Passenger car and light-truck tires
Suspension systems
Travel publications
Truck tires
Two-wheel tires

Selected Brands

BF Goodrich	Riken
Encore	Siamtyre
Euromaster	Taurus
Kleber	TyreMaster
Kronprinz	Uniroyal
Michelin	

Selected Subsidiaries

Compagnie Financière Michelin (93%, Switzerland)
Manufacture Française des Pneumatiques Michelin (96%)
Michelin Aircraft Tire Corporation (93%, US)
Michelin Americas Research & Development Corporation (93%, US)
Michelin Asia (Hong-Kong) Ltd. (93%)
Michelin Corporation (93%, US)
Michelin Investment Holding Company Limited (93%, Bermuda)
Michelin North America, Inc. (93%, US)
Norsk Michelin Gummi A/S (93%, Norway)
Société d'Exportation Michelin
Spika SA
Taurus Rubber Company Ltd (93%, Hungary)
Transityre France SA (93%)

COMPETITORS

Bandag
Bridgestone
Continental AG
Cooper Tire & Rubber
Goodyear
Sime Darby
Toyo Tire & Rubber
Vredestein
Yokohama Rubber

HISTORICAL FINANCIALS

Company Type: Public

Income Statement

FYE: December 31

	REVENUE ($ mil.)	NET INCOME ($ mil.)	NET PROFIT MARGIN	EMPLOYEES
12/02	16,398	609	3.7%	126,285
12/01	13,973	262	1.9%	127,467
12/00	14,887	376	2.5%	128,122
12/99	13,859	155	1.1%	130,434
12/98	15,289	669	4.4%	127,241
12/97	12,110	647	5.3%	123,254
12/96	13,615	553	4.1%	119,780
12/95	13,467	570	4.2%	115,000
12/94	12,595	242	1.9%	117,776
12/93	10,690	(620)	—	124,575
Annual Growth	4.9%	—	—	0.2%

2002 Year-End Financials

Debt ratio: 70.4%
Return on equity: 13.4%
Cash ($ mil.): 1,267
Current ratio: 1.80
Long-term debt ($ mil.): 3,196

Net Income History

Euronext Paris: ML

Millea Holdings

The Big Bang lit a fire under Tokio Marine and Fire Insurance, Japan's oldest and largest property & casualty insurance company. In the battle for size, Tokio Marine has merged with Nichido Fire & Marine to create Millea Holdings. The merger creates the largest insurance sales network in Japan. The company provides marine, fire, property & casualty, personal accident, and auto insurance. Through a joint venture with online brokerage bigwig Charles Schwab, Millea Holdings offers securities. The firm is allied with the Mitsubishi industrial group.

The ailing Japanese economy has hurt Millea, but it hopes to draw more customers by selling on the Internet (including overseas travel insurance) and offering express service for accidents. It has also expanded its lines to include such products as Lady Guard, insurance for women that covers the costs of damage caused by stalkers. Auto insurance, the company's main line of business, still accounts for more than half of sales.

Millea hopes to strengthen cross-selling, closely aligning its life insurance units (including Tokio Marine Life and Nichido Life). The proposed merger of Asahi Mutual into Millea has been postponed.

HISTORY

After the US forced Japan to open to trade in 1854, Western marine insurers began operating there. In 1878 Japan's government organized backers for a Japanese marine insurance firm. Tokio Marine and Fire was founded the next year.

Tokio grew quickly, insuring trading companies like Mitsubishi and Mitsui; it soon had offices in London, Paris, and New York. Increased competition in the 1890s forced it to curtail its foreign operations and begin using brokers in most other countries.

Victory in the Russo-Japanese War of 1904-05 buoyed the country, but the economy slowed as it demobilized. Businesses responded by forming cooperative groups known as *zaibatsu*. Tokio Marine and Fire was allied with the Mitsubishi group.

Before WWI, Tokio expanded by adding fire, personal accident, theft, and auto insurance, and it continued to buy foreign sales brokers. Japan's insurance industry consolidated in the 1920s, and the company bought up smaller competitors. The 1923 Tokyo earthquake hit the industry hard, but Tokio's new fire insurance operations had little exposure.

Most of Tokio Marine's foreign operations were seized during WWII. In 1944 Tokio merged with Mitsubishi Marine Insurance and Meiji Fire Insurance. Business grew in WWII, but wartime destruction left Tokio with nothing to insure and no money to pay claims.

After the war Tokio slowly recovered and resumed overseas operations. Although the US had dismantled the *zaibatsu* during occupation, Tokio Marine allied once again with Mitsubishi when Japan's government rebuilt most of the old groups as *keiretsu*.

During the 1950s and 1960s, the company grew its personal lines, adding homeowners coverage. Domestic business slowed during the 1970s and 1980s, and Tokio boosted operations overseas. It added commercial property/casualty insurer Houston General Insurance (a US company sold in 1997), Tokio Reinsurance, and interests in insurance and investment management firms.

In the 1980s the firm invested heavily in real estate through *jusen* (mortgage companies). Japan's overheated real estate market collapsed in the early 1990s, dumping masses of nonperforming assets on *jusen* and their investors (the country's major banks and insurers, including Tokio Marine).

Deregulation began in 1996, and economic recession soon followed. In 1998 Tokio Marine joined other members of the Mitsubishi group, including Bank of Tokyo-Mitsubishi and Meiji Life Insurance, to form investment banking, pension, and trust joint ventures. The firm also formed its own investment trust and allied with such foreign financial companies as BANK ONE and United Asset Management to develop new investment products. Brokerage Charles Schwab Tokio Marine Securities, a joint venture, was launched in 1999. That year Tokio consolidated its foreign reinsurance operations into Tokio Marine Global Re in Dublin, Ireland, and kicked off a business push that included reorganizing its agent force and planning for online sales.

Tokio Marine merged with Nichido Fire and Marine in 2002, creating Millea Holdings.

EXECUTIVES

Chairman: Tomio Higuchi
President: Kunio Ishihara
EVP: Katsuo Handa
Executive Managing Director: Yukitero Noji
Managing Director: Yasuo Yaoita
Auditors: KPMG

LOCATIONS

HQ: Millea Holdings, Inc.
   Otemachi First Sq., West Tower, 1-5-1 Otemachi,
   Chiyoda-ku, Tokyo 100-0004, Japan
Phone: +81-3-6212-3341   **Fax:** +81-3-6212-3343
Web: www.millea.co.jp

Millea Holdings has operations in about 40 countries on five continents.

PRODUCTS/OPERATIONS

2003 Premiums

	% of total
Voluntary auto	49
Compulsory auto	13
Fire and allied lines	13
Personal accident	9
Hull and cargo	3
Other	13
Total	**100**

Selected Subsidiaries

First Insurance Company of Hawaii, Ltd.
Nichido Investment (Luxembourg) S.A.
The Nichido Life Insurance Co., Ltd.
The Tokio Marine and Fire Insurance Company (Hong
   Kong) Limited
The Tokio Marine and Fire Insurance Company
   (Singapore) Pte. Limited
Tokio Marine Brasil Seguradora S.A.
The Tokio Marine Capital Research Ltd.
The Tokio Marine Career Service Co., Ltd.
Tokio Marine Europe Insurance Limited
Tokio Marine Global Re Limited
The Tokio Marine Life Insurance Co., Ltd.
Tokio Millennium Re Ltd.
Trans Pacific Insurance Company

COMPETITORS

AEGON	HCC Insurance
Aioi	ING
Allianz	Kemper Insurance
AIG	Mitsui Sumitomo
Aviva	Insurance
AXA	Nippon Life Insurance
CIGNA	Nipponkoa
CNA Financial	Sompo Japan Insurance
General Re	Travelers
The Hartford	

HISTORICAL FINANCIALS

Company Type: Public

Income Statement

FYE: March 31

	ASSETS ($ mil.)	NET INCOME ($ mil.)	INCOME AS % OF ASSETS	EMPLOYEES
3/03	92,212	3,200	3.5%	6,700
3/02	63,581	1,208	1.9%	6,700
3/01	65,435	754	1.2%	6,588
3/00	76,146	794	1.0%	13,616
3/99	63,445	1,205	1.9%	13,751
3/98	58,629	1,147	2.0%	15,294
3/97	61,077	952	1.6%	14,029
3/96	73,235	806	1.1%	14,000
3/95	79,361	1,021	1.3%	14,000
3/94	70,904	1,933	2.7%	14,900
Annual Growth	**3.0%**	**5.8%**	**—**	**(8.5%)**

2003 Year-End Financials

Equity as % of assets: 25.9%	Dividends
Return on assets: 4.1%	Yield: 0.0%
Return on equity: 15.0%	Payout: —
Long-term debt ($ mil.): 1,506	Market value ($ mil.): 11,421
No. of shares (mil.): 371	Sales ($ mil.): 18,441

Stock History

NASDAQ: MLEA

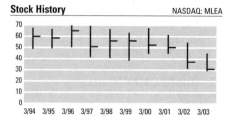

	STOCK PRICE ($) FY Close	P/E High/Low		PER SHARE ($) Earnings	Dividends	Book Value
3/03	30.75	15	10	8.61	0.00	64.37
3/02	37.29	30	17	3.90	0.34	0.06
3/01	50.25	25	19	2.44	0.40	0.07
3/00	52.44	26	18	2.56	0.30	0.08
3/99	56.13	16	10	3.89	0.00	0.07
3/98	56.00	18	11	3.71	0.70	0.06
3/97	50.75	22	14	3.07	0.32	0.06
3/96	65.00	27	20	2.60	0.38	0.07
3/95	58.36	20	15	3.30	0.34	0.07
3/94	59.75	59	43	6.25	0.32	0.07
Annual Growth	**(7.1%)**	**—**	**—**	**3.6%**	**—**	**114.0%**

Mizuho Financial Group

Mizuho means "golden ears of rice" in Japanese, but in the banking world it means the first bank with a trillion dollars in assets. Since surpassed by Citigroup as the largest financial services company in the world, #2 Mizuho Financial Group is the parent of Mizuho Holdings, which includes the intergrated operations and assets of The Dai-Ichi Kangyo Bank, Fuji Bank, and Industrial Bank of Japan (IBJ). The merger and integration, which is occurring under the anxious eye of regulators at the Japanese Financial Services Agency, is the ultimate example of consolidation among Japanese banks trying to streamline and cope with massive loan defaults.

The banks' assets and operations have been chopped to pieces and rolled together along divisional lines. The reorganization has resulted in the creation of at least four major operating units: from Dai-Ichi Kangyo comes Mizuho Bank for the retail market and from Fuji Bank comes Mizuho Corporate Bank for commercial banking. Mizuho Securities provides investment and securities services and Mizuho Trust & Banking (of which Mizuho Financial owns a majority) offers trust services.

Mizuho Financial plans to cut its staff by more than a quarter and to close 30% of its branches by 2006. At the urging of government regulators, Mizuho may accelerate its restructuring efforts. The company's 2002 launch was marred by problems with its newly integrated computer system.

Internationally, the bank earns about half of its revenue from the US, followed by Asia with 30%, and Europe about 20%. Mizuho is expanding into Hong Kong and mainland China to profit from Chinese growth and the export of Japanese production facilities from their home market.

Bad corporate loans have been at the heart of Japan's banking problems, in part because the country's post-war economy focused on rebuilding industries, rather than building retail operations. Accordingly Mizuho Financial hopes to increase its retail and mid-level banking activities in coming years. The bank also plans to expand its nascent securities, investment, trust, and asset management activities. But critics contend that such a massive concentration of banking operations exposes the company to a menacingly large array of risks; they also warn that, should Mizuho or any other banking company of similar size fail, it could jeopardize the entire industry.

HISTORY

Of the three banks that formed Mizuho Holdings, Industrial Bank of Japan (IBJ) is the youngest, founded in 1902. Fuji Bank started in 1880 and Dai-Ichi Kangyo's roots reach back to 1872.

By the late 1990s Japanese banks faced the challenges of a fossilized banking system, chained together by the *keiretsu* cross-shareholding system that hindered companies' agility in the marketplace. Other economic stresses included the Asian financial crisis, which left banks holding thousands of bad loans. In 1997 the Big Bang of banking reform was supposed to free lending institutions to restructure for greater competition, with presumably sounder business models. The industry's reliance on government-sponsored bailouts underscored the need for change.

IBJ, Dai-Ichi Kangyo Bank, and Fuji Bank (none of them excessively chummy within their respective *keiretsu*) saw an opportunity to consolidate, strengthen their business through combined forces, and streamline their operations by closing redundant branches, agencies, and divisions.

Mizuho Holdings was formed in 1999 and placed atop the three banks as their new parent company. While Mizuho's $1.3 trillion in assets made it the largest bank in the world at the time, its copious debts weren't to be ignored, either (though the bank waived the nearly $1 billion in debt of troubled retailer Sogo in 2001).

Also in 2001, other Japanese banks followed the lead of IBJ, Dai-Ichi Kangyo, and Fuji by joining with peers in the quest for size. Sumitomo Bank and Sakura Bank merged to form Sumitomo Mitsui Financial Group; and Sanwa Bank, Tokai Bank, and Toyo Trust and Banking combined to create UFJ Holdings.

Initially, the CEOs of the three banks that comprised Mizuho were tapped as co-CEOs of the company, but they resigned in 2002 after the banks' consolidation was marred by PR gaffes and computer glitches that caused customers to be double-billed, created a logjam of money transfers, and crashed thousands of ATMs. Terunobu Maeda was named the sole CEO of Mizuho later that year.

EXECUTIVES

President and CEO: Terunobu Maeda
Deputy President, Head of IT, Systems, and Operations Group, and CIO: Seiji Sugiyama
Managing Director, Head of Financial Control and Accounting Group, and CFO: Mitsuru Machida

Managing Director, Head of Strategic Planning Group, Head of Audit and Compliance Group, Chief Strategy Officer, and Chief Compliance Officer: Jun Kawada

Managing Executive Officer, Head Of Risk Management Group, Head of Human Resources, General Manager of Post-Retirement Counseling, Chief Risk Officer, and Chief Human Resources Officer:
Takashi Tsukamoto

Executive Officer: Yoshiaki Sugita

President and CEO, Mizuho Bank: Tadashi Kudo

President and CEO, Mizuho Trust and Banking:
Hiroaki Etoh

President and CEO, Mizuho Corporate Bank:
Hiroshi Saito

President, Mizuho Securities: Yoshio Osawa

Auditors: Shin Nihon & Co.

LOCATIONS

HQ: Mizuho Holdings, Inc.
Marunouchi Center Bldg.,
1-6-1 Marunouchi, Chiyoda-ku,
Tokyo 100-0005, Japan
Phone: +81-3-5224-1111   **Fax:** +81-3-3215-4616
Web: www.mizuho-fg.co.jp

PRODUCTS/OPERATIONS

2003 Sales

	$ mil.	% of total
Interest income	16,566.0	58
Fee & commission income	4,078.1	14
Gain on sales of bonds	2,297.1	8
Trading income	2,034.3	7
Gains on sales of stock and other securities	631.1	2
Foreign exchange transactions	618.5	2
Fiduciary income	461.4	2
Other	2,032.0	7
Total	**28,718.5**	**100**

2003 Assets

	$ mil.	% of total
Cash & due from banks	65,498.0	6
Trading assets	82,764.8	7
Securities	198,725.5	18
Loans and bills discounted	577,488.5	52
Other assets	193,892.4	17
Total	**1,118,369.2**	**100**

COMPETITORS

Bank of Yokohama
Mitsubishi Tokyo Financial
Mitsui Trust
Shinsei Bank
Shizuoka Bank
Sumitomo Mitsui
Sumitomo Trust and
 Banking
UFJ Holdings

HISTORICAL FINANCIALS

Company Type: Public

Income Statement

FYE: March 31

	ASSETS ($ mil.)	NET INCOME ($ mil.)	INCOME AS % OF ASSETS	EMPLOYEES
3/03	1,118,369	(19,835)	—	27,900
3/02	1,140,744	(7,358)	—	30,262
3/01	1,293,914	1,672	0.1%	32,068
Annual Growth	**(7.0%)**	**—**	**—**	**(6.7%)**

2003 Year-End Financials

Equity as % of assets: 2.9%   Long-term debt ($ mil.): 109,734
Return on assets: —   Sales ($ mil.): 28,719
Return on equity: —

Net Income History   Exchange: Tokyo

Molson Inc.

Molson hopes to break the deadlock resulting from its sudsy rivalry with Interbrew's Labatt. Both breweries control nearly 45% of the Canadian beer market. To get a leg up, Molson plans to tap its international resources, adding Brazilian import Marca Bavaria to its product lineup. Molson owns 80% of Brazil's Cervejarias Kaiser brewery, having sold a minority stake to Heineken. The company also works closely with Coors to better reach US markets and sell Coors Light in Canada. Molson's mix includes about 20% of the Montreal Canadiens, the most successful ice hockey team in NHL history.

The company's purchase of Brazil's Kaiser in 2002 has increased the company's market share to about 18% in Brazil (the world's #4 market); Molson is now the second largest brewer in Brazil, but finds it must carefully manage its new assets. In 2003, it closed Kaiser's 75-year-old Ribeirao Preto brewery, eliminating 140 jobs to reduce overcapacity.

In the US, Molson hopes to take advantage of its partnership with Coors to rebuild its Molson Golden and Molson Ice brands, (Coors owns nearly half of Molson USA; Molson owns nearly half of Coors Canada). Molson will watch signs of US growth closely as the number of US beer drinkers far exceeds Molson's domestic market.

HISTORY

In 1786 John Molson founded in Montreal what would become North America's oldest brewery. In 1797 Molson added a lumberyard, and in 1809 he launched the *Accommodation*, Canada's first steamboat, to make runs between Montreal and Quebec City. Brewing sales stalled during the second half of the 1800s, and in 1897 Fred and Herbert, the fourth generation of Molsons to run the brewery, began to revitalize the company. By 1900 sales had increased by 40%.

When a temperance movement swept through Canada during the 1910s, Molson and its fellow Quebec-based brewers started an anti-prohibition campaign. Quebec's citizens voted overwhelmingly against prohibition. Molson got a boost from Americans who came to drink in Montreal during the US Prohibition.

Sales took off again following WWII, and by 1950 the company was making 1.5 million bottles of beer a day. Molson opened a brewery in Toronto in 1955 and acquired Sick's Brewery (five breweries in Canada and two in the US, 1958), Fort Garry Brewery (Winnipeg, 1959), and Newfoundland Brewery (1962).

As part of a diversification program, in 1971 Molson acquired several home improvement retailers, including Aikenhead Hardware (converted

to Home Depot stores in 1994) and Beaver Lumber. In 1978 it bought the Montreal Canadiens hockey team, which began playing in 1917.

In 1988 Molson merged its brewing operations with Carling O'Keefe Breweries (a subsidiary of Australian brewer Elders IXL, now called Foster's Brewing). Each company took a 50% stake in the venture, called Molson Breweries; their respective stakes were reduced to 40% as Miller Brewing bought 20% in 1993.

In 1996 Molson sold Diversey (most of the company went to Unilever). It moved the Canadiens hockey team from the Montreal Forum to its own Molson Centre in 1996. Toronto corporate lawyer James Arnett became CEO in 1997.

Now committed to brewing, Molson sold its Réno-Dépôt home improvement stores to Castorama in 1997. Molson and Foster's also bought back and split Miller Brewing's 20% stake in Molson Breweries that year. In 1998 Molson bought back Foster's stake — Molson is now the only large Canadian-owned brewer — and its 25% interest in Coors Canada. (Its stake is now about 50%.) Also in 1998 Molson sold its 25% interest in Home Depot Canada to The Home Depot.

Its Molson Breweries unit was renamed Molson Canada in 1999. Also that year the company sold its 130 Beaver Lumber outlets. In 2000 Daniel J. O'Neill succeeded Arnett as president and CEO of the corporation.

Molson bought back its brands in the US from its Molson USA partnership with Foster's later that year; it then reorganized Molson USA, selling a 49.9% stake in that business to Coors for $65 million. The deal, finalized in January 2001, called for Coors to distribute its brands in the US and to develop the light beer segment in Canada. In December 2000 Molson purchased the Bavaria beer brand from the #3 global brewer, AmBev, for $213 million.

In June 2001 the company sold the Molson Centre and 80.1% of the Canadiens to George Gillett Jr., a Colorado businessman, and his family who paid about $190 million.

In 2002 Molson acquired Brazil's #2 brewer, Kaiser, for $765 million.

EXECUTIVES

Chairman: Eric H. Molson, age 64
Deputy Chairman: R. Ian Molson, age 47
President, CEO, and Director: Daniel J. O'Neill, age 50
EVP and CFO: Brian Burden
EVP, Molson Inc.; President and CEO, Cervejarias Kaiser SA: Robert Coallier
SVP, Business Development and Innovation: Peter L. Amirault
SVP, Chief Legal Officer, and Secretary: Marie Giguère
SVP, Human Resources: Bernard Cormier
SVP, Quality Brewing: Gregory L. Wade
VP and Controller: Brian J. Bidulka
VP, Corporate Affairs: Sylvia Morin
VP, Investor Relations: Danielle Dagenais
VP, Quality and Distributor Development: Geoff Molson
President, Molson USA: David Perkins
President, Ontario/West Region: Les Hine
President, Quebec/Atlantic Region, Molson Canada: Raynald H. Doin
Treasurer: Stuart B. Preston
Auditors: PricewaterhouseCoopers LLP

LOCATIONS

HQ: 1555 Notre Dame St. East, Montreal,
Quebec H2L 2R5, Canada
Phone: 514-521-1786   **Fax:** 514-598-6866
US HQ: 1658 Cole Blvd., Bldg. 6, Ste. 100,
Golden, CO 80401
US Fax: 303-462-1513
Web: www.molson.com

2003 Sales

	% of total
Canada	80
Brazil	17
US	3
Total	**100**

PRODUCTS/OPERATIONS

Selected Brands

Molson
Black Ice
Brador
Canadian (Golden, Ice, Light)
Cream Ale
Diamond
Dry (Smooth Dry)
Exel
Export and Ex Light
Golden
Grand North
Ice
Light
Red Jack
Special Dry
Spring Bock
Stock Ale
Ultra
XXX

Other Owned, Licensed, and Distributed Brands
A Marca Bavaria
Artic (malt-based lemonade)
Black Horse
Black Label
Carling (Black Label)
Coors (regular and Light)
Corona
Dave Nichol's Personal Selection (Dave's, Dave's Lemon
Lager, Dave's Scotch Ale)
Foster's Lager (Canada)
Heineken (regular and Lager)
Laker
Laurentide
Miller (Genuine Draft regular and light, High Life, Lite,
Milwaukee's Best; Canada)
Murphy's Irish Stout and Irish Amber
O'Keefe
O'Keefe Extra Old Stock
Old Vienna
Pilsner
Red Dog
Rickard's (Pale Ale, Honey Brown)
Tornade (malt-based lemonade)
Toronto's OwnA Marca Bavaria

Major Group Operations

Brewing
Bavaria (80%, Brazil)
Coors Canada (49.9%, brewing and distribution)
Cervejarias Kaiser (80%, Brazil)
Molson Canada
Molson USA (50.1%)

Sports and Entertainment
Molson Centre (21,400-seat arena)
Molstar Sports & Entertainment (produces NHL games
for Canadian television)
Montreal Canadiens (NHL team)

COMPETITORS

Adolph Coors
Anchor Brewing
Anheuser-Busch
Big Rock Brewery
Boston Beer
Boston Bruins
Constellation Brands
Diageo
Gambrinus
Genesee

Heineken
Interbrew
Kirin
Miller Brewing
Grupo Modelo
Ottawa Senators
Pabst
Pyramid Breweries
Sleeman Breweries

HISTORICAL FINANCIALS

Company Type: Public

Income Statement

FYE: March 31

	REVENUE ($ mil.)	NET INCOME ($ mil.)	NET PROFIT MARGIN	EMPLOYEES
3/03	1,709	212	12.4%	5,400
3/02	1,318	111	8.4%	5,900
3/01	1,178	85	7.2%	3,800
3/00	1,736	(30)	—	3,600
3/99	1,403	112	8.0%	4,100
3/98	1,091	78	7.2%	4,500
3/97	1,072	24	2.3%	5,100
3/96	1,061	(225)	—	5,100
3/95	2,063	62	3.0%	18,870
3/94	2,144	91	4.2%	14,700
Annual Growth	**(2.5%)**	**9.9%**	**—**	**(10.5%)**

2003 Year-End Financials

Debt ratio: 114.2%
Return on equity: 29.5%
Cash ($ mil.): 8

Current ratio: 0.54
Long-term debt ($ mil.): 802

Net Income History

Toronto: MOL

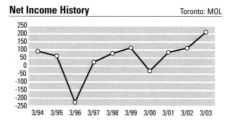

Moore Wallace Incorporated

Moore Wallace (formerly Moore Corporation) recognizes there is more than one information medium. The company offers print management services through its three segments, its largest being Forms and Labels (business forms, labels, electronic print management). Other divisions include Commercial (printing business communications, direct marketing services) and Outsourcing (print and mail services, electronic statements, database management services).

Moore Wallace markets primarily in North America to government agencies and a variety of industries, including finance and telecommunications. More than three-fourths of the company's sales come from the US.

A decrease in demand for paper products prompted Moore Wallace to invest in electronic systems and services and document-management services. The company has also been investing in commercial printing operations. It plans to acquire Payment Processing Solutions, a processor of printed customer statements.

Following mounting losses and unsuccessful restructurings, Moore Wallace agreed in 2003 to a buyout bid from US printing giant R. R. Donnelley; the resulting company will be the #1 commercial printer in North America.

HISTORY

Moore Wallace traces its origins to 1879, when UK-born printer Samuel Moore met salesclerk John Carter in Toronto. Carter had an idea to bind together multiple sets of receipts with a single sheet of carbon paper between, rescuing salespeople from fumbling with separate sets of forms. Moore bought the idea, hired Carter, patented the product, and in 1882 formed Grip Printing and Publishing Company to produce the Paragon Black Leaf Counter Check Book.

As the forms business grew, Moore bought Kidder Press (1899), maker of the printing presses he used, and created box and form maker F.N. Burt (1909). In 1925 Moore's organization began selling inexpensive, single-use carbon paper to be bound into sets of business forms, eliminating handling entirely. The product proved popular and led to the development of snap-apart forms. The US government's use of carbon copies resulted in their acceptance as legal documents in business, boosting sales. In 1929 Moore began consolidating his namesake business and took it public as Moore Corporation.

By WWII all modern organizations were hooked on forms. Following the war, Moore grew globally. It formed Toppan Moore (Japan), a joint venture with Toppan Printing (sold in 1997). Samuel Moore died in 1948.

In the 1970s and 1980s, Moore entered direct marketing, image processing, and database management but failed in its efforts to diversify into US computer supply retailing (MicroAge stores).

With declining sales and a $78 million loss in 1993, the company restructured, cutting 3,000 jobs and closing several plants. Moore began buying companies that would give it entry into new technology markets, including Computer Resources Trust (1993, Australia's largest business forms company) and an 18% stake — now 12% — in JetForm (1994, software and electronic forms).

Moore repeated its overhauls in 1994, closing nine plants and cutting more than 1,900 jobs. However, it was still making acquisitions in the 1990s, including Peak Technologies (bar-code system distribution).

Ed Tyler became CEO in 1998 and initiated yet another restructuring; to combat stiff competition from new technology and outdated manufacturing facilities, the company closed 10 plants and divested itself of its European forms and labels business and operations in Australia, New Zealand, and China. The restructuring contributed to a $548 million loss in 1998.

In 1999 Moore entered into a joint venture to provide printing and design services to Argentina's postal department and purchased a 40% stake in Quality Color Press, an Edmonton, Alberta-based print management firm.

The growing availability of business forms on the Internet and other market forces took a $66 million bite out of the company's bottom line in 2000. Robert Burton became CEO late that year. As part of its strategy for divesting non-core businesses, Moore sold Colleagues (a British direct marketing company) in March 2001 and the Phoenix Group (integrated marketing and customer relationship management services) in November. Also in 2001 Moore moved its administrative offices to Stamford, Connecticut, and cut 3,000 jobs.

Moore made two acquisitions in 2002. Its acquisition of Document Management Services, a unit of IBM Canada, boosted its opportunities in the outsourcing print market. It also acquired The Nielsen Company, a privately held commercial printer that produces annual reports, brochures, and other printed materials for FORTUNE 500 companies.

Non-executive chairman Mark Angelson took over as CEO in January 2003. A few months later the company acquired Wallace Computer Services (May). Moore Corporation then changed its name to Moore Wallace.

EXECUTIVES

Chairman: Alfred C. Eckert III, age 55
CEO and Director: Mark A. Angelson, age 52
President and COO: Thomas W. Oliva, age 45, $837,583 pay
SEVP: James R. Sulat, age 52
EVP, Business Integration: Thomas J. Quinlan III, age 40, $723,333 pay
EVP, Business and Legal Affairs:
Theodore J. Theophilos
EVP and CFO: Mark S. Hiltwein, age 39, $741,667 pay
SVP, CTO: Kenneth E. O'Brien
SVP, Tax: William F. Paparella, age 53
SVP, Controller: Richard T. Sansone
EVP, Direct Sales: Thomas G. Brooker, age 43
EVP, Business Communication Services:
James E. Kersten
EVP, Corporate Sales: Robert C. Nelson
EVP, Labels: Wayne E. Richter, age 45
EVP, Forms, Tops, Customer Service: James R. Riffe
EVP, Logistics and Distribution: Daniel J. Scapin
Group President, Commercial and Direct Mail:
Dean E. Cherry, $812,583 pay
SVP, Marketing and Business Development:
John E. Berger
SVP, Human Resources, Moore Wallace North America:
Andrew B. Panega
VP, Human Resources: Lorien O. Gallo
Auditors: Deloitte & Touche LLP

LOCATIONS

HQ: 6100 Vipond Dr., Mississauga, Ontario L5T 2X1, Canada
Phone: 905-362-3100   **Fax:** 905-565-9757
Web: www.moorewallace.com

Moore Wallace has operations in Europe, Latin America, and North America.

2002 Sales

	$ mil.	% of total
North America		
US	1,607.4	79
Canada	208.2	10
International	222.4	11
Total	**2,038.0**	**100**

PRODUCTS/OPERATIONS

2002 Sales

	$ mil.	% of total
Forms and labels	1,125.8	55
Commercial	596.1	29
Outsourcing	316.1	16
Total	**2,038.0**	**100**

Selected Products and Services

Forms and Labels
Custom continuous forms, cut sheets, and multipart forms
Electronic forms and services
Integrated form-label application
Logistics, warehouse, and inventory management
Pressure-sensitive labels
Print services
Proprietary label products
Security documents
Self-mailers

Commercial
Annual reports
Catalogs
Corporate image and product brochures
Creation and production of personalized mail
Database management and segmentation services
Digital color printing
Direct marketing program development
Market inserts
Post-processing equipment
Printers, applicators, and software products and solutions
Promotional materials
Response-analysis services
Variable-imaged bar codes

Outsourcing
Bill and service notifications
Insurance policies
Investment, banking, credit card, tax and year-end financial statements
Licenses
Special notices
Telecommunication cards

COMPETITORS

American Banknote	New England Business
Avery Dennison	Service
Corporate Express	Northstar Computer
Deluxe	Forms
Ennis Business Forms	Pitney Bowes
Equifax	ProQuest
infoUSA	R. R. Donnelley
John Harland	Standard Register
Merrill	Workflow Management
Nashua	Xerox
NCR	

HISTORICAL FINANCIALS

Company Type: Public

Income Statement

FYE: December 31

	REVENUE ($ mil.)	NET INCOME ($ mil.)	NET PROFIT MARGIN	EMPLOYEES
12/02	2,038	73	3.6%	11,800
12/01	2,155	(358)	—	11,500
12/00	2,258	(66)	—	16,200
12/99	2,425	93	3.8%	15,812
12/98	2,718	(548)	—	17,135
Annual Growth	**(6.9%)**	**—**	**—**	**(8.9%)**

2002 Year-End Financials

Debt ratio: 49.0%
Return on equity: 20.8%
Cash ($ mil.): 140
Current ratio: 1.16
Long-term debt ($ mil.): 188
No. of shares (mil.): 112
Dividends
  Yield: 0.0%
  Payout: —
Market value ($ mil.): 1,017

Stock History

NYSE: MWI

12/93 12/94 12/95 12/96 12/97 12/98 12/99 12/00 12/01 12/02

	STOCK PRICE ($) FY Close	P/E High/Low		PER SHARE ($) Earnings	Dividends	Book Value
12/02	9.10	23	12	0.64	0.00	3.42
12/01	9.50	—	—	(4.21)	0.10	2.87
12/00	3.06	—	—	(0.75)	0.20	7.06
12/99	6.06	12	6	1.05	0.20	7.60
12/98	11.00	—	—	(6.19)	0.57	6.90
12/97	15.13	39	23	0.59	0.94	12.72
12/96	20.50	15	11	1.50	0.94	15.49
12/95	18.75	9	7	2.68	0.94	14.90
12/94	18.88	17	13	1.22	0.94	13.71
12/93	19.13	—	—	(0.78)	0.94	13.19
Annual Growth	**(7.9%)**	**—**	**—**	**—**	**—**	**(13.9%)**

Munich Re

Some companies live with risk. Münchener Rückversicherungs-Gesellschaft Aktiengesellschaft (Munich Re), on the other hand, *thrives* with risk. Coverage includes fire, life, motor, liability, and other types on both facultative (individual risks) and treaty (groups of risks) bases. The firm owns about 90% of ERGO Versicherungsgruppe, putting it second only to Allianz in Germany's direct insurance market. Through American Re, Munich Re enjoys greater access to US markets. As the world's largest reinsurer, the company operates in some 150 countries.

Europe is its biggest market (about 75% of premiums) and the company plans expansion through acquisitions there.

As insurance clients seek less expensive ways to manage risk, reinsurance markets have stagnated. In response, Munich Re moved into direct insurance. Continuing its expansion, Munich Re has also entered the asset management game, forming MEAG Munich ERGO AssetManagement, a joint venture with ERGO.

Uber-insurer Allianz AG owns 21% of Munich Re, which in turn owns 21% of Allianz. Other major shareholders include some of Germany's top banks: HypoVereinsbank and Dresdner Bank. Deutsche Bank has sold its stake in the company.

The company is hoping to continue the growth of its primary insurance segment (80% of business comes from Germany), focusing on personal lines.

HISTORY

Investors Carl Thieme and Theodor Cramer-Klett founded Munich Re in 1880. Within a month Munich Re opened offices in Hamburg, Berlin, Vienna, and St. Petersburg, establishing treaties with German and Danish insurers. In 1888 Munich Re went public; two years later, it opened an office in London and helped finance the creation of Allianz, which would soon come to dominate the German insurance industry. In 1892 the firm opened a branch in the US (it incurred severe losses from the 1906 San Francisco earthquake).

WWI interrupted Munich Re's UK and US operations. The company recovered after 1918, only to be hobbled again by the Great Depression. In 1933 Munich Re executive Kurt Schmitt became minister of economic affairs for the Nazis. Objecting to the evolving policies of National Socialism, he left after a year, returning to Munich Re, where he became chief executive in 1938.

Hitler's ignition of WWII wasn't quite the boom Munich Re needed; its international business was again disrupted. After the war, the Allies further limited overseas operations. Because of his involvement with the Nazi government, Schmitt was replaced by Eberhard von Reininghaus in 1945. The division of Germany further hampered the company's recovery.

Jump-started by the Marshall Plan in 1950, the West German *Wirtschaftswunder* (economic miracle) kicked into high gear, as the devastated country rebuilt. Relaxation of occupation-era trading limits also helped as the company rebuilt its foreign business. By 1969, Munich Re's sales topped DM 2 billion. Amid the global oil crisis and a rash of terrorist acts in Germany, the firm reported its first-ever reinsurance loss in 1977.

German reunification in 1990 provided new markets for Munich Re, but advantages from new business in the East were wiped out by claims arising from that year's harsh winter.

In 1992 an investigation by the German Federal Cartel Office prompted a realignment in the insurance business — Allianz ceded its controlling interests in three life insurers (Berlinische Lebensversicherung, Hamburg-Mannheimer Versicherungs, and Karlsruher Lebensversicherung) to Munich Re, bringing it into direct insurance. Munich Re took over Deutsche Krankenversicherung (DKV) in 1996. Also that year Munich Re acquired American Re.

During the 1990s, reinsurance sales dwindled as competition increased, forcing lower premiums, and alternatives to insurance and reinsurance became more common. Munich Re looked to direct insurance, particularly individual property/casualty and life insurance, to compensate. In 1997 it merged Hamburg-Mannheimer and DKV with another insurer, Victoria AG, to form ERGO Versicherungsgruppe. Within a year, ERGO's insurance income accounted for half of all revenues.

Munich Re and ERGO launched asset management firm MEAG Munich ERGO Asset-Management in 1999. That year Munich Re experienced its worst year ever after natural disasters hit its reinsurance business hard. To recoup its losses, the next year the firm expanded both its reinsurance and primary insurance operations into key markets in Europe, North and South America, and Asia. Also in 2000, Munich Re bought CNA Financial's life reinsurance operations. Together with Swiss Re, the company launched Inreon, an online reinsurance exchange, in 2001.

As one of the companies hit hardest financially by the World Trade Center tragedy, Munich Re paid out some $2 billion in claims.

EXECUTIVES

Chairman Supervisory Board: Ulrich Hartmann, age 65
Deputy Chairman Supervisory Board: Herbert Bach
Chairman Board of Management: Hans-Jürgen Schinzler, age 63
Member Board of Management, Finance, General Services, Company Structure, and Organization: Heiner Hasford, age 54
Member Board of Management, Accounting, Controlling, Taxes, and Information Technology: Jörg Schneider
Member Board of Management, Asia, Australia, and Africa: Karl Wittmann
Member Board of Management, Corporate Underwriting/Global Clients: Stefan Heyd
Member Board of Management, Europe 1 and Corporate Communications: Christian Kluge
Member Board of Management, Europe 2 and Latin America: Nikolaus von Bomhard
Member Board of Management, Life, Health, and Personnel: Detlef Schneidawind
Member Board of Management, North America; Chairman and CEO, American Re: John P. Phelan
Auditors: Bayerische Treuhandgesellschaft AG

LOCATIONS

HQ: Münchener Rückversicherungs-Gesellschaft Aktiengesellschaft
Königinstrasse 107, D-80802 Munich, Germany
Phone: +49-89-38-91-0   **Fax:** +49-89-39-90-56
US HQ: American Re Corporation, 555 College Rd. East, Princeton, NJ 08543-5241
US Phone: 609-243-4200   **US Fax:** 609-243-4257
Web: www.munichre.com

Munich Re operates in some 150 countries worldwide.

PRODUCTS/OPERATIONS

2002 Assets

	$ mil.	% of total
Cash	2,867	1
Real estate	10,322	5
Other securities	112,649	55
Receivables	9,298	5
Loans	13,252	6
Other	57,502	28
Total	**205,890**	**100**

2002 Sales

	$ mil.	% of total
Premiums	38,052	84
Investment income	5,875	13
Other	1,408	3
Total	**45,335**	**100**

Selected Subsidiaries

Asset Management
ERGO Trust
MEAG MUNICH ERGO

Reinsurance
American Re Corporation (US)
American Re-Insurance Company (US)
Great Lakes Reinsurance (UK) PLC
Münchener Rück Italia S.p.A.
Munich American Reassurance Company (US)
Munich Reinsurance Company of Africa Limited (South Africa)
Munich Reinsurance Company of Australasia Limited (Australia)
Munich Reinsurance Company of Canada
New Reinsurance Company (Switzerland)

Direct Insurance
ERGO Versicherungsgruppe AG (92%)
D.A.S. Deutscher Automobil Schutz Allgemeine Europäische Reiseversicherung AG
Karlsruher Lebensversicherung AG (54%)
Rechtsschutz-Versicherungs-AG (62%)
D.A.S. Deutscher Automobil Schutz Versicherungs-AG (62%)
DAS Legal Expenses Insurance Company Limited (62%, UK)
D.A.S. Nederlandse Rechtsbijstand Verzekeringsmaatschappij N.V. (39%, the Netherlands)
DKV Deutsche Krankenversicherung AG (63%)
dkv International S.A. (63%, Belgium)
Hamburg-Mannheimer Versicherungs-AG (63%)
Hamburg-Mannheimer Sachversicherungs-AG (63%)
VICTORIA Lebensversicherung AG (63%)
VICTORIA Krankenversicherung AG (63%)
VICTORIA MERIDIONAL Compañía Anónima de Seguros y Reaseguros, S.A. (61%, Spain)
VICTORIA-Seguros de Vida, S.A. (62%, Portugal)
VICTORIA-Seguros S.A. (62%, Portugal)
VICTORIA-VOLKSBANKEN Versicherungs-AG (46%, Austria)

COMPETITORS

Allianz
AXA
Bâloise-Holding
Converium Reinsurance
Everest Re
GE Global Insurance Holding
General Re
Hannover Re
Nippon Life Insurance
Reinsurance Group of America
Swiss Re
Transatlantic Holdings
Winterthur

HISTORICAL FINANCIALS

Company Type: Public

Income Statement

FYE: December 31

	ASSETS ($ mil.)	NET INCOME ($ mil.)	INCOME AS % OF ASSETS	EMPLOYEES
12/02	205,890	1,133	0.6%	41,396
12/01	178,979	221	0.1%	38,317
12/00	182,263	1,648	0.9%	27,489
12/99	181,139	1,141	0.6%	33,245
12/98	140,670	714	0.5%	23,948
12/97	90,370	332	0.4%	18,021
12/96	81,416	321	0.4%	16,343
12/95	84,746	199	0.2%	16,218
12/94	68,563	121	0.2%	17,325
12/93	57,431	99	0.2%	16,943
Annual Growth	**15.2%**	**31.1%**	**—**	**10.4%**

2002 Year-End Financials

Equity as % of assets: 7.1%   Long-term debt ($ mil.): 21,666
Return on assets: 0.6%   Sales ($ mil.): 45,335
Return on equity: 7.1%

Net Income History   German: MUV

National Australia Bank

National Australia Bank (NAB) is down under, up over, and all around. The largest of Australia's top four banks (the others are Westpac Banking, Australia and New Zealand Banking Group, and Commonwealth Bank of Australia), NAB also owns banks in Asia, Ireland, New Zealand, and the UK. The company offers retail banking (deposits, credit cards, mortgages, and other loans) and such business banking services as loans, leases, and foreign exchange. Subsidiaries of the company provide such services as leasing, trustee services, international trade finance, and asset management.

Almost half of NAB's sales come from outside Australia. Abroad, NAB owns regional banks Northern Bank (Northern Ireland), Yorkshire Bank (England), Clydesdale Bank (Scotland), and National Irish Bank (Ireland). NAB has retreated from the US, selling Michigan National Bank to ABN AMRO and unloading troubled mortgage lender HomeSide International in a sale to Washington Mutual. Closer to home are its Bank of New Zealand and Hong Kong-based National Australia Bank Asia, which primarily offers trade financing and foreign exchange.

NAB has diversified to defend against potential economic downturns that could zap individual units. Since the government banned consolidation among Australia's top four banks, the company has been taking advantage of market deregulation and consolidation abroad. The bank cut some 2,000 jobs in fiscal year 2002, mostly in back office operations.

HISTORY

Formed in 1858 in Melbourne, National Bank of Australasia (NBA) just missed the peak of the Victoria gold rush. The bank expanded across the territory and was one of the first to lend to farmers and ranchers using land deeds as security. In the late 1870s, drought imperiled Victoria. Seeking greener pastures, NBA entered New South Wales in 1885, then headed into Western Australia. Economic instability continued; in 1893 the bank experienced its first panic and was shuttered for eight weeks. NBA reopened only to close a quarter of its branches between 1893 and 1896.

During the Australian commonwealth's early years, Western Australia was the bank's salvation as the economies in Victoria and South Australia stagnated. NBA helped fund Australia's WWI efforts through public loans. A postwar consolidation wave in banking swept up NBA, which made acquisitions in 1918 and 1922.

Overdue farm and ranch loans weakened the bank during the Depression. As WWII raged, the Commonwealth Bank (established in 1912) took greater control of Australia's banks. With competition among banks primarily limited to branch growth, NBA acquired Queensland National Bank in 1948 and Ballarat Banking Co. in 1955. The bank diversified into consumer finance through acquisition. In the 1960s Australia experienced an economic boom as immigration and industrialization grew. The boom went bust in the 1970s as the world sunk into recession. Still under the Commonwealth Bank's tight control, the banks watched business that had once been theirs lost to building societies, merchant banks, and credit unions.

The 1980s brought banking deregulation. To vie with foreign banks entering Australia, NBA in 1981 merged with Commercial Banking Co. of Sydney and became the National Commercial Banking Corp. of Australia in 1982. (It took its present name in 1984.) Throughout the 1980s the bank diversified and moved into the US and Japan. It invested in property and made loans to foreign countries. All too quickly, though, property values sank and countries defaulted on loans.

To fight recession, NAB looked abroad for opportunities. In 1987 it bought Clydesdale Bank, Northern Bank, and National Irish Bank from Midland Bank Group (now part of HSBC Holdings). Three years later, NAB bought Yorkshire Bank, then turned the four banks around by linking them and tightening loan operations. In 1992 it bought the troubled Bank of New Zealand, again tightening loan operations. Three years later NAB claimed Michigan National in the US.

After the mid-1990s economic recovery, NAB bought HomeSide to try to adapt the US mortgage firm's efficient operations for all its banks.

NAB in 2000 bought Lend Lease's MLC fund management group. It also announced plans to launch a separate stock for its European businesses, fueling speculation it might be on the prowl to buy or merge with a large UK bank. The Australian Competition and Consumer Commission that year accused NAB of credit card transaction price-fixing; the bank faces a possible fine of nearly $6 million.

The next year NAB sold US-based Michigan National to ABN AMRO, providing the Australian bank with some greenbacks to fuel growth elsewhere. The following year it sold HomeSide to Washington Mutual.

EXECUTIVES

Chairman: Charles Allen
Managing Director, CEO, and Executive Director: Francis J. Cicutto, age 51, $1,369,801 pay
CFO: Richard E. McKinnon, age 52
CIO: Ian R. Crouch, age 49, $266,078 pay
Executive General Manager, Corporate Development: Michael T. (Mike) Laing
Executive General Manager, Risk Management: Christopher D. Lewis, age 43
Executive General Manager, Financial Services Australia: Ian G. MacDonald, age 48
Executive General Manager, People and Culture: Peter A. McKinnon, age 48
Executive General Manager, Office of the CEO and Acting Executive General Manager, Financial Services Great Britain and Ireland: Ross E. Pinney, age 54
Executive General Manager, Wholesale Financial Services: Ian F. Scholes, age 48
Executive General Manager, Wealth Management: Peter B. Scott, age 48, $639,971 pay
Executive General Manager, Financial Services New Zealand; CEO, Bank of New Zealand: Peter Thodey, age 52
General Manager, Corporate Finance: Graham Maloney
CEO, Northern Bank and National Irish Bank: Donald Price, age 49
Company Secretary: Garry F. Nolan, age 55
Group General Counsel: David M. Krasnostein, age 48
Auditors: KPMG

LOCATIONS

HQ: National Australia Bank Limited
Fl. 24, 500 Bourke St., Melbourne 3000, Australia
Phone: +61-3-8641-4200   **Fax:** +61-3-8641-4927
US HQ: 200 Park Ave., 34th Fl.,
New York, NY 10166-0001
US Phone: 212-916-9500   **US Fax:** 212-983-1969
Web: www.national.com.au

2002 Sales

	$ mil.	% of total
Australia	7,654	53
Europe	3,487	24
US	1,820	13
New Zealand	1,191	8
Asia	249	2
Total	**14,401**	**100**

PRODUCTS/OPERATIONS

Selected Subsidiaries

Bank of New Zealand
Clydesdale Bank (UK)
NAB Asia (Hong Kong)
National Irish Bank
Northern Bank (UK)
Yorkshire Bank (UK)

COMPETITORS

Abbey National
Allied Irish Banks
Australia and New Zealand Banking
Bank of Ireland
Barclays
Commonwealth Bank of Australia
HBOS
HSBC Holdings
Lloyds TSB
Northern Rock plc
Royal Bank of Scotland
St.George Bank
Westpac

HISTORICAL FINANCIALS

Company Type: Public

Income Statement

FYE: September 30

	ASSETS ($ mil.)	NET INCOME ($ mil.)	INCOME AS % OF ASSETS	EMPLOYEES
9/02	204,921	1,832	0.9%	46,642
9/01	184,774	1,027	0.6%	49,710
9/00	186,582	1,758	0.9%	47,000
9/99	165,813	1,841	1.1%	51,566
9/98	149,266	1,194	0.8%	46,300
9/97	146,428	1,610	1.1%	46,392
9/96	137,665	1,666	1.2%	47,178
9/95	108,028	1,446	1.3%	52,567
9/94	93,153	1,264	1.4%	43,053
9/93	75,592	728	1.0%	43,053
Annual Growth	**11.7%**	**10.8%**	**—**	**0.9%**

2002 Year-End Financials

Equity as % of assets: 6.0%	Dividends
Return on assets: 0.9%	Yield: 4.1%
Return on equity: 15.6%	Payout: 67.5%
Long-term debt ($ mil.): 13,063	Market value ($ mil.): 27,836
No. of shares (mil.): 307	Sales ($ mil.): 14,401

Stock History

NYSE: NAB

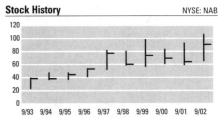

	STOCK PRICE ($) FY Close	P/E High/Low		PER SHARE ($) Earnings	Dividends	Book Value
9/02	90.68	19	12	5.50	3.71	41.01
9/01	63.81	31	20	3.01	3.46	50.84
9/00	69.38	15	11	5.54	3.54	38.25
9/99	73.81	16	10	5.93	3.44	40.72
9/98	59.94	20	14	4.09	3.15	31.44
9/97	77.13	15	10	5.50	3.43	30.78
9/96	52.88	9	7	5.69	3.27	33.48
9/95	44.38	9	7	5.18	2.93	29.16
9/94	38.25	10	8	4.71	2.18	26.53
9/93	38.50	14	8	2.82	0.82	21.54
Annual Growth	**10.0%**	**—**	**—**	**7.7%**	**18.3%**	**7.4%**

NEC Corporation

NEC has three arms and plenty of muscle. The company's IT Solutions business makes high-end computers (servers and supercomputers) and peripherals (monitors and projectors), and it wrestles with Fujitsu for the top spot among Japanese PC makers. Its Electron Devices division makes electronics ranging from transistors to display modules, and competes with Toshiba for the second spot among semiconductor makers (both companies trail Intel). The company sells broadband and wireless networking equipment through its Network Solutions group. NEC also runs one of Japan's largest Internet service providers (BIGLOBE).

Not wanting to be pigeonholed as a PC maker, centenarian NEC has followed industry suit and recast itself as a provider of Internet products and services. Citing efforts to sharpen its focus, NEC realigned its vast empire into three in-house companies. (It later scrapped the in-house structure, retaining the three groups as product divisions.) Other structural changes within NEC include the reorganization of its PC operations, job cuts, and the formation of joint ventures for its monitor and dynamic RAM (DRAM) operations with Mitsubishi and Hitachi, respectively. NEC plans to take its DRAM joint venture, Elpida Memory, public, thereby reducing its stake in the company and the volatile memory sector.

HISTORY

A group of Japanese investors, led by Kunihiko Iwadare, formed Nippon Electric Company (NEC) in a joint venture with Western Electric (US) in 1899. Starting as an importer of telephone equipment, NEC soon became a maker and a major supplier to Japan's Communications Ministry. Western Electric sold its stake in NEC in 1925. The company became affiliated with the Sumitomo *keiretsu* (industrial group) in the 1930s and went public in 1949.

After Nippon Telegraph and Telephone (NTT) was formed in 1952, NEC became one of its four leading suppliers. The post-WWII need to repair Japan's telephone systems and the country's continuing economic recovery resulted in strong demand from NTT for NEC's products. In the 1950s and 1960s NTT business represented over 50% of sales, even though NEC had expanded overseas, diversified into home appliances, and formed a computer alliance with Honeywell (US). ITT (US), which had begun acquiring shares in the company decades earlier and owned as much as 59% of NEC, sold its stake in the 1960s.

In the 1970s Honeywell's lagging position in computers hurt NEC; the company recovered through in-house development efforts and a mainframe venture with Toshiba. In 1977 CEO Koji Kobayashi articulated his revolutionary vision of NEC's future as an integrator of computers and communications through semiconductor technology.

NEC invested heavily in R&D and expansion, becoming the world's largest semiconductor maker in 1985. Despite its proprietary operating system, NEC garnered over 50% of the Japanese computer market in the 1980s. NEC entered into a mainframe computer partnership with Honeywell and France's Groupe Bull in 1987.

By the early 1990s NEC had lost its status as world's largest semiconductor maker to Intel. NEC bought 20% of US computer maker Packard Bell in 1995. The following year NEC merged most of its PC business outside Japan with that company, creating Packard Bell NEC. Also in 1996 NEC created US subsidiary Holon Net Corp. to make hardware and software for Internet and intranet markets.

NEC took control of Packard Bell NEC in 1998, upping its stake to 53%. A sluggish Japanese economy and slumping memory prices contributed to NEC's drop in income for fiscal 1998. A defense contract scandal involving overbilling and improper hiring by an NEC unit forced the resignation of chairman Tadahiro Sekimoto and, later, president Hisashi Kaneko.

New president Koji Nishigaki, the first at NEC without an engineering background, led a sweeping reorganization to cut 10% of the company's workforce — 15,000 employees — over three years. He revamped NEC operations around Internet application hardware, software, and services. In 1998 NEC formed a rare pact with a Japanese rival, allying with Hitachi to consolidate memory chip operations. The restructuring of Packard Bell NEC (NEC by then owned 88%) helped cause a $1.3 billion loss for fiscal 1999, NEC's worst-ever drop. NEC folded up its Packard Bell NEC division later that year, imposing layoffs of about 80% of its staff, divesting it from the US retail market, and excising the historic Packard Bell brand name.

NEC restructured again in 2000, splitting into more autonomous units and streamlining its PC operations. That year the company launched an aggressive spending program in a move to lead the broadband mobile networking market. In early 2001 NEC ended a long-running dispute with Cray, investing $25 million in the company and granting distribution rights to its vector supercomputers in North America — a deal contingent upon Cray's dropping an antidumping suit that led to heavy import taxes being placed on NEC supercomputers sold in the US.

In 2002 NEC announced plans to spin off its semiconductor operations and form joint ventures for other divisions comprising its NEC Electron Devices business.

EXECUTIVES

Chairman: Hajime Sasaki
Vice Chairman: Koji Nishigaki, age 65
President: Akinobu Kanasugi, age 62
SEVP: Mineo Sugiyama
EVP: Toshiro Kawamura
EVP: Kazuhiko Kobayashi
EVP: Shigeo Matsumoto
EVP: Hiroshi Takakuta
EVP: Kaoru Yano
SVP: Yukio Doi
SVP: Kazumasa Fujie
SVP: Yasushi Kaito
SVP: Makoto Maruyama
SVP: Tsutomu Nakamura
SVP: Kelichi Shimakura
SVP: Shunichi Suzuki
SVP: Taiji Suzuki
Associate SVP: Yoshio Omori
Associate SVP: Hideki Teranishi
Associate SVP: Nobuhito Yagi
Auditors: Ernst & Young

LOCATIONS

HQ: Nippon Denki Kabushiki Kaisha
7-1, Shiba 5-chome, Minato-ku,
Tokyo 108-8001, Japan
Phone: +81-3-3454-1111 **Fax:** +81-3-3798-1510
Web: www.nec.com

NEC operates a network of 60 plants and more than 300 sales offices in Japan. The company operates through subsidiaries and affiliates in about 40 countries.

2003 Sales by Origin

	$ mil.	% of total
Japan	32,877	83
Other countries	6,911	17
Total	**39,788**	**100**

PRODUCTS/OPERATIONS

2003 Sales

	$ mil.	% of total
IT solutions	17,649	39
Network solutions	13,359	30
Electron devices	7,938	18
Leasing	324	1
Other	5,607	12
Adjustments	(5,089)	—
Total	**39,788**	**100**

Selected Products

IT Solutions
PCs
   Desktop
   Handheld
   Notebook
Peripherals
   CD-ROMs
   Monitors
   Projectors
Servers
Supercomputers

Network Solutions
Broadcasting equipment
Control servers
Fiber-optic devices
Gateways
Lasers
Mobile networking and communications devices
Multiplexers
Network management applications
Postal automation systems
Routers and switches
Satellite systems

Electron Devices
Application-specific components
Discrete devices
Flat-panel displays
Integrated circuits
Memory
Microprocessors
Optoelectronics
Radio-frequency and microwave devices

COMPETITORS

Acer	Mitsubishi Electric
AMD	Motorola
Alcatel	Nokia
Apple Computer	Nortel Networks
Canon	Oki Electric
CASIO COMPUTER	Philips Electronics
Cisco Systems	Ricoh
Dell	Samsung Electronics
EDS	Samsung
Ericsson	SANYO
Fuji Photo	Seiko Epson
Fujitsu	Sharp
Hewlett-Packard	Siemens
Hitachi	Sony
Intel	STMicroelectronics
IBM	Sun Microsystems
Lucent	Texas Instruments
Matsushita	Toshiba
Micron Technology	Unisys
Microsoft	

HISTORICAL FINANCIALS

Company Type: Public

Income Statement

FYE: March 31

	REVENUE ($ mil.)	NET INCOME ($ mil.)	NET PROFIT MARGIN	EMPLOYEES
3/03	39,788	(208)	—	145,807
3/02	38,446	(2,352)	—	142,000
3/01	43,099	451	1.0%	150,000
3/00	48,461	101	0.2%	154,787
3/99	40,334	(1,339)	—	157,800
3/98	36,851	311	0.8%	152,450
3/97	39,907	739	1.9%	151,966
3/96	41,095	721	1.8%	152,719
3/95	43,326	406	0.9%	147,994
3/94	35,096	65	0.2%	143,320
Annual Growth	1.4%	—	—	0.2%

2003 Year-End Financials

Debt ratio: 280.0%	No. of shares (mil.): 1,656
Return on equity: —	Dividends
Cash ($ mil.): 2,918	Yield: 0.6%
Current ratio: 1.08	Payout: —
Long-term debt ($ mil.): 8,507	Market value ($ mil.): 5,482

Stock History

NASDAQ: NIPNY

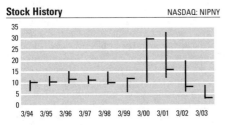

	STOCK PRICE ($) FY Close	P/E High/Low		PER SHARE ($) Earnings	Dividends	Book Value
3/03	3.31	—	—	(0.13)	0.02	1.83
3/02	8.35	—	—	(1.42)	0.27	2.57
3/01	15.88	116	45	0.28	0.06	4.40
3/00	29.69	498	174	0.06	0.05	1.16
3/99	11.93	—	—	(0.84)	0.05	0.93
3/98	10.15	82	54	0.18	0.05	1.01
3/97	11.33	31	24	0.42	0.05	1.03
3/96	11.65	36	24	0.42	0.05	1.06
3/95	10.50	50	35	0.26	0.08	1.18
3/94	10.33	219	137	0.05	0.08	1.00
Annual Growth	(11.9%)	—	—	—	(14.3%)	7.0%

Nestlé S.A.

With instant coffee, baby formula, and the bottled water to mix them with, Nestlé's crunch is in more than just chocolate. The world's #1 food company, Nestlé is the world leader in coffee (Nescafé) and bottled water (Perrier). The 2001 purchase of Ralston Purina made it a top player in the pet food business. Ranging from kitty kibble to pasta, chocolate, and dairy products, its largest global brands include Buitoni, Friskies, Maggi, Nescafé, Nestea, and Nestlé. In addition to food products, Nestlé owns about 75% of Alcon Inc. (ophthalmic drugs, contact lens solutions, and equipment for ocular surgery) and has a large indirect stake in cosmetic giant L'Oreal.

The company also makes eye care products. It is forming a 50-50 joint venture with L'Oréal to produce nutritional supplements aimed at improving skin, hair, and nails. Other joint ventures include Cereal Partners Worldwide, with General Mills.

Nestlé has long been an international company. Many of its brands are unique to particular countries, with products tailored to local tastes. Seeking to further strengthen its position in the worldwide ice cream market, in 2003 Nestlé agreed to acquire the ice cream and related products of the Mövenpick Group, a Swiss food company. The acquisition will bring Nestlé licensing agreements with companies in Egypt, Finland, Germany, Norway, Sweden, and Saudi Arabia.

Also in 2003, in an effort to increase its confectionery sales, Nestlé formed a 50-50 joint venture with Colgate-Palmolive to develop and market functional confectionery products, including gum and candy that, for example, will whiten teeth and fight plaque.

For the future, the company sees itself expanding into more specialty nutritional foods and bringing more of L'Oréal under its roof. Nestlé has about 500 factories in more than 70 countries.

HISTORY

Henri Nestlé purchased a factory in Vevey, Switzerland, in 1843 that made products ranging from nut oils to rum. In 1867 he developed a powder made from cow's milk and wheat flour as a substitute for mother's milk. A year earlier Americans Charles and George Page had founded the Anglo-Swiss Condensed Milk Company in Cham, Switzerland, using Gail Borden's milk-canning technology.

In 1875 Nestlé sold his eponymous company, then doing business in 16 countries. When Anglo-Swiss launched a milk-based infant food in 1878, Nestlé's new owners responded by introducing a condensed-milk product. In 1905, a year after Nestlé began selling chocolate, the companies ended their rivalry by merging under the Nestlé name.

Hampered by limited milk supplies during WWI, the company expanded into regions less affected by the war, such as the US. In 1929 it acquired Cailler, the first company to mass-produce chocolate bars, and Swiss General, inventor of milk chocolate.

An investment in a Brazilian condensed-milk factory during the 1920s paid an unexpected dividend when Brazilian coffee growers suggested the company develop a water-soluble "coffee cube." Released in 1938, Nescafé instant coffee quickly became popular.

Other new products included Nestlé's Crunch bar (1938), Quik drink mix (1948), and Taster's Choice instant coffee (1966). Nestlé expanded during the 1970s with acquisitions such as Beringer Brothers wines (sold in 1995), Stouffer's, and Libby's.

Moving beyond foods in 1974, Nestlé acquired a 49% stake in Gesparal, a holding company that controls the French cosmetics company L'Oréal. It acquired pharmaceutical firm Alcon Laboratories three years later.

Helmut Maucher was named chairman and CEO in 1981. He began beefing up Nestlé's global presence. Boycotters had long accused Nestlé of harming children in developing countries through the unethical promotion of infant formula, and Maucher acknowledged the ongoing boycott by meeting with the critics and setting up a commission to police adherence to World Health Organization guidelines.

Nestlé bought Carnation in 1985. Maucher doubled the company's chocolate business in 1988 with the purchase of UK chocolate maker Rowntree (Kit Kat). Also in the 1980s Nestlé acquired Buitoni pastas.

The company expanded in the 1990s with the purchases of Butterfinger and Baby Ruth candies, Source Perrier water, Alpo pet food, and Ortega Mexican foods. Company veteran Peter Brabeck-Letmathe succeeded Maucher as CEO in 1997. He cleaned out Nestlé's pantry by selling noncore businesses (Contadina tomato products, Libby's canned meat products) but restocked with San Pellegrino (mineral water) and Dalgety's Spillers (pet food) in 1998.

By 1999 the company started rolling out its Nestlé Pure Life bottled water. That year Nestlé merged its US novelty ice-cream unit with operations of Pillsbury's Häagen-Dazs to form Ice Cream Partners USA.

In 2000 Nestlé purchased snack maker PowerBar. In 2001 Nestlé bought Ralston Purina for $10.3 billion, making it the world's largest pet food maker. To win FTC approval, the companies agreed to sell Meow Mix and Alley Cat dry cat food brands to Hartz Mountain. In a deal that gives Nestlé a 99-year license to use the Häagen-Dazs brand in the US, the company agreed to pay $641 million to General Mills (which bought Pillsbury from Britain's Diageo) for the other half of Ice Cream Partners.

In 2002 Nestlé acquired German ice-cream maker Schoeller Holding Group, as well as US food company, Chef America, maker of Hot Pockets. It spun off eyecare subsidiary, Alcon Laboratories, but retained about 75% ownership of it. Nestlé and Cadbury Schweppes made a joint $10.5 billion bid for Hershey Foods in 2002 but Hershey called the sale off later that year.

In 2003 the company added to its bottled-water business by acquiring Hutchison Whampoa's Powwow. It also acquired Clear Water, a bottled-water home-and-office delivery company located in Russia.

While Nestlé already owned 30% of US ice cream powerhouse Dreyer's, in 2002 it proposed a merger of its US ice cream businesses. After months of antitrust scrutiny the deal was authorized in 2003 but required both parties to dispose of overlapping businesses. Nestlé sold most of its frozen-dessert distribution operations to CoolBrands International. At its completion, the deal gave Nestlé 67% of Dreyer's.

In 2003 the Nestlé USA unit sold its Ortega brand Mexican food products to B&G Foods.

EXECUTIVES

Chairman: Rainer E. Gut, age 70
Vice Chairman and CEO: Peter Brabeck-Letmathe, age 59
EVP, Zone Americas; and Chairman, Nestlé Mexicio: Carlos E. Represas, age 58
EVP, Chairman and CEO Nestlé Waters: Frits van Dijk, age 56
EVP, Asia, Oceania, Africa, Middle East: Michael W. O. Garrett, age 61
EVP, Europe: Lars Olofsson, age 51
EVP, Finance, Control, Legal, Tax, Purchasing, Export; and CFO: Wolfgang H. Reichenberger, age 50
EVP, Pharmaceutical and Cosmetic, Human Rresources, Corporate Affairs and Nestlé España S.A., Market Research: Francisco Castañer, age 59
EVP, Strategic Business Units and Marketing: Frank Cella, age 63
EVP, Technical, Production, Environment, and Research and Development: Werner J. Bauer, age 52
Deputy EVP, GLOBE Programme leader: Chris Johnson, age 42
Deputy EVP, Nurtition Strategic Business: Luis Cantarell, age 51
CEO, Nestlé Japan: Jose Lopez
Manager, HealthCare, Nestlé Nutrition: Eric Van Der Loo
General Secretary: Bernard Daniel
Investor Relations: Roddy Child-Villiers
Media Relations: François-Xavier Perroud
Managing Director, Malaysia: Sullivan O'Carroll
Maket Head, Nestlé Canada: Ed Marra
Market Head, Nestlé Germany: Paul Bulcke
Auditors: KPMG Klynveld Peat Marwick Goerdeler SA

LOCATIONS

HQ: Avenue Nestlé 55, CH-1800 Vevey, Switzerland
Phone: +41-21-924-21-11   **Fax:** +41-21-924-28-13
US HQ: 800 N. Brand Blvd., Glendale, CA 91203
US Phone: 818-549-6000   **US Fax:** 818-549-6952
Web: www.nestle.com

Nestle operates about 500 factories in more than 70 countries.

2002 Sales

	% of total
Food	
The Americas	33
Europe	32
Africa, Asia & Oceania	17
Other	18
Total	**100**

PRODUCTS/OPERATIONS

2002 Sales

	% of total
Beverages	26
Milk products, nutrition & ice cream	26
Prepared dishes & cooking aids	18
Petcare	12
Chocolate & confectionery	12
Pharmaceuticals	6
Total	**100**

Selected Products

Beverages
Chocolate-based and malted drinks (Milo, Nescau, Nesquik)
Instant coffee (Nescafé, Taster's Choice)
Mineral water (Arrowhead, Calistoga, Contrex, Perrier, San Pellegrino, Vittel)
Roasted coffee (Bonka, Loumidis, Zoégas)
Tea, fruit juices, and cereal drinks (Nestea, Libby's, Caro)

Milk Products, Nutrition, and Ice Cream
Breakfast cereals (Nestlé)
Coffee creamer (Coffee-Mate)
Ice cream (Camy, Dairy Farm, Frisco, Häagen-Dazs, Nestlé, Schoeller Holding Group)
Infant foods and dietetic products (Cérélac, Guigoz, Lactogen, Nan, Nestlé, Nestum)
Milk products (Carnation, La Lechera, Nespray, Nido)

Chocolate and Confectionery
Aero
Baby Ruth
Butterfinger
Cailler
Galak/Milkybar
KitKat
Lifesavers
Lion
Nestlé
Rolo
Smarties
Willy Wonka

Pet Product
Alpo
Beggin' Strips
Beneful
Dog Chow
Fancy Feast
Felix
Fit & Trim
Friskies
Kitten Chow
Mighty Dog
Pro Plan
Puppy Chow
Purina O.N.E.
Purina Right Bites
Purina Special Care
Purina Veterinary Diets
secondnature
T Bonz
Tender Vittles
Tidy Cats
Whisker Lickin's

Pharmaceuticals
Contact lens solutions (Opti-Free)
Instruments and equipment for ocular surgery
Ophthalmic therapeutic drugs (Patanol)

Prepared Dishes and Cooking Aids
Delicatessen products (Herta)
Frozen prepared dishes (Buitoni, Maggi, Stouffer's)
On-the-go foods (Croissant Pockets, Hot Pockets, Lean Pockets)
Pasta and Italian foods (Buitoni)

COMPETITORS

Abbott Labs
Allergan
Barilla
Bausch & Lomb
Brach's
Cadbury Schweppes
Campbell Soup
Lindt & Sprüngli
Colgate-Palmolive
ConAgra
Danone
Ferrara Pan Candy
Goya
Hershey
Heinz
Kraft Foods
Kraft Foods International
Kraft Foods North America
Mars
Novartis
Parmalat
PepsiCo
Procter & Gamble
Revlon
Russell Stover
Sara Lee Beverage
Sara Lee
Suntory
Tchibo Holding
Thorntons
Unilever
World's Finest Chocolate

HISTORICAL FINANCIALS

Company Type: Public

Income Statement

FYE: December 31

	REVENUE ($ mil.)	NET INCOME ($ mil.)	NET PROFIT MARGIN	EMPLOYEES
12/02	64,258	5,451	8.5%	254,199
12/01	50,624	3,993	7.9%	229,765
12/00	50,522	3,576	7.1%	224,541
12/99	46,924	2,969	6.3%	230,929
12/98	52,031	3,112	6.0%	231,881
12/97	48,061	2,750	5.7%	225,808
12/96	44,835	2,521	5.6%	221,144
12/95	48,934	2,528	5.2%	220,172
12/94	43,479	2,484	5.7%	212,687
12/93	38,620	1,940	5.0%	209,755
Annual Growth	**5.8%**	**12.2%**	**—**	**2.2%**

2002 Year-End Financials

Debt ratio: 30.3%
Return on equity: 24.1%
Cash ($ mil.): 10,300
Current ratio: 1.05
Long-term debt ($ mil.): 7,602

Net Income History

OTC: NSRGY

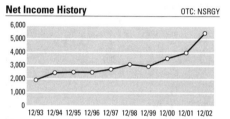

The News Corporation

Rupert Murdoch's News Corporation is truly a global media and entertainment empire. The company, which is one of the world's largest media conglomerates, publishes scores of newspapers (including *The Times* of London) and books (through units such as HarperCollins). The company's 81%-owned Fox Entertainment Group has significant entertainment holdings, including FOX Broadcasting (TV network with 200 US affiliates) in the US, Twentieth Century Fox, and the Los Angeles Dodgers. It also owns 35 US TV stations and cable and satellite operations in Asia, Australia, Europe, and Latin America. More than 75% of News Corp.'s sales are from its US businesses. Murdoch's family controls about 30% of the company.

A mogul with satellites in his sights, Murdoch has finally emerged as the winning bidder for General Motors' (GM) stake in Hughes Electronics, the owner of satellite TV company, DIRECTV. News Corp. will pay GM and Hughes shareholders a total of $6.6 billion for a 34% stake in Hughes. Once the deal is completed, News Corp. will transfer its Hughes interest to Fox Entertainment. Murdoch has had his eye on DIRECTV for a long time, and spent the better part of a year fighting the satellite company's chief rival, EchoStar, from acquiring its competitor. EchoStar and Hughes did reach a merger agreement in 2002, but antitrust authorities quashed the deal. Wall Street, however, is apprehensive about placing the DIRECTV stake with Fox, as it will add $4.5 billion in debt to the subsidiary's books.

The DIRECTV deal furthers News Corp.'s desire to be a global satellite television powerhouse. The company's other important purchase was the 2003 buy of Vivendi Universal's Italian pay-TV unit, Telepiú. News Corp. has combined Telepiú with its Stream unit (which was co-owned with Telecom Italia) into a new firm called Sky Italia. (News Corp owns about 80% of the combined company; Telecom Italia owns the rest.) News Corp. is also one of the few companies to have a satellite TV presence in tightly controlled China.

News Corp. has also placed the Los Angeles Dodgers on the selling block, claiming that it is no longer a valuable asset to the company. It has struck a deal to sell the team to an investment group led by real estate developer Frank McCourt.

Additional News Corp. shareholders include Liberty Media, with a 19% stake.

HISTORY

In 1952 Rupert Murdoch inherited two Adelaide, Australia, newspapers from his father. After launching the *Australian,* the country's first national daily, in 1964, Murdoch moved into the UK market. He bought tabloid *News of the World,* a London Sunday paper, in 1968, and London's *Sun* the next year. In 1973 Murdoch hit the US, buying the *San Antonio Express-News* and founding the *Star* tabloid. He followed this up in 1976 by buying the *New York Post.* Murdoch formed News Corporation in Australia in 1979.

Moving upmarket in 1981, Murdoch bought the London *Times* and 40% of Collins Publishers, a London book publisher. After buying the *Chicago Sun-Times* in 1983 (sold 1986), Murdoch bought 13 US travel, hotel, and aviation trade magazines from Ziff-Davis, as well as film studio Twentieth Century Fox in 1985. In 1986 Murdoch bought six Metromedia stations and launched FOX Broadcasting, the first new US TV network since 1948.

Print was not forgotten, however, and in the late 1980s News Corp. picked up US book publisher Harper & Row as well as Triangle Publications (*TV Guide* and other magazines). It also bought textbook publisher Scott, Foresman and the rest of Collins Publishers.

In 1996 Murdoch launched the Fox News Channel, an all-news cable channel. The next year, News Corp.'s Fox Kids joint venture bought Pat Robertson's International Family Entertainment.

In 1998 the company bought the Los Angeles Dodgers and stakes in the new Los Angeles-area Staples Center sports arena. Also that year News Corp. spun off part of Fox Entertainment in one of America's largest IPOs, raising $2.7 billion.

That year News Corp. sold *TV Guide* to Tele-Communications Inc.'s (now AT&T Broadband & Internet) United Video Satellite Group (now Gemstar-TV Guide International) for $800 million in cash and a 21.5% interest in Gemstar-TV Guide International (later boosted to 42%). The company also bought the 50% of FOX/Liberty Networks (now Fox Sports Networks) it didn't own and transferred ownership to Fox Entertainment. The deal gave Liberty an 8% stake (later 19%) in News Corp. The company also broke into the coveted German pay-TV market through BSkyB's agreement to buy 24% of KirchGruppe's (since renamed TaurusHolding) Kirch PayTV (completed in 2000). In 1999 News Corp. bought an 11% stake in Healtheon/WebMD (now simply

WebMD), but the stake was later divested. That same year the company bought a 10% stake of wireless ISP OmniSky.

In 2000 Murdoch placed all of the company's satellite holdings into a new entity, Sky Global Networks. (News Corp. folded Sky Global back into its operations in 2002 when it failed in its initial bid to buy DIRECTV.) Also that year News Corp. agreed to buy TV station owner Chris-Craft and bought a stake in China's state-owned telecom operator Netcom.

In 2001, along with partner Saban, News Corp. sold the Fox Family Channel to Disney for about $5.2 billion. In mid-2001 the FCC approved the company's $4.8 billion purchase of Chris-Craft. The deal gave News Corp. an additional 10 TV stations.

EXECUTIVES

Chairman and CEO, News Corporation and Fox Entertainment Group: K. Rupert Murdoch, age 72, $12,008,000 pay
President and COO, News Corporation and Fox Entertainment Group: Peter Chernin, age 52, $16,104,000 pay
Deputy COO: Lachlan K. Murdoch, age 32, $2,603,000 pay
SEVP and CFO, News Corporation and Fox Entertainment Group: David F. DeVoe, age 56, $9,254,000 pay
SEVP and Group General Counsel, News Corporation and Fox Entertainment Group: Arthur M. Siskind, age 64, $3,165,000 pay
EVP; CEO, British Sky Broadcasting: James R. Murdoch, age 30, $2,100,000 pay (prior to promotion)
EVP Human Resources: Ian Moore
EVP Investor Relations and Corporate Communications: Gary L. Ginsberg, age 39
Chairman, President, and CEO, NDS: Abraham (Abe) Peled, age 55
Chairman and CEO, Fox News Channel: Roger Ailes, age 63, $8,456,000 pay
Chairman and CEO, Fox Television Stations: Mitchell Stern, age 49, $3,845,000 pay
Chairman and CEO, Los Angeles Dodgers: Robert A. Daly
Chairman and CEO, News America Marketing: Paul V. Carlucci
Co-Chairman, Fox Filmed Entertainment: James N. (Jim) Gianopulos, age 51, $3,491,000 pay
Co-Chairman, Fox Filmed Entertainment: Thomas E. (Tom) Rothman, age 48, $3,491,000 pay
Chairman, Fox Sports Networks; Chairman and CEO, Fox Sports Television Group: David Hill, age 57, $3,500,000 pay
Chairman, FOX Television Entertainment Group: Sandy Grushow, $3,751,000 pay
President and CEO, Fox Networks Group: Anthony J. (Tony) Vinciquerra, age 49
President and CEO, FX Networks: Peter Liguori
President and CEO, HarperCollins: Jane Friedman
Auditors: Ernst & Young LLP

LOCATIONS

HQ: The News Corporation Limited
   2 Holt St., Sydney 2010, Australia
Phone: +61-2-9288-3000   **Fax:** +61-2-9288-3292
US HQ: 1211 Avenue of the Americas,
   New York, NY 10036
US Phone: 212-852-7059   **US Fax:** 212-852-7145
Web: www.newscorp.com

News Corp. has operations worldwide.

2003 Sales

	$ mil.	% of total
US	15,273	76
Europe	3,215	16
Australia/Asia	1,608	8
Total	**20,096**	**100**

PRODUCTS/OPERATIONS

2003 Sales

	$ mil.	% of total
Television	5,426	27
Filmed entertainment	5,225	26
Newspapers	3,216	16
Cable network programming	2,613	13
Book publishing	1,407	7
Magazines/Inserts	1,005	5
Direct broadcast satellite televison	200	1
Other	1,004	5
Total	**20,096**	**100**

Selected Operations

Books, Magazines, and Inserts
Gemstar-TV Guide International (42%, US)
HarperCollins Publishers (general-interest and religious books, US)
InsideOut (Australia)
News America Marketing
The Weekly Standard (US)

Cable and Satellite TV Properties
British Sky Broadcasting (36%, UK)
China Network Systems (20%, 18 cable systems)
Fox Cable Networks Group
   FX (general interest cable channel)
   Fox Movie Channel (pay television network)
   Fox Sports Networks (interests in regional cable sports networks, Madison Square Garden, Radio City Music Hall, the New York Knicks, and New York Rangers)
Fox News Channel
Fox Sports Australia (50%)
Hathway Cable and Datacom (26%)
Hughes Electronics (34%)
   DIRECTV (Satellite television service)
   Hughes Network Systems (telecommunications equipment)
   PanAmSat (81%, satellite communications network operations)
Phoenix Satellite Television (38%, Asia)
Sky Italia (80%)
Sky Latin America
Sky PerfecTV! (8%, Japan)

Filmed Entertainment
Blue Sky Studios
Fox 2000 Pictures
Fox Searchlight Pictures
Fox Television Studios
Twentieth Century Fox Film
Twentieth Century Fox Home Entertainment
Twentieth Century Fox Television

Newspapers
The Advertiser (South Australia)
The Australian
The Courier Mail (42%; Queensland, Australia)
The Daily Telegraph (New South Wales, Australia)
Gold Coast Bulletin (Queensland, Australia)
Herald Sun (Victoria, Australia)
Independent Newspapers Ltd. (44%; 100 daily and weekly newspapers in New Zealand, Australia, and the US; New Zealand)
The Mercury (Tasmania, Australia)
New York Post (US)
News of the World (UK)
The Sun (UK)
Sunday Herald Sun (Victoria, Australia)
Sunday Mail (42%, South Australia)
The Sunday Telegraph (New South Wales, Australia)
Sunday Territorian (Northern Territory, Australia)
The Sunday Times (UK)
The Times (UK)

Television
Balkan News Corporation (Europe)
FOX Broadcasting Company (television network, US)
Fox Television Stations
STAR (Asia)
Cine Canal (23%, Latin America)
Premium Movie Partnership (20%, Australia and New Zealand)
Telecine (13%, Latin America)

Other
Broadsystem Ventures (database management system, UK)
Convoys Group
Festival Records (record label, Australia)
Los Angeles Dodgers (professional baseball organization)
National Rugby League (50%, Australia)
News Outdoor Group (75%)
Newspoll (50%)
NDS (78%, pay-TV scrambling services)
Sky Radio (93%)
UTV Software Communications (20%)
The Wireless Group (19%)

COMPETITORS

Advance Publications	Pearson
Bertelsmann	Reed Elsevier Group
CANAL+	Sony
Cox Enterprises	Thomson Corporation
Hachette Filipacchi Médias	Time Warner
Hollinger	Tribune
Liberty Media	Viacom
McGraw-Hill	VUE
NBC	Vivendi Universal
New York Times	Walt Disney
Northern & Shell	

HISTORICAL FINANCIALS

Company Type: Public

Income Statement

FYE: June 30

	REVENUE ($ mil.)	NET INCOME ($ mil.)	NET PROFIT MARGIN	EMPLOYEES
6/03	20,096	1,215	6.0%	37,000
6/02	16,344	(6,738)	—	33,800
6/01	13,047	1,880	14.4%	31,400
6/00	13,421	1,149	8.6%	30,000
6/99	14,292	714	5.0%	50,000
6/98	11,716	1,040	8.9%	28,220
6/97	10,727	537	5.0%	26,500
6/96	10,285	802	7.8%	27,250
6/95	8,641	969	11.2%	26,600
6/94	8,468	973	11.5%	25,845
Annual Growth	10.1%	2.5%	—	4.1%

2003 Year-End Financials

Debt ratio: 38.9%
Return on equity: 6.0%
Cash ($ mil.): 4,532
Current ratio: 1.60
Long-term debt ($ mil.): 8,328
No. of shares (mil.): 1,332
Dividends
  Yield: 0.2%
  Payout: 7.6%
Market value ($ mil.): 40,316

Stock History

NYSE: NWS

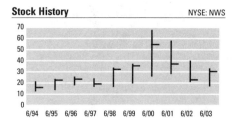

	STOCK PRICE ($) FY Close	P/E High/Low	PER SHARE ($) Earnings	Dividends	Book Value
6/03	30.27	35 19	0.92	0.07	16.30
6/02	22.93	— —	(5.48)	0.06	16.77
6/01	37.15	— —	(1.11)	0.07	37.54
6/00	54.50	60 23	1.52	0.08	38.62
6/99	35.31	38 21	0.97	0.07	35.69
6/98	32.13	29 15	1.15	0.04	35.98
6/97	19.25	39 28	0.61	0.09	33.99
6/96	23.50	41 30	0.49	0.04	26.15
6/95	22.63	13 8	1.84	0.07	22.24
6/94	16.07	23 14	1.02	0.05	20.63
Annual Growth	7.3%	— —	(1.1%)	3.8%	(2.6%)

Nikon Corporation

Paul Simon may still have a Nikon camera and still love to take a photograph, but Nikon's focus extends far wider than that. Though well-known for its cameras, lenses, and other consumer optical products, Nikon vies with national rival Canon and Netherlands-based ASML Holding to be the world's top producer of photolithography steppers — crucial equipment used to etch circuitry onto semiconductor wafers and LCD panels. The company makes a broad range of other products, including binoculars, eyewear, surveying instruments, microscopes, industrial equipment, and electronic imaging equipment. Nikon is part of the huge Mitsubishi *keiretsu*, a group of businesses linked by cross-ownership.

The range of Nikon's products offers a snapshot of the optical world. Its cameras have caught images from every manned space flight since Apollo 13. Its microscopes are used in schools and cell biology research laboratories, and its eye examination equipment and prescription glasses and sunglasses are fixtures in opticians' offices worldwide.

Nikon has adjusted operations in an effort to become more nimble in the face of sluggish stepper sales. It has reorganized into more-autonomous divisions, an arrangement under which the parent corporation serves as a holding company.

HISTORY

Lensmaker Nippon Kogaku KK formed in 1917 with the merger of three large Japanese optical glassmakers. Nippon Kogaku started selling binoculars in 1921; the company introduced its first microscope four years later.

In 1932 the company adopted the brand name Nikkor for its lenses, which were attached to other manufacturers' cameras. By WWII the company had diversified into cameras, microscopes, binoculars, surveying equipment, measuring instruments, and eyeglass lenses. During this time the Japanese government bought nearly all of the company's products. Nippon Kogaku began using the Nikon brand name on its cameras in 1946.

The company introduced its first commercially available pocket camera in the early 1950s, but few of Nikon's cameras made it out of Japan. The world would not begin to appreciate the quality of Nikon's products until photojournalists began using them in the Korean War.

Continuing a European expansion in the 1960s, the company opened subsidiaries in Switzerland (1961) and the Netherlands (1968). The company, in conjunction with undersea explorer Jacques Cousteau and a partner, introduced an underwater camera system in 1963. The 1970s were years of further development: The company introduced high-precision coordinate measuring instruments (1971) and sunglasses (1972), among other products. During the late 1970s Canon passed Minolta and Nikon as the world's top seller of cameras, setting off a battle that has seesawed ever since.

In 1980 the company developed its first stepper system for the semiconductor industry. By 1984 Nikon controlled 53% of the Japanese step-

per market. Nippon Kogaku changed its name in 1988 to Nikon Corporation.

The company further broadened its geographic scope in the early 1990s, opening subsidiaries in South Korea (1990), Thailand (1990), Hungary (1991), Italy (1993), and Singapore (1995). When demand for chips dropped in the early 1990s, so did Nikon's sales: the company lost money in fiscal 1993 and fiscal 1994. It restructured its unprofitable camera division, cutting staff by a third to save cash.

In 1997 Shoichiro Yoshida, a Nikon designer since the 1950s who became a proponent of the company's stepper business, was named president, replacing Shigeo Ono, who became chairman. A slumping Asian market and declining prices for chips caused demand for steppers to fall and left the company with slack earnings for fiscal 1998 and 1999. Rebounds in the markets for digital cameras and semiconductor equipment led Nikon back into the black in 2000.

In 2001 the company expanded its semiconductor equipment offerings by entering the market for chemical mechanical polishing (CMP) equipment. In June of that year Ono retired as chairman; Yoshida replaced him.

EXECUTIVES

Chairman and CEO: Shoichiro Yoshida
Vice Chairman and CFO: Kenji Enya
President and COO: Teruo Shimamura
EVP; President, Business Administration Center: Yasujiro Hara
Senior Managing Director; President, Precision Equipment Company: Michio Kariya
Managing Director; President, Corporate Strategy Center: Masami Kurosawa
Managing Director; President, Office of Corporate Technology Management; President, Core Technology Center; General Manager, Production Technology Headquarters, Core Technology Center: Takashi Tamori
Senior Executive Officer; VP, Business Administration Center: Mamoru Kajiwara
Senior Executive Officer; President, Imaging Company: Makoto Kimura
Executive Officer; Divisional President, Office of Management Strategy: Norio Miyauchi
Executive Officer; VP, Imaging Company; and General Manager, Development Management Department, Imaging Company: Naoki Tomino
Executive Officer; Chairman, Nikon-Essilor: Yoichi Nishida
Executive Officer; President, Instruments Company: Yuichi Umeda
Executive Officer; President, Nikon Europe: Hideshi Hirai
President and CEO, Nikon Americas: Hideo Fukuchi
President and CEO, Nikon Inc.: Jack Abrams
Manager, Human Resources, Nikon Inc. (US): Heidi Heyden
Auditors: Deloitte Touche Tohmatsu

LOCATIONS

HQ: Fuji Bldg., 2-3 Marunouchi 3-chome, Chiyoda-ku, Tokyo 100-8331, Japan
Phone: +81-3-3214-5311   **Fax:** +81-3-3216-1454
US HQ: 1300 Walt Whitman Rd., Melville, NY 11747-3064
US Phone: 631-547-4200   **US Fax:** 631-547-0362
Web: www.nikon.com

Nikon has subsidiaries in Canada, China, the Czech Republic, France, Germany, Hong Kong, Hungary, Italy, Malaysia, the Netherlands, Singapore, South Korea, Sweden, Switzerland, Taiwan, Thailand, the UK, and the US.

2003 Sales

	$ mil.	% of total
Asia/Pacific		
Japan	1,499.6	38
Other countries	249.9	6
North America	1,324.0	34
Europe	839.5	22
Total	**3,913.0**	**100**

PRODUCTS/OPERATIONS

2003 Sales

	% of total
Imaging Products	55
Precision Equipment	27
Instruments	10
Other	8
Total	**100**

Products

Imaging Products
Camera lenses
Compact cameras
Digital cameras
Film scanners
Single-lens reflex (SLR) cameras

Precision Equipment
Semiconductor and liquid crystal display (LCD) steppers

Instruments
Biological and industrial microscopes
Inspection equipment
Measuring instruments
Medical imaging systems
Ophthalmic instruments

Other
Binoculars
Eyeglasses
Sunglasses
Surveying instruments
Telescopes

COMPETITORS

ASML	Fuji Photo
Canon	Olympus
Eastman Kodak	Pentax
FSI International	Ultratech

HISTORICAL FINANCIALS

Company Type: Public

Income Statement				FYE: March 31
	REVENUE ($ mil.)	**NET INCOME** ($ mil.)	**NET PROFIT MARGIN**	**EMPLOYEES**
3/03	3,913	(68)	—	13,184
3/02	3,641	(45)	—	14,328
3/01	3,831	166	4.3%	13,894
3/00	3,524	74	2.1%	11,946
3/99	2,567	(153)	—	—
3/98	2,797	63	2.2%	—
3/97	3,062	161	5.3%	—
3/96	3,103	173	5.6%	—
3/95	3,333	18	0.5%	—
3/94	2,396	(42)	—	—
Annual Growth	**5.6%**	**—**	**—**	**3.3%**

2003 Year-End Financials

Debt ratio: —
Return on equity: —
Cash ($ mil.): 198

Current ratio: 1.53
Long-term debt ($ mil.): 1,158

Net Income History   Exchange: Tokyo

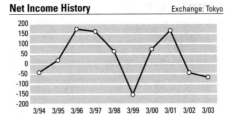

Nintendo Co.

It's not a game, boy, it's serious business, and Nintendo Co. knows it. One of the Big Three video game console makers, Nintendo makes the GameCube console, which battles with Microsoft's Xbox for second place in its industry (Sony's PlayStation 2 is the world's top game system). In the handheld console segment, however, Nintendo's Game Boy system remains the leader. The newest model, Game Boy Advance, boasts a bigger screen, better speed, and enhanced graphics. By the end of 2002 more than 25 million Game Boy Advance units had been sold. Nintendo is also the game software market leader; hit series include *Pokemon*, *Super Mario*, and *The Legend of Zelda*.

Nintendo (which, loosely translated, means "leave luck to heaven") once ruled the golden age of the video game industry until more powerful machines introduced by SEGA (in 1989) and Sony (in 1994) pared down its kingdom (SEGA has since stopped making console systems). Microsoft entered the gaming hardware market in 2001, leaving Nintendo with a shrinking piece of the pie. The company plans to broaden its previous focus on kids and to concentrate its efforts on its games, in contrast to competitors Sony and Microsoft, which are developing increasingly complex multimedia systems.

HISTORY

Nintendo Co. was founded in 1889 as the Marufuku Company to make and sell *hanafuda*, Japanese game cards. In 1907 the company began producing Western playing cards. It became the Nintendo Playing Card Company in 1951 and began making theme cards under a licensing agreement with Disney in 1959.

During the 1950s and 1960s, Hiroshi Yamauchi took the company public and diversified into new areas (including a "love hotel"). The company took its current name in 1963. Nintendo began making toys at the start of the 1970s and entered the budding field of video games toward the end of the decade by licensing Magnavox's Pong technology. Then it moved into arcade games. Nintendo established its US subsidiary, Nintendo of America, in 1980; its first hit was *Donkey Kong* ("silly monkey") and its next was *Super Mario Bros.* (named after Nintendo of America's warehouse landlord).

The company released Famicom, a technologically advanced home video game system, in Japan in 1983. With its high-quality sound and graphics, Famicom was a smash, selling 15.2 million consoles and more than 183 million game cartridges in Japan alone. Meanwhile, in 1983 and 1984, the US home game market crashed,

sending pioneer Atari up in flames. Nintendo persevered, successfully launching Famicom in the US in 1986 as the Nintendo Entertainment System (NES).

To prevent a barrage of independently produced, low-quality software (which had contributed to Atari's demise), Nintendo established stringent licensing policies for its software developers. Licensees were required to have approval of every game design, buy the blank cartridges from the company, agree not to make the game for any of Nintendo's competitors, and pay Nintendo royalties for the honor of developing a game.

As the market became saturated, Nintendo sought new products, releasing Game Boy in 1989 and the Super Family Computer game system (Super NES in the US) in 1991. The company broke with tradition in 1994 by making design alliances with companies like Silicon Graphics. After creating a 32-bit product in 1995, Nintendo launched the much-touted N64 game system in 1996. It also teamed with Microsoft and Nomura Research Institute on a satellite-delivered Internet system for Japan. Price wars between the top contenders continued in the US and Japan.

In 1998 Nintendo released Pokemon, which involves trading and training virtual monsters (it had been popular in Japan since 1996), in the US. The company also launched the video game *The Legend of Zelda: Ocarina of Time*, which sold 2.5 million units in about six weeks. Nintendo issued 50 new games for 1998, compared to Sony's 131.

Nintendo announced in 1999 that its next-generation game system, Dolphin (later renamed GameCube), would use IBM's PowerPC microprocessor and Matsushita's DVD players.

In early 2000 the company bought a 3% stake in convenience store operator Lawson in hopes of using its online operations to sell video games. Nintendo also teamed with advertising agency Dentsu to form ND Cube, a joint company that will develop game software for mobile phones and portable machines.

In September 2001 Nintendo launched its long-awaited GameCube console system (which retailed at $100 less than its console rivals, Sony's Playstation 2 and Microsoft's XBox); the system debuted in North America in November. In addition, the company came out with Game Boy Advance, its newest handheld model with a bigger screen and faster chip.

In May 2002 Nintendo formed a business alliance with game software developer Namco Ltd for the development and sales of games for the GameCube platform. In October 2002 the European Union fined Nintendo $165 million for colluding with seven of its distributors to limit the cross-border flow of its products in a scam to raise prices. Nintendo said it would file an appeal.

In April 2003 Nintendo cut its royalty rates (charged to outside game developers), in an effort to enhance its video game titles portfolio. In late 2003 the company bought a stake (about 3%) in game developer and toy maker Bandai, a move expected to solidify cooperation between the two companies in marketing game software.

EXECUTIVES

Chairman: Atsushi Asada, age 70
President: Satoru Iwata, age 43
Senior Managing Director/General Manager, Corporate Analysis and Administration: Yoshihiro Mori
Senior Managing Director/General Manager, Entertainment Analysis & Development Division: Shigeru Miyamoto
Senior Managing Director/General Manager, Integrated Research and Development: Genyo Takeda
Senior Managing Director/General Manager, Licensing: Shinji Hatano
Managing Director/General Manager, Finance and Information Systems: Masaharu Matsumoto
Managing Director/General Manager, General Affairs: Eiichi Suzuki
Managing Director/General Manager, Manufacturing: Nobuo Nagai
Managing Director/General Manager, Nintendo Europe: David Gosen
President, Nintendo of America: Tatsumi Kimishima
Auditors: ChuoAoyama Audit Corporation

LOCATIONS

HQ: Nintendo Co., Ltd.
11-1 Kamitoba hokotate-cho, Minami-ku, Kyoto 601-8501, Japan
Phone: +81-756629600   **Fax:** +81-756629620
US HQ: 4820 150th Ave. NE, Redmond, WA 98052
US Phone: 425-882-2040   **US Fax:** 425-882-3585
Web: www.nintendo.co.jp

Nintendo Co. has offices and plants in Japan and major subsidiaries in Australia, Canada, France, Germany, the Netherlands, Spain, and the US.

2003 Sales

	$ mil.	% of total
Japan	4,024.2	56
Americas	2,070.3	29
Europe	1,011.2	14
Other	45.5	1
Adjustments	2,947.9	—
Total	**4,203.3**	**100**

PRODUCTS/OPERATIONS

Game Consoles and Hardware

Game Boy
Game Boy Advance
Game Boy Player
GameCube
Nintendo 64
Super Nintendo Entertainment System (Super NES)
Wavebird

Selected Games

Banjo-Kazooie
Diddy Kong Racing
Donkey Kong series
GoldenEye 007
Ken Griffey Jr.'s Slugfest
Pokemon series
Star Wars Episode I Racer
Super Mario series
Yoshi series
Zelda series

COMPETITORS

Acclaim Entertainment	Radica Games
Atari	SEGA
Bandai	Sony
Electronic Arts	Take-Two
LucasArts	THQ
Microsoft	Vivendi Universal
Midway Games	Publishing

HISTORICAL FINANCIALS

Company Type: Public

Income Statement

FYE: March 31

	REVENUE ($ mil.)	NET INCOME ($ mil.)	NET PROFIT MARGIN	EMPLOYEES
3/03	4,203	561	13.4%	2,977
3/02	4,183	803	19.2%	3,073
3/01	3,661	765	20.9%	2,937
3/00	5,279	531	10.1%	2,806
3/99	4,806	721	15.0%	2,463
3/98	4,015	629	15.7%	—
3/97	3,378	529	15.7%	—
3/96	3,302	558	16.9%	—
3/95	4,803	481	10.0%	—
3/94	4,726	512	10.8%	—
Annual Growth	**(1.3%)**	**1.0%**	**—**	**4.9%**

2003 Year-End Financials

Debt ratio: 0.0%
Return on equity: 7.8%
Cash ($ mil.): 6,316
Current ratio: 5.21
Long-term debt ($ mil.): 1

Net Income History

Pink Sheets: NTDOY

Nippon Life Insurance

There's competition "nippon" at this company's heels. Nippon Life Insurance, one of Japan's Big Three life insurers (along with Dai-Ichi Mutual Life and Sumitomo Life), leads the Japanese market. A door-to-door sales corps peddles its plain-vanilla products, including individual and group life and annuity products. Deregulation has allowed the company to move into such areas as corporate and residential lending. Other activities include real estate development and management and a variety of educational and philanthropic projects. The majority of the company's overseas activities focus on providing coverage to Japanese companies and citizens abroad. In the US, Nippon Life collaborates with Principal Financial.

As the Japanese economy struggles to recover, Nippon Life has grappled with declining individual sales as consumers cut back on expenditures. To attract customers, the company continues to broaden its sales channels, adding Internet and telephone sales and allowing customers to access loans directly through ATMs.

With deregulation in the financial services industry boosting competition, the company is expanding its offerings to include nursing/medical services and a 401(k)-like pension plan. Nippon Life is also partnering with such firms as Deutsche Bank and Sakura Bank (now part of Sumitomo Mitsui Banking Corporation) to offer investment trusts, personal lending, and other services. The

company has merged its Nissay General subsidiary with Dowa Fire & Marine in order to boost sales, create computer systems for insurance services, and rationalize agency networks.

HISTORY

Nippon Life, known as Nissay, was a product of the modernization that began after US Commodore Perry opened Japan's ports to foreigners in 1854. Industry and trade were Japan's first focus, but financial infrastructure soon followed. The country's first insurer (Meiji Mutual) opened in 1881. In 1889 Osaka banker Sukesaburo Hirose founded Nippon Life as a stock company. It grew and opened branches in Tokyo (1890) and Kyushu (1895).

In the 20th century, the company developed a direct sales force and began lending directly to businesses. Lending remained the backbone of its asset strategy through most of the century. The insurance market in Japan grew quickly until the late 1920s but had already slowed by the eve of the Depression.

After WWII the company reorganized as a mutual and began mobilizing an army of women to build its sales of installment-premium, basic life policies. In 1962 the company began automating its systems and established operations in the US (1972) and UK (1981).

As interest rates rose in the wake of oil price hikes in the 1970s, the company began offering term life and annuities and slowly moved to diversify its asset holdings from mostly government bonds (whose yields declined as rates rose) to stocks. This movement accelerated in the 1980s, as the businesses that traditionally borrowed from Nippon Life turned directly to capital markets to raise money through debt issues. Seeking to replace its shrinking lending business, the company began investing in US real estate and businesses whose values rose in the mid-1980s. The company reached its zenith in 1987; it owned about 3% of all the stocks on the Tokyo Exchange, held more real estate than Mitsubishi's real estate units, and had bought 13% of US brokerage Shearson Lehman from American Express.

By the end of the year, thanks to the US stock market crash, the value of the Shearson investment had fallen 40%. But the company felt confident enough of its importance as the world's largest insurance company (by assets) to crow its intentions to strong-arm Japan's Ministry of Finance into letting it diversify into trust and securities operations.

Then its bubble burst. In 1989 real estate crashed, and the stock market lost more than half its value. Japan's economy failed to improve, and Nippon Life was left struggling with non-performing loans and assets whose value had declined. The company suffered further from policy cancellations and from the Ministry of Finance's focus on buoying banks. In 1997 the ministry asked Nippon Life to convert its subordinated debt from Nippon Credit Bank (now Aozora Bank) to stock. That year Nippon Life formed an alliance with Marsh & McLennan's Putnam Investments subsidiary to help manage its assets; the relationship deepened in 1998 when they began developing investment trust products.

The next year Nippon Life faced a shareholder lawsuit over its involvement in the collapse of Nippon Credit Bank; the company claims the Ministry of Finance tricked it into bailing out the bank, even though it was beyond rescue. In 2001 the company merged its Nissay General subsidiary with Dowa Fire & Marine, creating nonlife insurer Nissay Dowa.

EXECUTIVES

Chairman: Josei Itoh, age 74
President: Ikuo Uno, age 68
EVP: Mitsuhiro Ishibashi, age 61
EVP: Wataru Taguchi, age 57
Senior Managing Director: Shingo Okada, age 58
Senior Managing Director: Kunie Okamoto, age 59
Senior Managing Director: Eitaro Waki, age 58
Managing Director: Takao Arai, age 55
Managing Director: Mitsutoshi Kimura, age 61
Managing Director: Takashi Mitsukubo, age 56
Managing Director: Takashi Minagawa, age 56
Managing Director: Tetsuro Taki, age 54
Managing Director: Sadao Kato, age 54
Managing Director: Isao Takehara, age 56
Managing Director: Keizo Tsutsui, age 55
Managing Director: Shunsuke Wada, age 55
Auditors: ChuoAoyama Audit Corporation

LOCATIONS

HQ: Nippon Seimei Hoken Kabushiki Kaisha
   (Nippon Life Insurance Company)
   3-5-12, Imabashi, Chuo-ku, Osaka 541-8501, Japan
Phone: +81-6-6209-5525   **Fax:** +81-3-5510-7340
US HQ: Nippon Life Insurance Company of America,
   512 5th Ave., New York, NY 10175
US Phone: 212-682-3000   **US Fax:** 212-682-3002
Web: www.nissay.co.jp

Nippon Life has operations in China, Germany, Hong Kong, Japan, the Philippines, Singapore, the UK, and the US.

PRODUCTS/OPERATIONS

2003 Sales

	% of total
Premiums	73
Investment income	18
Other	9
Total	**100**

Selected Subsidiaries & Affiliates

DG PanAgora Asset Management GmbH (Germany)
Nippon Life Insurance Company of America
Nippon Life Insurance Company of the Philippines
Nissay Asset Management Corporation
Nissay Deutsche Asset Management Europe Limited
   (Germany)
Nissay Dowa General Insurance Company, Limited
Nissay Information Technology Co., Ltd
NLI International Inc. (US)
NLI Properties Central, Inc. (US)
NLI Properties East, Inc. (US)
NLI Properties UK Limited (real estate investment)
NLI Properties West, Inc. (US)
PanAgora Asset Management, Inc. (US)
PanAgora Asset Management Limited (UK)

COMPETITORS

Allianz
Asahi Mutual Life
AXA
AXA Life Insurance
Daido Life Insurance
Dai-ichi Mutual Life
Gibraltar Life Insurance
ING
Meiji Life Insurance
Millea Holdings
Mitsui Mutual Life
Sumitomo Life
Taiyo Life
Yasuda Mutual Life

HISTORICAL FINANCIALS

Company Type: Mutual company

Income Statement

FYE: March 31

	ASSETS ($ mil.)	NET INCOME ($ mil.)	INCOME AS % OF ASSETS	EMPLOYEES
3/03	366,426	943	0.3%	72,784
3/02	343,097	2,100	0.6%	72,895
3/01	350,340	2,367	0.7%	60,000
3/00	411,477	3,594	0.9%	60,000
3/99	360,772	888	0.2%	—
3/98	317,199	1,954	0.6%	75,851
3/97	323,424	2,547	0.8%	86,695
3/96	363,895	3,023	0.8%	—
3/95	423,815	3,078	0.7%	—
3/94	337,898	2,949	0.9%	—
Annual Growth	**0.9%**	**(11.9%)**	**—**	**(2.9%)**

2003 Year-End Financials

Equity as % of assets: 4.2%   Long-term debt ($ mil.): —
Return on assets: 0.3%   Sales ($ mil.): 62,197
Return on equity: 5.1%

Net Income History

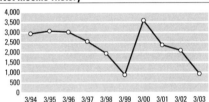

Nippon Steel Corporation

When it comes to steel, Nippon Steel rates as Japan's heavy lifter. The company manufactures steel plates, sheets, pipes, and tubes, as well as specialty, processed, and fabricated steel products. Nippon Steel's annual crude steel output is roughly 3 million metric tons. The company's operations include engineering, construction, chemicals, nonferrous metals, ceramics, electronics, information and communications, and urban development. Nippon Steel also provides energy, finance, and insurance services. With sales and profits down because of a weak Japanese economy and antidumping petitions in the US, Nippon Steel plans to place more emphasis on its engineering and energy businesses.

The worst Japanese recession since the end of WWII has dampened demand for most of Nippon Steel's products and services, depressing both sales and profits. Steel products in particular have suffered. The company plans to keep steel operations as its core business and has formed separate cooperative alliances with steel giants POSCO (South Korea) and Nippon Metal Industry (Japan). It also plans to expand its engineering and energy businesses.

The company has announced that it will form an alliance with Kobe Steel to cut costs by joining the procurement of raw materials and the use of storage facilities. Hoping to strengthen its environment-related operations overseas, Nippon Steel plans to cooperate with POSCO in such areas

as plastic recycling, water treatment, and soil purification. Nippon Steel has been contracted by POSCO Engineering & Construction, a POSCO engineering subsidiary, to provide gasified melting furnaces, which reduce dioxin emissions.

The company signed an agreement with Baosteel to produce steel sheets for cars made in China's burgeoning vehicle market.

HISTORY

As Japan prepared for war, the government in 1934 merged Yawata Works, its largest steel producer, and other Japanese steelmakers into one giant company — Japan Iron & Steel. During postwar occupation, Japan Iron & Steel was ordered to dissolve. Yawata Iron & Steel and Fuji Iron & Steel emerged from the dissolution, and with Western assistance the Japanese steel industry recovered from the war years. In the late 1960s Fuji Steel bought Tokai Iron & Steel (1967), and Yawata Steel took over Yawata Steel Tube Company (1968).

Yawata and Fuji merged in 1970 and became Nippon Steel, the world's largest steelmaker. In the 1970s the Japanese steel industry was criticized in the US; American competitors complained that Japan was "dumping" low-cost exports. Meanwhile, Nippon Steel aggressively courted China.

The company diversified in the mid-1980s to wean itself from dependence on steel. It created a New Materials unit in 1984, retraining "redundant" steelworkers to make silicon wafers and forming an Electronics Division in 1986. Nippon Steel began joint ventures with IBM Japan (small computers and software), Hitachi (office workstations), and C. Itoh (information systems for small and midsize companies) in 1988 as increased steel demand for construction and cars in Japan's "bubble economy" took the company to new heights.

In an atmosphere of economic optimism, the company spent more than four times the expected expense to build an amusement park capable of competing with Tokyo Disneyland. The company plowed ahead, spending more than ¥15 billion on the park. Space World amusement park opened on the island of Kyushu in 1990. The company's bubble burst that year.

In response, Nippon Steel cut costs and intensified its diversification efforts by targeting electronics, information and telecommunications, new materials, and chemicals markets. Seeking to remake its steel operations, the company began a drastic, phased restructuring in 1993 that included a step most Japanese companies try to avoid — cutting personnel. A semiconductor division was organized that year as part of the company's diversification strategy.

Upgrading its steel operations, Nippon Steel and partner Mitsubishi in 1996 introduced the world's first mass-production method for making hot-rolled steel sheet directly from smelted stainless steel. Profits were hurt that year by a loss-making project in the information and communications segment and by a steep decline in computer memory-chip prices.

The company began operation of a Chinese steelmaking joint venture, Guangzhou Pacific Tinplate, in 1997. The next year its Singapore-based joint venture with Hitachi, Ltd., began mass-producing computer memory chips in hopes of stemming semiconductor losses. But falling prices convinced Nippon Steel to get out of the memory chip business and in 1999 it sold its semiconductor subsidiary to South Korea's United Microelectronics.

That year the US imposed antidumping duties on the company's steel products. The next year Nippon Steel agreed to form a strategic alliance with South Korea-based Pohang Iron and Steel (POSCO), at that time the world's #1 steel maker. The deal calls for the exploration of joint ventures, shared research, and joint procurement, as well as increased equity stakes in each other (at 2%-3%). Also in 2000 Nippon Steel agreed to provide Sumitomo Metal Industries and Nisshin Steel Co. with stainless steel products.

Early in 2001 Nippon Steel formed a cooperative alliance — focused on automotive sheet products — with French steel giant Usinor (now a part of Arcelor). At the end of the year, Nippon Steel decided to form an alliance with Kobe Steel to pare down costs and share in distribution and production facilities. In 2002 the company continued its series of comprehensive alliances by forming alliances with Japanese steelmaker Nippon Metal Industry to exchange its semi-finished stainless steel technologies and with POSCO to build environment-related businesses.

The company reported a huge loss of ¥51.69 billion for fiscal 2003 due to securities valuation losses and group restructuring charges. The steelmaker expects to recover profitability in the current fiscal year, however, through cutting costs and steel price increases.

EXECUTIVES

Honorary Chairman: Takashi Imai
President and Representative Director: Akira Chihaya
EVP and Representative Director (HR): Makoto Kihara
EVP and Representative Director: Iwao Koyama
EVP and Representative Director: Okitsugu Mantani
President and Representative Director: Akio Mimura
EVP and Representative Director: Tetsuro Ohashi
EVP and Representative Director: Tetsuo Seki
Managing Director: Nobuyoshi Fujiwara
Managing Director: Makoto Haya
Managing Director: Takashi Hirao
Managing Director: Seiki Miyamoto
Managing Director: Motoyoshi Nishikawa
Managing Director: Haruhiko Okumura
Managing Director: Hideki Saito
Managing Director: Yasushi Sawada
Managing Director: Jujiro Yagi
Managing Director: Toshio Yonezawa
Auditors: ChuoAoyama Audit Corporation

LOCATIONS

HQ: Shin Nippon Seitetsu Kabushiki Kaisha
6-3 Otemachi 2-chome, Chiyoda-ku,
Tokyo 100-8071, Japan
Phone: +81-3-3242-4111 **Fax:** +81-3-3275-5607
US HQ: 10 E. 50th St., 29th Fl., New York, NY 10022
US Phone: 212-486-7150 **US Fax:** 212-593-3049
Web: www.nsc.co.jp

Nippon Steel has operations in the Americas, Asia, Australia, and Europe. Its principal subsidiaries are in Australia, Brazil, China, Germany, Singapore, Thailand, the UK, and the US.

2003 Sales

	$ mil.	% of total
Japan	17,841	78
Other countries	5,099	22
Total	**22,940**	**100**

PRODUCTS/OPERATIONS

2003 Sales

	$ mil.	% of total
Steelmaking & steel fabrication	16,528	67
Chemicals & nonferrous materials	2,889	12
Engineering & construction	2,293	9
Systems solutions	1,277	5
Urban development	878	4
Other businesses	660	3
Adjustments	(1,585)	—
Total	**22,940**	**100**

Selected Products and Services

Steelmaking and Steel Fabrication
Fabricated and processed steels
Pig iron and ingots
Pipes and tubes
Plates and sheets
Sections
Specialty sheets

Chemicals, Nonferrous Metals, and Ceramics
Aluminum products
Ammonium sulfate
Cement
Ceramic products
Coal tar
Coke
Ferrite
Metallic foils
Semiconductor bonding wire
Silicon wafers
Slag products
Titanium products
Transformers

Engineering and Construction
Building construction
Civil engineering
Marine construction
Plant and machinery
Technical cooperation

Urban Development
Condominiums
Theme parks

Electronics, Information/Communications, and LSIs
Communications services
Computers and equipment
Data processing
Systems development and integration

Other Operations
Services
  Energy services
  Financial services
  Insurance services
Transportation
  Loading and unloading
  Marine and land transportation
  Warehousing

COMPETITORS

Arcelor
Bechtel
BHP Steel
Corus Group
Fluor
Hitachi
International Steel Group
Ito-Yokado
JFE Holdings
Kobe Steel
Marubeni
Mitsubishi Corporation
News Corp.
POSCO
Samsung
ThyssenKrupp
TUI
United States Steel
Vale do Rio Doce
Yamato Kogyo

HISTORICAL FINANCIALS

Company Type: Public

Income Statement

FYE: March 31

	REVENUE ($ mil.)	NET INCOME ($ mil.)	NET PROFIT MARGIN	EMPLOYEES
3/03	22,940	(431)	—	49,400
3/02	19,461	(214)	—	50,463
3/01	21,772	210	1.0%	52,247
3/00	25,407	106	0.4%	40,000
3/99	23,167	96	0.4%	35,000
3/98	23,120	45	0.2%	35,500
3/97	24,729	28	0.1%	—
3/96	27,550	509	1.8%	—
3/95	33,288	(46)	—	—
3/94	26,759	(527)	—	—
Annual Growth	**(1.7%)**	**—**	**—**	**6.8%**

2003 Year-End Financials

Debt ratio: 140.2%
Return on equity: —
Cash ($ mil.): 660
Current ratio: 0.81
Long-term debt ($ mil.): 9,234

Net Income History   Exchange: Tokyo

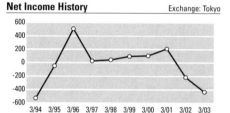

Nippon Telegraph and Telephone

Nippon Telegraph and Telephone (NTT) has executed an AT&T-style breakup into two local carriers and a long-distance provider — but unlike Ma Bell's gang, this family is sticking together. The world's #1 telecommunications firm, NTT is a holding company for regional local phone companies NTT East and NTT West, which enjoy de facto monopolies in their markets, and long-distance carrier NTT Communications, which faces growing competition. NTT also operates a leading ISP, and it owns 63% of Japan's dominant cellular carrier, NTT DoCoMo. The firm has made international investments, too, throughout the Pacific Rim and the US. NTT remains 46%-owned by the state.

While the Japanese government has restructured this telecom Godzilla, the telecom market has worked other changes. Combined sales from data transport, Internet services, and mobile phone operations have eclipsed conventional wireline voice revenue; in contrast to the high-growth cellular market, NTT's number of fixed lines in service (at 50 million) is on the decline. The company has announced plans for a new business unit, NTT Resonant, that will focus on the development of video communications and broadband portal services.

NTT's international holdings include Hong

Kong's HKNet, a 15% stake in Philippine Long Distance Telephone, and Australia-based Davnet Telecommunications (Davtel), which it has renamed NTT Australia IP. In the US, NTT owns Web-hosting company Verio and an 8% stake in fixed wireless carrier Teligent.

But as a result of the economic downturn NTT took a write-down of around $4.5 billion on its Verio acquisition in 2001 and shifted more than 25% of its workers to lower-paying positions.

HISTORY

In 1889 the Japanese Ministry of Communications began telephone service, operated as a monopoly after 1900. In 1952 the ministry formed Nippon Telegraph and Telephone Public Corporation (NTT). Regulated by the Ministry of Posts and Telecommunications, NTT was charged with rebuilding Japan's war-ravaged phone system. Another company, Kokusai Denshin Denwa (now KDD), was created in 1953 to handle international phone service.

Japanese authorities cast NTT in the image of AT&T but prohibited it from manufacturing to encourage competition among equipment suppliers. Nonetheless, NTT bought most equipment from favored Japanese vendors. By the late 1970s NTT was a large bureaucracy, perceived as inefficient and corrupt. NTT's president quipped that the only equipment the firm would buy overseas was telephone poles and mops, but in 1981 NTT was forced to allow US companies to bid. The phone firm spent heavily in the 1980s, installing a nationwide fiber-optic network and high-speed ISDN lines.

In 1985 Japan privatized NTT as a precursor to deregulation. At its IPO, NTT became the world's most valuable public company. NTT International was established to provide overseas telecom engineering, and NTT Data Communications Systems, Japan's largest systems integrator, was formed in 1988.

As Japan's stock market bubble burst in 1990, NTT chose AT&T, Motorola, and Ericsson to develop a digital mobile phone system and the next year formed NTT Mobile Communications Network (NTT DoCoMo) as its mobile carrier. Following the deregulation of Japan's cellular market, NTT launched its Personal Handyphone Service (PHS) in 1995.

The Japanese government unveiled a plan to break up NTT in 1996, a year before the World Trade Organization spearheaded a historic agreement to open international telecom markets. Meanwhile, the government forced NTT to allow rivals to connect to its new, all-digital systems. Overseas, NTT made its first significant investment in the US by buying a 12.5% stake in local carrier Teligent (later reduced).

In 1998 tiny Tokyo Telecommunications Net (a Tokyo Electric Power affiliate) offered discount phone rates, spurring NTT to do the same. NTT spun off DoCoMo in the world's largest IPO at the time.

NTT lost its 1999 bidding war with the UK's Cable and Wireless for International Digital Communications. That year NTT split into three carriers, two near-monopoly regional local phone providers — NTT East and NTT West — and a long-distance and international carrier called NTT Communications. Unlike AT&T's breakup in 1984, this split featured a holding company — the new NTT — that owns the three carriers. Criticized for continuing to promote last-generation ISDN as the key to high-speed Internet access, NTT in 1999 began to test

higher-speed digital subscriber line (DSL) service and planned to cut 21,000 jobs at NTT West and NTT East over three years.

The company pressed forward with international investments, taking a 49% stake in HKNet of Hong Kong and a 49% stake in Davnet Telecommunications, a subsidiary of Australia's Davnet Limited (both were later increased to 100%). In 2000 the Japanese government said it would sell another 6% of NTT. That year NTT paid $5.5 billion for the 90% of US Web-hosting firm Verio that it didn't already own.

EXECUTIVES

President: Norio Wada, age 63
SEVP, Information Strategy: Haruki Matsuno, age 66
SEVP, Technological Strategy, and Director of Broadband Promotion Office: Hiromi Wasai, age 57
SEVP and CFO: Toyohiko Takabe, age 56
EVP: Satoru Miyamura, age 57
SVP: Yuji Inoue, age 55
SVP: Shin Hashimoto, age 54
SVP: Masaki Mitsumura, age 54
SVP: Hiroo Unoura, age 54
Chief Executive Counselor and Member of the Board: Jun-ichiro Miyazu, age 67
President, NTT East: Satoshi Miura, age 59
President, NTT West: Michitomo Ueno, age 59
President, NTT Communications: Masanobu Suzuki, age 62
President, NTT DoCoMo: Keiji Tachikawa, age 64
President, NTT DATA: Tomokazu Hamaguchi
President and CEO, NTT Resonant Inc.: Michio Takeuchi
COO, NTT America division of NTT Communications Corporation: Dave Ryan
Director of Sales, Northeast Region, NTT America division of NTT Communications Corporation: Philip Mogerman
Auditors: PricewaterhouseCoopers

LOCATIONS

HQ: Nippon Denshin Denwa Kabushiki Kaisha (Nippon Telegraph and Telephone Corporation) 3-1, Otemachi 2-chome, Chiyoda-ku, Tokyo 100-8116, Japan
Phone: +81-3-5205-5581   **Fax:** +81-3-5205-5589
US HQ: 101 Park Ave., 41st Fl., New York, NY 10178
US Phone: 212-661-0810   **US Fax:** 212-661-1078
Web: www.ntt.co.jp

Nippon Telegraph and Telephone operates principally in Japan. The company also operates or has investments in operations throughout the Pacific Rim — including in Australia, Hong Kong, Malaysia, the Philippines, Singapore, and Taiwan — as well as in Europe, Latin America, and the US.

PRODUCTS/OPERATIONS

2003 Sales

	$ mil.	% of total
Regional communications services	34,135	37
Wireless services	33,224	37
Long-distance & international services	8,192	9
Data communications services	5,462	6
Other revenues	10,013	11
Total	**91,026**	**100**

Selected Subsidiaries and Affiliates

HKNet Company Limited (49%, ISP, Hong Kong)
Internet Initiative Japan Inc. (32%)
Nippon Telegraph and Telephone East Corporation (NTT East, regional telecommunications)
Nippon Telegraph and Telephone West Corporation (NTT West, regional telecommunications)
NTT Australia IP Pty Ltd (formerly Davnet Telecommunications Pty Ltd. (Davtel), Australia)
NTT Communications Corporation (long-distance and international telecommunications)

NTT DATA Corporation (54%, systems integration and network services)
NTT DoCoMo (63%, mobile telecommunications)
NTT Resonant Inc. (development of video communications and broadband portal services)
Philippine Long Distance Telephone (PLDT, 15%)
Teligent, Inc. (8%, fixed wireless carrier, US)
Verio Inc. (corporate Internet services, US)

COMPETITORS

Asia Netcom	Kansai Electric
AT&T	KDDI
BT	Microsoft
Cable & Wireless	NEC
Equant	SOFTBANK
Fujitsu	Telstra
Infonet	Tokyo Electric
Internet Initiative Japan	Tokyo Telecommunication
Japan Telecom	WorldCom

HISTORICAL FINANCIALS

Company Type: Public

Income Statement

FYE: March 31

	REVENUE ($ mil.)	NET INCOME ($ mil.)	NET PROFIT MARGIN	EMPLOYEES
3/03	91,026	1,945	2.1%	207,363
3/02	86,734	(6,276)	—	213,062
3/01	92,098	4,340	4.7%	222,000
3/00	97,956	2,821	2.9%	224,000
3/99	80,411	4,582	5.7%	224,000
3/98	71,591	1,625	2.3%	226,000
3/97	71,143	2,028	2.9%	230,000
3/96	74,610	2,582	3.5%	231,000
3/95	69,569	960	1.4%	235,000
3/94	56,536	403	0.7%	248,000
Annual Growth	**5.4%**	**19.1%**	**—**	**(2.0%)**

2003 Year-End Financials

Debt ratio: 102.3%	No. of shares (mil.): 3,186
Return on equity: 4.3%	Dividends
Cash ($ mil.): 10,942	Yield: 1.2%
Current ratio: 1.05	Payout: 32.8%
Long-term debt ($ mil.): 48,054	Market value ($ mil.): 54,105

Stock History

NYSE: NTT

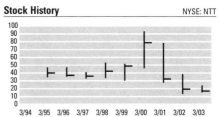

	STOCK PRICE ($) FY Close	P/E High/Low		PER SHARE ($) Earnings	Dividends	Book Value
3/03	16.98	35	24	0.61	0.20	14.74
3/02	19.35	—	—	(1.60)	0.21	13.67
3/01	32.28	57	21	1.37	0.23	17.02
3/00	78.81	104	53	0.89	0.39	17.92
3/99	48.75	35	22	1.44	0.09	15.35
3/98	42.31	103	67	0.51	0.00	13.01
3/97	35.88	63	53	0.64	0.10	13.53
3/96	37.00	46	36	1.01	0.11	15.40
3/95	39.94	64	49	0.72	0.00	18.01
Annual Growth	**(10.1%)**	**—**	**—**	**(2.1%)**	**—**	**(2.5%)**

Nissan Motor

Nissan Motor, Japan's #2 auto manufacturer after Toyota and just ahead of Honda, is back in the black after a patch of bad road. Nissan's models include Maxima and Sentra cars, Altima and Infiniti upscale sedans, Frontier pickups, the 350Z sports car, and Xterra and Pathfinder SUVs. In 1999 French automaker Renault took a 37% stake in Nissan, and installed president and CEO Carlos Ghosn (nicknamed "Le Cost Cutter" based on his talent for turning red ink black) who has since returned the company to profitability after years of losses. Renault now owns almost 45% of Nissan.

Under the watchful eye of Ghosn, Nissan steered into financial recovery by closing inefficient factories, reducing its workforce, curbing purchasing costs, and sharing operations with Renault. The results are compelling — the company is enjoying its best financial results in its history. On the product end, Nissan has introduced the Murano in the US. An urban SUV, the Murano features the first North American application of Nissan's continuously variable transmission (CVT). Nissan also has revived its revered Z car series with the introduction of the 350 Z. Also in 2003 Nissan entered the full-size truck market, traditionally dominated by Detroit, with the introduction of the massive Titan. To further strengthen the ties between the two companies, Nissan has taken a 15% stake in Renault, and the French carmaker has increased its stake in Nissan to 44%.

Despite its dramatic success, Nissan isn't satisfied. The company has announced Nissan 180, a three-year plan that aims to produce an additional one million units annually by the end of fiscal 2004 while reducing automotive debt to zero.

HISTORY

In 1911 US-trained Hashimoto Masujiro established Tokyo-based Kwaishinsha Motor Car Works to repair, import, and make cars. Kwaishinsha made its first car, sporting its DAT ("fast rabbit" in Japanese) logo, in 1913. Renamed DAT Motors in 1925 and suffering from a strong domestic preference for American cars, the company consolidated with ailing Jitsuyo Motors in 1926. DAT introduced the son of DAT in 1931 — the Datsun minicar ("son" means "damage or loss" in Japanese, hence the spelling change).

Tobata Casting (cast iron and auto parts) bought Datsun's production facilities in 1933. Tobata's Yoshisuke Aikawa believed there was a niche for small cars, and the car operations were spun off as Nissan Motors that year.

During WWII the Japanese government limited Nissan's production to trucks and airplane engines; Nissan survived postwar occupation, in part, due to business with the US Army. The company went public in 1951 and signed a licensing agreement the next year with Austin Motor (UK), which put it back in the car business. A 40% import tax allowed Nissan to compete in Japan even though it had higher costs than those of foreign carmakers.

Nissan entered the US market in 1958 with the model 211, using the Datsun name; it established Nissan Motor Corporation in Los Angeles in 1960. Exports rose as factory automation led to higher quality and lower costs. In the 1970s Nissan expanded exports of fuel-efficient cars

such as the Datsun B210. The company became the leading US car importer in 1975.

The company's name change in the US from Datsun to Nissan during the 1980s confused customers and took six years to complete. In 1986 Nissan became the first major Japanese carmaker to build its products in Europe. It launched its high-end Infiniti line in the US in 1989.

Nissan and Japanese telecom firm DDI Corporation set up cellular phone operations in 1992. Japan's recession resulted in a $450 million loss the next year. The company cut costs in 1993 and sold $200 million in real-estate holdings in 1994.

Nissan suffered its fourth straight year of losses, posting an $834 million loss for 1996. Fiscal 1997 brought profits for Nissan — its first since 1992 — in part the result of cost-cutting moves, sales to countries with currencies stronger than the yen, and the launching of new models. In 1998 Nissan made plans to cut production in Japan by 15% over five years, and it received a $827 million loan from the government-owned Japan Development Bank to restructure its debt.

Suffering under an estimated $30 billion in debt in 1999, Nissan invited major carmakers to buy into the company. Renault took a 37% stake and a 15% stake (later increased to 23%) in affiliate Nissan Diesel Motor for $5.4 billion. The stake gave Renault veto power and enabled it to install its chief cost-cutter, Carlos Ghosn, as chief operating officer. Ghosn began plans to slash the number of suppliers, close five plants, and cut its workforce by 14% by 2002. Meanwhile, Nissan sold its interests in nine mobile-phone companies and its powder metallurgy business.

In 2000 Nissan sold its stake in Fuji Heavy Industries. That year Ghosn became president of Nissan; Nissan's former president, Yoshikazu Hanawa, remained as CEO and chairman. Nissan also announced that it was developing a full-sized truck for the US market and that it and Renault were combining their European sales and marketing operations. Late in the year the company announced plans to build a $930 million manufacturing plant in the US.

Ghosn was named CEO (in addition to president) in 2001. Later in 2001 Nissan announced it would take a 15% stake in Renault while the French carmaker would increase its stake in Nissan to 44%. These steps, along with the French government's decision to reduce its interest in Renault from 44% to 25%, are aimed at further strengthening the bond between the two companies. In 2002 Nissan and Renault completed their planned equity swap.

EXECUTIVES

Honorary Chairman: Yoshikazu Hanakawa
Co-Chairman, President, CEO, and Representative Director: Carlos Ghosn, age 48
Co-Chairman, EVP, Purchasing and Administration for Affiliated Companies, and Representative Director: Itaru Koeda
Vice Chairman, External and Government Affairs: Takeshi Isayama
EVP, Global Sales and Marketing, North American Operations and Global Aftersales Business: Norio Matsumura
EVP, Manufacturing, Supply Chain Management, Industrial Machinery, and Marine: Tadao Takahashi
EVP, Planning and Design, European Operations: Patrick Pélata
EVP, Research, Technology and Engineering Development, and Cost Engineering: Nobuo Okubo
Auditors: Shin Nihon & Co.

LOCATIONS

HQ: Nissan Jidosha Kabushiki Kaisha
(Nissan Motor Co., Ltd.)
17-1, Ginza 6-chome, Chuo-ku,
Tokyo 104-8023, Japan
Phone: +81-3-3543-5523   **Fax:** +81-3-5565-2228
US HQ: 18501 S. Figueroa St., Gardena, CA 90248
US Phone: 310-771-5631   **US Fax:** 310-516-7967
Web: www.nissan-global.com

Nissan Motor Co. has manufacturing operations in China, Egypt, Indonesia, Iran, Japan, Kenya, Malaysia, Pakistan, the Philippines, South Africa, Spain, Taiwan, Thailand, the UK, the US, Vietnam, and Zimbabwe.

2003 Sales

	% of total
North America	42
Japan	38
Europe	14
Other regions	6
Total	**100**

PRODUCTS/OPERATIONS

Selected Products

Infiniti
FX35/FX45
G35 coupe
G35 sedan
I35
M45
Q45

Nissan
350 Z
Altima
Frontier
Maxima
Murano
Pathfinder
Quest
Titan
Sentra
SE-R
Xterra

Selected Subsidiaries and Affiliates

Calsonic Kansei Corporation
JATCO TransTechnology Ltd.
Nissan Canada Inc.
Nissan Diesel Motor Co., Ltd.
Nissan Europe NV (The Netherlands)
Nissan Mexicana, SA de CV
Nissan Motor Acceptance Corporation
Nissan Motor Co. (Australia) Pty. Ltd.
Nissan North America, Inc. (US)
Unisia JECS Corporation

COMPETITORS

BMW
Brunswick
DaimlerChrysler
Deere
Fiat
Ford
Fuji Heavy Industries
GE
General Motors
Honda
Isuzu
Kia Motors
Lockheed Martin
Mazda
NACCO Industries
Peugeot
Saab Automobile
Suzuki Motor
Toyota
Volkswagen
Volvo
Yamaha

HISTORICAL FINANCIALS

Company Type: Public

Income Statement

FYE: March 31

	REVENUE ($ mil.)	NET INCOME ($ mil.)	NET PROFIT MARGIN	EMPLOYEES
3/03	56,905	4,126	7.3%	127,625
3/02	46,588	2,799	6.0%	125,099
3/01	49,110	2,670	5.4%	133,833
3/00	56,388	(6,456)	—	136,397
3/99	54,380	(229)	—	143,681
3/98	49,732	(106)	—	137,201
3/97	53,701	627	1.2%	135,331
3/96	56,973	(834)	—	139,856
3/95	67,402	(1,918)	—	145,582
3/94	56,319	(844)	—	143,310
Annual Growth	0.1%	—	—	(1.3%)

2003 Year-End Financials

Debt ratio: 88.7%
Return on equity: 30.3%
Cash ($ mil.): 2,249
Current ratio: 1.27
Long-term debt ($ mil.): 13,360
No. of shares (mil.): 2,233
Dividends
Yield: 1.5%
Payout: 10.3%
Market value ($ mil.): 29,723

Stock History

NASDAQ (SC): NSANY

	STOCK PRICE ($) FY Close	P/E High/Low		PER SHARE ($) Earnings	Dividends	Book Value
3/03	13.31	9	7	1.95	0.20	6.75
3/02	14.36	11	5	1.39	0.11	5.40
3/01	12.69	21	11	0.67	0.00	3.88
3/00	8.13	—	—	(3.40)	0.00	4.47
3/99	7.50	—	—	(0.18)	0.00	8.25
3/98	7.94	—	—	(0.08)	0.00	7.73
3/97	11.88	74	43	0.25	0.11	8.70
3/96	15.38	—	—	(0.66)	0.12	10.19
3/95	14.75	—	—	(0.76)	0.12	13.14
3/94	16.00	—	—	(0.34)	0.11	12.21
Annual Growth	(2.0%)	—	—	—	6.9%	(6.4%)

Nissho Iwai-Nichimen Holdings

Trading in all kinds of places is Nissho Iwai-Nichimen Holdings' calling. The company is a merger of two Japanese trading powerhouses, Nissho Iwai and Nichimen. Its Nissho Iwai unit deals in a variety of products, from information technology to agricultural commodities and consumer goods. Nissho Iwai's machinery division, which distributes industrial machinery, is its biggest revenue producer. Other activities include automobile export and distribution, air-craft sales, and logistics. The Nichimen unit operates in seven major business areas: plastics and chemicals, construction; foodstuffs; forest products; machinery; metals; and textiles. Nichimen's top revenue producer is its plastics and chemicals group.

Rough economic conditions in Japan and the disastrous performance of both Nissho Iwai and Nichimen prompted the merger to form Nissho Iwai-Nichimen Holdings. With a fresh infusion of cash from banks and investors, the new holding company hopes to benefit from the synergy of the merger. It already has plans to slash the workforce of the combined companies by 4,000 and consolidate overlapping subsidiaries to cut costs.

HISTORY

The Nissho and Iwai companies got their acts together as Nissho Iwai in 1968, but each company dates back to the middle of the 19th century. In 1863, Bunsuke Iwai opened a shop in Osaka to sell imported goods such as glass, oil products, silk, and wine. The Meiji government, which came to power in 1868, encouraged modernization and industrialization, a climate in which Iwai's business flourished. In 1877 Iwajiro Suzuki established a similar trading concern, Suzuki & Co., that eventually became Nissho.

After cotton spinning machines were introduced in Japan in the 1890s, both Iwai and Suzuki imported cotton. Iwai began to trade directly with British trader William Duff & Son (an innovation in Japan, where the middleman, or *shokan*, played the paramount role in international trade). Iwai became the primary agent for Yawata Steel Works in 1901 and was incorporated in 1912. Meanwhile, Suzuki, solely engaged in the import trade, emerged as one of the top sugar brokers in the world and established an office in London.

To protect itself from foreign competition, Iwai established a number of companies to produce goods in Japan, including Nippon Steel Plate (1914) and Tokuyama Soda (1918). Stagnation after WWI forced Suzuki to restructure. In 1928 the company sold many of its assets to trading giant Mitsui and reorganized the rest under a new name, Nissho Co.

Both Iwai and Nissho subsequently grew as they helped fuel Japan's military expansion in Asia in the 1930s. But Japan's defeat in WWII devastated the companies. When the occupation forces broke up Mitsui and other larger trading conglomerates, both companies took advantage of the situation to move into new business areas. In 1949 Nissho established Nissho Chemical Industry, Nissho Fuel, and Nijko Shoji (a trading concern). It also opened its US operations, Nissho American Corp., in 1952.

Poor management by the Iwai family led the company into financial trouble in the 1960s and prompted the Japanese government to instruct the profitable Nissho to merge with Iwai in 1968.

In 1979 Nissho Iwai was accused of funneling kickbacks from US aircraft makers to Japanese politicians. The scandal led to arrests, the resignation of the company's chairman, and the suicide of another executive. Nissho Iwai exited the aircraft marketing business in 1980.

Despite Japan's recession in the 1990s, Nissho Iwai managed to make some significant investments. In 1991 the company teamed up with the Russian government to develop a Siberian oil refinery. A year later Nissho acquired a stake in courier DHL International, and in 1995 it set up a unit to process steel plates in Vietnam.

However, in the late 1990s rough economic conditions caught up with the firm. It dissolved its NI Finance unit (domestic financing) in 1998 after its disastrous performance. The *sogo shosha* (large trading firm) also began a major restructuring effort to get back on track.

In 1999 Nissho Iwai sold its headquarters, its 5% stake in DHL International, and its stake in a Japanese ISP, Nifty. CEO Masatake Kusamichi resigned. He was replaced by Shiro Yasutake, who took charge of the firm's restructuring. In 2000, the company's ITX Corp. acquired five IT-related affiliates of Nichimen Corp.

As part of the group's streamlining efforts, in 2001 Nissho Iwai spun off its nonferrous marketing unit (Alconix) and agreed to merge the group's LNG operations with Sumitomo's LNG business. The next year Hidetoshi Nishimura replaced Yasutake as CEO.

In 2003 Nissho Iwai merged with the smaller Nichimen Corp. to form Nissho Iwai-Nichimen Holdings. Hidetoshi Nishimura, President and CEO of Nissho Iwai, and Toru Hambayashi, President of Nichimen, became co-CEOs of the new holding company.

EXECUTIVES

Chairman and Co-CEO: Toru Hambayashi
President and Co-CEO: Hidetoshi Nishimura
EVP: Masaki Hashikawa
Director and Senior Managing Executive Officer: Katsuhiko Kobayashi
Director and Senior Managing Executive Officer: Kenichi Minami
Director and Senior Managing Executive Officer: Hiroshi Takeda
Executive Officer: Akio Dobashi
Executive Officer: Kunihide Izumi, age 60
Executive Officer: Katsuyuki Sumida
Executive Officer: Hiroyuki Tanabe
Executive Officer: Shinichi Taniguchi
Auditors: Asahi & Co.

LOCATIONS

HQ: Nissho Iwai-Nichimen Holdings Corporation
1-23 Shiba 4-Chome, Minato-ku,
Tokyo 108-8408, Japan
Phone: +81-3-5446-3600   **Fax:** +81-3-5446-1542
US HQ: 1211 Avenue of the Americas,
New York, NY 10036
US Phone: 212-704-6500   **US Fax:** 212-704-6543
Web: www.nn-holdings.com

PRODUCTS/OPERATIONS

Nissho Iwai Corporation 2003 Sales

	% of total
Machinery	22
Energy & mineral resources	19
Overseas subsidiaries	15
Foods & consumer products	11
Metals	11
Chemicals & housing materials	8
Information technology	6
Construction & urban development	4
Other businesses	4
Total	**100**

Nichimen Corporation 2003 Sales

	% of total
Plastics & chemicals	51
Machinery & metals	19
Foodstuffs	10
Construction & forest products	9
Textiles	8
Others	3
Total	**100**

Selected Subidiaries

Nichimen Corporation
Nissho Iwai Corporation
Nissho Iwai-Nichimen Shared Service Corporation

COMPETITORS

ITOCHU	TOMEN
Kanematsu	Toyota Tsusho
Marubeni	

HISTORICAL FINANCIALS

Company Type: Public

Income Statement

FYE: March 31

	REVENUE ($ mil.)	NET INCOME ($ mil.)	NET PROFIT MARGIN	EMPLOYEES
3/03	54,296	(1,021)	—	25,161

Nokia Corporation

Wireless wizard Nokia has cast its spell on the mobile handset market. The company is the world's #1 maker of cell phones (ahead of such rivals as Motorola, Siemens, and Samsung among many others). Nokia is also aiming for the top of the nascent mobile Internet market. Its products are divided between two divisions: mobile phones (wireless voice and data devices for personal, business, and entertainment uses) and networks (wireless switching and transmission equipment used by carriers). Nokia's other products include set-top boxes, home satellite systems, wireless network software, and cell phone displays. The company's Nokia Ventures division invests in technology-related startups.

One of Europe's largest companies by market capitalization, Nokia has set its sights on becoming the leader in third generation (3G) wireless network equipment. It will take a steady stream of commitments from major providers worldwide if Nokia is to maintain momentum and gain significantly on market leader Ericsson.

In an effort to jumpstart slowing handset sales as the cell phone market in the West and Japan flirts with saturation, Nokia has teamed with other phone makers and wireless service providers to develop a common global standard for 3G phone software. The effort is backed by Motorola, Sony Ericsson, and Japan's NTT DoCoMo.

Nokia has emphasized home and business communications through products such as wireless networks and interactive TV set-top boxes.

Effective at the beginning of 2004, the company will be organized into four primary business units: mobile phones, multimedia, networks, and enterprise solutions.

HISTORY

Nokia got its start in 1865 when engineer Fredrik Idestam established a mill to manufacture pulp and paper on the Nokia River in Finland. Although Nokia flourished within Finland, the company was not well known to the rest of the world until it attempted to become a regional con-

glomerate in the early 1960s. French computer firm Machines Bull selected Nokia as its Finnish agent in 1962, and Nokia began researching radio transmission technology. In 1967, with the encouragement of Finland's government, Nokia merged with Finnish Rubber Works (a maker of tires and rubber footwear, formed in 1898) and Finnish Cable Works (a cable and electronics manufacturer formed in 1912) to form Nokia Corporation.

The oil crisis of 1973 created severe inflation and a large trade deficit for Finland. Nokia reassessed its heavy reliance on Soviet trade and shifted its focus to consumer and business electronics. Nokia's basic industries — paper, chemicals, electricity, and machinery — were modernized and expanded into robotics, fiber optics, and high-grade tissues.

The company acquired a 51% interest in the state-owned Finnish telecom company in 1981 and named it Telenokia. The next year Nokia designed and installed (in Finland) the first European digital telephone system. Also in 1982 Nokia acquired interests in Salora, Scandinavia's largest maker of color televisions, and Luxor, the Swedish state-owned electronics and computer firm.

Nokia acquired control of Sahkoliikkeiden, Finland's largest electrical wholesaler, in 1986. It then created the largest information technology (IT) group in Scandinavia, Nokia Data, by purchasing Ericsson's Data Division in 1988. Sales soared, but profits plunged because of stiff price competition in consumer electronics.

To raise cash, the company sold Nokia Data to IT services company ICL in 1991 and bought UK mobile phone maker Technophone, which had been #2 in Europe, after Nokia. Under the leadership of Jorma Ollila (appointed CEO in 1992 and chairman in 1999), Nokia intensified its focus on telecommunications and sold its noncore power (1994), televisions, and tire and cable machinery (1995) units.

It also began selling digital phones at the end of 1993. The company expected to sell 400,000; it shipped 20 million in 1995. The company rode the phones' success to a billion-dollar profit in 1997.

Nokia sold more than 40 million mobile phones in 1998 to surpass Motorola and became the world's #1 mobile phone company. Extending its push into Internet capability, Nokia that year bought several small companies that develop e-commerce and telephony technologies. In 1999 Nokia penned deals to put its wireless application protocol (WAP) software into Hewlett-Packard's and IBM's network servers.

The company, which also unveiled several WAP-enabled phones designed to access the Internet, widened its lead as the world's top seller of mobile phones, and made several acquisitions to strengthen its Internet protocol networks business.

Although Nokia was leaps and bounds ahead of its rivals with digital phones and dominated the European global system for mobile communications (GSM) market, it lagged in the US market, where many big carriers adopted QUALCOMM's CDMA standard. Nokia in 2000 began to cover the bases for the third generation by offering products to bridge the gap between generations.

In 2001 Nokia added Internet security appliances to its product line-up with the acquisition of Ramp Networks. Later that year, as part of an initiative to build up its line of network infrastructure products, the company bought US-based router maker Amber Networks. Nokia began working with other equipment makers and wireless service providers that year to develop a

global standard for 3G phone software. The company also outsourced the management of some of its infrastructure operations centers in the US, China, and Singapore to Hewlett-Packard.

Nokia, in 2002, formed a subsidiary, Vertu, to sell "luxury" mobile phones and accessories made of precious metals.

EXECUTIVES

Chairman and CEO: Jorma Ollila, age 53, $2,904,949 pay
Vice Chairman: Paul J. Collins, age 67
President: Pekka Ala-Pietilä, age 46, $978,173 pay
EVP; General Manager, IP Mobility, Nokia Networks: JT Bergqvist, age 46
EVP and CFO: Olli-Pekka Kallasvuo, age 50, $844,622 pay
EVP, Nokia Mobile Software: Pertti Korhonen, age 42
EVP; CTO, Nokia Mobile Phones: Yrjö Neuvo, age 60
EVP, Corporate Relations and Trade Policy: Veli Sundbäck, age 57
EVP, Nokia Mobile Phones: Anssi Vanjoki, age 47
SVP, Corporate Communications: Lauri Kivinen
SVP; General Manager, Enterprise Solutions: Mary T. McDowell
SVP, Human Resources: Hallstein Moerk
SVP, Mobile Software: Niklas Savander
VP, Investor Relations, US: Ulla James
VP and General Cousel: Ursula Ranin
President, Nokia Mobile Phones: Matti Alahuhta, age 51, $931,744 pay
President, Nokia Networks: Sari Baldauf, age 48, $563,438 pay
President, Nokia Inc.: Kari-Pekka (K-P) Wilska
Director, Corporate Communications, Americas: Megan Matthews
Director, Investor Relations, US: Bill Seymour
Auditors: SVH Pricewaterhouse Coopers Oy

LOCATIONS

HQ: Keilalahdentie 4, FIN-00045 Espoo, Finland
Phone: +358-7180-08000 **Fax:** +358-7180-38226
US HQ: 6000 Connection Dr., Irving, TX 75039
US Phone: 972-894-5000 **US Fax:** 972-894-5050
Web: www.nokia.com

Nokia sells its products in more than 130 countries. The company has manufacturing plants in 10 countries and research and development centers in 15 countries.

PRODUCTS/OPERATIONS

Operations

Mobile Phones
Analog mobile cellular phones
Digital mobile cellular phones
Handheld telephone/personal organizers
Phone accessories (batteries, cases, chargers)

Networks
Base station site products
Corporate network products
  Base stations
  Messaging platforms
  Wireless local-area network (LAN) systems
  Wireless access systems
Fault-tolerant network routers
Fixed network switching systems
Internet protocol (IP) network switching systems
Microwave radios
Mobile radio systems
Network, messaging, and multimedia services and software
Radio base station controllers
Radio network controllers
Services
  Network planning and building
  Network operations development and management
  Wireless location
Wireless network nodes, gateways, switches, and servers

Selected Subsidiaries

Beijing Nokia Hang Xing Telecommunications Systems Co. Ltd (69%, China)
Beijing Capitel Nokia Mobile Telecommunications Ltd (50%, China)
Dongguan Nokia Mobile Phones Company Ltd (70%, China)
Nokia do Brazil Technologia Ltda (100%, Brazil)
Nokia Finance International B.V. (100%, financial services, the Netherlands)
Nokia France S.A. (100%, France)
Nokia GmbH (100%, Germany)
Nokia Inc. (100%, US)
Nokia Italia Spa (100%, Italy)
Nokia Komárom Kft (100%, Hungary)
Nokia TMC Limited (100%, South Korea)
Nokia UK Limited (100%, UK)

COMPETITORS

Alcatel
Cisco Systems
ECI Telecom
Ericsson
Fujitsu
GE
Harris Corp
Kyocera
Lucent
Marconi
Microsoft
Mitsubishi Electric
Motorola
NEC
Nortel Networks
Oki Electric
Openwave Systems
Pace Micro
Panasonic Mobile Communications
Philips Electronics
Pioneer
QUALCOMM
Robert Bosch
Sagem
Samsung Electronics
Samsung
SANYO
Scientific-Atlanta
Siemens
Sony Ericsson Mobile
Tellabs
Toshiba

HISTORICAL FINANCIALS

Company Type: Public

Income Statement

FYE: December 31

	REVENUE ($ mil.)	NET INCOME ($ mil.)	NET PROFIT MARGIN	EMPLOYEES
12/02	31,526	3,551	11.3%	51,748
12/01	27,801	1,961	7.1%	53,849
12/00	28,608	3,709	13.0%	60,000
12/99	19,954	2,601	13.0%	51,177
12/98	15,553	2,043	13.1%	44,543
12/97	9,702	1,154	11.9%	36,647
12/96	8,446	745	8.8%	31,723
12/95	8,400	509	6.1%	31,948
12/94	6,368	632	9.9%	28,600
12/93	4,079	132	3.2%	25,800
Annual Growth	25.5%	44.2%	—	8.0%

2002 Year-End Financials

Debt ratio: 0.0%
Return on equity: 27.4%
Cash ($ mil.): 1,571
Current ratio: 2.09
Long-term debt ($ mil.): 0
No. of shares (mil.): 4,788
Dividends
  Yield: 1.5%
  Payout: 32.0%
Market value ($ mil.): 74,213

Stock History

NYSE: NOK

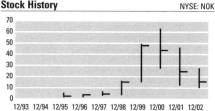

	STOCK PRICE ($) FY Close	P/E High/Low	PER SHARE ($) Earnings	Dividends	Book Value
12/02	15.50	36 14	0.75	0.24	3.13
12/01	24.53	111 31	0.41	0.25	2.30
12/00	43.50	81 36	0.77	0.20	2.17
12/99	47.77	89 28	0.55	0.12	1.60
12/98	15.05	37 10	0.46	0.00	1.23
12/97	4.34	25 13	0.26	0.00	0.83
12/96	3.60	2 1	2.31	0.04	0.71
12/95	2.44	54 22	0.12	0.00	0.66
Annual Growth	30.2%	— —	29.9%	—	25.0%

Nomura Holdings, Inc.

Nomura Holdings is the parent company of Nomura Securities, Japan's #1 brokerage house ahead of Daiwa Securities and Nikko Cordial. Nomura Securities offers a variety of retail and institutional brokerage, corporate and governmental underwriting, asset management, and mergers and acquisitions services. Its primary business is individual and corporate trading services in its home market. Increased competition and deregulation have caused sagging commissions, but the firm has countered by trying to bolster its M&A business. Nomura merged its M&A and Securities divisions in February 2002.

Rocked by recession in Asia and stung by bribery and racketeering scandals, Nomura buckled down, reorganized, and is slowly emerging from its gloom. Although primarily focused on domestic retail services, the company also offers fixed income and equity trading, investment banking, merchant banking, and asset management, with operations in more than 20 countries.

Deregulation of Japanese financial markets has created new competition, and the firm has watched commissions — traditionally its prime source of revenues — tumble. In response to decreased M&A activity and the anemic Japanese economy, Nomura made significant organizational changes in its securities, M&A, and asset management operations. In addition to trying to boost its M&A-associated stock and securities transactions, the company has tried to become more involved in the management of its M&A clients.

HISTORY

Tokushichi Nomura started a currency exchange, Nomura Shoten, in Osaka in 1872 and began trading stock. His son, Tokushichi II, took over and in 1910 formed Nomura's first syndicate to underwrite part of a government bond issue.

It established the Osaka Nomura Bank in 1918. The bond department became independent in 1925 and became Nomura Securities. The company opened a New York office in 1927, entering stock brokerage in 1938.

The firm rebuilt and expanded retail operations after WWII. It encouraged stock market investing by promoting "million ryo savings chests," small boxes in which people saved cash (ryo was an old form of currency); when savings reached 5,000 yen, savers could buy into investment trusts. Nomura distributed more than a million chests in 10 years.

Nomura followed clients overseas in the 1960s, helped underwrite a US issue of Sony stock and opened a London office. It became Japan's leading securities firm after a 1965 stock market crash decimated rival Yamaichi Securities. The firm grew rapidly in the 1970s, ushering investment capital in and out of Japan and competing with banks by issuing corporate debt securities.

As the Japanese economy soared in the 1980s, it opened Nomura Bank International in London (1986) and bought 20% of US mergers and acquisitions advisor Wasserstein Perella (1988, sold 2001).

Then the Japanese economic bubble burst. Nomura's stock toppled 70% from its 1987 peak and underwriting plummeted. In 1991 and 1992, amid revelations that Nomura and other brokerages had reimbursed favored clients' trading losses, the firm was accused of manipulating stock in companies owned by Japanese racketeers. Nomura's chairman and president — both named Tabuchi — resigned, admitting no wrongdoing.

The firm trimmed staff and offices and focused on its most efficient operations. From 1993 to 2000, it seesawed from red to black to red again.

Junichi Ujiie became president after 1997's payoff scandal; he restructured operations to prepare for Japan's financial deregulation. Nomura invested in pub chain Inntrepreneur and William Hill, a UK betting chain. It also created an entertainment lending unit to lend against future royalties or syndication fees, and spun off a minority stake in its high-risk US real estate business, which ceased lending altogether the next year.

In 1998 Nomura was dealt a double blow when Asian economies collapsed and Russia defaulted on its debts; incurring substantial losses, the firm refocused on its domestic market and reduced overseas operations. That year it teamed with Industrial Bank of Japan for derivatives sales in the UK and pension plan consulting in Japan.

In 1999 Nomura bailed out its ailing property subsidiary Nomura Finance, crippled by the sinking Japanese real estate market. It also invested heavily in UK real estate and bought 40% of the Czech beer market with South African Breweries.

The next year the firm agreed to buy the business services arm of Welsh utilities firm Hyder; it also bought 114,000 flats in Germany with local government authorities, its first European deal outside the UK. Also in 2000 Nomura sold its assets in pachinko parlors and "love" hotels, Japanese cultural traditions with less-than sparkling reputations. British authorities that year fined Nomura traders in relation to charges of trying to rig Australia's stock market in 1996.

The company made two big deals in the UK in 2001, buying hotel chain Le Méridien and becoming the nation's largest pub owner via the purchase of some 1,000 locations from Bass. Also that year Nomura bought a stake in Thomas Weisel Partners to increase its participation in M&A action between US and Japanese firms. The following year, the company decided to sell the network of more than 4,100 pubs to a consortium of private investors for almost $3 billion.

Meanwhile, a dispute with the Czech Republic over the seizure of Investicni a Postovni Banka, a Czech bank in which Nomura acquired a 46% stake in 1998, resulted in both sides seeking billions of dollars in damages.

EXECUTIVES

Chairman: Junichi Ujiie, age 58
President and CEO: Nobuyuki Koga, age 53
Deputy President and COO: Hiroshi Toda, age 52
Deputy President and Co-COO; President & CEO, Nomura Asset Management: Kazutoshi Inano, age 50
CFO; Head of Global Treasury and Controller: Akira Maruyama
Head of Global Risk Management, IR, IT & Operations: Kenichi Watanabe, age 51
General Manager, Investor Relations: Koichi Ikegami
Head of Global Corporate Communications: Masanori Itatani
Head of Global Fixed Income: Yasuo Agemura
Head of Global Research: Kenichi Fukuhara
Head of Global Wholesale: Takumi Shibata
Head of Global Equity: Hiroshi Tanaka
Head of Global Investment Banking: Noriyuki Ushiyama
Head of Domestic Retail: Takashi Yanagiya, age 52
Regional Management of Americas Region: Hideyuki Takahashi
Head of Administration, Nomura Holdings America: Lawrence Wagner
Executive Managing Director, Head of Equity: Bill Mumma
Managing Director, Head of US Equity Sales and Trading: Anthony Abenante
Regional Management of Europe Region: Hiromi Yamaji
Auditors: Shin Nihon & Co.

LOCATIONS

HQ: 1-9-1, Nihonbashi, Chuo-ku, Tokyo 103-8011, Japan
Phone: +81-3-5255-1000   **Fax:** +81-3-3278-0420
US HQ: 2 World Financial Center, Bldg. B, New York, NY 10281-1198
US Phone: 212-667-9300   **US Fax:** 212-667-1058
Web: www.nomura.com

Nomura Holdings operates in more than 25 countries. Nomura Securities Co. has almost 130 branch offices.

PRODUCTS/OPERATIONS

Selected Subsidiaries

Banque Nomura France
The Capital Company of America, LLC
Nomura Advisory Services (Malaysia) Sdn. Bhd.
Nomura Asia Holding N.V. (the Netherlands)
Nomura Asia Ltd. (Hong Kong)
Nomura Asset Capital Corp. (US)
Nomura Asset Management Co., Ltd.
Nomura Australia Ltd.
Nomura Bank (Deutschland) GmbH (Germany)
Nomura Bank International PLC (UK)
Nomura Bank (Luxembourg) S.A.
Nomura Bank (Switzerland) LTD.
Nomura Canada Inc.
Nomura Corporate Research and Asset Management Inc. (US)
Nomura Europe Finance NV (the Netherlands)
Nomura Europe Holdings PLC (UK)
Nomura Finance Co., Ltd.
Nomura Futures (Hong Kong) Ltd.
Nomura Futures (Singapore) Pte. Ltd.
Nomura Global Funding PLC (UK)
Nomura Holding America Inc. (US)
P.T. Nomura Indonesia
Nomura International (Hong Kong) Ltd.
Nomura International PLC (UK)
Nomura International Trust Co. (US)
Nomura Investment Banking (Middle East) E.C. (Bahrain)
Nomura Investor Relations Co., Ltd.

Nomura Italia S.I.M.p.A. (Italy)
Nomura Realty Advisors, Inc. (US)
Nomura Satellite Communications Co., Ltd.
Nomura Securities (Hong Kong) Ltd.
Nomura Securities Hungary Ltd.
Nomura Securities Philippines, Inc.
Nomura Securities (Singapore) Pte. Ltd.
Nomura Singapore Limited
The Nomura Trust & Banking Co., Ltd.

COMPETITORS

Bank of America
Barclays
Bear Stearns
Boom Securities
Charles Schwab
Citigroup
Credit Suisse First Boston
Daiwa
Deutsche Bank
Goldman Sachs
HSBC Holdings
Lehman Brothers
Merrill Lynch
Nikko Cordial
UBS
UBS Financial Services

HISTORICAL FINANCIALS

Company Type: Public

Income Statement

FYE: March 31

	REVENUE ($ mil.)	NET INCOME ($ mil.)	NET PROFIT MARGIN	EMPLOYEES
3/03	7,122	1,016	14.3%	14,385
3/02	13,756	1,266	9.2%	14,500
3/01	10,286	1,438	14.0%	15,000
3/00	10,788	1,380	12.8%	15,581
3/99	5,525	(3,920)	—	13,770
3/98	7,582	323	4.3%	9,888
3/97	7,901	(736)	—	9,938
3/96	8,015	758	9.5%	10,306
3/95	6,235	(510)	—	10,440
3/94	6,611	482	7.3%	10,948
Annual Growth	0.8%	8.6%	—	3.1%

2003 Year-End Financials

Debt ratio: 119.1%
Return on equity: 7.8%
Cash ($ mil.): —
Current ratio: —
Long-term debt ($ mil.): 16,562
No. of shares (mil.): 1,966
Dividends
Yield: 0.0%
Payout: —
Market value ($ mil.): 20,308

Stock History

NYSE: NMR

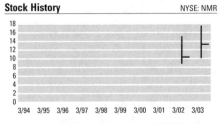

3/94 3/95 3/96 3/97 3/98 3/99 3/00 3/01 3/02 3/03

	STOCK PRICE ($) FY Close	P/E High/Low	PER SHARE ($) Earnings	Dividends	Book Value
3/03	10.33	435 255	0.52	0.00	7.08
3/02	13.24	23 14	0.64	0.00	6.15
Annual Growth	(22.0%)	— —	(18.8%)	—	15.0%

Norsk Hydro

Norsk Hydro is at home in Norwegian waters. Norway's largest publicly traded industrial company, Norsk Hydro has aluminum, energy, and chemical interests. Light metals (aluminum) is its largest business segment, accounting for a third of sales. Norsk Hydro's 2002 acquisition of VAW Aluminum boosted the company to #3 among global aluminum producers. Its oil and energy operations boast 2 billion barrels of reserves and are focused on its home turf. A third business segment, Hydro Agri makes nitrate and other fertilizers. The Norwegian government owns 45% of Norsk Hydro.

Norsk Hydro's light metals unit produces aluminum and the raw materials to make aluminum extruded sections and sheets, which are sold to the building and automotive industries worldwide. The company also produces aluminum rolled products, automotive structures, and magnesium for the automotive, packaging, transportation, and building industries. The unit trades its aluminum products internationally.

Norsk Hydro's oil and energy segment explores primarily on the Norwegian continental shelf, but it also has operations off the coasts of Angola and Canada as well as in Russia, Libya, and the Gulf of Mexico. The company has refining operations and markets its products through a network of more 1,800 stations in Sweden, Norway, Denmark, and the Baltics. (The non-Swedish service stations are operated through a joint venture with Texaco.)

Hydro Agri produces and sells ammonia and other fertilizers, including nitrate fertilizers (civil explosives), urea (glue production), and complex fertilizers. The company also produces natural gas and chemicals under such names as hydrogas, hydro chemicals, and hydro oleochemicals used in the production of soft drinks and beer, refrigeration, and freezing and packaging of foods.

Despite the weakened secondary aluminum market, Norsk Hydro says it plans to invest in new facilities in Europe and America over the next five years. The company has strengthened its Light Metals unit by acquiring VAW Aluminum from Germany's E.On AG for around $2.8 billion. That deal made Norsk Hydro the world's #3 aluminum company (behind Alcoa and Alcan) and enabled it to expand its product base in Europe and the US, especially to key customers in the automobile industry.

The company has made a deal with Comalco, a subsidiary of Rio Tinto, to purchase alumina (the raw material to make aluminum) beginning with 300,000 tonnes in 2005 and increasing to 500,000 tonnes in 2006-2030. Norsk Hydro is also investing about $240 million to expand production at its Brazilian-based Alunorte (alumina) plant, which it has close to 35% ownership.

HISTORY

Norwegian entrepreneurs Sam Eyde and Kristian Birkeland began Norsk Hydro-Elektrisk Kvaelstofaktieselskap (Norwegian Hydro-Electric Nitrogen Corp.) in 1905. The company used electricity generated from waterfalls to extract nitrogen from the air to produce fertilizer.

After WWII the Norwegian government seized German holdings in Norsk Hydro and took a 48% stake in the company. It grew to be the largest chemical firm in Scandinavia. In 1965, when Norway granted licenses for offshore petroleum exploration, the company formed partnerships with foreign companies. These included Phillips Petroleum, which spurred the North Sea boom in 1969 when its drilling rig Ocean Viking struck oil in the giant Ekofisk field, and Elf Aquitaine, which oversaw the Frigg discovery in 1971. The Norwegian state increased its share of Norsk Hydro to 51% in 1972.

The company also branched out with hydroelectric-powered aluminum processing at its Karmoy Works (1967) and with a fish-farming subsidiary, Mowi (1969). During much of the 1970s, it focused on oil and gas development, which added to the treasury and helped finance growth, often through acquisitions.

Norsk Hydro pushed into the European fertilizer market by buying Dutch company NSM in 1979; during the 1980s it acquired interests in fertilizer operations in France, Sweden, and the UK. In petrochemicals it expanded by buying two British PVC makers. Norsk Hydro-controlled Hydro Aluminum merged with ASV, another Norwegian aluminum company, in 1986, and the company consolidated its aluminum holdings two years later.

Hydro served as operator in the Oseberg field, which began production in 1988 and grew rapidly to become a major source of oil and gas. In 1990 it bought 330 Danish gasoline stations from UNO-X; in 1992 it purchased Mobil Oil's Norwegian marketing and distribution system. Two years later Norsk Hydro merged its oil and marketing operations in Norway and Denmark with Texaco's.

A weak world economy and increased competition limited its revenues in 1992 and 1993. The company countered slumping sales by selling noncore subsidiaries, including pharmaceutical unit Hydro Pharma (1992) and chocolate maker Freia Marabou (1993).

Norsk Hydro expanded further during the early 1990s, acquiring fertilizer plants in Germany, the UK, and the US, as well as W. R. Grace's ammonia plants in Trinidad and Tobago. The firm acquired Fisons' NPK fertilizer business in 1994. The company agreed to an asset swap with Petro-Canada in 1996, becoming a partner in oil and gas fields off the east coast of Canada. That year Norsk Hydro bought UNO-X's Swedish gas station operations.

The Norwegian government's stake in Norsk Hydro was reduced from 51% to about 45% in 1999 when the company and state-owned Statoil made a deal to take over Saga Petroleum, Norway's leading independent oil producer, to keep it out of foreign hands.

In light of major losses in 1999 by Hydro Agri, the company made plans in 2000 to close several European nitrogen fertilizer operations. However, it agreed to modernize and expand its Hydro Aluminum Sunndal facility, to make it the largest aluminum plant in Europe. That year the company also sold Saga UK (North Sea assets) to Conoco, and its fish-farming unit to Dutch company Nutreco.

In 2001 the company acquired a stake in Soquimich, an industrial minerals company in Chile, and majority control of Slovakian aluminum producer Slolvalco.

Norsk Hydro sold its VAW FlexPac to Alcan for about $545 million in 2003.

EXECUTIVES

Chairman: Egil Myklebust, age 61
Deputy Chairman: Borger A. Lenth, age 65
President and CEO: Eivind Reiten, age 50

EVP, Corporate Human Resources: Alexandra Bech, age 38
EVP and CFO: John Ove Ottestad, age 5
EVP, Agri: Thorleif Enger, age 60
EVP, Aluminium: Jon-Harald Nilsen, age 52
EVP, Oil and Energy: Tore Torvund, age 51
SVP and General Counsel: Odd I. Biller, age 54
SVP, Accounting: Idar Eikrem, age 40
SVP, Corporate Communications: Henrik Andenaes, age 53
SVP, Corporate Finance: Ida Helliesen, age 56
SVP, Corporate Tax: Jørgen Kristian Andersen, age 51
SVP, Exploration and Production International: Morten Ruud, age 50
President Automotive, Hydro Aluminum: Dieter J. Braun
President, Energy: Riedar Saether, age 60
President, Hydro Aluminum Metal Products: Svein Richard Brandtzæg, age 45
President, Hydro Aluminum North America: Martin Carter, age 39
President, Norsk Hydro America: Odd S. Gullberg, age 63
President, Petrochemical Division: Anders Hermansson
President, Primary Metals: Truls Gautesen, age 62
President Rolled Products, Hydro Aluminium: Andreas Schütte
Auditors: Deloitte & Touche AS

LOCATIONS

HQ: Norsk Hydro ASA
Bygdøy allé 2, N-0240 Oslo 2, Norway
Phone: +47-22-53-81-00   **Fax:** +47-22-53-27-25
Web: www.hydro.com

Norsk Hydro sells its products in Europe, including Norway, and in Asia, North America, and other regions. It has oil and gas exploration and production operations along the Norwegian continental shelf, as well as in Angola, Canada, Iran, Libya, Russia, and the UK.

2002 Sales

	$ mil.	% of total
Europe		
EU		
Germany	2,786	12
UK	2,654	11
Norway	2,129	9
France	2,089	9
Sweden	1,494	6
Italy	1,137	5
Denmark	864	4
The Netherlands	736	3
Spain	691	3
Other EU countries	1,490	6
Switzerland	940	4
Other countries	979	4
Americas		
US	2,150	9
Canada	461	2
Other countries	893	4
Asia	1,293	6
Africa	589	2
Australia & New Zealand	88	1
Total	**23,463**	**100**

PRODUCTS/OPERATIONS

2002 Sales

	% of total
Hydro Aluminum	40
Hydro Oil & Energy	32
Hydro Agri	20
Other	8
Total	**100**

Selected Operations

Hydro Aluminum
Hydro Aluminum Automotive
Hydro Aluminum Extrusion
Hydro Aluminum Metal Products
Hydro Aluminum Rolled Products and Wire Rod
Hydro North America
Hydro Primary Metals

Hydro Oil & Energy
Hydro Energy
Hydro Exploration and Development Norway
Hydro Exploration and Production International
Hydro Oil Marketing
Hydro Operation and Production Norway
Hydro Technology and Projects

Hydro Agri
Hydro Agri Operations
Korn-og Foderstof Kompagniet

Other
Hydro Petrochemicals
Pronova as

COMPETITORS

Alcan
Alcoa
BASF AG
Bayer AG
BayWa
BHP Billiton Ltd
BP
Cargill
Cebeco-Handelsraad
Sinopec Group
ConAgra
Devon Energy
DuPont
Eni
E.ON
SEPI
Exxon Mobil
Farmland Industries
FPC
IMC Global
ICI
Kemira
Occidental Petroleum
Pechiney
PETROBRAS
PDVSA
PEMEX
Repsol YPF
Royal Dutch/Shell Group
Statoil
TOTAL

HISTORICAL FINANCIALS

Company Type: Public

Income Statement

FYE: December 31

	REVENUE ($ mil.)	NET INCOME ($ mil.)	NET PROFIT MARGIN	EMPLOYEES
12/02	23,463	1,262	5.4%	—
12/01	17,099	883	5.2%	35,563
12/00	17,693	1,577	8.9%	38,166
12/99	12,804	427	3.3%	37,900
12/98	12,827	494	3.9%	40,000
12/97	13,069	707	5.4%	38,000
12/96	13,167	963	7.3%	35,400
12/95	12,606	1,128	8.9%	28,305
12/94	10,554	597	5.7%	32,400
12/93	8,293	399	4.8%	32,500
Annual Growth	**12.3%**	**13.7%**	**—**	**1.1%**

2002 Year-End Financials

Debt ratio: 40.7%
Return on equity: 13.1%
Cash ($ mil.): 859
Current ratio: 1.39
Long-term debt ($ mil.): 4,450
No. of shares (mil.): 258
Dividends
Yield: 2.7%
Payout: 24.9%
Market value ($ mil.): 11,456

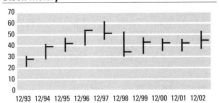

	STOCK PRICE ($)	P/E		PER SHARE ($)		
	FY Close	High/Low		Earnings	Dividends	Book Value
12/02	44.41	11	8	4.90	1.22	42.35
12/01	42.00	13	10	3.41	0.05	32.38
12/00	42.06	8	6	6.02	0.96	30.14
12/99	42.75	27	19	1.73	1.86	28.42
12/98	34.19	24	14	2.16	0.00	27.74
12/97	51.00	20	15	3.08	0.98	27.12
12/96	53.63	13	10	4.21	0.79	24.72
12/95	41.88	9	7	4.91	0.68	25.64
12/94	39.13	15	11	2.74	0.42	19.93
12/93	28.00	16	11	1.94	0.37	14.72
Annual Growth	5.3%	—	—	10.8%	14.2%	12.5%

Nortel Networks

Nortel Networks is telecom's North (American) star. The company, one of the top global telecom equipment makers in North America makes core switching, wireless, and optical systems for telephone carriers and data service providers worldwide. Nortel's wireline and enterprise network equipment includes systems for digital voice and data switching, routing, and call center communications. Wireless products include cellular base stations and controllers. The company makes such long-haul fiber optic products as multiplexers and optical switches. Customers include global communications carriers; regional, local, and wireless phone carriers; and corporations.

A global telecom market collapse has driven Nortel to outsource operations and close plants. The company, led by CEO Frank Dunn, has also exited non-core markets and cut staff to reduce spending. Nortel focused largely on selling equipment for metropolitan networks as spending on long-haul optical networks slowed to a trickle.

Nortel, which experienced slipping wireless sales in Europe and North America, looked to developing areas like China to land additional contracts. The company's wireless product segment accounted for 40% of sales in 2002. Nortel is pushing Ethernet technology — adapted from local area networks — for use in metro networks as a cheaper alternative to existing optical products. The company has plans to sell its fixed wireless network access equipment business to Airspan.

HISTORY

Nortel Networks traces its lineage to 1880, when Bell Telephone Company of Canada was established in Montreal four years after the invention of the telephone. In 1882 the Northern Electric and Manufacturing Co. was founded to produce Bell Canada's mechanical equipment. Northern Electric pooled its resources with elec-

trical wire maker Imperial Wire & Cable to form the Northern Electric Co. in 1914. AT&T's manufacturing subsidiary Western Electric owned 44% of the company.

During the 1930s the company created an electronics division and purchased a majority interest in Amalgamated Electric (1932). In the mid-1950s, the US Justice Department forced Western Electric to sell its interest in Northern Electric, and Bell Canada purchased most of the shares. In 1958 the company formed Northern Electric Laboratories to push research and development.

During the 1960s Northern Electric began supplying switching gear overseas. In 1971 the company merged its Northern Electric Laboratories with Bell Canada's R&D unit to form Bell Northern Research. (Northern Electric retained 70% ownership, while Bell Canada owned the remaining 30%.)

Northern Electric remained wholly owned by Bell Canada until 1973, when that company began reducing its stake. In 1976 Northern Electric changed its name to Northern Telecom and became the first equipment company to introduce a digital switch. When AT&T approved use of the switch in its equipment in 1981, Northern Telecom's growth took off.

Paul Stern became CEO in 1989 as the company thrived on its digital switch sales. The former IBM executive focused on cutting costs in lieu of technical advancement, and customer dissatisfaction built as the company failed to develop the software in its switching systems. Directors forced Stern out and replaced him with Jean Monty as CEO in 1992, just before Northern Telecom suffered a loss of nearly $900 million for 1993.

Monty acted quickly, calming customers, revamping the software, and selling underused divisions and factories. In 1996 the company acquired data networking maker Micom Communications. The next year Monty was succeeded by COO John Roth, who began to lead Nortel down a path to expansion.

In 1998 Northern Telecom bought Bell Canada's 30% stake in Bell Northern Research, which had been renamed Nortel Technology Limited. Also that year the company boosted its networking expertise through such acquisitions as Bay Networks. The Bay Networks deal, worth $6.7 billion, led to a loss that year and prompted the 1999 name change to Nortel Networks.

The change was pivotal for the company, transforming it from a staid seller of simple telephone systems to a fast-moving Internet supplier. That year Nortel acquired Shasta Networks (network management products for Internet service providers). It also continued to beef up its business offerings by acquiring systems integrator Periphonics, which it would later combine with 2000 acquisition Clarify to offer high-margin business software and services.

Nortel increased its purchasing pace in 2000 to boost fiber optics and software holdings. The company bought optical equipment startups Qtera, CoreTek, and Xros; it also purchased communication service activation software maker Architel Systems. Later that year Nortel acquired Web switch maker Alteon WebSystems and Internet access equipment maker Sonoma Systems.

As sales of telecom gear slowed that year Nortel made moves to focus its unwieldy operations; it outsourced some semiconductor operations, a large part of its manufacturing, and its information technology services. Bell Canada parent

BCE distributed to its shareholders most of its 40% stake in Nortel in 2000.

In 2001 the company announced and then postponed plans to take its fiber-optic components business public. Amid an economic downturn Nortel laid off 30,000 employees and scaled back its digital subscriber line operations. Frank Carlucci (chairman since March 2000) stepped down that year. CFO Lynton Wilson took the chair and Roth stepped down as president and CEO in late 2001. Former CFO Frank Dunn was named CEO and Roth assumed the vice chairman role.

Nortel decided that year to cut an additional 20,000 employees. It also sold its Clarify customer service software business (originally purchased for $2.1 billion) to Amdocs for $200 million.

In 2002 Nortel restructured its fiber optic business, cutting jobs and selling some of its optical components assets (advanced tunable lasers, transmitters, receivers, and amplifiers) to Bookham Technology.

EXECUTIVES

President and CEO: Frank A. Dunn, age 49, $825,000 pay
CFO: Douglas C. Beatty, age 48
CTO: D. G. (Greg) Mumford, age 56
SVP, Global Human Resources: William J. Donovan, age 45
Chief Legal Officer: Nicholas J. DeRoma, age 56, $526,000 pay
CIO: Albert Hitchcock, age 38
President, Global Operations: Chahram Bolouri, age 48, $510,000 pay
President, Enterprise Networks: Malcolm Collins
President, Wireless Networks: Pascal Debon, age 56, $537,143 pay
President, The Americas: Gary R. Donahee, age 56, $528,000 pay
President, Asia Pacific: John Joseph Giamatteo, age 36
President, Caribbean and Latin America (CALA): Dion C. Joannou, age 37
President and CEO, Nortel Networks China: Robert Yu Lang Mao, age 59
President, Optical Networks: Brian W. McFadden, age 49
President, Europe, Middle East, and Africa: Stephen C. Pusey, age 41
President, Enterprise Accounts: Steven L. Schilling, age 48
President, Wireline Networks: Sue Spradley, age 42
President, Global Alliances: Masood A. Tariq, age 52
COO, China: Yuan Hao-Lin
Corporate Secretary: Deborah J. Noble, age 42
Treasurer: Katharine B. Stevenson, age 40
Corporate Communications, North America: Tina Warren
Auditors: Deloitte & Touche LLP

LOCATIONS

HQ: Nortel Networks Corporation
 8200 Dixie Rd., Ste. 100, Brampton,
 Ontario L6T 5P6, Canada
Phone: 905-863-0000 **Fax:** 905-863-8408
US HQ: 2221 Lakeside Blvd.,
 Richardson, TX 75082-4399
US Phone: 972-684-1000
Web: www.nortelnetworks.com

Nortel Networks operates 229 facilities in about 150 regions worldwide.

2002 Sales

	$ mil.	% of total
US	5,336	51
EMEA	2,574	24
Canada	675	6
Other regions	1,975	19
Total	**10,560**	**100**

PRODUCTS/OPERATIONS

Selected Products

Wireless
Base station transceivers and controllers
Core networking equipment
Gateway support nodes
Home location registers
Mobile switching centers

Enterprise
Call center communications systems (Symposium)
Digital telephone switching systems (Meridian, Norstar)
Interactive voice response systems (Directory Assistance, Periphonics)
Network management software (Preside, Optivity)

Wireline
Circuit to packet voice network systems
Voice and data communications systems for service providers and large enterprises (Succession)
Packet switching and routing
Data network access aggregation nodes (Shasta)
Data routers (Bay)
Data switching platforms for Internet-based virtual private networks (Contivity)
Ethernet data switches (Baystack, Business Policy)
Multi-service switches (Passport)
Voice and data communications systems for small to mid-sized businesses (Business Communications Manager)

Optical and long-haul
Dense wavelength division multiplexing equipment
Repeaters
Transmission terminals
Network management software (Preside)
Optical Ethernet (OPTera)
Optical networking components
Optical switching equipment
Synchronous optical transmission systems
SDH-based products (TN-X line)
SONET-based products (SDMS TransportNode)
SONET/SDH (OPTera Connect DX)

COMPETITORS

3Com	Harris Corp
ADC Telecommunications	Hitachi
ADVA	Huawei Technologies
Agere Systems	JDS Uniphase
Alcatel	Juniper Networks
Amdocs	Lucent
Avaya	Marconi
BroadSoft	Motorola
CIENA	NEC
Cisco Systems	Nokia
Corning	Panasonic Mobile
Enterasys	Communications
Ericsson	Redback Networks
Extreme Networks	Samsung
Foundry Networks	Siemens
Fujitsu	Sonus Networks
Genesys	Sycamore Networks

HISTORICAL FINANCIALS

Company Type: Public

Income Statement

FYE: December 31

	REVENUE ($ mil.)	NET INCOME ($ mil.)	NET PROFIT MARGIN	EMPLOYEES
12/02	10,560	(3,585)	—	36,960
12/01	17,511	(27,302)	—	53,600
12/00	30,275	(3,470)	—	94,500
12/99	22,217	(170)	—	76,700
12/98	17,575	(537)	—	75,052
12/97	15,449	829	5.4%	73,000
12/96	12,847	623	4.8%	68,000
12/95	10,672	473	4.4%	63,715
12/94	8,874	408	4.6%	57,054
12/93	8,148	(878)	—	60,293
Annual Growth	2.9%	—	—	(5.3%)

2002 Year-End Financials

Debt ratio: 189.7%
Return on equity: —
Cash ($ mil.): 3,861
Current ratio: 1.21
Long-term debt ($ mil.): 3,719
No. of shares (mil.): 3,850
Dividends
 Yield: 0.0%
 Payout: —
Market value ($ mil.): 6,199

Stock History

NYSE: NT

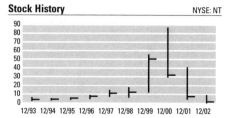

	STOCK PRICE ($) FY Close	P/E High/Low		PER SHARE ($) Earnings	Dividends	Book Value
12/02	1.61	—	—	(0.93)	0.00	0.51
12/01	7.50	—	—	(8.56)	0.04	1.50
12/00	32.06	—	—	(1.17)	0.08	9.40
12/99	50.50	—	—	(0.08)	0.08	4.54
12/98	12.50	—	—	(0.25)	0.06	4.36
12/97	11.09	36	19	0.39	0.07	2.61
12/96	7.73	28	17	0.30	0.06	2.35
12/95	5.38	24	17	0.23	0.06	1.90
12/94	4.17	24	16	0.20	0.05	1.69
12/93	3.86	—	—	(0.45)	0.05	1.54
Annual Growth	(9.3%)	—	—	—	—	(11.5%)

Novartis AG

Although it's based in Switzerland, Novartis has been aggressive in attacking illnesses. The company's prescription drugs include treatments for nervous system and ophthalmic disorders, cardiovascular diseases, and cancer; it also makes dermatological products and drugs to prevent organ transplant rejection. Novartis' consumer health unit includes such brands as Gerber baby foods, ExLax, Maalox, Tavist, and Theraflu. The CIBA Vision unit makes eye drops, contact lenses (Focus), and contact lens solutions. Its animal health unit offers parasite control products (Sentinel) and pharmaceuticals for pets and farm animals.

To more narrowly focus on pharmaceuticals, Novartis sold most of its food and beverage portfolio to Associated British Foods and the remainder is still on the auction block, but Novartis is keeping the adorable Gerber baby and her line of products. Novartis is also consolidating its 14 generic drug brands under the visible and respected Sandoz name. Novartis is also expanding its animal health line through acquisitions; the company bought two animal vaccine companies in the US.

The company also boasts a healthy drug pipeline. Novartis is gleeful over Gleevec, a bioengineered drug that "turns off" a rare form of leukemia and cancerous gastrointestinal tumors by inhibiting tumor growth. The drug, approved by the FDA in near-record time, may be useful in treating other cancers. Novartis' pipeline includes other drugs that inhibit tumor growth. Based on the strength of this new technology, the company aims to become a oncology drug kingpin. Other drugs awaiting

approval include osteoarthritis treatment Prexige, and transplant aid Certican.

Responding to consumer criticism over costly drugs, Novartis joined with six other druggernauts (including Aventis and GlaxoSmithKline) to offer drug discounts to low-income, elderly patients in the US through the Together Rx program. Critics slam the program as an attempt to stave off federal drug price limits, which would cut into profits.

HISTORY

Johann Geigy began selling spices and natural dyes in Basel, Switzerland, in 1758. A century later the Geigy family began producing synthetic dyes. About that time Alexander Clavel also entered the synthetic dye trade in Basel, forming the Gesellschaft fur Chemische Industrie Basel (Ciba). Ciba was Switzerland's #1 chemical firm at century's end.

After WWI, Ciba, Geigy, and Sandoz (a Basel synthetic dye maker founded in 1886) formed the Basel AG cartel to compete with German rival I.G. Farben. Basel used its profits to diversify into pharmaceuticals and other chemicals and to gain a foothold in the US. In 1929 Basel merged with German and, later, French and British counterparts, but WWII shattered the so-called Quadrapartite Cartel in 1939, leaving only Basel AG intact.

Basel scientist Paul Muller won a Nobel Prize in 1948 for inventing DDT. Basel AG voluntarily dissolved itself back into its component parts in 1951.

Ciba, Geigy, and Sandoz continued to diversify. Finding new markets in agricultural chemicals, Geigy had passed Ciba in sales by 1967. That year Sandoz bought the Wander group of companies (dietetic products). Ciba and Geigy merged in 1970 and began a series of US acquisitions, including Funk Seeds in 1974. Sandoz bought Minneapolis-based Northrup, King & Co. (1976) and Dutch seed company Zaadunie (1980).

Ciba-Geigy and US biotech company Chiron started a joint venture in 1986 to produce and market genetically engineered vaccines (Ciba-Geigy acquired 50% of Chiron in 1994). Sandoz also bought shares in US biotechnology companies, including Genetic Therapy and SyStemix, in 1991. It bought Gerber (founded 1927) in 1994.

Ciba-Geigy and Sandoz rejoined to form Novartis in 1996. To win approval for the merger, Sandoz (whose Daniel Vasella became CEO of the new company) sold its corn herbicide and US animal health businesses. Novartis spun off its specialty chemicals unit in 1997 and bought Merck's insecticide and fungicide operations.

In 1998 the company merged its OTC health and nutrition businesses into a new consumer health division, and in the following year sold several units, including cracker maker Wasa, to focus the new division's operations. Chairman Alex Krauer, who had overseen the formation of Novartis, stepped down that year, leaving the post to Vasella.

To boost its market share, CIBA Vision bought colored contact lens maker Wesley Jessen VisionCare in 2000. Novartis spun off its crop protection and seed units, merging them with AstraZeneca's Agrochemicals unit to create Syngenta.

Novartis Ophthalmics split off from the CIBA Vision division to become a separate eye health care unit under the Pharmaceutical Division of Novartis in 2001. The firm's joint venture with BioTransplant successfully cloned genetically altered pigs whose organs would be more suitable for human transplants. Attempting to refine the company's focus on pharmaceuticals, Novartis made several acquisitions in 2002, including two animal vaccine companies, Grand Laboratories and Immtech Biologies, and generic manufacturer Lek Pharmaceuticals, while divesting its food and beverage division.

EXECUTIVES

Chairman and CEO: Daniel L. Vasella, age 49, $2,102,042 pay
Vice Chairman: Helmut Sihler, age 73
Vice Chairman: Hans-Jörg Rudloff, age 62
CFO: Raymond Breu, age 58, $648,630 pay
Head of Human Resources: Norman C. Walker, age 50, $432,420 pay
Head of Legal and General Affairs: Urs Bärlocher, age 60, $475,662 pay
Head of Pharmaceuticals Research: Mark C. Fishman, age 52
CEO, Novartis Pharma: Thomas Ebeling, age 44, $1,513,470 pay
CEO, Novartis Consumer Health: Paul Choffat, age 53, $540,525 pay
CEO, Novartis Pharma Schweiz: Theodor Sproll, age 45
Head of Investor Relations: Karen J. Huebscher
Head of Investor Relations, North America: Kamran Tavangar
Secretary: Max Kaufmann
Head, Oncology Business Unit: David Epstein, age 41
Head, Generics Business Unit: Christian Seiwald, age 47
Head, Transplantation and Immunology Business Unit: Anthony Rosenberg, age 49
Head, Opthalmics Business Unit: Flemming Ørnskov, age 45
Head, Animal Health Business Unit: Kurt T. Schmidt, age 45
Head, Infant and Baby Business Unit: Frank Palantoni, age 45
Head, Medical Nutrition Business Unit: Michel Gardet, age 45
Head, CIBA Vision: Joseph T. Mallof, age 51
Auditors: PricewaterhouseCoopers AG

LOCATIONS

HQ: Lichtstrasse 35, CH-4056 Basel, Switzerland
Phone: +41-61-324-1111   **Fax:** +41-61-324-8001
US HQ: 608 5th Ave., New York, NY 10020
US Phone: 212-307-1122   **US Fax:** 212-246-0185
Web: www.novartis.com

Novartis has operations in more than 140 countries.

2002 Sales

	% of total
Americas	51
Europe	33
Asia, Africa & Australia	16
Total	**100**

PRODUCTS/OPERATIONS

Selected Products

Pharmaceuticals
Apligraf (bi-layered skin substitute)
Aredia (cancer treatment)
Cibacen (hypertension drug)
Cibadrex (hypertension drug)
Comtan (treatment for Parkinson's disease)
Diovan (hypertension drug)
Elidel (eczema treatment)
Estalis (estrogen treatment)
Estraderm TTS (estrogen treatment)
Exelon (treatment of Alzheimer's disease)
Famvir (antiviral treatment for herpes)
Femara (advanced breast cancer treatment)
Focalin (attention deficit/hyperactivity disorder treatment)
Foradil (asthma drug)

Gleevec (leukemia and gastrointestinal tumor treatment)
Lamisil (antifungal)
Leponex/Clozaril (schizophrenia drug)
Lescol (cholesterol drug)
Lotrel (hypertension drug)
Miacalcic (osteoporosis drug)
Neoral/Sandimmun (transplant rejection preventative; also treatment for rheumatoid arthritis, psoriasis, and atopic dermatitis)
Rescula (glaucoma treatment)
Ritalin (attention deficit/hyperactivity disorder and narcolepsy treatment)
Sandostatin LAR (acromegaly, cancer treatment)
Simulect (prophylaxis to prevent transplant rejection)
Starlix (Type 2 diabetes treatment)
Tegretol (epilepsy, acute and bipolar affective disorders drug)
Trileptal (epilepsy drug)
Visudyne (wet form of age-related macular degeneration treatment)
Voltaren/Emulgel (antirheumatic)
Zaditen (allergic conjunctivitis drug)
Zelmac (irritable bowel syndrome treatment)
Zelnorm (irritable bowel syndrome treatment)
Zometa (cancer treatment)

Consumer Health
Desenex (athlete's foot remedy)
Dulcolax (laxative)
ExLax (laxative)
Gas-X (antacid)
Gerber (baby foods)
Habitrol (smoking cessation agent)
Lamisil AT Cream (athlete's foot treatment)
Maalox (antacid)
Nicotinell (smoking cessation patch)
Ocléa (fruit juice morning drink)
Optalidon (analgesic)
Resource (standard and disease-specific nutritional supplements)
Tavist (allergy medication)
Theraflu (flu treatment)
Triaminic (cough and cold remedy)
Voltaren (topical analgesic)

Eye Care
AOSept (contact lens cleaning system)
Focus (contact lenses)
Focus Dailies (disposable contact lenses)
SOLO-care (contact lens disinfecting solution)
Animal Health
Capstar (antiflea treatment)
Endex (liver fluke and gastrointestinal roundworm treatment for sheep and cattle)
Fasinex (liver fluke treatment for sheep and cattle)
Fortekor (treatment for canine heart failure)
Interceptor (canine heartworm prevention and intestinal worm treatment)
Lopatol (canine treatment for intestinal worms)
Neocidol (control agent for mites, lice, and blowflies on sheep)
Protrol (cockroach control agent)
Sentinel/Program Plus (canine and feline flea treatment)
Tetramutin (treatment for bacterial infections in pigs)
Tiamutin/Dynamutilin (treatment for bacterial and mycoplasmal infections in pigs and poultry)

COMPETITORS

Abbott Labs	GlaxoSmithKline
Allergan	Johnson & Johnson
Altana	Merck
AstraZeneca	Milnot Company
Aventis	Perrigo
Bausch & Lomb	Pfizer
Bayer AG	Roche
Bristol-Myers Squibb	Sanofi-Synthélabo
Eli Lilly	Schering
Essilor International	Schering-Plough
Genentech	Wyeth

HISTORICAL FINANCIALS

Company Type: Public

Income Statement

FYE: December 31

	REVENUE ($ mil.)	NET INCOME ($ mil.)	NET PROFIT MARGIN	EMPLOYEES
12/02	23,151	5,224	22.6%	73,000
12/01	19,335	4,239	21.9%	71,116
12/00	21,832	4,395	20.1%	68,000
12/99	20,418	4,188	20.5%	81,854
12/98	22,990	4,398	19.1%	82,449
12/97	21,408	3,578	16.7%	87,000
12/96	27,009	1,718	6.4%	116,178
12/95	31,138	3,652	11.7%	133,959
12/94	12,128	1,325	10.9%	60,304
12/93	10,144	1,146	11.3%	52,500
Annual Growth	**9.6%**	**18.4%**	**—**	**3.7%**

2002 Year-End Financials

Debt ratio: 9.7%
Return on equity: 19.4%
Cash ($ mil.): 5,813
Current ratio: 2.52
Long-term debt ($ mil.): 2,736

No. of shares (mil.): 2,475
Dividends
Yield: 1.4%
Payout: 25.6%
Market value ($ mil.): 90,906

Stock History

NYSE: NVS

	STOCK PRICE ($) FY Close	P/E High/Low		PER SHARE ($) Earnings	Dividends	Book Value
12/02	36.73	22	17	2.03	0.52	11.45
12/01	36.50	29	20	1.64	0.50	10.01
12/00	44.75	27	21	1.68	0.00	344.91
Annual Growth	**(9.4%)**	**—**	**—**	**9.9%**	**—**	**(81.8%)**

Novo Nordisk

Novo Nordisk can tell diabetics where to stick it. The company is one of the world's leading producers of insulin. In addition, Novo Nordisk also offers a line of diabetes education and training materials and services to doctors and patients under the name NovoCare. Other health care products include women's hormone-replacement products primarily treating menopause (such as Activelle), human growth hormones (including Norditropin SimpleXx), and drugs for hemophilia (like blood clotter NovoSeven). Through a subsidiary, The Novo Nordisk Foundation controls about 70% of the voting power in Novo Nordisk.

Novo Nordisk has bought out the remaining shares in its Brazilian subsidiary, Biobrás, and delisted the company. In addition, the company owns about 40% of ZymoGenetics, a Seattle-based biotechnology company.

The company is pursuing new drugs in its areas of core competency, including diabetes, hemophilia, and organ transplantation. Novo Nordisk holds research alliances with such companies as Abbott Laboratories, Boehringer Ingelheim, and Schering AG.

HISTORY

Novo Nordisk was formed by the 1989 merger of Danish insulin producers Novo and Nordisk.

Soon after Canadian researchers extracted insulin from pancreas of cattle, Danish researcher August Krogh (winner of the 1920 Nobel Prize in physiology) and physician Marie Krogh, his wife, teamed up with H. C. Hagedorn, also a physician, to found Nordisk Insulinlaboratorium. One of their lab workers was an inventor named Harald Pedersen, and in 1923 Nordisk hired Pedersen's brother, Thorvald, to analyze chemicals. The relationship was unsuccessful, however, and the brothers left the company.

The Pedersens decided to produce insulin themselves and set up operations in their basement in 1924. Harald also designed a syringe that patients could use for their own insulin injections. Within a decade their firm, Novo Terapeutisk Laboratorium, was selling its product in 40 countries.

Meanwhile, Nordisk introduced a slow-acting insulin in 1936. NPH insulin, launched in the US in 1950, soon became the leading longer-acting insulin. Nordisk later became a major maker of human growth hormone.

During WWII Novo produced its first enzyme, trypsin, used to soften leather. It began producing penicillin in 1947 and during the 1950s developed Heparin, a trypsin-based drug used to treat blood clots. The company unveiled more industrial enzymes in the 1960s.

In 1981 Novo began selling its insulin in the US through a joint venture with E. R. Squibb (now part of Bristol-Myers Squibb). The next year Novo was the first to produce human insulin (actually a modified form of pig insulin), and in 1983 Nordisk introduced the Nordisk Infuser, a pump that constantly released small quantities of insulin. Two years later Novo debuted the NovoPen, a refillable injector that looked like a fountain pen.

Novo was the world's #2 insulin maker (and the world's largest maker of industrial enzymes) when it merged with #3, Nordisk, in 1989. By combining their research and market share, they were better able to complete globally with then-#1 Eli Lilly. After the merger, Novo Nordisk introduced the NovoLet, the world's first prefilled, disposable insulin syringe.

Novo Nordisk introduced drugs for depression (Seroxat, 1992), epilepsy (Gabitril, 1995), and hemophilia (NovoSeven, 1995). The company entered a joint marketing alliance with Johnson & Johnson subsidiary LifeScan, the world's #1 maker of blood glucose monitors, in 1995. It also began working with Rhône-Poulenc Rorer on estrogen replacement therapies.

Eli Lilly raised a new challenge in 1996 with the FDA approval of Humalog (the US's first new insulin product in 14 years), which is absorbed faster, giving users more flexibility in their injection schedule. (Novo Nordisk's own fast-acting insulin product, NovoLog, received FDA approval four years later.) A 1998 marketing pact with Schering-Plough signaled Novo Nordisk's desire to boost sales of its diabetes drugs in the US, where Eli Lilly has historically dominated.

In 2000 Novo Nordisk split its health care and enzymes businesses; the split left Novo Nordisk with all the health care operations, while a new company, Novozymes, was formed to carry out the enzyme business. In 2002 Novo Nordisk focused its operations even further by spinning off its US-based biotechnology firm, ZymoGenetics; it retained about 40% of its stake in the company.

EXECUTIVES

Chairman: Mads Øvlisen, age 63
Vice Chairman: Kurt Anker Nielsen, age 58
President and CEO: Lars Rebien Sørensen, age 49
EVP and CFO: Jesper Brandgaard, age 40
EVP and COO: Kåre Schultz, age 42
EVP and Chief of Staffs: Lars A. Jørgensen, age 55
EVP and Chief Science Officer:
 Mads Krogsgaard Thomsen, age 42
EVP, Stakeholder Relations: Lise Kingo, age 42
Member, Senior Management Board, Discovery:
 Peter Kurtzhals
Member, Senior Management Board, Development:
 Hans Glise
Member, Senior Management Board, Europe:
 Klaus Ehrlich
Member, Senior Management Board, International Marketing: Jesper Høiland
Member, Senior Management Board, International Operations: Witte Rijnberg
Member, Senior Management Board, Japan and Oceania: Roger Moore
Member, Senior Management Board, Legal Affairs:
 Ole Ramsby
Member, Senior Management Board, North America:
 Martin Soeters
Member, Senior Management Board, Regulatory Affairs: Peter Bonne Eriksen
VP, Diabetes Sales, Managed Care, and Government Operations, US: Michael J. Dwyer
Auditors: PricewaterhouseCoopers

LOCATIONS

HQ: Novo Nordisk A/S
 Novo Allé, 2880 Bagsvaerd, Denmark
Phone: +45-4444-8888 **Fax:** +45-4449-0555
US HQ: 405 Lexington Ave., Ste. 6400,
 New York, NY 10017-6401
US Phone: 212-867-0123 **US Fax:** 212-867-0298
Web: www.novonordisk.com

Novo Nordisk has production facilities in Brazil, China, Denmark, France, Japan, South Africa, and the US.

2002 Sales

	% of total
Europe	53
Japan	21
North America	12
Other regions	14
Total	**100**

PRODUCTS/OPERATIONS

Selected Products

Activelle (hormone therapy)
Estrofem (hormone therapy)
FlexPen (prefilled insulin injector)
InDuo (combination blood glucose monitor and insulin injection system)
InnoLet (insulin device for people with poor eyesight and reduced manual dexterity)
Innovo (electronic insulin doser)
Nordiject (injection system)
Norditropin (recombinant human growth hormone)
Novofem (hormone therapy)
NovoFine (needles)
NovoLet (prefilled disposable syringe)
Novolin (insulin)
Novolin PenFill
NovoNorm/Prandin (oral diabetic treatment)
NovoPen (durable injection system)
NovoRapid (NovoLog in the US; fast-acting insulin analogue)
NovoSeven (hemophilia treatment)
Vagifem (hormone therapy)

COMPETITORS

Abbott Labs
Akzo Nobel
Amylin Pharmaceuticals
Aventis
Baxter
Bayer AG
Becton Dickinson
Bristol-Myers Squibb
Eli Lilly
GlaxoSmithKline
Medtronic MiniMed
Merck
Novartis
Pfizer
Roche
Sankyo Co
Wyeth

HISTORICAL FINANCIALS

Company Type: Public

Income Statement

FYE: December 31

	REVENUE ($ mil.)	NET INCOME ($ mil.)	NET PROFIT MARGIN	EMPLOYEES
12/02	3,554	578	16.3%	18,005
12/01	2,839	461	16.2%	16,141
12/00	2,595	385	14.8%	13,752
12/99	2,833	326	11.5%	15,184
12/98	2,812	378	13.4%	14,857
12/97	2,481	324	13.1%	14,175
12/96	2,502	303	12.1%	13,395
12/95	2,474	282	11.4%	12,997
12/94	2,223	235	10.6%	12,847
12/93	1,935	211	10.9%	11,648
Annual Growth	7.0%	11.9%	—	5.0%

2002 Year-End Financials

Debt ratio: 3.6%
Return on equity: 20.5%
Cash ($ mil.): 201
Current ratio: 2.31
Long-term debt ($ mil.): 116
No. of shares (mil.): 355
Dividends
 Yield: 1.3%
 Payout: 22.4%
Market value ($ mil.): 10,251

Stock History

NYSE: NVO

12/93 12/94 12/95 12/96 12/97 12/98 12/99 12/00 12/01 12/02

	STOCK PRICE ($) FY Close	P/E High/Low		PER SHARE ($) Earnings	Dividends	Book Value
12/02	28.90	25	13	1.65	0.37	9.12
12/01	40.10	35	26	1.33	0.32	13.81
12/00	35.40	41	22	1.12	0.24	11.24
12/99	25.85	31	21	0.91	0.22	14.16
12/98	26.60	33	21	1.02	0.00	15.57
12/97	28.85	34	20	0.86	0.00	14.11
12/96	18.70	23	16	0.81	0.07	14.34
12/95	13.70	18	12	0.75	0.07	13.87
12/94	9.50	18	14	0.63	0.05	11.52
12/93	9.90	18	14	0.56	0.06	9.38
Annual Growth	12.6%	—	—	12.8%	22.4%	(0.3%)

NTT DoCoMo

The Japanese yen for mobile phones means business for NTT DoCoMo. Formerly NTT Mobile Communications Network, the wireless spinoff of Nippon Telegraph and Telephone (NTT), the mobile phone carrier has about 44 million subscribers to its digital network. (It is one of the world's largest mobile phone operators by subscribers, behind #1 Vodafone.) Nearly 38 million customers subscribe to DoCoMo's i-mode service, which provides Internet access from mobile phones. The company also offers paging, maritime and in-flight phone services, and sells handsets and pagers. NTT owns 62% of DoCoMo.

DoCoMo (which means "anywhere") corners nearly 60% of the Japanese market for mobile phones through its eight majority-owned regional operating subsidiaries. It has announced plans to take full ownership of these units and consolidate them.

The company has scored big with the rollout of its popular i-mode service. It became the first company in the world to offer the third-generation mobile phone service with a 2001 debut in Tokyo.

DoCoMo is now building a presence in Europe. In 2001 the pair teamed up with Telecom Italia Mobile to introduce i-mode services in Europe. It also joined Hutchison Whampoa and Dutch phone company KPN in an alliance to bid on European next-generation mobile phone licenses and the company paid $4.5 billion for a 15% stake in KPN's wireless unit, KPN Mobile (the stake was reduced to 2.2% when DoCoMo declined to subscribe to additional shares offered). The company also has licensed its i-mode technology to the telecom unit of French construction group Bouygues, to Italy's Wind, and to Telefónica Móviles in Spain, and it has reorganized its European holdings under a single subsidiary, DoCoMo Europe Ltd.

DoCoMo has staked its claim in the US, too, by paying $9.8 billion for a 16% stake in AT&T Wireless. It also is planning new services for all its markets, through a joint venture it is forming in 2004 with Sony to develop mobile phones equipped with Sony's smart-card technology.

HISTORY

Formed in 1952 by the Japanese Ministry of Communications to rebuild Japan's war-ravaged phone system, Nippon Telegraph and Telephone (NTT) enjoyed a monopoly on phone services for more than four decades.

NTT first went into mobile communications with a maritime phone service in 1959, and in 1968 the company began offering paging services. Other telecommunications services followed: car phone service (1979), in-flight phone service (1986), and mobile phone service (1987).

In 1991 NTT established a subsidiary to adopt these wireless segments: It launched operations in 1992 as NTT Mobile Communications Network under the leadership of NTT executive Kouji Ohboshi. The firm quickly took on the DoCoMo nickname. The year closed with slightly more than a million analog mobile phone users in Japan — a market DoCoMo shared with upstart telecom companies DDI and IDO (later bought by DDI). Paging service was more popular, and DoCoMo won more than 3 million customers.

DoCoMo in 1993 launched digital mobile phone service based on a scheme called PDC (personal digital cellular) — a system incompatible with the digital standards that would take root in Europe and the US. Liberalization of the cellular phone market in 1994 triggered unexpected growth: Customers who previously had to lease mobile phones from the network operators could now buy them at retail stores. Further competition emerged in 1995 with the launch of personal handyphone services, or PHS (parent company NTT was among the companies providing PHS), but DoCoMo's subscriber count passed 3.5 million mobile phone users — about half the market.

DoCoMo's pager business peaked in 1996 before commencing a long-term decline; the mobile phone market, where DoCoMo had more than 8 million subscribers, overtook it. The company launched a satellite-based mobile phone system that year to serve customers beyond the range of cell sites, reaching ships and mountainous regions.

Financial crises rocked the Pacific Rim in 1997, and Japan's Fair Trade Commission rocked NTT by ordering it to cut its 95%-ownership of DoCoMo. Customers continued to flock to mobile phones despite economic turmoil, and DoCoMo passed the 15 million-subscriber mark. In 1998 DoCoMo gave hope to Japan's low-flying market when it left the nest: Its mammoth IPO raised more than $18 billion.

Meanwhile, DDI (now KDDI) had become the first Japanese carrier to launch a digital mobile phone network based on CDMA (code division multiple access) technology. Though DoCoMo still used PDC, it redoubled its efforts to help develop and standardize a next-generation, wideband version of CDMA.

In 1999 DoCoMo took over NTT's unprofitable PHS unit and rolled out a high-speed data service over the PHS network. It also launched its i-mode service, which gave customers Internet access on a specialized handset. To promote such new data services, DoCoMo launched a joint venture in Japan with Microsoft (Mobimagic). That year it acquired a 19% stake in the telecom unit of Hong Kong's Hutchison Whampoa.

The next year DoCoMo became the largest shareholder in America Online Japan when it acquired a 42% stake.

EXECUTIVES

President and CEO: Keiji Tachikawa, age 64
SEVP and Managing Director, Global Business Division: Shiro Tsuda, age 58
SEVP: Toyotaro Kato, age 63
SEVP and Managing Director, Marketing Division: Masao Nakamura, age 59
EVP and Managing Director, Mobile Multimedia Division: Kimio Tani, age 56
EVP, CFO, and Managing Director, Accounting and Finance Division: Masayuki Hirata, age 56
EVP, CTO, and Managing Director, Research and Development Division: Kota Kinoshita, age 56
EVP and Managing Director, Network Division: Kunio Ishikawa, age 55
EVP and Managing Director, Corporate Marketing Division: Kunio Ushioda, age 57
EVP; General Manager, Kanagawa Branch: Noboru Inoue, age 55
EVP and Managing Director, i-mode Business Division: Kei-ichi Enoki, age 54
EVP and Managing Director, General Affairs Department: Yasuhiro Kadowaki, age 55
SVP and Managing Director, Corporate Citizenship Office: Kunito Abe, age 58
SVP and Managing Director, Research and Development Planning: Takanori Utano, age 54
SVP and Managing Director, Ubiquitous Business Department: Tamon Mitsuishi, age 54
SVP and Managing Director, Public Relations Department: Takashi Sakamoto, age 54
SVP and Managing Director, Corporate Marketing Department I: Shuro Hoshizawa
SVP and Managing Director, Personnel Development Department: Yoshiaki Noda, age 54
SVP and Managing Director, Sales Promotion Department: Bunya Kumagai, age 51
Auditors: Asahi & Co.

LOCATIONS

HQ: NTT DoCoMo, Inc.
11-1 Nagatacho-2-chome, Chiyoda-ku,
Tokyo 100-6150, Japan
Phone: +81-3-5156-1111 **Fax:** +81-3-5156-0271
US HQ: 461 Fifth Ave., 24th Fl., New York, NY 10017
US Phone: 212-696-0974 **US Fax:** 212-994-7219
Web: www.nttdocomo.com

PRODUCTS/OPERATIONS

2003 Sales

	$ mil.	% of total
Wireless services	36,850	90
Equipment sales	3,881	10
Total	**40,731**	**100**

Selected Services

Cellular
i-mode (wireless Internet access)
In-flight telephone
Mobile multimedia
Personal Handyphone System (PHS, wireless voice and data transmission service)
Quickcast (paging)
Satellite mobile communications
Third-generation (3G) wireless (W-CDMA)
World Call (direct international calling)

Selected Affiliates

AT&T Wireless Services Inc. (AWE, 16%, US)
DoCoMo AOL, Inc. (43%)
DoCoMo Europe Ltd.
Hutchison 3G HK Holdings Ltd. (24%)
Hutchison 3G UK Holdings Ltd. (20%)
Hutchison Telephone Company Ltd. (24%, Hong Kong)
KG Telecommunications Co. (21%, Taiwan)
KPN Mobile N.V. (2%, Netherlands)

COMPETITORS

BT	Orange
Cellco Partnership	Optus
China Mobile (Hong Kong)	SK Telecom
Cingular Wireless	Sprint PCS
Deutsche Telekom	Telstra
France Telecom	Vodafone
Japan Telecom	Vodafone K.K.
KDDI	

HISTORICAL FINANCIALS

Company Type: Public

Income Statement

FYE: March 31

	REVENUE ($ mil.)	NET INCOME ($ mil.)	NET PROFIT MARGIN	EMPLOYEES
3/03	40,731	1,800	4.4%	23,310
3/02	38,939	(876)	—	19,700
3/01	37,194	3,200	8.6%	18,015
3/00	35,246	2,390	6.8%	10,098
3/99	26,181	1,720	6.6%	9,342
3/98	19,735	907	4.6%	7,557
3/97	15,856	232	1.5%	6,901
3/96	11,535	199	1.7%	6,323
3/95	9,324	190	2.0%	5,945
Annual Growth	**20.2%**	**32.5%**	**—**	**18.6%**

2003 Year-End Financials

Debt ratio: 34.9%
Return on equity: 6.6%
Cash ($ mil.): 5,767
Current ratio: 1.56
Long-term debt ($ mil.): 10,262

No. of shares (mil.): 5,017
Dividends
  Yield: 0.2%
  Payout: 11.1%
Market value ($ mil.): 94,621

Stock History

NYSE: DCM

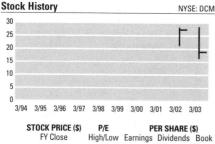

3/94 3/95 3/96 3/97 3/98 3/99 3/00 3/01 3/02 3/03

	STOCK PRICE ($) FY Close	P/E High/Low	PER SHARE ($) Earnings	Dividends	Book Value
3/03	18.86	67 39	0.36	0.04	5.87
3/02	27.36	— —	(0.17)	0.00	4.94
Annual Growth	(31.1%)	— —	—	—	18.7%

Oki Electric Industry Company

Oki Electric Industry is plugged into a variety of products. The company has three core businesses: information systems, telecommunication systems, and electronic devices. Its information products include printers and facsimile machines offered through its Oki Data subsidiary, as well as automated teller machines, terminals, banking systems, and security systems. The company's electronics operations (represented by Oki Semiconductor in the US) produce integrated circuits, microprocessors, and audiovisual products. Oki's telecom products include network equipment, switching systems, and computer telephony integration systems.

The company generates about half of sales from its information systems segment; the company's electronics operations account for about 20% of sales. In order to combat a slumping telecommunications market and worldwide downturn in information technology spending, Oki Electric has realigned its operations. The company's restructuring efforts include a shift away from hardware sales to broader service offerings such as network design, installation, and maintenance.

HISTORY

Engineer Kibataro Oki founded Meikosha in Tokyo in 1881 to produce telephones (only five years after they were invented). Meikosha was soon producing telegraphs, bells, and medical equipment. Its main factory adopted the name Oki Electric Plant in 1889, and the marketing division began operating under the name Oki & Company in 1896.

In 1907, a year after the founder's death, the Oki groups were united as a limited partnership.

Divided again in 1912, they were recombined in 1917 as Oki Electric Co. Oki continued to expand its product line to include automatic switching equipment (1926) and electric clocks (1929).

The manufacturer produced communications equipment for the Japanese military during WWII, but after the war it started working on the teleprinter and added consumer goods such as portable stoves. The company adopted its present name, Oki Electric Industry Company, in 1949.

Oki entered the semiconductor and computer industries in the 1950s, joining Fujitsu, Hitachi, Mitsubishi, Nippon Electric Co., and Toshiba as one of Japan's Big Six electronics makers by 1960. It then began developing overseas businesses, particularly in Latin America, where it built communications networks in Honduras (1962) and Bolivia (1966) and radio networks in Brazil (1971).

In 1970 Oki formed a computer software unit. The company was a major telecommunications equipment supplier for the Japanese government until the mid-1970s, when the government increased its purchases from other companies. Former Nippon Telegraph and Telephone executive Masao Miyake took over as president, initiating a dramatic reorganization into 15 business units.

Oki started building PCs in 1981. It consolidated its US operations as Oki America in 1984. A new financial crisis followed in the mid-1980s when the bottom fell out of the semiconductor market — Oki's earnings plummeted into the red in 1986. However, by the end of the decade Oki had become a major provider of automated teller machines (ATMs) and bank computer systems; growth in the Japanese financial industry sparked a ninefold increase in Oki's sales in 1989. In 1994 Oki established subsidiary Oki Data Corp. to handle printer and fax machine operations.

Plunging memory prices and higher taxes stymied Oki's recovery in fiscal 1998, so the company halted mass random-access memory (RAM) production and closed an assembly and testing facility. Oki shifted its semiconductor focus to large-scale integrated circuits, and placed more emphasis on its information systems segment, which had seen increasing sales.

Further battered by a weak Asian economy, Oki restructured in 1999. That year the company bought Toshiba's ATM operations. It also launched an access control system that uses a person's iris for identification and payment services.

In 2000 Oki announced plans to establish (along with NTT Data, NTT DoCoMo, Microsoft and others) Payment First Corporation, an Internet payment company.

Responding to poor market conditions, Oki announced in 2001 that it would reduce its workforce by about 10% over two years. The company also agreed to sell its automotive electronics division to Keihin Corporation.

EXECUTIVES

President and CEO: Katsumasa Shinozuka
SEVP: Hajime Maeda
EVP: Yutaka Maeda
EVP: Katsuhiko Sano
EVP: Kazuo Tanaka
EVP and CTO: Masayoshi Ino
EVP, Financial Solutions Company: Tateo Yamane
EVP, Financial Solutions Company; General Manager, Financial Solutions Division: Shigeru Yamamoto
EVP, Network Systems Company: Yutaka Asai
EVP, System Solutions Company; General Manager, Network Application Division: Masayoshi Matsushita
Chief Information Officer: Tadao Murase

President, Financial Solutions Company: Takashi Hattori
President, Network Systems Company: Hideichi Kawasaki
President, Silicon Manufacturing Company and General Manager, Production Division: Hironori Kitabayashi
President, Silicon Solutions Company: Akira Kamo
President, Systems Solutions Company: Kazushige Matsui
General Manager, Accounting and Control Division: Keiichi Fukumura
General Manager, Human Resources Division: Kei Takenaka
General Manager, Research and Development Center: Harushige Sugimoto
General Manager, Strategic Marketing Division: Tatsuro Muraoka
Auditors: Shin Nihon & Co.

LOCATIONS

HQ: Oki Denki Kogyo Kabushiki Kaisha
  (Oki Electric Industry Company, Limited)
  7-12, Toranomon 1-chome, Minato-ku,
  Tokyo 105-8460, Japan
Phone: +81-3-3501-3111   **Fax:** +81-3-3581-5522
US HQ: 785 N. Mary Ave., Sunnyvale, CA 94085-2909
US Phone: 408-720-1900   **US Fax:** 408-720-1918
Web: www.oki.com

2003 Sales

	% of total
Japan	72
Europe	8
North America	7
Other regions	13
Total	**100**

PRODUCTS/OPERATIONS

2003 Sales

	% of total
Information systems	53
Electronic devices	19
Telecommunications	15
Other	13
Total	**100**

Selected Products

Information Systems
Automated teller machines
Point-of-sale terminals
Printers
Terminals
Video delivery software

Electronic Devices
Large-scale integrated circuits
Memory chips
Microprocessors
Optical components
Telecommunications and voice synthesis circuits

Telecommunications Systems
ATM (asynchronous transfer mode) switches
Computer telephony integration
ISDN terminals
Key telephone systems
Fiber-optic communications products
Modems
PBX systems
Radio equipment
Teleconferencing systems
Video/audio encoders/decoders

COMPETITORS

Canon	NCR
CASIO COMPUTER	NEC
Cisco Systems	NTT DATA
Dell	Ricoh
Diebold	Samsung
Fuji Xerox	SANYO
Fujitsu	Seiko Epson
Hewlett-Packard	Sharp
Hitachi	Siemens
IBM	Sony
Konica Minolta	Symbol Technologies
Kyocera	Toshiba
Lexmark International	VeriFone
Matsushita	Wincor Nixdorf
MICROS Systems	Xerox
Mitsubishi Electric	

HISTORICAL FINANCIALS

Company Type: Public

Income Statement				FYE: March 31
	REVENUE ($ mil.)	NET INCOME ($ mil.)	NET PROFIT MARGIN	EMPLOYEES
3/03	4,885	(55)	—	22,520
3/02	4,558	(257)	—	23,597
3/01	5,860	71	1.2%	25,626
3/00	6,348	11	0.2%	25,444
3/99	5,652	(398)	—	23,425
3/98	5,746	(61)	—	23,968
3/97	5,915	26	0.4%	21,355
3/96	6,977	230	3.3%	21,718
3/95	7,591	373	4.9%	23,568
3/94	6,341	(170)	—	22,585
Annual Growth	(2.9%)	—	—	(0.0%)

2003 Year-End Financials

Debt ratio: —
Return on equity: —
Cash ($ mil.): 244

Current ratio: 1.25
Long-term debt ($ mil.): 1,415

Net Income History　　　　Exchange: Tokyo

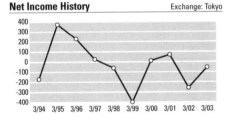

Olivetti S.p.A.

These days, Olivetti pushes keypads, not keyboards. The maker of the first Italian typewriter has sold its PC business and is making its mark in telecommunications. Olivetti once controlled 55% of former monopoly Telecom Italia, the peninsular nation's #1 fixed-line and mobile phone operator. But a 2003 reorganization turned the tables and now Olivetti is a subsidiary of Telecom Italia. Olivetti hasn't completely exited the office equipment business, however. Olivetti subsidiaries continue to offer office and document management products, imaging devices and Internet appliances (Olivetti Tecnost), as well as information technology systems (Tecnost Sistemi).

Once typecast by its typewriters, Olivetti began redefining itself with its 1999 hostile takeover of Telecom Italia. Then Olivetti itself became the subject of a takeover bid. A holding company controlled by tire maker Pirelli and the Benetton family took over Olivetti in 2001 by buying out a group led by former Olivetti CEO Roberto Colaninno. After Colaninno stepped down, Montedison veteran Enrico Bondi and Pirelli's Carlo Buora were named co-CEOs (Bondi resigned from the board in 2002). Then, to make the corporate structure a little easier to understand, and to capitalize on the core telecom strategy, which was bringing in more than 95% of revenues, Olivetti and Telecom Italia traded places, with the telecom firm now the parent entity.

Apart from the company's telecom interests and its office services divisions, Olivetti is expanding its Internet and business network services, and the company is developing call center services.

Prior to restructuring, Olivetti's largest shareholder was Olimpia (29%), a company owned by Pirelli, Edizione Holding (the Benetton family's holding company), and other investors.

HISTORY

Inspired by a trip to the US, Camillo Olivetti founded Olivetti in 1908 to produce the first Italian-made typewriter (introduced in 1911). After diversifying into office furniture, teleprinters, and adding machines, the company went public in 1932.

Camillo's son Adriano led Olivetti into computers, and in 1959 the company developed Italy's first mainframe. That year Olivetti bought control of ailing US typewriter maker Underwood, which later became Olivetti Corporation of America (OCA).

Following Adriano's death, the Olivetti family relinquished direct management of the firm, and in 1964 a consortium of bankers bought Olivetti. The firm, slow to switch from mechanical to electric office equipment in the 1960s, saw earnings stagnate.

Former Fiat executive Carlo De Benedetti bought 14% of the firm in 1978 (increased to 20% in 1988) and became CEO. De Benedetti slashed debt while increasing spending on research and development. Olivetti introduced its first electronic typewriter in 1978.

OCA had suffered through more than a decade of losses, and in 1982 De Benedetti sold it to Dallas-based ATM maker Docutel for a 46% stake in that company. In 1985 Olivetti bought the rest of Docutel and used it to establish a new US unit, Olivetti USA.

The company unveiled its first PC in 1982, a year after IBM rolled out its first desktop machine. AT&T bought a 25% stake in Olivetti the next year, and Toshiba bought 20% of Olivetti's Japanese operations in 1985. De Benedetti hoped AT&T and Toshiba would boost Olivetti's global market share, but competition from lower-priced PCs hurt the company.

In Europe Olivetti expanded further, buying 80% of the UK's Acorn Computers Group (1985); Volkswagen's ailing office-products maker, Triumph-Adler (1986); and bank automation firms Bunker Ramo (1986) and I.S.C. Systems (1989). However, world demand for minicomputers had softened by the late 1980s, and in 1991 Olivetti posted its first loss in 13 years.

De Benedetti was convicted in 1992 of bankruptcy fraud in the scandal surrounding the 1982 collapse of Banco Ambrosiano. (His conviction was thrown out in 1998.) In 1995 Olivetti formed fixed-line operator Infostrada to rival Telecom Italia and its 36%-owned Omnitel Pronto venture (formed in 1989) began offering mobile phone service. De Benedetti, pressured to resign in 1996, chose Francesco Caio as his successor. But Caio clashed with De Benedetti and quit after 70 days. Roberto Colannino, another executive close to the former CEO, replaced him. That year Olivetti sold part of its stake in Omnitel Pronto: Mannesmann and Bell Atlantic (now Verizon) each bought 5.8%.

In 1997 venture capitalists bought Olivetti's PC business. That year Olivetti and Mannesmann formed OliMan as a telecom holding company for Omnitel Pronto and Infostrada; the German firm got a 25% stake. Wang Laboratories bought Olivetti's Olsy computer services business in 1998 in a multimillion-dollar deal that gave Olivetti an almost 19% stake in Wang (later reduced to about 16%). Mannesmann upped its ownership in OliMan to 49% in 1999, and OliMan expanded its stake in Omnitel.

Olivetti paid $33 billion in a successful hostile takeover of larger rival Telecom Italia in 1999. To help raise cash, it sold its stakes in Omnitel Pronto and Infostrada to Mannesmann (later acquired by Vodafone) and agreed to sell its 80%-owned Ricerca subsidiary to Getronics. Plans to transfer Telecom Italia's 60% stake in Telecom Italia Mobile to Tecnost, Olivetti's acquisition vehicle, in exchange for Tecnost stock were abandoned after shareholders voiced disapproval. The next year Olivetti bought the 26% of Tecnost it didn't already own and merged the two companies. In 2001 the company changed the name of its Lexicon unit to Olivetti Tecnost.

EXECUTIVES

Chairman: Antonio Tesone, age 80
Deputy Chairman and CEO: Marco Tronchetti Provera, age 55, $132,355 pay (partial-year salary)
Deputy Chairman: Gilberto Benetton, age 62, $12,032 pay (partial-year salary)
Administration Department: Mario Ferrero, age 54
Finance Department: Luigi Premoli, age 43
Human Resources: Angelo Landriani, age 52
Legal Affairs: Loris Bisone, age 55
Auditors: Reconta Ernst & Young S.p.A.

LOCATIONS

HQ: Via Jervis 77, 10015 Ivrea, Torino, Italy
Phone: +39-0125-52-00　　**Fax:** +39-0125-52-2524
US HQ: 379 Campus Dr., 2nd Fl., Somerset, NJ 08875
US Phone: 732-627-9977　　**US Fax:** 732-627-9928
Web: www.olivetti.it

The Olivetti group of subsidiaries and affiliates has operations in Argentina, Austria, Belgium, Bolivia, Brazil, Canada, Chile, China, Colombia, Costa Rica, Cuba, the Czech Republic, Ecuador, France, Germany, Greece, Hong Kong, Hungary, India, Ireland, Israel, Italy, Japan, Kenya, Luxembourg, Mexico, the Netherlands, Nigeria, Panama, Peru, Poland, Portugal, Puerto Rico, Romania, Russia, San Marino, Serbia and Montenegro, South Africa, Spain, Sweden, Switzerland, Turkey, the UK, Ukraine, the US, and Venezuela.

PRODUCTS/OPERATIONS

2002 Sales

	% of total
Telecom Italia Group	97
Olivetti Tecnost Group	3
Total	**100**

Selected Subsidiaries and Affiliates

Olivetti Multiservices S.p.A. (facility and property management services)
Olivetti Tecnost S.p.A. (office and document management products)
DomusTech S.p.A. (63%, automated IT services for residential customers)
GoToWeb S.p.A. (Internet services for small to midsized businesses)
Tecnost Sistemi S.p.A. (specialized information technology [IT] systems and office products)
Webegg S.p.A. (50%, IT services for the Internet)

COMPETITORS

Alcatel	IBM
Canon	Matsushita
Danka	Océ
Hewlett-Packard	Ricoh
Imagistics	Xerox

HISTORICAL FINANCIALS

Company Type: Subsidiary

Income Statement

FYE: December 31

	REVENUE ($ mil.)	NET INCOME ($ mil.)	NET PROFIT MARGIN	EMPLOYEES
12/02	33,447	(810)	—	104,370
12/01	29,179	(2,737)	—	116,020
12/00	28,357	(885)	—	120,973
12/99	30,157	4,974	16.5%	129,073
12/98	4,345	150	3.5%	17,000
12/97	3,753	9	0.2%	22,659
12/96	5,492	(603)	—	26,277
12/95	6,208	(1,008)	—	30,120
12/94	5,568	(417)	—	33,867
12/93	5,028	(271)	—	35,171
Annual Growth	23.4%	—	—	12.8%

2002 Year-End Financials

Debt ratio: 290.4%
Return on equity: —
Cash ($ mil.): 4,639

Current ratio: 1.11
Long-term debt ($ mil.): 35,430

Net Income History

5,000	
4,000	
3,000	
2,000	
1,000	
0	
-1,000	
-2,000	
-3,000	

12/93 12/94 12/95 12/96 12/97 12/98 12/99 12/00 12/01 12/02

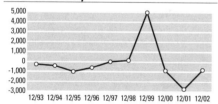

OMV

Oil and chemicals group OMV is Austria's largest industrial company. It explores for natural gas and crude oil, refines crude oil, and imports, transports, and stores gas. A leading oil and gas company in Central and Eastern Europe, OMV has proved reserves of 338 million barrels of oil equivalent. With petroleum products marketed through OMV gas stations and direct distributors, OMV has a 14% retail market share in Central and Eastern Europe. The company also manufactures plastics (it owns geotextile producer Polyfelt) and chemicals (fertilizers and melamine). OMV's largest shareholders are Aus-

trian state holding company ÖIAG (35%) and the International Petroleum Investment Company (IPIC) of Abu Dhabi (20%).

OMV has exploration activities in Austria as well as internationally (including Australia, Libya, Pakistan, and the UK), OMV has gathered some 338 million barrels of oil equivalent in proved reserves.

The bulk of OMV's sales come from refining and marketing. It has two refineries with a capacity of 270,000 barrels of oil equivalent per day. Petroleum products are marketed through more than 1,100 OMV filling stations and direct distributors. Its natural gas network, serving about 90% of Austria's natural gas demand, draws gas supplies from Russia, Norway, and Germany, as well as from domestic reserves.

Subsidiary Agrolinz Melamin is the Austrian leader in plant nutrients and the world's #2 producer of melamine (a synthetic resin used to manufacture flooring and furniture) behind DSM Chemicals North America. OMV also makes nonwoven geotextiles for engineering materials through its Polyfelt unit and owns 25% of Danish polyolefin producer Borealis.

Austria's gas market, now dominated by OMV, is slated for full competition; OMV is among state-controlled companies set for full privatization.

The company moved into Bosnia-Herzegovina in 2003, opening nine gas stations.

HISTORY

Oil exploration began in Austria in the 1920s, largely as joint ventures with foreign firms such as Shell and Socony-Vacuum. Full-scale production did not get underway until 1938, when the Anschluss (the absorption of Austria by Germany) paved the way for Germany to exploit Austria's natural resources to fuel its growing war machine. In the division of spoils following WWII, Russia gained control of Austria's oil reserves.

The Russian-administered oil assets were transferred to the new Austrian government in 1955, which authorized the company Österreichische Mineralölverwaltung (ÖMG) in 1956 to control state oil assets. ÖMG, state-controlled by the Austrian Mineral Oil Administration, set about building a major refinery in 1960 and acquiring marketing companies Martha and ÖROP in 1965.

In 1968 ÖMG became the first Western company to sign a natural gas supply contract with Russia. In 1974 it commissioned the Trans-Austria Gas Pipeline, which enabled the supply of natural gas to Italy. That year ÖMG changed its named to ÖMV Aktiengesellschaft (ÖMV became OMV in 1995 for international markets).

During the 1970s OMV expanded its crude supply arrangements, tapping supplies from Iran, Iraq, Libya, and other Middle Eastern countries. It moved into oil and gas exploration in the mid-1980s, forming OMV Libya (acquiring 25% of Occidental's Libyan production) and OMV UK.

With Austria moving toward increasing privatization, in 1987 about 15% of OMV's shares were sold to the public. The government sold a further 10% two years later. In 1989 OMV acquired PCD Polymere. With the aim of merging state-owned oil and chemical activities, OMV acquired Chemie Linz in 1990. The company also opened its first OMV-branded service station that year. In 1994 OMV reorganized itself as an integrated oil and gas group based in Central Europe, with international exploration and production activities, and with other operations in the chemical and petrochemical sectors.

In 1995 OMV acquired TOTAL-AUSTRIA, expanding its service stations by 59. The company introduced OMV lubricants to the Greek market in 1996. It also expanded its OMV service station network in Hungary to 66 stations after acquiring 31 Q8 (Kuwait) sites. In 1997 the Stroh Company's retail network in Austria was merged into OMV.

Expanding its retail network even further, OMV acquired BP's retail network in the Czech Republic, Slovakia, and Hungary in 1998. It also sold its stake in Chemie Linz and acquired a 25% stake in major European polyolefin producer Borealis, which in turn acquired PCD Polymere. In 1999 the company pushed its retail network into Bulgaria and Romania. That year OMV also acquired Australian company Cultus Petroleum.

OMV and Shell agreed to develop North Sea fields together in 2000. That year OMV also formed a joint venture with Italy's Edison International to explore in Vietnam and acquired more than 9% of Hungarian rival MOL. It upped that stake to 10% in 2001. The company also made a bid that year for 18% of Poland's largest refiner, PKN Orlen.

In 2002 OMV opened its first gas station in Serbia and Montenegro. It also announced plans to increase its German gas station count from 79 to 151 with the purchase of 32 Royal Dutch/Shell Group units and the planned acquisition of 40 stations from Martin GmbH & Co.

In 2003 the company acquired Preussag Energie's exploration and production assets for $320 million.

EXECUTIVES

Chairman, Supervisory Board: Peter Michaelis, age 57
Deputy Chairman, Supervisory Board:
Mohamed Naser Al Khaily
Chairman of the Executive Board and CEO:
Wolfgang Ruttenstorfer, age 53
Deputy Chairman of the Executive Board and VP, Refining and Marketing and Plastics: Gerhard Roiss, age 51
CFO: David C. Davies, age 48
VP, Exploration and Production: Helmut Langanger, age 53
Investor Relations: Brigitte H. Juen
Auditors: KPMG Alpen-Treuhand GmbH

LOCATIONS

HQ: OMV Aktiengesellschaft
Otto-Wagner-Platz 5, A-1090 Vienna, Austria
Phone: +43-1-404-40-0   **Fax:** +43-1-404-40-20091
Web: www.omv.com

OMV has exploration operations in Albania, Australia, Austria, Libya, Pakistan, Sudan, Tunisia, the UK, and Vietnam, and marketing operations across Central and Eastern Europe, including Austria, Bulgaria, the Czech Republic, Germany, Hungary, Romania, Serbia and Montenegro, Slovakia, and Switzerland. The company operates refineries in Schwechat, Austria, and Burghausen, Germany, and has chemicals and plastics plants in Austria, Italy, and Malaysia.

2002 Sales

	% of total
Europe	
Austria	57
Croatia, Czech Republic, Hungary, Slovakia & Slovenia	21
Germany	13
Other EU countries	4
Other countries	3
Other regions	2
Total	**100**

PRODUCTS/OPERATIONS

2002 Sales

	% of total
Refining & marketing	64
Gas	19
Exploration & production	10
Chemicals & plastics	6
Other	1
Total	**100**

Selected Subsidiaries and Affiliates

Refining and Marketing
Abu Dhabi Petroleum Investments L.L.C. (25%, United Arab Emirates)
Adria-Wien Pipeline Gesellschaft m.b.H (55%)
AUSTRIA Mineralöl GmbH
CRODUX proizvodno, trgovacko i usluzno d.o.o. (Croatia)
International Consortium Bulgaria AD (20%)
OMV — International Services Ges. m.b.H
VIVA Tankstellenbetriebs-GmbH
WÄRME-ENERGIE VORARLBERG Beratung- und Handels GmbH (80%)

Gas
ADRIA LNG STUDY COMPANY LIMITED (20%, Malta)
Baumgarten-Oberkappel Gasleitungsgesellschaft m.b.H (51%)
Ferngas Beteiligungs-Aktiengesellschaft (68%)
GWH Gas- und Warenhandelsgesellschaft m.b.H. (50%)
Trans-Austria-Gasleitung Gesellschaft m.b.H. (51%)

Exploration and Production
OMV (ALBANIEN) offshore Exploration GmbH
OMV AUSTRALIA PTY LTD
OMV OF LIBYA LIMITED (UK)
OMV Oil Exploration GmbH
OMV Oil Production GmbH
OMV (PAKISTAN) Exploration Gesellschaft m.b.H.
OMV PEX ÖI und Gas Exploration Gesellschaft m.b.H. (OPEX)
OMV (SUDAN) Exploration GmbH
OMV (U.K.) Limited

Chemicals and Plastics
Agrolinz Magyarország Kft. (Hungary)
Agrolinz Melamin GmbH
Agrolinz Melamin Italia S.r.l. (Italy)
Borealis A/S (50%, Denmark)
Chemiepark Linz Services Gesellschaft m.b.H (48%)
POLYFELT Gesellschaft m.b.H.

COMPETITORS

BP	MOL
DSM	PKN ORLEN
Eni	Royal Dutch/Shell Group
Exxon Mobil	UNIPETROL
Hellenic Petroleum	

HISTORICAL FINANCIALS

Company Type: Public

Income Statement

FYE: December 31

	REVENUE ($ mil.)	NET INCOME ($ mil.)	NET PROFIT MARGIN	EMPLOYEES
12/02	3,285	231	7.0%	2,849
12/01	3,056	299	9.8%	2,985
12/00	4,436	305	6.9%	5,757
12/99	5,215	195	3.7%	5,953
12/98	5,508	198	3.6%	6,360
12/97	6,591	180	2.7%	7,934
Annual Growth	**(13.0%)**	**5.1%**	**—**	**(18.5%)**

2002 Year-End Financials

Debt ratio: 0.0%
Return on equity: 12.8%
Cash ($ mil.): 36
Current ratio: 1.68
Long-term debt ($ mil.): 0

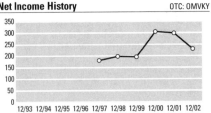

Otto Versand

Otto Versand has the mail-order business in the bag. The world's largest mail-order company sells merchandise in more than 20 countries through about 90 subsidiaries. Customers order through more than 600 print catalogs yearly, as well as through CD-ROM catalogs and the Internet. The firm sells products ranging from clothing to appliances to sporting goods. Otto Versand also owns a majority stake in the Crate & Barrel housewares chain, and it owns travel agencies in Germany. The company controls Actebis Holding, a major computer distributor in Europe. The family of executive board chairman Michael Otto owns the majority of the company and separately controls US catalog company Spiegel.

Otto Versand has grown largely through its acquisitions and diversification tactics (entering non-mail-order businesses). The firm does about 50% of its business in Germany, and customers there can get same-day delivery of many of Otto Versand's wares.

HISTORY

East German refugee Werner Otto founded Otto Versand (German for "dispatch") in Hamburg, West Germany, in 1949. It distributed its first catalog in 1950; 300 hand-bound copies offered only shoes, but in 28 styles. Instead of being required to pay upon delivery, customers received bills with their orders; this was new for mail orders. By 1956 the firm employed 500 people; by 1958 the catalog had expanded to 200 pages, offering low-cost women's fashions and other products to 200,000 potential customers.

In 1963 Otto Versand began taking phone orders. Its catalog grew to 800 pages and one million copies by 1967. The following year it published the Post Shop Magazine, its first special-interest catalog, which targeted fashion-conscious youth. In 1969 Otto Versand formed Hanseatic Bank to offer customers monthly payment plans; three years later it formed the Hermes Express Package delivery service.

The firm began a shopping spree in the 1970s by investing in mail-order companies 3 Suisses International (France, 1974), Heinrich Heine (luxury clothes and household goods, West Germany, 1974) and Hanau (West Germany, 1979).

Werner's son Michael succeeded him as chairman in 1981, and in 1982 he led the acquisition of low-cost women's apparel firm Spiegel. Michael immediately revamped Spiegel into an upscale retailer. The ownership of Spiegel was restructured in 1984, but the Otto family remained in control of the US company.

Throughout the 1980s the firm continued investing in European companies (entering the UK in 1986 and Austria in 1988) and began Otto-Sumisho in Japan (a joint venture, 1986). Its combined catalog circulation reached 200 million in 1987.

Otto Versand launched 24-hour delivery service in 1990; that year it expanded to the Polish market by forming joint venture Otto-Epoka. In 1991 it began 24-hour phone sales and acquired a majority stake in Grattan (the UK's fourth-largest mail-order firm). Acquisitions continued during the early and mid-1990s, including Margareta (Hungary), Postalmarket (Italy's largest mail-order firm), and Otto-Burlingtons (Germany-India joint venture).

Otto Versand acquired a majority stake in Reiseland's 60 travel agencies in 1993 and bought two UK collection agencies in 1994. In 1994 it became Germany's first mail-order firm to offer an interactive CD-ROM catalog.

The firm bought a majority stake in US housewares retailer Crate & Barrel in 1998 and bought German computer wholesaler Actebis Holding. It then formed Zara Deutschland, a joint venture in Germany (with Spain's Inditex), to sell clothing in a new chain of outlets. Otto Versand added to its travel business (about 140 locations) in 1998 with the purchase of 25 offices from American Express Germany. It closed Postalmarket that year because of problems with the Italian postal service.

In 1999 Otto Versand acquired the Freemans catalog business (nearly $900 million in 1998 sales) from the UK's Sears PLC. The deal nearly doubled the company's UK mail-order market share, from 8% to 15%. In late 1999 the firm formed a joint venture with Harrods to sell fancy English goods online.

In early 2000 Otto Versand set up a joint venture with America Online (now part of Time Warner) and Deutsche Bank 24 to offer online banking, Internet service, and PCs. In October 2001 the company entered into a joint venture with US Internet travel service provider Travelocity.com to form Travelocity Europe.

EXECUTIVES

Supervisory Board Chairman: Hans Jörg Hammer
Executive Board Chairman and CEO: Michael Otto, age 60
CFO: Michael E. Crüesemann
COO: Peer Witten, age 56
General Manager, Merchandise (Hardware): Diethard Gagelmann
General Manager, Marketing, Advertising, and E-Commerce: Rainer Hillebrand
General Manager, Merchandise (Textiles): Gert Rietz, age 55
Chief Human Resources Officer: Hans-Otto Schrader, age 46
CIO: Wolfgang Linder, age 54
Deputy General Manager, Planning and Controlling: Winfried Zimmermann
Auditors: KPMG Deutsche Treuhand-Gesellschaft AG

LOCATIONS

HQ: Otto Versand Gmbh & Co.
Wandsbeker Strasse 3-7, 22179 Hamburg, Germany
Phone: +49-40-64-61-0 **Fax:** +49-40-64-61-85-71
Web: www.otto.de

PRODUCTS/OPERATIONS

Selected Subsidiaries

3 Suisses France
Actebis Holding
Crate & Barrel (majority stake)
Grattan
Handelsgesellschaft Heinrich Heine GmbH
Hanseatic Bank GmbH
Otto-Sumisho (51%)
Reiseland GmbH (75%)

COMPETITORS

Amazon.com	Lands' End
Bed Bath & Beyond	Lillian Vernon
Blair	Linens 'n Things
Direct Marketing	Littlewoods
Fast Retailing	L.L. Bean
Federated	METRO AG
GUS	Pier 1 Imports
Hammacher Schlemmer &	Pinault-Printemps-
Co.	Redoute
Hanover Direct	Provell
J. C. Penney	Schickedanz
Karstadt	Williams-Sonoma
Vendex	

HISTORICAL FINANCIALS

Company Type: Private

Income Statement

FYE: Last day in February

	REVENUE ($ mil.)	NET INCOME ($ mil.)	NET PROFIT MARGIN	EMPLOYEES
2/03	15,083	141	0.9%	65,854
2/02	12,461	125	1.0%	79,137
2/01	13,636	192	1.4%	75,962
2/00	12,741	266	2.1%	71,350
2/99	15,535	288	1.9%	50,055
2/98	13,364	201	1.5%	41,476
2/97	12,439	249	2.0%	46,500
2/96	16,876	—	—	41,221
2/95	13,176	—	—	39,817
2/94	11,300	—	—	—
Annual Growth	**3.3%**	**(9.0%)**	**—**	**6.5%**

2003 Year-End Financials

Debt ratio: 67.1%
Return on equity: 11.8%
Cash ($ mil.): 277

Current ratio: 1.89
Long-term debt ($ mil.): 857

Net Income History

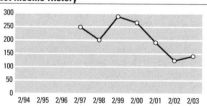

Pearson plc

There's nothing fishy about information from Pearson. The media giant is a leading provider of financial information and business news with such titles as the salmon-colored *The Financial Times,* the 50%-owned *The Economist* and its 60% stake in US-based Interactive Data Corporation (formerly Data Broadcasting, which sold its 34% stake in MarketWatch.com to Pearson). The company's Pearson Education unit is the world's top educational publisher through imprints Scott Foresman, Addison Wesley Longman, and Prentice Hall. Pearson also publishes trade books through its Penguin Group (Penguin, Putnam, Viking).

In addition to printed works, the company is making significant Internet investments, including the *Financial Times* Web site (FT.com) and online educational services. Pearson had been active in television through its 22% interest in RTL Group, a merger of Pearson's TV assets with Bertelsmann and Audiofina's CLT-Ufa, but sold its stake to Bertelsmann in 2001.

Under CEO Marjorie Scardino, Pearson has shed many of its non-media assets — which once included Madame Tussaud's wax museums — and is moving to strengthen its printed content brands. In 2000 it launched a German version of *The Financial Times* with Bertelsmann's Gruner + Jahr, and bought children's book publisher Dorling Kindersley (now part of Penguin Group). Spain's Telefónica owns about 5% of the company (which it wants to divest).

HISTORY

In 1844 Samuel Pearson became a partner in a small Yorkshire building firm. When he retired in 1879 his grandson Weetman took over, moving the company to London in 1884. The business enjoyed extraordinary success — building the first tunnel under New York's Hudson River and installing Mexico City's drainage system. By the 1890s the company (incorporated as S. Pearson & Son in 1897) was the world's #1 contractor.

In the 1920s the company bought newspapers and engaged in oil exploration. Weetman died in 1927, and so did the construction business. His heirs then bought into several unrelated businesses. Pearson bought control of *The Financial Times* newspaper in 1957, a deal that also brought it 50% of *The Economist* (*The Financial Times* had acquired half of *The Economist* in 1928). The company later added stakes in vintner Chateau Latour (1963, sold 1988) and publisher Longman (1968). The firm went public in 1969.

During the 1970s Pearson bought Penguin Books (1971) and Madame Tussaud's (1978). In 1989 it added Addison-Wesley (educational publisher, US) and Les Echos (financial newspaper publisher, France).

Concentrating on media interests, the company bought Thames Television in 1993 and Grundy Worldwide (game shows and soap operas) in 1995. It acquired HarperCollins Educational Publishing from News Corp. in 1996, as well as US publisher Putnam Berkley from MCA, gaining such authors as Tom Clancy and Amy Tan. By the mid-1990s, however, Pearson's holdings still lacked focus, and earnings were depressed. Marjorie Scardino, a Texan who had been CEO of The Economist Group since 1992, replaced Frank Barlow in 1997, becoming the first woman to lead a major UK company. She

rounded out Pearson's TV holdings with the purchase of All American Communications that year.

In 1998 Pearson bought Simon & Schuster's reference and educational publishing divisions from Viacom for $4.6 billion and sold Tussaud's amusement business. In 1999 Pearson shed $58 million in college textbooks and instructional programs to John Wiley & Sons.

As part of a long-term plan to build *The Financial Times* brand online, Pearson bought 60% of Data Broadcasting Corporation (now called Interactive Data Corporation) in 2000, and began to cross-promote the FT.com Web site with MarketWatch.com (Data Broadcast sold its 34% stake in MarketWatch to Pearson in 2001) as part of a $35 million marketing campaign. Pearson also bought troubled UK publisher Dorling Kindersley for nearly $500 million and later combined the firm with its Penguin unit.

Later in 2000, Pearson combined its TV operations with CLT-Ufa, co-owned by German media company Bertelsmann and Audiofina, into a new publicly traded broadcasting firm called RTL Group. Pearson took a 22% stake in RTL. In addition, Pearson bought educational test processing firm National Computer Systems (now NCS Pearson). In 2001 Pearson expanded its educational operations, announcing plans for a joint venture with Telefónica to distribute online educational content in Latin America. That year the company also formed a joint venture with an arm of Chinese state television to produce programming for a Chinese audience. In late 2001 Pearson sold its stake in RTL to Bertelsmann.

EXECUTIVES

Chairman: Lord Dennis Stevenson, age 57, $441,072 pay
Chief Executive: Marjorie M. Scardino, age 56, $1,279,912 pay
CFO: Rona A. Fairhead, age 41, $774,683 pay
CIO: William B. (Bill) Gauld, age 49
Director for People; Chairman, Financial Times Group: David Bell, age 56, $755,437 pay
Director of Global Communications and President, Pearson Inc.: John Fallon, age 40
Director of Global Communications: Luke Swanson
Chairman and CEO, Pearson Education: Peter Jovanovich, age 54, $1,554,179 pay
Chairman and CEO, The Penguin Group: John C. Makinson, age 48, $1,119,522 pay
Managing Director, Financial Times Group: Olivier Fleurot
Auditors: PricewaterhouseCoopers LLP

LOCATIONS

HQ: 80 Strand, London WC2R ORL, United Kingdom
Phone: +44-20-7010-2000 **Fax:** +44-20-7010-6060
US HQ: 1330 Avenue of the Americas, New York, NY 10019
US Phone: 212-641-2400 **US Fax:** 212-641-2500
Web: www.pearson.com

2002 Sales

	$ mil.	% of total
North America	5,059	73
Europe	675	10
UK	662	9
Asia/Pacific	401	6
Other countries	165	2
Total	**6,962**	**100**

PRODUCTS/OPERATIONS

2002 Sales

	$ mil.	% of total
Pearson Education	4,442	64
Penguin Group	1,350	19
Financial Times Group	1,170	17
Total	**6,962**	**100**

Selected Operations

Pearson Education
Elementary education
  Computer Curriculum
  Pearson Learning
  Scott Foresman
  Silver Burdett Ginn
FT Management (business education and management development)
Higher education
  Addison Wesley Longman
  Allyn & Beacon
  Prentice Hall College
Macmillan Computer Publishing
  BradyGAMES
  Macmillan Online
  Macmillan Software
  Que
  Sams
NCS Pearson (educational test processing)
Secondary education
  Globe Fearon
  Prentice Hall

Financial Times Group
Business Day & Financial Mail (50%; South Africa)
The Economist Group (50%)
  CFO
  The Economist
  The Journal of Commerce
  Roll Call
The Financial Times
Financial Times Deutschland (with Gruner + Jahr)
FT asset Management
FT.com (financial news)
FTSE International (market indices, with London Stock Exchange)
Interactive Data Corp. (60%; US)
Les Echos (France)
MarketWatch.com (34%; US)
Recoletos (79%; Spain)
  Expansion (financial and business news)
  Marca (sports news)

Penguin Group

Avery	Penguin
Berkley Books	Penguin Business
Dorling Kindersley	Penguin Classics
Dutton	Penguin Reference
Frederick Warne	Plume
Hamish Hamilton	Puffin
Ladybird	Viking
Michael Joseph	

COMPETITORS

1mage	Prometric
Compass Learning	ProQuest
Daily Mail and General Trust	Random House
	Reed Elsevier Group
Dow Jones	Reuters
Educational Testing Service	Scan-Optics
	Simon & Schuster
HarperCollins	Sylvan Learning
John Harland	Thomson Corporation
John Wiley	Time
Knowledge Universe	Touchstone Applied
Learning Tree	Science
McGraw-Hill	Verlagsgruppe Georg von
Moody's	Holtzbrinck
New Horizons Worldwide	Vivendi Universal
New York Times	Publishing
News Corp.	Washington Post
PLATO Learning	Wolters Kluwer

HISTORICAL FINANCIALS

Company Type: Public

Income Statement

FYE: December 31

	REVENUE ($ mil.)	NET INCOME ($ mil.)	NET PROFIT MARGIN	EMPLOYEES
12/02	6,962	(179)	—	30,359
12/01	6,152	(569)	—	29,027
12/00	5,792	268	4.6%	24,688
12/99	5,384	485	9.0%	20,000
12/98	3,973	625	15.7%	18,400
12/97	3,783	63	1.7%	18,306
12/96	3,714	410	11.0%	17,383
12/95	2,836	404	14.3%	19,422
12/94	2,425	349	14.4%	17,215
12/93	1,950	219	11.2%	15,514
Annual Growth	**15.2%**	—	—	**7.7%**

2002 Year-End Financials

Debt ratio: 52.0%	No. of shares (mil.): 802
Return on equity: —	Dividends
Cash ($ mil.): 927	Yield: 4.0%
Current ratio: 1.87	Payout: —
Long-term debt ($ mil.): 2,799	Market value ($ mil.): 7,496

Stock History

NYSE: PSO

12/93 12/94 12/95 12/96 12/97 12/98 12/99 12/00 12/01 12/02

	STOCK PRICE ($) FY Close	P/E High/Low	PER SHARE ($) Earnings	Dividends	Book Value
12/02	9.35	— —	(0.22)	0.37	6.71
12/01	12.28	— —	(0.57)	0.35	6.53
12/00	23.56	85 62	0.36	0.00	7.58
Annual Growth	**(37.0%)**	— —	—	—	**(5.9%)**

Peninsular and Oriental Steam Navigation

It's all hands on deck as The Peninsular and Oriental Steam Navigation Company (P&O) reorganizes to battle stiff competition. The Eurotunnel torpedoed P&O's cross-Channel ferry dominance, prompting it to merge ferry operations with rival Stena Line. Still, the company has other resources. Subsidiary P&O Ports is one of the world's leading port operators, with stakes in about two dozen container terminals and cargo-handling and other operations in more than 80 ports. P&O's cold logistics unit provides temperature-controlled warehousing and distribution services. P&O also owns 50% of one of the world's largest container shippers, P&O Nedlloyd.

P&O expects its port operations to benefit from the trend toward containerization of freight. The company plans to increase its cargo handling ca-

pacity at its existing terminals — notably at the Qingdao terminal in China — and to bid for new port concessions. At the same time, P&O is working to cut costs in its ferry operations.

The company has expanded its cold logistics business in the US, particularly in California and Texas, and it is working to integrate those acquisitions. It has sold off its contract logistics operations.

P&O's interests in container shipping companies complement its port business. But the container shipping business is highly cyclical, and P&O intends to sell part of its interest in P&O Nedlloyd. In addition, P&O has sold most of its investment properties.

HISTORY

In 1815 Scotsman Arthur Anderson joined the London office of shipbroker Brodi Willcox. They formed a partnership in 1822 and built a business based on trade between Britain and the Iberian Peninsula. Their ships ran guns and transported troops for the royalists during the Portuguese and Spanish civil wars of the 1830s.

The two men teamed up with Irish shipowner Richard Bourne in 1835 to establish the Peninsular Steam Navigation Company, which offered regular trading service between London and ports in Spain, Portugal, and Gibraltar. Two years later Bourne won a contract to carry mail by sea between England and Spanish and Portuguese ports. The company extended its mail routes to the Mediterranean, and in 1840 a contract for monthly mail deliveries to Alexandria, Egypt, allowed it to raise enough money to incorporate as a limited liability company, the Peninsular and Oriental Steam Navigation Company.

The firm began offering cruises in the 1840s and continued to add mail routes, including Suez/Calcutta (1843), Hong Kong (1845), and Sydney (1852). P&O's mail and passenger steamships provided vital logistical support to the expansion of the British Empire.

Between 1914 and 1946 P&O acquired several other shipping firms, including the British India Steam Navigation Company and the New Zealand Shipping Company. The company operated nearly 500 ships in the 1920s.

During WWII, P&O lost 182 ships that were drafted as troop carriers and cargo vessels. After the war, as aircraft took away its passenger and mail income, P&O added cruise ships and various forms of cargo ships, from containers to tankers.

By the 1970s P&O was involved in nearly every kind of merchant shipping. In 1974 it further diversified with the purchase of Britain's #4 construction company (at that time), Bovis Construction. Jeffrey Sterling joined P&O as chairman in 1983.

Two years later the firm acquired its chairman's Sterling Guarantee Trust, which owned US commercial properties and London's Earls Court and Olympia exhibition halls. In the late 1980s and early 1990s chairman Sterling kept the company on a course of expansion: P&O bought Sitmar Cruises in 1988, formed P&O Asia in 1992, and acquired interests in Chinese container terminals.

But P&O had hit the business doldrums. To put some wind in its sails, P&O and rival Royal Nedlloyd merged their container shipping lines into P&O Nedlloyd Container Line in 1996 and spun off faltering Bovis Homes (residential construction) the next year. In 1998 it combined its ferries with those of Stena Line in order to compete against the Eurotunnel. P&O's Grand

Princess, the biggest cruise ship in the world at the time, also came into service that year.

In 1999 P&O began jettisoning noncore businesses. It sold Bovis Construction to real estate group Lend Lease; it also sold Earls Court and Olympia. The next year the company spun off its cruise line business as P&O Princess Cruises (expanded in 1999 with the acquisition of Germany's Aida). P&O had announced plans to add privately held Festival to its cruise line offerings before the spinoff, but a slump in the price of P&O's stock forced the company to call off the $400 million acquisition.

Also in 2000 P&O pulled the IPO of bulk shipping unit Associated Bulk Carriers (ABC), citing poor market conditions. Instead the company sold 50% of ABC to Eurotower Holdings and turned over the company's management to Zodiac Maritime Agencies. (P&O sold its remaining 50% stake in ABC to Eurotower Holdings in 2003.)

In 2002 P&O bought Stena Line's 40% stake in the companies' combined ferry business.

EXECUTIVES

Chairman: Lord Sterling of Plaistow, age 68, $556,553 pay
Managing Director: Sir Bruce MacPhail, age 64, $1,040,931 pay
Executive Chairman, P&O Ports; Group Managing Director, P&O Nedlloyd Container Line: Robert B. Woods, age 57, $603,066 pay
CFO: Nick Luff, age 36
Executive Director, Commercial and Legal Affairs and Company Secretary: R. Michael Gradon, age 44, $412,202 pay
Executive Director, Communications and Strategy: Peter Smith, age 51, $340,027 pay
Managing Director, P&O Ferries: Russ Peters, age 55
COO, P&O Ports: Alistair Baillie
Commercial Director, P&O Nedlloyd: Tom Boardley
Auditors: KPMG Audit Plc

LOCATIONS

HQ: The Peninsular and Oriental
Steam Navigation Company
79 Pall Mall, London SW1Y 5EJ, United Kingdom
Phone: +44-20-7930-4343 **Fax:** +44-20-7930-8572
US HQ: 19840 Rancho Way, Dominguez Hills, CA 90221
US Phone: 310-632-6265 **US Fax:** 310-632-8887
Web: www.pogroup.com

PRODUCTS/OPERATIONS

Selected Subsidiaries and Affiliates

Ferries
Larne Harbour Ltd. (harbor operator, Ireland)
P&O European Ferries (Irish Sea) Ltd.
P&O European Ferries (Portsmouth) Ltd.
P&O Ferries Ltd.
P&O North Sea Ferries BV (Holland)
P&O North Sea Ferries Ltd. (England)
Three Quays International Ltd. (marine consultancy and project management services)

Ports
Asian Terminals Inc. (84%, container terminals and stevedoring, Philippines)
Container Terminals Australia Ltd. (90%)
Nhava Sheva International Container Terminal Ltd. (95%, container terminals, India)
Partrederiet International Offshore Services ANS (50%, offshore maritime services, Norway)
P&O Maritime Services Pty. Ltd. (offshore services, ships agency, and chartering, Australia)
P&O Polar Australia Pty. Ltd. (Antarctic research and resupply services)
P&O Ports Ltd. (container terminals, stevedoring, and international port management, Australia)
P&O Ports North America Inc. (stevedoring and passenger terminal services)

Shekou Container Terminals Ltd. (25%, container terminals, China)
Southampton Container Terminals Ltd. (51%, container terminals)
Terminales Rio de la Plata SA (53%, container terminal and stevedoring, Argentina)
Tilbury Container Services Ltd. (34%, container terminal operations)

Cold Logistics
Pacific Cold Storage Inc. (US)
P&O Cold Logistics Argentina SA (freezer, handling, and cold storage of consumables)
P&O Cold Logistics Ltd. (freezing, handling, and cold storage of consumables, Australia)

COMPETITORS

A.P. Møller — Maersk
COSCO Group
Crowley Maritime
DFDS
Eurotunnel
Evergreen Marine
Hanjin Shipping
Hutchison Whampoa
Kuehne & Nagel
Mitsui O.S.K. Lines
Neptune Orient
NYK Line
Sea Containers
Stevedoring Services of America
Stolt-Nielsen

HISTORICAL FINANCIALS

Company Type: Public

Income Statement

FYE: December 31

	REVENUE ($ mil.)	NET INCOME ($ mil.)	NET PROFIT MARGIN	EMPLOYEES
12/02	4,292	(288)	—	30,194
12/01	3,593	173	4.8%	26,891
12/00	5,888	102	1.7%	41,853
12/99	9,920	650	6.6%	62,674
12/98	9,806	451	4.6%	68,333
12/97	9,762	549	5.6%	69,533
12/96	12,047	426	3.5%	71,205
12/95	10,182	366	3.6%	66,924
12/94	9,372	374	4.0%	61,467
12/93	8,490	595	7.0%	51,755
Annual Growth	(7.3%)	—	—	(5.8%)

2002 Year-End Financials

Debt ratio: 92.8%
Return on equity: —
Cash ($ mil.): 106
Current ratio: 1.26
Long-term debt ($ mil.): 1,942

Net Income History

London: PO

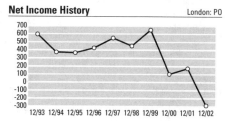

PETROBRAS

PETRÓLEO BRASILEIRO (PETROBRAS) isn't brash, but it is Brazil's largest industrial company. It engages in exploration for oil and gas and in production, refining, purchasing, and transportation of oil and gas products. The company has proved reserves of 10.5 billion barrels of oil equivalent and operates 10 refineries, 10,000 miles of pipeline, and more than 7,000 gas stations. Subsidiary Petrobras Distribuidora is

Brazil's leading retailer of oil products and fuel alcohol. Petrobras Internacional operates the company's worldwide exploration, production, and marketing services. Other units produce petrochemicals and natural gas. The Brazilian government owns 32% of PETROBRAS and 56% of its voting shares.

Petrobras Internacional, also known as Braspetro, conducts international exploration in Angola, Kazakhstan, Nigeria, the UK, the US, and Latin America.

Although most of PETROBRAS' wells are onshore, the bulk of its production comes from offshore operations; the company is recognized as a leader in offshore drilling technology and deepwater wells. To boost its natural gas operations, PETROBRAS is investing $2 billion to build a pipeline from gas fields in Bolivia to Brazil. The company also plans to triple production outside Brazil to 300,000 barrels per day by 2005 and is eyeing a major acquisition to boost its Gulf of Mexico assets.

HISTORY

"O petróleo é nosso!"
"The oil is ours!" proclaimed the Brazilian nationalists' slogan in 1953, and President Getúlio Vargas approved a bill creating a state-run monopoly on petroleum discovery, development, refining, and transport. The same year that PETRÓLEO BRASILEIRO (PETROBRAS) was created, a team led by American geologist Walter Link reported that the prospects of finding petroleum in Brazil were slim. The report outraged Brazilian nationalists, who saw it as a ploy for foreign exploitation. PETROBRAS proved it could find oil, but Brazil continued to import crude oil and petroleum products. By 1973 the company produced about 10% of the nation's needs.

When oil prices soared during the Arab embargo, the government, instead of encouraging exploration for domestic oil, pushed PETROBRAS into a program to promote alcohol fuels. The company was forced to raise gasoline prices to make the more costly gasohol attractive to consumers. During the 1979 oil crunch the price of gasohol was fixed at 65% of gasoline. But during the oil glut of the mid-1980s, PETROBRAS' cost of making gasohol was twice what it cost to buy gasoline — in other words, PETROBRAS lost money.

PETROBRAS soon began overseas exploration. In 1980 it found an oil field in Iraq, an important trading partner during the 1980s. The company also drilled in Angola and, through a 1987 agreement with Texaco, in the Gulf of Mexico.

In the mid-1980s PETROBRAS began production in the deepwater Campos basin off the coast of Rio de Janeiro state. Discoveries there in 1988, in the Marlim and Albacora fields, more than tripled its oil reserves. It plunged deep into the thick Amazon jungle in 1986 to explore for oil, and by 1990 Amazon wells were making a significant contribution to total production. That year, to ease dependence on imports, PETROBRAS launched a five-year, $16.9 billion plan to boost crude oil production. It also began selling its mining and trading assets.

Before the invasion of Kuwait, Brazil relied heavily on Iraq, trading weapons for oil. After the invasion spawned increases in crude prices, PETROBRAS raised pump prices but, yielding to the government's anti-inflation program, still did not raise them enough to cover costs. It lost $13 million a day.

The company sold 26% of Petrobras Distribuidora to the public in 1993 and privatized several of its petrochemical and fertilizer subsidiaries. A 1994 presidential order, bent on stabilizing Brazil's 40%-per-month inflation, cut the prices of oil products. In 1995 the government loosened its grip on the oil and gas industry and allowed foreign companies to enter the Brazilian market. In the wake of this reform, PETROBRAS teamed up with a Japanese consortium to build Brazil's largest oil refinery.

In 1997 PETROBRAS appealed a $4 billion judgment from a 1992 shareholder lawsuit; the suit alleged PETROBRAS had undervalued shares during the privatization of the loss-making Petroquisa affiliate. (The appeal was granted in 1999.)

As part of an effort to boost oil production, PETROBRAS also began to raise money abroad in 1999. The next year PETROBRAS and Spanish oil giant Repsol YPF agreed to swap oil and gas assets in Argentina and Brazil in a deal worth more than $1 billion.

In 2000 the company announced plans to change its corporate name to PETROBRAX, but fierce political and popular reaction forced the company to abort this plan in 2001. In an even greater public relations disaster that year, one of PETROBRAS' giant rigs sank off of Brazil and 10 workers were killed. In 2001 PETROBRAS announced that it was going to spend as much as $3 billion to buy an oil company in order to increase its production in the Gulf of Mexico.

In 2002 the company expressed an interest in buying Argentina's major oil company (YPF) from Spanish/Argentine energy giant Repsol YPF. That year PETROBRAS bought control (59%) of Argentine energy company Perez Companc in a deal valued at $1 billion. PETROBRAS also reported its first oil find in Argentina in 2002.

EXECUTIVES

Chairman: Dilma Vana Rousseff
CEO: José Eduardo de Barros Dutra, age 46
Director Finance and Investor Relations: José Sérgio Gabrielli de Azevedo
Director Exploration and Production: Guilherme de Oliveira Estrella
Director Gas and Energy: Ildo L. Sauer
Director International: Nestor C. Cervero
Director Services: Renato de Souza Duque
Director Supply: Rogério A. Manso da Costa Reis
Accounting: Marcos A. Silva Menezes
Corporate Strategy: Ceslo F. Lucchesi
Corporate Exploration and Production: Carlos A. Pereira de Oliveira
Corporate Finance and Treasury: Almir Guilherme Barbassa
Financial Planning and Risk Management: Gustavo Tardin
Internal Audit: Gerson Luiz Gonçalves
Logistics and Planning: Carlos A. Martins de Souza
Management Systems Development: Afonso C. Granato Lopes
Materials: João C. Soares Nunes
Petrochemicals: Carlos A. de Meira Fontes
Refining: Eider Castro de Andrade Prudente de Aquino
Secretary General: Euler Pinto Coelho
President Petrobras Distribuidora: Luiz Rodolfo Landim Machado
HR: Heitor Cordero Chagas de Oliveira
Legal Affairs: Milton Antonio de Almeida Mala
Auditors: PricewaterhouseCoopers

LOCATIONS

HQ: PETRÓLEO BRASILEIRO S.A. — PETROBRAS
Avenida República do Chile 65, sala 401 E,
20031-912 Rio de Janeiro, Brazil
Phone: +55-21-2534-1510   **Fax:** +55-21-2534-6055
US HQ: 750 Lexington Ave., 43rd Fl.,
New York, NY 10022
US Phone: 212-829-1517   **US Fax:** 212-832-5300
Web: www.petrobras.com.br

PETRÓLEO BRASILEIRO S.A. — PETROBRAS explores for oil and gas in Brazil, as well as in Angola, Argentina, Bolivia, Colombia, Cuba, Ecuador, Equatorial Guinea, Kazakhstan, Nigeria, Peru, Trinidad and Tobago, the UK, and the US.

PRODUCTS/OPERATIONS

2002 Sales

	% of total
Refining & marketing	48
Distribution	38
Exploration & production	10
Gas & energy	4
Total	**100**

Selected Subsidiaries

Petrobras Distribuidora SA (BR; distribution and marketing of petroleum products, fuel alcohol, and natural gas)
Petrobras Gás SA (Gaspetro, management of the Brazil-Bolivia pipeline and other natural gas assets)
Petrobras Internacional SA (Braspetro; overseas exploration and production, marketing, and services)
Petrobras Química SA (Petroquisa, petrochemicals)
Petrobras Transporte SA (Transpetro, oil and gas transportation and storage)

COMPETITORS

Ashland	Lyondell Chemical
BHP Billiton Ltd	Marathon Oil
BP	Norsk Hydro
ChevronTexaco	Occidental Petroleum
Devon Energy	PDVSA
Eni	PEMEX
Exxon Mobil	Royal Dutch/Shell Group
Imperial Oil	Sunoco
Kerr-McGee	TOTAL
Koch	Unocal

HISTORICAL FINANCIALS

Company Type: Public

Income Statement

FYE: December 31

	REVENUE ($ mil.)	NET INCOME ($ mil.)	NET PROFIT MARGIN	EMPLOYEES
12/02	22,612	2,311	10.2%	49,049
12/01	24,549	3,491	14.2%	38,483
12/00	26,955	5,342	19.8%	38,908
12/99	16,358	727	4.4%	35,891
12/98	14,914	1,150	7.7%	38,225
12/97	17,425	1,353	7.8%	41,200
12/96	17,483	644	3.7%	43,468
12/95	15,178	580	3.8%	46,226
12/94	19,931	1,645	8.3%	50,295
12/93	20,244	687	3.4%	56,900
Annual Growth	**1.2%**	**14.4%**	**—**	**(1.6%)**

2002 Year-End Financials

Debt ratio: 136.5%
Return on equity: 20.5%
Cash ($ mil.): 3,301
Current ratio: 1.47
Long-term debt ($ mil.): 12,694
No. of shares (mil.): 1,086
Dividends
  Yield: 0.0%
  Payout: —
Market value ($ mil.): 16,226

Stock History   NYSE: PBR

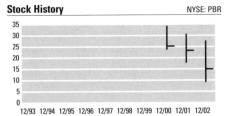

12/93 12/94 12/95 12/96 12/97 12/98 12/99 12/00 12/01 12/02

	STOCK PRICE ($) FY Close	P/E High/Low		PER SHARE ($) Earnings	Dividends	Book Value
12/02	14.94	13	4	2.13	0.00	8.56
12/01	23.30	10	6	3.21	0.00	12.20
12/00	25.25	7	5	4.92	0.00	23.19
Annual Growth	**(23.1%)**	**—**	**—**	**(34.2%)**	**—**	**(39.2%)**

Petróleos de Venezuela S.A.

American motorists rely on Petróleos de Venezuela S.A. (PDVSA), one of the top exporters of oil to the US. The state-owned company has proved reserves of 77.9 billion barrels of oil — the most outside the Middle East — and 147.6 trillion cu. ft. of natural gas. PDVSA's exploration and production take place in Venezuela, but the company also has refining and marketing operations in the Caribbean, Europe, and the US. Subsidiary CITGO Petroleum supplies gasoline to 13,540 US retail outlets. PDVSA also makes Orimulsion, a coal alternative made from bitumen. Management protests of government policies in 2002 prompted disruption of production, two major strikes, and the temporary ouster of the country's president.

Outside of Venezuela, PDVSA refines, markets, and transports petroleum products in Belgium, Germany, Sweden, the Caribbean, the UK, and the US.

On the domestic front, PDVSA's BITOR subsidiary mines Venezuela's extensive bitumen reserves, turning the tarlike ooze into Orimulsion, a patented fuel marketed as an alternative to coal for electric generating plants.

In a move that requires foreign investment, PDVSA is expanding its production of petrochemicals, gas, and Orimulsion. However, investors will step carefully: Venezuelan President Hugo Chavez's tightening state control over the oil company's operations has led to management unrest and major political instability.

In 2003 the government threatened to split the company in two as a way to break the striking managers' hold on the company, and to restore full production. The strike led to a third of the workforce being laid off by February 2003.

HISTORY

Invited by dictator Juan Vicente Gomez, Royal Dutch/Shell looked for oil in Venezuela just before WWI. After the war US companies plunged in. Standard Oil of Indiana began Creole Petroleum in 1920 to explore in Venezuela, selling the company in 1928 to Standard of New Jersey.

When the Venezuelan government threatened to nationalize its oil industry in 1938, the foreign oil companies agreed to pay more taxes and royalties. But in 1945 Venezuela set a pattern for the rest of the world's oil-rich nations when it decreed it was a 50% partner in all oil operations. Venezuela was pivotal to OPEC's creation in 1960, and the next year the government created the Venezuelan Petroleum Corporation (CVP). CVP was granted the nation's unassigned petroleum reserves. By the early 1970s CVP produced about 2% of the nation's oil.

President Carlos Andres Perez nationalized oil holdings in 1975, paying only $1 billion for foreign-owned oil assets and creating Petróleos de Venezuela S.A. (PDVSA) to hold the properties. Venezuela formed stand-alone PDVSA subsidiaries: Shell operations became Maraven, Creole became Lagoven, and smaller companies combined into Corpoven. (All units were merged into PDVSA in 1998.)

Free of debt and buoyed by high crude prices in the late 1970s and early 1980s, PDVSA formed ventures (Ruhr Oel) with Germany's Veba Oel and Sweden's Nynas Petroleum. In the US, PDVSA bought 50% of CITGO, the former refining and marketing arm of Cities Service Co., from Southland in 1986 (and the rest in 1990). PDVSA also bought a 50% stake in a Unocal refinery in 1989 to create joint venture UNO-VEN.

After the 1991 Gulf War, Venezuela increased its own production despite OPEC oil quotas. The next year PDVSA opened some marginal fields to foreign investment for the first time since the industry's 1975 nationalization.

Venezuelan President Rafael Caldera named Luis Giusti president of the company in 1994, and the next year Venezuela's oil industry was opened to foreign investment. In 1996 PDVSA began building a $1.5 billion plastics plant with Mobil (later Exxon Mobil). PDVSA and Unocal finally ended UNO-VEN the next year when UNO-VEN CEO David Tippeconnic took over as head of CITGO.

The rush for Venezuelan oil rights was on by 1997; one week's worth of bidding brought in $2 billion from top international oil companies. Meanwhile, PDVSA searched for facilities to refine the heavy crude, striking deals with Phillips Petroleum (later renamed ConocoPhillips) in 1997 and Amerada Hess in 1998.

PDVSA's profits took a hit in 1998 when oil prices fell to record lows. Concerns arose about the firm's direction that year after populist Hugo Chavez was elected as Venezuela's president. Chavez and his allies sought to retain state control over PDVSA's resources and to keep a closer check on foreign partners.

In 1999 PDVSA, suffering from a devastated domestic economy, decided to expand its downstream operations globally. As part of that plan, it formed a Houston-based crude and products marketing firm, PDVSA Trading.

Tightening his control of the company, in 2000 Chavez appointed army generals to head up both PDVSA (Gen. Guaicaipuro Lameda) and CITGO (Gen. Oswaldo Contreras Maza). The appointments followed a management shake-up and an oil workers' strike.

In 2001 PDVSA with other oil partners announced that it had secured $1.1 billion in funding to develop an extra-heavy crude production project in the Hamaca region of the Orinoco basin.

Tightening his control on the company, in 2002 Chavez replaced Lameda as PDVSA's top executive with banker Gaston Parra. However,

growing management discontent with Chavez's board of directors led to a major strike and a serious disruption of the company's oil production.

The strike spread into other industries and led to violence and a revolt by some military leaders. Pedro Carmona, president of Venezuela's top business association, was appointed to lead a civilian junta in the run-up to national elections. But Chavez refused to step down, and within a few days loyalist troops brought him back to power. In a move to make peace with PDVSA managers, Chavez removed Parra and other controversial appointees from the company's board. He then announced that he would appoint Alí Rodríguez, the former oil minister and head of OPEC, to take over the reins at PDVSA. Venezuela's energy minister (Alvaro Silva Calderon) was appointed to complete Rodríguez's term as OPEC's top executive.

However, continued political turmoil led to another major strike in 2002.

EXECUTIVES

President and CEO: Alí Rodríguez Araque
Executive Director, Exploration, Production, and Upgrade: Luis Vielma Lobo
Executive Director Finance and CFO: Luis Dávila, age 47
Deputy Director, Production: Marco Rossi
Deputy Director, Production: Fuenmayor Iván
Chairman, CITGO Petroleum: Aires Barreto
Managing Director, Production: Carlos Machado
Managing Director, Exploration: Richard Aymard
Manager, Corporate Affairs: Alejandro Almaral
CEO Bitor: Alfredo Riera
CEO, PDVSA Gas: Fernando Puig
CEO, Interven: Karl Mazeika
CEO, Intevep: César Jiménez
Managing Director PDV UK: Vicenzo Paglione
Managing Director, Bitor: Mauricio Di Girolamo
General Manager, Production (Western Division): Luis Matheus
Director, Pequiven: Armando Izquierdo
Auditors: KPMG Alcaraz Cabrera Vázquez

LOCATIONS

HQ: Edificio Petroleos de Venezuela, Avenida Libertador, La Campiña, Apdo. 169, Caracas 1010-A, Venezuela
Phone: +58-2-708-4111   **Fax:** +58-2-708-4661
US HQ: One Warren Place, 6100 S. Yale Ave., Tulsa, OK 74136
US Phone: 918-495-4000   **US Fax:** 918-495-4511
Web: www.pdvsa.com.ve

Petróleos de Venezuela has exploration and production operations in Venezuela and conducts refining and marketing there and in Belgium, Germany, Sweden, the Caribbean, the UK, and the US.

PRODUCTS/OPERATIONS

Selected Subsidiaries and Affiliates

PDVSA Exploration and Production
Bitumenes Orinoco, SA (BITOR, bitumen and Orimulsion) Carbozulia, SA (coal)
CVP
PDVSA Exploration
PDVSA Orinoco Belt
PDVSA Production

PDVSA Manufacturing and Marketing
Deltaven
Intevep, SA (research and support)
PDV Marina
PDVSA Gas
PDVSA Refining

Other
CIED
CITGO Petroleum Corp. (refining, marketing, and petrochemicals; US)
Palmaven, SA (agricultural assistance and conservation projects)
PDVSA Services
PDVSA Trading (crude oil and products marketing; US)
Pequiven, SA (petrochemicals)
SOFIP

COMPETITORS

BHP Billiton Ltd	Marathon Oil
BP	NIOC
ChevronTexaco	Norsk Hydro
ConocoPhillips	Occidental Petroleum
Devon Energy	PETROBRAS
Eni	PEMEX
Exxon Mobil	Royal Dutch/Shell Group
Imperial Oil	Saudi Aramco
Kerr-McGee	Sunoco
Koch	TOTAL
Lyondell Chemical	

HISTORICAL FINANCIALS

Company Type: Government-owned

Income Statement

FYE: December 31

	REVENUE ($ mil.)	NET INCOME ($ mil.)	NET PROFIT MARGIN	EMPLOYEES
12/02	42,580	2,590	6.1%	45,683
12/01	46,250	3,993	8.6%	46,425
12/00	53,680	7,216	13.4%	45,520
12/99	32,648	2,818	8.6%	50,000
12/98	25,526	663	2.6%	50,821
12/97	34,801	4,505	12.9%	51,677
12/96	33,855	4,382	12.9%	53,200
12/95	26,041	3,614	13.9%	53,500
12/94	22,157	2,074	9.4%	53,600
12/93	21,275	1,089	5.1%	52,218
Annual Growth	**8.0%**	**10.1%**	**—**	**(1.5%)**

2002 Year-End Financials

Debt ratio: 17.4%
Return on equity: 7.0%
Cash ($ mil.): 3,475

Current ratio: 1.48
Long-term debt ($ mil.): 6,494

Net Income History

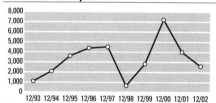

Petróleos Mexicanos

Petróleos Mexicanos (PEMEX) not only fuels Mexico's automobile engines, the state-owned oil company also fuels the nation's economy, accounting for some one-third of the Mexican government's revenues and 7% of its export earnings. The integrated company's operations, spread throughout Mexico, range from exploration and production to refining and petrochemicals. PEMEX's P.M.I. Comercio Internacional subsidiary manages the company's trading operations outside the country. The company has proved reserves of 17.2 billion barrels of oil and 15 trillion cu. ft. of natural gas.

PEMEX's refining operations convert crude oil into gasoline, jet fuel, diesel, fuel oil, asphalts and lubricants. In 2002 PEMEX-Refining produced 1.28 million barrels per day of refined products, up from 1.27 million barrels per day in 2001. PEMEX's Gas and Basic Petrochemicals unit processes natural gas and natural gas liquids, and ships and sells natural gas and liquefied petroleum gas throughout Mexico. It also produces several basic petrochemical feedstocks.

Long recognized as the tangible expression of Mexican nationalism, PEMEX has faced popular opposition in its bid to follow other Latin American state oil companies and privatize some operations. PEMEX is, however, working to become more responsive to market conditions and expand its international scope.

HISTORY

Histories of precolonial Mexico recount the nation's first oil business: Natives along the Tampico coast gathered asphalt from naturally occurring deposits and traded with the Aztecs.

As the 20th century began, Americans Edward Doheny and Charles Canfield struck oil near Tampico. Their success was eclipsed in 1910 by a nearby well drilled by British engineer Weetman Pearson, leader of the firm that became Pearson PLC.

President Porfirio Díaz had welcomed foreign ownership of Mexican resources, but revolution ousted Díaz, and the 1917 Constitution proclaimed that natural resources belonged to the nation. Without enforcing legislation, however, foreign oil companies continued business as usual until a 1925 act limited their concessions. During a bitter labor dispute in 1938, President Lázaro Cárdenas expropriated foreign oil holdings — the first nationalization of oil holdings by a non-Communist state. Subsequent legislation created Petróleos Mexicanos (PEMEX).

Without foreign capital and expertise, the new state-owned company struggled, and Mexico had to import petroleum in the early 1970s. But for many Mexicans, PEMEX remained a symbol of national identity and economic independence. That faith was rewarded in 1972 when a major oil discovery made PEMEX one of the world's top oil producers again. Ample domestic oil supplies and high world prices during the Iranian upheaval in the late 1970s fueled a boom and a government borrowing spree in Mexico. Between 1982 and 1985 PEMEX contributed more than 50% of government revenues.

When oil prices collapsed in 1985, Mexico cut investment in exploration, and production dropped. To decrease its reliance on oil, Mexico began lowering trade barriers and encouraging manufacturing, even allowing some foreign ownership of petrochemical processing.

Elected in 1988, President Carlos Salinas de Gortari began to reform PEMEX. Labor's grip on the company was loosened in 1989 when a union leader was arrested and jailed after a gun battle. In 1992, after a PEMEX pipeline explosion killed more than 200 people in Guadalajara, four of its executives and several local officials were sent to prison, amid public cries for company reform.

President Ernesto Zedillo appointed Adrián Lajous Vargas head of PEMEX in 1994. Under the professorial Lajous, PEMEX began to adopt modern business practices (such as trimming its bloated payroll), look for more reserves, and improve its refining capability. Lajous tried to sell some petrochemical assets in 1995, but had to modify the scheme the next year after massive public protests by the country's nationalists. Still, PEMEX began selling off natural gas production, distribution, and storage networks to private companies.

Though oil prices were dropping, in 1998 Mexico finally upped PEMEX's investment budget and PEMEX dramatically increased exploration and production. In spite of 2000's looming national election (elections traditionally had caused bureaucrats to keep a low profile to protect their jobs), Lajous again fanned the flames of the opposition: In 1998 he signed a major deal to sell Mexican crude to Exxon's Texas refinery, and in 1999 a four-year-old PEMEX/Shell joint venture announced it would expand its US refinery.

In 1999 Lajous resigned and was replaced by Rogelio Montemayor, a former governor. The next year Vicente Fox was elected as Mexico's new president, the country's first non-Institutional Revolutionary Party (PRI) leader in seven decades. He announced plans to replace PEMEX's politician-staffed board with professionals — Montemayor was among the casualties — and modernize the company, but he ruled out privatizing PEMEX as politically unfeasible.

Fox subsequently appointed Raúl Muñoz, formerly with Dupont Mexico, to lead PEMEX.

EXECUTIVES

Chairman: Ernest M. Rebolledo
General Director: Raúl Muñoz Leos
Director Corporate Administration:
Julio Camelo Martínez
Director Corporate Finance: José Juán Suárez Coppel
Director Corporate Industrial Safety Systems:
Rafael Fernández de la Garza
Director Corporate Operations:
José A. Ceballos Soberanis
Director Corporate Strategic Planning:
Roberto Osegueda Villaseñor
Director Corporate Administration:
Carlos De la Garza Mijares
General Counsel: José César Nava Vázquez
Auditors: PricewaterhouseCoopers

LOCATIONS

HQ: Avenida Marina Nacional 329, Colonia Huasteca, 11311 México, D.F., Mexico
Phone: +52-55-5722-2500   **Fax:** +52-55-5531-6321
Web: www.pemex.com

PRODUCTS/OPERATIONS

2002 Sales

	% of total
Refining	53
Exploration & production	27
Gas & basic petrochemicals	13
Petrochemicals	2
Other (subsidiaries)	5
Total	**100**

Major Subsidiaries

PEMEX Exploración y Producción (petroleum and natural gas exploration and production)
PEMEX Gas y Petroquímica Básica (natural gas, liquids from natural gas, and ethane processing)
PEMEX Petroquímica (petrochemical production)
PEMEX Refinación (refining and marketing)
P.M.I. Comercio Internacional (international trading)

COMPETITORS

Ashland	Marathon Oil
BHP Billiton Ltd	Norsk Hydro
BP	Occidental Petroleum
ChevronTexaco	PETROBRAS
Devon Energy	PDVSA
Eni	Royal Dutch/Shell Group
Exxon Mobil	Sunoco
Imperial Oil	TOTAL
Koch	Unocal

HISTORICAL FINANCIALS

Company Type: Government-owned

Income Statement

FYE: December 31

	REVENUE ($ mil.)	NET INCOME ($ mil.)	NET PROFIT MARGIN	EMPLOYEES
12/02	45,944	(2,910)	—	137,134
12/01	46,249	(3,519)	—	134,852
12/00	49,592	(2,084)	—	135,091
12/99	36,361	(1,921)	—	132,496
12/98	20,891	(1,108)	—	131,433
12/97	28,566	1,003	3.5%	121,220
12/96	29,403	2,091	7.1%	120,945
12/95	20,584	1,283	6.2%	119,928
12/94	17,870	625	3.5%	119,928
12/93	26,686	959	3.6%	106,951
Annual Growth	**6.2%**	**—**	**—**	**2.8%**

Net Income History

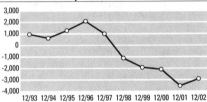

Peugeot Citroën

PSA Peugeot Citroën has regained its space under L'Arc de Triomphe, besting rival Renault to claim the top spot in the battle for auto sales in France. The best-selling auto brand in its home country, Peugeot is #2 behind Volkswagen in passenger car and commercial vehicle sales in Europe. Peugeot makes cars and light commercial vehicles under the Peugeot and Citroën brands. It also offers parts (Faurecia), transportation and logistics (Gefco), and financial services (Banque PSA Finance) for dealers and customers. Other products include motorbikes, scooters, and light-armored vehicles. The Peugeot family controls nearly 42% of the voting stock.

In an era of automotive industry consolidation, Peugeot prefers partnerships over mergers. To compete and stay solo, the company focuses on efficiently rolling out new models and technologies and keeping down expenses through alliances with low-cost car component makers. Peugeot, which has agreed to a joint venture with Toyota to build small cars in Europe, is also trying to broaden its markets. Europe accounts for 90% of sales.

HISTORY

In 1810 brothers Frédéric and Jean-Pierre Peugeot made a foundry out of the family textile mill in the Alsace region of France and invented the cold-roll process for producing spring steel. Bicycle production began in 1885 at the behest of avid cyclist Armand Peugeot, Jean-Pierre's grandson.

Armand turned to automobiles and built Peugeot's first car, a steam-powered three-wheeler, in 1889. A gas-fueled Peugeot tied for first place in the 1894 Paris-Rouen Trials, the earliest auto race on record. That year the budding carmaker built the first station wagon, followed in 1905 by the first compact, the 600-pound "Le Bébé."

Peugeot built factories in France, including one in Sochaux (1912) that remains the company's main plant. It made the first diesel passenger car in 1922. The 1929 introduction of the reliable 201 model was followed by innovations such as synchromesh gears in 1936. The company suffered heavy damage in WWII, but quickly bounced back and began expanding overseas after the war.

In 1954 CEO Roland Peugeot rebuffed a board proposal calling for global expansion that would place the company in competition with US automakers. By 1976 the French government had persuaded Peugeot to merge with Citroën.

André Citroën founded his company in 1915, and in 1919 it became the first in Europe to mass-produce cars. Citroën hit the skids during the Depression and in 1934 handed Michelin a large block of stock in lieu of payment for tires. Citroën never fully recovered, though by 1976 the company's line ranged from the 2CV minicar (discontinued 1990) to limousines.

In 1978 Peugeot bought Chrysler's aging European plants and withering nameplates, including Simca (France) and Rootes (UK). Peugeot changed the nameplates to Talbot but sales continued to slide. It lost nearly $1.2 billion from 1980 to 1984.

Jacques Calvet took over as CEO in 1984. He cut 30,000 jobs and spent heavily on modernization. Aided by the strong launch of the 205 superminicar, Peugeot returned to profitability in 1985, and by 1989 had halved its production break-even point. In the 1980s Peugeot inked production deals with Renault (industrial vehicles, motors, gearboxes) and Fiat (light trucks) and introduced a reasonably priced electric van in 1990.

Peugeot withdrew from the US in 1991 after five years of declining sales. A year later Renault and Peugeot developed electric cars and set up servicing centers throughout France. Citing an economic slump in 1993, Peugeot suffered its first loss ($239 million) since 1985. A French government incentive to replace cars over 10 years old boosted 1994 sales.

Peugeot and rival Renault together introduced a V6 engine in 1996. Jean-Martin Folz replaced Calvet as chairman and CEO in 1997; restructuring charges contributed to company losses that year. In 1998 the company began building Peugeots and Citroëns in the same plants and created its Faurecia unit when its ECIA subsidiary merged with car parts maker Bertrand Faure. In an effort to capitalize on the growing South American car market, the company purchased more than 80% of Argentina's Sevel, and built a plant in Brazil. In 1999 the company sold its flight systems supplier, SAMM, to TRW's Lucas Aerospace unit.

With demand for its cars falling steeply in South America due to the region's continuing economic crisis, Peugeot restructured its Brazil operations in 2000 and formed a new subsidiary, Citroën do Brasil.

In 2001 Peugeot announced that it was building a new engine plant in Brazil and agreed to produce a subcompact car for the European market with Toyota. The following year Peugeot formed an alliance with BMW to develop and build a line of small diesel engines for use in vehicles made by both companies.

EXECUTIVES

Chairman, Supervisory Board: Thierry Peugeot
Vice Chairman, Supervisory Board: Jean Boillot, age 77
Chairman, Managing Board and Executive Committee: Jean-Martin Folz, age 56
Member, Managing Board and Executive Committee; Director, Citroën Marque: Claude Satinet
Member, Managing Board and Executive Committee; Director, Peugeot Marque: Frédéric Saint-Geours
Member, Executive Committee; Director, Employee Relations and Human Resources: Jean-Luc Vergne
Member, Executive Committee; Director, Finance, Control, and Performance: Yann Delabrière
Member, Executive Committee; Director, Group Strategy and Products: Jean-Marc Nicolle
Member, Executive Committee; Director, Innovation and Quality: Robert Peugeot
Member, Executive Committee; Director, Manufacturing and Components: Roland Vardanega
Member, Executive Committee; Director, Platforms, Technical Affairs, and Purchasing: Gilles Michel
Director, Corporate Communications: Liliane Lacourt
Director, Executive Development: Jean-Louis Grégoire
Director, External Relations: Xavier Fels
Director, Legal Affairs: Jean-Claude Hanus
Auditors: PricewaterhouseCoopers

LOCATIONS

HQ: PSA Peugeot Citroën S.A.
  75, avenue de la Grande-Armée, 75116 Paris, France
Phone: +33-1-40-66-55-11   **Fax:** +33-1-40-66-54-14
US HQ: 150 Clove Rd., Little Falls, NJ 07424
US Phone: 973-812-4444   **US Fax:** 973-812-2280
Web: www.psa-peugeot-citroen.com

PSA Peugeot Citroën has manufacturing operations in Argentina, Brazil, Chile, Egypt, France, Iran, Italy, Kenya, Morocco, Nigeria, Poland, Portugal, Russia, Spain, Turkey, the UK, and Uruguay.

2002 Sales

	$ mil.	% of total
Europe		
Western Europe	48,931	86
Other countries	2,345	4
Latin America	1,344	2
Other regions	4,434	8
Total	**57,054**	**100**

PRODUCTS/OPERATIONS

2002 Sales

	$ mil.	% of total
Automobile	47,397	76
Automotive equipment	10,640	17
Transportation & logistics	2,853	5
Other	1,082	2
Adjustments	(4,918)	—
Total	**57,054**	**100**

Selected Subsidiaries

Automobiles Citroën
Automobiles Peugeot
Banque PSA Finance
Faurecia (72%, automotive components)
Gefco (transportation services)

COMPETITORS

BMW	Mazda
Bridgestone	Nissan
Caterpillar	Renault
DaimlerChrysler	Renco
Fiat	Saab Automobile
Ford	Suzuki Motor
General Motors	Toyota
Honda	Volkswagen
Isuzu	Yamaha
Kia Motors	

HISTORICAL FINANCIALS

Company Type: Public

Income Statement

FYE: December 31

	REVENUE ($ mil.)	NET INCOME ($ mil.)	NET PROFIT MARGIN	EMPLOYEES
12/02	57,054	1,771	3.1%	198,600
12/01	45,763	1,498	3.3%	192,500
12/00	41,601	1,235	3.0%	172,400
12/99	38,072	779	2.0%	165,800
12/98	39,394	565	1.4%	156,500
12/97	31,137	(461)	—	140,200
12/96	32,997	140	0.4%	139,100
12/95	33,459	347	1.0%	139,900
12/94	31,140	581	1.9%	139,800
12/93	24,562	(239)	—	143,900
Annual Growth	**9.8%**	**—**	**—**	**3.6%**

2002 Year-End Financials

Debt ratio: 95.7%   Current ratio: 1.30
Return on equity: 17.2%   Long-term debt ($ mil.): 11,023
Cash ($ mil.): 9,578

Net Income History

OTC: PEUGY

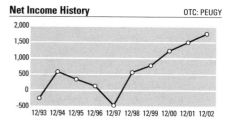

Philips Electronics

Koninklijke ("Royal") Philips Electronics, the world's third-largest consumer electronics maker, wants consumers to change the channel when it comes to #1 Sony and #2 Matsushita. Philips makes TVs, VCRs, CD and DVD players, phones, pagers, and other electronic gadgets. Its brands include Marantz, Norelco, and Magnavox, although the company plans to put more emphasis on its Philips brand. The company also makes lightbulbs (#1 worldwide), electric shavers (#1), picture tubes, small appliances, components, medical systems, PC monitors, and semiconductors. Philips has been dumping noncore businesses, such as its stake in music giant PolyGram, and acquiring and forming joint ventures in its core sectors.

Philips' medical systems unit (with its Marconi acquisition) is now the world's second largest.

Philips owns about 19% of Taiwan Semiconductor Manufacturing. In the last decade Philips has eliminated jobs, shut down plants, and sold off struggling business units to maintain its competitive edge. In January 2003 the company announced its intention to sell its Business Communications Group (voice communication solutions) to Gores Technology Group.

HISTORY

Gerard Philips (later joined by brother Anton) founded Philips & Co. in the Dutch city of Eindhoven in 1891. Surviving an industry shakeout, Philips prospered as a result of Gerard's engineering and Anton's foreign sales efforts. The company had become Europe's #3 light bulb maker by 1900. It adopted the name Philips Gloeilampenfabrieken (light bulb factory) in 1912.

The Netherlands' neutrality during WWI allowed Philips to expand and integrate into glass manufacturing (1915) and X-ray and radio tubes (1918). The company set up its first foreign sales office in Belgium in 1919; it started building plants abroad in the 1930s to avoid trade barriers and tariffs.

During WWII Philips created US and British trusts to hold majority interests in North American Philips (NAP) and in Philips' British operations. Following the war, the company established hundreds of subsidiaries worldwide. It repurchased its British businesses in 1955; NAP operated independently until it was reacquired in 1987.

The company started marketing televisions and appliances in the 1950s. Philips introduced audiocassette, VCR, and laser disc technology in the 1960s but had limited success with computers and office equipment. Despite its development of new technologies, in the 1970s Philips was unable to maintain market share against an onslaught of inexpensive goods from Japan. Meanwhile, NAP acquired Magnavox (consumer electronics, US) in 1974. NAP also purchased GTE Television in 1981 and Westinghouse's lighting business in 1983. In 1986 it provided $60 million in seed money to start Taiwan Semiconductor Manufacturing with the Taiwanese government.

Philips' successful PolyGram unit (formed in 1972) went public in 1989 and bought record companies Island (UK) that year and A&M (US) the next. In 1991 the company changed its name to Koninklijke ("Royal") Philips Electronics.

Ill-timed product introductions contributed to huge losses in the early 1990s. Philips cut some 60,000 jobs and sold money-losing businesses, including its computer business. Cor Boonstra, a former Sara Lee executive, was named chairman and president in 1996. The company sold its cellular communications business in 1996 to AT&T and merged its systems integration unit with BSO/Origin to form Origin B.V.

Continuing to focus on core businesses, it sold its 75% stake in PolyGram to Seagram and bought US-based medical instruments maker ATL Ultrasound in 1998. Also that year, Philips sold its optoelectronics unit to Uniphase Corp.

The company formed an alliance with Sun Microsystems and Sony in 1999 to develop appliances that use the Internet. Philips then launched a hostile takeover of microchip maker VLSI Technology and, after negotiations, bought VLSI for nearly $1 billion. It also bought a 50% stake in flat-panel display maker LG LCD, a subsidiary of LG Group, for $1.6 billion; it was renamed LG.Philips LCD Co.

In 2000 the company formed TriMedia Technologies with Sony to create embedded processor core designs and software. Also that year, Philips divested its 24% stake ($3.8 billion) in semiconductor equipment maker ASML Holding. In late 2000 Philips bought 60% of top medical transcription service MedQuist, and agreed to buy Adac Laboratories (nuclear imaging technology) for $426 million.

In April 2001, amid a large decline in profits, Philips announced plans to trim its semiconductor spending by up to 50%. Also that month Boonstra retired and COO Gerard Kleisterlee became chairman and president. In August 2001 Philips completed its acquisition of the Healthcare Solutions Group of Agilent Technologies for $1.7 billion, and in October the firm acquired Marconi Medical Systems, a distributor of medical imaging systems.

Since 2001, Philips has cut more than 35,000 jobs; the reductions are the result of support staff job eliminations and the sale of non-core businesses (Communication, Security, and Imaging unit to Robert Bosch GmbH; contract manufacturing services to Jabil Circuit; health care products group to Platinum Equity Holdings). The company also dissolved its components division (maker of screens for mobile phones and optical storage products) and transferred Mexican production of computer monitors to China.

In January 2003 Fidelio Acquisition Company (an investor firm led by Philips, along with Sony Corporation of America) acquired InterTrust Technologies, a manufacturer of digital copy-protection software, for $450 million.

EXECUTIVES

Chairman, Management Board, President, and CEO: Gerard J. Kleisterlee, age 56
Vice Chairman, Management Board, EVP, and CFO: Jan H. M. Hommen, age 60
EVP and CTO: Ad Huijser, age 57
EVP; CEO, Philips Consumer Electronics: Gottfried Dutiné
EVP: Arthur P. M. van der Poel, age 54
SVP and Chief Marketing Officer: Andrea Ragnetti, age 43
SVP and Chief Legal Officer: Arie Westerlaken, age 57
SVP Corporate Strategy and Regions and Countries: Jan P. Oosterveld, age 59
SVP Human Resources Management: Tjerk Hooghiemstra, age 47
SVP; CEO, Domestic Appliances and Personal Care: Ad Veenhof, age 58
SVP; CEO, Philips Medical Systems: Jouko Karvinen
SVP; CEO, Semiconductors: Scott McGregor, age 47
President and CEO, Philips Lighting: Theo van Deursen, age 57
President and CEO, Philips Lighting North America: Erik Bouts
CEO, Philips Consumer Electronics Business Groups: Frans van Houten
CEO, Philips Consumer Electronics Global Sales and Services: Rudy Provoost
CEO, Philips Domestic Appliances and Personal Care: Johan van Splunter
CIO: Daniel Hartert
Head of Media Relations: Jeremy Cohen
Auditors: KPMG Accountants N.V.

LOCATIONS

HQ: Koninklijke Philips Electronics N.V.
Breitner Center, Amstelplein 2, 1096 BC
Amsterdam, The Netherlands
Phone: +31-20-59-77-777   **Fax:** +31-20-59-77-070
US HQ: 1251 Avenue of The Americas,
New York, NY 10020-1104
US Phone: 212-536-0500   **US Fax:** 212-536-0827
Web: www.philips.com

Koninklijke Philips Electronics has operations in more than 60 countries.

2002 Sales

	$ mil.	% of total
US	9,883	30
China	2,636	8
Germany	2,450	7
France	1,988	6
Netherlands	1,583	5
UK	1,579	4
Other countries	13,302	40
Total	**33,421**	**100**

PRODUCTS/OPERATIONS

2002 Sales

	$ mil.	% of total
Consumer electronics	10,156	29
Medical systems	7,200	21
Lighting	5,118	15
Semiconductors	4,845	14
Components	2,573	7
DAP	2,409	7
Other	2,520	7
Adjustments	(1,400)	—
Total	**33,421**	**100**

Selected Products

Consumer Electronics
Audio systems (CD-recordable/rewritable)
Business communication systems
DVD players
Fax machines
LCD monitors
LCD projectors
Mobile phones
PC cameras
Phones
Portable audio systems
Remote controls
Security systems
Set-top boxes
Speakers
Speech processing systems
Televisions
TV/VCR combos
VCRs

Medical Systems
Computed Tomography
Imaging IT
Magnetic Resonance
Nuclear Medicine
Ultrasound
X-ray equipment (radiography, universal R/F, cardiovascular, surgery)

Lighting
Automotive
Batteries
Lamps
Lighting electronics
Luminaries

Semiconductors
Consumer systems
Discrete semiconductors
MultiMarket products
Telecom terminals

Components
Display
Large display systems
Mobile display systems
Optical storage

Domestic Appliances & Personal Care Products

Beard trimmers	Hair dryers
Blenders	Kettles
Coffee makers	Shavers
Depilators	Steam irons
Electric toothbrushes	Thermometers
Food processors	Toasters
Hair clippers	Vacuums

COMPETITORS

AMD
Alcatel
Apple Computer
Bose
Canon
Eastman Kodak
Ericsson
Fuji Photo
Fujitsu
GE
Gillette
Harman International
Hitachi
IDT International
Infineon Technologies
Intel
Kyocera
LG Electronics
LSI Industries
Marconi
Matsushita
Mitsubishi Electric
Motorola
NEC
Nokia
Oki Electric
OSRAM
Pioneer
Rockwell Automation
Samsung
SANYO
Sharp
Siemens
Siemens
Solectron
Sony
STMicroelectronics
Texas Instruments
THOMSON
Toshiba

HISTORICAL FINANCIALS

Company Type: Public

Income Statement

FYE: December 31

	REVENUE ($ mil.)	NET INCOME ($ mil.)	NET PROFIT MARGIN	EMPLOYEES
12/02	33,421	(3,367)	—	170,087
12/01	28,824	(2,321)	—	188,643
12/00	35,658	9,043	25.4%	219,429
12/99	31,748	1,816	5.7%	226,874
12/98	35,521	7,060	19.9%	233,686
12/97	37,737	2,829	7.5%	264,685
12/96	39,725	(339)	—	272,270
12/95	40,115	1,654	4.1%	263,554
12/94	35,129	1,224	3.5%	253,000
12/93	30,283	1,012	3.3%	252,214
Annual Growth	1.1%	—	—	(4.3%)

2002 Year-End Financials

Debt ratio: 46.6%
Return on equity: —
Cash ($ mil.): 1,951
Current ratio: 1.21
Long-term debt ($ mil.): 6,819

No. of shares (mil.): 1,276
Dividends
  Yield: 1.8%
  Payout: —
Market value ($ mil.): 22,559

Stock History

NYSE: PHG

	STOCK PRICE ($) FY Close	P/E High/Low		PER SHARE ($) Earnings	Dividends	Book Value
12/02	17.68	—	—	(2.64)	0.31	11.46
12/01	29.11	—	—	(1.82)	0.32	12.91
12/00	36.25	8	5	6.82	1.18	15.94
12/99	34.80	26	13	1.35	0.24	11.32
12/98	17.45	42	17	5.02	0.26	11.58
12/97	15.59	20	9	2.04	0.22	6.79
12/96	10.31	36	24	0.25	0.26	5.86
12/95	9.25	11	6	1.15	0.18	6.51
12/94	7.57	9	6	0.95	0.06	6.33
12/93	5.32	7	3	0.81	0.00	5.42
Annual Growth	14.3%	—	—	—	—	8.7%

Pinault-Printemps-Redoute

Pinault-Printemps-Redoute (PPR) might have its roots in timber, but its branches spread far and wide. The company sells to businesses and consumers through four divisions that operate worldwide: retail, including department stores (Printemps) and catalogs (Redcats); business-to-business operations, which distribute electrical equipment (its biggest-selling product line) and building materials; and its financial division operates France's #3 consumer credit group. PPR is also the world's third-largest luxury group via its 67% stake in Italian luxury goods company Gucci Group, and several perfume lines (including Yves Saint Laurent). Founder François Pinault's investment firm, Artémis, owns 57% of PPR.

PPR's retail division accounts for more than 40% of sales. It includes the world's #3 catalog merchant, Redcats, with distribution in the US and Europe. The division also operates three large retail chains: Conforama, France's #1 appliance retailer; Printemps, Paris' #1 department store; and Fnac books and music stores. The company's other major division distributes directly to businesses. It includes a 73% stake in Rexel (electrical equipment), Pinault Bois & Matériaux (lumber and building supplies), and Guilbert (office supplies and furniture).

PPR is transforming itself from a conglomerate to a focused retail group. To that end, the company is selling non-retail assets to shore up its balance sheet to fund its $4 billion offer for the rest of Gucci. (The two men credited with the turnaround at Gucci — Domenico De Sole, the CEO, and Tom Ford, its creative director — are leaving the company in April 2004, after failing to agree to a new contract with PPR.)

Office Depot has agreed to acquire Guilbert, and PPR is set to sell its timber wholesale business to the UK's Wolseley plc. PPR's financial division provides store credit cards and insurance, but PPR has agreed to sell this division off in parts (to Agricole and BNP Paribas).

Self-made billionaire and founder François Pinault has a cache of prestigious businesses, including auction house Christie's.

HISTORY

Sixteen-year-old François Pinault left school in 1952 to join the family timber business. He took over the firm when his father died in 1963; that year the company was renamed Pinault Group. Pinault diversified the company into wood importing and retailing, eventually building a flourishing enterprise. In 1973 Pinault began to show his talent for the art of the deal. Sensing the demand for timber was peaking, he sold 80% of the business, buying it back two years later at an 85% discount.

During the 1970s Pinault bought struggling timber businesses and turned them around. (He was helped, in part, by a policy of the French government that subsidized purchases of failing companies in order to preserve jobs.) Pinault purchased bankrupt wood panel manufacturer Isoroy in 1986 for a token fee. In 1987 he bought ailing paper company Chapelle Darblay, selling it three years later at a 40% profit. By 1988, when it filed to go public on the Paris exchange, Pinault Group was a vertically integrated timber manufacturing, trading, and distribution company.

Pinault began to diversify outside the timber industry in the 1990s. It acquired electrical equipment distributor CFAO (Compagnie Française de l'Afrique Occidentale) in 1990, the Conforama furniture chain in 1991, and Au Printemps (owner of Printemps stores and 54% of catalog company Redoute) in 1992. The firm then became the Pinault-Printemps Group. The purchase of Au Printemps left the company heavily in debt, and it sold some of its noncore assets during the early 1990s.

In 1993 the group reorganized into four divisions: retail, business-to-business, financial services, and international trade. That year Pinault-Printemps bought a majority stake in Groupelec and merged it with electrical equipment subsidiary CDME, forming Rexel. In 1994 the company completed its acquisition of Redoute. After renaming itself Pinault-Printemps-Redoute (PPR), it bought a majority stake in French book and music retailer Fnac (buying the rest in 1995). In 1995 Rexel head Serge Weinberg took over the company after CEO Pierre Blayau ran afoul of Pinault over strategy. PPR added West African pharmaceuticals distributor SCOA in 1996. While Rexel gobbled up 11 companies in Europe and the US that year, PPR launched a new chain of women's lingerie stores called Orcanta and started its own venture capital fund.

PPR acquired Becob, France's #3 building materials distributor, in 1997. Expanding globally, Redcats (Redoute's new name) launched the Vertbaudet (children's wear) and Cyrillus (sportswear) catalogs in the UK that year.

In 1998 PPR bought a majority stake in Guilbert, the European leader in office supplies and furniture, and a 44% stake in Brylane, the US's #4 mail-order company. PPR also opened a new store format in France called Made in Sport (sporting goods). In addition, it began offering phone cards through subsidiary Kertel.

PPR bought the remainder of Brylane in 1999 and also launched a new division to oversee the online efforts of its various businesses. Later that year, PPR sparked a string of legal battles between it and LVMH when it purchased 42% of luxury goods maker Gucci. (The move thwarted LVMH's efforts to take over Gucci by diluting LVMH's stake in the firm.) In early 2000 PPR bought France's largest computer retailer, Surcouf.

In March 2001 a Dutch court granted a request by LVMH and ordered an investigation into the legality of the alliance of PPR and Gucci. In a deal to end years of litigation, PPR purchased LVMH's stake in Gucci for $806.5 million in October 2001, increasing its ownership to 53.2%.

The company sold Yves Saint Laurent's haute couture division to French dressmaking company SLPB Prestige Services in March 2002. Guilbert's mail-order business was sold to US office supplies retailer Staples in October for $815 million.

EXECUTIVES

Chairman of the Management Board and CEO: Serge Weinberg, age 52
COO: Denis Olivennes, age 42
Corporate Secretary and CFO: Patrice Marteau, age 55
VP Auditing: Alessandro Reitelli
VP Corporate Affairs: Thomas Kamm, age 41
VP Corporate Communications: Vincent de La Vaissière, age 40
VP Corporate Development: Philippe Klocanas
VP Human Resources: François Potier, age 55
VP Strategy and Planning: Frédéric Obala
Chairman of the Management Board, Conforama: Per Kaufmann, age 47
Chairman of the Management Board, France Printemps: Laurence Danon
Chairman and CEO, CFAO: Alain Viry
Chairman and CEO, Credit and Financial Services Division: Alain van Groenendael, age 39
Chairman and CEO, Fnac: Jean Paul Giraud, age 57
Chairman and CEO, Gucci Group: Domenico De Sole, age 59
President and CEO, Pinault Bois & Materiaux: Patrick Bérard
Chairman and CEO, Redcats: Thierry Falque-Pierrotin, age 42
Chairman and CEO, Rexel: Jean-Charles Pauze, age 56
CEO, PPR Interactive: Jean-François Nebel, age 37
COO, Rexel: Yves Barraquand
Financial Communications: David Newhouse
Auditors: Deloitte Touche Tohmatsu; KPMG Audit

LOCATIONS

HQ: 18, place Henri-Bergson, 75381 Paris, France
Phone: +33-1-44-90-61-00   **Fax:** +33-1-44-90-62-25
Web: www.pprgroup.com

PRODUCTS/OPERATIONS

Operations

Business-to-Business
CFAO (distribution of automobiles, motorcycles, pharmaceuticals, and consumer goods in Africa and French territories)
Guilbert S.A. (office supplies and furniture, Belgium, France Germany, Italy, Spain, and the UK)
Pinault Bois & Matériaux (distribution of lumber and building supplies, France)
Rexel (73%; distribution of electrical equipment; Australia, China, Europe, New Zealand, South America, and the US)

Retail
Conforama (furniture and appliances; Croatia, France, Italy, Luxembourg, Portugal, Spain, and Switzerland)
Fnac (electronics, books, music; Belgium, Brazil, France, Italy, Monaco, Portugal, Spain, Switzerland, and Taiwan)
Printemps (department stores in France)
Redcats (catalogs, including Brylane, Daxon, Ellos, and Redoute)

Credit and Financial Services
Finaref (store cards, consumer credit, and family-based insurance)

Other Holdings
Gucci Group N.V. (67%, leather goods and apparel)

COMPETITORS

C&A
Carrefour
Casino Guichard
Consolidated Electrical
Galeries Lafayette
Graybar Electric
IKEA
Kingfisher
LVMH
Manutan
METRO AG
Otto Versand
Pier Import Europe
Virgin Group
Vivarte

HISTORICAL FINANCIALS

Company Type: Public

Income Statement

FYE: December 31

	REVENUE ($ mil.)	NET INCOME ($ mil.)	NET PROFIT MARGIN	EMPLOYEES
12/02	28,692	1,666	5.8%	113,453
12/01	24,624	667	2.7%	115,935
12/00	23,308	722	3.1%	110,862
12/99	19,042	630	3.3%	89,178
12/98	19,272	593	3.1%	81,073
12/97	14,866	476	3.2%	64,135
12/96	15,363	395	2.6%	57,241
12/95	15,848	309	1.9%	59,299
12/94	13,265	227	1.7%	60,843
12/93	10,691	86	0.8%	50,586
Annual Growth	**11.6%**	**38.9%**	**—**	**9.4%**

2002 Year-End Financials

Debt ratio: 113.5%   Current ratio: 1.25
Return on equity: 27.7%   Long-term debt ($ mil.): 7,908
Cash ($ mil.): 7,351

Net Income History

Euronext Paris: PP

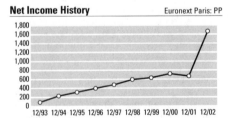

Pioneer Corporation

Pioneer takes you on a journey of sight and sound. A leading maker of consumer and commercial electronics, about 40% of its sales come from car electronics (stereos, speakers, navigation systems), which are sold to retailers and automobile manufacturers. Pioneer also makes video equipment (flat-screen TV monitors, DVD players, and DVD recorders) and audio products (stereo receivers, home-theater speaker systems, and surround-sound receivers). It also produces audiovisual software (music, movies, and games in DVD, DVD-ROM, CD, and CD-ROM formats). Pioneer has nearly 40 manufacturing facilities worldwide.

The company is placing more energy on newer products, especially in the DVD and plasma display arenas (areas expected to have long-term growth). Pioneer is also focusing efforts on its car navigation systems, a category which has grown to become a major revenue and profit source for the company. Pioneer has been streamlining its manufacturing operations and trimming its workforce; at the same time the company has expanded production in China, a growing, and therefore, attractive market for Pioneer product sales and manufacturing. The company is considering selling its DVD and video software operations in order to focus on its audiovisual equipment business.

The company — Pioneer Kabushiki Kaisha in Japanese — was the first to give us the laser disc (LD), car CD players, and car navigation devices that use a satellite-based global positioning system (GPS).

HISTORY

Nozomu Matsumoto, son of a Christian missionary, first heard high-fidelity speakers in 1932; nothing made in Japan compared in quality. In 1938 he founded Fukuin Shokai Denki Seisakusho (Gospel Electric Works) in Osaka to repair radios and speakers. It later began making these items. Matsumoto designed the company's trademark — a tuning fork overlaying the symbol for the ohm (a unit for measuring electrical resistance) — and chose the brand name Pioneer to reflect the company's spirit.

The firm introduced turntables and amplifiers in 1955 and hi-fi receivers in 1958. By the 1960s Pioneer Electronic was Japan's #1 audio equipment maker. It introduced the world's first stereo with speakers separate from the control unit in 1962 and the world's first car stereo in 1963. Subsidiaries opened in the US and Europe in 1966.

Convinced that laser disc (LD) technology was the wave of the future, Pioneer started work on a LD video player in 1972. Pioneer was listed on the NYSE four years later. It partnered with DiscoVision Associates (DVA, a partnership between IBM and Music Corporation of America) in 1977 to form Universal Pioneer Corporation (UPC). Home LD players appeared in the US in 1980 and in Japan in 1981. But consumers wanted machines that could record, not just play, and demand for LDs remained sluggish; Pioneer's competitors let it have the LD business to itself.

Matsumoto's eldest son, Seiya, became president in 1982. Two years later Pioneer introduced the world's first car CD system; it also created a

LD/CD player, perhaps hoping customers would react better to LD products if they were combined with other features. Pioneer branched into office automation, introducing the Write-Once Read-Many (WORM) optical memory disk in 1985. In 1989 it bought DVA, by then a leading optical-disk research firm with more than 1,400 patents. Also that year it formed Pioneer Trimble with US-based Trimble Navigation to develop a computerized car navigation system.

Pioneer sold its joint venture record company Warner-Pioneer to partner Warner (now Time Warner) in 1989, but it took another stab at the US entertainment business the next year when it bought 10% of theatrical filmmaker Carolco Pictures (*Basic Instinct*). But like many high-profile Japanese investments in the US, Carolco turned sour: It filed for Chapter 11 bankruptcy protection in 1995, leading Pioneer to write off its investment.

With sales not meeting expectations, in 1996 Pioneer replaced Seiya as president with his in-law Kaneo Ito (former head of Pioneer's Europe sales network); Seiya became chairman and his brother Kanya was made vice chairman. The company reentered the entertainment business with the 1996 launch of Pioneer Music Group. In 1997 Pioneer restructured itself into three separate operating units: Home Entertainment, Mobile Entertainment, and Business Systems; it added a Display Products unit the following year.

In 1999 the company opted for a simpler moniker, removing the word "electronic" from its name. Chairman Seiya died that year and was replaced by brother Kanya. With price wars and slow sales in its software business eroding profits, Pioneer announced in 1999 a three-year plan to cut more than 2,500 jobs. In 2000 Pioneer started making TV set-top boxes for digital cable. In 2001 Pioneer established two production subsidiaries in China to generate DVD pickups (the lens that converts the laser reflection into digital info), DVD-R/RW drives, and car electronics products.

EXECUTIVES

Chairman: Kanya Matsumoto, age 73
President: Kaneo Ito, age 67
EVP: Yoshimichi Inada, age 67
EVP: Katsuhiro Abe, age 67
Senior Managing Director; President, Pioneer Home Entertainment Company: Akira Niijima, age 59
Senior Managing Director: Takashi Kobayashi, age 63
Managing Director; EVP, Pioneer Home Entertainment Company: Tadahiro Yamaguchi, age 57
Managing Director; General Manager, Environmental Preservation Division: Satoshi Matsumoto, age 49
Director; General Manager, External Relations Division: Hiroshi Aiba, age 63
Director; President, Pioneer China Holding Company: Shinji Yasuda, age 58
Director; General Manager, Production, Management, and Coordination Division and Procurement Center: Koichi Shimizu, age 59
Senior Executive Officer; President, Pioneer North America: Kazunori Yamamoto, age 61
Senior Executive Officer: Shungo Minato, age 60
Senior Executive Officer; EVP, Pioneer Home Entertainment Company; General Manager, Display Business Division, Pioneer Home Entertainment Company: Masaru Saotome, age 59
Senior Executive Officer; President, Mobile Entertainment Company: Tamihiko Sudo, age 56
Senior Executive Officer; International Business Division; General Manager, Components Division: Hajime Ishizuka, age 56
Senior Executive Officer; General Manager, Research and Development Group and Corporate Research & Development Laboratories: Osamu Yamada, age 59
Senior Executive Officer, Business Systems Division: Kiyoshi Uchida

Executive Officer; General Manager, Personnel Division: Osamu Takada, age 55
Executive Officer; General Manager, Corporate Communications Division: Masao Kawabata, age 55
Auditors: Deloitte Touche Tohmatsu

LOCATIONS

HQ: 4-1, Meguro 1-chome, Meguro-ku, Tokyo 153-8654, Japan
Phone: +81-3-3495-6774   **Fax:** +81-3-3495-4301
US HQ: 2265 E. 220th St., Long Beach, CA 90810
US Phone: 310-952-2210   **US Fax:** 310-952-2199
Web: www.pioneer.co.jp

Pioneer has nearly 40 manufacturing facilities in Asia, Europe, and North America. Its products are sold around the world.

2003 Sales

	$ mil.	% of total
Japan	2,484.2	42
North America	1,633.4	27
Europe	1,106.4	19
Other regions	711.5	12
Total	**5,935.5**	**100**

PRODUCTS/OPERATIONS

2003 Sales

	$ mil.	% of total
Car Electronics	2,342.4	39
Home Electronics	1,906.2	32
Patent Licensing	104.8	2
Other	1,582.1	27
Total	**5,935.5**	**100**

Selected Products

Home Electronics Products
DVD players
DVD recorders
Equipment for cable-TV systems
Laser disc players
Plasma displays
Stereo components
Stereo systems

Car Electronics Products
Car audio products
Car navigation systems

Other Products
DVR-R/RW drives
DVD-ROM drives

COMPETITORS

Aiwa
Anam Electronics
Audiovox
Bang & Olufsen
Bose
Boston Acoustics
Digital Video
Emerson Radio
Fujitsu
Harman International
Kenwood
LG Electronics
Matsushita
Mitek Corp.
Philips Electronics
Polk Audio
Robert Bosch
Rockford
Samsung Electronics
SANYO
Scientific-Atlanta
Sony
THOMSON
Toshiba
Universal Electronics

HISTORICAL FINANCIALS

Company Type: Public

Income Statement

FYE: March 31

	REVENUE ($ mil.)	NET INCOME ($ mil.)	NET PROFIT MARGIN	EMPLOYEES
3/03	5,936	134	2.3%	34,656
3/02	5,029	61	1.2%	31,220
3/01	5,053	148	2.9%	28,871
3/00	5,627	123	2.2%	27,414
3/99	4,701	10	0.2%	23,647
3/98	4,241	47	1.1%	20,470
3/97	4,456	20	0.5%	19,962
3/96	4,779	(94)	—	19,378
3/95	5,728	(13)	—	18,341
3/94	4,973	64	1.3%	18,341
Annual Growth	**2.0%**	**8.5%**	**—**	**7.3%**

2003 Year-End Financials

Debt ratio: 10.1%
Return on equity: 5.1%
Cash ($ mil.): 1,187
Current ratio: 2.01
Long-term debt ($ mil.): 268

No. of shares (mil.): 175
Dividends
  Yield: 0.6%
  Payout: 16.0%
Market value ($ mil.): 3,640

Stock History

NYSE: PIO

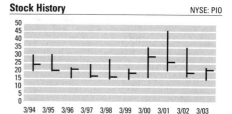

	STOCK PRICE ($) FY Close	P/E High/Low	Earnings	Dividends	Book Value
3/03	20.75	29 20	0.75	0.12	15.12
3/02	18.90	102 49	0.34	0.12	14.49
3/01	25.75	55 25	0.82	0.11	15.13
3/00	29.19	50 23	0.69	0.08	16.41
3/99	18.63	425 298	0.05	0.04	14.42
3/98	16.19	105 58	0.26	0.00	13.93
3/97	16.75	217 145	0.11	0.02	14.07
3/96	21.00	— —	(0.52)	0.12	15.55
3/95	20.25	— —	(0.08)	0.21	18.47
3/94	24.00	331 224	0.35	0.19	16.79
Annual Growth	**(1.6%)**	**— —**	**8.8%**	**(5.0%)**	**(1.2%)**

Pirelli & C. SpA

Hold the phone! Pirelli is de-emphasizing its core tire and cable businesses and jumping feet first into the telecommunications game. Presently Pirelli has three core businesses: energy cables, telecom cables, and tires. Pirelli has two cable divisions, energy and telecommunications. In the energy cables line are low-, medium-, and high-voltage power cables and building wire products. The telecommunications family of products includes fiber-optic copper communication cables. Where the rubber meets the road, Pirelli makes tires for cars, industrial and commercial vehicles, motorcycles, and farm machinery.

In an attempt to better reflect the company's new direction, Pirelli has reorganized and added a telecom cables and systems division. The company has also merged all of the activities currently conducted through Pirelli S.p.A. with Pirelli & C. (including Pirelli & C. Real Estate); the company's legal name is now Pirelli & C. SpA.

Pirelli became a global leader in power cables after buying US-based General Cable's BICC General division. Pirelli boosted its cash reserves by selling two niche optical units and began eyeing investments, settling on the Telecom Italia deal (and the mobile TIM unit) with Benetton in 2001. Pirelli controls 60% of Olimpia SpA, a company created to take over Olivetti SpA, which is a holding company that controls Telecom Italia. If it passes regulatory scrutiny, the deal will give Pirelli and the Benetton family a 23% controlling stake in Olivetti.

HISTORY

After fighting for Italian unification with Garibaldi in the 1860s, Giovanni Battista Pirelli observed that France, not Italy, was providing rubber tubes for an Italian ship salvage attempt. The young patriot reacted by founding Pirelli & Co. in Milan, Italy, in 1872 to manufacture rubber products. In 1879 Pirelli began making insulated cables for the rapidly growing telegraph industry, and by 1890 he was making bicycle tires. Pirelli introduced his first air-filled automobile tire in 1899.

Foreign expansion began when Pirelli opened cable factories in Spain (1902), the UK (1914), and Argentina (1917). The company set up Societe Internationale Pirelli (SIP) in Switzerland in 1937 and consolidated all non-Italian operations within it. After WWII the group expanded along with the growth in worldwide auto sales. Pirelli began production in Turkey and Greece in 1962, and six years later it set up cable plants in Peru.

Pirelli's first radial tires (early 1970s) backfired when they wore out too quickly. In 1971 the company swapped stock with tire maker Dunlop (UK). Although the firms engaged in joint research and development (R&D), they never consolidated production.

Pirelli S.p.A., the Italian operating company, and SIP became holding companies in 1982 by transferring their operating units into the jointly owned Pirelli Societe Generale (Switzerland). That year Pirelli started producing fiberoptic cables.

Heavy spending on R&D and new equipment bolstered the newly unified tire business, and the 1986 purchase of Metzeler Kautscuk (Germany) made Pirelli one of the world's largest motorcycle tire manufacturers.

Pirelli S.p.A. became an operating company in 1988 when it bought SIP's Pirelli Societe Generale holdings. It launched a hostile bid for Firestone through Pirelli Tyre, but was outbid by Bridgestone. Pirelli settled for the much smaller Armstrong Tire. In 1989 Pirelli sold nearly 24% of Pirelli Tyre to the public.

In 1990 Pirelli proposed an unusually complex and convoluted merger with Continental AG (Germany) designed to leave Pirelli in control. Continental declined, but negotiations continued throughout 1991 until Continental terminated the talks after learning of Pirelli's deteriorating financial condition.

Pirelli became a top power-cable maker with operations in more than 20 countries in 1998 by acquiring Germany-based Siemens' power cable unit in a $277 million deal.

In 1999 Pirelli agreed to ally with Cooper Tire and Rubber, including an arrangement whereby Cooper would distribute and sell Pirelli tires for passenger cars and light trucks in the US,

Canada, and Mexico. In return, Pirelli agreed to sell Cooper tires in South America. Additionally, Pirelli Cables Australia acquired Metal Manufacturers Ltd's energy cable business to strengthen its market share down under.

In 1999 Pirelli unveiled a compact, computerized manufacturing system designed to cut the cost of tire production about 25%, while raising tire quality. In 2000 Pirelli sold its terrestrial optical systems business to Cisco Systems for about $2.15 billion; Cisco agreed to invest $100 million in Pirelli's optical components and undersea cable transmissions divisions. Also in 2000 the company sold its fiber-optic telecommunications business to Corning for about $3.6 billion.

In 2001 the company separated energy cables and systems from its telecom business to focus on new growth and reached an alliance agreement with Alloptic to develop network fiber-optic solutions for commercial and home markets. In a surprise July announcement, Pirelli announced that it and the Benetton family had agreed to buy the 23% controlling stake in Olivetti — controlled by Roberto Colaninno, the CEO of both Olivetti and Telecom Italia. Pirelli sold its enamelled wire holdings in late 2002 to Investitori Associati, an Italy-based investment group. After merging its operating company (Pirelli SpA) and holding company (Pirelli & C. SpA) in 2003, the company changed its name to Pirelli & C. SpA.

EXECUTIVES

Chairman and CEO: Marco Tronchetti Provera
Deputy Chairman: Alberto Pirelli
General Manager, Finance and Administration, and Managing Director: Carlo Orazio Buora, age 57
Managing Director and General Manager: Giovanni Ferrario
Secretary to the Board: Sergio Lamacchia
General Manager, Administration and Control: Claudio De Conto
General Manager, Finance: Luciano Gobbi
General Manager, Cables and Systems Sector — Energy: Valerio Battista
General Manager, Cables and Systems Sector — Telecom: Kevin Riddett
General Manager, Tires Sector: Francesco Gori
CIO: Dario Scagliotti
Director, Investor Relations: Roberto Rivellino
Investor Relations: Massimiliano Cominelli
Assistant Investor Relations: Annaluisa Weber
Auditors: PricewaterhouseCoopers; PricewaterhouseCoopers SpA

LOCATIONS

HQ: V.le Sarca, 222, 20126 Milan, Italy
Phone: +39-02-64421   **Fax:** +39-02-6442-4686
US HQ: 300 George St., New Haven, CT 06511
US Phone: 203-784-2200   **US Fax:** 203-784-2408
Web: www.pirelli.com

Pirelli has cable and tire manufacturing facilities around the globe.

2002 Sales

	$ mil.	% of total
Europe		
Italy	1,613	23
Other countries	2,892	41
Oceania, Africa & Asia	953	13
Central & South America	816	12
North America	766	11
Adjustments	(425)	—
Total	**6,615**	**100**

PRODUCTS/OPERATIONS

2002 Sales

	$ mil.	% of total
Energy cables & systems	3,167	48
Tires	2,994	45
Telecommunication cables	491	7
Adjustments	(37)	—
Total	**6,615**	**100**

Selected Products

Energy Cables and Systems
Building wire
Low-, medium-, and high- voltage utility cables
Submarine cables

Tires
Automobile (passenger car, SUV, and truck)
Motorcycle

Telecommunication Cable
Cable assemblies and hardware
Fiber-optic cables
Indoor/outdoor cable

Selected Subsidiaries

Metzeler Reifen GmbH (Germany)
MKM Magyar Kabel Muvek RT (Hungary)
Pirelli Cables and Systems Inc. (Canada)
Pirelli Cables and Systems LLC (USA)
Pirelli Cables Australia Ltd. (Australia)
Pirelli Câbles et Systèmes S.A. (Italy)
Pirelli Cables SAIC (Argentina)
Pirelli Cabos S.A. (Brazil)
Pirelli General plc (UK)
Pirelli Kabel und Systeme Holding GmbH (Germany)
Pirelli Neumaticos S.A. (Spain)
Pirelli Pneumatici S.p.A. (Italy)
Pirelli Pneus S.A. (Brazil)
Pirelli Reifenwerke GmbH (Germany)
Pirelli Tire LLC (USA)
Pirelli UK Tyres Ltd (UK)
Power Cables Malaysia Sdn Bhd (Malaysia)
PT Pirelli Cables Indonesia (Indonesia)
Tianjin Top Power Cables Co. Ltd (China)
Türk Pirelli Lastikleri A.S. (Turkey)

COMPETITORS

Alcatel	Michelin
Ansell	Nexans Hellas
Bandag	Nexans
Bridgestone	Nokia
Cable Design Technologies	Nortel Networks
CIENA	Sime Darby
CommScope	Southwire
Continental AG	Sumitomo Electric
Corning	Superior Essex
Goodyear	Volex
Lucent	

HISTORICAL FINANCIALS

Company Type: Public

Income Statement

FYE: December 31

	REVENUE ($ mil.)	NET INCOME ($ mil.)	NET PROFIT MARGIN	EMPLOYEES
12/02	6,615	(640)	—	36,079
12/01	6,652	73	1.1%	39,127
12/00	7,040	3,420	48.6%	41,914
12/99	6,619	307	4.6%	40,103
12/98	6,580	324	4.9%	36,226
12/97	6,395	261	4.1%	36,211
12/96	6,746	255	3.8%	36,534
12/95	6,862	162	2.4%	38,106
12/94	6,040	68	1.1%	40,588
12/93	5,501	(36)	—	42,132
Annual Growth	**2.1%**	**—**	**—**	**(1.7%)**

2002 Year-End Financials

Debt ratio: 33.4%
Return on equity: —
Cash ($ mil.): 544

Current ratio: 1.43
Long-term debt ($ mil.): 1,536

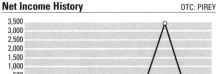
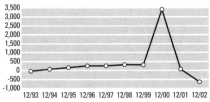

Net Income History   OTC: PIREY

Placer Dome

When an Ontario prospector slipped and fell in 1909, he dislodged a clump of moss to reveal a dome-shaped rock sparkling with gold. Thus began the chain of events that led to the creation of Placer Dome, the world's fifth-largest gold mining company. Placer Dome produces about 3.5 million ounces of gold (75% of sales) a year and has nearly 53 million ounces in reserves. It also produces around 4 million ounces of silver and more than 425 million pounds of copper annually. Placer Dome has interests in 17 mines in Australia, the Americas, Papua New Guinea, and South Africa. In early 2003 Placer Dome acquired Australia's AurionGold.

Even as Placer Dome wraps up operations at played-out mines in Australia, Papua New Guinea, and Montana, acquisitions are helping the company grow. In early 2003 it won a protracted battle for Australia's AurionGold, increasing its total annual production by about a million ounces. Placer Dome paid a pricey $1 billion for the Getchell Gold mine in Nevada in 1999 only to see gold prices languish; recent higher gold prices have allowed the company to start production at that difficult site. Placer Dome has also pinpointed new deposits at the Granny Smith mine in Australia and has penned production deals with other leading miners, including Barrick Gold, Newmont Mining, and Kinross.

HISTORY

Placer Dome was formed by the 1987 amalgamation of three Canadian mining firms: Dome Mines Ltd. (the famed gold-studded dome of rock that gave the company its name was found in 1909; the business incorporated the next year), Placer Development Ltd. (1926), and Campbell Red Lake Mines (1944). The merger formed North America's largest gold-mining firm. When Australian mining companies moved to take over Placer and Dome in the 1980s, Placer engineered the merger.

Upon consolidation, Placer Dome began acquiring new operations using gold loans, in which the company borrowed gold from its lenders' reserves to make acquisitions and then repaid the loans in gold obtained from its mining operations. It bought Consolidated TVX Mining Corp. in the late 1980s. The company increased its interest in Nevada's Cortez Gold Mine joint venture in 1991 and bought half of Chile's Compañía Minera Zaldívar in 1992. That year

Placer Dome's sales topped $1 billion for the first time.

In 1993 mining veteran John Willson became president and CEO and melded the company into an organization focused on regional operations. He also narrowed Placer Dome's primary focus to mining gold.

The company began production at two new mines in 1996, the Musselwhite in northern Ontario and the Pipeline in Nevada. That year a major spill of 4 million tons of tailings at Placer Dome's 40%-owned Marcopper mine in the Philippines led to a $43 million charge (the company sold its stake in Marcopper in 1997; in 2001 it agreed to fund further clean-up). In addition, Placer Dome began protracted battles, one to acquire Papua New Guinea-based Highlands Gold, the other to operate the Las Cristinas mine in Venezuela.

The Highlands Gold acquisition evolved into a hostile takeover bid. In Venezuela, Crystallex International Corporation disputed Placer Dome's claim to Las Cristinas, believed to be one of the richest gold deposits in South America. Placer Dome eventually won the court battle.

Also in 1997 both the Pipeline and Musselwhite mines in North America began producing their first gold. That year Placer Dome completed its takeover of Highlands Gold, including a 50% stake in Papua New Guinea's Porgera mine.

Weak gold prices and writedowns for mining interests led to a big loss for Placer Dome in 1997. The company continued, nevertheless, to add mining properties. In 1998 it bought 51% of the Aldebaran copper-gold property in Chile, as well as the Can Can mine (also in Chile) with joint-venture partner PVX Gold. The next year Placer Dome bought a 50% share in the undeveloped South Deep gold deposit in South Africa (Western Areas Ltd. owns the rest) and Getchell Gold (two mines in central Nevada) for about $1 billion. Low metal prices caused Placer Dome to put operations at its Las Cristinas mine on hold (it was later sold). Later in 1999 gold prices increased on the promise from 15 European central banks to limit the sale of gold reserves.

In 2000 Willson retired, and Jay Taylor, an EVP and 20-year company veteran, replaced him as president and CEO. That year's loss, caused in part by charges related to the company's lowering of long-term gold price assumptions and adjustments to asset values, was laid at the door of lowered gold prices. Placer Dome finished sinking the world's deepest vent shaft, at its South Deep mine in South Africa, in 2001. That year the company won a bid for the Pueblo Viejo mine in the Dominican Republic. It later put development at its Getchell mine on hold and took a $292 million write-off; production at Getchell was restarted in 2002.

EXECUTIVES

Chairman Emeritus: Fraser M. Fell
Chairman: Robert M. Franklin
President, CEO, and Director: Jay K. Taylor, age 55
EVP and CFO: Rex J. McLennan
EVP, Secretary, and General Counsel: J. Donald Rose
EVP, Strategic Development: Geoffrey A. Handley
EVP, Asia-Pacific: Peter Tomsett
EVP, Canada: George E. Pirie
EVP, South Africa: George Paspalas
EVP, United States and Latin America:
 William M. (Bill) Hayes
SVP, Human Resources: Jennifer A. Gordon
SVP, Project Development: Peter W. Harris
VP, Corporate Relations: Joseph L. (Joe) Danni
VP, Design and Construction: Martyn A. Creaney
VP, Evaluations, Strategic Development Group:
 Alfred Hills

VP, Research and Technology: Marilyn P. A. Hames
VP, Safety and Sustainability: Keith Ferguson
VP and Controller: Bruce B. Nicol
VP, Associate General Counsel, and Assistant Secretary:
 Geoffrey Gold
Auditors: Ernst & Young LLP

LOCATIONS

HQ: Placer Dome Inc.
 Ste. 1600, Bentall IV, 1055 Dunsmuir St.,
 Vancouver, British Columbia V7X 1P1, Canada
Phone: 604-682-7082   **Fax:** 604-682-7092
Web: www.placerdome.com

Placer Dome operates mines in Australia, Canada, Chile, Papua New Guinea, South Africa, and the US.

2002 Sales by Origin

	$ mil.	% of total
US	296	24
Chile	276	22
Australia	205	16
Canada	169	13
Papua New Guinea	166	13
South Africa	60	5
Metal hedging & other	87	7
Total	**1,259**	**100**

PRODUCTS/OPERATIONS

Selected Properties

Australia
Granny Smith Mine
Henty Mine
Kalgoorlie West
Kanowna Belle
Osborne Mine (copper)

Canada
Campbell Mine
Dome Mine
Musselwhite Mine (68%)
Porcupine Mine (51%)

Chile
La Coipa Mine (50%, gold and silver)
Zaldívar Mine (copper)

Dominican Republic
Pueblo Viejo (in development)

Papua New Guinea
Misima Mine (80%, gold and silver)
Porgera Mine (75%)

South Africa
South Deep Mine (50%)

US
Bald Mountain Mine
Cortez Mine (60%)
Donlin Creek project (30%)
Getchell Mine
Golden Sunlight Mine

COMPETITORS

AngloGold	Harmony Gold
Antofagasta	Kennecott
Apollo Gold	Kinross Gold
ASARCO	Lihir Gold
Ashanti Goldfields	Lonmin
Barrick Gold	METALEUROP
BHP Billiton Ltd	Newmont Mining
Brascan	Peñoles
Cambior	Phelps Dodge
Codelco	Rio Tinto
Doublestar	Southern Peru Copper
Freeport-McMoRan	Teck Cominco
Copper & Gold	Trelleborg
Gold Fields Limited	Umicore
Goldcorp	Vale do Rio Doce
Grupo México	WMC Resources

HISTORICAL FINANCIALS
Company Type: Public

Income Statement
FYE: December 31

	REVENUE ($ mil.)	NET INCOME ($ mil.)	NET PROFIT MARGIN	EMPLOYEES
12/02	1,259	111	8.8%	11,950
12/01	1,266	(180)	—	11,100
12/00	1,442	(358)	—	12,000
12/99	1,315	60	4.6%	12,000
12/98	1,279	105	8.2%	7,300
12/97	1,209	(249)	—	8,400
12/96	1,157	(65)	—	8,300
12/95	1,029	74	7.2%	8,000
12/94	899	105	11.7%	6,231
12/93	917	107	11.7%	6,231
Annual Growth	3.6%	0.4%	—	7.5%

2002 Year-End Financials

Debt ratio: 16.1%
Return on equity: 6.4%
Cash ($ mil.): 539
Current ratio: 1.49
Long-term debt ($ mil.): 345

No. of shares (mil.): 409
Dividends
Yield: 0.9%
Payout: 33.3%
Market value ($ mil.): 4,701

Stock History
NYSE: PDG

	STOCK PRICE ($) FY Close	P/E High/Low		PER SHARE ($) Earnings	Dividends	Book Value
12/02	11.50	49	26	0.30	0.10	5.88
12/01	10.91	—	—	(0.59)	0.10	4.88
12/00	9.63	—	—	(1.14)	0.10	5.56
12/99	10.75	109	57	0.16	0.10	7.73
12/98	11.50	50	22	0.36	0.10	6.79
12/97	12.69	—	—	(1.06)	0.30	6.52
12/96	21.75	—	—	(0.27)	0.30	7.24
12/95	24.13	95	59	0.31	0.30	6.45
12/94	21.75	64	41	0.44	0.27	6.41
12/93	24.88	57	25	0.45	0.22	6.36
Annual Growth	(8.2%)	—	—	(4.4%)	(8.4%)	(0.9%)

Polski Koncern Naftowy ORLEN

Crudely moving into the private market, Polski Koncern Naftowy ORLEN (PKN) is the largest refiner and distributor of oil in Poland. Two former state monopolies, Petrochemia Plock (Poland's largest refinery) and Centrala Produktow Naftowych (Poland's #1 petroleum distributor), merged in 1999 to create PKN. The company also owns stakes in two other refineries (its total capacity is 600,000 barrels per day) and has some 1,945 retail sites, about a third of Poland's gas stations. It also has gas stations in Germany. PKN owns a 75% stake in chemical maker Anwil and has holdings in several other Polish companies.

The company also manufactures liquefied propane-butane gas (LPG) for use at industrial plants and for heating public buildings. Other PKN products include plastics used in foils, containers, bottles, cable insulation, and auto parts; asphalts for construction of roads, airports, and sports facilities; and basic industrial and engine oils.

The state floated 30% of PKN in 1999, and in 2000 it sold an additional 42% to the public. That year the company added ORLEN to its name. To meet German antitrust regulations for its merger with Veba Oel, in late 2002 BP sold some 494 gas stations in Germany to PKN.

HISTORY

The merger between Petrochemia Plock, Poland's largest refiner and petrochemicals maker, and CPN (Centrala Produktow Naftowych), the nation's largest motor fuel distributor, created Polski Koncern Naftowy (PKN) in 1999.

Poland's oil industry stretches back to the late 1800s, when five refineries were built in the nation's southern region. The Polish Oil Monopoly was formed in 1944 to oversee the country's oil distribution operations; it assumed the CPN name a year later.

While the rest of the world increasingly turned to oil as an energy source after WWII, Poland continued to rely on coal, and its oil industry grew slowly. CPN was split up into 17 regional branches in 1955. The branches controlled local operations, and the head office in Warsaw handled pricing and purchasing.

In the late 1950s the Soviet Union began building the Friendship pipeline to deliver crude oil to East Germany and Poland. The Polish government responded by forming Petrochemia to develop a refinery next to the pipeline in the city of Plock.

The Petrochemia refinery began producing refined products in 1964; four years later it began processing crude oil to make fuels, lubricants, and bitumen. The refinery also began making products such as detergents and plastics from processed refinery gases and other hydrocarbons. It added petrochemicals in 1970.

Because of the oil industry's slow growth in Poland, the country managed to avoid some of the impact of the 1970s energy crisis. (Even as late as 1995, oil accounted for only 17% of Poland's energy consumption.) But it was forced to pay higher prices for Russian crude. In 1975 the government decided to expand its refining operations and created a second major refiner, Rafineria Gdanska, to focus on motor oils.

Locked behind the Iron Curtain, Poland was not able to build its oil operations until the early 1990s. In 1992 Petrochemia began expanding its refinery facilities to reach a production capacity of 820,000 barrels per day within 10 years.

After Communism's demise, the Polish government began planning the privatization of its oil operations. After several plans were adopted and discarded in the early 1990s, the government finally decided in 1996 to split CPN up among the nation's refineries. Holding company Nafta Polska was formed that year to own 75% stakes in Poland's refineries and in CPN and carry out the privatization process.

In 1997 CPN was stripped of its fuel depots and rail transport operations, which were placed under the Nafta Polska umbrella. Displeased with the plan to carve up CPN, the distributor's management rallied against the government's plan. The Polish government gave in and went back to the drawing board.

A successful plan was formed in 1998: to merge Petrochemia and CPN. The companies were combined in 1999, and 30% of the new PKN was floated on the Warsaw and London stock exchanges. The next year the government spun off an additional 42% stake. The company also added ORLEN to its name (combining the Polish words for eagle and energy).

Also in 2000 the government began preparing to float Refineria Gdanska. PKN hoped to get a piece of its regional rival, but the state left PKN out of the bidding to encourage competition.

EXECUTIVES

Chairman: Maciej Gierej
Vice Chairman: Jan Waga
President: Zbigniew Wrobel, age 50
VP and CFO: Jecek Strzelecki, age 54
VP Sales: Slawomir Golonka, age 46
VP Development and Production: Janusz Wisniewski, age 43
VP Human Resources and Management Systems: Andrzej Ernest Macenowicz, age 56

LOCATIONS

HQ: Polski Koncern Naftowy S.A.
ul. Chemików 7, 09-411 Plock, Poland
Phone: +48-24-365-00-00   **Fax:** +48-24-365-40-40
Web: www.orlen.pl

Polski Koncern Naftowy ORLEN has a major refinery in Plock, Poland; stakes in two refineries in southern Poland; and a network of gas stations in Poland and Germany.

PRODUCTS/OPERATIONS

Selected Subsidiaries

Petrolot Sp. z o.o. (51%, distribution of aviation fuels)
Petroprofit Sp. z o.o. (85%; distribution of fuels, radiator fluids, and plastics)
Rafineria Nafty Jedlicze SA (75%, refining)
Rafineria Trzebinia SA (77%, refining)
Zaklady Azotowe Anwil SA (75%, chemical manufacturing)

COMPETITORS

BP	OMV
Exxon Mobil	Royal Dutch/Shell Group
LUKOIL	Statoil
MOL	

HISTORICAL FINANCIALS
Company Type: Public

Income Statement
FYE: December 31

	REVENUE ($ mil.)	NET INCOME ($ mil.)	NET PROFIT MARGIN	EMPLOYEES
12/02	4,398	110	2.5%	17,818
12/01	4,278	94	2.2%	17,582
12/00	4,498	218	4.8%	13,342
12/99	3,206	228	7.1%	14,169
12/98	3,202	225	7.0%	—
Annual Growth	8.3%	(16.4%)	—	7.9%

2002 Year-End Financials

Debt ratio: 4.8%
Return on equity: 5.3%
Cash ($ mil.): 46

Current ratio: 1.07
Long-term debt ($ mil.): 105

Net Income History Warsaw: PKN

```
250
200
150
100
 50
  0
  12/93 12/94 12/95 12/96 12/97 12/98 12/99 12/00 12/01 12/02
```

Porsche

Still going strong a century after its founder began designing autos, Dr. Ing. h.c. F. Porsche's cars have handled more curves than Wilt Chamberlain. Porsche has streamlined production and now makes three model lines: the Boxster, the 911 models, and the Cayenne SUV. Can't afford a new Cayenne? Porsche also offers watches, luggage, and tennis rackets bearing its name. Porsche also offers consulting services to other companies involved in auto and furniture manufacturing, mechanical and electronic engineering, and construction. Descendants of the founding family control Porsche.

Since his arrival in the early 1990s, CEO Wendelin Wiedeking has transformed Porsche from a money-loser into a profitable carmaker by streamlining both the company's operations and its product line. The new Cayenne, introduced for the 2003 model year, has helped offset sagging sales of the aging 911 and Boxster models in the US. Porsche also introduced the Carrera GT in 2003.

Porsche has plans to nearly double North American sales within the next few years. Although the company is considering the addition of a fourth model, Porsche plans to reach a sales volume of 50,000 units in North America with only the 911, Boxster, and Cayenne models. To achieve this goal, Porsche plans to add as many as 15 new dealers in the US and Canada and increase its marketing budget.

HISTORY

Ferdinand Porsche was 25 when a battery-powered car with a motor he had designed was unveiled at the Paris Exposition in 1900. Six years later, Porsche was hired by Daimler Motor. During his rise to chief engineer at Daimler, he designed the famous Mercedes-Benz S-series.

Frustrated by the conservative nature of his employer, Porsche quit and opened an engine-design company bearing his name in 1931. The next year Josef Stalin offered to make Porsche the head of the Soviet Union's auto industry. Porsche turned Stalin down.

In 1933 Hitler announced his intention to build a widely affordable "volkswagen" (people's car). Soon Porsche was designing the vehicle that would become the Volkswagen Beetle. During WWII Porsche continued work on the Volkswagen project and also provided advice on increasing Germany's factory production. After the war, Ferdinand and his son Ferry were imprisoned for two years in France for allegedly abusing French laborers. Father and son were compelled to work on the Renault line of automobiles. After his release, Ferdinand reportedly burst into tears and exclaimed, "My Beetle!" when he saw his Volkswagen cars populating the streets in Germany.

By 1948 Ferdinand and Ferry had developed a Porsche sports-car prototype based on the Volkswagen. It was named the 356 because it was the 356th project undertaken at the Porsche design office. In 1950 the first Porsche 356 rolled off the assembly line in Stuttgart. Ferdinand Porsche lived just long enough to see his sports cars become highly sought by the rich and famous. He died in 1951.

In 1952 Ferry designed the Porsche emblem, which combined the Porsche name and the Stuttgart and Wurttemberg coats of arms. Porsches won hundreds of races during the 1950s, and the car's popularity grew. (James Dean was driving his brand-new Porsche when he was killed in 1955.)

By the 1960s Ferry Porsche decided to build an entirely new Porsche model that didn't rely so heavily on the Beetle's design. The company unveiled the Type 911 Porsche in 1964 and discontinued the 356 the next year. In 1973 the company went public under the Porsche AG name.

The company flourished in the 1980s, due largely to its cars' popularity in the US. By 1986 Porsche was producing almost 50,000 cars a year, with about 60% of them destined for the US market. Models introduced in the late 1980s included the 912, the 924, and the 928.

Porsche's fortunes crashed in the early 1990s, when the company faced tough competition and a recession priced many consumers out of the sports-car market. In 1992 the company sold only 23,060 cars — 4,100 of those in the US. That year Wendelin Wiedeking, an engineering and manufacturing expert, was brought in as CEO. He cut costs, in part, by convincing most workers to reduce the number of hours they worked each day and eliminating overtime. Wiedeking also updated the 911 and initiated development of the Boxster.

Introduced in 1996, the $40,000 Boxster was an instant hit — its first year of production sold out in advance. In 1998 the company initiated plans to produce a luxury SUV in partnership with Volkswagen. Porsche launched the Boxster S, featuring a 250-hp engine, in 1999. The next year Porsche announced that its Cayenne SUV — which shares a platform with Volkswagen's SUV — would hit the market in 2003.

Early in 2002 Porsche announced its next product launch — the Carrera GT. Production of the Carrera GT began the following year.

EXECUTIVES

Chairman of the Supervisory Board: Helmut Sihler, age 73
Deputy Chairman of the Supervisory Board: Hans Baur
Chairman, President, and CEO of the Executive Board: Wendelin Wiedeking, age 49
CFO: Holger P. Härter
Director, Production and Logistics: Michael Macht
Director, Research and Development: Wolfgang Dürheimer, age 45
Director, Sales and Marketing: Hans Riedel
Personnel Director, Human Resources: Harro Harmel
President and CEO, Porsche Cars North America: Peter Schwarzenbauer
Auditors: Ernst & Young

LOCATIONS

HQ: Dr. Ing. h.c. F. Porsche AG
Porscheplatz 1, 70435 Stuttgart, Germany
Phone: +49-711-911-0   **Fax:** +49-711-911-5777
US HQ: 980 Hammond Dr., Ste. 1000, Atlanta, GA 30328
US Phone: 770-290-3500   **US Fax:** 770-290-3706
Web: www.porsche.com

Porsche operates main production facilities in Zuffenhausen, Germany, and in Finland.

2002 Sales

	$ mil.	% of total
North America	1,974	41
Germany	1,102	23
Other regions	1,700	36
Total	**4,776**	**100**

PRODUCTS/OPERATIONS

Selected Vehicles

Boxter
Boxter S
911 Carrera Coupe and Cabriolet
911 Carrera 4 Cabriolet
911 Carrera 4S
911 GT2
911 Targa
911 Turbo

COMPETITORS

BMW
DaimlerChrysler
Fiat
Ford
General Motors
Honda
Mazda
Nissan
Peugeot
Renault
Saab Automobile
Saleen
Volkswagen

HISTORICAL FINANCIALS

Company Type: Public

Income Statement

FYE: July 31

	REVENUE ($ mil.)	NET INCOME ($ mil.)	NET PROFIT MARGIN	EMPLOYEES
7/02	4,776	454	9.5%	10,143
7/01	3,883	236	6.1%	9,752
7/00	3,440	194	5.6%	9,320
7/99	3,363	204	6.1%	8,712
7/98	2,767	156	5.6%	8,151
7/97	2,233	75	3.4%	7,959
7/96	1,912	32	1.7%	7,107
7/95	1,880	1	0.1%	6,847
7/94	1,475	(96)	—	6,970
7/93	1,098	(137)	—	7,133
Annual Growth	**17.7%**	**—**	**—**	**4.0%**

2002 Year-End Financials

Debt ratio: —
Return on equity: —
Cash ($ mil.): 1,421
Current ratio: 3.25
Long-term debt ($ mil.): 312

Net Income History OTC: PSEPF

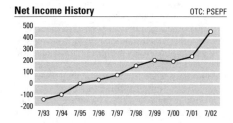

```
500
400
300
200
100
  0
-100
-200
  7/93 7/94 7/95 7/96 7/97 7/98 7/99 7/00 7/01 7/02
```

POSCO

POSCO steeled itself against unfavorable market conditions in its neck of the woods, but things are looking up. The company makes hot- and cold-rolled steel products (plate steel, stainless steel, electrical steel, and wire rods), which it sells to the auto and shipbuilding industries. It produces about 28 million tons of steel a year and ships it worldwide. Subsidiaries include POSCO Engineering & Construction (which builds steel plants, steel-related infrastructure, and energy facilities) and POSDATA (systems integration). The South Korean government has privatized its remaining stake in POSCO, ending the company's 30-year steelmaking monopoly in that country.

Unfortunately for POSCO, South Korea has little native iron ore, and the company has had to look for iron elsewhere. To that end, POSCO has developed about 18 joint ventures, including six in China and others in Australia, Brazil, Canada, Indonesia, Myanmar, South Africa, Thailand, the US, and Venezuela.

The late 1990s economic slowdown in Asia and an excessive world steel supply caused POSCO to suspend or halt projects in China and Indonesia while reducing shipments to the US (the latter in an effort to reduce trade frictions). Even as the price of steel rebounds as most Asian economies recover and steel demand increases, POSCO continues to tighten its belt. The company plans to reduce or sell its low-profit operations such as its minimills and to concentrate on higher-margin specialized products needed by automotive, electrical, and electronics manufacturers. POSCO has also formed an alliance with long-time rival Nippon Steel and plans to establish agreements with other steelmakers in China and Europe. The company also intends to diversify into the energy distribution business, bioscience, and other emerging high-tech areas.

In 2002 POSCO's largest export market was China, which represented around 30% of volume of steel products such as cold-rolled and stainless steel.

HISTORY

After the Korean War, South Korea, the US, and its allies wanted to rebuild South Korea's infrastructure as quickly as possible. Steel was given a high priority, and before long about 15 companies were making various steel products. Quality was a problem, though, as the companies used dated production processes.

With the backing of Korean president Chung Hee Park, momentum for a large steel plant grew in the late 1960s. In 1967 the South Korean government and Korean International Steel Associates (KISA) — a consortium of seven Western steelmakers — signed an agreement that called for the completion of an integrated mill by 1972. Pohang Iron & Steel Co. (POSCO), the operating company, was incorporated in 1968. Efforts to raise the necessary capital failed, however, and KISA was dissolved in 1969.

Undaunted, the Koreans turned to the Japanese, who arranged loans covering most of the mill's costs and the early phases of planning and construction. The Japanese also transferred the technology needed to run such a plant. Slow and deliberate planning resulted in a plant far away from Seoul (part of a plan to locate industries throughout the country) and a design that lent itself to future expansion. The first stage, including a blast furnace and two steel converters, was completed in 1973. By the time the fourth stage of construction began in 1979, the Koreans had gained enough confidence to take over many of the tasks. When the last stage was completed in 1981, the plant had an annual capacity of 8.5 million tons.

To ensure steel of acceptable quality, POSCO focused first on plain high-carbon steel for general construction, rather than on specialized (and difficult to produce) varieties. The company gradually broadened its specialized offerings.

In 1985 POSCO began construction on a second integrated steel plant located in Kwangyang. That plant was also built in four stages; its annual production capacity, when it was completed in 1992, was 11.4 million tons. By 1987 POSCO was exporting almost 3 million tons of steel a year and using its knowledge to assist in plant construction projects in other countries.

By the mid-1990s POSCO was exporting 6 million tons of steel annually. The South Korean government sold a 5% stake in POSCO to the public in 1998 and vowed to open up the primary steelmaking industry to competition. However, facing a severe downturn in steel demand that year because of sluggishness in Asian and domestic markets, the company canceled two projects in China and suspended two in Indonesia. In 1999 POSCO merged its two subsidiaries, Pohang Coated Steel and Pohang Steel Industries, to create Pohang Steel Co. That same year POSCO Machinery & Engineering, POSEC-HAWAII, and P.T. Posnesia Stainless Steel Industry were joined to form POSCO Machinery Co. The South Korean government continued selling off its 13% stake in 1999.

In 2000 POSCO sold its 51% stake in telecommunications company Shinsegi Telecom to SK Telecom in exchange for cash and a 6.5% stake in SK Telecom. It also formed a strategic alliance — exploration of joint ventures, shared research, and joint procurement — with Nippon Steel, the world's #1 steel maker. The deal also calls for each to take increased equity stakes (2% or 3%) in the other. After about 30 years of government control, the South Korean government sold its remaining shares of POSCO in 2001.

In June 2002 Chairman Yoo was indicted for influencing POSCO subsidiaries and contractors to buy inflated shares of Tiger Pools International (South Korea's sole sports lottery business) for Kim Hong-Gul, the third son of South Korean President Kim Dae-Jung. That same year Pohang Iron & Steel Co. officially changed its company name to POSCO to try and strengthen brand recognition.

In 2003 Chairman Yoo resigned ahead of the company's shareholder meeting amid his possible involvement in illegal stock transactions.

EXECUTIVES

Chairman: Lee Ku-Taek, age 57
President: Kang Chang-Oh
SEVP and General Superintendent, Kwangyang Works: Han Soo-Yang, age 58
SEVP and General Superintendent, Pohang Works: Lee Won-Pyo, age 59
SEVP: Choi Kwang-Woong, age 58
EVP and Deputy General Superintendent, Pohang Works: Lee Youn, age 55
EVP, Process Innovation Dept. and PI Enablement Dept.: Ryoo Kyeong-Ryul, age 55
EVP, Beijing Office: Kim Dong-Jin, age 56
EVP, Corporate Communications: Yoon Seok-Man, age 54
EVP, Corporate Strategic Planning: Cho Sung-Sik, age 52
EVP, Finance Division: Hwang Tae-Hyun
EVP, General Administration Dept., Public Service Dept.: Kim Jung-Won, age 59
EVP, Human Resources Center: Choi Jong-Tae
Auditors: Samil Accounting Corporation

LOCATIONS

HQ: POSCO Center, 892 Daechi-4-dong, Kangnam-ku, Seoul, South Korea
Phone: +82-2-3457-0114   **Fax:** +82-54-220-6000
US HQ: 2 Executive Dr., Ste. 805, Fort Lee, NJ 07024
US Phone: 201-585-3060   **US Fax:** 201-585-6001
Web: www.posco.co.kr

POSCO operates subsidiary companies in Australia, Brazil, Canada, China, Germany, Hong Kong, Indonesia, Japan, Myanmar, Russia, Singapore, South Africa, South Korea, Thailand, Turkey, the UK, the US, and Vietnam.

2002 Sales

	% of total
Asia/Pacific	
South Korea	66
China	15
Japan	4
Other countries	7
North America	3
Europe	1
Middle East	1
Other regions	3
Total	**100**

PRODUCTS/OPERATIONS

2002 Production

	Metric tons	% of total
Hot-rolled	11,461	38
Cold-rolled	9,503	31
Plates	3,060	10
Wire rods	2,808	9
Stainless steel	1,394	5
Galvanized steel	589	2
Other	1,518	5
Total	**30,333**	**100**

Selected Subsidiaries and Affiliates

Changwon Specialty Steel Co., Ltd. (99%, specialty steel)
Dalian POSCO-CFM Coated Steel Co., Ltd. (59%, coated-steel manufacturing, China)
Davey Distington Ltd. (54%, engineering)
IBC Corporation (58%, rent)
Pohang Steel America Corp. (99.9%, steel trading, US)
Pohang Steel Australia Pty., Ltd. (95%, ore mining)
Pohang Steel Canada Ltd. (95%, coal mining)
Pohang Steel Industries Co., Ltd. (coated steel)
POSCO Asia Co., Ltd. (57%, steel trading, Hong Kong)
POSCON Co., Ltd. (97%, electric control devices)
POSDATA Co., Ltd. (computer system development)
POSCO Machinery & Engineering Co., Ltd. (steel work maintenance)
POSCO Research Institute (99.8%, economic research and consulting)
POSCO Venezuela Compañía Anónima (POSVEN, 59%, steel manufacturing)
POSCO Engineering & Construction Co., Ltd. (97%)
POSCO International Osaka Inc. (95%, Japan)
POSEC-Europe, Ltd. (97%, engineering, UK)
POSEC-HAWAII Inc. (97%, construction and rent, US)
POS-Energy Co., Ltd. (99.9%)
POSLILAMA Steel Structure Co., Ltd. (68%, Vietnam)
POSMETAL Co., Ltd. (48%, steel processing, Japan)
POS-THAI Steel Service Center Co., Ltd. (39%, steel sales)
POS-Tianjin Coil Center Co., Ltd. (67%, steel sales)
PT. Posnesia Stainless Steel Industry (70%, stainless steel sales, Thailand)
Seung Kwang Co., Ltd. (94%, athletic facilities)
Shanghai POSEC Real Estate Development Co., Ltd. (97%, rent, China)
SHUNDE Pohang Coated Steel Co., Ltd. (80%, China)

VSC-POSCO Steel Corp. (40%, Vietnam)
Zhangjiagang Pohang Stainless Steel Co., Ltd. (80%, China)
Zhangjiagang POSCO Coated Steel Co., Ltd. (90%, China)

COMPETITORS

Arcelor
Bechtel
Corus Group
Fluor
Hitachi
JFE Holdings
Kobe Steel
LTV
Marubeni
Nippon Steel
Samsung
Shanghai Baosteel
ThyssenKrupp
Toyota Tsusho
United States Steel

HISTORICAL FINANCIALS

Company Type: Public

Income Statement

FYE: December 31

	REVENUE ($ mil.)	NET INCOME ($ mil.)	NET PROFIT MARGIN	EMPLOYEES
12/02	12,101	918	7.6%	27,100
12/01	9,989	644	6.4%	25,000
12/00	10,873	1,289	11.9%	26,261
12/99	11,181	1,368	12.2%	27,949
12/98	11,288	790	7.0%	28,500
12/97	6,795	430	6.3%	29,161
12/96	11,381	698	6.1%	—
12/95	11,140	1,222	11.0%	—
12/94	10,561	472	4.5%	—
12/93	8,564	365	4.3%	—
Annual Growth	3.9%	10.8%	—	(1.5%)

2002 Year-End Financials

Debt ratio: 28.3%
Return on equity: 10.6%
Cash ($ mil.): 225
Current ratio: 1.36
Long-term debt ($ mil.): 2,692
No. of shares (mil.): 327
Dividends
Yield: 1.9%
Payout: 17.1%
Market value ($ mil.): 8,086

Stock History

NYSE: PKX

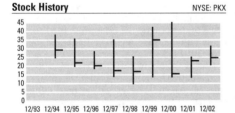

12/93 12/94 12/95 12/96 12/97 12/98 12/99 12/00 12/01 12/02

	STOCK PRICE ($) FY Close	P/E High/Low		PER SHARE ($) Earnings	Dividends	Book Value
12/02	24.73	11	7	2.80	0.48	29.12
12/01	23.00	13	7	1.97	0.47	23.75
12/00	15.56	12	4	3.78	0.39	19.22
12/99	35.00	12	4	3.57	0.00	20.73
12/98	16.88	12	5	2.10	0.00	17.99
12/97	17.44	30	12	1.15	0.00	11.56
12/96	20.25	15	10	1.88	0.25	20.66
12/95	21.88	11	6	3.25	0.04	20.78
12/94	29.25	—	—	0.25	0.21	17.51
Annual Growth	(2.1%)	—	—	35.3%	10.9%	6.6%

Pricewaterhouse Coopers

Not merely the firm with the longest one-word name, PricewaterhouseCoopers (PwC) is also the world's largest accountancy, formed when Price Waterhouse merged with Coopers & Lybrand in 1998, passing then-leader Andersen. The firm has offices around the world, providing clients with services in three lines of business: Assurance and Business Advisory Services (including financial and regulatory reporting), Tax and Legal Services, and Corporate Finance and Recovery. The company serves some of the world's largest businesses, as well as smaller firms.

PwC puts its heft to good use: Global clients make up about 40% of the firm's sales. Its bottom line, though, changed significantly in 2002, when PwC sold its consulting arm to IBM. A separation had been under consideration for years in light of SEC concerns about conflicts of interest when firms perform auditing and consulting for the same clients. The collapse of Enron and concomitant downfall of Enron's auditor and PwC's erstwhile peer Andersen undoubtedly hastened plans to spin off PwC's consultancy via an IPO, which was scrapped in favor of the IBM deal.

Like the other members of the (now) Big Four, PwC picked up business and talent as scandal-felled Andersen was winding down its operations in 2002. The former Andersen organization in China and Hong Kong joined PwC, accounting for about 70% of the approximately 3,500 Andersen alumni that came aboard.

In 2003 former client AMERCO (parent of U-Haul) sued PwC for $2.5 billion, claiming negligence and fraud in relation to a series of events that led to AMERCO restating its results.

HISTORY

In 1850 Samuel Price founded an accounting firm in London and in 1865 took on partner Edwin Waterhouse. The firm and the industry grew rapidly, thanks to the growth of stock exchanges that required uniform financial statements from listees. By the late 1800s Price Waterhouse (PW) had become the world's best-known accounting firm.

US offices were opened in the 1890s, and in 1902 United States Steel chose the firm as its auditor. PW benefited from tough audit requirements instituted after the 1929 stock market crash. In 1935 the firm was given the prestigious job of handling Academy Awards balloting. It started a management consulting service in 1946. But PW's dominance slipped in the 1960s, as it gained a reputation as the most traditional and formal of the major firms.

Coopers & Lybrand, the product of a 1957 transatlantic merger, wrote the book on auditing. Lybrand, Ross Bros. & Montgomery was formed in 1898 by William Lybrand, Edward Ross, Adam Ross, and Robert Montgomery. In 1912 Montgomery wrote *Montgomery's Auditing*, which became the bible of accounting.

Cooper Brothers was founded in 1854 in London by William Cooper, eldest son of a Quaker banker. In 1957 Lybrand joined up to form Coopers & Lybrand. During the 1960s the firm expanded into employee benefits and internal control consulting, building its technology ca-

pabilities in the 1970s as it studied ways to automate the audit process.

Coopers & Lybrand lost market share as mergers reduced the Big Eight accounting firms to the Big Six. After the savings and loan debacle of the 1980s, investors and the government wanted accounting firms held liable not only for the form of audited financial statements but for their veracity. In 1992 the firm paid $95 million to settle claims of defrauded investors in MiniScribe, a failed disk-drive maker. Other hefty payments followed, including a $108 million settlement relating to the late Robert Maxwell's defunct media empire.

In 1998 Price Waterhouse and Coopers & Lybrand combined PW's strength in the media, entertainment, and utility industries, and Coopers & Lybrand's focus on telecommunications and mining. But the merger brought some expensive legal baggage involving Coopers & Lybrand's performance of audits related to a bid-rigging scheme involving former Arizona governor Fife Symington.

Further growth plans fell through in 1999 when merger talks between PwC and Grant Thornton International failed. The year 2000 began on a sour note: An SEC conflict-of-interest probe turned up more than 8,000 alleged violations, most involving PwC partners owning stock in their firm's audit clients.

As the SEC grew ever more shrill in its denunciation of the potential conflicts of interest arising from auditing companies that the firm hoped to recruit or retain as consulting clients, PwC saw the writing on the wall and in 2000 began making plans to split the two operations. As part of this move, the company downsized and reorganized many of its operations.

The following year PwC paid $55 million to shareholders of MicroStrategy Inc., who charged that the audit firm defrauded them by approving the client firm's inflated earnings and revenues figures.

EXECUTIVES

Global Chairman: Andrew Ratcliffe
Global CEO and Global Board Member: Samuel A. DiPiazza Jr.
Global CFO: Geoffrey E. Johnson
Managing Partner, Global Markets: Willem L.J. Bröcker
Managing Partner, Global Operations: Amyas C.E. Morse, age 53
Global General Counsel; Acting US General Counsel: Lawrence Keeshan
Global Human Capital Leader: Amy DiGeso, age 49
Global Risk Management Leader: Ian Brindle
Global Consumer and Industrial Products Leader: Thomas W. Cross
Global Industries, Markets and Strategic Planning Leader: Rocco J. Maggiotto
Global Services Leader: Bruce W. Hucklesby
Global Assurance and Business Advisory Services Leader: J. Frank Brown, age 45
Global Financial Services Leader: Jeremy Scott
Global Geography Leader: Paul Batchelor
Global Tax and Legal Services Leader: Paul J.M. van Leent
Global Human Resources Solutions Leader: John Kaplan
Territory/Regional Leader, US; Chairman and Senior Partner (US): Dennis M. Nally
Tax Leader (US): Rick Berry
Human Resources, Learning, and Education Leader (US): Bob Daugherty
Marketing Leader (US): Dean Kern

LOCATIONS

HQ: 1301 Avenue of the Americas, New York, NY 10019
Phone: 646-471-4000   **Fax:** 646-394-1301
Web: www.pwcglobal.com

PricewaterhouseCoopers has offices in about 140 countries.

2003 Sales

	% of total
Europe	46
North America & Caribbean	37
Asia	9
Australasia & Pacific Islands	4
South & Central America	2
Middle East & Africa	2
Total	**100**

PRODUCTS/OPERATIONS

2003 Sales

	$ mil.	% of total
Assurance & business advisory services	8,983	61
Tax & legal services	4,293	29
Corporate finance & recovery	1,165	8
Discontinued operations	148	1
Other	94	1
Total	**14,683**	**100**

Selected Services

Audit, Assurance, and Business Advisory Services
Accounting and regulatory advice
Attest and related services
Audit
Corporate training
Performance measurement and corporate reporting
Public services audit and advisory
Specialized services for growing and middle market companies

Financial Advisory (called Corporate Finance & Recovery outside the US)
Business recovery services
Corporate finance
Dispute analysis and investigations (forensics)
Specialized services relating to infrastructure, government, and utilities
Valuation and strategy

Global Risk Management Solutions
Audit and compliance services
Behavioral transformation (services related to human resources)
Operational advisory
Risk and value management
Security and technology services
Sustainability services

Global Tax Services
Customs and duties
E-business services
Finance and treasure
Global VAT solutions
Global visa solutions
International assignment solutions
Mergers and acquisitions
Personal financial services
Tax compliance and outsourcing
Transfer pricing

Selected Industry Specializations

Consumer and Industrial Products and Services
Automotive
Energy and utilities
Industrial products
Pharmaceuticals
Retail and consumer
Services (including public sector)
Financial Services
Banking and capital markets
Insurance
Investment management
Real estate
Technology, InfoComm, and Entertainment
Entertainment and media
Information and communications
Technology

COMPETITORS

Bain & Company	Hewitt Associates
BDO International	KPMG
Booz Allen	Marsh & McLennan
Boston Consulting	McKinsey & Company
Deloitte Touche Tohmatsu	Towers Perrin
Ernst & Young	Watson Wyatt
H&R Block	

HISTORICAL FINANCIALS

Company Type: Partnership

Income Statement

FYE: June 30

	REVENUE ($ mil.)	NET INCOME ($ mil.)	NET PROFIT MARGIN	EMPLOYEES
6/03	14,683	—	—	122,820
6/02	13,800	—	—	124,563
6/01	24,000	—	—	160,000
6/00	21,500	—	—	150,000
6/99	15,300	—	—	155,000
Annual Growth	**(1.0%)**	**—**	**—**	**(5.7%)**

Revenue History

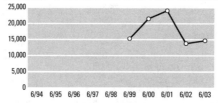

Prudential plc

The Man from the Pru no longer surfs the sidewalk, he surfs the Internet. The company (known for its Man from the Pru sales agent) is one of the UK's biggest insurers, offering life insurance and savings products to customers in the UK, Europe, the US, and Asia. Prudential's UK businesses include life insurer Scottish Amicable and its Prudential Banking division. Products include pensions, investment bonds, and personal loans. In the US Prudential already owns Jackson National Life, which offers annuities and life insurance. Asian operations are headed by Prudential Corporation Asia. Other businesses include fund management (M&G) and real estate.

The bank's publicly listed Egg offers telephone and Internet banking services, as well as mortgages and VISA credit cards, and is expanding into online brokerage.

Prudential's planned buy of American General, in hopes of capturing the lucrative annuities market, fell through. It dropped its bid, and American General embraced American International Group, leaving the Pru with a $600 million break-up fee. The company is still searching for potential US acquisitions. Overhauling its UK operations, Prudential has abolished its direct sales force (some 2,000 people), concentrating on sales by phone and through the Internet.

The firm has been remaking itself in the image of a company that can be all things financial to all people; it has divested noncore operations to concentrate on life insurance, group pensions, and with-profit bonds. In a further attempt to bolster its slumping domestic operations, the company has sold its general insurance business to Swiss insurer Winterthur (a subsidiary of Credit Suisse) and is cutting another 2,000 people. The move also includes dropping its Scottish Amicable products, which was rebranded under the Prudential name.

HISTORY

Actually, prudence almost killed Prudential before it ever got started. Founded in 1848 as Prudential Mutual Assurance Investment and Loan Association, the firm initially insured middle-class customers. The Dickensian conditions of the working poor made them too risky for insurers. Unfortunately the company found few takers of the right sort, and by 1852 Prudential was in peril.

Two events saved Prudential: The House of Commons pressed for insurance coverage for all classes, and Prudential's own agents pushed for change. The company expanded into industrial insurance, a modest coverage for the working poor. In 1864, to quell criticism of the insurance industry, Prudential brought in independent auditors to confirm its soundness. This soon became a marketing tool and business took off. The Pru, as it came to be known, became the leading industrial insurer by the 1880s. It covered half the country's population by 1905. The firm's salesmen were known for making personal visits to customers (the "Man from the Pru" became a ubiquitous icon in the 1940s and was revived in 1997).

During the two world wars Prudential boosted its reputation by honoring the policies of war victims when it could have legally denied them. Between wars the company added fire and accident insurance in Europe.

In 1969 it bought Mercantile and General Reinsurance Company from Swiss Re.

In 1982, under the direction of CEO Brian Corby, the Pru reorganized product lines and in 1985 entered the real estate business. In 1986 it entered the US market by buying US-based Jackson National Life. The 1980s were volatile for insurance companies, especially in the wake of Britain's financial deregulation in 1986.

Prudential, which had considered selling Mercantile and General Reinsurance in the early 1990s, sold the reinsurer back to Swiss Re in 1996. It also formed Prudential Bank and created an Asian emerging-market investment fund that year.

In 1997 Prudential bought Scottish Amicable. Insurance regulators reprimanded the company for mis-selling financial products that year.

In 1998 Jackson National bought a California

savings and loan, enabling it to sell investment products in the US. Also that year the Pru sold its Australian and New Zealand businesses, and Prudential Bank launched its Internet bank Egg (now larger than any US online bank). In 1999 Prudential bought investment manager M & G Group and announced plans to cut more than 5,000 jobs by 2002 to reduce costs.

The company changed its name to Prudential plc and began talks with the Prudential Insurance Company of America to resolve confusion of their similar names as they expand into new markets. The Pru in 1999 joined forces with the Bank of China to offer pension and asset management in Hong Kong.

In 2000 the company announced plans to sell a chunk of its institutional fund management business as well as its traditional balanced pension business to Deutsche Bank. That year the company spun off 20% of its Internet banking business, Egg. Also in 2000 the company agreed to start an insurance joint venture in China with state-owned investment vehicle CITIC Group.

Entering the Japanese life insurance market, Prudential bought Orico Life in 2001.

EXECUTIVES

Chairman: David C. Clementi, age 53
Group Chief Executive and Board Member:
 Jonathan Bloomer, age 49
Group Finance Director and Board Member:
 Philip Broadley, age 42
Chief Executive, The M&G Group and Board Member:
 Michael McLintock, age 42
Chief Executive, Prudential Asia and Board Member:
 Mark Tucker, age 45
Chief Executive, UK and European Insurance and Board Member: Mark Wood, age 49
Chief Executive, Egg plc: Paul Gratton, age 43
President and CEO, Jackson National Life and Board Member: Clark P. Manning Jr.
Group Corporate Relations Director: Geraldine Davies
Group Human Resources Director: Jane Kibbey
Group Legal Services Director and Secretary:
 Peter Maynard
Investor Relations Director: Rebecca Burrows
Vice Chairman and COO, Jackson National Life:
 Mike Wells
EVP and Chief Distribution Officer, Jackson National Life: Clifford Jack
EVP, Information Technology: George Napoles
EVP, Corporate Development: Jim Sopha
Auditors: KPMG Audit Plc

LOCATIONS

HQ: Laurence Pountney Hill,
 London EC4R 0HH, United Kingdom
Phone: +44-20-7220-7588 **Fax:** +44-20-7548-3850
US HQ: Jackson National Life, 1 Corporate Way,
 Lansing, MI 48951
US Phone: 517-381-5500 **US Fax:** 517-706-5517
Web: www.prudential.co.uk

2002 Sales

	% of total
UK insurance operations	64
US operations	24
Prudential Asia	11
Prudential Europe	1
Total	**100**

PRODUCTS/OPERATIONS

Selected Subsidiaries

Egg plc (79%, Internet banking)
Jackson National Life Insurance Co. (life insurance, annuities; US)
M&G Investment Management Ltd.
Prudential Annuities Ltd. (insurance)
The Prudential Assurance Co. Ltd.

Prudential Assurance Co. Singapore (Pte) Ltd.
 (insurance)
Prudential Banking plc (banking)

COMPETITORS

Abbey National	Legal & General Group
AEGON	MetLife
Alliance & Leicester	Millea Holdings
Allianz	Mitsui Sumitomo
Allstate	Insurance
AMB Generali	Munich Re
AIG	New York Life
Generali	Nippon Life Insurance
Aviva	Prudential
AXA	Royal & Sun Alliance
Britannic group	Insurance
Canada Life	Sompo Japan Insurance
Citigroup	State Farm
ERGO	Winterthur
HBOS	Woolwich
ING	Zurich Financial Services

HISTORICAL FINANCIALS

Company Type: Public

Income Statement

FYE: December 31

	ASSETS ($ mil.)	NET INCOME ($ mil.)	INCOME AS % OF ASSETS	EMPLOYEES
12/02	245,207	724	0.3%	21,930
12/01	228,287	566	0.2%	23,047
12/00	231,681	1,029	0.4%	21,942
12/99	243,514	876	0.4%	22,372
12/98	196,742	1,460	0.7%	22,200
12/97	178,525	1,381	0.8%	22,100
12/96	134,445	2,412	1.8%	22,187
12/95	116,109	1,175	1.0%	23,064
12/94	102,638	347	0.3%	25,500
12/93	96,262	585	0.6%	21,114
Annual Growth	**10.9%**	**2.4%**	**—**	**0.4%**

2002 Year-End Financials

Equity as % of assets: 2.4%
Return on assets: 0.3%
Return on equity: 12.4%
Long-term debt ($ mil.): 172,355
No. of shares (mil.): 1,001

Dividends
 Yield: 6.1%
 Payout: 115.1%
Market value ($ mil.): 13,882
Sales ($ mil.): 39,630

Stock History

NYSE: PUK

	STOCK PRICE ($) FY Close	P/E High/Low	PER SHARE ($) Earnings	Dividends	Book Value
12/02	13.87	33 14	0.73	0.84	5.91
12/01	23.43	58 27	0.57	0.80	5.77
12/00	31.88	135 102	0.24	0.27	6.07
Annual Growth	**(34.0%)**	**— —**	**74.4%**	**76.4%**	**(1.3%)**

Publicis Groupe

Advertising is *la joie de vivre* for Publicis. One of the world's largest advertising and media services conglomerates, the company offers a variety of communication services, including creative advertising, media and campaign planning, marketing, and public relations. The company's three global networks: Publicis Worldwide, Saatchi & Saatchi, and Leo Burnett Worldwide represent the bulk of the company's advertising operations (advertising accounts for 56% of revenue). Publicis acquired Bcom3 Group in 2002, creating the world's fourth-largest ad holdings company. Publicis' counts Coca Cola, Nestlé, and Procter & Gamble among its clients.

While always a leading ad firm in Europe, Publicis rose to global prominence after a string of acquisitions in 2000. Many of its targets were located in the US, including DeWitt Media and Chicago's Frankel & Co. Publicis secured its standing when it bought Saatchi & Saatchi for $1.9 billion. This did not stop it from negotiating new deals, however. In 2001 it merged Optimedia with Zenith to create one of the world's largest media services firms (Publicis owned 75% of the merged operation and acquired the remainder after WPP's acquisition of Cordiant).

In 2002 Publicis acquired Bcom3 Group for $3 billion to make it the fourth-largest advertising group worldwide. With the addition of Bcom3's Starcom MediaVest Group to Publicis' own Zenith Optimedia, Publicis controls the largest media buying and planning group in the world. The merger also creates a significant size gap between Publicis and the sixth-largest ad group Havas Advertising (Dentsu is fifth but through its partnership with Bcom3 won't be competing geographically with the new company). As a result of the acquisition, Publicis is undergoing a structural reorganization; the company is eliminating D'Arcy Masius Benton & Bowles and is integrating Leo Burnett Worldwide into its operations. (It acquired both D'Arcy and Leo Burnett when it completed the Bcom3 takeover).

In addition to its advertising and media services operations, Publicis' third business line offers a variety of marketing services on a global basis. The Specialized Agencies and Marketing Services (SAMS) group includes such services as public relations (Pangea), direct marketing (Frankel), interactive marketing (Semaphore), multicultural (Burrell), and a slew of other services and agencies. SAMS accounts for about one quarter of Publicis' revenue.

Elisabeth Badinter, supervisory board chair and daughter of late founder Marcel Bleustein-Blanchet, controls about 35% of Publicis (through her stake in Somarel). Dentsu, as a result of its investment in Bcom3, now owns 15% of the combined company.

HISTORY

In 1926 Marcel Bleustein, then 19 years old, started France's first advertising agency, which he called Publicis (a takeoff on "publicity" and "six"). He launched his own radio station, Radio Cite, after the French government banned all advertising on state-run stations, and by 1939 he had expanded into film distribution and movie theaters. With the outbreak of WWII, Bleustein fled to London to serve with the Free French Forces.

Having adopted the name Bleustein-Blanchet, he returned to France following the liberation and revived his advertising business. In 1958 he bought the former Hotel Astoria on the Champs-Elysées and opened the first Le Drugstore. The original structure burned in a 1972 fire, and legend has it that Bleustein-Blanchet tapped Maurice Lévy to lead the company after he found Lévy salvaging records amid the ruins.

To expand its business, Publicis formed an alliance — Chicago-based Foote, Cone & Belding Communications (FCB) — in 1988. The partnership soured five years later, however, when Publicis acquired France's Groupe FCA. (FCB claimed the acquisition was a breach of contract and countered by establishing a new holding company for itself, True North Communications.) Bleustein-Blanchet died in 1996, and his daughter, Elisabeth Badinter, was named chair of the supervisory board.

In 1997 Publicis and True North divided their joint network, Publicis Communications, with True North getting the European offices and Publicis getting Africa, Asia, and Argentina. Later that year Publicis attempted a $700 million hostile bid for the 81.5% of True North it didn't already own to stop True North's acquisition of Bozell, Jacobs, Kenyon & Eckhardt. The bid failed, and Publicis' stake in True North was reduced to 11%. (True North was later acquired by Interpublic Group in 2001.)

The company gained new ground in the US through its acquisitions of Hal Riney & Partners and Evans Group in 1998. That year Lévy helped sooth a bitter feud among the descendants of Marcel Bleustein: Elisabeth Badinter had battled with her sister Michele Bleustein-Blanchet over Bleustein-Blanchet's desire to sell her stake in Publicis' holding company. Lévy's solution allowed Bleustein-Blanchet to sell her shares and left Badinter with control of the company.

Continuing its US expansion, in 1999 Publicis bought a 49% stake in Burrell Communications Group (one of the largest African-American-owned ad agencies in the US).

In 2000 the company bought advertising outfit Fallon McElligott (now Fallon Worldwide), marketing firm Frankel & Co., and media buyer DeWitt Media (which was merged into Optimedia). Publicis capped off the year by acquiring Saatchi & Saatchi for about $1.9 billion. Along with the deal, it inherited Saatchi's 50% of media buying unit Zenith Media (jointly owned by Cordiant Communications). In 2001 it merged Optimedia and Zenith, with Publicis owning 75% of the new business.

2002 was a big year for Publicis and the ad industry in general; the decision to acquire Bcom3 catapulted the company into the really big leagues and created a distinct size difference between the top 4 advertising conglomerates and everyone else.

EXECUTIVES

Chairman, Management Board and CEO: Maurice Lévy, age 59
President and COO: Roger A. Haupt, age 56
CFO: Jean-Michel Etienne
CEO, Saatchi & Saatchi: Kevin J. Roberts, age 54
Board Member and Chairman, Saatchi & Saatchi: Robert Louis Seelert, age 61
Board Member and Director, Property Division: Henri-Calixte Suaudeau, age 67
Board Member; Chairman and CEO, Médias & Régies Europe: Simon Badinter, age 35
Chairman, Fallon Worldwide: Patrick (Pat) Fallon
Chairman and CEO, Publicis in US: Susan Gianinno, age 54
Chairman and CEO, Starcom MediaVest Group: Jack Klues, age 45

President and CEO, Specialized Agencies and Marketing Services: John Farrell
CEO, Zenith Optimedia Group: John Perriss
COO, Publicis Worldwide: Rick Bendel
Managing Director: Bruno Desbarats-Bollet, age 60
Managing Director and EVP Publicis Worldwide: Bertrand Siguier, age 62
Worldwide Creative Director, Publicis Worldwide: David B. Droga, age 34
Director Investor Relations: Pierre Benaich
Manager Administration: Fran Class
Corporate Communications: Eve Magnant
Auditors: Ernst & Young Audit; Mazars & Guérard

LOCATIONS

HQ: Publicis Groupe S.A.
133, avenue des Champs-Elysées,
75008 Paris, France
Phone: +33-1-44-43-70-00   **Fax:** +33-1-44-43-75-25
Web: www.publicis.fr

Publicis has about 180 offices in more than 100 countries.

PRODUCTS/OPERATIONS

2002 Sales

	$ mil.	% of total
North America	1,360	44
Europe	1,305	43
Other Countries	408	13
Total	**3,073**	**100**

Selected Operations and Agencies

Advertising
Beacon Communications
Fallon Worldwide
Kaplan Thaler Group
Leo Burnett Worldwide
Publicis Worldwide
Saatchi & Saatchi Worldwide

Media Services
Médias & Régies Europe
Starcom MediaVest Group
ZenithOptimedia

Specialized Agencies and Marketing Services Group (SAMS)
Frankel (sales promotion and direct marketing)
iLeo (interactive marketing)
Lapiz (multicultural marketing)
Medicus Group (health care marketing)
Nelson Communications (health care marketing)
Pangea PR (public relations)
Publicis Dialog (sales promotion and direct marketing)
Publicis Sanchez & Levitan (multicultural marketing)
Rowland Companies (public relations)
Semaphore (interactive marketing)
Van Sluis (public relations)

Selected Clients

Allied Domecq
Club Med
Coca-Cola
Fiat
L'Oréal
McDonald's
Nestlé
Pharmacia Upjohn
Procter & Gamble
Siemens

COMPETITORS

Aegis Group
Grey Global
Hakuhodo
Havas
Incepta
Interpublic Group
Omnicom
WPP Group

HISTORICAL FINANCIALS

Company Type: Public

Income Statement

FYE: December 31

	REVENUE ($ mil.)	NET INCOME ($ mil.)	NET PROFIT MARGIN	EMPLOYEES
12/02	3,073	154	5.0%	35,681
12/01	2,169	135	6.2%	20,592
12/00	1,667	119	7.1%	16,000
12/99	1,052	96	9.1%	10,362
12/98	993	55	5.6%	8,709
12/97	725	39	5.3%	7,363
12/96	716	35	4.9%	6,038
12/95	744	6	0.9%	6,000
12/94	644	5	0.8%	5,540
12/93	532	4	0.7%	4,690
Annual Growth	**21.5%**	**51.8%**	**—**	**25.3%**

2002 Year-End Financials

Debt ratio: 131.1%
Return on equity: 16.8%
Cash ($ mil.): 906
Current ratio: 1.02
Long-term debt ($ mil.): 2,068
No. of shares (mil.): 183
Dividends
Yield: 1.0%
Payout: 21.6%
Market value ($ mil.): 3,842

Stock History

NYSE: PUB

12/93 12/94 12/95 12/96 12/97 12/98 12/99 12/00 12/01 12/02

	STOCK PRICE ($) FY Close	P/E High/Low		PER SHARE ($) Earnings	Dividends	Book Value
12/02	20.96	34	16	1.02	0.22	8.60
12/01	26.00	38	15	0.96	0.17	1.87
12/00	33.63	35	24	1.08	0.00	2.05
Annual Growth	**(21.1%)**	**—**	**—**	**(2.8%)**	**—**	**105.1%**

Qantas Airways

Some Australians go on walkabout; others fly about on Qantas Airways, Australia's #1 airline and a leader in international flights to and from the country. Including code-sharing agreements, Qantas flies to about 140 destinations in Australia and 33 other countries, and it operates a regional airline. Qantas' fleet includes nearly 200 aircraft. Qantas is also part of the global marketing alliance Oneworld, which is led by code-sharing partners British Airways and American Airlines, among others. Other Qantas operations include catering and tourism.

Qantas' Australian regional airline QantasLink flies more than 60 planes to more than 55 domestic destinations. With the demise of its Australian rival Ansett, Qantas is attempting to expand its domestic network. It is also developing e-commerce operations devoted to travel and transport.

Qantas has an extensive code-sharing agreement with British Airways; they coordinate their scheduling, sales, and marketing and share facilities such as airport lounges. Qantas has offered to acquire a 23% stake in Air New Zealand, which has been approved by the New Zealand government. Should the deal happen, the New Zealand government's stake in the airline would drop from 82% to 64%.

To try to curb continued losses, the airline has announced plans to operate a low-fare carrier called JetStar, for which Qantas plans on purchasing 23 new Airbus jets.

HISTORY

Ex-WWI pilots Wilmot Hudson Fysh and Paul McGinness and stockman Fergus McMaster founded Queensland and Northern Territory Aerial Services (Qantas) in 1920 to provide an air link between Darwin in the Northern Territory and the railheads in Queensland. In 1922 Qantas began carrying airmail over a 577-mile route between Charleville and Cloncurry, and by 1930 it covered northeastern Australia with air routes. Qantas moved its headquarters to Sydney in 1938.

Qantas and Imperial Airways (predecessor of British Airways, or BA) formed Qantas Empire Airways in 1934 to fly the last leg of a London-to-Australia mail route (Singapore to Brisbane). Qantas bought the British share of Qantas Empire in 1947 (when Qantas made its first Sydney-London flight) and was subsequently nationalized.

By 1950 the airline served most major cities in the Pacific Rim. Qantas inaugurated a route to Johannesburg (1952) and opened the Southern Cross route, previously operated by British Commonwealth Pacific Airlines, to San Francisco and Vancouver via Honolulu (1953).

In 1958 Qantas offered the first complete round-the-world service. (Pan Am had started a similar service in 1957 but was barred by the US government from crossing North America.) It bought 29% of Malayan Airways in 1959 and added several European destinations in the 1960s, including Frankfurt (1966) and Amsterdam (1967). Founder Fysh retired as chairman in 1966, and the airline took its present name in 1967.

Tourism in Australia boomed in the 1970s. Competition from foreign (especially US) airlines initially hurt Qantas, contributing to a $4 million loss in 1971 (its second since 1924). But in 1973 annual boardings jumped 28%. Qantas' Aussie passengers flew some 4,217 miles per journey — the longest average trip of any airline.

In 1987 Qantas bought a stake in Fiji's Air Pacific. Later acquisitions included Australia-Asia Airlines (1989) and 20% of Air New Zealand (1990; sold 1997). Qantas enjoyed record profits in 1989, but a strike by domestic pilots paralyzed Australia's tourist industry that year, hurting Qantas in 1990.

The Australian airline industry was deregulated in the early 1990s, and Qantas formed regional carrier Airlink in 1991. The next year it merged with Australia Airlines, and in 1993 the Australian government sold BA a 25% stake in Qantas. Still, the airlines' 1994 attempt to set prices and services together was rejected by Australian authorities.

Because Australian privatizations had deluged the stock exchange with issues, Qantas delayed its IPO until 1995. Also that year Qantas and BA got approval for a joint service agreement that allowed them to operate some facilities together.

The carrier began code-sharing with American Airlines in 1995; three years later Qantas joined the Oneworld global marketing alliance, led by American and BA. In 1998 and 1999 Qantas and BA began combining their operations in Hong Kong, Indonesia, Malaysia, Singapore, and Thai-

land. The airline expanded its code-sharing with affiliate Air Pacific in 2000, even as it braced for competition at home from Virgin Atlantic's new Australian low-fare carrier.

Unable to gain regulatory approval, Qantas dropped its bidding war with rival Ansett to acquire regional carrier Hazelton Airlines in 2001. That year Qantas agreed to acquire Impulse Airlines, an ailing Australian low-fare carrier. The company also entered negotiations with Air New Zealand to buy Ansett, but Qantas decided against a purchase of its troubled Australian rival. Air New Zealand subsequently shut down Ansett's operations.

Also in 2001 two Qantas employees were killed when a plane on which they were traveling crashed into the north tower of the World Trade Center. The next year Qantas began negotiations to acquire a stake in Air New Zealand.

EXECUTIVES

Chairman: Margaret Jackson
CEO: Geoff Dixon, age 62
CFO: Peter Gregg, age 47
Chief Executive, Australian Airlines: Denis Adams, $805,000 pay
Executive General Manager and Chief Information Officer: Fiona Balfour
Executive General Manager, Aircraft Operations: David Forsyth, $566,880 pay
Executive General Manager, Airline Strategy and Network Management: Paul Edwards, $468,066 pay
Executive General Manager, Finance and Deputy CFO: Grant Fenn
Executive General Manager, Human Resources: Kevin Brown
Executive General Manager, Sales and Marketing: John Borghetti, $977,014 pay
Executive General Manager, Subsidiary Businessess: Narendra Kumar
Group General Manager, Government and International Relations: David Hawes
Group General Manager, Public Affairs: Michael Sharp
General Counsel and Company Secretary: Brett Johnson
Auditors: KPMG

LOCATIONS

HQ: Quantas Airways Limited
Qantas Centre, Level 9, Bldg. A,
203 Coward St., Mascot,
New South Wales 2020, Australia
Phone: +61-2-9691-3636　　**Fax:** +61-2-9691-3339
US HQ: 841 Apollo St., Ste. 400, El Segundo, CA 90245
US Phone: 310-726-1400　　**US Fax:** 310-726-1484
Web: www.qantas.com.au

Qantas serves about 140 destinations in Australia and about 33 other countries.

PRODUCTS/OPERATIONS

2003 Sales

	% of total
Passenger	79
Tours & travel	6
Contract	5
Freight	4
Other	6
Total	**100**

Selected Partners

Air Pacific
Alaska Airlines
American Airlines
Asiana
British Airways (BA)
EVA Airways
Finnair
Japan Airlines
Vietnam Airlines

COMPETITORS

Air New Zealand	Lufthansa
All Nippon Airways	Northwest Airlines
Cathay Pacific	SAS
Continental Airlines	Singapore Airlines
Delta	UAL
DHL	UPS
FedEx	Virgin Atlantic Airways
KLM	

HISTORICAL FINANCIALS

Company Type: Public

Income Statement

FYE: June 30

	REVENUE ($ mil.)	NET INCOME ($ mil.)	NET PROFIT MARGIN	EMPLOYEES
6/03	7,585	229	3.0%	34,872
6/02	6,380	241	3.8%	33,044
6/01	5,196	212	4.1%	31,632
6/00	5,437	309	5.7%	29,217
6/99	5,585	279	5.0%	23,411
6/98	5,005	188	3.7%	30,000
6/97	5,850	189	3.2%	30,080
6/96	5,982	194	3.2%	29,627
6/95	5,088	128	2.5%	28,565
6/94	4,809	114	2.4%	26,791
Annual Growth	**5.2%**	**8.1%**	**—**	**3.0%**

2003 Year-End Financials

Debt ratio: 102.5%	Current ratio: 0.83
Return on equity: —	Long-term debt ($ mil.): 3,595
Cash ($ mil.): 81	

Net Income History

Australian: QAN

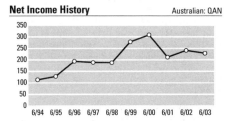

Quebecor Inc.

Quebecor Inc. has one hand on the printing press, the other on media. Subsidiary Quebecor World is one of the world's top commercial printers. Its main products include books, advertising inserts, and directories, as well as a number of magazines such as *Time*. The company's Sun Media subsidiary is Canada's #2 newspaper publisher, with some 190 regional papers and magazines. Its Vidéotron Itée subsidiary is Canada's third-largest cable company. Its TVA Group subsidiary owns the dominant TV network in Quebec. The founding Péladeau family controls 62% of the company.

Quebecor World's purchase of rival World Color Press in 1999 pushed it into position as the world's third-largest commercial printer (behind Dai Nippon Printing and Toppan Printing). Through 160 printing plants in 15 countries, the company makes advertising inserts, books, and magazines, as well as catalogs for North American retailers.

Quebecor also has operations in book publishing (Éditions CEC, among others) and music retail (Archambault superstores). In the Internet realm, the company operates an Internet portal (canoe.com), as well as several other Web sites. It also owns a 57% stake in e-services firm nurun (formerly Informission Group). The company has also made a foray into radio with several station acquisitions in 2002.

HISTORY

In 1950 law student Pierre Péladeau borrowed $1,500 from his mother so he could buy a small Montreal newspaper called *Le Journal de Rosemont*. This became the base for Péladeau's publishing empire. Within a few years he had established five other weekly newspapers and his first printing firm.

Péladeau seized the opportunity presented to him in 1964 by a strike at the major Montreal paper *La Presse*. He assembled a team from his various weeklies and, according to company legend, had the tabloid *Le Journal* on the streets within three days.

Quebecor went public in 1972 and expanded beyond Quebec, branching out into a variety of communication concerns. But by the late 1980s, the company had refocused on its core printing businesses.

Quebecor purchased printing plants in New Jersey and Michigan in 1985. Péladeau teamed with Robert Maxwell in 1987 to form Mircor to buy a stake in forestry concern Donohue. The company took a major step into the international arena when it bought the printing group BCE PubliTech in 1988, making the company the #1 commercial printer in Canada.

In 1990 Maxwell sold his US printing plants (with state-of-the-art printing presses) to Péladeau, who formed Quebecor Printing (USA) around the new assets. Maxwell subsequently bought a 26% stake in the new company for $100 million.

Maxwell died mysteriously in 1991 followed by revelations of deceptive finances and shady business dealings by the Maxwell empire. This allowed Péladeau to buy back all of Maxwell's shares in Quebecor at bargain-basement prices.

In the 1990s Quebecor continued expanding, buying a bookbinding and publishing company in Mexico (Gráficas Monte Alban, 1991), three US printing plants (1993), France's largest commercial printer (Group Jean Didier, 1995), and a UK printer (1995). Quebecor Printing went public in 1995, which reduced the parent company's interest to less than 50%. Quebecor also set up its multimedia unit and expanded it by acquiring 50% of Sierra Creative Communications and 25% of multimedia software publisher Micro-Intel (1996).

A Quebecor-controlled consortium in 1997 acquired Télévision Quatre Saisons, which operates three Canadian TV stations and the Quatre Saisons TV network license. (The company sold the network and related stations in 2001.) Péladeau died from heart failure that year.

In 1999 Quebecor bought Sun Media, which made the company the #2 Canadian newspaper publisher. It later sold a 30% stake in Sun Media to a group of private investors for $260 million. In 1999 Quebecor Printing acquired World Color Press. Also that year Pierre Karl Péladeau, the founder's second son, took over as president and CEO. Péladeau family members have filed a flood of lawsuits against one another and the executor of Pierre Péladeau's estate in a battle for control of family assets, including the company.

Quebecor sold its controlling stake in market pulp, lumber, and newsprint producer Donohue to rival Abitibi-Consolidated in 2000. Also that year the company restructured into two operating units: Quebecor Printing (changing its name to Quebecor World) and Quebecor Media. Later in 2000 Quebecor and Caisse de Dépôt et Placement du Québec (Quebec's public-pension agency) won a bidding war with Rogers Communications for the acquisition of Le Groupe Vidéotron, Canada's #3 cable TV operator, with an offer of $3.6 billion. Le Groupe Vidéotron's broadcasting company TVA Group was part of the deal, but was not finalized until 2001 after Quebecor completed the sale of its TQS network, which had been required by regulators.

In 2001 the company bought the 30% of Sun Media that it didn't already own. That year it also bulked up its Latin American holdings with the purchase of Grupo Serla, a school book text printer in Mexico, and 75% of Grafica Melhoramentos, a Brazilian book publisher. That year Quebecor also agreed to buy the European printing facilities of Hachette Filipacchi Médias. In 2002 the company merged its Publicor and TVA Publishing operations under the TVA Publishing name.

EXECUTIVES

Chairman: Jean Neveu
Vice Chairman: Erik Péladeau
President, CEO, and Director: Pierre K. Péladeau
EVP and CFO: Jacques Mallette
EVP Corporate Affairs: Luc Lavoie
VP Human Resources: Julie Tremblay
VP Legal Affairs and Secretary: Louis Saint-Arnaud
VP Taxation and Real Estate: Marc Doré
VP and Treasurer: Marc D'Souza
Director, Corporate Services; Assistant Corporate Secretary: Claudine Tremblay
President, Videotron Iteé: Robert Depatie
Auditors: KPMG LLP

LOCATIONS

HQ: 612 Saint-Jacques St., Montreal, Quebec H3C 4M8, Canada
Phone: 514-877-9777   **Fax:** 514-877-9757
US HQ: 980 Washington St., Ste. 222, Dedham, MA 02026
US Phone: 781-410-2000   **US Fax:** 781-410-2192
Web: www.quebecor.com

Quebecor has operations in Argentina, Austria, Belgium, Brazil, Canada, Chile, Colombia, Finland, France, Mexico, Peru, Spain, Sweden, the UK, and the US.

2002 Sales

	$ mil.	% of total
North America	6,209	82
Europe	978	13
Latin American	182	2
Other	250	3
Total	**7,619**	**100**

PRODUCTS/OPERATIONS

Selected Operations

Quebecor Media Inc.
  Archambault Group (music store chain in Canada)
  Book publishing
  Le Super Club Vidéotron Itée (video store chain in Canada)
  Netgraphe Inc. (portals and e-commerce sites)
  nurun Inc. (57%, Web development and e-commerce consulting)
  Sun Media Corporation (newspaper publishing)
  TVA Group (TV network in Quebec)
  TVA Publishing (magazine publishing)
  Vidéotron Itée (third-largest cable company in Canada)
  Vidéotron Télécom Itée (telecommunications services)
Quebecor World Inc. (commercial printing)

Selected Publications

The Calgary Sun
Clin d'oeil
Décoration Chez-Soi
The Edmonton Sun
Femme
Filles d'Aujourd'hui
Le Journal de Montréal
Le Journal de Québec
Les idées de ma maison
The London Free Press
The Ottawa Sun
The Toronto Sun
The Winnipeg Sun

COMPETITORS

ACG Holdings
Applied Graphics
Arandell
Banta
BCE
Bell Globemedia
Cadmus Communications
CBC
Cancom
CanWest Global
  Communications
COGECO Inc.
Courier
Dai Nippon Printing
EBSCO
Hachette Filipacchi Médias
Hollinger
Pearson
Quad/Graphics
Rogers Communications
R. R. Donnelley
Segerdahl
Shaw Communications
Toppan Printing
Torstar
Valassis
Vertis

HISTORICAL FINANCIALS

Company Type: Public

Income Statement

FYE: December 31

	REVENUE ($ mil.)	NET INCOME ($ mil.)	NET PROFIT MARGIN	EMPLOYEES
12/02	7,619	58	0.8%	50,000
12/01	7,312	(152)	—	54,000
12/00	7,282	724	9.9%	57,000
12/99	7,490	333	4.4%	60,000
12/98	5,486	112	2.0%	39,000
12/97	4,898	100	2.0%	37,000
12/96	4,562	107	2.3%	33,700
12/95	4,070	137	3.4%	28,900
12/94	2,834	63	2.2%	25,900
12/93	2,324	56	2.4%	20,600
Annual Growth	**14.1%**	**0.4%**	**—**	**10.4%**

2002 Year-End Financials

Debt ratio: 384.2%
Return on equity: 4.6%
Cash ($ mil.): 270
Current ratio: 0.81
Long-term debt ($ mil.): 3,603

Net Income History

Toronto: QBR.A

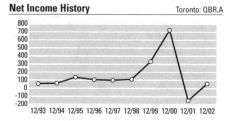

The Rank Group

Leisure and entertainment are highly rated by this company. The Rank Group owns a diverse portfolio of hospitality and leisure business around the world. The company has major UK gaming holdings, including more than 120 Mecca Bingo clubs and 30 Grosvenor Casinos. It also operates some 35,000 gaming machines (a business it is selling) and offers online gaming and sports betting through a number of Internet sites. In addition to its gaming businesses, Rank owns the Hard Rock Cafe franchise of restaurants, live entertainment venues, and hotels. The rest of the firm's business is focused on media services through its Deluxe subsidiary, one of the world's leading film processing and postproduction firms.

While Rank has received criticism in the past for its wide-ranging, and seemingly incongruent, holdings, the company's diversity has saved it from at least some of the ravages of the current economy. Its Hard Rock division has been hit by the slump in tourism while its UK gaming businesses, especially those located in the London area, have continued to remain popular. Meanwhile, the film services business at Deluxe has been very good owing to the recent slate of blockbusters passing through its labs, including *Star Wars Episode II*, *Spider Man*, and *Die Another Day*.

Rank added to its gaming business in 2003 when it acquired online betting site Blue Square for about $100 million. That same year the company formed a joint venture with resort operator Sol Meliá to develop new luxury Hard Rock hotels. The effort, backed by $1 billion for Becker Ventures, comes after a boardroom row that ended in the abrupt departure of Hard Rock chief Peter Beaudrault.

HISTORY

The Rank Group grew out of a sense of strong conviction. Joseph Arthur Rank was a devout Methodist who saw films as a way to spread the message of his religion. Leaving the successful family milling business, he started a production company in 1934 called British National Films. Later Rank acquired General Film Distributors, Pinewood Studios, and the Odeon theater chain. By 1941, Rank's entertainment holdings were so vast that many saw him as a monopolist. But after WWII the British film business deteriorated as American films flooded into the country. Television and an emerging leisure industry also took their toll in the 1950s.

With the holding company recast as The Rank Organisation in 1955, J. Arthur Rank and his managing director, John Davis, set about searching for alternative businesses. Rank formed a joint venture with the Haloid Company (now Xerox) in 1956 to market photocopying equipment. Later called Rank Xerox, the joint venture eventually dwarfed the profits of Rank's other operating units. Davis became chairman in 1962 (Rank died in 1972) and invested in a diverse but underperforming group of businesses, including bingo parlors, hotels, and dance halls. The pitiful results of his efforts were exposed in the late 1970s as Rank Xerox's earnings receded under growing competition in the copier market. Investors forced Davis to step down in 1977.

Michael Gifford was installed as chief executive in 1983 and immediately began cutting overhead and dumping businesses, which increased profits. Rank joined with MCA to create the Universal Studios Florida theme park (now part of Universal Parks & Resorts) in 1988 and acquired Mecca Leisure Group's bingo parlors, casinos, hotels, and clubs in 1990. It also bought the rights to a number of Hard Rock Cafes (originally established in London in 1971).

Rank named former ICI chief Sir Denys Henderson as its new chairman in 1994, and two years later Andrew Teare became Rank's new CEO. Teare led Rank's buyout of Hard Rock co-founder Peter Morton that year and installed former schoolteacher Jim Berk as Hard Rock's CEO. Teare also restructured Rank into four divisions (Film and Entertainment Services, Hard Rock, Holidays, and Leisure) and changed its name to The Rank Group.

The company sold its Rank Xerox stake back to Xerox for about $1.5 billion in 1997. After reporting more disappointing results, however, Teare left the company the next year. Mike Smith, former head of Ladbroke's (now Hilton Group) betting and gaming division, came in as CEO in 1999. Peter Beaudrault replaced Berk at Hard Rock that year.

Smith's restructuring efforts led to the sale of Rank's nightclub business to Northern Leisure in 1999. The Odeon theater chain went to UK buyout specialist Cinven for $450 million and Pinewood Studios was sold for about $100 million in 2000. Rank later sold its 50% stake in Universal Studios Orlando to Blackstone Capital Partners for $275 million, while its UK holiday resorts went to Bourne Leisure for $1 billion. In 2001 Henderson stepped down as chairman; former Avis Europe chairman Alun Cathcart was tapped as his replacement.

Early in 2003 Beaudrault left his post at Hard Rock as the theme restaurant chain posted declining sales.

EXECUTIVES

Chairman: W. Alun Cathcart, $240,585 pay
Chief Executive; Interim CEO, Hard Rock Cafe International: Mike Smith, age 56, $1,180,470 pay
Finance Director: Ian Dyson, age 41, $667,222 pay
Investor Relations Director: Peter Reynolds
Group Human Resources Director: Christine Ray, age 55
Company Secretary: Charles Cormick, age 52
Managing Director, Gaming Division: David Boden, age 46
Managing Director, Leisure Machine Services: Wes Mulligan
Managing Director, Interactive Gaming: Martin Belsham
President, Deluxe Laboratories: Cyril Drabinsky, age 45
President and CEO, Deluxe Media Services: Peter Pacitti, age 45
Compliance Director, Gaming Division: Alan Armstrong
Commercial Director, Blue Square: Ed Andrewes
Commercial Director, Gaming Division: Nigel Sibley
Finance Director, Gaming Division: David Walcott
Human Resources Director, Gaming Division: Sue Waldock
Operations Director, Gaming Division: Peter McCann
Marketing, Blue Square: Susie Hollands
Online Marketing, Blue Square: Jonathan Raab
Public Relations, Blue Square: Ed Pownall
Auditors: PricewaterhouseCoopers LLP

LOCATIONS

HQ: The Rank Group PLC
6 Connaught Place,
London W2 2EZ, United Kingdom
Phone: +44-20-7706-1111   **Fax:** +44-20-7262-9886
Web: www.rank.com

2002 Sales

	% of total
North America	48
UK	41
Other regions	11
Total	**100**

PRODUCTS/OPERATIONS

2002 Sales

	$ mil.	% of total
Deluxe	1,130	48
Gaming	761	32
Hard Rock	389	17
US Holidays	69	3
Total	**2,349**	**100**

2002 Operating Income

	$ mil.	% of total
Deluxe	143	39
Gaming	168	46
Hard Rock	44	12
US Holidays	13	3
Total	**368**	**100**

Selected Operations

Deluxe
Distribution and fulfillment
DVD manufacturing (Electric Switch)
Film processing (Deluxe Film Laboratories)
Post-production facilities and services
Video duplication (Deluxe Video Services)

Gaming
Blue Square (Internet and phone gambling)
Grosvenor Casinos (Belgium and UK)
Mecca Bingo (Spain and UK)
Rank Leisure Machine Services (gaming machines)

Hard Rock
Hard Rock Cafes
Hotels & Casinos
Hard Rock Casino (London)
Hard Rock Casino (Manchester)
Hard Rock Hotel (Bali, Indonesia)
Hard Rock Hotel (Orlando, Florida)
Hard Rock Hotel (Pattaya, Thailand)
Hard Rock Hotel & Casino (Las Vegas)

US Holidays
Resorts USA (Bushkill, Pennsylvania)
Fairway Villas (timeshare resort)
Fernwood Hotel and Resort
Tree Tops Villas (timeshare resort)
Outdoor World (15 campgrounds in seven states)

Other Interests
Portofino Bay Hotel (25%; Orlando, Florida)
Royal Pacific Resort Hotel (25%; Orlando, Florida)
Universal Studios Japan (10%; theme park)

COMPETITORS

Ascent Media
Camelot
Clear Channel Entertainment
Coral Eurobet
Harrah's Entertainment
Hilton Group
HOB Entertainment
Hooters
Laser-Pacific Media
Lucas Digital
Mandalay Resort Group
MGM Mirage
Park Place Entertainment
Planet Hollywood
Stanley Leisure
THOMSON
Trump Hotels & Casinos
William Hill

HISTORICAL FINANCIALS

Company Type: Public

Income Statement

FYE: December 31

	REVENUE ($ mil.)	NET INCOME ($ mil.)	NET PROFIT MARGIN	EMPLOYEES
12/02	2,360	220	9.3%	21,862
12/01	1,991	184	9.2%	20,955
12/00	2,682	(479)	—	37,057
12/99	3,298	110	3.3%	43,081
12/98	3,414	(181)	—	45,600
12/97	3,323	319	9.6%	43,698
12/96	3,569	(58)	—	43,478
12/95*	4,054	814	20.1%	—
10/94	3,597	275	7.6%	—
10/93	3,121	249	8.0%	—
Annual Growth	(3.1%)	(1.4%)	—	(10.8%)

*Fiscal year change

2002 Year-End Financials

Debt ratio: 66.5%
Return on equity: 22.3%
Cash ($ mil.): 134
Current ratio: 2.06
Long-term debt ($ mil.): 753

No. of shares (mil.): 297
Dividends
  Yield: 5.2%
  Payout: 66.7%
Market value ($ mil.): 2,421

Stock History

NASDAQ (SC): RANKY

10/93 10/94 12/95 12/96 12/97 12/98 12/99 12/00 12/01 12/02

	STOCK PRICE ($) FY Close	P/E High/Low	PER SHARE ($) Earnings	Dividends	Book Value
12/02	8.15	15 11	0.63	0.42	4.06
12/01	6.65	14 8	0.52	0.39	2.88
12/00	4.75	— —	(1.47)	0.36	2.81
12/99	6.13	14 8	0.27	0.60	4.95
12/98	7.50	— —	(0.44)	0.52	5.65
12/97	11.25	44 31	0.35	0.69	5.99
12/96	15.00	— —	(0.23)	0.62	7.35
12/95*	14.63	8 6	1.90	0.30	7.57
10/94	13.13	23 17	0.59	0.14	6.15
10/93	10.00	19 13	0.55	0.67	5.31
Annual Growth	(2.2%)	— —	1.5%	(5.1%)	(2.9%)

*Fiscal year change

Reckitt Benckiser plc

With a cart full of products, Reckitt Benckiser is cleaning up. The company is the world's leading household cleaning products maker. Its brands include air fresheners (Airwick), household cleaners (Lysol, Easy-Off), laundry products (Woolite), furniture polishes (Old English), and dishwashing detergents (Electrasol). It also makes over-the-counter pharmaceuticals such as analgesics, antiseptics, flu remedies, and gastrointestinal medications (Gaviscon) and offers products for hair removal, denture cleaning, and pest control (d-Con). Reckitt is also the maker of

French's mustard. The company was created by the merger of UK-based Reckitt & Colman and The Netherlands' Benckiser.

The company sells products in 180 countries worldwide. Reckitt Benckiser has divested about 75 minor brands, allowing the company to focus on its key brands in the areas of fabric care, surface care, dishwasher products, health and personal care, and home care.

In late 2002 the company lost a bid for Pfizer's Schick-Wilkinson Sword shaving products (the world's second-largest razor maker behind Gillette) to Energizer Holdings.

Reckitt, admitting that launching entirely new brands in the fast-moving consumer goods niche is risky and expensive, is looking for acquisition opportunities. SSL International (the maker of Durex condoms and Dr. Scholl footcare products) was approached by Reckitt in mid-2003.

HISTORY

Reckitt & Colman's roots can be traced to Jeremiah Colman, who bought a flour mill near Norwich, England, in 1804. In 1823 his nephew James joined the company, and their business was incorporated as J. and J. Colman. Jeremiah died in 1851 and James' son, also named Jeremiah, became a partner, taking over the operations when his father died in 1854. The company moved to Carrow that year.

Colman worked to make the Carrow facilities as self-sufficient and waste-free as possible. The factory had its own foundry, print shop, paper mill (to make containers), and fire brigade. By-products from the milling process were sold to farmers for cattle feed and fertilizer. The company continued to expand, adding wheat flour and using the leftover starch from milling operations to make laundry bluing.

In 1903 the mill acquired Keen, Robinson & Co., a manufacturer of spices. J. and J. Colman got a lock on British mustard sales in 1912 when it acquired its only major competitor, Joseph Farrow & Company. A year later it joined another rival, starch maker Reckitt & Sons, in a joint venture in South America. The joint venture between Colman and Reckitt was a success, and in 1921 they pooled their overseas operations.

The two companies created Reckitt & Colman Ltd. in 1938 to manage their operations, although each company maintained a separate listing on the London Stock Exchange. In 1954 they formally merged into a single entity.

Reckitt & Colman formed its US subsidiary in 1977, and during the 1980s it made a number of acquisitions (Airwick air fresheners, Gold Seal bath products) to expand its presence in the US.

In 1990 the firm picked up such brands as Black Flag (insecticide), Woolite (fabric care), and Easy-Off (oven cleaner) when it bought Boyle-Midway from American Home Products.

The company gained the Lysol brand in 1994 when it bought L&F Household from Eastman Kodak. To help finance the $1.6 billion deal, Reckitt & Colman sold its flagship Colman Mustard unit to Unilever. Its French's operations in the US (mustard, Worcestershire sauce) were its only remaining food business.

Michael Colman, the last active family member, stepped down as chairman in 1995. In 1996 it sold its US personal products unit.

In 1998 Reckitt & Colman bought certain cleaning products brands, including Spray'n Wash and Glass Plus, from S.C. Johnson & Son for about $160 million. CEO Vernon Sankey re-

signed in 1999, and Michael Turrell became the acting chief executive.

Johann A. Benckiser founded Benckiser in 1823 in the Netherlands to make industrial chemicals. The company launched Calgon Water Softener in 1956 and released Calgonit automatic dishwashing detergent in 1964. From 1982 to 1992 a number of acquisitions expanded the company's market in Central Europe and North America. By 1999 Benckiser's products were sold in 45 countries, including Eastern Europe, Asia, and the Middle East.

After the merger in December 1999, Alan Dalby, former chairman of Reckitt & Colman, was named chairman of Reckitt Benckiser (he retired in 2001). Bart Becht, previously CEO of Benckiser, was named CEO of the new company. In 2000 Reckitt Benckiser announced plans to unload 75 brands to focus on more growth-oriented brands.

As part of an effort to expand its presence in the Asia/Pacific region, Reckitt Benckiser bought Korean household products maker Oxy Co. (Oxy Clean fabric treatment) in 2001.

In 2002 the company won FDA approval to market Subutex and Suboxone in the US. Both are drugs for the treatment of opiate dependence. They are available in 24 other countries.

EXECUTIVES

Director: Peter Harf, age 56
CEO: Bart Becht, age 46, $3,802,847 pay
CFO and Director: Colin Day, age 47, $1,331,237 pay
EVP, Americas: Ken Stokes, age 47
EVP, Category Development: Elio Leoni-Sceti, age 37
EVP, Rest of World: Freddy Caspers, age 41
EVP, Supply: Alain Le Goff, age 50
EVP, Western Europe: Erhard Schoewel, age 54
SVP, Human Resources: Frank Ruether, age 50
SVP, Information Services: Tony Gallagher, age 47
SVP, Investor Relations and Corporate Communications: Tom Corran
Secretary: Elizabeth Richardson
Auditors: PricewaterhouseCoopers

LOCATIONS

HQ: 103-105 Bath Rd.,
Slough SL1 3UH, United Kingdom
Phone: +44-1753-217-800   **Fax:** +44-1753-217-899
US HQ: 1655 Valley Rd., Wayne, NJ 07474-0977
US Phone: 973-633-3600   **US Fax:** 973-633-3633
Web: www.reckittbenckiser.com

2002 Sales

	% of total
Western Europe	43
North America	32
Asia/Pacific	11
Latin America	5
Other regions	9
Total	**100**

PRODUCTS/OPERATIONS

2002 Sales

	% of total
Fabric care	25
Surface care	22
Home care	15
Dishwashing	14
Health & personal care	13
Other	11
Total	**100**

Selected Brands

Fabric Care	Home Care
Ava	Air Care
Calgon	Airwick
Cherie	d-Con
Colon	Haze
Dosia	Mortein
Napisan	Pest Control
Oxy Clean	Wizard
Resolve	
Spray'n Wash	**Dishwashing**
Vanish	Calgonit
	Electrasol
Surface Care	Finish
Brasso	Jet-Dry
Dettox	
Easy Off	**Health and Personal Care**
Harpic	Dettol
Lime-A-Way	Disprin
Lysol	Gaviscon
Old English	Immac
	Kukident
	Lemsip
	Steradent
	Veet

COMPETITORS

Alticor	Colgate-Palmolive
Blyth	Dial
Boots Group	Henkel
Chattem	Johnson & Johnson
Church & Dwight Canada	Procter & Gamble
Church & Dwight	S.C. Johnson
Clorox	Unilever

HISTORICAL FINANCIALS

Company Type: Public

Income Statement

FYE: December 31

	REVENUE ($ mil.)	NET INCOME ($ mil.)	NET PROFIT MARGIN	EMPLOYEES
12/02	5,663	654	11.6%	22,300
12/01	4,990	517	10.4%	22,400
12/00	4,780	469	9.8%	18,900
12/99	4,937	(59)	—	20,200
12/98	5,128	410	8.0%	21,400
12/97	3,624	356	9.8%	16,500
12/96	3,933	558	14.2%	17,425
12/95	3,573	504	14.1%	18,739
12/94	3,240	128	4.0%	18,700
12/93	3,096	249	8.0%	21,000
Annual Growth	6.9%	11.3%	—	0.7%

2002 Year-End Financials

Debt ratio: 34.8%
Return on equity: 34.6%
Cash ($ mil.): 672

Current ratio: 0.93
Long-term debt ($ mil.): 670

Net Income History

London: RB

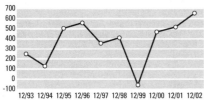

Reed Elsevier

Finding legal, business, scientific, or educational information is a cinch thanks to Reed Elsevier Group plc. Its Reed Business unit publishes business-to-business titles worldwide. Reed Elsevier's legal publishing operations fall under the LexisNexis banner, offering online, CD-ROM, and hard copy legal, corporate, and government information. Reed Elsevier Group also publishes scientific and medical information; its educational materials are published through units including Harcourt Education. Reed Elsevier PLC and Reed Elsevier NV each own 50% of Reed Elsevier Group.

The company also operates event organizer Reed Exhibition Companies.

No slouch in scientific publishing, Reed Elsevier Group issues thousands of scientific and medical journals and millions of research articles through Elsevier Science and ScienceDirect, its online scientific information service. Its Reed Educational & Professional Publishing unit produces the company's educational materials, an area Reed Elsevier Group rapidly expanded through its $4.5 billion acquisition of US-based Harcourt General (now called Harcourt Education) in 2001. To gain antitrust clearance for the deal, Reed Elsevier Group sold Harcourt's higher education, corporate training, and assessment businesses to Canada's Thomson Corporation.

HISTORY

Newsprint manufacturer Albert E. Reed & Co. was named after its founder in 1894. It went public in 1903. For the next 50 years, Reed grew by buying UK pulp and paper mills. Reed began making packaging materials in the 1930s and added building products in 1954. The company expanded into New Zealand (1955), Australia (1960), and Norway (1962).

Chairman Sir Don Ryder radically altered the company in the 1960s and 1970s, leading Reed into other paper-related products and into the wallpaper, paint, and interior-decorating and do-it-yourself markets. Reed bought International Publishing, Mirror Group Newspapers, and 29% of Cahners Publishing in 1970 (buying the remaining 71% in 1977). By 1978 Ryder's strategy proved flawed. Coordinating so many companies was difficult, and, strapped for cash, Reed dumped most of its Australian businesses.

The company sold the Mirror Group to Robert Maxwell in 1984 and divested the remainder of its nonpaper and nonpublishing companies by 1987 to focus on publishing. It bought Octopus Publishing (1987), the UK's TV Times (1989), News Corp.'s Travel Information Group (1989), and Martindale-Hubbell (1990).

Reed International merged its operations with those of Elsevier, the world's leading scholarly journal publisher, in 1993. Five Rotterdam booksellers and publishers founded Elsevier in 1880. It took its name from a famous Dutch family publishing company, which had operated from the late 16th century to the early 18th century.

Elsevier entered the scientific publishing market in the 1930s, and following WWII diversified into trade journals and consumer manuals. The company made its first US acquisition, Congressional Information Service, in 1979. The company fended off a takeover bid by Maxwell in 1988 by planning a merger with UK publisher Pearson; Maxwell was thwarted, the merger ul-

timately failed, and Elsevier later sold its Pearson stock. Elsevier bought Maxwell's Pergamon Press in 1991.

Reed and Elsevier were both listed on the NYSE in 1994. Reed Elsevier built its US presence that year with its purchase of Mead's LexisNexis online service. The company acquired Tolley, a UK tax and legal publisher, and a 50% interest in Shepard's, a US legal citation service in 1996. Reed Elsevier sold IPC Magazines (now IPC Media) for $1.4 billion in 1998 to an investment group led by venture capitalists Cinven. Later that year the company bought Matthew Bender and the remaining 50% of Shepard's from Times Mirror.

Crispin Davis, the former head of Aegis Group, became CEO in 1999. The firm reorganized Cahners that year, laying off several hundred employees and consolidating magazine operations. It also boosted its scientific publishing profile by unveiling Web-based scientific information service ScienceDirect. Reed Elsevier purchased educational publisher Harcourt General in 2001 to boost its market share in the US. The company had to sell some of Harcourt's businesses (including the higher education and corporate training operations) to Thomson Corporation in order to ease antitrust concerns.

In 2002 the company's US Cahners Business Information unit changed its name to Reed Business. That year the company also changed its name to Reed Elsevier Group plc.

EXECUTIVES

Chairman: Morris Tabaksblat, age 65
CEO: Crispin Davis, age 53
CFO: Mark Armour, age 48
CEO, LexisNexis Group and Director: Andrew Prozes
CEO, Reed Business Group and Director: Gerard van de Aast, age 44
CEO, Reed Business Information US: Jim Casella
President, Media Division: Tad Smith
President, New Product Information Division, Reed Business Information: Colin Ungaro
Director of Human Resources: Jean-Luc Augustin
EVP, Licensing and Electronic Development, Media Division: William McGorry
Auditors: Deloitte & Touche

LOCATIONS

HQ: Reed Elsevier Group plc
25 Victoria St.,
London SW1H 0EX, United Kingdom
Phone: +44-20-7222-8420   **Fax:** +44-20-7227-5799
US HQ: 125 Park Ave., 23rd Fl., New York, NY 10017
US Phone: 212-309-5498   **US Fax:** 212-309-5480
Web: www.reedelsevier.com

Reed Elsevier has offices in Asia, Australia, Canada, Europe, India, Latin America, New Zealand, South Africa, the UK, and the US.

PRODUCTS/OPERATIONS

Selected Operations

Business publishing
Reed Business
Reed Exhibition Companies (trade shows)

Education publishing and testing
Harcourt Education
Harcourt Educational Assessment
Reed Educational & Professional Publishing

Legal publishing
LexisNexis

Scientific publishing
Elsevier Science
Health Sciences
ScienceDirect (Web site)

COMPETITORS

Advance Publications	Reuters
American Lawyer Media	Thomson Corporation
Bertelsmann	Time Warner
Cadmus Communications	United Business Media
Dow Jones	Verlagsgruppe Georg von
Informa Group	Holtzbrinck
John Wiley	Vivendi Universal
McGraw-Hill	Publishing
Pearson	VNU
Penton Media	Wolters Kluwer
PRIMEDIA	

HISTORICAL FINANCIALS

Company Type: Joint venture

Income Statement

FYE: December 31

	REVENUE ($ mil.)	NET INCOME ($ mil.)	NET PROFIT MARGIN	EMPLOYEES
12/02	8,052	290	3.6%	36,800
12/01	6,617	183	2.8%	34,600
12/00	5,625	49	0.9%	28,900
12/99	5,480	(102)	—	27,700
12/98	5,293	1,281	24.2%	26,100
12/97	5,637	343	6.1%	27,600
12/96	5,744	1,028	17.9%	25,800
12/95	5,247	794	15.1%	30,400
12/94	4,703	700	14.9%	30,000
12/93	4,861	661	13.6%	25,700
Annual Growth	5.8%	(8.7%)	—	4.1%

2002 Year-End Financials

Debt ratio: 72.8%
Return on equity: 6.8%
Cash ($ mil.): 914
Current ratio: 0.64
Long-term debt ($ mil.): 3,104

Net Income History

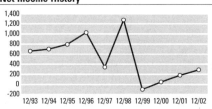

1,400	
1,200	
1,000	
800	
600	
400	
200	
0	
-200	

12/93 12/94 12/95 12/96 12/97 12/98 12/99 12/00 12/01 12/02

Renault S.A.

In Renault's road race against rival Peugeot Citroën to be France's dominant automaker, second place will have to deux. Renault S.A. manufactures a range of small to midsize cars (including Clio, Megane, Twingo, and Scenic) and light commercial vehicles (Kangoo Express, Traffic, and Master). Renault has joined the consolidation trend by taking a 44% stake in Japan's #3 automaker, Nissan Motor, and a 23% stake in its truck-making affiliate Nissan Diesel Motor. The French government controls 26% of the company.

With the Nissan deal and by taking a 93% stake in Automobile Dacia (Romania's leading automaker), Renault made it clear that it doesn't intend to be left in the international slow lane. The company also has purchased a 70% stake in South Korea-based Samsung Motors' automobile business. Renault sold its Renault V.I. subsidiary and its Mack Trucks unit to Volvo in return for a 20% stake in the Swedish truck-

maker. To firm up ties between the two companies, Nissan has taken a 15% stake in Renault, and Renault has increased its share of Nissan from 37% to 44%. The plan also reduced the French government's stake in Renault to 26% from 44% through a public offering.

HISTORY

In the Paris suburb of Billancourt in 1898, 21-year-old Louis Renault assembled a motorized vehicle with a transmission box of his own design. Louis and his brothers, Marcel and Fernand, established Renault Freres and produced the world's first sedan in 1899. Marcel died in a racing accident (1903) and Fernand left the business (1908), leaving Louis in sole possession of the company. He renamed it La Société Louis Renault in 1908.

In 1914 a fleet of 600 Paris taxis shuttled French troops to fight the Germans in the Battle of the Marne. Renault also built light tanks and airplane engines. Between world wars Renault expanded into trucks, tractors, and aircraft engines. Renault sustained heavy damage in WWII, but Louis Renault operated the remaining Paris facilities for the Germans during their occupation of France. After the liberation of Paris, he was accused of collaboration and died in prison while awaiting trial in 1944. The de Gaulle government nationalized Renault in 1945 and gave the company its present name.

Worldwide economic growth aided Renault's postwar comeback. The company achieved its greatest success in high-volume, low-cost cars such as the 4 CV in the late 1940s and 1950s, the Renault 4 in the 1960s and 1970s, and the Renault 5 in the 1970s and 1980s.

In 1979 Renault acquired 46% of American Motors Corporation (AMC). In the early 1980s AMC fared poorly, and Renault suffered from a worldwide slump in auto sales, an aging product line, and stiff competition from Japanese carmakers. Decreasing sales, an unwieldy bureaucracy, and above-average wages contributed to a $1.5 billion loss in 1984.

Georges Besse took over Renault in 1985, and trimmed employment by 20,000. When Besse was assassinated by terrorists in 1986, Raymond Levy assumed his role and continued his policies, laying off 30,000 more workers and selling AMC to Chrysler (1987).

Renault and Volvo agreed to extensive cross-ownership and cooperation in 1990. In 1994 Renault swapped its 25% stake in Volvo's car division for the latter's 45% stake in Renault's troubled truck unit. (Volvo sold its remaining 11% stake in 1997.)

The French government reduced its share of the firm from 80% to 52% in 1995 and to 44% the following year. In 1997 it shut down a Belgian plant that employed more than 3,000 workers and fired a similar number of employees in France. Renault paid a $13 million civil penalty to the EPA in 1998 to settle allegations that its Mack unit cheated on its diesel engine emissions tests.

Renault and Fiat struck several deals in 1999. They combined their bus-making operations under the name Irisbus and their foundry operations into jointly owned Teksid. Renault sold a 51% stake in Renault Automation to Fiat's Comau robotics unit. Also that year Renault bought a 51% stake in Romanian automaker, Automobile Dacia SA, and paid $5.4 billion for a 37% stake in Nissan and a 15% (later increased to 23%) stake in truck affiliate Nissan Diesel Motor.

Early in 2000 the company announced that it would spend around $100 million to build an SUV factory in Brazil and announced plans to trim almost $3 billion in costs between 2001 and 2003. The same year Renault agreed to buy a 70% stake in Samsung Motors' automobile business for around $550 million. It also sold its Mack truck unit to AB Volvo in exchange for a 15% stake in the Swedish truck maker. Renault plans to buy another 5% of Volvo on the open market. Renault and Nissan also announced plans to save about $1 billion by combining their European sales and marketing operations.

Later in 2001 Renault announced plans to further strengthen ties with Nissan. The plan would increase Renault's stake in Nissan to 44% while granting Nissan a 15% stake in Renault. The French Finance ministry also announced that it would reduce the French government's stake in Renault from 44% to 25% through a future public offering. The two deals were completed in 2002.

EXECUTIVES

Chairman and CEO: Louis Schweitzer, age 61
EVP and CFO: Shemaya Lévy, age 56
EVP, Corporate Communications; Chairman and CEO, Renault F1 Team: Patrick Faure, age 57
EVP, Group Human Resources and Corporate Secretary General: Michel de Virville, age 58
EVP, Industry and Technology: Pierre-Alain de Smedt, age 59
EVP, Product and Strategic Planning and International Operations: Georges Douin, age 58
EVP, Sales and Marketing: François Hinfray, age 49
SVP, Advanced Vehicle Engineering and Research: Jacques Lacambre
SVP, Advisor to the Chairman: Tsutomu Sawada
SVP and CIO: Jean-Pierre Corniou
SVP, Corporate Communications: Patrick Bessy
SVP, Corporate Controller: Alain-Pierre Raynaud
SVP, Corporate Design: Patrick le Quément
SVP, International Operations: Luc-Alexandre Ménard
SVP, Quality: Jean-Louis Ricaud
SVP, Strategy and Marketing: Benoit Marzloff
SVP, Supplier Relations; Chairman and CEO, Renault Nissan Purchasing Organization: Jean-Baptiste Duzan
SVP, Vehicle Engineering Development: Michel Faivre-Duboz
Chairman and CEO, RCI Banque SA: Philippe Gamba
Auditors: Deloitte Touche Tohmatsu; Ernst & Young Audit

LOCATIONS

HQ: 13-15 Quai Le Gallo, 92513 Boulogne-Billancourt, France
Phone: +33-1-41-04-50   **Fax:** +33-1-41-04-51-49
US HQ: Mack Trucks, Inc., 2100 Mack Blvd., Allentown, PA 18105-5000
US Phone: 610-709-3011   **US Fax:** 610-709-2405
Web: www.renault.com

Renault has manufacturing operations in Argentina, Brazil, France, Portugal, Slovenia, Spain, Turkey, and the US.

2002 Sales

	$ mil.	% of total
Europe		
France	14,586	38
Other EU countries	16,940	45
Other Europe	2,204	6
Americas	1,494	4
Asia/Pacific	2,325	6
Africa	535	1
Total	**38,084**	**100**

PRODUCTS/OPERATIONS

2002 Sales

	$ mil.	% of total
Automobiles	36,113	95
Sales financing	1,971	5
Total	**38,084**	**100**

Selected Products

Automobiles	Megane Hatchback
Clio	New Clio V6
Clio Saloon	New Kangoo
Clio Sport	Scenic
Espace	Scenic II
Express	Scenic 4X4
Kangoo 4X4	Twingo
Laguna	Vel Satis
Laguna Estate	
Megane II Hatch	**Light Commercial**
Megane II Sport Hatch	**Vehicles**
Megane Cabriolet	Master
Megane Classic	New Kangoo Express
Megane Coupe	Trafic
Megane Estate	

COMPETITORS

BMW	Mazda
CNH Global	Peugeot
DaimlerChrysler	Peugeot Motors of
Fiat	America, Inc.
Ford	Saab Automobile
General Motors	Suzuki Motor
Honda	Tata Group
Isuzu	Toyota
Kia Motors	Volkswagen

HISTORICAL FINANCIALS

Company Type: Public

Income Statement

FYE: December 31

	REVENUE ($ mil.)	NET INCOME ($ mil.)	NET PROFIT MARGIN	EMPLOYEES
12/02	38,084	2,050	5.4%	132,351
12/01	32,200	931	2.9%	140,417
12/00	37,829	1,017	2.7%	166,114
12/99	37,851	538	1.4%	159,608
12/98	43,396	1,560	3.6%	138,321
12/97	34,659	905	2.6%	141,315
12/96	35,177	(1,003)	—	140,905
12/95	37,495	436	1.2%	139,950
12/94	33,453	681	2.0%	138,279
12/93	28,676	181	0.6%	139,733
Annual Growth	**3.2%**	**31.0%**	**—**	**(0.6%)**

2002 Year-End Financials

Debt ratio: 95.7%
Return on equity: 19.2%
Cash ($ mil.): 3,515

Current ratio: 1.25
Long-term debt ($ mil.): 11,861

Net Income History

Euronext Paris: RNO

Repsol YPF

The sun shines on Repsol YPF, Spain's largest oil company. A fully integrated oil and gas company, it has proved reserves of 5.3 billion barrels of oil equivalent, mostly in Latin America, the Middle East, and North Africa. The company owns 99% of YPF, Argentina's #1 oil company, and has operations in 28 countries. Repsol YPF has five refineries in Spain (as well as stakes in five Latin American refineries) and produces chemicals, plastics, and polymers. It sells gas under the brands Campsa, Petronor, and Repsol at more than 3,650 service stations in Spain and has 2,970 stations in Argentina and elsewhere. It is Spain's #1 seller of liquefied petroleum gas. Spanish bank La Caixa owns 10% of the company.

The company acquired its current name and expanded its reserves significantly with the 1999 purchase of YPF, Argentina's leading oil company. To comply with its agreement with Argentina's government to divest 11% of the company's refining and marketing assets in Argentina, Repsol YPF shed 700 of its stations and a refinery in a $1 billion asset swap with Brazil's Petrobras.

Through 24%-owned affiliate Gas Natural, the company is the second-largest stakeholder in Spanish natural gas supplier Enagas. Deregulation has forced Repsol YPF to reduce its Enagas stake and open up 65% of the gas sold in Spain to competition. For growth, Repsol YPF has targeted Latin America. Besides YPF, the company owns a 99% stake in Argentine oil company Astra and has interests in oil and gas assets (including refineries) in other Latin American countries.

HISTORY

Repsol YPF, officially created as Repsol in 1987, is actually the result of efforts that began as early as the 1920s to organize Spain's fragmented energy industry.

Following an era of dependency on foreign investment prior to and during Francisco Franco's dictatorship (1939-75), Spain began reorganizing its energy industry. In 1979 it set up the Instituto Nacional de Hidrocarburos, which in 1981 incorporated all public-sector firms involved in gas and oil under one government agency.

Repsol was formed six years later to provide central management to a Spanish oil company that could compete in the unified European market. The government chose the name Repsol, after a well-known brand of Spanish lubricant products. The firm was charged with pursuing a global strategy to bring together all levels of the industry.

In 1989 Repsol offered 26% of the firm on the Madrid and New York stock exchanges, raising over $1 billion. That year Repsol increased its marine fleet with the purchase of the Naviera Vizcaina shipping company and bought Carless Refining & Marketing, a UK business with a chain of 500 service stations operating mainly under the Anglo brand. Although Spain was opening its doors to foreign investment, the Spanish government maintained control over the country's energy industry, including a tightly guarded distribution network under state-controlled Campsa. Campsa oversaw a marketing/logistics system of pipelines, storage terminals, and sales outlets.

The European Community demanded that Spain open its markets to other EC members, forcing Campsa in 1991 to divide its 3,800 gasoline stations among its four major shareholders: Cepsa (Spain's largest private refiner), Petromed, Ertoil, and Repsol. Repsol gained 66% of the logistical network and use of the Campsa brand name.

Repsol and Spanish bank La Caixa merged their interests in natural gas in 1992 to create Gas Natural, a new gas distributor. That year the Spanish government began reducing its majority holding, and by 1996 its stake had dwindled to 10%. (It sold its remaining stock in 1997.)

Expanding its South American operations, Repsol acquired control of Argentinian oil company Astra CAPSA and a Peruvian oil refinery in 1996. That year Repsol purchased a 30% stake in the Tin Fouye Tabankort field in Algeria.

In 1999 Repsol paid $2 billion for a 15% stake in giant oil company YPF, which was auctioned off by Argentina's government. After acquiring another 83% of YPF for $13.2 billion, Repsol changed its name to Repsol YPF. To help pay down debt incurred in the acquisition, Repsol YPF sold its UK North Sea oil and gas operations to US independent Kerr-McGee for $555 million in 2000. That year the company (as part of its commitment to Argentina's government after acquiring YPF) agreed to swap some of its Argentine refining and marketing assets for Brazilian oil and gas operations owned by Petrobras.

In 2002 Repsol YPF sold oil and gas assets in Indonesia to CNOOC for about $585 million. That year Argentina's economic crisis had the cash-strapped company eyeing other asset sales as well.

EXECUTIVES

Chairman and CEO, Repsol YPF and YPF: Alfonso Cortina de Alcocer, age 59
Vice Chairman: Manuel González Cid
Vice Chairman: Antonio Hernández-Gil Alvarez Cienfuegos
Vice Chairman: José Vilarasau Salat
COO and Consejero Delegado: Ramon Blanco Balin
CFO: Carmelo de las Morenas López
EVP Exploration and Production: Miguel Ángel Remón Gil
EVP Refining and Marketing: Juan Sancho Rof
Director Assistant to the Chairman: Jose Manuel Revuelta Lapique
Director External Relations: Antonio Gomis Sáez
Director Human Resources: Jesus Fernández de la Vega Sanz
Director Legal Affairs: Rafael Piqueras Bautista
Director Planning and Control: Luis Mañas Antón
Director Real Estate Activities and General Services: Fernando Cid Garcia
Director Shared Services: Enrique Locutura Rupérez

LOCATIONS

HQ: Repsol YPF, S.A.
Paseo de la Castellana, 278, 28046 Madrid, Spain
Phone: +34-91-348-81-00 **Fax:** +34-91-348-28-21
Web: www.repsol-ypf.com

Repsol YPF has operations in 28 countries in Africa, Asia, the Caribbean, Europe, Latin America, and the Middle East.

PRODUCTS/OPERATIONS

2002 Sales

	% of total
Refining & marketing	75
Exploration & production	13
Gas & electricity	7
Chemicals	5
Total	**100**

COMPETITORS

Anadarko Petroleum	Murphy Oil
Apco Argentina	Noble Energy
BHP Billiton Ltd	Norsk Hydro
BP	Occidental Petroleum
Devon Energy	Petrobras Energía
Endesa	PETROBRAS
Eni	PDVSA
Exxon Mobil	PEMEX
Iberdrola	Pioneer Natural Resources
Imperial Oil	Royal Dutch/Shell Group
Kerr-McGee	TOTAL
Koch	Unión Fenosa
Marathon Oil	Unocal

HISTORICAL FINANCIALS

Company Type: Public

Income Statement

FYE: December 31

	REVENUE ($ mil.)	NET INCOME ($ mil.)	NET PROFIT MARGIN	EMPLOYEES
12/02	38,325	2,050	5.3%	30,110
12/01	38,908	914	2.3%	35,452
12/00	43,080	2,287	5.3%	37,387
12/99	26,537	1,020	3.8%	29,262
12/98	21,740	1,025	4.7%	23,762
12/97	21,057	827	3.9%	21,440
12/96	21,344	918	4.3%	19,560
12/95	20,962	970	4.6%	18,878
12/94	18,019	735	4.1%	18,797
12/93	15,140	560	3.7%	18,797
Annual Growth	10.9%	15.5%	—	8.3%

2002 Year-End Financials

Debt ratio: 69.1%
Return on equity: 15.1%
Cash ($ mil.): 205
Current ratio: 1.24
Long-term debt ($ mil.): 9,859
No. of shares (mil.): 1,221
Dividends
  Yield: 1.4%
  Payout: 10.7%
Market value ($ mil.): 15,969

Stock History

NYSE: REP

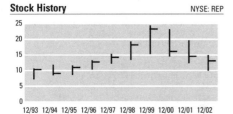

12/93 12/94 12/95 12/96 12/97 12/98 12/99 12/00 12/01 12/02

	STOCK PRICE ($) FY Close	P/E High/Low		PER SHARE ($) Earnings	Dividends	Book Value
12/02	13.08	9	6	1.68	0.18	11.69
12/01	14.53	26	17	0.75	0.44	10.61
12/00	16.13	12	8	1.91	0.41	11.68
12/99	23.25	22	14	1.10	0.48	10.64
12/98	18.19	17	12	1.13	0.44	7.85
12/97	14.17	16	13	0.92	0.44	6.73
12/96	12.70	13	10	1.00	0.40	7.25
12/95	10.95	11	9	1.00	0.28	6.02
12/94	9.07	14	11	0.82	0.21	4.96
12/93	10.28	17	12	0.63	0.21	4.09
Annual Growth	2.7%	—	—	11.5%	(1.7%)	12.4%

Reuters Group

Reuters, one of the world's top providers of news and financial information, helps the public stay informed on the business of business. It culls data from some 240 exchanges, over-the-counter markets, and contributing subscribers and distributes it through various products to nearly 500,000 users globally. Reuters also provides news to online, broadcast, and print media. Subsidiary Instinet, which the company spun off in 2001 (it still owns 63%), serves the equities and fixed income markets as the world's top electronic agency brokerage. Reuters has acquired most of the operations of former rival Bridge Information Systems and has purchased financial information provider Multex.com.

Several deals and combinations in recent years have changed the face and fate of Reuters. The company teamed with rival Dow Jones in 1999 to create the Dow Jones Reuters Business Interactive joint venture (operating under the name Factiva) and with Microsoft to develop joint Internet initiatives. It has increased its US presence through the purchase of several Bridge Information Systems businesses, including Bridge's North American share-trading operations. Reuters' purchase of Multex.com resulted in its launch of Multex 360, an advanced research and analysis product offering for portfolio managers and analysts.

Reuters has struggled post-September 11 both from the economic slowdown as well as from a $14 million loss in assets during the World Trade Center collapse. The company has also been losing ground to rival Bloomberg. As a cost-cutting measure, the company has eliminated more than 2,000 jobs since Tom Glocer became CEO in 2001. It plans to cut 3,000 more by 2006. The company has unveiled a redesign of its Reuters.com site that includes e-mail newsletters and tools for investors, such as stock quotes, market analyses, and portfolio management software.

Reuters is controlled by the Reuters Founders Share Company, an organization created in 1984 to ensure Reuters' independence.

HISTORY

In 1849 German news correspondent Paul Julius Reuter seized the chance to scoop his competitors by using carrier pigeons to bridge the telegraph gap between Aachen, Germany, and Brussels. He moved to London in 1851 and began telegraphing stock quotes between Paris and London. In 1865 Reuter's Telegram Co. was organized as a limited company.

Reuter ceded management to his son Herbert in 1878 and died in 1899. Herbert made the disastrous decision to establish Reuter's Bank in 1913. Two years later, under the strain of WWI anti-German sentiment and the death of his wife, Herbert committed suicide. Successor Roderick Jones changed the company's name to Reuters Ltd. and took it private in 1916 to avoid a hostile takeover. Reuters advanced into new technology by using radios and teleprinters in the 1920s. By 1925 The Press Association owned a majority of the company; it ousted Jones in 1941, displeased with his relationship to the British government. In an attempt to uphold Reuters' independence, The Reuters Trust was created that year.

Reuters established international bureaus during the 1940s and 1950s, but its owners' focus on the bottom line limited the scale of expansion. The company partnered with Ultronic Systems Corporation in 1964 to launch Stockmaster, a financial data transmission system. Nine years later Reuters introduced its Monitor electronic marketplace to track the foreign exchange market. Monitor Dealing, introduced in 1981, enabled dealers to trade currencies online.

The company went public in 1984 as Reuters Holdings PLC, and with the new capital, it accelerated acquisitions. It bought Visnews (now Reuters Television, 1985), Instinet (1986), TIBCO (1994), and Quotron (1994). The company also acquired a new CEO during this time when Peter Job, a journalist who joined Reuters in 1963, was named to the top spot in 1991. In 1994 the company launched Reuters Television for financial markets. The following year it agreed to make its information available on the Internet via IBM's infoMarket service. In 1997 the FBI began investigating whether Reuters illegally used information from rival Bloomberg (the case was dropped two years later).

With competition from the Internet nipping at its heels, Reuters restructured in 1998 to refocus along product lines (which led to the creation of holding company Reuters Group PLC). Its acquisition of Lipper Analytical Services' mutual fund business that year extended its financial information reach. In 1999 Reuters and Dow Jones & Company launched a joint venture combining their online news databases. Reuters also established the Reuters New Media International unit to oversee its Internet operations.

In 2000 Reuters and telecommunications firm Equant launched Radianz, a joint venture (51%-owned by Reuters) to offer secure business-to-business Internet and telecommunications service. It also announced joint ventures with online investment information provider Multex.com (to launch an Internet portal for European investors) and wireless communications firm Aether Systems (to provide wireless data application in Europe) and allied with Microsoft to develop a series of online products. It also purchased The Yankee Group from fellow financial information provider Primark.

Job retired as CEO in 2001 and was replaced by Tom Glocer, the second American and first non-journalist (he's a lawyer) to hold the position. During his first week on the job, Glocer announced that the company would cut about 1,800 jobs by the end of 2002. As part of that initiative, the company closed its financial television services, cutting 45 jobs in the process.

Also in 2001 Reuters took Instinet public (it now owns about 63%) and bought several US-focused operations from the bankrupt Bridge Information Systems. It also transferred its corporate venture fund, Greenhouse Fund, to a newly formed fund management firm (RVC).

In 2002 Reuters launched an instant-messaging service, Reuters Messaging, for traders and investors. Also that year the company struck a deal with VNU to distribute entertainment news stories from *Billboard* and *The Hollywood Reporter*. In late 2002 the company purchased foreign exchange transaction technology specialist AVT Technologies to form the Reuters Automated Dealing Technologies business unit for delivering Reuters automated dealing and limit order management offerings.

EXECUTIVES

Chairman: Sir Christopher A. Hogg, age 67, $421,826 pay
CEO and Director: Thomas H. (Tom) Glocer, age 43, $2,290,369 pay
CFO and Director: David J. Grigson, age 48, $994,418 pay
Chairman, Radianz: David G. Ure, age 55
Editor-in-Chief: Geert Linnebank, age 46
Head of Risk Management and General Counsel: Stephen F. Mitchell, age 43
Director, Human Resources: Chris Verougstraete
CTO: Michael (Mike) Sayers, age 49
President, Coporates and Media: Chris Ahearn
President, Business Program: Graham Albutt, age 49
President, Investment Banking and Brokerage: Isaak Karaev, age 55
CIO: Gregory Meekings
Managing Director, Europe, Middle East, and Africa: Christopher Hagman, age 44
Managing Director, Asia: Marc Dualé
Secretary: Rosemary Martin
Chairman, Instinet and Director: Ian C. Strachan, age 61
President and CEO, Dow Jones Reuters Business Interactive: Clare Hart
President and CEO, The Yankee Group: Brian Adamik
CEO, Reuters America: Phillip Lynch
Director of Corporate Communications: Simon Walker
Head of Investor Relations: Miriam McKay
Auditors: PricewaterhouseCoopers LLP

LOCATIONS

HQ: Reuters Group PLC
85 Fleet St., London EC4P 4AJ, United Kingdom
Phone: +44-20-7250-1122   **Fax:** +44-20-7542-4064
US HQ: 3 Times Square, New York, NY 10036
US Phone: 646-223-4000
Web: www.reuters.com

Reuters operates in 220 cities throughout 94 countries.

2002 Sales

	% of total
Europe, Middle East & Africa	48
The Americas	38
Asia/Pacific	14
Total	**100**

PRODUCTS/OPERATIONS

Selected Products

Multex 360 (research and analysis for portfolio managers and analysts)
Reuters 3000 Xtra (desktop information system)
Reuters DataScope (data management system)
Reuters Dealing 3000 (workstation for foreign exchange markets)
Reuters Messaging (instant messaging for traders and investors)

Selected Subsidiaries and Joint Ventures

Dow Jones Reuters Business Interactive (50%, Factiva online financial news database)
Instinet Corporation (63%, electronic brokerage services for securities professionals)
Lipper Analytical Services (mutual fund and global fund data)
Multex.com (financial information provider)
Radianz (51%, global financial communications)
TIBCO (50%, systems integration and software development)

COMPETITORS

Agence France-Presse
Associated Press
Bloomberg
CDA/Weisenberger
CSK
Dow Jones
D&B
Financial Times
Hoover's
LexisNexis
MarketWatch.com
McGraw-Hill
Misys
Morningstar
NASD
NYSE
Pearson
Quick Corp.
SunGard
Telekurs
Thomson Corporation
UPI
Value Line

HISTORICAL FINANCIALS

Company Type: Public

Income Statement

FYE: December 31

	REVENUE ($ mil.)	NET INCOME ($ mil.)	NET PROFIT MARGIN	EMPLOYEES
12/02	5,761	(651)	—	17,414
12/01	5,657	67	1.2%	19,429
12/00	5,371	795	14.8%	18,082
12/99	5,049	687	13.6%	16,546
12/98	5,032	637	12.7%	16,938
12/97	4,760	644	13.5%	16,119
12/96	4,990	841	16.8%	15,478
12/95	4,198	643	15.3%	14,348
12/94	3,614	543	15.0%	12,718
12/93	2,773	442	16.0%	11,306
Annual Growth	**8.5%**	**—**	**—**	**4.9%**

2002 Year-End Financials

Debt ratio: 71.2%
Return on equity: —
Cash ($ mil.): 255
Current ratio: 0.91
Long-term debt ($ mil.): 569
No. of shares (mil.): 239
Dividends
  Yield: 5.7%
  Payout: —
Market value ($ mil.): 4,107

Stock History

NASDAQ: RTRSY

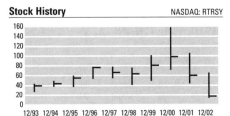

	STOCK PRICE ($) FY Close	P/E High/Low		PER SHARE ($) Earnings	Dividends	Book Value
12/02	17.20	—	—	(2.80)	0.98	3.35
12/01	59.99	373	160	0.28	2.74	6.77
12/00	98.50	47	22	3.35	1.52	6.92
12/99	80.81	35	17	2.88	1.57	4.10
12/98	63.38	28	16	2.65	1.21	2.61
12/97	66.25	32	23	2.40	1.48	9.72
12/96	76.50	25	18	3.12	1.04	7.67
12/95	55.13	25	16	2.40	0.99	5.26
12/94	43.88	47	38	1.02	0.66	4.02
12/93	39.50	27	17	1.60	0.56	3.47
Annual Growth	**(8.8%)**	**—**	**—**	**—**	**6.4%**	**(0.4%)**

Ricoh Company

Ricoh isn't content to just play the role of copycat, and it hopes a little networking will improve its image. One of the world's leading manufacturers of copiers and supplies, Ricoh also makes fax machines, personal computers, and printers. Other products from the company, which has more than 400 subsidiaries and affiliates worldwide, include digital cameras, semiconductors, printed circuit boards, scanners, and recordable and rewritable CDs and DVDs. Among Ricoh's US-based subsidiaries are office equipment specialists Lanier Worldwide and Savin.

Ricoh continues to concentrate on its networked imaging and connectivity products, which include laser printers, copiers, and document management software and systems. The company has also announced plans to expand past its core office products into related services, including systems customization, integration, consulting, and facilities management. The company's copiers and supplies account for about half of its sales.

HISTORY

Ricoh began in 1936 as the Riken Kankoshi Company making photographic paper. With founder Kiyoshi Ichimura at the helm, the company soon became the leader in Japan's sensitized-paper market. It changed its name to Riken Optical Company in 1938 and started making cameras. Two years later it produced its first camera under the Ricoh brand.

By 1954 Ricoh cameras were Japan's #1 sellers and were also popular abroad. The next year the company entered the office machine market with its compact mimeograph machine. Ricoh followed that in 1960 with an offset duplicator.

Ricoh built its business in the 1960s with a range of office machines, including reproduction and data processing equipment and retrieval systems. The company began establishing operations overseas, including US subsidiary Ricoh Industries U.S.A. in 1962. The US unit started marketing cameras but found greener pastures in the copier industry, where Ricoh's products were sold under the Pitney Bowes and Savin brand names. The company changed its name to Ricoh Company in 1963. Two years later Ricoh entered the emerging field of office computers and introduced an electrostatic copier. In 1968 Ichimura died, and Mikio Tatebayashi took over as president for the next eight years.

During the 1970s Ricoh debuted the first high-speed fax machine and began consolidating its network outside Japan. In 1973 it established Ricoh Electronics, its second US subsidiary, to assemble copier supplies and parts, making it the first Japanese company to manufacture copiers in the US. It released a plain-paper copier in 1975, followed the next year by a daisy wheel printer and its first word processor. Tatebayashi passed away in 1976 and was replaced by Takeshi Ouye as president. Subsidiary Rapicom was established in 1978 in Japan to develop fax products.

Throughout the 1970s Savin and Pitney Bowes continued to brand and sell Ricoh-made products in the US, but in the early 1980s Ricoh started marketing products under its own name. It introduced a PC and its first laser printer in 1983. By the next year Ricoh had 7% of the US copier market. Other products introduced in the 1980s included a color copier, minicomputers developed with AT&T, and (in Japan) a digital copier that could also be used as an input/output station for electronic filing systems. Ricoh's overseas sales continued to grow in the late 1980s and for a while exceeded its domestic sales. In 1983 Ouye turned over leadership of the company to Hiroshi Hamada.

Ricoh founded Tailien Optical (Shenzhen) Co. Ltd. in 1992 to make compact camera parts. As the 1990s progressed, the company increasingly pushed products based on digital technologies.

Ricoh won licensing fees from Samsung Electronics in a 1995 dispute over fax machine patents. Seeking to boost international sales, it bought marketing firms Savin in the US and Gestetner Holdings (later renamed NRG Group) in Europe that year. The next year Hamada became chairman and CEO, and Masamitsu Sakurai took over as president.

The company's push during the mid-1990s to increase overseas sales paid off. Amid an Asian economic crisis, Ricoh's overall sales remained relatively stable, while sales of its copiers outside Japan increased 20% and 9% for 1998 and 1999, respectively.

In 2000 the company reorganized its US operations and consolidated its European distribution centers. Early the following year Ricoh boosted its push into the US market with its acquisition of office equipment supplier Lanier Worldwide for about $250 million. Despite shaky world economic conditions, in fiscal 2002 Ricoh saw growth in sales and profits, with strong overseas sales making up for slightly lowered revenues from Japan.

EXECUTIVES

Chairman: Hiroshi Hamada
President, CEO, and COO: Masamitsu Sakurai
Deputy President: Tatsuo Hirakawa
Deputy President: Haruo Kamimoto
Executive Managing Director: Koichi Endo
Executive Managing Director: Masayuki Matsumoto
Executive Managing Director: Naoto Shibata
Executive Managing Director: Masami Takeiri
Managing Director: Kazunori Azuma
Managing Director: Makoto Hashimoto
Managing Director: Shiroh Kondoh
Managing Director: Kiyoshi Sakai
Managing Director: Kazuo Togashi
Managing Director: Katsumi (Kirk) Yoshida
EVP: Zenji Miura
EVP: Terumoto Nonaka
EVP: Tadatoshi Sakamaki
EVP: Hiroshi Tategami
Auditors: KPMG

LOCATIONS

HQ: Ricoh Company Ltd.
  15-5, Minami-Aoyama 1-chome, Minato-ku, Tokyo 107-8544, Japan
Phone: +81-3-3479-3111 **Fax:** +81-3-3403-1578
US HQ: 5 Dedrick Place, West Caldwell, NJ 07006
US Phone: 973-882-2000 **US Fax:** 973-882-2506
Web: www.ricoh.com

Ricoh Company has more than 400 subsidiaries and affiliates worldwide. The company has manufacturing plants in China, France, Hong Kong, Japan, South Korea, Taiwan, the UK, and the US.

2003 Sales

	% of total
Japan	52
Europe	20
The Americas	20
Other regions	8
Total	**100**

PRODUCTS/OPERATIONS

2003 Sales

	% of total
Office equipment	
Imaging	50
Network input/output	27
Network system	11
Other	12
Total	**100**

Selected Products

Imaging Solutions
Diazo copiers
Digital duplicators
Digital monochrome and color copiers
Fax machines
Imaging supplies and consumables
Wide-format copiers

Network Input/Output Systems
Printing systems
  Laser printers
  Multifunction printer/fax/copier/scanner devices
Other input/output systems
  CD and DVD recordable and rewritable discs and drives
  Scanners

Network System Solutions
Document management software
Networking and applications software
Network systems
Personal computers
Servers
Services and support

Other
Digital cameras and other photographic equipment
Measurement equipment
Printed circuit boards
Semiconductors

COMPETITORS

3M	Imagistics
A.B.Dick	Matsushita
Canon	NEC
CASIO COMPUTER	Nikon Corporation
Danka	Oki Electric
Eastman Kodak	SANYO
Fuji Photo	Seiko Epson
Fuji Xerox	Sharp
Hewlett-Packard	Toshiba
Hitachi	Xerox
IKON	

HISTORICAL FINANCIALS

Company Type: Public

Income Statement

FYE: March 31

	REVENUE ($ mil.)	NET INCOME ($ mil.)	NET PROFIT MARGIN	EMPLOYEES
3/03	14,505	605	4.2%	74,600
3/02	12,608	465	3.7%	74,209
3/01	12,177	421	3.5%	74,200
3/00	13,716	397	2.9%	67,300
3/99	11,972	257	2.1%	65,000
3/98	10,546	226	2.1%	63,600
3/97	10,631	234	2.2%	60,200
3/96	10,377	204	2.0%	50,000
3/95	11,789	215	1.8%	50,000
3/94	9,424	93	1.0%	48,000
Annual Growth	**4.9%**	**23.2%**	**—**	**5.0%**

2003 Year-End Financials

Debt ratio: —
Return on equity: —
Cash ($ mil.): 1,672
Current ratio: 1.40
Long-term debt ($ mil.): 2,886

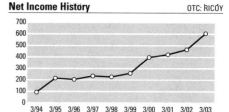

Net Income History OTC: RICOY

Robert Bosch

Robert Bosch is one of the world's top makers of automobile components. Bosch's automotive offerings include antilock braking and fuel-injection systems, auto electronics, starters, and alternators. The company also makes industrial machinery and hand tools and owns 50% of Bosch-Siemens Hausgerate, a European appliance maker. Bosch's Blaupunkt unit is a major manufacturer of car audio equipment. Subsidiary Bosch Rexroth makes electric, hydraulic, and pneumatic machinery for applications ranging from automotive to mining. The Robert Bosch Stiftung, a charitable organization, owns 92% of the company; the Bosch family owns 8%.

The stagnating German economy has helped keep Robert Bosch in low gear, while the increased value of the Euro undermined the company's progress in North America and Asia. However, despite the negative outlook for 2003, Bosch remains optimistic about the long-term potential for growth, particularly in China.

HISTORY

Self-taught electrical engineer Robert Bosch opened a Stuttgart workshop in 1886 and the following year produced the world's first alternator for a stationary engine. In 1897 his company built the first automobile alternator. Later electrical automotive product launches included spark plugs (1902), starters (1912), and regulators (1913). Bosch believed in treating employees well and shortened their workday to eight hours (extraordinary for 1906).

US operations begun in 1909 were confiscated during WWI as part of a trade embargo against Germany. Bosch survived the German depression of the 1920s, introduced power tools (1928) and appliances (1933), and bought Blaupunkt (car radios, 1933). Industrial and military demand for the company's products continued from the 1930s until WWII. Bosch died in 1942 and left 90% of his company to charity.

Bosch suffered severe damage in WWII, and its US operations were again confiscated. It rebuilt after the war and enjoyed growing demand for its appliances and automotive products as postwar incomes increased worldwide. In 1963 Hans Merkle took the helm. Believing fuel efficiency and pollution control would be important issues in the future, Bosch invested heavily to develop automotive components that would raise gas mileage and lower emissions. The company made the world's first electronic fuel-injection (EFI) system in 1967. That year Bosch and Siemens (West Germany) formed Bosch-Siemens Hausgerate to make home appliances.

The oil crisis of the 1970s increased awareness

of fuel efficiency and benefited sales of EFI systems. Buying a plant in Charleston, South Carolina, Bosch re-entered the US in 1974 to make fuel-injection systems. It introduced the first antilock braking system in 1978.

A 1984 strike against Bosch in Germany disrupted automobile production throughout Europe. In the late 1980s the company developed technology for multiplexing (employing one wire to replace many by using semiconductor controllers) in automobiles, established it as an industry standard, and licensed it to chip makers Intel (US), Philips (the Netherlands), and Motorola (US). Throughout the 1980s and into the 1990s, Bosch acquired various telecommunications companies.

In 1993 Bosch's sales dropped for the first time since 1967. In response, the company cut its workforce. In 1996 Bosch bought Emerson's half of joint venture S-B Power Tool Co., which makes Bosch, Dremel, and Skil brand tools. Further consolidating its position as a world leader in braking systems, Bosch also purchased AlliedSignal's struggling light-vehicle braking unit. The company sold its private mobile radio business to Motorola in 1997 and, to speed its business for mobile phones, bought Dancall Telecom (a maker of mobile-phone handsets) from UK-based Amstrad.

In 1998 the company's Bosch-Siemens Hausgerate joint venture opened a plant in the US and bought Masco's Thermador unit (cooktops, ovens, and ranges). In 1999 Bosch sold its US-based telecom unit to a joint venture of Motorola and Cisco Systems. The next year UK-based General Electric Company (now Marconi) bought the German operations of Bosch's telecom unit.

Early in 2000 the company sold its mobile-phone business to Siemens AG. That year the company's joint venture with Siemens bought Rexroth AG (Atecs Mannesmann AG's automation and packaging technology group) for about $9.2 billion. The new division was named Bosch Rexroth AG. In 2001 Bosch bought out Siemens' stake in Bosch Rexroth and consolidated its operations as a wholly owned subsidiary.

EXECUTIVES

Chairman, Supervisory Council: Ing.
Wolfgang Eychmuller
Deputy Chairman, Supervisory Council: Walter Bauer
Chairman, Management Board: Hermann Scholl
Deputy Chairman, Management Board:
Tilman Todenhöfer
Senior Director; President, Thermotechnology:
Joachim Berner
Senior Director; EVP, USA: Reiner Beutel
Senior Director; President, Energy and Body Systems:
Beda-Helmut Bolzenius
Senior Director; President, Diesel Systems:
Ulrich Dohle
Senior Director; SVP, Original Equipment Sales:
Dieter Eichler
Senior Director; President, Automotive Aftermarket:
Eugen Konrad
Senior Director; President, Car Multimedia:
Wolfgang Malchow
Senior Director; EVP, USA: John Moulton
Senior Director; President, Power Tools: Uwe Raschke
Senior Director; EVP, USA: David D. Robinson
Senior Director; President, Gasoline Systems:
Ludwig Walz
Senior Director; EVP, USA: Hans-Joachim Weckerle
Senior Director; President, Bosch Rexroth:
Winfried Witte
Auditors: Ernst & Young Deutsche Allgemeine
Treuhand AG

LOCATIONS

HQ: Robert Bosch GmbH
Robert-Bosch-Platz 1,
D-70839 Gerlingen-Schillerhöhe, Germany
Phone: +49-711-811-0 **Fax:** +49-711-811-6630
US HQ: 2800 S. 25th Ave., Broadview, IL 60155
US Phone: 708-865-5200 **US Fax:** 708-865-6430
Web: www.bosch.com

2002 Sales

	$ mil.	% of total
Europe		
EU	21,844	60
Other countries	1,954	5
Americas	7,712	21
Asia, Africa & Australia	5,149	14
Total	**36,659**	**100**

PRODUCTS/OPERATIONS

Selected Divisions and Products

Automotive Technology
Automotive aftermarket
Automotive electronics
Car multimedia
Chassis systems
Diesel systems
Energy and body systems
Gasoline systems

Consumer Goods and Building Technology
Broadband networks
Household appliances
Power tools
Security systems
Thermotechnology (gas-fired hot water heating systems)

Industrial Technology
Automation technology
Packaging technology

COMPETITORS

American Standard	Johnson Controls
Black & Decker	Key Safety Systems
BorgWarner	Lucent
DaimlerChrysler	Maytag
Dana	Motorola
Donnelly	Nokia
Eaton	Pioneer
Electrolux AB	Prestolite Electric
Emerson Electric	Siemens
Federal-Mogul	Snap-on
Fiat	Stanley Works
Ford	Tenneco Automotive
GE	Textron
General Motors	ThyssenKrupp
Honeywell International	Valeo
Hughes Electronics	Whirlpool
Ingersoll-Rand	Yamaha
ITT Industries	

HISTORICAL FINANCIALS

Company Type: Private

Income Statement

FYE: December 31

	REVENUE ($ mil.)	NET INCOME ($ mil.)	NET PROFIT MARGIN	EMPLOYEES
12/02	36,659	681	1.9%	224,341
12/01	30,143	576	1.9%	220,999
12/00	30,058	1,300	4.3%	196,880
12/99	28,103	463	1.6%	194,889
12/98	30,029	507	1.7%	188,017
12/97	26,143	926	3.5%	180,639
12/96	26,490	322	1.2%	176,481
12/95	24,930	383	1.5%	156,771
12/94	22,251	330	1.5%	156,464
12/93	18,674	245	1.3%	164,506
Annual Growth	**7.8%**	**12.0%**	**—**	**3.5%**

2002 Year-End Financials

Debt ratio: 28.5%
Return on equity: 8.4%
Cash ($ mil.): 6,796
Current ratio: 3.93
Long-term debt ($ mil.): 2,548

Net Income History

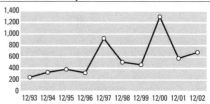

Roche Group

Roche is on a roll. The company operates three segments: pharmaceuticals, diagnostics, and consumer health. Roche's prescription drugs include antibiotic Rocephin; obesity treatment Xenical; AIDS drug Invirase; acne medication Roaccutan/Accutane; and Tamiflu, which is used to prevent and treat influenza. Consumer health products include vitamins, the analgesic Aleve, and antacid Rennie. Roche has invested heavily in diagnostics, including advanced DNA tests, to become one of the top companies in the diagnostics field. Descendants of the founding Hoffmann and Oeri families own just over half of the company.

The company, which is narrowing its focus on health care, sold its vitamins and fine chemicals business to DSM in 2003. The sale did not include vitamin supplements, which are part of Roche's consumer health care line, including Redoxon and Supradyn. In 2000 Roche spun off Givaudan, a leader in fragrances and flavors, and BASILEA Pharmaceutica, its biotech division focused on infectious disease and skin disorder drugs.

The company is also acquiring to achieve its goals. Roche also owns almost 60% of Genentech, one of the world's largest biotech companies, and bought a majority stake in Japan's Chugai Pharmaceutical, expanding the company's foothold in the world's second-most valuable drugs market.

The bulk of Roche's research and development efforts are aimed at oncology, HIV/AIDS, diabetes, and central nervous system disorders. The company maintains several development alliances with other companies to beef up its pipeline.

HISTORY

Fritz Hoffmann-La Roche, backed by family wealth, began making pharmaceuticals in a lab in Basel, Switzerland, in 1894. At the time, drug compounds were mixed at pharmacies and lacked uniformity. Hoffmann was not a chemist, but saw the potential for mass-produced, standardized, branded drugs.

By WWI, Hoffman had become successful, selling Thiocal (cough medicine), Digalen (digitalis extract), and other products on four continents. During the war, the Bolsheviks seized the firm's St. Petersburg, Russia, facility, and its Warsaw plant was almost destroyed. Devastated, Hoffmann sold company shares outside the family in 1919 and died in 1920.

As WWII loomed, Roche divided its holdings between F. Hoffman-La Roche and Sapac, which held many of Roche's foreign operations. US operations became more important during the war. Roche synthesized vitamins C, A, and E (eventually becoming the world's top vitamin maker) and built plants and research centers worldwide.

Roche continued to develop such successful products as tranquilizers Librium (1960) and Valium (1963), the world's best-selling prescription drug prior to antiulcer successors Tagamet (SmithKline Beecham, now part of GlaxoSmithKline) and Prilosec (AstraZeneca). Roche made its first fragrance and flavor buy, Givaudan, in 1963.

In the 1970s, after several governments accused it of price-gouging on Librium and Valium, Roche agreed to price restraints. The company was fined for vitamin price-fixing in 1976. It was also rapped that year for its slow response to an Italian factory dioxin leak that killed thousands of animals and forced hundreds of families to evacuate.

Roche became one of the first drugmakers to sell another's products when it agreed to sell Glaxo's Zantac ulcer treatment in the US in 1982. The move let Roche maintain its large US sales force at the time when Valium went off patent, decimating the company's drug sales.

Roche acquired a product pipeline when it bought a majority stake in genetic engineering firm Genentech in 1990. In 1994 it bought the struggling Syntex, solidifying its position in North America. The company gained Aleve and other products in 1996 when it bought out its joint venture with Procter & Gamble and also acquired Cincinnati-based flavors and fragrances firm Tastemaker.

In its biggest acquisition ever, Roche bought Corange in 1998 for $10.2 billion; its subsidiary Boehringer Mannheim was renamed Roche Molecular Biochemicals. In 1999 Roche announced it had located the gene that causes osteoarthritis. The company began to market anti-obesity pharmaceutical Xenical in the US that year, despite reports of some unpleasant side effects.

Also in 1999 Roche agreed to a record-setting fine to end a US Justice Department investigation into Roche's role in an alleged vitamin price-fixing cartel; in 2000 it agreed to pay out again (to 22 states) to settle a lawsuit regarding the cartel. A related European Union probe the following year also found Roche guilty and levied heavy fines against the firm. In 1999 and 2000 Roche squeezed cash out of its high-flying biotech progeny; it bought the 33% of Genentech it didn't own in 1999, then raised a total of almost $8 billion by reselling 42% of the firm in three offerings in 1999 and 2000.

Influenza drug Tamiflu failed to win European Union approval in 2000, but breast cancer drug Herceptin was OK'd there. Also that year the company spun off its fragrances and flavors unit Givaudan SA, and two long-time Roche leaders, chairman Fritz Gerber and CFO Henri Meier, retired (both remain on Roche's board, with Gerber acting as Honorary Chairman).

In 2001 rival Swiss pharmaceuticals firm Novartis bought a 20% stake in Roche from financier Martin Ebner's BZ Gruppe Holding. The company sold its vitamins and fine chemicals business in 2003.

EXECUTIVES

Honorary Chairman: Fritz Gerber, age 73
Chairman and CEO: Franz B. Humer, age 56, $5,426,871 pay
Vice Chairman: Rolf Hänggi, age 59
Vice Chairman: Andres F. Leuenberger, age 64
CFO and Controller: Erich Hunziker, age 49
Corporate Services: Daniel Villiger, age 47
Diagnostics Division: Heino von Prondzynski, age 53
Research: Jonathan K.C. Knowles, age 55
Pharmaceuticals Division: William M. Burns, age 55
Roche Consumer Health: Richard Laube, age 46
Vitamins and Fine Chemicals Division: Markus Altwegg, age 61
President and CEO, Hoffmann-La Roche:
George B. Abercrombie
Secretary: Pierre Jaccoud
Auditors: PricewaterhouseCoopers AG

LOCATIONS

HQ: Grenzacherstrasse 124, CH-4070 Basel, Switzerland
Phone: +41-61-688-1111   **Fax:** +41-61-691-9391
US HQ: 340 Kingsland St., Nutley, NJ 07110-1199
US Phone: 973-235-5000   **US Fax:** 973-235-7605
Web: www.roche.com

Roche sells its products in more than 150 countries.

2002 Sales

	% of total
North America	40
Europe	37
Asia	13
Latin America	7
Other regions	3
Total	**100**

PRODUCTS/OPERATIONS

Selected Consumer Health Products

Gastrointestinal
Citrosodina (neutralizer of excess acid)
Rennie (antacid with calcium and magnesium carbonate)
Rennie Deflatine (relief from bloatedness, trapped wind, and fullness after food)
Rennie Duo (treats heartburn and acid indigestion)
Transipeg (restores bowel regularity in cases of constipation)

Pain relief
Aleve (analgesic)

Skin and hair care
Bepanthen Cream (treatment of minor burns and stressed skin)
Bepanthen Nasal Ointment (treatment of dry and crusted nasal mucosa)
Bepanthen Ointment (ointment for baby skin and breast care)
Bepanthen Plus (disinfects and heals minor wounds)
Bepanthol Body Lotion (treatment of irritated and reddened skin)
Bepanthol Handbalm (daily care of dry and sensitive hands)
Bepanthol Intensive Body Lotion (treatment of very dry and sensitive skin)
Bepanthol Lipcream (protects and cares for dry and chapped lips)
Golden Millet (extract used to keep hair healthy and firmly anchored at their roots)
Gyn-Hydralin (line of mild feminine hygiene products)
Oceral (treatment of fungal infections)
Priorin (capsules that deliver essential nutrients directly to hair roots)
Vagitrol (treatment of yeast infections)

Vitamins and minerals
Berocca (minerals and a high concentration of all B-Group vitamins and vitamin C)
Elevit ProNatal (prenatal multivitamin)
Redoxon (vitamin C supplement)
Supradyn (multivitamin)

Selected Diagnostic Products

Laboratory systems
COBAS INTEGRA line (sample selective analysers)
COBAS INTEGRA Reagents
Elecsys line (sample selective, multi-batch, bench top heterogeneous immunoassay analysers)
Elecsys Reagents
ROCHE/Hitachi line (clinical chemistry analysers)
ROCHE/Hitachi System Reagents

Molecular biochemicals
Fugene (chemical reagent for the introduction of foreign DNA and RNA into cells)
LightCycler (temperature-controlled fluorimeter)
Lumi-Imager (analysis and documentation of non-radioactively labeled biomolecules)
MagNA Pure LC (isolates nucleic acids)
RTS 500 (expression system for preparative-scale protein production)

Molecular systems
AMPLICOR CT/NG Test (detects Chlamydia trachomatis and Neisseria gonorrhea in both males and females)
AMPLICOR HBV MONITOR Test (quantifies the amount of circulating hepatitis B DNA in serum or plasma)
AMPLICOR HCV Test (detects hepatitis C viral RNA in serum or plasma)
AMPLICOR HIV-1 MONITOR Test and AMPLICOR HIV-1 MONITOR Test version 1.5 (quantitate and monitor HIV-1 viral load levels)
AMPLICOR HIV-1 Test (detects HIV-1 DNA in leukocyte preparations)
COBAS AMPLICOR Analyzer (amplification and detection of DNA and RNA targets)
COBAS AMPLICOR HIV-1 MONITOR (HIV-1 viral load testing)

Patient care
Accu-Chek Systems (sensor technology meters for the quantitative determination of blood glucose)
Accutrend Systems (reflectance photometers for determining levels of various chemicals in the blood)

Selected Prescription Pharmaceuticals

Anesthesia and sedation
Dormicum (anesthetic)

Cancer
Furtulon (colon cancer)
Herceptin (breast cancer, Genentech)
Kytril (cancer)
Mabthera (non-Hodgkin's lymphoma)
Roferon-A (cancer)
Xeloda (breast cancer)

Cardiovascular diseases
Activase (heart attack, pulmonary embolism, and stroke)
Dilatrend (high blood pressure, angina pectoris, and chronic heart failure)
NeoRecormon (anemia)
Rapilysin (heart attack)

Central nervous system
Lexotanil (anxiety and tension)
Dermatology
Roaccutan/Accutane (severe acne)

Infectious diseases
Cymevene/Cytovene (cytomegalovirus infection in immunocompromised patients)
Fortovase (HIV)
Pegasys (hepatitis C)
Roferon-A (hepatitis B and C)
Tamiflu (influenza)
Valcyte (HIV, cytomegalovirus)
Viracept (HIV)

Inflammatory and autoimmune diseases
Madopar (Parkinson's disease)
Nutropin/Protropin (growth hormone deficiency)
Pulmozyme (cystic fibrosis)
Metabolic disorders
Rocaltrol (osteoporosis)
Xenical (obesity)

Transplantation
CellCept (prevention of acute rejection)
Zenapax (prevention of acute rejection)

COMPETITORS

Abbott Labs	Eli Lilly
Amgen	GlaxoSmithKline
AstraZeneca	Johnson & Johnson
Aventis	Merck
Bayer AG	Novartis
Bristol-Myers Squibb	Pfizer
Chiron	Schering-Plough
Dade Behring	Wyeth
Diagnostic Products	

HISTORICAL FINANCIALS

Company Type: Public

Income Statement

FYE: December 31

	REVENUE ($ mil.)	NET INCOME ($ mil.)	NET PROFIT MARGIN	EMPLOYEES
12/02	21,423	(2,902)	—	69,659
12/01	15,638	2,210	14.1%	63,717
12/00	17,791	5,366	30.2%	64,758
12/99	17,326	3,623	20.9%	67,695
12/98	17,885	3,185	17.8%	66,707
12/97	12,885	2,937	22.8%	51,643
12/96	11,834	2,890	24.4%	48,972
12/95	12,754	2,921	22.9%	50,497
12/94	11,271	2,186	19.4%	61,381
12/93	9,617	1,665	17.3%	56,082
Annual Growth	9.3%	—	—	2.4%

2002 Year-End Financials

Debt ratio: 68.1%	Current ratio: 2.01
Return on equity: —	Long-term debt ($ mil.): 10,210
Cash ($ mil.): 2,472	

Net Income History

OTC: RHHVF

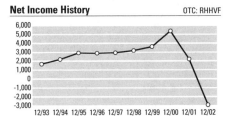

Rogers Communications

Canada is tuned in to Rogers Communications. The company is the nation's #1 cable TV operator with some 2.3 million subscribers throughout New Brunswick, Newfoundland, and Ontario, and it owns more than 270 video stores. In addition, the company owns 56% of Rogers Wireless (which operates under the Rogers AT&T Wireless brand), one of Canada's largest mobile phone operators. Rogers' media operations include 43 radio stations, two Toronto TV stations, business and consumer publications, and Internet holdings. CEO Ted Rogers controls about 91% of the voting stake in the company.

This Mr. Rogers is redrawing the lines of his neighborhood. The company, which formerly operated in British Columbia, has swapped its western systems for rival Shaw Communications' eastern operations.

In fact, Rogers is looking to become a one-stop communications shop for many of its neighbors. The company's cable unit provides broadband Internet access to about 640,000 customers, and its networks are being upgraded for telephony services.

After winning spectrum licenses in all major areas of Canada, Rogers Wireless plans to upgrade its network and convert it to the GSM (global system for mobile communications) standard.

Rogers also plans to roll out a video-on-demand service through its video stores. The company is considering the sale of its Rogers Media unit, which operates the radio stations and TV stations, and produces more than 60 publications, including consumer magazines and trade publications. Jumping into the Web, it invests in interactive media and Internet initiatives, including financial portal Quicken.ca.

Microsoft has a minority stake in Rogers Communications.

HISTORY

Edward Rogers, at age 21, transmitted Canada's first radio signal across the Atlantic in 1921. He invented the first alternating current (AC) radio tube in 1925, which revolutionized the home-receiver industry.

Son of a wealthy businessman, Rogers founded Rogers Majestic in Toronto in the mid-1920s to make his radio tubes. He also established several radio stations, including CFRB ("Canada's First Rogers Batteryless"), which later commanded the country's largest audience.

In 1931 Rogers won the first experimental license to broadcast TV, but his businesses were sold when he died in 1939. His son Ted Rogers Jr. was only five at the time, but even as a youngster he showed business acumen, buying up shares of Standard Broadcasting. In his twenties he bought CHFI, a Toronto radio station that pioneered FM broadcasting.

Rogers moved into cable TV and in 1967 was awarded licenses for Toronto, Brampton, and Leamington. Rogers Cable TV expanded when it bought Canadian Cablevision (1979) and Premier Cablevision (1980). With the takeover of UA-Columbia Cablevision in 1981, Rogers became Canada's largest cable operator.

The firm also began pushing cellular phone service through subsidiary Rogers Cantel in 1985. (The carrier won a license for nationwide coverage in 1992.) In 1986 all of Rogers' holdings were combined to form Rogers Communications.

Rogers acquired a stake in telecom company Unitel in 1989. When it received permission to sell long-distance in 1992, Unitel geared up to take on monopoly Bell Canada. However, the venture wasn't successful, and Rogers walked away from its 32% stake in 1995.

Meanwhile, in 1994 Rogers acquired rival cable TV and publishing firm Maclean-Hunter. The next year it acquired Shaw Communications' Vancouver cable system and began providing Internet access. After selling its 62% stake in Toronto Sun Publishing to management in 1996, Rogers extended its Internet content operations, including a partnership with Intuit to develop a financial Web site.

Expenses related to cable network upgrades and Cantel's development created operating losses for several years. To raise cash, in 1998 Rogers sold subsidiary Rogers Telecom to local phone startup MetroNet Communications and sold its home-security unit to Protection One. That year it turned its first profit in the 1990s.

In 1999 Microsoft paid $400 million for a 9% stake in the company; Rogers agreed to use Microsoft set-top box software and offer Microsoft's Web services to its customers. Also in 1999 AT&T and British Telecommunications (now BT Group) together bought a 33% stake in Cantel; Rogers' stake fell to 51%.

The next year Rogers agreed to buy Quebec cable operator Videotron. But media firm Quebecor, backed by pension fund manager Caisse, weighed in with a rival bid, and Rogers collected a breakup fee of about $160 million when Videotron terminated the companies' deal.

Also in 2000 Rogers purchased an 80% stake in the Toronto Blue Jays baseball team for $112 million. The next year Rogers gained another 75,000 cable subscribers with the acquisition of Cable Atlantic.

The company in 2001 offered to buy up the 16% of Rogers Wireless shares held by the public, but shareholders rejected the deal.

EXECUTIVES

Chairman, Rogers Communications; Vice Chairman, Rogers Wireless: H. Garfield (Gar) Emerson
Vice Chairman: Philip B. Lind
President and CEO; Chairman, Rogers AT&T Wireless: Edward S. (Ted) Rogers, age 69, $1,266,434 pay
President and Co-CEO, Rogers Cable: Edward S. Rogers Jr., age 33
SVP Cable Communications; President and CEO, Rogers Cable: John H. Tory, age 47, $708,302 pay
EVP and COO, Rogers Cable: Dean T. MacDonald
SVP Media; President and CEO, Rogers Media: Anthony P. Viner, $1,313,648 pay
SVP Wireless Telecommunications; President and CEO, Rogers Wireless Communications: Nadir H. Mohamed, age 47, $785,266 pay
VP Business Economics: David J. Watt
VP Business Performance: Richard Wong
VP Communications: Jan L. Innes
VP Convergence: Thomas A. Turner Jr.
VP Corporate Development: Bruce D. Day, age 47
VP Finance and CFO: Alan D. Horn
VP Human Resources: Donald B. (Don) Burt
VP Investor Relations: Bruce M. Mann
VP Sales and Distribution: Douglas Perry
VP Regulatory: Kenneth G. (Ken) Engelhart
VP Technology: Roger D. Keay
VP Strategic Planning and Venture Investments: Melinda M. Rogers
VP and Treasurer: M. Lorraine Daly
VP and Group Controller: Gregory J. (Greg) Henderson
VP and General Counsel: David P. Miller, $410,347 pay
VP and Associate General Counsel: Graeme H. McPhail
VP and Assistant General Counsel: E. Jennifer Warren
VP Business Development: Alexander R. Brock
CIO; President, Rogers Shared Services: Ronan D. McGrath, $1,100,518 pay
Assistant Secretary: Daphne Evans
Auditors: KPMG LLP

LOCATIONS

HQ: 333 Bloor St. East, Toronto, Ontario M4W 1G9, Canada
Phone: 416-935-7777   **Fax:** 416-935-3538
Web: www.rogers.com

Rogers Communications has cable TV operations in New Brunswick, Newfoundland, and Ontario; video retail stores in Alberta, British Columbia, Manitoba, Nova Scotia, Ontario, Saskatchewan, and the Yukon Territory; and broadcast, print, and Internet content operations across Canada.

PRODUCTS/OPERATIONS

2002 Sales

	% of total
Wireless	45
Cable	37
Media	18
Total	**100**

Selected Services

Wireless
Cellular
Data
Digital PCS
Paging

Cable Systems
Cable television
Cable modem Internet access
Digital cable television
Premium channels
Video retail stores (Rogers Video)

Media
Home shopping channel
New media (interactive media and the Internet)
Publishing (directories and magazines)
Radio and television broadcasting (16 FM and 14 AM
   stations, the multicultural CFMT-TV station, and
   minority interests in two other cable TV stations)

Selected Subsidiaries

Rogers Cable Inc.
Rogers Wireless Communications Inc. (56%)
Rogers Media Inc.
Rogers Broadcasting
Rogers iMedia
Rogers Publishing
Rogers Telecommunications Ltd.
Toronto Blue Jays Baseball Club (80%)

COMPETITORS

Aliant	Fundy Communications
Alliance Atlantis	Microcell
Communications	Telecommunications
Astral Media	Nextel
AT&T	Persona (Canada)
BCE	Quebecor
Bell Globemedia	Shaw Communications
Call-Net Enterprises	Teleglobe
CBC	Telemedia
Cancom	Tele-Metropole
CanWest Global	TELUS
Communications	Thomson Corporation
CHUM	Torstar
Cogeco Cable	Transcontinental
COGECO Inc.	Viacom
Corus Entertainment	

HISTORICAL FINANCIALS

Company Type: Public

Income Statement

FYE: December 31

	REVENUE ($ mil.)	NET INCOME ($ mil.)	NET PROFIT MARGIN	EMPLOYEES
12/02	2,747	198	7.2%	14,900
12/01	2,458	(273)	—	13,500
12/00	2,337	94	4.0%	12,700
12/99	2,148	581	27.0%	11,612
12/98	1,834	410	22.4%	10,010
12/97	1,885	(377)	—	10,300
12/96	1,812	(203)	—	16,425
12/95	1,975	(208)	—	14,000
12/94	1,604	(120)	—	13,300
12/93	1,008	(217)	—	6,540
Annual Growth	**11.8%**	**—**		**9.6%**

2002 Year-End Financials

Debt ratio: 550.0%	No. of shares (mil.): 215
Return on equity: 22.7%	Dividends
Cash ($ mil.): 17	Yield: 0.0%
Current ratio: 0.47	Payout: —
Long-term debt ($ mil.): 3,614	Market value ($ mil.): 2,017

Stock History

NYSE: RG

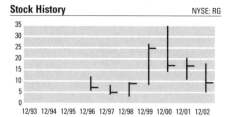

12/93 12/94 12/95 12/96 12/97 12/98 12/99 12/00 12/01 12/02

	STOCK PRICE ($) FY Close	P/E High/Low		PER SHARE ($) Earnings	Dividends	Book Value
12/02	9.38	33	10	0.53	0.00	4.15
12/01	16.80	—	—	(1.51)	0.00	7.23
12/00	17.00	119	50	0.29	0.03	7.89
12/99	24.75	10	3	2.55	0.00	5.05
12/98	8.88	5	2	1.89	0.00	(0.15)
12/97	4.88	—	—	(2.22)	0.00	(2.03)
12/96	7.13	—	—	(1.26)	0.00	0.19
Annual Growth	**4.7%**	**—**	**—**	**—**	**—**	**67.7%**

Rolls-Royce plc

Rolls-Royce plc doesn't make luxury cars — Volkswagen owns those operations — but it can provide serious horsepower. The company is the second-largest aircraft engine maker in the world, behind General Electric's GE Aircraft Engines division. Rolls-Royce's aerospace business makes commercial and military gas turbine engines for military, airline, and corporate aircraft customers worldwide. In the US, the company makes engines for regional and corporate jets, helicopters, and turboprop aircraft. Rolls-Royce also constructs and installs power generation systems and is one of the world's largest makers of marine propulsion systems.

Rolls-Royce's 1999 purchase of Vickers made it a world leader among makers of marine propulsion systems. That diversification may help, because repercussions from the terrorist attacks of September 11 have hurt Rolls-Royce's civil aerospace operations, which account for nearly half the company's sales. While engine deliveries have dropped, the company hopes to increase sales in the spare parts and aftermarket services arena. It has also sold off some noncore operations, including its Vickers Defence Systems unit. German carmaker BMW owns 10% of Rolls-Royce.

Rolls-Royce has used joint ventures to increase its global presence — more than 80% of its business is done outside the UK. Rolls-Royce shares its name with the luxury auto, but the two parted ways when the British government split them in 1971.

HISTORY

In 1906 automobile and aviation enthusiast Charles Rolls and engineer Henry Royce unveiled the Silver Ghost, an automobile that earned Rolls-Royce a reputation as maker of the best car in the world.

A year after Rolls' 1910 death in a biplane crash, Royce suffered a breakdown. From his home Royce continued to design Rolls-Royce engines such as the Eagle, Rolls-Royce first aircraft engine, in 1914, and other engines used to power airplanes during WWI — but management of the company fell to Claude Johnson, who remained chief executive until 1926.

Although the company returned to primarily making cars after WWI, its engines were used in several history-making flights and, in 1931, set world speed records for land, sea, and air. Rolls-Royce bought the Bentley Motor Company that year. In 1933 it introduced the Merlin engine, which powered the Spitfire, Hurricane, and Mustang fighters of WWII. Rolls-Royce began designing a jet engine in 1938 and over the years it pioneered the turboprop engine, turbofan, and vertical takeoff engine.

Realizing that it had to break into the lucrative US airliner market to stay alive, Rolls-Royce bought its main British competitor, Bristol-Siddley Engines in 1966. With Bristol-Siddley came its contract to build the engine for the Anglo-French Concorde in 1976 and a US presence.

Lockheed ordered the company's RB211 engine for its TriStar in 1968, but Rolls-Royce underestimated the project's technical and financial challenges and entered bankruptcy in 1971. The British government stepped in and nationalized the aerospace division and sold the auto group. The RB211 entered service on the TriStar in 1972 and on the Boeing 747 in 1977.

Rolls-Royce was reprivatized in 1987. In a diversification effort two years later, the company bought mining, marine, and power plant specialist Northern Engineering Industries. In the early 1990s the aerospace market was hurt by military spending cutbacks and a recession; the company cut over 18,000 jobs.

A joint venture with BMW launched the BR710 engine for Gulfstream and Canadair's long-range business jets in 1990. The company bought Allison Engine in 1995.

The company sold Parsons Power Generation Systems to Siemens in 1997. Also that year it won a contract to supply Trent 892 engines for Boeing 777 jets being built for American Airlines in a deal worth $1 billion.

In 1998 the British government approved a repayable investment of about $335 million in the company to develop a new model of Trent aircraft engines. Narrowing its focus, the company sold its power transmission and distribution business to Austria-based VA Technologie.

Rolls-Royce pumped up its gas and oil equipment business in 1999 by buying the rotating compression equipment unit of Cooper Cameron, and it became one of the world leaders in marine propulsion by acquiring Vickers. The company then bought the aero and industrial engine repair service of First Aviation Services and took full control of its aircraft-engine joint venture with BMW; in return BMW received a 10% stake in Rolls.

In 2000 subsidiary Rolls-Royce Energy Systems India Private was awarded its first order: producing a Bergen gas engine for Garden Silk Mills for powering a textile plant in India. That year Rolls-Royce won a contract to supply engines for Israel's El Al airline's Boeing 777s. Late in 2000 it was reported that the company would cut about 5,000 jobs over three years.

Early in 2001 Rolls-Royce sold most of its Vickers Turbine Components business. In October the company cut about 11% of its workforce in response to the world-wide crisis in the commercial jet business.

In 2002 the company announced that it had inked a 10-year, $2 billion deal to supply engines to Gulfstream Aerospace. In 2003 Sir Ralph Robins, who had been executive chairman for more than a decade, retired from his post. That year Rolls-Royce sold its Vickers Defence Systems unit, which made tanks and armored vehicles, to Alvis Plc.

EXECUTIVES

Chairman: D. Euan Baird, age 65
Non-Executive Deputy Chairman and Senior Independent Non-Executive Director: Lord Moore, age 65
Chief Executive: John E. V. Rose, age 50, $1,152,094 pay
COO: John P. Cheffins, age 55, $496,000 pay
Finance Director: Andrew B. Shilston, age 47
Company Secretary: Charles E. Blundell, age 51
Director, Engineering and Technology: Michael G. Howse, age 60, $364,000 pay
Director, Human Resources: John R. Rivers, age 55
Director, Procurement: Chris J. Hole, age 56
President and CEO, Rolls-Royce North America: James M. Guyette, age 57, $851,670 pay
President, Civil Aerospace: Mike Terrett, age 46
President, Corporate Aircraft; EVP, Airlines Americas, Rolls-Royce North America Inc.: Ian C. Aitken
President, Defence Aerospace: Colin H. Green, age 54, $769,872 pay
President, Defense North America: Steve Dwyer
President, Energy: Tom Curley, age 47
President, Helicopters: Stuart Mullan, age 39
President, Marine: Saul Lanyado, age 55
Managing Director, Airlines: Charles Cuddington, age 53
Managing Director, Defence (Europe): Andy Stevens, age 45
Chairman, Rolls-Royce Deutschland: Axel Arendt, age 54
Auditors: KPMG Audit Plc

LOCATIONS

HQ: 65 Buckingham Gate, London SW1E 6AT, United Kingdom
Phone: +44-20-7222-9020 **Fax:** +44-20-7227-9178
US HQ: 14850 Conference Center Dr., Ste. 100, Chantilly, VA 20151
US Phone: 703-834-1700 **US Fax:** 703-709-6087
Web: www.rolls-royce.com

Rolls-Royce has operations in about 15 different countries and sells its products around the world.

PRODUCTS/OPERATIONS

Selected Products and Services

Aircraft engines
Diesel engines
Engine support services
Gas turbine systems
Industrial power plants
Marine equipment
Nuclear submarine propulsion systems
Overhaul and repair services
Ship engines
Shiplift systems

COMPETITORS

AAR	Honeywell International
ABB Inc.	Ishikawajima-Harima
Bechtel	Kawasaki Heavy Industries
Cummins	Marubeni
DaimlerChrysler	McDermott
Emerson Electric	Peter Kiewit Sons'
Fiat	Pratt & Whitney
Fluor	Siemens
GE Aircraft Engines	Snecma
Halliburton	Textron
Hitachi	Volvo

HISTORICAL FINANCIALS

Company Type: Public

Income Statement

FYE: December 31

	REVENUE ($ mil.)	NET INCOME ($ mil.)	NET PROFIT MARGIN	EMPLOYEES
12/02	9,283	85	0.9%	39,200
12/01	9,182	154	1.7%	43,300
12/00	8,753	124	1.4%	46,600
12/99	7,669	459	6.0%	40,900
12/98	7,458	428	5.7%	42,000
12/97	7,149	370	5.2%	42,600
12/96	7,290	(80)	—	42,600
Annual Growth	4.1%	—	—	(1.4%)

2002 Year-End Financials

Debt ratio: 51.0%
Return on equity: 2.7%
Cash ($ mil.): 1,152
Current ratio: 1.43
Long-term debt ($ mil.): 1,665

Net Income History

OTC: RYCEY

Royal Ahold N.V.

A real prince of international food and beverage retailing, Royal Ahold owns, services, or has interests in about 5,600 supermarkets, hypermarkets, discount stores, and specialty stores across Asia, Europe, and the Americas. While it is one of the reigning retailers in the world, it is also a leading supermarket operator in the US (mainly on the East Coast under names such as BI-LO, Giant Food, and Stop & Shop) and owns food distributor U.S. Foodservice. It also runs liquor and beauty care stores; institutional food supplier Deli XL; and Schuitema, a Dutch food distributor (73%-owned). Other interests include online food retailer Peapod and a 50% stake in top Scandinavian food seller ICA AB.

Royal Ahold gets about 90% of its revenue from food. In the Netherlands, the company owns or franchises the Albert Heijn supermarket chain (the country's largest, with about 700 stores), as well as nearly 500 Gall & Gall liquor stores, and some 425 Etos health and beauty care stores. Its other European holdings include ICA AB, with more than 3,000 outlets. It US operations account for nearly 75% of the company's sales. The

company is restructuring operations at four of its six US supermarket chains.

Like its Dutch ancestors, Royal Ahold took to the high seas to find new opportunities outside its small home. Often working with local partners, Royal Ahold developed grocery chains in Indonesia, Malaysia, and Thailand. But a $1.1 billion accounting scandal, most of it at U.S. Foodservice, and economic weakness in Latin America are causing the global food retailer to retrench by selling its Asian and Latin American holdings — among others — to reduce debt and focus on more-stable markets. To that end, it has sold the Chilean and Peruvian operations of its supermarket chain Santa Isabel, and will also divest its holdings in Argentina and Brazil.

As a result of the massive accounting scandal that led to the resignation of the CEO and CFO and almost bankrupted the company, IKEA veteran Anders C. Moberg joined Royal Ahold as acting CEO. A national outcry over Moberg's multimillion-dollar pay package — as the retailer cuts hundreds of jobs at its flagship Albert Heijn supermarket chain — led to the resignation of Chairman Hendrikus "Henny" de Ruiter and the overhaul of Moberg's compensation.

Central to Moberg's recovery plan is raising 2.5 billion from asset sales and restoring profitability at U.S. Foodservice. Underperforming US assets, including Bruno's and Bi-Lo, are more likely to be sold than solid performers like Stop & Shop.

HISTORY

Albert Heijn and his wife took over his father's grocery store in Ootzaan, Netherlands, in 1887. By the end of WWI, the company had 50 Albert Heijn grocery stores in Holland, and by the end of WWII, it had almost 250 stores. In 1948 the company went public.

It opened its first self-service store in 1952 and its first supermarket in 1955. Growing into the #1 grocer in the Netherlands, Albert Heijn opened liquor and cosmetic stores in 1973. (It changed its name to Ahold that year to better reflect its range of businesses.) Ahold expanded outside the Netherlands in 1976 when it founded supermarket chain Cadadia in Spain (sold, 1985).

Ahold entered the US in 1977 by purchasing BI-LO and furthered its expansion in 1981 by adding Pennsylvania-based Giant Food Stores. In 1987, in honor of its 100th anniversary, Ahold was granted the title Koninklijke (Dutch for "royal"). In 1988 it bought a majority stake in Dutch food wholesaler Schuitema.

The company added New York-based Tops Markets in 1991. That year Royal Ahold founded food retailer and distributor Euronova (now called Ahold Czech Republic), and in 1992 it acquired 49% of Portuguese food retailer Jerónimo Martins Retail. In 1993 Cees van der Hoeven was promoted to chief executive and Royal Ahold was listed on the NYSE.

Other acquisitions included New England grocery giant The Stop & Shop Companies in 1996. That year saw the beginning of several Asian joint ventures that gave Royal Ahold stores in Singapore, Malaysia, and Thailand. In 1998 it added Maryland-based grocer Giant Food Inc. (unrelated to Royal Ahold's Giant Food Stores).

Royal Ahold's moves in 1999 included the purchase of several Spanish supermarket chains (with a total of about 200 stores); the purchase of Dutch institutional food wholesaler Gastronoom; and the acquisition of 50% of Sweden's top food seller, ICA AB. In Central America it acquired half of La Fragua, an operator of supermarkets and discount stores.

In 2000 Royal Ahold acquired Spanish food retailer Kampio; #2 and #4 food service distributors U.S. Foodservice and PYA/Monarch; US convenience store chains Sugar Creek and Golden Gallon; and all of the voting stock of Brazilian retailer Bompreço. In June the firm bought a 51% stake in online grocer Peapod. Royal Ahold took over food retailer Superdiplo, which runs more than 300 stores in Spain (and the Canary Islands), in late 2000.

Chicago-based Peapod became a wholly owned Royal Ahold subsidiary in 2001. The retailer also expanded its bricks-and-mortar US presence in 2001 by purchasing Alliant Exchange, parent of Alliant Foodservice, which distributes food to more than 100,000 customers, and Bruno's Supermarkets, which operates more than 180 stores in the Southeast.

Royal Ahold reported its first net loss in nearly 30 years in the second quarter of 2002. In late 2002 subsidiary U.S. Foodservice agreed to buy Allen Foods, a major independent foodservice distributor in the Central Plains region.

In 2003 CEO Cees van der Hoeven and CFO A. Michiel Meurs resigned following an announcement that the grocery giant would restate its financial results by at least $500 million because of accounting irregularities at U.S. Foodservice. Chairman Henny de Ruiter became acting CEO of the company and Dudley Eustace was named interim-CFO. Later that year IKEA veteran Anders C. Moberg became acting CEO; de Ruiter remained chairman. Soon after, Ahold said it would restate earnings downward by $880 million. Further accounting investigations uncovered about $29 million in irregularities at the company's Tops Markets US subsidiary.

Adding to its woes, in July the Public Prosecutor in Amsterdam launched a criminal investigation into possible falsification of accounts by the company. In October 2003, Royal Ahold published its long-awaited 2002 results revealing a $1.27 billion loss, which the retailer attributed to special charges related to overstated profits at U.S. Foodservice. de Ruiter resigned and was succeeded by Karel Vuursteen, previously a board member.

EXECUTIVES

Chairman: Karel Vuursteen
President and CEO: Anders C. Moberg, age 53
CFO: Hannu Ryöppönen, age 51
EVP, Europe: Jan G. Andreae, age 57
EVP, and Liaison Officer, Latin America and Asia:
 M. P. M. (Theo) de Raad, age 58, $1,783,866 pay
Executive Board: Dudley G. Eustace, age 67
EVP; President and CEO Ahold USA Retail Operations:
 William J. (Bill) Grize, age 57, $3,460,826 pay
Corporate Secretary: Norbert L. J. (Nol) Berger, age 50
SVP, Accounting and Control: Joost L.M. Sliepenbeek, age 40
SVP, Finance and Fiscal Affairs: André Buitenhuis, age 56
SVP, Corporate Communications: Sharon Christians, age 52
SVP, Legal Affairs and General Counsel:
 A. H. P. M. (Ton) van Tielraden, age 48
SVP, Communications: Hans Gobes, age 65
CEO, U.S. Foodservice: Lawrence S. Benjamin, age 47
President and CEO, Albert Heijn: Dick Boer
President and CEO, BI-LO and Bruno's Supermarkets:
 Dean Cohagan
President and CEO, Giant Food Inc.:
 Richard A. (Dick) Baird
President and CEO, Giant Food Stores:
 Anthony (Tony) Schiano

President and CEO, Peapod Inc.: Marc C. van Gelder, age 42
President and CEO, Schuitema: Jan Brouwer
President and CEO, Stop & Shop: Marc E. Smith
Chief Human Resources Officer: James (Jim) Lawler, age 44
Auditors: Deloitte & Touche Accountants

LOCATIONS

HQ: Koninklijke Ahold N.V.
 Albert Heijnweg 1,
 1507 EH Zaandam, The Netherlands
Phone: +31-75-659-9111   **Fax:** +31-75-659-8350
US HQ: 14101 Newbrook Dr., Chantilly, VA 20151
US Phone: 703-961-6000   **US Fax:** 703-961-6077
Web: www.ahold.com

Royal Ahold operates or has interest in supermarkets and specialty stores in Asia (Thailand), Europe (Baltic States, Belgium, the Czech Republic, Denmark, the Netherlands, Norway, Poland, Portugal, Slovakia, Spain, and Sweden), Latin America (Argentina, Brazil, Costa Rica, El Salvador, Guatemala, Honduras, Nicaragua, and Peru), and the US.

2002 Sales

	% of total
US	74
Europe	22
Latin America	3
Asia	1
Total	**100**

2002 Stores

	No.
Europe	3,351
US	1,635
Latin America	507
Asia/Pacific	113
Total	**5,606**

PRODUCTS/OPERATIONS

2002 Sales

	% of total
Retail	69
Food service	31
Real estate & other	—
Total	**100**

Selected Operations and Brands

Retail
Albert (supermarkets, Czech Republic)
Albert Heijn (supermarkets, the Netherlands)
BI-LO (supermarkets, US)
Bompreço (supermarkets and hypermarkets, Brazil)
Bruno's (supermarkets, US)
Disco (supermarkets, Argentina)
Etos (health and beauty stores, the Netherlands)
Feira Nova (hypermarkets, Portugal)
Gall & Gall (liquor stores, the Netherlands)
Giant-Carlisle (supermarkets, US)
Giant-Landover (supermarkets, US)
Hypernova (hypermarkets, Czech Republic and Poland)
ICA (50%, supermarkets, Scandinavia)
Jerónimo Martins (49%, supermarkets and hypermarkets, Portugal)
La Fragua (50%; supermarkets; Guatemala, El Salvador, Honduras)
Max (supermarkets, Poland)
Pingo Doce (supermarkets, Portugal)
Prima (mini-hypermarkets, Czech Republic)
Schuitema (73%, wholesale supplier, the Netherlands)
Sesam (supermarkets, Poland)
Stop & Shop (supermarkets, US)
Superdiplo (supermarkets, Spain)
Supermercados (supermarkets, Spain)
Tops (supermarkets, US)
TOPS (supermarkets; Thailand)

Food Service
U.S. Food Service
PYA/Monarch (US)
Deli XL (the Netherlands, Belgium)

Other
Ahold Real Estate (real estate development; the Netherlands, US)
Peapod (online grocery shopping, US)
Statoil (50%, gasoline stations, Scandinavia)

COMPETITORS

Albertson's	Kroger
ALDI	Laurus
Auchan	Lidl & Schwarz Stiftung
Carrefour	Meijer
Casino Guichard	METRO AG
Delhaize	NorgesGruppen
Eroski	Red Apple Group
Golub	Ruddick
A&P	Safeway
Hannaford Bros.	Shaw's
IGA	Tengelmann
ITM Entreprises	Wal-Mart
Kooperativa Förbundet	Winn-Dixie

HISTORICAL FINANCIALS

Company Type: Public

Income Statement   FYE: Sunday nearest December 31

	REVENUE ($ mil.)	NET INCOME ($ mil.)	NET PROFIT MARGIN	EMPLOYEES
12/02	65,836	(1,269)	—	341,909
12/01	59,354	993	1.7%	404,453
12/00	49,449	1,052	2.1%	377,000
12/99	33,811	758	2.2%	309,000
12/98	30,946	639	2.1%	235,248
12/97	24,961	461	1.8%	218,446
12/96	20,891	362	1.7%	191,267
12/95	18,431	284	1.5%	139,839
12/94	16,694	236	1.4%	127,668
12/93	13,947	177	1.3%	119,027
Annual Growth	**18.8%**	**—**	**—**	**12.4%**

2002 Year-End Financials

Debt ratio: 414.2%   No. of shares (mil.): 931
Return on equity: —   Dividends
Cash ($ mil.): 1,052   Yield: 5.2%
Current ratio: 0.86   Payout: —
Long-term debt ($ mil.): 11,067   Market value ($ mil.): 11,853

Stock History   NYSE: AHO

12/93 12/94 12/95 12/96 12/97 12/98 12/99 12/00 12/01 12/02

	STOCK PRICE ($) FY Close	P/E High/Low		PER SHARE ($) Earnings	Dividends	Book Value
12/02	12.73	—	—	(1.41)	0.66	2.94
12/01	29.39	30	23	1.10	0.60	5.70
12/00	32.50	23	15	1.39	0.49	2.89
12/99	29.94	37	22	1.14	0.37	3.31
12/98	37.00	34	23	1.09	0.00	2.89
12/97	26.13	37	23	0.87	0.00	2.92
12/96	20.56	26	16	0.82	0.26	2.73
12/95	13.69	18	13	0.78	0.00	3.74
12/94	10.20	16	12	0.65	0.00	3.55
12/93	8.28	18	14	0.51	0.00	3.15
Annual Growth	**4.9%**	**—**	**—**	**—**	**—**	**(0.7%)**

Royal Bank
of Canada

Royal Bank of Canada sits enthroned as Canada's banking monarch. That nation's largest financial institution, which also goes by RBC Financial Group, is a leading provider of personal deposit products, residential mortgages, consumer and business loans, and wealth management services. The company also offers insurance and corporate and investment banking. In addition to more than 1,100 domestic locations, the bank has approximately 100 offices in the Caribbean and some two dozen additional countries. Its US operations include brokerage firm RBC Dain Rauscher and RBC Centura Banks, which operates some 250 branches in the Southeast.

Other subsidiaries include investment dealer RBC Capital Markets (formed by the fusion of RBC Dominion Securities and equity capital markets division Dain Rauscher Wessels in 2001) and discount brokerage Action Direct. RBC Global Private Banking aims to compete internationally through local partnerships.

The company is looking to increase its presence outside Canada, particularly in the US, where it also owns Chicago-based mortgage lender RBC Mortgage and South Carolina-based Liberty Life Insurance. Significantly, RBC Centura Banks gives RBC Financial an anchor in the technology-rich Research Triangle Park area in North Carolina, but the company has expressed its desire to use Atlanta as its base of operations for further expansion in the southeastern US. To this end, it bought Atlanta-area bank Eagle Bancorp. RBC Centura also purchased Florida's Admiralty Bancorp. Other south-of-the-border acquisitions by RBC Financial include Tucker Anthony Sutro, a Boston-based brokerage.

Beyond North America, RBC provides foreign exchange services and import/export services for multinational clients. The bank has set out to become a leader in wealth management, acquiring and adding services to attract high-net-worth clients (and the fees it can charge them for handling their assets).

HISTORY

Royal Bank of Canada (RBC) has looked south of the border ever since its 1864 creation as Merchants Bank in Halifax, Nova Scotia, a port city bustling with trade spawned by the US Civil War. After incorporating in 1869 as Merchants Bank of Halifax, the bank added branches in eastern Canada. Merchants opened a branch in Bermuda in 1882. Gold strikes in Canada and Alaska in the late 1890s pushed it into western Canada.

Merchants opened offices in New York and Cuba in 1899 and changed its name to Royal Bank of Canada in 1901. RBC moved into new Montreal headquarters in 1907 and grew by purchasing such banks as Union Bank of Canada (1925). In 1928 it moved into the 42-story Royal Bank Building, then the tallest in the British Empire.

The bank faltered during the Depression but recovered during WWII. After the war RBC financed the expanding minerals and oil and gas industries. When Castro took power in Cuba, RBC tried to operate its branches under communist rule but sold out to Banco Nacional de Cuba in 1960.

RBC opened offices in the UK in 1979 and in West Germany, Puerto Rico, and the Bahamas in 1980. As Canada's banking rules relaxed, RBC bought Dominion Securities in 1987. The US Federal Reserve approved RBC's brokerage arm for participation in stock underwriting in 1991.

In 1992 the bank faced a $650 million loss after backing the Reichmann family's Olympia & York property development company, which failed under the weight of its UK projects. The next year an ever-diversifying RBC bought Royal Trustco, Canada's #2 trust company, and Voyageur Travel Insurance, its largest retail travel insurer. A management shakeup in late 1994 ended with bank president John Cleghorn taking control of the company.

In 1995 RBC listed on the New York Stock Exchange and the next year joined with Heller Financial (an affiliate of Japan's Fuji Bank) to finance trade between Canada and Mexico. It began offering PC home banking in 1996 and Internet banking in 1997. That year RBC became one of the world's largest securities-custody service providers with its acquisition of The Bank of Nova Scotia's institutional and pension custody operations.

The company and Bank of Montreal agreed to merge in 1998, but Canadian regulators, fearing the concentration of banking power seen in the US, rejected the merger. In response, the bank trimmed its workforce and orchestrated a sale-leaseback of its property portfolio (1999).

In the late 1990s RBC grew its online presence by purchasing the Internet banking operations of Security First Network Bank (now Security First Technologies, 1998); the online trading division of Bull & Bear Group (1999); and 20% of AOL Canada (1999). It also bought several trust and fiduciary services businesses from Ernst & Young.

In 2000 it acquired US mortgager Prism Financial (now RBC Mortgage) and the Canadian retail credit card business of BANK ONE. RBC also sold its commercial credit portfolio to U.S. Bancorp and bought the insurance subsidiaries of South Carolina-based Liberty Corporation to boost its US operations. The company agreed to pay a substantial fine after institutional asset management subsidiary RT Capital Management came under scrutiny from the Ontario Securities Commission for alleged involvement in illegal pension fund stock manipulation. RBC ended up selling RT Capital to UBS AG the following year.

Also in 2001 RBC made another US purchase: North Carolina's Centura Banks (now RBC Centura Banks). It sold Bull & Bear Securities to JB Oxford Holdings of Los Angeles.

EXECUTIVES

Chairman: Guy Saint-Pierre
President and CEO: Gordon M. Nixon
Vice Chairman and CFO: Peter W. Currie
Vice Chairman and Chief Risk Officer:
  Suzanne B. Labarge
Vice Chairman, RBC Global Services and CIO:
  Martin J. (Marty) Lippert
Vice Chairman, RBC Banking: James T. Rager
Vice Chairman, RBC Capital Markets:
  Charles M. (Chuck) Winograd
SEVP, Human Resources and Public Affairs:
  Elisabetta Bigsby
EVP and General Counsel: David Allgood
EVP, Government and Community Affairs:
  Charles S. (Charlie) Coffey
EVP, Sales, RBC Banking; President and CEO, Royal Mutual Funds: Anne Lockie
EVP, Ontario: Gay Mitchell
EVP, RBC Banking: Rod S. Pennycook

Chairman, RBC Dominion Securities: Anthony S. Fell
Chairman and CEO, RBC Dain Rauscher: Irving Weiser
President and CEO, RBC Investments: Peter Armenio
President, RBC Centura Banks: Shauneen Bruder
Auditors: Deloitte & Touche LLP

LOCATIONS

HQ: 200 Bay St., Toronto, Ontario M5J 2J5, Canada
Phone: 416-974-5151   **Fax:** 416-955-7800
US HQ: 1 Liberty Plaza, New York, NY 10006
US Phone: 212-428-6200   **US Fax:** 212-428-2329
Web: www.rbc.com

PRODUCTS/OPERATIONS

Selected Subsidiaries

Atlantis Holdings Limited (Barbados)
Connor Clark Ltd.
RBC Alternative Assets, L.P.
RBC Action Direct Inc.
RBC Capital Investment Holdings (USA) Inc.
RBC Capital Partners Limited
RBC Capital Trust
RBC Centura Banks, Inc.
  RBC Centura Bank
RBC Finance B.V. (the Netherlands)
  Royal Bank of Canada Holdings (UK) Limited
    Royal Bank of Canada Europe Limited (UK)
  RBC Holdings (Channel Islands) Limited
    Royal Bank of Canada (Channel Islands) Limited
RBC Global Services Australia Pty Limited
RBC Investment Management (Asia) Limited (Hong Kong)
Royal Bank of Canada Financial Corporation
Royal Bank Holding Inc.
  Investment Holdings (Cayman) Limited
    Royal Bank of Canada (Barbados) Limited
    Royal Bank of Canada (Caribbean) Corporation (Barbados)
  RBC Dominion Securities Limited
    RBC Dominion Securities Inc.
    RBC Alternative Assets, Inc.
  R.B.C. Holdings (Bahamas) Ltd.
    Finance Corporation of Bahamas Limited (75%)
    Royal Bank of Canada Reinsurance (Cayman) Limited
    Royal Bank of Canada Insurance Company Ltd. (Barbados)
  RBC Holdings (USA) Inc.
    RBC Dain Rauscher Corp. (US)
    RBC Dominion Securities Corporation (US)
    RBC Holdings (Delaware) Inc. (US)
    RBC Insurance Holding (USA) Inc.
    Liberty Life Insurance Company (US)
  RBC Insurance Holdings, Inc.
    RBC Life Insurance Company
  RBC Mortgage Company
  Royal Bank Realty Inc.
Royal Bank Mortgage Corporation
Royal Mutual Funds Inc.
Royal Trust Corporation of Canada
The Royal Trust Company

COMPETITORS

Bank of America	FMR
Bank of Montreal	Goldman Sachs
Scotiabank	HSBC Holdings
BANK ONE	J.P. Morgan Chase
Barclays	Laurentian Bank
BB&T	Mellon Financial
BCE	Merrill Lynch
Bear Stearns	National Bank of Canada
CIBC	Nomura Securities
Citigroup Global Markets	TD Bank
Citigroup	UBS
Deutsche Bank	UBS Financial Services
First Citizens BancShares	

HISTORICAL FINANCIALS

Company Type: Public

Income Statement
FYE: October 31

	ASSETS ($ mil.)	NET INCOME ($ mil.)	INCOME AS % OF ASSETS	EMPLOYEES
10/02	242,006	1,773	0.7%	59,549
10/01	226,370	1,519	0.7%	57,568
10/00	193,076	1,450	0.8%	49,232
10/99	185,761	1,173	0.6%	60,168
10/98	177,783	1,182	0.7%	60,035
10/97	173,814	1,192	0.7%	50,719
10/96	163,011	1,069	0.7%	54,700
10/95	137,206	943	0.7%	49,011
10/94	127,957	864	0.7%	49,208
10/93	124,889	227	0.2%	52,745
Annual Growth	7.6%	25.6%	—	1.4%

2002 Year-End Financials

Equity as % of assets: 4.6%
Return on assets: 0.8%
Return on equity: 16.7%
Long-term debt ($ mil.): 4,246
No. of shares (mil.): 665

Dividends
Yield: 2.7%
Payout: 37.3%
Market value ($ mil.): 23,464
Sales ($ mil.): 14,916

Stock History
NYSE: RY

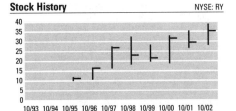

10/93 10/94 10/95 10/96 10/97 10/98 10/99 10/00 10/01 10/02

	STOCK PRICE ($) FY Close	P/E High/Low	PER SHARE ($) Earnings	Dividends	Book Value
10/02	35.27	15 11	2.52	0.94	18.13
10/01	29.50	16 12	2.24	0.89	16.98
10/00	31.63	15 9	2.23	1.08	14.49
10/99	21.59	17 12	1.69	0.61	13.65
10/98	23.00	19 11	1.72	0.59	12.48
10/97	26.84	16 9	1.75	0.54	11.96
10/96	16.50	11 7	1.53	0.25	12.44
10/95	11.25	9 8	1.31	0.00	10.74
Annual Growth	17.7%	— —	9.8%		7.8%

Royal Dutch/Shell Group of Companies

Royal Dutch/Shell sits on an oil and gas throne that is slightly higher than those of Exxon Mobil and BP. The world's #1 oil and gas group has proved reserves of 10.1 billion barrels of oil and 53.4 trillion cu. ft. of gas. The Group, a unique joint venture between Royal Dutch Petroleum (60%) and "Shell" Transport and Trading (40%), generates sales mainly from oil products, but it also makes chemicals, transports natural gas,

trades gas and electricity, and develops renewable energy sources. It operates more than 46,000 gas stations worldwide. Most of the oil giant's crude is produced in Nigeria, Oman, the UK, and the US. Royal Dutch/Shell owns or has interests in about 50 refineries worldwide.

The Anglo/Dutch entity has restructured to stay competitive. Gone are the decentralized committees that ruled the company's once byzantine bureaucracy; they have been replaced by divisional chiefs who report to the CEO.

The Group is expanding through acquisitions. Its purchases have included UK independent Enterprise Oil and US-based Pennzoil-Quaker State. In 2002 Royal Dutch/Shell and China National Offshore Oil Corporation got the go-ahead for building a $4.3 billion petrochemicals plant in southern China, the largest foreign investment in that country. In another major move, in 2003 Royal Dutch/Shell signed a $5 billion deal to build a plant in Qatar to convert natural gas into liquid fuel.

HISTORY

In 1870 Marcus Samuel inherited an interest in his father's London trading company, which imported seashells from the Far East. He expanded the business and, after securing a contract for Russian oil, began selling kerosene in the Far East.

Standard Oil underpriced competitors to defend its Asian markets. Samuel secretly prepared his response and in 1892 unveiled the first of a fleet of tankers. Rejecting Standard's acquisition overtures, Samuel created "Shell" Transport and Trading in 1897.

Meanwhile, a Dutchman, Aeilko Zijlker, struck oil in Sumatra and formed Royal Dutch Petroleum in 1890 to exploit the oil field. Young Henri Deterding joined the firm in 1896 and established a sales force in the Far East.

Deterding became Royal Dutch's head in 1900 amid the battle for the Asian market. In 1903 Deterding, Samuel, and the Rothschilds created Asiatic Petroleum, a marketing alliance. With Shell's non-Asian business eroding, Deterding engineered a merger between Royal Dutch and Shell in 1907. Royal Dutch shareholders got 60% control; "Shell" Transport and Trading, 40%.

After the 1911 Standard Oil breakup, Deterding entered the US, building refineries and buying producers. Shell products were available in every state by 1929. Royal Dutch/Shell joined the 1928 "As Is" cartel that fixed prices for most of two decades.

The post-WWII Royal Dutch/Shell profited from worldwide growth in oil consumption. It acquired 100% of Shell Oil, its US arm, in 1985, but shareholders sued, maintaining Shell Oil's assets had been undervalued in the deal. They were awarded $110 million in 1990.

After the 1990-1991 Persian Gulf crisis, Shell sold a major California refinery to Unocal in 1991 and its US coal mining unit to Zeigler Coal in 1992.

Management's slow response to two 1995 controversies — environmentalists' outrage over the planned sinking of an oil platform and human rights activists' criticism of Royal Dutch/Shell's role in Nigeria — spurred a major shakeup. It began moving away from its decentralized structure and adopted a new policy of corporate openness.

In 1996 Royal Dutch/Shell and Exxon formed a worldwide petroleum additives venture. Shell Oil joined Texaco in 1998 to form Equilon Enterprises, combining US refining and marketing operations in the West and Midwest. Similarly, Shell Oil, Texaco, and Saudi Arabia's Aramco combined downstream operations on the US's East Coast and Gulf Coast as Motiva Enterprises.

In 1999 Royal Dutch/Shell and the UK's BG plc acquired a controlling stake in Comgas, a unit of Companhia Energética de São Paulo and the largest natural gas distributor in Brazil, for about $1 billion.

In 2000 the company sold its coal business to UK-based mining giant Anglo American for more than $850 million. To gain a foothold in the US power marketing scene, Royal Dutch/Shell formed a joint venture with construction giant Bechtel (called InterGen). The next year the company agreed to combine its German refining and marketing operations with those of RWE-DEA. Royal Dutch/Shell tried to expand its US natural gas reserves in 2001 by making a $2 billion hostile bid for Barrett Resources, but the effort was withdrawn after Barrett agreed to be acquired by Williams for $2.5 billion.

In 2002, in connection with Chevron's acquisition of Texaco, Royal Dutch/Shell acquired ChevronTexaco's stakes in the underperforming US marketing joint ventures Equilon and Motiva. That year the company, through its US Shell Oil unit, acquired Pennzoil-Quaker State for $1.8 billion.

Also that year Royal Dutch/Shell acquired Enterprise Oil for $5 billion, plus debt. In addition it purchased RWE's 50% stake in German refining and marketing joint venture Shell & DEA Oil (for $1.35 billion).

EXECUTIVES

Chairman of the Committee of Managing Directors and Group Managing Director; Chairman and Managing Director, Shell Transport; Chairman, Shell Oil: Sir Philip B. Watts, age 58, $2,598,269 pay

Vice Chairman of the Committee of Managing Directors and Group Managing Director; President and CEO, Royal Dutch Petroleum, Chief Executive Chemicals: Jeroen van der Veer, age 56, $2,352,176 pay

Group Managing Director and CEO, Exploration and Production: Walter van de Vijver, $499,472 pay

Group Managing Director; Managing Director Royal Dutch Petroleum: Malcom Brinded, age 56, $839,397 pay

Group Managing Director; CEO Global Oil Products: Rob J. Routs

Group Managing Director, The "Shell" Transport and Trading Company; Finance Director and CFO: Judith G. Boynton, age 46

Group Director, Human Resources: John D. Hofmeister

Group Director, International Directorate: John Withrington

Group Director, Legal: Beat Hess, age 54

Chairman and CEO, Shell Nigeria: Chris Finlayson

CEO Shell Canada: Linda Cook

Chief Executive, Renewables: Karen de Segundo

Chief Executive, Shell Hydrogen: Don Huberts

Group Chief Information Officer: Michael Rose

President, Shell Trading: Mike Warwick

President and CEO, Shell Exploration & Production Company: Raoul Restucci

Treasurer: Neil Gaskell

Taxation: Patrick J. Ellingsworth

Auditors: KPMG Accountants N.V.; PricewaterhouseCoopers

LOCATIONS

HQ: Koninklijke Nederlandsche Petroleum Maatschappij
(Royal Dutch Petroleum Company)
30 Carel van Bylandtlaan,
2596 HR The Hague, The Netherlands
Phone: +31-70-377-9111   **Fax:** +31-70-377-3115
HQ: The "Shell" Transport and Trading Company, p.l.c.
Shell Centre, London SE1 7NA, UK
Phone: +44-20-7934-4000   **Fax:** +44-20-7934-8060
US HQ: One Shell Plaza, 910 Louisiana St.,
Houston, TX 77002
US Phone: 713-241-6161   **US Fax:** 713-241-4044
Web: www.shell.com

Royal Dutch/Shell operates in more than 145 countries.
It has major oil and gas interests in Argentina, Australia,
Bangladesh, Brunei, Canada, China, Colombia, Denmark,
Egypt, Gabon, Germany, Kazakhstan, Malaysia, the
Netherlands, New Zealand, Nigeria, Norway, Oman,
Pakistan, Peru, the Philippines, Russia, Syria, United
Arab Emirates, the UK, the US, and Venezuela.

2002 Sales

	$ mil.	% of total
Eastern Hemisphere		
Europe	65,137	36
Other regions	33,322	19
Western Hemisphere		
US	62,632	35
Other regions	18,340	10
Total	**179,431**	**100**

PRODUCTS/OPERATIONS

2002 Sales

	$ mil.	% of total
Oil & gas	220,172	93
Chemicals	14,659	6
Other	767	1
Adjustments	(56,167)	—
Total	**179,431**	**100**

COMPETITORS

7-Eleven	Kerr-McGee
Amerada Hess	Koch
Ashland	Lyondell Chemical
BHP Billiton Ltd	Marathon Oil
BP	Norsk Hydro
Celanese	Occidental Petroleum
ChevronTexaco	PETROBRAS
Dow Chemical	PDVSA
Eastman Chemical	PEMEX
DuPont	Repsol YPF
Eni	Sinopec Shanghai
Exxon Mobil	Petrochemical
Forum Energy	Sunoco
Huntsman International	TOTAL
ICI	Unocal
Imperial Oil	

HISTORICAL FINANCIALS

Company Type: Joint venture

Income Statement

FYE: December 31

	REVENUE ($ mil.)	NET INCOME ($ mil.)	NET PROFIT MARGIN	EMPLOYEES
12/02	179,431	9,419	5.2%	111,000
12/01	135,211	10,852	8.0%	91,000
12/00	149,146	12,719	8.5%	90,000
12/99	105,366	8,584	8.1%	96,000
12/98	93,692	350	0.4%	102,000
12/97	128,115	7,753	6.1%	105,000
12/96	128,313	8,886	6.9%	104,000
12/95	109,872	6,919	6.3%	106,000
12/94	94,830	6,267	6.6%	106,000
12/93	95,173	4,497	4.7%	117,000
Annual Growth	**7.3%**	**8.6%**	**—**	**(0.6%)**

2002 Year-End Financials

Debt ratio: 11.3%
Return on equity: 16.2%
Cash ($ mil.): 1,556
Current ratio: 0.74
Long-term debt ($ mil.): 6,817

Net Income History

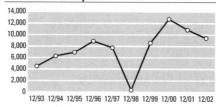

Royal KPN N.V.

Spawned from one of the Old World's state-
owned postal and telephone monopolies —
Dutch PTT — Royal KPN faces a new world of
technology and competition. At home the company (which is 19%-owned by the government
after it sold a 12% stake in 2003) has nearly
10 million fixed-line phone customers. Its mobile
division, KPN Mobile, has more than 5 million
domestic subscribers and another 10 million internationally. Through its ownership of several
European ISPs, KPN also provides Internet access
to more than 2 million customers and it offers
business network services and data transport.

While KPN remains the dominant telecom operator in the Netherlands, it also is extending its
European data communications network, including the purchase of some assets from
KPNQwest, its bankrupt joint venture formed in
1999 with US-based Qwest Communications,
which operated a pan-European data communications network with connections to North
America. The venture was dissolved in 2002, another victim of the over-development of broadband infrastructure and a general economic
downturn in the telecom sector.

KPN Mobile, in which Japanese wireless operator NTT DoCoMo has taken a 15% stake, has
holdings in mobile phone providers in Belgium,
Germany, and Indonesia.

But rough economic times and the company's
sizable debt have led KPN to seek the sale of
many of its international holdings, including its
stakes in US-based Infonet, Ireland's eircom,
Czech phone company Ceský Telecom, and Hungarian mobile phone operator Pannon GSM.

In 2002 KPN began searching for a buyer for
its stake in the European wireless services joint
venture formed in 2000 with NTT DoCoMo and
Hutchison Whampoa. The next year the company sold its directory unit to private equity firm
3i Group and investment bank Veronis Suhler
Stevenson Partners in a deal valued at $503 mil-
lion. Also in 2003 the company sold its 16% stake
in Ukrainian Mobile Communications for
$55 million to Mobile Telesystems of Russia.

HISTORY

Royal KPN is a descendant of the Dutch PTT —
a traditional European state-owned postal, telegraph, and telephone monopoly. The PTT traces
its roots to the 1700s, when the Dutch provinces
began taking over postal operations from the

---

cities. Under Napoleonic rule in 1799, mail delivery was organized under one national service.

In 1877 postal and telegraph services were assigned to the new Ministry for Water, Commerce,
and Industry. The operation became an independent administration, called Postal Services
and Telegraphy (P&T), in 1893.

The telephone made its Dutch debut in 1881
with Netherlands Bell Telephone, and several
private operators and the P&T soon entered the
business. After building its first local phone exchange in 1911, the P&T became the Staats
Bedrijf der Posterijen, Telegraphie & Telephony
(PTT) in 1928. In 1941 during the Nazi occupation, all independent phone operators were
folded into the PTT.

After WWII, business began to boom for the
PTT, which had fully automated its phone systems by 1962. Despite inflation and the government's practice of siphoning off PTT funds in
the 1970s, the company stuck to a course of investment and new services. It launched a packet
data network in 1982 and an analog mobile
phone network in 1985.

Following years of debate, the PTT became an
independent corporation called PTT Netherland
NV in 1989, but the state was its only shareholder. Momentum had been building within
Europe for liberalizing telecom services, and the
door was opened to competition for some postal
and telecom services. Fearing competition from
the likes of British Telecom (now BT Group),
PTT joined Sweden's Televerket (renamed Telia
in 1993) to form Unisource, a global communications provider. Swisscom joined Unisource in
1993, and AT&T began working with the venture
the next year.

Meanwhile, KPN launched a digital GSM
(global system for mobile communications) mobile phone network in 1994, and Dutch mobile
use began to take off. The company, now called
Koninklijke PTT Nederland NV (or KPN; *Koninklijke* means "royal") launched its long-awaited
IPO that year; the state sold a 30% share. Also in
1995 the firm began offering Internet access.

KPN's mail delivery and logistics businesses
were finally spun off in 1998 as TNT Post Group
(KPN had bought express carrier TNT in 1996).
The company began to focus squarely on telecom
and adopted the name Royal KPN. AT&T abandoned the unsuccessful Unisource venture that
year, and the others decided to sell its assets.
Wireless subsidiary KPN Mobile was formed in
1999 and took a 77% interest in German GSM
operator E-Plus (BellSouth bought the remaining 23%, then sold it to KPN in 2002).

KPN announced it would take KPN Mobile
public in 2001 and entered merger talks with
Belgacom, Belgium's leading telecom company,
but the companies could not come to terms.

Also in 2001 KPN raised $4.6 billion in a pub-
lic offering that reduced the Dutch government's
stake in the company to 35%.

EXECUTIVES

Chairman of the Supervisory Board:
A. H. J. (Ton) Risseeuw, age 67
Vice Chairman of the Supervisory Board:
Dudley G. Eustace, age 67
Chairman of the Management Board and CEO:
A. J. (Ad) Scheepbouwer, age 59, $3,703,481 pay
Member of the Management Board and CFO:
J. M. (Maarten) Henderson, age 55, $650,313 pay
**Member of the Management Board; Managing Director,
Fixed Networks Division:** Leo Roobol, age 47,
$601,072 pay
**Member of the Management Board, CEO, Mobile
Division:** Guy J. M. Demuynck, age 52

CFO, Mobile Division: Ed Kraaijenzank, age 44
CTO, Mobile Division: Horst Lennertz, age 61
EVP, Mobile Division, and CEO, BASE (Belgium):
Stan P. Miller
EVP, Mobile Division, and CEO, E-Plus (Germany):
Uwe Berghiem
EVP, Mobile Division, and CEO, The Netherlands:
Cees H.W.M. van den Heijkant
EVP Corporate Development, Mobile Division:
M. W. (Mark) de Jong
Director of Finance, Fixed Division: M. L. G. Tigelaar
Manager, Business Market, Fixed Networks Division:
T. R. Veraar
Manager, Consumer Markets, Fixed Networks Division:
Cees P. Bosman
Manager, Corporate Market, Fixed Networks Division:
F. A. M. de Goede
Manager, Strategy and Business Development, Fixed Networks Division: J. Wildeboer
Manager, Wholesale and Operations, Fixed Network Operator, Fixed Networks Division: Eelco Blok
Auditors: PricewaterhouseCoopers N.V.

LOCATIONS

HQ: Koninklijke KPN N.V.
Maanplein 5, 2516 CK The Hague, The Netherlands
Phone: +31-70-343-43-43   **Fax:** +31-70-332-44-85
US HQ: 494 8th Ave., 23rd Fl., New York, NY 10001
US Phone: 212-560-9898   **US Fax:** 212-560-0770
Web: www.kpn.com

Royal KPN N.V. operates primarily in the Netherlands, but it also owns stakes in telecom operators in Belgium, the Czech Republic, Germany, Indonesia, and the Ukraine. The company's KPNQwest venture operates a network serving 10 European cities in Belgium, France, Germany, the Netherlands, and the UK.

PRODUCTS/OPERATIONS

2002 Sales

	$ mil.	% of total
Fixed Networks Division	6,865	44
Mobile Division	5,461	35
Business Solutions	2,028	13
Other revenues	1,248	8
Adjustments	(2,175)	—
Total	**13,427**	**100**

Selected Subsidiaries and Affiliates

KPN Mobile Holding B.V.
  KPN Mobile N.V. (85%, mobile telecommunications)
    BASE N.V./S.A. (mobile telecommunications, Belgium)
    E-Plus Mobilfunk GmbH & Co KG (mobile telecommunications, Germany)
    Hutchison 3G UK Holdings Ltd. (15%, mobile telecommunications)
    KPN International B.V.
    KPN Mobile The Netherlands B.V.
KPN Telecom B.V.
  Euroweb International Corp. (53%, ISPs, US)
  Infonet Services Corporation (18%, data network operator, US)
  PanTel Rt. (75%, telecommunications, Hungary)
  Proclare (10%)
KPN Telecommerce B.V.
  KPN Consumer Internet and Media Services B.V.
  Planet Media Group N.V.
  SNT Group N.V. (51%, call center operations)
  XS4ALL Holding B.V.
KPN Vastgoed & Facilities B.V.
Volker Wessels Netwerk Bouw B.V. (45%)

COMPETITORS

Belgacom	Tele2
BT	TeliaSonera
COLT Telecom	UGC Europe
Deutsche Telekom	VersaTel Telecom
Energis	International
Equant	Vodafone
France Telecom	Vodafone Libertel
MATÁV	WorldCom
TDC	

HISTORICAL FINANCIALS

Company Type: Public

Income Statement

FYE: December 31

	REVENUE ($ mil.)	NET INCOME ($ mil.)	NET PROFIT MARGIN	EMPLOYEES
12/02	13,427	(10,022)	—	38,118
12/01	11,461	(6,680)	—	49,121
12/00	12,725	1,765	13.9%	47,688
12/99	9,177	832	9.1%	38,550
12/98	9,377	802	8.5%	36,073
12/97	15,191	1,328	8.7%	34,257
12/96	12,246	1,413	11.5%	34,494
12/95	12,344	1,403	11.4%	35,004
12/94	10,720	1,173	10.9%	36,367
12/93	9,001	913	10.1%	—
Annual Growth	**4.5%**	**—**		**0.6%**

2002 Year-End Financials

Debt ratio: 280.5%
Return on equity: —
Cash ($ mil.): 2,791
Current ratio: 0.86
Long-term debt ($ mil.): 13,284
No. of shares (mil.): 2,491
Dividends
  Yield: 0.0%
  Payout: —
Market value ($ mil.): 15,992

Stock History

NYSE: KPN

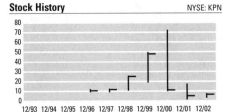

	STOCK PRICE ($) FY Close	P/E High/Low		PER SHARE ($) Earnings	Dividends	Book Value
12/02	6.42	—	—	(4.14)	0.00	1.90
12/01	5.06	—	—	(5.24)	0.00	4.74
12/00	11.13	40	6	1.79	0.49	15.64
12/99	48.00	57	22	0.87	0.56	6.67
12/98	25.13	30	13	0.85	0.21	7.24
12/97	11.62	8	7	1.41	0.27	9.26
12/96	10.61	8	6	1.53	0.74	9.90
Annual Growth	**(8.0%)**	**—**	**—**	**—**	**—**	**(24.0%)**

RWE AG

RWE doesn't stand for Runs With Electricity, but it could. Through its subsidiaries, the energy conglomerate provides electricity, gas, water, and environmental services to more than 100 million residential and business customers, primarily in Europe and North America; it is also one of Germany's top two electricity suppliers (along with E.ON). The holding company for more than 500 energy and industrial interests, RWE also owns two major UK-based utilities: #3 global water supplier Thames Water and UK electricity and gas supplier Innogy. RWE owns oil and gas exploration and production company RWE-DEA; other business interests include companies engaged in mining, construction, and environmental services.

As Germany's old industrial controls continue to tumble like Berlin's famous wall in the face of European Union-wide deregulation, RWE is doing its best to cope with the chaos of a new order by restructuring its regional energy businesses. RWE's former German utility unit, RWE Energie, lost its regional monopoly status because of deregulation, and RWE has responded by splitting its domestic power generation, distribution, and supply operations into new units.

To do battle in an increasingly competitive utility industry, RWE is also acquiring stakes in other European utilities, including its 2002 purchases of Innogy and Czech Republic gas supplier Transgas. RWE has also acquired North American utility American Water Works, which was combined with the US operations of Thames Water, for $4.6 billion in cash and $4 billion in assumed debt.

RWE is selling noncore assets to reduce debt associated with its expansion efforts. The company divested its refinery and service station interests in 2002; it also plans to sell its 40% stake in construction and civil engineering firm HOCHTIEF and its 50% interest in Heidelberger Druckmaschinen, one of the world's largest printing-press makers.

RWE's minority shareholders include German municipal governments and insurer Allianz.

HISTORY

Founded at the end of the 19th century, RWE mirrored the industrialization of Germany in its growth. It was formed as Rheinisch-Westfalisches Elektrizitatswerk in 1898 by Erich Zweigert, the mayor of Essen, and Hugo Stinnes, an industrialist from Mulheim, to provide electricity to Essen and surrounding areas. The company began supplying power in 1900.

Stinnes persuaded other cities — Gelsenkirchen and Mulheim — to buy shares in RWE in 1905. In 1908 RWE and rival Vereinigte Elektrizitatswerk Westfalen (VEW) agreed to divide up the territories that each would supply.

Germany's coal shortages, caused by WWI, prompted RWE to expand its coal operations, and it bought Rheinische Aktiengesellschaft fur Braunkohlenbergbau, a coal producer, in 1932. RWE also built a power line network, completed in 1930, to connect the populous north Germany with the south. By 1939, as WWII began, the company had plants throughout most of western Germany. However, the war destroyed much of the company's infrastructure, and RWE had to rebuild.

RWE continued to rely on coal for most of its fuel needs in the 1950s, but in 1961 RWE and Bayern Atomkraft sponsored the construction of a demonstration nuclear reactor, the first of several such projects, at Gundremmingen. The Gundremmingen plant was shut down in 1977, and to replace it RWE built two 1,300-MW reactors that began operation in 1984.

RWE began to diversify, and in 1988 it acquired Texaco's German petroleum and petrochemical unit, which became RWE-DEA. By 1990 RWE's operations also included waste management and construction. RWE reorganized, creating RWE Aktiengesellschaft as a holding company for group operations.

RWE-DEA acquired the US's Vista Chemical in 1991, and RWE's Rheinbraun mining unit bought a 50% stake in Consolidation Coal from DuPont. (The mining venture went public in 1999 as CONSOL Energy.) RWE led a consortium that acquired major stakes in three Hungarian power companies in 1995.

Hoping to play a role in Germany's telecommunications market, RWE teamed with VEBA in 1997 to form the o.tel.o joint venture, and RWE and VEBA gained control of large German mobile phone operator E-Plus. The nation's telecom market was deregulated in 1998, but Mannesmann and former monopoly Deutsche Telekom proved to be formidable competitors. In 1999 RWE and VEBA sold o.tel.o's fixed-line business (along with the o.tel.o brand name) and cable TV unit Tele Columbus. The next year the companies sold their joint stake in E-Plus.

Faced with deregulating German electricity markets, RWE Energie had begun restructuring as soon as the market opened up in 1998. It agreed to buy fellow German power company VEW in a $20 billion deal which closed in 2000. RWE also joined with insurance giant Allianz and France's Vivendi in a successful bid for a 49.9% stake in state-owned water distributor Berliner Wasserbetriebe (Vivendi later spurned an RWE offer to buy its energy businesses).

After taking advantage of deregulating markets in Germany, RWE moved to pick up other European utilities: It acquired UK-based Thames Water in 2000 and bought a majority stake in Dutch gas supplier Intergas the next year. In 2002 the company issued an exchange offer to acquire UK electricity supplier Innogy for a total of about $4.4 billion in cash and $3 billion in assumed debt. It also completed a $3.7 billion purchase of Czech Republic gas supplier Transgas.

In a move to further streamline operations, RWE sold its 50% stake in refinery and service station subsidiary Shell & DEA Oil to Deutsche Shell and Shell Petroleum.

EXECUTIVES

Chairman of the Supervisory Board: Friedel Neuber
Chairman of the Executive Board, President, and CEO; Chairman, Innogy and Thames Water:
Harry J. M. Roels, age 55
EVP and CFO: Klaus Sturany, age 57
EVP Human Resources and Law: Jan Zilius, age 57
EVP Multi Energy; President and CEO, RWE Power:
Gert Maichel, age 57
Chairman and CEO, HOCHTIEF: Hans-Peter Keitel, age 54
Chairman of the Board of Management, RWE-DEA Aktiengesellschaft für Mineraloel und Chemie:
Georg Schöning, age 54
Group Chief Executive,Thames Water:
William J. (Bill) Alexander, age 56
CEO, Innogy: Brian M. Count
Auditors: PwC Deutsche Revision AG

LOCATIONS

HQ: Opernplatz 1, D-45128 Essen, Germany
Phone: +49-201-12-00 **Fax:** +49-201-12-15199
Web: www.rwe.com

RWE operates in Europe, mainly in Germany. It also has a presence in Africa, Asia, Australia, and the US.

2002 Sales

	% of total
Europe	
Germany	60
Other countries	27
US	9
Asia	3
Africa	1
Total	**100**

PRODUCTS/OPERATIONS

2002 Sales

	% of total
Electricity	51
Gas	12
Financial investments	9
Water	6
Environmental services	5
Discontinued operations & other	17
Total	**100**

Selected Subsidiaries

Energy
CONSOL Energy Inc. (72%, coal mining, US)
Innogy Holdings plc (electricity and gas supply, UK)
RWE Gas AG (natural gas transportation, distribution, storage, procurement, and sales)
RWE Net AG (electricity transmission and distribution system operations)
RWE Plus AG (electricity supply)
RWE Power AG (electricity generation)
RWE Rheinbraun AG (coal mining and coal-fired power generation)
RWE Trading GmbH (wholesale energy commodity sales)

Petroleum and Chemicals
RWE-DEA AG (oil and gas exploration, production, and storage)

Financial Holdings
HOCHTIEF AG (40%, construction and civil engineering)
Heidelberger Druckmashinen AG (50%, printing systems)

Environmental Services
RWE Umwelt AG (waste disposal and recycling)

Water
Thames Water plc (water and wastewater services, UK)
American Water Works Company, Inc. (water and wastewater services, US)

COMPETITORS

ABB
BASF AG
Bechtel
BP
Centrica
Electricité de France
Endesa
Enel
E.ON
Exxon Mobil
Fluor
mg technologies
Philipp Holzmann
Powergen
Royal Dutch/Shell Group
Schneider
Severn Trent
Siemens
Suez
ThyssenKrupp
United Utilities
Vattenfall
Veolia Environnement

HISTORICAL FINANCIALS

Company Type: Public

Income Statement

FYE: December 31

	REVENUE ($ mil.)	NET INCOME ($ mil.)	NET PROFIT MARGIN	EMPLOYEES
12/02	45,579	1,101	2.4%	131,765
12/01*	26,592	550	2.1%	155,634
6/01	48,182	1,073	2.2%	163,720
6/00	45,618	1,154	2.5%	155,697
6/99	41,772	1,186	2.8%	155,576
6/98	40,226	1,223	3.0%	145,467
6/97	35,109	748	2.1%	136,115
6/96	35,887	784	2.2%	132,658
6/95	46,059	787	1.7%	137,331
6/94	35,105	581	1.7%	117,958
Annual Growth	**2.9%**	**7.4%**	**—**	**1.2%**

*Fiscal year change

2002 Year-End Financials

Debt ratio: 212.4%   Current ratio: 1.81
Return on equity: 16.2%   Long-term debt ($ mil.): 14,315
Cash ($ mil.): 2,246

Net Income History

Pink Sheets: RWEOY

SABMiller plc

It's Miller time at South African Breweries (SAB). SAB's 2002 purchase of Miller Brewing has earned it a new name, SABMiller plc, and new status as the world's second-largest brewer, behind Anheuser-Busch. The company, which has operations in more than 40 countries, dominates South African brewing with 98% of the market on the strength of Africa's best-selling beer, Castle Lager. It brews other regional brands, including Hansa Pilsener and Ohlssons. SABMiller also makes wines, spirits, and fruit drinks as well as bottles Coca-Cola and Schweppes products. Miller's former parent Altria Group (formerly Philip Morris Companies) owns 23% of SABMiller.

Apartheid kept SAB from investing overseas in the 1980s; so it grew by purchasing a diverse range of businesses at home. After sanctions were lifted in the early 1990s, the company bulked up on foreign breweries. It now has major operations in Africa, China, India, Central Europe, and Central America. It owns more than 100 breweries in about 25 countries, not including Miller's facilities.

Similar to rival Anheuser-Busch, Miller is particularly interested in growing its base in China. Miller now has investments in both the Harbin Brewery Group and China Resources Breweries. SAB shed most of its nonbrewing units, and is combining its Southern Sun Hotels group with its Tsogo Sun casino operations to create Tsogo Sun Holdings, which will be 51%-owned by

Tsogo Investments, a consortium of black empowerment groups in South Africa.

The company also hopes to give Miller a boost with additional advertising and global marketing. As part of that effort, it plans to sell Miller Genuine Draft throughout Central Europe. For example, Birra Peroni will launch Miller Genuine Draft in Italy toward the end of 2003.

HISTORY

British sailor Frederick Mead purchased the Castle Brewery in Johannesburg in 1892, about 15 years after gold was discovered in South Africa. Mead took his brewing operation public as South African Breweries (SAB) in 1895. The company began making its flagship Castle Lager three years later and survived the Anglo-Boer War (1899-1902) as South Africa's fastest-growing nonindustrial firm. Mead died in 1915.

The brewer acquired the Grand Hotel in Cape Town in 1921 and a stake in Schweppes (carbonated drinks) in 1925. In the late 1940s SAB began an extensive expansion program involving its breweries, small hotels, and pubs. In 1951 it acquired the Hotel Victoria in Johannesburg. An increase in beer taxes during the 1950s led SAB to start producing liquors. With beer demand slackening, South Africa's three largest brewers — SAB, Ohlsson's, and United Breweries — merged in 1956. The new company, which took the SAB name, controlled about 90% of the beer market. Beer taxes continued to pressure sales, and in 1960 SAB acquired control of Stellenbosch Farmers' Winery to extend its product range. In 1962 the restriction prohibiting alcohol consumption by blacks was lifted, opening an enormous market. SAB continued to extend its range of beer brands during the 1960s by adding licenses to brew Amstel and Carling Black Label.

Further diversifying, SAB formed Barsab (an investment venture with Thomas Barlow & Sons) in 1966. The company launched its hotel division, Southern Sun Hotels, three years later by merging its hotels with those owned by the Sol Kerzner family. The Barsab venture was dissolved in 1973, leaving SAB with furniture and footwear businesses. The following year it acquired the South African bottling business of Pepsi (converted to Coca-Cola in 1977). The company added the beer interests of the Rembrandt Group and a 49% stake in Appletiser, a fruit drinks company, in 1979. (It gained control of it in 1982.)

SAB moved into apparel retailing with its purchase of the Scotts Stores group (1981) and Edgars stores (1982). Antiapartheid sanctions forced the company to grow at home. After forming a joint venture with Ceres Fruit Juices (1986), SAB made a number of investments in South Africa, including Lion Match Company (1987), Da Gama Textiles (1989), and Plate Glass (1992).

As sanctions eased in the 1990s, the company expanded internationally. It acquired stakes in breweries in Hungary (1993), Tanzania and China (1994), and Poland and Romania (1996). Graham Mackay (now CEO) became managing director in 1996.

Before moving its main listing to the London Stock Exchange in 1999, SAB sold its Amalgamated Retail unit (furniture, appliances), Lion Match Company, and a large stake in Edgars. It then bought controlling interests in Czech brewers Pilsner Urquell and Radegast to become the largest brewer in Central Europe and sold its 68% interest in Plate Glass to Dibelco (a D'Ieteren and Copeba joint venture). Bevcon

(a consortium of three South African companies) sold its 27% interest in SAB in 1999.

The continuing woes of the South African economy in 2000 continued to fuel SAB's desire to expand its international base. In 2001 SAB announced a new joint venture in the Sichuan province of China; the move cemented the company's position as the #2 brewer in China (behind Tsingtao) with 25 breweries. The company also became the first international brewer with a presence in Central America, spending more than $500 million on breweries in Honduras and El Salvador.

In July 2002 SAB bought Miller Brewing from Philip Morris (now Altria Group) for $5.6 billion, making it the world's second-largest brewer. SAB then changed its name to SABMiller plc. SABMiller moved into Western Europe in June 2003 with the $270 million purchase of Italian brewer Birra Peroni.

EXECUTIVES

Chairman: Jacob Meyer Kahn, age 63
Chief Executive: Ernest Arthur (Graham) Mackay, age 53, $1,425,600 pay
CFO: Malcolm Ian Wyman, age 56, $812,592 pay
Organization Development Director:
Richard L. (Pete) Lloyd, age 57, $584,496 pay
Managing Director, Beer South Africa:
Tony van Kralingen
Managing Director, SAB Europe: Michael H. Simms, age 52, $484,704 pay
Managing Director, SAB Africa and Asia:
André C. Parker, age 50, $54,989 pay
President and CEO, Miller Brewing Company:
Norman J. Adami, $355,826 pay
Chief Executive, SAB Soft Drinks: Alan Clark
Global Marketing Chief: Mark Sherrington, age 45
Communications Executive: Briony Gilbert
Head of Corporate Communications: Ciaran Baker
Head of Financial Media: Nigel Fairbrass
Head of Investor Relations: Anna Salzman
Investor Relations: Caroline Metcalf
Marketing Manager, Ubevco: Tim Jackson
Public Relations Manager, South Africa: Loraine Harris
Group Corporate Accountability Manager, South Africa:
Alison Ramsden
Auditors: PricewaterhouseCoopers LLP

LOCATIONS

HQ: 1 Stanhope Gate,
London W1k 1AF, United Kingdom
Phone: +44-20-7659-0100 **Fax:** +44-20-7659-0111
Web: www.sabmiller.com

SABMiller has brewing operations in Africa, Central Europe, Central and North America, China, India, and Italy. It also owns hotels and casinos in Africa.

2003 Sales

	$ mil.	% of total
North America	3,465	42
South Africa	1,903	23
Europe	1,621	20
Africa/Asia	781	9
Central America	525	6
Total	**8,295**	**100**

PRODUCTS/OPERATIONS

Selected Brands

Beer Africa
Amstel (licensed from Heineken)
Carling Black Label
Castle (Draught, Lager, Lite, Milk Stout)
Dooley's
Hansa Pilsener
Heineken (imported)
Lion Lager (licensed from Heineken)
Ohlsson's
Redd's
Rhino

Beer Asia
Blue Sword
Green Leave
Haywards
Knock Out
Shenyang
Snow
Yingshi
Zero Clock

Beer Central America
Budweiser (license)
Golden Light
Heineken (license)
Port Royal
Suprema

Beer Europe
Dorada
Dreher
Itala Pilsen
Keller
Miller
Peroni
Tourtel

Beer North America
Hamm's
Doppelbock
Magnum
Miller
Milwaukee's Best
Olde English
Red Dog
SKYY Blue
Southpaw Light

Soft Drinks
Appletiser
Coca-Cola brands
Grapetiser
Just Juice
Schweppes brands

Other
Valpre (spring water)

COMPETITORS

Anadolu	Heineken
Anheuser-Busch	Interbrew
Asahi Breweries	Kirin
Asia Pacific Breweries	Lion Nathan
AmBev	Marriott International
Yanjing	MGM Mirage
Budvar	Nestlé
Carlsberg	PepsiCo
China Internet Global Alliance	Grolsch
Diageo	Tsingtao

HISTORICAL FINANCIALS

Company Type: Public

Income Statement

FYE: March 31

	REVENUE ($ mil.)	NET INCOME ($ mil.)	NET PROFIT MARGIN	EMPLOYEES
3/03	8,295	296	3.6%	42,402
3/02	3,185	250	7.9%	33,230
3/01	3,304	328	9.9%	31,327
3/00	4,135	456	11.0%	34,365
3/99	4,683	305	6.5%	49,099
3/98	6,436	240	3.7%	81,000
3/97	6,542	479	7.3%	105,000
3/96	6,301	435	6.9%	106,900
Annual Growth	**4.0%**	**(5.4%)**	**—**	**(12.4%)**

2003 Year-End Financials

Debt ratio: 18.2%   Current ratio: 0.45
Return on equity: 6.9%   Long-term debt ($ mil.): 1,130
Cash ($ mil.): 561

Net Income History

Pink Sheets: SBMRY

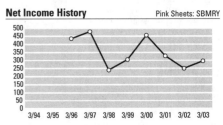

Compagnie de Saint-Gobain

Compagnie de Saint-Gobain is in a glass by itself. The materials mega-group controls more than 1,000 companies with operations in three sectors. Its Housing Products businesses (about half of sales) make and distribute building materials (roofing, mortars, wall facing) and pipe. The group's Glass Products operations make containers, flat glass, and insulation and reinforcements. Its High-Performance Materials unit includes ceramics, plastics, and abrasives businesses. Saint-Gobain is a world leader in many of its business segments. The operation dates to the 1660s, when it provided glass for Versailles; today it makes 30 billion glass containers a year and provides insulation for 20% of all US homes.

Saint-Gobain is growing through acquisitions, geographic expansion, and product development. The company has targeted Eastern Europe and Latin America as emerging areas ripe for growth. It will also open a major ceramic research facility in France.

The company's market value has suffered since its 2001 announcement that it would set aside funds for possible asbestos-related claims. Saint-Gobain pledged further funding for 2003 and 2004 to deal with asbestos litigation in the US.

HISTORY

Originally called Dunoyer, Saint-Gobain (named after the factory location) was founded in 1665 by order of the Sun King, Louis XIV, who needed mirrors to adorn his palaces. Because Venice had the monopoly on glass, Louis lured Venetian artisans to Paris. Some were poisoned by Italian assassins, but enough remained to teach Parisians their secrets. Saint-Gobain glass decorates the Palace of Versailles' Hall of Mirrors.

With its decreed glass monopoly in France, the company grew steadily until the French Revolution interrupted its prosperity. By the early 1800s, however, Saint-Gobain was shining again. It set up a sales office in New York in 1830 and its first foreign subsidiary in Germany in 1857. Under chemist Joseph Gay-Lussac's direction, Saint-Gobain began dabbling in chemicals in the mid-1800s.

Expanding to Italy (1889) and Spain (1904), the firm was Europe's leading glassmaker by 1913. Saint-Gobain pioneered the production of tempered security glass in the 1920s; it diversified into glass fiber in the 1930s.

Pilkington, a UK competitor, developed a glass-making method in 1959 that obviated the need for polishing and therefore slashed production costs. Saint-Gobain refit its factories to use the Pilkington method to keep its 50% EC market share. In 1968 the shareholding Suez Group forced Saint-Gobain to merge with Pont-à-Mousson (now Saint-Gobain Canalisation), then the world's leading iron pipe maker. The merger led to a much-needed restructuring that included selling Saint-Gobain's chemical interests.

The company acquired a majority interest in US building material maker CertainTeed in 1976. In 1982 it was forced to divest some of its interests when it was nationalized by France's new socialist government. Despite nationalization the company grew steadily during the 1980s, investing in Compagnie Générale des Eaux, the world's largest drinking-water distributor.

In 1986, after a change in France's political climate, Saint-Gobain became the first company to be reprivatized. Three years later it purchased Générale Française de Céramique (clay tile) and controlling interest in Vetri (glass containers, Italy).

Saint-Gobain bought Norton (the world's leader in abrasives) and UK glassmaker Solaglas in 1990. With the 1991 purchases of German glassmakers GIAG and Oberland, Saint-Gobain became the world's #1 glass manufacturer within a year.

After the recession of the early 1990s, Saint-Gobain sold its paper and packaging interests to Jefferson Smurfit in 1994, raising more than $1 billion for acquisitions. With Ball Corporation, it formed a glass container joint venture, Ball-Foster Glass, in 1995; the next year it bought Ball's stake. Acquisitions in 1997 included industrial ceramics firms in Germany and France and UK abrasives maker Unicorn International. In 1998 Saint-Gobain bought Bird Corp. (roofing materials, US) and CALMAR (plastic pump sprayers, US). The next year it bought US-based Furon, which was absorbed into a new unit, Saint-Gobain Performance Plastics.

In 2000, Saint-Gobain acquired Meyer International (a UK building materials supplier), Raab Karcher (a German building materials distributor), and US-based polymer specialist Chemfab. The following year Saint-Gobain bolstered its ceiling systems operations with the acquisition of the Maars Group's metal ceiling grid business. In 2002 Saint-Gobain acquired the 25% of France-based Lapeyre SA (doors, windows, cabinetry) stock it didn't own.

EXECUTIVES

Chairman and CEO: Jean-Louis Beffa, age 61
COO: Gianpaolo Caccini
SVP: Phillippe Crouzet
SVP: Emile François
SVP: Jean-François Phelizon
SVP; President, Ceramics and Plastics, and Abrasives Divisions: Christian Streiff
SVP; President, Flat Glass Division: Jacques Aschenbroich
SVP; President, Building Materials Distribution Division: Pierre-André de Chalendar
VP, External Relations: Nicole Grisoni-Bachelier
VP, Corporate Planning: Laurent Guillot
VP, Research: Jean-Claude Lehmann
President, Reinforcements Division: Roberto Caliari
President, Insulation Division: Peter R. Dachowski
President, Building Materials Division: Martin H. Ellis
President, Containers Division: Jerome Fessard
President, Pipe Division: Claude Imauven
Corporate Secretary: Bernard Field
Auditors: Befec-Price Waterhouse; SECEF

LOCATIONS

HQ: Les Miroirs, 18 Avenue d'Alsace, 92096 La Défense, France
Phone: +33-1-47-62-30-00   **Fax:** +33-1-47-78-45-03
US HQ: 750 E. Swedesford Rd., Valley Forge, PA 19482-0101
US Phone: 610-341-7000   **US Fax:** 610-341-7797
Web: www.saint-gobain.com

Saint-Gobain has more than 1,000 subsidiaries in some 45 countries worldwide.

2002 Sales

	$ mil.	% of total
Europe		
France	9,893	30
Other countries	13,696	42
North America	7,112	22
Other regions	2,300	6
Adjustments	(1,271)	—
Total	**31,730**	**100**

PRODUCTS/OPERATIONS

2002 Sales

	$ mil.	% of total
Housing products		
Building distribution	11,479	36
Building materials	3,222	10
Pipe	1,409	4
Glass		
Flat glass	4,635	14
Containers	4,272	13
Insulation & reinforcements	3,489	11
High-performance materials		
Ceramics, plastics, & abrasives	3,812	12
Adjustments	(588)	—
Total	**31,730**	**100**

Principal Segments and Products

Housing Products
Building materials distribution
　Joinery services
　Sanitation equipment
　Windows
Building materials manufacturing
　Decking
　Fences
　Railing
　Siding
　Windows
Cement-glass composites
Clay products
　Bricks
　Tiles
Industrial concrete
Mortar
Pipes
Reinforced cement
Roofing materials
　Asphalt shingles
　Terracotta tiles

Glass
Containers
　Bottles
　Jars
Flat glass
Glass fiber
Glazed glass
Insulation

High-Performance Materials
Abrasives
Industrial ceramics

COMPETITORS

3M	Imerys
Anchor	Johns Manville
Asahi Glass	Kyocera
Ball Corporation	Lafarge SA
BayWa	mg technologies
Corning	Owens Corning
CRH	Owens-Illinois
Danone	Pilkington
Franz Haniel	PPG
Gerresheimer Glas	Showa Denko
Glaverbel Group	Tetra Laval
Guardian Industries	USG
Hanson	Vitro

HISTORICAL FINANCIALS

Company Type: Public

Income Statement

FYE: December 31

	REVENUE ($ mil.)	NET INCOME ($ mil.)	NET PROFIT MARGIN	EMPLOYEES
12/02	31,730	1,090	3.4%	172,357
12/01	26,920	1,005	3.7%	173,329
12/00	27,132	1,428	5.3%	171,125
12/99	23,113	1,235	5.3%	164,698
12/98	20,797	1,280	6.2%	117,287
12/97	17,850	938	5.3%	107,968
12/96	17,464	826	4.7%	111,701
12/95	14,323	858	6.0%	89,852
12/94	13,958	679	4.9%	80,909
12/93	12,082	222	1.8%	92,348
Annual Growth	11.3%	19.3%	—	7.2%

2002 Year-End Financials

Debt ratio: 55.1%
Return on equity: 9.7%
Cash ($ mil.): 1,266
Current ratio: 1.44
Long-term debt ($ mil.): 6,538

Net Income History

Euronext Paris: SGO

Samsung Group

Samsung Group has reason to sing. The *chaebol* (industrial group) has surpassed its former archrival, the erstwhile Hyundai Group, to become the #1 business group in South Korea. Samsung's flagship unit is Samsung Electronics, which is the world's top maker of dynamic random-access memory (DRAM) and other memory chips, as well as a global heavyweight in all sorts of electronic gear including LCD panels, DVD players, and cellular phones. Other affiliated companies include credit card unit Samsung Card, Samsung General Chemicals, Samsung Life Insurance, Samsung Securities, and trading arm Samsung Corporation.

Forced into action by the Korean economic crisis of the late 1990s, Samsung has worked to whittle away its debt and shed noncore operations. (The company's holdings have fallen from 61 affiliates to about 35.)

Lee Kun-Hee, son of Samsung's founder, has dissolved much of the central management structure, including his post as the group's chairman, in his revamp of the group. He now chairs Samsung Electronics.

HISTORY

In 1936 Japan-educated Lee Byung-Chull began operating a rice mill in Korea, then under Japanese rule. By 1938 Lee had begun trading in dried fish and had incorporated as Samsung (Korean for "three stars"). WWII left Korea fairly unscathed, and by war's end Samsung had transportation and real estate adjuncts.

The Korean War, however, destroyed nearly all of Samsung assets. Left with a brewery and an import business for UN personnel, Lee reconstructed Samsung in South Korea. He formed the highly profitable Cheil Sugar Company, then the country's only sugar refiner, in 1953. Textile, banking, and insurance ventures followed.

A 1961 political coup brought Park Chung Hee to power in South Korea. Lee, wealthy and tied to the former government, was accused of illegal profiteering. A 1966 smuggling case involving one of Lee's sons led to another scandal, but charges were dropped when Lee gave the government an immense fertilizer plant. Despite the political change, Samsung still grew, diversifying into paper products, department stores, and publishing.

In 1969, with help from SANYO, Lee established Samsung Electronics, which benefited from the government's export drive and low wage rates. By disassembling Western-designed electronics, Samsung Electronics figured out how to produce inexpensive black-and-white televisions and, later, color TVs, VCRs, and microwave ovens. It manufactured such products under private labels for corporations including General Electric and Sears. In concert with the government's industrialization push, the *chaebol* also began making ships (1974), petrochemicals (1977), and aircraft engines (1977). By the 1980s Samsung was exporting electronics under its own name.

When Lee died in 1987, his son Lee Kun-Hee assumed control. After years of importing technology and spending freely on R&D, in 1990 Samsung became a world leader in chip production. Encouraged by the government, Samsung agreed to cooperate with fellow *chaebol* Goldstar (now LG Group) to obtain foreign technology to develop liquid crystal displays. In 1994 Lee, a longtime car lover, announced plans to form Samsung Motors.

In 1996 Lee was caught in a corruption scandal and got a two-year suspended sentence for bribery. The next year Asian financial markets crashed. Nonetheless Samsung bought the remaining 50.1% of struggling PC maker AST (it had bought a 49.9% share in 1996) but exited the US consumer PC market. Even as the bottom fell out of the Korean auto market, Samsung Motors began delivering its first cars in 1998. To lessen its debt, the group sold Samsung Heavy Industries' construction-equipment business to Sweden's Volvo and sold Samsung Electronics' power-device unit to Fairchild Semiconductor. Also in 1998 the South Korean government fined several *chaebol*, including Samsung, a collective $93 million for illegally funneling money to weaker subsidiaries.

Samsung sold the ailing AST to Beny Alagem, former head of Packard Bell NEC, in 1999. The following year Samsung sold a 70% stake in struggling Samsung Motors to France-based Renault.

EXECUTIVES

Chairman, Samsung Electronics: Lee Kun-Hee, age 61
Vice Chairman and CEO, Samsung Electronics: Yun Jong-Yong
President and CEO, Samsung Corporation: Pae Chong-Yeul
President and CEO, Samsung Engineering: Jung Yeon-Joo
President and CEO, Samsung General Chemicals: Ko Hong-Sik
President and CEO, Samsung Heavy Industries: Kim Jing-Wan
President and CEO, Samsung Techwin: Lee Joong-Koo

President and CEO, Shilla Hotels & Resorts: Lee Man-Soo
CEO, Samsung BP Chemicals: Lee Jae-Han
CEO, Samsung Corning: Lee Suk-Jai
CEO, Samsung Electro-Mechanics: Kang Ho-Moon
CEO, Samsung Fine Chemicals: Lee Yong-Soon
CEO, Samsung Fire & Marine Insurance: Lee Soo-Chang
CEO, Samsung Life Insurance: Bae Ho-Wan
CEO, Samsung Networks: Park Yang-Kyu
CEO, Samsung Petrochemical: Her Tae-Hak
CEO, Samsung Securities: Hwang Young-Key
Director, Samsung Medical Center: Choi Kyoo-Wan
Director, Samsung Economics Research Institute: Choi Woo-Sock
VP, Samsung Human Resources Development Center: Ko In-Soo

LOCATIONS

HQ: 250, 2-ga, Taepyung-ro, Chung-gu, Seoul 100-742, South Korea
Phone: +82-2-727-7114   **Fax:** +82-2-751-2083
US HQ: 105 Challenger Rd., Ridgefield Park, NJ 07660
US Phone: 201-229-5000   **US Fax:** 201-229-5080
Web: www.samsung.com

Samsung Group has operations in more than 50 countries around the world.

PRODUCTS/OPERATIONS

Selected Operations

Chemicals
Samsung BP Chemicals Co., Ltd.
Samsung Fine Chemicals Co., Ltd.
Samsung General Chemicals Co., Ltd.
Samsung Petrochemical Co., Ltd.

Electronics
Samsung Corning Co., Ltd. (TV picture-tube glass)
Samsung Electro-Mechanics Co., Ltd. (electronic components)
Samsung Electronics Co., Ltd. (semiconductors, consumer electronics)
Samsung SDI Co. Ltd.
Samsung SDS Co., Ltd. (systems integration, telecommunications)

Financial and Insurance
Samsung Capital Co., Ltd.
Samsung Card Co., Ltd. (loans, cash advances, financing)
Samsung Fire & Marine Insurance Co., Ltd.
Samsung Life Insurance Co., Ltd.
Samsung Life Investment Trust Management Co., Ltd.
Samsung Securities Co., Ltd.
Samsung Venture Investment Co., Ltd.

Other
Cheil Communications, Inc. (advertising)
Cheil Industries Inc. (textiles)
S1 Corporation (security systems)
Samsung Advanced Institute of Technology
Samsung Corporation (general trading)
Samsung Engineering Co., Ltd.
Samsung Everland Inc. (amusement parks)
Samsung Heavy Industries Co., Ltd. (machinery, vehicles)
Samsung Lions (pro baseball team)
Samsung Techwin Co., Ltd. (fine machinery including semiconductor equipment)
The Shilla Hotels & Resorts Co., Ltd.

COMPETITORS

DuPont	Millea Holdings
Ericsson	Motorola
Fujitsu	NEC
Hitachi	Nokia
Hyundai Corporation	Northrop Grumman
IBM	Philips Electronics
ITOCHU	SANYO
Kyobo Life Insurance	Sharp
LG Group	SK Group
Marconi	Sony
Marubeni	Ssangyong
Matsushita	Toshiba
Micron Technology	

HISTORICAL FINANCIALS

Company Type: Group

Income Statement

FYE: December 31

	REVENUE ($ mil.)	NET INCOME ($ mil.)	NET PROFIT MARGIN	EMPLOYEES
12/02	116,800	8,900	7.6%	175,000
12/01	98,700	4,500	4.6%	175,000
12/00	119,500	7,300	6.1%	174,000
12/99	93,500	2,200	2.4%	161,000
12/98	72,000	201	0.3%	193,000
12/97	57,199	173	0.3%	267,000
12/96	94,654	164	0.2%	256,000
12/95	87,000	3,802	4.4%	233,000
12/94	63,900	1,681	2.6%	206,000
12/93	51,300	521	1.0%	191,000
Annual Growth	**9.6%**	**37.1%**	**—**	**(1.0%)**

Net Income History

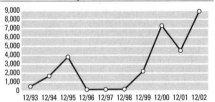

San Miguel Corporation

Filipinos filling out their grocery lists often turn to San Miguel — they don't have much other choice. San Miguel Corporation (SMC) is the largest beverage and food firm in the Philippines, selling its more than 200 product lines produced in more than 100 area factories. The company brews and distributes beer, including San Miguel Pale Pilsen and Red Horse, and controls more than 90% of the Philippine beer market. It enjoys similar dominance of the soft drink market thanks to its 65% stake in bottler Coca-Cola Philippines (The Coca-Cola Company owns the remaining 35%) and its 2001 purchase of the Cosmos Bottling Corporation. Wrapping things up is San Miguel's can, bottle, and container business.

SMC's food and agribusiness subsidiaries make a variety of meat products, animal feeds, coconut products, and dairy goods, while its packaging operations produce glass containers,

aluminum cans, corrugated cartons, metal caps, and crowns. SMC also manages real estate.

The company says it plans to expand into Australia, China, Indonesia, Malaysia, Taiwan, Thailand, and Vietnam.

Chairman Eduardo Cojuangco says he owns less than 10% of the company; however, others report he owns as much as 20% of SMC and controls the voting rights of another 27% through the United Coconut Planters Bank. These shares are under government sequestration (but still controlled by Cojuangco); the Filipino government believes the shares were gained through corrupt use of a levy imposed on farmers during the administration of Ferdinand Marcos.

HISTORY

La Fabrica de Cerveza de San Miguel, a brewery, was opened by Don Enrique Barretto y de Ycaza in Manila in 1890. By 1900 the European-styled beers of San Miguel were outselling imported brands five to one. The company became a corporation in 1913. By WWI the brewery was selling beer in Hong Kong, Shanghai, and Guam.

Andres Soriano y Roxas joined San Miguel in 1918 and in the 1920s established the Royal Soft Drinks Plant (1922), the Magnolia Ice Cream Plant (1925), and the first non-US national Coca-Cola bottling and distribution franchise (1927). After WWII, the company added additional facilities and factories as it continued to modernize and expand operations.

In the 1960s the firm changed its name to San Miguel Corporation (SMC). After the death of Andres in 1964, his son Andres Soriano Jr. became president. He modernized and decentralized operations into product segments. SMC continued to diversify in the 1970s.

A family feud erupted in 1983 when members of the controlling Soriano and Zobel families engaged in a proxy battle. Enrique Zobel realized that he could not win and sold all of his shares (about 20% of SMC) to Eduardo Cojuangco, a Ferdinand Marcos crony and president of United Coconut Planters Bank. Upon Soriano's death in 1984, Cojuangco became chairman, thus securing the company within Marcos' sphere of influence.

During the 1986 election, Cojuangco ordered all company employees to vote for Marcos. Cojuangco's estranged cousin Corazon Aquino won, and her government seized assets associated with Marcos and his followers, including Cojuangco's share of SMC. Cojuangco fled the country with Marcos, and Andres Soriano III became CEO. Cojuangco returned to the Philippines in 1989 to reclaim his share of the company.

SMC sold Coca-Cola Bottlers Philippines to Sydney-based Coca-Cola Amatil (CCA) in 1995 in exchange for a 25% stake in CCA. In mid-1998, immediately following Cojuangco-backed Joseph Estrada's election as president of the Philippines, Andres Soriano III stepped down and Cojuangco returned to SMC's helm.

In 1999 SMC withdrew plans to sell its remaining 21.5% of CCA, but in April 2000 again decided to divest its stake. SMC and a company it majority owns, La Tondeña Distillers, jointly bought Filipino juice maker Sugarland. SMC bought Australian brewer J. Boag & Son in June 2000 and the next month Estrada announced the government's plan to sell a 27% stake in SMC.

After Estrada's ouster in early 2001, his successor, President Gloria Arroyo, said the government would seize 47% of the company's shares

controlled by United Coconut Planters Bank (27%) and Cojuangco (20%). In March San Miguel agreed to buy the Philippines' largest processed-meat maker, Pure Foods. The company bought 65% of bottler Coca-Coca Phillipines from CCA in July; SMC surrendered its stake in CCA as part of the deal.

SMC acquired 83% of rival RFM's Cosmos Bottling, the Philippines' #2 soft drink company, in August 2001, further consolidating their domestic beverage dominance. In September the company transferred its 49% stake in Sugarland to La Tondeña Distillers, which then became the sole owner of the juice maker.

In 2002 Japanese brewer Kirin paid $530 million for 15% of San Miguel. Following an announced expansion plan into Asia, the company purchased a Thailand industrial complex for $20 million in September 2003.

EXECUTIVES

Chairman and CEO: Eduardo M. Cojuangco Jr.
Vice Chairman, President, and COO: Ramon S. Ang
CFO and Treasurer: Ferdinand K. Constantino
SVP, Corporate Human Resources: David Santos
SVP, Corporate Planning and Development: Maria Belen C. Buensuceso
SVP, Corporate Quality Management: Alberto A. Manlapit
SVP, Corporate Technical Services: Lubin B. Nepomuceno
VP, Corporate Affairs: Ira Daniel B. Maniquis
VP, Corporate Human Resources: Emiliano B. Canonigo Jr.
VP, Corporate Marketing: Minerva Lourdes B. Bibonia
President, San Miguel Beer Division: Faustino F. Galang
President, San Miguel Pure Foods Company: Enrique A. (Ricky) Gomez Jr.
President, San Miguel Packaging Products: Alberto O. Villa-Abrille Jr.
President, San Miguel Properties Inc.: Jeronimo Kilayko
President, La Tondeña Distillers: Arnaldo L. Africa
President, Coca-Cola Bottlers Philippines: Genaro V. Lapez
Corporate Secretary and General Counsel: Francis H. Jardeleza
Auditors: SyCip Gorres Velayo & Co.

LOCATIONS

HQ: 40 San Miguel Ave., PO Box 271, Mandaluyong City, Metro Manila 1550, Philippines
Phone: +63-2-632-3000   **Fax:** +63-2-632-3099
Web: www.sanmiguel.com.ph

San Miguel Corporation has manufacturing plants in China, Hong Kong, Indonesia, the Philippines, Vietnam, and other countries in Southeast Asia. The company's beers are sold in some 20 countries in the Americas, Asia, and Australia.

2002 Sales

	% of total
Philippines	90
China	6
Indonesia	1
Australia	1
Vietnam	1
Others	1
Total	**100**

PRODUCTS/OPERATIONS

2002 Sales

	% of total
Beverage	64
Food	31
Packaging	5
Total	**100**

Selected Products and Brands

Beverages
Beer, Multinational
  Ander Bir (licensed)
  Blue Ice
  Cerveza Negra
  Gold Eagle
  Miller Genuine Draft (licensed)
  Red Horse
  San Mig Light
  San Miguel (Draft Beer, Pale Pilsen, Super Dry)
Beer, Regional
  China (Blue Star, Double Happiness Beer, Dragon
    Beer, Guang's Draft, Kirin, Pineapple Beer, Valor)
  Hong Kong (Bruck, Eagle High, Knight, Lowenbrau
    — licensed, San Miguel Dark)
  Indonesia (Anker Stout — licensed, Carlsberg —
    licensed)
  Vietnam (Bock)
Bottled Water
  Distilled Drinking Water (FIRST, Wilkins)
  Mineral Water (VIVA!)
Juice Drinks
  Cordial Lime Juice
  Magnolia (Fruit Drinks, FunChum, Junior Juice, Ice
    Tea)
  Zip Juice
Nonalcoholic malt beverages
  Cali (Shandy, 10, Ice)
  Guang's Pineapple Shandy (China)
  San Miguel NAB
  Shanta Super Shandy (Indonesia)
Wines and Spirits
  Gin (Ginebra San Miguel, Oxford London Dry Gin —
    licensed)
  Rum (Añejo, Tondeña, San Miguel)

Food and Agribusiness
Dairy
Dari Creme
Star
Meat (beef, chicken, pork)
Longanisa
Magnolia
Moby
Valiente

Real Estate
Bel Adea
Buenavista Homes
Country Mile Homes
The Enterprise Center
Greenwoods
HOC Realty Inc.
HQ Business Centers
The Legacy
Lexington
Maravilla
Primavera Hills
San Miguel Properties Corp.
Villa de Calamba
Wedge Woods

COMPETITORS

Amcor	Diageo
Anheuser-Busch	Foster's
Asahi Breweries	Heineken
Asia Brewery	Interbrew
Bacardi USA	International Paper
Benguet	Kirin
Cadbury Schweppes	Lion Nathan
Cargill	Mercian
Carlsberg	Nestlé
CBR Brewing	PepsiCo
ConAgra	Tsingtao
Danone	Tyson Foods

HISTORICAL FINANCIALS

Company Type: Public

Income Statement

FYE: December 31

	REVENUE ($ mil.)	NET INCOME ($ mil.)	NET PROFIT MARGIN	EMPLOYEES
12/02	2,536	124	4.9%	27,259
12/01	2,353	125	5.3%	26,697
12/00	1,771	137	7.7%	14,864
12/99	1,881	150	8.0%	14,511
12/98	1,911	629	32.9%	15,923
12/97	1,699	75	4.4%	18,444
12/96	3,232	232	7.2%	28,544
12/95	3,027	223	7.4%	31,485
12/94	2,790	484	17.3%	30,965
12/93	2,209	146	6.6%	32,832
Annual Growth	1.5%	(1.9%)	—	(2.0%)

2002 Year-End Financials

Debt ratio: 13.2%
Return on equity: 8.0%
Cash ($ mil.): 532

Current ratio: 2.22
Long-term debt ($ mil.): 239

Net Income History

OTC: SMGBY

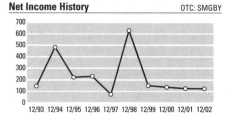

Santander Central Hispano

Santander Central Hispano (SCH) is a leader in the running of Spanish banks. It offers retail banking in Spain, as well as other European countries and in Latin America. Its subsidiaries, including Chile's Banco Santander-Chile (which acquired fellow Santander holding Banco Santiago), Argentina's Banco Río de la Plata, and Mexico's Grupo Financiero Santander Mexicano, also make it a top banking group in Latin America, where it is active in more than a dozen countries. SCH also offers asset management, wholesale banking, private banking, and other financial services through subsidiaries.

Roughly 85% of the company's net income comes from its retail banking operations in Spain, other countries in Europe, and Latin America. It owns about 10% of Royal Bank of Scotland and together the two banks participate in joint venture partnerships throughout Europe. SCH still does business under three names: Banco Santander, BCH, and Banesto, which SCH plans to rebrand.

SCH, which formed when Banco Central Hispano joined with Banco Santander in 1999, hasn't achieved the efficiency it hoped for. Tension between the two executive boards ended with Emilio Botín-Sanz's ouster of Ángel Corcóstegui. The Botín family is firmly in control, which makes corporate governance advocates fret.

HISTORY

Banco Santander Central Hispano (BSCH) was created by the 1999 merger of Banco Santander and Banco Central Hispano (BCH).

In 1857 a group of Basque businessmen formed Banco Santander to finance Latin American trade. The emergence of Cantabria as a leading province after WWI helped the bank expand, first regionally, then nationally.

The Botín family has been closely identified with the bank for decades. Before his death in 1923, Emilio Botín served as a board member, then for a few years as chairman. The post was held by his son Emilio Botín-Sanz de Sautuola from 1950 to 1986, when *his* son Emilio Botín Ríos (known as Don Emilio) took over.

Spanish banks were spared the worst of the Great Depression (thanks to their isolation and the country's shunning the gold standard), but Spain's civil war was draining. In the early 1940s Santander expanded into Madrid and other major Spanish cities and merged with a few rivals. In the 1950s and 1960s, as interest rates were controlled and mergers halted, banks competed by building branch networks and investing overseas, particularly in Latin America. In 1965 Santander joined with Bank of America to form Bankinter (it divested most of its stake by the mid-1990s).

Tight economic controls were relaxed in the 1970s after Franco's death. Despite global recession, Santander continued to invest in Latin America through the mid-1980s.

In the late 1980s Santander prepared to compete in a deregulated Spain and Europe, forming alliances with Royal Bank of Scotland, Kemper (now part of Zurich Financial Services), and Metropolitan Life Insurance. In 1989 the bank jumpstarted competition by introducing Spain's first high-interest account.

In the 1990s Santander focused on home. Spurned by Banco Hispano Americano, Santander acquired a 60% stake in the ailing Banco Español de Crédito (Banesto). Banesto became wholly owned in 1998. The bank took a hit when Latin America plunged into an economic crisis that year. With profit margins falling, the bank merged with BCH in 1999.

BCH was formed by the 1991 merger of Banco Central and Banco Hispano Americano (BHA). BHA was established in 1900 by investors in Latin America; Central was founded in 1919. The mixed banks offered both commercial and investment banking; they funded industrialization and investment in Latin America and became two of Spain's largest banks before the civil war.

After the war BHA sold its Latin American assets when the currency dried up, while Central used mergers and acquisitions to expand across Spain. Isolated from WWII by Franco, the two banks used their dual strategies to fund overseas investment and domestic branch growth.

After Franco's death, the banks faced increased competition at home and abroad. Central bought BHA in 1991 to remain competitive as Spain entered the European Economic Community in 1992.

Following the merger, BCH trimmed 20% of its branches, fired some 10,000 employees, and sold unprofitable holdings. Focused on Latin America, the bank took small stakes in small banks. Losing its edge, BCH merged with Santander in 1999.

In 2000 BSCH focused on expanding in Europe and Latin America. Among its European moves was its alliance with Société Générale to buy investment fund management firms, particularly in the US. In Latin America the bank bought Brazil's Banco Meridional, Banco do Estado de São Paulo (Banespa), and Grupo Financiero Serfin, Mexico's #3 bank. Critics question the $5 billion price tag BSCH paid for Banespa, charging that the formerly state-run bank was overvalued in 2001. Executive in-fighting saw ex-Santander chairman Emilio Botín triumph over ex-BCH chairman José María Amusátegui for control of BSCH's helm. Soon after, the bank dropped the word "Banco" to be known simply as Santander Central Hispano (SCH). The following year the bank sold off its shares of Germany's Commerzbank and France's Société Générale.

EXECUTIVES

Chairman: Emilio Botín-Sanz
First Vice Chairman: Jaime Botín-Sanz
Second Vice Chairman and CEO: Alfredo Saenz Abad
Third Vice Chairman: Matías Rodríguez Inciarte
Chairman, Banesto: Ana P. Botín-Sanz
EVP, Finance: Francisco G. Roldán
EVP, Global Wholesale Banking: José M. Arrojo
EVP, Europe, Finance Companies, and Quality: Juan Rodríguez Inciarte
EVP, Internal Auditing: David Arce Torres
EVP, Latin America: Francisco Luzón López
EVP, Commercial Banking: Enrique García Candelas
EVP, Equity Stakes: Joan David Grimà
EVP, Portugal: Antonio Horta Osorio
EVP, Communications and Economic Studies: Juan M. Cendoya
EVP, Resources and Costs: José Antonio Aróstegui
General Secretary: Ignacio Benjumea
Auditors: Deloitte & Touche

LOCATIONS

HQ: Santander Central Hispano S.A.
Plaza de Canalejas,1, 28014 Madrid, Spain
Phone: +34-91-558-11-11   **Fax:** +34-91-522-66-70
Web: www.gruposantander.com

2002 Sales

	% of total
Interest	77
Net fees & commissions	15
Group transactions	4
Other	4
Total	**100**

2002 Assets

	% of total
Cash & equivalents	14
Government securities	8
Bonds	10
Stocks	4
Loans	50
Other	14
Total	**100**

COMPETITORS

BBVA	Bankinter
Banco Comercial Português	BBVA Banco BHIF
	Deutsche Bank
Banco de Galicia y Buenos Aires	Dresdner Bank
	Espírito Santo
Banco de la Nación	HSBC Holdings
Banco do Brasil	Itaúsa
Banco Popular	J.P. Morgan Chase
Bank of America	

HISTORICAL FINANCIALS

Company Type: Public

Income Statement

FYE: December 31

	ASSETS ($ mil.)	NET INCOME ($ mil.)	INCOME AS % OF ASSETS	EMPLOYEES
12/02	340,516	2,360	0.7%	104,178
12/01	319,208	2,216	0.7%	114,927
12/00	328,620	2,127	0.6%	126,757
12/99	258,439	1,587	0.6%	95,442
12/98	181,777	1,392	0.8%	73,964
12/97	171,353	1,086	0.6%	72,740
12/96	149,954	919	0.6%	—
12/95	135,243	837	0.6%	—
12/94	114,269	759	0.7%	—
12/93	73,098	465	0.6%	—
Annual Growth	**18.6%**	**19.8%**	**—**	**7.4%**

2002 Year-End Financials

Equity as % of assets: 6.5%	Dividends
Return on assets: 0.7%	Yield: 3.8%
Return on equity: 11.1%	Payout: 54.0%
Long-term debt ($ mil.): 99,316	Market value ($ mil.): 33,617
No. of shares (mil.): 4,768	Sales ($ mil.): 32,524

Stock History

NYSE: STD

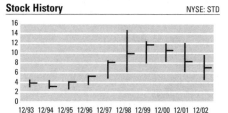

12/93 12/94 12/95 12/96 12/97 12/98 12/99 12/00 12/01 12/02

	STOCK PRICE ($) FY Close	P/E High/Low	Earnings	PER SHARE ($) Dividends	Book Value
12/02	7.05	19 9	0.50	0.27	4.66
12/01	8.30	24 13	0.49	0.26	4.37
12/00	10.56	24 17	0.50	0.23	4.31
12/99	11.69	29 19	0.43	0.19	2.68
12/98	9.88	32 14	0.45	0.00	2.56
12/97	8.14	21 13	0.39	0.00	2.30
12/96	5.29	15 10	0.36	0.16	2.44
12/95	4.10	13 8	0.33	0.12	2.80
12/94	3.18	15 10	0.28	0.50	2.40
12/93	3.88	13 9	0.35	0.12	1.53
Annual Growth	**6.9%**	**— —**	**4.0%**	**9.4%**	**13.2%**

SANYO Electric Co., Ltd.

"Sanyo" means "three oceans," and when it comes to consumer and commercial electronics, SANYO covers the waterfront. The electronics powerhouse has nearly 170 subsidiaries worldwide. From electric bicycles to semiconductors, SANYO manufactures products both innovative and prosaic. Its companies make a variety of electrical devices and appliances, including industrial and commercial equipment (refrigerated supermarket cases), audio and video equipment (DVD players, TVs, digital cameras), semiconductors, communications equipment (cellular phones, computers), batteries, and home appliances (microwave ovens, air conditioners).

Japan accounts for about 70% of the corporation's sales. SANYO is focused on developing environment-friendly products such as solar cells, rechargeable batteries, and CFC-free refrigerators and air-conditioning units. The company also is placing particular emphasis on developing multimedia products, such as digital cameras and liquid-crystal displays (LCDs).

To remain competitive in the explosive high-tech environment, the company is forming alliances with leading technology developers, including a five-member consortium to address 3-D technology (ITOCHU, NTT DATA, Sharp, and Sony); an initiative with Samsung (home-use air conditioners); and a joint venture with International Rectifier (technologies for energy-efficient appliances).

HISTORY

"Sanyo" means "three oceans" in Japanese. Toshio Iue, SANYO's first CEO, had the Pacific, Atlantic, and Indian Oceans in mind — he wanted to turn the company into an international enterprise. SANYO was formed after WWII when the Allies broke Matsushita Electric into two companies. Toshio, brother-in-law to Matsushita founder Konosuke Matsushita, took charge of SANYO, which then made bicycle lamps.

By 1949 the company was producing radios, and in the 1950s it diversified into refrigerators, fans, and washing machines. In 1953 a Japanese household appliances rush began, and SANYO led washing machine sales. By the end of the decade, the company was Japan's leading exporter of transistor radios.

To raise money, in 1959 SANYO created Tokyo SANYO Electric, in which it took a 20% stake. The company established its first factory abroad, in Hong Kong, in 1961 and created Cadnica, a durable rechargeable battery.

The 1970s oil crisis drew SANYO into alternative energy development, and the company continued its energy research when the crisis had passed. In 1973 SANYO joined forces with Emerson Electric (US) to bail out Emerson's Fisher electronics subsidiary. (SANYO bought Fisher in 1978.) SANYO began shifting its focus from appliances to high-tech products in the mid-1970s. It started making color TVs in the US in 1976. Although sales slowed when SANYO initially opted to develop VCRs using the ill-fated Betamax format, they rose tremendously in the 1970s, from $71 million in 1972 to $855 million in 1978.

SANYO and Tokyo SANYO Electric merged in 1986. A high yen forced the company to move much of its manufacturing outside Japan; that year it made more products abroad than any other Japanese company. By then the country's leading TV maker, SANYO formed a joint venture with Sears to manufacture TVs. SANYO also developed the world's first CFC-free refrigeration system, a version of which was installed in New York's Guggenheim Museum.

In 1993 SANYO set a world record for solar energy conversion efficiency. The company strengthened its electronic components and solar businesses two years later by establishing SANYO Electronic Components and SANYO Solar Industries. In 1997 SANYO introduced the highest-output home-use solar cells, capable of producing 160 watts of electricity.

SANYO in 1998 formed a pact with IBM to make semiconductors using Big Blue's energy saving copper circuit technology. The next year SANYO allied with Philips to develop semiconductors and related products. Weakness in the

Asian economy, a slowdown in US sales, and overall decreased demand hammered SANYO's earnings for fiscal 1999.

Also in 1999 SANYO teamed up with Eastman Kodak to develop flat-panel displays based on next-generation organic electroluminescent technology. The company announced several product developments, including an advanced battery for hybrid-fuel vehicles and an air-conditioning and refrigeration compressor that uses carbon dioxide instead of Freon. It signed a deal with Turbolinux to equip 20,000 medical workstations with the company's version of the Linux operating system — the largest enterprise deployment of Linux thus far.

Amidst charges of knowingly selling defective solar cell systems, president Sadao Kondo resigned in 2000. He was replaced by Yukinori Kuwano. In 2001 SANYO acquired Toshiba's nickel metal hydride battery business, solidifying its position as one of the world's leading battery manufacturers.

In January 2002 the company formed an alliance with China's largest consumer electronic maker, Haier Group, whereby SANYO sells its products through Haier's outlets and service centers and, in turn, selected Haier goods are sold in Japan.

SANYO's three-year initiative (launched in 2001) resulted in the sale of the troubled vending machine manufacturing operations (2002). The initiative also led to the restructuring of the company's Home Appliance business, including shifting production of home-use air conditioners to China. In April 2003 SANYO further reorganized; resulting in four business groups (Consumer Group, Commercial Group, Component Group, and Service Group), each corresponding to a customer base.

In January 2003 SANYO and Eastman Kodak agreed to jointly fund production of full-color organic light emitting diode (OLED) displays; OLED displays feature full-motion images viewable from very wide angles. In the same year SANYO turned wholly owned SANYO Electric Software Co. into a 50/50 joint venture with NTT DATA.

EXECUTIVES

Chairman and CEO: Satoshi Iue
President and COO: Yukinori Kuwano
EVP and CFO: Yoichiro Furuse
EVP and Chief Marketing Officer: Toshimasa Iue
Executive Officer: Eiji Kotobuki
Executive Officer: Sunao Okubo
Executive Officer: Hiromoto Sekino
Executive Officer: Tadahiko Tanaka
Senior Officer: Satoshi Inoue
Senior Officer: Osamu Kajikawa
Senior Officer: Hiroshi Ono
Senior Officer: Yasusuke Tanaka
Senior Officer: Fusao Terada
Auditors: PricewaterhouseCoopers

LOCATIONS

HQ: San'yo Denki Kabushiki Kaisha
5-5 Keihan-Hondori, 2-chome, Moriguchi, Osaka 570-8677, Japan
Phone: +81-6-6991-1181   **Fax:** +81-6-6991-6566
US HQ: 2055 Sanyo Ave., San Diego, CA 92154
US Phone: 619-661-1134   **US Fax:** 619-661-6795
Web: www.sanyo.co.jp

SANYO Electric has nearly 120 subsidiaries worldwide, and operates manufacturing facilities in more than 20 countries (located primarily in Asia, as well as in North America and Europe).

2003 Sales

	$ mil.	% of total
Japan	13,270	70
Asia	2,561	14
North America	2,092	11
Other	1,026	5
Total	**18,949**	**100**

PRODUCTS/OPERATIONS

2003 Sales

	$ mil.	% of total
A/V information and communications equipment	7,561	40
Electronic devices	3,700	20
Batteries	2,386	13
Home appliances	2,156	11
Industrial and commercial equipment	1,583	8
Other	1,563	8
Total	**18,949**	**100**

Selected Products

A/V Information and Communications Equipment
Automotive stereo components
CDs
CD-R/RW systems
Cellular phones
Color TVs
Digital memory players
Digital cameras
DVD players
DVD-ROM systems
Fax machines
High-definition TV systems
Liquid crystal display (LCD) projectors
Medical computer systems
Personal Handyphone System (PHS) phones and base stations
Portable navigation systems
VCRs
Video cameras

Batteries
Alkaline batteries
Manganese batteries
Lithium batteries
Lithium-ion rechargeable batteries
Nickel-cadmium rechargeable batteries
Shavers
Solar cells

Electronic Devices
BIP-LSIs
CCD
Electronic components
LCDs
LEDs
Laser diodes
MOS-LSIs
Organic semiconductive condensers
Thick-film integrated circuits (ICs)
Transistors and diodes

Home Appliances
Air conditioners
Clothes dryers
Compressors for freezers, refrigerators, and air conditioners
Dehumidifiers
Dishwashers and dryers
Electric fans
Electric and kerosene heating equipment
Electronic and electric products for bicycles
Freezers
Home-use pumps
Massage loungers
Medical sterilizing equipment
Microwave ovens
Motor-assisted bicycles
Refrigerators
Small kitchen appliances (toasters, rice cookers, electromagnetic cookers)
Ultralow-temperature freezers
Vacuum cleaners
Washing machines

Industrial and Commercial Equipment
Absorption chillers and heaters
Automatic chip mounters
Beverage dispensers
Commercial freezers and refrigerators
Gas-engine heat-pump air conditioners
Golf cart systems
Ice makers
Package air conditioners
Prefabricated freezers
Refrigerated/freezer/supermarket showcases
Water coolers

COMPETITORS

AMD	Mitsubishi Electric
Apple Computer	Motorola
Canon	National Semiconductor
CASIO COMPUTER	NEC
Daewoo Electronics	Nokia
Dell	Oki Electric
Electrolux AB	Philips Electronics
Energizer Holdings	Pioneer
Fujitsu	Pitney Bowes
GE	Ricoh
Gillette	Samsung Electronics
Hewlett-Packard	Seiko Epson
Hitachi	Sharp
Intel	Siemens
IBM	Sony
Kyocera	THOMSON
LG Electronics	Toshiba
Matsushita	United Technologies
Maytag	Whirlpool

HISTORICAL FINANCIALS

Company Type: Public

Income Statement

FYE: March 31

	REVENUE ($ mil.)	NET INCOME ($ mil.)	NET PROFIT MARGIN	EMPLOYEES
3/03	18,949	(607)	—	79,025
3/02	15,881	13	0.1%	80,500
3/01	18,073	340	1.9%	86,009
3/00	19,002	205	1.1%	83,519
3/99	15,687	(216)	—	77,071
3/98	14,581	93	0.6%	67,887
3/97	14,889	143	1.0%	67,827
3/96*	4,949	(35)	—	56,612
11/95	17,081	153	0.9%	—
11/94	17,124	115	0.7%	—
Annual Growth	1.1%	—	—	4.9%

*Fiscal year change

2003 Year-End Financials

Debt ratio: 121.3%
Return on equity: —
Cash ($ mil.): 2,665
Current ratio: 1.11
Long-term debt ($ mil.): 4,863

No. of shares (mil.): 371
Dividends
  Yield: 1.8%
  Payout: —
Market value ($ mil.): 5,080

Stock History

NASDAQ (SC): SANYY

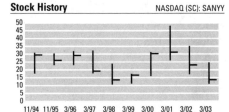

11/94	11/95	3/96	3/97	3/98	3/99	3/00	3/01	3/02	3/03

STOCK PRICE ($) FY Close	P/E High/Low	PER SHARE ($) Earnings	PER SHARE ($) Dividends	PER SHARE ($) Book Value
3/03	13.69	— —	(1.63)	0.25	10.81
3/02	22.99	580 292	0.06	0.00	12.10
3/01	31.25	54 30	0.89	0.25	14.06
3/00	30.25	57 30	0.54	0.22	16.77
3/99	16.63	— —	(0.56)	0.11	15.22
3/98	13.50	98 46	0.24	0.19	14.57
3/97	19.13	86 49	0.37	0.06	160.36
3/96*	29.13	— —	(0.09)	0.12	19.58
11/95	26.00	77 60	0.39	0.21	20.18
11/94	29.50	105 62	0.29	0.19	18.62
Annual Growth	(8.2%)	— —	—	3.1%	(5.9%)

*Fiscal year change

SAP

SAP's plans to dominate the software world are more than a little enterprising. The company is the leading provider of enterprise resource planning (ERP) software used to integrate back-office functions such as distribution, accounting, human resources, and manufacturing. Nearly 20,000 companies such as ChevronTexaco, Sony, and GM use its software. SAP continues to shift its huge customer base to its mySAP products, which are Web-based software platforms used for a variety of enterprise functions. SAP has leveraged its prominent position in the ERP market to expand into related fields, including supply chain and customer relationship management (CRM).

SAP has methodically transitioned towards incorporating Web-based capabilities into its product lines; the company's mySAP Business Suite products now account for about 75% of software sales.

While the company's huge installed base of customers provides a steady stream of recurring licensing and service revenue, SAP has come under pressure from investors to pursue new areas of growth. With its legacy ERP software industry maturing, the company has intensified its efforts in the CRM software arena, battling head to head with CRM leader Siebel Systems, as well as with Oracle and PeopleSoft.

Partially in response to Microsoft's expanding presence in the enterprise software market, SAP has also released a scaled-down version of its software designed specifically for small and mid-sized businesses, as well as new software development tools and services for its strategic partners in Europe. The company has also announced plans to expand its ERP business in fledgling, unsaturated markets in Latin America and Asia (with a particular emphasis on China).

Three of SAP's founders — Hasso Plattner, Dietmar Hopp, and Klaus Tschira — control about 35% of the company.

HISTORY

Software engineers Hasso Plattner, Hans-Werner Hector, Dietmar Hopp, and Klaus Tschira started SAP in 1972 when the project they were working on for IBM was moved to another unit. The four agreed to write a program for IBM customer Imperial Chemical Industries,

and SAP (named for the IBM project they left — Systems, Applications, and Projects) was formed.

Set up in a cornfield, the group worked nights on borrowed computers until business picked up. While rival software companies made many products to automate the various parts of a company's operations, these engineers decided to make a single system that would tie a corporation together. In 1973 they launched an instantaneous accounting transaction processing program called R/1. By 1981, with 200 customers already on board, they had adapted the program to create R/2, mainframe software that linked external databases and communication systems.

The company went public in 1988. That year Plattner began a project to create software for the computer network market. In 1992, as sales of its R/2 mainframe software lagged, SAP introduced its R/3 software.

Still basically a stranger outside Europe, SAP built a technology development center that year in California to attract attention from Silicon Valley. To support its push into the US, the company launched a $2 million advertising campaign in 1993; sales soared, and by 1995 the US had become SAP's largest market.

In 1996 Hector decided to sell holdings amounting to about 10% of SAP's stock, a move that possibly undermined hostile takeover barriers; he left the company after a dispute with Hopp.

The next year SAP moved to the NYSE; longtime executive Henning Kagermann was named co-chairman along with Plattner. In 1999 the company expanded on the Internet, unveiling a Web-based exchange (mySAP.com) supporting online transactions and other services. The company's long-standing resistance to employee stock options weakened in 2000 when SAP approved an option program to offset the loss of more than 200 key US managers in an 18-month period.

Later that year SAP launched a US subsidiary (SAP Markets) and increased its minority stake in software maker Commerce One.

In 2001 SAP acquired enterprise portal software provider Top Tier Software, renaming it SAP Portals. The company also invested additional money in Commerce One, raising its ownership stake to about 20%.

In 2002 the company reabsorbed its SAP Portals and SAP Markets subsidiaries, integrating their offerings into its mySAP product family.

Plattner stepped down in 2003, leaving Kagermann in sole control of the chairman and CEO positions.

EXECUTIVES

Chairman and CEO: Henning Kagermann
Executive Board, Finance and Administration: Werner Brandt
Executive Board, Global Field Operations: Leo Apotheker
Executive Board, Human Resources and mySAP: Claus E. Heinrich
Executive Board, Information Technology Infrastructure: Gerhard Oswald
Executive Board, mySAP and Global Research: Peter Zencke
Executive Board, Technology Strategy: Shai Agassi
Extended Management Board: Leslie Hayman
Extended Management Board, Global Initiatives: Wolfgang Kemna
Extended Management Board, Global Marketing: Martin Homlish
Extended Management Board, SAP NetWeaver Development: Klaus Kreplin
Extended Management Board, Strategic Research and Development: Peter J. Kirschbauer

Extended Management Board, Technology Development: Karl-Heinz Hess
President and CEO, SAP America: William R. (Bill) McDermott, age 41
Auditors: KPMG Deutsche Treuhand-Gesellschaft AG

LOCATIONS

HQ: SAP Aktiengesellschaft
Neurottstrasse 16, 69190 Walldorf, Germany
Phone: +49-6227-74-7474   **Fax:** +49-6227-75-7575
US HQ: 3999 West Chester Pike,
Newtown Square, PA 19073
US Phone: 610-661-1000   **US Fax:** 610-355-3106
Web: www.sap.com

SAP has offices in more than 50 countries.

2002 Sales

	% of total
Europe, Middle East & Africa	55
Americas	34
Asia Pacific	11
Total	**100**

PRODUCTS/OPERATIONS

2002 Sales

	% of total
Maintenance	33
Software	31
Consulting	30
Training & other	6
Total	**100**

Selected mySAP Software

Business intelligence
Customer relationship management
E-commerce
Enterprise resource planning
Financials and accounting
Human resources management
Logistics
Product life cycle management
Supply chain management

Market-Specific Applications

Consumer goods
SAP Consumer Products
SAP Retail

Discrete manufacturing
SAP Aerospace & Defense
SAP Automotive
SAP Engineering & Construction
SAP High Tech

Financial services and service providers
SAP Banking
SAP Insurance
SAP Service Provider

Process industries
SAP Chemicals
SAP Mill Products
SAP Mining
SAP Oil & Gas
SAP Pharmaceuticals

Public sector
SAP Healthcare
SAP Higher Education & Research
SAP Public Sector

Utilities and communications
SAP Media
SAP Telecommunications
SAP Utilities

Selected Services

Application hosting
Business consulting
Implementation
Maintenance
Training

COMPETITORS

Ariba	Lawson Software
Baan	Manugistics Group
Epicor Software	MAPICS
i2 Technologies	Microsoft
Intentia	Oracle
IBM	PeopleSoft
J.D. Edwards	Siebel Systems

HISTORICAL FINANCIALS

Company Type: Public

Income Statement

FYE: December 31

	REVENUE ($ mil.)	NET INCOME ($ mil.)	NET PROFIT MARGIN	EMPLOYEES
12/02	7,786	534	6.9%	29,374
12/01	6,534	517	7.9%	28,878
12/00	5,881	596	10.1%	24,480
12/99	5,146	605	11.8%	21,699
12/98	5,073	629	12.4%	17,323
12/97	3,346	515	15.4%	12,856
12/96	2,415	367	15.2%	9,202
12/95	1,875	281	15.0%	6,857
12/94	1,182	181	15.3%	5,229
12/93	634	84	13.2%	3,648
Annual Growth	32.1%	22.9%	—	26.1%

2002 Year-End Financials

Debt ratio: 0.4%	No. of shares (mil.): 1,246
Return on equity: 18.5%	Dividends
Cash ($ mil.): 1,206	Yield: 0.7%
Current ratio: 4.80	Payout: 30.2%
Long-term debt ($ mil.): 12	Market value ($ mil.): 24,293

Stock History

NYSE: SAP

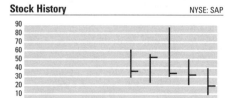

12/93 12/94 12/95 12/96 12/97 12/98 12/99 12/00 12/01 12/02

	STOCK PRICE ($) FY Close	P/E High/Low	PER SHARE ($) Earnings	Dividends	Book Value
12/02	19.50	91 23	0.43	0.13	2.42
12/01	31.93	120 52	0.41	0.00	2.21
12/00	33.69	90 32	0.95	0.00	1.85
12/99	52.06	57 25	0.96	0.00	6.15
12/98	36.06	120 59	0.50	0.00	5.36
Annual Growth	(14.2%)	— —	(3.7%)	—	(18.0%)

SAS AB

Danes, Norwegians, and Swedes travel the world via SAS. In addition to serving more than 90 destinations directly, the airline owns stakes in several Scandinavian regional carriers. The company's Rezidor SAS Hospitality subsidiary operates about 185 hotels in 40 countries. The former Scandinavian Airlines System, a consortium made up of three companies controlled by the governments of Denmark, Norway, and Sweden, respectively, was restructured into a single, publicly traded company, SAS AB, in 2001. The Swedish government owns 21% of the new SAS,

and the governments of Denmark and Norway each own 14%.

Key to its continued success in the deregulated skies is the formation of the Star Alliance, whose members include Air Canada, All Nippon Airway, Lufthansa, Thai Airways, United Airlines, and VARIG of Brazil. The marketing alliance allows the carriers to pool frequent-flyer programs and share booking and airport facilities, and many of the members have signed code-sharing deals with one another. The Star Alliance extends SAS's offerings to nearly 730 destinations in about 125 countries worldwide. In addition, SAS controls Spanish carrier Spanair.

And SAS hasn't neglected local markets: The company has acquired Norwegian carriers Braathens and Widerøe and taken ownership stakes in regional airlines Cimber Air (Denmark), Skyways (Sweden), and Air Botnia (Finland). SAS also has been optimizing its fleet, phasing out older aircraft as it buys new Boeing 737s and widebody airliners from Airbus.

HISTORY

The national airlines of Sweden (ABA), Norway (DNL), and Denmark (DDL) first met in 1938 to negotiate joint service to New York. The plan was delayed by WWII but kept alive in Sweden, where banker Marcus Wallenberg founded Svensk Interkontinental Luftrafik (SILA), a private airline that in 1943 replaced ABA as Sweden's international carrier. With SILA's financial backing, the yet-to-be-formed Scandinavian Airlines System (SAS) obtained the necessary landing concessions to open a Stockholm-New York air route in 1945. SAS was formed in 1946.

After opening service to South America (1946), Southeast Asia (1949), and Africa (1953), SAS inaugurated the world's first commercial polar route in 1954. It formed charter airline Scanair in 1961 and Danish domestic carrier Danair, through a joint venture, in 1971.

Deregulation of US airlines (1978) signaled the demise of nationally protected airlines. SAS seemed ill-equipped to adapt and reported its first loss in 18 years in 1980. Jan Carlzon, former head of Swedish airline Linjeflyg, became SAS's president in 1981. By targeting businessmen as the airline's most stable market and substituting an economy-rate business class for first-class service on European flights, Carlzon had turned SAS's losses into profits by the end of 1982.

The company bought about 25% of Airlines of Britain Holdings in 1988, gaining a foothold at London's Heathrow Airport. Another purchase that year brought SAS nearly 10% of Continental Airlines Holdings. In 1989 the airline signed agreements that provided route coordination and hub-sharing with Swissair, Finnair, LanChile, and Canadian Airlines International.

SAS tried in the early 1990s to merge with KLM, Swissair, and Austrian Airlines to create a new international carrier, but that effort failed in 1993, leading to the replacement of Carlzon. New CEO Jan Stenberg consolidated the group, shed noncore businesses, and cut 15,000 jobs. By late 1994 SAS had sold SAS Service Partner (catering, its largest nonairline unit), Diners Club Nordic, and most of the SAS Leisure Group. By spinning off its 42% stake in LanChile and creating a new Latvian airline with Baltic International, SAS focused its air routes in Scandinavia, Western Europe, and the Baltic region.

The SAS trading subsidiary was folded into the airline unit in 1994. Through its hotel unit, SAS allied itself with Radisson Hotels to expand its

presence in Europe, the Middle East, and Asia. In 1997 the company joined UAL's United Airlines, Lufthansa, VARIG, and others to form the Star Alliance. In 1998 SAS acquired Finland's Air Botnia.

New code-sharing agreements in 1999 included deals with Singapore Airlines and Icelandair. SAS agreed to sell half its 40% stake in British Midland to Lufthansa, paving the way for British Midland to join the Star Alliance.

SAS boosted its cargo services in 2000 when it partnered with giants Lufthansa Cargo and Singapore Airlines to harmonize their cargo handling and information technology services.

The SAS consortium was restructured into a single publicly traded company, SAS AB, in 2001. That year SAS and Danish carrier Maersk Air were fined by the European Commission for agreeing not to compete on certain Scandinavian routes. SAS EVP Vagn Sørensen accepted responsibility for the illegal agreement and resigned. A month later SAS's board of directors also resigned, and a new board was elected at an extraordinary shareholders' meeting held later that year.

Also in 2001 Scandinavian Airlines flight SK 686 crashed while attempting to take off from Milan's Linate airport, killing all 110 on board. The following year, SAS joined with Deutsche Lufthansa and Singapore Airlines to form WOW, a global cargo alliance.

EXECUTIVES

Chairman: Egil Myklebust, age 61
Vice Chairman: Jacob Wallenberg, age 47
President and CEO: Jørgen Lindegaard
EVP and CFO: Gunilla Berg
EVP, Corporate Administration and Support: Bernhard Rikardsen
EVP, Airline Support and Airline-Related Businesses: John S. Dueholm
SVP and COO: Sören Belin
Auditors: Deloitte & Touche AB

LOCATIONS

HQ: Frösundaviks Allé 1, Solna,
S-195 87 Stockholm, Sweden
Phone: +46-8-797-00-00   **Fax:** +46-8-797-16-03
Web: www.scandinavian.net

SAS serves nearly 90 destinations in about 30 countries; with Star Alliance partners it serves nearly 730 destinations in more than 120 countries. The company also operates hotels in about 40 countries.

PRODUCTS/OPERATIONS

Selected Subsidiaries and Affiliates

AirBaltic (47% Latvian airline)
Braathens (Norwegian airline)
British Midland PLC (20%, British airline)
Commercial Aviation Leasing Ltd. (49%)
Gronlandsfly A/S (38%)
Polygon Insurance (31% Channel Islands)
Rezidor SAS Hospitality A/S (hotels)
Spanair S.A. (74%, Spanish airline)
Widerøe (Norwegian airline)

COMPETITORS

Accor	Granada
Aer Lingus	Hilton Group
Air France	Hyatt
Alitalia	Iberia
AMR	KLM
A.P. Møller — Maersk	Marriott International
British Airways	Ryanair
Cathay Pacific	Brussels Airlines
Continental Airlines	Starwood Hotels & Resorts
Delta	Air Portugal
Finnair	Virgin Atlantic Airways

HISTORICAL FINANCIALS

Company Type: Public

Income Statement

	REVENUE ($ mil.)	NET INCOME ($ mil.)	NET PROFIT MARGIN	EMPLOYEES
12/02	7,423	(15)	—	35,506
12/01	4,866	(101)	—	30,972
12/00	5,049	227	4.5%	30,939
12/99	4,869	198	4.1%	28,863
12/98	5,054	349	6.9%	27,071
12/97	4,919	282	5.7%	25,057
12/96	5,166	261	5.0%	23,607
12/95	5,318	355	6.7%	22,731
12/94	4,968	294	5.9%	28,425
12/93	4,679	(71)	—	37,330
Annual Growth	5.3%	—	—	(0.6%)

2002 Year-End Financials

Debt ratio: 142.6%
Return on equity: —
Cash ($ mil.): 120

Current ratio: 0.82
Long-term debt ($ mil.): 2,475

Net Income History

Stockholm: SAS

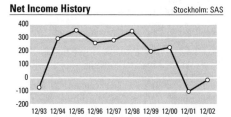

Schneider Electric SA

If Schneider Electric sees a light at the end of the tunnel, the company probably put it there. The company is one of the world's largest manufacturers of equipment for electrical distribution and industrial control and automation. Schneider helps power generators distribute electricity. It also designs automation systems for the automobile and water-treatment industries; builds infrastructure for airports, road and rail networks, and port facilities; and manages electric power in residential, industrial, and commercial buildings. Schneider sells its products to the construction, electric power, industrial, and infrastructure markets. Subsidiary Square D conducts Schneider's North American operations.

Schneider will attempt to increase the size of its voice-data holdings through selective acquisitions. The company will also look to expand its industrial automation offerings by means of its Transparent Factory (a system that allows real time data to be delivered from the factory floor via the Internet). The company is also working with THOMSON multimedia to develop powerline communication (PLC) technologies, which use a building's electrical wiring to transmit digital data to and from devices such as DVD and MP3 players. An attempt to expand its low-voltage offering through the acquisition of Legrand, a

French electrical products maker, was blocked by EU regulators. Schneider has received a reported $3.69 billion from Kohlberg Kravis Roberts and Wendel Investissement for Legrand.

HISTORY

Schneider Electric's predecessor was founded in 1782 to make industrial equipment. After the upheavals of the French Revolution and the Napoleonic Wars, the company came under the control of brothers Adolphe and Eugene Schneider in 1836. Within two years they had built the first French locomotive (the country's first rail line had opened in 1832).

The company became one of France's most important heavy-industry companies, branching into a variety of machinery and steel operations. However, the country's industrial development continued to trail that of Britain and Germany due to recurrent political strife, including the revolutions of 1848 and the Franco-Prussian War. France also possessed fewer coal and iron deposits.

During WWI Schneider was a key part of France's war effort. It entered the electrical contracting business in 1929 and fought off nationalization attempts in the mid-1930s.

The blitzkrieg of 1939 brought much of France under Nazi occupation, and the Schneider factories that were not destroyed were commandeered by the Germans. After the war, the company rebuilt, aided by the French government. It was restructured as a holding company, and its operating units were split into three subsidiaries: civil and electrical engineering, industrial manufacturing, and construction. Charles Schneider, the last family member to lead the company, died in 1950.

In 1963 Schneider concluded an alliance with the Empain Group of Belgium, and by 1969, three years after Schneider went public, the two companies merged to become Empain-Schneider. During this period the company made numerous noncore acquisitions, entering such fields as ski equipment, fashion, publishing, and travel.

Schneider began reorganizing in 1980. This effort entered its final phase in 1993 with a major recapitalization that saw the merger of its former parent company, Société Parisienne d'Entreprises et de Participations, with Schneider SA and the issue of new stock to existing stockholders. The company also streamlined operations. Merlin Gerin (acquired in 1975) and Télémecanique (1988) became Schneider Electric in Europe, and their North American operations were merged into Square D after its acquisition in 1991.

Schneider's 1994 takeover of two Belgian subsidiaries led Belgium's government to charge CEO Didier Pineau-Valencienne with fraud in the valuation of the stock. (A Belgian newsmagazine reported in 1997 that Belgian authorities turned down an offer to settle out of court.)

In 1996 Schneider established the Schneider Electric (China) Investment Co. in Beijing, China's first totally French-owned firm. The next year the company sold Spie Batignolles, its electrical contracting subsidiary. Cost-cutting measures and strong sales in France and North America combined to boost the company's 1998 income.

In 1999 Schneider agreed to pay $1.1 billion for Lexel, a joint venture owned by Finland's Ahlstrom and Denmark's NKT Holding, to broaden its electrical equipment offerings for the

household. Also that year the company changed its name to Schneider Electric and changed its main subsidiary's name to Schneider Electric Industries. Looking to add more machinery makers to its list of customers, the company acquired the French-based Crouzet Automatismes and Switzerland-based Positec in 2000.

Although Schneider announced in early 2001 that it would buy Legrand (a deal valued at about $6.4 billion), EU regulators blocked the acquisition in October of the same year. As part of the UN's "Oil for Food" program, Schneider received an order from Iraq in 2002 for nearly 16,000 circuit breakers to be used in that country's power grid. In early 2003 the company's North American division and the US-based Leviton Manufacturing inked a joint technology agreement to develop prototype voice-data-image products.

EXECUTIVES

Chairman and CEO; Chairman and CEO, Schneider Electric Industries SA: Henri Lachmann, age 65
EVP, European Operating Division: Christian Wiest, age 53
EVP, Developments — Industry: Marcel Torrents, age 54
EVP, Finance and Control: Antoine Giscard d'Estaing, age 42
EVP, Strategy — Markets: Eric Pilaud, age 46
EVP, Human Resources and Corporate Communication: Jean-François Pilliard, age 54
EVP, International Operating Division: Jean-Pascal Tricoire, age 40
President and CEO, North American Operating Division: Chris C. Richardson, age 59
President and COO, U.S. Business: David D. Petratis
Director, Communication: Gérard Fauconnet
Director, NEW2004 Program: Carlos Siria
Director, Schneider Electric Ventures: Jean Netter
Director, Specialist Business Units (Bergher Lahr, Crouzet, Ensys, Infra+, Num, Selectron): Guy Lemarchand
Director, Sustainable Development: Gilles Vermot-Desroches
Legal Affairs: Pedro Salazar
Auditors: Barbier Frinault & Autres; Ernst & Young; PricewaterhouseCoopers Audit ZAO

LOCATIONS

HQ: 43-45 boulevard Franklin-Roosevelt, 92500 Rueil-Malmaison, France
Phone: +33-1-41-29-8500 **Fax:** +33-1-41-51-8020
Web: www.schneider-electric.com

Schneider Electric has about 150 manufacturing and marketing facilities in 130 countries.

2002 Sales

	% of total
Europe	51
North America	29
Other regions	20
Total	**100**

PRODUCTS/OPERATIONS

Selected Operations and Products

Merlin Gerin (circuit breakers, panelboards, and remote installation management equipment)
Modicon (programmable logic controllers)
Square D (electrical distribution and industrial control equipment, US)
Télémecanique (industrial automation products and systems)

COMPETITORS

ABB	GE Industrial Systems
Alcatel	GE
ALSTOM	Johnson Controls
Beghelli	Legris
Eaton	Mitsubishi Electric
Electricité de France	Siemens
EMCOR	Siemens Energy &
Emerson Electric	Automation
Endress+Hauser	Technology Research
Finmeccanica	Transtector
Fluor	

HISTORICAL FINANCIALS

Company Type: Public

Income Statement

FYE: December 31

	REVENUE ($ mil.)	NET INCOME ($ mil.)	NET PROFIT MARGIN	EMPLOYEES
12/02	9,496	442	4.7%	74,814
12/01	8,706	(874)	—	66,144
12/00	9,129	589	6.4%	72,144
12/99	8,437	484	5.7%	67,510
12/98	8,899	477	5.4%	60,780
12/97	7,901	366	4.6%	61,499
12/96	11,779	252	2.1%	63,000
12/95	12,104	166	1.4%	92,700
12/94	10,486	127	1.2%	89,762
12/93	9,522	68	0.7%	91,458
Annual Growth	(0.0%)	23.0%	—	(2.2%)

2002 Year-End Financials

Debt ratio: 22.1%
Return on equity: 5.7%
Cash ($ mil.): 3,369
Current ratio: 2.44
Long-term debt ($ mil.): 1,807

Net Income History

Euronext Paris: SU

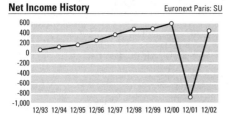

Scottish Power

With more power in England than Bonnie Prince Charlie, Scottish Power is a hero in the UK's deregulated energy market. One of the largest multi-utilities in the country, the company supplies electricity and natural gas to 3.6 million customers and generates 5,000 MW of capacity through its Scottish Power UK unit, which also markets and trades energy. Scottish Power's Infrastructure Division operates the company's regulated domestic power transmission and distribution assets. Across the Atlantic, Scottish Power owns PacifiCorp, which generates and distributes electricity to 1.5 million customers in the western US.

Subsidiary PPM Energy, formerly a part of PacifiCorp, markets and trades energy, operates renewable energy projects, and provides related services in the US.

The company has been divesting noncore businesses and cutting staff to concentrate on its energy operations. It has spun off its 50.1% stake in

Thus (formerly Scottish Telecom), which offers telecom services for businesses and is one of the UK's top ISPs, to its shareholders. Scottish Power has also sold its Southern Water subsidiary, which provides water and wastewater services to 2.8 million customers in southern England.

HISTORY

The UK power industry was nationalized in 1947, and two regional state-controlled boards were charged with generating, transmitting, and distributing electricity in Scotland. The two monopolies were the North of Scotland Hydro-Electric Board (formed in 1943) and the South of Scotland Electricity Board (SSEB, formed in 1955). In keeping with the deregulation trend that swept the UK in the 1980s, Scottish Power was formed in 1989 to assume the non-nuclear operations of SSEB, and Hydro-Electric (now part of Scottish and Southern) took the northern board's assets. Scottish Power had to prepare for competition, which began in a limited form in 1990.

Scottish Power's initial assets included six coal, gas, and hydropower plants that served southern Scotland and Northumberland, including Glasgow and much of Scotland's industrial base. The company, which went public in 1991, also inherited 73 retail outlets that sold consumer electronic and electrical goods. It expanded this retail business across the UK in the 1990s.

The company teamed with SeaWest of the US and Japan's Toman in the early 1990s to set up Europe's largest wind farm, in Wales. It set up other wind-energy plants in Northern Ireland, Scotland, and England; by the mid-1990s Scottish Power was the largest wind-farm operator in the UK.

In 1993 the company moved into telecommunications. Running fiber-optic lines alongside its high-voltage power lines between Glasgow and Edinburgh, the company's Scottish Telecom unit (established in 1994) provided high-speed voice and data services to several major businesses.

With opportunities for growth limited by the relatively small population base in southern Scotland, the company sought to expand through geographic and business diversification. In 1995 it became the first UK power firm to buy a rival when it acquired Manweb, a regional electricity company that served northwestern England and North Wales. The next year the company became the first British electricity firm to buy a water company when it acquired Southern Water, a water supply and wastewater services firm based in England's South Coast. Scottish Power disposed of many of Southern Water's noncore businesses in 1997.

In 1998 Scottish Power boosted its telecom business with the purchase of Demon Internet, then the UK's largest independent ISP. Also that year, after merger talks with two US electric utilities failed, Scottish Power agreed to acquire PacifiCorp, a major utility in the US Pacific Northwest. The deal was completed in 1999.

With the BBC, Scottish Telecom launched a free Internet service, Freebeeb.net, in 1999. That year Scottish Telecom's name was changed to Thus, and the company floated a 49.9% stake in the unit. The company also announced a restructuring plan that would cut jobs and divest noncore businesses. In 2000 Scottish Power announced plans to join the Royal Bank of Scotland in offering bundled services, including banking, utilities, and telecommunications. Also in 2000 it divested PacifiCorp's Powercor Australia unit.

In 2001 Scottish Power agreed to sell its retail appliance business to Powerhouse Retail. It also restructured into three business units: UK power generation and supply, infrastructure (asset management and water supply), and US operations (PacifiCorp). Later that year, the company announced plans to spin off its remaining stake in Thus; the demerger was completed in 2002.

Scottish Power also sold its Southern Water unit to First Aqua, a private investment firm backed by the Royal Bank of Scotland, for $2.9 billion in 2002.

EXECUTIVES

Chairman: Charles Miller Smith, age 63, $335,016 pay
Chief Executive; Chairman, PacifiCorp: Ian M. Russell, age 50, $784,080 pay
Finance Director: David Nish, age 43, $498,960 pay
Executive Director UK: Charles Berry, age 51, $427,680 pay
Executive Director Corporate Strategy and Development: Simon Lowth, age 41
Executive Director; President and CEO, PacifiCorp: Judith A. (Judi) Johansen, age 45
Group Director Commercial and Legal: James Stanley, age 48
Group Director Corporate Communications: Dominic Fry, age 43
Group Director Human Resources; SVP Human Resources and Director, PacifiCorp: Michael J. Pittman, age 50
Group Director Infrastructure: Ronnie Mercer, age 59
Group Company Secretary: Andrew Mitchell, age 51
CEO, PPM Energy: Terry F. Hudgens, age 48
Group Media Relations Manager: Colin McSeveny
Media Relations Manager: Simon McMillan
Media Relations Manager, Wales and North West England: Anne Benson
Head of Investor Relations: Andrew Jamieson
Head of UK Community Affairs and Manweb: Gaynor Kenyon
Public Relations Executive: Jane Holmes
Auditors: PricewaterhouseCoopers LLP

LOCATIONS

HQ: Scottish Power plc
1 Atlantic Quay, Glasgow G2 8SP, United Kingdom
Phone: +44-141-248-8200 **Fax:** +44-141-248-8300
US HQ: 825 NE Multnomah, Portland, OR 97232
US Phone: 503-813-5000 **US Fax:** 503-813-7247
Web: www.scottishpower.plc.uk

Scottish Power primarily operates in the UK and the US.

PRODUCTS/OPERATIONS

2003 Sales

	$ mil.	% of total
US		
PacifiCorp	3,930	47
PPM Energy	450	5
UK		
Scottish Power UK	3,377	41
Infrastructure Division	494	6
Discontinued operations	42	1
Total	**8,293**	**100**

Selected Subsidiaries

Infrastructure Division
SP Distribution plc (regulated distribution assets)
SP Manweb plc (regulated distribution assets)
SP Transmission plc (regulated transmission assets)
PacifiCorp (electricity generation and distribution, US)
PPM Energy, Inc. (formerly PacifiCorp Power Marketing, wholesale power generation and marketing, US)

UK Division
Scottish Power UK plc (electricity generation, electricity and gas supply, and energy marketing)

COMPETITORS

British Energy
Centrica
Edison International
Innogy
International Power
MidAmerican Energy
National Grid Transco
PG&E

Portland General Electric
Powergen
Puget Energy
Questar
Scottish and Southern
Energy
United Utilities
Viridian Group

HISTORICAL FINANCIALS

Company Type: Public

Income Statement

FYE: March 31

	REVENUE ($ mil.)	NET INCOME ($ mil.)	NET PROFIT MARGIN	EMPLOYEES
3/03	8,293	763	9.2%	13,825
3/02	9,000	(1,407)	—	16,162
3/01	9,000	436	4.8%	21,981
3/00	6,557	1,502	22.9%	24,114
3/99	5,225	810	15.5%	16,032
3/98	5,229	284	5.4%	15,099
3/97	4,821	690	14.3%	15,018
3/96	3,465	452	13.0%	11,359
Annual Growth	13.3%	7.8%	—	2.8%

2003 Year-End Financials

Debt ratio: 103.0%
Return on equity: 10.8%
Cash ($ mil.): 1,050
Current ratio: 1.18
Long-term debt ($ mil.): 7,550

No. of shares (mil.): 464
Dividends
 Yield: 7.8%
 Payout: 112.7%
Market value ($ mil.): 11,131

Stock History

NYSE: SPI

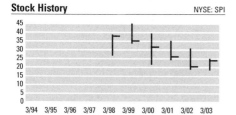

	STOCK PRICE ($) FY Close	P/E High/Low		PER SHARE ($) Earnings	Dividends	Book Value
3/03	23.99	15	11	1.66	1.87	15.80
3/02	20.45	—	—	(3.06)	1.63	14.68
3/01	26.22	30	21	0.95	1.70	18.18
3/00	31.69	9	5	4.32	2.83	21.95
3/99	35.19	17	13	2.71	1.73	10.46
3/98	37.94	14	10	0.96	0.00	9.54
Annual Growth	(8.8%)	—	—	11.6%	—	10.6%

Securitas AB

Securitas profits from the lack of caritas in human nature. The world's largest security services company provides security guards, alarm systems, and cash transportation services to banks, retailers, large corporations, small businesses, and residential customers in more than 30 countries, mainly in Europe and North America. Securitas' purchase of US security firms Pinkerton's and Burns International Services, now included in its Security Services USA division, has given it a dominant position in the US security

guard services market. The company, founded in 1934, is 28%-owned by Swedish firm Säkl.

Securitas operates through five divisions: Security Services USA, Security Services Europe, Security Systems, Direct, and Cash Handling Services. Its Security Services divisions account for more than 75% of sales. The three other divisions account for the rest. The company holds a 10% share of the security market in Europe and 8% of the security market in the US.

Securitas' Cash Handling division handles monetary flows — overseeing cash transport, cash-processing services, ATMs, and night deposit boxes. The company has expanded its cash-handling operations in the US through the acquisitions of Loomis Fargo and Armored Motor Services of America.

Securitas is conquering a fragmented industry replete with individual investigators and mom-and-pop security firms. In an effort to strengthen its position in the western US, Securitas has acquired Lincoln Security, a security guard service provider based in California. Through its Security Services Europe division, the company has acquired Spanish-based Ebro Vigilancia & Seguridad.

HISTORY

Securitas established its first outpost in 1934, in Helsingborg, Sweden, when Erik Philip-Sörensen bought Hälsingborgs Nattvakt and renamed it Securitas. Erik was following in the footsteps of his father, who in 1901 had established a small Danish guard company as part of the ISS Group of security companies. Securitas was housed within ISS as well.

Sörensen spent the next two decades establishing and acquiring more Swedish firms and adding them to the Securitas family. He also added to his own family two sons, Sven and Jörgen, who would figure into Securitas' future. Jörgen began establishing new branches in Belgium and the UK in the late 1950s. The companies were combined into one company, Group 4, in 1968.

In 1974, two years after the Securitas name was finally branded onto all of the firm's security companies, the elder Sörensen retired. Sven and Jörgen bid against ISS for control of the company and won. Seven years later they divided the company equally: Sven took half of the Securitas operations in Sweden, and Jörgen assumed control of the international businesses (which became Group 4 Securitas).

In 1983 Sven sold Securitas. Jörgen bought back some of the Swedish operations, but by 1985 the rest of the company had ended up in the hands of Swedish investment firm Investment AB Latour (now chaired by Gustaf Douglas, also vice chairman of Securitas). Melker Schörling became president in 1987.

The new owners trimmed away all companies that weren't directly related to guard services and alarm systems. Securitas then began an acquisition rampage in 1988 with the purchase of Swedish lock manufacturer Assa. Not content with the lovely lakes and fjords of Sweden, Securitas bought companies in Denmark, Norway, and Portugal and set up new operations in Hungary.

Securitas went public in 1991 and soon bought US lock maker Arrow; it began cutting a wider swath through Europe. With its 1992 purchase of security firm Protectas, Securitas gained operations in Austria, France, Germany, and Switzerland; it bought more firms in Spain in 1992 and in Finland in 1993. To streamline fur-

ther, Securitas merged its lock manufacturing operations with those of Finland's Metra, creating Assa-Abloy. It spun off the new company in 1994 but retained a 45% stake. Securitas made more acquisition raids in Estonia, Poland, and the UK in 1996.

In 1997 Securitas created Securitas Direct to handle its domestic and small-scale alarms business; the division quickly became active throughout Scandinavia, as well as in France, Spain, and Switzerland. That year the company made more acquisitions in France and Sweden. In 1998 Securitas made two significant purchases: Raab Karcher Sicherheit, the market leader in industrial guarding services in Germany, and Proteg, France's security market leader (Securitas sold Proteg's fire protection divisions to Williams PLC in 1999).

The grand-daddy of acquisitions was still to come. In early 1999 Securitas bought 150-year-old US security firm Pinkerton's in a bid to create the largest security firm in the world. Securitas took over Pinkerton's operations in the Czech Republic, Germany, Portugal, and the UK. The next year Securitas made several US acquisitions, including its purchase of Burns International Services for $650 million.

Securitas' takeover of US companies didn't stop with Pinkerton's and Burns. In 2001 the company became the second-largest cash-handling services provider in the US when it bought the remaining 51% of Loomis Fargo. (Securitas had previously acquired 49% of Loomis as part of the Burns deal).

Securitas continued expanding in 2002, but this time the company focused outside the US, buying security companies in the Netherlands and Canada. In 2003, it returned its focus to the US by acquiring Lincoln Security, a security guard service provider operating in California, Nevada, and Oregon. It also acquired Armored Motor Services of America. Later that year, Securitas expanded its offering in Spain with the acquisition of Ebro Vigilancia & Seguridad.

EXECUTIVES

Chairman: Melker Schörling
Vice Chairman: Gustaf Douglas
President and CEO: Thomas Berglund
EVP and CFO: Håkan Winberg
EVP; Chairman, Security Services USA; Country President, USA: Don W. Walker
SVP Investor Relations: Henrik Brehmer
President and CEO, Globe Aviation Services Corporation: Ronald J. Harper
President, B&M: Hans Mulder
President, Strategic and Account Support Development: Brad Van Hazel
President, VNV: Gustave Long
Divisional President, Cash Handling Services Europe: Johan Eriksson
Divisional President, Cash Handling Services USA: James B. (Jim) Mattly
Divisional President, Direct Europe: Dick Seger
Divisional President, Security Services Europe: Tore K. Nilsen
Divisional President, Security Services USA: Santiago Galaz
Divisional President, Security Systems: Juan Vallejo
Divisional President, Security Systems USA: Björn Lohne
Auditors: PricewaterhouseCoopers AB

LOCATIONS

HQ: Lindhagensplan 70, Box 12307, SE-102 28
Stockholm, Sweden
Phone: +46-8-657-74-00   **Fax:** +46-8-657-70-72
Web: www.securitasgroup.com

Securitas has operations in Argentina, Austria, Belgium,
Canada, the Czech Republic, Denmark, Estonia, Finland,
France, Germany, Hungary, Ireland, Mexico, the
Netherlands, Norway, Poland Portugal, Spain, Sweden,
Switzerland, the UK, and the US.

2002 Sales

	% of total
US	55
France	8
Germany	7
Spain	5
Sweden	5
Netherlands	4
Belgium	3
Norway	3
Canada	2
Great Britain	2
Portugal	2
Finland	1
Switzerland	1
Mexico	1
Poland	1
Total	**100**

PRODUCTS/OPERATIONS

2002 Sales

	% of total
Security Services USA	42
Security Services Europe	34
Cash Handling Services	16
Security Systems	5
Direct	3
Total	**100**

Selected Subsidiaries

Securis N.V. (Belgium)
Securitas A/S (Norway)
Securitas Canada Limited
Securitas Cash Handling Services Holding AB (Sweden)
Securitas C.I.T. Sp. z.o.o. (Poland)
Securitas CR s.r.o. (Czech Republic)
Securitas Deutschland Holding GmbH (Germany)
Securitas Eesti Ltd. (Estonia)
Securitas France Holding S.A.
Securitas Holding A/S (Norway)
Securitas Holding UK Limited
Securitas Holdings Inc. (US)
Securitas Hungária RT
Securitas Nordic Holding AB
Securitas Polska Sp. z.o.o. (Poland)
Securitas S.A. (Portugal)
Securitas Seguridad España S.A. (Spain)
Securitas Services Holding Ltd. (UK)
Securitas Services International B.V. (Norway)
Securitas Serviços e Tecnologia de Segurança SA
(Portugal)
Securitas Treasury Ireland Limited
Securitas Werttransporte GmbH (98%, Austria)

COMPETITORS

Allied Security
Chubb plc
Command Security
Group 4 Falck
Initial Security
Prosegur
Securicor
TransNational Security
Tyco Fire and Security
   Services
Wackenhut

HISTORICAL FINANCIALS

Company Type: Public

Income Statement

FYE: December 31

	REVENUE ($ mil.)	NET INCOME ($ mil.)	NET PROFIT MARGIN	EMPLOYEES
12/02	7,508	170	2.3%	203,070
12/01	5,710	112	2.0%	207,799
12/00	4,334	90	2.1%	202,794
12/99	3,008	94	3.1%	115,946
12/98	1,692	64	3.8%	66,420
12/97	1,360	56	4.1%	40,567
12/96	1,332	56	4.2%	36,689
12/95	1,098	52	4.7%	26,799
12/94	922	33	3.5%	27,051
Annual Growth	30.0%	22.9%	—	28.7%

2002 Year-End Financials

Debt ratio: 97.7%
Return on equity: 13.8%
Cash ($ mil.): 86
Current ratio: 1.06
Long-term debt ($ mil.): 1,303

Net Income History

Stockholm: SECUB

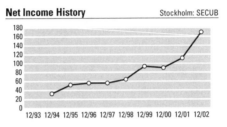

Seiko Corporation

Seiko is way beyond its tradition of marking time — whether it's wristwatches, clocks, or timing devices for athletic events (like the 2002 Olympics in Utah). The corporation serves as a holding company for subsidiaries such as Seiko Watch, maker of watches such as the Kinetic and Thermic series that generate power by the movement of the owner's wrist or body heat. It also makes mass-market watch brands Pulsar and Lorus. Seiko's other timepieces range from small bedside alarm clocks to large-scale public clocks. Its other subsidiaries include Seiko Epson, Seiko Instruments, and Seiko Optical Products. The Hattori family controls Seiko.

Watches and clocks account for 70% of sales, but Seiko companies such as Seiko Epson and Seiko Instruments offer other products including computers, computer components and peripherals, plus jewelry, eyeglasses and other optical products, toiletries, sporting goods, and camera components.

HISTORY

Kitaro Hattori started in the jewelry business at age 13. In 1881, at age 21, he set up K. Hattori & Co. in Tokyo's Ginza district to import clocks. As increasing railroad traffic created a demand for accurate timepieces, Hattori started making wall clocks at his Seikosha factory in 1892. Pocket watches followed in 1895, alarm clocks in 1899, and table clocks in 1902. Hattori

began exporting clocks to China and opened his first foreign branch, in Shanghai, in 1913.

Hattori first used the name "Seiko" (Japanese for "precision") on a watch in 1924. The Seikosha plant started producing camera shutters six years later. Daini Seikosha, the predecessor to Seiko Instruments, was set up as an independent watch manufacturer in 1937. Production shifted during WWII from timepieces to time fuses and ammunition. In 1942 Daiwa Kogyo, which later became Seiko Epson, was established.

By 1953 K. Hattori had restored itself to its prewar position in the Japanese watch market, with a 55% market share. The company attacked the US market in the 1960s by initially offering jewel-lever watches in the midrange market with an average price of $50 and then expanding to the upper and lower ends of the market. This expansion was aided by K. Hattori's selection as the official timekeeper for the 1964 Tokyo Olympics. The company launched the world's first quartz wall clock in 1968 and the first analog quartz watch (the Seiko Astron) the following year.

During the 1970s K. Hattori expanded globally, establishing subsidiaries in Asia, Europe, and North and South America. The company broadened its quartz technology by offering the world's first women's quartz watch in 1972 and the first digital watch with an LCD the next year. K. Hattori introduced the first black-and-white TV watch in 1982. To promote the Seiko brand, the company changed its name to Hattori Seiko Co. the following year. In 1984 it marketed the world's first computer wristwatch and the first battery-operated LCD pocket color television.

The company changed its name to Seiko Corporation in 1990. The next year it introduced the Seiko Perpetual Calendar, a watch capable of tracking dates for more than 1,000 years. Also in 1991 Seiko acquired American Telephone and Electronics (AT&E) — its partner in a wristwatch pager joint venture — after AT&E filed for bankruptcy, and it established a joint venture with DEC to market PCs in Japan.

The official timekeeper for the Olympics in 1992 (Barcelona, Spain) and 1994 (Lillehammer, Norway), Seiko was outbid by rival SMH (Swatch watchmaker) for the 1996 Olympics. In 1997 it secured the timekeeping position for the 2002 Utah Olympics; it also was timekeeper for the Nagano, Japan, Olympics in 1998. Also in 1998 Seiko began selling the Ruputer, a wristwatch/PC that exchanges data with a PC and stores files. In 1999 the company formed SII Marketing International with Fossil to sell the companies' lower-priced watches in Wal-Marts and other discount outlets.

Seiko spun off its watch operations as Seiko Watch in 2001 and set itself up as a holding company for its six independent companies. To combat competition from Chinese and Swiss watch companies, Seiko and rival Citizen Watch — already cooperating on shipments — began combining other operations in early 2002, including purchasing and supplying parts.

EXECUTIVES

Honorary Chairman: Reijiro Hattori
Chairman: Katsumi Yamamura
President: Koichi Murano
Executive Director, Finance and Accounting:
   Kunio Maeda
Director, Legal and Intellectual Property and Corporate
   Communications: Takamitsu Muto
Auditors: Asahi & Co.

LOCATIONS

HQ: 1-7-1 Kyobashi, Chuo-ku,
Tokyo 104-8831, Japan
Phone: +81-3-3563-8292   **Fax:** +81-3-3563-8495
US HQ: 1111 MacArthur Blvd., Mahwah, NJ 07430
US Phone: 201-529-5730   **US Fax:** 201-529-0132
Web: www.seiko.co.jp

PRODUCTS/OPERATIONS

Selected Watch Brands

Arctura	Pulsar
The Grand Blue	Rivoli
Kinetic	Ruputer
Lorus	Seiko
Premier	Sportura
Presage	Vivace

Selected Operations

Ohara Inc. (precision optical glass, ceramics, glass
ceramics)
Seiko Clock Inc. (clocks)
Seiko Epson Corp. (printers, computers, LCD modules
and projectors, color TVs, semiconductors, crystal
devices, watches, corrective lenses, precision assembly
robots, electronic devices and components)
Seiko Jewelry Co., Ltd. (jewelry, including brands such
as Royal Asscher Diamond of the Netherlands and
Nina Ricci of France)
Seiko Optical Products Co., Ltd. (eyeglass lenses, frames,
sunglasses, other optical products)
Seiko Precision Inc. (camera components, clock systems,
printers, machine tools)
Seiko Service Center Co., Ltd.
Seiko S-Yard Co., Ltd. (golf clubs, electric shavers,
metronomes, musical instrument tuners, stop watches
and timing equipment, health and exercise products)
Seiko Time Systems Inc. (system clocks, sports-timing
equipment, display devices)
Seiko Watch Corporation (watches, watch movements)
Wako Co. Ltd. (watches, jewelry, luxury goods for men
and women, interior ornaments, arts and crafts,
eyeglasses, foodstuffs)

COMPETITORS

Bausch & Lomb	IDT International
Bulova	Loews
CASIO COMPUTER	Luxottica
Citizen Watch	Movado Group
E. Gluck	Olympus
Egana	Oregon Scientific
Fossil	Pentax
Franklin Electronic	Swatch
Publishers	Swiss Army Brands
Gucci	Three-Five Systems
Highway Holdings	Timex

HISTORICAL FINANCIALS

Company Type: Public

Income Statement

FYE: March 31

	REVENUE ($ mil.)	NET INCOME ($ mil.)	NET PROFIT MARGIN	EMPLOYEES
3/03	1,892	45	2.4%	7,009
3/02	1,743	(76)	—	6,711
3/01	2,064	16	0.8%	—
3/00	2,618	(13)	—	—
3/99	2,527	(114)	—	—
3/98	2,638	51	1.9%	—
3/97	3,072	8	0.3%	—
3/96	3,189	(104)	—	—
3/95	3,823	(108)	—	—
3/94	3,258	(61)	—	—
Annual Growth	(5.9%)	—	—	4.4%

2003 Year-End Financials

Debt ratio: 820.1%   Current ratio: 1.12
Return on equity: 68.9%   Long-term debt ($ mil.): 724
Cash ($ mil.): 179

Net Income History

Exchange: Tokyo

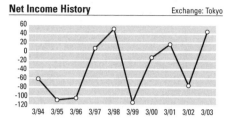

Seiko Epson Corporation

For Seiko Epson, timing isn't everything, but
it's important. Seiko Epson (also called Epson) is
a manufacturing arm of Seiko Group, the internationally known watchmaker. In addition to
watches, Seiko Epson makes information-related
products such as desktop and portable computers;
electronic devices and components, including
semiconductors and LCDs; and a variety of other
products, such as lenses, motors, and magnets. A
top printer manufacturer, Seiko Epson produces
dot matrix, ink jet, laser, and thermal printers, as
well as printer components. Heirs of Seiko's
founder, Kitaro Hattori, control the company.

Seiko Epson is one of the two manufacturing
arms of Seiko Group. (Seiko Instruments is the
group's other manufacturer; a third sister company, Seiko Corporation, markets watches under
the Seiko and Pulsar brand names and sells
clocks and optical equipment.) Although watchmaking and precision products constitute the
company's smallest segment (6% of sales), Seiko
Epson has no plans to wind down its most dated
business. The skills gleaned from watchmaking,
including miniaturization and precision timing,
have given rise to the company's other, more
profitable lines. The company's computer and peripheral products account for about 70% of sales.

HISTORY

In 1881, 21-year-old Kitaro Hattori, who had
begun working in the jewelry trade at age 13,
opened a Tokyo watch shop and called it K. Hattori & Co. In 1892 Hattori started a factory in
Seikosha to manufacture wall clocks and, later,
watches and alarm clocks. K. Hattori & Co. went
public in 1917. In 1924 it began using the Seiko
brand on its timepieces. Kitaro's son Ganzo
formed Daini Seikosha Co., precursor of Seiko
Instruments, in 1937.

The company formed Daiwa Kogyo Ltd., a
maker of mechanical watches, in 1942; it would
later become Seiko Epson. Developments included self-winding watches (1955) and transis-
torized table clocks (1959).

A big break came for the company in 1964,
when it developed crystal chronometers and
printing timers for the Tokyo Olympics' official
timekeepers. It was the first time a precision time-
piece and a printer had been combined. Based on

that technology, in 1968 Seiko Epson debuted the
EP-101, the first commercially successful miniature printer (used primarily with calculators).

During the late 1960s Seiko Epson entered
the semiconductor field when it began developing LSIs (large-scale integrated circuits) for its
watches. The company introduced the world's
first quartz watch in 1969 and the first quartz
digital watch in 1973. It soon expanded into liquid crystal display (LCD) technology. It formed
its US affiliate, Epson America, in 1975. With
the advent of the PC in the 1970s, Seiko Epson
also began working on computer printers. It released its first dot matrix model in 1978. The
next year the company introduced the Alba and
Pulsar watch brands.

The company's European headquarters, in the
Netherlands, opened in 1980. Seiko Epson debuted the first laptop computer, the HX-20, in
1982; a high-quality daisy wheel printer and LCD
color TV in 1983; and an ink jet printer in 1984.
In 1985 it began making contact lenses. Reijiro
Hattori, grandson of the company's founder, took
the helm in the late 1980s.

In 1990 Seiko baptized the Scubamaster, a
computerized diver's watch featuring a dive
table. The next year it introduced a wrist-
watch/pager. That year it added color printers to
its line. Seiko Epson unveiled digital cameras
for use with PCs and Macs in 1996. The next year
Lattice Semiconductor invested $150 million
with Seiko Epson to build a new semiconductor
wafer factory.

In 1998 the company made its US semiconductor manufacturing subsidiary, Epson Electronics America, an independent firm. It also
formed an ink jet printer joint venture in China.
That year the company entered the personal
digital assistant (PDA) market with a line of
PDAs that use the satellite-based Global Positioning System.

In 1999 Seiko Epson acquired Pacific Metals
Co.'s metal powder operations, a complement to
metal injection molding subsidiary Injex.

With profit margins from its printers shrinking, in 2000 the company announced plans to
consolidate its printer operations in China, Indonesia, and Singapore, and to expand its LCD
products line. The following year Seiko Epson
agreed to form a joint venture with IBM to produce logic chips for cell phones, handheld computers, and other devices.

EXECUTIVES

Chairman: Hideaki Yasukawa
Vice Chairman: Yasuo Hattori
President: Saburo Kusama
EVP: Seiji Hanaoka
EVP: Toshio Kimura
EVP: Norio Niwa
Managing Director: Masao Akahane
Managing Director: Kenji Kubota
Managing Director: Masayuki Morozumi
Managing Director: Masayoshi Omae
Managing Director: Yasumasa Otsuki
Managing Director: Torao Yajima

LOCATIONS

HQ: 3-3-5 Owa, Suwa, Nagano 392-8502, Japan
Phone: +81-266-52-3131   **Fax:** +81-266-53-4844
US HQ: 3840 Kilroy Airport Way, Long Beach, CA 90806
US Phone: 562-981-3840
Web: www.epson.com

Seiko Epson has more than a dozen plants in Japan, as well as manufacturing and sales operations in the Americas, Asia, Australia, Europe, and New Zealand. The company has regional headquarters in China, the Netherlands, and the US.

PRODUCTS/OPERATIONS

Selected Products

Information equipment
Computers
LCD projectors
Printers
Scanners
Visual instruments

Electronic devices
Crystal devices
LCDs
Semiconductors

Precision products
Optical devices
Watches

COMPETITORS

Acer	LSI Logic
Bausch & Lomb	Matsushita
Canon	NEC
CASIO COMPUTER	Océ
Citizen Watch	Oki Electric
Dell	Ricoh
Fujitsu	Samsung
Hewlett-Packard	SANYO
Hitachi	Sharp
Intel	Sony
IBM	Swatch
Kyocera	Toshiba
Lexmark International	Xerox

HISTORICAL FINANCIALS

Company Type: Private

Income Statement

FYE: March 31

	REVENUE ($ mil.)	NET INCOME ($ mil.)	NET PROFIT MARGIN	EMPLOYEES
3/03	11,034	348	3.2%	73,797
3/02	9,605	145	1.5%	68,786
3/01	10,615	728	6.9%	69,743
3/00	10,995	635	5.8%	42,500
3/99	8,760	—	—	41,500
3/98	6,125	—	—	44,000
3/97	5,032	—	—	31,000
3/96	5,603	—	—	—
3/95	5,903	—	—	—
3/94	4,327	—	—	—
Annual Growth	11.0%	(18.2%)	—	15.6%

Net Income History

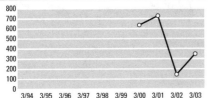

Sharp's business is pointed at the electronic components market. Best known for its consumer electronics, the company is a leading maker of electronic components and computer hardware and peripherals. Its flagship components business includes liquid crystal displays (LCDs, used in everything from airplane cockpits to PCs to pinball machines), flash memory, integrated circuits, and laser diodes used in optical data drives. Sharp also makes PCs, printers, fax machines, and cell phones; consumer audio and video products, such as CD and DVD players, televisions, and video cameras; and a variety of appliances, such as air conditioners, refrigerators, and vacuum cleaners.

Sharp has suffered in the global economic downturn along with most other electronics companies. Weak demand from manufacturers has hurt its components business, and electronics equipment sales have fallen as consumers, especially in Japan (which accounts for more than half of sales), have curtailed purchases. Sharp's bottom line has also been hit by losses on investments, specifically those in the Japanese banking sector.

To turn the situation around, Sharp plans to focus on new and more advanced products for consumers, such as LCD televisions, next generation handsets, and home networking products. On the components side, the company sees demand for advanced LCDs increasing as new handheld devices come into the mainstream. It is also positioning itself to capitalize on rising consumer demand in China.

HISTORY

Tokuji Hayakawa got started in manufacturing in 1912 when he established Hayakawa Electric Industry to make a type of belt buckle he had designed. Three years later he invented the first mechanical pencil, named the Ever-Sharp, which was a commercial success. After an earthquake leveled much of Tokyo in 1923, including Hayakawa's business, he moved to Osaka and sold the rights to his pencil to finance a new factory. He introduced Japan's first crystal radio sets in 1925 and four years later debuted a vacuum tube radio.

Following WWII, Hayakawa Electric developed an experimental TV, which it began mass-producing in 1953. The company was ready with color TVs when Japan initiated color broadcasts in 1960. Hayakawa Electric grew tremendously during the 1960s, introducing microwave ovens (1962), solar cells (1963), the first electronic all-transistor-diode calculator (1964), and the first gallium arsenide LED (1969). The firm opened a US office in 1962.

In 1970 the company began to make its own microchips and changed its name to Sharp Corporation, a nod to the name of its first product. It began mass production of LCDs in 1973. Sharp later introduced the first electronic calculator with an LCD (1973), solar-powered calculators (1976), and a credit card-sized calculator (1979).

The company began producing VCRs in the early 1980s, and in 1984 Sharp introduced its first color copier. That year the firm introduced a fax machine and began concentrating its mar-

keting efforts on small businesses (while its competitors were scrambling for large corporate accounts). Haruo Tsuji became president in 1986. He restructured the company and concentrated research on LCDs. Sharp blitzed the market with a new line of creative products in the late 1980s, including a high-definition LCD color TV (1987) and a notebook-sized PC (1988).

Sharp introduced a cordless pocket telephone in 1992 that operated continuously for over five hours, as well as a low-cost high-definition television (HDTV). That year the company announced strategic alliances with Apple to build the Newton personal digital assistant (which flopped) and with the Shanghai Radio and Television to make air conditioners, fax machines, copiers, and printers (Shanghai Sharp Electronics began production in 1994). During the mid-1990s Sharp's ViewCam camcorder and Zaurus personal digital assistant were both big sellers.

In 1996 Sharp formed partnerships with Alcatel, Advanced Micro Devices, Fujitsu, Intel, and Nanjing Panda Electronics (China's second-largest TV maker). More joint ventures followed in 1997, including a partnership with Sony to develop flat-panel displays.

Katsuhiko Machida became president in 1998 as the company attempted to pump younger blood into its veins; Tsuji became company adviser. That year the company restructured around three business areas: home appliances and consumer electronics, information and communications, and components. Restructuring in its LCD operations reduced profits by 80% in 1999. The company rebounded the next year, but a downturn in the global economy and competitive pricing in the LCD business again put Sharp's profits under pressure in 2001. The company reduced its workforce and simplified its organizational structure, reorganizing its operations from 42 divisions into just 24.

EXECUTIVES

President: Katsuhiko Machida
SEVP; CTO, Information and Communication Systems Business: Shigeo Misaka
SEVP; Chief General Administration Officer: Hiroshi Saji
SEVP, LCD Business; Group General Manager, Mie-Kameyama Production Group: Zempei Tani
Senior Executive Director; Group General Manager, Human Resources Group: Akihiko Kumagai
Senior Executive Director; Group General Manager, Sales and Marketing Group, Electronic Components and Devices: Terumasa Yoneda
Senior Executive Director; Group General Manager, International Business Group: Toshishige Hamano
Senior Executive Director; Group General Manager, Electronic Components Group: Keiichi Miyata
Senior Executive Director; Group General Manager, Domestic Sales and Marketing Group: Masaaki Ohtsuka
American Operations; CEO, North and South American Operations: Toshiaki Urushisako
Executive Director; Group General Manager, IT Strategic Planning: Yoichi Sakai
Executive Director; Group General Manager, Corporate Research and Development Group: Kenji Ohta
Director; General Manager, Management Planning Board: Takashi Nakagawa
Director; Group General Manager, Digital Document Systems Group: Yoshiaki Ibuchi
Director; Group General Manager, Corporate Accounting and Control Group: Tetsuo Ohnishi
Auditors: Asahi & Co.

LOCATIONS

HQ: 22-22 Nagaike-cho, Abeno-ku,
Osaka 545-8522, Japan
Phone: +81-6-6621-1221 **Fax:** +81-6-6627-1759
US HQ: Sharp Plaza, Mahwah, NJ 07430-2135
US Phone: 201-529-8200 **US Fax:** 201-529-8425
Web: www.sharp.co.jp

Sharp has operations in 30 countries worldwide.

2003 Sales

	$ mil.	% of total
Asia/Pacific		
Japan	8,823	53
Other countries	2,258	13
The Americas	2,811	17
Europe	1,962	12
Other regions	861	5
Total	**16,715**	**100**

PRODUCTS/OPERATIONS

2003 Sales

	$ mil.	% of total
Audio/video equipment	6,228	37
Electronics		
LCDs	2,893	18
Integrated circuits	1,041	6
Other components	1,547	9
Information equipment	3,138	19
Home appliances	1,868	11
Total	**16,715**	**100**

Selected Products

Audio/Video Equipment
Audio amplifiers
Compact disc players
Digital cameras
DVD players
High-definition televisions
Liquid crystal display DVD televisions
Liquid crystal display televisions
Liquid crystal display video projectors
Video cameras

Communication and Information Equipment
Calculators
Digital copiers
Fax machines
Mobile business tools
Personal computers
Printers

Electronic Components
Flash memory
Integrated circuits
Laser diodes and other optoelectronic devices
Radio-frequency components
Satellite broadcasting components
Solar cells and other photovoltaic devices

Home Appliances
Air conditioners
Microwave ovens
Refrigerators
Vacuum cleaners
Washing machines

COMPETITORS

AMD	Kyocera
Canon	LG Electronics
CASIO COMPUTER	Matsushita
Dell	Motorola
Eastman Kodak	NEC
Electrolux AB	Oki Electric
Ericsson	Philips Electronics
Fuji Photo	Pioneer
Fuji Xerox	Ricoh
Fujitsu	Samsung Electronics
GE	SANYO
Hewlett-Packard	Seiko Epson
Hitachi	Siemens
Intel	Sony
IBM	Toshiba
Konica Minolta	Xerox

HISTORICAL FINANCIALS

Company Type: Public

Income Statement

FYE: March 31

	REVENUE ($ mil.)	NET INCOME ($ mil.)	NET PROFIT MARGIN	EMPLOYEES
3/03	16,715	272	1.6%	46,633
3/02	13,599	85	0.6%	46,518
3/01	15,934	305	1.9%	49,101
3/00	17,580	267	1.5%	49,748
3/99	14,655	39	0.3%	57,521
3/98	13,456	186	1.4%	47,981
3/97	14,464	392	2.7%	46,900
3/96	15,391	432	2.8%	44,789
3/95	18,690	514	2.8%	43,949
3/94	14,775	309	2.1%	42,883
Annual Growth	1.4%	(1.4%)	—	0.9%

2003 Year-End Financials

Debt ratio: 28.7%
Return on equity: 30.7%
Cash ($ mil.): 3,194
Current ratio: 1.36
Long-term debt ($ mil.): 2,161

Net Income History

OTC: SHCAY

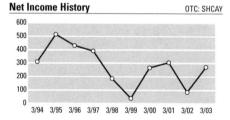

Shiseido Company

If your face is a canvas, Shiseido wants to be the paint. Shiseido, Japan's largest cosmetics company, produces makeup and skin care products for men and women. It also makes toiletries, sun care products, fragrances, professional salon hair care products, pharmaceuticals, and fine chemicals. Upscale brands include Shiseido and Clé de Peau Beauté. Mid- and mass-market brands include Ayura and Nars. Other interests include the Ginza chain of upscale fashion boutiques; and specialty fragrance, hair, and skin care salons. The company also has an Institute of Beauty Sciences which researches the rela-

tionship between "cosmetic behavior" and psychology. About three-quarters of Shiseido's sales come from Japan.

For years the company focused on the high end of the cosmetics market, selling the same merchandise in every store and insisting that all items be sold by in-store consultants. But faced with an ugly Japanese retail market Shiseido now offers different lines to different types of stores, is focusing on improving operations at the sales counter, is putting profits ahead of revenue, and is looking overseas for growth opportunities. To that end the makeup maker is targeting middle-income consumers in China, where it is already the market leader for prestige cosmetics. Shiseido opened its first store in Shanghai recently and plans to open a total of five stores in Shanghai and Beijing in 2004.

Part of Shiseido's expansion plan is a multi-brand approach that targets specific customer categories; the company is also seeking growth through mergers and acquisitions.

HISTORY

Yushin Fukuhara, former head pharmacist for the Japanese admiralty, established Japan's first modern drugstore, Shiseido Pharmacy, in 1872. Attracted by the store's Western-style products and format, the customers were the nobility and the rich. Shiseido manufactured Japan's first toothpaste in 1888 and introduced its first cosmetics product (Eudermine, a skin lotion) in 1897. Fukuhara opened the country's first soda fountain in 1902.

Yushin's son, Shinzo, created Shiseido's first extensive makeup lines, introducing flesh-toned face powder in 1906 and a fragrance line in 1918. Under Shinzo's influence, cosmetics replaced drugs as Shiseido's mainstay.

Shiseido began franchise operations in 1923 and business boomed. The firm went public that year; in 1927 Shinzo became president. During WWII the company couldn't make cosmetics, only medicines, and many of Shiseido's factories were destroyed. This led to near-bankruptcy in 1945, but Shiseido rebounded the next year, thanks to nail enamel.

In 1951 it introduced its de Luxe high-end cosmetics line, and by 1956 it had become the #1 Japanese cosmetics firm. With a 1962 move into Hong Kong, Shiseido began overseas operations. It steadily expanded its international business by setting up subsidiaries across the world (including one in New York City in 1965).

In the 1970s Shiseido failed at marketing its products in the US, and at home its market share was slipping. Seen as being out of touch with the young, it was also hampered by strict product development laws that caused delays in getting products to market. In the mid-1980s it developed a successful US marketing strategy that included selling exclusive product lines in high-end department stores such as Macy's; it also made several acquisitions, including Zotos (hair products, US, 1988).

The firm's first prescription-only drug, an ophthalmological treatment used in certain types of cataract surgery and cornea transplants, was launched in 1993. In 1996 it announced a biological compound that retards skin aging by preventing oxidization. The company bought the Helene Curtis salon hair care business in the US and Canada from Unilever that year. In 1997 Shiseido bought Helene Curtis Japan salon hair operations and a New Jersey factory, which more than doubled its North American production.

Also in 1997 Akira Gemma (a Shiseido veteran of nearly four decades) became CEO, and the company expanded to Croatia, the Czech Republic, Hungary, and Vietnam. It bought the professional salon products business of the US's Lamaur Corporation in 1998.

Shiseido opened a New York City flagship store in 1998 and began selling cosmetics in Russia in 1999. It also began selling soap, shampoo, and baby powder in 1999 under the wildly popular Hello Kitty name, licensed from Japanese media firm Sanrio. Late that year Shiseido introduced Clé de Peau Beauté to international markets as its top-of-the-line beauty brand.

Looking to expand its foreign brands portfolio, in June 2000 Shiseido bought the Sea Breeze line of facial products from Bristol-Myers Squibb; it also acquired 75% of French cosmetics firm and aromatherapy specialists Laboratoires Decléor. In September the company announced an agreement with Intimate Brands (owner of Victoria's Secret and Bath & Body Works) to develop a new prestige beauty products line.

In June 2001 Morio Ikeda took over for Gemma as president and CEO; Gemma was named chairman.

In 2002 Shiseido, together with Limited Brands, introduced a new retail beauty company called aura science. One of 10 outlets planned to open in major US cities, the first aura science store was opened in Columbus, Ohio, in April of that year.

In the fall of 2003 the introduction of two new fragrances under the brand name FCUK (French Connection United Kingdom) by Shiseido's Zirh International subsidiary was met with vocal protest from some consumers.

EXECUTIVES

Chairman: Akira Gemma
President and CEO: Morio Ikeda
VP, Corporate Senior Executive Officer:
 Shigeo Shimizu
Corporate Senior Executive Officer: Osamu Hosokawa
Corporate Senior Executive Officer: Tadakatsu Saito
Corporate Executive Officer: Kohei Mori
Corporate Executive Officer: Takeshi Ohori
Corporate Officer: Masaaki Komatsu
Corporate Officer: Shinzo Maeda
Senior Corporate Auditor: Kazunari Moriya
Corporate Auditor: Isao Isejima
Auditors: ChuoAoyama Audit Corporation

LOCATIONS

HQ: Shiseido Company, Limited
 5-5, Ginza 7-chome, Chuo-ku,
 Tokyo 104-0061, Japan
Phone: +81-3-3572-5111   **Fax:** +81-3-3289-1235
US HQ: 900 3rd Ave., New York, NY 10022
US Phone: 212-805-2300   **US Fax:** 212-688-0109
Web: www.shiseido.co.jp/e

2003 Sales

	% of total
Japan	75
Europe	10
Americas	8
Asia & Oceania	7
Total	**100**

PRODUCTS/OPERATIONS

2003 Sales

	% of total
Cosmetics	78
Toiletries	11
Other	11
Total	**100**

Selected Brands

Mass Market
Aquair
Super Mild

Middle Market
Aspril
Ayura
Uno

Prestige
Aupres
Carita
Shiseido

High Prestige
Clé de Peau Beauté

Other Operations

Chromatography products (chemical analysis equipment)
Fine chemicals (photochromic titanium dioxide pigment)
Ginza fashion boutiques
Laboratoires Decléor (French cosmetics and aromatherapy products)
Shiseido Pharmaceutical Co., Ltd.
Zotos International, Inc. (research and development facilities)

COMPETITORS

Alberto-Culver
Alticor
Avon
Bath & Body Works
Beiersdorf
Body Shop
Chanel
Colgate-Palmolive
Estée Lauder
Henkel
Kao
L'Oréal
Mary Kay
Procter & Gamble
Revlon
Shu Uemura
Unilever
Wella
Yves Saint-Laurent Groupe

HISTORICAL FINANCIALS

Company Type: Public

Income Statement

FYE: March 31

	REVENUE ($ mil.)	NET INCOME ($ mil.)	NET PROFIT MARGIN	EMPLOYEES
3/03	5,184	204	3.9%	25,202
3/02	4,448	(172)	—	25,021
3/01	4,711	357	7.6%	24,959
3/00	5,655	145	2.6%	24,495
3/99	5,073	87	1.7%	23,688
3/98	4,666	127	2.7%	22,718
3/97	4,754	155	3.3%	22,045
3/96	5,229	163	3.1%	22,305
3/95	6,243	132	2.1%	23,355
3/94	5,345	143	2.7%	—
Annual Growth	(0.3%)	4.1%	—	1.0%

2003 Year-End Financials
Debt ratio: 12.5%   Current ratio: 1.66
Return on equity: 7.4%   Long-term debt ($ mil.): 370
Cash ($ mil.): 859

Net Income History   OTC: SSDOY

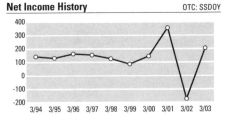

Siemens AG

Thinking globally and acting locally is more than semantics for Siemens. The company is Europe's largest electronics and electrical engineering firm and has operations worldwide in the industrial automation and control, information and communications, lighting, medical, power transmission, and transportation sectors. Siemens' Information and Communications Networks division (ICN), a leading global manufacturer of telecom network equipment including mobile phones, is its top revenue maker. Siemens is also active in the semiconductor sector through a minority stake in chip maker Infineon Technologies.

The company, captained by CEO Heinrich von Pierer, has navigated through a two-year restructuring to focus on six core areas. However, Siemens is still bailing to keep from sinking — it has announced over 35,000 layoffs (with more expected) and about 50 affiliated companies are up for sale. Kohlberg Kravis Roberts has purchased seven noncore subsidiaries — including Mannesmann Plastics Machinery, Stabilus, Demag Cranes & Components, and Gottwald Port Technology — and reorganized them into a new company, Demag Holding (in which Siemens retained a 19% stake).

Siemens' Information and Communications division has been hurt by an industry slump and reduced by the sale of Unisphere Networks to Juniper Networks in 2002. Siemens' Power Generation unit is also suffering due to a decrease in demand for gas turbines, especially in the US.

On the whole Siemens has been focusing on the US. Just over half of sales comes from business in Europe, but the US is now the company's largest market over Germany. The company has gained a listing on the New York Stock Exchange and reorganized its US operations as Siemens Corporation.

HISTORY

In 1847 electrical engineer Werner von Siemens and craftsman Johann Halske formed Siemens & Halske. The firm's first major project linked Berlin and Frankfurt with the first long-distance telegraph system in Europe (1848). In 1870 it completed a 6,600-mile telegraph line from London to Calcutta, India, and in 1874 it made the first transatlantic cable, linking Ireland to the US.

The company's history of firsts includes Europe's first electric power transmission system (1876), the world's first electrified railway (1879), and one of the first elevators (1880). In 1896 it patented the world's first X-ray tube and completed the first European subway, in Budapest, Hungary.

By the next century it had formed lightbulb cartel Osram with German rivals AEG and Auer (1919) and created a venture with Furukawa Electric called Fuji Electric (1923). It developed radios and traffic lights in the 1920s and began producing electron microscopes in 1939.

Siemens & Halske played a critical role in Germany's war effort in WWII and suffered heavy losses. During the 1950s it recovered by developing data processing equipment, silicates for semiconductors, and the first implantable pacemaker. It moved into the nuclear industry in 1959 when its first reactor went into service at Munich-Garching. In 1966 the company reincorporated as Siemens AG. It formed joint ventures with Bosch (BSH Bosch und Siemens Hausgeräte, appliances, 1967) and AEG (Kraftwerk Union, nuclear power, 1969), among others. AEG dropped out of Kraftwerk Union (now Siemens Power Generation) in 1977.

In 1981 Karlheinz Kaske became the first CEO from outside the von Siemens family. Under his lead the firm entered joint ventures with Philips, Intel, and Advanced Micro Devices. In 1988 and 1989 it made several buys, including Bendix Electronics (US), and was a willing buyer when IBM wanted to unload Rolm (then the #1 maker of PBXs). It had acquired all of Rolm's businesses by 1992. That year Heinrich von Pierer replaced Kaske as CEO.

The 1990s saw more consolidation: Siemens and German computer maker Nixdorf combined computer businesses to form Siemens Nixdorf Informationssysteme (SNI, 1990); the firm acquired Sylvania's North American lamp business from GTE and merged it with the Osram companies in North America to form Osram Sylvania (1993).

The Asian economic crisis combined with other factors to make 1998 the worst year in the company's 150-year history. That year Siemens sold its defense electronics operations to British Aerospace (now BAE SYSTEMS) and Daimler-Benz (now DaimlerChrysler) and bought CBS's power generation business (formerly Westinghouse Electric).

SNI's operations were juggled in a 1999 revamping of the company's information and communications units. That year Siemens held an IPO for its passive components and electron tubes unit. It spun off its semiconductor operations into Infineon Technologies, but kept a 71% stake after Infineon's IPO in 2000. Siemens also sold its electromechanical components unit to Tyco International and its fiber-optic cable and hardware businesses to Corning.

In 2000 BSH paid $9.2 billion for the engineering and automotive parts unit Atecs Mannesmann. Also that year Siemens boosted its IT Service unit in the US by purchasing information services company ENTEX , and it agreed to merge its nuclear business with Framatome's.

Siemens shares began trading on the New York Stock Exchange in 2001. The slump in the telecommunications industry hurt Siemens that year, and the company announced plans to cut 9,700 jobs. It also came close to posting its first loss since 1992.

Late in 2001 Siemens cut its stake in Infineon Technologies to less than 50%, and in 2002 it announced an additional 6,500 jobs to be cut from its telecom unit. The company continued to trim from its information and communications holdings with the July 2002 sale of Unisphere Networks to Juniper Networks. Later that year, the company sold seven noncore businesses (including Mannesmann Plastics Machinery, Stabilus, Demag Cranes Components, and Gottwald Port Technology) to buyout firm Kohlberg Kravis Roberts for $1.7 billion.

EXECUTIVES

Chairman, Supervisory Board: Karl-Hermann Baumann, age 68
President and CEO: Heinrich von Pierer, age 62
EVP and CFO: Heinz-Joachim Neubürger, age 50
EVP, Automation and Drives and Industrial Solutions and Services, Asia and Australia: Klaus Wucherer, age 59
EVP, Corporate Personnel: Peter Pribilla, age 62
EVP: Edward G. Krubasik
EVP: Jürgen Radomski, age 62
EVP, Power Generation and Power Transmission and Distribution, Latin America: Uriel J. Sharef, age 59
SVP; Group President, Information and Communication Mobile: Rudi Lamprecht, age 55
SVP, Corporate Technology: Claus Weyrich, age 59
SVP, Corporate Development: Heinrich v. Pierer
VP and CIO: Jan D. Dressel, age 43
VP and Controller: Charles Herlinger
President and CEO, Siemens Financial Services: Herbert Lohneiss
President and CEO, Siemens Corporation and Information and Communication Networks: George Nolen, age 47
President and CEO, Infineon Technologies: Ulrich Schumacher, age 45
Director, Corporate Communications: Eberhard Posner
Auditors: KPMG Deutsche Treuhand-Gesellschaft AG

LOCATIONS

HQ: Wittelsbacherplatz 2, D-80333 Munich, Germany
Phone: +49-89-636-3300 **Fax:** +49-89-636-342-42
US HQ: Citicorp Center, 153 East 53rd St., New York, NY 10022-4611
US Phone: 212-258-4000 **US Fax:** 212-767-0580
Web: www.siemens.de

2002 Sales

	% of total
Europe	
Germany	21
Other countries	32
Americas	
US	24
Other countries	5
Asia-Pacific	12
Other countries	6
Total	**100**

PRODUCTS/OPERATIONS

Selected Subsidiaries and Associated Companies

Information and Communications
Information and Communication Networks
  Siemens Information and Communication Networks, Inc. (US)
Information and Communication Mobile (ICM)
  Fujitsu Siemens Computers (Holding) B.V. (50%, Netherlands)
  Siemens Information and Communication Products LLS (US)
Siemens Business Services (SBS)
  Entex IT Service, Inc. (US)
  Siemens Business Services AG (Switzerland)
  Siemens Business Services GmbH & Co. OHG
  Siemens Business Services GmbH (Austria)
  Siemens Business Services Limited (UK)
  Siemens Business Services LLC (US)
  Siemens Business Services S.A. (Belgium)
  Siemens Informatica S.p.A. (51%, Italy)
  Siemens Itron Business Services SA (60%, Argentina)

Automation and Drives
Siemens Automation and Drives
  Siemens Elektromotory s.r.o. (Czech Republic)
  Siemens Energy & Automation, Inc. (US)
Siemens Industrial Solutions and Services
  Siemens Westinghouse Technical Services Company, Inc. (US)
Siemens Production and Logistics Systems (PL)
  Siemens ElectroCom GmbH & Co.
  Siemens ElectroCom International, Inc. (US)
Siemens Building Technologies (SBT)
  Siemens Building Technologies AG
  Siemens Building Technologies Inc. (US)
  Siemens Gebäudetechnik GmbH & Co. OHG

Power
Siemens Power Generation
  Framatome ANP (34%, France)
  Siemens Power Corporation (US)
  Siemens Westinghouse Power Corporation (US)
Siemens Power Transmission and Distribution
  Siemens Power Transmission & Distribution, LLC (US)

Transportation
Siemens Automotive
  Siemens Automotive Corp. (US)
  Siemens Automotive S.A. (France)
Siemens Transportation Systems
  Matra Transport International S.A. (95%, France)
  Siemens Duewag Schienenfahrzeuge GmbH
  Siemens SGP Verkehrstechnik Ges.m.b.H. (Austria)
  Siemens Transportation Systems, Inc. (US)

Medical
Siemens Medical Solutions
  Acuson Corp. (US)
  Siemens-Elema AB (Sweden)
  Siemens Medical Solutions, USA, Inc. (US)

Lighting
Osram GmbH
Osram Opto Semiconductors GmbH & Co. OHG

Semiconductors
Infineon Technologies AG (less than 50%)
Infineon Technologies North America Corp. (US)

Other
Demag Holding s.a.r.l (19%)

COMPETITORS

ABB
Agilent Technologies
Alcatel
Bull
Cap Gemini
Cisco Systems
Cooper Industries
Ericsson
GE
Harris Corp
Hitachi
Honeywell ACS
Intel
IBM
Johnson Controls
Koor
Lucent
Marconi
Matsushita
Mitsubishi Electric
Motorola
NEC
Nokia
Nortel Networks
Oki Electric
Philips Electronics
Samsung
SANYO
Schneider
Sharp
Tellabs
Texas Instruments
Toshiba

HISTORICAL FINANCIALS

Company Type: Public

Income Statement

FYE: September 30

	REVENUE ($ mil.)	NET INCOME ($ mil.)	NET PROFIT MARGIN	EMPLOYEES
9/02	82,865	2,561	3.1%	426,000
9/01	86,208	2,069	2.4%	450,000
9/00	68,387	7,820	11.4%	430,200
9/99	73,049	1,987	2.7%	443,000
9/98	70,323	548	0.8%	416,000
9/97	60,718	1,481	2.4%	386,000
9/96	61,796	1,960	3.2%	379,000
9/95	62,181	1,460	2.3%	373,000
9/94	54,571	1,141	2.1%	382,000
9/93	49,953	1,103	2.2%	391,000
Annual Growth	5.8%	9.8%	—	1.0%

2002 Year-End Financials

Debt ratio: 43.5%
Return on equity: 10.9%
Cash ($ mil.): 11,043
Current ratio: 1.27
Long-term debt ($ mil.): 10,103

No. of shares (mil.): 890
Dividends
 Yield: 0.0%
 Payout: —
Market value ($ mil.): 29,924

Stock History

NYSE: SI

	STOCK PRICE ($) FY Close	P/E High/Low	PER SHARE ($) Earnings	Dividends	Book Value
9/02	33.61	24 11	2.88	0.00	26.06
9/01	38.40	34 14	2.34	0.00	26.56
Annual Growth	(12.5%)	— —	23.1%	—	(1.9%)

Sime Darby Berhad

Malaysia's oldest and largest conglomerate, Sime Darby started in rubber and stretched. Its core business activities include the distribution of autos (BMW, Ford, Land Rover) and heavy equipment (Caterpillar); tire manufacturing; oil palm and rubber plantations; production of edible oils; residential and commercial property development; and the construction and operation of power plants. Sime Darby's general trading arm distributes a wide range of products, including advanced composite materials, auto parts, and sealants. The company also has stakes in hotels, hypermarkets, and medical facilities.

Amid continued economic weakness in many of the Asian nations in which it does business, Sime Darby has worked to control costs and to limit acquisitions to companies that operate in its core business areas.

HISTORY

William Sime, a 37-year-old Scottish adventurer, convinced Henry Darby, a wealthy 50-year-old English banker, that money could be made in rubber, a product that had just been introduced to Malaya from Brazil. Together they established Sime, Darby & Co., Ltd., in 1910 to manage about 500 acres of rubber estates in the jungles of Malacca, Malaya. To overcome local hostility to their venture, the pair maintained close links with the Chinese business community.

Riding a rubber boom, Sime, Darby became a managing agent for other plantations before moving into general trading. In 1915 it set up a branch office in Singapore and formed a London office for marketing. To clear jungle and meet growing demand for rubber, in 1929 Sime, Darby bought Sarawak Trading, which held a franchise for Caterpillar earth-moving equipment. In 1936 Sime, Darby moved its headquarters to Singapore.

In 1958 Sime Darby Holdings Ltd. was incorporated in England as successor to Sime, Darby & Co., Ltd. When demand for rubber softened in the 1960s, it was one of the first plantations to diversify into palm oil and cocoa production. It acquired the Seafield Estate and Consolidated Plantations in the 1970s, becoming a dominant force in Malaysian plantations while it started processing crops into finished products. Success of the switch to oil palms allowed the conglomerate's autocratic British CEO, Denis Pinder, to gobble up numerous firms. In 1973 allegations appeared in newspapers about improprieties at "Slime Darby." Pinder ended up in Changi prison on misdemeanor charges. The mysterious death of Sime Darby's outside auditor, found stabbed in his bathtub, was ruled a suicide.

After Pinder's successor upset Malaysians by investing in unsuccessful European ventures, Pernas (the Malaysian government trading corporation) bought Sime Darby shares on the London Stock Exchange and demanded an Asian majority be placed on the board. Outmaneuvered, the British lost control of Sime Darby in 1976. The only man acceptable as chairman to both Asian and British board members was Tun Tan Siew Sin, a former Malaysian finance minister and son of Tun Tan Cheng Lock, one of Malaysia's founding fathers. The firm, reincorporated in Malaysia as Sime Darby Berhad in 1978, moved its head office to Kuala Lumpur in 1979.

Sime Darby acquired the tire-making operations of B.F. Goodrich Philippines in 1981 and the Apple Computer franchise for southeast Asia in 1982. It bought an interest in United Estates, a Malaysian property development firm, two years later. In 1989 Sime Darby bought Dur-A-Vend, a UK condom wholesaler marketing a product called Jiffy with the slogan "Do it in a Jiffy." Sime Darby moved into tourism in 1991, acquiring Sandestin Resorts in Florida.

Expanding its financial portfolio in 1996, Sime Darby acquired control of United Malayan Banking (breaking it up into Sime Bank and SimeSecurities). The next year it consolidated its travel-related holdings into its Sime Wings unit. Hurt by regional financial turmoil, Sime Darby in 1999 sold Sime Bank and SimeSecurities to Malaysian financier Tan Sri Rashid Hussain.

In 1999 it divested Sandestin Resorts, LEC Refrigeration, and its 7% stake in British chemical firm Elements. Despite its streamlining, the firm could not resist picking up power generation assets as the power industry restructured. In 2000 it increased its stake in Port Dickson Power to

60%. Sime Darby also sold its insurance operations that year.

In 2003 Sime Darby sold a 30% stake in its tire business to Continental AG. Continental has an option to purchase an additional 21% in the future.

EXECUTIVES

Chairman: Tan Sri Dato' Seri Ahmad Sarji bin Abdul Hamid, age 65
Deputy Chairman: Tunku Tan Sri Dato' Seri Ahmad bin Tunku Yahaya, age 74
Group Chief Executive: Tan Sri Nik Mohamed bin Nik Yaacob, age 53
Group Finance Director: Martin G. Manen, age 48
Managing Director, Consolidated Plantations Berhad and Divisional Director, Plantations Division: YBhg Datuk Syed Tamin Syed Mohamed
Managing Director, DMIB Berhad and Sime Tyres International, and Divisional Director, Tyre Manufacturing: Tuan Haji Ahmad Zubir bin Haji Murshid
Managing Director, Hastings Deering (Australia) Limited: James C. Sheed
Managing Director, Sime Darby China Limited: Tan Wan Hong
Managing Director, Sime Darby Motor Holdings Limited and Divisional Director, Motor Distribution Operations: Marc Alexander Singleton
Managing Director, Sime Engineering Services Berhad: Tuan Haji Md Ja'far bin Abdul Carrim
Managing Director, Sime Singapore Limited: Yip Jon Khiam
Managing Director, Sime UEP Properties Berhad and Divisional Director, Property Development: YBhg Dato' Mohamed bin Haji Said
Managing Director, Tractors Malaysia Holdings Berhad and Divisional Director, Heavy Equipment and Motor Vehicle Distribution: Oh Teik Tatt
Director Human Resources: Datuk Othman Yusoff
Group Secretary and Tax Controller: Nancy P. Y. Yeoh
Joint Group Secretary and Senior Legal Advisor: Puan Saleha binti M Ramly
Regional Director, Malaysia Region II: Encik Mohamed Nor bin Abdul Hamid
Auditors: PricewaterhouseCoopers

LOCATIONS

HQ: Wisma Sime Darby, 21st Fl., Jalan Raja Laut, 50350 Kuala Lumpur, Malaysia
Phone: +60-3-2691-4122   **Fax:** +60-3-2698-7398
Web: www.simenet.com/home.html

2003 Sales

	$ mil.	% of total
Malaysia	1,373	38
Hong Kong	695	19
Australia	568	16
Singapore	464	13
China	150	4
Other regions	362	10
Total	**3,612**	**100**

PRODUCTS/OPERATIONS

2003 Sales

	$ mil.	% of total
Motor vehicle distribution	1,222	34
Heavy equipment distribution	766	21
Plantations	373	11
Tire manufacturing	218	6
Property	189	5
Energy	191	5
General trading, services & other	653	18
Total	**3,612**	**100**

COMPETITORS

Ansell	Hutchison Whampoa
Bridgestone	Jardine Matheson
Cummins	Joy Global
DaimlerChrysler	Komatsu
General Motors	Marubeni
Goodyear	Michelin
Hopewell Holdings	Swire Pacific
HSBC Holdings	

HISTORICAL FINANCIALS

Company Type: Public

Income Statement

FYE: June 30

	REVENUE ($ mil.)	NET INCOME ($ mil.)	NET PROFIT MARGIN	EMPLOYEES
6/03	3,612	213	5.9%	27,484
6/02	3,164	202	6.4%	26,384
6/01	3,147	162	5.2%	26,000
6/00	2,888	203	7.0%	27,000
6/99	2,608	216	8.3%	29,000
6/98	2,924	(131)	—	36,000
6/97	4,349	323	7.4%	37,000
6/96	4,321	278	6.4%	32,000
6/95	3,854	216	5.6%	32,000
6/94	3,153	186	5.9%	32,000
Annual Growth	1.5%	1.5%	—	(1.7%)

2003 Year-End Financials

Debt ratio: 22.6%
Return on equity: 10.7%
Cash ($ mil.): 626

Current ratio: 2.31
Long-term debt ($ mil.): 474

Net Income History

OTC: SIDBY

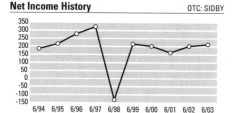

Singapore Airlines Limited

With its wine selection, fine cuisine, and sarong-clad flight attendants, Singapore Airlines (SIA) has tried to cultivate a reputation for superior service. The carrier boasts a fleet of more than 90 aircraft (one of the youngest among international carriers) and flies to more than 60 cities in 33 countries. It also belongs to the Star Alliance airline marketing network, which includes United Airlines, Lufthansa, and SAS. SIA units include regional carrier SilkAir, a pilot school, and repair and maintenance facilities. In addition, it owns a 49% stake in the UK's Virgin Atlantic Airways. SIA plans to form a low-fare carrier in 2004. The Singapore government owns 57% of SIA through Temasek Holdings.

The company's Singapore Airport Terminal Services (SATS) subsidiary provides catering, security, and cargo handling to other airlines, and it owns stakes in similar ventures outside Singapore. SIA sold minority stakes in SATS and in

maintenance and repair unit SIA Engineering. Other SIA operations include cargo carrier SIA Cargo and property investment.

SIA remained a relative bright spot during Asia's economic downturn and in the post-September 11 environment. The carrier continued to invest in its operations and aircraft. With a rich balance sheet, the firm had been itching to take a stake in a foreign airline. After aborted attempts to buy into South African Airways and Ansett Australia, SIA acquired its 49% of UK carrier Virgin Atlantic.

The war in Iraq and SARS (Singapore was listed on the World Health Organization's list of affected countries) have given the airline new challenges to face, and SIA has found itself scaling back capacity by about 30%, freezing recruitment, and halting expansion plans. Since being removed from the list, SIA is looking to take advantage of an airline industry that has many competitors filing for bankruptcy and struggling to stay aloft.

While ruling out turning its regional carrier SilkAir into a budget carrier, SIA has begun to consider developing a separate, low-cost airline.

HISTORY

Singapore Airlines (SIA) was formed as Malayan Airways in 1937 but did not begin scheduled service until 1947, when the Mansfield & Co. shipping line used it to link Singapore with other Malayan cities. The airline added service to Vietnam, Sumatra, and Java by 1951 and opened routes to Borneo, Brunei, Burma, and Thailand by 1958.

Meanwhile, British Overseas Airways Corporation (BOAC, predecessor of British Airways) bought 10% of Malayan in 1948 and raised its stake to 30% in 1959. Australia's Qantas Airways also took a 30% stake in Malayan that year. In 1963 the governments of Singapore, Malaya, Sarawak, and Sabah merged to form Malaysia, inspiring Malayan to change its name to Malaysian Airways. Singapore seceded from the federation in 1965 but joined Malaysia to buy control of the airline from BOAC and Qantas in 1966, changing the name to Malaysia-Singapore Airlines.

The carrier extended service to Bombay, Melbourne, Rome, and London in 1971 and then to Osaka, Athens, Zurich, and Frankfurt in 1972. That year managerial disagreements led Malaysia and Singapore to dissolve the company to form two separate national airlines: The domestic network went to the Malaysian Airline System, and international routes went to SIA. Joe Pillay of Singapore's ministry of finance became SIA's first chairman. The government owned 82%, and employees held 17%.

SIA initiated such now well-known amenities as free drinks, hot towels, and headsets in 1972, thereby gaining a reputation for outstanding service. By 1974 it served 25 cities worldwide. It added flights to Auckland and Paris in 1976, Tehran and Copenhagen in 1977, and San Francisco, its first US destination, in 1978.

In 1985 the Singapore government reduced its stake in SIA to 63%. The company joined Cathay Pacific and Thai International in 1988 to form Abacus, a computer reservation system for Asia/Pacific carriers.

The next year SIA bought stakes in Delta Air Lines and Swissair; the three created a route network reaching 82 countries. The Singapore airline also snagged a 40% stake in Royal Air Cambodge from the Cambodian government in

1993. In 1995 SIA ordered 77 Boeing 777s for delivery between 1997 and 2004.

The US and Singapore governments signed an "open skies" agreement in 1997 (the first between the US and an Asian nation), allowing unlimited flights between the two countries, but SIA canceled its alliance with Delta and Swissair in favor of one with Germany's Lufthansa.

A December 1997 crash of a new SilkAir 737 killed all 104 people on board; investigators speculated that the crash was an act of suicide by the pilot. (Two years later SIA agreed to pay each family settlements of up to $195,000.) The Asian crisis added to the airline's woes, but SIA was able to cut costs when the government reduced contributions to the national pension plan and the Singapore airport lowered landing fees.

In 1999 SIA implemented code-sharing with SAS, and soon SIA announced it would join SAS in the global Star Alliance marketing network. After failed attempts to buy into South African Airways and Australia Ansett, SIA bought a 49% stake in UK carrier Virgin Atlantic for some $960 million, acquired 25% of Air New Zealand (reduced to 7% in 2001), and joined the Star Alliance in 2000. Also that year 82 passengers died when Singapore Airlines flight SQ006 crashed into debris on an out-of-service runway.

SIA spun off its cargo operations, SIA Cargo, in 2001. Later in the year SIA Cargo formed an alliance with Lufthansa Cargo, SAS, and Deutsche Post.

In the airline industry downturn that followed the September 11, 2001, attacks on the US, SIA was forced to tighten its belt. By the next year, however, nearly all of the service that the carrier had suspended had been restored. The airline was forced to cut jobs, including more than 180 pilots and some 415 ground crew, in 2003 because of decreased demand for air travel as well as global fears of SARS, a mysterious virus with the highest reported incidents coming from Asian countries. SIA also had to cut back nearly 360 flights per week.

EXECUTIVES

Chairman: Koh Boon Hwee, age 51
Deputy Chairman and Deputy CEO:
Cheong Choong Kong, age 60
CEO: Chew Choon Seng
SEVP Commercial: Michael T. J. Ngee
SEVP Technical and Human Resources:
Bey Soo Khiang
EVP Marketing and the Regions: Huang Cheng Eng
SVP Finance and Administration: Teoh Tee Hooi
SVP Information Technology: Goh Choon Phong
SVP Corporate Affairs and Secretary: Mathew Samuel
SVP Engineering: Mervyn Sirisena
SVP Flight Operations: Raymond Ng
SVP Human Resources: Loh Meng See
SVP Marketing: Tan Chik Quee
Secretary: Foo Kim Boon
Auditors: Ernst & Young

LOCATIONS

HQ: Airline House, 25 Airline Rd., 819829, Singapore
Phone: +65-6541-4885   **Fax:** +65-6542-3002
US HQ: 5670 Wilshire Blvd., Ste. 1800,
Los Angeles, CA 90036
US Phone: 323-934-8833   **US Fax:** 323-934-4482
Web: www.singaporeair.com

2003 Sales

	% of total
East Asia	49
Europe	21
Southwest Pacific	13
Americas	10
West Asia & Africa	7
Total	**100**

PRODUCTS/OPERATIONS

2003 Sales

	% of total
Airline operations	82
Airport terminal services	8
Engineering services	7
Other	3
Total	**100**

2003 Aircraft Fleet

Type	No.
Boeing 777	44
Boeing 747	32
Airbus A310	8
Airbus A319	4
Airbus A320	4
Airbus A340	3
Total	**95**

Selected Subsidiaries and Affiliates

SIA Engineering Company Limited (87%, engine
  maintenance and repair)
SIA Properties (Pte) Ltd. (building services)
SilkAir (Singapore) Private Limited (regional airline)
Singapore Airlines Cargo Private Limited
Singapore Airport Terminal Services Limited (87%)
SATS Airport Services Pte. Ltd.
SATS Catering Pte. Ltd.
SATS Security Services Private Ltd.
Singapore Aviation and General Insurance Company
  (Pte) Limited
Singapore Flying College Pte. Ltd.
Virgin Atlantic Limited (49%, holding company for
  Virgin Atlantic Airways, UK)

COMPETITORS

AMR	Delta
British Airways	Japan Airlines
Cathay Pacific	KLM
China Airlines	Korean Air
China Eastern Airlines	Malaysian Airlines
China Southern Airlines	Northwest Airlines
Continental Airlines	Qantas

HISTORICAL FINANCIALS

Company Type: Public

Income Statement

FYE: March 31

	REVENUE ($ mil.)	NET INCOME ($ mil.)	NET PROFIT MARGIN	EMPLOYEES
3/03	5,934	601	10.1%	30,243
3/02	5,123	343	6.7%	29,316
3/01	5,510	858	15.6%	28,336
3/00	5,182	678	13.1%	27,513
3/99	4,506	597	13.3%	27,906
3/98	4,786	641	13.4%	27,516
3/97	4,998	714	14.3%	27,241
3/96	4,893	728	14.9%	26,326
3/95	4,645	650	14.0%	24,722
3/94	3,975	511	12.8%	24,337
Annual Growth	**4.6%**	**1.8%**	**—**	**2.4%**

2003 Year-End Financials

Debt ratio: 17.6%
Return on equity: 10.6%
Cash ($ mil.): 463

Current ratio: 0.68
Long-term debt ($ mil.): 1,061

Net Income History

Singapore: SIAL

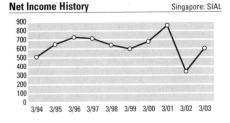

Sinopec Shanghai Petrochemical

China's own entry into the world of giant chemical companies, Sinopec Shanghai Petrochemical Company, is one of that country's largest producers of ethylene, a crucial ingredient in the manufacture of synthetic fibers, resins, and plastics. It also makes petroleum-based fuels and oils and other intermediate petrochemicals such as benzene. The company, which operates primarily within China (most of its revenues are from Eastern China), has joint ventures with US firm Dow Chemical and Japan's ITOCHU Corporation. China Petroleum & Chemical (Sinopec), which is controlled by the Chinese government, owns about 55% of Shanghai Petrochemical.

In anticipation of China's admission to the World Trade Organization, Shanghai Petrochemical Company has been overhauling its production facilities. The upgrades have enabled the company to process 10 million tons of crude oil per year, along with 1 million tons of ethylene and other synthetic fiber materials. The current quality of Chinese ethylene is generally inferior to that produced in developed countries. The upgrades have allowed the company to produce world-class polyethylene and polypropylene, which it can use domestically and sell on the world market.

HISTORY

The Mao-inspired Cultural Revolution of the 1960s restored the aging leader's political grip, but it also caused immense economic disruptions in China, including a virtual shutdown of foreign trade. In the early 1970s party reformists led by Zhou Enlai and Deng Xiaoping advocated improved contact with the outside world and the restoration of foreign trade, giving the Chinese economy access to much-needed technology. In 1972, the year President Nixon's visit to China restored Sino-US ties, China began contracting for plant and equipment imports, especially in the petrochemical areas of chemical fertilizers for agriculture and artificial fibers for industrial use. That year Shanghai Petrochemical Company was founded as China's first large petro-

chemical enterprise, using imported equipment and technology.

Under Sinopec's control, Shanghai Petrochemical fit squarely into the government's Four Modernizations policy (agriculture, industry, technology, and defense). Other factors in the firm's growth were the booming economies of the coastal cities in the east and south, made possible by economic liberalization policies that encouraged foreign investment. The Guangdong province in the south led the way as Hong Kong enterprise migrated there in the 1980s in search of lower wages and overhead. The expansion of industrial output there and in other provinces resulted in greatly increased demand for petrochemicals.

Emboldened by growth and further reforms in the oil industry, Sinopec restructured Shanghai Petrochemical in 1993 and listed it on the Hong Kong and New York stock markets. (It was the first Chinese company listed on the New York Stock Exchange.) The company formed a joint venture with US-based agribusiness giant Continental Grain in 1995 to build a liquid petroleum gas plant and teamed up with British Petroleum (now BP) to build an acrylonitrile plant. The company entered a joint venture with Union Carbide (purchased by Dow Chemical) in 1996 to build a polymer emulsion plant in China. Shanghai Petrochemical increased its market share for acrylics with its 1997 purchase of the Zhejiang Acrylic Fibre Plant, then a producer of about 40% of China's total acrylic-fiber output. Annual production grew to 130,000 tons by 1999.

Three broad-reaching events have hammered the company's profits: the Asian economic crisis, the decrease of Sinopec's subsidy on crude oil, and a global oversupply of petrochemicals. In 1997 Shanghai Petrochemical's product-mix adjustments, combined with cost cutting, offset some of the increased crude costs and lower prices. The company announced in 1998 that the Chinese government planned to crack down on the smuggling of foreign petrochemicals and help the domestic market. The firm remains vulnerable to policy changes, however. Additionally, consolidation of the Chinese petrochemical industry could translate into lost jobs. The company continued to modernize its facilities and increase its capacity in 2000 when it moved to upgrade operations in order to become a world-class production base for petrochemicals and derivatives.

EXECUTIVES

Chairman, Supervisory Committee: Du Chongjun,
  age 48
Chairman and President: Lu Yiping, age 57
Vice Chairman: Xu Kaicheng, age 46
CFO: Han Zhihao, age 52
VP: Rong Guangdao, age 47
VP: Wu Haijun, age 40
VP: Feng Jianping, age 49
VP: Yin Jihai, age 45
VP: Zhang Zhiliang, age 49
Company Secretary: Zhang Jingming, age 44
Auditors: KPMG

LOCATIONS

HQ: Sinopec Shanghai Shiyou Huagong Gufen Youxien
  Gongsi (Sinopec Shanghai Petrochemical
  Company Limited)
  48 Jinyi Rd., Jinshan District,
  Shanghai 200540, China
Phone: +86-21-5794-3143   **Fax:** +86-21-5794-0050
Web: www.spc.com.cn

PRODUCTS/OPERATIONS

2002 Sales

	% of total
Petroleum products	29
Intermediate petrochemicals	26
Resins & plastics	20
Synthetic fibers	11
Other	14
Total	**100**

Selected Products

Petroleum Products
Diesel
Gasoline
Jet oil
Residual oil

Intermediate Petrochemicals
Benzene
Butadiene
Ethylene
Ethylene glycol
Ethylene oxide

Resins and Plastics
LDPE film and pellets
Polyester chips
PP pellets
PVA

Synthetic Fibers
Acrylic staple
Acrylic top
Polyester filament-POY
Polyester staple
pp fiber
PVA fiber

COMPETITORS

DuPont	Royal Dutch/Shell Group
ExxonMobil Chemical	Tianjin Bohai Chemical
FPC	Yizheng Chemical
ICI American	Zhenhai Refining &
Jilin Chemical	Chemical
Marubeni	

HISTORICAL FINANCIALS

Company Type: Public

Income Statement

FYE: December 31

	REVENUE ($ mil.)	NET INCOME ($ mil.)	NET PROFIT MARGIN	EMPLOYEES
12/02	2,624	111	4.2%	31,489
12/01	2,370	14	0.6%	32,081
12/00	2,406	104	4.3%	33,911
12/99	1,696	73	4.3%	35,826
12/98	1,294	29	2.2%	38,000
12/97	1,429	88	6.1%	38,000
12/96	1,434	122	8.5%	38,000
12/95	1,423	256	18.0%	38,000
12/94	1,111	177	15.9%	39,000
12/93	1,305	150	11.5%	39,000
Annual Growth	**8.1%**	**(3.3%)**	**—**	**(2.3%)**

2002 Year-End Financials

Debt ratio: 32.8%	No. of shares (mil.): 72
Return on equity: 6.7%	Dividends
Cash ($ mil.): 201	Yield: 0.0%
Current ratio: 0.99	Payout: —
Long-term debt ($ mil.): 555	Market value ($ mil.): 1,076

Stock History

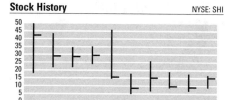

NYSE: SHI

			12/93	12/94	12/95	12/96	12/97	12/98	12/99	12/00	12/01	12/02

	STOCK PRICE ($) FY Close	P/E High/Low		PER SHARE ($) Earnings	Dividends	Book Value
12/02	14.95	11	6	1.50	0.00	23.46
12/01	9.03	90	37	0.19	0.73	22.12
12/00	9.63	13	6	1.45	0.60	22.65
12/99	15.06	25	7	1.01	0.36	21.22
12/98	8.50	44	13	0.40	0.00	20.80
12/97	15.56	38	12	1.20	0.00	20.82
12/96	29.38	19	13	1.80	1.56	19.68
12/95	28.50	9	6	3.90	2.54	17.55
12/94	28.88	17	9	2.54	1.04	16.69
12/93	42.25	16	6	3.11	0.00	20.47
Annual Growth	**(10.9%)**	**—**	**—**	**(7.8%)**	**—**	**1.5%**

Sodexho Alliance, SA

Sodexho Alliance has a lot of mouths to feed. The company is the world's #2 contract food service provider (after Compass Group), with operations in more than 70 countries. Its clients include corporations, colleges, hospitals, and public institutions. Besides food service, Sodexho Alliance also provides facilities management (grounds keeping, laundry), service vouchers, remote site management (including offshore rigs), and river pleasure cruises. In 2001 Sodexho Alliance bought Sodexho Marriott Services (one of the largest food service companies in the US) to serve as its North American subsidiary and renamed the firm Sodexho, Inc. Chairman and CEO Pierre Bellon and his family own about 40% of the company.

The company's client list spans the globe, and includes France's Peugeot and Total Fina, Sweden's Ericsson, the UK's Unilever, and Germany's Ministry of Foreign Affairs. Food service operations account for some 90% of the company's business. Sodexho Alliance is the largest such operator in North America through Sodexho, Inc.

Through its Sodexho Pass subsidiary, the company's service vouchers (passes, coupons, and smart cards for food, transportation, medical care, and employee and social benefits) are used in Europe and Latin America. It operates a fleet of more than 40 boats for river and harbor dinner cruises in cities such as Boston, Chicago, London, New York, Paris, Philadelphia, Seattle, and Washington, DC. In 2002 the company announced it had detected accounting and management errors in its UK operations, causing the value of its stock to fall by nearly one-third.

HISTORY

The Bellon family had been luxury ship hospitality specialists since the turn of the century, 60 years before Pierre Bellon founded Sodexho in 1966. By 1971 Bellon had his first contract outside of France to provide food service to a Brussels hospital. Sodexho continued to expand its services into the late 1970s, entering remote site management in Africa and the Middle East in 1975 and starting its service vouchers segment in Belgium and Germany in 1978.

Sodexho jumped the pond in 1980, expanding its businesses to North and South America. The company went public on the Paris Bourse exchange in 1983. Two years later it bought Seiler, a Boston vending machine company-turned-restaurateur. Sodexho then bought San Francisco's Food Dimensions in 1987. After beefing up its American operations with four other US acquisitions, the company merged Food Dimensions and Seiler in 1989. Sodexho's US river cruise company, Spirit Cruises — an echo of the Bellon family's original calling — was also included in the merger. The merged US companies were renamed Sodexho USA in 1993.

The 1990s proved an era of growth and acquisitions for Sodexho. The company expanded into Japan, Africa, Russia, and five Eastern European countries in 1993. The company acquired a 20% stake in Corrections Corporation of America the following year and virtually doubled its size with the acquisition of the UK's Gardner Merchant in 1995. The largest catering company in that region, Gardner Merchant had holdings that spanned Australia, the Far East, northern Europe, the UK, and the US — generally markets where Sodexho did not have a strong presence. That year the company also acquired Partena, a Swedish security and care company, from Volvo's Fortos.

Gardner Merchant's US business was officially merged with Sodexho USA in 1996 to make it the #4 food service company in the US. Also that year Sodexho acquired Brazilian service voucher company Cardapio. After a year of legal wrangling, Sodexho also lost a fight for control of Accor's Eurest France to rival caterer Compass Group, and sold off its minority interest. The next year Sodexho acquired 49% of Universal Ogden Services, renamed Universal Services, an American remote site manager. To signify its efforts to maintain the individuality of the companies it acquires, Sodexho changed its name to Sodexho Alliance in 1997.

Marriott International merged its food service branch with Sodexho's North American food service operations in 1998. With a 48% stake, Sodexho Alliance became the largest shareholder; former Marriott International stockholders took the rest, with the Marriott family controlling 9%. Before the merger, Sodexho USA was less than one-fourth the size of Marriott International's food service division. Sodexho acquired GR Servicios Hoteleros in 1999, thereby becoming the largest caterer in Spain. The following year it agreed to merge its remote site management operations with Universal Services and rename it Universal Sodexho.

In 2001 its initial $900 million bid to buy the 52% of Sodexho Marriott Services it didn't already own was rebuffed by its subsidiary's shareholders. Sodexho Alliance made a better offer (about $1.1 billion) and finally reached an agreement to purchase the rest of Sodexho Marriott Services. The deal was completed later that year and Sodexho Marriott Services changed its name to Sodexho, Inc. Also that year the company agreed to pay some $470 million for French rival Sogeres and US-based food management firm Wood Dining.

In April 2002 the company replaced its UK management team because of poor performance there.

EXECUTIVES

Chairman and CEO: Pierre Bellon, age 73
Vice Chairman: Remí Baudin, age 73
CFO: Siân H. Jones
CEO Continental Europe and Executive Committee VP: Jean-Michel Dhenain
CEO Sodexho, Inc. (North America) and Executive Committee VP: Michel Landel
CEO Sodexho UK and Ireland: Mark Shipman
COO Sodexho Group and Director: Patrice Douce, age 61
SVP and CIO: Phillippe Taillet
SVP Corporate Communications: Clodine Pincemin
SVP Human Resources: Elisabeth Carpentier
Investor Relations: Jean-Jacques Vironda
Media Relations: Jerome Chambin
Auditors: Befec-Price Waterhouse

LOCATIONS

HQ: 3, avenue Newton,
78180 Montigny-le-Bretonneux, France
Phone: +33-1-30-85-75-00   **Fax:** +33-1-30-43-09-58
US HQ: 9801 Washingtonian Blvd.,
Gaithersburg, MD 20878
US Phone: 301-987-4431   **US Fax:** 301-987-4068
Web: sodexho.com

Sodexho Alliance has operations in 74 countries.

2002 Sales

	% of total
North America	52
Continental Europe	29
UK/Ireland	14
Other regions	5
Total	**100**

PRODUCTS/OPERATIONS

2002 Sales

	% of total
Business & industry	44
Education	24
Health care	18
Seniors	6
Remote site management	5
Service vouchers & cards	2
River & harbor cruises	1
Total	**100**

COMPETITORS

Accor
ARAMARK
Compass Group
Delaware North
HDS Services
HMSHost
Host America

HISTORICAL FINANCIALS

Company Type: Public

Income Statement

FYE: August 31

	REVENUE ($ mil.)	NET INCOME ($ mil.)	NET PROFIT MARGIN	EMPLOYEES
8/02	12,378	198	1.6%	315,141
8/01	10,891	126	1.2%	313,469
8/00	9,490	165	1.7%	285,986
8/99	9,521	139	1.5%	269,973
8/98	6,933	123	1.8%	250,000
8/97	4,843	88	1.8%	152,000
8/96	4,922	135	2.7%	141,118
8/95	3,635	56	1.5%	115,669
8/94	2,076	117	5.7%	55,000
8/93	1,812	39	2.2%	50,339
Annual Growth	**23.8%**	**19.6%**	**—**	**22.6%**

2002 Year-End Financials

Debt ratio: 112.3%
Return on equity: 8.7%
Cash ($ mil.): 578
Current ratio: 1.08
Long-term debt ($ mil.): 2,644
No. of shares (mil.): 159
Dividends
Yield: 0.0%
Payout: —
Market value ($ mil.): 4,691

Stock History

NYSE: SDX

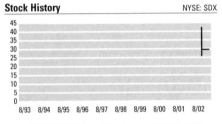

	STOCK PRICE ($) FY Close	P/E High/Low	PER SHARE ($) Earnings	Dividends	Book Value
8/02	29.50	35 22	1.20	0.00	14.80

SOFTBANK CORP.

SOFTBANK's bottom line is getting a little soft. Full-throttle investing by founder, president, and CEO Masayoshi Son has molded SOFTBANK through aggressive investments in a variety of Internet ventures. Under Son's tutelage, (he is hailed by many as the Bill Gates of Japan), the holding company has extended its investment reach across e-commerce, financial services, Internet infrastructure, information technology-related distribution services, publishing and marketing, and technology services. Son is selling its shares of E*TRADE for cash to put into its high-speed Internet access business in Asia, as times are looking tight for the rising Son.

With stakes in more than 100 Internet-related companies, the debt-heavy SOFTBANK is looking to prune some of its less profitable holdings (including Medialive International, formerly Key3 Media). SOFTBANK expanded into banking when it joined a consortium that purchased Japan's failed Nippon Credit Bank (later renamed Aozora). A stockmarket darling during the "Internet bub-

ble" of the late 1990s, SOFTBANK has seen its stock price and bottom line take a beating.

The bedrock of the company's Internet holdings is its less than 10% stake in Yahoo!, but SOFTBANK's Internet investments also include stakes in ventures such as E*TRADE and Morningstar Asset Management. The firm also owns nearly half of Aozora Bank (formerly Nippon Credit Bank), but is considering selling it. It has ceased new investments in Latin America and Europe and is looking to sell off some of its assets.

In an attempt to create a larger domestic market for its e-commerce and Internet companies, SOFTBANK has moved into the broadband Internet connection market, providing asymmetric digital subscriber line (ADSL) services. Son owns about 40% of the company.

HISTORY

Ethnic Korean Masayoshi Son grew up in Japan using the name Yasumoto to conform with the Japanese policy of assimilation. In the early 1970s, the 16-year-old came to the US and began using his Korean name. Son entered the University of California at Berkeley and, while there, invented the prototype for the Sharp Wizard handheld organizer.

Bankrolled by the nearly $1 million that Sharp paid him for his patent, Son returned to Japan and founded software distributor SOFTBANK in 1981. The company got its first big break when it inked a distribution agreement with Joshin Denki, one of Japan's largest consumer electronics retailers, that year. Son used this agreement to gain exclusive distribution rights for much of the software he distributed.

SOFTBANK went public in 1994. That year, as part of an evolving plan to control digital data delivery, Son bought the trade show division of Ziff-Davis Publishing, augmenting it in 1995 with the purchase of COMDEX, the trade show operations of the Interface Group. The next year SOFTBANK bought the rest of Ziff-Davis. It also bought 80% of Kingston Technology (sold 1999) and a stake in Yahoo! — which laid the cornerstone for its Internet empire.

SOFTBANK accelerated its Internet investment pace in 1997, taking stakes in dozens of Web companies. That year it filed suit against Yell Publishing, a Japanese firm that published a book accusing SOFTBANK of issuing phony financial statements, among other improprieties.

In 1998 the firm moved into financial services, entering a joint venture with E*TRADE Group to offer online stock trading in Japan. SOFTBANK also took Ziff-Davis public (it retained a majority stake).

Internal changes marked 1999 when SOFTBANK merged with MAC, Son's private asset management company, and transformed itself into a holding company focused on Internet-related companies. It teamed with the National Association of Securities Dealers to create a Japanese version of the Nasdaq stock market (launched in 2000; closed in 2002). SOFTBANK also partnered with Microsoft and Tokyo Electric Power to launch SpeedNet, a Japanese Internet service provider.

In 2000 the nearly decimated Ziff-Davis announced it would transform its online arm, ZDNet, from a tracking stock into a stand-alone company and adopt the ZDNet name; later CNET Networks bought both companies instead. That year SOFTBANK formed venture capital funds focusing on areas such as Latin America, Japan, Europe, the UK, and emerging markets.

The company reorganized in 2000 and placed most of its non-Japan-based holdings under a new unit called SOFTBANK Global Ventures. Sharpening its focus on Internet investments, SOFTBANK sold its stake in anti-virus software maker Trend Micro. Branching into banking, SOFTBANK headed a consortium that paid $932 million for Japan's failed Nippon Credit Bank. SOFTBANK's share of the bank (renamed Aozora) stood at nearly 49%. The firm's stock price tumbled in 2000, and it considered taking several holding companies public.

In 2001 Cisco bought a nearly 2% stake in SOFTBANK in exchange for the firm's 12% stake in the hardware company's Japanese unit. The company also sold its SOFTBANK Forums Japan, an Internet trade show company, to Key3Media Group. In 2002 Nasdaq Japan announced its plans to close, after two loss-making years. SOFTBANK owned 43%.

EXECUTIVES

President and CEO: Masayoshi Son, age 45
President and CEO, SOFTBANK Finance Corp.:
 Yoshitaka Kitao
President and CEO, SOFTBANK EC Holdings:
 Ken Miyauchi
VC, SOFTBANK Holdings: Ronald D. Fisher, age 55
Auditors: ChuoAoyama Audit Corporation

LOCATIONS

HQ: 24-1, Nihonbashi Hakozakicho, Chuo-ku,
 Tokyo 103-8501, Japan
Phone: +81-3-5642-8000   **Fax:** +81-3-5543-0431
US HQ: 1188 Centre St., Newton Center, MA 02459
US Phone: 617-928-9300   **US Fax:** 617-928-9301
Web: www.softbank.co.jp

SOFTBANK has operations in Asia, Australia, Europe, Latin America, and the US.

PRODUCTS/OPERATIONS

2003 Sales

	% of total
e-Commerce	60
Broadband infrastructure	10
e-Finance	6
Technology services	6
Internet culture	5
Media & marketing	4
Broadmedia	3
Other	6
Total	**100**

Selected Holdings

E-Commerce
AIP Bridge CORP.
BluePlanet Corp.
BridalConcierge Corp.
CarPoint K.K.
CMnet corporation
CreativeBank Corporation
Diamond.Com Corporation
eBEST Corp.
EC RESEARCH CORP.
e-Career CORP.
eEntry Corporation
e-express CO.,LTD
eselect Corp.
e-Shopping! Books CORP.
e-Shopping! Cargoods CORP.
e-Shopping! Information CORP.
e-Shopping! Toys CORP.
e-Shopping! Wine CORP.
Eupholink,Inc
GWP Japan Corporation
Nihon Ariba K.K.
ONSALE Japan K.K.
SmartFirm Corp.

SOFTBANK COMMERCE CORP.
SOFTBANK EC HOLDINGS CORP.
SOFTBANK Frameworks Corporation
SOFTBANK MOBILE CORP.
Style Index Corporation
Tavigator Inc.
Vector Inc.
VerticalNet Japan Corp.

Financial Services
Aozora Bank, Ltd.
ASCOT CO., LTD.
AtWork Corporation
B toB Technology Corporation
BB Technologies Corporation
BRAIN.COM, INC.
BROADBAND TECHNOLOGY CORP.
Cognotec Japan K.K
Commerce Technology Corp.
Commodity Co.,Ltd
CyberCash K.K.
E*Advisor Co., Ltd.
E*FINANCE SCHOOL CORPORATION
E*TRADE Japan K.K.
E*TRADE SECURITIES CO., LTD.
EC Architects Corporation
E-cosmos,Inc.
E-Loan Japan K.K.
E-Real Estate Co.,Ltd.
GlobalCenter Japan Corp.
GOODLOAN Co.,Ltd.
HousePortal Co.,Ltd.
INSWEB Japan K.K.
Internet Infrastructure
IP REVOLUTION Inc.
Morningstar Japan K.K.
Office Work Corporation
OnLine IR Co.,Ltd.
SF REALTY Co.,Ltd.
SOFT TREND CAPITAL Corp.
SOFTBANK FINANCE CORPORATION
SOFTBANK MOBILE TECHNOLOGY CORP.
SOFTBANK Networks Inc.
SOFTBANK Ventures, Inc.
SophiaBank Limited
SpeedNet Inc.
Web Portal Co.,Ltd.
Yahoo Japan Corporation

Media
Akamai Technologies Japan K.K.
ALISS-NET Co.,Ltd.
Computer Channel Corporation
Digital Club Corporation
Digital Media Factory Inc.
J SKY SPORTS Corporation
Nihon Eiga Satellite Broadcasting Corp.
SKY Perfect Communications Inc.
SOFTBANK Broadmedia Corporation
Xdrive Japan K.K.
YesNoJAPAN Corporation

Publishing
Aplix.NET Inc.
BARKS K.K.
Click2learn Japan K.K.
COM-PATH, Inc.
cyber communications inc.
DirektPlanet Co.,Ltd.
Englishtown Limited
iWeb Technologies Japan K.K.
JaJa Entertainment Inc.
Key3Media Events Japan, Inc.
Rivals Japan Corporation
SOFTBANK Media & Marketing Corp.
Softbank Publishing Inc.
SOFTBANK ZDNet Inc.
WebMD Japan K.K.

COMPETITORS

Accel Partners	idealab
Alloy Ventures	Internet Capital
Benchmark Capital	Internet Initiative Japan
CMGI	Kleiner Perkins
CSK	Safeguard Scientifics
Flatiron Partners	Sequoia Capital
Fujitsu	Shikoku Electric
Hummer Winblad	Trinity Ventures

HISTORICAL FINANCIALS

Company Type: Public

Income Statement

FYE: March 31

	REVENUE ($ mil.)	NET INCOME ($ mil.)	NET PROFIT MARGIN	EMPLOYEES
3/03	3,171	(834)	—	8,000
3/02	2,876	(669)	—	8,000
3/01	2,891	290	10.0%	7,400
3/00	4,011	80	2.0%	7,000
3/99	4,434	315	7.1%	6,865
3/98	3,858	77	2.0%	7,743
3/97	2,906	73	2.5%	5,600
3/96	1,595	54	3.4%	4,375
3/95	1,119	24	2.1%	909
3/94	624	9	1.5%	630
Annual Growth	**19.8%**	**—**	**—**	**32.6%**

Net Income History

Exchange: Tokyo

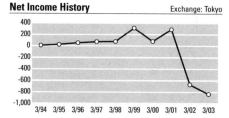

Sony Corporation

All eyes are on Sony — or, more likely, on its high-profit PlayStation home video game systems. Playstation 2 dominates the game console market with about 70% of global sales (Nintendo's GameCube and Microsoft's Xbox control about 15% each). Sony, the world's #1 consumer electronics firm (ahead of Matsushita), also makes a host of other products, including PCs, digital cameras, Walkman stereos, and semiconductors. The company's TVs, stereos, and other consumer electronics account for more than 60% of sales. Sony's entertainment assets include recorded music and video (Epic and Columbia), motion pictures, DVDs, and TV programming (Columbia TriStar).

In addition Sony sells mobile phones via a joint venture with Ericsson. Along with Time Warner, Sony also owns a 15% stake in music club Columbia House.

Though the PlayStation still dominates the game machine scene, sales of other electronics (DVD recorders, TVs, and computers) and music have seen a drop. Weak consumer demand and price wars, along with charges incurred while streamlining operations, have significantly hurt Sony's market value.

Sony has launched a restructuring effort planned through 2006; the cost-cutting plan will reduce headcount by 20,000 (about 13% of its workforce), combine operating divisions, and shift component sourcing to low-cost markets such as China. Sony also plans to drastically reduce (by nearly 90%) the number of parts used in manufacturing its consumer electronics products.

Sony is emphasizing digital content, semiconductors (aimed at improving product innovation), and products that merge electronics and game technologies. The company is developing PSP, a Walkman-like device with DVD-quality video (to launch in late 2004), and PSX, which combines electronics and game technology (released in Japan in 2003, and to launch in the US and Europe in 2004).

To gain an edge over competitors, Sony is spending about $1.67 billion during the next three years to build a cutting-edge semiconductor plant in Japan. The firm is also working with Matsushita and other electronics manufacturers to develop software that uses the Linux operating system to run home electronics.

In an effort to combat losses in a weakening music industry, Sony plans to merge its music division with BMG; the new company (Sony BMG) would become the #2 player (after Universal Music).

HISTORY

Akio Morita, Masaru Ibuka, and Tamon Maeda (Ibuka's father-in-law) started Tokyo Telecommunications Engineering in 1946 with funding from Morita's father's sake business. The company produced the first Japanese tape recorder in 1950. Three years later Morita paid Western Electric (US) $25,000 for transistor technology licenses, which sparked a consumer electronics revolution in Japan. His firm launched one of the first transistor radios in 1955, followed by the first Sony-trademarked product, a pocket-sized radio, in 1957. The next year the company changed its name to Sony (from "sonus," Latin for "sound," and "sonny," meaning little man). It beat the competition to newly emerging markets for transistor TVs (1959) and solid-state videotape recorders (1961).

Sony launched the first home video recorder (1964) and solid-state condenser microphone (1965). Its 1968 introduction of the Trinitron color TV tube began another decade of explosive growth. Sony bet wrong on its Betamax VCR (1976), which lost to rival Matsushita's VHS as the industry standard. However, 1979 brought another success, the Walkman personal stereo.

Pressured by adverse currency rates and competition worldwide, Sony used its technology to diversify beyond consumer electronics and began to move production to other countries. In the 1980s it introduced Japan's first 32-bit workstation and became a major producer of computer chips and floppy disk drives. The purchases of CBS Records in 1988 ($2 billion) and Columbia Pictures in 1989 (a $4.9 billion deal, which included TriStar Pictures) made Sony a major force in the rapidly growing entertainment industry.

The firm manufactured Apple's PowerBook, but its portable CD player, Data Discman, was successful only in Japan (1991). In the early 1990s Sony joined Nintendo to create a new kind of game console, combining Sony's CD-ROM drive with the graphic capabilities of a workstation. Although Nintendo pulled out in 1992,

Sony released PlayStation in Japan (1994) and in the US (1995) to great success. Two years later, in a joint venture with Intel, it developed a line of PC desktop systems.

In 1998 Sony shipped its first digital, high-definition TV to the US, folded TriStar into Columbia Pictures, merged its Loews Theatres unit with Cineplex Odeon, and launched its Wega flat-screen TV. Philips, Sun Microsystems, and Sony formed a joint venture in early 1999 to develop networked entertainment products. Also in 1999 Nobuyuki Idei became CEO, and the company introduced a Walkman with the capability to download music from the Internet.

In 2000 Sony formed PlayStation.com Japan to sell game consoles and software online; it also introduced its 128-bit PlayStation 2, which plays DVD movies and connects to the Internet.

In early 2001 Sony started an online bank with Japan's Sakura Bank and JP Morgan Chase. Adverse market conditions in 2001, aggravated by the September 11 attacks, led Sony Pictures Entertainment to consolidate its two domestic television operations, folding Columbia TriStar Network Television into Columbia TriStar Domestic Television (CTDT).

In the course of the fiscal year ending March 2002, Sony laid off about 13,700 employees, primarily in its electronics and music businesses. In an attempt to capitalize on the strength of its own brand, Sony renamed its Columbia TriStar Domestic Television (CTDT) and Columbia TriStar International Television (CTIT) divisions in 2002, designating them as Sony Pictures Television (SPT) and Sony Pictures Television International (SPTI), respectively.

In 2003 Sony adopted a US-style corporate governance model (made possible by a revision in Japan's Commercial Code) and acquired CIS Corp., a Japanese information system consulting firm. In an effort to cut costs through manufacturing consolidation, Sony closed its audio equipment plant in Indonesia that year.

EXECUTIVES

Honorary Chairman: Norio Ohga, age 73
Chairman and Group CEO: Nobuyuki Idei, age 66
Vice Chairman and Group Chief Production Officer: Minoru Morio, age 64
President and Group COO: Kunitake Ando, age 61
SEVP and Group CIO: Akira Kondoh, age 58
SVP and Group CFO: Takao Yuhara
SVP; Senior General Manager, Intellectual Property Division; Chairman, Sony Chemicals Corporation: Yoshihide Nakamura
Executive Deputy President and Group Chief Strategy Officer, Personal Solutions Business Group and Network Application and Content Service Sector: Teruhisa Tokunaka
Executive Deputy President; COO, Home Network Company, Game Business Group, and Broadband Network Company; President, Semiconductor Solutions Network Company; President and CEO, Sony Computer Entertainment: Ken Kutaragi, age 53
Corporate SEVP and Group General Counsel: Teruo Masaki, age 60
Corporate EVP and Co-CTO; President, Sony Computer Science Laboratories; Co-CTO Electronics, Sony Group: Mario Tokoro, age 56
Corporate EVP, Human Resources and General Affairs: Kenichiro Yonezawa, age 61
Corporate EVP; President, Network Application and Content Service Sector: Masayuki Nozoe, age 54
Corporate EVP; President, Semiconductor Network Company; Electronics Co-Chief Quality Officer, Sony Group: Takeo Minomiya, age 59
Corporate EVP, Public Relations, Corporate External Relations, and Brand Strategy: Mitsuru Ohki, age 59

Corporate SVP and Electronics Chief Marketing Officer; President and COO, Sony Electronics: Fujio Nishida, age 54
Chairman and CEO, Sony Music Entertainment: Andrew R. (Andy) Lack, age 56
Chairman and CEO, Sony Pictures Entertainment: Michael Lynton
Chairman and CEO, Sony Corporation of America; Chairman, Sony Electronics: Sir Howard Stringer, age 61
President, Sony Music Entertainment US: Don Ienner, age 52
Auditors: PricewaterhouseCoopers

LOCATIONS

HQ: 7-35, Kitashinagawa, 6-chome, Shinagawa-ku, Tokyo 141-0001, Japan
Phone: +81-3-5448-2111 **Fax:** +81-3-5448-2244
US HQ: 550 Madison Ave., New York, NY 10022-3211
US Phone: 212-833-6800 **US Fax:** 212-833-6956
Web: www.sony.net

Sony has its main manufacturing plants in Japan, as well as in China, Malaysia, Mexico, Spain, the UK, and the US; it sells its products worldwide.

2003 Sales

	$ mil.	% of total
US	20,033	32
Japan	17,449	28
Europe	13,883	22
Other regions	10,915	18
Total	**62,280**	**100**

PRODUCTS/OPERATIONS

2003 Sales

	$ mil.	% of total
Electronics	37,861	61
Game	7,802	13
Pictures	6,690	11
Music	4,659	7
Financial Services	4,272	7
Other	996	1
Total	**62,280**	**100**

Selected Products

Audio
Car audio
Car navigation systems
Home audio
Portable audio

Video
Digital still cameras
DVD players/recorders
Video cameras
Video decks

Televisions
CRT televisions
LCD televisions
PC projectors
Plasma televisions
Projection televisions
Set-top boxes

Information and Communications
Broadcast and professional-use equipment
Computer displays
PCs
PDAs
Printers

Semiconductors
CCDs
LCDs
Other semiconductors

Components
Audio/video/data recording media
Batteries
CRTs
Data recording systems
Optical pickups

Entertainment
Home video and DVDs
Motion pictures
Recorded music and music videos
Television programming

Network Services
Games
Interactive programming
Online content
Video-on-demand
Wireless entertainment

Insurance
Auto insurance
Life insurance

Other
Aiwa products
Banking
Entertainment robots
Mobile phones

COMPETITORS

Amazon.com
Apple Computer
Bertelsmann
Bose
Canon
Daewoo Electronics
Dell
EMI Group
Fujitsu
Harman International
Hewlett-Packard
Hitachi
IDT International
Intel
IBM
Kyocera
LG Electronics
Lung Cheong
Matsushita
Microsoft
Mitek Corp.
Mitsubishi Electric
Motorola
NEC
Nintendo
Nokia
Philips Electronics
Pioneer
Robert Bosch
Samsung
SANYO
SEGA
Sharp
Sharp Electronics
THOMSON
Time Warner
Toshiba
Viacom
VUE
Walt Disney

HISTORICAL FINANCIALS

Company Type: Public

Income Statement

FYE: March 31

	REVENUE ($ mil.)	NET INCOME ($ mil.)	NET PROFIT MARGIN	EMPLOYEES
3/03	63,264	978	1.5%	161,100
3/02	57,117	115	0.2%	168,000
3/01	58,518	134	0.2%	181,800
3/00	63,082	1,149	1.8%	189,700
3/99	57,109	1,505	2.6%	177,000
3/98	51,178	1,682	3.3%	173,000
3/97	45,670	1,125	2.5%	163,000
3/96	43,326	512	1.2%	151,000
3/95	44,758	(3,296)	—	138,000
3/94	36,250	149	0.4%	130,000
Annual Growth	6.4%	23.3%	—	2.4%

2003 Year-End Financials

Debt ratio: 35.4%
Return on equity: 5.3%
Cash ($ mil.): 6,036
Current ratio: 1.30
Long-term debt ($ mil.): 6,835
No. of shares (mil.): 925
Dividends
  Yield: 0.6%
  Payout: 20.0%
Market value ($ mil.): 32,511

Stock History

NYSE: SNE

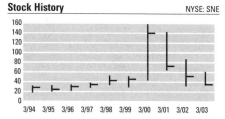

	STOCK PRICE ($) FY Close	P/E High/Low		PER SHARE ($) Earnings	Dividends	Book Value
3/03	35.13	60	35	1.00	0.20	20.86
3/02	51.70	1,072	410	0.13	0.20	19.36
3/01	72.25	143	66	0.15	0.35	20.14
3/00	140.06	127	36	1.24	0.20	22.70
3/99	45.66	31	18	1.65	0.10	18.70
3/98	42.53	28	19	1.83	0.00	16.90
3/97	34.56	30	24	1.25	0.10	15.32
3/96	30.38	53	36	0.63	0.12	14.74
3/95	24.44	—	—	(3.92)	0.22	15.14
3/94	28.19	147	91	0.21	0.20	17.27
Annual Growth	2.5%	—	—	18.9%	0.0%	2.1%

Statoil ASA

Statoil (formerly Den norske stats oljeselskap) is Norway's oil and gas exploration, production, transport, refining, and marketing giant. Statoil operates in 25 countries, focusing its upstream activities on the Norwegian continental shelf, the North Sea, the Caspian Sea, Western Africa, and Venezuela. It has proved reserves of 3.7 billion barrels of oil equivalent. It runs 1,500 service stations in Scandinavia, Ireland, Poland, Russia, and the Baltic states. Statoil also has a stake in petrochemicals venture Borealis. A bribery scandal involving an Iranian oil contract forced the resignation of the chairman, CEO, and another top executive in 2003. The Norwegian government owns almost 81% of Statoil.

The company manages the state's direct financial interest (known as SDFI) in oil and gas partnerships active on the Norwegian continental shelf. It also owns the world's largest offshore gas platform, the Aasgard B off Norway's west coast. In addition, Statoil supplies electricity in Norway and Sweden.

To focus on its core areas Statoil has divested its US exploration and production operations, although the US is still a major market for the company's exports: Statoil ships about 500,000 barrels of oil per day to the US and Canada. It is also a major exporter to Asia.

Cost overruns in the Aasgard field toppled most of Statoil's management in 1999. The company is gearing up for growth by reorganizing into four main segments and divesting up to 20% of its assets.

In 2002 Statoil agreed to sell its oil and gas assets in the Danish North Sea to Dong, the Danish state oil company, for about $120 million.

That year the company also agreed to buy the Polish unit of Sweden's Preem Petroleum, which owns 79 gas stations in Poland.

In 2003 Statoil sold its Navion unit to shipping group Teekay, for about $800 million. That year it also announced plans to acquire two Algerian natural gas projects from BP for $740 million.

HISTORY

To exert greater control over exploration and production of the Norwegian continental shelf (NCS), the government of Norway set up Den norske stats oljeselskap (Statoil) in 1972.

A decade earlier three geologists had visited Norway on behalf of Phillips Petroleum (later renamed ConocoPhillips) to apply for sole rights to explore on the NCS. The government initially refused drilling rights to foreign companies, and in 1963 Norway claimed sovereignty over the NCS. Two years later the government began allowing exploration. Phillips' major discovery in the Ekofisk field in 1969 prompted Norway to set up its own oil company. After Statoil's formation in 1972, the company garnered funds to expand through taxation of multinationals, production limits, leasing contracts, and other measures.

In 1974 a giant discovery was made in the North Sea's Statfjord field, and Statoil was given a 50% stake. A year later Statoil began exploring for oil and gas, exporting oil, and commissioning its first subsea oil pipeline, the Norpipe, which extended to the UK. In 1986 Statoil's gas pipeline system, the Statpipe, began transporting gas from the North Sea to the mainland.

Moving into retailing, Statoil acquired Esso's service stations and other downstream operations in Sweden and Denmark in 1985 and 1986. The next year, cost overruns stemming from the extension of Statoil's Mongstad oil refinery led to the ousting of the company's first president, Arve Johnsen, and many of his deputies. Harald Norvik was appointed CEO in 1988.

In 1990 Statoil and BP teamed up to develop international operations, and in 1992 Statoil acquired BP's service stations in Ireland. Statoil and Neste Chemicals (later part of Industri Kapital) formed the Borealis petrochemicals group in 1994.

The company in 1995 acquired Aran Energy, moving into exploration offshore Ireland and the UK. Statoil brought its field projects in China and Azerbaijan onstream in 1997. That year Statoil spun off its shipping operations as Navion, partly owned by Norway's Rasmussen group. It also contracted with Kvaerner to build a giant offshore gas platform for Aasgard field in the Norwegian Sea.

The Aasgard field project resulted in cost overruns in 1999, again leading to a Statoil board shakeup and CEO resignation. Norvik, who had advocated partial privatization of Statoil, was replaced by Olav Fjell, former head of Norway's Postbanken (who resigned in 2003). That year Statoil helped Norsk Hydro take over rival Saga in return for some of Saga's assets.

As part of a major restructuring in 2000, Statoil sold most assets of US unit Statoil Energy. Political opposition that year postponed Statoil's plans for partial privatization, but the government proceeded with an IPO in 2001, raising about $3 billion.

EXECUTIVES

Chairman: Jannik Lindbaek, age 62
Acting CEO: Inge K. Hansen, age 57
EVP and Acting CFO: Eldar Saetre, age 47
EVP Communications and Public Affairs:
Elisabeth Berge, age 49
EVP Exploration and Production Norway:
Henrik Carlsen, age 57
Acting EVP International Exploration and Production:
Ottar I. Rekdal, age 54
EVP Manufacturing and Marketing: Erling Øverland,
age 51
EVP Natural Gas: Peter Mellbye, age 54
EVP Technology: Terje Overvik
SVP Corporate Audit: Svein Andersen
SVP Corporate Services: Randi Grung Olsen
SVP Group Finance: Jon A. Jacobsen
SVP Health, Safety, and the Environment:
Stig Bergseth
SVP Human Resources: Kjølv E. Egeland
SVP Information and Communication Technology:
Ole A. Jørgensen
SVP Legal Affairs: Jacob S. Middelthon
VP Country Analysis and Social Responsibility:
Geir Westgaard
VP Investor Relations: Mari Tiømøe
VP Public Affairs: Wenche Skorge
VP Promotion and Media: Hans Aasmund Frisak
Auditors: Ernst & Young AS

LOCATIONS

HQ: Forusbeen 50, N-4035 Stavanger, Norway
Phone: +47-51-99-00-00 **Fax:** +47-51-99-00-50
US HQ: 225 High Ridge Rd., Stamford, CT 06905
US Phone: 203-978-6900 **US Fax:** 203-978-6952
Web: www.statoil.com

Statoil has operations in Angola, Azerbaijan, Belgium, China, Denmark, Estonia, France, Germany, Ireland, Kazakhstan, Latvia, Lithuania, Malaysia, Nigeria, Norway, Poland, Russia, Singapore, Sweden, the UK, the US, Venezuela, and Vietnam.

PRODUCTS/OPERATIONS

2002 Sales

	% of total
Refining & marketing	71
Exploration & production	21
Natural gas	8
Total	**100**

COMPETITORS

BP	Royal Dutch/Shell Group
Exxon Mobil	TOTAL
Norsk Hydro	

HISTORICAL FINANCIALS

Company Type: Public

Income Statement

FYE: December 31

	REVENUE ($ mil.)	NET INCOME ($ mil.)	NET PROFIT MARGIN	EMPLOYEES
12/02	34,874	2,426	7.0%	17,115
12/01	25,720	1,919	7.5%	16,686
12/00	25,925	1,822	7.0%	16,800
12/99	17,415	423	2.4%	18,000
12/98	14,131	36	0.3%	18,133
12/97	16,915	585	3.5%	16,777
12/96	16,775	828	4.9%	15,171
Annual Growth	**13.0%**	**19.6%**	**—**	**2.0%**

2002 Year-End Financials

Debt ratio: 57.5%	No. of shares (mil.): 2,166
Return on equity: 34.7%	Dividends
Cash ($ mil.): 965	Yield: 4.0%
Current ratio: 0.98	Payout: 29.5%
Long-term debt ($ mil.): 4,724	Market value ($ mil.): 17,914

Stock History

NYSE: STO

12/93 12/94 12/95 12/96 12/97 12/98 12/99 12/00 12/01 12/02

	STOCK PRICE ($) FY Close	P/E High/Low		PER SHARE ($) Earnings	Dividends	Book Value
12/02	8.27	8	6	1.12	0.33	3.79
12/01	6.55	8	7	0.92	0.00	2.66
Annual Growth	**26.3%**	**—**	**—**	**21.7%**	**—**	**42.4%**

ST

The list of European chip makers starts with ST. STMicroelectronics (ST) is one of the world's largest and most respected semiconductor companies; it is the #1 Europe-based chip maker (ahead of Infineon) and the #1 maker of analog chips (just ahead of Texas Instruments). ST makes many types of discrete devices (such as transistors and diodes) and integrated circuits (ICs), including microcontrollers, memory chips, and application-specific and custom ICs. It sells to manufacturers in the telecommunications, computer, consumer electronics, industrial, and automotive markets. (ST chips are in half of all cars on the road.) Top clients include Nokia, Robert Bosch, Schlumberger, Scientific-Atlanta, and Sony.

ST focuses on intensive product development, especially in close concert with key long-term strategic allies such as Nokia, Seagate Technology, and Alcatel. The company has also expanded its product range through a series of small, complementary acquisitions. Its product breadth lends to its expertise in SOC (system-on-a-chip) ICs, which integrate disparate functions onto a single device.

The company, which employs a highly decentralized organizational structure that reflects its global reach, has also won many awards for its commitments to manufacturing quality, environmental responsibility, and employee satisfaction. Its top-flight management has been credited with helping ST to avoid the dismal losses and big layoffs experienced by many chipmakers during the brutal industry downturn of 2001 and 2002.

Through a complex structure of holding companies, French-government-controlled companies AREVA Group and France Telecom together own 18% of ST. Italian aerospace and military supplier Finmeccanica also owns 18%. (All three companies have pared their stakes, and France Telecom is planning further divestments.)

HISTORY

SGS-THOMSON (ST) was formed through the 1987 merger of SGS Microelettronica, a state-owned Italian chip maker, and the nonmilitary electronics arm of Thomson-CSF (now Thales). Included in the deal were two US oper-

ations: SGS Semiconductor in Phoenix and Texas-based Thomson Components-Mostek (acquired by Thomson in 1986 from United Technologies).

Microelettronica was part of Finmeccanica, formed in 1948 as the engineering subsidiary of the (now liquidated) Italian state industrial holding company IRI.

Thomson SA got its start shortly before the turn of the century, when a group of French businessmen acquired patents from General Electric predecessor Thomson-Houston Electric and created Compagnie Française Thomson-Houston to produce power generation equipment.

Both Thomson and Microelettronica were struggling at the time of their merger. Pasquale Pistorio, a Motorola veteran who became head of SGS in 1980, was named president of the new company. To jump-start the organization, he closed and sold factories, trimmed management, and shifted jobs to the Mediterranean and Asia.

ST lost $300 million in its first two years of operation, made a small profit in 1989, then stumbled again as recession spread across Europe. To secure ST's market presence, Pistorio began making acquisitions and forging alliances with major chip buyers such as Alcatel, Hewlett-Packard, and Sony. By 1993 ST had become the world's #1 maker of erasable programmable read-only memories (EPROMs). Profits soared to $160 million, and the company bought Tag Semiconductors, a maker of low-cost chips, from US conglomerate Raytheon. ST went public in 1994.

Thomson sold off its stake in ST in 1997 and SGS-THOMSON changed its name to STMicroelectronics in 1998. The company formed development deals with Philips Electronics (for advanced chip manufacturing processes) in 1997 and with Mitsubishi (for flash memory chips) in 1998.

In 1999 ST bought Adaptec's Peripheral Technology Solutions group, which makes chips for disk drives; Vision Group, a developer of image sensors; and Arithmos, a maker of ICs for digital displays.

In 2000 ST acquired the Canada-based semiconductor fabrication operations of Nortel Networks for about $100 million. The deal included a six-year supply agreement worth at least $2 billion. The following year, though, ST announced that a sluggish chip industry would lead it to close the former Nortel fab as part of an overall reduction in its capital spending; later in 2001 ST announced that it would close a fab in California as well.

Early in 2002 the company announced that it planned to sell its small PC graphics chip business. Later that year ST bought Alcatel Microelectronics from French telecom giant Alcatel for about $345 million. In a related transaction, ST resold Alcatel's mixed-signal chip business to AMI Semiconductor (the operating unit of AMIS Holdings).

EXECUTIVES

Chairman: Bruno Steve, age 61
Vice Chairman: Jean-Pierre Noblanc, age 64
President and CEO: Pasquale Pistorio, age 67
VP and CFO: Carlo Ferro
VP and Treasurer: Piero Mosconi, age 63
Group VP and General Manager, DVD Division:
Bob Krysiak
Group VP and General Manager, Smartcard ICs Division: Reza Kazerounian
Group VP and Managing Director, ST Malta:
Gene Gretchen
Group VP, Central Research and Development and Director, Design Automation: Philippe Magarshack

Group VP, Corporate Communications:
Carlo E. Ottaviani
Group VP, Operations and Technology: Orio Bellezza
VP and General Manager, Advanced System Technology:
Andrea Cuomo, age 49
VP and General Manager, Memory Products Group:
Carlo Bozotti, age 50
VP and General Manager, Set-Top Box Division:
Christos Lagomichos, age 48
VP and Deputy General Manager, Telecommunications, Peripheral, and Automotive Groups; General Manager, Telecommunications Group: Johan Danneels, age 53
VP, Americas Region; President and CEO, STMicroelectronics, Inc.: Richard J. (Dick) Pieranunzi, age 64
VP, Central Research and Development: Joël Monnier, age 58
VP, Corporate Relations: Lynn Morgen
VP, Distribution Sales, North America: John North
VP, Strategic Planning and Human Resources:
Alain Dutheil, age 58
Director, US Media Relations: Michael Markowitz
Auditors: PricewaterhouseCoopers N.V.

LOCATIONS

HQ: STMicroelectronics
39 Chemin du Champ des Filles, Plan-Les-Ouates, 1228 Geneva, Switzerland
Phone: +41-22-929-29-29   **Fax:** +41-22-929-29-00
US HQ: 1310 Electronics Dr., Carrollton, TX 75006-5039
US Phone: 972-466-8445   **US Fax:** 972-466-8387
Web: www.st.com

STMicroelectronics has operations in more than 30 countries.

2002 Sales

	$ mil.	% of total
Asia/Pacific		
Japan	275	4
Other countries	2,748	43
Europe	1,832	29
North America	919	15
Other regions	544	9
Total	**6,318**	**100**

PRODUCTS/OPERATIONS

2002 Sales by Division

	$ mil.	% of total
Telecommunications, Peripherals & Automotive	3,074	49
Memory	1,055	17
Discrete & Standard ICs	1,055	17
Consumer & Microcontrollers	1,026	16
Other	108	1
Total	**6,318**	**100**

Selected Products

Telecommunications, Peripherals, and Automotive
Telecommunications
  Wireless telecommunications
  Wireline telecommunications
Peripherals and automotive
  Audio and automotive
  Data storage
  Industrial and power supplies
  Printers

Memory
Electrically erasable programmable read-only memories (EEPROMs)
Erasable programmable read-only memories (EPROMs)
Flash memory
Nonvolatile random-access memories (NVRAMs)
Smart card ICs

Discrete and Standard ICs
Discrete power devices
Power transistors
Radio-frequency (RF) products (used in avionics, telecom, and television broadcasting equipment)
Standard linear and logic ICs

Consumer and Microcontrollers
Consumer electronics
  DVD (decoder/host processor chips)
  Imaging and display (modules and sensors for flat-panel displays, monitors, and video cameras)
  Set-top box (decoders and integrated tuner/demodulator/error correction chips)
  TV (application-specific microcontrollers)
Microcontrollers (8- and 16-bit)

COMPETITORS

AMD	Maxim Integrated
Agere Systems	Products
Agilent Technologies	Motorola
Analog Devices	National Semiconductor
Atmel	NEC Electronics
Broadcom	ON Semiconductor
Cypress Semiconductor	Philips Semiconductors
Fairchild Semiconductor	QUALCOMM
Fujitsu	Renesas
Infineon Technologies	Samsung Electronics
Intel	Sharp
IBM Microelectronics	Texas Instruments
International Rectifier	Toshiba
LSI Logic	

HISTORICAL FINANCIALS

Company Type: Public

Income Statement

FYE: December 31

	REVENUE ($ mil.)	NET INCOME ($ mil.)	NET PROFIT MARGIN	EMPLOYEES
12/02	6,318	429	6.8%	43,170
12/01	6,357	257	4.0%	40,300
12/00	7,813	1,452	18.6%	43,650
12/99	5,056	547	10.8%	34,500
12/98	4,248	411	9.7%	29,182
12/97	4,019	407	10.1%	28,728
12/96	4,122	626	15.2%	25,468
12/95	3,554	527	14.8%	25,523
12/94	2,640	363	13.8%	21,800
12/93	2,038	160	7.9%	19,898
Annual Growth	**13.4%**	**11.6%**	**—**	**9.0%**

2002 Year-End Financials

Debt ratio: 40.0%
Return on equity: 6.6%
Cash ($ mil.): 2,562
Current ratio: 2.77
Long-term debt ($ mil.): 2,797
No. of shares (mil.): 888
Dividends
  Yield: 0.2%
  Payout: 8.3%
Market value ($ mil.): 17,316

Stock History

NYSE: STM

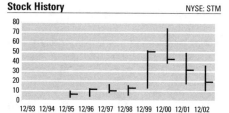

	STOCK PRICE ($) FY Close	P/E High/Low		PER SHARE ($) Earnings	Dividends	Book Value
12/02	19.51	75	23	0.48	0.04	7.88
12/01	31.67	168	62	0.29	0.00	6.83
12/00	42.81	47	25	1.58	0.00	6.88
12/99	50.43	83	22	0.62	0.00	5.24
12/98	13.00	32	12	0.48	0.00	4.77
12/97	10.17	34	17	0.49	0.00	3.96
12/96	11.66	16	6	0.75	0.00	3.91
12/95	6.70	14	6	0.67	0.00	3.21
Annual Growth	**16.5%**	**—**	**—**	**(4.7%)**	**—**	**13.7%**

Stora Enso Oyj

Forest products company Stora Enso Oyj's roots reach back more than 700 years. Stora Enso produces a wide range of paper and wood products such as magazine paper, newsprint, fine papers, packaging boards, and sawn timber. The company also makes graphic products, office papers, and wallpaper base. Stora Enso acquired US-based Consolidated Papers (now Stora Enso North America) to move past International Paper as the world's #1 paper and board producer. The Finnish State and Sweden's Knut and Alice Wallenberg Foundation each control about 24% of Stora Enso.

Stora Enso has long been a major player in Europe, where it derives about 70% of sales and is the #1 producer of newsprint and sawn softwood timber; Stora Enso acquired Consolidated Papers to gain market share in America. The company continues to focus on its core paper (magazine, newsprint, fine) and timber businesses (packaging boards, lumber) while divesting periphery businesses such as specialty paper, off-site energy generation, and packaging paper.

Finland is reducing its stake from 24% to around 11% as part of its privatization program.

HISTORY

Stora Kopparbergs Bergslag's ancestors were mining Kopperberg Mountain in Sweden as long ago as 1288. The mountain housed a copper mine that Swedish nobles and German merchants managed as a cooperative. By the 17th century King Karl IX instituted German mining methods to increase production. Copper became Sweden's largest export, accounting for 60% of the country's gross national product.

Copper production slowed after two cave-ins in 1655 and 1687, and exploitation of the region's timber and iron ore resources began. By the early 1800s the company was producing pig and bar iron. In 1862 all of the company's activities were combined to form Stora Kopparbergs Bergslag. The role of copper became less important as the company consolidated its iron works and ventured into forest products. The firm reorganized as a limited liability company in 1888.

By 1915 Stora Kopparbergs had firmly established pulp and paper mills, as well as iron and steel works concentrated along the Dalalven River Basin. The company's activities revolved around these facilities for the next 60 years.

During the 1960s Stora Kopparbergs was hurt by low bulk commodity prices and increased competition. The company, feeling the crunch of the oil crisis, sold its holdings in steel and mining between 1976 and 1978. With its purchase of Billerud (forestry), the company became Sweden's largest industrial concern in 1984. Stora Kopparbergs shortened its name to Stora, meaning "great" or "large" in Swedish, to commemorate the event.

Stora went on a shopping spree in the late 1980s and early 1990s to compete with its giant US rivals. At home it bought Papyrus and Swedish Match; abroad it acquired Feldmuhle Nobel of Germany and France's Les Paperteies de la Chapelle-Darblay. In 1998 Stora established operations in China through a joint venture. The company also merged with Finnish forest products company Enso Gutzeit Oyj to form Stora Enso Oyj that year.

Hans Gutzeit founded a sawmill in 1872 on

the Finnish island of Kotka. Gutzeit bought Utra Wood Co. to eliminate competition and was incorporated in Finland as Aktiebolaget W. Gutzeit & Co. in 1896. The company constructed a pulp mill to use waste wood from the Kotka sawmill, and in 1912 it purchased rival sawmill Enso Trasliperi Aktiebolaget to increase its access to hydropower.

In 1917 the Russian Revolution marked the disappearance of a major market, and Finland's declaration of independence from Norway halted production. Gutzeit's Norwegian shareholders sold the company to the new Finnish state in 1919. In 1924 the company was renamed Enso-Gutzeit.

Enso-Gutzeit went from 400,000 hectares (99 acres) of forestlands in 1913 to 523,000 hectares (129 acres) in 1939. Russia attacked Finland that year, and in the armistice, Finland ceded land on which Enso-Gutzeit had many of its operations. However, post-war devastation in the former Russia created Soviet demand for the company's building products.

In the 1950s and 1960s the company added a paper mill, a box factory, bleaching plants, and pulp mills. It entered Canada through a 50% stake (obtaining full ownership in 1979) in Eurocan Pulp & Paper in 1970.

Enso-Gutzeit took part in a 1980s Finnish consolidation trend by buying rival A. Ahlstrom Oy's pulp and paper mills. The company merged with Veitsiluoto in 1996 to form Enso Oy. Two years later Enso Oy merged with Stora to form Stora Enso.

Stora Enso bought US-based Consolidated Papers (now Stora Enso North America) for $4.9 billion in 2000. The next year Stora Enso dissolved its pulp division by reallocating the mills to divisions that use pulp in their operations. In 2002 the company sold 300,000 acres of forestland, primarily in Wisconsin and Michigan, to paper maker Plum Creek Timber Company for about $140 million. The same year Finland announced that it was reducing its stake in Stora Enso to 10.8%.

EXECUTIVES

Chairman: Claes Dahlbäck
Vice Chairman: Krister Ahlström
CEO and Director: Jukka Härmälä
Deputy CEO and Director: Björn Hägglund
SEVP and CFO, Accounting, and Legal Affairs: Esko Mäkeläinen
SEVP, Corporate Support and Northern European Forest Units: Yngve Stade
SEVP, Fine Paper: Jussi Huttunen
SEVP, Magazine Paper: Bernd Rettig
SEVP, Newsprint: Lars Bengtsson
SEVP, Packaging Boards Country Manager, Finland: Pekka Laaksonen
SEVP, Timber Products: Arno Pelkonen
SEVP, Stora Enso North America: Kai Korhonen
EVP, Asia Pacific: Seppo Hietanen
EVP, Corporate Communications: Kari Vainio
EVP, Corporate Strategy Investments and Business Planning: Magnus Diesen
EVP, Human Resources and TQM: Christer Ågren
EVP, Market Services and Information Technology: Nils Grafström
SVP, Investor Relations: Keith B. Russell
SVP, Legal Affairs: Jyrki Kurkinen
SVP, Stora Enso North America: John Bergin
Auditors: SVH Pricewaterhouse Coopers Oy

LOCATIONS

HQ: Kanavaranta 1, PO Box 309, FIN-00101 Helsinki, Finland
Phone: +358-2046-131   **Fax:** +358-2046-21471
Web: www.storaenso.com
Stora Enso Oyj has operations in Europe, Asia, and North America.

2002 Sales

	% of total
Europe	81
US	15
Canada	2
China	1
Other regions	1
Total	**100**

PRODUCTS/OPERATIONS

2002 Sales

	% of total
Fine paper	21
Packaging board	21
Magazine paper	21
Forest	13
Newsprint	11
Timber products	8
Merchants	5
Other	—
Total	**100**

Selected Products

Book paper	Graphic board
Business forms	Graphic paper
Cartonboards	Kraft papers
Coreboards and tubes	Laminated papers
Corrugated boxes	Liquid packaging boards
Digital papers	Magazine paper
Directory paper	Newsprint
Document papers	Paper-grade pulp
Envelope papers	Sawn boards
Fluff pulp	Scholastic paper
Food service boards	

COMPETITORS

Abitibi-Consolidated	Norske Skog
Boise Cascade	Smurfit-Stone Container
International Paper	UPM-Kymmene
Kinnevik	Weyerhaeuser
Myllykoski Paper	

HISTORICAL FINANCIALS

Company Type: Public

Income Statement

FYE: December 31

	REVENUE ($ mil.)	NET INCOME ($ mil.)	NET PROFIT MARGIN	EMPLOYEES
12/02	13,426	(233)	—	42,461
12/01	13,386	918	6.9%	42,932
12/00	12,259	1,352	11.0%	41,785
12/99	10,734	759	7.1%	40,226
12/98	12,240	223	1.8%	40,987
12/97	5,371	106	2.0%	19,870
12/96	5,575	224	4.0%	19,094
12/95	6,424	398	6.2%	19,298
12/94	5,017	243	4.8%	19,334
12/93	3,517	(27)	—	18,753
Annual Growth	**16.0%**	**—**	**—**	**9.5%**

2002 Year-End Financials

Debt ratio: 55.5%	No. of shares (mil.): 900
Return on equity: —	Dividends
Cash ($ mil.): 177	Yield: 3.8%
Current ratio: 1.82	Payout: —
Long-term debt ($ mil.): 4,753	Market value ($ mil.): 9,412

Stock History   NYSE: SEO

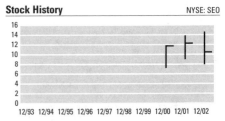

12/93 12/94 12/95 12/96 12/97 12/98 12/99 12/00 12/01 12/02

	STOCK PRICE ($) FY Close	P/E High/Low		PER SHARE ($) Earnings	Dividends	Book Value
12/02	10.46	—	—	(0.26)	0.40	9.52
12/01	12.26	13	9	1.02	0.00	9.82
12/00	11.75	7	4	1.66	0.00	8.86
Annual Growth	**(5.6%)**	**—**	**—**	**—**	**—**	**3.6%**

Suez

Having dredged up success from the Suez to the sewers, Suez is channeling its efforts into utility operations around the world. The company operates in more than 130 countries and provides electricity, natural gas, water, and waste management services. Suez's Tractebel unit is a leading global independent power producer and Belgium's top utility holding company. Its water business, ONDEO, is the world's second-largest, behind the water unit of Veolia Environnement (formerly Vivendi Environnement). Its SITA unit is one of Europe's top waste management firms.

Tractebel owns nearly 49,000 MW of electric generating capacity, procures and transmits natural gas, and distributes and trades energy. Suez's ONDEO unit provides water and wastewater services to about 125 million people and 60,000 businesses. Suez has restructured its operations by combining its ONDEO, SITA, and Degrémont (water treatment plant construction) units under the Suez Environment banner.

Suez is divesting noncore assets, including interests in manufacturing, construction, and financial services companies, to reduce debt. The company has sold subsidiary Nalco (formerly ONDEO Nalco) to a consortium of US equity firms (Blackstone Group, Apollo Management, and Goldman Sachs) in a $4.4 billion deal. It has also agreed to sell a 75% stake in its UK water utility, Northumbrian Water, to a group of institutional investors, and it is selling its remaining communications assets.

The energy conglomerate was formed by the 1997 merger of Compagnie de Suez (builder of the Suez Canal) and water treatment and engineering giant Lyonnaise des Eaux.

HISTORY

The first canal in Egypt was dug in the 13th century BC, but it was Napoleon who revived the idea of a shorter trade route to India: a canal through Egypt linking the Gulf of Suez with the Mediterranean. Former French diplomat and engineer Ferdinand de Lesseps formed Compagnie Universelle du Canal Maritime de Suez in 1858 to build and eventually operate the canal, which opened 11 years later. Egypt's modernization had pushed it into debt and increased its ties to the

British government, which, by 1875, had acquired a 44% stake in the company.

For more than 80 years the Suez Canal was a foreign enclave, protected by the British Army since 1936. After Egypt's puppet government fell, and as Gamal Abd Al-Nasser assumed power in 1956, British troops exited the Canal Zone, which Egypt quickly nationalized. Israel, Britain, and France attacked, but the United Nations arranged a truce and foreign forces withdrew, leaving the Suez in Egypt's control.

With no canal to operate, Universelle du Canal Maritime de Suez became Compagnie Financière de Suez in 1958. A year later it created a bank (which became Banque Indosuez in 1974).

In 1967 Financière de Suez became the largest shareholder in Société Lyonnaise des Eaux et de L'Eclairage, a leading French water company. Formed in 1880, Lyonnaise des Eaux had stakes in water (Northumbrian Water) and energy (Elyo). After France's energy firms were nationalized in 1946, Lyonnaise des Eaux dipped deeper into the water industry by acquiring Degrémont (now Ondeo-Degrémont) in 1972. It also purchased stakes in waste management (SITA, 1970) and heating systems (Cofreth, 1975).

In the 1980s Lyonnaise des Eaux expanded in Spain, the UK, and the US, and diversified into cable TV (1986) and broadcast TV (1987). It merged with construction firm Dumez in 1990.

Meanwhile, Financière de Suez became a financial power when it won a controlling stake in Société Générale de Belgique (SGB) in 1988 and bought Groupe Victoire in 1989. But the two buys left the firm (renamed Compagnie de Suez in 1990) deeply in debt.

Losing money, Compagnie de Suez disposed of Victoire (1994) and then the valuable Banque Indosuez (1996). In 1996 the company bought a controlling stake in Belgium's top utility, Tractebel. Compagnie de Suez and Lyonnaise des Eaux merged in 1997 to create Suez Lyonnaise des Eaux. The following year Suez Lyonnaise acquired the rest of SGB and bought the European and Asian operations of waste management giant Browning-Ferris Industries; it also began divesting noncore operations.

Suez Lyonnaise in 1999 expanded its core businesses, primarily in the US. The company bought Calgon (water treatment, US) and Nalco Chemical (water treatment chemicals, US), then merged Calgon into Nalco (now Ondeo Nalco).

In 2000 Suez Lyonnaise bought United Water Resources and acquired the rest of SITA. Through its Elyo subsidiary, Suez Lyonnaise bought out minority shareholders in US-based Trigen Energy. The company also merged its construction unit, Groupe GTM, with French rival VINCI; Suez Lyonnaise then sold the VINCI shares that it received from the transaction.

The next year the company shortened its name to Suez as part of a global rebranding effort. It also united its water services operations under the ONDEO brand. In 2002 Suez made Tractebel a wholly owned subsidiary by purchasing the remaining publicly held shares. Also in 2002, Suez sold minority stakes in communications equipment manufacturer Sagem, steelmaker Arcelor, and motorway operator Autopistas Concesionaria Española (ACESA).

Suez divested most of its 11% stake in Belgian insurance firm Fortis for nearly $2 billion in 2003. It also sold its 79% stake in cable company Coditel that year.

EXECUTIVES

Chairman and CEO: Gérard Mestrallet, age 54
Vice Chairman: Baron Albert Frère, age 77
Vice Chairman: Jean Gandois, age 73
SEVP and COO; Chairman of the General Management Committee and CEO, Tractebel; Chairman, Electrabel: Jean-Pierre Hansen, age 55
SEVP Business Strategy and Development: Patrick Buffet
SEVP International Affairs and Institutional Relations: Yves-Thibault de Silguy
EVP Finance and CFO: Gérard Lamarche, age 41
EVP Communications: Valérie Bernis
EVP Human Resources; Vice Chairman, Electrabel: Emmanuel van Innis, age 56
EVP Operational Assistance: Jérôme Tolot, age 50
EVP Electricity and Gas Europe; Executive Director Electricity and Gas Europe, Tractebel; CEO, Electrabel: Willy Bosmans, age 56
EVP Electricity and Gas International; Executive Director Electricity and Gas International, Tractebel; CEO, Tractebel Electricity and Gas International: Dirk Beeuwsaert
EVP Environmental Local Services; Chairman and CEO, Suez Environment: Jacques Pétry
Group SVP Organization and Central Services and Chief Risk Officer: Henry Masson, age 51
General Secretary and Group Ethics Officer: Patrick Ouart, age 43
Chairman and CEO, ONDEO-Degrémont: Jean-Louis Chaussade
Auditors: Barbier Frinault & Autres; Deloitte Touche Tohmatsu — Audit

LOCATIONS

HQ: 16, rue de la Ville l'Evêque, 75008 Paris, France
Phone: +33-1-40-06-64-00   **Fax:** +33-1-40-06-66-10
Web: www.suez.fr

2002 Sales

	$ mil.	% of total
Europe		
Belgium	11,393	24
France	10,472	22
UK	3,977	8
Other EU countries	11,116	23
Other European countries	1,408	3
North America	4,894	10
South America	2,204	4
Asia & Oceania	1,967	4
Middle East	977	2
Total	**48,408**	**100**

PRODUCTS/OPERATIONS

2002 Sales

	$ mil.	% of total
Energy	31,034	64
Environment local services	13,589	28
Environment industrial services	3,108	7
Other	677	1
Total	**48,408**	**100**

Major Business Operations

Energy
Tractebel (Belgium)
Distrigas (47%)
Electrabel (50%)
Fluxys (47%)

Environment
Degrémont
ONDEO
Lyonnaise des Eaux France
United Water Resources (US)
SITA

Communications
Noos (50%)

COMPETITORS

ACEA	National Grid Transco
AWG	Philadelphia Suburban
Bouygues	RWE
Brambles	SABESP
CANAL+	Scottish Power
Covanta	Séché Environnement
Dragados	Severn Trent
Electricité de France	Thames Water
EnBW	United Utilities
Eni	Vattenfall
E.ON	Veolia Environnement
France Telecom	Waste Management

HISTORICAL FINANCIALS

Company Type: Public

Income Statement

FYE: December 31

	REVENUE ($ mil.)	NET INCOME ($ mil.)	NET PROFIT MARGIN	EMPLOYEES
12/02	48,408	(906)	—	198,750
12/01	37,755	1,860	4.9%	188,050
12/00	32,602	1,808	5.5%	173,200
12/99	31,682	2,719	8.6%	222,000
12/98	36,595	2,402	6.6%	210,100
12/97	31,743	669	2.1%	175,000
12/96	17,509	258	1.5%	116,290
12/95	20,089	185	0.9%	118,770
12/94	18,731	199	1.1%	151,873
12/93	15,801	136	0.9%	120,038
Annual Growth	**13.2%**	—	—	**5.8%**

2002 Year-End Financials

Debt ratio: 326.6%
Return on equity: —
Cash ($ mil.): 6,263
Current ratio: 1.45
Long-term debt ($ mil.): 36,282
No. of shares (mil.): 1,007
Dividends
Yield: 3.6%
Payout: —
Market value ($ mil.): 17,801

Stock History

NYSE: SZE

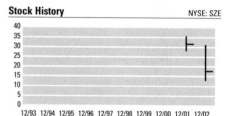

12/93 12/94 12/95 12/96 12/97 12/98 12/99 12/00 12/01 12/02

	STOCK PRICE ($) FY Close	P/E High/Low	PER SHARE ($) Earnings	Dividends	Book Value
12/02	17.67	— —	(0.91)	0.64	11.03
12/01	31.53	19 15	1.85	0.00	12.96
Annual Growth	**(44.0%)**	— —	—	—	**(14.9%)**

Suzuki Motor Corporation

Suzuki Motor Corporation has its shoulder to the wheel. The company is Japan's #1 minicar producer as well as its #3 motorcycle manufacturer (behind Honda and Yamaha). Suzuki's US cars and SUVs include the Aerio and the Grand Vitara; motorcycles include the Bandit, Katana, and Marauder. Suzuki's nonvehicle products include generators, outboard marine engines, and prefabricated housing. The company operates in more than 190 countries. Suzuki has partnered to make cars with General Motors and has agreed to develop motorcycles and ATVs with Kawasaki.

General Motors has invested in several Asian auto companies (including Isuzu Motors and Subaru maker Fuji Heavy Industries) to gain a better foothold in that market. GM took a 20% stake in Suzuki in a deal that gave the latter $600 million and strengthened cooperation in the development of small cars.

Suzuki and Kawasaki lag far behind Honda and Yamaha, which together account for 85% of the Japanese motorcycle market. The Suzuki/Kawasaki deal is aimed at closing the domestic market share gap while making further inroads to the lucrative Chinese market. Suzuki also has taken a 15% stake in troubled Korean carmaker GM Daewoo Auto & Technology (formerly Daewoo Motor). GM, Suzuki, and Shanghai Automotive Industry Corp. together control 67% of GM Daewoo. The deal is anticipated to give GM and Suzuki a better footing in the Asian market.

Suzuki's nonvehicle product lines (electric wheelchairs, generators, prefabricated houses, and outboard motors) have shrunk from representing 20% of total sales to making up less than 5%.

HISTORY

In 1909 Michio Suzuki started Suzuki Loom Works in Hamamatsu, Japan. The company went public in 1920 and continued producing weaving equipment until the onset of WWII, when it began to make war-related products.

Suzuki began developing inexpensive motor vehicles in 1947, and in 1952 it introduced a 36cc engine to motorize bicycles. The company changed its name to Suzuki Motor and launched its first motorcycle in 1954. Suzuki's entry into the minicar market came in 1955 with the Suzulight, followed by the Suzumoped (1958), a delivery van (1959), and the Suzulight Carry FB small truck (1961).

Suzuki's triumph in the 1962 50cc-class Isle of Man TT motorcycle race started a string of racing successes that brought international prominence to the Suzuki name. The company established its first overseas plant in Thailand in 1967.

In the 1970s Suzuki met market demand for motorcycles with large engines. Meanwhile, a mid-1970s recession and falling demand for low-powered cars in Japan led the minicar industry there to produce two-thirds fewer minicars in 1974 than in 1970. Suzuki responded by pushing overseas, beginning auto exports, and expanding foreign distribution. In 1975 it started producing motorcycles in Taiwan, Thailand, and Indonesia.

Suzuki boosted capacity internationally throughout the 1980s through joint ventures. Motorcycle sales in Japan peaked in 1982, then tapered off, but enjoyed a modest rebound in the late 1980s. In 1988 the company agreed to handle distribution of Peugeot cars in Japan.

Suzuki and General Motors began their long-standing relationship in 1981 when GM bought a small stake in Suzuki. The company began producing Swift subcompacts in 1983 and sold them through GM as the Chevy Sprint and, later, the Geo Metro. In 1986 Suzuki and GM of Canada jointly formed CAMI Automotive to produce vehicles, including Sprints, Metros, and Geo Track-

ers (Suzuki Sidekicks), in Ontario; production began in 1989.

Although sales via GM increased through 1990, US efforts with the Suzuki nameplate faltered shortly after Suzuki formed its US subsidiary in Brea, California, in 1986. A 1988 *Consumer Reports* claim that the company's Samurai SUV was prone to rolling over devastated US sales. The next year Suzuki's top US executives quit, apparently questioning the company's commitment to the US market.

Suzuki established Magyar Suzuki, a joint venture with Hungarian automaker Autokonszern Rt., C. Itoh & Co., and International Finance Corporation in 1991 to begin producing the Swift sedan in Hungary. The company expanded a licensing agreement with a Chinese government partner in 1993, becoming the first Japanese company to take an equity stake in a Chinese car-making venture. The next year Suzuki introduced the Alto van, Japan's cheapest car, at just over $5,000, and the Wagon R miniwagon, which quickly became one of Japan's top-selling vehicles.

In a case that was later overturned, a woman was awarded $90 million from Suzuki after being paralyzed in a Samurai rollover in 1990. The company sued Consumers Union, publisher of *Consumer Reports,* in 1996, charging it had intended to fix the results in the 1988 Samurai testing.

GM raised its 3% stake in Suzuki to 10% in 1998. The company teamed up with GM and Fuji Heavy Industries (Subaru) in 2000 to develop compact cars for the European market. It was also announced that GM would spend about $600 million to double its stake in Suzuki to 20%. In 2001 Suzuki announced that it had agreed to cooperate with Kawasaki in the development of new motorcycles, scooters, and ATVs.

The following year Suzuki agreed to take control of Maruti Udyog Ltd., the state-owned India-based car manufacturer, in an $80 million rights issue deal. Additional shares will be made available in a public offering.

EXECUTIVES

Chairman and CEO: Osamu Suzuki
President and COO: Hiroshi Tsuda
EVP: Sokichi Nakano
Senior Managing Director: Osamu Matsuoka
Senior Managing Director: Shunichi Wakuda
Managing Director: Takao Hirosawa
Managing Director: Sadayuki Inobe
Managing Director: Akio Kosugi
Managing Director: Shinzo Nakanishi
Managing Director: Takashi Nakayama
Managing Director: Akihiro Sakamoto
Managing Director: Junzo Sugimori
Managing Director: Kazuyoshi Suzuki
Managing Director: Yasuhiro Yamada
Auditors: Seimei Audit Corporation

LOCATIONS

HQ: 300 Takatsuka, Hamamatsu,
  Shizuoka 432-8611, Japan
Phone: +81-53-440-2061   **Fax:** +81-53-440-2776
US HQ: 3251 E. Imperial Hwy., Brea, CA 92821-6795
US Phone: 714-996-7040   **US Fax:** 714-524-8499
Web: www.globalsuzuki.com

Suzuki Motor Corporation operates major subsidiaries in Australia, Austria, Cambodia, Canada, Colombia, France, Germany, Hungary, India, Indonesia, Italy, Myanmar, New Zealand, Pakistan, the Philippines, Poland, Spain, Thailand, the UK, and the US. It distributes its products in more than 190 countries.

2003 Sales

	$ mil.	% of total
Asia		
Japan	9,388	56
Other countries	2,257	13
North America	2,525	15
Europe	2,459	15
Other regions	187	1
Total	**16,816**	**100**

PRODUCTS/OPERATIONS

2003 Sales

	$ mil.	% of total
Automobiles	13,503	80
Motorcycles	2,902	17
Other products	411	3
Total	**16,816**	**100**

Selected Products

Cars, Minicars, and SUVs	Intruder 1400
Aerio Sedan	Intruder LC1500
Aerio SX	Intruder Volusia
Alto	Katana 600
Carry	Katana 750
Forenza	Marauder 1600
Grand Vitara	RM85
Ignis	RM125
Ignis Sport	RM250
Jimny	Savage 650
Verona	SV650
Vitara V6	
Wagon R	**All Terrain Vehicles**
XL-7	Eiger 400 2X4
	Eiger 400 4X4
Motorcycles	Eiger 400 Automatic 2X4
Bandit 1200S	Eiger 400 Automatic 4X4
DR650SE	Ozark 250
DR-Z250	QuadSport Z400
DR-Z400	Twin Peaks 700 4X4
DR-Z400E	Vinson 500 4X4
DR-Z400S	
DR-Z125L	**Other Products**
GS500F	Electro-scooters
GSX-R600	General-purpose engines
GSX-R750	Generators
GSX-R1000	Motorized wheelchairs
GZ250	Outboard motors
Hayabusa	Prefabricated houses
Intruder 800	

COMPETITORS

BMW
Bombardier
Brunswick
DaimlerChrysler
Delco Remy
Dover
Ek Chor China Motorcycle
Fiat
Ford
General Motors
Harley-Davidson
Honda
Hyundai Motor
Invacare
Isuzu
Kawasaki Heavy Industries
Kohler
Mazda
Nissan
Peugeot Motors of
  America, Inc.
Piaggio
Renault
Saab Automobile
Toyota
Triumph Motorcycles
Volkswagen
Volvo
Yamaha Motor

HISTORICAL FINANCIALS

Company Type: Public

Income Statement FYE: March 31

	REVENUE ($ mil.)	NET INCOME ($ mil.)	NET PROFIT MARGIN	EMPLOYEES
3/03	16,816	259	1.5%	13,920
3/02	12,577	169	1.3%	14,260
3/01	12,668	160	1.3%	14,460
3/00	14,418	255	1.8%	14,800
3/99	12,223	205	1.7%	14,760
3/98	11,188	227	2.0%	14,610
3/97	12,136	271	2.2%	13,873
3/96	12,877	248	1.9%	14,650
3/95	14,539	232	1.6%	13,455
3/94	11,942	148	1.2%	13,218
Annual Growth	3.9%	6.4%	—	0.6%

2003 Year-End Financials

Debt ratio: 8.7%
Return on equity: 5.1%
Cash ($ mil.): 1,488
Current ratio: 1.25
Long-term debt ($ mil.): 473

Net Income History OTC: SZKMF

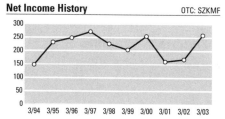

The Swatch Group Ltd.

Swatch is worth watching. The Swatch Group (formerly Société Suisse de Microélectronique & d'Horlogerie) is the world's second-largest watchmaker (after Citizen Watch). Its watches range from low-priced, collectible Swatch and Flik Flak to premium-priced Longines, Blancpain, and Omega brands. Swatch watches are sold at some 15,000 retailers worldwide, plus at more than 500 Swatch stores, about 1,000 shop-in-shops, and some 140 kiosks. Its Dress Your Body subsidiary makes jewelry. Chairman Nicolas Hayek's family controls about 37% of The Swatch Group.

The Swatch Group holds 25% of the world's watch market.

The company, which has more than 100 subsidiaries and affiliated units, also makes watch components and private-label watches. In addition, it makes semiconductors, quartz oscillators, and industrial lasers, among other items, for industries such as telecommunications and medical electronics. It also provides timing and scoring services at major sporting events such as the Olympic Games.

HISTORY

The Swatch Group was first established when watchmakers ASUAG and SSIH were merged in 1983. ASUAG was founded in 1931 in Switzerland to make watches. By the late 1970s ASUAG

had acquired some 100 family-owned companies, many of which were operating independently and inefficiently. When it merged with SSIH, ASUAG owned the Longines and Rado brands and made watch components.

Watchmaker SSIH was formed in 1930 with the merger of brands Tissot and Omega (which traced its history to 1848). SSIH and other Swiss watchmakers were struggling by the late 1970s. The market was flooded with cheaper watches made in Japan and Hong Kong that used quartz technology (a technology invented — but ignored — by the Swiss). SSIH had licensed out its prestigious Omega brand to other manufacturers in various countries, hurting that brand's reputation.

With both ASUAG and SSIH on the verge of bankruptcy, Swiss banks named Nicolas Hayek (then the CEO of consulting firm Hayek Engineering) to advise the companies on their futures. He recommended that ASUAG and SSIH merge and then mass-produce a low-cost watch and sell it globally at a set price. The two companies merged in 1983, forming SMH (Société Suisse de Microélectronique & d'Horlogerie); its headquarters were ASUAG's in Biel, Switzerland.

SMH had sales of about $1.1 billion with losses of some $124 million in 1983. That year it introduced the Swatch watch amid some resistance and objections that the watch would ruin the Swiss image of makers of high-quality, premium-priced watches. But Swatch watches became fashion statements and pop-culture icons in the 1980s and Hayek, who spearheaded the turnaround, became a Swiss business hero. Hayek and a group of investors bought a controlling 51% stake of SMH, and he became CEO in 1985.

In 1992 the company bought Blancpain (luxury watches) and Frederic Piguet (luxury watch components). By 1993 SMH had expanded into semiconductor chips, pagers, and telephones. The next year it formed a joint venture (19%-owned by SMH) called Micro Compact Car (MCC) with Daimler-Benz to make a battery-and-gasoline powered Swatchmobile.

Because of difficulty in translating its name into other languages, the company changed its name in 1998 to The Swatch Group. That year it also sold its 19% stake in MCC to Daimler-Benz. In 1999 Swatch bought Groupe Horloger Breguet, a manufacturer of mechanical timepieces since 1775, and Swiss watch case maker Favre & Perret. In 2000 the growing company pocketed German luxury watchmaker Glashütter, among others. Acquisitions in 2001 included two Greek companies, Aliki Perri and Alikonia. Swatch bought Swiss watch dial maker Rubattel & Weyermann in 2002. Later that year Hayek retired as CEO, but remained chairman; his son Nicolas became CEO.

EXECUTIVES

Chairman: H. C. Nicolas G. Hayek Sr., age 74
CEO: G. Nicolas (Nick) Hayek Jr., age 48
SVP and CFO: Edgar Geiser
SVP, Human Resources and General Counsel: Hanspeter Rentsch
Company Secretary: Roland Bloch
Corporate Treasurer: Thomas Dürr
Assistant CFO and Investor Relations: Pia Tschannen
Head of Public Relations: Beatrice Howald
Assistant Public Relations: Sandra Obergsell
Auditors: PricewaterhouseCoopers Ltd.

LOCATIONS

HQ: Faubourg du Lac 6, CH-2501 Biel, Bern, Switzerland
Phone: +41-32-343-68-11   **Fax:** +41-32-343-69-11
US HQ: 1200 Harbor Blvd., Weehawken, NJ 07086
US Phone: 201-271-1400   **US Fax:** 201-271-4633
Web: www.swatchgroup.com

The Swatch Group sells its products worldwide. It has more than 150 manufacturing facilities, plus other operations in 50 countries throughout the world.

PRODUCTS/OPERATIONS

Selected Products and Brands

Watches
Basic Range
  Flik Flak
  Swatch
High Range
  Longines
  Rado
Middle Range
  Calvin Klein
  Certina
  Hamilton
  Mido
  Pierre Balmain
  Tissot
Prestige
  Blancpain
  Breguet
  Glashüte Original/Union
  Jaquet-Droz
  Léon Hatot
  Omega
Private Label
  Endura

Jewelry
Dress Your Body

Retailing
Les Boutiques

Selected Electronic Systems Operations

Asulab (research and development of watches and components and microtechnical products)
EM Microelectronic-Marin (semiconductors, LCDs)
Lasag (industrial lasers)
Micro Crystal (watch crystals, miniature oven oscillators, crystals for telecommunications, medical electronics, aerospace, automotive, and computer industries)
Microcomponents SA (precision micromechanical parts and components for automotive, electrical appliance, and watchmaking industries; miniaturized stepping motors)
Oscilloquartz (quartz crystal oscillators for telecommunications)
Renata (batteries for cellular phones, hearing aids, and other electronics)
SMH Immeubles SA (real estate)
Swiss Timing Ltd. (timing and scoring for major sporting events)

COMPETITORS

Benetton
Bulgari
CASIO COMPUTER
Citizen Watch
E. Gluck
Fossil
Guess
Hermès
Loews
LVMH
Rolex
Movado Group
Richemont
Seiko
Tiffany
Timex

HISTORICAL FINANCIALS

Company Type: Public

Income Statement

FYE: December 31

	REVENUE ($ mil.)	NET INCOME ($ mil.)	NET PROFIT MARGIN	EMPLOYEES
12/02	2,835	356	12.6%	20,327
12/01	2,420	301	12.4%	19,665
12/00	2,563	404	15.8%	17,719
12/99	2,279	282	12.4%	17,751
12/98	2,311	260	11.2%	18,000
12/97	2,032	225	11.1%	17,729
12/96	2,024	209	10.3%	16,459
12/95	2,220	237	10.7%	17,082
12/94	1,978	241	12.2%	16,363
12/93	1,861	296	15.9%	15,039
Annual Growth	4.8%	2.1%	—	3.4%

2002 Year-End Financials

Debt ratio: 0.3%
Return on equity: 15.8%
Cash ($ mil.): 619

Current ratio: 3.96
Long-term debt ($ mil.): 9

Net Income History

Pink Sheets: SWGAF

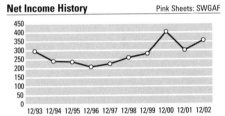

Swire Pacific

Swire Pacific has interests in airlines, beverages, and manufacturing, but the *hong* (general trading company) bases its prosperity on property in Hong Kong, where it holds some prime commercial real estate. The company's airline holdings include stakes in Cathay Pacific Airways and regional Chinese carrier Dragonair. Swire Pacific has extensive interests in apparel, sugar, and other manufacturing operations and is a major Coca-Cola bottler in southern China. Joint ventures include a paint factory and sporting goods stores. The firm is controlled by its founding family, through UK-based John Swire & Sons, which owns 28% of Swire Pacific and more than 50% of its voting stock.

Despite regional economic turmoil, Swire Pacific is committed to building new office space in Hong Kong and to investing in Cathay Pacific. Not wanting to be shut out when the UK gave up control of Hong Kong, Swire Pacific over the years has assiduously allied itself with Chinese interests through joint ventures in Hong Kong and Taiwan and on the mainland.

HISTORY

John Swire began a Liverpool trading company in 1816. By the time he died in 1847, the company, John Swire & Sons, derived much of its revenues from the US cotton trade. One of Swire's sons, John Samuel Swire, refocused the company on Chinese tea and textiles during the US Civil War. Unhappy with his representatives in Asia, Swire went to Shanghai and in 1866 partnered

with customer Richard Butterfield. Butterfield & Swire (B&S) took *Taikoo* ("great and ancient") as a Chinese name. Butterfield soon left, but his name lived on with the company until 1974.

By 1868 B&S had offices in New York and Yokohama, Japan; it added a Hong Kong office two years later. The firm created China Navigation Company in 1872 to transport goods on the Yangtze River; the shipping line served all the major Pacific Rim ports by the late 1880s. Hong Kong-based Taikoo Sugar Refinery began operations in 1884.

The third John Swire took over B&S in 1898 and built the Taikoo Dockyard in Hong Kong. The company's Chinese operations were eventually devastated by the Japanese attack on China in 1937, WWII, and the Communist takeover in 1949. However, the company had rebuilt in Hong Kong, and in 1948 it bought control of Cathay Pacific, a Hong Kong airline with six DC-3s.

In the 1950s and 1960s the Swire family expanded the airline and established airport and aircraft service companies. Swire Pacific, the holding company for most of the family's Hong Kong interests, went public in 1959. It won the Coca-Cola bottling franchise for Hong Kong in 1965. The fifth generation of Swires, John and Adrian, took command of parent company John Swire & Sons in 1968 (Adrian became chairman in 1987). The Taikoo Dockyard merged its business with Hongkong & Whampoa Dockyard in 1972.

The 1984 agreement to return Hong Kong to Chinese control in 1997 plunged the colony into uncertainty. Capital flight and free-falling real estate values gave Swire an opportunity to pick up properties at bargain prices.

Meanwhile, Cathay Pacific had become a major Pacific carrier. In 1987 Swire sold about 12% of the airline to CITIC, China's state-owned overseas investment company. (CITIC later increased its share.) Three years later Swire bought 35% of Hong Kong's Dragonair, also partly owned by CITIC, and gave it Cathay Pacific's Shanghai and Beijing routes.

In the 1990s Swire's financial results and property values fluctuated along with confidence about the consequences of China's takeover. In 1997 Swire expanded its Chinese operations, acquiring the rights to distribute Volvo cars in China and Hong Kong. As Asian financial markets collapsed, Swire sold its insurance-underwriting businesses to focus on core operations. Adrian Swire stepped down that year, relinquishing the John Swire & Sons chairmanship to a nonfamily member, Edward Scott.

To expand its dwindling undeveloped property base, in 1998 a Swire-led consortium bought a reclaimed waterfront site on Hong Kong Island. Reflecting a rebounding economy, in 1999 the company sold more than 274,000 sq. ft. of Hong Kong office space to Time Warner and Cable & Wireless HKT.

In 2000 Swire sold health care and medical products trading unit Swire Loxley to diversified Chinese company CITIC Pacific. In 2001 Swire Properties announced plans to build a major retail, office, and hotel project in Guangzhou in a joint venture with the Guangzhou Daily Group.

That year Swire sold its 49% stake in Carlsberg Brewery Hong Kong Ltd., in order to focus on its growing regional soft drinks operations. The company sold its 49% stake in Schneider Swire Ltd. to joint venture partner Schneider Electric Industries in 2002. Also that year Swire agreed to sell its controlling stake in its Coca-Cola bottling plant in Dongguan, China, to Coca-Cola.

EXECUTIVES

Chairman, Swire Pacific, Cathay Pacific Airways, and Swire Properties: James W. J. Hughes-Hallett, age 52
Finance Director: M. Cubbon, age 44
Director, Aviation Division; Deputy Chairman and CEO, Cathay Pacific Airways; Chairman, Hong Kong Aircraft Engineering: D. M. Turnbull, age 46
Director, Property Division; Managing Director, Swire Properties: K. G. Kerr, age 49
Chairman, Taiwan Operations: Davy Ho, age 54
Auditors: PricewaterhouseCoopers

LOCATIONS

HQ: Swire Pacific Limited
35th Fl., 2 Pacific Place,
88 Queensway, , Hong Kong
Phone: +852-2840-8098   **Fax:** +852-2526-9365
Web: www.swirepacific.com

2002 Sales

	% of total
Hong Kong	50
Other Asia	23
North America	21
Shipping	6
Total	**100**

PRODUCTS/OPERATIONS

2002 Sales

	% of total
Bottling	32
Rent	31
Goods	23
Services	7
Sales of property	7
Total	**100**

Selected Subsidiaries

AHK Air Hong Kong Ltd. (34%, cargo airline)
Cathay Pacific Airways Ltd. (46%)
Crown Can Hong Kong Ltd. (45%)
Hong Kong Aircraft Engineering Company (HAECO, 45%)
Hong Kong Dragon Airlines Ltd. (16%)
Hongkong United Dockyards Ltd. (50%)
ICI Swire Paints Ltd. (40%)
Reebok Hong Kong Ltd. (67%, marketing and distribution of footwear, apparel, and accesssories)
Swire Beverages Holdings Ltd.
Swire Coca-Cola HK Ltd. (88%, soft drink production and distribution)
Swire Coca-Cola Taiwan Ltd. (79%, soft drink production and distribution)
Swire Pacific Holdings Inc. (US)
Swire Pacific Offshore Holdings Ltd. (holding company, Bermuda)
Swire Pacific Ship Management Ltd. (ship personnel management)
Swire Properties Ltd.
Swire Resources Ltd (general trading and retailing)
Taikoo Motors Ltd. (automobile distribution)
Waylung Waste Collection Ltd. (50%)

COMPETITORS

AMR	Marks & Spencer
China Southern Airlines	Northwest Airlines
Hopewell Holdings	PepsiCo
HSBC Holdings	Qantas
Hutchison Whampoa	Sime Darby
ITOCHU	Singapore Airlines
Japan Airlines	UAL
Jardine Matheson	WBL Corporation
Kumagai Gumi	Wing Tai Holdings

HISTORICAL FINANCIALS

Company Type: Public

Income Statement

FYE: December 31

	REVENUE ($ mil.)	NET INCOME ($ mil.)	NET PROFIT MARGIN	EMPLOYEES
12/02	1,951	693	35.5%	58,000
12/01	1,948	528	27.1%	55,000
12/00	1,929	499	25.8%	60,000
12/99	2,170	571	26.3%	60,000
12/98	2,182	228	10.4%	58,000
12/97	3,163	862	27.2%	60,000
12/96	4,847	990	20.4%	56,000
12/95	6,939	835	12.0%	37,000
12/94	6,155	719	11.7%	35,000
12/93	5,278	603	11.4%	30,000
Annual Growth	(10.5%)	1.6%	—	7.6%

2002 Year-End Financials

Debt ratio: 7.7%
Return on equity: 7.6%
Cash ($ mil.): 61
Current ratio: 0.47
Long-term debt ($ mil.): 683

Net Income History

OTC: SWRAY

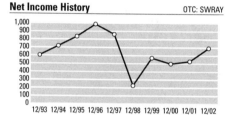

Tata Group

Founded as a textile trader more than a century ago, the Tata Group now includes enough businesses to blanket India. The nation's largest industrial conglomerate, Tata runs about 80 companies in seven main business sectors: chemicals, communications and IT, consumer products, energy, engineering, materials, and services. Two of its largest operations are steelmaking, through Tata Steel (Tisco), and vehicle manufacturing, through Tata Engineering. Tata is restructuring its vast empire to reduce hierarchy, focus on profitable operations, and increase efficiency. The group is managed through holding company Tata Sons, which controls the Tata brand.

Although a recessionary economy has hurt India's heavy industries, Tata has offset downturns with operations such as IT unit Tata Consultancy Services (TCS). The group is working to expand its telecommunications businesses.

The Tata family's ownership stakes in group companies are managed through Tata Sons, the group's principal investment holding company, of which the family owns about 3%. Much of the rest is held by charitable trusts established by the Tata family; more than 60% of Tata Sons' profits are channeled into philanthropic trusts. Tata Sons generally holds only minority stakes in the group's companies but maintains control with the support of other investors, including state-owned financial institutions.

HISTORY

Jamsetji Tata, a Parsi (Zoroastrian) from Bombay, started a textile trading company in 1868. He began in textile manufacturing, then embarked on a mission to industrialize India. Before his death in 1904 Tata had built the Taj Mahal Hotel in Bombay and set in motion plans to create a hydroelectric power plant, a forum for technical education and research in India, and a steel mill to supply rapidly expanding railroads.

Jamsetji's son Dorabji carried on. Dorabji found a jungle site for the steel mill, renamed the area Jamshedpur after his father, and in 1907 established Tata Iron and Steel Company (Tisco). Three years later Tata Hydro-Electric Power went on line. By 1911 Jamsetji's plans were realized when the Indian Institute of Science opened.

The British chairman of the Railway Board promised "to eat every pound of steel rail" Tata made. Tata shipped 1,500 miles of rail to British troops in Mesopotamia during WWI.

Six years after Dorabji's death in 1932, J. R. D. Tata, the son of Dorabji's cousin, took over the family empire. India's first licensed pilot, J. R. D. had started Tata Airlines, later nationalized as Air India. He started Tata Chemicals in 1939. After WWII and Indian independence, the government built a state-owned steel industry but allowed Tata's mills to operate through a grandfather clause. Inefficient government operations led to high fixed prices for steel, and Tata profited.

Tata Engineering & Locomotive Co. (Telco), founded in 1945 to make steam locomotives, entered truck production in 1954 by collaborating with Daimler-Benz (now DaimlerChrysler). With help from Swiss firm Volkart Brothers, the company also started the Voltas manufacturing conglomerate. In 1962 Tata joined James Finlay of Scotland to create Tata-Finlay, now Tata Tea.

For a long time India's socialist government and unwieldy bureaucracy hampered Tata. The group was reluctant to pay bribes for licenses to enter new fields, and red tape and trade restrictions discouraged expansion abroad. A 1970 antitrust law ended the "managing agency" system, in which Tata Sons had held interests in subsidiaries and Tata Industries managed them for a fee; the subsidiaries became independently managed.

J. R. D. retired as chairman in 1991, and his nephew Ratan Tata took control of the company. In 1994 Tata formed a major alliance with Daimler-Benz to assemble cars. A Tata IBM joint venture in 1997 launched the first computer operating system in Hindi, India's national language (Tata sold its IBM stake in 1999).

Not every new venture flew. In 1998 Tata dropped a proposal to start an Indian airline that hadn't won government approval after three years. In 2000 Tata Tea bought UK tea bag maker Tetley, an acquisition that made Tata the world's largest tea producer. In 2001 Tata made plans to sell its pharmaceuticals unit (Rallis India) and float 10% of its information technology unit (TCS). That year Tata joined Singapore Airlines in bidding for a 40% stake in Air India being offered by the Indian government. Later in the year, however, Singapore Airlines withdrew and the deal fell through.

In 2002 Tata acquired a 25% stake in telecom giant Videsh Sanchar Nigam Ltd. (VSNL), from the Indian government. Tata said it would combine its Tata Teleservices unit with VSNL. In 2003 Tata International formed an alliance with Turbo Genset Company Limited (UK) to develop and distribute generational products and solutions used in the power generation industry.

EXECUTIVES

Chairman: Ratan N. Tata, age 65
Executive Office Member and Finance Director, Tata Sons; Director-In-Charge, Tata Financial Services: Ishaat Hussain
Executive Office Member and Human Resource Director, Tata Sons: R. Gopalakrishnan
Executive Office Member, Tata Sons: Kishor Chaukar
President, Tata Indicom Enterprise Business Unit: Ajay Pandey
CEO and SVP, Indian Hotels International Division: Rajiv Gujral
CEO, Tata Quality Management Services: Jehangir Ardeshir
EVP, Human Resources: Satish Pradhan
SVP Finance and Secretary, Tata Sons: Farokh N. Subedar
Managing Director, Tata Chemicals: Prasad Menon
Managing Director, Tata Power: Firdose Ardeshir Vandrevala
Managing Director, Tata Services: Tehmuras Rustom Doongaji
Managing Director, Tata Steel: B. Muthuraman, age 57
Executive Director Commercial Vehicle Business Unit, Tata Motors: Ravi Kant
Executive Director Finance and Corporate Affairs, Tata Motors: Praveen P. Kadle
Executive Director, Tata Power: Prabhakar Keshaorao Kukde
Managing Director, Tata Honeywell: Vinayak Deshpande, age 45
Managing Director, Tata Power: Firdose Vandrevala
General Manager, Media Relations, Tata Sons: Camille Miranda Gonsalves

LOCATIONS

HQ: Tata Sons Limited, Bombay House, 24, Homi Mody St., Fort Mumbai, Mumbai 400 001, India
Phone: +91-22-5665-8282 **Fax:** +91-22-204-8187
US HQ: 101 Park Ave., New York, NY 10178
US Phone: 212-557-7979 **US Fax:** 212-557-7987
Web: www.tata.com

PRODUCTS/OPERATIONS

Selected Operations

Engineering
Automotive
 Tata Auto Component Systems
 Tata Cummins
 Tata Engineering
 Telco Construction Equipment Co.
 Tata Holset
Engineering products
 Stewarts and Lloyds of India
 TAL Manufacturing Solutions
 Tata Construction and Projects
 Tata Korf Engineering Services
 Tata Projects
 TCE Consulting Engineers
 VoltasEngineering services

Chemicals
Rallis India
Tata Chemicals
Tata Pigments

Communications and IT
Nelco
Tata Honeywell

Information Technology
Nelito Systems
Tata Consultancy Services (TCS)
Tata Elxsi
Tata Infotech
Tata Interactive Systems
Tata TechnologiesTelecommunications
Tata Cellular
Tata Internet Services
Tata Telecom
Tata Teleservices
VSNL

Consumer Products

Tata Ceramics
Tata Coffee Limited
Tata McGraw Hill Publishing Company
Tata Tea
Tata Tetley
Titan Industries
Trent

Energy

Tata BP Solar India
Tata Electric Companies

Materials

Composites
  Tata Advanced Materials
Metals
  Tata Steel (Tisco)
  Tata Metaliks
  Tata Refractories
  Tata Ryerson
  Tata Sponge Iron
  Tata SSL
  Tinplate Company of India

Services

Hotels and property development
  Indian Hotels Company (Taj Group)
  Information Technology Park
  Tata Housing Development Company
Financial services
  Tata-AIG General Insurance
  Tata-AIG Life Insurance
  Tata-AIG Risk Management
  Tata Investment Corporation
  Tata TD Waterhouse Asset Management
International operations
  Tata International
Other services
  Tata Economic Consultancy Services
  Tata Services
  Tata Strategic Management Group

COMPETITORS

Accor	Infosys Tech
Birla	James Finlay
Caterpillar	Nippon Steel
Fluor	Procter & Gamble
Ford	Reliance Industries
Four Seasons Hotels	Ritz-Carlton
GE	RPG
General Motors	Steel Authority of India
Hilton	Suzuki Motor
Hindustan Lever	Toyota
Hyatt	Wipro
Indian Oil	

HISTORICAL FINANCIALS

Company Type: Group

Income Statement

FYE: March 31

	REVENUE ($ mil.)	NET INCOME ($ mil.)	NET PROFIT MARGIN	EMPLOYEES
3/03	10,943	—	—	210,443
3/02	9,816	—	—	218,443
3/01	8,585	—	—	225,318
3/00	7,959	—	—	250,000
3/99	7,541	—	—	255,000
3/98	8,407	—	—	262,000
Annual Growth	5.4%	—	—	(4.3%)

Revenue History

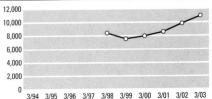

Tate & Lyle PLC

Even a kid would get a rush out of the business of Tate & Lyle — even if only a sugar rush. With operations on four continents, it is one of the world's largest producers of white and raw sugar, including leading brands Tate & Lyle (UK), Redpath (Canada), and Alcântara (Portugal). Tate & Lyle also makes sugar by-products such as molasses (used in animal feed). The company also makes starches used in foodstuffs and packaging, and it produces Sucralose, a low-calorie sweetener sold under the name Splenda. In 2001 Tate & Lyle sold part of its US sugar business, including the top-selling Domino brand.

In addition to sugar products, the company uses grains, wheat, and corn to make citric acids (used in foods and beverages), starches (used in foodstuffs and packaging), and sweeteners (corn syrup, fructose, and others used in beverages, baked goods, and pharmaceuticals).

As part of its strategy to jettison noncore or underperforming businesses, in 2002 Tate & Lyle agreed to sell its French monosodium glutamate production unit, Orsan S.A., to Ajinomoto. That year it announced plans for ingredients based on xanthan gum and related biological products made from carbohydrate feedstock.

Archer Daniels Midland owns about 16% of Tate & Lyle.

HISTORY

Henry Tate founded Henry Tate & Sons in 1869 and the next year began building a sugar refinery in Liverpool. Tate was noted for his philanthropy, and in 1896 he provided the money to found the Tate Gallery. When he died three years later, he left the business to his sons. In 1903 William Henry Tate took the company public, although only 17 investors, primarily family members, put up money for the company.

Abram Lyle founded his sugar company in 1881 when he bought Odam's and Plaistow Wharves, on the River Thames, to build a sugar refinery. While Tate focused on sugar cubes, Lyle concentrated on a sugary concoction called Golden Syrup.

WWI saw an interruption in raw beet sugar imports from Germany and Austria, and in 1918 the two companies began discussing a merger. Although they combined, creating Tate & Lyle in 1921, they kept separate sales organizations into the 1940s. Seeking new sources of sugar, Tate & Lyle began investing abroad. In 1937 it created the West Indies Sugar Company and built a processing plant in Jamaica.

Although WWII brought sugar rationing (1940) and both of Tate & Lyle's London factories were severely damaged by bombs, there was great demand for the company's inexpensive syrup. Following the war, a movement to nationalize Tate & Lyle failed. In the 1950s Tate & Lyle expanded, buying Rhodesian Sugar Refineries (1953, now ZSR) and Canada & Dominion Sugar Company (1959, later Redpath Industries). It added United Molasses in 1965.

Tate & Lyle acquired the only other independent British cane refiner, Manbre and Garton, in 1976. That year it entered the US market when it bought Refined Sugars. The company added Portuguese sugar refiner Alcntara in 1983; US beet refiner Great Western Sugar Company in 1985; and Staley Continental (now A E Staley Manufacturing), a major producer of high-

fructose corn syrup, in 1988. It sold Staley's food service business to SYSCO that year and bought Amstar Sugar Corporation (which became Domino Sugar). Tate & Lyle launched Sucralose, a low-calorie sweetener, in 1991 in cooperation with Johnson & Johnson. The company began investing millions in emerging markets in 1990 through acquisitions and joint ventures, including Mexico's Occidente in 1995. Although operations in Ukraine and Bulgaria were abandoned the next year, Tate & Lyle continued with new ventures in Vietnam and India.

Larry Pillard became CEO in 1996. Sucralose was approved for use in the US in 1998. The company reported disappointing profits that year due in part to low sugar prices in the US. Also in 1998 Tate & Lyle purchased the food ingredients division of Bayer AG's Haarmann & Reimer unit, renaming it Tate & Lyle Citric Acid. The deal made Tate & Lyle the only global producer of citric acid.

In 1999 Tate & Lyle sold its 61% share of Industrias de Maiz SA (Argentina). Sugar prices in the US remained low due to bumper harvests, which affected the company's 1999 bottom line. In 2000 it sold Bundaberg, its Australian sugar company, to Société Financière de Sucres and its US grain unit to J. D. Heiskell & Company. Later that year it sold Rumenco, an animal-feed supplement maker, to an industry consultant, and UMT, its feed milling equipment business, to Andritz. Also in 2000 the company attained full ownership of Europe's Amylum (sweeteners and starches).

In 2001 Tate & Lyle sold off the Domino brand to a group of investors led by Flo-Sun, Inc., chairman Alfonso Fanjul and his brother, J. Pepe Fanjul. As US sugar prices remained weak, during 2002 the company sold its Western Sugar business to Rocky Mountain Sugar Growers Cooperative. During the same year, the company sold its 51% stake in Zambia Sugar to Illova Sugar and its 15% stake in East Asia Properties to East Asia Sugar Investment Ltd. It also exited the sugar business in China with the sale of Well Pure to a group of Chinese investors.

In 2003 the company sold United Molasses Co. and UM Canada to Westway Holdings. That year Tate & Lyle formed a joint venture with Igene Biotechnology to develop fermented astaxanthin, a pigment used in aquaculture (specifically, to make farmed fish more red in color).

EXECUTIVES

Non-Executive Chairman: Sir David Lees, age 66, $303,653 pay
CEO: Iain Ferguson, age 47
COO: Stanley Musesengwa, age 50
Group Finance Director: Simon Gifford, age 56, $742,738 pay
Group President, Manufacturing & Technology: Loren Luppes
CEO, Amylum Group: Frank Karsbergen
CEO, European Cane Sugar: Mark White
CEO, European Cereal Sweeteners & Starches: Clive Rutherford
President, North American Cereal Sweeteners & Starches; President, AE Staley: D Lynn Grider
President, North American Sugar: Silvio Allamandi
President, Support & Efficiency Services: Pat Mohan
Group Director, Human Resources and Director, Human Resources Europe: Jan Broekaert
Managing Director, International Division: Stuart Strathdee, age 51, $460,469 pay
Director, Corporate Relations: Chris Fox
General Counsel and Secretary: Robert (Rob) Gibber
Head, Investor Relations: Mark Robinson
Auditors: PricewaterhouseCoopers LLP

LOCATIONS

HQ: Sugar Quay, Lower Thames St.,
London EC3R 6DQ, United Kingdom
Phone: +44-20-7626-6525   **Fax:** +44-20-7623-5213
US HQ: 2200 E. El Dorado St., Decatur, IL 62521
US Phone: 217-423-4411   **US Fax:** 217-421-2216
Web: www.tate-lyle.co.uk

PRODUCTS/OPERATIONS

Selected Brands

Alcntara (Portugal)
Amylum (Europe)
Lyle's Golden Syrup
Redpath (Canada)
Splenda (calorie-free sweetener)
Tate & Lyle (UK)

Selected Products

Animal feed (molasses)
Corn sweeteners (dextrose, fructose, glucose, high
   fructose corn syrup, maltodextrin)
Fermentation products (amino acid, citric acid, ethanol,
   monosodium glutamate, polyols, potable alcohol)
Starches and starch derivatives
Sugar (beet, cane, raw, white)

Selected Subsidiaries and Affiliates

A E Staley Manufacturing Co. (corn sweeteners and
   starches, US)
Alcntara Refinarias — Açucares, SA (sugar refining,
   Portugal)
Amylum UK Limited (corn sweeteners and starches)
Hansa Melasse — Handelsgesellschaft mbH (molasses,
   Germany)
Melitalia SpA (molasses, Italy)
Mexama, SA de CV (citric acid, Mexico)
Nordisk Melasse A/S (molasses, Denmark)
Orsan Guangzhou Gourmet Powder Company Limited
   (glutamate producer, China)
Tate & Lyle Citric Acid (global producer of citric acid)

COMPETITORS

Ag Processing	Florida Crystals
American Crystal Sugar	Genesee
ADM	Greencore
Associated British Foods	Imperial Sugar
Beghin-Say	Onex
Cargill	Penford
Corn Products	PPB Group
International	Südzucker AG
CSM	U.S. Sugar
Danisco	

HISTORICAL FINANCIALS

Company Type: Public

Income Statement

FYE: March 31

	REVENUE ($ mil.)	NET INCOME ($ mil.)	NET PROFIT MARGIN	EMPLOYEES
3/03	4,985	208	4.2%	7,018
3/02	5,623	168	3.0%	8,503
3/01	5,872	(382)	—	17,465
3/00*	8,987	293	3.3%	20,085
9/98	6,992	211	3.0%	21,494
9/97	7,504	164	2.2%	21,435
9/96	8,063	272	3.4%	21,281
Annual Growth	(7.7%)	(4.4%)	—	(16.9%)

*Fiscal year change

2003 Year-End Financials

Debt ratio: 53.7%	Current ratio: 1.48
Return on equity: 13.5%	Long-term debt ($ mil.): 855
Cash ($ mil.): 271	

Net Income History

OTC: TATYY

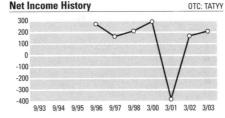

Tatung Co.

This company can make sure you stay connected, stay cool, and cook a perfect bowl of rice. Tatung manufactures computer products (PCs, servers, monitors, workstations), appliances (air conditioners, refrigerators, rice cookers), industrial goods (cable and wire, transformers, motors), and medical devices (blood pressure monitors, electrical massage devices, thermometers). The company also offers product development, prototyping, and logistics services. The family-run company maintains a close relationship with Tatung University and Tatung Senior High School, institutions endowed by Tatung's founder, Shan-Chih Lin.

Tatung has subsidiaries in more than a dozen countries. Taiwan-based subsidiaries include Tatung OTIS Elevator (a joint venture with US-based elevator maker Otis Elevator), Chunghwa Picture Tubes (cathode-ray tube and LCD products), and San Chih Semiconductor (silicon wafers). Its US operations include Tatung Company of America (displays and appliances), Tatung Science and Technology (SPARC workstations and servers), and Tatung Telecom Corporation (telecommunications equipment). Tatung also has operations in Canada, Mexico, Europe, and other areas of Asia.

HISTORY

Shan-Chih Lin founded a construction company, the Shan-Chih Business Association, in 1918. Projects during its 30-year lifespan included the Taiwanese government's Building of the Executive Yuan, which houses the country's ministry offices.

The company entered heavy industry in 1946 when it began repairing railway cars. It diversified into electric products in 1949 with fans, which it started exporting five years later. In 1950 the company changed its name to Tatung ("great harmony").

Because he believed strongly in the importance of education, when Lin retired in 1942, he donated 80% of his assets to the Hsieh-Chih Association for the Development of Industry, which went on to administer scholarships, awards, the Tatung Institute of Technology, and the Hsieh-Chih Industrial Publishing Company. The philanthropist's bequest established the Tatung Schools-Company, made up of the Institute of Technology and Tatung High School. This education-industry cooperative provides hands-

on training in Tatung factories and offices. The Institute of Technology was founded in 1956.

During the 1960s Tatung expanded further into home appliances and electronics, adding refrigerators (1961), air conditioners (1964), and televisions (1964) to its product line. Taiwan Telecommunication was formed in 1966.

Lin died in 1971. In 1972 Lin's grandson, Lin Weishan (W. S.) was named president; he began expanding Tatung's operations overseas. Tatung established US subsidiary Tatung Co. of America that year, initially to make electric fans. In 1973 Tatung formed a joint venture with Japanese computer maker Fujitsu. Tatung would go on that decade to establish offices in Japan (1975) and Korea (1979).

The company's joint venture with US company Otis Elevator was formed in 1983. Tatung continued to expand overseas during the 1980s, establishing subsidiaries in the UK (1981) and Germany (1985). During that period the company continued to move production overseas, shipping the finished goods back to Taiwan as imports.

Tatung's profits slipped in the early 1990s as Taiwan's economy slowed, but the company rebounded, signing a deal with Packard Bell (folded into NEC) in 1991 to supply the computer marketer with 100,000 PCs a month. In 1994 the company formed an alliance with telecommunications company QUALCOMM to develop cellular phone systems for Taiwan.

The following year Tatung subsidiary Chunghwa Picture Tubes began making large picture tubes for Toshiba. Tatung started making computer motherboards in 1996.

To keep pace with Internet use, the company in 1997 introduced an Internet access set-top box. Sales were down that fiscal year, a result of the Asian economic crisis and falling cathode-ray tube prices. In 1998 Tatung unveiled a DVD player and its PC Cinema, a PC combining TV, computer, and telephone functions with Internet access.

In 1999 Chunghwa Picture Tubes opened Taiwan's first factory to build thin-film transistor LCDs. The subsidiary's chairman was indicted later that year for allegedly investing foreign capital to manipulate parent Tatung's stock. In 2000 Tatung spun off its information and communications department as a separate company, Tatung System Technologies.

Tatung jumped on the mobile computing bandwagon in 2001, introducing a tablet PC. Bucking the downsizing trend in the electronics industry, the company expanded its production capacity in China and Europe the next year.

EXECUTIVES

Chairman: Lin Tingsheng
President: Lin Weishan
Chairman, President, and CEO, Tatung Co. of America: Lun Kuan Lin
CFO, Tatung Co. of America: Michael Lai
CIO, Tatung Co. of America: Chris Chu
VP, Sales, Tatung Co. of America: Mike Lee
Marketing Director: Greg Hwang
Production Director: H. H. Lin
Public Relations Manager: Ming Ho
Public Relations Specialist: Angela Shih

LOCATIONS

HQ: 22 Chungshan North Rd., Sec. 3, Taipei, Taiwan
Phone: +886-22-592-5252   **Fax:** +886-22-592-1813
US HQ: 2850 El Presidio St., Long Beach, CA 90810
US Phone: 310-637-2105   **US Fax:** 310-637-8484
Web: www.tatung.com.tw

Tatung has operations in Cambodia, Canada, China, Hong Kong, Indonesia, Japan, Mexico, the Netherlands, Singapore, South Korea, Taiwan, Thailand, the UK, and the US.

PRODUCTS/OPERATIONS

Selected Products

Computers and Communications
Monitors
PCs
Peripherals
Servers
Silicon wafers
Workstations

Consumer Products
Air conditioners and dehumidifiers
Appliances
Compressors
Microwave ovens
Refrigerators
Rice cookers
Office furniture and office furniture systems
Televisions and video displays

Industrial Equipment
Copper rods
Cyclos
Elevators
Industrial castings
Motors
Switch gears
Transformers
Varnishes and varnish thinners
Wire and cable (including communications and power cable)

COMPETITORS

Acer	Mitsumi Electric
CASIO COMPUTER	NEC
Dell	Oki Electric
Dover	Philips Electronics
Electrolux AB	Pioneer
Emerson Electric	Samsung
Fuji Electric	SANYO
Fujitsu	Sharp
GE	Siemens
Hewlett-Packard	Sony
Hitachi	Sumitomo Electric
IBM	Sun Microsystems
Kyocera	Taiwan Semiconductor
Legend Group	Toshiba
Lennox	United Microelectronics
LG Group	United Technologies
Marconi	Whirlpool
Marubeni	Yamaha
Matsushita	Zenith
Maytag	

HISTORICAL FINANCIALS

Company Type: Public

Income Statement

FYE: December 31

	REVENUE ($ mil.)	NET INCOME ($ mil.)	NET PROFIT MARGIN	EMPLOYEES
12/02	4,327	(146)	—	35,000
12/01	3,891	(247)	—	20,000
12/00	4,133	107	2.6%	20,671
12/99	4,471	148	3.3%	35,000
12/98	2,921	(14)	—	
12/97	2,160	123	5.7%	19,570
12/96	3,040	270	8.9%	20,671
12/95	3,104	242	7.8%	19,491
12/94	2,466	205	8.3%	17,869
12/93	2,041	132	6.4%	26,000
Annual Growth	8.7%	—	—	3.4%

2002 Year-End Financials

Debt ratio: 95.4%
Return on equity: —
Cash ($ mil.): 707

Current ratio: 1.12
Long-term debt ($ mil.): 1,061

Net Income History

Exchange: Taiwan

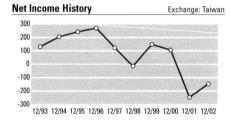

| 12/93 | 12/94 | 12/95 | 12/96 | 12/97 | 12/98 | 12/99 | 12/00 | 12/01 | 12/02 |

TDK Corporation

While TDK is best known for blank audiotapes and CDs, the company actually records most of its sales through manufacturing electronic materials and components. TDK is a major supplier of such materials as ferrite magnets, transformer and inductor cores, and multilayer chip capacitors. Other components include voltage-controlled oscillators and noise reduction filters, as well as a variety of semiconductors. The company also makes magnetic recording heads used in computer disk drives, optical media, and DVD software. Subsidiary TDK Mediactive makes a number of video games for PCs and game consoles.

Nearly 30% of TDK's sales come from Japan, while customers in the rest of Asia account for more than 40% of the company's business.

TDK, like other high tech firms, has suffered the ravages of the deep slump in the electronics market. Sales of components have fallen off as manufacturers have reacted to the weak demand for PCs, mobile phones, and other electronics gear. Meanwhile, price pressures from competitors in China and Taiwan, especially in the recordable media sector, have added to TDK's woes and contributed to losses in 2002. In response, the company has announced long term plans to reduce its workforce and consolidate its manufacturing operations to cut costs. It also

plans to pull out of underperforming business lines and has targeted home electronic appliances, high-speed networks, and auto electronics for growth.

HISTORY

Kanzo Saito, who had previously raised rabbits for their fur, took out a patent in 1935 on ferrite, a type of ceramic made mainly from iron oxide that held promise for electronics applications. (Japan's Yogoru Kato is credited with inventing the material.) Saito founded Tokyo Denkikagaku Kogyo K.K. (TDK) to pioneer the mass production of ferrite and output rose quickly as developers found countless new uses for the substance. Saito handed over the presidency of the company in 1946 to Teiichi Yamazaki, who expanded TDK's portfolio into products such as magnetic recording tape (1952).

The company's global thrust began when it opened a Los Angeles office in 1959. Two years later it was listing shares on the Tokyo Stock Exchange. TDK branched into cassette tapes in 1966 and electromagnetic wave absorbers in 1968, the year the company opened its first overseas manufacturing center in Taiwan.

During the 1970s TDK launched operations in Australia, Europe, and South America. It began listing its shares on the New York Stock Exchange in 1982. That year the company also introduced a solar battery. In 1983 TDK officially changed its name to TDK Corporation.

In 1987 Hiroshi Sato was appointed president of the company. TDK bought integrated circuit maker Silicon Systems in 1989 (sold in 1996 to Texas Instruments) as Sato began to modernize the company's offerings and organization. With a conservative management style, he'd often wait to see how other companies fared in new markets before committing TDK, prompting the industry to label him the "gambler who follows someone else." During his tenure, Sato gave the company solid footholds in niches such as optical disks, high-density heads, and cellular phone components.

To reverse falling profits in 1992, Sato made plans to eliminate managers by playing on the Japanese sense of honor — he asked them to accept pay cuts and work on standby at home until their retirement, expecting that they would simply resign. Sato was forced to scuttle the plan amid international outcries and depleted morale.

The company revamped its organization in 1994 around four operating divisions. That year it began producing high-end magnetic heads in China, but poor demand and a weakened yen hurt sales and profits. Meanwhile, TDK had become the global leader in magnetic tape manufacturing.

The company bought UK-based communications equipment maker Grey Cell Systems in 1997, thereby gaining a European presence in the data transmission market. In 1998 Sato and Yamazaki retired and Hajime Sawabe was tapped as CEO. After a sluggish Japanese economy caused earnings to decline in 1999, TDK restructured its product lines again the next year and acquired California-based Headway Technologies, a maker of giant magnetoresistive heads used in computer disk drives.

Competitive pricing in the CD-R market led to losses for TDK's recording media business in 2001, prompting the company to close many of its manufacturing plants and outsource its blank tape and CD manufacturing.

EXECUTIVES

President and CEO: Hajime Sawabe, age 61
SVP and General Manager, Administration Group and Environment: Jiro Iwasaki, age 58
SVP and General Manager, China Business Development: Hirokazu Nakanishi, age 59
SVP and General Manager, Circuit Devices Business: Kiyoshi Ito, age 59
SVP and General Manager, Data Storage and Thin Film Technology Components Business: Takehiro Kamigama, age 45
SVP and General Manager, Electronic Components Sales and Marketing: Shinji Yoko, age 55
SVP and General Manager, Intellectual Properties Center, Materials Research Center, and Information Technology Research Center: Takeshi Nomura, age 51
Corporate Senior Officer and General Manager, Ferrite and Magnet Products Business: Katsuhiro Fujino, age 59
Corporate Senior Officer and General Manager, SCM Group: Takeshi Ohwada, age 59
Corporate Officer, General Manager, Capacitors Group, and Deputy General Manager, Circuit Devices Business Group: Takaya Ishigaki, age 50
Corporate Officer and General Manager, Akita General Affairs: Yoshitomo Suzuki, age 59
Corporate Officer and General Manager, Corporate Communications: Michinori Katayama, age 57
Corporate Officer and General Manager, Corporate Research and Development Center: Kenryo Namba, age 56
President and CEO, TDK Semiconductor: Den Suzuki
President, TDK U.S.A.: Kenichi Aoshima, age 57
Corporate Communications, TDK U.S.A.: Francis J. Sweeney, age 52
Auditors: KPMG

LOCATIONS

HQ: 1-13-1 Nihonbashi, Chuo-ku, Tokyo 103-8272, Japan
Phone: +81-3-5201-7102   **Fax:** +81-3-5201-7114
US HQ: 901 Franklin Ave., Garden City, NY 11530
US Phone: 516-535-2600   **US Fax:** 516-294-8318
Web: www.tdk.co.jp

TDK has operations in Australia, Brazil, China, France, Hong Kong, Hungary, Italy, Luxembourg, Malaysia, the Philippines, Poland, Singapore, South Korea, Sweden, Taiwan, Thailand, the UK, and the US.

2003 Sales

	$ mil.	% of total
Asia		
Japan	1,379	27
Other countries	2,133	42
Americas	884	17
Europe	656	13
Middle East & Africa	22	1
Total	**5,074**	**100**

PRODUCTS/OPERATIONS

2003 Sales

	$ mil.	% of total
Electronics		
Recording devices	1,467	29
Electronic materials	1,408	28
Electronic devices	939	19
Semiconductors & others	124	2
Recording media & systems	1,136	22
Total	**5,074**	**100**

Selected Products

Data Storage
Magnetic heads (hard disk drives)
Thermal printing heads

Electronic Components
Anechoic chambers
Capacitors
Converters
Cores and magnets
Electrodes
Ferrite electromagnetic wave absorbers
Inductors and coils
Noise filters
Optical isolators
Oscillators
Power supplies
PTC/NTC thermistors
Sensors
Transformers
Uninterrupted Power Supply (UPS)
Varistors

Recording Media and Systems
Audio tape
Computer-aided instruction software
Magnetic tape (computers)
MiniDiscs
PC cards and peripherals
Removable media
Video tape

Semiconductors
Modem ICs
Networking ICs
Set-top box ICs

Other
Factory automation systems
MPEG-4 based streaming server software
Organic EL displays
Solar cells

COMPETITORS

AVX	Philips Electronics
EPCOS	Pioneer
Fuji Photo	Samsung
Fujitsu	Solectron
Hitachi	Sony
Imation	Toshiba
Kyocera	Vishay Intertechnology
Matsushita	Yamaha
Murata Manufacturing	

HISTORICAL FINANCIALS

Company Type: Public

Income Statement

FYE: March 31

	REVENUE ($ mil.)	NET INCOME ($ mil.)	NET PROFIT MARGIN	EMPLOYEES
3/03	5,074	100	2.0%	31,705
3/02	4,324	(194)	—	32,249
3/01	5,564	355	6.4%	37,251
3/00	6,363	479	7.5%	34,321
3/99	5,589	380	6.8%	31,305
3/98	5,278	442	8.4%	29,747
3/97	5,006	486	9.7%	28,055
3/96	5,108	261	5.1%	29,070
3/95	5,605	150	2.7%	27,276
3/94	4,507	54	1.2%	26,830
Annual Growth	**1.3%**	**7.1%**	**—**	**1.9%**

2003 Year-End Financials

Debt ratio: 0.0%
Return on equity: 2.2%
Cash ($ mil.): 1,421
Current ratio: 4.01
Long-term debt ($ mil.): 1

No. of shares (mil.): 133
Dividends
  Yield: 0.9%
  Payout: 48.0%
Market value ($ mil.): 5,082

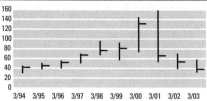

	STOCK PRICE ($) FY Close	P/E High/Low		Earnings	Dividends	Book Value
3/03	38.32	76	44	0.75	0.36	34.80
3/02	53.50	—	—	(1.46)	0.49	33.05
3/01	65.90	59	20	2.67	0.56	38.66
3/00	131.50	40	21	3.59	0.52	39.91
3/99	80.75	32	20	2.85	0.18	33.02
3/98	76.75	29	21	3.32	0.45	29.63
3/97	67.25	19	14	3.65	0.23	28.71
3/96	51.88	28	21	1.97	0.23	28.84
3/95	45.13	43	34	1.14	0.43	32.62
3/94	41.75	110	77	0.42	0.39	28.09
Annual Growth	**(0.9%)**	**—**	**—**	**6.7%**	**(0.9%)**	**2.4%**

Telecom Italia

Former state monopoly Telecom Italia is facing up to its increasing competition. Italy's #1 fixed-line operator and #1 wireless provider (through 55%-owned Telecom Italia Mobile), the company also holds stakes in telecommunications operations, especially mobile phone carriers, outside Italy, mainly in Europe and Latin America. It operates a leading ISP (Tin.it) but has sold its nearly 62% stake in directories unit SEAT Pagine Gialle to an investor group in a deal valued at $3.55 billion. The company then created a new media division: Telecom Italia Media. Telecom Italia also provides information technology. Former rival Olivetti controlled 55% of Telecom Italia before a complex merger arrangement in 2003.

Once the subsidiary, Telecom Italia is now the parent company after the merger with Olivetti, its former parent. The restructuring is intended to simplify a corporate structure that was at best confusing: Olivetti, through its Tecnost unit, acquired a controlling 55% stake in Telecom Italia in 1999. Two years later, tire maker Pirelli and the Benetton family teamed up to take control of Olivetti. Olivetti's largest shareholder is Olimpia, a company owned by Pirelli and the Benetton Group, among others.

Because Telecom Italia accounted for more than 95% of the revenues of Olivetti, the reorganization also hopes to focus on the core business of Telecom Italia. The merger was met with favor among market watchers and some shareholders although a group of international investors opposed the restructuring.

To reduce debt, the new management team has announced plans to sell off Telecom Italia's fixed-line assets outside Italy. The company also has sold its stake in Spanish joint venture Auna and has agreed to sell satellite unit Telespazio to Finmeccanica.

Telecom Italia has teamed up with Rupert Murdoch's News Corp. to develop Sky Italia; the Italian firm will own 20% of the direct broadcast satellite provider and News Corp. will own 80%. The new venture gained a kick-start when the two firms teamed to buy Italian pay-TV business Telepiu from Vivendi Universal in a cash and debt assumption deal that was valued at $871 million. The deal includes agreements to drop disputes between Telepiu and News Corp.'s Italian pay-TV unit Stream. Telecom Italia also has acquired the Ebisnews unit from e.Biscom for an undisclosed amount. It later bought TMNews, which distributes Associated Press news and other content to media and corporate subscribers.

HISTORY

After gaining political power in Italy, Benito Mussolini began a program of nationalization, focusing first on three major banks and their equity portfolios. Included were three local phone companies that became the core of Societa Finanziaria Telefonica (STET), created in 1933 to handle Italy's phone services under the state's industrial holding company, Istituto per La Ricostruzione Industriale (IRI).

Germany and Italy grew closer in the years leading up to WWII, and Italian equipment makers entered a venture with Siemens to make phone equipment. STET came through the war with most of its infrastructure intact and a monopoly on phone service in Italy. Siemens' properties, along with those of other equipment makers, were taken over by another company, TETI, which was nationalized and put under STET's control in 1958. This expanded STET's monopoly to include equipment manufacturing.

Italy's industries were increasingly nationalized under IRI. Companies within the IRI family forged alliances with each other and with independent companies, which frequently were absorbed into STET.

STET's scope expanded during the 1960s and 1970s to include satellite and data communications, but its monopoly was undermined by new technologies such as faxes, PCs, and teleconferencing. In the technology race among equipment makers, STET fell behind. And in a satellite communications era, STET's status as a necessary long-distance carrier was threatened. Despite these pressures, change did not come easily to STET. State monopolies maintained popular support, not only on nationalistic grounds but also because of labor's strong anticompetitive stance.

Anticipating privatization, however, IRI reorganized STET in 1994 and poured new capital into the company. STET's five telecom companies — SIP (domestic phone operator), Italcable (intercontinental), Telespazio (satellite), SIRM (maritime), and Iritel (domestic long distance) — were merged into one, Telecom Italia. Its mobile phone business was spun off as Telecom Italia Mobile (TIM) in 1995.

To end political feuding, the government abruptly replaced the heads of STET and Telecom Italia in 1997. Telecom Italia was merged with STET, which took the Telecom Italia name and was privatized that year. Berardino Libonati became chairman, and Franco Bernabe, formerly CEO of oil company ENI, took the helm as CEO. The company had begun taking stakes in foreign telecom companies, including Mobilkom Austria, Spanish broadcaster Retevision, and — as European Union competition began in 1998 — Telekom Austria.

Erstwhile rival Olivetti launched a hostile takeover bid for Telecom Italia in 1999. Though Telecom Italia tried to fend off the smaller firm with various maneuvers, including a proposed

merger with Deutsche Telekom, Olivetti gained 55% of Telecom Italia. Olivetti CEO Roberto Colaninno took over as chairman and CEO.

That year Telecom Italia sold 50% of Stream, its pay-TV unit, to an investor group led by News Corp. And in a venture with Lockheed Martin and TRW, Telecom Italia planned to develop a $3.5 billion global broadband satellite system called Astrolink.

The company also announced plans to spin off and sell a stake in its ISP, Tin.it. In 2000, however, Telecom Italia instead combined Tin.it with SEAT Pagine Gialle, a yellow page publisher and Internet portal operator (spun off from the parent company and sold in 2003). Also that year the company sold off 81% of its telecom equipment unit, Italtel, and its 49% stake in installations firm Sirti.

In 2001 Colaninno and several other Telecom Italia officials were named as suspects in an investigation of whether the company had violated accounting, conflict-of-interest, and share-manipulation laws. Colaninno was replaced when tire maker Pirelli and Edizione Holding, the parent company of the Benetton Group acquired a 23% stake in Olivetti.

EXECUTIVES

Chairman: Marco Tronchetti Provera, age 55
Vice Chairman: Gilberto Benetton, age 62
Managing Director: Carlo Orazio Buora, age 57
Managing Director and CEO, Wireline:
  Riccardo Ruggiero, age 43
Head of the Telecom Italia Group Mobile Business Unit; Managing Director (CEO), Telecom Italia Mobile: Marco De Benedetti, age 44
Head of Information Technology Market Business Unit; Managing Director (CEO) of Finsiel:
  Guiseppe Nino Tronchetti Provera, age 35
Head of Human Resources: Gustavo Emanuele Bracco, age 55
Head of Finance, Administration, and Control:
  Enrico Parazzini, age 59
Head of Information Technology Group; Managing Director, IT Telecom: Arrigo Andreoni, age 59
Head of Purchasing: Germano Spreafico, age 51
Head of Communication and Image:
  Gian Carlo Rocco di Torrepadula
Head of Corporate and Legal Affairs: Aldo Cappuccio, age 54
Head of Internet and Media: Paolo Dal Pino, age 40
Head of IN. TEL. AUDIT: Armando Focaroli, age 58
Head of Mergers and Acquisitions: Francesca Di Carlo, age 40
Head of Public and Economic Affairs:
  Riccardo Perissich, age 61
Head of Public and Regulatory Affairs: Andrea Camanzi, age 54
Head of Latin America Operations: Oscar Cristianci, age 61
General Counsel: Francesco Chiappetta, age 43
Auditors: Reconta Ernst & Young S.p.A.

LOCATIONS

HQ: Telecom Italia S.p.A.
  Corso d'Italia 41, 00198 Rome, Italy
Phone: +39-06-368-81   **Fax:** +39-06-368-83388
Web: www.telecomitalia.it

Telecom Italia operates principally in Italy but has interests in subsidiaries and affiliates in Argentina, Austria, Bolivia, Brazil, Canada, Chile, Costa Rica, Cuba, the Czech Republic, Ecuador, France, Germany, Greece, Hong Kong, Hungary, India, Ireland, Israel, Kenya, Luxembourg, Mexico, the Netherlands, Nigeria, Poland, Portugal, Romania, Russia, San Marino, Serbia and Montenegro, Spain, Switzerland, the UK, Ukraine, and the US.

2002 Sales

	$ mil.	% of total
Europe		
Italy	25,862	81
Other countries	2,235	7
Americas		9
Central & South	2,874	
North	319	1
Australia, Africa & Asia	639	2
Total	**31,929**	**100**

PRODUCTS/OPERATIONS

2002 Sales

	$ mil.	% of total
Wireline	17,750	51
Mobile	11,485	33
Internet & Media	2,123	6
Information technology (IT)	2,053	6
International	1,392	4
Adjustments	(2,874)	—
Total	**31,929**	**100**

COMPETITORS

AT&T
BellSouth Latin America
BT
Cable & Wireless
Canon
Danka
Deutsche Telekom
e.Biscom
France Telecom
Cegetel
Hewlett-Packard
Hutchison Whampoa
Imagistics
IBM
Ricoh
Swisscom
Telefónica
Tiscali
Vodafone Omnitel
Wind Telecomunicazioni
WorldCom
Xerox

HISTORICAL FINANCIALS

Company Type: Public

Income Statement

FYE: December 31

	REVENUE ($ mil.)	NET INCOME ($ mil.)	NET PROFIT MARGIN	EMPLOYEES
12/02	31,929	(338)	—	101,713
12/01	27,468	(1,843)	—	109,956
12/00	25,424	1,784	7.0%	114,669
12/99	25,989	1,666	6.4%	122,662
12/98	29,302	2,317	7.9%	122,300
12/97	24,203	1,475	6.1%	127,451
12/96	24,153	1,033	4.3%	126,381
12/95	23,588	921	3.9%	132,548
12/94	20,822	719	3.5%	139,346
12/93	17,325	590	3.4%	136,184
Annual Growth	**7.0%**	**—**	**—**	**(3.2%)**

2002 Year-End Financials

Debt ratio: 166.0%   Current ratio: 0.89
Return on equity: —   Long-term debt ($ mil.): 15,773
Cash ($ mil.): 1,376

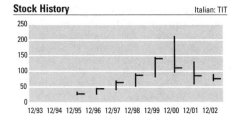

	STOCK PRICE ($) FY Close	P/E High/Low		PER SHARE ($) Earnings	Dividends	Book Value
12/02	75.98	—	—	(0.50)	4.23	12.79
12/01	85.50	—	—	(2.52)	2.75	16.48
12/00	110.31	50	23	4.20	2.76	22.29
12/99	140.00	76	43	1.90	1.08	22.01
12/98	87.00	29	17	3.12	0.00	25.80
12/97	64.00	35	21	1.98	0.00	22.78
12/96	44.38	25	15	1.80	0.57	19.73
12/95	27.88	19	15	1.74	0.00	20.54
Annual Growth	15.4%	—	—	—	—	(6.5%)

Telefónica CTC Chile

Once a telecommunications dictator, Compañía de Telecomunicaciones de Chile is now battling to keep its top ranking in a highly competitive market. Known as Telefónica CTC Chile, the former state monopoly has more than 2.7 million phone lines in service and provides long-distance calling through subsidiaries Telefónica Mundo 188 and Globus (formerly VTR Larga Distancia). It also provides data transmission, directory services, and public phones. Its mobile communications subsidiary (Telefónica Móvil) is the largest wireless provider in Chile and the company owns 35% of Sonda, Chile's largest information systems provider. Spain's Telefónica owns 44% of Telefónica CTC Chile.

Telefónica CTC Chile controls almost 90% of the local phone access market and handles more than a third of the long-distance market.

Having one of the world's first all-digital networks, CTC is well equipped to handle Chile's telecom needs, though competition is fierce. There is a lot of room for growth in Chile, where the lack of phone lines has aided the wireless market: Telefónica CTC Chile's mobile subsidiary has more than 1 million cellular customers.

Restructuring in the face of the telecom slump, the company in 2002 cut 900 jobs and reorganized into three main business units: consumer and small business customers, major business, and mobile services. It also sold a 25% stake in Sonda to Sonda founder Andres Navarro in a deal valued at $37.5 million. The deal also gave Navarro an option to acquire the remaining 35% stake held by CTC.

HISTORY

Telecommunications in Chile began in 1880, four years after Alexander Graham Bell's invention of the telephone, with the establishment of Compañía de Teléfonos de Edison in Valparaiso.

The International Telephone and Telegraph Corporation (ITT) bought the company's 26,205 phones in 1927. Three years later the Compañía de Teléfonos de Chile S.A. (CTC) was formed to acquire local phone companies. CTC became ITT's largest phone company in South America by gaining a 50-year concession that controlled 92% of Chile's phones. CTC became very valuable to ITT; by 1962 it provided about 12% of ITT's total profits. CTC was ITT's last phone property in South America to escape nationalization. In 1970 ITT CEO Harold Geneen, fearing that the election of Marxist Salvador Allende as president would lead to CTC's nationalization, met clandestinely with CIA officials to discuss how to prevent Allende's inauguration.

Allende won the election. The Chilean government assumed management control of CTC in 1971 but to delay having to compensate ITT, did not formally expropriate CTC. During sensitive negotiations over compensation, internal ITT memos that discussed the anti-Allende plans came to light. Allende offered a mere $12 million for CTC, about $141 million less than CTC was worth.

Allende was killed in a 1973 coup led by General Augusto Pinochet, who was to run Chile under a cruel military dictatorship for the next 17 years. Pinochet agreed to pay ITT's price for CTC, and in 1974 the Corporación de Fomento de la Producción (CORFO, or Corporation for the Promotion of Production) bought the 80% of the company that had been owned by ITT.

CORFO sold 30% of its CTC shares to Bond Corporation Chile in 1988. A subsidiary of Telefónica de España (today Telefónica), the Spanish telephone monopoly, bought Bond Chile stock in 1990 and changed Bond Chile's name to Telefónica Internacional Chile. Later that year CTC became the first South American company to be listed on the NYSE.

In 1994 Chile became the first Latin American country to allow all comers to offer fixed-line phone service. Although deregulation increased competition and slashed long-distance prices in 1994, other regulatory changes expanded CTC's protected local calling areas. CTC increased local call prices as much as 70%. That year CTC acquired 80% of Intercom, Chile's largest cable TV company.

The company changed its name to Compañía de Telecomunicaciones de Chile S.A. in 1995 and won the right to expand service to all regions of Chile. In 1996 CTC merged its cable operations with those of Metropolis to form Metropolis-Intercom, a cable TV company with over 40% of the market; it also merged its cellular operations with those of VTR-Celular, forming Startel, to achieve national coverage. That year CTC joined a Telefónica-led consortium that won a 35% stake in telecom company Companhia Riograndense de Telecomunicações in Brazil's first privatization auction.

In 1998, the year Pinochet retired, CTC received government approval to acquire VTR Larga Distancia, Chile's #4 long-distance carrier, despite regulatory concerns over the possible stifling of competition. A year later CTC sold its Internet division to Telefónica (as part of that company's Terra Networks subsidiary) and acquired 60% of Sonda, Chile's largest information systems provider. It also began using the brand name Telefónica CTC Chile. The next year the company announced the sale of its cable TV assets. In 2001 CTC created a new subsidiary to explore opportunities with fixed wireless local loop technology.

EXECUTIVES

Chairman: Bruno Phillippi, age 58
Vice Chairman: Jose Maria Alvarez-Pallete, age 39
CEO: Claudio Muñoz, age 40
CFO; General Manager, T-Gestiona: Julio Covarrubias, age 45
Corporate Manager, Consumer and Small Business Communications; General Manager, CTC Equipos: Velko Petric, age 39
Corporate Manager, Customer Services and Sales: Diego Barros, age 49
Corporate Manager, Human Resources: Mauricio Malbrán, age 48
Corporate Manager, Internal Auditing: Marcel Mancilla, age 43
Corporate Manager, Network Services: Franco Faccilongo, age 47
Corporate Manager, Regulation: Humberto Soto, age 44
Chief Accounting Officer and Corporate Manager, Planning and Control: Rafael Zamora, age 38
CIO and Corporate Manager, Systems: Oscar Márquez, age 49
General Manager, Telefónica Empresas: Ricardo Majluf, age 57
General Manager, Telefónica Móvil: Oliver Flogel, age 31
General Counsel and Secretary: Cristián Aninat, age 47
Head of Investor Relations: Sofía Chellew
Auditors: Deloitte & Touche

LOCATIONS

HQ: Compañía de Telecomunicaciones de Chile S.A.
 Avenida Providencia 111, Piso 2, Santiago, Chile
Phone: +56-2-691-2020   **Fax:** +56-2-691-7881
Web: www.ctc.cl

PRODUCTS/OPERATIONS

2002 Sales

	$ mil.	% of total
Fixed telephone	527	44
Mobile telecommunications	288	24
Corporate communications & data	120	10
Long-distance	108	9
Information system services (Sonda)	84	7
Other revenues	71	6
Total	**1,198**	**100**

Selected Services

Data transmission
Directory advertising
Domestic and international long distance
Equipment sales
Fixed wireless communications
Information technology systems
Interconnections
Line installations and connections
Local phone service
Mobile communications
Paging
Public telephones
Radio trunking

Selected Subsidiaries and Affiliates

Compañía de Telecomunicaciones de Chile — Equipos y Servicios de Telecomunicaciones S.A. (99.9%; equipment maintenance, line installation and services, and public phones)
Compañía de Telecomunicaciones de Chile Globus 120 S.A. (99.9%, long-distance services)
Compañía de Telecomunicaciones de Chile Inalambrica S.A. (fixed wireless services)
Compañía de Teléfonos de Chile — Transmisiones Regionales S.A. (188 Telefónica Mundo, 99%, long-distance services)

Empresas de Tadetas Inteligentes, S.A. (20%, calling cards)
Sociedad Nacional de Procesamiento de Datos S.A. (Sonda, 35%, information technology)
Tecnonáutica S.A. (Internet products and services)
Telefónica Empresas CTC Chile S.A. (99.9%, corporate telecommunications services)
Telefónica Gestión de Servicios Compartidos Chile S.A. (T-Gestiona, 99.9%, professional services)
Telefónica Móvil de Chile S.A. (Telefónica Móvil, 99.9%, wireless communications)

COMPETITORS

AT&T Latin America
BellSouth Latin America
Chilesat Corp
Entel
TIM
TELECOM (Colombia)

HISTORICAL FINANCIALS

Company Type: Public

Income Statement

FYE: December 31

	REVENUE ($ mil.)	NET INCOME ($ mil.)	NET PROFIT MARGIN	EMPLOYEES
12/02	1,198	(25)	—	4,571
12/01	1,352	6	0.5%	7,720
12/00	1,479	(199)	—	9,250
12/99	1,604	(115)	—	9,933
12/98	1,602	237	14.8%	8,985
12/97	1,439	312	21.6%	8,802
12/96	1,274	354	27.8%	8,982
12/95	1,037	268	25.9%	9,170
12/94	1,014	226	22.3%	9,354
12/93	967	235	24.3%	9,000
Annual Growth	2.4%	—	—	(7.3%)

2002 Year-End Financials

Debt ratio: 72.2%
Return on equity: —
Cash ($ mil.): 23
Current ratio: 1.18
Long-term debt ($ mil.): 1,289

No. of shares (mil.): 239
Dividends
Yield: 0.0%
Payout: —
Market value ($ mil.): 2,295

Stock History

NYSE: CTC

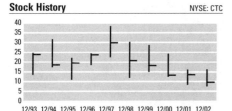

12/93 12/94 12/95 12/96 12/97 12/98 12/99 12/00 12/01 12/02

	STOCK PRICE ($) FY Close	P/E High/Low		PER SHARE ($) Earnings	Dividends	Book Value
12/02	9.59	—	—	(0.02)	0.00	7.46
12/01	13.46	397	215	0.04	0.00	8.01
12/00	13.19	—	—	(0.83)	0.00	8.94
12/99	18.25	—	—	(0.48)	0.00	9.21
12/98	20.69	30	12	1.00	0.00	10.68
12/97	29.88	27	16	1.40	0.00	9.57
12/96	23.76	15	11	1.65	0.59	8.98
12/95	19.47	13	7	1.64	0.41	7.93
12/94	18.50	36	20	0.88	0.78	6.90
12/93	23.94	24	13	1.03	0.36	6.25
Annual Growth	(9.7%)	—	—	—	—	2.0%

Telefónica, S.A.

Spain's onetime phone monopoly, Telefónica, is still the telecommunications *jefé* among Spanish- and Portuguese-speaking populations worldwide. The company operates about 43 - million fixed lines, including about 19 million in Spain. Its wireless unit, Telefónica Móviles, has about 19 million subscribers in Spain among about 48 million overall. Telefónica also is the largest shareholder in the Terra Lycos Internet portal, and the company provides ADSL broadband access to more than 1 million subscribers. Other operations include call centers and directory publishing. Chase Manhattan Bank and Banco Bilbao Vizcaya Argentaria (owning about 7% and 6%, respectively) are Telefónica's largest shareholders.

Spain's dominant phone company is like a latter-day conquistador. Telefónica is seeking its fortune in Latin America where it has made acquisitions and formed partnerships to extend its holdings in both wire-line and wireless operations. It's also building an undersea fiber-optic cable to connect the US and Latin America.

At home Telefónica de España, the company's domestic operations, provides phone and data transmission services. Other operations include call centers, directory publishing, and public telephony. Telefónica also provides pay TV to about 700,000 subscribers in Spain, as well as 350,000 in Peru.

Although it's a leading telecom provider in some Latin American markets, such as Brazilian and Mexican mobile telecommunications, Telefónica has fallen victim to volatile currency and political issues in others. In addition, the company is facing increased competition at home, prompting Telefónica de España to cut nearly a third of its workforce by 2008. The company also is straightening out its media holdings by selling its Antena 3 broadcast TV station, merging its Via Digital pay-TV service with rival Sogecable, and seeking to buy the stake in Terra Lycos it doesn't already own.

HISTORY

When a 1923 military coup brought General Miguel Primo de Rivera to power in Spain, the government-run phone system was in shambles. More than half of the country's 90,000 lines did not work. With little cash in the government coffers, Primo de Rivera sought foreign assistance.

Supported by National City Bank (now Citigroup), US-based ITT bought three private Spanish phone companies, later combining them to form Compañía Telefónica Nacional de España. The ITT unit gained the state phone concession in 1924, and the government agreed not to reclaim the system for 20 years. But when Franco came to power in 1939, he froze Telefónica's assets. ITT tried to sell the company to German buyers in 1941 but backed out when the US State Department objected. The Spanish government nationalized Telefónica in 1945, keeping 41% of its shares.

Long-distance service was introduced in 1960, satellite communications in 1967, and international service in 1971. Still, when Spain entered the European Union (EU) in 1986, Telefónica was unprepared for the increase in demand for services, and complaints rose.

The company purchased a minority stake in Compañía de Teléfonos de Chile in 1990, and a

Telefónica-led consortium won a bid to manage the southern half of ENTEL, Argentina's former state phone system. The company acquired a majority stake in Peru's telecom monopoly in 1994 and a year later joined Unisource, a European telecom consortium.

The Spanish government at first defied the EU's directive to break up its telecom monopoly. But in 1994 the government announced it would meet the EU's 1998 deadline for opening telecom markets; in exchange Telefónica won permission to begin new businesses when competition arrived.

Flamboyant former investment banker Juan Villalonga took over as chairman in 1996. The boyhood friend of Spain's prime minister began expanding Telefónica's presence in Latin America with several acquisitions in 1997. They included 35% of Brazil's Companhia Riograndense de Telecomunicaçes (CRT); a large stake in Multicanal, Argentina's #1 cable company (sold in 1998 to Grupo Clarin); and 35% of satellite TV service Vía Digital.

That year Telefónica broke off with Unisource and allied with British Telecom (now BT Group) and MCI (now WorldCom), only to have the alliance break up when MCI agreed to be bought by WorldCom (1998). Meanwhile, the Spanish government had finished divesting its interest in the company in 1997 (retaining a golden share), and competition came to Spain the next year. The company revamped its corporate structure, cut 10,000 jobs, and became Telefónica S.A. It also won fixed-line phone company Telesp and a cellular company in Brazil's auction of the former national phone company, Telebras.

In 1999 Telefónica sold to the public part of its Internet unit, Terra Networks (formerly Telefónica Interactiva). The next year it took near-total ownership of four of its Latin American units: Telefónica de Argentina, Telefónica del Perú, Telesp, and Tele Sudeste Celular (it later sold its stake in CRT to meet regulatory approval) and separated the mobile and data operations to reorganize by business units.

To expand its multimedia offerings, Telefónica bought Netherlands-based independent TV producer Endemol for $5.3 billion in 2000 and formed Telefónica Media. After dropping out of the UK wireless license auction, the company teamed up with Finland's Sonera (later acquired by Telia) to win a license in the German auction. But when merger talks with Dutch telecom carrier Royal KPN broke down, Villalonga resigned over disagreements on the direction of the company.

In 2001 Telefónica combined its Brazilian mobile telephone holdings with those of Portugal Telecom to form market leader Brasilcel. Telefónica then spent $2.7 billion in Mexico in 2001 and 2002 to buy four wireless operators and a 65%-stake in a fifth (Pegaso PCS) to achieve #2 in that market.

EXECUTIVES

Executive Chairman and CEO: César Alierta Izuel
General Manager Corporate Strategy and Regulation: Luis Lada Díaz
Secretary: Antonio Jesús Alonso Ureba
General Manager Media, Marketing and Content Division: Luis Abril Pérez
General Director Corporate Finances; CFO: Santiago Fernandez Valbuena
General Manager Internal Auditing and Communication: Calixto Ríos Pérez
General Manager Resources: Antonio Palacios Esteban
General Manager Human Resources: Oscar Maraver Sánchez-Valdepeñas

General Manager and Assistant to the Chairman:
Francisco de Bergia González
Corporate General Manager: Guillermo Fernández-Vidal
General Manager Corporate Development:
Angel Vilá Boix
General Manager of Corporate Marketing and Content:
Kim Faura Batlle
CIO: Luis Furnells Abaunz
CEO, Atento: Alberto Maria Horcajo Aguirre
CEO, Emergia and Telefónica DataCorp:
Eduardo Caride
CEO, Telefónica de España: Julio Linares López
CEO, Telefónica Latinoamericana (Latam):
José María Alvarez-Pallete López
CEO, Telefónica Móviles: Antonio Viana-Baptista, age 45
CEO, Terra-Lycos: Joaquim Agut Bonsfills
CEO, T.P.I.Páginas Amarillas: Belén Amatriaín Corbi

LOCATIONS

HQ: Gran Vía 28, 28013 Madrid, Spain
Phone: +34-91-584-47-00   **Fax:** +34-91-531-93-47
Web: www.telefonica.com

In addition to Spain, Telefónica's areas of operation
include 42 countries in Africa, Asia, Europe, Latin
America, and North America.

PRODUCTS/OPERATIONS

2002 Sales

	$ mil.	% of total
Telefónica de España	10,116	33
Telefónica Móviles	8,584	28
Telefónica Latinoamericana	7,357	24
Telefónica Data	1,533	5
Admira Media	1,227	4
Terra-Lycos	613	2
Other revenues	1,226	4
Total	**30,656**	**100**

Selected Subsidiaries and Affiliates

Admira Media Group (formerly Telefónica Media Group,
content, entertainment, and media production and
distribution services)
Antena 3 de televisión, S.A. (47%, TV broadcasting)
Uniprex, S.A. (Onda Cera, radio broadcasting)
DTS Distribuidora de Televisión Digital, S.A. (Via Digital,
49%, satellite pay TV)
Endemol Entertainment Holding N.V. (99%, television
production, The Netherlands)
Pearson plc (5%, publishing, UK)
Atento N.V. (data center operations and customer
relation management, The Netherlands)
Emergia Holding N.V. (submarine fiber-optic cable
operations)
Portugal Telecom, SGPS, S.A. (7%, telecommunications
services)
Telefónica Data Group (data transmissions)
Telefónica Latinoamericana (formerly Telefónica
Internacional, non-wireless international
telecommunications holdings)
Cia. Anónima N. de Teléfonos de Venezuela, C.A.
(CANTV, 7%, fixed-line telecommunications)
Telefónica CTC Chile (44%, fixed-line
telecommunications and pay TV)
Telefónica de Argentina, S.A. (98%, fixed-line
telecommunications)
Telefónica del Perú, S.A.A. (97%, fixed-line
telecommunications and pay TV)
Telesp Participaçes, S.A. (87%, fixed-line
telecommunications, Brazil)
Telefónica Móviles, S.A. (92%, wireless
telecommunications services)
Brasilcel N.V. (50%, joint venture)
Celular CRT Participaçes, S.A. (49%, wireless
telecommunications, Brazil)
Tele Leste Celular Participaçes, S.A. (Bahia Celular, 19%,
cellular services, Brazil)
Tele Sudeste Celular Participaçes, S.A. (Rio Celular, 84%,
cellular service, Brazil)
Telesp Celular Participaçes, S.A. (65%, cellular service,
Brazil)
Médi Telecom (29%, wireless telecommunications,
Morocco)

NewComm Wireless Puerto Rico (49.9%)
Telefónica Centroamérica Guatemala (92%, wireless
telecommunications)
Telefónica Móviles El Salvador (84%, wireless
telecommunications)
Telefónica Móviles México, S.A. de C.V. (92%, wireless
telecommunications)
Telefónica Sociedad Operadora de Servicios de
Telecomunicaciones en España, S.A. (Telefónica de
España, fixed-line telecommunications services in
Spain)
Telefónica Publicidad e Información, S.A. (TPI-Paginas
Amarillas, 60%, directory publishing and advertising)
Terra-Lycos Group (72%, Internet portal operations)

COMPETITORS

AT&T	IFX
Auna	Jazztel
Bell Canada	Portugal Telecom
BellSouth Latin America	SBC Communications
BT	Sogecable
Cable & Wireless	Spantel
Cableuropa	Telecom Italia
CycleLogic	Telmex
Deutsche Telekom	Vodafone
France Telecom	WorldCom
Global Crossing	

HISTORICAL FINANCIALS

Company Type: Public

Income Statement

FYE: December 31

	REVENUE ($ mil.)	NET INCOME ($ mil.)	NET PROFIT MARGIN	EMPLOYEES
12/02	30,656	(5,857)	—	152,845
12/01	28,424	1,875	6.6%	161,527
12/00	27,941	2,353	8.4%	148,707
12/99	23,168	1,821	7.9%	118,778
12/98	20,476	1,533	7.5%	101,809
12/97	15,601	1,255	8.0%	92,022
12/96	15,288	1,222	8.0%	92,148
12/95	14,297	1,094	7.7%	69,570
12/94	13,162	856	6.5%	72,207
12/93	12,203	1,079	8.8%	74,340
Annual Growth	**10.8%**	**—**	**—**	**8.3%**

2002 Year-End Financials

Debt ratio: 118.2%	No. of shares (mil.): 1,620
Return on equity: —	Dividends
Cash ($ mil.): 571	Yield: 0.0%
Current ratio: 0.72	Payout: —
Long-term debt ($ mil.): 21,108	Market value ($ mil.): 43,049

Stock History

NYSE: TEF

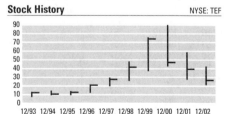

	STOCK PRICE ($) FY Close	P/E High/Low		PER SHARE ($) Earnings	Dividends	Book Value
12/02	26.57	—	—	(3.56)	0.00	11.02
12/01	39.28	48	23	1.21	0.00	14.78
12/00	47.06	61	29	1.47	0.00	16.49
12/99	74.18	48	24	1.58	0.00	12.65
12/98	41.54	35	19	1.37	0.00	14.23
12/97	27.38	26	18	1.10	0.34	12.62
12/96	20.82	18	11	1.17	0.40	13.65
12/95	12.59	12	9	1.06	0.36	12.20
12/94	10.56	17	12	0.82	1.58	11.03
12/93	12.23	—	—	1.15	0.40	14.34
Annual Growth	**9.0%**			**—**	**—**	**(2.9%)**

Teléfonos de México

Telmex is no longer a monopoly, but it's still Mexico's #1 telecom company, offering local and long-distance service over more than 14.4 million access lines. Telmex has spun off its Telcel subsidiary (Mexico's leading wireless carrier with more than 7 million subscribers) and most of its international investments to form América Móvil, which in turn owns a stake in Latin American wireless joint venture Telecom Americas. Telmex also owns a stake in Prodigy, the US-based ISP, and Spanish-language portal T1msn, a partnership with Microsoft. Grupo Carso Telecom, a holding company controlled by Mexican billionaire Carlos Slim Helú, owns a controlling stake in Telmex.

After a decade of facing competition, Teléfonos de México (Telmex) continues to control about two-thirds of Mexico's long-distance market and more than 90% of the phone local traffic. But competitors — and the US government — have sought an end to what they claim are monopolistic practices by the telecom giant.

Telmex reached a tentative agreement with rivals backed by AT&T and WorldCom that would end a dispute over access to the Mexican telecommunications market. The wrangling had led the US to file a complaint against Mexico before the World Trade Organization.

US-based SBC Communications owns a 7.5% stake in Telmex.

HISTORY

Mexican Telephone and Telegraph, backed by investors allied with AT&T, received a government concession to operate in Mexico City in 1903. Two years later a Swedish consortium led by equipment maker Ericsson also won a concession, and it became Empresa de Teléfonos Ericsson in 1909.

In 1915 Mexican Telephone and Telegraph was nationalized. The company languished after WWI, but the Ericsson enterprise thrived. In 1925 International Telephone and Telegraph (ITT), led by telecom pioneer Sosthenes Behn, won the concession to operate Mexican Telephone and Telegraph. ITT expanded operations nationwide and linked to AT&T's system in the US. In 1932 ITT won control of Ericsson.

Teléfonos de México (Telmex) was created after WWII to buy the ITT and Ericsson subsidiaries in Mexico. Private investors bought Telmex in 1953, but it remained under close state regulation until the government bought 51% of the voting shares in 1972. Phone service grew slowly, and the government continually raised the long-distance tax until it accounted for half of Telmex's revenues. By the 1980s the government was using Telmex funds for unrelated programs.

The 1985 earthquakes heavily damaged Telmex's facilities, and it was forced to modernize and expand in the rebuilding stage. To improve the inefficient enterprise, President Carlos Salinas announced in 1989 that Telmex would be privatized. The following year a consortium that included Grupo Carso, SBC Communications, and France Telecom won voting control of Telmex. (France Telecom sold its stake in 2000).

Telmex bought a 49% stake in Empresas Cablevision's Mexican cable business in 1995, and the next year it teamed with Sprint to offer business telecom services in the US and Mexico. After long-distance competition began in 1997, Telmex surrendered about a quarter of its market share. Many customers, angered over years of unexplained hang-ups and incorrect billings, switched providers. Also that year Telmex and Sprint formed another venture to resell long-distance service to Mexican Americans. However, the venture had to gain approval from the FCC, and regulators insisted that Telmex lower the high termination fees charged to US long-distance providers. Telmex agreed to do so, and the venture won approval in 1998. Telmex also invested in US ISP Prodigy in 1998.

Meanwhile, Telmex maintained a de facto monopoly over local service until 1999 when MAXCOM, backed by Grupo Radio Centro, entered the market. Telmex gained strength in other communications arenas, receiving additional radio spectrum for mobile and PCS wireless services, joining SBC to buy Cellular Communications of Puerto Rico, and buying Miami-based Topp Telecom (prepaid cellular service) and Dallas-based CommSouth (prepaid local service). It bought out Sprint's share of their joint venture and took a 1% stake ($100 million) in Williams Communications Group (now WilTel Communications), the US-based fiber-optic firm. It also began managing Guatemalan phone company TELGUA and the next year acquired a controlling stake.

Also in 2000 Telmex and Microsoft introduced T1msn, a Spanish-language Internet portal (T1msn acquired the Spanish-language portal Yupi in 2001). Telmex also formed a joint venture with Bell Canada International and SBC to expand operations in South America.

EXECUTIVES

Chairman: Carlos Slim Helú
Vice Chairman: Juan Antonio Pérez Simón
Vice Chairman and CEO: Jaime Chico Pardo, age 52
Secretary and General Counsel:
  Sergio F. Medina Noriega
Director, Corporate Market: Isidoro Ambe Attar
Director, Finance and Administration:
  Adolfo Cerezo Pérez
Director, Human Resources: Jaime Pérez Gómez
Director, Investments and Strategic Development:
  Andrés R. Vazquez del Mercado Benshimol
Director, Legal Affairs: Javier Mondragón Alarcón
Director, Mass Market: Patricio (Patrick) Slim Domit
Director, Operational Support: Héctor Slim Seade
**Director, Strategic Alliances, Communication, and
  Institutional Relations:** Arturo Elías Ayub
Director, Systems and Processes:
  Oscar Von Hauske Solís
Director, Technical and Long Distance:
  Eduardo Gómez Chibli
Dean of Inttelmex: Javier Elguea Solís
Division Director, Telnor: Luis Villanueva Gómez
Auditors: Mancera, S.C.

LOCATIONS

HQ: Teléfonos de México, S.A. de C.V.
  Parqué Vía 190, Colonia Cuauhtémoc,
  06599 México, D.F., Mexico
Phone: +52-55-5703-3990   **Fax:** +52-55-5545-5550
Web: www.telmex.com.mx

Teléfonos de México (Telmex) has operations in Brazil, Guatemala, Mexico, Puerto Rico, and the US.

PRODUCTS/OPERATIONS

2002 Sales

	$ mil.	% of total
Local service	5,144	47
Long-distance		
Domestic	2,845	26
International	876	8
Interconnections	1,532	14
Other revenues	547	5
Total	**10,944**	**100**

Selected Services

Calling cards
Internet access
Local fixed-line access
National and international fixed-line long-distance
Network engineering
Pay phones
Telephone directories
Wireless data networking

Selected Subsidiaries

Anuncios en Directorios (Seccion Amarilla (ADSA),
  directory publishing)
Red Uno (corporate telecommunications services)
Telbip (paging services)
Telcel (cellular communications)
Telnor (telecom services in the states of Baja California
  and Sonora)
UniNet (data network support)

COMPETITORS

Alestra
America Online Latin
  America
Avantel
Bell Canada
CycleLogic
IMPSAT
Iusacell
Movil@ccess
Quepasa.Com
Telefónica
Yahoo!

HISTORICAL FINANCIALS

Company Type: Public

Income Statement

FYE: December 31

	REVENUE ($ mil.)	NET INCOME ($ mil.)	NET PROFIT MARGIN	EMPLOYEES
12/02	10,944	1,897	17.3%	63,775
12/01	12,140	2,570	21.2%	67,550
12/00	10,670	2,757	25.8%	66,928
12/99	10,182	2,656	26.1%	72,321
12/98	7,903	1,657	21.0%	54,425
12/97	7,529	1,593	21.2%	54,758
12/96	6,714	1,478	22.0%	62,317
12/95	5,428	1,209	22.3%	62,777
12/94	5,914	1,591	26.9%	63,246
12/93	7,923	2,900	36.6%	62,977
Annual Growth	**3.7%**	**(4.6%)**	**—**	**0.1%**

2002 Year-End Financials

Debt ratio: 90.0%
Return on equity: 33.0%
Cash ($ mil.): 1,391
Current ratio: 1.13
Long-term debt ($ mil.): 5,340
No. of shares (mil.): 639
Dividends
  Yield: 3.6%
  Payout: 814.3%
Market value ($ mil.): 20,430

Stock History

NYSE: TMX

12/93 12/94 12/95 12/96 12/97 12/98 12/99 12/00 12/01 12/02

	STOCK PRICE ($) FY Close	P/E High/Low		PER SHARE ($) Earnings	Dividends	Book Value
12/02	31.98	296	189	0.14	1.14	9.28
12/01	35.02	11	7	3.56	1.04	8.43
12/00	26.53	13	7	3.56	0.96	7.35
12/99	33.08	10	3	3.44	0.60	17.20
12/98	14.31	8	5	2.10	0.62	13.85
12/97	16.48	9	5	1.90	0.22	13.48
12/96	9.70	7	5	1.61	0.46	12.80
12/95	9.37	10	5	1.25	0.46	10.64
12/94	12.05	15	7	1.51	0.74	10.62
12/93	19.85	7	5	2.73	0.48	11.25
Annual Growth	**5.4%**	**—**	**—**	**(28.1%)**	**10.1%**	**(2.1%)**

Grupo Televisa

With its television, radio, and publishing interests, Grupo Televisa is *número uno* in the Latin media world. The firm is Mexico's #1 TV broadcaster with four networks and almost 230 affiliated stations (about 190 are company-owned). It also has a 51% stake in cable joint venture Cablevisión and a 60% stake in Innova, which operates the SKY direct-to-home satellite system (of which Televisa owns 30%). The company's publishing unit, Editorial Televisa, is a leading producer of Spanish-language magazines. Televisa also owns three soccer teams, a sports stadium, and 50% of 17 Mexican radio stations. Through holding company Televicentro, the family of chairman and CEO Emilio Azcárraga Jean controls 51% of Televisa.

While a leader in many of its business segments, Televisa has been moving to strengthen its position on the balance sheet. Cost cutting and payroll reduction efforts have proved successful. It also expanded its operations into cyberspace, launching the Spanish-language portal EsMas.com in 2000 and buying Mexican e-commerce site Submarino.com in 2001.

The company's dominance in the Mexican television market was evidenced by the successful launch of Mexico's first reality TV program, Big Brother (produced by Televisa's new television partnership with Europe's Endemol), as well as strong ratings for the 2002 World Cup. It also floated about half of Cablevisión to the public and entered the live entertainment business through the purchase of 40% of OCESA Entretenimiento. Televisa has cut some costs by selling its music recording operations to US-based Hispanic broadcaster Univision Communications (in which Televisa has a 15% stake), and 50% stake in its radio operations to Grupo Prisa.

HISTORY

Credited with launching the Golden Age of Mexican cinema in the 1940s via his Churrubusco Studios, Emilio Azcárraga Vidaurreta was a radio pioneer who also owned one of Mexico's first TV channels. He joined fellow TV channel owners Rómulo O'Farrill (a newspaper publisher) and Guillermo Camarena (an inventor) to form one network, Telesistema Mexicana, in 1954. When Azcárraga Vidaurreta died in 1972, his son Emilio Azcárraga Milmo took the reins of the company, dubbed it Grupo Televisa, and began his long stint as chairman. His aggressive style earned him the nickname "El Tigre" (The Tiger).

Azcárraga Milmo saw Mexican television as an escape for the nation's middle and lower classes. He nurtured stars for soap operas (called *telenovelas*) and variety shows and insisted upon the actors' loyalty in return. Grupo Televisa started producing feature films for markets in Mexico and abroad in 1978. It also ran cable TV and music recording businesses and a regional TV network that it bought in 1982. The company used its news programs to support Mexico's Institutional Revolutionary Party (PRI).

A 1990 attempt to start a sports newspaper in the US (*The National*) met with failure (it closed after a year, leaving the company with heavy debts). Azcárraga Milmo bought out the other principal investors in 1990 and reorganized Televisa into a holding company, taking it public in 1991. The company launched its Skytel paging service in Mexico in 1992 and bought a minority stake in US-based Univision. The Mexican government privatized the Televisión Azteca network in 1993, giving Televisa its first taste of competition in the TV broadcast market.

Televisa joined Brazil's Organizações Globo and TCI (now AT&T Broadband) in 1995 to develop direct-to-home (DTH) satellite television. (News Corp. joined the venture, now called SKY, in 1997.) The company also pared its staff by 12% and divested some of its lesser operations, including the sale of 49% of its cable TV businesses to telephone giant Teléfonos de México (Telmex).

A month before his death in 1997, Azcárraga Milmo installed his 29-year-old son, Emilio Azcárraga Jean, as president and CEO of the company. The company sold half of its stake in Univision the next year and slashed more jobs. Holding company Grupo Televicentro sold a 9% stake in Televisa in 2000 and used the proceeds to pay off debt. It also sold its newspaper, *Ovaciones*, in 2000. Later that year Televisa consolidated its ownership of publishing unit Editorial Televisa.

A plan to merge its radio stations with those of Grupo Acir was foiled when Mexican competition authorities ruled against it. But the next year the company was able to strike a deal to sell 50% of its radio station subsidiary to Grupo Prisa. Also that year the company eliminated 730 jobs in response to falling advertising revenue. It again increased its stake in Univision from 6% to 15%. The company agreed to form a television production company in a joint venture with Endemol in 2001.

In 2002 the company sold its Fonovisa Records regional music label to Univision for $210 million.

EXECUTIVES

Chairman, President, and CEO: Emilio Azcárraga Jean, age 35
Vice Chairwoman: Asunción Aramburuzabala Larregui
EVP: Jaime Dávila Urcullu
EVP and CFO: Alfonso de Angoitia Noriega
Deputy to the President: Bernardo Gómez Martínez
VP Broadcasting and Telesistema: Felix J. Araujo Ramírez
VP Human Resources: Gustavo Pérez Ríos
VP Sales and Marketing: Alejandro Quintero Iñíguez
VP Television: José A. Bastón Patiño
CEO, Radio Division: Raul R. Gonzales
CEO, Cablevision: Xavier Von Bertrab
CEO, Innova: Pablo Vázquez Oria
Managing Director, Editorial Televisa: Eduardo Michelsen
Deputy to the President: Bernardo Gomez
Investor Relations: Alberto Islas
Auditors: PricewaterhouseCoopers

LOCATIONS

HQ: Grupo Televisa S.A.
Avenida Chapultepec 28, 06724 México, D.F., Mexico
Phone: +52-55-5224-5000 **Fax:** +52-55-5261-2494
Web: www.televisa.com

Grupo Televisa owns about 190 television stations and 17 radio stations in Mexico.

PRODUCTS/OPERATIONS

2002 Sales

	% of total
Television broadcasting	64
Publishing	8
Programming licensing	6
Publishing distribution	6
Cable television	5
Programming for pay television	3
Radio	1
Other	7
Total	**100**

Selected Operations

Paging Systems
Skytel (51%)
Publishing and Internet
EsMas.com (internet service provider and portal)

Magazines
Eres (teen interests)
Furia Musical (music magazine)
Muy Interesante (science and culture)
Tele Guía (television program guide)
TV y Novelas (weekly entertainment magazine)
Vanidades (women's magazine)

Radio and Television
Cable Television
Cablevisión (51%)
Direct-To-Home Satellite
Innova (60%)
SKY (30%, Latin America and Caribbean basin)

Radio
Sistema Radiópolis (50%, 17 stations throughout Mexico)

Television Broadcasting
Channel 2
Channel 4
Channel 5
Channel 9
Univision Communications (15%, US)

Sports and Entertainment
Azteca Stadium (Mexico City)
OCESA Entretenimiento (40%, Mexican live entertainment promoter)
Soccer teams
América
Necaxa
Real San Luis

COMPETITORS

Bertelsmann
Cisneros Group
DIRECTV
Corporación Interamericana de Entretenimiento
MVS
Radio Centro
Telemundo
Time Warner
TV Azteca

HISTORICAL FINANCIALS

Company Type: Public

Income Statement

FYE: December 31

	REVENUE ($ mil.)	NET INCOME ($ mil.)	NET PROFIT MARGIN	EMPLOYEES
12/02	2,075	71	3.4%	12,600
12/01	2,147	147	6.8%	13,700
12/00	2,164	(82)	—	20,000
12/99	1,892	112	5.9%	19,900
12/98	1,699	77	4.5%	15,400
12/97	1,756	740	42.1%	19,900
12/96	1,460	(76)	—	20,700
12/95	1,147	122	10.7%	20,700
12/94	1,982	167	8.4%	21,600
12/93	1,926	261	13.6%	23,600
Annual Growth	0.8%	(13.5%)	—	(6.7%)

2002 Year-End Financials

Debt ratio: 66.1%
Return on equity: 3.7%
Cash ($ mil.): 155
Current ratio: 1.38
Long-term debt ($ mil.): 1,285
No. of shares (mil.): 442
Dividends
Yield: 0.0%
Payout: —
Market value ($ mil.): 12,357

Stock History

NYSE: TV

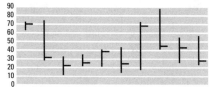

12/93 12/94 12/95 12/96 12/97 12/98 12/99 12/00 12/01 12/02

	STOCK PRICE ($) FY Close	P/E High/Low	PER SHARE ($) Earnings	Dividends	Book Value
12/02	27.93	122 52	0.46	0.00	4.39
12/01	43.18	55 27	0.98	0.00	4.38
12/00	44.94	— —	(0.56)	0.00	3.80
12/99	68.25	328 83	0.00	0.00	46.12
12/98	24.69	270 93	0.16	0.00	43.05
12/97	38.69	25 14	1.59	0.00	41.42
12/96	25.63	— —	(0.16)	0.00	25.52
12/95	22.50	108 40	0.30	0.07	25.56
12/94	31.75	184 72	0.40	0.36	35.35
12/93	70.00	126 111	0.57	0.00	25.58
Annual Growth	(9.7%)	— —	(2.4%)	—	(17.8%)

TeliaSonera AB

An expert at cold calling, TeliaSonera (formerly Telia) offers telecom services in the chilly Nordic and Baltic regions. With its acquisition of Finnish carrier Sonera in 2002, the company operates 8.6 million fixed lines and it has about 9.8 million mobile phone subscribers. Facing growing competition since Sweden deregulated its telecom industry in 1993, TeliaSonera has responded by traveling abroad. Its network facilities reach the European continent, the Americas, and Asia. The company has telecom investments in nearly 30 countries, including the Baltic states and major European markets. The Kingdom of Sweden owns 45% of TeliaSonera; the Republic of Finland owns about 19%.

The company is structured in five business areas: mobile, international carrier, networks, Internet services, and equity holdings. It also is reaching out to other countries with carrier services, using its fiber-optic network to reach the European continent and the US. The company's Internet protocol (IP) backbone connects Europe, the Americas, and Asia; TeliaSonera has investments in telecom ventures in nearly 30 countries but the company has said it considers its international operations as financial assets rather than core business elements, including its 37% stake in Turkish telecom Turkcell.

Most of TeliaSonera's growth is driven by its mobile phone services. It provides wireless phone services in Denmark, Norway, and Sweden, but it has been required to sell its Telia Mobile Finland wireless unit as a condition of the merger. The company also boasts 15.9 million mobile customers in Turkey, Russia, and the Baltic region. It has agreed to buy the 35% stake in Omnitel of Lithuania from Motorola in a deal valued at $117 million that would increase TeliaSonera's stake in the Lithuanian mobile operator to 90%.

The company also is pulling its wireless customers online using SMS (short messaging service) and WAP (wireless application protocol) technologies, and it has teamed up with Microsoft to offer e-mail access via mobile phones. TeliaSonera is the leading ISP in the Baltic and Nordic regions with 1.5 million subscribers. Other TeliaSonera activities include directory publishing and telecom equipment sales, and the carrier also sells wholesale capacity on its networks to other carriers. Following the merger that created TeliaSonera, the company said it would eliminate as many as 1,500 jobs with 700 workers eliminated in Sweden.

After Telia's proposed merger with Norway's Telenor fell through in 1999, the company began tweaking its strategy to become a strong global player. But conditions within the telecom industry has forced the company to revamp its international carrier strategy, cutting 400 jobs within the unit and trimming back its operations.

Telia did acquire Norwegian mobile phone operator NetCom ASA and in 2002 it bought the UK operations of bankrupt Canadian network operator 360networks and acquired defunct KPNQwest's network in France.

HISTORY

Telia's wires go back to 1853 when the Swedish government created Kongl. Elektriska Telegraf-Verket to operate a telegraph line linking Stockholm and Uppsala. The next year it opened a line that reached the main European continent; the company became Telegrafverket in 1860.

Just a year after the telephone was invented in 1876, the firm installed its first phone line. The 1880s saw private phone companies sprout up in Sweden's larger cities, and by 1900 Telegrafverket had installed some 62,000 telephones. Even though Sweden was open to telecom competition, the company became a de facto monopoly in 1918 when it bought the country's largest exchange, Stockholms Allmanna Telefon. In 1921 Telegrafverket began laying its first long-distance cable.

Telegrafverket began automating its phone systems in the 1930s. After WWII, the company entered a major growth period: More than 110,000 new telephone users were connected in 1947 alone. Also in the mid-1940s, Telegrafverket launched one of the world's first mobile phone networks (closed radio).

Renamed Televerket, the firm continued to grow rapidly in the 1960s and 1970s and introduced data communications services in 1965. It teamed up with equipment maker Ericsson in 1970 to form Ellemtel, an R&D concern that developed the first all-digital public switching system. (Ellemtel ceased operations in 1999.) Televerket began moving into satellite services in 1970, when INTELSAT installed an earth station in the Nordic region. In the early 1980s it rolled out several new services, including cable TV, cellular, and international packet switching.

Meanwhile, the company began losing its monopoly status in the 1980s and lost its government funding in 1984. Fearing competition from giants such as AT&T and British Telecom (now BT Group), the company in 1991 joined the Netherlands' Royal KPN to form Unisource, a global telecommunications provider; Swisscom joined the group two years later. Sweden's telecom deregulation was completed in 1993, and the firm became Telia. That year it ventured into the Baltic states.

AT&T teamed up with Unisource in 1994 to provide services to multinationals. In 1995 Telia began providing Internet access and announced it was installing an overlay Internet protocol (IP) backbone. Moving into the Americas in 1997, Telia led a consortium that secured rights to offer cellular service in Brazil. Unisource never took off, and, after AT&T jumped ship in 1998, Telia and its partners began divesting the venture's assets. In 2000 the Swedish government floated 30% of Telia. A restructuring in 2001 created five new business areas.

EXECUTIVES

Chairman: Tapio J. A. Hintikka, age 61, $55,030 pay
Vice Chairman: Carl Bennet, age 52
President and CEO: Anders Igel, age 52, $323,929 pay
CFO: Kim Ignatius, age 47
Group VP, Corporate Communications: Michael Kongstad, age 43
Group VP, Corporate Human Resources: Rune Nyberg, age 54
Group VP, Corporate Legal Affairs, and General Counsel: Jan Henrik Ahrnell, age 44
Group VP, Corporate Networks and Technology: Lars-Gunnar Johansson, age 59
Head of Marketing, Products, and Services: Terje Christoffersen
President, TeliaSonera Finland: Anni Vepsäläinen, age 40
President, TeliaSonera International: Harri Koponen, age 41
President, TeliaSonera Norway, Denmark, and the Baltic countries: Kenneth Karlberg, age 49
President, TeliaSonera Sweden: Marie Ehrling, age 48
VP, TeliaSonera International: Aimo Eloholma, age 54
Auditors: Ernst & Young AB

LOCATIONS

HQ: Mårbackagatan 11, SE-123 86 Farsta, Sweden
Phone: +46-8-713-1000   **Fax:** +46-8-713-3333
Web: www.teliasonera.com

2002 Sales

	% of total
Europe	
Sweden	75
Norway	9
Denmark	5
Finland	4
Baltic region	1
Other Europe regions	3
Other countries	3
Total	**100**

PRODUCTS/OPERATIONS

2002 Sales

	$ mil.	% of total
Network (fixed-line) services	3,155	46
Mobile (wireless) services	2,332	34
Internet services	514	7
International carrier services	446	7
Other revenues	411	6
Total	**6,858**	**100**

Selected Subsidiaries and Affiliates

AB Lietuvos Telekomas (60%, fixed-line telecommunications, Lithuania)
AS Eesti Telekom (49%, fixed-line telecommunications, Estonia)
EMT (formerly AS Eesti Mobiiltelefon, 49%, wireless telecommunications, Estonia)
Latvijas Mobilais Telefons SIA (60%, wireless telecommunications, Latvia)
NetCom AS (telecommunications services, Norway)
Sonera Carrier Networks Ltd. (Finland)
Sonera Corporation (telecommunications services, Finland)
Svenska UMTS-nät AB (50%, %, wireless telecommunications, UMTS joint venture with Tele2)
Telefos AB (49%, holding company)
Telia Mobile AB (wireless telecommunications)
Telia Internet Services AB
Telia Online AB
Telia Partner AB (business telecommunications services)
TeliaSonera Holding (holding company for non-core investments)
TeliaSonera International
Fintur Holdings B.V. (59%, wireless telecommunications in Azerbaijan, Georgia, Kazakhstan, and Moldova, Netherlands)
Lattelekom SIA (49%, fixed-line telecommunications, Latvia)
MegaFon (44%, wireless telecommunications, Russia)
Turkcell Iletisim Hizmetleri A.S. (37%, wireless telecommunications, Turkey)
UAB Omnitel (55%, wireless telecommunications, Lithuania)
TeliaSonera International Carrier AB (Internet protocol-based data transport)
TeliaSonera International Carrier UK Ltd.
TeliaSonera Sverige AB (IT services)
Tilts Communications A/S

COMPETITORS

AT&T	Sprint
BT	TDC
Cable & Wireless	Tele2
Deutsche Telekom	Telenor
Equant	UGC Europe
France Telecom	Vodafone
Infonet	WorldCom
KPN	

HISTORICAL FINANCIALS

Company Type: Public

Income Statement   FYE: December 31

	REVENUE ($ mil.)	NET INCOME ($ mil.)	NET PROFIT MARGIN	EMPLOYEES
12/02	6,858	(930)	—	29,173
12/01	5,411	177	3.3%	17,149
12/00	5,742	1,092	19.0%	29,868
12/99	6,114	495	8.1%	30,643
12/98	6,324	554	8.8%	31,320
12/97	5,868	346	5.9%	30,500
12/96	6,474	338	5.2%	34,192
12/95	6,167	336	5.4%	33,065
12/94	5,110	301	5.9%	32,593
12/93	4,231	377	8.9%	34,090
Annual Growth	5.5%	—	—	(1.7%)

2002 Year-End Financials

Debt ratio: 29.5%	No. of shares (mil.): 935
Return on equity: —	Dividends
Cash ($ mil.): 326	Yield: 0.0%
Current ratio: 0.85	Payout: —
Long-term debt ($ mil.): 3,704	Market value ($ mil.): 16,831

Stock History

NASDAQ: TLSN

12/93 12/94 12/95 12/96 12/97 12/98 12/99 12/00 12/01 12/02

	STOCK PRICE ($) FY Close	P/E High/Low	PER SHARE ($) Earnings	Dividends	Book Value
12/02	18.00	— —	(1.49)	0.00	13.42

Telstra Corporation

With Telstra's telecommunications services, Matilda can waltz all across Australia and stay connected from Down Under to Dallas. Australia's #1 carrier, the former monopoly provides traditional phone services to more than 8.7 million residential and small business lines. Telstra also has more than 4 million mobile phone customers and is the country's leading ISP. Dancing into international markets, Telstra has teamed up with PCCW to form a pan-Asian Internet protocol backbone network. It also provides pay TV and directory services. The Australian government owns 50.1% of Telstra and has initiated efforts to sell that stake.

Telstra operates a digital GSM (global system for mobile communications) network and a second digital network based on CDMA (code division multiple access) technology for wireless communications. Online, the carrier provides Internet access to more than 650,000 subscribers and has developed remote access via satellite. The firm also owns 50% of pay TV operator Foxtel.

The company's Telstra International unit oversees Telstra's operations in Australasia. Telstra International has telecom facilities in Hong Kong, Singapore, and in New Zealand, where it is combining its operations with those of cable TV operator Austar United to form Telstra Saturn. It also has agreed to buy Clear Communications, the New Zealand unit of BT Group (formerly British Telecommunications), in a deal worth about $182 million. Its Reach alliance with PCCW (formerly Pacific Century CyberWorks), Asia's largest international carrier of voice, private line, and Internet protocol data services, attained nominal profits but has been forced to seek a debt restructuring deal.

Telstra also has sales and service operations in Europe and in the US, where it has opened new offices in Chicago, Dallas, and Los Angeles.

Deregulation has crashed over the Great Barrier Reef: Telstra now provides wholesale services to some 50 licensed operators. With competition in every arena, it is focusing on the Internet and mobile phone markets. To trim costs in the face of rising competition, Telstra has announced 10,000 job cuts (nearly 20% of its workforce) since 2000.

HISTORY

When Australia gained independence in 1901, telecommunications were assigned to the new state-owned Postmaster-General's Department (PMG). Engineer H. P. Brown, who had managed the UK's telegraph and telephone system, became head of PMG in 1923. He set up research labs that year, oversaw the first overseas call to London in 1930, and streamlined operations until his reign ended in 1939.

During WWII Australia quickly expanded its communications infrastructure to assist the Allied Front in the South Pacific. Following the war, the government formed the Overseas Telecommunications Commission (OTC) in 1946 to handle international operations independent of PMG.

Even as new technology connected the continent and boosted the productivity of PMG, its postal operations steadily recorded losses in the postwar era. In 1974 a Royal Commission recommended that postal and telecom services be split. Australian Telecommunications Commission (Telecom Australia) was launched in 1975 (OTC retained overseas services); it turned a profit in its first year.

Looking to connect residents in the outback, the firm signed Japan's Nippon Electric (now NEC) in 1981 to set up a digital radio transmission system; by the next decade it connected some 50,000 outback users. Also in 1981 Telecom Australia took a 25% stake in government-owned satellite operator AUSSAT and launched nationwide paging and mobile phone service in Melbourne and Sydney.

Renamed Australian Telecommunications in 1989, the carrier got its first whiff of competition as others were allowed to provide phone equipment. Two years later Optus Communications began competing with Telecom Australia; for the privilege it was forced to buy the unsuccessful AUSSAT. Long-distance competition began in 1991, and mobile phone competition began in 1992. In response, Telecom Australia merged with OTC to become the Australian and Overseas Telecommunications Corporation (AOTC). AT&T's Frank Blount became CEO to lead the transition.

AOTC became Telstra Corporation in 1993 and launched a digital wireless GSM-based network. It joined with Rupert Murdoch's News Corp. to form pay TV operator Foxtel in 1995.

That year Telstra teamed with Microsoft to create ISP On Australia. Microsoft dropped out in 1996, but Telstra kept the service (Big Pond) and its portal (renamed Telstra.com in 1999). The government fully deregulated telecommunications and sold a third of Telstra to the public in 1997.

Kerry Packer's Publishing and Broadcasting bought a 25% stake in Foxtel in 1998. The next year Telstra posted an Australian record-setting profit, former Optus CEO Ziggy Switkowski succeeded Blount, and the government floated an additional 17% stake.

EXECUTIVES

Chairman: Robert C. Mansfield, age 51, $146,059 pay
Deputy Chairman: John T. Ralph, age 69, $73,030 pay
CEO and Managing Director: Zygmunt E. (Ziggy) Switkowski, age 53, $1,350,061 pay
Group Managing Director, Finance and Administration, and CFO: John Stanhope
Group Managing Director, Telstra Consumer and Marketing, and President, International: David Moffatt, age 40, $951,695 pay
Group Managing Director, Corporate and Human Relations: Bill Scales
Group Managing Director, Infrastructure Services: Michael Rocca
Group Managing Director, Telstra Country Wide: Douglas C. (Doug) Campbell, $673,467 pay
Group Managing Director, Telstra Mobile: David Thodey
Group Managing Director, Telstra Technology, Innovation, and Products: Ted N. Pretty, $957,950 pay
Group Managing Director, Telstra Wholesale, Media, Legal, and Regulatory, and Group General Counsel: Bruce J. Akhurst, $599,423 pay
Manager, Investor Relations: Mark Dehring
Group Managing Director, Corporate Development: John Allerton, age 46
Auditors: Ernst & Young; Auditor General of Melbourne

LOCATIONS

HQ: Telstra Corporation Limited
Level 41, 242 Exhibition St.,
Melbourne 3000, Australia
Phone: +61-3-9634-6400   **Fax:** +61-3-9632-3215
Web: telstra.com

PRODUCTS/OPERATIONS

2003 Sales

	% of total
Fixed-line	39
Mobile	18
Data, text, & Internet	14
Directory services	6
Intercarrier services	6
Customer premises equipment	1
Other revenues	
Controlled entities	9
Other sales & services	7
Total	**100**

Selected Services

Audio, video, and Internet conferencing
Cable TV
Data transmission
E-mail
Enhanced fax products and services
Freecall (toll-free 1-800 phone service)
Internet access
Mobile phone service
Prepaid telephony
Satellite transmission

COMPETITORS

Asia Netcom
Hutchison Whampoa
NTT
Pacific Internet
PowerTel

Optus
Telecom Corporation of
  New Zealand
Vodafone
WorldCom

HISTORICAL FINANCIALS

Company Type: Public

Income Statement

FYE: June 30

	REVENUE ($ mil.)	NET INCOME ($ mil.)	NET PROFIT MARGIN	EMPLOYEES
6/03	13,732	2,274	16.6%	42,064
6/02	11,310	2,050	18.1%	44,977
6/01	9,641	2,070	21.5%	48,317
6/00	11,267	2,161	19.2%	53,055
6/99	11,616	2,305	19.8%	52,840
6/98	10,441	1,865	17.9%	57,234
6/97	11,935	1,207	10.1%	66,109
6/96	12,009	1,817	15.1%	76,522
6/95	10,001	1,245	12.4%	—
Annual Growth	4.0%	7.8%	—	(8.2%)

2003 Year-End Financials

Debt ratio: 72.8%
Return on equity: 24.9%
Cash ($ mil.): 871
Current ratio: 0.99
Long-term debt ($ mil.): 7,525

No. of shares (mil.): 2,573
Dividends
  Yield: 5.1%
  Payout: 84.4%
Market value ($ mil.): 38,214

Stock History

NYSE: TLS

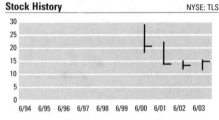

	STOCK PRICE ($) FY Close	P/E High/Low		PER SHARE ($) Earnings	Dividends	Book Value
6/03	14.85	17	13	0.90	0.76	4.01
6/02	13.30	19	15	0.80	0.58	3.07
6/01	13.89	28	17	0.80	0.49	2.62
6/00	20.69	30	19	0.85	0.00	2.69
Annual Growth	(10.5%)	—	—	1.9%	—	14.3%

Tengelmann

American shoppers know the Tengelmann Group best through its majority-owned A&P (Great Atlantic & Pacific Tea Company) supermarkets. Some 760 A&P-owned stores in Canada and the US make up only part of Tengelmann, one of the world's largest food retailers (along with German rivals METRO AG and REWE-Zentral). The group has nearly 7,200 supermarkets, drugstores, and general stores, mostly in Europe under such names as Tengelmann and Kaiser's (supermarkets and drugstores), Obi (do-it-yourself supply stores), Plus (a discount food chain), and Skala-Coop (retail department stores). The company also makes candy and chocolate. Chairman and former CEO Erivan Haub's family owns the company.

Haub's youngest son, Christian, runs the group's troubled A&P business; the eldest, Karl-Erivan, leads Tengelmann's European operations.

While Tengelmann is expanding its Plus and Obi chains in Europe, the company has closed or sold at least 600 of its Tengelmann and Kaiser's supermarkets, lessening its dependence on food retailing. The German retailer recently sold 69 of its KD chemist's shops to beauty retail chain Rossmann and closed another 50. Rossmann, which is 40% owned by Hutchison Whampoa, will run the remaining 320 KD shops for Tengelmann.

The international divisions of the company's Plus, Obi, and textile discounter Kik chains are growing rapidly. Tengelmann estimates Obi, which currently has about 125 stores internationally and 342 in its home market, will have 100 stores in China in 10 years through its partnership with the Haier Group.

Business outside of Germany accounts for more than 55% of the group's sales.

HISTORY

William and Louise (Scholl) Schmitz founded Wilh. Schmitz Scholl in Mulheim, Germany, in 1867, importing goods and processing coffee. In 1893 the Schmitz's sons opened their first retail store, selling groceries, sweets, coffee, tea, and cocoa. The family called the store Tengelmann, after employee Emil Tengelmann, to avoid the social stigma then attached to grocers in Germany.

The company rebuilt after WWII left many of its stores in ruins. The man who would guide the company through much of its growth was still a youngster at this time. In 1952 Erivan Haub, the great-grandson of William and Louise Schmitz, was 20 when he was sent to the US for three years to learn the ropes at supermarkets in California and Illinois. He saw that US grocery stores, unlike most in Germany, let consumers serve themselves. Haub passed this practice along to his relatives, and Tengelmann Group opened its first self-serve stores in Germany soon afterward. Haub developed a fondness for the US during this trip that has not faded: His children were born in America to give them citizenship; St. Joseph's University in Philadelphia named its business school after Haub to recognize the family's contributions.

Haub took over as head of the company in 1969 after his uncle's death. First on his shopping list was acquisitions. He bought Kaiser's Kaffee-Geschaft, a troubled German supermarket chain, two years later, then converted some of the stores into the discount Plus format. Tengelmann came to the rescue in 1979 when it agreed to buy more than half of the troubled US supermarket chain Great Atlantic & Pacific Tea Company (A&P). Haub turned the grocer around by focusing on acquisitions and revamping older store formats.

International expansion marked the tone of Tengelmann in the 1990s. Using its Plus discount chain as a vehicle, Tengelmann branched out into East Germany and other countries once part of the communist bloc, such as Hungary and Poland. Germany, with its stiff competition and strict laws limiting acquisitions and requiring shops to close early on weeknights, paled in comparison as a growth opportunity to the hungry environments in the East.

Tengelmann enraged Holocaust survivors in 1991 when it proposed building a Kaiser's supermarket on part of the Ravensbrueck Nazi concentration camp site, where approximately 92,000 women and children were killed. The

company canceled its plans after worldwide protests, although the local community, in need of jobs, had supported the idea.

Heavy competition among German retailers hammered profits in 1995. Haub announced plans to cut costs and restructure the company. The changes included modifying the Plus store format from discounter to neighborhood convenience store; Haub continued to back new deep-discount chain Ledi. Tengelmann entered a partnership in 1998 with the Pam group of Venice, merging its Italian supermarkets with Pam's. It also bought 165 German Tip discount stores from competitor Metro. The youngest Haub son, Christian, was promoted to CEO of A&P in 1998. He is also chairman of A&P's board of directors.

In the midst of a restructuring, in 2000 the company announced its would sell or close at least 600 of the poorly performing Tengelmann and Kaiser's stores. Meanwhile, it is extending its Obi do-it-yourself stores into Latvia, Slovakia, and Finland.

In 2002 Tengelmann restructured its troubled A&P operations, which posted a $72 million loss for the fiscal year ending in February 2002.

EXECUTIVES

Chairman: Erivan Haub
Chairman of Holding Management Board; CEO, Europe: Karl-Erivan W. Haub
Managing Director of Finance: Jens-Jürgen Böckel
Managing Director, Food Retail: Peter Zühlsdorff
Chairman, President and CEO, A&P: Christian W. E. Haub
Personnel Director, Tengelmann/Kaiser's Headquarters: Bernd Ahlers

LOCATIONS

HQ: Tengelmann Group
Wissollstrasse 5-43,
45478 Mülheim an der Ruhr, Germany
Phone: +49-208-5806-7601   **Fax:** +49-208-5806-6401
Web: www.tengelmann.de

Tengelmann has stores in Austria, Canada, China, the Czech Republic, Denmark, Germany, Hungary, Italy, Latvia, Poland, Portugal, Slovenia, Spain, Switzerland, and the US.

2003 Sales

	% of total
Germany	43
North America	42
Rest of Europe	15
Total	**100**

2003 Stores

	No.
Germany	5,203
Rest of Europe	1,223
North America	760
Total	**7186**

PRODUCTS/OPERATIONS

Selected Store Operations

The Great Atlantic & Pacific Tea Company (56%, A&P grocery store chain)
Interfruct Cash & Carry
Kaiser's (grocery and drugstore chain)
KD (drugstores)
KiK (discount clothing and textile stores)
OBI (do-it-yourself supply, hardware, and appliance retailer)
Plus (grocery and goods discount store chain)
Skala Co-Op (department stores; property management)
Tengelmann (grocery store chain)
Wissoll (chocolate and candy maker)

COMPETITORS

ALDI	Vendex
Schlecker	Lidl & Schwarz Stiftung
AVA AG	METRO AG
Carrefour	Praktiker
Casino Guichard	REWE-Zentral
Delhaize	Royal Ahold
Edeka Zentrale	SPAR Handels
Home Depot	Tesco
ITM Entreprises	Wal-Mart
Kingfisher	

HISTORICAL FINANCIALS

Company Type: Private

Income Statement

FYE: April 30

	REVENUE ($ mil.)	NET INCOME ($ mil.)	NET PROFIT MARGIN	EMPLOYEES
4/03*	29,511	—	—	183,638
6/02	28,227	—	—	183,396
6/01	22,626	—	—	186,000
6/00	30,800	—	—	200,000
6/99	28,820	—	—	200,000
6/98	29,430	—	—	200,000
6/97	30,005	—	—	200,000
6/96	33,000	—	—	200,000
6/95	36,116	—	—	200,000
Annual Growth	(2.5%)	—	—	(1.1%)

*Fiscal year change

Revenue History

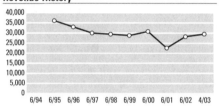

Tesco PLC

Tesco is proof of the good a little dressing-up can do. The company runs nearly 1,100 supermarkets, hypermarkets, and convenience stores in the UK (where it is the #1 food retailer), Ireland, Central Europe, and Asia. Built on the "pile it high and sell it cheap" philosophy of founder Sir Jack Cohen, Tesco abandoned its discount format, with its downmarket image, for a variety of dressier mid-market formats. Its operations include convenience and gasoline retailing (Tesco Express), small urban stores (Tesco Metro), hypermarkets (Tesco Extra), and financial services. A global leader in online grocery sales, it owns a 35% stake in Safeway's GroceryWorks.

Unlike its online competition Tesco.com is profitable (with a 65% share of the UK internet grocery market) and has expanded beyond its homebase to South Korea, as well as the US. Tesco is also expanding its bricks-and-mortar presence, most recently with plans to open six new supermarkets and a distribution center in the Irish Republic. Since 1993 the company has grown significantly outside the UK: It has more than 300 stores (including hypermarkets) in other countries. Tesco's recent acquisition of C Two-Network, a small Japanese convenience store operator, marks its entry into the world's second-largest consumer market, and pits the British food giant against Wal-Mart Stores, which owns a controlling stake in Seiyu.

Although food has been the cornerstone of Tesco's operations, the company is actively expanding its nonfood offerings, including clothing, gasoline, travel, financial services (through a joint venture with the Royal Bank of Scotland), and even residential phone service. Tesco plans to launch "Tesco Telecom" in the summer of 2003. Tesco is also challenging rivals J Sainsbury and Wal-Mart-owned ASDA on the fashion front with an exclusive agreement with US clothing brand Cherokee to supply fashions to its stores.

To strengthen its presence in the convenience store market Tesco bought T&S Stores and is converting 450 of T&S's 862 outlets to the Tesco Express banner. The acquisition gives Tesco about 5% of the convenience store market in Britain. UK competition authorities have barred Tesco from bidding for fourth-ranked Safeway plc, which is the target of a takeover bid from Wm Morrison Supermarkets.

HISTORY

With WWI behind him, in 1919 Jack Cohen invested his serviceman's gratuity in a grocery stall in London's East End. He introduced his first private-label product, Tesco Tea, in 1924 — the name was the combination of the initials of his tea supplier (T. E. Stockwell) and the first two letters of Cohen's last name. By the late 1920s Cohen had several stalls, and in 1929 he opened his first store, under the Tesco name, in Edgeware, London.

Cohen founded Tesco Stores Limited in 1932. During the rest of the decade, the company added more than 100 stores, mainly in London. Cohen visited the US in 1935, studying its self-service supermarkets, and returned to England with a plan of using a similar "pile it high and sell it cheap" format. Delayed by WWII, Tesco opened its first American-styled store in 1947 and went public that year as Tesco Stores Holdings. By 1950 the company ran 20 self-service stores.

Tesco grew primarily through acquisitions during the 1950s and 1960s, adding about 600 stores. By the early 1970s, however, competition and a recession battered Tesco. Managing director Ian MacLaurin initiated radical changes, including abandoning trading stamps and, to shed its down-market image, refurbishing stores with a more upscale decor. A price-slashing initiative in 1977 dramatically increased Tesco's market share within a year. Because cheap brands were best-sellers, Tesco began creating its own private-label brands. The company also started closing unprofitable stores while opening superstores, some with gas stations.

In 1979, the year Sir Jack Cohen died, Tesco entered Ireland by buying Three Guys (abandoning the effort in 1986). In 1983 the company became Tesco, and two years later it named MacLaurin as chairman. By 1991 Tesco was the UK's largest independent gasoline retailer.

Looking for new opportunities, in 1992 Tesco introduced small urban stores called Tesco Metro and the next year began expanding outside England, acquiring stores in France and Scotland. In 1994 it acquired an initial 51% stake in Global, a 43-store grocery chain in Hungary. That year it also opened Tesco Express (combination convenience stores and gas stations).

Tesco acquired 31 Stavia stores in Poland in 1995; a year later it added 13 Kmart stores in the Czech Republic and Slovakia. Tesco returned to Ireland in 1997 by acquiring 109 Associated British Food stores. It also launched its financial services division that year and named John Gardiner as chairman (replacing the retiring MacLaurin) and Terry Leahy as CEO. In 1998 the retailer purchased 75% of food retailer Lotus, with 13 stores in Thailand. The following year Tesco partnered with Samsung to develop Homeplus hypermarkets in South Korea.

By 2000, Tesco's profitable online shopping business was one of the world's most successful, and the company made it a separate subsidiary, Tesco.com. To build on that success, Tesco bought a 35% stake in GroceryWorks, a subsidiary of the US Safeway grocery chain, in June 2001.

In March 2002, Tesco acquired the travel company First Class Leisure and renamed the business Tesco Freetime. The acquisition was yet another move by the supermarket chain to expand beyond groceries. Tesco became the market leader in the fragmented Polish food retailing arena by acquiring German hypermarket operator HIT in July 2002. In early 2003 Tesco completed the acquisition of the British convenience store chain T&S Stores. In July it acquired a 95% stake in Japanese convenience store operator C Two-Network.

EXECUTIVES

Chairman: John A. Gardiner, age 66, $519,537 pay
Deputy Chairman: David E. Reid, age 56, $1,097,273 pay
Chief Executive and Board Member: Terry P. Leahy, age 47, $1,392,529 pay
Commercial and Trading Director and Board Member: John Gildersleeve, age 59, $968,099 pay
Non-food Commercial and Trading Director: Richard Brasher, age 42
Finance Director and Board Member: Andrew T. Higginson, age 46, $793,500 pay
Logistics and IT Director, and Board Member: Philip A. Clarke, age 43, $762,271 pay
Marketing, E-Commerce, Property and Republic of Ireland, and Board Member: Tim Mason, age 46, $735,300 pay
Operations Director: John Browett, age 39
Retail and UK Distribution Director and Board Member: David T. Potts, age 46, $725,364 pay
Secretary and Board Member: Rowley S. Ager, age 57, $681,359 pay
Corporate Affairs Director: Lucy Neville-Rolfe, age 50
Human Resources Director: Clare Chapman, age 42
International Corporate Affairs Director: Peter Bracher
Produce Director: Steve Murrells
Technology Director: Colin Cobain
Chief Executive, Tesco.com: Laura Wade-Gery, age 38
Chief Executive, Tesco Clothing: John Hoerner, age 61
Director, IT Strategic Development: Philip Robbins-Jones
Director, Marketing, Tesco.com: David Clements
Investor Relations: Steve Butler
Auditors: PricewaterhouseCoopers

LOCATIONS

HQ: Tesco House, Delamare Rd., Cheshunt, Hertfordshire EN8 9SL, United Kingdom
Phone: +44-1992-632-222   **Fax:** +44-1992-630-794
Web: www.tesco.com

Tesco has nearly 1,100 stores in the Czech Republic, Hungary, Ireland, Malaysia, Poland, Slovakia, South Korea, Taiwan, Thailand, and the UK.

Selected Subsidiaries and Joint Ventures

Ek-Chai Distribution System Co. Ltd. (99%, Lotus stores in Thailand)
Global T.H. (99%, Kaposvar and Tesco stores in Hungary)
Samsung Tesco. Co. Limited (81%, Homeplus stores in South Korea)
Shopping Centres Limited (50%, property investment)
Tesco Home Shopping Limited (60%, mail order)
Tesco Ireland Limited (Tesco stores)
Tesco Personal Finance Group Limited (credit cards, savings accounts, loans, online banking, insurance)
Tesco Polska Sp. Z o.o. (Czestochowa stores in Poland)
Tesco Stores CR a.s. (Tesco stores in the Czech Republic)
Tesco Stores SR a.s. (Tesco stores in Slovakia)
Tesco.com (online sales)

COMPETITORS

ALDI
ASDA
Big Food
Boots Group
BP
Budgens
Carrefour
Cooperative Group
Dunnes Stores
Exxon Mobil
First Quench
Gap
J Sainsbury
John Lewis
Marks & Spencer
METRO AG
NEXT plc
Royal Ahold
Royal Dutch/Shell Group
Safeway plc
Somerfield
SPAR Handels
Wm Morrison
 Supermarkets
Woolworths Group

HISTORICAL FINANCIALS

Company Type: Public

Income Statement

FYE: Last Saturday in February

	REVENUE ($ mil.)	NET INCOME ($ mil.)	NET PROFIT MARGIN	EMPLOYEES
2/03	41,615	1,495	3.6%	270,800
2/02	33,575	1,178	3.5%	247,374
2/01	30,277	1,107	3.7%	225,388
2/00	29,666	1,064	3.6%	215,216
2/99	27,451	970	3.5%	198,342
2/98	29,273	832	2.8%	185,580
2/97	24,379	846	3.5%	153,198
Annual Growth	9.3%	10.0%	—	10.0%

2003 Year-End Financials

Debt ratio: 62.1%
Return on equity: 16.5%
Cash ($ mil.): 1,008
Current ratio: 0.45
Long-term debt ($ mil.): 6,398

Net Income History

OTC: TSCDY.PK

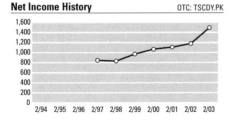

The Thomson Corporation

Niche information is The Thomson Corporation's niche. The company provides specialized information (such as legal and financial data) online and through CD-ROMs, computer software, and print products. Thomson has been divesting almost all of its traditional media assets in favor of electronic products. It sold most of its 130 daily and non-daily newspapers, as well as its 20% stake in Canadian media giant Bell Globemedia, a firm it founded with telecommunications company BCE. It bought several Harcourt General businesses (after Harcourt was sold to Reed Elsevier Group) and also owns business information firm Dialog. The Thomson family owns about 73% of the company.

Thomson's makeover into an electronic-based information provider has been successful for the company. It intends to dramatically increase Internet-related sales and the purchases of rival information provider Primark (for about $1 billion), investor research firm Carson Group, and NewsEdge (which it folded into the Dialog business) were part of that strategy. The deals also cemented its presence in North America and helped it expand into Europe and Asia. Even though it initially benefited from its participation in the creation of Bell Globemedia, Thomson decided the venture didn't fit well into its stable of assets.

The company has leveraged its growing educational and Internet properties by investing with a consortium of several schools worldwide to launch an online university. (The new business is called U21global.) The university targets Asian and Latin American markets and focuses on awarding business and information technology degrees.

Thomson has agreed to sell its dental, veterinary, and medical economics publishing units to Advanstar Communications for $135 million.

HISTORY

Having failed at farming and auto parts distribution, Roy Thomson left Toronto for the hinterlands of Ontario and started a radio station in 1930. He purchased the *Timmons Press*, a gold-mining town newspaper, in 1934. Thomson bought other town papers, venturing outside Ontario in 1949 and into the US in 1952.

The Thomson Newspaper empire grew rapidly during the 1950s. In 1953 Thomson moved to the UK, where he bought the *Scotsman* (Edinburgh). When commercial TV broadcasting began in the UK, Thomson started Scottish Television (1957) and merged it with the UK's Kemsley Newspapers, publisher of the *Sunday Times*, to create the International Thomson Organization in 1959.

International Thomson bought the *Times* of London (1967) and entered the travel business. The next year J. Paul Getty invited International Thomson into a North Sea oil drilling venture. The consortium struck oil in 1973, just as the OPEC oil embargo took hold. Oil accounted for the bulk of International Thomson's profits by 1976, when Thomson died. His son, Kenneth, took over as chairman. In 1978 a public holding company was created to house International Thomson's operations.

Using oil earnings to expand and diversify its publishing interests, the company sold the *Times* in 1981 and began shopping for specialty publishers with subscription-based revenues, which would be less vulnerable to recession. Purchases included American Banker and Bond Buyer (financial publications, 1983), Gale Research (library reference materials, 1985), and several online information providers. The company then completed the sale of its oil and gas holdings.

Thomson Newspapers and International Thomson merged to become The Thomson Corporation in 1989, and in 1991 it bought Maxwell's Macmillan Professional and Business Reference Publishing. The company grouped its newspapers in regional clusters.

The firm bought law and textbook publisher West Publishing in 1996. Continuing its selective divestment of newspapers, the company sold 43 daily papers in the US and Canada in 1996.

In 1998 Thomson veteran Richard Harrington became CEO. Also that year Thomson bought tax return software maker Computer Language Research as well as a pair of tax and law publishing units from UK's Pearson. It also bought Knight Ridder's Technimetrics financial information unit and spun off its travel group business.

In 2000 Thomson announced it would sell its newspapers to focus on the Internet. The company bought Sylvan Learning Systems' Prometric division, which provides computer-based testing services, and Wave Technologies International, a provider of multimedia instructional products. Thomson also bought the online data services division of Dialog. Thomson also acquired rival financial data provider Primark for $1 billion.

Thomson joined forces in 2001 with Canadian telecommunications giant BCE to create media firm Bell Globemedia, with Internet, newspapers, and broadcasting assets worth about $2.7 billion. (It sold its interest in the company two years later.) Also that year it bought the higher education and corporate training businesses of Harcourt General from Reed Elsevier Group plc (formerly Reed Elsevier plc) and acquired business content provider NewsEdge.

Thomson started trading on the New York Stock Exchange in mid-2002. Later that year it beefed up its Internet education group with the purchase of certain e-learning assets from McGraw-Hill. In 2003 the company purchased Techstreet, a digital content company focused on technical information.

EXECUTIVES

Chairman: David K. R. Thomson, age 44
Deputy Chairman: W. Geoffrey Beattie
President, CEO, and Director:
 Richard J. (Dick) Harrington, age 55, $3,040,800 pay
CEO, Thomson Financial; Director:
 David H. (Dave) Shaffer, age 59, $2,315,150 pay
 (prior to title change)
EVP, CFO, and Director: Robert D. (Bob) Daleo, age 52, $1,748,460 pay
EVP Executive Development and Corporate Affairs: James C. (Jim) Smith, age 42
SVP Finance: David J. Hulland
SVP Human Resources: John J. Raffaeli Jr.
SVP and Director of Taxes: Joseph J.G.M. Vermeer
SVP and General Counsel: Deirdre Stanley, age 37
SVP and Treasurer: Stephane Bello, age 40
VP Corporate Communications: Janey M. Loyd
Secretary: David W. Binet
President and CEO, Lifelong Learning Group:
 Alex Brnilovich
President and CEO, Medstat: Laurence J. Hagerty
President and CEO, Thomson Healthcare:
 Richard A. (Rick) Noble

President and CEO, Thomson Learning:
Ronald H. Schlosser, age 53
President and CEO, Thomson Legal & Regulatory:
Brian H. Hall, age 54, $1,649,250 pay
President and CEO, Thomson Scientific and Healthcare: Robert C. Cullen
President and COO, Thomson Financial:
Sharon Rowlands
President, Thomson Financial Banking and Brokerage Group: Louis Eccleston
President, Thomson Financial Corporate Group:
Kevin Marcus
President, Thomson Financial Investment Management Group: Suresh Kavan
President, Thomson Financial Research: Bob Bulik
Auditors: PricewaterhouseCoopers LLP

LOCATIONS

HQ: Toronto-Dominion Bank Tower,
66 Wellington Street West, Toronto,
Ontario M5K 1A1, Canada
Phone: 416-360-8700   **Fax:** 416-360-8812
US HQ: Metro Center, 1 Station Place,
Stamford, CT 06902
US Phone: 203-969-8700   **US Fax:** 203-977-8354
Web: www.thomson.com

2002 Sales

	$ mil.	% of total
US	6,358	81
Europe	1,029	13
Asia/Pacific	271	3
Canada	180	2
Other countries	77	1
Adjustments	(159)	—
Total	**7,756**	**100**

PRODUCTS/OPERATIONS

2002 Sales

	$ mil.	% of total
Legal & regulatory	2,961	38
Learning	2,290	30
Financial	1,543	20
Scientific & healthcare	780	10
Other	201	2
Adjustments	(19)	—
Total	**7,756**	**100**

Selected Operations

Thomson Financial
AutEx (global securities market tracking)
BASELINE (financial information & software for
   portfolio managers)
Datastream International (current & historical economic
   & financial information, UK)
First Call (real-time broker research)
Vestek Systems, Inc. (investment information services &
   applications software)

Thomson Learning
Education Direct (distance learning)
Gale Group (academic and business reference material)
NETg (information technology training)
Prometric (computer based testing)
Wadsworth (higher education textbooks)

Thomson Legal & Regulatory
Australian Digest
Checkpoint (online tax research library)
Elite Information Group (business management
   software)
FindLaw (Web portal of legal resources)
Foundation Press (law school publications)
Thomson & Thomson (trademark information)
West Group (legal information)

Thomson News & Business
Dialog (business information and news service)
Dialog DataStar
Dialog NewsEdge
Dialog NewsRoom
Dialog Profound
Dialog TradStat

Thomson Scientific & Healthcare
ISI (global research online)
MICROMEDIX (drug information)
Physician's Desk Reference
Thomson Derwent (patent and scientific data)

COMPETITORS

Addison-Wesley
American Lawyer Media
Berkshire Hathaway
Bloomberg
COMTEX
Dow Jones
D&B
Encyclopædia Britannica
IHS Group
infoUSA
John Wiley
Kaplan
LexisNexis
McGraw-Hill
Pearson
Pinnacor
ProQuest
Reed Elsevier Group
Reuters
Scholastic Library
   Publishing
Solucient
United Business Media
Wolters Kluwer
W.W. Norton

HISTORICAL FINANCIALS

Company Type: Public

Income Statement   FYE: December 31

	REVENUE ($ mil.)	NET INCOME ($ mil.)	NET PROFIT MARGIN	EMPLOYEES
12/02	7,756	615	7.9%	42,000
12/01	7,237	776	10.7%	44,000
12/00	6,514	1,223	18.8%	39,330
12/99	5,752	532	9.2%	32,500
12/98	6,269	3,665	58.5%	48,000
12/97	8,753	578	6.6%	48,400
12/96	7,719	581	7.5%	47,800
12/95	7,262	793	10.9%	48,600
12/94	6,197	416	6.7%	48,250
12/93	5,693	270	4.7%	46,400
Annual Growth	**3.5%**	**9.6%**	**—**	**(1.1%)**

2002 Year-End Financials

Debt ratio: 41.0%
Return on equity: 7.6%
Cash ($ mil.): 709
Current ratio: 0.94
Long-term debt ($ mil.): 3,487
No. of shares (mil.): 651
Dividends
   Yield: 2.0%
   Payout: 57.0%
Market value ($ mil.): 17,405

Stock History   NYSE: TOC

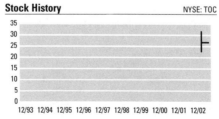

12/93 12/94 12/95 12/96 12/97 12/98 12/99 12/00 12/01 12/02

	STOCK PRICE ($) FY Close	P/E High/Low	PER SHARE ($) Earnings	Dividends	Book Value
12/02	26.73	34 24	0.93	0.53	13.75

ThyssenKrupp

How do you say "giant engineering and steel company" in German? Try "ThyssenKrupp." The company — a product of a 1999 merger between Thyssen AG, (pronounced "TISS-in") and Fried. Krupp AG Hoesch-Krupp — is one of the largest steel producers in the world. ThyssenKrupp operates worldwide through eight business units: steel (carbon steel and stainless steel), elevators, technology (machine tools, large-diameter bearings, and industrial doors), automotive (parts, sub-assemblies, and modules), materials (tailor-made materials), services (environmental services, mechanical engineering, and scaffolding services), real estate, and another catch-all unit that houses businesses such as its shipbuilding operations.

Although its combined interests range from elevators to shipbuilding, the company relies heavily on the cyclical steel market; hence, ThyssenKrupp has put on hold its plans to spin off the steel unit. The company also plans to scrap its dual-management structure to speed decision-making processes. ThyssenKrupp is focusing on expansion in Eastern Europe, Latin America, and Southeast Asia.

The company's steel unit plans on investing about $794 million over the next couple of years, mainly in its plants and equipment. ThyssenKrupp's largest investment will go towards its tinplate manufacturing business, which supplies the food and beverage industries. The company will be disposing of some assets but speculations are that its steel, auto parts and elevator businesses will be kept.

ThyssenKrupp is about to complete a joint venture with DaimlerChrysler to build steering systems. ThyssenKrupp will have about a 60% stake in the joint venture and Daimler will have the other 40%. The company will have an option to buy Daimler's position in 2005.

The Krupp Foundation owns about 19% of the company.

HISTORY

Formed separately in the 1800s, both Thyssen and Krupp flourished in their early years under family control. Friedrich Krupp opened his steel factory in 1811. He died in 1826 and left the nearly bankrupt factory in the hands of his 14-year-old son Alfred, who turned the business around. At the first World's Fair in 1851, Alfred unveiled a steel cannon far superior to earlier bronze models.

Twenty years later, August Thyssen founded a puddling and rolling mill near Mulheim. He bought small factories and mines, and by WWI, he ran Germany's largest iron and steel company. During the world wars the resources of both companies were turned toward war efforts.

Post-WWII years were tough for both companies. Thyssen was split up by the Allies, and when it began production again in 1953, it consisted of one steel plant. In the Krupp camp, Alfred's great-grandson Alfried was convicted in 1948 of using slave labor during WWII. Released from prison in 1951, Alfried rebuilt Krupp. After near ruin following WWII, both companies emerged and enjoyed a resurgence, along with the German economy, in which they prospered and expanded during the 1950s.

By the 1980s Thyssen's businesses included ships, locomotives, offshore oil rigs, specialty steel, and metals trading and distribution. Krupp continued to grow, and in 1992 it took over engineering and steelmaking concern Hoesch AG. (Eberhard Hoesch had begun making railroad tracks in the 1820s. The company grew and expanded into infrastructure and building products.)

The new Fried. Krupp AG Hoesch-Krupp bought Italian specialty steelmaker Acciai Speciali Terni, chemical plant builder Uhde, and South African shipper J.H. Bachmann. Its automotive division formed a joint venture in Brazil and added production sites in China, Mexico, Romania, and the US.

In 1997 Thyssen expanded in North America with its $675 million acquisition of Giddings & Lewis (machine tools, US) and the purchase of Copper & Brass Sales (metals processing and distributing).

Krupp attempted a hostile takeover of Thyssen in 1997. The takeover failed, but the companies soon agreed to merge their steel operations to form Thyssen Krupp Stahl. Bigger plans were in the works, and in 1998 the two companies agreed to merge. That year Thyssen sold its Plusnet fixed-line phone business to Esprit Telecom Group.

In 1999 Krupp's automotive division (Krupp Hoesch Automotive) bought Cummins' Atlas Crankshaft subsidiary. Thyssen also bought US-based Dover's elevator business for $1.1 billion. Krupp and Thyssen completed their merger in 1999. The company planned to spin off its steel operations, but held off due to its success in 2000. ThyssenKrupp did, however, sell its Krupp Kunststofftechnik unit (plastic molding machines) for about $183 million. To speed corporate decision-making, the company made plans to scrap its dual-management structure in 2001.

Early in 2001 ThyssenKrupp agreed to buy 51% of Fiat unit Magneti Marelli's suspension-systems and shock-absorbers business. It also has the option of buying the remainder after 2004. In 2002 the company formed alliances with NKK and Kawasaki Steel to share its steel sheet making technologies while expanding its business with Japanese automotive makers in Europe.

EXECUTIVES

Chairman, Supervisory Board: Gerhard Cromme
Vice Chairman, Supervisory Board; Chairman, Executive Board, ThyssenKrupp Steel AG; Chairman, Supervisory Board, ThyssenKrupp Technologies AG: Ulrich Middelmann, $950,785 pay
Chairman, Executive Board: Ekkehard D. Schulz, age 60, $1,217,029 pay
CFO and Controller: A. Stefan Kirsten, $130,473 pay
Chairman, Executive Board, ThyssenKrupp Technologies AG, Technologies Segment: Eckhard Rohkamm, age 60, $760,667 pay
President, Krupp Hoesch Automotive of America: Craig Shetler, age 39
CFO, Krupp Hoesch Automotive of America: Heinz Bizenberger, age 61
Member, Supervisory Board, ThyssenKrupp Automotive AG, and Regional Manager IG Metall North Rhine-Westphalia: Peter Gasse, age 48
Member, Executive Board; Chairman, Executive Board, ThyssenKrupp Automotive AG: Jürgen Harnisch, age 60
Member, Executive Board, ThyssenKrupp Technologies AG: Heinrich Igelbüscher, age 58
Member, Executive Boards of ThyssenKrupp AG, Thyssen Umformtechnik + Guss GmbH, Bo-chum, and ThyssenKrupp Automotive AG; CEO, The Budd Company: Wolfram Mörsdorf, age 53
Member, Board of Management; Chairman, Executive Board, ThyssenKrupp Technologies: Olaf Berlien, age 40
Executive Board Chairman, ThyssenKrupp Materials: Edwin Eichler

Executive Board Member and Labor Director: Ralph Labonte
Director Central Bureau/Public Relations, Automotive: Viktor Braun
Director Corporate Communication: Jürgen Claassen
Auditors: KPMG Deutsche Treuhand-Gesellschaft AG; PwC Deutsche Revision AG

LOCATIONS

HQ: ThyssenKrupp AG
August-Thyssen-Strasse 1,
40221 Düsseldorf, Germany
Phone: +49-211-824-0   **Fax:** +49-211-824-38512
Web: www.thyssenkrupp.com

ThyssenKrupp operates worldwide; it has current operations centered in Europe and North America.

2002 Sales

	$ mil.	% of total
EU		
Germany	12,706	35
Other countries	8,817	25
US	7,776	21
Other regions	6,702	19
Total	**36,001**	**100**

PRODUCTS/OPERATIONS

2002 Sales

	$ mil.	% of total
Steel	8,077	23
Material services	8,050	22
Technology	5,918	16
Automotive	5,461	15
Elevators	4,835	13
Services	3,262	9
Corporate	229	1
Real estate	169	1
Total	**36,001**	**100**

COMPETITORS

Allegheny Technologies	Magna International
Arcelor	MAN
Bechtel	Marubeni
BHP Steel	mg technologies
Cargill	Nippon Steel
Corus Group	Otis Elevator
Dana	POSCO
Descours & Cabaud	Robert Bosch
HBG	RWE
Ingersoll-Rand	Schindler Holding
Ingersoll-Rand Industrial Solutions	Siderar
	Siemens
Ispat	Sumitomo Metal
ITOCHU	Industries
JFE Holdings	Tenneco Automotive
Kobe Steel	Tower Automotive
LNM Group	United States Steel
LTV	United Technologies

HISTORICAL FINANCIALS

Company Type: Public

Income Statement

FYE: September 30

	REVENUE ($ mil.)	NET INCOME ($ mil.)	NET PROFIT MARGIN	EMPLOYEES
9/02	36,001	212	0.6%	191,254
9/01	34,572	605	1.7%	193,516
9/00	32,710	463	1.4%	193,316
9/99	31,734	284	0.9%	184,770
9/98	26,013	1,309	5.0%	116,174
9/97	23,058	1,233	5.3%	127,873
9/96	25,327	229	0.9%	122,659
9/95	27,407	543	2.0%	126,987
9/94	22,544	58	0.3%	131,863
9/93	20,497	(608)	—	141,009
Annual Growth	6.5%	—	—	3.4%

2002 Year-End Financials

Debt ratio: 62.9%   Current ratio: 1.34
Return on equity: 2.6%   Long-term debt ($ mil.): 5,115
Cash ($ mil.): 923

Net Income History   German: TKA

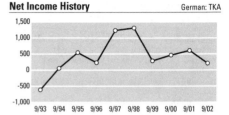

The Tokyo Electric Power Company

Japan Inc. would grind to a halt without Tokyo Electric Power Company (TEPCO), which supplies power to more than 27 million customers in Tokyo, Yokohama, and the rest of the Kanto region. One of the world's largest electric utilities, TEPCO has a generating capacity of more than 60,000 MW, produced by fossil fuel, nuclear, and hydroelectric power sources. Through interests in telecom businesses, the company offers telephony and Internet services; it also provides construction services and has international consulting and power generation operations.

Although public confidence has been shaken by a rash of accidents within Japan's nuclear industry, the firm promotes the use of nuclear power as an earth-friendly energy source. Apropos of this mission, TEPCO owns the world's largest nuclear plant and plans to build a bigger one. However, TEPCO is struggling to restore its credibility after the Japanese government shut down one of its nuclear plants for one year (from November 2002 to November 2003) as punishment for the company's admittance of falsifying safety data to cover up faults at several of its nuclear facilities.

In the face of further deregulation (large customers who account for about 30% of Japan's electricity market may now choose their suppliers), TEPCO is diversifying its operations. The company owns a major stake in local and long-distance phone company Tokyo Telecommunication Network (TTNet), and its POWEREDCOM venture (with nine other Japanese electric utilities) offers data communications services through the utilities' fiber-optic networks. TTNet and POWEREDCOM have announced plans to merge their operations. TEPCO is also entering the natural gas business.

HISTORY

The Tokyo Electric Power Company (TEPCO) descended from Tokyo Electric Light, which was formed in 1883. In 1887 the company switched on Japan's first power plant, a 25-KW fossil fuel generator. Fossil fuels were the main source of electricity in Japan until 1912, when long-distance transmission techniques became more efficient, making hydroelectric power cheaper.

In 1938 Japan nationalized electric utilities, despite strong objections from Yasuzaemon Matsunaga, a leader in Japan's utility industry and former president of the Japan Electric Association. After WWII Matsunaga championed public ownership of Japan's power companies, which helped in 1951 to establish the current system of 10 regional companies, each with a service monopoly. Tokyo Electric Power was the largest. That year it was listed on the Tokyo Stock Exchange and was regulated by the Ministry of International Trade and Industry. (The ministry has regulated electric utilities since 1965.)

Fossil fuel plants made a comeback in Japan in the postwar era because they could be built more economically than hydroelectric plants. When the OPEC oil embargo of the 1970s demonstrated Japan's dependence on foreign oil, TEPCO increased its use of liquefied natural gas (LNG) and nuclear energy sources. (It brought its first nuke online in 1971.) In 1977 it formed the Energy Conservation Center to promote conservation and related legislation.

To further reduce its oil dependence TEPCO joined other US and Japanese firms in building a coal gasification plant in California's Mojave Desert in 1982. Two years later TEPCO announced it would begin building its first coal-burning generator since the oil crisis. It established Tokyo Telecommunication Network (TTNet), a partnership to provide telecommunications services, in 1986 and TEPCO Cable TV in 1989.

As part of its interest in alternative energy systems, TEPCO established a global environment department in 1990 to conduct R&D on energy and the environment. Its environmental program has included reforestation and fuel cell research.

Liberalization in 1995 allowed Japan's electric utilities to buy power from independent power producers; TEPCO quickly lined up 10 suppliers. The company proceeded with energy experimentation in 1996, trying a 6,000-KW sodium-sulfur battery at a Yokohama transformer station. The next year the company announced that it would become the first electric utility to sell liquefied natural gas as part of its energy mix, and finished building the world's largest nuclear plant.

To gain experience in deregulating markets, TEPCO invested in US power generating company Orion Power in 1999. (It agreed to sell its 5% stake to Reliant Energy in 2001.) At home the firm joined Microsoft and SOFTBANK to form SpeedNet, which provides Internet access over TTNet's network. In 2000 TEPCO got its first taste of deregulation when large customers (accounting for about a third of the market) began choosing their electricity suppliers. Also in 2000 TEPCO joined a group of nine Japanese electric companies to create POWEREDCOM.

In 2001 TEPCO joined up with Sumitomo and Electricité de France to build Vietnam's first independent power plant.

EXECUTIVES

Chairman: Shigemi Tamura
President: Tsunehisa Katsumata
EVP, General Accounting, Planning, and International: Katsutoshi Chikudate
EVP: Ryoichi Shirato
EVP: Teruaki Masumoto
EVP: Yukinori Ichida
EVP: Takashi Murata
Managing Director: Hisao Naito
Managing Director: Yoshihisa Morimoto

Managing Director: Susumu Shirakawa
Managing Director: Takashi Hayashi
Managing Director: Takuya Hattori
Managing Director: Kenji Fushimi
Managing Director: Yuichi Hayase
Managing Director: Katsumi Mizutani
Auditors: Shin Nihon & Co.

LOCATIONS

HQ: Tokyo Denryoku Kabushiki Kaisha
(The Tokyo Electric Power Company, Incorporated)
1-3, Uchisaiwai-cho 1-chome, Chiyoda-ku,
Tokyo 100-8560, Japan
Phone: +81-3-4216-1111   **Fax:** +81-3-4216-2539
US HQ: 1901 L St. NW, Ste. 720, Washington, DC 20036
US Phone: 202-457-0790   **US Fax:** 202-457-0810
Web: www.tepco.co.jp

The Tokyo Electric Power Company provides electricity in Japan's Kanto region, which includes Tokyo and Yokohama. It also has independent power projects in Australia, Taiwan, the United Arab Emirates, the US, and Vietnam.

PRODUCTS/OPERATIONS

2003 Sales

	% of total
Electricity	91
Information & telecommunications	2
Other	7
Total	**100**

2003 Generation Fuel Mix

	% of total
Fossil fuel	56
Nuclear	25
Hydroelectric	19
Total	**100**

Selected Subsidiaries and Affiliates

Japan COM Company, Limited (65%, fuel supply)
POWEREDCOM, Inc. (33%, telecommunications)
SpeedNet Inc. (77%, telecommunications)
TEPCO CABLE TELEVISION Inc. (86%, cable television)
TEPCO LOGISTICS CO., LTD. (80%, transportation and services)
TEPCO HOME SERVICE CO., LTD. (facilities construction and maintenance)
Toden Kogyo Co., Ltd. (facilities construction and maintenance)
Toden Real Estate Co., Inc. (property management)
Tokyo Densetsu Services Co., Ltd. (facilities construction and maintenance)
The Tokyo Electric Generation Company, Incorporated (power generation)
Tokyo Electric Power Environmental Engineering Company, Incorporated (facilities construction and maintenance)
Tokyo Electric Power Services Company, Limited (facilities construction and maintenance)
Tokyo Telecommunication Network Company, Incorporated (TTNet, 39%, telecommunications)

COMPETITORS

Chubu Electric Power
Chugoku Electric Power
Hokkaido Electric Power
Hokuriku Electric Power
Internet Initiative Japan
Japan Telecom
Jinpan International
Kansai Electric
KDDI
Korea Electric Power
Kyushu Electric Power
NTT
Osaka Gas
Shikoku Electric
Tohoku Electric Power
Tokyo Gas

HISTORICAL FINANCIALS

Company Type: Public

Income Statement

FYE: March 31

	REVENUE ($ mil.)	NET INCOME ($ mil.)	NET PROFIT MARGIN	EMPLOYEES
3/03	41,045	1,379	3.4%	39,619
3/02	39,358	1,521	3.9%	40,725
3/01	41,622	1,646	4.0%	42,000
3/00	48,258	829	1.7%	43,000
3/99	42,720	818	1.9%	42,700
3/98	39,664	1,017	2.6%	42,672
3/97	40,703	659	1.6%	43,166
3/96	47,121	483	1.0%	43,448
3/95	57,798	1,000	1.7%	43,122
3/94	45,947	603	1.3%	41,967
Annual Growth	**(1.2%)**	**9.6%**	**—**	**(0.6%)**

2003 Year-End Financials

Debt ratio: 321.6%
Return on equity: 7.8%
Cash ($ mil.): 675
Current ratio: 0.24
Long-term debt ($ mil.): 60,269

Net Income History

Exchange: Tokyo

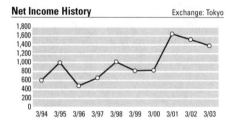

Tokyo Electron

Let me tell you about TEL. Tokyo Electron Limited (TEL) is the world's #2 manufacturer of semiconductor production equipment (well behind #1 Applied Materials). TEL's chip making systems include chemical vapor deposition, thermal processing, etching, cleaning, and probing equipment. The company also makes liquid crystal display (LCD) production equipment, and distributes other companies' chip making equipment, computer systems, networking products, and software in Japan. Subsidiary Tokyo Electron Device distributes chips, boards, and software made by companies including Advanced Micro Devices, Agilent, Motorola, and Microsoft.

Chip production equipment accounts for more than three-quarters of TEL's sales, and customers outside Japan account for more than half of sales.

Like its customers and competitors, TEL suffered through a dismal year in 2001 — by all accounts the worst year in the history of the chip industry — and again in 2002. To counter these conditions, and to give itself more flexibility for future market ups and downs, TEL restructured its operations. Among other measures, it merged production plants, closed field offices, and let go many of its contract workers. It has also sold its physical vapor deposition (PVD) product line to Metron Technology.

HISTORY

Frustrated by the unreliable semiconductor production equipment their employer, Nissho Trading Co. (now Nissho Iwai-Nichimen), was importing from the US, Tokuo Kubo and Toshio Kodada quit their jobs at Nissho in 1963 and founded Tokyo Electron Laboratories (TEL). Tokyo Broadcasting System provided some initial backing.

At first about half of the company's sales came from importing US semiconductor equipment. The other half came from exporting Japanese electronics such as car radios. In 1968 TEL and US-based diffusion furnace maker Thermco Systems (later acquired by Allegheny International) formed TEL-Thermco Engineering Co. (now Tokyo Electron Tohoku Ltd. Sagami Plant). TEL followed with other joint ventures, paying royalties to manufacture other companies' products in Japan.

The company's US unit, TEL America (now Tokyo Electron America), was established in 1972. In 1978 Tokyo Electron Laboratories was renamed Tokyo Electron Limited (also TEL).

TEL went public in 1980. In 1981 the company formed a joint venture with GenRad (later acquired by Teradyne) to make test systems in the US. In 1988 TEL acquired Thermco's stake in their joint venture.

The company began a major international expansion in 1993, setting up shop in South Korea. In the following years it expanded into Germany, Italy, the UK, and Taiwan. In 1996 TEL managing director Tetsuro Higashi was named president.

In 1997 TEL delivered the first of its 300mm wafer production equipment. The next year the company acquired the semiconductor equipment division (now part of Tokyo Electron Arizona) of Sony's Material Research Corp. Also in 1998 TEL formed Tokyo Electron EE Limited to refurbish and upgrade semiconductor manufacturing equipment.

The company formed its French subsidiary in 1999. That year TEL and AlliedSignal (now Honeywell International) formed a joint venture to develop chip making equipment. Also in 1999 rival Tegal won a permanent injunction against TEL to stop US sales of some of TEL's wafer etching equipment; legal wrangling over patent issues continued between the two companies through 2000.

In 2000 TEL acquired US-based Supercritical Systems, a maker of semiconductor cleaning devices. The next year the company bought Timbre Technologies, a US-based maker of metrology tools used in chip production.

In 2002 the company expanded its reach into China — which many industry watchers project as the next great market for the chip industry — when it opened a support office there.

EXECUTIVES

Chairman: Tetsuro (Terry) Higashi
Vice Chairman: Tetsuo (Tom) Tsuneishi
President and CEO: Kiyoshi (Ken) Sato
EVP, Administration: Mamoru Hara
SVP, Sales: Mitsuru Onozato
SVP, Technology and Marketing: Ryuichi Komatsubara
VP and General Manager, Field Engineering; President, Tokyo Electron FE: Jinzaburo Sakamoto
VP and General Manager, Manufacturing: Hisashi Shirahada
VP and General Manager, Human Resources, Finance, Accounting, Order Process, and Business Support Center: Noriyuki Kuga

VP & General Manager, General Affairs, Accounting, Administration, Fuchu Technology Center, and Osaka Branch Office and Director, General Affairs Department: Yoshiteru Harada
VP and General Manager, IT Center: Takao Kodama
VP & General Manager, Clean Track Business Unit: Hikaru Ito
VP & General Manager, Etch Systems Business Unit: Takashi Ito
VP and General Manager, Thermal Processing Systems Business Unit and President, Tokyo Electron Tohoku Ltd.: Yasuyuki Kuriki
VP and General Manager, Business Development and Account Management, North America and Europe: Kiyoshi Sunohara
VP and General Manager, Marketing: Yoichi Ishikawa
President, Tokyo Electron America: Barry R. Rapozo
Auditors: Masatoshi Yoshino, Eiji Miyashita, Fumihiko Sugiura

LOCATIONS

HQ: Tokyo Electron Limited
TBS Broadcast Center,
3-6 Akasaka 5-chome, Minato-ku,
Tokyo 107-8481, Japan
Phone: +81-3-5561-7000 **Fax:** +81-3-5561-7400
US HQ: 2400 Grove Blvd., Austin, TX 78741-1000
US Phone: 512-424-1000 **US Fax:** 512-424-1001
Web: www.tel.com

Tokyo Electron Limited has operations in China, France, Germany, Ireland, Israel, Italy, Japan, the Netherlands, South Korea, Taiwan, the UK, and the US.

2003 Sales

	% of total
Japan	41
Other countries	59
Total	**100**

PRODUCTS/OPERATIONS

2003 Sales

	% of total
Semiconductor production equipment	79
Electronic components	17
Computer network equipment	4
Total	**100**

Selected Products

Production Equipment
Liquid crystal displays
  Coater/developers
  Plasma etcher/ashers
Semiconductors
  Carrierless cleaners
  Coater/developers
  Metal chemical vapor deposition (CVD) systems
  Oxidation/diffusion furnaces and LP-CVD systems
  Plasma etchers
  Scrubbers
  Spin-on dielectric coaters
  Wafer probers
  Wafer-level burn-in and test systems

Distributed Products
Data management software
Film metrology tools
Lithography process management software
Semiconductor manufacturing yield management
  software
Semiconductors and board-level products
Storage area network (SAN) equipment
Wafer inspection systems

COMPETITORS

Amtech Systems	Hitachi
Applied Materials	Lam Research
ASM International	Novellus
Electroglas	Semitool
FSI International	Tegal
Future Electronics	Trikon
Genus	Veeco Instruments

HISTORICAL FINANCIALS
Company Type: Public

Income Statement
FYE: March 31

	REVENUE ($ mil.)	NET INCOME ($ mil.)	NET PROFIT MARGIN	EMPLOYEES
3/03	3,843	(347)	—	10,053
3/02	3,150	(150)	—	10,171
3/01	5,730	491	8.6%	10,236
3/00	4,177	188	4.5%	8,946
3/99	2,603	16	0.6%	8,576
3/98	3,424	226	6.6%	8,242
3/97	3,496	242	6.9%	6,988
3/96	3,752	229	6.1%	6,148
3/95	2,910	89	3.1%	5,410
3/94	1,846	38	2.1%	4,896
Annual Growth	**8.5%**	**—**	**—**	**8.3%**

2003 Year-End Financials

Debt ratio: 27.8%
Return on equity: —
Cash ($ mil.): 442
Current ratio: 2.22
Long-term debt ($ mil.): 586

Net Income History
Exchange: Tokyo

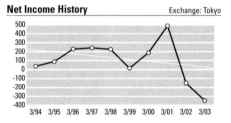

Tomkins PLC

Not so long ago, whether you wanted to pack some heat or merely pack some lunch, multinational conglomerate Tomkins had a subsidiary that could make your day. But the company has sold its food manufacturing operations and subsidiary Smith & Wesson in order to reshape itself as a global engineering group. Tomkins companies make and distribute automotive products, industrial power systems, plumbing components, windows, doors, valves, and other construction products. In the US, Tomkins' marquee names include Gates (automotive belts and hoses) and Trico (wiper blades).

In keeping with its new focus on core operations, Tomkins sold its Gates Consumer and Industrial (carpet padding and accessories, diving suits, and commercial rubber compounds) division to the Rutland Fund for about $35 million in cash. US operations account for about 70% of sales.

HISTORY

Tomkins was founded in 1925 as the F. H. Tomkins Buckle Company, a maker of buckles and fasteners. Tomkins continued to develop within this niche market for the next six decades. In 1983 Gregory Hutchings acquired a 23% stake in the company. Hutchings, who at age 24 had started his own construction business, had won a reputation as a go-getter when he caught the eye of Lords Hanson and White; he was hired by the Hanson Group in 1980 as its chief acquisition scout. In 1984 Hutchings became Tomkins'

CEO and set about acquiring manufacturing companies in the UK and the US.

The company acquired Ferraris Piston Service (auto components) and Hayters (a garden tool manufacturer) that year, followed by Pegler-Hattersley (plumbing fixtures) in 1986, Smith & Wesson (guns) in 1987, and Murray Ohio (lawn mowers and bicycles) the next year. In 1992 the company acquired Rank Hovis McDougall, a leading UK baker and food manufacturer.

Tomkins made only eight major purchases between 1983 and 1993, as Hutchings worked to put his acquisitions on a sound financial footing, upgrading plants and equipment and giving each company the autonomy to become efficient.

In 1994 Tomkins bought Outdoor Products and Dynamark Plastics from Noma Industries of Canada. Outdoor Products complemented the Murray Ohio operations, and injection molder Dynamark Plastics fit into Tomkins' industrial products portfolio.

Two years later the company acquired Gates, a US maker of belts and hoses, with operations in 15 countries; the move gave Tomkins access to new markets in Latin America and Southeast Asia. That year Tomkins acquired the hose operations of Nationwide Rubber Enterprises, making Gates the leading manufacturer of curved hose in Australia. In 1997 Tomkins acquired US firm Stant Corp., a leading maker of windshield wipers, fuel tank caps, and other auto accessories, to further complement Gates' product lines.

Besides acquisitions, Tomkins regularly disposed of companies that no longer fit its strategic plan. It sold Inchbrook Printers in 1996 and Ferraris Piston Service, the first business purchased by Tomkins under Hutchings' leadership, in 1997. In a symbolic break with its past, Tomkins sold F. H. Tomkins Buckle in 1998.

That year Tomkins made another automotive equipment acquisition when it bought US-based Schrader-Bridgeport; it also bought Martine Spécialités, a supplier of frozen patisserie products. In 1999 the company acquired ACD Tridon, a Canadian manufacturer of automotive parts.

In 2000 Smith & Wesson settled more than a dozen lawsuits with US cities attempting to collect damages for handgun violence cases. Breaking rank with other handgun makers, the company agreed to install child-safety locks on its guns and ensure that gun sellers conduct background checks.

Tomkins moved to exit the food manufacturing business in 2000, selling Red Wing and agreeing to sell the European operations of Ranks Hovis McDougall. Hutchings resigned that year in the midst of an investigation of his spending practices (including his use of corporate jets and the presence of Hutchings' wife and housekeeper on the company payroll), and chairman David Newlands took over. That year the company sold its bicycle, snowblower, and mowing machinery businesses (Hayter and Murray). In 2001 Tomkins sold Smith & Wesson to US-based Saf-T-Hammer, a manufacturer of gun safety equipment, for $15 million.

In 2002 Tomkins sold its Gates Consumer and Industrial (GCI) division to the Rutland Fund for about $35 million in cash. GCI's products include carpet padding and accessories, diving suits, and commercial rubber compounds. Also that year Jim Nicol took over as CEO. The following year Tomkins sold its Milliken Valve Company, Inc. subsidiary to the Henry Pratt Company for $7.3 million in cash.

EXECUTIVES

Non-Executive Chairman: David B. Newlands, age 56, $500,417 pay
CEO: Jim Nicol, age 49
CFO: Ken Lever, age 48
Chairman, Tomkins Corporation: Anthony J. (Tony) Reading, age 59
President, The Gates Rubber Company: Richard Bell, age 51
President, Air Systems Components Division: T.J. O'Halloran, age 55
General Counsel: G.S. Pappayliou, age 49
Secretary: N.C. Porter, age 51
Auditors: Deloitte & Touche

LOCATIONS

HQ: East Putney House, 84 Upper Richmond Rd., London SW15 2ST, United Kingdom
Phone: +44-20-8871-4544 **Fax:** +44-20-8877-9700
Web: www.tomkins.co.uk

2002 Sales

	% of total
US	70
Europe	
UK	6
Other countries	9
Other regions	15
Total	**100**

PRODUCTS/OPERATIONS

2002 Sales

	% of total
Industrial & automotive	60
Engineered & construction products	24
Air systems components	16
Total	**100**

Subsidiaries and Affiliates

Industrial & Automotive
Gates Air Springs (US)
Schrader Bridgeport (automotive electronics, tire valves and gauges; US)
Schrader Electronics (remote tire pressure measuring systems; US)
Standard-Thomson Corporation (automotive thermostats; US)
Stant Manufacturing Inc. (gas caps, closure caps; US)
The Gates Rubber Company (automotive belts, hoses, pulleys; US)
Trico Products Corporation (wiper systems, signal flashers; US)

Engineered and Construction Products
Aquatic Whirlpools (whirlpool baths; US)
Dearborn Mid-West Conveyor Company (heavy-duty conveyor systems, US)
Dexter Axle (axles and wheels for trailers, US)
Hattersley Newman Hender Ltd. (cast-iron and bronze valves)
Lasco Bathware (fiberglass and acrylic baths and whirlpools, US)
Lasco Fittings (PVC pipe fittings, US)
Pegler Ltd. (nonferrous faucets, valves, and plumbing fittings)
Philips Products (aluminum and vinyl windows, vinyl-clad steel doors, ventilation devices; US)
Ventline (bathroom fans, exhaust hoods, roof vents; US)

Air Systems Components
Hart & Cooley (heating, ventilation, and air-conditioning components, US)
Lau (centrifugal fans and propellers, US)
Penn Ventilation (HVAC components, US)
Ruskin Air Management Ltd (air handling products and louvers, US)
Ruskin (air, fire, and smoke dampers; louvers and fiberglass products; US)

COMPETITORS

Applied Industrial Technologies	Goodyear
Bridgestone	Tenneco Automotive
Continental AG	United Technologies

HISTORICAL FINANCIALS

Company Type: Public

Income Statement

FYE: December 31

	REVENUE ($ mil.)	NET INCOME ($ mil.)	NET PROFIT MARGIN	EMPLOYEES
12/02*	3,380	190	5.6%	39,596
4/02	4,916	273	5.6%	40,670
4/01	5,875	96	1.6%	52,755
4/00	8,722	164	1.9%	70,039
4/99	8,600	491	5.7%	66,927
4/98	8,442	545	6.5%	65,300
4/97	7,451	459	6.2%	54,496
4/96	5,431	338	6.2%	46,096
4/95	6,006	335	5.6%	46,096
4/94	4,931	273	5.5%	43,714
Annual Growth	**(4.1%)**	**(3.9%)**	**—**	**(1.1%)**

*Fiscal year change

2002 Year-End Financials

Debt ratio: 53.3%
Return on equity: 37.6%
Cash ($ mil.): 577
Current ratio: 1.69
Long-term debt ($ mil.): 266
No. of shares (mil.): 193
Dividends
  Yield: 5.0%
  Payout: 69.7%
Market value ($ mil.): 2,361

Stock History

NYSE: TKS

	STOCK PRICE ($) FY Close	P/E High/Low		PER SHARE ($) Earnings	Dividends	Book Value
12/02*	15.30	15	7	1.09	0.76	8.36
4/02	12.22	21	14	0.76	0.50	8.67
4/01	8.81	13	7	0.20	1.16	7.70
4/00	12.19	11	6	0.47	1.41	4.45
4/99	17.63	17	9	1.42	0.94	3.99
4/98	23.06	18	11	1.52	0.94	5.71
4/97	18.00	15	11	1.34	0.73	7.81
4/96	17.00	16	12	1.14	0.59	5.57
4/95	15.38	14	11	1.13	0.55	5.38
4/94	15.75	19	14	0.92	0.42	4.88
Annual Growth	**(0.3%)**	**—**	**—**	**1.9%**	**6.8%**	**6.2%**

*Fiscal year change

Tommy Hilfiger

From the blacktop to the golf course, designer Tommy Hilfiger has the streets covered. His namesake casual wear is worn by rap, rock, teen, and sports stars and fans, and, these days, many of them are women. Tommy (to those in the know) designs, sources, makes, and markets men's and women's sportswear and denim wear, as well as athletic wear, children's wear, and accessories. Through extensive licensing deals (almost 40 product lines), Tommy also offers products such as fragrances, belts, bedding, home furnishings, and cosmetics. The company's clean-cut clothing is sold in major department and specialty stores as well as some 165 Tommy Hilfiger shops and outlets.

Disparaged by some as a triumph of merchandising rather than design, Hilfigerwear features traditional styles often decorated with nothing more than the company's red, white, and blue logo. Tommy Hilfiger licenses its name and logo to such companies as Hartmarx, Jockey, Jones Apparel, Movado, and Stride Rite for everything from handbags and watches to shoes.

The big three US department store chains — Federated, May, and Dillard's — account for almost 40% of sales. Although Tommy Hilfiger's products have often been viewed as geared towards men, the company in 2002 sold more than half of its goods to women. Hilfiger sources its products mainly from manufacturers in Asia and India.

In 2003 Tommy Hilfiger began producing men's leather outerwear through a licensing agreement with Winlit Group. Licenses for men's underwear and loungewear, meanwhile, have run out, and the company has brought production in-house.

Begun in 2000, initial efforts to combat counterfeiting and trademark infringements received their first payoff in May 2003, when Hilfiger prevailed in a suit against budget store chain Goody's Family Clothing.

HISTORY

Teenage clotheshorse Tommy Hilfiger once bought trendy clothes in New York City then resold them from the trunk of his car in his hometown of Elmira, New York. In 1969, while a senior in high school, he opened a boutique. By the mid-1970s Hilfiger had seven stores in upstate New York operating under The People's Place name. Hilfiger designed items for the shops, but the chain went bankrupt during the recession of the late 1970s. He briefly designed jeans for Jordache in the early 1980s.

Hilfiger launched an independent menswear collection in 1984 as a licensee of Murjani International, headed by Mohan Murjani (who also backed Gloria Vanderbilt). The line received a good bit of notoriety from a 1985 ad campaign that called Hilfiger one of "the four great American designers for men" along with Ralph Lauren, Perry Ellis, and Calvin Klein.

Eventually outgrowing Murjani, in 1989 Hilfiger partnered with Joel Horowitz, Lawrence Stroll, and Hong Kong-based manufacturer Silas Chou, part of one of Hong Kong's most established textile and apparel families. Hilfiger retained control of design. Their company, Tommy Hilfiger, went public in 1992.

Sales were helped even more when rapper Snoop Doggy Dog hosted *Saturday Night Live* in 1994 wearing a rugby shirt emblazoned with a Tommy Hilfiger logo. Much of the sales increase was credited to fans of the artist (and other Hilfiger-clad musicians) who loyally outfitted themselves head-to-toe in Tommy Hilfiger. Horowitz, Hilfiger COO, moved up to the CEO spot that year. In 1995 the company licensed sister company Pepe Jeans USA to make and distribute its jeans and womenswear in the US. The women's clothing line debuted the next year, as did a line of men's athletic shoes through licensee Stride Rite.

In 1997 Tommy Hilfiger opened its first flagship store in Beverly Hills, California, and a small store in London. The following year the company added licensing agreements for women's hosiery and home furnishings; it also began offering men's dress shoes and women's shoes through Stride Rite. In addition, in 1998 the company purchased its Canadian distributor and Pepe Jeans USA, which held the license for womenswear and jeans. The deal gave Hilfiger, chairman Chou, Horowitz, and director Stroll (who together controlled the affiliates) nearly 20% in Tommy Hilfiger. Stroll was also named co-chairman that year.

Tommy Hilfiger began targeting older women in late 1998, offering designer-priced suits and other conservative clothing sans his flashy logo. The company also reached a deal with Estée Lauder Companies to market a line of cosmetics.

Discounter Wal-Mart Stores agreed in 1999 to pay $6.4 million to settle a claim it was selling counterfeit Tommy Hilfiger merchandise. In early 2000, after the stock had lost two-thirds of its value in six months, the company scrapped plans for its upscale women's label and began considering acquisitions to bolster its share price. It later closed its London flagship store. In 2001 Tommy Hilfiger closed its remaining flagship store in Beverly Hills. To penetrate selected markets not served by its department store distribution, the company announced plans in mid-2001 to open around 35 new stores by the middle of 2002.

Tommy Hilfiger bought its European licensee, T.H. International, in July 2001 for $200 million. In October 2002 namesake founder Tommy Hilfiger was named chairman (later honorary chairman), replacing longtime founding chairman Silas Chou.

EXECUTIVES

Principal Designer and Honorary Chairman: Thomas J. (Tommy) Hilfiger, age 52, $22,360,000 pay
Chairman: Joel J. Horowitz, age 52, $10,715,678 pay
President and Director: David F. Dyer, age 54
EVP, Finance and Operations, and Assistant Secretary; COO, Tommy Hilfiger U.S.A.: Joel H. Newman, age 61, $1,350,000 pay
SVP, CFO, and Treasurer: Joseph (Joe) Scirocco, age 46
SVP, Operations: Arthur Bargonetti, age 69
VP and Corporate Controller; SVP and Corporate Controller, Tommy Hilfiger U.S.A.: James P. (Jim) Reilly, age 39
VP, Communications: George Kolasa
VP, Human Resources: Bettina Havrilla
President, Tommy Kids: Michael Spillane
President, Licensing, Tommy Hilfiger U.S.A.: Lynn Shanahan
President, Men's Sportswear and Jeans: David McTague
President, Missy Sportswear, Junior Jeans, and TH Women: Christa Michalaros
President of Production: JoAnne Bies
President, Worldwide Marketing and Communications, Tommy Hilfiger U.S.A.: Peter Connolly
Secretary: Lawrence T. S. Lok, age 47
Auditors: PricewaterhouseCoopers LLP

LOCATIONS

HQ: Tommy Hilfiger Corporation
9/F Novel Industrial Building
850-870 Lai Chi Kok Rd., Cheung Sha Wan, Kowloon, Hong Kong
Phone: +852-2216-0668　　**Fax:** +852-2312-1368
US HQ: 25 W. 39th St., New York, NY 10018
US Phone: 212-840-8888　　**US Fax:** 212-548-1818
Web: www.tommy.com

Tommy Hilfiger's products are sold in Asia, Europe, and North and South America.

2003 Sales

	$ mil.	% of total
US	1,497	79
Europe	276	15
Canada	91	5
Other	24	1
Total	**1,888**	**100**

PRODUCTS/OPERATIONS

2003 Sales

	$ mil.	% of total
Wholesale	1,420	75
Retail	405	22
Licensing	63	3
Total	**1,888**	**100**

Selected Licensing Partners

Aramis, Inc. (fragrances)
Bestform Intimates (women's intimate apparel)
FAO Schwartz (dolls)
Hartmarx (men's suits)
Jantzen (women's swimwear)
Jockey International (men's underwear)
Lantis Eyewear Corporation (sunglasses)
Mountain High Hosiery (socks and women's hosiery)
Movado Group, Inc. (watches)
Oxford Industries (men's dress shirts and golfwear)
Revman Industries, Inc. (linens, bedding, and bath products)
Russell-Newman, Inc. (robes and sleepwear)
Strellson AG (men's tailored clothing, Europe)
Swank (men's accessories)
The Stride Rite Corporation (footwear)
Victoria & Co. Ltd. (jewelry)

COMPETITORS

Abercrombie & Fitch	Limited Brands
American Eagle Outfitters	Liz Claiborne
Benetton	L.L. Bean
Calvin Klein	Nautica Enterprises
Diesel	NIKE
Donna Karan	Oxford Industries
Esprit Holdings	Perry Ellis International
Fruit of the Loom	Phat
FUBU	Phillips-Van Heusen
Gap	Polo Ralph Lauren
Armani	Quiksilver
Gucci	Reebok
Guess	Salant
Haggar	Sara Lee Branded
Hugo Boss	Spiegel
J. Crew	Tropical Sportswear
Kenneth Cole	Viewpoint
Levi Strauss	Warnaco Group

HISTORICAL FINANCIALS

Company Type: Public

Income Statement

FYE: March 31

	REVENUE ($ mil.)	NET INCOME ($ mil.)	NET PROFIT MARGIN	EMPLOYEES
3/03	1,888	(514)	—	5,400
3/02	1,877	135	7.2%	4,900
3/01	1,881	131	7.0%	4,100
3/00	1,977	172	8.7%	2,600
3/99	1,637	174	10.6%	3,000
3/98	847	113	13.4%	1,820
3/97	662	86	13.1%	1,570
3/96	478	62	12.9%	—
3/95	321	41	12.7%	—
3/94	227	25	11.1%	—
Annual Growth	**26.5%**	**—**	**—**	**22.9%**

2003 Year-End Financials

Debt ratio: 33.6%
Return on equity: —
Cash ($ mil.): 421
Current ratio: 2.22
Long-term debt ($ mil.): 350

No. of shares (mil.): 91
Dividends
Yield: 0.0%
Payout: —
Market value ($ mil.): 655

Stock History

NYSE: TOM

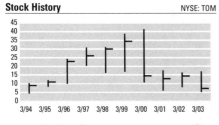

	STOCK PRICE ($)	P/E		PER SHARE ($)		
	FY Close	High/Low		Earnings	Dividends	Book Value
3/03	7.23	—	—	(5.68)	0.00	11.52
3/02	14.35	11	6	1.49	0.00	16.67
3/01	12.85	12	4	1.43	0.00	15.16
3/00	14.50	23	6	1.80	0.00	13.47
3/99	34.44	21	9	1.86	0.00	11.58
3/98	30.03	21	11	1.50	0.00	6.91
3/97	26.13	27	18	1.14	0.00	5.34
3/96	22.94	29	12	0.83	0.00	4.08
3/95	11.00	21	15	0.56	0.00	2.97
3/94	8.97	26	12	0.39	0.00	—
Annual Growth	(2.4%)	—	—	—	—	18.5%

The Toronto-Dominion Bank

The Toronto-Dominion Bank wants to score financial TDs at home and abroad. Also known as TD Financial Group, Canada's third-largest bank provides consumer, corporate, and government banking services, including deposit accounts, credit cards, mortgages, trusts, estate planning, and investment management. Toronto-Dominion also offers financial and advisory services to businesses at home and abroad. Subsidiary TD Waterhouse is a leading online discount brokerage in Canada, the UK, and the US. Other operations include TD Asset Management (mutual funds) and TD Securities (investment banking, equities, and foreign exchange).

After the government nixed Toronto-Dominion's planned merger with Canadian Imperial Bank of Commerce, the company is pursuing more international expansion south of the border in the US, and across the Pacific with brokerage DBS TD Waterhouse Direct, a partnership with DBS Group that operates in Singapore and Hong Kong. Toronto-Dominion has invaded the US by linking its online trading customers to its online Waterhouse National Bank and cross-selling deposit, loan, and other banking services.

Toronto-Dominion suffered its first-ever annual loss during fiscal year 2002. Write-downs on loans to telecommunications, technology, and energy firms contributed mightily to the dismal results.

The company's plans to hitch a ride on the Wal-Mart gravy train have been derailed. Arrangements to open bank branches in some US-based Wal-Mart stores were squelched by regulators enforcing the banking and commerce barrier. Toronto-Dominion also announced it will close all of its existing branches (more than 100 in all) inside Canadian Wal-Marts by 2006 as part of a broader restructuring.

HISTORY

The Bank of Toronto was established in 1855 by flour traders who wanted their own banking facilities. Its growth encouraged another group of businessmen to found the Dominion Bank in 1869. Dominion emphasized commercial banking and invested heavily in railways and construction.

As the new nation expanded westward, both banks established branch networks. They helped fund Canada's primary industries — dairy, mining, oil, pulp, and textiles. True to its pioneering spirit, a Bank of Toronto official claimed to be the first to have set up a branch office with the help of aviation (in Manitoba in the 1920s).

The demand for agricultural products and commodities dropped after WWI, but production continued full throttle, creating a world grain glut that helped trigger the stock market crash of 1929. Both the Bank of Toronto and Dominion Bank contracted during the 1930s. After growing during and subsequent to WWII, The Bank of Toronto and Dominion Bank decided to increase their capital base, merging into a 450-branch bank in 1955.

In the 1970s TD opened offices in Bangkok, Beirut, and Frankfurt, among other cities abroad. During the 1980s it was active in making loans to less-developed countries. After the deregulation of the Canadian securities industry in 1987, CEO Richard Thomson reduced international lending and began focusing on brokerage activities. The strategy paid off when several Latin American countries fell behind on their loans in the late 1980s.

As the North American economy slowed in the early 1990s, TD's nonperforming loans increased and, with it, its loan loss reserves. The bank still made acquisitions, including Central Guaranty Trust (1993) and Lancaster Financial Holdings (1995, investment banking). It worked to build its financial services, expanding its range of service offerings and geographic coverage and buying New York-based Waterhouse Investor Services (1996); 97% of Australia-based Pont Securities (1997); and California-based Kennedy, Cabot & Co. (1997). In 1998 the bank sold its payroll services to Ceridian, and its Waterhouse Securities unit bought US discount brokerage Jack White & Co.

That year the government nixed TD's merger with Canadian Imperial on the same day it voided the Royal Bank of Canada/Bank of Montreal deal. The banks believed the consolidation necessary to stave off foreign banks' encroachment into Canada, but the government had domestic anti-competition concerns: Though Canada has one-tenth the population of the US, its five top banks all ranked in the top 15 in North America.

In 1999 TD bought Trimark Financial's retail trust banking business and spun off part of Waterhouse Investor Services (now TD Waterhouse Group). That year the bank ramped up its focus on Internet banking; the company's Web site sells competitors' products, as well as TD's.

Not giving up on acquisition-fueled growth, in 2000 the company bought CT Financial Services (now Canada Trust) from British American Tobacco. As a condition for government approval, TD had to sell its MasterCard credit portfolio (sold to Citibank Canada) and a dozen southern Ontario branches (to Bank of Montreal). TD is also shopping for a US bank and has teamed up with Commerce One to launch TDMarketSite, a business-to-business (B2B) Web site.

In 2001 TD finished integrating Canada Trust's retail operations into its own.

EXECUTIVES

Chairman: John M. Thompson, age 60
President, CEO, and Director: W. Edmund (Ed) Clark, age 55, $664,937 pay
Vice Chairman; President, TD Canada Trust: Andrea S. Rosen, $625,030 pay
Vice Chairman, Risk Management: Thomas R. (Tom) Spencer
Vice Chairman, Corporate Operations: Fredric J. Tomczyk, $1,000,279 pay
EVP, Marketing: T. Christian Armstrong
EVP and CFO: Daniel A. Marinangeli
EVP, General Counsel, and Secretary: Christopher A. Montague
EVP, Corporate Development: J. David Livingston
EVP; Chairman and CEO, TD Securities: Robert E. Dorrance, age 49
EVP; President and CEO, TD Waterhouse USA: Frank J. Petrelli
EVP; President, TD Securities: Michael W. MacBain
EVP, Retail Product Group: Bernard T. Dorval
EVP, Commercial Banking: Michael A. Foulkes
EVP, Wealth Management Canada: William H. Hatanaka
EVP, Retail Distribution: Timothy D. Hockey
EVP and Chief Investment Officer: Robert F. MacLellan
EVP, Credit Asset Management: Bharat Masrani
SVP, Group Human Resources: Brian J. Haier
SVP, Group Corporate and Public Affairs: Kerry A. Peacock
Auditors: Ernst & Young LLP; PricewaterhouseCoopers LLP

LOCATIONS

HQ: Toronto-Dominion Centre, King St. West and Bay St., Toronto, Ontario M5K 1A2, Canada
Phone: 416-982-8222 **Fax:** 416-982-5671
US HQ: 31 W. 52nd St., New York, NY 10019
US Phone: 212-468-0610
Web: www.td.com

PRODUCTS/OPERATIONS

Selected Subsidiaries

Canada
1390017 Ontario Limited
1390018 Ontario Limited
Commercial Mortgage Origination Company of Canada
Cotyledon Capital Inc.
CT Financial Assurance Company
First Nations Bank of Canada (89%)
Meloche Monnex Inc.
Meloche Monnex Insurance & Financial Services Inc.
Meloche Monnex Financial Services Inc.
Security National Insurance Company
Primmum Insurance Company
TD General Insurance Company
TD Assurance Agency, Inc.
Newcrest Holdings Inc.
TD Asset Finance Corp.
TD Asset Management Inc.
TD Capital Canadian Private Equity Partners Ltd.
TD Capital Management L.P. (41%)
TD Capital Group Limited
TD Capital Trust
TD Futures Inc.
TD Investment Management Inc.
TD Investment Services Inc.
TD Life Insurance Company
TD MarketSite Inc.
TD Mortgage Corporation
Canada Trustco Mortgage Company
The Canada Trust Company
Canada Trustco International Limited (Barbados)

CT Corporate Services Inc.
TD Waterhouse Bank N.V. (the Netherlands)
Truscan Property Corporation
TD Pacific Mortgage Corporation
TD Mortgage Investment Corporation
TD Nordique Inc.
TD Parallel Private Equity Investors Ltd.
TD Realty Limited
TD Securities Inc.

United States
TD North American Limited Partnership
TD Waterhouse Group, Inc.
CTUSA, Inc.
TD Bank USA, F.S.B.
National Investor Services Corp.
TD Waterhouse Advertising, Inc.
TD Waterhouse Asset Management, Inc.
TD Waterhouse Bank, N.A.
Waterhouse Mortgage Services, Inc.
TD Waterhouse Canada, Inc.
TD Waterhouse Capital Markets, Inc.
TD Waterhouse European Acquisition Corporation
TD Waterhouse Holdings (Australia) Pty Ltd
TD Waterhouse Investor Services, Inc.
Toronto Dominion Holdings (U.S.A.), Inc.
TD Equity Options, Inc.
TD Options Acquisition, Inc.
TD Securities (USA) Inc.
Toronto Dominion Capital (U.S.A.), Inc.
Toronto Dominion Investments, Inc.
Toronto Dominion (New York), Inc.
Toronto Dominion (Texas), Inc.

Other
Carysforth Investment Limited (70%) (Cayman Islands)
Haddington Investments Ltd. (70%) (Cayman Islands)
TD Asset Management Limited (UK)
TD Asset Management (Luxembourg) S.A.
TD Capital Canadian Private Equity Partners (Barbados) Ltd.
TD European Finance Limited (UK)
TD Financial International Ltd. (Bermuda)
TD Reinsurance (Barbados) Inc.
TD Haddington Services B.V. (the Netherlands)
Belgravia Securities Investments Limited (67%, Cayman Islands)
TD Guernsey Services Limited (UK)
TD European Funding Limited (61%, UK)
TD Ireland
TD Global Finance (Ireland)
TD Securities (Japan) Inc.
TD Waterhouse Investor Services (UK) Limited
TD Waterhouse Investor Services (Europe) Limited (UK)
TD Waterhouse Pacific Ltd. (Mauritius)
Toronto Dominion Australia Limited
Toronto Dominion Securities Pty. Limited (Australia)
Toronto Dominion International Inc. (Barbados)
The TD Bermuda Trust
TD Trust (Bermuda) Limited
Toronto Dominion Investments B.V. (the Netherlands)
TD Bank Europe Limited (UK)
Toronto Dominion Holdings (U.K.) Limited
TD Securities Limited (UK)
Toronto Dominion Finance (UK) Limited
Toronto Dominion International Limited
Toronto Dominion (United Kingdom) Limited
Toronto Dominion Jersey Holdings Limited (UK)
Toronto Dominion (South East Asia) Limited (Singapore)

COMPETITORS

Ameritrade	FleetBoston
Bank of Montreal	FMR
Scotiabank	Jones Financial
CIBC	Companies
Charles Schwab	Laurentian Bank
Credit Suisse First Boston (USA), Inc.	Morgan Stanley
	National Bank of Canada
Desjardins	Quick & Reilly
E*TRADE Financial	RBC Financial Group

HISTORICAL FINANCIALS

Company Type: Public

Income Statement

FYE: October 31

	ASSETS ($ mil.)	NET INCOME ($ mil.)	INCOME AS % OF ASSETS	EMPLOYEES
10/03	207,419	816	0.4%	41,934
10/02	178,502	(49)	—	51,000
10/01	181,367	871	0.5%	51,000
10/00	173,879	673	0.4%	44,798
10/99	145,739	2,026	1.4%	30,636
10/98	117,808	726	0.6%	29,236
10/97	116,351	773	0.7%	28,001
10/96	93,919	683	0.7%	26,815
10/95	80,930	591	0.7%	25,413
10/94	73,718	475	0.6%	25,705
Annual Growth	12.2%	6.2%	—	5.6%

2003 Year-End Financials

Equity as % of assets: 4.2%
Return on assets: 0.4%
Return on equity: 10.1%
Long-term debt ($ mil.): 4,464
No. of shares (mil.): 656

Dividends
  Yield: 2.3%
  Payout: 66.1%
Market value ($ mil.): 21,847
Sales ($ mil.): 11,849

Stock History

NYSE: TD

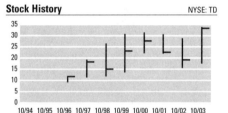

10/94 10/95 10/96 10/97 10/98 10/99 10/00 10/01 10/02 10/03

	STOCK PRICE ($) FY Close	P/E High/Low		PER SHARE ($) Earnings	Dividends	Book Value
10/03	33.29	29	15	1.15	0.76	15.15
10/02	19.13	—	—	(0.16)	0.71	12.97
10/01	22.51	23	17	1.30	1.09	13.44
10/00	27.56	31	22	1.02	0.92	13.02
10/99	23.06	9	4	3.33	0.48	12.64
10/98	15.00	22	10	1.18	0.45	9.30
10/97	18.25	15	9	1.26	0.41	8.73
10/96	11.69	11	9	1.11	0.09	8.25
Annual Growth	16.1%	—	—	0.5%	35.6%	9.1%

Toshiba Corporation

In the electronics world, Toshiba makes everything under the sun. The company may be best known for portable computers (it's a perennial contender for #1 worldwide), but its product portfolio also includes a full range of personal and professional computing systems (storage devices, peripherals), telecommunications and medical equipment (cell phones, X-ray machines), industrial machinery (power plant reactors, elevators), consumer appliances (microwaves, DVD players), electronic components (electron tubes, batteries), and semiconductors. Its portfolio also includes air traffic control and railway transportation systems. Toshiba sells about 75% of its products in Asia.

Feeling the pressure of a harsh Japanese economy, falling semiconductor prices, and a stagnant PC market, Toshiba continues to restructure its operations, moving away from less profitable segments such as industrial equipment and toward information technology. It has also announced its intention to begin spinning off some of its in-house companies. The company has made significant workforce reductions, with a particular emphasis on streamlining its domestic operations.

Toshiba has pulled out of the commodity DRAM (dynamic random-access memory) business, and is instead focused on specialty memory products. It merged its LCD operations with those of Matsushita, forming Toshiba Matsushita Display Technology. The company has also formed an alliance with rival Fujitsu that will focus on system-on-chip (SOC) operations, leaving the door open for wider semiconductor product integration in the future.

HISTORY

Two Japanese electrical equipment manufacturers came together in 1939 to create Toshiba. Tanaka Seizo-sha, Japan's first telegraph equipment manufacturer, was founded in 1875 by Hisashige Tanaka, the so-called Edison of Japan. In the 1890s the company started making heavier electrical equipment such as transformers and electric motors, adopting the name Shibaura Seisakusho Works in 1893. Seisakusho went on to pioneer the production of hydroelectric generators (1894) and X-ray tubes (1915) in Japan.

The other half of Toshiba, Hakunetsusha & Company, was founded by Ichisuke Fujioka and Shoichi Miyoshi as Japan's first incandescent lamp maker (1890). Renamed Tokyo Electric Company (1899), the company developed the coiled filament lightbulb (1921), Japan's first radio receiver and cathode-ray tube (1924), and the internally frosted glass lightbulb (1925). In 1939 it merged with Shibaura Seisakusho to form Tokyo Shibaura Electric Company (Toshiba).

Toshiba was the first company in Japan to make fluorescent lamps (1940), radar systems (1942), broadcasting equipment (1952), and digital computers (1954). Production of black-and-white televisions began in 1949. Even so, through the 1970s the company was considered an also-ran, trailing other Japanese business groups, known as keiretsu, partly because of its bureaucratic management style.

Electrical engineer Shoichi Saba became president in 1980. Saba invested heavily in Toshiba's information and communications segments. The company became the first in the world to produce the powerful one-megabit DRAM chip (1985). That year it unveiled its first laptop PC. In the meantime Saba (named chairman 1986) pushed Toshiba into joint ventures to exchange technology with companies such as Siemens and Motorola.

But in 1987 Toshiba incurred the wrath of the US government. A subsidiary sold submarine sound-deadening equipment to the USSR, resulting in threats of US sanctions and a precipitous decline in its stock price and in US sales. Chairman Saba and president Sugichiro Watari resigned in shame.

Toshiba in 1992 bought a $500 million stake in Time Warner (the stake was reduced in 1998). In 1996 the company appointed marketing and multimedia specialist Taizo Nishimuro as president, breaking its tradition of filling the position with an engineer from its heavy electrical operations.

In 1997 Toshiba and IBM formed joint venture Dominion Semiconductor to develop memory chips. (IBM sold its stake to Toshiba in 1999.) The next year the company looked to boost earnings by cutting its workforce and allying with other manufacturers such as GE and Fujitsu in development deals. But continued semiconductor price declines, and sluggish demand in Japan, caused the company to record its first annual loss in more than two decades.

Nishimuro made plans to cut 5,000 jobs, and streamlined Toshiba's 15 divisions to eight in-house companies. Toshiba in 1999 agreed to take a $1 billion charge to settle a class-action lawsuit alleging some manufacturers supplied potentially corrupt disk drives in its portable computers — even though no Toshiba customer complaints were filed.

In 2000 Nishimuro stepped down as CEO. SVP and Information and Industrial Systems and Services subsidiary president Tadashi Okamura assumed the post. Nishimuro filled the vacant chairman's seat. Toshiba announced another restructuring effort in 2001, which included plans to reduce its workforce, shift manufacturing to overseas plants, and withdraw from unprofitable businesses. The following year it sold its DRAM manufacturing plant, Dominion Semiconductor, to Micron Technology.

EXECUTIVES

Chairman: Taizo Nishimuro
President and CEO: Tadashi Okamura
SEVP: Takeshi Iida
SEVP: Yasuo Morimoto
SEVP: Makoto Nakagawa
EVP: Yuji Kiyokawa
EVP: Tadashi Matsumoto
EVP: Takeshi Nakagawa
EVP: Atsutoshi Nishida
SVP: Makoto Azuma
SVP: Tsuyoshi Kimura
SVP: Shigeo Koguchi
SVP: Susumu Kohyama
SVP: Masaki Matsuhashi
SVP: Tsutomu Miyamoto
SVP: Yoshihiro Nitta
SVP: Masao Niwano
SVP: Sadazumi Ryu
SVP: Yoshiaki Sato
SVP: Toshitake Takagi
Auditors: Ernst & Young

LOCATIONS

HQ: 1-1, Shibaura 1-chome, Minato-ku, Tokyo 105-8001, Japan
Phone: +81-3-3457-4511   **Fax:** +81-3-3455-1631
US HQ: 1251 Avenue of the Americas, 41st Fl., New York, NY 10020
US Phone: 212-596-0600   **US Fax:** 212-593-3875
Web: www.toshiba.com

2003 Sales

	% of total
Asia	
Japan	59
Other countries	15
North America	15
Europe	9
Other regions	2
Total	**100**

PRODUCTS/OPERATIONS

2003 Sales

	% of total
Digital media	26
Electronic devices & components	20
Social infrastructure	15
Information & communication	14
Home appliances	10
Power systems	8
Other	7
Total	**100**

Selected Products

Computers, peripherals, and information equipment
CD-ROM and DVD-ROM drives
Copiers
DVD players
Fax machines
Hard disk drives
Notebook PCs
LCD projectors
Media cards (SD Memory Card, SmartMedia)

Electronic components
Display devices and components
Semiconductors

Elevators and escalators

Home appliances
Air-conditioners
Batteries
Compressors
Lighting
Ventilating fans

Information and industrial systems
Air traffic
Broadcasting
Computer networking
Industrial
Labor-saving
Railway transportation
Space
Technology and manufacturing equipment
Telecommunications

Medical systems

Power systems

COMPETITORS

Acer	Matsushita
Alcatel	Mitsubishi Electric
Canon	Motorola
CASIO COMPUTER	NEC
Dell	Nokia
Electrolux AB	Oki Electric
Emerson Electric	Philips Electronics
Ericsson	Pioneer
Fuji Photo	Ricoh
Fujitsu	Samsung Electronics
Gateway	Samsung
GE	SANYO
Hewlett-Packard	Seiko
Hitachi	Sharp
Ingersoll-Rand	Siemens
Intel	Sony
IBM	Sun Microsystems
Kyocera	Unisys
Lucent	

HISTORICAL FINANCIALS

Company Type: Public

Income Statement

FYE: March 31

	REVENUE ($ mil.)	NET INCOME ($ mil.)	NET PROFIT MARGIN	EMPLOYEES
3/03	47,192	154	0.3%	165,776
3/02	40,666	(1,915)	—	176,398
3/01	47,111	761	1.6%	188,042
3/00	54,493	(265)	—	198,000
3/99	44,504	(117)	—	198,000
3/98	41,020	55	0.1%	186,000
3/97	44,605	542	1.2%	186,000
3/96	48,410	843	1.7%	186,000
3/95	56,199	516	0.9%	190,000
3/94	45,070	118	0.3%	175,000
Annual Growth	**0.5%**	**3.0%**	**—**	**(0.6%)**

2003 Year-End Financials

Debt ratio: 154.5%   Current ratio: 1.00
Return on equity: 3.1%   Long-term debt ($ mil.): 7,360
Cash ($ mil.): 2,729

Net Income History   Pink Sheets: TOSBF

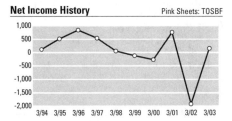

TOTAL S.A.

TOTAL, one of the world's largest integrated oil companies, explores for, develops, and produces crude oil and natural gas; refines and markets oil; and trades and transports both crude and finished products. Operating in more than 100 countries, the company has reserves of 11.2 billion barrels of oil equivalent. It operates 28 refineries and 16,700 service stations, mostly in Europe and Africa. The company's ATOFINA unit is a major chemical producer. TOTAL FINA was formed in 1999 when France's TOTAL bought Belgium-based PetroFina. It became TOTAL FINA ELF in 2000 with the acquisition of French rival Elf Aquitaine. The company renamed itself as TOTAL S.A. in 2003.

TOTAL gas stations operate under the Premier, FINA, and Elf brands. ATOFINA produces monomers, polymers, and specialty chemicals such as adhesives, inks, paints, resins, and rubbers. TOTAL also owns 26% of drugmaker Sanofi-Synthélabo, gained in the Elf acquisition.

The old TOTAL had been exiting mature markets in favor of high-growth regions when it joined the industry consolidation (Exxon and Mobil, BP and Amoco) spurred by the slump in oil prices. The enlarged company has integrated the operations of its acquisitions and is looking to further cut costs where there are overlaps. In 2003 TOTAL announced plans to acquire Mobil Gas, the UK industrial and commercial gas marketing business of Exxon Mobil.

That year a number of former Elf executives

and state officials were named in a corruption scandal that implicated the former French oil giant in influence peddling and bribery in the early 1990s.

HISTORY

A French consortium formed the Compagnie Française des Pétroles (CFP) in 1924 to develop an oil industry for the country. Lacking reserves within its borders, France had a 24% stake in the Turkish Petroleum Company (TPC), acquired from Germany in 1920 as part of the spoils from WWI. When oil was discovered in Iraq in 1927, the TPC partners (CFP; Anglo-Persian Oil, later BP; Royal Dutch/Shell; and a consortium of five US oil companies) became major players in the oil game.

In 1929 France acquired a 25% stake in CFP (raised to 35% in 1931) but ensured the company's independence from government control. CFP began establishing refining and transporting capabilities, and by the start of WWII it was a vertically integrated petroleum company.

With France's occupation by Germany during WWII, CFP was effectively blocked from further expansion, and its stake in Iraq Petroleum (formerly the TPC) was held by its partners until the end of the war. In 1948, over French protests, the US partners ended the "Red Line" agreement, a pact that limited members' competition in that Middle Eastern region.

After WWII, CFP diversified its sources for crude, opening a supply in 1947 from the Venezuelan company Pantepec and making several major discoveries in colonial Algeria in 1956. It also began supplying crude to Japan, South Korea, and Taiwan in the 1950s. To market its products in North Africa and France and other European areas, it introduced the brand name TOTAL in 1954. It began making petrochemicals in 1956.

Algeria in 1971 became North Africa's first major oil-producing country to nationalize its petroleum industry. This was not as dire a blow to CFP as it could have been; by that time the company got only about 20% of its supplies from Algeria. Exploration had paid off, with discoveries in Indonesia in the 1960s and, in the early 1970s, the North Sea.

CFP joined Elf Aquitaine in 1980 to buy Rhône-Poulenc's petrochemical segment. Ten years later it purchased state-owned Orkem's coating business (inks, resins, paints, and adhesives).

In 1985 the company had adopted its brand name as part of its new name, TOTAL Compagnie Française des Pétroles, shortened in 1991 to TOTAL. The firm was listed on the NYSE that year. The French government began reducing its stake in TOTAL in 1992 (ultimately to less than 1%). The company expanded reserves with stakes in fields in Argentina, the Caspian Sea, and Colombia.

In 1995, the year Thierry Desmarest became CEO, TOTAL contracted to develop two large oil and gas fields in Iran, despite US pressure not to do business there. The next year TOTAL led a consortium (including Russia's Gazprom and Malaysia's Petronas) in a $2 billion investment in Iran's gas sector, just days after selling its 55% stake in its North American arm, Total Petroleum, to Ultramar Diamond Shamrock — insulating TOTAL from the threat of US sanctions.

TOTAL bought Belgium's Petrofina, an integrated oil and gas company, for $11 billion in 1999 and became TOTAL FINA. Within days the new TOTAL FINA launched a $43 billion hostile bid for rival Elf Aquitaine. Elf made a counter-bid, but TOTAL FINA wound up acquiring 95% of Elf in 2000 for $48.7 billion and became TOTAL FINA ELF. The new company gained control of the remainder of Elf later that year.

In 2001 the company, in collaboration with Pertamina and Unocal Indonesia, agreed to invest $500m to boost its production of liquefied gas in Indonesia by 14%. That year the company also acquired generating assets in Argentina from AES for $370 million. Also that year an explosion in a TOTAL FINA ELF subsidiary's petrochemical and fertilizer plant in southern France killed 29 people and injured a further 2,500.

EXECUTIVES

Chairman and CEO: Thierry Desmarest, age 58
Vice Chairman; President, Chemicals: François Cornélis
EVP and CFO: Robert Castaigne
EVP; President, Exploration and Production: Chrisophe de Margerie
EVP; President, Refining and Marketing: Jean-Paul Vettier
EVP; President, Strategy and Risk Assessment: Bruno Weymuller
EVP; President, Upstream: Jean-Luc Vermeulen
EVP; President Gas and Power: Yves-Louis Darricarrére
SVP Executive Career Management: Michel Bonnet
SVP Human Resources and Corporate Communications: Jean-Jacques Guilbaud
SVP; President Trading and Shipping: François Groh
SVP Acrylics, PMMA, and Chlorochemicals, Chemicals Division : Philippe Goebel
SVP Administration, Refining and Marketing Division: Pierre Klein
SVP Northern Europe, Exploration and Production Division: Michel Bénézit
SVP Africa, Exploration and Production Division: Jean Privey
SVP Hutchinson, Mapa Spontex, and Technical Polymers: Pierre-Christian Clout
EVP and COO, TOTAL Holdings USA, Inc.: Otto Takken
VP Investor Relations: Ladislas Paszkiewicz
Auditors: KPMG Audit

LOCATIONS

HQ: 2 place de la Coupole, La Défense 6, 92400 Courbevoie, France
Phone: +33-1-47-44-58-53   **Fax:** +33-1-47-44-58-24
US HQ: 444 Madison Ave, 42nd Fl., New York, NY 10022
US Phone: 212-922-3030   **US Fax:** 212-922-3074
Web: www.totalfinaelf.com

TOTAL has operations in more than 100 countries.

2002 Sales

	% of total
Europe	
France	20
Other countries	35
North America	12
Africa	4
Other regions	29
Total	**100**

PRODUCTS/OPERATIONS

2002 Sales

	% of total
Downstream	59
Upstream	24
Chemicals	17
Total	**100**

Selected Subsidiaries and Affiliates

ATOFINA
ATOFINA Chemicals, Inc. (US)
ATOFINA Petrochemicals, Inc. (US)
Ato Findley (adhesives)
Bostik (adhesives)
Hutchinson (seals, gaskets, and other rubber products)
Elf Aquitaine
Compañia Española de Petróleos, S.A. (45%; integrated oil and gas firm; Spain)
FINA, Inc. (refining and marketing, chemicals, US)
Sanofi-Synthelabo (26%; pharmaceuticals)

COMPETITORS

Akzo Nobel
Anglo American
Ashland
BASF AG
BHP Billiton Ltd
BP
ChevronTexaco
ConocoPhillips
Devon Energy
DuPont
Eni
Exxon Mobil
Imperial Oil
Kerr-McGee
Lyondell Chemical
Norsk Hydro
Occidental Petroleum
PETROBRAS
PDVSA
PEMEX
PPG
Royal Dutch/Shell Group
Unocal

HISTORICAL FINANCIALS

Company Type: Public

Income Statement

FYE: December 31

	REVENUE ($ mil.)	NET INCOME ($ mil.)	NET PROFIT MARGIN	EMPLOYEES
12/02	107,698	6,240	5.8%	121,469
12/01	93,870	6,826	7.3%	122,025
12/00	107,890	6,502	6.0%	123,303
12/99	42,566	1,534	3.6%	127,252
12/98	28,507	1,038	3.6%	57,166
12/97	31,720	1,263	4.0%	54,391
12/96	34,062	1,089	3.2%	57,555
12/95	27,696	458	1.7%	53,000
12/94	25,612	634	2.5%	49,772
12/93	23,037	504	2.2%	49,772
Annual Growth	**18.7%**	**32.3%**	**—**	**10.4%**

2002 Year-End Financials

Debt ratio: 31.6%
Return on equity: 19.5%
Cash ($ mil.): 5,216
Current ratio: 1.24
Long-term debt ($ mil.): 10,668
No. of shares (mil.): 1,374
Dividends
Yield: 2.3%
Payout: 35.7%
Market value ($ mil.): 98,268

Stock History

NYSE: TOT

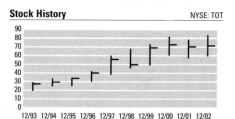

	STOCK PRICE ($) FY Close	P/E High/Low		PER SHARE ($) Earnings	Dividends	Book Value
12/02	71.50	18	13	4.68	1.67	24.57
12/01	70.24	16	12	4.92	1.46	21.82
12/00	72.69	18	13	4.60	1.13	21.68
12/99	69.25	33	23	2.18	0.88	20.45
12/98	49.75	32	22	2.12	0.00	25.27
12/97	55.75	23	15	2.58	0.00	23.14
12/96	40.25	18	14	2.27	0.64	24.13
12/95	34.00	35	26	0.98	0.61	23.34
12/94	29.50	24	19	1.37	0.51	21.97
12/93	27.13	25	18	1.14	0.00	20.47
Annual Growth	**11.4%**	**—**	**—**	**17.0%**	**—**	**2.0%**

Toyota Motor Corporation

Toyota Motor Corporation, Japan's largest and the world's #4 carmaker by sales (after General Motors, Ford, and DaimlerChrysler), has a driving ambition to become greener. The company makes a hybrid-powered (gas and electric) sedan — the Prius — that is already being snapped up in US and European markets. Its gas-powered cars, pickups, minivans, and SUVs include such models as the Camry, Celica, Corolla, 4Runner, Echo, Land Cruiser, Sienna, the luxury Lexus line, and a full-sized pickup truck, the V-8 Tundra. Toyota also makes forklifts and manufactured housing, and offers consumer financial services.

Recognizing that it depends, perhaps too heavily, on domestic production, Toyota is focusing on expanding its global manufacturing capability. The company has opened new vehicle plants in India (1999) and France (2001). Toyota also opened a new compact car plant in China late in 2002 and has plans for a new small car plant in the Czech Republic (2005) and a truck bed plant in Mexico (2004). Additionally, Toyota opened its 10th US plant in Alabama in 2003 (engines). Toyota will open its 11th US plant in San Antonio, Texas in 2006.

While growing its worldwide production base, Toyota has committed itself to leading the charge toward the development of alternative-fuel vehicles, primarily powered by fuel cells. Toyota also is expanding its financial services operations.

HISTORY

In 1926 Sakichi Toyoda founded Toyoda Automatic Loom Works. In 1930 he sold the rights to the loom he invented and gave the proceeds to his son Kiichiro Toyoda to begin an automotive business. Kiichiro opened an auto shop within the loom works in 1933. When protectionist legislation (1936) improved prospects for Japanese automakers, Kiichiro split off the car department, took it public (1937), and changed its name to Toyota.

During WWII the company made military trucks, but financial problems after the war caused Toyota to reorganize in 1950. Its postwar commitment to R&D paid off with the launch of the four-wheel-drive Land Cruiser (1951); full-sized Crown (1955); and the small Corona (1957).

Toyota Motor Sales, U.S.A., debuted the Toyopet Crown in the US in 1957, but it proved underpowered for the US market. Toyota had better luck with the Corona in 1965 and with the Corolla (which became the best-selling car of all time) in 1968. By 1970 Toyota was the world's fourth-largest carmaker.

Toyota expanded rapidly in the US. During the 1970s the oil crisis caused demand for fuel-efficient cars, and Toyota was there to grab market share from US makers. In 1975 Toyota displaced Volkswagen as the US's #1 auto importer. Toyota began auto production in the US in 1984 through NUMMI, its joint venture with GM. The Lexus line was launched in the US in 1989.

Because of the European Community's restrictions on Japanese auto imports until the year 2000, Toyota's European expansion slowed. Toyota responded in 1992 by agreeing to distribute cars in Japan for Volkswagen and also by establishing an engine plant (later moved to full auto production) in the UK.

The sport utility vehicle (SUV) mania of the 1990s spurred Toyota's introduction of luxury minivans and light trucks. Hiroshi Okuda, a 40-year veteran with Toyota and the first person from outside the Toyoda family to run the firm, succeeded Tatsuro Toyoda as president in 1995. The next year Toyota consolidated its North American production units into Cincinnati-based Toyota Motor Manufacturing North America.

In 1997 Toyota introduced the Prius, a hybrid electric- and gas-powered car. The next year Toyota boosted its stake in affiliate Daihatsu (minivehicles) to about 51% and started Toyota Mapmaster (51%-owned), to make map databases for car navigation systems.

Okuda became chairman in 1999, replacing Shoichiro Toyoda, and Fujio Cho became president. Also that year Toyota agreed to form a joint venture with Isuzu to manufacture buses, and it announced plans to invest $800 million to boost US auto production by 16% (200,000 vehicles) to about 1.45 million.

In 2000 Toyota launched the WiLL Vi, a sedan aimed at young people. It announced that it was building an online replacement parts marketplace with i2 Technology and that it was forming a financial services company (Toyota Financial Service) and a brokerage firm (Toyota Financial Services Securities Corp.). Toyota also made plans to buy a 5% stake in Yamaha (the world's #2 motorcycle maker) and raised its stake in truck maker Hino Motors from about 20% to almost 34%. International developments included Toyota's agreement with the Chinese government to produce passenger cars for sale in China. The cars are to be built by Tianjin Toyota Motor Corp., a joint venture between Chinese carmaker Tianjin Automobile Xiali and Toyota.

Early in 2001 Toyota opened a new plant in France. Later that year, the company formed an agreement with PSA Peugeot Citroen to begin joint car production in Europe by 2005. Toyota also increased its stake in Hino Motors to 50%.

With partners Toyoda Gosei, Ltd. and Horie Metal Co., Ltd., Toyota formed a joint venture in 2002 to manufacture resin fuel tank systems.

EXECUTIVES

Honorary Chairman: Shoichiro Toyoda
Chairman: Hiroshi Okuda
Vice Chairman: Kosuke Ikebuchi
Vice Chairman: Iwao Isomura
President: Fujio Cho
EVP, Business Development, IT and ITS, Housing, Government and Public Affairs, Purchasing, Tokyo Head Office, e-Toyota: Katsuaki Watanabe
EVP, Corporate Planning, Research, Legal, General Administration and Human Resources, Finance and Accounting, and Information Systems: Ryuji Araki, age 63
EVP, Domestic Sales Operations: Kazushi Iwatsuki
EVP, International Government and Industrial Affairs, and Overseas Planning Operations Group: Katsuhiro Nakagawa
EVP, Product Management, Research & Development, and Quality Control: Akihiko Saito
EVP, Production & Transportation, Production Engineering, TQM Promotion, and Environmental Affairs: Kosuke Shiramizu
EVP, Overseas Operations Groups: Yoshio Ishizaka, age 63
Senior Managing Director, General Administration and Human Resources Group and Information Systems Group: Akio Matsubara
Senior Managing Director, Production Engineering Group and Manufacturing Group: Yasuhito Yamauchi
Director; President, Toyota Motor Europe; President, Toyota Motor Engineering Manufacturing Europe: Shuhei Toyoda
President and CEO, Toyota Motor Manufacturing North America: Atsushi Niimi
President, Toyota Motor Manufacturing Kentucky, Inc.: Gary L. Convis
President, Toyota Technical Center, USA: Tadashi Tadashi
Auditors: PricewaterhouseCoopers

LOCATIONS

HQ: Toyota Jidosha Kabushiki Kaisha
   1, Toyota-cho, Toyota, Aichi 471-8571, Japan
Phone: +81-565-28-2121   **Fax:** +81-565-23-5800
US HQ: 9 W. 57th St., Ste. 4900, New York, NY 10019
US Phone: 212-223-0303   **US Fax:** 212-759-7670
Web: www.toyota.co.jp/en

Toyota Motor operates more than 60 manufacturing facilities in 26 countries throughout the world.

2003 Sales

	$ mil.	% of total
Japan	90,230	53
North America	51,737	31
Europe	13,310	8
Other regions	12,868	8
Adjustments	(39,180)	—
Total	**128,965**	**100**

2003 Unit Sales

	No. (thou.)	% of total
Asia		
Japan	2,218	36
East & Southeast Asia	462	8
North America	1,982	32
Europe	776	13
Oceania	203	3
Central & South America	161	3
Other regions	311	5
Total	**6,113**	**100**

PRODUCTS/OPERATIONS

2003 Sales

	$ mil.	% of total
Automotive	119,063	90
Financial services	6,031	5
Other	6,616	5
Adjustments	(2,745)	—
Total	**128,965**	**100**

Selected Products and Services

Selected Models
4Runner (SUV, Latin America and North America)
Avalon (full-sized sedan; Asia, Middle East, North America, and Oceania)
Camry (midsized sedan; Africa, Asia, Europe, Latin America, Middle East, North America, and Oceania)
Camry Solara (midsized coupe; North America)
Celica (sports car; Asia, Europe, Latin America, North America, and Oceania)
Corolla (compact sedan; Africa, Asia, Europe, Latin America, Middle East, North America, and Oceania)
Echo (compact coupe; North America)
Highlander (SUV, North America)
Hilux (pickup truck; Africa, Asia, Europe, Latin America, Middle East, and Oceania)
Land Cruiser (SUV; Africa, Asia, Europe, Latin America, Middle East, and Oceania)
Lexus (luxury sedan)
MR2 Spyder (sports car; Asia, Europe, Middle East, North America, and Oceania)
Prius (gas/electric hybrid compact sedan, Asia, Europe and North America)
RAV4 (SUV; Africa, Asia, Europe, Latin America, Middle East, North America, and Oceania)

Sienna (minivan, North America)
Tacoma (pickup truck, North America)
Tundra (pickup truck, North America)

Other Products
Factory automation equipment
Forklifts and other industrial vehicles
Housing products

COMPETITORS

BMW	Kubota
Caterpillar	Marubeni
DaimlerChrysler	Mazda
Deere	Nissan
Fiat	Peugeot Motors of
Ford	America, Inc.
Fuji Heavy Industries	Renault
General Motors	Saab Automobile
Honda	Saturn
Ingersoll-Rand	Suzuki Motor
Isuzu	Volkswagen
Kia Motors	Volvo
Komatsu	

HISTORICAL FINANCIALS

Company Type: Public

Income Statement

FYE: March 31

	REVENUE ($ mil.)	NET INCOME ($ mil.)	NET PROFIT MARGIN	EMPLOYEES
3/03	128,965	6,247	4.8%	264,096
3/02	107,443	4,177	3.9%	246,702
3/01	106,030	5,447	5.1%	215,648
3/00	119,656	4,540	3.8%	214,631
3/99	105,832	3,747	3.5%	183,879
3/98	88,473	3,442	3.9%	159,035
3/97	98,741	3,112	3.2%	150,736
3/96	101,120	2,424	2.4%	146,855
3/95*	95,828	1,557	1.6%	142,645
6/94	95,032	1,277	1.3%	110,534
Annual Growth	3.5%	19.3%	—	10.2%

*Fiscal year change

2003 Year-End Financials

Debt ratio: 58.1%	No. of shares (mil.): 1,805
Return on equity: 11.0%	Dividends
Cash ($ mil.): 13,245	Yield: 1.1%
Current ratio: 1.22	Payout: 29.0%
Long-term debt ($ mil.): 34,422	Market value ($ mil.): 81,135

Stock History

NYSE: TM

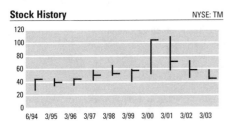

	STOCK PRICE ($) FY Close	P/E High/Low		PER SHARE ($) Earnings	Dividends	Book Value
3/03	44.95	33	25	1.76	0.51	32.82
3/02	58.15	31	20	2.28	0.38	29.87
3/01	70.75	37	20	2.92	0.45	31.00
3/00	104.00	43	22	2.42	0.34	34.73
3/99	57.25	30	21	1.98	0.37	29.37
3/98	52.75	36	28	1.80	0.16	23.98
3/97	50.50	36	27	1.62	0.33	24.15
3/96	44.50	36	29	1.24	0.27	26.74
3/95*	39.75	56	43	0.81	0.28	31.70
6/94	44.63	66	41	0.68	0.29	26.33
Annual Growth	0.1%	—	—	11.1%	6.5%	2.5%

*Fiscal year change

TUI AG

Once a steel and mining conglomerate, TUI (formerly Preussag) now makes a living on the road. Its tourism business, which is the largest in Europe, serves about 22 million customers and accounts for nearly 60% of the company's sales. TUI operates more than 3,700 travel agencies, more than 280 hotels, and about 80 tour operators, as well as some 90 airplanes through six airlines. TUI's service division provides various support services for travelers, including airport reception, brochures, medical support, and departure assistance. State-owned Westdeutsche Landesbank owns 33% of TUI.

To reposition itself as a tourism company, TUI has sold its operations in such areas as building engineering, metals trading, and real estate.

TUI acquired leading UK tour operator Thomson Travel Group in 2001. To get European Commission approval for the deal, it sold a majority stake in tour operator Thomas Cook to rival C&N Touristik. TUI has introduced "World of TUI" as a global brand for its tourism business.

HISTORY

TUI was founded in Berlin in 1923 as Preussische Bergwerks-und Hutten-Aktiengesellschaft (Prussian Mine and Foundry Company) to operate former state-owned mining companies, saltworks, and smelters. Despite outmoded equipment and a war-shattered economy, the company prospered. So in 1929 the Prussian parliament combined Preussag with Hibernia and Preussischen Elektrizitats to form the state-run VEBA group, hoping to stimulate foreign investment. It didn't.

WWII left Preussag a shell of its former self. In 1952, as restrictions on steel production were lifted and industry rebounded, Preussag relocated to Hanover. After taking steps to reestablish itself, Preussag made a public offering in 1959; VEBA kept about 22%.

A worldwide steel glut that lasted through the 1960s forced Preussag to diversify. Acquisitions included railroad tank car and transport agent VTG and shipbuilding and chemical companies. The company also formed oil exploration unit Preussag Energie in 1968. In 1969 VEBA finally sold its remaining stake in Preussag to Westdeusche Landesbank (WestLB).

When the 1970s oil crisis drove up steel costs, Preussag began international ventures to counter falling revenues at home. But the 1980s brought PR disasters. The European Commission fined Preussag and five other zinc producers for antitrust violations in 1984.

In 1989 Preussag reorganized into a holding company with four independent units: coal, oil, natural gas, and plant construction. But it was about to take a sharp business turn. Michael Frenzel, who had managed WestLB's industry holdings, became CEO in 1994 in the midst of another steel recession. Frenzel was determined to shift Preussag away from its rusting past and toward services and technology. In 1997 it acquired container shipping and travel firm Hapag-Lloyd, which had a 30% stake in Touristik Union International (TUI). By the end of 1998 it was Europe's top tourism group after buying the rest of TUI, First Reisebuero Management, and a 25% stake in the UK's Thomas Cook (raised to 50.1% in 1999).

As part of its restructuring, Preussag traded its plant engineering units and half of its shipbuilding unit (HDW) to Babcock Borsig for a 33% stake in that company in 1999. Preussag then made plans to transfer another 25% of HDW to Sweden's Celsius in a deal (along with Babcock Borsig) to merge Celsius' Kockums submarine shipyards with HDW. That year Hapag-Lloyd and TUI were merged into Hapag Touristik Union (renamed TUI Group in 2000); VTG merged with Lehnkering, a 126-year-old freight forwarding group, becoming VTG-Lehnkering.

The group also acquired a stake in French package tour leader Nouvelles Frontières and sold a metals trading unit, W. & O. Bergmann, to Enron. By 2002 the company had sold off most of its non-tourism operations, changed its name to TUI, and restructured its business to focus primarily on tourism.

EXECUTIVES

Chairman: Michael Frenzel, age 56
Executive Director, Finance and Accounting: Rainer Feuerhake, age 59
Executive Director, Human Resources and Legal: Peter Engelen, age 47
Executive Director, Tourism Platforms: Sebastian Ebel
Director, Source Market Central and Managing Director, TUI Deutschland GmbH: Volker Boettcher
Director, Source Market North and CEO, TUI Northern Europe: Peter Rothwell
Director, Source Market West and President, Nouvelles Frontieres: Eric Debry
Auditors: PwC Deutsche Revision AG

LOCATIONS

HQ: Karl-Wiechert-Allee 4, D-30625 Hanover, Germany
Phone: +49-511-566-00   **Fax:** +49-511-566-1098
Web: www.tui.com

With operations worldwide, TUI maintains offices in Austria, Belgium, Germany, Ireland, the Netherlands, Poland, Scandinavia, Spain, Switzerland, and the UK.

COMPETITORS

Accor	Kuoni Travel
American Express	Lufthansa
BTI Canada	MyTravel
Carlson	REWE-Zentral
Carnival	Rosenbluth International
Club Med	Royal Caribbean Cruises
First Choice	Thomas Cook AG

HISTORICAL FINANCIALS

Company Type: Public

Income Statement

FYE: December 31

	REVENUE ($ mil.)	NET INCOME ($ mil.)	NET PROFIT MARGIN	EMPLOYEES
12/02	22,710	34	0.1%	70,299
12/01*	21,080	307	1.5%	69,550
9/00	19,212	291	1.5%	79,959
9/99	18,739	368	2.0%	57,673
9/98	21,003	322	1.5%	66,563
9/97	15,083	205	1.4%	62,601
9/96	16,401	164	1.0%	66,226
9/95	18,461	260	1.4%	65,227
9/94	14,972	183	1.2%	69,712
9/93	14,249	144	1.0%	73,319
Annual Growth	5.3%	(15.0%)	—	(0.5%)

*Fiscal year change

2002 Year-End Financials

Debt ratio: 83.1%
Current ratio: 0.54
Return on equity: 1.2%
Long-term debt ($ mil.): 2,533
Cash ($ mil.): 384

Net Income History   German: PRS

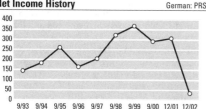

UBS AG

One of the largest investment managers in the world, UBS has offices in some 50 nations — but primarily in Europe and North America — that provide financial services through four major segments. Its UBS Wealth Management & Business Banking, UBS Wealth Management Americas, and UBS Global Asset Management divisions serve institutional investors and high-net-worth individuals by offering mutual funds, asset management, corporate finance, and estate planning. UBS Investment Bank provides securities underwriting, mergers acquisitions advice, fixed-income products, and foreign exchange. The company also provides traditional banking services in its home country of Switzerland.

UBS' Investment Bank unit has taken control of Enron's infamous wholesale energy trading business. The acquisition has prompted fears that the bank has become an unwitting host body in which Enron's questionable trading practices can survive.

UBS is looking to catapult itself higher into the echelons of global finance. To beef up its asset management segment, the company bought RT Capital Management (renamed Brinson Canada), the institutional asset management business of RBC Financial Group. It also hopes to cash in on wealthy individuals by expanding its private banking services in Europe. The bank's hopes for a successful European private equities business have been scuttled by the poor condition of consumer industries, industrial products, and computer firm stocks.

A shake-up of management, including the resignation of UBS Warburg chairman Markus Granziol, has brought on a more youthful generation of leadership.

HISTORY

Businessmen in Winterthur, Switzerland, formed the Bank of Winterthur in 1862 to serve trading interests, finance railroads, and operate a warehouse. In 1912 the bank merged with the Bank of Toggenburg (formed in 1863) to create Schweizerische Bankgesellschaft — Union Bank of Switzerland (UBS).

It expanded in Switzerland, buying smaller banks and adding branches. After growing in the post-WWI era, it was hit hard by the Depression. UBS benefited from Switzerland's neutrality in WWII, gaining deposits from both Jews and Nazis. In 1946 the bank opened an office in New York. Expansion in Switzerland continued after the war with the purchase of Eidgenossische Bank of Zurich.

UBS continued its acquisitions in the 1950s; by 1962 it had 81 branches. Other purchases included Interhandel, a cash-rich Swiss financial concern (1967), and four savings banks (1968). In 1967 it opened a full-service office in London, and during the 1970s established several securities underwriting subsidiaries abroad.

International financial markets became supercharged in the 1980s, and UBS resolved to catch up with its domestic peers in international operations. As London prepared for financial deregulation in 1986, UBS bought brokerage house Phillips & Drew.

The firm's UK brokerage business was hit hard by the 1987 US stock market crash; over the next two years losses continued, prompting an overhaul of the London operations. Then its US operations were jarred by the collapse of the junk bond market in 1990. The next year UBS set up offices in Paris, Singapore, and Hong Kong and took over Chase Manhattan's (now J.P. Morgan Chase) New York money management unit.

Meanwhile, the firm continued to expand within Switzerland, buying five more banks to boost market share and fill in gaps in its branch network. These buys left UBS with overlapping operations and a bloated infrastructure when recession hit. Falling real estate values left the bank with a heavy load of nonperforming loans.

In 1994 profits plummeted. Stockholder Martin Ebner, dissatisfied with the performance of president Robert Studer, tried to obtain control of UBS; failing that, he sought to have Studer charged with criminal fraud. In 1996 he almost thwarted Studer's election to the chairmanship.

UBS launched a multiyear reorganization in 1994 by consolidating its consumer credit operations. The next year it joined with Swiss Life/Rentenanstalt to offer insurance products through its bank network.

In 1996, after rebuffing Credit Suisse Group's merger bid, UBS began an even more draconian reorganization, cutting domestic branches and writing down billions of francs in bad loans, leading to UBS' first loss ever (with another the next year). In 1998 the company merged with Swiss Bank Corp. then cut 23% of its staff. Later that year the bank lost $1.6 billion in the stumbling Long-Term Capital Management hedge fund, prompting chairman Mathis Cabiallavetta to resign.

As UBS struggled to swallow Swiss Bank in 1999, it retreated somewhat from riskier markets, began selling some $2 billion in real estate, and sold its 25% stake in Swiss Life/Rentenanstalt. Looking to bulk up, the firm that year bought Bank of America's European and Asian private banking operations and Allegis Realty Investors, a US real estate investment management firm.

In 2000 UBS reorganized yet again and bought US broker Paine Webber (now UBS Paine Webber). UBS's integration of Paine Webber continued into the next year. Also in 2001 chairman Marcel Ospel was criticized for UBS's handling of Swissair's cash crisis, which resulted in the air fleet's grounding.

EXECUTIVES

Chairman: Marcel Ospel, age 53
Vice Chairman: Alberto Togni, age 65
President and CEO: Peter A. Wuffli, age 46
Deputy CEO: Stephan Haeringer, age 57
Chairman and CEO, UBS Warburg: John P. Costas, age 46

Chairman and CEO, UBS Global Asset Management: John A. Fraser, age 52
CEO, UBS PaineWebber: Joseph J. (Joe) Grano Jr., age 55
Chairman, UBS Wealth Management and Business Banking: Georges Gagnebin, age 57
CEO, UBS Wealth Management and Business Banking: Marcel Rohner, age 39
Chairman, UBS America: Donald B. Marron, age 68
Chairman and CEO, Asia Pacific: Clive Standish, age 50
President and COO, UBS Paine Webber: Mark B. Sutton, age 49
CEO, Americas, UBS Global Asset Management: Brian Storms
President, UBS PaineWebber Services: Robert H. Silver
Group Chief Communications Officer: Mark Branson
Group Treasurer: Rolf Enderli
Group Head of Human Resources: Thomas Hammer
Group General Counsel: Peter Kurer, age 54
Global Head of Strategic Planning and Business Development, UBS Warburg: Regina A. Dolan
Global Head of Equities, UBS Warburg: Alan C. Hodson
Auditors: Ernst & Young Ltd.

LOCATIONS

HQ: Bahnhofstrasse 45, CH-8098 Zurich, Switzerland
Phone: +41-1-234-4100   **Fax:** +41-1-234-3415
US HQ: 10 E. 50th St., New York, NY 10022
US Phone: 212-574-3000   **US Fax:** 212-713-3680
Web: www.ubs.com

PRODUCTS/OPERATIONS

2002 Sales

	% of total
Interest	62
Net fee & commission income	29
Net trading & other income	9
Total	**100**

2002 Assets

	% of total
Cash & equivalents	40
Trading account	31
Positive relacement values	7
Net loans	18
Other	4
Total	**100**

COMPETITORS

Bank of America	HSBC Holdings
Barclays	J.P. Morgan Chase
CIBC	Mitsubishi Tokyo Financial
Citigroup	Mizuho Financial
Credit Suisse	RBC Financial Group
Deutsche Bank	

HISTORICAL FINANCIALS

Company Type: Public

Income Statement   FYE: December 31

	ASSETS ($ mil.)	NET INCOME ($ mil.)	INCOME AS % OF ASSETS	EMPLOYEES
12/02	855,248	2,560	0.3%	69,000
12/01	756,365	3,001	0.4%	69,985
12/00	673,847	4,828	0.7%	71,000
12/99	616,330	3,956	0.6%	49,058
12/98	684,673	2,197	0.3%	48,011
12/97	396,564	(89)	—	27,611
12/96	324,091	(258)	—	29,153
12/95	335,081	1,458	0.4%	29,071
12/94	249,417	1,233	0.5%	28,882
12/93	209,107	1,524	0.7%	27,500
Annual Growth	**16.9%**	**5.9%**	**—**	**10.8%**

2002 Year-End Financials

Equity as % of assets: 3.3%	Dividends
Return on assets: 0.3%	Yield: 0.0%
Return on equity: 9.4%	Payout: —
Long-term debt ($ mil.): 153,936	Market value ($ mil.): 55,777
No. of shares (mil.): 1,159	Sales ($ mil.): 46,157

Stock History

NYSE: UBS

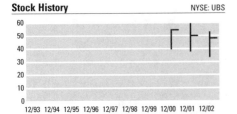

12/93 12/94 12/95 12/96 12/97 12/98 12/99 12/00 12/01 12/02

	STOCK PRICE ($) FY Close	P/E High/Low	PER SHARE ($) Earnings	Dividends	Book Value
12/02	48.12	25 16	2.08	0.00	24.36
12/01	50.00	25 16	2.37	0.30	20.50
12/00	54.41	14 10	3.93	0.86	21.72
Annual Growth	(6.0%)	— —	(27.2%)	—	5.9%

Unilever

Unilever has universal appeal. One of the largest producers of packaged consumer goods, Unilever operates in 150 countries in Asia, Africa, North America, the Middle East, Western Europe, and Latin America. The company's brand names for fragrances, frozen foods, soap, and tea include Calvin Klein, Birds Eye, Dove, and Lipton. Unilever is part of the Unilever Group owned by the Netherlands-based Unilever N.V. and UK-based Unilever PLC. Unilever has two global divisions, Home & Personal Care and Food.

Unilever foods account for more than half of sales. Brands range from the widely recognized, such as Hellmann's mayonnaise (acquired in the $24 billion purchase of Bestfoods in 2000), to locally marketed products, such as Italy's Findus frozen foods.

The Unilever line of home and personal care products include deodorants (Axe, Degree), hair care products (Suave, ThermaSilk), prestige fragrances (Lagerfeld, Very Valentino), and skincare (Lever 2000, Pond's). Its other familiar goods include Q-Tips, Vaseline, and laundry and cleaning products such as all, Wisk, and Surf.

In the wake of rival Procter & Gamble's purchase of Wella hair products, Unilever was rumored to have interest in acquiring Germany's Beiersdorf, primarily known for its Nivea skin products. However, Unilever has made no public move to buy the company. Rather, Unilever says it's now in the fourth year of a five-year growth strategy that focuses on supporting a smaller number of global brands and selling under-performing businesses. For example, in early 2003 Unilever sold its Unipamol Malaysia and Pamol Plantations oil plantations and later sold its Ven den Bergh Oils business. Also, after selling its men's toiletry brand, Brut, and some minor cheese operations in Germany, Unilever sold its Bestfood's Ambrosia and Brown & Polson to Premier Foods in late 2003.

Also in 2003 Church & Dwight agreed to purchase Unilever's oral care brands in the US and Canada. Products included in the deal are Mentadent toothpaste and toothbrushes, Pepsodent and Aim toothpaste, and exclusive licensing rights to Close-Up toothpaste. In late 2003 Unilever announced it intended to sell four of its home care brands (Rit, Niagara, Final Touch, Sunlight) to Lehman Brothers Merchant Banking Group, an affiliate of Lehman Brothers Holdings.

HISTORY

After sharpening his sales skills in the family wholesale grocery business, Englishman William Lever formed a new company in 1885 with his brother James. Lever Brothers introduced Sunlight, the world's first packaged, branded laundry soap. Sunlight was a success in Britain, and within 15 years Lever Brothers was selling soap worldwide. Between 1906 and 1915 it grew mostly through acquisitions. Needing vegetable oil to make soap, the company established plantations and trading companies around the world. During WWI Lever began using its vegetable oil to make margarine.

Rival Dutch butter makers Jurgens and Van den Berghs were pioneers in margarine production. In 1927 they created the Margarine Union, a cartel that owned the European market. The Margarine Union and Lever Brothers merged in 1930, but for tax reasons formed two separate entities: Unilever PLC in London and Unilever N.V. in Rotterdam, the Netherlands.

Despite the Depression and WWII, Unilever expanded, acquiring US companies Thomas J. Lipton (1937) and Pepsodent (1944). Unilever benefited from the postwar boom in Europe, the increasing use of margarine, new detergent technologies, and the growing use of personal care products.

Although product development fueled some growth, acquisitions (at one time running at the rate of one per week) played a major role in shaping Unilever. These included Birds Eye Foods in the UK (1957) and, in the US, Good Humor (1961), Lawry's Foods (1979), Ragu (1986), Chesebrough-Ponds (1987), Calvin Klein Cosmetics (1989), Faberge/Elizabeth Arden (1989), and Breyers ice cream (1993).

In 1995 Unilever began cutting its global workforce by 7,500. The following year it bought hair care and deodorant maker Helene Curtis. Unilever shed its specialty chemicals operations in 1997. In 1998 the company sold its Plant Breeding International Cambridge (PBIC) business to Monsanto.

In 2000 Unilever bought US weight-management firm Slim-Fast Foods for $2.3 billion and ice-cream maker Ben & Jerry's. As part of its previously announced brand-reduction strategy, Unilever also that year sold its European bakery supplies business to CSM. Later that same year, the company bought Bestfoods for $24 billion, which would result in putting Bestfoods' US baking business (Entenmann's, Oroweat bread) up for sale. George Weston's offer of $1.77 billion won the bidding war for Bestfoods' US baking business. Unilever also owns the rights to the game show Wheel of Fortune.

In 2001 Unilever sold its Elizabeth Arden fragrance and skin care business to French Fragrances. Also in 2001 the company sold some of its dry soup and sauce brands to Campbell Soup to meet regulatory approval for the Bestfoods' purchase.

Also in 2001, it sold its North American seafood businesses (the Gorton's brand in the US and BlueWater in Canada) to seafood conglomerate Nippon Suisan Kaisha. The company sold Unipath, which produces the Clearblue home pregnancy test, to Inverness Medical Innovations in December 2001.

In 2002 Unilever sold its retail dry cleaning and laundry-related business to ZOOTS-The Cleaner Cleaner and its institutional and industrial cleaning business, DiverseyLever, to Johnson Wax Professional. It also sold 19 of its North American food brands (including Argo and Kingsford cornstarches, Karo corn syrup, Mazola corn oil, and Henri's salad dressings) to a subsidiary of Associated British Foods plc. The company sold its Iberia Foods business to the Brooklyn Bottling Group. It also sold its international specialty oils and fats business Loders Croklaan Group.

In 2003 Unilever sold its French frozen-products company Fridedoc to home-vending company Toupargel. Unilever sold its Brut brand of male personal care products, including fragrance, antiperspirant, and deodorant products, to Helen of Troy. The agreement gives Helen of Troy ownership of the brand in the Americas, Canada, Mexico, Puerto Rico, and elsewhere in Latin America; Unilever retains ownership in Europe, Africa, Australia, Asia, and the Middle East.

EXECUTIVES

Chairman, Unilever PLC; Vice Chairman, Unilever N.V.: Niall FitzGerald, age 57, $2,605,270 pay

Chairman, Unilever N.V.; Vice Chairman, Unilever PLC: Antony Burgmans, age 56, $1,969,133 pay

Director, Corporate Development: Clive Butler, age 57, $1,523,704 pay

Director, Finance: Rudy Markham, age 57, $1,481,834 pay

Director, Global Foods: Patrick Cescau, age 54, $1,862,998 pay

Director, Home and Personal Care: Keki Dadiseth, age 57, $1,514,481 pay

Director, Skin Care Research and Development: Michael Cheney

President and CEO, Bestfoods North America and President and CEO, Slimfast Worldwide: John Rice, age 51

President, Home and Personal Care North America, Global Prestige Business: Charles Strauss, age 60, $2,125,000 pay

President, Unilever Bestfoods North America: Neil Beckerman, age 47

Joint Secretary and General Counsel: Stephen Williams, age 55

Director, Public Relations, Unilever United States: Nancy L. Goldfarb

Group Treasurer: Henning Rehder, age 49

Personnel Director: André van Heemstra, age 55, $1,096,178 pay

Chief Auditor: James Duckworth, age 58

Head of Investor Relations: Howard Green

Corporate Communications: Paul Wood

Auditors: PricewaterhouseCoopers

LOCATIONS

HQ: Unilever PLC, Unilever House, Blackfriars, London EC4P 4BQ, United Kingdom
Phone: +44-20-7822-5252   **Fax:** +44-20-7822-6907
HQ: Unilever N.V., Weena 455, 3013 AL Rotterdam, The Netherlands
Phone: +31-10-217-4000   **Fax:** +31-10-217-4798
US HQ: 390 Park Ave., New York, NY 10022-4698
US Phone: 212-906-4240   **US Fax:** 212-906-4666
Web: www.unilever.com

2002 Sales

	% of total
Europe	41
North America	26
Asia/Pacific	16
Latin America	11
Africa & Middle East	6
Total	**100**

PRODUCTS/OPERATIONS

2002 Sales

	% of total
Foods	
Savory & dressings	19
Ice cream & frozen foods	15
Spreads & cooking	13
Health & wellness/beverages	8
Personal care	26
Home care & professional cleaning	18
Other	1
Total	**100**

Selected Brands

Culinary (Calvé, Colmans, Hellman's, Knorr, Lipton Cup-a-Soup, Ragu, Skippy)
Deodorants (Axe, Brut, Degree, Dove, Rexona)
Fragrances (Brut, Calvin Klein, House of Cerruti, House of Valentino, Lagerfeld)
Frozen foods (Birds Eye, Findus)
Hair care (Organics, Suave, SunSilk, ThermaSilk)
Household care (Cif, Domestos)
Ice cream (Ben & Jerry's, Breyers, Good-Humor, Klondike, Magnum, Popsicle, Solero)
Laundry (all, Ala, Comfort, Omo, Snuggle, Surf, Wisk)
Personal wash (Dove, Lever 2000, Lux, Pond's, Q-tips, Vaseline)
Professional cleaning (DiverseyLever)
Salad dressing (Wish-Bone)
Spreads and cooking products (Becel, Country Crock, I Can't Believe It's Not Butter!, Promise, Rama)
Tea-based beverages (Lipton)
Weight management (Slim-Fast)

COMPETITORS

Alberto-Culver
Alticor
Avon
Beiersdorf
Campbell Soup
Cereol
Church & Dwight
Clorox
Coca-Cola
Colgate-Palmolive
ConAgra
Dairy Farmers of America
Danone
Del Monte Foods
Dial
Estée Lauder
General Mills
Gillette
Johnson & Johnson
Kao
Kraft Foods
L'Oréal
LVMH
Mars
McBride
MedPointe
Nestlé
PepsiCo
Procter & Gamble
Reckitt Benckiser
Revlon
Sara Lee Household
S.C. Johnson
Shiseido
Tata Group
Uniq

HISTORICAL FINANCIALS

Company Type: Joint venture

Income Statement

FYE: December 31

	REVENUE ($ mil.)	NET INCOME ($ mil.)	NET PROFIT MARGIN	EMPLOYEES
12/02	50,698	2,236	4.4%	247,000
12/01	45,914	1,638	3.6%	279,000
12/00	44,813	1,041	2.3%	261,000
12/99	43,636	3,165	7.3%	255,000
12/98	47,532	3,432	7.2%	265,000
12/97	46,693	5,568	11.9%	270,000
12/96	50,403	2,420	4.8%	306,000
12/95	48,881	2,285	4.7%	308,000
12/94	47,580	2,500	5.3%	304,000
12/93	39,962	1,860	4.7%	294,000
Annual Growth	**2.7%**	**2.1%**	**—**	**(1.9%)**

2002 Year-End Financials

Debt ratio: 190.6%
Return on equity: 36.0%
Cash ($ mil.): 2,365

Current ratio: 0.79
Long-term debt ($ mil.): 11,483

Net Income History

United Business Media PLC

United Business Media (UBM) is a house divided between publishing and business services. Formerly United News & Media, the company's holdings include high-tech publisher CMP Media (*InformationWeek, Windows Developer Journal, Communication Systems Design*) and market research firms such as RoperASW (formerly Audits & Surveys), Allison Fisher, Strategic Marketing Corporation, and Mediamark Research. Other businesses include news service PR Newswire, classified publishers (Dalton's, Exchange & Mart, Auto Exchange), and broadcaster Channel 5 (35%).

After regulators blocked a merger deal with UK broadcaster Carlton Communications in 2000, UBM has been on a selling spree to refocus and reorganize its business. The company sold its consumer magazines and the US operations of exhibitor Miller Freeman, as well as its UK newspapers and photo archive business, Visual Communications Group. It also disposed of its 20% stake in UK television network ITV, selling it to Granada for $2.6 billion. UBM returned about half the proceeds to its shareholders and has earmarked the rest for possible acquisitions. The company also cut about 900 jobs in 2001.

HISTORY

United Business Media traces its roots back to United Newspapers, formed in 1918 after British Prime Minister David Lloyd George, stung by criticism of his war strategy in the *Daily Chronicle*, persuaded a group of Liberal party supporters to buy the newspaper. The company later acquired *Lloyd's Weekly News* (founded in 1842) and went public in 1925. William Harrison bought a controlling interest in United Newspapers and merged it with his Provincial Newspapers in 1929. Burdened by debt, United Newspapers merged the *Daily Chronicle* with the *Daily News* in 1930 to produce the *Daily News and Chronicle*, but sold its stake in the paper in 1936. With most of its printing activities located outside London, United Newspapers fared better than its London-based rivals during WWII.

Following the war, Harold Drayton bought a third of the company in 1946 and became chairman in 1948. The company accelerated its acquisitions during the 1960s, buying regional newspapers, weekly papers, and periodicals. After a period of consolidation in the 1970s, David Stevens took over the leadership and launched an expansion drive in 1981. United Newspapers made several acquisitions, including Gralla (a US publisher and promoter of trade shows), Miller Freeman, and PR Newswire, as well as newspaper group Fleet Holdings and the Hong Kong International Trade Fair Group. Reflecting its expanded interests, the company changed its name to United News & Media in 1995.

In 1996 United News & Media merged with financial services group MAI. Founded in 1974 as the J.H. Vavasseur Group, MAI was headed by Clive Hollick (later Lord Hollick), who had helped the struggling company turn its fortunes around. The deal added several operations to United News & Media, including NOP Research Group, two Independent Television broadcast licenses, and interests in financial services. Following the merger with United News & Media, Hollick became United News' chief executive, and Stevens continued as chairman.

In 1997 the company sold its stake in Yorkshire Tyne-Tees Television and acquired HTV (the ITV license in Wales and western England) and Telecom Library (US magazines and trade shows). It finished disposing of its regional newspapers in 1998 and became an equal partner in Internet venture LineOne that year. A renewed focus on its media businesses led United News to spin off its financial services unit (Garban) in late 1998.

The next year Sir Ronald Hampel succeeded Stevens as chairman and the company bought US-based high-tech publisher CMP Media. Later that year, United News agreed to merge with rival broadcasting firm Carlton Communications in a deal worth $12.6 billion. Regulators, however, blocked the proposed merger in 2000. Following the collapse of the merger deal, United News began shedding businesses, selling its consumer magazine business, UAP, to Trader Publishing for $520 million and Visual Communications Group to Getty Images. It also sold most of Miller Freeman to VNU and its Express Newspapers subsidiary to Northern & Shell. At the end of 2000, Granada Media (now Granada plc) agreed to pay $2.6 billion for United News' stake in ITV. The company later changed its name to United Business Media.

In 2001 it bought US auto market researcher Allison-Fisher International. It also purchased

Roper Starch Worldwide, a marketing and consulting firm, which it combined with its Audits & Surveys Worldwide unit to create RoperASW. The company also cut about 900 jobs that year.

EXECUTIVES

Chairman: E. Geoffrey (Geoff) Unwin, age 60
Group Chief Executive and Director:
 Lord Clive R. Hollick, age 57
CFO: Nigel Wilson, age 46
COO and Director: Malcolm Wall, age 46
Executive Director: Charles Gregson, age 55
CIO: Matthew Graham-Hyde
President and CEO, CMP Media: Gary Marshall
President and CEO, Mediamark Research:
 Kathleen D. (Kathi) Love
CEO, RoperASW: Edward B. Keller
Chief Executive, Channel 5: Jane Lighting
Head of Treasury: Peter Wrankmore
Director of Communications: Michael Waring
Auditors: PricewaterhouseCoopers

LOCATIONS

HQ: Ludgate House, 245 Blackfriars Rd.,
 London SE1 9UY, United Kingdom
Phone: +44-20-7921-5000   **Fax:** +44-20-7928-2717
US HQ: 32 Union Sq. East, New York, NY 10003
US Phone: 212-358-6750   **US Fax:** 212-358-6755
Web: www.unitedbusinessmedia.com

PRODUCTS/OPERATIONS

2002 Sales

	$ mil.	% of total
Professional media	767	60
Market research	342	27
News distribution	170	13
Total	**1,279**	**100**

Selected Operations

Consumer media
Channel 5 (35%)

Market research
Allison Fisher International (US)
Market Measures Interactive (US)
Medimark Research (US)
NOP Research Group
RoperASW (US)
Strategic Marketing Corporation (US)

News distribution
PR Newswire (Europe)
PR Newswire (US)

Professional media
CMP Asia
CMP Information
CMP Media (US)
United Advertising Publications

Selected Magazine Titles

Communication Systems Design
EE Times
Game Developer
InformationWeek
MSDN Magazine
Network Computing
Network Magazine
VARBusiness
Wall Street & Technology
Windows Developer Network

COMPETITORS

ACNielsen
Advanstar
Arbitron
CNET Networks
Information Resources
International Data Group
Jupitermedia
MediaLve International
PGI
PRIMEDIA
Reed Elsevier Group
Reuters
Taylor Nelson
Thomson Corporation
VNU
Ziff Davis Media

HISTORICAL FINANCIALS

Company Type: Public

Income Statement

FYE: December 31

	REVENUE ($ mil.)	NET INCOME ($ mil.)	NET PROFIT MARGIN	EMPLOYEES
12/02	1,279	(385)	—	11,180
12/01	1,358	(827)	—	5,609
12/00	2,953	2,741	92.8%	13,459
12/99	3,508	(170)	—	15,000
12/98	3,659	516	14.1%	15,096
12/97	3,728	539	14.5%	18,150
12/96	3,409	261	7.7%	18,318
12/95	1,659	106	6.4%	13,573
12/94	1,591	151	9.5%	13,333
12/93	1,345	148	11.0%	11,850
Annual Growth	**(0.6%)**	**—**		**(0.6%)**

2002 Year-End Financials

Debt ratio: 276.2%
Return on equity: —
Cash ($ mil.): 156
Current ratio: 1.44
Long-term debt ($ mil.): 940

No. of shares (mil.): 168
Dividends
 Yield: 1.6%
 Payout: —
Market value ($ mil.): 713

Stock History

NASDAQ: UNEWY

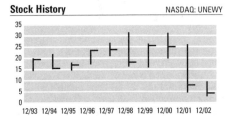

	STOCK PRICE ($) FY Close	P/E High/Low		PER SHARE ($) Earnings	Dividends	Book Value
12/02	4.25	—	—	(2.31)	0.07	2.03
12/01	7.92	—	—	(4.29)	0.53	5.32
12/00	25.00	—	—	10.94	0.76	14.30
12/99	25.50	—	—	(0.69)	0.82	4.14
12/98	18.13	22	11	2.03	1.13	5.70
12/97	23.75	18	15	1.84	0.00	(4.07)
12/96	23.38	22	16	1.07	0.85	(1.97)
12/95	17.00	20	17	0.87	0.51	2.83
12/94	15.50	17	12	1.24	0.73	3.95
12/93	19.50	15	11	1.34	0.98	5.07
Annual Growth	**(15.6%)**	—	—	**—**	**(25.4%)**	**(9.7%)**

Veolia Environnement

Veolia Environnement (formerly Vivendi Environnement) holds water — as well as waste management, energy, and transportation — operations. The company's Veolia Water (formerly Vivendi Water) unit, which provides water and wastewater services to more than 110 million people and 40,000 businesses in about 100 countries, is the world's largest water company. Subsidiary Onyx is one of the world's leading waste management companies, and Dalkia operates global cogeneration facilities and heating and cooling systems. Connex is a top European provider of bus, light-rail, and rail transport. Vivendi Universal owns about 20% of Veolia Environnement.

The firm's Veolia Water unit includes USFilter, a leading water-treatment equipment manufacturer. Waste management subsidiary Onyx serves 76 million people and 272,000 companies and treats 54 million tons of waste per year.

Veolia Environnement merged its Dalkia unit with the energy services operations of Electricité de France (EDF) in 2001. EDF holds 34% of Dalkia while Veolia Environnement holds the rest; holdings will eventually be split 50-50. The company is weighing its options with regard to its 26% stake in Spanish construction group Fomento de Construcciones y Contratas (FCC); it either wants to increase its stake and slim down the unit to focus on FCC's environmental and energy services operations or sell its FCC stake altogether.

Veolia Environnement continues to expand through global acquisitions and outsource-management contracts. It is also selling some noncore assets, including a 17% stake in US water company Philadelphia Suburban and a 34% stake in US power producer Sithe Energies.

The company consists of the water, waste, energy, and transport businesses of the former Vivendi group. The group spun off Veolia Environnement (then called Vivendi Environnement), sold a minority stake to the public, and renamed itself Vivendi Universal in 2000. To raise cash, Vivendi Universal reduced its stake in Veolia Environnement from 63% to about 20% in 2002, and it plans to sell its remaining shares in 2004.

The company changed its name to Veolia Environnement in 2003 to signify the break with Vivendi Universal. Veolia is derived from "Aeolus," the keeper of the winds in Greek mythology.

HISTORY

Vivendi Environnement, spun off from the Vivendi group in 2000, dates back to the 19th century. The group originated in 1853 as Compagnie Générale des Eaux in Paris. The company irrigated farmlands and subsequently supplied water. By 1860 Paris had granted the company a 50-year contract to provide the city's water. In 1880 it moved beyond France to provide water in Venice, Italy. Operations in Turkey (Istanbul) and Portugal (Oporto) followed.

Compagnie Générale des Eaux extended its water network in 1924, and by WWII it supplied half of all urban households in France. After the war the company expanded into household waste collection (1953) and operation of household waste incineration and compost plants (1967). Wastewater treatment activities began in 1972.

The next decade Compagnie Générale des Eaux dove into diversification. It increased its holding in energy-conversion systems operator Compagnie Générale de Chauffe to 100% (making it France's leading energy company) in 1980. That year it merged its wastewater treatment subsidiaries to create Omnium de Traitement et de Valorisation (OTV). Its waste operations were further augmented through the takeover of Compagnie Générale d'Entreprises Automobiles (CGEA), a transport and waste management firm. The company also ventured into telecommunications, pay-TV, and construction (it gained a controlling stake in builder SGE in 1988 but disposed of its interest in the firm, now known as VINCI, in 2000).

CGEA bid and won control of several British Rail lines in 1996 by taking advantage of the UK's rail privatization scheme. Operating under the name Connex, the company began to run trains throughout southeastern England, the UK's largest commuting area.

In 1998 the company changed its name to Vivendi — the group (which came to include mobile phone provider Cegetel and a stake in the Havas media company) transferred the Compagnie Générale des Eaux name to its water business. Vivendi also organized its Compagnie Générale de Chauffe and Sithe subsidiaries into a single energy division, named Dalkia. In 1999 Sithe Energies bought 23 thermal power plants from US utility GPU (now FirstEnergy) and became the leading independent power producer in the northeastern US.

Vivendi continued its charge into the US that year. The group acquired waste services company Superior Services (then the US's fourth-biggest solid waste company). Its purchase of USFilter transformed Vivendi into the world's largest water company and marked the biggest acquisition of a US firm by a French company.

The ever-evolving Vivendi transformed into a global media company and renamed itself Vivendi Universal in 2000. It bought Seagram and French pay-TV provider CANAL+ and spun off its water, waste management, transportation, and energy operations (Vivendi Environnement) after turning down German utility RWE's $28 million offer to buy the business.

Vivendi Environnement's waste operations grew after snapping up operations in Brazil, Hong Kong, and Mexico from Waste Management. In 2001 the company merged its Dalkia energy operations with the energy services operations of Electricité de France (EDF).

In 2002 Vivendi Universal reduced its stake in Vivendi Environnement from 63% to about 20%; the following year Vivendi Environnement changed its name to Veolia Environnement.

EXECUTIVES

Chairman of the Supervisory Board:
Jean-René Fourtou, age 64
Chairman of the Management Board and CEO:
Henri Proglio, age 53
SEVP, COO, and CFO: Jérôme Contamine, age 45
Managing Director, Energy Services Division:
Olivier Barbaroux, age 47
Managing Director, Transportation Division:
Stéphane Richard, age 41

Managing Director, Waste Management Division:
Denis Gasquet, age 49
Managing Director, Water Division: Antoine Frérot, age 44
Managing Director; President and CEO, USFilter:
Andrew D. (Andy) Seidel, age 40
VP US Investor Relations: Brian Sullivan
Director Investor Relations: Nathalie Pinon
Auditors: Barbier Frinault & Cie; RSM Salustro Reydel

LOCATIONS

HQ: 36-38, Avenue Kléber, 75116 Paris, France
Phone: +33-1-71-75-00-00   **Fax:** +33-1-71-71-15-45
Web: www.veoliaenvironnement.com

Veolia Environnement has operations in more than 100 countries and territories in Africa, the Asia/Pacific region, Europe, Latin America, the Middle East, and North America.

2002 Sales

	% of total
Europe	
France	43
UK	8
Other European countries	25
US	16
Other regions & countries	8
Total	**100**

PRODUCTS/OPERATIONS

2002 Sales

	$ mil.	% of total
Water	13,962	44
Waste management	6,448	20
Energy	4,801	15
Transport	3,594	12
Other	2,787	9
Total	**31,592**	**100**

Selected Operations

Water
Veolia Water (formerly Vivendi Water)
Générale des Eaux
United States Filter Corporation (USFilter)
Culligan
Veolia Water Systems

Waste Management
CGEA Onyx
Onyx Environmental Group Plc (UK)
Onyx North America Corp.
Renosol
Société d'Assainissement Rationnel et de Pompage (SARP)
SARP Industries

Energy
Dalkia (66%)

Transport
CGEA Connex
Connex Transport Ltd (formerly Connex Rail Ltd, UK)

Other
FCC (26%, Spain)

COMPETITORS

American States Water	SABESP
AWG	Scottish Power
Bechtel	Severn Trent
Bouygues	Shanks
SNCF	Stagecoach
Earth Tech	Suez
Electricité de France	Thames Water
Kelda	United Utilities
Middlesex Water	United Water Resources
Northumbrian Water	Vattenfall
Group	Waste Management
Pennon	Welsh Water

HISTORICAL FINANCIALS

Company Type: Public

Income Statement

FYE: December 31

	REVENUE ($ mil.)	NET INCOME ($ mil.)	NET PROFIT MARGIN	EMPLOYEES
12/02	31,592	356	1.1%	302,283
12/01	25,647	(1,982)	—	295,286
12/00	24,858	579	2.3%	215,376
12/99	41,914	1,441	3.4%	275,000
12/98	37,034	1,308	3.5%	235,610
12/97	29,729	959	3.2%	193,300
Annual Growth	**1.2%**	**(18.0%)**	**—**	**9.4%**

2002 Year-End Financials

Debt ratio: 204.0%
Return on equity: 6.1%
Cash ($ mil.): 2,502
Current ratio: 1.00
Long-term debt ($ mil.): 13,563

No. of shares (mil.): 405
Dividends
Yield: 5.9%
Payout: 139.8%
Market value ($ mil.): 9,442

Stock History

NYSE: VE

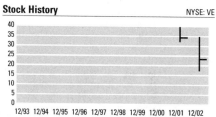

40			
35			
30			
25			
20			
15			
10			
5			
0			
	12/93 12/94 12/95 12/96 12/97 12/98 12/99 12/00 12/01 12/02		

	STOCK PRICE ($) FY Close	P/E High/Low	PER SHARE ($)		
			Earnings	Dividends	Book Value
12/02	23.31	35 18	0.98	1.37	16.41
12/01	34.25	— —	(5.80)	0.00	14.60
Annual Growth	**(31.9%)**	**— —**	**—**	**—**	**12.4%**

Virgin Group

Led by adventurous founder, chairman, and owner Sir Richard Branson, Virgin Group gets around. The group's travel operations, led by 51%-owned Virgin Atlantic Airways, are among its biggest breadwinners. Virgin Atlantic is complemented by its pan-European and Australian low-fare cousins, Virgin Express and Virgin Blue. Virgin Group also operates two UK rail franchises and sells tour packages. The group's Virgin Megastores sell music, videos, and computer games. Other Virgin Group operations include balloon flights, beverages, bridal stores, cosmetics, financial services, health clubs, Internet services, mobile phone services, publishing, and a record label.

Branson has made Virgin Group's name one of the most recognizable brands in the world by plastering it on everything from airplanes to cola. But with the airline industry slumping, Virgin Group is looking for new growth opportunities, and the company believes it may have found one in the US mobile phone market.

In addition, Branson has announced plans to raise cash by selling stakes in several group companies to the public by 2010. Australian airline Virgin Blue is expected to be the first to be floated.

HISTORY

Always one to revel in competition, Richard Branson got his start in the business world at the age of 17, dropping out of boarding school to pursue his magazine, *Student*, in 1968. Two years later he was on to a new challenge when he started Virgin — a mail-order record company named for his lack of experience at such things. After a postal strike the next year put a damper on that enterprise, Branson opened the first Virgin record store. Continued success led to a recording studio and record label that went on to sign several popular British rock bands in the 1970s, including the Sex Pistols, Genesis, and the Rolling Stones.

With his entertainment businesses flourishing in the early 1980s, Branson sought a new adventure and found it in the airline industry, another business he knew very little about. Virgin Atlantic Airways took off in 1984 with one plane and one transatlantic route. Growing steadily, Virgin Atlantic became one of the world's most profitable airlines in the 1980s. The company added Virgin Holidays (tours) to its travel group in 1985.

Branson collected all his businesses (except the travel operations) into a new company called Virgin Group and took it public in 1986. Despite the company's continued growth and profits, the market slashed its value after the crash of 1987, and a frustrated Branson bought it all back the following year. Virgin sold its smaller UK record stores in 1988 to focus on the development of its Megastores concept. It also entered the hotel business that year.

Virgin started Britain's first national commercial rock radio station in 1992. Branson sold the Virgin Music Group (a decision he still regrets) to THORN EMI that year for about $1 billion. He used the proceeds to build Virgin Atlantic. By the early 1990s the airline had added to its fleet and had new routes, including flights to Asia. It also took on British Airways and won a libel suit in 1993.

The company debuted Virgin Cola in 1994 and bought 25% of the Our Price record store chain with WH Smith (it purchased the rest in 1998). Virgin acquired MGM Cinemas (the UK's largest theater operator) and introduced its financial services business in 1995. Meanwhile it added dozens of new Megastores around the world in the mid-1990s. Virgin got back into the recording business in 1996 when it launched the V2 record label. It also bought low-fare Euro Belgian Airlines (renamed Virgin Express).

Virgin looked to keep itself on the right track in 1997 when it got into the rail business. Realizing that the right track might be the Internet, Branson has pushed the group toward the age of e-commerce and online services with Virgin.com. Mobile phone sales (at its existing retail locations) entered the company's cornucopia in 1999. In late 1999 Virgin agreed to sell its cinema chain to Vivendi (now Vivendi Universal), raising funds for other online and retail ventures. It launched a major Australian airline (Virgin Blue) in 2000.

That year Branson's bid to wrest the operation of UK's national lottery from current contract holder Camelot Group came up short. The National Lottery Commission extended Camelot's contract for seven years. Later in 2000 the company sold 49% of Virgin Atlantic to Singapore Airlines.

In 2001 Virgin agreed to sell Virgin Sun (package holidays) to rival travel firm First Choice Holidays. Also that year the company sold its 16 French Megastores, as well as some international rights to the Virgin brand, to France's Lagardère.

Virgin Mobile in 2002 began offering prepaid wireless service in the US in conjunction with Sprint PCS.

EXECUTIVES

Chairman, President, and CEO: Sir Richard Branson, age 53
Director Financial Control: Susannah Parden
Group Brand Marketing Director: Ashley Stockwell
IT Services Director: Gareth Lewis
General Counsel: Helena Samaha
Auditors: KPMG

LOCATIONS

HQ: Virgin Group Ltd.
120 Campden Hill Rd.,
London W8 7AR, United Kingdom
Phone: +44-20-7229-1282   **Fax:** +44-20-7727-8200
Web: www.virgin.com

Virgin Group has operations in Africa, Asia, Australia, Europe, and North America.

PRODUCTS/OPERATIONS

Major Operations

Virgin Active (45%, health clubs)
Virgin Arcadia Productions (video production)
Virgin Airship & Balloon company (commercial hot air balloon for advertising and other contracts)
Virgin Atlantic Airways (51%, international airline)
Virgin Balloon Flights (passenger balloons)
Virgin Biz Net (website creation and other online services for small businesses)
Virgin Blue (Australian low-fare airline)
Virgin Books (book publishing)
Virgin Bride (bridal emporium)
Virgin Cars (car purchasing website)
Virgin Cola (beverage brands)
Virgin Cosmetics (more than 500 products for men and women available in the UK)
Virgin Direct (financial services)
Virgin Energy (25%, utility bill payment program)
Virgin Express (pan-European low-fare airline)
Virgin Holidays (UK-based tour operator)
Virgin Limobike (motorcycle passenger service)
Virgin Limousines (Northern California limo service)
Virgin Megastores (retail music, movies, and computer games)
Virgin Mobile (mobile phone services)
Virgin Money (financial information)
Virgin Net (online entertainment, sports and leisure service)
Virgin One (banking services)
Virgin Student (online community)
Virgin Trains (passenger trains)
Virgin Travelstore (online travel agency)
Virgin Vouchers (voucher program)
V2 Music (record label)
V.SHOP (entertainment stores)

COMPETITORS

Accor	MyTravel
Air France	News Corp.
AMR	Pearson
Bertelsmann	PepsiCo
British Airways	Rank
Coca-Cola	Sony
EMI Group	Starwood Hotels & Resorts
HMV	Time Warner
Japan Airlines	UAL
KLM	Viacom
Lufthansa	Vivendi Universal
Marriott International	Walt Disney
MTS	

HISTORICAL FINANCIALS

Company Type: Private

Income Statement

FYE: January 31

	ESTIMATED REVENUE ($ mil.)	NET INCOME ($ mil.)	NET PROFIT MARGIN	EMPLOYEES
1/03	7,000	—	—	36,000
1/02	6,500	—	—	34,000
1/01	6,000	—	—	32,000
1/00	5,200	—	—	30,000
1/99	4,941	—	—	25,000
1/98	5,000	—	—	24,000
1/97*	4,003	—	—	20,000
10/96	3,254	—	—	10,000
10/95	2,800	—	—	10,000
10/94	2,500	—	—	9,000
Annual Growth	12.1%	—	—	16.7%

*Fiscal year change

Revenue History

Vivendi Universal S.A.

Vivendi Universal is tired of entertaining. The firm that evolved from a water utility into the world's #3 media company (behind Time Warner and Disney) has had its Hollywood dreams dashed. In 2000 it bought Seagram (owner of Universal Music and Universal Studios) and the 51% of European pay-TV provider CANAL+ that it didn't already own. The firm also owns 70% of telecom provider Cegetel and 20% of Veolia Environnement, the world's #1 water distributor. It also bought the entertainment assets of InterActiveCorp (formerly USA Interactive), which it combined with Universal Studios into the 86%-owned Vivendi UNIVERSAL Entertainment (VUE). Vivendi Universal is selling VUE to television network NBC.

Despite Vivendi Universal's impressive array of entertainment assets, the firm desperately needed to increase its US distribution capabilities. To that end, it bought 10% of EchoStar for $1.5 billion to help fund the satellite TV giant's purchase of rival DIRECTV. However, the combination was rejected by US authorities on antitrust grounds and the companies terminated the merger agreement. Vivendi Universal sold the 10% stake back to EchoStar for $1 billion.

Maverick Frenchman Jean-Marie Messier (former CEO and chairman) wanted to sell his company as the entertainment house of the future that would combine entertainment content with wireless distribution capabilities, but after several run-ins with the board Messier was forced to resign.

He was replaced by drug maker Aventis' vice chairman Jean-René Fourtou. Fourtou's new management team wasted no time planning Vivendi Universal's recovery. It sold all of Vivendi Universal Publishing, with the exception of educational publisher Houghton Mifflin (which was sold to investment firms Thomas H. Lee and Bain Capital in a separate deal), to Lagardère. The company instead exercised an option to buy BT Group's stake in Cegetel, which brings Vivendi Universal's holding in the French telecommunications giant to 70%.

The company is transferring the majority of its CANAL+ Group operations to CANAL+ SA, the publicly traded entity that owns the French CANAL+ pay-TV channel. Vivendi will retain a 49% stake in the company.

After the company posted the largest one-year loss in French corporate history in 2002 (about $25 billion), Vivendi Universal conceded it would have to find a buyer for most of its US entertainment assets so it can focus on telecommunications and CANAL+. (Universal Music is not for sale.) After intense negotiations with several suitors, Vivendi Universal chose broadcast network NBC as the buyer. The new NBC Universal will be 80%-owned by NBC parent GE, and 20%-owned by Vivendi Universal.

JP Morgan owns a 10% stake in the company.

HISTORY

Authorized by an imperial decree, Compagnie Générale des Eaux was founded in 1853 by investors such as the Rothschild family and Napoleon III's half-brother to irrigate French farmland and supply water to towns. It won contracts to serve Lyons (1853), Nantes (1854), Paris (1860), and Venice (1880).

After WWI Générale des Eaux created water engineering firm Société Auxiliaire de Distribution d'Eau (Sade, 1918) and extended its water distribution network to several areas of France. By 1953 the company had added trash collection to its services. In the 1960s it began managing district heating networks and waste incineration/composting plants. The company moved into construction in 1972. By the time Guy Dujouany became chairman in 1976, water distribution accounted for less than half of the company's sales.

Dujouany began an expansion drive in the 1980s. In 1980 Générale des Eaux became France's #1 private energy management firm when it bought Générale de Chauffe. Also that year it expanded its wastewater and waste management businesses and moved into transportation, buying Compagnie Générale d'Entreprises Automobiles (CGEA). The company also entered communications in the 1980s; it took a 15% stake in pay-TV provider CANAL+ (1983) and created mobile phone unit Société Francaise de Radiotelephonie (SFR, 1987).

Générale des Eaux's took its water services global in the 1990s. Dujouany stepped down in 1996, and the new helmsman, Jean-Marie Messier, dumped noncore businesses. In 1997 the company launched telecom provider Cegetel and increased its stake in publisher Havas to 30%. In 1998 the firm bought the rest of Havas and took the name Vivendi — representing vivacity and mobility.

Its purchase of USFilter in 1999 made Vivendi the world's largest water company; it also bought US waste management company Superior Services. Bulking up its media holdings, it added US firm Cendant Software (educational software and games) and bought French film producer Pathé. Vivendi sold most of Pathé's assets but kept

stakes in BSkyB and CANAL+'s CanalSatellite digital-TV unit. The company sold $985 million worth of real estate to Unibail and its hotel and restaurant businesses to Accor, the French hotels group.

In 2000 Vivendi and Vodafone launched an Internet portal, Vizzavi. Vivendi brought its environmental services businesses together under the Vivendi Environnement umbrella and sold a minority stake in the new company to the public. Later that year Vivendi bought Seagram and the portion of CANAL+ that it didn't already own in a $34 billion deal. The combined company became Vivendi Universal, one of the world's leading entertainment companies. To gain European Commission approval for the Seagram acquisition, Vivendi Universal is slowly unloading its stake in BSkyB. Vivendi Universal also sold Seagram's liquor business for $8.1 billion to Diageo and Pernod Ricard.

In 2001 the company struck the biggest deal in its short history by agreeing to buy the entertainment assets of USA Networks. The deal closed the following year and Vivendi combined Universal Studios with the USA business — which includes film and TV production and cable channels — into a new company called Vivendi UNIVERSAL Entertainment.

Vivendi Universal sold a 20% stake (later reduced to a 20% stake) in Vivendi Environnement. (In 2003, the company changed its name to Veolia Environnement to distance itself from Vivendi Universal.)

The company struck a deal with Marvel Enterprises in 2002 to license the comic book publisher's characters for online games. At the end of the year Vivendi Universal completely exited the publishing business by selling Vivendi Universal Publishing (now named Editis) to Lagardère for $1.2 billion, and Houghton Mifflin to Thomas H. Lee and Bain Capital for $1.6 billion. The sales were part of Vivendi Universal's $10 billion asset fire sale put in place by Fourtou.

EXECUTIVES

Chairman and CEO: Jean-René Fourtou, age 64
COO: Jean-Bernard Levy, age 48
SEVP and CFO: Jacques Espinasse, age 60
SEVP Human Resources: Andrew J. Kaslow, age 53
SEVP Social Policies: Jean-François Colin
SEVP Divestitures, Mergers, and Acquisitions: Robert de Metz, age 51
EVP Divestitures, Mergers, and Acquisitions: Régis Turrini, age 44
EVP and General Counsel: Jean-François Dubos, age 58
EVP Corporate Communications: Michel Bourgeois
EVP Labor Relations: Pierre Allain
EVP Investor Relations: Daniel Scolan
EVP US Asset Monitoring and and Deputy CFO: Hubert Joly, age 43
President and COO, Vivendi UNIVERSAL Entertainment: Ron Meyer
Chairman, Universal Pictures: Stacey Snider, age 40
Chairman and CEO, Cegetel: Frank Esser, age 45
Chairman and CEO, Universal Music Group: Douglas (Doug) Morris
Chairman and CEO, Universal Parks & Resorts: Thomas L. (Tom) Williams
Chairman and CEO, Veolia Environnement: Henri Proglio, age 53
Chairman, CANAL+ Group; Chairman and CEO, CANAL+ SA: Bertrand Méheut
President and COO, Universal Music Group: Zach Horowitz
President and COO, Universal Pictures: Rick Finkelstein
Auditors: RSM Salustro Reydel

LOCATIONS

HQ: 42 avenue de Friedland, 75380 Paris, France
Phone: +33-1-71-71-10-00   **Fax:** +33-1-71-71-11-79
US HQ: 800 Third Ave., New York, NY 10012
US Phone: 212-572-7000   **US Fax:** 212-753-9301
Web: www.vivendiuniversal.com

Vivendi Universal operates in about 100 countries.

PRODUCTS/OPERATIONS

Selected Subsidiaries and Affiliates

Environmental Services
Veolia Environnement (20%)
  Energy
    Dalkia (66%)
  Transport
    CGEA-Connex
    Connex Australia
    Connex Transport AB (Scandinavia)
    Connex Transport UK
    Connex Verkehr (Germany)
  Waste management
    CGEA-Onyx
    FCC (50%, Spain)
  Water
    Philadelphia Suburban (17%, US)
    Veolia Water
      Culligan
      General Utilities plc (UK)
      Générale des Eaux
      OTV/Vivendi Water Systems
      United States Filter Corporation (USFilter)

Media & Communications
Antennes Tonna (51%, cable and satellite equipment manufacturing)
CANAL+ Group
  CANAL+ SA (49%)
  CANAL+ France
  CANAL+ Television (pay TV, Nordic countries)
  StudioCanal (film production)
Cegetel (70%)
Expand (35%, TV production)
France Loisirs
Groupe Anaya
Sogecable (21%, pay TV, Spain)
UGC (39%)
Universal Music Group
Vivendi UNIVERSAL Entertainment (86%)
  Universal Parks & Resorts (US)
Universal Pictures
Universal Television Group
  SCI-FI Channel (cable network featuring science fiction, horror, and fantasy programming)
  Universal Television Distribution
  Universal Television Production
USA Network (general entertainment cable network)
Vivendi Universal Net
  EMusic.com
  GetMusic.com
  RollingStone.com

COMPETITORS

American States Water
Bertelsmann
Electricité de France
Enron
France Telecom
Kelda
News Corp.
Pennon
RWE
Sony
Suez
Technip
Terra Lycos
Thames Water
Time Warner
Viacom
Walt Disney
Waste Recycling

HISTORICAL FINANCIALS

Company Type: Public

Income Statement

FYE: December 31

	REVENUE ($ mil.)	NET INCOME ($ mil.)	NET PROFIT MARGIN	EMPLOYEES
12/02	61,075	(24,473)	—	61,815
12/01	51,125	(12,119)	—	381,504
12/00	40,138	2,165	5.4%	290,000
12/99	43,774	1,438	3.3%	275,000
12/98	37,034	1,308	3.5%	234,800
12/97	27,858	899	3.2%	193,300
12/96	31,623	373	1.2%	217,300
12/95	32,713	(751)	—	221,157
12/94	28,985	627	2.2%	215,281
12/93	24,395	541	2.2%	204,307
Annual Growth	10.7%	—	—	(12.4%)

2002 Year-End Financials

Debt ratio: 74.6%
Return on equity: —
Cash ($ mil.): 7,662
Current ratio: 0.69
Long-term debt ($ mil.): 10,981

No. of shares (mil.): 1,069
Dividends
  Yield: 5.5%
  Payout: —
Market value ($ mil.): 17,172

Stock History

NYSE: V

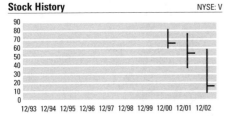

12/93 12/94 12/95 12/96 12/97 12/98 12/99 12/00 12/01 12/02

	STOCK PRICE ($) FY Close	P/E High/Low	PER SHARE ($) Earnings	Dividends	Book Value
12/02	16.07	— —	(22.51)	0.89	13.78
12/01	53.79	— —	(0.12)	0.90	30.16
12/00	65.31	25 19	3.20	0.00	49.39
Annual Growth	(50.4%)	— —	—	—	(47.2%)

VNU N.V.

This company has a nose for industry news and information. VNU has remade itself as the leading market research and business information publishers in the world. Holdings include the US-based ACNielsen (it flagship marketing information business) and Nielsen Media Research (media measurement and information). The company's Business Information segment consists of such industry rags as *Adweek, Billboard,* and *The Hollywood Reporter* and includes trade show and conference production. VNU also publishes European business and telephone directories. To focus on business information and services, the company sold its consumer magazine operations and its educational publishing unit in 2001.

VNU has become one of the world's leading suppliers of business information, with operating units collecting and disseminating marketing and media information and industry news in 100 countries around the world. Formerly known more for its publishing operations, the company has significantly grown its media mea-

surement and market research segment through the acquisitions of US-based Nielsen Media Research and ACNielsen in 2000 and 2001, respectively. Other operations include trade show production (acquired Miller Freeman in 2001), and various directory publishers. Despite the global business offerings of the company the US accounts for more than 50% of sales.

With its focus on information products and business services, VNU is paring away its non-core operations. In 2001 it sold its consumer titles to Finnish newspaper publisher SanomaWSOY for about $1.1 billion (one of the largest acquisitions ever by a Finnish company). Also that year it sold its educational publishing unit to the unit's management team (backed by UK venture capital firm 3i Group). As VNU divested itself of its consumer publishing operations the company has been reinvesting in its European directory services with a focus on smaller countries.

In 2002 VNU struck a deal with Reuters through which Reuters will distribute stories from VNU's *Billboard* and *The Hollywood Reporter* publications, making VNU the sole third-party provider of entertainment content for Reuters.

HISTORY

VNU was formed in 1964 through the merger of Dutch mass-market consumer publishing companies Cebema ('sHertogenbosch) and De Spaarnestad (Haarlem). The newly formed company acquired regional newspaper publisher Het Nieuwsblad van het Zuiden and book publisher Het Spectrum in 1967. The next year it acquired magazine publisher NRM and Smeets, one of the largest offset printers in Europe. The company's buying spree pumped up sales and profits but also created an unwieldy organization. During the early 1970s VNU hired US management consultant McKinsey & Company to help streamline its operations.

Acquisitions continued through the 1970s, including trade journal publisher Intermediair (1973) and Belgian bookbinder Reliure Industrielle de Barchon (1974). In the late 1970s the company began moving into professional publishing, and in 1980 VNU acquired the publishing units of Computing Publications and Business and Career Publications. In 1985 Joep Brentjens was appointed chairman of VNU. That year the company began to focus on expanding into the US and bought financial information provider Disclosure. It later acquired New Jersey-based Hayden Publishing (1986, sold in 1989). Back at home, VNU became the #1 regional newspaper publisher in The Netherlands when it bought Audet in 1988. The next year the company made its first foray into television, buying stakes in Belgian station VTM and Dutch TV station RTL 4. (Both investments were sold in 1998.)

In 1990 the company entered the eastern European market with *Moscow Magazine*. As part of a plan to focus on publishing, VNU sold its printing operations to Koninklijke De Boer Boekhoven in 1993. The next year it acquired US-based BPI Communications (*Billboard, Adweek*) and Bill Communications (*Beverage World*). VNU sold Disclosure in 1995 and bought SRDS, a business information provider, as part of its strategy to increase its US market share of business information services (professional newsletters, magazines, directories, trade shows).

In 1997 VNU acquired Czech consumer magazine publisher Kwety Ceske and a 50% stake in RCV Entertainment (later boosted to full-

ownership), a Netherlands-based film, video, and TV program distributor. The company paid $2.1 billion for a directories unit of ITT the next year. After acquiring venerable *Editor & Publisher Magazine* in 1999, VNU made its biggest US investment when it agreed to buy TV ratings firm Nielsen Media Research for $2.5 billion (completed in 2000).

Rob van den Bergh, a 20-year company veteran, was appointed chairman of VNU in 2000. That year the company entered into a joint venture with Germany's Gatrixx to create localized financial portals in Europe and bought Netherlands-based Internet portal Startpagina (starting page). It also sold its VNU Dagbladen newspaper publishing division. Later in 2000 VNU acquired trade show unit Miller Freeman from United News & Media (now United Business Media).

At the beginning of 2001 VNU took another major step with its $2.3 billion acquisition of US market research firm ACNielsen. It also announced plans to get out of the consumer magazine and educational publishing business. Later that year it sold its consumer titles to SanomaWSOY (Finland) for about $1.1 billion and its educational publishing business to a management group.

EXECUTIVES

Chairman, Supervisory Board: Aad G. Jacobs, age 66
Chairman, Executive Board: R. F. van den Bergh, age 52
Executive Director and CFO: Franz J. G. M. Cremers, age 51
Executive Director; Chairman and CEO, VNU Media Measurement & Information; Vice Chairman, ACNielsen: Michael P. Connors, age 47
Chief Legal Officer: Earl H. Doppelt
Chairman, Nielsen Media Research: John A. Dimling, age 64
Chairman and CEO, Media Measurement Division International: R. McCann
CEO, VNU Business Media Europe: R. H. Bakker
CEO, VNU World Directories: E. G. M. Penninx
President and CEO, VNU Business Media: Michael Marchesano
President and CEO, Internet Measurement Division: William R. (Bill) Pulver, age 43
President and CEO, Nielsen Media Research, USA: Susan D. Whiting
President and CEO, Nielsen Entertainment: Andrew Wing
Secretary: T. C. M. van Kampen
Corporate Development: Thomas A. Mastrelli, age 55
Controller: Ad van Schaik
Corporate Communications And Investor Relations: R. de Meel
Human Resources and Management Development Director Europe: Jeremy Lancaster
Human Resources and Management Development, USA: Georgina Challis
Information and Communication Technology: M. O'Toole
Auditors: Ernst & Young

LOCATIONS

HQ: Ceylonpoort 5-25,
  2037 AA Haarlem, The Netherlands
Phone: +31-23-546-34-63   Fax: +31-23-546-39-38
US HQ: 770 Broadway, New York, NY 10003-9595
US Phone: 646-654-5000   US Fax: 646-654-5001
Web: www.vnu.com

2002 Sales

	$ mil.	% of total
US and Canada	2,354	53
The Netherlands	288	6
Other European Countries	1,330	30
Rest of the World	509	11
Total	**4,481**	**100**

PRODUCTS/OPERATIONS

2002 Sales

	$ mil.	% of total
Marketing & media information	2,074	46
Media measurement & information	1,082	24
Business information	812	18
Directories	513	12
Total	**4,481**	**100**

Selected Operations and Operating Units

Business Information
VNU Business Publications USA
  Adweek
  Billboard
  The Hollywood Reporter
  National Jeweler
  Progressive Grocer
VNU Expositions
VNU eMedia

Marketing Information
ACNielsen
Claritas
Spectra Marketing Systems
MediaPlan
Solucient (36% ownership)

Media Measurement & Information
Nielsen Media Research
Broadcast Data Systems
SoundScan
BookScan
VideoScan

Directories
Promedia
Gouden Gids
Golden Pages
Páginas Amarelas (75%)
Verizon Information Services (40%)
Telkom Directory Services (33%)

COMPETITORS

Arbitron	NFO WorldGroup
Bertelsmann	Reed Elsevier Group
Bonnierforetagen	RoperASW
Consodata	Synovate
Crain Communications	Taylor Nelson
GfK	Thomson Corporation
Information Resources	United Business Media
International Data Group	Vivendi Universal
IPSOS	Publishing
Kantar Group	Wolters Kluwer
McGraw-Hill	

HISTORICAL FINANCIALS

Company Type: Public

Income Statement

FYE: December 31

	REVENUE ($ mil.)	NET INCOME ($ mil.)	NET PROFIT MARGIN	EMPLOYEES
12/02	4,481	178	4.0%	37,590
12/01	4,274	708	16.6%	36,796
12/00	3,187	752	23.6%	18,720
12/99	2,829	247	8.7%	14,591
12/98	2,848	294	10.3%	12,059
12/97	1,935	207	10.7%	12,123
12/96	1,949	186	9.5%	10,462
12/95	1,897	268	14.1%	9,285
12/94	1,601	119	7.4%	9,919
12/93	1,187	74	6.3%	8,367
Annual Growth	**15.9%**	**10.2%**	**—**	**18.2%**

2002 Year-End Financials

Debt ratio: 69.4%
Return on equity: 3.9%
Cash ($ mil.): 550
Current ratio: 0.98
Long-term debt ($ mil.): 3,337

Net Income History

Euronext Amsterdam: VNU

12/93 12/94 12/95 12/96 12/97 12/98 12/99 12/00 12/01 12/02

Vodafone Group

Customers have voted with their phones to make Vodafone Group the world's top wireless phone services provider (by subscribers) — with more than 122.7 million. Vodafone Group has grown rapidly through acquisitions and has advanced toward its goal of creating a pan-European wireless network. The company, formerly known as Vodafone AirTouch, owns stakes in wireless carriers around the globe. Vodafone companies are leading mobile phone operators in the US (45%-owned Verizon Wireless), Germany (D2), and the UK (Vodafone). The company is uniting its far-flung affiliates under the Vodafone brand.

The Vodafone Group owns stakes in operating affiliates in Europe, the Americas, the Asia Pacific region, the Middle East, and Africa.

Besides leading the mobile carrier market in the UK, the company's acquisitions include Germany's Mannesmann, which had controlled the #1 network in Germany (D2) and the #2 network in Italy (Omnitel). Vodafone also owns stakes in wireless carriers in several other European countries, including France, the Netherlands, and Spain.

On the other side of the Atlantic, Vodafone Group has combined its US wireless operations (acquired when the company bought AirTouch in 1999) with those of Bell Atlantic and GTE to form Verizon Wireless, the #1 US wireless provider. Verizon Wireless is 45%-owned by Vodafone Group and 55%-owned by Verizon Communications (formed when Bell Atlantic bought GTE).

Wanting a pause to catch its breath, perhaps, Vodafone Group said it would shift its focus from growing through acquisitions to developing existing businesses. But the shopping respite didn't last long. The company expanded its wireless data offerings and took full ownership in the Vizzavi Internet portal, buying out France's Vivendi Universal, its original 50% partner. It also sought to buy the stakes held in French operator Cegetel by SBC and BT Group and offered to buy Vivendi Universal's stake, but Vivendi Universal exercised its option to strengthen its control of the French company. In 2003 the company agreed to buy UK-based Project Telecom in a deal valued at about $250 million. It also reached an agreement to buy Singlepoint, the fast-growing UK independent service provide, from Caudwell Holdings, in a deal valued at $650 million.

Vodafone Group has announced plans to con-

solidate its holdings both in Asia and Europe, including an agreement to sell Japan Telecom's fixed-line assets and the acquisition of outstanding stakes in subsidiaries in Sweden, Portugal, and the Netherlands. It has sold its 74% stake in Mexico's Grupo Iusacell, held jointly with Verizon Communications, to Movilccess in a deal valued at $7.4 million. It also is selling its 21% stake in Indian regional operator RPG Cellular Services.

Vodafone Group also has teamed up with US-based software giant Microsoft to develop mobile Web services and standards.

HISTORY

Vodafone was formed in 1983 as a joint venture between Racal Electronics (a UK electronics firm) and Millicom (a US telecom company), and was granted one of two mobile phone licenses in the UK. It launched service in 1985 as a Racal subsidiary. Vodafone and Cellnet, the other licensee, were swamped with demand. In 1988 Racal offered 20% of Vodafone to the public; three years later the rest of the firm was spun off to become Vodafone Group.

Vodafone moved beyond the UK in the 1990s. By 1993 it had interests in mobile phone networks in Australia, Greece, Hong Kong, Malta, and Scandinavia.

For a time Vodafone and Cellnet, a joint venture of British Telecom (now BT Group) and Securicor, enjoyed a duopoly in the UK. Regulators elected not to impose price controls, and the pounds rolled in. But in 1993 a new wireless provider, One 2 One, launched a digital network in London. Vodafone countered that year with its own GSM (global system for mobile communications) digital network.

With increasing competition at home, Vodafone continued to expand in 1994. It launched or bought stakes in operations in Fiji, Germany, South Africa, and Uganda.

Digital service took on a larger role in Vodafone's UK business, and by 1997 some 85% of new subscribers were opting for digital GSM. In 1998 Vodafone sold its French service provider, Vodafone SA, and bought digital cellular carrier BellSouth New Zealand. It also expanded into Egypt by buying a minority stake in Misrfone, marking the largest British investment in Egypt since the Suez Canal.

In 1999 Vodafone prevailed in a brief bidding war with Bell Atlantic (now Verizon) to buy AirTouch Communications for about $60 billion. Vodafone's Chris Gent took over as CEO of the new company, Vodafone AirTouch. The prize for Vodafone: entry into the lucrative US market, plus the opportunity to consolidate minority interests in European wireless carriers.

Vodafone AirTouch moved to significantly boost its European footprint in 1999 by launching a $131 billion hostile takeover bid for Germany's Mannesmann. The company acquired Mannesmann for about $180 billion in stock in 2000 and agreed to sell the conglomerate's engineering operations and its UK mobile phone unit, Orange. (France Telecom bought Orange for $37.5 billion later that year.) Vodafone AirTouch also announced plans for an IPO for Italian fixed-line carrier Infostrada, acquired in the Mannesmann deal, but the company instead agreed to sell Infostrada to Italian utility giant Enel. (The deal closed in 2001.)

Also in 2000 Vodafone AirTouch expanded its presence in the US, buying CommNet Cellular for $1.4 billion, then combining its US wireless operations with those of Bell Atlantic and GTE to form Verizon Wireless.

That year the company dropped AirTouch from its name and became Vodafone Group once again. It also continued its expansion push, investing in China Mobile (Hong Kong) and agreeing to buy Irish mobile phone operator Eircell in a deal that was completed in 2001. Also in 2001 Vodafone expanded its stakes in Japan Telecom and its J-Phone mobile phone operations by buying out rival BT Group; it also bought BT's remaining interest in Spain's Airtel.

EXECUTIVES

Chairman: Lord Ian MacLaurin of Knebworth, age 66, $684,288 pay
Deputy Chairman: Paul M. Hazen, age 61, $139,709 pay
CEO: Arun Sarin, age 48
Group COO and Director: Julian Horn-Smith, age 54, $2,290,939 pay
Group Financial Director and Director: Kenneth J. (Ken) Hydon, age 58, $1,891,771 pay
Chief Marketing Officer and Director: Peter R. Bamford, age 49, $1,888,920 pay
Group Personnel Director: Phillip (Phil) Williams, age 52
Group Strategy Director: Alan Harper, age 46
Chief Technology Officer and Director: Thomas Geitner, age 48, $1,455,537 pay
Chief Executive, Southern Europe, Middle East, and Africa Region; CEO, Omnitel Vodafone; and Director: Vittorio Amedeo Colao, age 41
Chief Executive, Central Europe Region: Jurgen von Kuczkowski, age 62
Chief Executive, Vodafone Asia Pacific Region: Brian Clark, age 54
Chief Executive, Americas Region: Tomas Isaksson, age 49
Chief Executive, Vodafone UK: Gavin Darby
Financial Director, Northern Europe, Middle East, and Africa: Edward (Ted) Langston
Company Secretary and Group Legal Director: Stephen R. Scott, age 49
President and CEO, Vodafone Sverige AB: Hans Kuropatwa
Auditors: Deloitte & Touche

LOCATIONS

HQ: Vodafone Group PLC
Vodafone House, The Connection, Newbury, Berkshire RG14 2FN, United Kingdom
Phone: +44-1635-33-251 **Fax:** +44-1635-45-713
Web: www.vodafone.com

Vodafone Group owns stakes in wireless carriers in Albania, Australia, Belgium, China, Egypt, Fiji, France, Germany, Greece, Hungary, Italy, Japan, Kenya, Malta, the Netherlands, New Zealand, Poland, Portugal, Romania, South Africa, Spain, Sweden, Switzerland, the UK, and the US.

2003 Sales

	$ mil.	% of total
Mobile telecommunications		
Europe		
Southern Europe	14,167	30
Northern Europe	11,414	24
Central Europe	8,777	18
Asia Pacific	8,557	18
Middle East & Africa	480	1
Americas	25	—
Other operations		
Asia Pacific	2,410	5
Europe	2,175	4
Total	48,005	100

PRODUCTS/OPERATIONS

Selected Subsidiaries and Affiliates

Belgacom Mobile S.A. (Proximus, 25%, wireless network operator, Belgium)
Cellco Partnership (Verizon Wireless, 45%, wireless network operator, US)
China Mobile (Hong Kong) Limited (2%, wireless network operator, China)
Europolitan Vodafone AB (formerly Europolitan Holdings AB, 99.1%, wireless network operator holding company, Sweden)
Groupe Cegetel (30%, telecommunications services and holding company, France)
Japan Telecom Holdings Co., Ltd. (67%, diversified telecommunications provider)
MobiFon S.A. (Connex GSM, 20%, wireless network operator, Romania)
Polkomtel S.A. (Plus GSM, 20%, wireless network operator, Poland)
Safaricom Limited (35%, wireless network operator, Kenya)
Swisscom Mobile S.A. (25%, wireless network operator, Switzerland)
Vodacom Group (Pty) Limited (35%, holding company, South Africa)
Vodafone AG (formerly Mannesmann AG, holding company, Germany)
Vodafone Albania Sh. A. (82%, wireless network operator)
Vodafone Americas Inc. (holding company, US)
Vodafone D2 GmbH (formerly Mobilfunk GmbH, wireless network operator, Germany)
Vodafone Egypt Telecommunications SAE (formerly Misrfone Telecommunications Company SAE, 60%, wireless network operator)
Vodafone España, S.A. (formerly Airtel Móvil S.A., wireless network operator, Spain)
Vodafone Europe B.V. (holding company, Netherlands)
Vodafone Fiji Limited (49%, wireless network operator)
Vodafone Holding GmbH (formerly Vodafone AG, holding company, Germany)
Vodafone Holdings Europe S.A. (holding company, Spain)
Vodafone Hungary Mobile Telecommunications Limited, (formerly V.R.A.M. Telecommunications Company Limited, 84%, wireless network operator, Hungary)
Vodafone Information Systems GmbH (billing, IT, and B2B services, Germany)
Vodafone International Holdings B.V. (holding company, Netherlands)
Vodafone Investments Luxembourg S. a. r.l. (holding company)
Vodafone Ireland Limited (formerly Eircell, wireless network operator)
Vodafone Libertel N.V. (wireless network operator, Netherlands)
Vodafone Limited (wireless network operator, UK)
Vodafone Malta Limited (wireless network operator)
Vodafone Network Pty Limited (wireless network operator, Australia)
Vodafone New Zealand Limited (wireless network operator)
Vodafone Omnitel N.V (formerly Omnitel Pronto Italia, 77%, wireless network operator, Italy)
Vodafone-Panafon Hellenic Telecommunications Company S.A. (64%, telecommunications and wireless network operator, Greece)
Vodafone Telecel Comunicaçes Pessoais, S.A. (94%, wireless network operator, Portugal)

COMPETITORS

AT&T Wireless	Nextel
Belgacom	NTT DoCoMo
BT	KPN
China Mobile (Hong Kong)	Sprint PCS
Cingular Wireless	TIM
Deutsche Telekom	Telefónica Móviles
France Telecom	Telstra

HISTORICAL FINANCIALS

Company Type: Public

Income Statement

FYE: March 31

	REVENUE ($ mil.)	NET INCOME ($ mil.)	NET PROFIT MARGIN	EMPLOYEES
3/03	48,005	(15,518)	—	66,667
3/02	32,561	(23,026)	—	70,800
3/01	21,267	(13,838)	—	56,800
3/00	12,545	776	6.2%	29,465
3/99	5,415	1,026	18.9%	12,642
3/98	4,130	700	16.9%	9,640
3/97	2,868	597	20.8%	6,051
3/96	2,140	473	22.1%	4,728
3/95	1,868	385	20.6%	—
3/94	1,263	364	28.8%	—
Annual Growth	49.8%	—	—	45.9%

2003 Year-End Financials

Debt ratio: 10.2%
Return on equity: —
Cash ($ mil.): 751
Current ratio: 0.60
Long-term debt ($ mil.): 20,822

No. of shares (mil.): 6,817
Dividends
Yield: 1.4%
Payout: —
Market value ($ mil.): 124,197

Stock History

NYSE: VOD

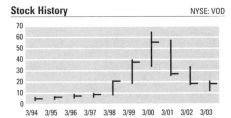

	STOCK PRICE ($) FY Close	P/E High/Low	Earnings	PER SHARE ($) Dividends	Book Value
3/03	18.22	— —	(2.28)	0.26	29.83
3/02	18.43	— —	(3.40)	0.22	27.38
3/01	27.15	— —	(2.25)	0.22	31.70
3/00	55.56	230 121	0.28	0.23	36.59
3/99	37.55	60 28	0.66	0.13	0.85
3/98	20.78	45 19	0.46	0.10	0.31
3/97	8.83	25 17	0.39	0.17	0.82
3/96	7.50	29 19	0.31	0.13	1.02
3/95	6.63	28 19	0.25	0.10	0.87
3/94	5.15	26 16	0.24	0.08	0.68
Annual Growth	15.1%	— —	—	14.0%	52.2%

Volkswagen AG

Volkswagen (VW) has given the "Love Bug" a makeover. Europe's #1 carmaker, VW revamped the Beetle (called the New Beetle) to scurry among its annual production of 5 million cars, trucks, and vans. Along with models such as Golf and Passat, VW owns a garage full of luxury carmakers — AUDI, Lamborghini, and Bentley. Other makes include SEAT (family cars, Spain) and SKODA (family cars, the Czech Republic). VW operates plants in Africa, the Americas, the Asia/Pacific region, and Europe. It also holds a 34% stake in Swedish truck maker Scania. VW's other interests include consumer financing and Europcar International (car rental).

Against the backdrop of declining economic growth in Europe, stagnant growth in the US, economic crisis in South America, worldwide automotive overcapacity, and high costs for raw materials, Volkswagen is still doing pretty well.

The company has managed to steer clear of automotive market potholes by cutting costs and implementing a module-based production strategy that involves sharing eleven major parts modules among several classes of vehicles. The company also has launched a major investment initiative in the Asia/Pacific region in anticipation of taking advantage of China's potentially huge automotive market. Volkswagen's right to use the Rolls-Royce brand expired in late 2002; fellow German competitor BMW has taken control of the nameplate. The German state of Lower Saxony controls about 14% of Volkswagen.

HISTORY

Since the early 1920s auto engineer Ferdinand Porsche (whose son later founded the Porsche car company) had wanted to make a small car for the masses. He found no backers until he met Adolf Hitler in 1934. Hitler formed the Gesellschaft zur Vorbereitung des Volkswagens (Company for the Development of People's Cars) in 1937 and built a factory in Wolfsburg, Germany. No cars were delivered during WWII, as the company produced military vehicles using the slave labor of Jews and Russian prisoners of war.

Following WWII British occupation forces oversaw the rebuilding of the bomb-damaged plant and initial production of the odd-looking "people's car" (1945). The British appointed Heinz Nordhoff to manage Volkswagen (1948) and then turned the company over to the German government (1949).

In the 1950s VW launched the Microbus and built foreign plants. Although US sales began slowly, by the end of the decade acceptance of the little car had increased. Advertising that coined the name "Beetle" helped carve VW's niche in the US.

VW sold stock to the German public in 1960. In 1966 it purchased Auto Union (AUDI) from Daimler-Benz. The Beetle became a counterculture symbol in the 1960s, and US sales took off. By the time of Nordhoff's death in 1968, the Beetle had become the best-selling car in history.

In the 1970s the Beetle was discontinued in every country except Mexico. VW lost heavily during the model-changeover period.

VW agreed to several deals in the 1980s, including a car venture in China (1984), the purchase of 75% of SEAT (1986; it bought the rest in 1990), and the merger of its suddenly faltering Brazilian unit with Ford's ailing Argentine operations to form Autolatina (1987).

In 1990 the company began building China's largest auto plant and acquired a 70% stake in Czech auto company SKODA. After suffering a $1.1 billion loss, the company put Ferdinand Piech in the driver's seat in 1993. Under his leadership the company cut costs and boosted sales by resuscitating the SEAT and SKODA brands and launching a bigger, more luxurious Passat sedan in 1997.

VW acquired Rolls-Royce Motor Cars, Vickers' Cosworth auto engines subsidiary, Italian sports-car maker Bugatti, and Italy's Automobili Lamborghini — all in 1998. Although less luxurious than VW's other pursuits, the New Beetle helped boost US sales that year. Also in 1998 VW established a $12 million fund to compensate the surviving 2,000 concentration-camp inmates forced to work as slave labor during WWII. However, the company was hit with a class-action lawsuit filed on behalf of Holocaust survivors anyway.

In 1999 chairman Ferdinand Piech announced an end to VW's acquisition binge, saying that growth would be driven from within; VW announced it would pour $31.5 billion into modernizing its factories through 2004. VW hoped to tap the market in China after getting approval in 1999 to sell a newly developed minicar there. That year it announced plans to invest $1 billion in its Mexico plant over the next five years.

Volkswagen expanded into heavy commercial vehicles in 2000 by purchasing a 34% stake in Swedish truck maker Scania (from holding company Investor). That year it also bought the 30% of SKODA that it didn't already own. Anticipating China's entry into the World Trade Organization, Volkswagen announced in 2001 that it would invest $1.7 billion in China and the Asia/Pacific region over the next five years. Later in the year — and half a world away — 12,500 workers at the company's Mexico plant went on strike for 19 days over a pay dispute.

In April 2002 former BMW head Bernd Pischetsrieder succeeded Piech as CEO.

The following year, in July, the final classic Beetle rolled off the VW assembly line in México. The final Beetle concluded a 70-year run of constant production.

EXECUTIVES

Chairman of the Supervisory Board:
 Ferdinand K. Piëch, age 65
Deputy Chairman, Supervisory Board: Klaus Zwickel, age 63
Chairman of the Board of Management:
 Bernd Pischetsrieder, age 55
Member of the Board of Management, Controlling and Accounting: Bruno Adelt, age 63
Member of the Board of Management, Group Strategy, Treasury, Legal Matters, and Organization:
 Jens Neumann, age 57
Member of the Board of Management, Human Resources: Peter Hartz, age 61
Member of the Board of Management, Procurement: Francisco Javier Garcia Sanz, age 45
Member of the Board of Management, Production: Folker Weissgerber, age 61
Member of the Board of Management, Sales and Marketing: Robert Büchelhofer, age 60
Member of the Board of Management; Chairman of the Board of Management, AUDI AG: Martin Winterkorn, age 55
Chairman, Automobili Lamborghini: Werner Mischke
Auditors: PwC Deutsche Revision AG

LOCATIONS

HQ: Brieffach 1848-2, 38436 Wolfsburg, Germany
Phone: +49-53-61-90   **Fax:** +49-53-61-92-82-82
US HQ: 3800 Hamlin Rd., Auburn Hills, MI 48326
US Phone: 248-340-5000
Web: www.volkswagen.de

Volkswagen AG operates 43 production facilities worldwide.

2002 Sales

	$ mil.	% of total
Europe		
Germany	25,022	27
Other countries	38,114	42
North America	18,108	20
Asia/Pacific	5,396	6
South America	3,493	4
Africa	997	1
Total	**91,130**	**100**

PRODUCTS/OPERATIONS

Selected Makes and Models

AUDI	**Skoda**
A4	Fabia
A6	Octavia
A8	Superb
allroad quattro	
TT Coupe	**Volkswagen**
TT Roadster	**(Commercial Vehicles)**
	Caddy
Bentley	Caravelle
Bentley Arnage R	LT
Bentley Arnage RL	Transporter
Bentley Arnage T	
Bentley Azure	**Volkswagen**
Bentley Continental GT	**(Passenger Vehicles)**
Bentley Continental R	Bora
Bentley Continental T	Golf
Mulliner Bentleys	Lupo
	New Beetle
Lamborghini	Passat
Murciélago	Passat W8
	Phaeton
Seat	Polo
Alhambra	Sharan
Arosa	Touareg
Ibiza	Touran
Leon	
Toledo	

COMPETITORS

BMW	Mazda
DaimlerChrysler	Nissan
Fiat	Peugeot
Ford	Porsche
Fuji Heavy Industries	Renault
General Motors	Saab Automobile
Honda	Suzuki Motor
Isuzu	Toyota

HISTORICAL FINANCIALS

Company Type: Public

Income Statement

FYE: December 31

	REVENUE ($ mil.)	NET INCOME ($ mil.)	NET PROFIT MARGIN	EMPLOYEES
12/02	91,130	2,708	3.0%	324,892
12/01	78,429	2,582	3.3%	322,070
12/00	80,553	1,941	2.4%	324,402
12/99	75,697	850	1.1%	306,275
12/98	80,089	1,338	1.7%	297,916
12/97	63,191	759	1.2%	279,892
12/96	64,459	424	0.7%	260,811
12/95	61,287	246	0.4%	259,342
12/94	51,656	96	0.2%	243,638
12/93	44,048	(1,172)	—	253,108
Annual Growth	**8.4%**	**—**	**—**	**2.8%**

2002 Year-End Financials

Debt ratio: 79.1%   Current ratio: 1.67
Return on equity: 11.5%   Long-term debt ($ mil.): 20,425
Cash ($ mil.): 6,476

Net Income History

German: VOW

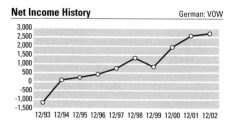

AB Volvo

Despite the fact that the word "Volvo" conjures up more visions of soccer moms than of burley truck drivers, AB Volvo has parked its car business. The company is now a leading maker of trucks as well as buses; marine, aircraft, and industrial engines; and construction equipment. The company's most widely known business — auto making — has been sold to #2 carmaker Ford Motor Company. The sale enables Volvo to focus on its remaining units, particularly trucks. Volvo's other interests include a stake in fellow Swedish truck maker Scania, and full control of the famous Mack Trucks brand.

Already a 31% owner of rival Swedish truck maker Scania, Volvo attempted to buy another 28% from Investor AB, but was thwarted by the EU Commission (the EU Commission has mandated that Volvo sell its Scania stake). The company doubled its truck making capacity when it agreed to grant Renault a 15% stake in Volvo in exchange for the French carmaker's Mack truck unit.

In the face of recession in the US and diminished demand in Western Europe, Volvo keeps on truckin'. To combat difficult market conditions, the company has consolidated its truck manufacturing operations in the US and Australia, combining the assembly of Mack and Volvo brands into the same plants. Volvo has also revamped its North American dealer networks for trucks and construction equipment in order to increase efficiencies and improve quality of service. Volvo has withdrawn from the unprofitable city bus market in the US, and has closed two bus plants.

HISTORY

Swedish ball bearing maker SKF formed Volvo (Latin for "I roll") as a subsidiary in 1915. It began building cars in 1926, trucks in 1928, and bus chassis in 1932 in Gothenburg. Sweden's winters and icy roads made the company keenly attentive to engineering and safety. Volvo bought an engine maker in 1931, and in 1935 reorganized as an independent company led by Assar Gabrielsson and Gustaf Larson.

Sweden's neutrality during WWII allowed Volvo to grow and move into component manufacturing and tractor production. Output in 1949 exceeded 100,000 units, 80% of which were sold in Sweden. The purchase of Bolinder-Munktell (farm machinery, diesel engines; Sweden; 1950) enhanced Volvo's position in the Swedish tractor market. Volvo introduced turbocharged diesel truck engines and windshield defrosters and washers in the 1950s. By 1956 car production had outstripped truck and bus output.

Aware that it was too small to compete in global markets, Volvo diversified (energy, industrial products, food, finance, and trading). Volvo increased its market share by purchasing several trucking and construction equipment companies that included White Motors' truck unit (US, 1981) and Leyland Bus (UK, 1986). In the 1980s Volvo acquired drug and biotechnology concern Pharmacia (now Pfizer) and Custos (investments, Sweden). The company consolidated its food and drug units with state-controlled holding company Procordia in 1990.

At that time, however, Volvo was facing stagnant sales. It embarked on the largest industrial undertaking in Swedish history, spending more than $2 billion to modernize plants and develop

a series of high-performance family sedans, which it introduced in 1991. Still, high costs and persistent recession in Europe kept the company in the red during the early 1990s.

Adding to its troubles, there was public outcry against a planned merger with French automaker Renault. The plan was abandoned in 1993, and the company sold its drug and consumer product interests (which had landed back in Volvo's lap when the government divested Procordia in 1993). These sales brought Volvo back into the black.

In 1997 Volvo sold its 11% stake in Renault left over from the abandoned merger. The next year the company strengthened its line of excavators and its Far Eastern presence by buying Samsung Heavy Industries' construction equipment unit. Volvo also bought Mexico's bus maker Mexicana de Autobuses and GM's share in Volvo GM Heavy Truck (now Volvo Trucks North America).

Anticipating a lower demand for cars, Volvo closed an assembly plant in Canada in 1998, and then in 1999 Volvo acquired a 13% stake (later upped to 25%) in rival truck maker Scania. To pay for its new focus on making heavy trucks, Volvo sold its auto brand and manufacturing operations in Sweden, Belgium, and the Netherlands to Ford Motor Company for $6.45 billion in 1999. Volvo then agreed to take a 20% stake in the truck and construction equipment operations of Japan's Mitsubishi Motors.

In 2000 Volvo boosted its stake in Scania to 46%, but its hope of acquiring a majority interest died when the EU rejected the $7.53 billion deal. Volvo then turned to France's Renault, and bought the company's Mack truck unit in exchange for a 15% stake in Volvo. Later in the year Volvo entered into talks with Volkswagen AG concerning the possible sale of Volvo's stake in Scania. The EU later thwarted the proposed deal, citing anti-competitive issues.

DaimlerChrysler bought out Volvo's 3.3% stake in Mitsubishi in 2001. The following year Volvo's Renault Trucks subsidiary inked a technology transfer deal with Chinese truckmaker Dong Feng Motors. The agreement clears the road for Dong Feng to equip its heavy- and medium-duty trucks with Renault engines.

EXECUTIVES

Chairman: Lars Ramqvist, age 65
President; CEO, Volvo Group: Leif Johansson
Deputy CEO and EVP: Lennart Jeansson
SVP; CFO, Volvo Group: Stefan Johnsson
SVP: Karl-Erling Trogen
SVP: Per Löjdquist
SVP; General Counsel, Volvo Group: Eva Persson
President, Volvo 3P: Torbjörn Holmström
President, Volvo Aero: Fred Bodin
President, Volvo Bus: Jan Engstrom
President, Volvo Construction Equipment: Tony Helsham
President, Volvo Financial Service: Salvatore L. Mauro
President, Volvo Penta: Staffan Jufors
President, Volvo Powertrain: Lars-Göran Moberg
President, Volvo Truck Corporation: Jorma Halonen
President, Volvo Trucks North America: Peter Karlsten
Auditors: PricewaterhouseCoopers

LOCATIONS

HQ: , S-405 08 Gothenburg, Sweden
Phone: +46-31-59-66-00   **Fax:** +46-31-54-57-72
US HQ: 7900 National Service Rd., Greensboro, NC 27409
US Phone: 336-393-2000   **US Fax:** 336-393-2900
Web: www.volvo.com

2002 Sales

	$ mil.	% of total
Europe		
Western Europe	10,396	48
Eastern Europe	899	4
Americas		
North America	6,069	29
South America	565	3
Asia	1,531	7
Other regions	1,188	5
Adjustments	821	4
Total	**21,469**	**100**

PRODUCTS/OPERATIONS

2002 Sales

	% of total
Trucks	65
Construction equipment	11
Buses	8
Aero	5
Financial services	5
Penta	4
Other	2
Total	**100**

COMPETITORS

Cummins
Freightliner
Fuji Heavy Industries
General Motors
Hino Motors
Isuzu
MAN
Mayflower
Navistar
Nissan
PACCAR
Rolls-Royce
Scania
Toyota

HISTORICAL FINANCIALS

Company Type: Public

Income Statement

FYE: December 31

	REVENUE ($ mil.)	NET INCOME ($ mil.)	NET PROFIT MARGIN	EMPLOYEES
12/02	21,469	161	0.7%	71,160
12/01	18,057	(140)	—	70,921
12/00	13,800	500	3.6%	54,270
12/99	14,665	3,780	25.8%	53,600
12/98	26,276	1,066	4.1%	79,820
12/97	23,229	1,310	5.6%	79,050
12/96	22,676	1,813	8.0%	70,330
12/95	25,641	1,385	5.4%	79,050
12/94	15,649	1,328	8.5%	75,549
12/93	13,339	(416)	—	73,641
Annual Growth	**5.4%**	**—**	**—**	**(0.4%)**

2002 Year-End Financials

Debt ratio: 59.3%
Return on equity: 1.9%
Cash ($ mil.): 1,023
Current ratio: 1.38
Long-term debt ($ mil.): 5,352

No. of shares (mil.): 419
Dividends
  Yield: 4.7%
  Payout: 205.3%
Market value ($ mil.): 6,942

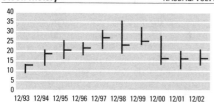

	STOCK PRICE ($)	P/E		PER SHARE ($)		
	FY Close	High/Low	Earnings	Dividends	Book Value
12/02	16.55	55 35	0.38	0.78	21.52
12/01	16.40	— —	(0.33)	0.78	19.38
12/00	16.50	23 12	1.19	0.80	23.59
12/99	25.25	4 3	8.80	0.61	25.95
12/98	23.31	15 8	2.42	0.00	19.02
12/97	27.00	11 7	2.90	0.00	17.31
12/96	21.75	6 5	3.91	0.60	18.14
12/95	20.59	8 5	3.02	0.46	16.51
12/94	18.75	6 4	3.19	0.17	9.80
12/93	12.93	— —	(1.07)	0.18	8.38
Annual Growth	2.8%	— —	—	17.7%	11.1%

Wal-Mart de México

Just call it Wal-Mex. Formerly known as Cifra, Wal-Mart de México is the numero uno retailer in Mexico, with nearly 600 stores or restaurants. These include Bodega discount stores and Superama supermarkets and hypermarkets; Suburbia apparel stores; and Vips, El Porton, and Ragazzi restaurants. It also runs about 125 Wal-Mart Supercenters and Sam's Club warehouses, which generate nearly 60% of the company's sales. Its stores are located in 55 cities throughout Mexico, although more than half are in and around Mexico City. Wal-Mart Stores first grabbed a stake in the company when it combined its Mexican stores (a joint venture with Cifra) with Cifra's stores. Wal-Mart Stores owns about 62% of Wal-Mart de México.

Wal-Mart has shaken up Mexico's grocery and department store sectors since entering the country in the 1990s. But its success has sparked a backlash; Mexican antitrust regulators launched an investigation into Wal-Mart de México's purchasing practices in May 2002, and the retailer has quit the country's supermarket and department store trade group because of the group's opposition to comparative advertising. Three of Mexico's largest supermarket chains — Grupo Gigante, Soriana, and Comerci — have formed purchasing and other alliances to better compete with Wal-Mex, which accounts for about 40% of the retail market in Mexico. Nevertheless the country's top mass merchandiser plans to invest more than $600 million by mid-2004 to open 61 new retail stores.

Wal-Mart de México contributes more than 25% of its parent company's international sales.

HISTORY

Spanish-born Jerónimo Arango Arias studied art and literature at several American universities without graduating. In his twenties he wandered around Spain, Mexico, and the US. He struck upon an idea after seeing a crowd waiting in line at the E. J. Korvette discount department store in New York City. Jerónimo called his two brothers, Plácido and Manuel, and convinced them to join him in a new business venture.

Borrowing about $250,000 from their father, a Spanish immigrant to Mexico successful in textiles, the three brothers opened their first Aurrerá Bolivar discount store in downtown Mexico City in 1958. Offering goods and clothing well below manufacturers' list prices, the store was an immediate hit with consumers but encountered hostility from competing Mexico City retailers. When local retailers threatened to boycott the Arangos' suppliers, the company turned to suppliers in Guadalajara and Monterrey.

In 1965 the Arango brothers formed a joint venture with Jewel Cos. of Chicago to open new Aurrerá stores. Jewel bought a 49% interest in the business a year later. Plácido and Manuel quit the business with their portion of the money, but Jerónimo stayed as head of the company, taking it public in 1976.

By 1981 almost a third of Jewel's earnings came from its operations in Mexico. But the next year the peso crashed, obliterating its earnings there. American Stores took over Jewel in 1984, and Jerónimo bought back Jewel's stake in the company (which was renamed Cifra that year).

With the Mexican economy staggering from the peso devaluation, weak oil markets, and a huge debt crisis, Jerónimo was taking a major risk. Although no new stores were opened, none were closed. Employees were expected to work longer, and those who left were not replaced. With Mexico's middle class hit hard, Jerónimo emphasized the Bodega Aurrerá no-frill warehouses, which discounted all kinds of nonperishable merchandise, from canned chili to VCRs.

Cifra and Wal-Mart Stores formed a joint venture in 1991 to open Club Aurrerá membership clubs similar to Sam's Club outlets. The two companies expanded the venture the next year to include the development of Sam's Club and Wal-Mart Supercenters in Mexico.

Remodeling began on Cifra's stores in 1992. The work was completed two years later, and the company was poised to take advantage of Mexico's much-improved economy.

However, devaluation struck again late in 1994. The resulting contraction of credit and rise in prices hit Mexican consumers hard, causing a 15% decline in Cifra's 1995 sales. But again it kept on as many employees as possible, transferring them to new stores that had been in development. Despite the hard times, Cifra opened 27 new stores (including 15 restaurants). The company was able to withstand the difficulties in part because it stayed debt-free.

Wal-Mart consolidated its joint venture into Cifra in 1997 in exchange for about 34% of that company; Wal-Mart later raised its stake to 51%. The cost-conscious companies combined the joint venture stores and Cifra's separate stores under one umbrella. Cifra opened 11 stores and eight restaurants that year.

Cifra opened nine stores and 17 restaurants in 1998; the next year it opened about 20 stores and nearly 25 restaurants. In early 2000 Cifra was renamed Wal-Mart de México. Shortly thereafter,

Wal-Mart upped its stake in Wal-Mart de México to about 61%.

In 2001 all the Aurrerá stores were converted to either Wal-Mart Supercenters or Bodega stores.

In November 2002 Eduardo Castro-Wright was promoted from COO to CEO of Wal-Mart de México, succeeding Cesareo Fernandez who retained the chairman's title. The retailer opened 50 new outlets in 2002.

In March 2003 Mexico's Federal Competition Commission closed an investigation of Wal-Mex's purchasing practices citing a lack of evidence that the retailer violated competition laws.

EXECUTIVES

Chairman: Cesareo Fernández Gonzalez
Vice Chairman: Héctor M. de Uriarte
President, CEO, and Director: Eduardo Castro-Wright, age 47
CFO and Director: Rafael Matute
EVP, Self-Service Division, and Director: Eduardo Solorzano
VP, Human Resources: José Angel Gallegos
VP, Investor Relations: Mariana Rodríguez
VP, Public Relations: Mercedes Aragones
VP, Sam's Club: José L. Laparte
VP, Suburbia: Alejandro Bustos
VP, Superama: Xavier Ezeta
VP, Vips: Sergio Larraguivel
VP, Wal-Mart Supercenter: Miguel Baltazar
Secretary: Enrique Ponzanelli
Director, Financial Planning: Federico Casillas
Auditors: Mancera, S.C.

LOCATIONS

HQ: Wal-Mart de México, S.A. de C.V.
Blvd. Manuel Avila Camacho 647,
Delegación Miguel Hidalgo,
11220 México, D.F., Mexico
Phone: +52-55-5283-0100   **Fax:** +52-55-5387-9240
Web: www.walmartmexico.com.mx

Wal-Mart de México operates 595 stores and restaurants in 55 cities throughout Mexico.

PRODUCTS/OPERATIONS

Selected Stores

Bodega (large, limited assortment discount warehouses)
El Portón (restaurants)
Ragazzi (Italian-style restaurants)
Sam's Club (membership-only warehouse outlets)
Suburbia (apparel stores)
Superama (supermarkets)
Vips (restaurants)
Wal-Mart Supercenters (discount hypermarkets)

COMPETITORS

Carrefour
Grupo Carso
Chedraui
Comerci
Costco Wholesale
El Puerto de Liverpool
Gigante
H-E-B
Safeway
Sanborns
Soriana

HISTORICAL FINANCIALS

Company Type: Public

Income Statement

FYE: December 31

	REVENUE ($ mil.)	NET INCOME ($ mil.)	NET PROFIT MARGIN	EMPLOYEES
12/02	10,097	472	4.7%	92,708
12/01	9,642	457	4.7%	84,607
12/00	7,661	370	4.8%	74,790
12/99	6,406	374	5.8%	70,700
12/98	6,009	281	4.7%	61,145
12/97	4,086	432	10.6%	57,649
12/96	2,947	257	8.7%	49,510
12/95	2,623	202	7.7%	47,129
12/94	3,165	236	7.5%	46,898
12/93	4,580	333	7.3%	39,934
Annual Growth	**9.2%**	**3.9%**	**—**	**9.8%**

2002 Year-End Financials

Debt ratio: 0.0%
Return on equity: 13.1%
Cash ($ mil.): 932

Current ratio: 1.39
Long-term debt ($ mil.): 0

Net Income History

OTC: WMMVY

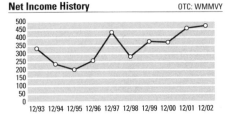

500
450
400
350
300
250
200
150
100
50
0

12/93 12/94 12/95 12/96 12/97 12/98 12/99 12/00 12/01 12/02

Waterford Wedgwood plc

Waterford Wedgwood is toasting (gently) its position as the world's premier maker of luxury crystal and fine china. The company's Waterford Crystal Group produces handcrafted crystal stemware, lamps, and giftware under the Waterford and Stuart brands. The Wedgwood Group makes fine bone china giftware and tableware under the Wedgwood brand. The company owns German ceramics makers Rosenthal (nearly 90% stake). In the US, it owns premium cookware maker All-Clad. Waterford Wedgwood also licenses its brands for non-crystal products such as linens and tea. Chairman Tony O'Reilly and his brother-in-law, deputy chairman Peter Goulandris, control about 27% of the company.

Not every company has a great-great-great-great-grandson of its founder sitting on the board of directors. And although Waterford Wedgwood has just that in Alan Wedgwood, it's Heinz ketchup king Tony O'Reilly who has given the firm its luster.

O'Reilly helped turn the company around after years of losses in the late 1980s and early 1990s. He outsourced product lines to cheaper manufacturers and licensed the company's popular brands to makers of products such as linens and writing instruments. Most of Waterford Wedgwood's sales are through department stores and specialty retailers. The firm owns more than 20% of UK ceramics maker Royal

Doulton and has offered to buy the remaining 10% stake in Rosenthal.

In response to the worldwide economic downturn and diminished interest in luxury goods, Waterford Wedgwood laid off nearly 15% of its workforce in 2002, and in 2003 announced plans to shut down two of its British factories and move production to Asia (eliminating another 1,000 jobs). Additionally, there is speculation that chairman Tony O'Reilly is trying to take the firm private. Reilly has denied that a buyout is in the works.

HISTORY

Waterford Wedgwood traces its roots back to two companies more than 200 years old. Josiah Wedgwood, an 18th-century English artisan, got his start as a potter bridging the gap between wooden bowls for the common people and fine porcelain for the rich. He developed a method of making ordinary clay look like porcelain and later developed fine ceramic ware incorporating neo-classical figures applied in a white cameo relief on a colored background — which became the signature product of Josiah Wedgwood and Sons.

Wedgwood operated as a family business for the next 176 years and may have indirectly contributed to Darwin's theory of evolution. Charles Darwin married into the Wedgwood clan and thus gained the financial security to pursue his scientific research on a full-time basis. Wedgwood did not have a non-family director on its board until 1945.

Around the same time that Wedgwood was gaining recognition in England, Quakers George and William Penrose founded a crystal glass-making business in 1783 in the Irish port city of Waterford. The two companies shared a reputation for quality and for exquisite craftsmanship. However, they both experienced the vagaries of fashion and financial difficulties.

Waterford went bankrupt in 1851 and remained inactive until its revival, aided by WWII refugees. With this new base of skilled artisans from Central Europe, it started operations again in 1947. The company quickly re-established the Waterford reputation. Profits rose steadily during the 1970s and early 1980s, with the US emerging as Waterford's primary market. In addition to consumer products, Waterford glassware has been used for the Boston Marathon Trophy and to hold President Reagan's jelly beans.

In 1986 Waterford borrowed heavily to acquire Wedgwood for $360 million, a move designed to allow both companies to cut costs by sharing marketing operations and by streamlining production. Waterford Wedgwood was still struggling in 1990 when Tony O'Reilly (the Irish-born chairman of US-based H.J. H.J. Heinz) and Morgan Stanley bought a 30% stake worth $125 million. That year the company launched its first new brand of crystal in 200 years, Marquis by Waterford. The line was a success, and by 1993 Waterford Wedgwood had returned to profitability.

The company acquired Stuart & Sons, the leading UK maker of premium crystal, in 1995 and introduced a best-seller, its Cornucopia fine bone china pattern. In 1996 Waterford Wedgwood also launched new licensed gift lines — pens and linens — and formed a strategic alliance with German luxury ceramics maker Rosenthal, in which it owned a 26% stake. In 1997, in a departure from tradition, the company introduced a line of china under the Waterford name.

In 1998 Waterford Wedgwood increased its

stake in Rosenthal to nearly 85%, making it the world's #1 producer of fine porcelain, and cut 1,500 jobs to reduce costs. In 1999 the company purchased US cookware-maker All-Clad for $110 million. Also in 1999 the company bought a 15% stake in ceramics maker Royal Doulton. Expanding its European presence, the company acquired German ceramics brand Hutschenreuther in August 2000 (integrated operations into Rosenthal business in 2003). In 2002 Waterford Wedgwood bought another 15% of Rosenthal, increasing its stake to nearly 90%. A month later the company solidified its commitment to new product lines with the acquisition of Ashling Corporation, a maker of luxury linens.

In 2003 Waterford Wedgwood acquired the Spring premium cookware business (Switzerland) and Cashs, a catalog and mail-order business (Ireland). In addition, Waterford Wedgwood upped its stake in Royal Doulton to nearly 22%.

EXECUTIVES

Chairman: Sir Anthony (Tony) O'Reilly
Deputy Chairman; Chairman, Waterford Wedgwood UK: Peter John Goulandris
CEO and Director: P. Redmond O'Donoghue
Group Finance Director and Director: Richard A. Barnes
Director; Co-chairman, All-Clad: Sam Michaels
Director; CEO, All-Clad: Peter B. Cameron
Director; CEO, Rosenthal: Ottmar C. Küsel
Director; CEO, Waterford Crystal: John Foley
Director; Co-chairman, All-Clad; President and CEO, Waterford Wedgwood USA: Christopher J. (Chris) McGillivary
Director; CEO, Wedgwood: Anthony (Tony) O'Reilly Jr.
SVP, Marketing and Sales, Wedgwood (USA): Moira Gavin
VP, Human Resources, Wedgwood (USA): Brian Smith
Company Secretary: Patrick J. Dowling
Auditors: PricewaterhouseCoopers

LOCATIONS

HQ: 1-2 Upper Hatch St., Dublin 2, Ireland
Phone: +353-147-81855   **Fax:** +353-147-84863
US HQ: 1330 Campus Pkwy., Wall, NJ 07719
US Phone: 732-938-5800   **US Fax:** 732-378-2120
Web: www.waterfordwedgwood.com

PRODUCTS/OPERATIONS

Selected Operations

All-Clad Inc.
Rosenthal AG
  Bulgari (licensed)
  Hutschenreuther
  Rosenthal
  Versace (licensed)
Waterford Crystal Group
  John Rocha at Waterford Crystal
  Marquis by Waterford Crystal
  Stuart
  Waterford
Wedgwood Group
  Coalport
  Sarah's Garden
  Wedgwood

COMPETITORS

ARC International	Newell Rubbermaid
Brown-Forman	Noritake
Carlsberg	Oneida
CRISAL	Pagnossin
Department 56	Richard Ginori 1735
Fitz and Floyd, Silvestri	Royal Doulton
Guy Degrenne	Syratech
Homer Laughlin	Taittinger
Lancaster Colony	Tiffany
Société du Louvre	Villeroy & Boch

HISTORICAL FINANCIALS

Company Type: Public

Income Statement

FYE: March 31

	REVENUE ($ mil.)	NET INCOME ($ mil.)	NET PROFIT MARGIN	EMPLOYEES
3/03*	1,037	2	0.2%	9,120
12/01	902	(40)	—	9,743
12/00	1,021	64	6.3%	9,671
12/99	888	58	6.5%	9,116
12/98	856	19	2.2%	—
12/97	596	9	1.5%	—
12/96	623	48	7.7%	—
12/95	551	39	7.0%	—
12/94	509	32	6.3%	—
12/93	450	13	2.8%	—
Annual Growth	9.7%	(18.6%)	—	0.0%

*Fiscal year change

2003 Year-End Financials

Debt ratio: 212.4%	No. of shares (mil.): 78
Return on equity: 0.9%	Dividends
Cash ($ mil.): 92	Yield: 9.2%
Current ratio: 2.56	Payout: 1,400.0%
Long-term debt ($ mil.): 462	Market value ($ mil.): 236

Stock History

NASDAQ: WATFZ

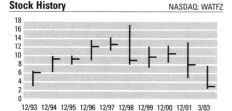

12/93 12/94 12/95 12/96 12/97 12/98 12/99 12/00 12/01 3/03

	STOCK PRICE ($) FY Close	P/E High/Low		PER SHARE ($) Earnings	Dividends	Book Value
3/03*	3.04	20	7	0.02	0.28	2.81
12/01	8.01	—	—	(0.54)	0.29	2.85
12/00	10.50	14	10	0.86	0.26	3.72
12/99	9.75	15	9	0.79	0.26	3.23
12/98	9.00	22	11	0.26	0.07	2.94
12/97	12.63	21	17	0.12	0.00	3.09
12/96	12.13	20	14	0.66	0.27	3.90
12/95	9.25	18	15	0.54	0.14	3.28
12/94	9.25	49	32	0.20	0.00	2.92
12/93	6.13	35	17	0.18	0.00	2.42
Annual Growth	(7.5%)	—	—	(21.7%)	—	1.7%

*Fiscal year change

Whitbread PLC

Whitbread wins the award for being one of the UK's leading hospitality and leisure groups. The company, which sponsors a prestigious UK book award, has operations ranging from restaurants to hotels to fitness clubs. Its restaurant division includes a 50% stake in Pizza Hut (UK) Ltd. (with US-based Yum! Brands), the operator and franchisor of about 500 pizza parlors. It also operates about 250 Brewers Fayre pub restaurants, more than 100 Brewsters family-friendly pubs, about 300 Costa Coffee outlets, and 40 T.G.I Friday's locations. Whitbread's hospitality operations include about 300 Travel Inn budget hotels and about 60 Marriott locations. The company also runs more than 50 David Lloyd Leisure fitness clubs.

Whitbread was one of the largest brewers and pub operators in the UK before selling its beer businesses to focus on hospitality and restaurants. Despite a challenging economy, the company is pressing ahead with expansion in all areas of its business. Whitbread is building more Travel Inn hotels and developing additional locations through Spirit Hotel, its 50%-owned joint venture with motorway hospitality operator RoadChef. During 2002 the company converted two dozen Swallow hotels to the Marriott brand; Whitbread sold its remaining Swallow sites along with the brand the following year.

Whitbread's restaurant division is focused on developing its best performing brands, with plans to expand its Pizza Hut network to 750 locations. It also has plans to expand both its Brewers Fayre and Brewsters chains into more suburban markets while renovating and updating its chain of 150 Beefeater pubs. Its Costa Coffee business, the leading coffee chain in the UK, is branching out through co-located shops in retail locations (WH Smith's, Virgin Megastores, and Madame Tussaud's) and through franchise agreements.

HISTORY

Samuel Whitbread became a brewer's apprentice in 1734 and learned his lessons well; in 1742 he began brewing beer at his own brewery. By 1750 he had built a new brewery and began producing porter in bulk. Whitbread had a head for business, as well as beer, acquiring other breweries and investing in new brewing techniques to increase the quality of his beers. The company prospered, despite an unlucky venture into politics by Samuel II; he opposed the war with Napoleon and committed suicide after Waterloo.

In the 1880s beer drinking declined, and Whitbread began buying up sinking pubs. But by WWI, the company started to concentrate on bottled beer sales in order to reduce its dependence on the tied pubs.

In 1944 W. H. Whitbread became chairman (the first Whitbread since founder Samuel) and took advantage of the aftermath of WWII to snap up less-robust rivals. The company first absorbed smaller breweries into its production and distribution operations but later made a living from taking over breweries and keeping their tied houses. The company went public in 1948 and had 10,000 pubs by 1970.

In the 1970s beer consumption fell yet again, and Whitbread started streamlining operations. It closed its original brewery in 1976. The company also began its shift from beer to other businesses, including acquiring a Pizza Hut franchise. It sold its wines and spirits business at the end of the 1980s.

The company continued to remake itself the next decade under the leadership of CEO Peter Jarvis. As more Britons began to eat out instead of going to the local pub for entertainment, Whitbread shifted with them, buying and developing restaurant concepts including its Beefeater Restaurant and Pub and family-friendly Brewers Fayre (complete with Charlie Chalk Fun Factories for kids). In 1995, even as it divested 400 underperforming pubs, Whitbread went shopping, buying David Lloyd Leisure and 16 Marriott hotels. The company later sold its Australian and Canadian Keg steak houses in 1995 and 1996, respectively, and expanded its Pizza Hut chain.

Whitbread bought Busy Bees day care centers and put them under its David Lloyd Leisure unit in 1997. That year Jarvis stepped down and was succeeded by David Thomas. A renewed focus on its core business that year also prompted the company to dispose of all pubs that served beer not brewed by Whitbread.

In 1998 Whitbread and Allied Domecq agreed to merge their retail beer and wine stores into a new company called First Quench. It also sold one of its five breweries, put another brewery on the market, and in the wake of the declining popularity of old-fashioned pubs, sold 253 of its pubs and 40 of its Beefeaters Restaurant & Pubs.

Whitbread's attempt to buy more than 3,500 UK pubs and restaurants from Allied Domecq for $3.8 billion failed in 1999. (Rival Punch Taverns had the winning bid.) Later that year the company sold off 75 pubs to Alehouse Company. In early 2000 the company bought Swallow Group, a hotel and pub operator, with plans to convert the Swallow locations to the Marriott brand. That same year Whitbread sold its brewery business to Interbrew.

Whitbread unloaded all 3,000 of its pubs in 2001, selling them to Deutsche Bank's Morgan Grenfell equity fund for $2.3 billion. (Later Morgan Grenfell set up The Laurel Pub Company.) During 2002 the company rebranded about two dozen of its Swallow hotels but sold the remaining 13 properties to REIT Asset Management the following year.

EXECUTIVES

Chairman: Sir John Banham, age 62, $269,938 pay
Chief Executive: David Thomas, age 59, $1,181,268 pay
Group Finance Director: David H. Richardson, age 51, $689,086 pay
Managing Director, Whitbread Restaurants: Bill F. C. Shannon, age 53, $804,818 pay
Managing Director, Whitbread Hotel Company: Alan Parker, age 56, $504,127 pay
Managing Director, David Loyd Leisure: Stewart Miller, age 50, $602,551 pay
Managing Director of TGI Friday, Whitbread Restaurants: Guy Parsons
Commercial Director of Merriot Hotels, Whitbread Hotel Company: Tony Dangerfield
Information Technology Director, Whitbread Restaurants: Ann Fraser
Director of Human Resources: Angie Risley
Director of Communications: Anna Glover
Communications Manager: Beverley Wilkins
Corporate Affairs Manager: Dan Waugh
Public Relations Manager: Mark Webb
Auditors: Ernst & Young LLP

LOCATIONS

HQ: CityPoint, 1 Ropemaker St., London EC2Y 9HX, United Kingdom
Phone: +44-20-7606-4455   **Fax:** +44-20-7615-1000
Web: www.whitbread.co.uk

2003 Sales

	$ mil.	% of total
UK	2,724	96
Other countries	111	4
Total	**2,835**	**100**

PRODUCTS/OPERATIONS

2003 Sales & Income

	$ mil.	% of total	$ mil.	% of total
Restaurants	1,618	55	156	33
Hotels				
Marriott/Swallow	619	21	113	24
Travel Inn	323	11	105	22
Health & fitness clubs	289	10	69	15
Beer & other drinks	104	3	26	6
Adjustments	(118)	—	—	—
Total	**2,835**	**100**	**469**	**100**

Selected Operations

Restaurants
Beefeater
Brewers Fayre
Brewsters
Costa Coffee
Pizza Hut
T.G.I. Friday's

Hotels
Courtyard by Marriott
Marriott Hotels
Renaissance
Travel Inn

Leisure clubs
David Lloyd Leisure clubs

Selected Partnerships and Investments

Britannia Soft Drinks (25%)
Morrison Street Hotel (Scotland, 40%)
Neptune Whitbread Hotel (20%)
Pizza Hut (UK) Ltd. (50%)
Poles (hotels, 26%)
Spirit Travel (hotels, 50%)

COMPETITORS

Best Western	J D Wetherspoon
City Centre Restaurants	Millennium & Copthorne
Compass Group	Hotels
De Vere	Mitchells & Butlers
Domino's Pizza UK	Papa John's
Enterprise Inns	PizzaExpress
Esporta	Punch Taverns
First Leisure	Spirit Group
Four Seasons Hotels	Starwood Hotels & Resorts
Greene King	Thistle Hotels
Hilton International	Wolverhampton & Dudley
Hyatt	Breweries
InterContinental Hotels	

HISTORICAL FINANCIALS

Company Type: Public

Income Statement

FYE: February 28

	REVENUE ($ mil.)	NET INCOME ($ mil.)	NET PROFIT MARGIN	EMPLOYEES
2/03	2,835	241	8.5%	55,315
2/02	2,859	(75)	—	61,470
2/01	3,743	285	7.6%	79,209
2/00	4,658	284	6.1%	73,058
2/99	4,745	398	8.4%	76,100
2/98	5,266	492	9.3%	81,375
2/97	4,925	402	8.2%	80,074
2/96	4,211	341	8.1%	70,594
Annual Growth	**(5.5%)**	**(4.8%)**	**—**	**(3.4%)**

2003 Year-End Financials

Debt ratio: 44.3%
Return on equity: 8.3%
Cash ($ mil.): 119

Current ratio: 0.49
Long-term debt ($ mil.): 1,390

Net Income History

London: WTB

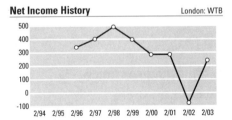

WMC Resources

WMC Resources gets a lot out of the Outback. The Australian mining giant is the world's third-largest miner of nickel, behind #1 Inco and #2 Norilsk Nickel. (Nickel is an important ingredient in stainless steel.) The company is also a top producer of copper. In addition, WMC owns Olympia Dam, a leading source of uranium used by power generators throughout the world. In 2002 WMC split off its aluminum segment (which owned a 40% stake in Alcoa subsidiary Alcoa World Alumina and Chemicals, one of the world's largest alumina producers) to form a new company, Alumina Ltd. WMC has mining operations in Australia, Asia, and the Americas.

Late in 2001, amid falling metal prices and a slumping economy, WMC entered talks with Alcoa. However, WMC eventually rejected the aluminum giant's takeover offer in favor of separating into two companies — WMC Resources Ltd. and Alumina Ltd.

HISTORY

William Sydney Robinson and his older brother helped finance the western Australia gold boom of the late 1800s and early 1900s. The brothers moved to London where William made a name as a stockbroker. When William returned to Australia in 1930, he formed Gold Mines of Australia. Three years later he formed Western Mining Corp. (WMC). The company began production at Kalgoorlie, on Australia's Golden Mile, in 1936. By the start of WWII, WMC had 10 mines in operation.

Most of the company's mines closed during WWII, but mining resumed in 1945. With gold prices fixed due to the war and with inflation high, WMC began exploring for copper, aluminum, iron ore, and nickel. The company formed Western Aluminum NL (WANL) in 1958 to develop a bauxite reserve in the Darling Range near Perth.

In 1960 WMC bought 50% of Three Springs Talc Pty. Ltd., and in 1961 WMC, Alcoa of America, and WMC's partners in WANL formed Alcoa of Australia Ltd. (later Alcoa World Alumina and Chemicals, or AWAC) to mine bauxite and refine aluminum. WMC discovered nickel at Kambalda in 1966. Nickel smelting operations started at nearby Kalgoorlie in 1972.

WMC discovered the Olympic copper-uranium-gold body at Roxby Downs in southern Australia in 1975. With gold prices up, expansion began at Kalgoorlie, Mount Magnet, and Norseman in 1976. The company expanded its interest in petroleum in 1978 with increased production at Durham Downs, Queensland, and Poolawanna, South Australia. The following year WMC's various interests were consolidated as Western Mining Corp. Holdings.

WMC acquired Queensland Phosphate in 1980. The company's operations expanded to Brazil in 1983 through a joint venture with Alcoa of America. In 1985 WMC bought a 50% stake in fertilizer importer and distributor Hi-Fert (it acquired the remainder in 1988). Development of the Olympic Dam uranium deposit began in 1985 in a joint venture with British Petroleum (now BP Amoco). WMC sold its interest in Kalgoorlie in 1987 and acquired the part of Mount Magnet that it didn't yet own. It also bought interests in several North American mines in 1988. WMC's gold production topped a million ounces

for the first time in 1989. That year it bought the Agnew Nickel Mine.

In 1992 WMC acquired the Mount Keith nickel deposit, and the next year it purchased British Petroleum's stake in Olympic Dam. During 1995-96 the company built the Goldfields Gas Transmission pipeline to supply natural gas to WMC power stations in southwestern Australia.

The company produced its 20 millionth ounce of gold in 1996. That year AWAC formed a 30-year agreement to supply China's Sino Mining Alumina with 400,000 tons of alumina annually. Also, WMC initiated a plan to develop a major fertilizer project at Phosphate Hill (Queensland). In 1997 WMC sold its petroleum operations (other than the Goldfields pipeline), expanded its alumina production in Texas and Brazil, and it began production at an aluminum refinery in the US Virgin Islands. Depressed metals prices affected revenues in 1998 and the company sold its interest in the Goldfields Gas Transmission project.

The company completed a major expansion of its Olympic Dam uranium mine and Queensland fertilizer facilities in 1999. WMC also added an important nickel discovery, dubbed West Musgrave, in Australia. In early 2001 WMC acquired the leases for Yakabindie nickel resource, also in Australia, from Rio Tinto. Later in 2001 the company sold the bulk of its gold mining operations to South Africa's Gold Fields for $232 million.

In late 2002 WMC changed its name to WMC Resources Ltd. after splitting off its aluminum business. The company acquired the Corridor Sands site in Mozambique in 2003, the world's largest undeveloped deposit of titanium mineral sands.

EXECUTIVES

Chairman: Tommie C-E Bergman, age 58
CEO and Director: Andrew G. Michelmore, age 50, $400,866 pay
Executive General Manager, Finance: Bruce R. Brook, $281,628 pay
Executive General Manager, Operations and Director: Alan K. Dundas, age 46, $381,105 pay
Executive General Manager, Business Strategy and Development: Michael Nossal
Executive General Manager, Group Services: Greg J. Travers, $297,262 pay
Chief Executive-Designate, Alumina Ltd.: John Marlay
General Manager, Legal and Secretary: Peter Horton
Corporate Affairs: David Griffiths
Auditors: PricewaterhouseCoopers LLP

LOCATIONS

HQ: WMC Resources Ltd.
 Level 16, IBM Centre, 60 City Rd.,
 Southbank, Victoria 3006, Australia
Phone: +61-3-9685-6000   **Fax:** +61-3-9686-3569
US HQ: 8008 E. Arapahoe Ct., Ste. 110,
 Englewood, CO 80112
US Phone: 720-554-8300   **US Fax:** 720-554-8370
Web: www.wmc.com.au

WMC has mining interests in Australia, Argentina, Brazil, Canada, Chile, China, Indonesia, Mongolia, the Philippines, and Peru.

2002 Sales

	% of total
Europe	30
Australia	21
Japan	12
North America	10
Taiwan	4
Other	23
Total	**100**

2002 Sales

	% of total
Nickel	53
Copper/Uranium	29
Fertilizers	17
Other	1
Total	**100**

COMPETITORS

Anglo American	Inco Limited
Barrick Gold	Norilsk Nickel
BHP Billiton Ltd	Newmont Mining
Cameco	Noranda
Grupo Carso	Phelps Dodge
COGEMA	Placer Dome
Freeport-McMoRan	Rio Tinto
Copper & Gold	Umicore
Gold Fields Limited	

HISTORICAL FINANCIALS

Company Type: Public

Income Statement FYE: December 31

	REVENUE ($ mil.)	NET INCOME ($ mil.)	NET PROFIT MARGIN	EMPLOYEES
12/02	1,395	13	0.9%	4,371
12/01	1,201	206	17.1%	4,634
12/00	1,706	425	24.9%	5,212
12/99	1,374	181	13.2%	5,143
12/98	1,054	104	9.8%	5,541
12/97*	643	64	10.0%	—
6/97	1,620	222	13.7%	—
6/96	1,846	308	16.7%	7,225
6/95	1,457	212	14.5%	6,885
6/94	1,093	81	7.4%	6,694
Annual Growth	**2.7%**	**(18.5%)**	**—**	**(4.6%)**

*Fiscal year change

2002 Year-End Financials

Debt ratio: 10.3%	No. of shares (mil.): 71
Return on equity: 0.6%	Dividends
Cash ($ mil.): 37	Yield: 0.0%
Current ratio: 0.59	Payout: —
Long-term debt ($ mil.): 208	Market value ($ mil.): 652

Stock History NYSE: WMC

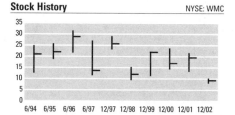

	STOCK PRICE ($) FY Close	P/E High/Low	PER SHARE ($) Earnings	Dividends	Book Value
12/02	9.25	247 206	0.04	0.00	28.69
12/01	19.50	30 19	0.72	0.76	8.94
12/00	16.88	15 10	1.51	0.75	9.47
12/99	21.88	34 18	0.64	0.15	10.78
12/98	12.00	42 27	0.36	0.00	9.93
12/97*	25.63	36 30	0.79	0.53	11.73
6/97	13.63	116 51	0.23	0.00	10.52
6/96	28.75	28 20	1.11	0.33	11.22
6/95	22.00	34 25	0.76	0.82	9.81
6/94	21.00	77 40	0.32	0.30	9.49
Annual Growth	**(8.7%)**	**— —**	**(20.6%)**	**—**	**13.1%**

*Fiscal year change

Wolters Kluwer

This publisher is focused on the basics in life: death and taxes. One of Europe's leading professional publishers, Wolters Kluwer disseminates information on tax and legal affairs, business information, medical and scientific data, and education through print and electronic formats. Among the company's publishing units are Facts & Comparisons, Nelson Thornes, and Wolters-Noordhoff. The company has divested the businesses that make up its professional training division. Wolters Kluwer has operations in 25 countries, primarily in Europe and North America.

The company distributes its information primarily in print form (about 70% of sales).

Under the direction of chairman Nancy McKinstry, the company is struggling to regain its financial health after battling a multi-year advertising slump. McKinstry has a three-year plan to turn the company around by focusing on key customer segments. She started the reorganization plan with an 8% cut in the company workforce announced in late 2003.

HISTORY

A pioneer of the Dutch publishing industry, J. B. Wolters founded his publishing house in 1836 to provide instructional material for Netherlands schools. The company later merged with educational publisher Noordhoff (founded in 1858). J. B. Wolters had no children, so the business went to his brother-in-law E. B. Horst in 1860. Dutch academic Anthony Schepman took over the management of Wolters-Noordhoff in 1917 and led the business' expansion. In 1920 it opened an office in the Dutch colony of Indonesia.

Wolters-Noordhoff and Information and Communication Union (ICU) merged in 1972. ICU had been formed by the 1970 merger of Samson (founded by Nicholaas Samson in 1883 to print government publications) and publisher A. W. Sijthoff. After the Wolters-Noordhoff-ICU merger, the resulting company initially took the ICU name, but in 1983 it became the Wolters Samson Group. That year it began exploring a merger with Kluwer.

Abele Kluwer, a former assistant schoolteacher, became a publisher in 1889. His publishing house specialized in educational products and children's books. The company expanded its range in the 1920s with a growing number of up-to-date publications regarding new laws, regulations, court decisions, and scholarly texts. Kluwer hired its first non-family managing director, J. M. Gorter, in 1957 and went public in 1967.

Reed Elsevier (now called Reed Elsevier Group plc) made a bid to acquire Kluwer in 1987, buying a minority stake in the company. The Anglo-Dutch concern was rebuffed by the subsequent merger of Wolters Samson with Kluwer that year, however, and was left with about a third of the shares in the new Wolters Kluwer. Despite Reed Elsevier's repeated advances to work closely with Wolters Kluwer, the company pursued an independent growth strategy. In 1990 it acquired J.B. Lippincott, a US health care publisher. That year Reed Elsevier sold its stake in the firm.

In the early 1990s Wolters Kluwer began acquiring several medium-sized European companies and in 1995 bought Commerce Clearing House (with roots dating back to 1892). In 1997

it agreed to an $8.8 billion acquisition deal from Reed Elsevier; however, the deal fell apart the following year. (Both companies blamed regulatory hurdles for the pact's failure.) Meanwhile, Wolters Kluwer bought Waverly (medical and scientific books and magazines) and Plenum Publishing (scientific and technical trade books and journals). It also bought Ovid Technologies, a provider of electronic information retrieval services to the academic, medical, and scientific markets.

The following year Wolters Kluwer acquired US professional information publisher Bureau of Business Practice and search and retrieval service Accusearch. In late 1999 internal candidate Casper van Kempen replaced C.J. Brakel as chairman; he was out six months later, having clashed with the board over the company's Web strategy. Deputy chairman Robert Pieterse was tapped to replace him. Also in 2000 Wolters Kluwer announced that it would invest some $240 million in Internet-related operations. The company divested itself of its professional training business that year. In 2001 the company bought Cutter Environment, a unit of Cutter Information, which was folded into its Aspen Publishers unit.

Wolters Kluwer sold the health calre book division of its Aspen Publishing unit, which specialized in health and legal books, in late 2002 to Jones and Bartlett Publishers. In addition, Wolters Kluwer sold its academic publishing unit (Kluwer Academic Publishers) for $582 million to two London-based equity firms. The company bought US financial services and information firm GainsKeeper Inc. in 2002.

Pieterse lefte the company in 2003 and was replaced by board member Nancy McKinstry.

EXECUTIVES

Chairman: Nancy McKinstry
CFO and Member, Executive Board:
  Boudewijn Beerkens
Member, Executive Board: Jean-Marc M. Detailleur
Member, Executive Board: Hugh J. Yarrington
SVP Human Resources: Kathy Baker
SVP Strategy: Andres Sadler
VP Corporate Communications: Peter Elbers, age 41
VP Investor Relations: Oya Yavuz
Business Development: C.J. Mellor
CEO, Education: Harry Sterk
CEO, Legal, Tax & Business Europe: Rolv Eide, age 49
President and CEO, International Health and Science:
  Christopher J. D. Ainsley, age 44
Corporate Media Relations: Caroline Wouters
Auditors: KPMG Accountants N.V.

LOCATIONS

HQ: Wolters Kluwer nv
  Apollolaan 153, P.O.Box 75248,
  NL-1070 AE Amsterdam, The Netherlands
Phone: +31-20-60-70-400   **Fax:** +31-20-60-70-490
US HQ: 161 N. Clark St., 48th Fl., Chicago, IL 60601
US Phone: 312-425-7000   **US Fax:** 312-425-7023
Web: www.wolters-kluwer.com

PRODUCTS/OPERATIONS

2002 Sales

		% of total
Legal, Tax & Business		
Europe		35
North America		34
Asia/Pacific		2
Health		21
Education		8
Total		**100**

2002 Sales

	% of total
Print	68
Electronic Sales	
CD-ROM	17
Internet	15
Total	**100**

Selected Publishing Units

Facts & Comparisons (health and science information, US)

Lippincott, Williams & Wilkins (educational, medical, and scientific information, US)

Nelson Thornes (educational information, UK)

Wolters-Noordhoff (educational information)

COMPETITORS

American Lawyer Media
Bertelsmann
Blackwell Publishing
BNA
Cadmus Communications
IHS Group
John Wiley
McGraw-Hill
Pearson
Reed Elsevier Group
Taylor & Francis
Thomson Corporation
Vivendi Universal
  Publishing
VNU

HISTORICAL FINANCIALS

Company Type: Public

Income Statement

FYE: December 31

	REVENUE ($ mil.)	NET INCOME ($ mil.)	NET PROFIT MARGIN	EMPLOYEES
12/02	4,082	344	8.4%	20,833
12/01	3,399	124	3.6%	19,766
12/00	3,450	319	9.3%	19,009
12/99	3,103	361	11.6%	17,452
12/98	3,214	363	11.3%	17,431
12/97	2,571	286	11.1%	15,385
12/96	2,497	277	11.1%	14,948
12/95	1,830	281	15.4%	8,993
12/94	1,578	220	14.0%	8,693
12/93	1,343	163	12.2%	8,052
Annual Growth	**13.1%**	**8.6%**	**—**	**11.1%**

2002 Year-End Financials

Debt ratio: 159.6%
Return on equity: 27.2%
Cash ($ mil.): 307
Current ratio: 1.24
Long-term debt ($ mil.): 2,086

Net Income History

OTC: WTKWY

Woolworths

Chow down under with Australia's #1 food retailer, Woolworths (also known as "Woolies"). The company operates about 1,500 supermarkets, general merchandise, and electronics stores in Australia and Tasmania. (Its nearly 700 supermarkets and 575 liquor stores account for about 85% of sales.) In addition, Woolworths sells gaso-

line and leverages its distribution network to provide wholesale merchandise for third-party supermarkets. Australia's #2 retailer (after Coles Myer), Woolworths' general merchandise discount stores operate under the Big W name. It also runs 150 Dick Smith Electronics stores and 16 Dick Smith Electronics Power-House superstores, and about 180 company-owned Tandy consumer electronics stores.

Woolworths (which has no relation to the five-and-dime chain once operated in the US) is trying not to choke on its own success, but it's hard to be humble. It has added gas pumps and banking to some supermarket locations, has opened Woolworths Metro (convenience stores), and acquired 72 Franklins supermarkets in 2001 (from a rival chain owned by Hong Kong-based Dairy Farm International Holdings). In a bid to fend off rival Coles Myer's entry into the food-and-fuel market, Woolworths has formed a joint venture with Caltex Australia to expand its network of discount fuel outlets to 450. Also, the retailer is in the midst of overhauling its supply chain operations to become a low-cost operator after studying systems at US retail giant Wal-Mart and the UK's Tesco.

Still hungry for acquisitions, CEO Roger Corbett has said Woolies would consider buying either of the Kmart or Target divisions from rival Coles Myer if they came up for sale. The company plans to add 25 supermarkets each year over the next two years. Woolworths' supermarkets operate under the flagship Woolworths and Safeway names.

HISTORY

Harold Percival Christmas first tried a mail-order dress business before opening the popular Frock Salon retail store. Christmas and his partners opened a branch store in the Imperial Arcade in Sydney in 1924, renaming it "Woolworths Stupendous Bargain Basement" and luring customers with advertisements calling it "a handy place where good things are cheap . . . you'll want to live at Woolworths." The company borrowed the name from Frank Woolworth's successful US chain, after determining that chain had no plans to open stores in Australia. Woolworths was listed on the Australian stock exchange in 1924.

Food sales came more than 30 years later. Woolworths opened its first freestanding, full-line supermarket in 1960, then diversified into specialty retail, buying the Rockmans women's clothing store chain the next year (sold, 2000). It expanded into discounting with the Big W chain in 1976 and further diversified when it bought 60% of the Dick Smith Electronics store chain in 1981 (buying the remainder in 1983).

The purchase of the Safeway grocery chain (the Australian operations of the US-based chain) put Woolworths on the top of the supermarket heap in 1985. But the company was hurting (it lost $13 million in 1985-86) because of a restructuring in the early 1980s that had weakened management by bulking up the front offices and dividing responsibilities. Woolworths got a shot in the arm from Paul Simons, who returned to the company in 1987 after running competitor Franklins. Simons cleaned house in the front offices, closed unprofitable stores, and began the successful "Fresh Food People" marketing strategy.

Industrial Equity Limited (IEL) bought the company in 1989; IEL then became part of the Adelaide Steamship group, which spun off Woolworths as a public company in 1993. The fol-

lowing year career Woolworths manager Reg Clairs took over as CEO, following the untimely death (on a golf course) in 1993 of Harry Watts, who was being groomed for the job. As a result, the company has an unwritten rule of avoiding CEOs older than 60.

Clairs took the company in a variety of new directions. Woolworths began supplying fresh food to neighbor Asia in 1995. The company added Plus Petrol outlets adjacent to Woolworths Supermarkets in 1996. It also started a superstore concept for its Dick Smith Electronics chain (Power House) that year. In 1997 the company launched its Woolworths Metro store chain, which targets commuters and other on-the-run shoppers in urban areas, and it aggressively jumped into wholesaling to independent grocers.

In late 1998 Clairs (who was turning 60 in 1999) stepped down and Roger Corbett took over as CEO. Woolworths also began offering banking services to its customers and bought Dan Murphy, a Victoria-based liquor chain, in 1998. It divested its Chisholm Manufacturing meat plants in 2000.

In 2001 Woolworths acquired two liquor store chains (Liberty Liquor, Booze Bros), more than 200 Tandy Electronics stores, and 72 Franklins supermarkets from Hong Kong-based Dairy Farm International Holdings (most of which were later converted to the Woolworths and Food for Less banners). It sold its Crazy Prices general merchandise stores, and began restructuring its liquor operations into four distinctive formats.

In June 2002 Woolworths exited the New Zealand market when it sold its supermarkets group there to Foodland Associated for $690 million.

Supermarket division chief Bill Wavish resigned in May 2003 (he is staying on as a consultant into 2004) and was replaced by former chief general manager of supermarket operations Tom Flood. Wavish was considered one of the top candidates to replace CEO Corbett. Also in 2003, the company discontinued its Australian Independent Wholesalers (AIW) operations.

EXECUTIVES

Chairman: James A. Strong, age 59
Group Managing Director, CEO, and Board Member: Roger C. Corbett, age 61, $919,171 pay
Director, Supermarket: Tom Flood, $276,605 pay
CFO: Tom Pockett
Director, General Merchandise, and General Manager Big W: Marty Hamnett
Chief General Manager, General Merchandise: K. R. (Dick) McMorron, $303,698 pay
Chief General Manager, Petrol and Free Standing Liquor: Naum J. Onikul, $276,115 pay
Chief General Manager, Supermarket Buying and Marketing: Bernie Brookes, $285,997 pay
General Manager, Business Development: Gary Reid
General Manager, Corporate Services and Secretary: Rohan K. S. Jeffs, $356,470 pay
General Manager, Dick Smith Electronics and Tandy: Greg Foran
General Manager, Human Resources: Julie Coates
General Manager, Information Technology: Steve Bradley
General Manager, Property: Peter Thomas
General Manager, Supermarket Operations: Peter Smith
General Manager, Supply Chain: Michael Luscombe, $285,997 pay
General Manager, Woolworths Academy: Judy Howard
Auditors: Deloitte Touche Tohmatsu

LOCATIONS

HQ: Woolworths Limited
540 George St., 5th Fl.,
Sydney NSW 2000, Australia
Phone: +61-2-9323-1555 **Fax:** +61-2-9323-1599
Web: www.woolworths.com.au

2003 Supermarkets

	No.
New South Wales & Australian Capital Territory	228
Victoria	175
Queensland	141
South Australia & Northern Territory	63
Western Australia	58
Tasmania	29
Total	**694**

PRODUCTS/OPERATIONS

2003 Sales

	% of total
Supermarkets	86
General merchandise	13
Wholesale	1
Total	**100**

Selected Operations

Food Stores
Safeway
Woolworths Metro
Woolworths Supermarkets

General Merchandise Stores
Big W

Liquor Operations
BWS (neighborhood stores)
Dan Murphy's (destination outlets)
First Estate (fine wine stores)
Woolworths Liquor (attached to supermarkets)

Specialty Retail
Dick Smith Electronics
Dick Smith Electronics PowerHouse
Tandy Electronics

Other
GreenGrocer.com.au (online grocery store)
Plus Petrol (gas stations)
Woolworths Ezy Banking
Woolworths HomeShop (online grocery and liquor store)

COMPETITORS

ALDI	Metcash Trading
BP	Metro Cash and Carry
Coles Myer	Pick'n Pay
Harris Scarfe Holdings	Royal Dutch/Shell Group
Harvey Norman Holdings	

HISTORICAL FINANCIALS

Company Type: Public

Income Statement

FYE: June 30

	REVENUE ($ mil.)	NET INCOME ($ mil.)	NET PROFIT MARGIN	EMPLOYEES
6/03	17,551	434	2.5%	145,000
6/02	13,791	317	2.3%	145,000
6/01	10,908	243	2.2%	140,000
6/00	12,278	176	1.4%	125,000
6/99	12,510	170	1.4%	120,000
6/98	10,366	172	1.7%	100,000
6/97	11,629	193	1.7%	100,000
6/96	11,007	184	1.7%	95,000
6/95	9,085	166	1.8%	87,000
6/94	8,365	146	1.7%	79,000
Annual Growth	**8.6%**	**12.9%**	**—**	**7.0%**

2003 Year-End Financials

Debt ratio: 40.2%
Return on equity: 46.9%
Cash ($ mil.): 192

Current ratio: 0.81
Long-term debt ($ mil.): 331

Net Income History

Australian: WOW

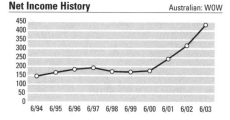

WPP Group

Who's down with WPP? Advertisers. Lots of advertisers. With some 1,400 offices in about 100 countries, WPP Group is the world's third-largest advertising and media services conglomerate (following The Interpublic Group #2 and Omnicom #1, based on worldwide revenues). Its global agency networks J. Walter Thompson, Ogilvy & Mather, and Y&R Advertising create advertising for clients such as American Express, Ford, and IBM. In addition to creative ads, WPP offers its clients an array of business services, including market research (The Kantar Group), media planning and buying (Mediaedge:cia and MindShare), and public relations (Hill & Knowlton and Burson-Marsteller).

Although WPP's advertising and media management business is the the company's single largest segment, WPP's marketing services account for 53% of its revenue. Consisting of Information, Insight & Consultancy; Public Relations and Public Affairs; and Branding, Identity, and Specialized Communications, WPP's marketing services have had mixed results in the face of a general economic downturn. Despite the mixed results in marketing services, WPP continues to rely on these areas for its future growth.

Like its rivals, WPP owes much of its growth to acquisitions. The firm reached the top industry position after its $4.7 billion acquisition of Young & Rubicam in 2000, but was eclipsed when Interpublic bought True North Communications.

While focused on integrating and aligning its new business units, WPP has kept its acquisitive eye open: the company offered to buy media services firm Tempus Group for $630 million in 2001, countering an offer from rival Havas Advertising. Havas later pulled out of the bidding due to the poor economy. WPP's attempts to withdraw its offer were not successful and eventually bought the company. In 2002 WPP bought a majority stake in Chinese public relations firm H-Line Worldwide, the company will fall under the umbrella of Ogilvy Public Relations Worldwide. The company also acquired Cordiant Communications the next year, increasing the company's presence in Asia and in healthcare marketing services through Cordiant's Healthworld operations.

HISTORY

WPP Group began as Wire and Plastic Products, a maker of grocery baskets and other goods founded in 1958 by Gordon Sampson (who retired from the company in 2000). Investors led by former Saatchi & Saatchi advertising executive (and current WPP CEO) Martin Sorrell bought the company in 1985 and began acquiring marketing firms under the shortened name of WPP. In 1987 Sorrell used revenue from these businesses (and a sizable loan) to buy US advertising warhorse J. Walter Thompson (JWT).

JWT was founded by William James Carlton as the Carlton & Smith agency in 1864. The New York City-based firm was bought by James Walter Thompson in 1877 and was later responsible for Prudential Insurance's Rock of Gibraltar symbol (1896). It began working for Ford (which is still a client) in 1943. JWT went public in 1969.

Following its acquisition of JWT, WPP formed European agency Conquest (now Red Cell) in 1988. The company (and its debt) grew the next year when it bought the Ogilvy Group (founded by David Ogilvy in 1948) for $860 million, making WPP the world's largest advertising company. But its acquisition frenzy also positioned the company for a fall in 1991, when depressed economies in the US and the UK slowed advertising spending. Saddled with debt, WPP nearly went into receivership before recovering the next year.

WPP began a period of controlled growth with no major acquisitions in 1993. It expanded internationally in 1994, opening new offices in South America, Europe, the Middle East, and Asia. Winning IBM's $500 million international advertising contract that year also aided WPP's financial recovery. However, this led to the loss of business from IBM's rivals, including AT&T, Compaq's European division (Compaq was purchased by Hewlett-Packard in 2002), and Microsoft.

By 1997 the company was again ready to flex its acquisition muscle. The firm bought 21 companies that year, including a stake in IBOPE (a market research firm in Latin America) and a share of Batey Holdings (the majority owner of Batey Ads, a prominent ad agency in the Asia/Pacific region). That year WPP also created its media planning unit MindShare.

More acquisitions followed in 1998, including a 20% stake in Asatsu (the #3 advertising agency in Japan). The next year the company bought Texas-based market research firm IntelliQuest Information Group, which was merged with WPP's Millward Brown unit. Along with its acquisitions, WPP snagged some significant new accounts in 1998 and 1999, lining up business with Kimberly-Clark, Merrill Lynch, and the embattled International Olympic Committee.

In 2000 the company bought US-based rival Young & Rubicam for about $4.7 billion — one of the largest advertising mergers ever. The move catapulted WPP to the top spot among the world's advertising firms. As if that wasn't enough, its MindShare unit later snagged the $700 million media planning account of consumer products giant Unilever. WPP also took a 49% stake in UniWorld Group, the largest African-American-owned ad agency in the US.

Hamish Maxwell, chairman since 1996, retired in 2001 and was replaced by Philip Lader, the former US ambassador to the UK. That year, however, WPP's top ranking was stolen away by Interpublic Group following its acquisition of True North Communications. It later sparked a bidding war with Havas Advertising when it offered $630 million to buy UK media services firm Tempus Group. WPP grudgingly completed its acquisition of Tempus in 2002. The following year the company acquired Cordiant Communications.

EXECUTIVES

Chairman: Philip Lader, age 57
Group Chief Executive and Executive Director: Sir Martin S. Sorrell, age 58, $1,261,000 pay
Group Finance Director and Executive Director: Paul Richardson, age 45
EVP Public Relations and Director: Howard G. Paster, $700,000 pay
Chief Talent Officer and Director: Beth Axelrod, age 40
Chairman and CEO, Hill and Knowlton: Paul Taaffe
Chairman and CEO, Ogilvy & Mather Worldwide: Shelly Lazarus, $1,010,000 pay
Chairman and CEO, Ogilvy Public Relations Worldwide: Robert (Bob) Seltzer
Chairwoman and CEO, Young & Rubicam; Chairwoman and CEO, Y&R Advertising: Ann Fudge
President and CEO, J. Walter Thompson: Peter A. Schweitzer, $750,000 pay
CEO, Branding & Identity, Healthcare, and Specialist Communications: John Zweig
CEO, The Kantar Group: David Jenkins
CEO, Group M: Irwin Gotlieb, $1,375,000 pay
CEO, Mindshare: Dominic Proctor
COO and CFO, J. Walter Thompson: Lewis J. (Lew) Trencher
Communications Director: Feona McEwan
Investor Relations Director: Francis S. Butera
Auditors: Deloitte & Touche LLP

LOCATIONS

HQ: WPP Group plc
27 Farm St., London W1J 5RJ, United Kingdom
Phone: +44-20-7408-2204 **Fax:** +44-20-7493-6819
US HQ: 125 Park Ave., 4th Fl.,
New York, NY 10017-5529
US Phone: 212-632-2200 **US Fax:** 212-632-2222
Web: www.wpp.com

2002 Sales

	$ mil.	% of total
United States	2,667	42
Continental Europe	1,498	24
United Kingdom	998	16
Other countries	1,135	18
Total	**6,298**	**100**

PRODUCTS/OPERATIONS

2002 Sales

	$ mil.	% of total
Advertising & media investment management	2,917	46
Branding, identity, health care & specialist communications	1,695	27
Information, insight & consultancy	965	15
Public relations & public affairs	721	12
Total	**6,298**	**100**

Selected Operations and Operating Units

Advertising and Media Services
J. Walter Thompson Company
Mediaedge:cia
Mindshare
Ogilvy & Mather Worldwide
Red Cell
Y&R Advertising

Health Care and Specialist Communications
Addison Corporate Marketing
Brand Union
BPRI
CommonHealth
Enterprise IG
Geppetto Group
Glendinning
icon brand navigation

Metro Group (production services)
PRISM Group (sports marketing)
RTC (relationship marketing)
Shire Health Group
VML
Wunderman (relationship marketing)

Information and Consultancy
Center Partners
Goldfarb Consultants
The Kantar Group
Millward Brown
Research International

Public Relations and Public Affairs
Burson-Marsteller
Cohn & Wolfe
Hill and Knowlton
Ogilvy Public Relations Worldwide
Robinson Lerer & Montgomery

COMPETITORS

Aegis Group
Bromley Communications
Dentsu
Grey Global
Hakuhodo
Harte-Hanks
Havas
Interpublic Group
Maxxcom
Omnicom
Publicis

HISTORICAL FINANCIALS

Company Type: Public

Income Statement

FYE: December 31

	REVENUE ($ mil.)	NET INCOME ($ mil.)	NET PROFIT MARGIN	EMPLOYEES
12/02	6,298	142	2.3%	50,417
12/01	5,856	395	6.7%	50,487
12/00	4,457	366	8.2%	55,000
12/99	3,511	279	8.0%	27,711
12/98	3,184	233	7.3%	25,589
12/97	2,885	192	6.6%	22,909
12/96	2,896	171	5.9%	21,166
12/95	2,412	107	4.4%	19,138
12/94	2,233	74	3.3%	19,198
12/93	2,117	34	1.6%	20,416
Annual Growth	**12.9%**	**17.2%**	**—**	**10.6%**

2002 Year-End Financials

Debt ratio: 38.2%
Return on equity: 2.5%
Cash ($ mil.): 1,111
Current ratio: 0.87
Long-term debt ($ mil.): 2,260

No. of shares (mil.): 231
Dividends
  Yield: 1.0%
  Payout: 62.9%
Market value ($ mil.): 8,768

Stock History

NASDAQ: WPPGY

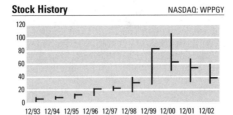

	STOCK PRICE ($) FY Close	P/E High/Low		PER SHARE ($) Earnings	Dividends	Book Value
12/02	37.88	94	49	0.62	0.39	25.59
12/01	53.90	38	19	1.75	0.32	23.97
12/00	62.81	50	24	2.12	0.28	30.56
12/99	83.13	46	16	1.82	0.25	3.32
12/98	30.88	25	11	1.56	0.21	1.02
12/97	22.56	21	16	1.19	0.18	(0.14)
12/96	21.47	19	10	1.14	0.14	0.13
12/95	12.69	19	11	0.71	0.08	(0.33)
12/94	8.44	4	3	2.55	0.08	(2.98)
12/93	6.41	7	2	1.26	0.95	(48.51)
Annual Growth	**21.8%**	**—**	**—**	**(7.6%)**	**(9.4%)**	**—**

Yamaha Corporation

Yamaha, the world's largest maker of musical instruments, is easy on the eardrums. The company makes conventional and electronic instruments, including a "silent" line of instruments. (The user tunes in with headphones; the line includes drums, cellos, and pianos, and muting systems for brass instruments.) Its musical instruments section sells pianos, synthesizers, and wind, string, and percussion instruments; it also runs music schools worldwide and teaches English in Japan. Other operations include making audio and home theater products (mixing boards, stereo systems, projectors), furniture, golf clubs, and specialty metals. Yamaha owns 28% of Yamaha Motor, the world's #2 motorcycle maker, behind Honda; Yamaha Motor also produces WaveRunners, snowmobiles, and golf carts.

In the face of a saturated market for pianos and full-sized keyboards in Japan, Yamaha is looking to the US and Europe, where the market is growing. Other growth areas include products for computers (PC speakers and routers), home theater equipment, and a system that lets cellular phone users pick from hundreds of ringer melodies.

HISTORY

Torakusu Yamaha first repaired medical instruments. But while repairing a broken organ, he decided he could make his own. His first attempt did not have good sound, but continuous work over a four-month period led to a new organ — completed in 1887 — that was highly praised. He established Yamaha Organ Manufacturing Company in 1889. In 1897, as production grew, Yamaha incorporated the company as Nippon Gakki (Japan Musical Instruments). Nippon Gakki began producing upright pianos in 1900 and grand pianos in 1902.

In 1920 the company diversified into the production of wooden airplane propellers (based on woodworking skills used in making pianos) and added pipe organs (1932) and guitars (1946) to its line of musical instruments. Genichi Kawakami, whose father had managed the company since 1927, took over in 1950.

The company formed its first overseas subsidiary, Yamaha de Mexico, in 1958. Under Kawakami's leadership, Nippon Gakki became the world's largest producer of musical instruments, developing Japan's first electronic organ, the Electone, in 1959. Kawakami conducted the company's movements into wind instruments (1965), stereos (1968), microchips (1971), and furniture (1975). He established the Yamaha Music Foundation in 1966 to oversee the company's music schools. By 1982 people in the Americas, Europe, and Asia could buy Yamaha-brand products locally.

Nippon Gakki undertook further diversification, particularly into customized chips for CD players. In 1983 it introduced a powerful, but affordable synthesizer. The company changed its name to Yamaha in 1987. It opened a facility in China two years later. Yamaha emphasized exports of electronic instruments and the production of integrated circuits.

Until 1992 three generations of the Kawakami family dominated Yamaha. After a failed attempt by heir apparent Hiroshi Kawakami to cut back

Yamaha's workforce through early retirement, the manufacturer's in-house labor union revolted. Kawakami was replaced by Seisuke Ueshima, a Yamaha veteran who set out to work on a combination of product innovation and corporate restructuring. Ueshima made a pact with the unions to keep most factory workers, lay off 30% of its Japanese administrative staff, and cut overseas employees.

In 1997 the company launched a joint licensing program with Stanford University for the Sondius-XG sound synthesis technology; the two institutions agreed to share royalties from the technology, which provides realistic sound quality for musical instruments and computer games.

Undergoing sluggish sales of electronic parts, in 1999 Yamaha stopped producing magnetic heads for hard disk drives, shut down a semiconductor plant, and trimmed its workforce by giving 11% of its employees early retirement. In 2000 the company introduced a bamboo guitar that could help slow the depletion of hardwoods and debuted its Super "Melo-Ring" for cellular phone users. Yamaha launched a high-resolution projector for home theater use in 2001. Genichi Kawakami, the 90-year-old former president of Yamaha, died in 2002.

In early 2003 the company decided to exit from the CD recorder market to focus more on high-end home theater systems.

EXECUTIVES

President and Representative Director: Shuji Ito
Senior Managing Director: Katsuhiko Kishida
Managing Director: Kunihiro Maejima
Director: Shinya Hanamoto
Director: Toru Hasegawa
Director: Hirokazu Kato
Director: Tsuneo Kuroe
Director: Tokihisa Makino
Director: Yoshihiro Umeda
Executive Officer, Music Group:
 Mitsuro (Mick) Umemura
President, Yamaha Corporation of North America:
 Yoshihiro Doi
Auditors: Shin Nihon & Co.

LOCATIONS

HQ: 10-1, Nakazawa-cho, Hamamatsu,
 Shizuoka 430-8650, Japan
Phone: +81-53-460-2141　　**Fax:** +81-53-464-8554
US HQ: 6600 Orangethorpe Ave., Buena Park, CA 90620
US Phone: 714-522-9011　　**US Fax:** 714-522-9961
Web: www.global.yamaha.com

2003 Sales

	% of total
Japan	62
North America	17
Europe	15
Other regions	6
Total	**100**

PRODUCTS/OPERATIONS

2003 Sales

	% of total
Musical instruments	55
AV-IT	16
Electronic equipment & metal products	12
Lifestyle-related products	9
Recreation	4
Other	4
Total	**100**

Musical Instruments
Digital musical instruments (portable keyboards, synthesizers)
Educational musical instruments (recorders, pianicas)
Percussion instruments
Pianos
String instruments (guitars, violins)
Wind instruments

AV-IT
Audio products (power amplifiers, stereo equipment)
Home theater systems
IT equipment (PC speakers, routers)

Electronic Equipment and Metal Products
Electronic devices
Electronic alloys and other specialty metals
Large-scale integration chips (LSIs)
Semiconductors
Thermoelectric materials

Lifestyle-Related Products
Bathtubs and washstands
Furniture
Parts for housing facilities
Sound equipment for housing facilities
System kitchens

Recreation
Management of leisure facilities
Golf courses
Sightseeing facilities
Ski resort

Other
Car interior parts
English schools
Golf equipment
Industrial robots
Molds and magnesium parts
Music schools

COMPETITORS

Allen Organ Company	Intel
Altec Lansing	D'Addario
Technologies	Kaman
A N D Music	Kawai
Arctic Cat	Kimball International
Baldwin Piano	Korg
Bombardier	Line 6
Brunswick	Loud Technologies
CASIO COMPUTER	Marshall Amplification
C. F. Martin & Co.	Matsushita
Creative Technology	NEC
E-MU / ENSONIQ	NTT
Ernie Ball	Pearl Corp.
Euphonix	Peavey Electronics
Fender Musical	Philips Electronics
Instruments	Pioneer
Fujitsu	Remo
G. Leblanc	Roland
Gibson Guitar	Seiko Epson
Honda	Shure
Hoshino (U.S.A.)	Sony

HISTORICAL FINANCIALS

Company Type: Public

Income Statement

FYE: March 31

	REVENUE ($ mil.)	NET INCOME ($ mil.)	NET PROFIT MARGIN	EMPLOYEES
3/03	4,379	150	3.4%	23,563
3/02	3,803	(78)	—	23,020
3/01	4,109	105	2.6%	22,277
3/00	5,003	(387)	—	21,599
3/99	4,733	(0)	—	9,044
3/98	4,577	101	2.2%	9,281
3/97	4,884	114	2.3%	9,324
3/96	4,952	88	1.8%	9,872
3/95	5,579	62	1.1%	10,812
3/94	4,341	(39)	—	10,676
Annual Growth	0.1%	—	—	9.2%

2003 Year-End Financials

Debt ratio: 13.5%　　　　　Current ratio: 1.40
Return on equity: 8.9%　　Long-term debt ($ mil.): 242
Cash ($ mil.): 383

Net Income History　　　　Exchange: Tokyo

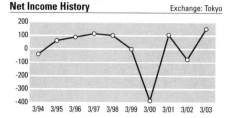

YPF, S.A.

The largest company in Argentina answers to a Spanish parent: Integrated oil company YPF is 99%-owned by Repsol YPF, Spain's largest oil concern (formerly Repsol). YPF has proved reserves of 3 billion barrels of oil equivalent. It produces, refines, and markets petroleum, natural gas, and petrochemicals. The company's three Argentine refineries have an annual capacity of 116.6 million barrels, 51% of Argentina's total refining capacity. YPF distributes oil to its 1,900 service stations in Argentina (29% of the country's total). Subsidiary YPF International has production interests in Indonesia, and also develops US oil and gas properties.

YPF also produces electricity and distributes LPG through interests in Bolivia, Brazil, Chile, Peru, and Russia.

Before its acquisition by Repsol, YPF had transformed itself from an inefficient state-owned firm into a streamlined international player. It has benefited from the Mercosur agreement, which set up an economic union in South America to promote regional trade.

HISTORY

An Argentine government team discovered oil while drilling for water in 1907. Determined to keep the oil under Argentine control, the government formed the world's first state-owned oil company, Direccion Nacional de los Yacimientos Petroliferos Fiscales (YPF), in 1922 to operate the newly discovered field. However, YPF lacked drilling equipment, capital, and staff; it found that the only way to increase domestic oil production was to allow in foreign oil companies. Although YPF's activities ebbed in the 1920s, it made major oil discoveries across Argentina in the 1930s.

A major turning point came with Juan Peron's rise to power in 1945. Peron extended state control over broad sections of the economy, including oil. He nationalized British and US oil holdings and gave YPF a virtual monopoly. In 1945 YPF accounted for 68% of the country's oil production; by 1955 it produced 84% of the national total. The company discovered a huge gas field two years later in western Argentina, making YPF — and Argentina — a major gas producer.

However, YPF's production failed to keep pace with the demands of the growing economy, and imports still dominated Argentina's oil market.

Over the next 30 years, YPF experienced radical swings in government policy as ultranationalist military regimes alternated with liberal, reformist governments. YPF grew into a bloated and inefficient conglomerate. Between 1982 and 1989, despite a World Bank-financed program to modernize YPF's refineries, the firm lost more than $6 billion.

In 1989 Carlos Menem became Argentina's president, and YPF was privatized as part of his economic reform plan to cut loose 50 state-owned companies. To prepare YPF for its IPO, the president brought in a former head of Baker Hughes, Jose Estenssoro, to draft a plan for privatization. The plan was so impressive that Menem gave him the job as CEO of the company in 1990. Estenssoro cut 87% of YPF's staff and sold off $2 billion of noncore assets. By 1993 YPF was profitable and went public as YPF Sociedad Anonima, selling 45% of its shares to raise $3 billion.

A year later YPF began expanding beyond Argentina by shipping crude oil to Chile through a new 300-mile pipeline. It bought woebegone Texas oil company Maxus Energy in 1995 and turned it around at great expense. Estenssoro and three other YPF executives died in a plane crash that year; in 1997 YPF selected Roberto Monti to head Maxus, to serve as its CEO.

In 1997 YPF and Astra C.A.P.S.A. — in which Spanish oil firm Repsol had a controlling stake — jointly purchased a 67% stake in Mexpetrol Argentina (an affiliate of Mexican state oil company PEMEX). Repsol was aggressively moving overseas. In 1998 Repsol lobbied hard to buy part of YPF; Spain's King Juan Carlos himself phoned up Menem to promote Repsol's interests.

A year later the Argentine government auctioned off a 15% stake in YPF to Repsol for $2 billion; Repsol then bought another 83% of the company for $13.2 billion. Repsol became Repsol YPF, and its chairman, Alfonso Cortina, took over as chairman and CEO of YPF, while Monti was named VC and COO.

Monti retired the next year, after Repsol YPF increased its stake in YPF from 98% to 99%.

EXECUTIVES

Chairman and CEO, Repsol YPF and YPF:
Alfonso Cortina de Alcocer, age 59
CFO: Carlos A. Olivieri
General Manager: Jose Maria Ranero Diaz
Director of General Exploration and Production, Latin America: Ruben Patritti
Director of General Refining and Marketing, Latin America: Pascual Olmos
Director of Legal Affairs: Alejandro Quiroga Lopez
Director of Human Resources: Luis Garcia
Director of External Relations: Fabian Falco
Director of Internal Audit, Latin America:
Jorge Genasetti
Controller: Gabriel Leiva

LOCATIONS

HQ: Avenida Presidente Roque Sáenz Peña 777, 1035 Buenos Aires, Argentina
Phone: +54-11-4329-2000   **Fax:** +54-11-4329-2113
Web: www.repsol-ypf.com

YPF's oil and gas interests in primarily located in Argentina, Indonesia, and the US.

PRODUCTS/OPERATIONS

Major Activities

Electricity generation
Oil and natural gas exploration and production
Refining, marketing, transportation, and distribution of oil and a range of petroleum products, derivatives, petrochemicals, and liquid petroleum gas

COMPETITORS

BP
Exxon Mobil
Imperial Oil
PETROBRAS
Petróleo Ipiranga
COPEC
PDVSA
PEMEX
Pioneer Natural Resources
Royal Dutch/Shell Group
TOTAL
Unocal

HISTORICAL FINANCIALS

Company Type: Public

Income Statement

FYE: December 31

	REVENUE ($ mil.)	NET INCOME ($ mil.)	NET PROFIT MARGIN	EMPLOYEES
12/02	5,833	995	17.1%	8,946
12/01	8,155	818	10.0%	8,900
12/00	8,674	1,231	14.2%	8,837
12/99	6,598	481	7.3%	9,000
12/98	5,501	589	10.7%	9,500
12/97	6,145	886	14.4%	10,000
12/96	5,944	845	14.2%	9,750
12/95	4,974	823	16.5%	9,350
12/94	4,403	564	12.8%	6,750
12/93	3,964	708	17.8%	7,500
Annual Growth	4.4%	3.9%	—	2.0%

2002 Year-End Financials

Debt ratio: 13.5%
Return on equity: 13.7%
Cash ($ mil.): 74
Current ratio: 1.89
Long-term debt ($ mil.): 812
No. of shares (mil.): 393
Dividends
  Yield: 9.2%
  Payout: 44.3%
Market value ($ mil.): 4,787

Stock History

NYSE: YPF

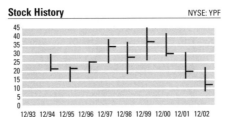

	STOCK PRICE ($) FY Close	P/E High/Low		PER SHARE ($) Earnings	Dividends	Book Value
12/02	12.17	9	3	2.53	1.12	15.35
12/01	19.75	15	8	2.08	4.22	21.55
12/00	29.94	12	8	3.49	0.88	23.53
12/99	36.94	33	20	1.35	0.66	20.89
12/98	27.94	22	11	1.64	0.66	20.43
12/97	34.19	15	10	2.48	0.42	19.66
12/96	25.25	11	8	2.31	0.60	18.08
12/95	21.63	10	6	2.30	0.60	16.73
12/94	21.38	19	13	1.60	0.80	15.10
Annual Growth	(6.8%)	—	—	5.9%	4.3%	0.2%

Zurich Financial Services

The gnomes hard at work at Zurich Financial Services are struggling. The slumping firm offers life and property & casualty insurance, financial planning, asset management, reinsurance, and other financial services through such brands as Farmers Group and Kemper (in the US), Allied Dunbar (the UK) and Eagle Star. Rolf Hüppi, legendary former chairman and CEO of Zurich Financial Services, stepped down while the company's asset management unit tumbled and investors pulled out. James Schiro, previously with PricewaterhouseCoopers, has been named as the new chief executive.

Since the merger that created it in 1998, ZFS has been working to simplify and expand its operations. The firm has streamlined its operations, including consolidating its 11 divisions into five (each headed by a CEO), and increasing its presence on the Internet. Its ownership structure has also been streamlined: Holding companies Zurich Allied and Allied Zurich (which owned 57% and 43% of the company, respectively) have merged and been absorbed into ZFS. Although it has operations in some 60 countries around the world, ZFS considers the US, the UK, and Switzerland its three "home" countries (together they account for about three-fourths of its sales).

The company has spun off reinsurance unit Converium (formerly Zurich Re), it is now an independent, separately listed, reinsurer; Zurich Financial plans to sell its entire stake in Converium. The company has sold troubled asset manager Zurich Scudder to Deutsche Bank (and bought Deutsche's life insurance operations in Italy, Spain, and Portugal), the money from the sale of Scudder has partly been spent on the acquisitions of German financial services company Bonnfinanz and mutual fund distributor DGV. Other sales include a large chunk of US-based Zurich Life to BANK ONE and its operations in Hungary, Poland, and Slovakia to Italian insurer Generali.

The write off of assets and strengthening of non-life reserves resulted in ZFS posting a $3.4 billion loss for 2002. The company laid off some 4,500 people by the end of 2003.

HISTORY

The roots of Zurich Financial Services (ZFS) stretch back to the 1872 founding of a reinsurer for Switzerland Transport Insurance. The company soon branched out into accident, travel, and workers' compensation insurance and changed its name to Transport and Accident Insurance plc Zurich in 1875 to reflect the changes. It began moving into such German cities as Berlin (the jumping-off point for its expansion into Scandinavia and Russia) and Stuttgart. The company exited marine lines in 1880; it later left the reinsurance business. It expanded into liability insurance and in 1894 changed its name to Zurich General Accident and Liability Insurance.

In 1912 Zurich moved into the US. It agreed in 1925 to provide insurance for Ford cars at favorable terms. Zurich's business was hit hard during WWII, and its wartime conduct would later come back to haunt it. In 1955 the company changed its name to Zurich Insurance.

Starting in the 1960s, Zurich began buying other insurers, including Alpina (1965, Switzerland), Agrippina (1969, Germany), and Maryland Casualty Group (1989, US). It also bought the property liability operations of American General.

In the early 1990s the company's strategy shifted. Being big wasn't enough; Zurich needed to find a focus. It began to specialize in such markets as life insurance in Switzerland, and to jettison such marginal or unprofitable business lines as commercial fire insurance in Germany.

In 1995 Zurich bought struggling Chicago-based asset manager Kemper and in 1997 bought lackluster mutual fund manager Scudder Stevens & Clark, forming Scudder Kemper. That year it also bought failed Hong Kong investment bank Peregrine Investment Holdings. In 1998 Zurich merged with the financial services businesses of B.A.T Industries.

The British-American Tobacco Co. was created in 1902 as a joint venture between UK-based Imperial Tobacco and American Tobacco.

As public disapproval of smoking grew in the 1970s, the company began diversifying; it changed its name to B.A.T Industries in 1976 and moved into insurance. In 1984 it rescued UK insurer Eagle Star from a hostile offer by German insurance giant Allianz. The next year it bought Hambro Life Assurance, renaming it Allied Dunbar. Moving into the large US market, B.A.T bought Farmers Insurance Group in 1988. (Farmers was founded in 1928 as an automobile insurer.)

While B.A.T battled the antismoking army of the 1990s, the insurance industry struggled with stagnant growth. The late 1990s were a bad time for Swiss insurance and banking firms as they, along with other European insurers, faced pressure to pay on insurance policies taken out by Holocaust victims. In 1998 Zurich became one of six Swiss insurers that agreed to pay on the life insurance policies.

That year Zurich and B.A.T's insurance units merged to create ZFS. The new company was immediately caught up in an investigation of insider trading relating to the merger. CFO Markus Rohrbasser resigned, disclosing that he had traded in Zurich Insurance stock before the merger. The firm reshuffled some of its holdings and sold Eagle Star Reinsurance.

In 1999 ZFS spun off its real estate holdings into PSP Swiss Property. At the turn of the century, it focused on expanding, buying mobile home insurer Foremost Group and the new business of insurer Abbey Life, which it merged into Allied Dunbar. In 2000, the holding companies formed to own ZFS (Zurich Allied and Allied Zurich) were merged into the firm.

Zurich Financial paid out some $900 million in 2001-2002 in claims related to the September 11 attacks.

EXECUTIVES

Chairman: Lodewijk Christiaan van Wachem, age 72
Vice Chairman: Philippe Pidoux
CEO: James J. (Jim) Schiro, age 57
COO: Peter Eckert, age 57
Group Finance Director: Patrick O'Sullivan, age 53
CEO, Life Insurance: Paul van de Geijn, age 57
CEO, North America Corporate Business Division: John Amore, age 54
CEO, North America Consumer and Latin America Business Division; Chairman and CEO, Farmers Group: Martin D. (Marty) Feinstein, age 54
CEO, Continental Europe Business Division: Axel P. Lehmann, age 43
CEO, UK, Ireland, Southern Africa, and Asia/Pacific Business Division: Alexander P. (Sandy) Leitch, age 55

CEO, UK, Ireland, and South Africa Insurance Division: Geoff Riddell
CEO, Global Asset Business Division: David L. Wasserman, age 48
CEO, Australia and Other Markets: Gunnar Stokholm, age 53
CEO, France: Berto Fisler
CEO, Latin America: Gastón Aguirre, age 52
CEO, Switzerland: Hans-Jürg Bernet, age 53
CEO, Spain: José Cela, age 58
CFO: Thomas Buess, age 45
Head of Corporate Communications: Doris Larmann
Head of Investor Relations: Pierre N. Guigui
General Counsel and Secretary: Monica Mächler-Erne, age 46
Auditors: PricewaterhouseCoopers AG

LOCATIONS

HQ: Mythenquai 2, 8022 Zurich, Switzerland
Phone: +41-1-625-2525   **Fax:** +41-1-625-3555
US HQ: Zurich North America, Zurich Towers, 1400 American Ln., Schaumburg, IL 60196
US Phone: 847-605-6000   **US Fax:** 847-605-6011
Web: www.zurich.com

Zurich Financial Services has operations in more than 60 countries throughout the world.

PRODUCTS/OPERATIONS

2002 Assets

	$ mil.	% of total
Cash	8,444	3
Bonds	102,498	36
Stocks	25,888	9
Mortgage loans	4,291	1
Receivables	10,654	4
Reinsurance assets	22,193	8
Separate account assets	58,059	20
Other	53,829	19
Total	**285,856**	**100**

2002 Sales

	$ mil.	% of total
Premiums & policy fees	31,367	75
Investment income	6,123	15
Management fees	2,353	6
Gain on disposal of businesses	498	1
Other	1,214	3
Losses on investments	(1,107)	—
Total	**40,448**	**100**

Selected Subsidiaries

AAS Zurich Latvia (non-life insurance)
Allied Dunbar Assurance (life insurance, UK)
Alpina (non-life insurance)
Centre Reinsurance International (Ireland)
Eagle Star Holdings (non-life insurance, UK)
Eagle Star Life Insurance Company (non-life insurance, China)
Eagle Star Malta (non-life insurance)
Empire Fire and Marine (non-life insurance, US)
Erbasei SpA (non-life insurance, Italy)
Farmers Group (management services, US)
Gresham Investment Trust (asset management, UK)
Kemper Corp. (life insurance, US)
Micoba Holdings (non-life insurance, Bahamas)
Peopleplus Insurance Company (non-life insurance, Canada)
SIAR (reinsurance, Italy)
South African Eagle Insurance (58%, non-life insurance)
Thai Zurich Insurance Co. (25%, non-life insurance, Thailand)
Turegum (reinsurance)
Zurich American Insurance Company (non-life insurance, US)
Zurich Brasil Seguros (life and non-life insurance, Brazil)
Zurich Eagle Insurance (non-life insurance, Singapore)
Zurich España (non-life insurance, Spain)
Zurich Eurolife (life insurance, Luxembourg)
Zürich Kosmos (life and non-life insurance, Austria)
Zurich Leven (life insurance, The Netherlands)

Zurich North America (Zurich U.S., Zurich Canada, and Universal Underwriters Group)
Zürich Rechtsschutz (non-life insurance, Germany)
Zurich Specialties London (non-life insurance, UK)
Zürich-Agrippina Beteiligungs-AG (non-life insurance, Germany)
ZURITEL (non-life insurance, France)

COMPETITORS

AEGON
Allianz
Allstate
AIG
Generali
Aviva
AXA
Citigroup
CNA Financial
ERGO
FMR
GEICO
General Re
ING
Liebherr International
Lloyd's of London
MetLife
Millea Holdings
Mitsui Sumitomo Insurance
Munich Re
New York Life
Nippon Life Insurance
Prudential
Prudential plc
Sompo Japan Insurance
State Farm
Sumitomo Life
Swiss Life
Swiss Re
Winterthur

HISTORICAL FINANCIALS

Company Type: Public

Income Statement

FYE: December 31

	ASSETS ($ mil.)	NET INCOME ($ mil.)	INCOME AS % OF ASSETS	EMPLOYEES
12/02	285,856	(3,430)	—	67,824
12/01	231,605	(387)	—	70,000
12/00	231,363	2,328	1.0%	72,930
12/99	221,178	3,260	1.5%	71,390
12/98	214,651	802	0.4%	68,876
12/97	191,807	2,142	1.1%	68,000
Annual Growth	**8.3%**	**—**	**—**	**(0.1%)**

2002 Year-End Financials

Equity as % of assets: 5.9%
Return on assets: —
Return on equity: —
Long-term debt ($ mil.): 11,808
Sales ($ mil.): 40,448

Net Income History

Swiss: ZURN

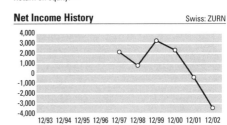

Hoover's Handbook of

World Business

The Indexes

Index by Industry

AEROSPACE & DEFENSE

Aerospace & Defense Parts Manufacturing
BAE SYSTEMS 53
Rolls-Royce plc 272

Aircraft Manufacturing
Airbus S.A.S. 29
Bombardier Inc. 67
European Aeronautic Defence and Space Company EADS N.V. 126

AUTOMOTIVE & TRANSPORT

Sime Darby Berhad 298

Auto Manufacturing
Bayerische Motoren Werke AG 60
DaimlerChrysler AG 104
Fiat S.p.A. 127
Honda Motor Co., Ltd. 150
Hyundai Motor Company 156
Isuzu Motors Limited 168
Koç Holding A.S. 182
Mazda Motor Corporation 204
Nissan Motor Co., Ltd. 224
PSA Peugeot Citroën S.A. 244
Dr. Ing. h.c. F. Porsche AG 253
Renault S.A. 264
Suzuki Motor Corporation 309
Toyota Motor Corporation 339
Volkswagen AG 350

Auto Parts Manufacturing
Robert Bosch GmbH 268
Tomkins PLC 332

Truck, Bus & Other Vehicle Manufacturing
AB Volvo 352

BANKING

Banking — Asia & Australia
National Australia Bank Limited 212

Banking — Canada
Bank of Montreal 54
Canadian Imperial Bank of Commerce 83
Royal Bank of Canada 275
The Toronto-Dominion Bank 335

Banking — Europe
Allied Irish Banks, p.l.c. 38
Crédit Agricole S.A. 100
Espírito Santo Financial Group S.A. 125
IntesaBci S.p.A. 165

UBS AG 341

Money Center Banks
ABN AMRO Holding N.V. 21
Barclays PLC 55
BNP Paribas 66
Credit Suisse Group 101
Deutsche Bank AG 111
HSBC Holdings plc 152
HVB Group (Bayerische Hypo- und Vereinsbank Aktiengesellschaft) 59
Mizuho Financial Group, Inc. 208
Santander Central Hispano S.A. 284

BEVERAGES

Alcoholic Beverages
Allied Domecq PLC 37
Bacardi Limited 52
Carlsberg A/S 86
Diageo plc 114
Foster's Group Limited 130
Heineken N.V. 144
Interbrew S.A. 164
Kirin Brewery Company, Limited 179
Molson Inc. 209
SABMiller plc 279
San Miguel Corporation 283

Non-Alcoholic Beverages
Cadbury Schweppes plc 81

BUSINESS SERVICES

Advertising & Marketing
Dentsu Inc. 109
Publicis Groupe S.A. 257
VNU N.V. 348
WPP Group plc 359

Commercial Printing
Dai Nippon Printing Co., Ltd. 102
Quebecor Inc. 259

CHEMICALS

Agricultural Chemicals
Agrium Inc. 27
Koor Industries Ltd. 184

Basic and Intermediate Chemical & Petrochemical Manufacturing
Sinopec Shanghai Petrochemical Company Limited 300

Paints, Coatings & Other Finishing Product Manufacturing
Akzo Nobel N.V. 30
Imperial Chemical Industries PLC 158

Plastic & Fiber Manufacturing
BASF Aktiengesellschaft 56
Bayer AG 57
Formosa Plastics Corporation 128

COMPUTER HARDWARE

Acer Inc. 23
Fujitsu Limited 134
Hitachi, Ltd. 148
NEC Corporation 214
Oki Electric Industry Company, Limited 235
Toshiba Corporation 336

Computer Peripherals
Canon Inc. 84
Logitech International S.A. 193
Ricoh Company, Ltd. 267
Seiko Epson Corporation 293

COMPUTER SERVICES

Computer Products Distribution & Support
Computacenter plc 96
Danka Business Systems PLC 105

Information Technology Services
Atos Origin S.A. 46
Bull 79
Cap Gemini Ernst & Young 85
Olivetti S.p.A. 236

COMPUTER SOFTWARE

Enterprise Resource Planning Software
SAP Aktiengesellschaft 287

CONSTRUCTION

Construction & Design Services
Bouygues SA 69
Hopewell Holdings Limited 151

Construction Materials
Hanson PLC 143

CONSUMER PRODUCTS MANUFACTURERS

Apparel
adidas-Salomon AG 24
Gucci Group N.V. 142

Index by Headquarters

Index of Executives

A

Aasmund Frisak, Hans 306
Abbott, Brian 194
Abe, Katsuhiro 249
Abe, Kunito 234
Abelló, Juan 64
Abenante, Anthony 228
Abercrombie, George B. 270
Abrams, Jack 218
Achenbach, Christoph 178
Acher, Franz-Josef 146
Achleitner, Paul 36
Ackermann, Josef 111
Adami, Norman J. 280
Adamik, Brian 267
Adams, Denis 259
Adams, George 179
Adams, Paul 75
Adams, Ralph G. 108
Adelt, Bruno 351
Adshead, John E. 172
Aelick, Ronald C. 162
Africa, Arnaldo L. 283
Agarwal, Bhikam C. 168
Agassi, Shai 287
Agemura, Yasuo 228
Ager, Rowley S. 327
Agnelli, Giovanni 157
Agnelli, Umberto 128, 157
Ågren, Christer 308
Agrusti, Raffaele 45
Aguirre, Gastón 363
Agut Bonsfills, Joaquim 321
Ahearn, Chris 267
Ahlers, Bernd 326
Ahlström, Krister 308
Ahrnell, Jan Henrik 324
Aiba, Hiroshi 249
Aiken, Philip S. 66
Ailes, Roger 217
Ainsley, Christopher J. D. 357
Airey, Dawn 77
Aitchinson, Duncan 86
Aitken, Ian C. 273
Akahane, Masao 293
Akers, Joseph A. 58
Akhurst, Bruce J. 325
Akikusa, Naoyuki 134
Al Khaily, Mohamed Naser 237
Alahuhta, Matti 226
Alangoya, Emine 182
Ala-Pietilä, Pekka 226
Alary, Pierre 68
Albutt, Graham 267
Alekperov, Vagit Y. 197
Alexander, Anthony 161
Alexander, Ralph C. 71
Alexander, William J. 279
Alexandre, Patrick 28
Alexandre, Vincent 136
Alierta Izuel, César 320
Alkemade, Bart 75
Allain, Pierre 347

Allamandi, Silvio 314
Allavena, Jean-Luc 189
Allen, Charles (National Australia Bank) 213
Allen, Charles Lamb (Granada) 141
Allen, David C. 71
Allen, Sharon L. 108
Allert, Richard H. 94
Allerton, John 325
Allgood, David 275
Almaral, Alejandro 243
Almassy, Stephen E. 124
Almond, Stephen 108
Alonso Ureba, Antonio Jesús 320
Alspaugh, Robert W. 185
Altwegg, Markus 270
Alvarez-Pallete, Jose Maria 319
Alvarez-Pallete López, José María 321
Amagai, Jiro 103
Amatriaín Corbi, Belén 321
Ambe Attar, Isidoro 322
Amemiya, Koichi 150
Amirault, Peter L. 209
Amore, John 363
Amundson, Garnet K. 27
Ananenkov, Alexander G. 138
Andenaes, Henrik 229
Andersen, Jørgen Kristian 229
Andersen, Kurt 63
Andersen, Per Brøndum 87
Andersen, Svein 306
Anderson, David J. 162
Anderson, Jeremy 47
Anderson, Toby 172
Anderson, William D. 62
Andersson, Bengt 117
Andersson, Rune 117
Ando, Kunitake 304
Andreae, Jan G. 274
Andreoni, Arrigo 318
Andrewes, Ed 261
Andrews, Steve 78
Andruchow, Al 118
Anesaki, Naomi 183
Ang, Ramon S. 283
Angelici, Bruno 46
Angelici, Carlo 34
Angelson, Mark A. 211
Aninat, Cristián 319
Ansell, Clive R. 78
Anzai, Fujio 169
Anzai, Takashi 171
Aoki, Satoshi 150
Aoshima, Kenichi 317
Aoyagi, Kazuhiro 183
Aoyagi, Matthew 193
Apotheker, Leo 287
Appel, Frank 112
Aragones, Mercedes 353
Arai, Takao 221
Arai, Yoshikazu 180
Arakawa, Shoshi 72
Araki, Ryuji 339
Aramaki, Koichiro 180

Aramburuzabala Larregui, Asunción 323
Araujo Ramírez, Felix J. 323
Arce Torres, David 285
Ardeshir, Jehangir 313
Arendt, Axel 273
Argus, Don R. 66
Ariza, Antonio 38
Armenio, Peter 275
Armour, Mark 263
Armstrong, Alan 261
Armstrong, J. Gregory 154
Armstrong, T. Christian 335
Arnault, Bernard 198
Arning, Robert F. 186
Aróstegui, José Antonio 285
Arrojo, José M. 285
Asada, Atsushi 220
Asai, Yutaka 235
Asami, Yasuo 72
Asano, Katsuhiko 180
Aschenbroich, Jacques 281
Ashcroft, Charles P. 118
Asheuer, Danielle 79
Ashton, Lynda 172
Aso, Kotaro 133
Atay, Ternel 182
Atkinson, Peter Y. 150
Augustin, Jean-Luc 263
Austin, Adam 97
Autheman, Marc-Antoine 100
Avery, Cecil 144
Avis, Alice 201
Axelrod, Beth 360
Axelrod, Mikhail A. 138
Aymard, Richard 243
Azcárraga Jean, Emilio 323
Azuma, Kazunori 268
Azuma, Makoto 337

B

Bach, Herbert 212
Bachmann, Peter W. 101
Bäck, Ragnar 123
Bacon, William Gordon 162
Badinter, Simon 258
Badke, Michael 178
Bahadur, Harsh 206
Bahlmann, Arnold 64
Bailey, Michael J. 96
Baillie, Alistair 241
Baird, D. Euan 273
Baird, Richard A. 274
Bakaj, Joseph 204
Baker, Ciaran 280
Baker, John 192
Baker, Kathy 357
Bakker, R. H. 348
Balbinot, Sergio 45
Baldauf, Sari 226
Balfour, Fiona 259

Bali, S. Ashish 108
Ball, Anthony 77
Baltazar, Miguel 353
Bamford, Peter R. 350
Bandier, Martin N. 118
Bang-Rae, Cho 191
Banham, John 355
Barat, Jean-Paul 172
Barbaroux, Olivier 116, 345
Barbassa, Almir Guilherme 242
Barber, R. G. 153
Barberis, Alessandro 128
Barberis, Joe 94
Barbosa, Fabio C. 21
Bargonetti, Arthur 334
Bark-Jones, Christopher 32
Barkov, Anatoly A. 197
Bärlocher, Urs 232
Barnes, Richard A. 354
Barnevik, Percy N. 45
Barraquand, Yves 248
Barrera de Irimo, Antonio 79
Barreto, Aires 243
Barrett, Matthew W. 56
Barrett, Stephen 186
Barros, Diego 319
Bart, Pierre 116
Bartlett, Rob 42
Barucq, Vincent 88
Bassil, Alain 28
Bastianello, Tito 45
Bastón Patiño, José A. 323
Batchelor, Paul 255
Bates, Deanna 77
Battista, Valerio 250
Bauccio, Fedele 96
Baudin, Remí 302
Baudouin, Jacques 100
Bauer, Bernd 64
Bauer, Sabine 25
Bauer, Walter 269
Bauer, Werner J. 216
Baumann, Ernst 61
Baumann, Karl-Hermann 297
Baur, Hans 253
Baxendale, Sonia A. 83
Baxter, Raymond A. 139
Bayegan, H. Markus 20
Bazire, Nicolas 198
Bazoli, Giovanni 166
Beattie, W. Geoffrey 328
Beatty, Douglas C. 230
Beauchet, Jacques 88
Beaudoin, Laurent 68
Beaufret, Jean-Pascal 33
Beaver, Dominic 136
Bébéar, Claude 50
Bec, Aline 100
Bech, Alexandra 229
Becht, Bart 262
Becker, Norbert R. 124
Beckerman, Neil 342
Beerkens, Boudewijn 357
Beeuwsaert, Dirk 309

Scheepbouwer, A. J. 277
Scheurle, Walter 112
Schiano, Anthony 274
Schiek, Lisa 142
Schilling, Steven L. 230
Schinzler, Hans-Jürgen 212
Schipporeit, Erhard 122
Schiro, James J. 363
Schlosser, Ronald H. 329
Schmidt, Hans Henrik 87
Schmidt, Kurt T. 232
Schmidt, Thomas 20
Schmidt-Holtz, Rolf 64
Schmittmann, Jan Peter 21
Schmoldt, Hubertus 122
Schneidawind, Detlef 212
Schneider, Jean-Luc 126
Schneider, Jörg 212
Schneider, Manfred 58
Schneier, Alan 108
Schoewel, Erhard 262
Scholes, Ian F. 213
Scholl, Hermann 269
Schöning, Georg 279
Schörling, Melker 291
Schorsch, Louis 168
Schrader, Hans-Otto 238
Schrempp, Jürgen E. 104
Schubert, Christian 57
Schug, Charles 136
Schulte, Hans-Jürgen 200
Schulte-Noelle, Henning 36
Schultz, Kåre 233
Schulz, Ekkehard D. 330
Schumacher, Ulrich 297
Schütte, Andreas 229
Schwarz, Randall J. 169
Schwarzenbauer, Peter 253
Schweitzer, Louis 264
Schweitzer, Peter A. 360
Schwenger, Bruce S. 54
Scirocco, Joseph 334
Scognamiglio, Vincenzo 63
Scolan, Daniel 347
Scotland, David 38
Scott, James 206
Scott, Jeremy 255
Scott, Peter B. (National Australia Bank) 213
Scott, Peter F. (Foster's) 131
Scott, Philip 49
Scott, Stephen R. 350
Scott, Timothy A. 159
Scott-Barrett, Hugh Y. 21
Scoular, Valerie 56
Scriven, John G. 20
Scully, Richard W. 131
Seelert, Robert Louis 258
Seger, Dick 291
Seidel, Andrew D. 345
Seike, Akira 186
Seistrup, Ivan 43
Seiwald, Christian 232
Seki, Koji 188
Seki, Tetsuo 222
Sekine, Shuichiro 108
Sekino, Hiromoto 286
Selden, Robin 193
Sellek, Roger 192
Sellière, Ernest-Antoine 86
Seltzer, Robert 360
Semenyaka, Alexander N. 138
Semtob, Patrick 79
Senior, Stuart 201
Seok-Man, Yoon 254
Sera, Nobuyoshi 173
Serletic, Matt 118
Servatius, Bernhard 51
Seymour, Bill 226
Shaffer, David H. 328
Shanahan, Lynn 334
Shannon, Bill F. C. 355
Shantz, Paul 39

Shaps, Simon 141
Sharef, Uriel J. 297
Sharifov, Vagit S. 197
Sharman, Mark 77
Sharp, Michael 259
Shattock, Matt 82
Shea, Peter 77
Shearer, Tony 96
Sheed, James C. 298
Shepard, Donald J. 26
Sheriff, Karen H. 62
Sherman, Frank 30
Sherrington, Mark 280
Shetler, Craig 330
Shibata, Naoto 268
Shibata, Takumi 228
Shields, Robert J. 154
Shiels, Stompie 194
Shigenaga, Takeshi 180
Shih, Angela 315
Shih, C.M. 162
Shih, Edith 155
Shih, Stan 24
Shilston, Andrew B. 273
Shimakura, Kelichi 214
Shimamura, Teruo 218
Shimizu, Juntaro 173
Shimizu, Koichi 249
Shimizu, Shigeo 296
Shimomura, Ryuichi 175
Shinmachi, Toshiyuki 173
Shinohara, Akira 169
Shinohara, Eisaku 187
Shinomoto, Manabu 148
Shinozuka, Katsumasa 235
Shioya, Keigo 133
Shipman, Mark 302
Shirahada, Hisashi 332
Shiraishi, Motoatsu 150
Shirakawa, Susumu 331
Shiramizu, Kosuke 339
Shirato, Ryoichi 331
Shohtoku, Yukio 203
Shoyama, Etsuhiko 148
Sibley, Nigel 261
Sicard, Daniel 89
Sichel, Olivier 132
Siddiqi, Mohammed 97
Sidlik, Thomas W. 104
Siguier, Bertrand 258
Sigurdsson, Arni 64
Sihler, Helmut 232, 253
Siler, Jim 167
Silva Menezes, Marcos A. 242
Silver, Robert H. 341
Simms, Michael H. 280
Simon, Nigel 137
Simpson-Bint, Jonathan 136
Singer, Robert 142
Singleton, David 53
Singleton, Marc Alexander 298
Siria, Carlos 289
Sirisena, Mervyn 299
Sirkis, Ronald B. 54
Siskind, Arthur M. 217
Sixt, Frank J. 155
Skorge, Wenche 306
Skou, Søren 43
Skov, Margrethe 87
Slater, Andrew 118
Slaven, Mark 97
Slechte, Jan J. 130
Sliepenbeek, Joost L.M. 274
Slim Domit, Patricio 322
Slim Helú, Carlos 322
Slim Seade, Héctor 322
Small, Francis 124
Smart, Tim 78
Smirnov, Alexander S. 197
Smith, Brian 354
Smith, Charles Miller 290
Smith, Chell 86
Smith, James C. 328

Smith, Jim 42
Smith, Marc E. 274
Smith, Mike 261
Smith, Paul A. 160
Smith, Peter (P&O) 241
Smith, Peter (Woolworths) 358
Smith, Richard 185
Smith, Tad 263
Smits, Peter 20
Snider, Stacey 347
Snollaerts, Etienne 89
Snowball, Patrick 49
Soares Nunes, João C. 242
Søderberg, Jess 43
Soeters, Martin 233
Soh, Tomomi 186
Solakoglu, Cengiz 182
Solard, Claude 92
Solomon, Stephen M. 20
Solorzano, Eduardo 353
Somerville, Penelope F. 54
Son, Masayoshi 303
Sono, Teisuke 187
Sonoda, Akira 72
Soo Khiang, Bey 299
Soo-Chang, Lee 282
Sood, Arvind 48
Soo-Ho, Lee 191
Soon-Won, Chung 156
Soo-Yang, Han 254
Sopha, Jim 257
Sørensen, Lars Rebien 233
Sorrell, Martin S. 360
Sorrentino, Rob 64
Soszyn, Peter 42
Soto, Humberto 319
Soursac, Thierry 48
Southwell, David A. 62
Specht, Uwe 146
Spencer, Thomas R. 335
Sperl, Andreas 29
Spiers-Lopez, Pernille 158
Spillane, Michael 334
Spinetta, Jean-Cyril 28
Spithill, Ronald 33
Spradley, Sue 23
Spreafico, Germano 318
Sprissler, Wolfgang 59
Sproll, Theodor 232
Stack, Robert J. 82
Stade, Yngve 308
Stalker, Robin 25
Stamminger, Erich 25
Stammler, Gebhard 178
Standish, Clive 341
Stanhope, John 325
Stanley, Deirdre 328
Stanley, James 290
Stanworth, Tony 179
Staunton, Henry 141
Steel, Gary 20
Steffen, Cennert 117
Stein, Jeffrey M. 185
Stein, Robert W. 124
Steineback, Lothar 146
Stenqvist, Asa 117
Sténson, Henry 123
Sterk, Harry 357
Stern, Jacques 23
Stern, Mitchell 217
Steve, Bruno 306
Stevens, Andy 273
Stevens, Ben 75
Stevenson, Barry 201
Stevenson, Dennis 239
Stevenson, Katharine B. 230
Stewart, Martin 77
Stewart, Shelley 167
Stitzer, H. Todd 82
Stockwell, Ashley 346
Stokes, Ken 262
Stokholm, Gunnar 363
Stolk, Marcel 193

Stone, Larry 78
Storck, Alfred 20
Storms, Brian 341
Storozhev, Yury 197
Stout, David M. 140
Stråberg, Hans 117
Strachan, Ian C. 267
Strathdee, Stuart 314
Strauss, Charles 342
Strauss-Wieczorek, Gerlinde 200
Street, Mike 73
Streiff, Christian 281
Streppel, Joseph B.M. 26
Stricker, Willy 93
Stringer, Howard 304
Stringham, P. E. 153
Strömqvist, Dag 30
Strong, James A. 358
Strzelecki, Jecek 252
Stubbins, Bill 30
Stubbs, Alan C. 162
Stubkjaer, Knud E. 43
Studzinski, John J. 153
Sturany, Klaus 279
Sturgell, Brian W. 32
Stutts, Jim 25
Suárez Coppel, José Juán 244
Suaudeau, Henri-Calixte 258
Subedar, Farokh N. 313
Sudo, Tamihiko 249
Sugimori, Junzo 310
Sugimoto, Harushige 235
Sugita, Yoshiaki 209
Sugiyama, Mineo 214
Sugiyama, Seiji 208
Suk-Jai, Lee 282
Sulat, James R. 211
Sullivan, Brian 345
Sumida, Katsuyuki 225
Sumie, Hiroshi 170
Sunderland, John M. 82
Sundström, Karl-Henrik 123
Sung-Sik, Cho 254
Sunohara, Kiyoshi 332
Sutherland, Peter D. 71
Sutton, Mark B. 341
Suzuki, Den 317
Suzuki, Eiichi 220
Suzuki, Kazuyoshi 310
Suzuki, Keisuke 72
Suzuki, Kuniaki 135
Suzuki, Masanobu 223
Suzuki, Minoru 102
Suzuki, Osamu 310
Suzuki, Shunichi 214
Suzuki, Taiji 214
Suzuki, Toshifumi 171
Suzuki, Yoshitomo 317
Suzuki, Yozo 90
Suzuki, Yuji 101
Svanberg, Carl-Henric 123
Svensson, Lars E. 123
Swan, Frank J. 131
Swanson, Luke 239
Swanson, Richard 142
Swartzman, Lisa R. 139
Sweeney, Francis J. 317
Swift, Nick 144
Switkowski, Zygmunt E. 325
Symonds, Jonathan 45

T

Taaffe, Paul 360
Tabaksblat, Morris 263
Tachikawa, Keiji 223, 234
Tadashi, Tadashi 339
Tae-Hak, Her 282
Tae-Hyun, Hwang 254
Taft, Claudia L. 186
Taguchi, Wataru 221

HOOVER'S 2004 EDITIONS

SAVE 25% when you order the Handbooks set directly from Hoover's

ONLY $495

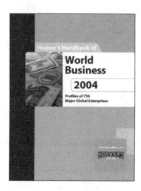

HOOVER'S HANDBOOK OF AMERICAN BUSINESS 2004

Profiles 750 of the largest and most important U.S. companies.

$205.00 • ISBN 1-57311-088-4
December 2003 • 1,232 pp. • Two volumes
NEW: Expanded to 8-1/2" x 11"

HOOVER'S HANDBOOK OF PRIVATE COMPANIES 2004

Includes coverage of 900 of the largest private U.S. business enterprises.

$165.00 • ISBN 1-57311-090-6
January 2004 • 732 pp.
NEW: Expanded to 8-1/2" x 11"

HOOVER'S HANDBOOK OF WORLD BUSINESS 2004

Features profiles of 300 of the most influential companies based outside the U.S.

$175.00 • ISBN 1-57311-089-2
March 2004 • 486 pp.
NEW: Expanded to 8-1/2" x 11"

HOOVER'S HANDBOOK OF EMERGING COMPANIES 2004

Covers 600 of America's most exciting growth companies and includes a combined index for the Hoover's Handbooks set.

$135.00 • ISBN 1-57311-091-4
April 2004 • 458 pp.
NEW: Expanded to 8-1/2" x 11"

HOOVER'S MASTERLIST OF U.S. COMPANIES 2004

This comprehensive selection of the 10,000 most important companies in America includes:

▶ 6,190 publicly traded companies, including all companies on the New York, American, and Nasdaq National Market exchanges, plus a selection of over-the-counter stocks
▶ 2,310 private companies, partnerships, and mutual companies
▶ 1,250 subsidiaries and business segments of large corporations
▶ 300 associations, foundations, cooperatives, universities, and non-profit organizations

$285.00 • 10th edition • ISBN 1-57311-087-6 • October 2003 • 1,872 pp. • 8-1/2" x 11" • Two volumes • Hardcover

REGIONAL VERSIONS OF HOOVER'S MASTERLIST NOW AVAILABLE!

Get the same valuable data as in *Hoover's MasterList of U.S. Companies* in a regional edition. Great for job seekers or others looking for local company information. Available November 2003 • 8-1/2" x 11" • Trade paper

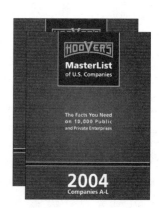

NEW! REGIONAL VERSIONS

Hoover's MasterList: California Edition 2004 • ITEM #HCA04 • est. 1,536 companies • $59 • ISBN 1-57311-094-9
Hoover's MasterList: Capital Area Edition 2004 (DC, MD, VA) • ITEM #HDC04 • est. 504 companies • $45 • ISBN 1-57311-095-7
Hoover's MasterList: Illinois Edition 2004 • ITEM #HIL04 est. • 558 companies • $45 • ISBN 1-57311-096-5
Hoover's MasterList: New York Metro Edition 2004 (CT, NJ, NY) • ITEM #HNY04 • est. 1,860 companies • $59 • ISBN 1-57311-097-3
Hoover's MasterList: Southeast Edition 2004 (AL, FL, GA) • ITEM #HSE04 • est. 768 companies • $45 • ISBN 1-57311-098-1
Hoover's MasterList: Texas Edition 2004 • ITEM #HTX04 • est. 678 companies • $45 • ISBN 1-57311-099-X

HOOVER'S INC. | 5800 AIRPORT BLVD. AUSTIN, TEXAS 78752
PHONE: 800-486-8666 | FAX: 512-374-4538 | E-MAIL: ORDERS@HOOVERS.COM | WWW.HOOVERSBOOKS.COM

HOOVER'S
Business Press